A Lawyer's Handbook: Volume 2

The Impact of Domestic Violence On Your Legal Practice

3rd Edition

**American Bar Association
Commission on Domestic & Sexual Violence**

ABA
AMERICAN BAR ASSOCIATION
Commission on
Domestic & Sexual Violence

ISBN 978-1-64105-243-6

For permission to reprint or adapt the contents of this publication, please contact:

American Bar Association Contracts & Copyrights
321 N. Clark Street
Chicago, IL 60654
(312) 988-6101
copyright@abanet.org

AUTHORS

(in alphabetical order)

Alicia Aiken

Sara Block

Sarah Bolling Mancini

Cassandra Brulotte

Hilary Chadwick

Alicia Clark

John Clune

Lori Cohen

Juanita Davis

Sarah Deer

Radha Desai

Margaret Drew

Nancy Durborow

Cecilia Friedman Levin

Terry Fromson

Lauren Groth

Drake Hagner

Lisa James

Diane Johnston

Angie Junck

Larisa Kofman

Debbie Lee

David Martin

Amanda Norejko

Protima Pandey

Maya Raghu

Robin Runge

Erika Sussman

Tia Katrina Taruc-Myers

Karen Merrill Tjapkes

Rob Valente

Katie VonDeLinde

Lydia Watts

Persis Yu

Jane Zhi

TABLE OF CONTENTS

Section Eight: Criminal Matters

Section One:
Introduction

Chapter One:
Introduction

I. Why All Lawyers Need to Know About Domestic Violence

All lawyers, regardless of their practice area, should know about domestic violence. In the United States, nearly twenty people are physically abused by their intimate partner each minute.[1] More than a third of women (35.6 percent) and more than a quarter of men (28.5 percent) in the United States have experienced physical or sexual violence and/or stalking by an intimate partner in their lifetime.[2] In addition, approximately a quarter of women (24.3 percent) and an eighth of men (13.8 percent) in the United States have experienced severe physical violence by an intimate partner in their lifetime.[3] A survey conducted by the National Network to End Domestic Violence in a twenty-four-hour period found that domestic violence programs in the United States served nearly 65,321 victims and answered more than 23,045 crisis calls in just that one day.[4]

---

[1] *Statistics*, Nat'l Coal. Against Domestic Violence, https://ncadv.org/statistics (last visited Apr. 22, 2018).

[2] Michele C. Black et al., Nat'l Ctr. for Injury Prevention & Control, National Intimate Partner and Sexual Violence Survey: 2010 Summary Report (Nov. 2011), *available at* https://www.cdc.gov/violenceprevention/pdf/nisvs_executive_summary-a.pdf.

[3] *Id.* Severe physical violence can refer to being hit with a fist or a hard object, beaten, or slammed against something. *Id.*

[4] *Frequently Asked Questions about Domestic Violence*, Nat'l Network to End Domestic Violence, https://nnedv.org/content/frequently-asked-questions-about-domestic-violence/ (last visited Apr. 22, 2018).

What is Domestic Violence?

This handbook uses the term "domestic violence" to encompass domestic violence, sexual assault, stalking, and dating violence.[5] While sexual violence and stalking can be committed by someone other than a partner, this book focuses primarily on intimate partner violence (IPV).

Domestic violence: Physical abuse, alone or in combination with sexual, economic or emotional abuse, stalking, or other forms of coercive control, by an intimate partner or household member, often for the purpose of establishing and maintaining power and control over the victim.

Sexual assault: Any type of non-consensual touching or sexual penetration, however slight. Sexual assault may be perpetrated by an intimate partner (including a spouse), a non-intimate person known to the victim, or a stranger.

Stalking: A course of conduct directed at a specific person that would cause a reasonable person to experience fear.

Dating violence: Physical abuse, alone or in combination with sexual, economic or emotional abuse, stalking, or other forms of coercive control, by a person who is or has been in a romantic or intimate relationship with the victim, often for the purpose of establishing and maintaining power and control over the victim.

The prevalence and frequency at which domestic violence is perpetrated in the United States every day results in the high likelihood that a client walking into an attorney's office will be either a victim of domestic violence or an abuser.

Lawyers may believe domestic violence is only relevant in family law, order of protection, and criminal law cases. This is far from true. Domestic violence intersects with many different areas of law, as described throughout this handbook. Throughout these areas of law, there may be relief available only to victims. Civil attorneys should, as a matter of habit, screen their clients for domestic violence and recognize the ways that the domestic violence may impact their cases.[6] By not understanding the implications domestic violence has on a victim's case, a lawyer runs the risk of violating professional and ethical

---

[5] These definitions are from A.B.A. Comm'n on Domestic & Sexual Violence, Standards of Practice for Lawyers Representing Victims of Domestic Violence, Sexual Assault and Stalking in Civil Protection Order Cases 1 (2007) [hereinafter Standards of Practice].

[6] See section III in this chapter (Screening for Domestic Violence).

obligations.[7] An attorney may also miss the opportunity to increase the safety of a client and the client's children.[8]

II. How to Use this Handbook

This book is not meant to be a treatise or instruction book on how to handle cases in an area of law; rather, this book is intended to be an issue-spotting aid for civil attorneys.

Civil attorneys who regularly represent victims of domestic violence may recognize that their clients have legal issues in other areas of law in which they do not normally practice. Civil attorneys who do not regularly represent victims of domestic violence may not understand how legal problems that arise in their area of practice could have a disparate impact on victims. This book is meant to help all civil attorneys recognize the various legal issues victims may encounter, and introduce the different forms of relief victims may seek through both the civil and criminal court systems. If an attorney does not have expertise to represent a client in the area of law, the attorney should make appropriate referrals to other legal and nonlegal resources.[9]

It is important for readers to be aware of changes in the law. The law is not static; it evolves as laws are created or revised, new precedents are set, and different administrations prioritize one thing over another. Therefore, the information in this book, including the weblinks and resources, may have changed since publication and no longer be current. Readers should also understand that laws may have different application and enforcement in different parts of the country, and be cognizant of other factors unique to their own jurisdiction.

---

[7] "Failure to recognize when a client or opposing party is or has been abused by a partner and failure to consider abuse in making strategic decisions are forms of legal malpractice." Margaret Drew, *Lawyer Malpractice and Domestic Violence: Are We Revictimizing Our Clients?*, 39 Fam. L.Q. 7 (2005). ABA Model Rule of Professional Conduct 1.1 requires attorneys to "provide competent representation to a client. Competent representation requires the legal knowledge, skill, thoroughness and preparation reasonably necessary for the representation." Model Rules of Prof'l Conduct r. 1.1 (Am. Bar Ass'n 2017). ABA Model Rule of Professional Conduct 1.6 states: "A lawyer may reveal information relating to the representation of a client to the extent the lawyer reasonably believes necessary to prevent reasonably certain death or substantial bodily harm." Model Rules of Prof'l Conduct r. 1.6 (Am. Bar Ass'n 2017). For a more in-depth discussion of the ABA model rules of professional conduct as they relate to domestic violence, see *Ethical Issues in Domestic Violence Law* in Section One of this manual.

[8] When representing a victim, the safety of the client and the client's children is paramount when considering case strategies and looking forward to possible case outcomes.

[9] For examples of legal and non-legal resources, see A.B.A. Comm'n on Domestic & Sexual Violence, *Client Counseling, Intake, and Referral, in* The Domestic Violence Civil Law Manual: Protection Orders and Family Law Cases (4th ed. 2017).

Readers will find advocacy tips scattered throughout the chapters of this handbook. These advocacy tips are aimed to be helpful for non-experts in each area of law. Again, this book is not intended for attorneys to handle cases in other areas of law themselves. Its purpose is to make civil attorneys aware of the legal issues that may affect their clients, and make appropriate referrals to legal and non-legal resources.

Each chapter in this handbook ends with an appendix, which may contain resources, referrals, rules, sample forms, and screening questions.

Definition of Terms[10]

Victim: A person who has been subjected to domestic violence, sexual assault, and/or stalking. We use the term "victim" throughout this handbook. Other terms used to describe a victim may include "survivor" or "client."

Abuser: A person who commits an act of domestic violence, sexual assault, and/or stalking against a victim. We use the term "abuser" throughout this book. Other terms used to describe an abuser may include "offender," "batterer," or "perpetrator."

Order of Protection: A civil court order, enforceable by law enforcement, intended to protect a victim and to stop the violent, dangerous, and/or harassing behavior of an abuser. An order of protection, if violated, can subject the abuser to criminal prosecution. We use the term "order of protection" throughout this book. Other terms used to describe an order of protection may include "civil protection order," "restraining order," or "protective order." However, in some jurisdictions these terms may have a distinct meaning and usage, and may not be enforceable by law enforcement.

III. Working with Victims of Domestic Violence

A. Screening for Domestic Violence

Given the prevalence of domestic violence and potential consequences on a client's case, all attorneys, regardless of their areas of practice, should screen their clients for domestic violence. Unless a client visits a lawyer for a domestic violence problem specifically, the topic may not come up without the attorney asking. This may be awkward and uncomfortable for a lawyer who does not normally practice domestic violence or family law. However, screening for domestic violence ensures that the representation of the client remains ethical

---

[10] These definitions are from STANDARDS OF PRACTICE, *supra* note 5.

and effective. Victims may have access to additional forms of relief and remedies that would not be available otherwise. Attorneys representing victims will also need to decide on case strategies that will best ensure the safety of the client. For these reasons, it is imperative that attorneys incorporate questions that identify domestic violence into their standard intakes.

The attorney should interview the client alone, and the attorney may inform the client that these questions are asked of all clients during the initial intake.[11] During the initial meeting, it is important that the lawyer advise the client of the lawyer's duty of confidentiality, in part because the abuser may have warned the victim not to disclose the domestic violence. If a client wishes to meet with the lawyer with another party present (a friend, a family member, the client's partner, or even the abuser), the lawyer should advise the client about the consequences of waiving the attorney-client privilege.[12]

Sample Screening Questions[13]

- Who makes decisions in your house? Are you comfortable with that arrangement?

- When you are with your partner, do you sometimes feel as if:
  - You are not safe?
  - You have to watch what you do and say?
  - Your relationship constantly has emotional highs and lows – but things are never just okay?

- Has your partner ever:
  - Told you where to go or what not to say?
  - Told you what to wear or what not to wear?
  - Told you how you could spend money or has withheld money from you?
  - Gotten in the way of you receiving medical care?
  - Prevented you from spending time with friends or family?
  - Spied on you, or accessed your email or cell phone without permission?

---

[11] These sample screening questions are from A.B.A. Comm'n on Domestic & Sexual Violence, Tool for Attorneys to Screen for Domestic Violence (2005), *available at* https://www.americanbar.org/content/dam/aba/administrative/domestic_violence1/20110419_cdv_screeningtool.authcheckdam.pdf.

[12] "A lawyer shall not reveal information relating to the representation of a client unless the client gives informed consent." Model Rules of Prof'l Conduct r. 1.6 (Am. Bar Ass'n 2017).

[13] Tool for Attorneys to Screen for Domestic Violence, *supra* note 11. For a more extensive discussion of client screening, including general screening techniques, see *Client Counseling, Intake, and Referral, supra* note 9.

- Has your partner ever:
  - Threatened you physically?
  - Pushed, hit, or held you down?
  - Taken the children without permission, threatened to never let them see you again, or otherwise harmed them?
  - Harmed your pets, destroyed your clothing, objects in your home or something you especially cared about?
  - Threatened to harm themselves if you break up with them?
  - Threatened to report you to an authority, such as immigration?
  - Refused to have safer sex or forced you to have sex against your will?

Victims of domestic violence may not want to disclose the abuse to their attorney for many reasons, including shame and embarrassment, social or cultural stigmas, fear that the abuser will find out about the disclosure, or a desire to protect the abuser. Immigrant victims without legal status, and victims with criminal records may also have reasons to not want to come forward.[14] Though attorneys should be diligent in screening for domestic violence, they should not pressure clients into disclosing or talking about domestic violence. Pressuring a client could endanger the client's safety and be a detriment to the attorney-client relationship. The attorney should inform the client that if there is domestic violence present, it is important for the attorney to know, as it may change the available remedies, and ultimate outcome of the case. The attorney should ensure the client that this topic may be revisited in the future if the client wishes.

---

[14] For more information on working with immigrant victims, see *Immigration Law and Domestic Violence* in Section Two of this manual. For more information on the immigration consequences of domestic violence, see *Immigration Consequences of Domestic Violence* in Section Two of this manual. For more information on the intersection of civil and criminal law in the domestic violence context, see *Domestic Violence: The Intersection of Criminal Law and Civil Law* in Section Eight of this manual.

If the Client Discloses Domestic Violence[15]	If the Client Identifies as an Abuser
• Do not attempt to provide your client with counseling, or tell them what you would do in their situation. • Provide information about resources in the community that may be helpful to your client, like a domestic violence helpline number; legal services; or local shelter. • Provide information about national resources to your client.[16] • Alert your client that violence—including the risk of death—escalates when a victim leaves an abusive relationship, and that the abuser may view the victim seeking legal help as a threat to their sense of power and control. • Impress upon your client the importance of safety planning.[17]	• Make sure that the abuser understands the legal system, and has realistic expectations of what will likely take place in the case. • Advise the abuser to discontinue any abusive behavior.[18] • Provide information about resources in the community available to abusers that will best meet their needs. Ideally, these programs should be recommended or endorsed by the local victim advocacy community and/or court. Speak with your client about the legal consequences of domestic violence, including information on federal firearms laws.[19] • Understand your ethical obligations. Provide your client with competent and effective representation, while considering the victim's safety.

---

[15] These points are from TOOL FOR ATTORNEYS TO SCREEN FOR DOMESTIC VIOLENCE, *supra* note 11.

[16] *See, e.g.,* THE NAT'L DOMESTIC VIOLENCE HOTLINE, http://www.thehotline.org/ (last visited Apr. 24, 2018); THE NAT'L SEXUAL ASSAULT HOTLINE, https://www.rainn.org/ (last visited Apr. 24, 2018).

[17] Safety planning is critical for clients who have been abused in the past or are still residing with their abusers. You or the client can contact the local domestic violence agency for resources related to remaining safe in the home, at work, or online. For more information on safety planning, see *Client Counseling, Intake, and Referral, supra* note 9.

[18] Remind your client of the negative impact domestic violence has on children in the household. For more information about the impact of domestic violence on children, see *Child Welfare and Domestic Violence* in Section Two of this manual.

[19] For more information on the connection between guns and domestic violence, see *Domestic Violence and Firearms* in Section One of this manual.

B. Communicating with Victims of Domestic Violence

Attorneys may encounter numerous difficulties when communicating and working with victims. It is not uncommon for victims to misremember or forget the details of incidents of domestic violence, an outcome of trauma that may make a victim appear less credible. Victims of trauma present a range of behaviors, from little emotional expression, to anger and defensiveness, to strong emotional reactions and the appearance of overreaction. Clients may also recant or return to a relationship with the abuser one or more times.[20] It is important for attorneys to educate themselves on the effects of trauma on victims, and what they can do to accommodate and meet their clients' needs.

You should be conscious of the verbal and nonverbal messages you convey when communicating with your clients.[21] When speaking, attorneys should be careful to avoid victim-blaming language in favor of language that holds perpetrators responsible for their actions. Attorneys should practice communication skills that assure clients that they are listened to and understood. These skills include active listening, asking open ended questions, and responding to and paraphrasing when appropriate.[22]

In addition, attorneys should be careful to set boundaries with their clients. This is beneficial for both the attorney and the client. From the outset, you should let your client know your professional limits and office policies (for example, you will respond to phone calls and emails within 48 hours), as well as your expectations of the client. In both your spoken and written communications, you should convey to the client the parameters of your representation and your role.

---

[20] On average, it takes a victim seven times to leave an abuser. *50 Obstacles to Leaving: 1-10*, THE NAT'L DOMESTIC VIOLENCE HOTLINE (June 10, 2013), http://www.thehotline.org/2013/06/10/50-obstacles-to-leaving-1-10/. Victims face many obstacles to leaving, including threats made by the abuser, cultural/religious reasons, the abuser controlling the household finances, the victim and abuser having children together, or the victim being elderly or having a disability. *Id.* "Leaving is often the most dangerous time for a victim of abuse, because abuse is about power and control." *"Why Don't They Just Leave?"*, THE NAT'L DOMESTIC VIOLENCE HOTLINE, http://www.thehotline.org/is-this-abuse/why-do-people-stay-in-abusive-relationships/ (last visited Apr. 23, 2018).

[21] U.S. DEP'T OF JUST. OFF. FOR VICTIMS OF CRIME, GAINING INSIGHT, TAKING ACTION: BASIC SKILLS FOR SERVING VICTIMS 9 (2005), *available at* https://ovc.gov/publications/infores/pdftxt/GainingInsight.pdf.

[22] *Id.*

Safely Communicating with Your Client[23]

- Find out the safest way to contact your client and the names of other individuals who will know how to reach them.

- Ask for your client when you call and speak only to your client about the case. Do not leave messages with other family members or on an answering machine or voicemail unless your client has told you this is safe.

- If questioned by family members or even the abuser, do not indicate that you are a lawyer; rather, give an innocuous reason for the call, such as selling a service.

- Avoid leaving your last name if you do leave a message.

- Always ask your client first if it is safe to talk. The abuser may be present, even if the abuser no longer lives with your client. Develop a system of coded messages to signal danger or the abuser's presence, or if you should call the police.

- Block identification of your number when calling your client.

- If your client fails to respond to your calls, make extensive (but confidential) efforts to confirm that your client is safe.

Attorneys should keep in mind that victims of domestic violence are not monolithic. Victims come from every racial, ethnic, and religious community; they are immigrants, persons with disabilities, persons with limited English proficiency, and members of the LGBTQ community. Attorneys may face unique challenges as they try to meet the needs of diverse victims, and this handbook attempts to address these considerations within the different legal topics.[24]

C. Attorney Safety and Self-Care

When representing a domestic violence victim, it is important to consider your own safety, as well as the importance of practicing self-care. Victims may refer to their abusers as having a "Dr. Jekyll and Mr. Hyde" personality; while an abuser may appear to be polite and well behaved, an abuser might become angry and violent without warning. Attorneys may also receive threats from their own clients

---

[23] These points are from TOOL FOR ATTORNEYS TO SCREEN FOR DOMESTIC VIOLENCE, *supra* note 11

[24] For a more extensive examination of unique considerations when working with marginalized victims, including teenaged victims, clients with disabilities, immigrant victims, clients who use interpreters, and LGBTQ victims, see *Client Counseling, Intake, and Referral, supra* note 9.

or third parties related to a case. It is therefore important for all attorneys to develop and implement policies to keep themselves and their offices safe. Some examples include making sure that your office parking lot is well lit, implementing a policy that staff members do not exit the building alone, and securing your office's reception area by installing surveillance cameras and ensuring that people cannot enter without a key or passcode. Attorneys should also make sure that their personal information cannot be located online; they should set their social media accounts to private and consider removing photographs of themselves from the Internet.[25]

Lawyers who represent victims may experience burnout, compassion fatigue, or vicarious trauma. The effects of these can be compounded for attorneys who work in offices lacking support or resources, or for attorneys who have high caseloads.[26] When left unaddressed, burnout, compassion fatigue, or vicarious trauma can lead to sleeplessness, anxiety, depression, isolation, and general pessimism about legal work.[27] It can also lead to ethical violations by the attorney, including failure to communicate with the client or failure to represent a client with reasonable diligence and promptness.[28]

Lawyers at risk of experiencing vicarious trauma should learn to recognize the signs and take steps to address symptoms that emerge. If possible, organizational changes should be made to prevent compassion fatigue and vicarious trauma. Such changes include reducing caseloads to make them manageable, encouraging staff to regularly discuss their high-trauma cases with colleagues and supervisors in a supportive atmosphere, and developing flexible leave policies and protocols. Attorneys can also practice personal self-care outside the office setting. This can involve taking time off without checking emails and voice messages, seeking and maintaining interpersonal relationships, and getting assistance or support from other people who work in the field, or from mental health professionals.

---

[25] It is also important to put into place office policies that consider the safety of the client. For example, safeguarding files and reminding personnel to always keep client information strictly confidential. *Client Counseling, Intake, and Referral, supra* note 9.

[26] Andrew P. Levin & Scott Greisberg, *Vicarious Trauma in Attorneys,* 24 Pace L. Rev. 245, 258 (2003). A study of domestic violence and family law attorneys, and public defenders conducted by Dr. Andrew P. Levin at Pace University found that "[c]ompared with mental health professionals and social service workers, attorneys were consistently higher on both secondary trauma and burnout scales." Andrew P. Levin, *Secondary Trauma and Burnout in Attorneys: Effects of Work with Clients Who are Victims of Domestic Violence and Abuse,* A.B.A. Comm'n on Domestic Violence eNewsl. (Winter 2008), *available at* https://www.americanbar.org/newsletter/publications/cdv_enewsletter_home/expertLevin.html.

[27] A.B.A. Comm'n on Domestic & Sexual Violence, *Introduction, in* The Domestic Violence Civil Law Manual: Protection Orders and Family Law Cases (4th ed. 2017).

[28] *See* Model Rules of Prof'l Conduct r. 1.3 (Am. Bar Ass'n 2017); Model Rules of Prof'l Conduct r. 1.4 (Am. Bar Ass'n 2017).

IV. Conclusion

It is important for all attorneys who represent clients to understand domestic violence and consider its impact on their cases. Given high rates of domestic violence perpetrated in the United States, it is very likely that any given client is a victim of domestic violence or an abuser. Failure to recognize the intersections between domestic violence with other seemingly unrelated areas of law could lead to attorneys violating their professional and ethical obligations, as well as further harm to their clients.

Attorneys can start by incorporating screening questions for domestic violence into their regular intakes. Knowing that a client is a victim may enhance the lawyer's representation because it could open the door to additional legal remedies for the client and their children. Screening for domestic violence may also give an attorney the opportunity to provide referrals to other legal and non-legal resources that will enhance their client's independence and/or ability to recover.

Representing victims of domestic violence can be rewarding, but challenging. Attorneys should take special care in developing and implementing safety policies for themselves and their offices. Attorneys should also educate themselves on the signs of burnout, compassion fatigue, or vicarious trauma, and the significance of self-care. The importance of self-care cannot be overstated, and is essential to the ethical and effective representation of victims.

Domestic violence has the potential to intersect with almost every area of legal practice. The intent of this handbook is to provide attorneys with an overview of the impact of domestic violence across different fields of law, and an introduction to legal strategies that may help their clients.

APPENDIX

The **ABA Commission on Domestic & Sexual Violence** hosts a website at https://www.americanbar.org/groups/domestic_violence.html that contains information and resources including:

- Technical Assistance

- Trainings & Events (including recordings from previous trainings)

- Statutory Summary Charts

- Listservs

- Podcasts

Publications:

For more information about these publications, visit https://shop.americanbar.org or https://www.americanbar.org/groups/domestic_violence/publications.html.

- **The Domestic Violence Civil Law Manual: Protection Orders and Family Law Cases**
    - A.B.A. Comm'n on Domestic & Sexual Violence, The Domestic Violence Civil Law Manual: Protection Orders and Family Law Cases (4th ed. 2017).

- **Standards of Practice for Lawyers Representing Victims of Domestic Violence, Sexual Assault and Stalking in Civil Protection Order Cases**
    - A.B.A. Comm'n on Domestic & Sexual Violence, Standards of Practice for Lawyers Representing Victims of Domestic Violence, Sexual Assault and Stalking in Civil Protection Order Cases (2007).

- **Comprehensive Issue Spotting: A Tool for Civil Attorneys Representing Victims of Domestic & Dating Violence, Sexual Assault & Stalking (2008).**
    - A.B.A. Comm'n on Domestic & Sexual Violence, Comprehensive Issue Spotting: A Tool for Civil Attorneys Representing Victims of Domestic & Dating Violence, Sexual Assault & Stalking (2008).

- **Tool for Attorneys Working with Lesbian, Gay, Bisexual, and Transgender (LGBT) Survivors of Domestic Violence**

- **What Rights Do I Have as an LGBT Victim of Domestic Violence?**

- **Tool for Attorneys to Screen for Domestic Violence**

- **Litigating for Deaf Clients**

- **Use of Electronic Evidence in Domestic Violence Litigation**

- **Confidentiality Tools for Attorneys**

ABA Model Rules of Professional Conduct:

MODEL RULES OF PROF'L CONDUCT (AM. BAR ASS'N 2017).

- https://www.americanbar.org/groups/professional_responsibility/publications/model_rules_of_professional_conduct/model_rules_of_professional_conduct_table_of_contents.html

Chapter Two:
Domestic Violence and Firearms:
A Lethal Connection

I. Introduction

Research is abundant and clear on the tragedy of firearms violence in domestic violence cases: actual use or threats to use firearms violence to exert coercive control over their intimate partners constitute one the most dangerous forms of control that abusers may employ.[1] An abuser's mere access to a firearm increases the risk of intimate partner homicide of women by five times.[2] And women are most often the victims of firearms violence; they are killed by intimate partners at twice the rate of men, making up approximately 70 percent of all intimate partner homicide victims.[3] Firearms play a devastating role in the high death rates of victims of domestic violence. A study published in the Journal of American Medical Association found domestic violence assaults involving a firearm were 12 times more likely to result in death than assaults with any other weapon or bodily force alone.[4]

---

[1] Evan Stark, *Re-presenting Battered Women: Coercive Control and the Defense of Liberty,* Violence Against Women: Complex Realities and New Issues in a Changing World (2012), *available at* http://www.stopvaw.org/uploads/evan_stark_article_final_100812.pdf; Susan B. Sorenson & Douglas J. Weibe, *Weapons in the Lives of Battered Women,* 94(8) Am. J. Pub. Health 1412 (Aug. 2004), *available at* https://www.ncbi.nlm.nih.gov/pmc/articles/PMC1448464/.

[2] Jacqueline C. Campbell et al., *Risk Factors for Femicide in Abusive Relationships: Results from a Multisite Case Control Study,* 93 Am. J. of Pub. Health 1089, 1092 (July 2003).

[3] Shannon Catalano et al., *Female Victims of Violence,* U.S. Dep't of Just. (Sept. 2009), *available at* https://www.bjs.gov/content/pub/pdf/fvv.pdf (last updated Oct. 23, 2009).

[4] Linda E. Saltzman et al., *Weapon Involvement and Injury Outcomes in Family and Intimate Assaults,* 267(22) J. Am. Med. Ass'n 3043 (1992).

In addition, not all incidents of firearms violence result in death. In fact, most abusers use firearms to make threats in order to control victims' behavior. A 2016 meta-analysis of research literature found that approximately 4.5 million American women alive today have been threatened by abusers with firearms; of those, one million had either been shot or shot at by their abusers.[5]

This chapter will discuss federal laws meant to limit abusers' access to firearms, and the role of lawyers in protecting the victimized partner from further abuse in order of protection and family law proceedings.

II. Federal Firearms Laws Regarding Firearms and Domestic Violence

A. The Federal Background Check System and Domestic Violence

The Brady Handgun Violence Prevention Act (Brady Act) was passed into law in 1993, authorizing the creation of a national system for conducting background checks on persons trying to purchase firearms.[6] The Brady Act created "prohibitors," which are conditions that block persons from purchasing firearms or ammunition from a federally licensed firearms dealer.[7]

---

[5]   Susan B. Sorenson & Rebecca A. Schut, *Nonfatal Gun Use in Intimate Partner Violence: A Systematic Review of the Literature*, TRAUMA, VIOLENCE, & ABUSE (Sept. 14, 2016).

[6]   Brady Handgun Violence Prevention Act, Pub. L. No. 103-159, 107 Stat. 1536 (1993).

[7]   18 U.S.C. § 922(g) (2011).

Brady Prohibitors

Who is prohibited from possessing or transferring firearms or ammunition under federal law? 18 U.S.C. § 922(g)

(1) Any person convicted in any court of a felony;

(2) Any person who is a fugitive from justice, having an open warrant against them;

(3) Any person who uses controlled substances (as defined at 21 U.S.C. § 802) illegally or is addicted to controlled substances;

(4) Any person who has been adjudicated as a "mental defective" or has been involuntarily committed by a court of law (generally found to be "a danger to self or others" or someone whose threats or acts of severe violence are related to mental health issues);

(5) Any person who is an undocumented immigrant in the U.S., or who is in the U.S. on a non-immigrant visa;

(6) Any person who has been dishonorably discharged from the military;

(7) Any person who has renounced their citizenship;

(8) Any person subject to a final protection order, so long as

    a. The person was provided full due process (mutual orders do not qualify);

    b. The order restrains such person from harassing, stalking, or threatening an intimate partner or the intimate partner's child(ren) or engaging in other conduct that would place an intimate partner in reasonable fear of bodily injury to the intimate partner or child; AND

    c. The order

        i. Includes a finding that such person represents a credible threat to the physical safety of the intimate partner or child; OR

        ii. The terms of the order explicitly prohibit the use, attempted use, or threatened use of physical force against the intimate partner or child that would reasonably be expected to cause bodily injury;

(9) Any person convicted in any court of a misdemeanor crime of domestic violence.

In domestic violence cases, the (g)(8) and (g)(9) prohibitors are most likely to cause a domestic violence offender to fail a background check, though other prohibitors may apply, depending on the facts of the case. The 18 U.S.C. § 922(g)(8) or "protection order prohibition" passed into law in the 1994 Violence Against Women Act (VAWA).[8] Two years later, Congress created 18 U.S.C. § 922(g)(9) to prohibit persons convicted of qualifying misdemeanor crimes of domestic violence (MCDV prohibition) from access to firearms or ammunition.[9]

The U.S. Attorney General established the National Instant Criminal Background Check System (NICS) within the Federal Bureau of Investigation (FBI) to implement these prohibitions. Any federally licensed firearms dealer may contact the FBI to obtain information on whether the sale, transfer, or return of a firearm to a particular person would violate federal gun prohibitions.[10] A federally licensed firearms dealer must submit the name and other information related to the person seeking to purchase a firearm or ammunition to NICS, at which point FBI personnel will search certain state-generated and federal databases to ascertain whether the person seeking to purchase the firearm or ammunition is subject to any of the prohibitors under federal law.

---

[8] Pub. L. 103-322, 108 Stat. 1796 (1994).

[9] Pub. L. 104-208, 110 Stat. 3009 (1996).

[10] FBI Services: National Instant Criminal Background Check System, https://www.fbi.gov/services/cjis/nics (last visited Apr. 16, 2018).

How does NICS work to keep firearms out of the hands of domestic violence offenders?

The FBI runs the databases that inform the background check system. For the system to work, states and the military must enter order of protection records and records documenting misdemeanor crimes of domestic violence into three federal databases:

National Crime Information Center (NCIC)

NCIC consists of 21 different databases containing information used by law enforcement. The following 3 contain information necessary to conduct a background check regarding the order of protection prohibition and the MCDV prohibition:

- The **Protection Order File (NCIC POF)** contains records identifying persons currently subject to protection orders.

- **Interstate Identification Index (Triple I)**
  Law enforcement agencies across the country depend on the state-generated criminal history records that go into Triple I. Records indicating a domestic violence offender has been convicted of a misdemeanor crime of domestic violence (or a misdemeanor crime involving physical force against an intimate partner) will be found in this database.

- **National Instant Criminal Background Check System Denied Transaction File (NICS, pronounced "nix")**
  As the name of the file indicates, records of denied firearms transactions are stored here.

While state courts have the authority to issue domestic violence orders of protection and convict domestic violence offenders of domestic violence misdemeanors (the predicate actions triggering the federal firearms prohibitions relating to domestic violence), state courts have no responsibility or authority under VAWA or any other federal law to enforce 18 U.S.C. § 922(g)(8) or (9). That rests with federal actors. Three federal agencies are involved in implementing and enforcing the federal firearms prohibitions relating to domestic violence offenders:

- **Bureau of Alcohol, Tobacco and Firearms (ATF)** agents are responsible for investigating potential violations of federal firearms laws; they are also responsible for searching for illegally possessed firearms and ammunition, as well as seizing them from prohibited persons.

- **Federal Bureau of Investigation (FBI)** personnel implement the federal background check system (NICS) and determine whether records searched indicate that a person is prohibited from possessing or purchasing a firearm or ammunition.

- **U.S. Attorneys** may prosecute persons who are in violation of federal firearms prohibitions.

Advocacy Tip: The combination of federal and state responses to firearms violence directed at intimate partners is the ideal way to relieve the terror of victims enduring firearms violence at the hands of their abusers. Yet a combined approach is not always the answer. There are times when a local response is better. Local law enforcement officers are more readily available to deal with emergency situations than ATF agents. But in other cases, federal agents may be better equipped to remove an abuser's terrifyingly large arsenal of weapons and ammunition. Where a state's laws regarding firearms and domestic violence are weak, a federal investigation and prosecution may result in a tougher sentence, giving the victim many more years of safety than local law would allow.

There are very clear limits to relying regularly on a federal response, not the least of which is the federal government's limited capacity to address all cases:

- There are not enough ATF agents to investigate every domestic violence offender who is in violation of federal law.

- There are not enough U.S. Attorneys available to prosecute all the cases that should properly be addressed.

- NICS has incomplete data because states are not able to upload required data from court records in real time.

- Domestic violence abusers can circumvent the federal background check system by purchasing firearms and ammunition at gun shows, through private sales or transfers between family members, or obtaining a firearm or ammunition via the internet.

B. The Role of the Civil Lawyer

The federal background check system relies on information generated by the state courts. As a civil lawyer litigating on behalf of the victim, you have an important role in advocating that the court enters the required information when issuing an order of protection. This will ensure that the FBI has the information needed to determine if the abuser is prohibited from possessing, purchasing, selling, or transferring firearms or ammunition under the federal firearms laws.

Although the federal firearms statute does not use the actual word "qualifying" in its description of conditions triggering the federal prohibitors, federal agencies charged with implementing the federal firearms laws use the word "qualifying" as a term of art to refer to the requisite provisions in protection orders that meet the requirements laid out in the statute.[11] Much of the information that the FBI relies on to determine whether an order of protection is "qualifying" should be contained in the four corners of the order of protection:

---

(1) The court must provide information on the order of protection or in the court record showing that the abuser had notice and an opportunity to be heard in a full hearing prior to the issuance of the order of protection.

Note: An order of protection issued after a default proceeding may still trigger the order of protection prohibition, so long as there is a record that the abuser was given notice of the scheduled hearing and subsequent to the hearing was served with the final order, even if the abuser failed to appear at the hearing.

Exceptions: The federal protection order prohibition does not apply to *ex parte* (temporary) orders of protection or mutual orders of protection, because they do not meet the due process requirements in the statute.

---

[11] The ATF has produced a helpful resource outlining these requirements. Bureau of Alcohol, Tobacco, Firearms & Explosives, *Protection Orders and Federal Firearms Prohibitions*, available at http://www.pcadv.org/Resources/atf-i-3310-2.pdf (last updated Sept. 2011).

(2) The court must make the following findings, or include the following prohibitions, on conduct in the order of protection related to the abuser's violent acts:

✔ One from Column A	✔ One from Column B
Ordered to refrain from: • Harassing, stalking, or threatening an intimate partner or the intimate partner's child, **Or** *Ordered to refrain from:* • Engaging in other conduct that would place an intimate partner in reasonable fear of bodily injury to the victim or the child.	*Finding of credible threat:* • To the physical safety of victim or their child, **Or** *Express prohibition on conduct:* • Order must prohibit use, attempted use, or threatened use of physical force against the victim or their child that would reasonably be expected to cause bodily injury.

(3) Orders of protection must state a qualifying relationship between the offender and victim.

To implement the protection order prohibition, the FBI looks at court-issued documents to identify if one of the following relationships required under federal law exists between the parties:
- current or former spouse
- cohabitant or former cohabitant
- the protected party has a child in common with the abuser
- the protected party is a child of either the victim or the abuser

(4) Other information that can be included in an order of protection that will help the FBI conduct a background check and help the ATF respond to a report that the abuser possesses or tried to purchase firearms in violation of federal firearms laws:
- The full name (including middle name) of the person subject to the protection order;
- A unique numeric identifier, such as a Social Security number or date of birth;
- A listing of firearms that the court has determined are owned or in the possession of the person subject to the protection order.

If all of the requirements outlined above are met, it is likely that the abuser's access to firearms will be limited for the duration of the order, because any attempt to possess or purchase a firearm or ammunition during that period will probably constitute a violation of federal law. Again, it is the role of the FBI to determine whether the order of protection contains the requisite elements to trigger the federal protection order prohibition.

Advocacy Tip: Most states, the military, and the tribes enter very few orders of protection or MCDV records into the NCIC files; therefore, many domestic violence offenders who might otherwise fail a background check are able to purchase firearms and ammunition. As a result, in very dangerous domestic violence cases involving firearms, it becomes very important that the lawyer representing the victim contact the Bureau of Alcohol, Tobacco and Firearms (ATF) on their tip line, to request assistance (1-800-ATF-GUNS (800-283-4867)).

III. Limiting Adjudicated Abusers' Access to Firearms for the Duration of the Order of Protection

The federal protection order prohibition is not the only way to limit abusers' access to firearms. There are many options under state law that are useful. The first place to begin is by talking with the victim about the victim's concerns regarding the abuser's access to firearms.

A. Discussing Firearms Remedies and Protections with the Victim

Whether you are representing a victim in a family law case or an order of protection case, once the victim has disclosed information relating to the abuser's threats and acts of firearms violence, you should discuss the various legal options that are available. Remember that a remedy you may think will make the victim safer may seem dangerous to the victim. The victim knows best how the abuser is likely to act, and how the abuser will respond to certain legal actions. It is important to offer the victim options and listen to the victim's reaction to those options.

Discuss the following with the victim:

- Is the victim afraid that the abuser may coerce, threaten, or harm the victim, the children, or family pets with a firearm?
  - Ask the victim to describe the incidents involving firearms threats or violence.
  - Ask the victim if there is any imminent danger.
  - Ask the victim what kinds of firearm(s) the abuser used.
    - Is the victim able to identify the firearm(s) by type of weapon (handgun, rifle, semiautomatic weapon) or make (i.e., Glock or Bushmaster)?
    - Does the victim know how many firearms the abuser has?
    - Does the abuser have friends or family who have given the abuser access to firearms in the past?

- Is the victim comfortable asking the court to order the abuser to surrender firearms to local law enforcement or a trusted third party?
  - If not, what is the victim concerned about?
  - Is there any way to do this that would make the victim feel safe?

- Is the victim comfortable asking the court to monitor the abuser after the surrender of the firearms to ensure that the abuser has not accessed additional firearms?
  - Is it better to have the court require the abuser to appear before the court to self-report compliance?
  - Is it better for law enforcement to come to the victim's home to check in with the victim?
  - Does the victim have any questions or concerns about safety issues if any of the above actions take place?

- What if the abuser threatens the victim with retaliation because of the removal of the firearms?
  - What are the victim's concerns?
  - Would it be better to respond to the retaliation through the legal system?
  - Would it be better to connect the victim with a shelter or identify another safe place to stay (family or friend) if retaliation is a concern?

- Is the abuser likely to go out and replace the firearms immediately, even if the abuser relinquishes the firearms or has them removed from the abuser's possession?
  - If so, would it be better to leave things as they are?
  - Would the victim like to connect with a local domestic violence victim services program to do safety planning if it is best to leave the abuser in continued possession of the firearms?

- A surprising number of victims possess their own firearms or wish to purchase a firearm for safety at the time when the victim is filing for an order of protection or contemplating living independently from the abuser. This is especially common where victims feel isolated and unable or unwilling to call law enforcement for help. You should be prepared to talk to the victim about the following:
  - Does the victim legally possess the firearm (has all required permits; passed a background check where required; knows that the firearm is not stolen or otherwise contraband)?
  - Does the victim know how to use the firearm?
    - Has the victim grown up using firearms and is familiar with using them?
    - If not, does the victim intend to obtain training in using firearms?
    - In either case, does the victim intend to regularly train/practice with the firearm, in order to be as proficient and as comfortable as possible using it in self-defense?

- Many victims will dismiss the idea of training/practice as unnecessary. Be prepared to help the victim understand why proficiency with firearms is so critically important and then help the victim identify good firearms training programs and practice ranges.

  ◦ How does the victim store the firearm?
    - Is it locked up away from the abuser and/or the children?
    - If not, why does the victim feel it must be readily available, and what alternative safeguards are in place to prevent the abuser or the children from getting access to the firearm before the victim does?

  ◦ Remind the victim that it is very easy for the abuser to take the firearm away from the victim and that it may be more dangerous to have an accessible firearm in the house than not to have one at all.

B. Discuss Possible Legal Remedies with the Victim

As the victim's attorney, you can help the victim learn about various legal remedies that the court may be able to provide to reduce the impact of firearms threats or violence. Explain these possible remedies fully, so that the victim understands what the court may order and what law enforcement can do.

Help the victim consider what to ask the court to do in either an order of protection or in a *pendente lite* order in a divorce or separation case, related to the firearms violence. For example, the court may:

- Order the abuser to identify any firearms that the abuser possesses or has easy access to (including firearms held by family or friends on behalf of the abuser) for the purpose of knowing the types and numbers of weapons the abuser must relinquish.

- Order the abuser to relinquish any firearms or ammunition in the abuser's possession to local law enforcement or to a safe third party within 24 to 48 hours.

- Order local law enforcement to enter abuser's residence and search for and seize any firearms or ammunition within.

- Order local law enforcement or third parties to accept the responsibility of storing the firearms in a way that keeps the abuser from accessing them.

- Order the abuser to refrain from attempting to possess, borrow, purchase, or otherwise gain access to any firearms or ammunition for the duration of the order.

- Tell the abuser the following and include it in writing in the order of protection or *pendente lite* order:

- ◦ "As a result of this order, it may be unlawful for you to possess or purchase a firearm, including a handgun or long gun, or ammunition, pursuant to federal law under 18 U.S.C. § 922(g)(8) [and state law]. If you have any questions whether these laws make it illegal for you to possess or purchase a firearm, you should consult a lawyer."

- Schedule a compliance review hearing within three to seven days, to ensure that the abuser has relinquished all firearms as required by the order of protection or *pendente lite* order.

- Order local law enforcement to conduct a safety check with victim three days after the seizure of any firearms or ammunition to ensure abuser has not engaged in any further threats or acts of firearms violence, and to ensure that abuser has not obtained additional firearms or ammunition.

- Prohibit the abuser from possessing, purchasing, transferring, or using in any other manner firearms or ammunition.

- Prohibit the abuser from accessing or using any firearms owned or possessed by third parties, including the abuser's family.

- Prohibit the abuser from asking others to share or obtain firearms on the abuser's behalf.

- Prohibit the abuser from using, possessing, or carrying firearms around the victim, children, or other vulnerable family members.

Advocacy Tip: In jurisdictions that severely limit the general public's possession of firearms or that require a permit or license to possess or carry a firearm, the abuser may refuse to answer questions about possessing firearms, in order to avoid charges of possessing a firearm illegally. In those cases, it can be helpful to talk with the victim before the hearing, to identify firearms that the victim knows are in the abuser's possession. The victim's attorney can provide this list to the court during the order of protection hearing, provided the victim feels that it is safe to do so.

Advocacy Tip: It is not uncommon for the abuser to fail to relinquish firearms voluntarily once the court hearing is concluded, so it is important that the order of protection contain a provision ordering or authorizing local law enforcement to remove firearms and/or ammunition from the abuser's possession if the abuser does not voluntarily relinquish the firearms within a set time period, such as 24 or 48 hours. And if the abuser attempts to defeat local law enforcement's attempts to remove the weapons at the end of that time period, be prepared to file a motion for contempt or to sanction the abuser for failing to relinquish the firearms. It is also helpful to file a motion to compel law enforcement to go to the abuser's residence in order to search for and remove any prohibited firearms.

Advocacy Tip: If the abuser is a law enforcement officer or serves in the military, federal law makes it possible for the abuser's supervisor to give the abuser a service weapon while the abuser is on duty. That still may pose a danger to the victim so, to the extent possible, work with the court and the abuser's supervisor to have the abuser assigned to duties that do not require carrying a weapon for the duration of the order.

IV. Safety Planning with the Victim

The most important part of safety planning is listening to the victim to find out what concerns exist. The victim is the expert regarding the abuser's behavior. Listen closely to the experiences the victim relates to you regarding firearms violence, so you can start thinking about remedies to suggest. Remember that it is up to you to offer the victim options for safety, but it is up to the victim to decide whether any of the options are safe. Unless you know that the victim or the victim's children, family, or friends are in immediate danger, refrain from forcing any options on the victim, no matter how logical the response seems to you. Be sure to offer to connect the victim with a victim services program that can help the victim put together a comprehensive safety plan.

A. Possible Points of Discussion with the Victim:

- Emergency issues
  - Addressing threats/imminent danger
  - Safety of children, other family members, friends, pets

- Has the victim experienced any episodes of firearms violence or threats?
  - Verbal threats
  - Using the firearm to threaten the victim
  - Shooting the firearm at the victim, the children, family, friends or pets
  - Threatening suicide or other self-harm with the firearm

Remember that some of the abuser's threats are subtle. Actions like cleaning a gun in front of the victim or purchasing a firearm may seem benign to someone not familiar with coercive control, but to a victim, the abuser may be sending a clear and threatening message. Explore the victim's experience of firearms violence to help both you and the victim hone in on the most emergent problems and identify the immediate and long-term remedies that will be needed:

- What incidents relating to firearms have made the victim feel unsafe?

- What is the victim most concerned about regarding abuser's use of firearms violence or threats?

- Does the abuser regularly use/access firearms (target practice, hunting, going to gun shows, etc.) in a way that reminds the victim that the abuser has firearms, even if the abuser does not actually engage in direct threats?

B. Working with the Victim to Develop a Personal Safety Plan

You can help the victim identify elements of the safety plan that may be unique to the victim's particular situation. In some cases, victims may find the following helpful:

- Identifying allies, such as relatives who would be willing to hold the abuser's firearms and deny the abuser access to them.

- Rehearsing what to do in an emergency, based on the abuser's previous use of firearms violence and threats, should future incidents arise.

- Identifying when the risk of serious injury or lethality is so high the victim should call law enforcement for help.

- Identifying local victim services programs that the victim can start working with to develop a comprehensive safety plan.

- Checking in with the victim regularly to evaluate and update the personal safety plan.

- Reminding the victim that sometimes the safest response to firearms threats or acts of violence is leaving the home/living space.

- Having the victim think about sleeping in a different room, preferably one that locks, away from where the abuser usually sleeps or away from the place where the abuser stores firearms.

- Helping the victim develop a plan to quickly access the phone to call for help.

- Deciding now what resources to safely use for help in future. For example, if the victim believes it would not be safe to talk aloud during an episode of firearms threats or violence by the abuser, then identify a friend to whom the victim can text an agreed-upon code word that signals to the friend to call law enforcement. Make sure the victim knows that the National Domestic Violence Hotline has confidential texting services and can reach out to law enforcement on their behalf.[12]

- Encouraging the victim to take pictures of weapons and save them in a safe place, like outside the home or in a protected email/online space. This will help law enforcement when there is an opportunity to remove the abuser's firearms and ammunition.

- Helping the victim develop a plan for safely documenting threats or acts of firearms violence to be used as evidence later.

---

[12] Victims can reach the National Domestic Violence Hotline by texting "love" to 22522, or accessing online chat services at http://www.thehotline.org.

- Helping the victim understand what resources local law enforcement or the ATF may be able to provide and helping the victim, where appropriate, contact local law enforcement or the ATF if you believe the abuser may possess firearms in violation of federal, tribal, or state law.

APPENDIX

Resources:

Bureau of Alcohol, Tobacco and Firearms, U.S. Department of Justice

- General information about federal firearms laws and domestic violence
  - https://www.atf.gov/file/62026/download

- ATF Victim Assistant Locator
  - https://www.atf.gov/contact/victim-witness-assistance-program

- ATF hotline numbers for reporting illegal firearms activity
  - https://www.atf.gov/contact/hotlines

Giffords Law Center to Prevent Gun Violence
http://lawcenter.giffords.org/

- Domestic Violence and Guns: State by State
  - http://lawcenter.giffords.org/resources/publications/domestic-violence-and-guns-state-by-state/#states

The National Domestic Violence Hotline
http://www.thehotline.org/
1-800-799-7233 | 1-800-787-3224 (TTY)

National Resource Center on Domestic Violence and Firearms (Battered Women's Justice Project)
Caselaw, State Laws, and Research
http://www.bwjp.org/our-work/projects/firearms-project.html

WomensLaw.org
State by State Compendium of Firearms Laws
https://www.womenslaw.org/

Chapter Three:
Ethical Issues in Domestic Violence Law

I. The Impact of Domestic Violence on Attorney Ethics

There are misconceptions in our culture that inaccurately cast trauma survivors as inherently poor decision-makers. It is important for all attorneys to remember that victims of domestic violence should be provided the same level of autonomy, decision-making, confidentiality, and zealous representation as any other client. ABA Model Rule of Professional Conduct 1.2 requires all lawyers to "abide by a client's decisions concerning the objectives of representation," and "consult with the client as to the means by which they are to be pursued."[1] Ethical lawyering of victims means giving honest advice about risks and benefits, and then allowing clients to make their own decisions about which risks to take, and which benefits to pursue.

A. Client Interviewing

Proper legal advice and zealous representation begins with an openness to hearing all the relevant facts that may impact your client: the client's wants and needs; the available remedies; and the possible settlement outcomes. In your practice, consider how you will facilitate clients feeling safe to share facts about domestic violence. Many attorneys do a brief screen with every single client who walks through the door to determine whether the client has experienced domestic violence.[2] Alternatively, an attorney can inform each client whenever a history of domestic violence could be relevant to a legal claim or defense, so that the client understands the benefits of disclosing to the attorney.

---

[1] MODEL RULES OF PROF'L CONDUCT r. 1.2 (AM. BAR ASS'N 2017).

[2] For additional information about the importance of screening all clients for domestic violence, see *Introduction* in Section One of this manual.

Most laypeople do not realize there are protections available beyond criminal prosecution or orders of protection. At the very least, attorneys should ask all clients an open-ended question during the intake or client interview about whether there is anything in the client's life that might impact the client's ability to fully participate in the case, communicate with the attorney, or make settlement decisions. Because it is not always obvious to a client that an attorney will respond well to information about domestic violence, attorneys must take affirmative steps to show clients that the disclosure will be helpful, and will be handled respectfully.

Just as all attorneys train for speaking in court or writing a brief, attorneys should consciously develop their client interviewing techniques. Listening to stories of trauma with empathy, and without judgment, is a learned skill. Additionally, it is particularly important that attorneys find the right balance between non-judgmental empathy and realistic assessments of credibility and case strength. Finally, attorneys should seek training on how to manage their personal responses to hearing about violence so that they can sustain their ability to work with victims over the span of a career. If you are uncertain how to handle an interview where a client discloses domestic violence, you should consider obtaining continuing education from your local bar association or local domestic and sexual violence service provider.[3]

B. Zealous Advocacy and Trauma-Informed Representation

Zealous representation requires an understanding of the law applicable to the facts, including remedies and defenses that are specific to victims.[4] Pay attention to statutory changes that offer protections to victims, and stay informed about common law that can be used to protect or defend those protections. At the very least, be prepared to issue spot and refer clients to other legal resources when the issues stray outside of your area of expertise. You should keep in mind that "domestic and sexual violence" is not a specialty. For example, if you handle personal injury cases, then it is within your province to develop tort claims that relate to the domestic violence your client may have suffered, although you may need to refer the client to another lawyer for help with their divorce or order of protection cases.

Absent law to the contrary, attorneys are required to follow client directions rather than make decisions based on the lawyer's perceptions of "best interests"

---

[3] The National Center on Domestic Violence, Trauma & Mental Health offers excellent, practical resources to improve your ability to provide Trauma-Informed Legal Advocacy. THE NAT'L CTR. ON DOMESTIC VIOLENCE, TRAUMA & MENTAL HEALTH, *Trauma-Informed Legal Advocacy (TILA) Project,* http://www.nationalcenterdvtraumamh.org/trainingta/trauma-informed-legal-advocacy-tila-project/ (last visited Apr. 24, 2018). There are lists containing all of the state and U.S. territory bar associations and domestic violence coalitions at the end of this manual.

[4] MODEL RULES OF PROF'L CONDUCT r. 1.1 (AM. BAR ASS'N 2017).

of the client.[5] Clients are typically presumed to have capacity to instruct their attorney, unless a court has determined otherwise. If you believe that a client has diminished capacity and there is a substantial risk of harm to the client, then you may take appropriate protective actions, but you should not just substitute your own decision-making for the client's.[6]

Some clients with diminished capacity may tell you they already have a guardian; be aware that guardianship comes in many different forms. Until you review the guardianship paperwork, you will not know if the court has taken away the client's decision-making power in the specific case you are helping them with. Additionally, many people confuse guardianship with power of attorney or representative payee (neither of which takes any decision-making power away from the client). The best practice is slowing down and reading any paperwork before you decide who makes the decisions for your client, knowing that it will never be you, the lawyer, deciding for the client what should happen in a case. As you assess whether you think a client has diminished capacity or needs protective measures, be cautious: your disagreement or discomfort with the client's choices is not enough to indicate diminished capacity. Distinguish between the client who is actually unable to take in information, and the client who makes decisions different from the ones you would make.

Your practice as a whole will be well-served if you employ a client-centered approach. A client-centered approach is especially effective in meeting the needs of victims. Just because a certain action increases the chances of winning legal relief does not automatically mean that the client will agree it is a good idea. Some legal strategies can significantly increase the danger of physical or emotional harm to the client. For that reason, resist telling clients that they "have" to disclose certain information if you mean that it is strategically helpful to disclose it.

If a client would be legally required to share certain information as part of a case, a client may prefer not to proceed with the case. If a client seems uncomfortable with proceeding with the case, you should discuss that option openly and without judgment. Choose language that truthfully communicates the options (and the risks), and ask open-ended questions designed to find out the client's informed choices. Often, if you ask the client, "What are you worried will happen?", you will be able to offer your client better information, or discover the client has a very good reason for being hesitant.

When a client approves certain legal strategies, lawyers should be alert to safety concerns that can arise in connection with case-related activities.

---

[5] MODEL RULES OF PROF'L CONDUCT r. 1.2 (AM. BAR ASS'N 2017).

[6] MODEL RULES OF PROF'L CONDUCT r. 1.14 cmt. (AM. BAR ASS'N 2017) (client with diminished capacity rule and comment). Consult and follow your local ethical rule about taking protective measures for a client with such diminished capacity.

For instance, service of process, settlement negotiations, or enforcement of orders can trigger new violence by an abuser. Filing of pleadings or conducting hearings can expose traumatic experiences to public scrutiny. Any scheduled appearance at court or for a deposition can give an assailant the opportunity to harm or harass the client. The lawyer has an ethical responsibility to (1) discuss the logistics of the event that is scheduled to happen, (2) ask the client what safety concerns they have in connection with that event, and (3) help the client strategize a safety plan for the event.[7] Clients are likely to want an even broader plan (beyond legal relief) for recovering from the violence they have experienced; thus, lawyers should be prepared to connect clients with community professionals such as victim service providers who can assist with needs related to safety planning (beyond the court case), access to resources, and mental health counseling.

> If you are uncertain about the resources available in your community for violence survivors, you or your client can contact the **National Domestic Violence Hotline** at 1-800-799-7233 or 1-800-787-3224 (TTY for Deaf/hard of hearing), or by using the live chat feature at http://www.thehotline.org/; or the **National Sexual Assault Telephone Hotline** at 1-800-656-HOPE (4673), or by using the live chat option at https://www.rainn.org/.

II. Communication between Attorneys and Clients

It is important for victims' attorneys to facilitate clear communication with their clients. Be conscious of your word choice, and avoid or explain legal jargon. Use basic reflection and active listening techniques to confirm that you understand what the client is telling you, and that you are using common terms to mean the same thing (e.g., does "partner" mean business partner or life partner?). "Active listening" means listening solely for the purpose of understanding, and temporarily setting aside any concerns about how you are going to respond to the client. "Reflection" means using the client's exact words to show you have heard the client, and to facilitate more information sharing. An example of reflection is: "You said that your boyfriend 'scares' you; can you tell me more about that?"[8]

Whenever English is not the client's native language, you need to offer the use of a qualified interpreter. Even though a client may be able to converse with you in English, an interpreter ensures that the client can fully understand your advice,

---

[7] MODEL RULES OF PROF'L CONDUCT r. 1.3 (AM. BAR ASS'N 2017); MODEL RULES OF PROF'L CONDUCT r. 1.4 (AM. BAR ASS'N 2017).

[8] If you are not familiar with the techniques for active listening, you can start by reading Artika Tyner, *Listening as an Effective Tool for Client Communication*, 6(3) A.B.A. GENERAL PRACTICE, SOLO & SMALL FIRM DIV. NEWSL. (Spring 2010), *available at* www.americanbar.org/newsletter/publications/law_trends_news_practice_area_e_newsletter_home/10_spring_lit_feat2.html.

and that you can fully understand the experience the client is sharing with you. If you cannot confirm that you and the client are communicating clearly, then you may be violating ABA Model Rule of Professional Conduct 1.4 Communication.[9]

Avoid the use of informal, untrained family or friend interpreters for two reasons: (1) being bilingual does not mean you have the skillset to interpret between languages; and (2) lay interpreters may have personal interests and relationships that interfere both with the accuracy of interpretation and the client's ability to speak freely. Similarly, do not assume that a bilingual professional working with the client (such as a social worker or advocate) will act as your interpreter with the client; that person is generally present to fulfill a different professional role. However, in the rare circumstance when you must use a person other than a professional interpreter in order to meet the client's needs, be sure to have a preliminary conversation with the interpreter about what you expect in terms of complete and accurate interpretation, non-disclosure of the conversation interpreted, and refraining from any editorializing by the interpreter.

III. Attorney/Client Confidentiality

There are several confidentiality issues that can arise when working with victims, specifically around (1) implied consent, (2) collaboration with other confidential professionals, and (3) third parties in the interview. You will want to teach your client about the actual boundaries of confidentiality and privilege and the kinds of sharing within confidentiality circles that you expect to be making (e.g., all staff at your organization). Help the client to make informed choices about whether and how to waive privilege rights, but always remember the decision remains with the client.

A. Implied Consent

Though attorneys are ethically allowed to rely on implied consent to disclose confidential information related to the case, it is a better practice to seek informed consent whenever possible.[10] Each client will have their own assessment of what is safe, dangerous, or requires safety planning. Explain to clients in advance which information you expect will be shared in a court pleading or a negotiation, and find out if the client agrees to have it shared. If the client does not, do not tell them that they "have to" disclose it; instead, discuss consequences, risks, and alternatives.

---

[9] "A lawyer shall explain a matter to the extent reasonably necessary to permit the client to make informed decisions regarding the representation." MODEL RULES OF PROF'L CONDUCT r. 1.4(b) (AM. BAR ASS'N 2017).

[10] "A lawyer shall not reveal information relating to the representation of a client unless the client gives informed consent, the disclosure is impliedly authorized in order to carry out the representation or the disclosure is permitted by paragraph (b)." MODEL RULES OF PROF'L CONDUCT r. 1.6(a) (AM. BAR ASS'N 2017).

If you unexpectedly discover that a disclosure would be helpful in court or in a negotiation, assess whether you can delay disclosure until you check in with your client. Slowing down and taking time to discuss and consider such a disclosure with your client is almost always helpful. However, there will be times when you are on the spot, need to make a disclosure, and are ethically allowed to rely on implied consent. In those cases, only disclose the minimum amount necessary to meet the goal in the moment, then notify the client as soon as possible. The process of balancing informed consent and implied consent is substantially easier if you inquire in advance about your client's privacy personality and how closely they want to monitor information disclosure.

B. Collaboration with Other Confidential Professionals

In working with a victim, there is a decent chance that you may find it necessary to communicate with another professional supporting the client: an advocate, a social worker, a therapist, or a doctor. If you think you should disclose confidential information to that professional, follow the recommendations discussed above around obtaining informed consent from the client. In order to help the client make an informed choice about sharing information with the other professional, be sure you clearly understand the other professional's legal confidentiality duties, privilege protections, and mandatory disclosure laws. Other privileged professionals can have very different exceptions to confidentiality.

Additionally, assess the impact in your jurisdiction of one privileged professional sharing information with a different kind of privileged professional. You cannot simply assume that because you both have "privilege," your privilege won't be waived by sharing information with the other privileged professional. The seminal case on lawyers sharing client communications with other professionals is *U.S. v. Kovel,* which protects privilege if the other professional is "reasonably necessary to facilitate communication between lawyer and client."[11] Unless your state law specifically holds that attorney-client privilege is protected when lawyers share client communications with other types of privileged professionals, there is a very good chance that disclosing client information will waive the privilege. A client may knowingly instruct you to waive the privilege, but neither you nor the client should be ignorant of the risk.

C. Third Parties Present in Client Interview

In a related issue, lawyers should be prepared to handle third parties who want to be present during client communications. Remember, the decision whether to waive privilege is the client's decision to make, not yours. If a client shows up at a meeting with a third party, follow this protocol: (1) ask to meet with the client briefly alone, (2) find out who the person is and what their role would be in the meeting, (3) assess the possible impact of the person on privilege, (4) inform the client of the consequences of having the other person in the room,

---

[11] U.S. v. Kovel, 296 F.2d 918 (2d Cir. 1961).

and (5) ask the client whether they would like the other person in the room. Avoid making assumptions about which people the client does or does not really want in on your conversation (e.g., don't have a "male relatives never, social workers always" standard).

If the client says, "No," to having the person present, then you can take responsibility for excluding the person from the meeting. If the client says, "Yes," then emphasize that the client can change their mind at any time during the meeting or for any future meeting.

During the meeting with a third-party present, proceed with care and pay attention to the dynamics. You might choose to defer some topics or ask the client for permission to talk alone for a few minutes later in the conversation. Third parties in interviews might complicate the interactions, but attorneys can be very clear during the meeting that the client is in charge and ask the third party to stay within the helpful role identified by the client. These measures will build the client's comfort in working with you, and increase trust that you are acting in your client's best interest.

IV. Mandatory/Discretionary Disclosures by Attorneys

When attorneys learn of domestic violence in a client's life, it often provokes a strong reaction for the attorney. Most attorneys will feel an impulse to "do something" in hopes of preventing future violence, especially if the client has children or is a minor. In those moments, it is vital to stay focused on your ethical rules and avoid acting on "gut instincts."

Make sure you know whether your jurisdiction makes lawyers mandatory reporters of child abuse or vulnerable adult abuse (and learn which other professionals are mandatory reporters in your jurisdiction as well). This will be highly variable from one state to the next. If you are unsure, check in with your bar association or ethics board. If you determine that you are a mandatory reporter, then learn what constitutes a reportable event and how you must report it. The presence of domestic violence in the life of a person who is also a parent is not necessarily a reportable child abuse event. If you learn you are not a mandatory reporter, then you still must follow attorney ethical rules around confidentiality and exceptions to confidentiality.

Every state has exceptions in the confidentiality rules that either require or allow a lawyer to make disclosures to prevent imminent, serious bodily harm. Though most states have adopted the ABA Model Rules of Professional Conduct, they may have adjusted the circumstances in Rule 1.6(b) when lawyers are allowed or required to disclose confidential client communications. If you think you may need to make such a disclosure, be prepared to check your local rule and confirm both what the standard is and what it requires or allows you to do.

In advance of encountering the situations described in this chapter, set up a procedure for how you will make decisions on ethical issues such as confidentiality and mandatory disclosures. If you are in a larger organization, you may have an ethics counsel or ethics committee you can consult. If you do not have access to that resource in-house, identify a confidential resource that you can turn to when you have to make difficult decisions about breaching confidentiality. You may enter into an agreement with a trusted colleague or have access to a state bar ethics line. Either way, avoid having to act alone when making emergency decisions about violating client privacy. The input of a colleague who does not have a direct relationship with the client is enormously helpful in reaching a decision that has a strong ethical foundation.

Regardless of whether you make a disclosure or find you are prohibited from making a disclosure about domestic violence, have a plan for communicating with the client about the issue. If you believe your client is in a dangerous situation—even the kind you would not disclose—your client will likely benefit from an opportunity to discuss it with you.

If you do disclose information about the domestic violence to outside authorities, your client will need assistance in planning for the consequences of that disclosure. That assistance is likely to include helping the client make sense of your actions, and possibly referring them to new counsel if attorney-client trust has been destroyed by the disclosure. A conversation about your disclosure will be less difficult if you have already educated the client about the boundaries of confidentiality at the beginning of the attorney/client relationship.

APPENDIX

Resources:

- **American Bar Association Model Rules of Professional Conduct**
  - https://www.americanbar.org/groups/professional_responsibility/publications/model_rules_of_professional_conduct/model_rules_of_professional_conduct_table_of_contents.html

- **Summary of U.S. State Laws Related to Advocate Confidentiality**
  - https://www.americanbar.org/content/dam/aba/uncategorized/cdsv-related/Advocate_Confidentiality_Chart_2_2014.authcheckdam.pdf

Specific Language Suggestions:

Language for screening every client for potential experience of domestic or sexual violence:

1. Use a framing statement so clients understand why you are asking this:
   a. "Because violence is so common in many people's lives, I have begun to check in with all of my clients about it. Is it okay if I ask you a few questions?"
      i. And if you are telling people this, make sure that it is true. Screening is not effective if you make assumptions certain people do not need the questions, and you only ask when you think you already know the answer is yes.
2. Ask a basic opening question to let the client know it is okay to tell you about domestic violence and that you are ready to be helpful:
   a. "Is there anything going on that makes you feel unsafe or afraid at home?"
   b. "Is there anyone in your life who threatens, scares or physically hurts you?"
   c. If yes to above, "Is there anyone in your life who makes you do things you don't want to sexually?"

Language for informing clients about potential legal relevance of domestic or sexual violence:

1. Frame it as a legal remedy that you could discuss more if the client thought it applied to their case or that it would be helpful:
   a. "Violence by one parent against another is something judges must consider in custody cases. Let me know if you think there is anything the judge should hear about violence in your relationship."
   b. "Most people do not know that our state allows victims of sexual assault to sue their rapist, even if it is a spouse, for money damages. I am happy to discuss those kinds of cases with you if you would like to know more."

c. "Last year, the legislature passed a law that prevents landlords for evicting people because of domestic violence. If you think that could be helpful to your case, we can discuss it more."

Language for encouraging to client to let you know about any barriers to working together:

1. "Is there anything going on in your life that might impact how we work together? Is there anything that affects your ability to talk to me freely, to make decisions, or makes you worried about how this case will go? Is there anything I can do to make it easier for us to work together?"

2. "What were you hoping a lawyer could do for you? Do you have any worries about working with a lawyer or pursuing this problem in the courts?"

Language for testing credibility without alienating the client:

1. Frame questions about inconsistencies as you trying to understand the story, rather than accusing the client of lying:
   a. "Earlier you said it happened on January 1, but then I heard you say it happened when you were picking your son up from school. That confuses me, since school is closed on New Year's Day. Can you help me understand?"

2. Tell the client how more explanation for a potential skeptic helps the client's case:
   a. "I worry that a judge will not understand why you moved across the country with someone who scared you. Can you talk more about what you were thinking and feeling when you made that move? That would help us make it clear to a judge."

Language for discussing whether to pursue the legal action, or whether to pursue a particular strategy:

1. Tell the client truthfully whether they "have" to do this or you think it is strategically advisable to do this.
   a. "Your husband filed for divorce. In the divorce, the judge is asking you to file a financial disclosure. You don't have the ability to stop the divorce case since your husband filed it. If you don't answer the financial disclosure, the judge could hold you in contempt of court or the judge could rule you are not entitled to receive any support. What worries you about answering the financial disclosure?"
   b. "You came in to me for help because your ex sexually assaulted you last week. I understand that you do not want to tell the court about the rape. If we do not disclose that recent event, I worry the judge will not believe that you need an order of protection right now. What are you worried will happen if you tell the judge about what your ex did last week?"

Language for discussing expectations with an interpreter and uncovering whether the interpreter understands their role:

1. "Please interpret everything that the client and I say without adding or taking anything away. That includes interpreting what I am saying now to you. I will pause so you can interpret that."
2. "Please let me know if you need me to slow down or take a break so that you can interpret a piece of the conversation."
3. "Would you like a pad and pen so you can take notes while interpreting?"
4. "What rules do you follow if someone asks you what the client and I discussed today?"
   a. "Do you agree not to discuss with anyone the things that you interpret today?"

Language for discussing the consequences of having a third party in your client interview:

1. "The law says that when you and I talk, the conversation is protected. We cannot be forced to testify about what we said in this conversation. If your friend sits in the room with us, then you, your friend, or I could all be forced to testify about what we discuss. I don't know if it would ever happen, but it is your choice whether you want to take that risk. What do you think?"

Language for explaining attorney disclosures of confidential communications:

1. "Before we start working together, I want you to know that everything you tell me stays between us and the other people who work in my law office, unless you want me to share it as part of your case. There are a few exceptions where I might have to share information even if you don't want me to, such as if you tell me someone is about to be seriously hurt, if I learn that you've used my services to commit a crime, or if there is a court dispute between you and me. Do you have any thoughts on what I've just told you?"
2. "What you just told me about 'wanting to end it all'—that is the kind of thing where I might need to get help for you. Can you tell me more about what you mean when you want to end it all?"

Section Two:
Specialized Advocacy and Litigation

Chapter Four:
Immigration Law and Domestic Violence

I. Introduction

Immigration law is immensely complicated and dynamic. Its processes and policies are ever-changing and complex, and though immigration law is federal in scope, procedures vary widely depending on the jurisdiction. In situations of domestic violence, abusers often manipulate the complexities of the immigration system to try to maintain power and control over victims. In express recognition of this, Congress created certain immigration benefits to help victims of domestic violence to obtain legal immigration status, which often leads to stability and safety.

This chapter will identify tactics of immigration-related abuse and discuss obstacles that immigrant victims face in accessing services and protection. It will also discuss various forms of immigration benefits for victims, some ways to address safety planning in the context of immigration enforcement, as well as some of the legal obligations of OVW-funded agencies that serve immigrant victims.

II. Barriers to Services and Immigration-Related Abuse

A. Barriers to Services

Immigrant victims of domestic violence often face linguistic, cultural, and economic obstacles when reaching out for assistance and protection. In 2013, the National Latin@ Network for Healthy Families and Communities (a project of Casa de Esperanza) and the National Domestic Violence Hotline conducted a survey which reported that 31 percent of Spanish-speaking respondents had encountered language barriers while accessing services.[1] Language access is central to the ability of victims to accurately tell their stories, and to understand what legal options and social services may be available to them.[2]

There are also cultural factors that affect a victim's decision to seek assistance. Victims in certain immigrant and refugee communities may not want to seek outside assistance, as domestic violence may be considered a private family matter.[3] Isolation from traditional support networks, religious views on family separation, unfamiliarity with U.S. laws, and the lack of culturally and linguistically appropriate services significantly impact an immigrant victim's ability and decision to reach out for help.[4] Similarly, a victim's capacity to reach out for help regarding domestic violence is affected by economic factors like the ability to legally work in the United States, and how to provide for themselves and their families. There are also institutional barriers that may impact an immigrant victim's ability to seek assistance from the police, courts, or service providers, including a victim's experience of racism, discrimination, and xenophobic or anti-immigrant sentiments within these institutions. While these social issues exist outside the context of domestic violence, abusers often exploit them to further isolate victims.[5]

B. Immigration-Related Forms of Abuse

Abusers often try to use a victim's lack of legal immigration status or dependent immigration status as a way to maintain control over victims. This can take may forms, including:

- Threatening victims that if they go to the police or the court, they will be arrested because they are undocumented;

---

[1] Nat'l Latin@ Network for Healthy Families & Communities & Nat'l Domestic Violence Hotline, Realidades Latinas: A National Survey on the Impact of Immigration and Language Access on Latina Survivors 5 (2013), *available at* http://www.nationallatinonetwork.org/images/files/NLNRealidades_ Latinas_The_Impact_of_Immigration_and_Language_Access_FINAL.pdf.

[2] Furthermore, service providers that receive government funding have additional legal responsibilities to provide meaningful language access. Title VI of the Civil Rights Act of 1964 prohibits discrimination based on national origin, and in 2000, President Clinton signed Executive Order 13166 expressly stating that those with limited English proficiency should have meaningful access to federally conducted and federally funded programs. Exec. Order No. 13,166, 65 Fed Reg. 159 (Aug. 16, 2000). Both Casa de Esperanza and Asian Pacific Institute on Gender-Based Violence have toolkits to help service providers create and implement a language access plan. The links to those resources are listed in the Appendix to this chapter.

[3] Kirsten Senturia, Marianne Sullivan, Sandy Ciske & Sharyne Shiu-Thornton, Cultural Issues Affecting Domestic Violence Service Utilization in Ethnic and Hard to Reach Populations, Final Report (Nov. 5, 2000), *available at* https://www.ncjrs.gov/pdffiles1/nij/grants/185357.pdf.

[4] *Id.* at 3.

[5] Jill M. Davies & Eleanor Lyon, Domestic Violence Advocacy: Complex Lives/Difficult Choices 98–99 (Claire M. Renzetti & Jeffrey L. Edleson, eds., 2d ed. 2014).

- Threatening to call "Immigration" on victims to get them arrested or deported;[6]

- Isolating victims from family or friends, or not allowing victims to learn English;

- Lying about filing paperwork for immigration benefits, or threats to withdraw paperwork;

- Hiding or destroying important documentation (passports, birth certificates);

- Coercing victims into doing something that would jeopardize their immigration status or ability to secure immigration status;

- Threatening to take away children to the abuser's country of origin, or otherwise to take custody away from an undocumented victim.[7]

A 2017 survey of more than 700 domestic violence and sexual assault advocates nationwide showed how much immigration-related concerns impacted immigrant victims' decisions to reach out for help from the police or the court system.[8] 78 percent of survey respondents indicated that immigrant victims reported having concerns about contacting the police, with one advocate stating: "Survivors are concerned that they will be detained if they make a police report or call 911. A 16-year-old survivor attempted suicide because she was concerned that her offender would report her and her family to [Immigration and Customs Enforcement] ICE."[9]

C. Enhancing Safety Planning

To meet these important concerns of victims, advocates should become familiar with victim safety planning in order to address the risk of immigration enforcement actions if the victim is undocumented.

---

[6] "Immigration" in this context usually refers to Immigration and Customs Enforcement or ICE, which is the agency within the Department of Homeland Security responsible for enforcement of immigration laws. Prior to the creation of the Department of Homeland Security in 2002, the term "Immigration" referred to "INS" or the Immigration and Nationality Service, the name of the agency then responsible for immigration-related enforcement matters.

[7] For more information, see the Futures without Violence Immigration Power and Control Wheel at *Forms of Domestic Violence that Women Experience: Immigrant Women,* Futures Without Violence, https://s3.amazonaws.com/fwvcorp/wp-content/uploads/20160121105935/Power-control-wheel-eng-4-w-description.pdf (last visited Apr. 24, 2018). *See also Immigrant Victims of Domestic Violence,* Nat'l Coal. Against Domestic Violence, http://www.ncdsv.org/images/NCADV_ImmigrantVictimsOfDV.pdf (last visited Apr. 24, 2018).

[8] Marium Durrani et al., Tahirih Just. Ctr., *2017 Advocate and Legal Service Survey Regarding Immigrant Survivors,* http://www.tahirih.org/wp-content/uploads/2017/05/2017-Advocate-and-Legal-Service-Survey-Key-Findings.pdf (last visited Apr. 24, 2018).

[9] *Id.*

Similar to the way that safety planning is conducted in the event there is an encounter with an abuser, advocates can help victims think through what steps should be taken if the victim is arrested or detained by immigration enforcement.[10] For example, advocates can help victims identify someone who can take temporary care of their children or pick up their paycheck if they are arrested and detained. Advocates can also provide victims with important "Know Your Rights" materials if immigration enforcement officials come to their homes, or if they are stopped in public or in their cars.[11] Attorneys and advocates should also ensure that victims do not carry fake documentation and that they have their attorney or advocate's business card with them in the event of emergencies. If victims have an application pending for an immigration benefit, they may also choose to carry a copy of their receipt notice.

Domestic violence service providers should ensure that their staff knows what to do in the event that immigration enforcement calls the agency or comes to the office or shelter. In addition to protecting the rights of the victims they serve, putting protocols in place can help ensure that the agency is in compliance with the confidentiality provisions that it may have as a recipient of federal funding under the Violence Against Women Act (VAWA) or the Family Violence Prevention and Services Act (FVPSA). Staff should remember that they cannot disclose personally identifying information about a client unless there is a release, a court order, or the disclosure is otherwise required by law.

Advocates should also become familiar with the VAWA confidentiality provisions that relate to immigration matters.[12] These protections are in place to protect victim information that has been filed with the Department of Homeland Security (DHS), and prevent DHS and other agencies from making an adverse

---

[10] For more information on immigration related safety planning, see *Family Preparedness Plan,* IMMIGRANT LEGAL RESOURCE CTR., https://www.ilrc.org/sites/default/files/resources/family_ preparedness_plan_v3-20170323.pdf (last visited Apr. 24, 2018). The Preparedness Plan is also available in Spanish: *Plan de Preparación,* IMMIGRANT LEGAL RESOURCE CTR., https://www.ilrc. org/sites/default/files/resources/plan_de_preparacion_familiar.v3.pdf (last visited Apr. 24, 2018), and Chinese: 家庭準備計劃, IMMIGRANT LEGAL RESOURCE CTR., https://www.ilrc.org/sites/default/files/ resources/family_preparedness_plan-chinese-ts_edit.pdf (last visited Apr. 24, 2018). *See also Know Your Rights: A Guide to Your Rights When Interacting with Law Enforcement,* CATHOLIC LEGAL IMMIGR. NETWORK, https://cliniclegal.org/resources/know-your-rights-law-enforcement (last visited Apr. 24, 2018). The Know Your Rights Guide is available in Spanish, Amharic, Chinese, and other languages. *Id.*

[11] Know Your Rights materials in multiple languages can be accessed at *Know Your Rights and What Immigrant Families Should Do Now,* IMMIGRATION LEGAL RESOURCE CTR. (Apr. 28, 2017), https:// www.ilrc.org/know-your-rights-and-what-immigrant-families-should-do-now. Know Your Rights materials can also be found at *Know Your Rights: Discrimination Against Immigrants and Muslims,* ACLU, https://www.aclu.org/issues/immigrants-rights/know-your-rights-discrimination-against-immigrants-and-muslims?redirect=feature/know-your-rights-immigration#immigration (last visited Apr. 24, 2018).

[12] 8 U.S.C. § 1367; INA § 239.

decision in a victim's case based solely upon information provided by the abuser or the abuser's family. There is also a VAWA confidentiality provision that requires ICE to certify that it complied with certain conditions if it conducts enforcement actions in places that victims are likely to go, including shelters, community organizations, and courthouses, if the victim is there for a criminal or civil matter related to the abuse they suffered.[13]

D. Protections Available to All Victims

In the United States, there are legal protections available for all victims of domestic violence, regardless of immigration status.

All victims may:

- Seek an order of protection;

- Obtain a divorce, custody, and support in a family court;

- Report a crime;[14]

- Receive emergency medical assistance.[15]

It is not only critical for immigrant victims to know that these protections are available regardless of immigration status, but also for domestic violence service providers to know as well. In 2016, the Department of Housing and Urban Development, Department of Justice, as well as the Department of Health and Human Services issued a joint letter reminding recipients of federal funds that they "should not withhold services based on immigration status when the services are necessary to protect life or safety."[16]

---

[13] *Violence Against Women Act (VAWA) Confidentiality Provisions at the Department of Homeland Security,* U.S. DEP'T OF HOMELAND SECURITY, *available at* http://www.asistahelp.org/documents/resources/VAWA_notice_PDF_FE347B89584A0.pdf (last visited Apr. 24, 2018).

[14] *Information on the Legal Rights Available to Immigrant Victims of Domestic Violence in the United States and Facts about Immigrating on a Marriage-Based Visa Fact Sheet,* U.S. CITIZENSHIP & IMMIGR. SERVICES, *available at* https://www.uscis.gov/news/fact-sheets/information-legal-rights-available-immigrant-victims-domestic-violence-united-states-and-facts-about-immigrating-marriage-based-visa-fact-sheet (last updated Jan. 11, 2011) [hereinafter *Marriage-Based Visa Fact Sheet*].

[15] For more information on immigrant access to benefit programs, see Michael K. Gusmano, *Undocumented Immigrants in the United States: U.S. Health Policy and Access to Care,* THE HASTINGS CTR. (Mar. 15, 2012), *available at* http://undocumentedpatients.org/issuebrief/health-policy-and-access-to-care/. Also, the National Immigration Law Center has extensive resources on economic supports for immigrants. *Overview of Immigrant Eligibility for Federal Programs,* NAT'L IMMIGR. L. CTR., https://www.nilc.org/issues/economic-support/table_ovrw_fedprogs/ (last updated Oct. 2011).

[16] Letter from Loretta E. Lynch, Att'y Gen. of the U.S., Sylvia M. Burwell, Sec'y of Health & Hum. Services & Julián Castro, Sec'y of Housing and Urb. Dev., to Recipients of Fed. Fin. Assistance (Aug. 5, 2016), *available at* https://www.hudexchange.info/resources/documents/HUD-HHS-DOJ-Letter-Regarding-Immigrant-Access-to-Housing-and-Services.pdf.

The aforementioned services include:

- Emergency shelter, and short-term housing assistance including transitional housing and rapid re-housing programs;

- Crisis counseling and intervention programs, including services and assistance relating to child protection, adult protective services, violence and abuse prevention, victims of domestic violence or other criminal activity; or treatment of mental illness or substance abuse;

- Soup kitchens or community food banks;

- Medical and public health services necessary to life or safety.[17]

Advocacy Tip: Service providers can partner with culturally specific organizations within their communities on outreach efforts to ensure that victims know that their programs are accessible regardless of one's immigration status. Recently, the Minnesota Coalition for Battered Women produced community flyers in more than 10 different languages indicating that their agencies are safe spaces for immigrants and refugees.[18]

---

[17] *Id.*

[18] "All Are Welcome" Campaign materials can be found at *All Are Welcome,* MINN. COAL. FOR BATTERED WOMEN, http://www.mcbw.org/immigration-resources (last visited Apr. 24, 2018).

> **International Marriage Broker Regulation Act (IMBRA): Helping Fiancés and Spouses Entering the U.S. Become Aware of Their Rights**
>
> IMBRA, enacted in 2006, was a critical step to addressing domestic violence issues in the fiancé visa process and regulate marriage broker agencies. One of its key provisions includes providing fiancés and spouses emigrating to the United States with a brochure about the rights of domestic violence victims and information about marriage based visas.[19] Some other key provisions include:
>
> - Prohibitions on international marriage broker agencies (IMBs) from providing any information about minors (under age eighteen);
>
> - Requiring that IMBs collect information regarding the U.S. citizen's criminal history, including searches of sex offender registries before releasing information about a foreign national client to the U.S. citizen;
>
> - Requiring that the U.S. citizen disclose criminal history related to domestic violence and other crimes, and that information be disclosed to the fiancé or spouse abroad;
>
> - Limiting how many and how often a U.S. citizen may submit a fiancé application.[20]

III. Benefits for Immigrant Victims of Domestic Violence

Congress enacted VAWA in 1994, which created the self-petitioning process for immigrant victims of domestic violence who had a certain relationship to a U.S. citizen (USC) or legal permanent resident (LPR) abuser. When VAWA was reauthorized in 2000, Congress created additional protections: the "T visa" for victims of human trafficking, and the "U visa" for victims of certain serious crimes, including domestic violence.

In creating these essential protections, Congress recognized that providing immigrant victims who "were experiencing domestic violence at home with protection against deportation allows them to obtain protection orders against their abusers and frees them to cooperate with law enforcement and prosecutors in criminal cases brought against their abusers and the abusers of their children without fearing that the abuser will retaliate by withdrawing or threatening withdrawal of access to an immigration benefit under the abuser's control."[21]

---

[19] *Marriage-Based Visa Fact Sheet, supra* note 14.

[20] *See Summary of the International Marriage Broker Regulation Act of 2005 (IMBRA),* TAHIRIH JUST. CTR., *available at* http://www.tahirih.org/wp-content/uploads/2015/06/IMBRA-Overview.pdf (last visited Apr. 24, 2018).

[21] Pub. L. No. 106-386, § 1502(a)(2).

This next section will provide an overview of humanitarian benefits available to victims of domestic violence including VAWA self-petitions, domestic violence waivers for conditional residents, U visas, T visas, and work authorization for abused spouses of certain nonimmigrant visa holders. What immigration benefits are available to victims is dependent on factors like where the domestic violence occurred, the immigration status of the abuser, whether there was a criminal investigation or prosecution of the case, and the client's own immigration or criminal history.[22] While this section provides a brief overview of the requirements and benefits of each form of relief, attorneys and advocates should consult with a knowledgeable immigration practitioner who specializes in these forms of relief in order to determine which benefits may apply in an individual client's case.

Notario Fraud

Immigration consultant fraud is pervasive, and can take several forms. Individuals may hold themselves out to be licensed attorneys when they are not, or pose as immigration officials. One form of immigration consultant fraud is "notario fraud." In some Spanish-speaking countries, the term "notario" can mean a licensed person who practices before the court. However, here in the U.S., scammers may apply for a "notary public license" and then rely on the false cognate to hold themselves out to be qualified and licensed professionals to give legal advice and help.[23]

---

[22] There are other humanitarian forms of relief that may be available to victims of domestic violence that go beyond the scope of this chapter, including Special Immigrant Juvenile Status (SIJS) and asylum claims for victims who may have fled domestic violence in their home countries. For more information on these forms of relief, please see the following immigration benefits for survivors chart: ASISTA, Freedom Network, Kids in Need of Defense & Tahirih Just. Ctr., Immigration Options for Victims of Crime, *available at* http://www.asistahelp.org/documents/resources/Immigration_Options_for_Victims_of__B13B63AC3B3D2.pdf (last updated June 26, 2016).

[23] For more information on how victims can prevent and identify immigration related fraud or "notario fraud," visit Ayuda's Project END (Ending Notario Deception): *Project END,* Ayuda, https://ayuda.com/get-help/legal-services/immigration-law/project-end/ (last visited Apr. 24, 2018). The website also includes materials advocates can utilize in their "Know Your Rights" and fraud prevention outreach work. *See also Fight Notario Fraud,* A.B.A. Comm'n on Immigr., https://www.americanbar.org/groups/public_services/immigration/projects_initiatives/fightnotariofraud.html (last updated June 2017).

A. VAWA Self-Petitions

VAWA self-petitions are available to immigrant victims who have a certain relationship to their abuser to obtain their own legal status so that they need not rely on an abusive partner to maintain or obtain immigration benefits. To be eligible for a VAWA self-petition, applicants must prove they have:[24]

(1) **A certain relationship to the abuser.** Victims must be married to, or the child of, a USC or LPR, or else the parent of an adult USC child.[25]

(2) **Suffered battery or extreme cruelty.** Battery refers to physical violence, while extreme cruelty is a general term which may encompass, but is not limited to, sexual, emotional, or psychological abuse.[26]

(3) **Shared a joint residence with the abuser.** Applicants must show that they lived with the abuser. Some documents that applicants can use to show this include: leases, utility bills, correspondence to both parties at the address, and declarations from the applicant and others who were aware that the victim and abuser resided together.

(4) **Good moral character.** Applicants must demonstrate that they have good moral character for at least three years prior to submitting the application. This is typically done through submitting a criminal background check and documents showing that the applicant is involved in the community.

(5) **For applications based on marriage, applicants must show that they entered into the marriage in good faith.** Generally, this means that applicants must show they entered into the marriage with the intention of establishing a life together with their spouse, and not solely for immigration benefits.

VAWA self-petitions provide a path to legal permanent residency without the need to rely on the abuser for status. They also allow a victim to receive work authorization upon approval. If your client is filing a VAWA self-petition on the basis of being an abused spouse of a USC or LPR, then they may include minor children (both in the United States and abroad) as derivatives on the application. The process and time frame by which applicants can obtain their legal permanent residency depends on whether the abuser was a USC or an LPR.[27]

---

[24] *Battered Spouses, Children & Parents,* U.S. Citizenship & Immigr. Services, *available at* https://www.uscis.gov/humanitarian/battered-spouse-children-parents (last updated Feb. 16, 2016).

[25] Legal permanent residents are also known as "green card holders."

[26] For more information, see 8 C.F.R. § 204.2(c)(1)(vi). *See also* Sally Kinoshita, *Extreme Cruelty: What It Is and How to Prove It,* ASISTA Newsl., Fall 2006, at 2–4, *available at* http://www.asistahelp.org/documents/resources/Fall_2006_Newsletter__2C990700B7BC0.pdf.

[27] If abusers are USCs, then applicants may be eligible to apply for residency sooner; if the abuser is an LPR, the process could take longer.

Advocacy Tips:

- Since the Supreme Court's 2013 decision *U.S. v. Windsor,* victims who are in same sex marriages to USCs and LPRs may also apply for VAWA self-petitions.[28]

- Victims may apply for a VAWA self-petition up to two years after the divorce from the abuser.

- Victims may apply even if the abusive LPR or USC spouse did not legally terminate a prior marriage. This "intended spouse" exception applies if a marriage ceremony was performed and the victim believed the marriage was valid.[29]

- Victims may file for a VAWA self-petition even if they are still residing with their abusers. These cases require additional levels of safety planning to ensure that a victim can safely obtain the needed documentation to support a VAWA self-petition.

- Attorneys and advocates can consider using the civil order of protection process or family court matters to obtain documentation that would support the requirements of the VAWA self-petition. For example, there could be a provision in an order of protection requiring abusers to turn over important documents like passports, copies of leases, insurance documents, taxes, or birth certificates of minor children. Furthermore, a finding of abuse in an order of protection could be useful documentation to support the victim's claim of battery or extreme cruelty.

B. Domestic Violence Waivers for Conditional Residents

Residency is conditional if immigrant spouses (and their minor children) obtain permanent resident status less than two years after their marriage to a USC or LPR spouse.[30] In order to receive a full 10 year legal permanent residency card,

---

[28] *Same-Sex Marriages,* U.S. CITIZENSHIP & IMMIGR. SERVICES, *available at* https://www.uscis.gov/family/same-sex-marriages (last updated Apr. 3, 2014).

[29] *See* INA § 101(a)(50). The term "intended spouse" means any alien who meets the criteria set forth in §§ 204(a)(1)(A)(iii)(II)(aa)(BB), 204(a)(1)(B)(ii)(II)(aa)(BB), or 240A(b)(2)(A)(i)(III).

[30] "Your permanent residence status is conditional if it is based on a marriage that was less than 2 years old on the day you were given permanent residence ... Your status is conditional, because you must prove that you did not get married to evade the immigration laws of the United States." *Remove Conditions on Permanent Residence Based on Marriage,* U.S. CITIZENSHIP & IMMIGR. SERVICES, *available at* https://www.uscis.gov/green-card/after-green-card-granted/conditional-permanent-residence/remove-conditions-permanent-residence-based-marriage (last updated Feb. 2, 2018) [hereinafter *Remove Conditions on Permanent Residence*].

the spouses need to file an application jointly to remove the conditions, with evidence showing they entered into the marriage in good faith.[31]

In recognition that a joint filing to remove the conditions may not always be possible, Congress enacted the Immigration Act of 1990, which created "waivers" to the joint filing requirement in cases of divorce, death, domestic violence, and extreme hardship.[32] To obtain the domestic violence-based waiver, applicants must show:

- That the qualifying marriage was entered into in good faith; and

- The applicant suffered battery or extreme cruelty.

Like the VAWA self-petition, the principal benefit to the domestic violence waiver is that conditional residents who are victims of domestic violence have an option to remove the conditions on their residency and obtain a full 10 year residency without reliance on an abusive spouse. Children who acquired conditional residency with their parent may also benefit from these provisions.[33]

C. U visas

U Nonimmigrant Status (U visa) was created with the dual purpose of strengthening the ability of law enforcement to investigate and prosecute criminal activity (including domestic violence), as well as providing essential protection to victims.[34] Applicants must show the following:

- They are victims of an enumerated qualifying crime;[35]

- They suffered substantial physical or emotional abuse due to victimization;

- They have information about the crime;

---

[31] The application is Form I-751, which must be submitted in the 90 days before the second year mark as a conditional resident. *Id. See I-751, Petition to Remove Conditions on Residence,* U.S. CITIZENSHIP & IMMIGR. SERVICES, *available at* https://www.uscis.gov/i-751 (last updated Apr. 12, 2018).

[32] Cecilia Olavarria & Moira Fisher Preda, *Additional Remedies Under VAWA: Battered Spouse Waiver, in* BREAKING BARRIERS: A COMPLETE GUIDE TO LEGAL RIGHTS AND RESOURCES FOR BATTERED IMMIGRANTS (Kathleen Sullivan, Leslye Orloff, NAT'L IMMIGRANT WOMEN'S ADVOCACY PROJECT eds., July 2013), *available at* http://library.niwap.org/wp-content/uploads/2015/IMM-Man-Ch3.5-BatteredSpouseWaiver-07.10.13.pdf.

[33] *Remove Conditions on Permanent Residence, supra* note 30.

[34] *See* Pub. L. No. 106-386, § 1513(a)(2)(A).

[35] INA § 101(a)(15)(U)(iii) lists all the U visa qualifying crimes: rape; torture; trafficking; incest; domestic violence; sexual assault; abusive sexual contact; prostitution; sexual exploitation; stalking; female genital mutilation; being held hostage; peonage; involuntary servitude; slave trade; kidnapping; abduction; unlawful criminal restraint; false imprisonment; blackmail; extortion; manslaughter; murder; felonious assault; witness tampering; obstruction of justice; perjury; fraud in foreign labor contracting (as defined in 18 U.S.C. § 1351); or attempt, conspiracy, or solicitation to commit any of the above mentioned crimes.

- They were, are, or will be helpful in the investigation or prosecution of the qualifying crime;

- The crime occurred in the U.S., or otherwise violated U.S. law;[36]

- They are admissible or eligible for a waiver.[37]

A required component of the U visa process is a signed certification form from a federal, state, or local law enforcement, prosecutor, judge, or other federal, state, or local authority investigating criminal activity.[38] These other investigative agencies can include Child Protective Services, state and federal Departments of Labor, as well as the Equal Employment Opportunity Commission, among other agencies.[39] The law enforcement certification confirms that a qualifying crime occurred, that the victim had information about the crime, and that the victim was, is, or will be helpful in the investigation or prosecution of the crime. The person who signs the certification form must be the head of the agency or someone designated by the head of the agency who serves in a supervisory role.[40]

The U visa process allows for victims and certain immediate family members (both in the United States and abroad) to receive a four-year visa, permitting them to remain and work in the United States.[41] After three years of continuously residing in the United States, U visa holders may apply to become legal permanent residents. There is a 10,000 cap on the number of U visas available annually for principal applicants, which has been met every year since 2010.[42] Even after the cap has been reached, the United States Citizenship and Immigration Services (USCIS) continues to accept and process U visa applications. If there is no visa available, but the application is approvable, USCIS will place victims and their eligible family members on a waitlist until such time that a visa becomes available. Once on the waitlist, victims and eligible family members in the United States may receive a two-year work permit which can be renewed until a U visa becomes available.

As of March 2018, there is an immense backlog in USCIS' processing of U visa applications, with more than 110,000 principal applications currently pending

---

[36] INA § 101(a)(15)(U); INA § 214(p).

[37] The inadmissibility waiver for U visas can be found at INA § 214(p)(6).

[38] INA § 214(p). The certification form is the I-918 Supplement B which can be found on the USCIS website. *Supplement B, U Nonimmigrant Status Certification,* U.S. CITIZENSHIP & IMMIGR. SERVICES, https://www.uscis.gov/sites/default/files/files/form/i-918supb.pdf (last updated Feb. 7, 2017).

[39] 8 C.F.R. § 214.14(a)(2)

[40] 8 C.F.R. § 214.14(a)(3).

[41] Keep in mind that in domestic violence or trafficking situations, perpetrators of the qualifying crime may not be included as derivatives on the application. 8 C.F.R. § 214.14(f).

[42] Eligible derivative family members are not counted against the U visa cap. INA § 214(p)(2)(B).

with USCIS.[43] At the time of this writing, USCIS is processing initial U visa applications that were filed on August 25, 2014.[44] This means that it may take more than 3.5 years for a U visa applicant to receive an initial review and be placed on the waitlist.

D. T visas

There often can be a strong connection between domestic violence and human trafficking, as some victims may be placed into commercial sex or labor trafficking situations by an intimate partner. Human trafficking is defined as "a form of modern-day slavery in which traffickers use force, fraud, or coercion to control victims for the purpose of engaging in commercial sex acts or labor services against his/her will."[45]

For trafficking situations involving commercial sex acts, trafficking occurs in two situations:

- If a commercial sex act is induced by force, fraud, or coercion; OR

- Situations in which the person induced to perform such act has not attained 18 years of age. In these cases, there is no need to show force fraud or coercion.[46]

Labor trafficking is defined as "the recruitment, harboring, transportation, provision, or obtaining of a person for labor or services, through the use of force, fraud, or coercion for the purposes of subjection to involuntary servitude, peonage, debt bondage, or slavery."[47]

Advocates should be familiar with red flags that indicate human trafficking, and incorporate them into their intake processes. For example, advocates can ask victims whether their abuser forced or tricked them to work long or unusual

---

[43] *Data Set: Form I-918 Application for Nonimmigrant Status*, U.S. CITIZENSHIP & IMMIGR. SERVICES, https://www.uscis.gov/tools/reports-studies/immigration-forms-data/data-set-form-i-918-application-u-nonimmigrant-status (last updated Jan. 19, 2018).

[44] See USCIS processing time information at *Check Case Processing Times,* U.S. CITIZENSHIP & IMMIGR. SERVICES, https://egov.uscis.gov/processing-times/ (last visited Apr. 24, 2018). To see current U visa processing times, select Vermont Service Center, then look for I-918 applications.

[45] *Human Trafficking,* NAT'L HUM. TRAFFICKING HOTLINE, https://humantraffickinghotline.org/type-trafficking/human-trafficking (last visited Apr. 24, 2018). For more information about sex trafficking and domestic violence, see *Sex Trafficking and Domestic Violence* in Section Eight of this manual. For more information about labor trafficking and domestic violence, see *Labor Trafficking and Domestic Violence* in Section Eight of this manual.

[46] 22 U.S.C. § 7102(9)(a).

[47] 22 U.S.C. § 7102(9)(b).

hours, whether they felt that they could leave their employment situation, or whether the abuser controlled their identity documents.[48]

The requirements for a T Nonimmigrant Status (T visa) are that applicants must show that they are:

- The victim of a "severe form of trafficking";

- Physically present in the U.S. on account of the trafficking;

- Assisting law enforcement officials in the investigation or prosecution of traffickers (exempted if under 18);

- Going to suffer extreme hardship upon removal;

- Admissible or eligible for a waiver.[49]

T visa applicants may also extend immigration benefits to certain family members, both in the United States or abroad. If granted, applicants receive a four-year visa which enables them to legally work and live in the United States. After three years of continuous presence, or after the Department of Justice certifies that the trafficking case has concluded, applicants may apply for their legal permanent residence.

There is a 5,000 cap on the number of T visas available annually for principal applicants. However, unlike U visas, that cap has never been met, meaning that there is currently no "waitlist" for T visa applicants. For this reason, additional screening for conditions of human trafficking may be beneficial for immigrant survivors of domestic violence.

E. Employment Authorization for Abused Spouses of Certain Nonimmigrant Visa Holders

VAWA Reauthorization of 2005 created protections for abused spouses of certain nonimmigrant visa holders if they or their child(ren) are victims of domestic violence. Specifically, INA § 106 grants abused spouses of A, E-3, G or H visa holders the ability to apply for work authorization if they or their child(ren) were subject to battery or extreme cruelty and currently reside in the United States.[50] To apply, victims must show:

---

[48] For a more complete listing of trafficking red flags, see *Recognizing the Signs,* NAT'L HUM. TRAFFICKING HOTLINE, https://humantraffickinghotline.org/human-trafficking/recognizing-signs (last visited Apr. 24, 2018).

[49] For more information on T visa requirements, see *Victims of Human Trafficking: T Nonimmigration Status,* U.S. CITIZENSHIP & IMMIGR. SERVICES, https://www.uscis.gov/humanitarian/ victims-human-trafficking-other-crimes/victims-human-trafficking-t-nonimmigrant-status (last updated Oct. 3, 2011).

[50] INA § 106.

- Marriage to an A, E-3, G or H visa holder (also eligible if the spouse dies, loses status due to an incident of domestic violence, or if the marriage was terminated within two years before the applicant filed for work authorization and there is connection between the termination and the domestic violence);

- That they entered the U.S. with a visa under the A, E-3, G or H visa provisions;

- That they or their child(ren) were subject to battery or extreme cruelty during the marriage and after being admitted to the U.S.;

- That they currently reside in the U.S.

If this application is approved, the abused spouse can receive a two-year work authorization which may be renewable.[51] It is important to note that this work authorization does not otherwise grant the victim any other legal immigration status.[52]

IV. Conclusion

This chapter provided an overview of immigration-related abuse, barriers that immigrant victims face in accessing services, and immigration benefits for victims of domestic violence. Given the complexity and variability of immigration law, it is critical to connect victims with knowledgeable and reputable immigration practitioners to help assess an individual victim's options for immigration relief.

---

[51] Policy Memorandum (PM-602-0130) from U.S. Citizenship & Immigr. Services on Eligibility for Employment Authorization for Battered Spouses of Certain Nonimmigrants (Mar. 8, 2016), *available at* https://www.uscis.gov/sites/default/files/USCIS/Laws/Memoranda/2016/2016-0308_PM-602-0130_Eligibility_for_Employment_Authorization_for_Battered_Spouses_of_Certain_Nonimmigrants.pdf.

[52] The special instructions for Form I-765V on the USCIS website explain: "Employment authorization is a benefit granted for a limited period of time and will not establish eligibility for or extend your lawful status in the United States. Receiving an Employment Authorization Document (EAD) will have no effect on your immigration status." *I-765V, Application for Employment Authorization for Abused Nonimmigrant Spouse,* U.S. Citizenship & Immigr. Services, https://www.uscis.gov/i-765v (last updated Feb. 14, 2017).

APPENDIX

Technical Assistance for Serving Immigrant Victims:

- **ASISTA Immigration Assistance**
  - www.asistahelp.org

- **Catholic Legal Immigration Network**
  - https://cliniclegal.org/ovw

- **National Immigrant Women Advocacy Project (NIWAP)**
  - http://www.niwap.org

Culturally-Specific Services Technical Assistance Providers:

- **Asian-Pacific Institute on Gender-Based Violence**
  - http://www.api-gbv.org/
  - **Asian-Pacific Institute on Gender-Based Violence Language Access Plan**
    https://www.api-gbv.org/resources/language-access-plan/

- **National Latin@ Network: A Project of Casa de Esperanza**
  - https://nationallatinonetwork.org/
  - **Casa de Esperanza Language Access Toolkits**
    https://nationallatinonetwork.org/learn-more/courts-language-access

- **Ujima: National Resource Center on Violence Against Women in the Black Community**
  - https://ujimacommunity.org/

Immigration Resources for Victims:

- **Immi** (an online resource developed by Immigration Advocates Network (IAN) and Probono Net)
  - https://www.immi.org

- **Immigration Advocacy Network Legal Services Directory**
  - https://www.immigrationadvocates.org/nonprofit/legaldirectory/

- **USCIS Resources for Victims of Crime** (including brochures in English, Spanish, Chinese, and Russian)
  - https://www.uscis.gov/tools/humanitarian-benefits-based-resources/resources-victims-human-trafficking-other-crimes

- **WomensLaw.org** (an online resource developed by the National Network to End Domestic Violence)
  - https://www.womenslaw.org/

- Directory of State and Local Programs
  http://www.womenslaw.org/gethelp_type.php?type_name=State%20 and%20Local%20Programs

Safety Planning Resources:

- **Appleseed Deportation Manual**
  - http://www.appleseednetwork.org/wp-content/uploads/2017/06/ MASTERDOC.DONOTEDIT.pdf

- **ASISTA Guidelines for Advocate Supporting Letter**
  - PDF:
    http://www.asistahelp.org/documents/filelibrary/documents/DV_ Advocate_Affidavit_Guidelines_8166176703E7B.pdf
  - Microsoft Word:
    http://www.asistahelp.org/documents/filelibrary/documents/Guidelines_ for_Victim_of_Crime_Advo_BB065957753D1.doc

- **CLINIC: Know Your Rights: A Guide to Your Rights When Interacting with Law Enforcement**
  - https://cliniclegal.org/resources/know-your-rights-law-enforcement

- **Immigrant Legal Resource Center Family Preparedness Plan**
  - https://www.ilrc.org/family-preparedness-plan.
  - Available in Spanish here: https://www.ilrc.org/plan-de-preparaci%C3%B3n-familiar

- **Immigrant Legal Resource Center Red Cards**
  - https://www.ilrc.org/red-cards

Other Materials:

- **APIGBV FAQ on Immigration Enforcement for Service Providers**
  - http://www.api-gbv.org/files/FAQs-ImmigrationEnforcementVictimServices Programs-byAPI-GBV_July2017.pdf

- **APIGBV Advisory for Victim Service Providers on Harboring Immigrant Survivors**
  - http://www.api-gbv.org/download/ADVISORY_VictimServicesPrograms-HarboringImmigrantSurvivors_byAPI-GBV_July2017.pdf

- **NNEDV Confidentiality Toolkit**
  - https://www.techsafety.org/confidentiality

Chapter Five:
The Child Welfare System and Domestic Violence

I. Introduction

One in every fifteen children live in homes in which domestic violence is occurring, such that between three and fifteen million children are exposed to domestic violence each year.[1] As a result, families experiencing domestic violence often come to the attention of the child welfare system because of concerns about the harm or risk of harm that the domestic violence may pose to the children, or because of the co-occurrence of child abuse or neglect. Following or alongside a child welfare intervention, these families may also find themselves involved in other systems from civil (orders of protection, domestic relations cases) to criminal (prosecutions for domestic violence related crimes). Each of these systems has a differing response to domestic violence, and as such, consistent cross-system coordination to children who have been exposed to domestic violence is lacking. In this complicated context, child welfare systems across the country grapple to effectively intervene into the lives of families experiencing domestic violence in ways that create safety, enhance wellbeing, and provide stability for children and families. To be effective, the goal of child

---

[1] Sherry Hamby et al., U.S. Dep't of Just. Off. of Just. Programs, Off. of Juvenile Just. & Delinquency Prevention, Children's Exposure to Intimate Partner Violence and Other Family Violence 3 (Oct. 2011), https://www.ncjrs.gov/pdffiles1/ojjdp/232272.pdf; *The Impact of Domestic Violence on Children*, A Report to the President of the American Bar Association from the ABA Center on Children and the Law (1994), http://library.niwap.org/wp-content/uploads/2015/FAM-Tool-ImpactDVChildren-8.94.pdf; *see also* Bonnie E. Carlson, *Children's Observations of Interpersonal Violence*, 1 Battered Women & Their Families 321, 321–342 (2000); Ernest N. Jouriles et al., *Estimating the Number of American Children Living in Partner-Violent Families*, 20 J. Fam. Psychol. 137, 137–142 (2006).

welfare interventions should be to strengthen, rather than weaken, the ability of the non-offending parent to parent in safety and stability; unfortunately, child welfare system interventions across the country fall short of meeting this objective.[2]

Effective interventions are difficult to achieve because many complex issues arise when a family experiencing domestic violence comes to the attention of the child welfare system. Although the vast majority of non-offending parents care deeply about their children and their safety, and have made sacrifices to ensure their wellbeing, the following questions arise during child welfare interventions.[3] What can be done to stop the abuser from battering the non-offending parent and harming the children? How can the non-offending parent and children be kept safe and remain protected? Do the children need to removed from one or both parents? What is the legal response when a non-offending parent wants to protect the children but is unable to do so? How have the children been impacted by the domestic violence and what do they need to recover from any harm they have experienced? Are the children "neglected" under the law due to witnessing domestic violence? If so, who is deemed responsible under the law for causing this neglect—the non-offending parent and/or the abuser? Ultimately, can children be protected without re-victimizing and blaming the non-offending parent?

---

[2] The term "non-offending parent" is used throughout this chapter to describe the adult victim of domestic violence. Other synonymous terms for non-offending parent are non-abusive parent, domestic violence victim/survivor, adult victim/survivor, survivor parent, and battered mother.

[3] Zoe N. Hilton, *Battered Women's Concerns About Their Children Witnessing Wife Assault*, 7 J. Interpersonal Violence 77, 77–86 (1992); *see also* Janice Humphries, *The Work of Worrying: Battered Women and Their Children*, 9 Scholarly Inquiry for Nursing Prac. 127, 127–145 (1995). It was concerns for their children that led almost one-third of the women in a study to remain with their abusive partners. Sarah M. Buel, *Family Violence and the Health Care System: Recommendations for More Effective Intervention*, 35 Hous. L. Rev. 109, 118 (1998). "Remaining with a batterer is not about being stupid, masochistic, or codependent. It is about not knowing to whom it is safe to disclose the abuse, not knowing what can be done if the shelter is full, not knowing what to do if the judge does not believe me, not knowing what to do if the shelter makes me quit my job so the batterer does not follow me back, not knowing what to do if the prosecutor does not treat my case seriously, not knowing what to do if I have no job skills and cannot pay the rent without him, not knowing what to do if he says he will kill me and my children if I leave him, not knowing what to do if he says he will find me wherever I go, not knowing whether the judge will give him custody of the children, and not knowing how I will stay alive in the process of fleeing." *Id.* These women stayed in order to ensure that their children would have food and a place to sleep at night. *See* Jeffrey L. Edleson & Susan Schechter, *In the Best Interest of Women and Children: A Call for Collaboration Between Child Welfare and Domestic Violence Constituencies* 9 (1994) (unpublished manuscript), *available at* http://www.bvsde.paho.org/bvsacd/cd67/wingsp.pdf. Also, some may have stayed because the batterer threatened to harm the children if she left. *Id.* Children influence the decision to stay or go because battered women know that attempting to leave a batterer, with children, is the one of the most significant factors associated with severe domestic violence and death.

With these questions in mind, attorneys working with clients who are interacting with the child welfare system have an important role to play in helping to ensure that the child welfare interventions lead to effective outcomes and do not negatively impact other litigation that may be ongoing in other systems. Attorneys may be representing the non-offending parent, the abuser, or a victim of domestic violence who directly harmed or abused the children. With any of these clients, the intersection with the child welfare system may occur, in part, in the following ways:

- The client may have called or is considering calling the state's child abuse and neglect hotline to report abuse or neglect from the abuser against the children.

- The client may be the subject of a child welfare investigation as the non-offending parent or the domestic violence abuser.

- The client may be in need of appealing a child welfare finding of abuse or neglect against them.

- There may be an ongoing or closed juvenile court case that involved the client and domestic violence.

This chapter will provide information and advocacy tips that will guide attorneys in obtaining clarity around answers to the complex questions above in order to navigate the child welfare system with a client whose family has experienced domestic violence. Specifically, this chapter will include an overview of child welfare systems. The chapter will then explore the intersection of child welfare and domestic violence from how families experiencing domestic violence come to the attention of child welfare to the social science research about the impact of domestic violence on children, to the national model for child welfare interventions involving domestic violence. Next, the chapter will explain child welfare investigations, including a description of the judicial stages of a dependency case related to domestic violence. Lastly, although some advocacy tips are included throughout, this chapter concludes with an extensive list of pointers for attorneys representing clients who have child welfare system involvement. Through these topics, attorneys will become better equipped to understand the intersection of child welfare and domestic violence, and the laws, procedure, and practice governing child welfare investigations and juvenile court proceedings related to domestic violence.

II. Overview of Child Welfare Systems

There is no federal child welfare system, and each state has the *parens patriae* duty to protect the safety and wellbeing of its children. Consequently, a child welfare agency exists in every state. Most child welfare systems are comprised of a state agency authorized by statute to act on behalf of children who are abused, neglected or in need of care, the juvenile court system, and other social service and public offices. The dual goals of any child welfare system are to ensure children's safety by protecting them from abuse and neglect, and to strengthen and preserve families. The main functions of most child welfare agencies are to: receive reports of abuse and neglect; maintain a registry of findings of abuse or neglect; provide services to at-risk families; remove children if they are in imminent risk of harm; and manage and administer foster care and reunification services to families with dependency cases. Despite these common elements, the structure, administration, laws, policies, procedures, and practices governing child welfare systems vary significantly across the country. The following provides a summary of the national landscape on important aspects of child welfare systems.

A. Department Structure

Each jurisdiction has a child welfare agency that is responsible for children/families services or child safety either in the form of an independent department or a division within a department.[4] The majority of states have established a centralized statewide administrative system;[5] nine states can be described as county-administered (though under the supervision of responsible state agencies);[6] and three are "hybrid" states, partially administered by the state and partially administered by counties.[7] Each child welfare agency has a functional unit at either at the state level or at the county level that is responsible for child abuse and neglect investigations.

---

[4] States identified with independent departments on children/family services or child safety are: Arizona, Connecticut, District of Columbia, Florida, Illinois, Indiana, Kansas, Louisiana, Massachusetts, Mississippi, New Mexico, Rhode Island, Tennessee, Texas, Utah, Vermont, Wisconsin, and Wyoming. CHILD WELFARE INFORMATION GETAWAY, STATE VS. COUNTY ADMINISTRATION OF CHILD WELFARE SERVICES (2018), https://www.childwelfare.gov/pubPDFs/services.pdf. States that have a departmental division or office responsible for children/family services or child safety are: Alabama, Alaska, Arkansas, California, Colorado, Delaware, Georgia, Hawaii, Idaho, Iowa, Kentucky, Maine, Maryland, Michigan, Minnesota, Missouri, Montana, Nebraska, Nevada, New Hampshire, New Jersey, New York, North Carolina, North Dakota, Ohio, Oklahoma, Oregon, Pennsylvania, South Carolina, South Dakota, Virginia, Washington, and West Virginia. *Id.*

[5] States identified with centralized administrative system are: Alabama, Alaska, Arizona, Arkansas, Connecticut, Delaware, District of Columbia, Florida, Georgia, Hawaii, Idaho, Illinois, Indiana, Iowa, Kansas, Kentucky, Louisiana, Maine, Massachusetts, Michigan, Mississippi, Missouri, Montana, Nebraska, New Hampshire, New Jersey, New Mexico, Oklahoma, Oregon, Rhode Island, South Carolina, South Dakota, Texas, Tennessee, Utah, Vermont, Washington, West Virginia, and Wyoming. *Id.*

[6] States identified as county administered are: California, Colorado, Minnesota, New York, North Carolina, North Dakota, Ohio, Pennsylvania, and Virginia. *Id.*

[7] "Hybrid" states are: Maryland, Nevada, and Wisconsin. *Id.*

B. Reporting System

Federal law requires that every state maintain a reporting system for child abuse and neglect in order to receive federal money.[8] Therefore, in each jurisdiction, there are established reporting systems for child abuse and neglect, and these reports typically initiate the child welfare intervention. Reports are usually made via a hotline, written report, or both. Thirty-five states utilize statewide hotlines;[9] eight states have multiple hotlines, each responsible for a specific region;[10] and three states adopted a written report system.[11] Five states have hotline report systems in conjunction with written report systems.[12]

C. Mandated Reporting

All states have statutes identifying persons who are required to report suspected child maltreatment to an appropriate agency, such as child protective services, a law enforcement agency, or a state's toll-free child abuse reporting hotline.[13] Although mandatory reporting professionals vary state by state, individuals designated as mandatory reporters typically have frequent contact with children and often include: social workers; teachers, principals, and other school personnel; physicians, nurses, and other health-care workers; counselors, therapists, and other mental health professionals; child care providers; medical examiners or coroners; and law enforcement officers.[14] Around 18 states have "universal reporting," which requires any person who suspects child abuse or neglect to report.[15]

---

[8] Federal Child Abuse Prevention and Treatment Act ("CAPTA"), 42 U.S.C.A. § 5106(g) (2016).

[9] States with statewide hotlines include: Arizona, Arkansas, Colorado, Connecticut, District of Columbia, Florida, Georgia, Hawaii, Idaho, Illinois, Indiana, Kansas, Louisiana, Maine, Maryland, Massachusetts, Michigan, Missouri, Montana, Nebraska, Nevada, New Hampshire, New Jersey, New Mexico, New York, Oregon, Oklahoma, Pennsylvania, Rhode Island, South Dakota, Utah, Vermont, Virginia, Washington, and West Virginia. Cover Memorandum of Nationwide Survey on Domestic Violence in Child Abuse and Neglect Investigations from Colleen Garlington, Kirkland & Ellis LLP to Sara Block, The Family Defense Center (April 2017) (on file with the author).

[10] States that have separate hotlines for different regions are: Alaska, California, Minnesota, North Carolina, Ohio, South Carolina, Wisconsin, and Wyoming. *Id.*

[11] States that have written report system for suspected child abuse and/or neglect are: Alabama, Mississippi (although a hotline system is available if certain conditions are satisfied), and North Dakota. *Id.*

[12] States that have both hotline reporting system and written report system are: Delaware, Iowa, Kentucky, Tennessee, and Texas. *Id.*

[13] *See generally* Child Welfare Information Getaway, Mandatory Reporters of Abuse and Neglect (2015), https://www.childwelfare.gov/pubPDFs/manda.pdf.

[14] *Id.* at 2.

[15] The following states have "universal" reporting: Delaware, Florida, Idaho, Indiana, Kentucky, Maryland, Mississippi, Nebraska, New Hampshire, New Mexico, North Carolina, Oklahoma, Rhode Island, Tennessee, Texas, and Utah. *Id.*

Advocacy Tip: Determine who is and is not a mandated reporter in your state. Share this information with your client and provide advice regarding potential risks of sharing information with mandated reporters. Lawyers should be cautious about whether they are mandated reporters. In some states, lawyers are statutorily designated as mandatory reporters, while other states include attorneys but make exceptions under certain circumstances.[16] In some states, domestic violence advocates are statutorily designated as mandated reporters, so it is important to inform clients of this obligation if they are receiving services from a domestic violence agency.[17] In addition, if someone has been appointed to represent the child in your client's case, such as a Court Appointed Special Advocate or guardian *ad litem*, be sure to determine whether this person is a mandated reporter and advise your client accordingly.

Advocacy Tip: If your client is contemplating calling the abuse and neglect hotline in the client's jurisdiction regarding the client's children, assist the client in considering the advantages and disadvantages, such as whether the client will also become a subject of the child welfare investigation or intervention, and whether any harm to the family could result.

D. Centralized Registry

Following a child welfare investigation, findings that abuse or neglect did or did not occur are made and documented in a registry. Nearly every state has a central registry for the purpose of maintaining child abuse and neglect records, and/or clearing prospective employees or volunteers who work with children.[18] Although the registries are not typically open to the public, certain employers have access to the information. As a result, certain findings of abuse or neglect against a person can impact their current or prospective employment, especially if the job is related to children. Non-offending parents who have child welfare findings of neglect against them can lose their jobs, making them potentially more dependent upon a wage earning abuser. For non-offending parents who are undocumented, a concern exists that findings of abuse or neglect contained on the registry may make them ineligible for certain immigration relief under the Violence Against Women Act and other special relief visas.

---

[16] Lisa Hansen, *Attorneys' Duty to Report Child Abuse*, 19 Am. Acad. of Matrimonial L. 59, 68 (2004).

[17] Domestic violence workers are mandated reporters in Alaska, Arizona, Arkansas, Connecticut, Maine, and South Dakota. Humane officers are mandated reporters in California, Colorado, Maine, Ohio, Virginia, and West Virginia. *Id.*

[18] *See* Child Welfare Information Gateway, Review and Expunction of Central Registries and Reporting Records 1 (2014), https://www.childwelfare.gov/pubPDFs/registry.pdf.

III. How and Why Child Welfare Cares About Children Exposed to Domestic Violence

Families experiencing domestic violence can come to the attention of a child welfare agency for various reasons. Sometimes families come to the attention of the agency solely because of domestic violence. In these circumstances, children may be witnessing domestic violence or could have been injured during an incident of domestic violence, including trying to protect the non-offending parent. These scenarios are coined as the "failure to protect" cases because the non-offending parent is blamed for choosing, remaining in, or continuing in an abusive relationship. Domestic violence can also be an underlying factor in a case that comes to the attention of child welfare for other reasons. These other reasons could include direct child abuse or intentional harm to a child; mental health or substance abuse issues; environmental neglect or "dirty house" circumstances;

or challenges meeting the needs of a medically complex child.[19] Domestic violence may co-occur with these other maltreatment indicators. In these cases, often the issues surrounding the domestic violence become the most complex and challenging for child welfare professionals to address effectively.

Child welfare systems care about children who are living in homes in which domestic violence is occurring because of the potential adverse impact that the domestic violence can have on children. It is imperative, however, to avoid a "one size fits all" approach by concluding that every child is at risk or has been harmed by witnessing domestic violence, because such assumptions inherently and inevitably miss opportunities for meaningful evaluation, engagement,

---

[19] Studies demonstrate a co-occurrence of domestic violence and child abuse. A majority of the studies conducted on the co-occurrence of domestic violence and child maltreatment reveal that there are adult and child victims in up to 60 percent of families experiencing domestic violence. H. Lien Bragg, U.S. Dep't of Health & Human Servs., Child Protection in Families Experiencing Domestic Violence (2003), http://secure.ce-credit.com/articles/100938/Child_Protection_domesticviolence.pdf. Children are physically abused in approximately 30 percent of the homes where the mother is the known victim of domestic violence. *Final recommendation Statement – Intimate Partner Violence and Abuse of Elderly and Vulnerable Adults: Screening*, U.S. Preventive Servs. Task Force, https://www.uspreventiveservicestaskforce.org/Page/Document/RecommendationStatementFinal/intimate-partner-violence-and-abuse-of-elderly-and-vulnerable-adults-screening (last updated Jan. 2013); see also Evan Stark, *The Battered Mother in the Child Protective Services Caseload: Developing an Appropriate Response*, 23 Women's Rts. L. Rep. 107, 109–111 (2002). Some studies find the correlation to be higher or lower. In 30 studies, 41 percent was the median co-occurrence of domestic violence and child maltreatment. As a corollary, research reveals that mothers are being battered in approximately half of the families where their children are being physically abused. Jeffrey L. Edleson, *The Overlap Between Child Maltreatment and Woman Battering*, 5 Violence Against Women 134, 134–154 (1999). Domestic violence was also identified in around 40 percent of families in which children died as a result of child abuse. Linda Spears, Nat'l Resource Ctr. on Domestic Violence, Building Bridges Between Domestic Violence Organizations and Child Protective Services 11 (2000), https://vawnet.org/sites/default/files/materials/files/2016-09/BCS7_cps.pdf. In 1993, the Oregon Department of Health reported that domestic violence was present in 41 percent of families experiencing child abuse and neglect resulting in critical injuries or death. *Id.* at 7. In addition, the Massachusetts Department of Social Services in 1994 found that in child abuse and neglect fatalities, 43 percent of the mothers identified themselves as victims of domestic violence. *Id.* Furthermore, in New York City, between 1990 and 1993, 55.6 percent of the families with child homicides had a documented history of domestic violence in the four years preceding the homicide. *Id.* These statistics do not indicate that child abuse or child fatalities are more likely to result when domestic violence is occurring but the correlation identifies domestic violence as a risk factor for child abuse. Children can also be injured while trying to protect the non-offending parent, hurt as an indirect victim during an incident of domestic violence targeted at the non-offending parent, or used as a tactic of the abuser's domestic violence. Research indicates that 80–90 percent of children living in homes with domestic violence are aware of the abuse. Catherine O'Malley et al., Child Exposure to Domestic Violence: An Exploration of Policy Defining it as Maltreatment (Aug. 2014), *available at* https://cvip.wustl.edu/outreach/Documents/Child%20Exposure%20to%20Domestic%20Violence%20August%202014.pdf (citing Children's Def. Fund, Domestic violence and its impact on children: Factsheet (2002)).

and intervention.[20] Each family and child is unique, especially as it relates to their experiences regarding domestic violence. An individualized child welfare approach is essential to an intervention that responds to the specific needs of the family and that leads to positive and sustainable outcomes.

Extensive research has focused on the impact that exposure to domestic violence can have on children. Jeffrey Edleson and Susan Schechter's critical social science research in this intersection found that the effect of the domestic violence impacts each child differently and established the following conclusions:

- The consequences that domestic violence has on children ranges from none to serious, such that some will experience short-term effects, some will endure long-term impacts, and some will demonstrate none at all.[21]

- Some children may exhibit low self-esteem; depression, anger, fear, anxiety, hypervigilance; eating and sleep disorders; bedwetting; vomiting; verbally and physically aggressive behaviors; guilt, when the child believes he or she is the cause of the abuse; poor academic performance; problems thinking and reasoning; lack of compliance with authority; adolescent alcohol and drug abuse; and dating violence.[22]

- The most important factor that influences the impact of the domestic violence on the child is past and ongoing quality of the child's relationship with the non-offending parent, including the non-offending parent's ability to mediate the intensity of the domestic violence incident, as well as stability of relationships the child has with people important to the child.[23]

- The safety and wellbeing of children is inextricably linked to the safety and wellbeing of the non-offending parent.

- Children in homes with domestic violence experience increased trauma when removed from the non-offending parent.

- The quality of children's relationships with the non-offending parent is the greatest predictor in their recovery from harm.[24] Children can overcome

---

[20] *See generally* Jeffrey L. Edleson, *Emerging Responses to Children Exposed to Domestic Violence*, VAWNET.ORG (July 2011), *available at* https://vawnet.org/sites/default/files/materials/files/2016-09/AR_ChildrensExposure.pdf. *See also* Jeffrey L. Edleson, *Should Childhood Exposure to Adult Domestic Violence Be Defined as Child Maltreatment under the Law?, in* PROTECTING CHILDREN FROM DOMESTIC VIOLENCE: STRATEGIES FOR COMMUNITY INTERVENTION 8, 20 (Peter G. Jaffe, Linda L. Baker & Alison J. Cunningham eds., 2004).

[21] Jeffrey L. Edleson, *Children's Witnessing of Adult Domestic Violence*, 14 J. INTERPERSONAL VIOLENCE 839 (1997).

[22] *See Id.*

[23] *Id.*

[24] SPEARS, *supra* note 19.

any problems within a relatively short time of experiencing safety with the non-offending parent.[25] Any harm from witnessing domestic violence will be significantly mitigated by remaining with the non-offending parent in a safe and stable environment.[26]

This pivotal research culminated in a publication that became the benchmark for child welfare interventions into the lives of families experiencing domestic violence. This national model is called *Effective Interventions In Domestic Violence and Child Maltreatment Cases: Guidelines for Policy and Practice*, and was published by the National Council of Juvenile and Family Court Judges (NCJFCJ) in 1999.[27] This well-respected and accepted publication is commonly referred to as *The Greenbook* and can be freely downloaded online.[28] Child welfare interventions that are inconsistent with this national model in policy and/ or practice can place children in greater risk of harm and will deter the non-offending parent from reaching out to systems of support in the future for help.

Advocacy Tip: Knowledge about the social science research and the tenets of *The Greenbook* is arsenal for your advocacy. Using the research and best practice model as a foundation for your advocacy while connecting your client's specific situation to the research and key tenets strengthens your arguments.

IV. Child Welfare Investigations and Juvenile Court

Advocacy Tip: Each state has laws, rules, procedures, policies, and practices that govern the operations of the child welfare system, including investigations and dependency cases in juvenile court. Become familiar with the relevant controlling authority for each stage of the client's child welfare involvement, from the investigation through the juvenile court case.

A. Investigations

The first step of the child welfare intervention is typically the investigation.[29] The investigation involves (1) gathering evidence and making a formal determination of whether child maltreatment has occurred, and (2) conducting ongoing assessments to determine if the children are safe.

---

[25] EDLESON, *supra* note 21.

[26] *Id.*

[27] NAT'L COUNCIL OF JUVENILE & FAMILY COURT JUDGES (NCJFCJ), EFFECTIVE INTERVENTIONS IN DOMESTIC VIOLENCE AND CHILD MALTREATMENT CASES: GUIDELINES FOR POLICY AND PRACTICE 17 (1999), https://www. rcdvcpc.org/the-greenbook.html [hereinafter *The Greenbook*].

[28] *Id.*

[29] In some states, rather than automatically assigning a case to an investigation after the hotline screening, a differential response approach is used in which a case can be assigned to either the investigation or alternative track, and cases involving domestic violence are often assigned to this alternative track.

Investigations typically are time limited, often to 45 or 60 days, and most states mandate a short time frame in which the child welfare professional must see the child, such as within 12 or 24 hours of the investigation assignment. During the investigation, the child welfare professional is supposed to gather information by interviewing the parents and children (when appropriate), observing the children, speaking to collateral contacts (teachers, doctors, law enforcement, friends/family with firsthand knowledge), and collecting documents (police reports, medical records, legal filings, etc.). Throughout this process, the worker is also assessing the child's safety and implementing interventions accordingly. At the end of the investigation, the parents will be notified of the result of the investigation, and any findings will be entered in the state's registry. In many states, parents are entitled to administrative appeal of these investigative findings.

Advocacy Tip: Determine Your Level of Involvement

During the investigation, as a lawyer, you can remain in the background in support of your clients, or you can directly communicate with the investigator. Discuss with your clients whether they want to advocate for themselves or if they want you to intervene on their behalf. Consider the potential reaction the investigator may have if you come in as a third party. With your client, you can:

1. Discuss strategies for maintaining a positive relationship with the investigator;
2. Assist clients in articulating their concerns to the investigator;
3. Assist clients in providing written documentation to the investigator;
4. Contact the investigator yourself; and/or
5. Contact the investigator's supervisor.

B. Investigative Determinations, Children's Exposure to Domestic Violence, and Precautionary Measures

Through the investigation, the child welfare professional will need to determine, under the law, whether the children are abused or neglected based upon their exposure to domestic violence, and if so, which parent(s) will have an abuse or neglect finding against them. In other words, does the child's exposure to domestic violence rise to the level of abuse or neglect and if so, does being in an abusive relationship make the non-offending parent also neglectful?

States vary drastically in how their laws and administrative rules define the legal connection between exposure to domestic violence and abuse and neglect. Within those states that have adopted an allegation system, only California (Los Angeles County), Florida, and Oklahoma have a maltreatment allegation specifically for domestic violence. Some states do not have a specific domestic violence allegation, but do identify domestic violence specifically in its rules regarding abuse and neglect allegation.[30] Most states, however, encompass exposure to domestic violence in an umbrella allegation of abuse or neglect.[31] Instructions regarding domestic violence cases are also contained in state procedures and policies. Thirty state agencies provide a domestic violence policy in the child welfare context.[32] It is important to become familiar with the relevant state laws and rules by looking at the state or local child welfare agency's website. Trends in definitions relating to children, non-offending parents, and abusers are summarized below.

Every state recognizes that exposure to domestic violence can cause a child to be abused or neglected, yet no state creates a *per se* rule that children who are exposed to domestic violence are abused or neglected. Rather, in order to determine whether exposure to domestic violence constitutes abuse or neglect to a child, child welfare agencies require the existence of harm or the risk of harm to the child. For instance, the procedures in the District of Columbia state that exposure to domestic violence, in and of itself, does not constitute abuse and neglect, but rather the impact of domestic violence on the children may lead to that finding.[33] The District of Columbia goes on to specify that domestic violence is considered child abuse and neglect when it "has resulted in actual physical or mental injury or specific risk of harm to the children."[34] Illinois, too, provides further guidance by requiring that the domestic violence pose a "real, significant, and imminent, risk of moderate to severe harm to the child."[35] Texas' policy echoes this stance by stating,

> [C]hild's exposure to domestic violence, in and of itself, does not constitute child abuse or neglect by the adult victim of domestic violence. Domestic violence that physically harms a child or puts the

---

[30] *The Greenbook, supra* note 27. The following states specifically mention domestic violence in their rules defining abuse and neglect: Arizona, Illinois, Nebraska, New Hampshire, New Jersey, Oklahoma, Oregon, Utah, Virginia, Washington. *Id.*

[31] *Id.* The following states do not have a specific abuse or neglect allegation for domestic violence and domestic violence cases are encompassed in general abuse and neglect: Alabama, Alaska, Connecticut, DC, Delaware, Hawaii, Idaho, Indiana, Kansas, Kentucky, Louisiana, Maine, Massachusetts, Michigan, Mississippi, Missouri, Montana, Nevada, New Mexico, New York, North Carolina, North Dakota, Ohio, Pennsylvania, South Carolina, North Dakota, Tennessee, Texas, Vermont, West Virginia, Wisconsin. *Id.*

[32] *Id.* These states include: Alaska, California (Los Angeles county), Connecticut, District of Columbia, Delaware, Florida, Georgia, Idaho, Indiana, Maine, Michigan, Minnesota, Missouri, Montana, New Hampshire, New Jersey, New Mexico, New York, North Carolina, North Dakota, Ohio (Cuyahoga County), Oregon, Pennsylvania (Philadelphia county), Tennessee, Texas, Utah, Vermont, Virginia, West Virginia, and Wisconsin. *Id.*

[33] D.C. Child & Family Servs. Agency, Investigations Procedural Operations Manual 85 (2013), https://cfsa.dc.gov/sites/default/files/dc/sites/cfsa/publication/attachments/Investigations-POM_0.pdf.

[34] *Id.*

[35] Ill. Adm. Code 89 § 300, Appendix B.

child at substantial risk of immediate harm, however, constitutes an allegation of child abuse or neglect.[36]

Based upon these rules and policies and in accordance with *The Greenbook's* guidance, an individualized assessment of the specific impact of domestic violence on each child is required. If the child is determined not to be abused or neglected, the investigative finding will be deemed "unfounded" or "unsubstantiated." If it is determined that the exposure to domestic violence has risen to the level of constituting child maltreatment, the child welfare professional must then determine the responsibility for such harm by each parent, guardian, or caretaker.

Investigative determinations will be made separately for each parent. In order to hold abusers accountable, investigative findings can be entered against them. Regarding the adult victim of domestic violence, a minority number of states take the position against indicating the non-offending parent for neglect, as in Maine's policy.[37] Similarly, Montana's policy instructs that "the child protection specialists should identify the offending parent appropriately and ensure that the non-offending parent is not blamed for the abuse that occurred and its impact on the children."[38] Similarly, Florida's "failure to protect" allegation requires verification of the domestic violence victim's active participation in the abuse of the child and is not appropriate as an allegation simply because the victim is still with the perpetrator or the perpetrator is still in the home."[39]

Other states emphasize that the critical factor in determining whether non-offending parents will be considered neglectful is the steps that they took to protect their children from the harm or risk of harm that the domestic violence created. In Cuyahoga County, Ohio, the policy requires child welfare professionals to "validate the non-offending parent's efforts to keep the children safe."[40] Further founded upon the lessons from the social science research and consistent with *The Greenbook* guidance, Illinois' administrative law states:

---

[36] Tex. Dep't of Family & Protective Servs., Disposition Guidelines for Domestic Violence Resource Guide 1 (2018), https://www.dfps.state.tx.us/handbooks/CPS/Resource_Guides/Disposition_Guidelines_for_Domestic_Violence_Resource_Guide.pdf.

[37] *Child Abuse and Neglect Findings*, Maine Off. of Child & Fam. Servs. (Jan. 1, 2015), http://www.maine.gov/dhhs/ocfs/cw/policy/iv__d-1__child_abuse_and_negle.htm.

[38] Child & Fam. Servs. Div., Mont. Dep't of Pub. Health & Human Servs., Domestic Violence Protocol Summary 3, https://dphhs.mt.gov/Portals/85/cfsd/documents/cfsdmanual/domesticviolence.pdf (citing Mont. Code Ann. § 41-3-102(23)(a)–(b) ("'Psychological abuse or neglect' . . . may not be construed to hold a victim responsible for failing to prevent the crime against the victim.")).

[39] *Id.* at A-18.

[40] Cuyahoga County Div. of Child & Fam. Servs., Policy Statement: Cases Involving Domestic Violence 2 (2015), http://cfs.cuyahogacounty.us/pdf_cfs/en-US/policies/2/20307.pdf.

> The adult victim of domestic violence, who is the non-offending parent or caregiver, is presumed to not be neglectful or to have created an environment injurious to the child so long as he or she has exercised precautionary measures to prevent or mitigate the real, significant and imminent risk of moderate to severe harm to the child.[41]

Illinois' "presumption against neglect" for non-offending parents is one of the most *Greenbook*-compliant rules in the country regarding the maltreatment status of the non-offending parent. Although not yet further defined, examples of "precautionary measures" could include, but are not limited to the following:

---

[41] ILL. ADMIN. CODE tit. 89 § 300, Appendix B (2018).

General Precautionary Measures	Domestic Violence Specific Precautionary Measures

• Attempts to stop the cause of the likelihood of harm
 	
• Takes steps to protect child from the likelihood of harm
 	
• Responds to any harm the child has experienced
 	
• Reaches out to support system
 	
• Utilizes social services to address needs in the family
 	
• Possesses and utilizes parenting skills
 	
• Maintains a healthy and loving relationship with the child
 	
• Attends to the child's emotional, psychological, physical, educational, and medical needs
 	
• Meets the child's medical, psychological, and educational needs, when appropriate
 	
• Maintains a healthy and loving parental relationship with the child
 	
• Provides stability—emotional, educational, relational, financial—for the child
 	
• Cooperates with current efforts to address stressors or risk factors in the home
 	
• Considers child's best interest
	• Uses knowledge about the abuser and the situation
	
	• Uses safety strategies for herself/himself and the child
	  ○ Takes preventative measures to keep the child safe in case an incident of domestic violence occurs (e.g., keeping coats and shoes near the child's bed in case the non-offending parent and child need to leave)
	  ○ Attempts to keep the child safe from harm during an incident of domestic violence (e.g., moving to a room where the child is not present; telling the child to leave the area where the domestic violence is occurring; instructing the child to seek outside help that the child can reasonably be expected to do; shielding the child from witnessing the domestic violence)
	
	• Discusses with the child a plan to maintain safety during an incident of domestic violence
	
	• Develops a domestic violence safety plan individually or with the assistance of an advocate
	
	• Physically defends herself/himself in attempt to stop the perpetrator of abuse from harming her/him or the child
	
	• Acknowledges the potential impact that domestic violence can have on the child
	
	• Utilizes a support system Attends individual therapy or domestic violence counseling
	
	• Seeks guidance from religious leadership
	
	• Calls the police
	
	• Seeks legal assistance
	
	• Obtains or attempts to obtain an order of protection or to initiate other legal proceedings
	
	• Ceases the relationship with the perpetrator of the domestic violence
	
	• Restricts the access of the perpetrator of domestic violence to the non-offending parent/adult victim and child

Because the non-offending parent cannot stop the abuser's choice to commit acts of domestic violence, the effort and willingness to try to keep the children safe and meet their needs should be the guiding principle for child welfare determinations.

Advocacy Tip: It is critically important that non-offending parents share helpful information with the child welfare worker in a coherent and organized way. Such helpful information includes the specific impact of the domestic violence on the child and the "precautionary measures" (protective steps) they exercised. Oftentimes, however, it is difficult for non-offending parents to generate a list of concrete "precautionary measures," because the steps they took to protect their children were a means of survival every day and not particularly noteworthy or significant from their perspective. To assist clients in thinking about these important factors, please use the "Risk of Harm" and "Precautionary Measures" worksheets, both of which are included in the appendix to this chapter. Please determine the most useful ways to use these worksheets with your clients, as well as the most constructive method of sharing the information with the child welfare professional.

Information can be conveyed verbally or in writing, and be cognizant of attorney-client and work product considerations.

C. Safety Determinations and Domestic Violence

In addition to determining the investigative finding, child welfare professionals continually evaluate the safety of the children throughout the investigation. If children are determined to be "unsafe," child welfare professional can do the following: (1) maintain the status quo, (2) provide interventions without judicial involvement, or (3) remove the children from the parents by taking protective custody.

Advocacy Tip: If the client is worried that the child welfare professional may determine that the children are "unsafe," proactively try to find a way to reduce the potential concern if this is consistent with the client's wishes. This could mean that the client temporarily lives somewhere else with the children, prohibits someone who could pose a risk from being in the home, or allows the children to stay with a relative or friend. The client could also be prepared to acknowledge the potential concern while explaining why the children's safety is not at risk.

If safety concerns exist, child welfare professionals can recommend conditions and provide services that can assist in keeping the non-offending parent and children safe, without judicial involvement. Such conditions may include getting an order of protection, going to a domestic violence shelter, engaging in domestic violence counseling, or prohibiting the abuser from living in the home. Any recommendations or conditions that child welfare professionals present are voluntary, such that non-offending parents and abusers are not required to comply. Although such interventions do not have the force of law, many parents, especially non-offending parents who may already feel powerless, perceive that they do not have an actual "choice" because of the power the child welfare professional and system yield. Nevertheless, conditions or services recommended by a child welfare professional are not mandatory (in contrast to a case plan approved by a judge that could result in significant legal consequences if not followed).

If the safety concerns cannot be ameliorated, children can be removed from their parents. Child welfare professionals have significant power because they, along with doctors and police officers, can remove children from their parents without a judge's order. This power should, however, only be exercised in emergency cases, where there is not time to get a judge's order. If the child welfare professional believes that the children are at "imminent risk of harm" by staying with the parents, and that "reasonable efforts could not prevent the removal," the child welfare professional can remove the children from the parents by taking "protective custody." If protective custody is taken, each state entitles the family to be in front of a juvenile court judge within a designated short period of time, such as 48 hours. For the days between protective custody and the first court hearing, the children will likely be placed with relatives, in a temporary foster home, or in a shelter. Most states have an assigned office that screens and initiates the dependency case, which is often the state's attorney, district attorney, or child welfare agency. If the case is not screened into juvenile court, the protective custody must end, and the children must be returned to their custodial parent. If the case is screened into court, the first court hearing will be in front of a judge who will determine if the case will proceed and where the children will be placed, which will be discussed in the following section.

Determining whether to remove children exposed to domestic violence from their homes requires several important considerations. There is general agreement that children function best if they can remain safely within their families, and this is increasingly true for child survivors of domestic violence.[42] Often, attempting to keep children safe by removing them from the non-offending parent is counterproductive.[43] Specifically, Cuyahoga County confirms that "[f]

---

[42] *The Greenbook, supra* note 27, at 19.

[43] Although keeping children with non-offending parents is the general benchmark, it is not always in the best interest of the children, as described in *The Greenbook*: "To link the safety of children to the safety of their mothers is the goal, although it may not always work in practice. Some battered mothers, for example, seriously maltreat their children or remain in violent relationships that are dangerous to their children despite repeated efforts to provide safety resources. Some batterers may not stop their violence despite intervention. In these cases, increasing the mother's safety may not enhance the child's. Obviously, when this occurs, the primary and pressing task must be child protection. However, in many cases, trying to make mothers safe does make children safer and offers children their best hope for stability." *Id.*

[43] *Id.*

rom the perspective of safety, healing from trauma, and stability, it is in the best interest of children to remain *safe and together* with the non-offending domestic violence survivors . . ."[44] Whenever possible, therefore, children exposed to domestic violence should remain with the non-offending parent in safety.[45] Research and practice have established, and as *The Greenbook* informs, the safety of children exposed to domestic violence is inextricably linked to the safety of their non-offending parent. It follows that if the non-offending parent is not in "imminent risk of harm"—the legal standard for "protective custody"—then the children are not in "imminent risk of harm." As such, achieving safety for the non-offending parent achieves safety for the children.[46] Before children are removed from the non-offending parent, the child welfare professional must make "reasonable efforts" to help the non-offending parent find safety, which in turn results in safety for the children.

D. Dependency Cases and Domestic Violence

In every state, families experiencing domestic violence may find themselves involved in a dependency case in the jurisdiction's juvenile court. Following the removal and the screening of the case, a dependency petition is filed, initiating the juvenile court case. Many people are involved in a dependency case, including typically the judge, court reporter, bailiff, court coordinator, state's attorney/district attorney, child welfare personnel and attorneys from the child welfare agency, attorneys for parents, and representation for the children. In most states, parents have a statutory right to an attorney at every phase of the dependency process, and one will be appointed if the parents' income qualifies.[47] It is best practice that parents are not appointed the same lawyer, especially if domestic violence is occurring. Children will also be represented, yet the model of representation varies among states between a child's attorney, guardian *ad litem*, and/or Court Appointed Special Advocate. State statutes define the relief being sought at each phase, and case law illustrates how cases involving domestic violence are resolved. The stages of a dependency case are summarized below, with advocacy suggestions throughout:

(1) **Temporary Custody/Shelter Care Hearing:** Before this hearing, determine if any relatives are able to care for the children. The client should be advised to comply with the case/service plan and visitation schedule that will be developed. In addition, the non-offending parent should be

---

[44] Cuyahoga County Div. of Child & Fam. Servs., *supra* note 40, at 1.

[45] *The Greenbook, supra* note 27, at 19.

[46] *Id.*

[47] Vivek Sankaran, *A National Survey On Parent's Right to Counsel in Termination of Parental Rights and Dependency Cases*, Youth Rts. Just., http://youthrightsjustice.org/Documents/SurveyParentRighttoCounsel.pdf (last visited May 8, 2018).

cautioned that remaining with the abusive partner will be a significant hindrance to regaining custody of the children.

(2) **Adjudication Hearing:** This hearing is most closely analogous to a trial, and includes testimony from all relevant witnesses. At this stage, calling an expert witness to testify may be helpful depending on the facts of the case. Because the judge needs to specify the acts or omissions of each parent regarding the finding, the non-offending parent will need to provide evidence of the protective steps or "precautionary measures" that were taken in order to keep the children safe or reduce the risk of harm the domestic violence posed. The expert witness can also provide an expert opinion about the "reasonableness" of these efforts.

(3) **Disposition Hearing:** The disposition hearing follows the adjudication and is best compared to a sentencing hearing, yet the outcome is not a loss of freedoms such as incarceration, but rather of the constitutional right to the care and custody of one's children. If the children are not returned to the non-offending parent at this stage, an argument for a permanency goal of "return home"/reunification should be made.

(4) **Permanency Hearings:** At least every six months, the court will evaluate the progress toward the permanency goal and determine if it has been met. During this time, the non-offending parent's attorney could advocate to increase visitation between the parent and the children.

(5) **Termination of Parental Rights:** If parents have not corrected the conditions that caused the case to come into the system, or if other grounds exist, a petition to terminate parental rights can be filed. If parental rights are terminated, parents and children lose their legal relationship to each other, and children lose their legal relationship with siblings and extended families. When addressing whether parental rights should be terminated involuntarily, most states require that a court determine 1) by clear and convincing evidence that the parent is unfit and 2) determine whether severing the parent-child relationship is in the child's best interests.[48] Although no state specifically designates "domestic violence" as a ground for unfitness, the parental rights of non-offending parents can be involuntarily terminated due to circumstances surrounding the domestic violence, in addition to federally outlined timeframes about the length of

---

[48] *See* Santosky v. Kramer, 455 U.S. 745 (1982) (setting the standard of proof in termination of parental rights proceedings at clear and convincing evidence); Child Welfare Information Gateway, Grounds for Involuntary Termination of Parental Rights (2016) 1, https://www.childwelfare.gov/pubPDFs/groundtermin.pdf#page=1&view=Introduction.

time children have been in substitute care.[49] Failing to complete services, or the continuation of the abusive relationship through the pendency of the dependency case, can form the basis of a termination determination.

A dependency case in juvenile court can last months to years depending upon the jurisdiction and circumstances. Child welfare interventions into the lives of families experiencing domestic violence, therefore, should prioritize effective front-end efforts that are trauma-informed, family-centered, and strength-based to help families find sustainable safety and stability.

V. *Advocacy Tips*

Equipped with the information in this chapter, the following are concrete suggestions that will enable attorneys to apply this knowledge to their practice in effective and practical ways.

- **Knowledge is power:** Become knowledgeable about your state's child welfare system structure. Pull the relevant statutes, rules, procedures, and policies regarding child welfare and domestic violence and mandated reporting in your state. Determine if your state child welfare agency has a domestic violence program that could be a resource for your client.

- **Keep your eye on the prize:** Encourage clients to articulate their priority or goal related to the child welfare involvement. Clients may feel that they have very little control over the process, but it can be helpful they articulate what the most important outcome would be to them. Some goals may be: avoid a child welfare abuse/neglect finding (which may impact employment or available immigration relief); ensure the abuser is held responsible; keep the children living with client and avoid removal; avoid placement with the abuser or abuser's family; and obtain services for client and the children. Clients may have more than one goal, but articulating their order of priorities will help guide decisions and strategic determinations throughout the investigation.

- **Write it down:** Encourage clients to keep a contact log of all communications, meetings, and conversations with the child welfare professional during the investigation and/or the dependency case. Advise clients to document voicemails left for and by the child welfare professional, and the dates and content of telephone conversations and in-person visits. Also encourage clients to provide supportive documents (such as letters of

---

[49] The Adoption and Safe Families Act, Pub. L. No. 105-89, amended title IV-E of the Social Security Act, which establishes guidelines that States must comply with as a condition for receiving Federal title IV-E funds. The Adoption and Safe Families Act (ASFA) requires State agencies to file a petition to terminate parental rights, with certain exceptions, when a child has been in foster care for 15 of the most recent 22 months.

support, police reports, medical records) to the child welfare worker, keep a copy for themselves, and document such exchanges in a document log. Examples of a contact log and document log are included in the appendix to this chapter. Encourage clients to keep track of all of the written notices, reports, and court orders received during the child welfare process.

- **It's a secret:** The client's address or other contact information can be kept confidential. While the child welfare professional will need to know where the client is living, especially if the children are living there as well, this information should not be released to anyone else without the client's consent and should be redacted from any reports; continually reminding the child welfare professional of this is important. The more people who become involved in the child welfare intervention, the more likely it is that other people could accidentally reveal the information, which could become a matter of life and death.

- **Keep it real:** Be honest with your client about the potential consequences of the choices they make. If you are representing non-offending parents, be realistic that the decision to maintain the relationship with an abuser, deny the abuse, or contact the abuser in secrecy will cause the child welfare professional to mistrust the client and will increase the probability of a neglect finding and removal of the children.

- **Call in the expert:** Experts can be very helpful at any stage of child welfare involvement. An expert can establish the impact of the domestic violence on the children, which is a necessary consideration in throughout the child welfare process. This expert should be someone who has the educational credentials and professional experience to provide a developmental or psychological assessment on children, and would ideally have some background in domestic violence practice. An expert is also helpful to provide an explanation of domestic violence, identify the non-offending parent and abuser, interpret acts of violence or force that the non-offending parent may have used, identify the protective steps the non-offending parent took, and determine whether these steps were reasonable under the circumstances. Enlisting the assistance of this expert during a child welfare investigation could provide a persuasive perspective to the child welfare professional. Expert reports and testimony about domestic violence could be helpful in an appeal of a child welfare abuse/neglect finding, or at any stage of a dependency case.

- **The art of persuasion:** Look for persuasive authority from other states that could be helpful. For instance, the *Nicholson* cases out of New York in the Second Circuit are the most expansive judicial exploration on the intersection of domestic violence and child welfare.[50] The progeny of cases held that children cannot be removed from non-offending parents when the sole allegation of harm is exposure to domestic violence, and that non-offending parents should not be deemed neglectful because they were victims of domestic violence.

- **"You say tomato, I say tomato:"** The judicial systems in every state lack a coordinated response to domestic violence, especially when children are involved. This means that each system provides varying types of legal remedies. Families may receive mixed messages about who is considered a victim, and the legal impact of children's exposure to domestic violence varies based upon the relief sought. The acknowledgment and understanding of this incongruent environment should direct your litigation strategy. For instance, in the non-offending parent's divorce case, a sound strategy may be to include an extensive history of domestic violence in pleadings and in testimony to argue that the children's exposure to the domestic violence harmed them. In a child welfare appeal or dependency case, however, minimizing the severity of the domestic violence and its effect on the children could be advantageous to the client. While it is difficult to reconcile these disparate approaches, it is important to anticipate future interventions or litigation that may ensue when determining the strategy in the present case. In addition, consider how interconnected the client's current case is with the child welfare system.

- **Help is on the way:** Connect your client with services such as domestic violence counseling. The state or local domestic violence coalitions likely have a database of domestic violence agencies and available services in each community. Every state also has a domestic violence hotline that can also be a useful way to connect with appropriate services. Be sure to advise your client about the confidentiality limitations and mandated reporting obligations of the service providers.

- **Know your limits:** Child welfare representation is a specialized practice. If you decide to take on child welfare representation—either informally by advising a client during a child welfare investigation, or formally during a dependency case or appeal of a child welfare abuse/neglect finding— consult with attorneys who have experience with these cases. If need be, refer your client to a lawyer with child welfare experience and if your client qualifies, refer them to local civil legal aid providers that have a child welfare practice area.

---

[50] In re Nicholson, 181 F. Supp. 2d 182, 182 (E.D.N.Y. 2002) (*Nicholson I*); Nicholson v. Williams, 203 F. Supp. 2d 153, 153 (E.D.N.Y. 2002) (*Nicholson II*).

Families experiencing domestic violence and the child welfare system require advocacy that is supportive, knowledgeable, strategic, calming, and holistic to ensure that the intervention strengthens, rather than weakens, the safety and stability of the family.

APPENDIX

"Risk of Harm" Worksheet

This worksheet will help you capture a complete picture of each of your children's overall wellbeing and how the exposure to domestic violence has impacted them. Some questions may not be relevant because of the age of your child(ren). You should fill out or think through these questions for each of your children.[51]

Child's Name: _____ Date of Birth: _____

Age at the time of the domestic violence incident giving rise to child welfare intervention:_____

Impact of Incident of Domestic Violence

Where was the child during the incident of domestic violence that gave rise to the child welfare investigation?

Was the child physically injured during the incident of domestic violence?

Did the child try to intervene during the incident of domestic violence?

How did the child react during the incident of domestic violence? (Be specific.)

Did you instruct your child about what to do during an incident of domestic violence? Was the child able to follow the plan?

Do you discuss the domestic violence with the child? How did the child respond? How does the child appear to be processing the abuse?

---

[51] Important Warning: If you choose to share this worksheet or the information contained on the worksheet, the information will not be kept confidential and there is a chance that the abuser will acquire access to the information.

Overall Wellbeing

Describe the personality of your child.

Describe the overall behavior of your child.

Describe the child's eating habits.

Describe how the child sleeps.

How does the child interact with peers/friends?

How is the child doing in school? Have the teachers identified any special or unmet needs of the child?

Is the child receiving any services (e.g., physical, emotional, speech, occupational therapy)?

In what ways has the domestic violence impacted the child?

Precautionary Measures/Protective Steps Worksheet

Use this worksheet as a place to think about all of the many ways you prioritized the needs of your children, protected them, and sacrificed for them despite the abuse you were experiencing.[52]

Below is a list of examples of "precautionary measures" or protective steps. You can circle the ones that apply to you and elaborate on the specifics. On the following pages, you can further explore the "precautionary measures" you have taken.

General Precautionary Measures/ Protective Steps	• Attempts to stop the cause of the likelihood of harm • Takes steps to protect child from the likelihood of harm • Responds to any harm the child has experienced • Reaches out to support system • Utilizes social services to address needs in the family • Possesses and utilizes parenting skills • Maintains a healthy and loving relationship with the child • Attends to the child's emotional, psychological, physical, educational, and medical needs • Meets the child's medical, psychological, and educational needs, when appropriate • Maintains a healthy and loving parental relationship with the child • Provides stability—emotional, educational, relational, financial—for the child • Cooperates with current efforts to address stressors or risk factors in the home • Considers child's best interest

---

[52] Important Warning: If you choose to share this worksheet or the information contained on the worksheet, the information will not be kept confidential and there is a chance that the abuser will acquire access to the information.

Domestic Violence Precautionary Measures/ Protective Steps	• Uses knowledge about the abuser and the situation
	
	• Uses safety strategies for herself/himself and the child
	  ○ Takes preventative measures to keep the child safe in case an incident of domestic violence occurs (e.g., keeping coats and shoes near the child's bed in case the non-offending parent and child need to leave)
	  ○ Attempts to keep the child safe from harm during an incident of domestic violence (e.g., moving to a room where the child is not; telling the child to leave the area where the domestic violence is occurring; instructing the child to seek outside help that the child can reasonably be expected to do; shielding the child from witnessing the domestic violence)
	
	• Discusses with the child a plan to maintain safety during an incident of domestic violence
	
	• Develops a domestic violence safety plan individually or with the assistance of an advocate
	
	• Physically defends herself/himself in attempt to stop the perpetrator of abuse from harming him/her or the child
	
	• Acknowledges the potential impact that domestic violence can have on the child
	
	• Utilizes a support system
	
	• Attends individual therapy or domestic violence counseling
	
	• Seeks guidance from religious leadership
	
	• Calls the police
	
	• Seeks legal assistance
	
	• Obtains or attempts to obtain an order of protection or to initiate other legal proceedings
	
	• Ceases the relationship with the perpetrator of the domestic violence
	
	• Restricts the access of the perpetrator of domestic violence to the non-offending parent/adult victim and child

Ensuring Overall Wellbeing

How would you describe your relationship with your child?

How does your child respond to you?

What do you enjoy doing with your child and what does your child enjoy doing with you?

What are your greatest strengths as a parent?

In what ways do you ensure that your child's needs are met (e.g., food, medical, academic, etc.)?

Is the child up to date on his/her immunizations? What is the contact information for the child's doctor?

Responding to the Domestic Abuse

What measures did you take to keep yourself safe during an incident of domestic violence?

What measures did you take to keep your children safe during the incident of domestic violence?

Did you have a safety plan? If so, did you communicate this safety plan to your child? Was the child able to follow the safety plan?

Describe your support system.

Have you reached out to governmental or social service supports? Medical? Religious? Police? Domestic violence agency?

Did you initiate or participate in legal proceedings related to the incident of domestic violence? Petition for an order of protection? Participate in a criminal prosecution? File for divorce?

Did you connect your child to therapeutic services because of the domestic violence?

Additional information about the steps you have taken to mitigate the risk of harm to your children posed by the domestic violence:

Contact Log

Name: _____ Case #: _____

Name of Investigator: _____ Phone #: _____

Name of Supervisor: _____ Phone #: _____

Date Investigation Began:Date Written Notice Received: _____

Date of Written Notice of Investigative Finding:_____

Due Date to File Appeal of Investigative Finding: _____

Date	Method of Contact	Initiated Contact	Received Contact	Notes about Conversation

Document Log

Please collect documents that would help demonstrate your child's wellbeing as well as the precautionary measures you have taken. Think about immunization records, medical records, police reports, legal filings, certifications of completion, letters of support, etc.

Document Type	Copy Obtained	Date given to Investigator

Chapter Six:
Understanding Elder Abuse and Working with Older Victims

I. Introduction

Elder abuse is the physical, psychological, or sexual abuse, neglect, abandonment, or financial exploitation of an older individual by another person or entity.[1] Elder abuse can occur in any setting (i.e., home, community, or facility), and includes intimate partner violence and stalking.[2] Older victims of domestic violence face a myriad of unique challenges when seeking help to end the harm they experience.

Civil attorneys can provide critical support to older clients who are victims of domestic violence to help them live free from harm. This chapter aims to help civil attorneys understand the unique dynamics of domestic violence for older adults and the barriers older victims face when seeking support and access to the civil legal system. This chapter will detail specific ways in which civil attorneys can enhance their work with older clients who are domestic violence victims, with particular emphasis on providing client-defined advocacy and advancing equity principles in their work.

---

[1] Marie-Therese Connolly, Bonnie Brandl & Risa Beckman, U.S. Dep't. of Just., The Elder Justice Roadmap: A Stakeholder Initiative to Respond to an Emerging Health, Justice, Financial and Social Crisis (2014).

[2] *Id.*

II. Domestic Violence and Older Victims

Incidences of elder abuse are significantly underreported, but research indicates that one in ten older adults experiences elder abuse.[3] Oftentimes, abusers perpetrate multiple forms of abuse at the same time.[4] Later life domestic violence occurs across all racial and ethnic demographics.[5] It can happen in facilities or other institutional settings. As our population continues to age into an older demographic, attorneys will increasingly be called up to work with an aging client base and must be prepared to do so effectively and with an understanding of who their older clients are, and the experiences they bring to each encounter with the lawyers and the civil legal system.

A significant portion of elder abuse is domestic violence.[6] Domestic violence in later life can be perpetrated by spouses and intimate partners as well as other family members, including adult children or grandchildren, and extended family. Abuse can also be perpetrated by caregivers, fiduciaries, and others in a position of trust. Abusers utilize an array of power and control tactics to manipulate and coerce older victims.[7] Oftentimes, abusers perpetrate harm against older victims out of greed or a sense of entitlement.[8] The abuser may also be dependent on an older victim for financial or other reasons.[9]

Given the complex dynamics of domestic violence and the behavior of abusers, any lawyer working with an older adult may encounter an older victim of domestic violence in their work. Lawyers may also encounter older victims of domestic violence through cases where the victim is not their client, or where domestic violence is not the presenting legal issue (i.e., family law, wills and estates, immigration law, etc.).

---

[3] Mark Lachs & Jacquelin Berman, Lifespan of Greater Rochester, Inc., Under the Radar: New York State Elder Abuse Prevalence Study (2011), *available at* https://ocfs.ny.gov/main/reports/Under%20 the%20Radar%2005%2012%2011%20final%20report.pdf; Ron Acierno et al., *Prevalence and Correlates of Emotional, Physical, Sexual, and Financial Abuse and Potential Neglect in the United States: The National Elder Mistreatment Study,* 100 Am. J. of Pub. Health, 292, 292-297 (Feb. 2010).

[4] Acierno, *supra* note 3.

[5] Melba Alexandra Hernandez-Tejada et al., *The National Elder Mistreatment Study: Race and Ethnicity Findings,* 25 J. of Elder Abuse & Neglect 281, 281–293 (2013).

[6] *Id.*; Lachs & Berman, *supra* note 3.

[7] Deb Spangler & Bonnie Brandl, *Abuse in Later Life: Power and Control Dynamics and a Victim-Centered Response,* 12 J. of the Am. Psychiatric Nurses Ass'n 322, 322–331 (2007). Also, for a visual representation of these dynamics, see Nat'l Clearinghouse on Abuse in Later Life & Wis. Coal. Against Domestic Violence, *Abuse in Later Life Power and Control Wheel, available at* http://www. ncall.us//FileStream.aspx?FileID=27 (last visited May 1, 2018).

[8] Lundy Bancroft, Why Does He Do That? Inside the Minds of Angry and Controlling Men (Berkley Publ'g Group, 2002); Evan Stark, Coercive Control: How Men Entrap Women in Personal Life (Oxford Un. Press, 2007).

[9] Stark, *supra* note 8.

Recognizing the multitude of contexts and reasons for which older victims seek access to the civil legal system is essential to providing support to older victims. Conversely, attorneys must understand that historical oppression and institutional biases may prevent some older victims (i.e., victims from marginalized communities or other vulnerable populations) from speaking to lawyers about the abuse they face and the concerns they may have about seeking legal services.

Attorneys must also be cognizant of other barriers older victims face when seeking legal services, including mandatory reporting requirements for abuse against older or vulnerable adults.[10] An older victim may fear retribution or a loss of autonomy or independence (i.e., being placed in a nursing home) if they report abuse to anyone, but especially if the person receiving the report is a mandatory reporter. You should learn about the mandatory reporting requirements for attorneys and others you work with in your jurisdiction and communicate upfront those requirements to an older client should you have reason to believe you may be required to report abuse. You may also be able to establish trust with a client by informing them that you are not a mandated reporter of abuse, if that is the case in your jurisdiction.

Older victims may also experience deep shame, guilt, or worry about the consequences of reporting abuse perpetrated by a child or grandchild. Older victims who are abused by long-term partners or spouses may hold generational, spiritual, or other values which lead them to seek an end to the abuse, but not necessarily the end of their relationship with their abuser. Older victims also face stigma and ageism when dealing with abuse and engaging support systems. Myths and misconceptions around who can be victims or abusers, and the invisibility of older victims, are difficult barriers to overcome as older victims seek to ameliorate the harm they experience.

---

[10] For more information on mandatory reporting requirements related to elder abuse in your jurisdiction, see ELDER JUST. INITIATIVE, DEP'T OF JUST., https://www.justice.gov/elderjustice/elder-justice-statutes-0 (last visited May 1, 2018).

Legal Capacity and Legal Competency

The issue of capacity or competency may arise in your work with some of your older clients who are victims of domestic violence. Understanding your role and responsibility in this context will be key to effectively and zealously advocating on behalf of your older client and their interests.

Competency (sometimes called legal capacity) is determination of legal status made by a judge, not a physician, and denoting a person's persistent legal ability or inability to make decisions. Until a person has been adjudicated as incompetent, they are presumed competent.[11] A person found to be incompetent will typically be placed under guardianship by the court.

Capacity (sometimes called clinical competency) is assessed by a physician, not a judge, and may rapidly fluctuate depending on various factors (i.e., a person could have full capacity in the mornings, but lose some capacity later in the day—a phenomenon known as "sundowning"). An assessment of capacity is a clinical opinion regarding a patient's ability to understand an informed consent discussion.[12]

In some situations, you may need to determine whether your client has the legal capacity to contract with you for your services and/or to carry out particular legal transactions. The ABA Model Rules for Professional Conduct provide some guidance to lawyers on ethical standards related to assessing capacity and what to do when a client's potential diminished capacity becomes an issue in your work with clients.

Client Lawyer Relationship
Rule 1.14 Client with Diminished Capacity

(a) When a client's capacity to make adequately considered decisions in connection with a representation is diminished, whether because of minority, mental impairment or for some other reason, the lawyer shall, as far as reasonably possible, maintain a normal client-lawyer relationship with the client.

---

[11] Amy Tao & Jeffrey S. Janofsky, *Capacity, Competency, and Guardianship, in* THE JOHNS HOPKINS PHIPPS PSYCHIATRY GUIDE (Matthew E. Peters, O. Joseph Bienvenu & Paul Nestadt eds., 2017).
[12] *Id.*

(b) When the lawyer reasonably believes that the client has diminished capacity, is at risk of substantial physical, financial or other harm unless action is taken and cannot adequately act in the client's own interest, the lawyer may take reasonably necessary protective action, including consulting with individuals or entities that have the ability to take action to protect the client and, in appropriate cases, seeking the appointment of a guardian ad litem, conservator or guardian.

(c) Information relating to the representation of a client with diminished capacity is protected by Rule 1.6. When taking protective action pursuant to paragraph (b), the lawyer is impliedly authorized under Rule 1.6(a) to reveal information about the client, but only to the extent reasonably necessary to protect the client's interests.[13]

III. Recognizing Domestic Violence

Given the many barriers that may prevent older victims from reporting abuse, attorneys need to be able to recognize risk factors and indicators for domestic violence. Attorneys must also be able to identify tactics of an abuser, which your clients may describe in your interactions with them, or that you may witness firsthand. With this knowledge, attorneys can employ strategies to help screen for domestic violence, identify coded disclosures, and encourage clients to safely report abuse.

Research shows that gender, social isolation, diminished health or mental capacity, incapacity or other impairment, and interdependence of the abuser and victim, are all factors which increase the likelihood an abuser will victimize an older adult.[14] Emotional distress or agitation; bruising or other untreated injuries; and an older client's reports of abuse are all indicators that domestic violence is occurring.[15]

---

[13] MODEL RULES OF PROF'L CONDUCT r. 1.14 (AM. BAR ASS'N 2009). For more information on the topic of capacity, including legal approaches to defining diminished capacity/incapacity, clinical capacity models, assessing your client's capacity, and guidance on making referrals for medical consultation for a more comprehensive assessment of capacity, please consult Am. Bar Ass'n & AM. PSYCHOLOGICAL ASS'N, ASSESSMENT OF OLDER ADULTS WITH DIMINISHED CAPACITY: A HANDBOOK FOR LAWYERS (2005), *available at* https://www.apa.org/pi/aging/resources/guides/diminished-capacity.pdf.

[14] Ron Acierno et al., *The National Elder Mistreatment Study: An 8-year Longitudinal Study of Outcomes,* 29 J. OF ELDER ABUSE & NEGLECT 254, 254–269 (2017).

[15] For more information on behavioral indicators of elder abuse and domestic violence, please see the National Clearinghouse on Abuse in Later Life's (NCALL's) Elder Abuse Behavioral Indicators chart in the appendix to this chapter.

In your work with older clients, an abuser may demand to accompany your client in meetings. They may speak for your client or attempt to dominate conversation, and they may refuse to let you speak privately with your client, or be hostile toward you. An abuser may claim to behave this way because they are concerned for your client or for the client's legal interests.

Abusers may seek to obtain powers of attorney, conservatorships, guardianships, or other legal and decision-making power over an older victim. Abusers may attempt to coerce an older victim to create, or modify, or otherwise nullify a will, trust, gift, or other transfer of estate assets or property in order to favor the abuser's desires and interests. Abusers may also attempt to use legal mechanisms to pressure a victim into creating a joint bank account or taking on unnecessary debt.

Sample Screening Questions[16]

- Do you feel safe at home or in your current living situation?
- Has anyone made you afraid, touched you in ways that you did not want, or hurt you physically?
- Have you relied on people for any of the following: bathing, dressing, shopping, banking, or meals?
- Do other people depend on you for financial or other needs?
- Has anyone prevented you from getting food, clothes, medication, glasses, hearing aids or medical care, or from being with people you wanted to be with?
- Have you been upset because someone talked to you in a way that made you feel shamed or threatened?
- Has anyone tried to force you to sign papers or to use your money against your will?

Your client's fears about physical safety, fears about access to basic needs and resources, or fear of retribution or loss of independence may cause them to be reluctant to share their experience with domestic violence. Coded disclosure can be a safe way to raise the topic, particularly during initial interviews. Some examples of coded disclosure include: "I don't want to make anyone mad," or "I just do whatever my spouse/child/grandchild says," or "Sometimes my spouse is rough with me." Any of these can be a way to open the door to further conversation. Be aware that disclosures may not happen during an initial intake or screening. Taking time to build trust and rapport will be essential to supporting your client to report abuse.

---

[16] Mark J. Yaffe et al., *Development and Validation of a Tool to Improve Physician Identification of Elder Abuse: The Elder Abuse Suspicion Index (EASI),* 20(3) J. of Elder Abuse & Neglect 276 (2008).

IV. Client-Defined Advocacy

Client-defined advocacy requires lawyers to develop a holistic understanding of the legal needs and perspective of a client and to contemplate the breadth of non-litigation options, legal rights and remedies, and victim services available to each client. It involves listening to your client, building a respectful rapport, and centering your client's experiences and strengths in your interactions and legal strategy. Client-defined advocacy also requires working in partnership with your client to construct a comprehensive approach and web of social supports to advance your client's interests and enhance their safety. Within this framework, successful outcomes are defined by clients, not by your values and opinions.

A critical component of client-defined advocacy is having clarity around who your client is and what their legal goals are, and communicating those facts to all parties. Consequently, you should meet with your client individually at intake and in subsequent meetings to ensure confidentiality and discuss why they are meeting with you, their legal concerns, client confidentiality, and your role in their legal case. Safety planning is also a component of client-defined advocacy. Working with your client to explore the confidential services and safety supports provided by domestic and sexual violence advocates will be vital to ensuring your client's wellbeing throughout the process of pursuing any remedies.

Finally, equity principles require you contemplate the differential impact of the civil legal system and institutional barriers on your client's experiences, and their perception of the appropriateness of different legal interventions. Working with your clients to craft an equitable approach to addressing their concerns, including exploring non-litigation alternatives, will have a positive impact their safety and wellbeing throughout your work together.

V. Non-Litigation and Litigation Legal Remedies

Mediation may be proposed as a method to resolve domestic violence. Generally, an abuser's desire to maintain power and control over their victim is inconsistent with the objectives of mediation. Mediation may provide an abuser with access to a victim and enhance the likelihood of violence. Should your client wish to explore this option, you should help them consider whether it would be a safe and effective tool to accomplish their goals.

Orders of protection can be an appropriate intervention in domestic violence cases. Circumstances in an older victim's life (i.e., the abuser is their partner, child, and/or caretaker) may require you to be creative in the remedies you pursue as part of the order (i.e., a prohibition against assaulting or threatening, but that allows parties to communicate). Working with your client to seek specific protections to include in the order of protection will be key to the long-term success of this remedy.

Older victims may choose to execute a "durable" power of attorney to name a trusted person to make decisions on their behalf. Be sure to screen for signs of abuse to ensure your client is making this designation freely and without coercion. You can also assist your client to revoke an already executed power of attorney to ensure that an abusive party no longer has the authority to make decisions for them.

The issue of legal guardianship and/or conservatorship may arise in your representation of an older client. A capable, well-intentioned guardian can protect an incapacitated victim from future harm by an abuser, or pursue perpetrator accountability on a victim's behalf. Conversely, there are serious risks to an older victim if an abusive person gains guardianship or conservatorship over their victim to exact power and control over them.

Finally, an older client may wish to pursue damages in civil court for injuries related to domestic violence.[17] If you think your client may have a claim for tort-related damages, you should discuss this option with them.

VI. Victim Services

Older victims can access a myriad of victim supports and services when dealing with domestic violence. Domestic and sexual violence programs provide crisis and long-term resources and supports, including 24-hour crisis lines, emergency shelter, peer-to-peer counseling, and support groups. Advocates provide confidential communications with abuse victims. Some programs have specialized services and supports to work with older victims, while others may not. It may be helpful to communicate to your client the scope of services provided by the local service provider, in advance of making a referral.

The Aging Network consists of thousands of private and public local service providers which coordinate access services, elder rights advocacy, community services, and in-home services to older adults. Services provided by the Aging Network often include benefits, financial, and legal assistance, prevention programs, health and wellness programs, transportation services, long-term care and in-home services, nutrition services, and information and referral assistance.

Adult Protective Services (APS) are state authorized entities that provide support to both older and at-risk vulnerable adults who are in danger of being abused or neglected, or who are unable to protect themselves. APS workers investigate reports and complaints of abuse, neglect, or exploitation. APS workers can make home visits and provide case management and referral services for community-based resources. Regardless of whether you are a mandatory reporter in your jurisdiction, you should learn about how APS

---

[17] For more information on domestic violence tort cases, see *Tort Law and Domestic Violence* in Section Three of this manual.

investigations work in your community so you can support your client and their safety through the investigatory process, while providing appropriate legal interventions and supports.

VII. Conclusion

As our population ages, older victims will increasingly seek the services of civil attorneys to help end the abuse they face. Lawyers are uniquely situated to respond to the needs of older victims of domestic violence. The confidential attorney-client relationship can be a safe and compassionate place for victims to disclose their experience with domestic violence and overcome barriers to receiving help. Once abuse is identified, attorneys can support survivors by providing responsive, client-defined advocacy that is rooted in equity principles. Exploring appropriate non-litigation and civil legal remedies and resources on behalf of older clients will enhance your client's safety and advance their legal interests. Attorneys should get to know the key community partners available in your area that can provide victim services and supports to your older clients. Each of these tools and strategies can improve an older victim's quality of life, increase perpetrator accountability, and empower older victims to live life free from abuse.

APPENDIX

NCALL Elder Abuse Behavioral Indicators[18]

A Victim May . . .	An Abuser May . . .
• Have injuries that do not match the explanation of how they occurred	• Minimize or deny the victim's injuries or complaints • Attempt to convince others that the victim is incompetent or crazy
• Have repeated "accidental injuries"	• Blame the victim for being clumsy or difficult
• Appear to be isolated	• Physically assault or threaten violence against the victim or victim's family, friends, pets, in home provider(s) or social worker • Forbid the victim from contacting family, friends, or service providers • Threaten or harass the victim • Stalk the victim
• Say or hint that she is afraid • Give coded communications about what is occurring	• Act overly attentive toward the victim • Act loving, kind, and compassionate to the victim, especially in presence of others
• Consider or attempt suicide	• Consider or attempt suicide
• Have a history of alcohol or drug abuse (including prescription drugs)	• Have a history of alcohol or drug abuse

---

[18] Excerpted and adapted with permission from BONNIE BRANDL ET AL., ELDER ABUSE: A MULTIDISCIPLINARY APPROACH (NEW YORK: SPRINGER, 2008).

• Be "difficult" or hard to get along with	• Refuse to allow an interview with the victim to take place without being present • Speak on behalf of the victim, not allow the victim to participate in the interview
• Have vague, chronic, non-specific complaints	• Say victim is incompetent, unhealthy or crazy
• Be emotionally and/or financially dependent on the abuser	• Be emotionally and/or financially dependent on the victim
• Miss appointments	• Cancel the victim's appointments or refuse to transport victim to appointments
• Delay seeking medical help	• Cover up the abuse by taking the victim to different doctors, hospitals, or pharmacies • Refuse to purchase needed prescriptions, medical supplies, and/or assistive devices
• Show signs of depression (mild or severe), stress, or trauma	• Turn family members against the victim • Talk about the victim as if he or she is not there or not a person (dehumanize victim)

Additional Resources:

- **ABA Commission on Law and Aging**
  The American Bar Association's Commission on Law and Aging examines
  and responds to law-related needs of older persons in the United States
  through policy development, education, and the provision of technical
  assistance. For more information on the Commission, please visit the
  website:
  - https://www.elderabusecenter.org/default.cfm_p_aba.html

- **National Resource Directory**
  The National Clearinghouse on Abuse in Later Life maintains a directory
  of programs that have created specialized services for older victims of
  abuse, especially those who are experiencing domestic violence, sexual
  assault, or stalking. To learn about services available for older clients in your
  community, please visit the Directory's website:
  - http://www.ncall.us/ncall-abuse-in-later-life-directory-map/

- **NCALL/ABA Webinar Series for Civil Attorneys**
  The National Clearinghouse on Abuse in Later Life and the American Bar
  Association Commission on Domestic & Sexual Violence with funding from
  the Office on Violence Against Women have created a five-part webinar
  series on Abuse in Later Life for civil attorneys, legal advocates and others
  who wish to gain a deeper understanding of Abuse in Later Life. To view
  modules from the series, please visit:
  - http://www.ncall.us/webinars-civil-legal-remedies/

Chapter Seven:
The Military and Domestic Violence

I. Background Information

A. Command Structure

Each branch of the military has different ranks and roles for their service members. It may be helpful to familiarize yourself with the branch of which your client and/or your client's partner/spouse is a member, but is not necessarily critical.[1] It may make you feel more comfortable knowing the relative rank and authority of your client, the abuser, the direct ranking officer (one right above the victim and/or abuser), the commander, etc.

One distinction that applies in all branches is the difference between enlisted personnel and officers. Generally speaking, enlisted personnel enter the military with a high school diploma or GED, and an officer comes into the military with a college degree or higher, or through one of the military academies. Enlisted personnel are of a lower rank and have an intermediary in their First Sergeant, who is the primary liaison with the commander on all matters concerning the enlisted corps. Someone could start as an enlisted member and be promoted into an officer rank.

---

[1] Branches of the military are Navy, Army, Air Force, Marines, Coast Guard; enlisted or officer; Active Duty, Veteran, Retired, Reserve, and National Guard. Throughout this chapter, the term "partner" is used to apply to a non-married couple. The marital status of the victim and abuser is relevant for the types of benefits and services available to the victim; there are far fewer for unmarried partners. However, if the abuser is the service member, the response of the military to allegations of domestic violence should be the same, whether the victim is a spouse or unmarried partner of the abuser.

It is also important to know the status of the service member(s) in your case. Are they active duty, reserve, guard, deployed, overseas, or in a combat zone? Each status may impact your case. If your client or the abuser are veteran or retired, one of the biggest issues is the benefits that the former service member and her/his family are receiving, and the impact of divorce on those benefits.

Advocacy Tip: Keep in mind that your client could be the service member or a civilian, and the abuser could be a civilian or a fellow service member. The combination (civilian victim/service member abuser; service member victim/ service member abuser; service member victim/civilian abuser) will likely impact how your client may decide to proceed with a case, and the services available to the victim and abuser.

B. DoD Policies Regarding Domestic Violence

The Department of Defense (DoD) is the Executive Branch department that oversees all branches of the military. From 2001 to 2003, the DoD was authorized to create the multidisciplinary joint military and civilian Defense Task Force on Domestic Violence (DTFDV). Over the period of three years, the DTFDV made a total of 194 recommendations for changes or improvements to the DoD response to domestic violence. The recommendations focused primarily on providing greater victim safety, enhanced offender accountability, and preventing abuse from occurring. Of those 194 recommendations, DoD agreed with 75 percent of them and turned most of those recommendations into formal Departmental and Service policies.[2] Many of the policies could provide attorneys working with victims with valuable tools for protecting the interests and safety of their clients.

C. MOUs Between Military Installations and Civilian Organizations

One of the DoD policies promulgated through the DTFDV is an encouragement that military installations in the United States enter into a Memorandum of Understanding (MOU) with victim-serving organizations that are in the geographic area of the installation. Some of the rationale behind the MOU is very practical, since jurisdictional issues can easily arise (see below) so having a pre-established understanding and cooperation between the military installation (including the military police) and the civilian police force can be very useful.[3]

---

[2] For a copy of the reports created by the DTFDV, see *The Military's Response to Domestic and Sexual Violence*, Nat'l Ctr. on Domestic & Sexual Violence, http://www.ncdsv.org/ncd_ militaryresponse.html (last visited May 8, 2018).

[3] For an example of a "standard" MOU between law enforcement agencies, see *Developing a Memorandum of Understanding Between the Installation Law Enforcement Office and Local Civilian Law Enforcement Agencies,* Nat'l Ctr. on Domestic & Sexual Violence, http://www.ncdsv.org/ images/DevelopinganMOUbetweenInstallationLECivilianLE.pdf (last visited May 4, 2018).

However, in some areas surrounding particularly large military bases (i.e., San Diego, San Antonio, Fort Bragg in North Carolina) there may be other MOUs and/or additional parties to an MOU, including local domestic violence shelters, hotlines, civilian legal service providers, etc. It is always helpful to call the military base that your client lives on or near to see if there are any MOUs in place, so that you are aware of any jurisdictional and service-provision agreements in place.

D. Military Culture

There are many aspects of military culture that distinguish it from the "civilian" lifestyle. Many aspects of military culture are things that members of the military community, including civilian family members, strongly embrace as empowering, special, distinct, and important to protect.

Military families understand that service impacts all members of the family. Everyone is expected to make sacrifices. With very short notice, the service member can be moved, deployed, ordered to a combat zone, etc., and the partner/spouse, children, and extended family members are expected to fully support that development. And, of course, the service member has almost no recourse to change those orders, even if the orders are inconvenient for the rest of the family.

E. Military Benefits

In part because of the demands made on military families, there are benefits that a service member and their spouses and children are entitled to receive, and other benefits that attach when the service member transitions to a veteran (having separated from service) or retirement status (having served for at least 20 years). Some of those benefits include: free housing on base; a housing stipend, if living in civilian housing; free health care; free counseling at Family Advocacy Programs that are in place throughout the military; purchasing discounts for food and other necessary items; moving assistance; pension, etc. Many of these benefits would diminish or be lost entirely if a civilian spouse and the service member abuser separate or divorce.

It is very important for a civilian spouse to consult with the JAG office and/or an experienced civilian family law attorney who specializes in representing military family members to assess what benefits can stay in place during separation, how a divorce can impact the military benefits, and how the length of the marriage can directly impact presumptions of pension allocation.

II. Key Legal Concepts, Terms, and Definitions

A. Defining Domestic Abuse and Domestic Violence in the Military

The DoD has developed the following definitions of domestic violence in the military:[4]

- **Domestic abuse** is (1) domestic violence or (2) a pattern of behavior resulting in emotional/psychological abuse, economic control, and/or interference with personal liberty that is directed toward a person of the opposite sex who is: (a) a current or former spouse; (b) a person with whom the abuser shares a child in common; or (c) a current or former intimate partner with whom the abuser shares or has shared a common domicile.

- **Domestic violence** is an offense under the United States Code, the Uniform Code of Military Justice (UCMJ), or state law that involves the use, attempted use, or threatened use of force or violence against a person of the opposite sex, or a violation of a lawful order issued for the protection of a person of the opposite sex, who is (a) a current or former spouse; (b) a person with whom the abuser shares a child in common; or (c) a current or former intimate partner with whom the abuser shares or has shared a common domicile.

DoD developed definitions that would apply to all of the first responders in military law enforcement and other agencies tasked with responding to domestic abuse in the military, including medical treatment facility (MTF) personnel, staff Judge Advocates (JAGs) who are attorneys on base who are likely to have been involved in similar cases and can help you navigate the legal jurisdictional and other issues, and Family Advocacy Program (FAP) clinical staff who are responsible for providing intervention and treatment services for families experiencing domestic abuse.[5] By creating the umbrella term "domestic abuse," which includes domestic violence as a subset, attention is drawn to the fact that domestic abuse also involves other behaviors that may not be addressed through

---

[4] *See Frequently Asked Questions About the Family Advocacy Program FY11 Domestic Abuse Data*, MILITARY ONESOURCE, http://download.militaryonesource.mil/12038/Project%20Documents/ Reports/FAP_FY11_DA_QA.pdf (last visited May 4, 2018); Kacy Mixon, *Domestic Violence: Definitions*, MILITARY FAMILIES LEARNING NETWORK (Jul. 23, 2013), https://militaryfamilies.extension. org/2013/07/23/domestic-violence-definitions/.

[5] More information about the Judge Advocate General's Corps (JAG) at the different military branches can be found at: U.S. NAVY JUDGE ADVOCATE GENERAL'S CORPS, http://www.jag.navy.mil/ (last visited Apr. 19, 2018); U.S. ARMY JUDGE ADVOCATE GENERAL'S CORPS, https://www.goarmy.com/jag. html (last visited Apr. 19, 2018); U.S. AIR FORCE JUDGE ADVOCATE GENERAL'S CORPS, http://www.afjag. af.mil/ (last visited Apr. 19, 2018); U.S. MARINE CORPS JUDGE ADVOCATE GENERAL'S CORPS, https://www. marines.com/becoming-a-marine/officer/marine-corps-law-program.html (last visited Apr. 19, 2018); and U.S. COAST GUARD JUDGE ADVOCATE GENERAL'S CORPS, https://www.uscg.mil/Resources/Legal/ (last visited Apr. 19, 2018). The chief attorney within each branch is called the "Judge Advocate General," however, individual JAG corps officers are often referred to as "JAGs."

the judicial process but that need to be addressed through intervention and treatment as soon as possible. Ideally, this helps to identify couples in need of services before the abuse has escalated to acts of physical violence.

Impact of NDAA

Legislation and policy questions regarding active duty, reserve, and guard members of the military are dictated by the DoD. The most frequent legislative means to make changes in laws impacting members of the military is the National Defense Authorization Act (NDAA), which is introduced with amendments every year. The NDAA includes the annual appropriations for the defense budget. This is relevant for your legal representation of a member of the military (other than veteran or retired) since the most recent legislative changes will most likely be passed through an amendment to the NDAA. For example, in the FY18 NDAA, there is an amendment that, if passed, would make non-consensual posting of explicit images a violation of the Uniform Code of Military Justice (UCMJ), the criminal code for members of the military.

B. Mandatory Reporting Requirements

The DoD response to domestic abuse is intended to enable commanders, military law enforcement, and the FAP to learn about incidents of domestic abuse as soon as they occur and to intervene to prevent further abuse. Current DoD policy requires all members of the military community to report known or suspected incidents of domestic abuse.[6] FAP or military law enforcement are usually the first to learn about incidents of domestic abuse. When a report of domestic violence is received, the incident is investigated by military law enforcement to determine whether the alleged violence occurred, and the investigative report is reviewed by the abuser's commander and a military attorney to determine whether a legal response under the UCMJ is warranted. In the case of any domestic abuse report, the victim (if he or she so desires, and is entitled to military benefits) and the abuser are clinically assessed by FAP to determine appropriate services for the victim and interventions/treatments for the abuser. The victim is entitled to military benefits if he or she is on active duty or has a military identification card.

Currently, victims do not have a confidential resource within the military other than chaplains. Although victim advocacy services are available at some military installations, military victim advocates do not have confidentiality. Civilian attorneys working with victims must realize that if they advise a client to contact FAP, a victim advocate on the installation, the victim or offender's

---

6 U.S. Dep't. of Def., Directive 6400.1, Family Advocacy Program (FAP) (June 23, 1992); U.S. Dep't. of Def., Directive 6400.1-M, Family Advocacy Program Standards and Self-Assessment Tool (Aug. 1992).

commander, or military law enforcement, such individuals or agency will initiate a full investigation and assessment of the situation that will involve contacting the abuser. If a client wants to speak to someone confidentially about their options for services/interventions, civilian attorneys should refer the victim to local civilian domestic violence services providers or civilian shelters. An attorney can contact the installation's FAP to learn more in general about the services and programs offered on the installation, and about the likely series of events that would generally follow a formal report of domestic abuse to FAP or military law enforcement.

C. Jurisdictional Issues

Jurisdiction over an incident of domestic abuse can be very complicated and is dependent on several factors: where the incident occurred (on or outside an installation); whether the abuser is a service member or a civilian; and whether the federal government, the state, or both, have legislative jurisdiction over the location where the incident occurred.

If the abuser is a civilian and the incident occurred off the installation, the state will have jurisdiction over the investigation, the prosecution, and any related civil lawsuit. For incidents occurring on an installation where the abuser is a civilian, jurisdiction over these matters will depend on who has legislative jurisdiction over the location where the incident occurred and agreements between military, state, and federal civilian authorities. While the military may investigate these on-installation incidents involving civilian offenders, only state or federal civilian authorities would have jurisdiction over the prosecution and over civil lawsuits.

If the abuser is a service member, regardless of where the incident occurs, the military authorities have jurisdiction to investigate and prosecute the offender under the UCMJ. If the incident occurred off the installation and the state has legislative jurisdiction over the location where the incident occurred, state authorities will also have jurisdiction to investigate and prosecute the offender. Normally, to avoid duplication of effort, military and civilian authorities will sign Memoranda of Understanding (MOUs) defining who will be responsible for investigation and prosecution of domestic violence cases involving service member offenders when jurisdiction is shared. If an MOU does not exist, civilian and military authorities will have to negotiate investigation and prosecution responsibilities on a case-by-case basis.

Although MOUs usually require civilian authorities to notify military authorities if a service member has been arrested in the civilian community, civilian attorneys cannot assume that the military will learn about an incident being investigated or prosecuted in the civilian community. If the victim wants the military to be aware of the case, her or his civilian attorney can be instrumental in ensuring that the civilian authorities share the information they have with their military counterparts, either by requesting that police reports be sent to the service member's commander or by encouraging the victim to contact military law enforcement or FAP directly.

It is often important for you, as the civilian attorney, to know which agencies have responsibility for the investigation and prosecution of an incident. To find out, contact the JAG on the victim's and/or abuser's installation.

D. Uniform Code of Military Justice (UCMJ)

The UCMJ is federal law enacted by Congress. The UCMJ defines the military justice system and lists criminal offenses under military law. A court-martial is the most severe sanction under the UCMJ.[7] A court-martial is a potential outcome for an abuser who has been convicted of a domestic violence offense, either in the military justice or civilian court system.

E. Enforceability of Civilian Orders of Protection on Military Installations

Although the Full Faith and Credit provisions of the Violence Against Women Act made civilian orders of protection (CPOs) enforceable in all U.S. states, territories, and on tribal lands, they did not make them enforceable on military installations. In 2002, the Armed Forces Domestic Security Act was enacted to address this issue.[8] Under the Armed Forces Domestic Security Act, a CPO has the same force and effect on military installations as it has in the state, U.S. territory, or tribal land that issued it.

As a result of the Armed Forces Domestic Security Act, civilian judges can take action against an individual who violates a CPO on a military installation located in the United States. DoD has issued a policy memorandum directing the Services to make a violation of a CPO by a service member punishable under Article 92 or any other applicable provision of the UCMJ. Civilians who violate orders of protection may also be barred from the installation.

F. Role of Military Victim Advocates

Across all branches of the military, there are FAPs, which employ victim advocates. Their role is similar to victim advocates in a civilian setting, and like victim advocates employed by civilian governmental agencies (like the police or prosecutor's office), there is no privilege or confidentiality between the victim and the advocate. This is important for your client to understand. In many states, there is a legislative privilege created between non-governmental advocates and victims as long as some criteria has been met (i.e., that the advocate has attended an enumerated number of hours of training by a domestic violence

---

[7] For an overview of the court-martial process, see *The Uniform Code of Military Justice (UCMJ)*, MILITARY.COM, https://www.military.com/join-armed-forces/the-uniform-code-of-military-justice-ucmj. html (last visited May 8, 2018).

[8] 10 U.S.C. § 1561(a).

agency), so that non-governmental advocates cannot be compelled to reveal confidences, testify, or turn over documents provided by the victim or regarding services provided to the victim, unless the victim explicitly and in writing waives that privilege.

If sexual assault has occurred, there are additional services and rights available to victims of sexual assault through the DoD's Sexual Assault Prevention and Response Office (SAPRO).[9] This office more regularly handles cases of non-intimate partner sexual assault, so be prepared for that distinction if your client wishes to report the sexual assault and obtain services through this office. A report made to SAPRO can be restricted, which means without identifying information about the abuser, or non-restricted, which identifies the abuser and means an investigation will ensue.

Which branch your client and/or the abuser is serving in may impact aspects of a case that results from the reporting of sexual assault. Both the Air Force and Army have established a Special Victims' Counsel Program, which provides an attorney to represent the victim in any military criminal proceeding related to the sexual assault.[10]

III. Other Considerations Related to the Military and Domestic Violence

A. The Impact of Domestic Violence on a Service member's Career

If a victim makes a report of domestic violence against a service member abuser, it is possible, even likely, to have an enormous impact on the career of the abuser. If the service member is convicted of a crime—either in civilian court or in the military justice system—it could result in at least an "other than honorable" discharge, which means the service member will not be able to convert to veteran status. If a civilian or military order of protection that meets the criteria set forth in 18 U.S.C. § 922 is issued against a service member, the abuser will not be allowed to possess a firearm per the Lautenberg Amendment of 1997, which means probable separation from the military since possessing a firearm is an integral part of being a member of the military.[11] Though the Lautenberg Amendment is a critically important policy to protect the safety and life of victims, some victims may not want to report, or even seek an order of

---

[9] *Victim Support Comes First*, VICTIM ASSISTANCE, http://www.sapr.mil/index.php/victim-assistance (last visited Apr. 19, 2018).

[10] For a history on the military's response to sexual assault, see Lorelei Laird, *Military Lawyers Confront Changes as Sexual Assault Becomes Big News*, A.B.A. J. (Sept. 2013), *available at* http://www.abajournal.com/magazine/article/military_lawyers_confront_changes_as_sexual_assault_becomes_big_news/.

[11] 8 U.S.C. § 922.

protection, due to the impact it could have on the abuser's career, livelihood, and benefits for the entire family.

If the victim is the service member, the victim may be very hesitant to make any kind of official report since the impact on one's career is unknown. Of course, there is no policy to sanction a service member victim, but many victims believe that the perception of their performance and/or ability to perform their role to the highest level will be detrimentally impacted if they reveal that they are a victim (even if the relationship has ended). In other words, being a victim is in contravention to what many service members believe they must project in order to survive and thrive in the military, one of strength, ability to persevere in the face of adversity, and unaffected by issues going on in one's personal life.

If the abuser is the service member, victims may hesitate or refuse to report due to the fear that a report will result in a possible end to the abuser's career, which not only impacts benefits and income, but could also compromise the victim's safety if the abuser feels like it is the victim's "fault" that his/her career has ended. In fact, victims have covered up about the cause of injuries or other "red flags" that would indicate that domestic violence is happening in order to avoid an inquiry. The cover up can then be used during a later civilian court process to impeach the witness or suggest that what the victim reports now is incorrect or fabricated.

Frequent Bias in Favor of Service Members

Similar to the civilian world, many police officers, judges presiding over a military tribunal, and commanders ("employers" in the civilian context) are not uniformly trained nor sensitive to issues common to victims. The focused training, designated prosecutors, and specialized courts that exist in some geographic areas in the civilian world are not nearly as comprehensive in the military context.

Many victims report being treated gruffly or with incredulity, particularly if the abuser is a service member, since service members are very often held in high regard, particularly if the service member shows up in uniform and with the support of their commander.

B. Representing Clients who are LGBT

Since the repeal in 2010 of "Don't Ask, Don't Tell," (DADT), lesbian, gay, and bisexual (LGB) folks can now openly serve in the military (transgender people were treated differently, see below). DADT was a DoD policy enacted under the Clinton Administration that all branches of the military would no longer ask if someone in the military is LGB, but that LGB folks could not serve openly. Prior to this policy, people were asked if they were LGB and if the answer was yes, they could not join or, if already in and were "outed," were subject to court-martial.

Since 2015, when marriage equality across the United States was achieved through the Supreme Court ruling in *Obergefell v. Hodges,* LGB folks serving in the military could also openly marry, and their spouses are fully recognized by the DoD and Veterans Affairs.[12] In May 2014, the ban on transgender people entering and openly serving in the military was lifted, and health services (such as hormone replacement therapy and surgery) are covered through military and veterans' health care.

In late 2017, the administration indicated that it would overturn the policy regarding transgender military personnel and return to a ban on transgender people serving in the military openly. As of the writing of this chapter, these efforts to overturn the policy have been legally challenged and transgender people are still able to serve and enter the military openly.

Despite these changes allowing LGBT folks to serve openly, there are still a lot of service members and veterans who served under DADT, and may still be fearful of being out if they believe it will impact their careers.

C. Accessing Records

If the victim is a civilian spouse and seeks services on base (i.e., calling the base police, getting counseling at the FAP, or makes a report to the base commander), the victim may find it difficult to access records of these services to support a civil case in civilian court. Due to the mandatory reporting policy, reports to military police, counselors, or the commander should result in some action against the service member. However, many victims may not feel comfortable or safe revealing the true nature of why they are seeking services, and therefore, may not be explicit that domestic violence, or some other crime, has occurred. Then, action is unlikely to be taken, and there may not be an "official" record created that can later be retrieved.

The military is a huge bureaucracy and since the civilian spouse is not a member of the military, there is no "standard" procedure for what forms and records should be kept, nor even how to access those records, particularly if the abuse happened over a long period of time and some of the incidents were in

---

[12] The Department of Veterans Affairs (VA) is a federal cabinet-level agency that administers extensive health care coverage to qualifying veterans and their dependent family members through veterans medical centers and outpatient clients. The VA also administers several non-healthcare benefits including disability compensation, vocational rehabilitation, education assistance, home loans, life insurance, and burial and memorial benefits to eligible veterans and family members at 135 national cemeteries.

the far past. The one exception should be access to a victim's medical records if medical attention was sought at a military health center.

Advocacy Tip: This does not mean you should not try to access the records, using your subpoena power to get copies of records. However, it may be difficult to determine who should be the subject of such a subpoena. The first place to turn, in these instances, is the JAG office at the service member's installation. If the records you are seeking are part of the service member abuser's personnel records, it will be very difficult to get these records without the consent of the abuser.[13] You can make an argument to a judge on why a subpoena should be issued to obtain the service member's records. If the subpoena is issued, it is likely that the judge will order the records be sent to chambers for review before sharing them with you or your client. If deemed not relevant, you and your client may never gain access to those records.

D. Impact of PTSD and TBI[14]

Compared to the civilian population, there are very high rates of post-traumatic stress disorder (PTSD) and traumatic brain injury (TBI) among active duty service members and veterans.[15] Both abusers and victims could have PTSD and/or TBI caused by combat-related stressors, or related to other abuse or trauma in their lives. If the abuser has a diagnosis of PTSD and/or TBI, the abuser is likely to garner sympathy and may even be "excused" for her or his violence as a side-effect of the PTSD and/or TBI. If the victim has been diagnosed with PTSD and/or TBI, regardless of the cause (combat or domestic violence), it is often used to discredit the victim as being unable to differentiate a true threat, artificially inflating the risk of harm, and unable to accurately remember facts and the sequence of events.

There is some evidence to suggest that people with PTSD and/or TBI are more prone to violence. This could be used in any defense of the abuser (in a criminal or civil context, both civilian and military), particularly if the violence started only after the event that caused the PTSD and/or TBI. In addition, many victims whose abusers have PTSD and/or TBI may feel that they must accept this new reality of violence, support the physically and emotionally injured service

---

[13]   The Privacy Act provides significant protections to the service member. For some relevant exceptions to an absolute bar on providing information about a service member, see *Privacy Act Statement & Security*, MILITARY ONESOURCE, http://www.militaryonesource.mil/privacy-act-statement-security (last visited Apr. 19, 2018).

[14]   For additional information, see *Combat-Related Post-Traumatic Stress Disorder (PTSD) and Intimate Partner Violence (IPV) Model*, BATTERED WOMEN'S JUST. PROJECT, http://www.bwjp.org/our-work/projects/military-and-veterans-advocacy-program/ptsd-and-ipv-model.html (last visited Apr. 19, 2018).

[15]   There is a common and incorrect misperception among the civilian world that all service members and veterans have PTSD.

member no matter what, and experience guilt if they are not able to handle this new role of caregiver and supporter.

IV. Legal Remedies and Other Relief Available to Victims

A. Military Protection Order

A Military Protection Order (MPO) is an order, similar in content to a CPO but issued by a commander to an active duty service member to both protect a victim of domestic violence and to regulate the behavior of the offending service member. A victim advocate, installation law enforcement agency, or FAP clinician may request a commander to issue an MPO. Commanders may tailor their orders to meet the specific needs of a victim. Among other things, an MPO may order the service member to surrender her/his government weapons custody card at the time of issuance of the order. Commanders can issue an MPO regardless of whether a CPO is already in place. If a civilian judge or magistrate has already issued a CPO, the MPO can be more restrictive but, ideally, will not contradict terms in the CPO. The DoD requires that each branch of the military have a policy in place that requires that all MPOs be issued in writing and that copies be provided to the victim, the offender, and installation law enforcement.

An MPO is difficult to enforce once the service member is assigned outside the command where the order was issued, because the new commander often does not know of its existence. If circumstances warrant the continuation of the MPO, the commander who issued the MPO should contact the new commander to advise him or her of the order. Although MPOs are enforceable by the issuing command regardless of whether they are violated on or off the installation, civilian law enforcement and civilian courts cannot enforce them because MPOs do not meet the due process requirements under the Full Faith and Credit provisions of the Violence Against Women Act.

A violation of an MPO constitutes a violation of Article 90, UCMJ, *Assaulting or Willfully Disobeying Superior Commissioned Officer*. Additionally, each branch of the military is required to have regulations in place making violation of an MPO a violation of Article 92, UCMJ, *Failure to Obey Order or Regulation*. Violating the UCMJ may result in non-judicial punishment, court-martial proceedings, or other disciplinary measures.

B. The Servicemembers Civil Relief Act[16]

In December 2003, the Servicemembers Civil Relief Act was signed into law, which completely replaced the Soldiers and Sailors' Civil Relief Act of 1940. The Servicemembers Civil Relief Act applies to all service members on active duty and provides them a wide range of protections, including the ability to request

---

[16] Servicemembers Civil Relief Act, Pub. L. No. 108-189, 117 Stat. 2835 (2003).

temporary suspension of civil judicial and administrative proceedings when their ability to participate in those proceedings is materially affected by their military duty. It does not apply to criminal proceedings.

Of particular note are the provisions regarding stays of proceedings, which were also in the former law, and are typically invoked when a service member is serving overseas or deployed out of state. The revised provisions apply to any civil action or proceeding in which the defendant is in military service (or within 90 days after termination of or release from military service), and in which the defendant has received notice of the action or proceeding. Under this section, a service member, upon application to the court that (1) demonstrates why military duty materially affects the service member's ability to appear, (2) states a date when an appearance can be made, and (3) includes a letter from the service member's commander confirming the service member's claim and stating that leave is currently not authorized, will be granted a stay of proceedings for not less than 90 days. Once the stay is granted, the service member may apply for an additional stay if military duty continues to materially affect her or his ability to appear.

This section of the law, as well as others regarding protections against default judgments and stays/vacations of executions of judgment, attachments and garnishments, may affect the ability of an attorney to provide quickly for a victim's economic security if an abuser's ability to appear at a hearing is materially affected by military duty. The law applies to all civil judicial and administrative hearings including those regarding orders of protection (although it does not affect a victim's ability to obtain an ex parte order), show cause, separation, divorce, support, child custody, eviction, and foreclosures.

C. The Transitional Compensation Program[17]

Victims may feel that they cannot leave their abuser or report the violence because doing so could mean losing the service member's income and the military medical and dental benefits that they need for themselves and their children. The Transitional Compensation Program provides for financial, health, and other benefits to family members who are being abused by a service member.

A victim may qualify to receive transitional compensation benefits if:

- She/he was married to or is a family member of a service member and was residing in the home of the now separated service member when the offense occurred;

---

[17] 10 U.S.C. § 1059; U.S. DEP'T OF DEF., INSTRUCTION 1342.24, TRANSITIONAL COMPENSATION FOR ABUSED DEPENDENTS (May 23, 1995).

- The service member has served at least 30 days on active duty; and

- The service member has been discharged administratively or by court-martial for dependent abuse, or sentenced to forfeiture of all pay and allowances by a court-martial for a dependent abuse offense.

To be eligible to apply for transitional compensation, the documented reason for the service member's separation from the service must be spousal abuse or child abuse. To learn whether a victim may be eligible to receive benefits under this program or to determine whether abuse will be the reason for a service member's separation from the service, the victim or the victim's attorney can contact the JAG office on the installation.

D. Financial Support

Military Service regulations require members to provide "adequate support" to their family members.[18] The Services expect their personnel to provide the amount of support specified in a court order. If there is not a court order, a written agreement between the parties will typically establish the amount of support required. In cases where there is not a court order or a written agreement, Army, Navy, and Marine Corps regulations provide specific guidance as to the amount of interim support. Under Air Force policy, a member's commander determines what is "adequate" under the circumstances.

E. Shipment of Household Goods

When a victim is living with a service member at an installation in another country or in the United States but is geographically isolated from a support system, returning to the United States or to the victim's family of origin can present extreme financial hurdles and a disincentive for leaving. Victim-spouses of service members, living either in the United States or abroad, may request compensation for shipment of household goods and a vehicle, if they choose to leave the service member. For a victim to be eligible to receive this benefit, a commander must make the following determinations:

- A service member has abused his/her spouse (or child),

- Counseling and safety planning were provided to the victim,

- The safety of the victim is at risk, and

- Relocation of the victim is advisable.

---

[18] ARMY REGULATION 608-99, FAMILY SUPPORT, CHILD CUSTODY, AND PATERNITY (Nov. 1, 1994); AIR FORCE INSTRUCTION 36-2906, PERSONAL FINANCIAL RESPONSIBILITY (Jan. 1, 1998); MARINE CORPS, MCO P5800.16A Ch. 15, DEPENDENT SUPPORT AND PATERNITY (Mar. 3, 2003); NAVY, MILPERSMAN 1754-030, SUPPORT OF FAMILY MEMBERS (Aug. 22, 2003).

However, shipment of household goods will only be provided if the parties have come to some written agreement about the division of property or if an order of a court of competent jurisdiction defines the allocation of property between the victim and the service member.

F. Child Custody and Divorce

A civilian court of competent jurisdiction must make child custody determinations; a military commander cannot make such a determination. Similarly, victims of domestic abuse must go through the civilian court system if they wish to pursue a divorce.

The division of retirement benefits accrued during military service (whether by the victim, abuser, or both) pursuant to a divorce is dictated by the Division of Retirement Benefits, Uniformed Services Former Spouses Protection Act (USFSPA), 10 USC § 1408. This is a fairly complex area of law that requires expertise. Advise your client to seek legal counsel from a family law attorney practicing in the jurisdiction where the divorce will be heard, who has this area of expertise.

V. Safety Planning

As is true in all cases involving victims of domestic violence, safety planning is critical. There are some unique consideration when representing a client who is, or is the partner or spouse of, a member of the military.

1. Access to firearms is present. There is no question about that. Access to firearms increases the possibility of fatality greatly. Many service members and family members of service members are very used to firearms being present and do not necessarily see it as an additional threat to safety. It is important to do extensive safety planning regarding what to do if a firearm is in the home, and/or if the abuser has unfettered access to a firearm.

2. The possible impact on an abuser's career if a report is made will increase the risk to the victim's safety, since this will threaten the abuser's livelihood and their chosen career path. Actions taken against the abuser due to a report of domestic violence could also alienate other family members who may be very connected to their identity as military family members, and/or also receiving benefits as a result of the abuser being a service member.

3. The community in which service members live is often very insular with strong connections between the service members and their families. A threat to that unity could result in other members of that community (other service members, other spouses, etc.) exerting pressure on the victim to reconcile with the abuser. This pressure is very real and influential on a victim's decision-making.

4. All branches of the military are required to report all domestic violence convictions from the military courts to the FBI so that the abuser will no longer be able to legally access firearms. The FBI enters that conviction in at least one of three databases that licensed gun dealers are required to consult before approving a gun purchase: National Instant Criminal Background Indexes (NICS), a computerized system designed to immediately determine if a person is disqualified from receiving or possessing firearms by conducting a search of available records; Interstate Identification Index (III), which pools all conviction records; and the National Crime Information Center (NCIC), a repository of justice-related records such as orders of protection and open arrest warrants. As a civilian attorney, you do not have access to these databases. However, you can and should contact the FBI to confirm that any domestic violence conviction of and/ or order of protection against the abuser in your case are in one or more of these databases. There is no simple way to perform this task. You will need to be creative and persistent. If you know of anyone who works in law enforcement (police officers, prosecutors), they may be able to assist you in this task.

APPENDIX

Learn About the Military Experience

In order to understand what your client has experienced as a member of, or partner/spouse of a member of the military, it is important to learn a little bit about the military experience. PsychArmor creates and provides free and concise webinars to educate the civilian world about what it means to serve in the military. Two that are most useful for your purposes are:

- *Veteran 201: Military Lingo and Discharges*:
  - https://psycharmor.org/courses/veteran-201-military-lingo-discharges/

- *Veteran 201: Military Families*:
  - https://psycharmor.org/courses/veteran-201-military-families/

Sample Screening Questions:

(1) Are you the service member, or your partner/spouse or both of you?

(2) What branch of the military?

(3) What is the rank and status of the service member(s)?

(4) Do you have children? Is the abuser the other parent (biological or adopted) of your children?

(5) Have you ever reported the domestic violence to anyone in the command? To an FAP? To a JAG?

(6) Have you ever spoken to the base chaplain about the domestic violence?

(7) Have you (or your children) ever received services from any of these places for the domestic violence?

(8) Do you have copies of or access to any records of those reports or services?

(9) Does the service member(s) have a diagnosis of PTSD and/or TBI?

(10) How long have you been married? (This is relevant only to discussions of pension allocation, which many spouses of service members will ask about since leaving the marriage will impact the amount of the pension to which s/he will receive upon the retirement of the service member. In other words, a victim may decide to stay in a marriage for a bit longer (or a lot longer) if it will impact the pension allocation greatly.)

(11) Where do you and your children currently live?

(12) Where would you live if you were no longer eligible for your current housing if you were to leave the abuser?

Other Resources:

I. Contact the nearest military installation **Family Advocacy Program** for information pertaining to:

    (a) Prevention programs

    (b) Victim advocacy services

    (c) Crisis intervention services

    (d) Batterer intervention and treatment

    (e) Support groups

    (f) Transitional Compensation

- It is critical to remember that any disclosure of identifying information about the service member will not be confidential. Inquiries of the FAP should be general in nature unless the client is fully aware of this lack of confidentiality and wishes to make a report.

II. Contact the nearest military installation **JAG Office** to get answers to military system legal questions (e.g. service of legal documents, court-martial proceedings, etc.)

- This communication is also not confidential.

III. For more general information, contact the **Department of Defense Family Advocacy Program** at 703-602-4990 x 4, which provides policy oversight to all FAPs across all service branches.

IV. For issues regarding sexual assault, if the abuser is a member of the military:

    (a) **Department of Defense (DoD) Sexual Assault Prevention and Response Office (SAPRO)**, http://www.sapr.mil/, 1-877-995-5247.

    (b) **DoD Safe Helpline,** https://safehelpline.org/.

V. For more guidance on many issues addressed in this chapter, or to connect to other civilian attorneys and advocates representing victims of domestic violence visit: http://www.bwjp.org/our-work/projects/military-and-veterans-advocacy-program.html. There are many additional resources available through this webpage.

Chapter Eight:
Native American Clients, Tribal Courts, and Domestic Violence

I. Introduction

American Indian and Alaska Native people are victimized at a much higher rate than any other group in the United States.[1] Research indicates that as many as 84 percent of all American Indian and Alaska Native women, and 81 percent of American Indian and Alaska Native men, will be physically and/or sexually assaulted in their lifetime.[2] The rate of violence against Two-Spirit (LGBT) Native people is also extremely elevated.[3]

There are many socio-legal reasons for the high rates of violence experienced by Native people. As an attorney, it is important to understand the role of federal Indian law in facilitating systems that make it less likely that Native people will be protected by the law. In recent decades, the powers of tribal justice systems have been weakened substantially. Federal statutory and case law have limited tribal

---

[1] There are a wide variety of opinions as to the appropriate terminology for indigenous peoples in the United States. Most federal law uses the term "Indian," but this term has fallen out of favor with academics, who often prefer "Native American." Most tribal citizens prefer to be identified by their tribal identity (e.g., Navajo, Tlingit, Lakota, Mohawk). In this chapter, the terms "Native," "Indian," and "tribal" are used interchangeably.

[2] André B. Rosay, Nat'l Inst. of Just., Violence Against American Indian and Alaska Native Women and Men: 2010 Findings From the National Intimate Partner and Sexual Violence Survey (2016), *available at* https://www.ncjrs.gov/pdffiles1/nij/249736.pdf.

[3] *See, e.g.,* Keren Lehavot, Karina L. Walters & Jane M. Simoni, *Abuse, Mastery, and Health Among Lesbian, Bisexual, and Two-Spirit American Indian and Alaska Native Women,* 15 Cult. Diversity & Ethnic Minority Psychol. 275 (2009). Two-Spirit is terminology often used to describe Native people who are lesbian, gay, bisexual, or transgender, or who otherwise do not adhere to a strict gender binary. *Id.*

jurisdiction, and in some cases, have supplanted tribal jurisdiction with that of the federal or state system.

Native people who live on or near their tribe's reservation (or service area) may choose to use the tribal justice system to address civil orders of protection, child custody, divorce, and related issues arising out of domestic violence. This chapter is designed to give you an introduction to representing domestic violence clients in tribal court.

II. What are Tribal Courts?

There are at least 300 tribal courts operating in the United States. Many of these are courts of limited jurisdiction (and may only hear child dependency cases, for example). Other tribal courts are courts of general jurisdiction, hearing both criminal and civil cases. Each tribal court is unique—and they emanate from the status of tribal nations as sovereign entities. Almost every tribal court in the United States is a court of record.

Many tribal governments have also revitalized traditional, non-adversarial systems to address certain disputes. "Peacemaking" is the most common name for these systems. These systems use traditional language, custom, and ceremony to help people resolve problems outside of an adversarial context. Typically, parties must request for their tribal court cases to be transferred to peacemaking. Not every tribal nation allows cases involving domestic violence to be transferred to peacemaking, but some do. Some advocates for Native victims have expressed concern about the use of certain peacemaking models for domestic violence, for many of the same concerns that advocates have about mediation in the Anglo-American system. If your client is involved in peacemaking or another form of traditional dispute resolution, you should encourage your them to consult local advocates for Native victims regarding what they can expect in the peacemaking system. Safety planning might be necessary if the process does not provide adequate protection for your client. The question of whether victims should participate in peacemaking systems can be an extremely sensitive matter. Attorneys are generally not allowed to participate in peacemaking.

Practicing in Tribal Courts

Most tribal courts will admit attorneys who are licensed to practice in state courts, but attorneys still need to apply for admission. A few tribes, like the Navajo Nation, require that attorneys take a cultural competency course and pass a tribal bar examination. Many tribal courts also allow lay advocates (non-lawyers) to become a member of the tribal bar after special training, thus allowing them to represent clients in tribal court proceedings.

If you live in an area near a tribal nation, you should contact the tribal court clerk to inquire about requirements for admission to the bar. Many tribes require a nominal fee to become licensed to practice in tribal court, and may ask you to attend a swearing-in ceremony or orientation before you enter your first appearance.

III. Applicable Laws

Tribal nations typically have their own statutes, though a few tribes have codified state or federal laws in particular areas such as criminal law or the rules of evidence. In some cases, the tribal laws may differ substantially from mainstream Anglo-American law; for example, some tribal codes allow for the admission of unwritten customary or traditional law. While many tribal nations post their statutes and rules online, in some cases you may need to request copies of tribal codes through the tribal court clerk.

Most tribal courts have a one-tier appellate process. A tribal supreme court issues decisions, much like state and federal courts. A few tribal nations post supreme court opinions on their websites and/or commercial databases, but in some cases, you may need to request copies of tribal supreme court opinions through the tribal court clerk.

As is the case with state and federal law, tribal governments vary in their statutory and judicial responses to domestic violence. Many tribal governments have passed very progressive victim-centered laws and have special provisions for victims. However, some tribal nations inherited their statutory codes from mid-20th Century state laws, which did not provide for comprehensive protection for victims. If the tribal nation has not updated their codes, you may encounter archaic laws which do not provide the kinds of protections you may be used to seeing in state courts.

IV. Tribal Court Jurisdiction

A complete explanation of how tribal jurisdiction will impact a domestic violence client is impossible in this short chapter. There are some common parameters explained below, but representing a Native client in tribal court can be extraordinarily complicated. It is recommended that you consult with an experienced Indian law attorney before representing your first client in tribal court.

Tribal jurisdiction has been curtailed by federal statutes and case law, meaning that tribal courts may not be able to preside over all cases involving domestic violence (particularly criminal cases). In many cases, state and/or federal courts may have concurrent jurisdiction over certain matters. Tribal jurisdiction is different for criminal and civil cases, and almost all questions turn on the Indian status of the parties (whether the parties are citizens of a tribal nation).

- If the victim and the abuser are both Native, and the domestic violence occurred on the reservation, then the tribal court will have jurisdiction over both criminal and civil matters related to domestic violence.

- If both the victim and the abuser are not Native, the tribal court cannot exercise criminal jurisdiction, even if the abuse occurs on the reservation. Depending on the location of the abuse and the tribal statutory law, the tribal court might be able to issue an order of protection against the abuser.

- If the victim is Native and the abuser is not Native, the tribal court may be able to exercise criminal jurisdiction over the abuser if the tribal nation is in compliance with the Violence Against Women Reauthorization Act of 2013 (Special Domestic Violence Criminal Jurisdiction).[4] The tribal nation may also have civil authority over both protection orders, dissolution matters, and child custody proceedings.

- If the victim is non-Native and the abuser is Native, the tribal court can exercise criminal jurisdiction. The tribal nation may also have civil authority over orders of protection, dissolution matters, and child custody proceedings.

- If the domestic violence incidents happen off-reservation, the tribal court may still retain jurisdiction, particularly in cases of child custody proceedings if the children are citizens of the tribe.

Most Native people do not live on reservations. In fact, the 2010 Census indicates that more Native people live in cities than ever before. Nonetheless, tribal citizens may maintain close cultural ties with their tribal nation. However, if the domestic violence incidents do not occur on the reservation, it is likely that the state court will have exclusive authority over criminal and civil matters.

The Indian Child Welfare Act (ICWA) is a federal law that requires state courts to refer child protection proceedings to the tribal court where the child is enrolled

---

[4] *See* Violence Against Women Reauthorization Act of 2013, Pub. L. No. 113-4, §§ 904, 908, 127 Stat. 54, 120–23, 125–26 (2013) (codified at 25 U.S.C. § 1304).

or eligible for enrollment.[5] ICWA does not apply in typical divorce custody cases. Instead, it applies to out-of-home placement (foster care and adoption). If your client is facing state child removal related to domestic violence, consult with an experienced ICWA attorney to determine the best course of action.

V. Client Safety

Native victims on reservations may experience numerous barriers to services, including geographic isolation, poverty, and a lack of transportation, telephone, and adequate housing. For example, some reservations do not have adequate numbers of law enforcement officers, and it could take hours before an emergency call is answered. In addition, many reservations do not have mobile phone coverage, meaning that victims do not have the ability to rely on a mobile phone for safety. Transportation can also be extremely difficult, and clients may have difficulty securing transportation to tribal or state court, or to your law office.

There are very few domestic violence shelters on reservations, meaning that many Native victims will need to find shelter in off-reservation shelters, which could be hundreds of miles away. Even if there is a local shelter, a victim may not feel safe if the community is particularly small and isolated. Some Native victims choose to find shelter off-reservation because it provides a greater likelihood of safety. However, many Native victims feel more comfortable working with Native advocates who understand their unique cultural and spiritual needs.

If your client is Native and their abuser is non-Native, this can present serious safety concerns in the context of criminal law. Typically, tribal courts do not have any criminal authority over non-Indians. However, some tribal nations have implemented the Violence Against Women Reauthorization Act of 2013 (Special Domestic Violence Criminal Jurisdiction), which allows tribal courts to exercise criminal jurisdiction over non-Indians who commit acts of domestic violence.[6] While considering your client's safety concerns, you should find out whether their tribe has implemented Special Domestic Violence Criminal Jurisdiction.

In many cases, a state court may have concurrent jurisdiction over civil matters. Ask your client whether they wish to go to tribal court or state court. There may be specific reasons why your client would prefer one over the other.

Pursuant to the Violence Against Women Act, tribal orders of protection must be enforced by state and local authorities off-reservation.[7] Likewise, tribal courts are also required to enforce orders of protection issued by state courts. However, there are still some jurisdictions that are out of compliance with federal law. In

---

[5] 25 U.S.C. ch. 21.

[6] *See* Violence Against Women Reauthorization Act of 2013, Pub. L. No. 113–4, §§ 904, 908, 127 Stat. 54, 120–23, 125–26 (2013) (codified at 25 U.S.C. § 1304).

[7] 18 U.S.C. § 2265.

such cases, Native victims may choose to obtain two orders of protection (one from tribal court and one from state court) to ensure their safety.

VI. *Advocacy Tips*

- Contact Native women's advocacy organizations, shelters, and coalitions, and ask about training opportunities so that you can become more familiar with the services available to Native women in the region.

- Cultivate a relationship with an experienced Indian law attorney. Because each tribal court is unique, you should seek out other attorneys who have practiced in the tribal court where you intend to practice.

- State and local bar association publications often have articles about the unique aspects of practicing in tribal courts in the region.

- Many states have a Native American bar association. Consider joining the local bar association to meet other attorneys who practice in tribal courts.

APPENDIX

Websites:

- **National American Indian Tribal Court Judges Association**
  - https://naicja.wildapricot.org/

- **National Congress of American Indians**
  - http://www.ncai.org/

- **National Indian Child Welfare Association**
  - https://www.nicwa.org/

- **National Indian Law Library**
  - https://www.narf.org/nill/

- **National Indigenous Women's Resource Center**
  - http://www.niwrc.org/

- **Southwest Center for Law and Policy**
  - http://www.swclap.org/

- **Tribal Law and Policy Institute**
  - http://www.home.tlpi.org/

- **Tribal Protection Order Resources**
  - http://tribalprotectionorder.org/

Books:

JUSTIN B. RICHLAND & SARAH DEER, INTRODUCTION TO TRIBAL LEGAL STUDIES (Jerry Gardner & Heather Valdez Singleton eds., 3d ed. 2016).

CARRIE E. GARROW & SARAH DEER, TRIBAL CRIMINAL LAW AND PROCEDURE (Jerry Gardner & Heather Valdez Singleton eds., 2d ed. 2015).

SHARING OUR STORIES OF SURVIVAL: NATIVE WOMEN SURVIVING VIOLENCE (Sarah Deer et al. eds., 2008).

Articles:

Rebecca A. Hart & M. Alexander Lowther, *Honoring Sovereignty: Aiding Tribal Efforts to Protect Native American Women from Domestic Violence,* 96 CALIF. L. REV. 185 (2008).

Loring Jones, *The Distinctive Characteristics and Needs of Domestic Violence Victims in a Native American Community,* 23 J. FAM. VIOLENCE 113 (2008).

Myrna S. Raeder, *Domestic Violence in Federal Court: Abused Women as Victims, Survivors, and Offenders,* 19 FED. SENT'G REP. 91 (2006).

Margaret Zhang, *Special Domestic Violence Criminal Jurisdiction for Indian Tribes: Inherent Tribal Sovereignty Versus Defendants' Complete Constitutional Rights,* 164 U. Pₐ. L. Rₑᵥ. 243 (2015).

Chapter Nine:
Domestic Violence on College Campuses

The recent surge in reporting of incidents of campus sexual violence, domestic violence, dating violence, and stalking has drastically increased the need for lawyers to understand both the psychological impacts of such violence, as well as the legal and administrative options available to these traditionally underserved and often misunderstood clients. Understanding the mental health, administrative, and legal options facing these victims is critical in responding to clients' varying needs. Practitioners should ensure that their clients understand all their options when they seek assistance

I. The Prevalence of Domestic Violence on College Campuses

In recent years, the prevalence of domestic violence on college campuses throughout the United States is well-documented. After decades of schools either ignoring or minimizing the harm of these incidents, student victims, civil rights lawyers, and advocacy groups have shined a light on recurrence of domestic violence faced by students at institutions of higher learning.

The most seminal statistic on sexual violence on college campuses comes from a 2007 study by the Department of Justice's National Institute of Justice, which found that one in five women and one in sixteen men will be sexually assaulted during their college career.[1] While some found this level of prevalence shocking, the likelihood is that the actual rates of college campus sexual assault are much higher. This is because less than 20 percent of sexual assault victims

---

[1] CHRISTOPHER P. KREBS ET AL., NAT'L INST. OF JUST., THE CAMPUS SEXUAL ASSAULT (CSA) STUDY FINAL REPORT (2007), *available at* https://www.ncjrs.gov/pdffiles1/nij/grants/221153.pdf.

on college campuses report their own assaults.[2] As a result, studies obtain only a limited sample of individuals who a) can identify the abuse, and b) choose to do so on anonymous questionnaires and other research study tools.

Dating violence is even more common during college years. Almost half (43 percent) of all college women who dated while in college have reported experiencing violent or abusive dating behaviors, including physical, sexual, technology-facilitated, verbal, or other controlling abuse.[3] And just over one in ten college women has experienced being stalked on campus.[4]

For most college students, the freedom of their first experience living alone brings with it a period of uncertainty, insecurity, and the need for acceptance. In conjunction, these dynamics make college students uniquely susceptible to becoming victims of domestic violence, thereby creating a heightened need for a strong legal community to help them.[5]

II. Federal Authority Governing Response to Domestic Violence on College Campuses

There are three main authorities that instruct schools in responding to domestic violence on campuses, and the rights of victims: Title IX, the Clery Act, and guidance from the Department of Education's Office of Civil Rights (OCR).[6]

A. Title IX

Title IX is a federal law that prohibits sex discrimination by educational institutions that receive federal funding, which includes almost all colleges and universities. Schools engage in discrimination when they know of gender-based harassment or violence, and fail to adequately respond. By its plain language, Title IX states:

---

[2] Sofi Sinozich & Lynn Langton, U.S. Dep't of Just., Rape and Sexual Assault Victimization Among College-Age Females, 1995–2013 (2014), *available at* https://www.bjs.gov/content/pub/pdf/rsavcaf9513.pdf.

[3] Knowledge Networks, 2011 College Dating Violence and Abuse Poll (2011), *available at* http://www.loveisrespect.org/pdf/College_Dating_And_Abuse_Final_Study.pdf.

[4] Bonnie S. Fisher, Francis T. Cullen & Michael G. Turner, U.S. Dep't of Just., The Sexual Victimization of College Women (2000), *available at* https://www.ncjrs.gov/pdffiles1/nij/182369.pdf.

[5] 84 percent of female survivors of assault report being sexually assaulted within the first four semesters that they are away at school. Krebs et al., *supra* note 1, at fn. 1. Because of the heightened risk that exists when women first arrive at college, this period of time has been labeled the "red zone" by researchers and advocates.

[6] Recently, a movement has taken afoot for individual states to pass their own legislation to give further guidance to schools on requirements in responding to domestic violence. Careful review of any applicable state laws is necessary in advising victims of domestic violence.

No person in the United States shall, on the basis of sex, be excluded from participation in, be denied the benefits of, or be subject to discrimination under any education program or activity receiving federal financial assistance.[7]

Though much attention has been given to incidents of campus rape, the broad language of Title IX encompasses all types of sexual or gender discrimination, including sexual harassment, any type of sexual assault, dating violence, domestic violence, or even bullying if motivated by gender. Title IX protections can apply to students, employees, and other persons who may suffer sex discrimination under an "educational program."

As a practical matter, this means that Title IX requires schools to ensure that their students are given the support that they need when they experience sexual assault, domestic violence, or any other type of gender-based discrimination on campus. This includes ensuring that students who experience domestic violence on campus: (1) can safely report the violence they experience; (2) receive support and accommodations to help them deal with the aftermath of these experiences; and (3) when they so choose, can participate in a fair disciplinary process against the perpetrators of this violence.

Notably, Title IX does not require that universities take any one specific action to address sexual assaults, sexual harassment, or any other forms of gender-based violence that occur on campus. Instead, schools are encouraged to act reasonably in responding to reports of violence and encourage an environment where students feel comfortable coming forward to report what has happened to them, thereby creating a safer environment for everyone involved. As discussed below, there are a wide range of campus procedures and proceedings that universities can implement to comply with their responsibilities under Title IX.[8]

B. The Clery Act

In addition to the requirements imposed by Title IX, a second piece of federal legislation, the Clery Act, also requires schools to: (1) maintain statistics about incidents of dating violence, domestic violence, sexual assault, and stalking; (2) provide prevention and awareness programs; and (3) assure certain minimum standards in preventing and addressing reports of violence.

The Clery Act requires schools to notify students and employees about the disciplinary processes available to deal with gender-based violence, as well as what protective measures (accommodations) can be put in place.[9] Additionally,

---

[7] Title IX of the Education Amendments of 1972, 20 U.S.C. § 1681 *et seq.*

[8] The Jeanne Clery Disclosure of Campus Security Policy and Campus Crime Statistics Act, 20 U.S.C. § 1092(f).

[9] 34 C.F.R. § 668.46(b)(11).

the Clery Act requires schools to provide a prompt, fair, and impartial disciplinary process by ensuring that: (1) matters are handled by specifically trained individuals; (2) the students involved have the advisor of their choice, including a lawyer if desired; (3) the parties involved are both given timely and equal access to information and procedures; and (4) the matter be resolved in a prompt and reasonable timeframe.[10]

C. Guidance from the Office of Civil Rights

OCR is tasked by Congress with the administrative enforcement of Title IX. In doing so, OCR publishes guidance on how schools should respond to domestic violence. Though OCR's guidance is not binding law, reviewing the latest guidance will help practitioners to evaluate whether a school's policies or practices are consistent with OCR's expectation.[11] If a school is believed to be in violation of this guidance, a complaint can be filed with OCR against the institution, which could result in the school being required to implement policy changes.[12] It is important to note that although a complaint to OCR can be a meaningful opportunity for a victim to correct a school's poor practices, doing so can rarely be done in a timeframe that would be of benefit to the complainant victim.

III. Procedures Taking Place on College Campuses

Historically, many campuses employed the practice of ignoring reports of domestic violence until they went away. The practical consequence of this approach was that victims of violence frequently ended up leaving these institutions after the campus environment became unendurable. In the past decade, frustration with this practice reached a tipping point and schools were publicly outed, sued, and disciplined for the mishandling of reports of domestic violence. Individuals today who experience domestic violence on college campuses have a very different experience. Though far from uniform, and with varying degrees of effectiveness, schools now have a more developed range of services and options available to victims.

As in all cases of violent crime, a practitioner's first responsibility is to ensure the physical safety of the individuals. Victims of domestic violence should be advised to call 911 if they feel threatened or unsafe. Additionally, victims should be aware of the safety and health resources available to them, including local law enforcement, campus police, the school's Title IX office, victim advocates, and

---

10 34 C.F.R. § 668.46(k).

11 *See Sex Discrimination Policy Guidance*, Dep't Educ. Off. C.R., https://www2.ed.gov/about/offices/list/ocr/frontpage/faq/rr/policyguidance/sex.html (last visited Apr. 18, 2018).

12 A complaint can be filed online with OCR. *OCR Complaint Forms – Electronic and PDF Versions*, Dep't Educ. Off. C.R., https://www2.ed.gov/about/offices/list/ocr/complaintintro.html (last visited Apr. 18, 2018).

campus and community based mental health counseling services. Support to a victim of trauma is critical. Victims who "go it alone" are less likely to successfully navigate the challenges of staying on campus, and more likely to suffer recurring mental health problems, feelings of hopelessness, or engage in self-harm.

Once the safety of the victim has been established, the focus should turn to addressing the victim's long-term needs, including: (1) how the victim can remain on campus and pursue their education; and (2) how to pursue disciplinary actions against the perpetrator (if the victim so chooses). While all schools are required to provide a disciplinary procedure to students, the structure of that process can differ, as discussed below. Even a process that moves with great speed may take two months or more to resolve. In the meantime, quite often the victims need measures to be put in place to accommodate them during the school's disciplinary process. Interim accommodations can be very useful and often necessary for the victim's continuation at the school.

Advocacy Tip: Though perhaps not legal authority, the school's own policies are in fact the primary "law of the land" in campus procedures. If there is one resource that will tell the practitioner and the client what to expect from the school's campus procedures and resources, it is the school policy.

A. Accommodations

All too often when schools fail to address the hostile environment that commonly follows campus domestic violence, the victim will end up abandoning their education altogether. Though seeking disciplinary action against an offender can be helpful in avoiding this outcome, the overriding focus should remain on the continuation of the education so long as that continuation is not at the expense of the victim's safety or emotional health.

Though accommodations alone may not be sufficient on a permanent basis to alleviate the difficultly of attending school with the abuser, they can in many cases be enough protection to keep the victim safe and in school until the resolution of the disciplinary process.

Categories of typical accommodations can be grouped as (1) no contact, (2) housing, and (3) academic:

(1) No Contact

Schools have widely varying practices for implementing no contact policies, ranging from only prohibiting direct contact to imposing campus bans on accused individuals whose cases may merit such treatment. The use of a "no contact" provision can be very useful depending on how the provision is applied. Some schools impose provisions that only prevent an accused student from physically contacting a victim or speaking directly to them. Such practices end up being of modest benefit to the victim as they still may walk the campus in constant fear of inadvertent contact with their abuser.

By contrast, effective no contact provisions can provide victims with relief such as: (1) requiring no direct or indirect contact of any kind with instruction that in the case of incidental contact, the accused must vacate the area; (2) providing the victim with the accused's class schedule so the victim may avoid those areas of campus; (3) providing a victim with an escort on campus; (4) giving the accused an escort from campus police when on campus; or (5) implementing a "soft" campus ban whereby the accused student is still allowed to enter campus but solely for the purpose of attending class or other approved purposes, with notice to the victim.

(2) Housing
Housing accommodations such as the ability to switch dormitories or move off campus can be some of the most useful tools that a school can provide to help a victim of domestic violence. In many cases, the accused abuser may live in the same building as the victim, attend an academic program close to the victim's housing, or even have friends on the victim's same floor. These scenarios can create a hostile environment in the one location where the victim most needs to feel safe from harassment or retaliation.

Though some schools may resist the requests of victims for housing accommodations as unnecessary, all reasonable requests should be considered. Many schools will proactively adjust the housing assignment of the accused student pending the outcome of the disciplinary hearing where the current housing assignment for the victim is a healthy and safe space. At a minimum, schools should prohibit the accused student from access to the victim's housing.

(3) Academic Accommodations
In the wake of domestic violence, victims can experience significant negative impacts to their academic performance.[13] The potential consequences range from inability to concentrate due to trauma to inability to attend class due to an overwhelming fear of running into the abuser. Schools can accommodate these issues by increasing excused absences, permitting extra time to complete assignments or testing, offering private testing rooms, permitting a student to drop classes past the normal drop deadline or, if the act of violence occurred in a prior semester, changing grades to either pass/fail or allowing a student to retake a class and replacing the poor grade. Without accommodations

---

[13] Carol E. Jordan, Jessica L. Combs & Gregory T. Smith, *An Exploration of Sexual Victimization and Academic Performance Among College Women*, 15(3) TRAUMA VIOLENCE ABUSE (July 2014).

from the institution, victims of domestic violence may fail out of school in the aftermath of the abuse.

B. Disciplinary Measures

For many victims, one of the goals in reporting domestic violence is the opportunity to see their offender disciplined and prevent other students from being harmed. The campus disciplinary process assists victims in these efforts. Though the specific disciplinary policies and practices differ greatly from school to school, all campuses essentially use one of two models. The first is the more traditional hearing model which resembles a trial type of adjudication. The second is an investigator model which uses a specially trained investigator to investigate the report and make findings and conclusions.[14] At all institutions, there is a process for the student or employee to have a meeting or phone call where the school provides information about the process, a copy of any relevant policies, and answer any questions the participant may have.

(1) The Disciplinary Hearing Model
The disciplinary hearing model will be familiar to many practitioners, as the process has the appearance of normal litigation. There are, however, several key distinctions:

- First, the role of the attorney in the hearing process is drastically different than in a court of law. At most institutions that employ the hearing model, an attorney is limited to acting as an advisor—assisting the participant through the process, but unable to actively participate in making arguments or giving opening or closing statements. Additionally, questioning of witnesses is often done by handing the hearing panel a list of questions from the participant, which severely limits the effectiveness of cross examination. Though not quite a "potted plant," it is rare that attorneys are able to proactively advocate for their clients. However, this does not mean that there is not a significant role for the attorney to play. Helping the participant in preparing for each stage of the hearing can be crucial to a participant's success.

- Second, there is no ability to subpoena witnesses. Student witnesses are often reluctant to get involved, and having a key student witness "no show" for a hearing is not uncommon. This means that assessing how to get the witness's testimony, whether in writing or by interview with the Title IX office, in front of the hearing panel *in advance* of the hearing can be critical if permitted.

---

[14] Occasionally, schools will use a hybrid of both models, where the investigator makes the initial findings and the participants have the right to appeal to a hearing board.

- Lastly, rather than a judge or jury, a disciplinary hearing panel is usually made up of three to five persons from the school community, including students. Depending on the school, the panelists may have little knowledge about domestic violence or trauma, or may be predisposed against complainant. Though the students who sit on the panel are usually mindful of the importance of their function and the sensitive nature of the material, the process is often uncomfortable for the complainant who must resume school with some of the same students from the panel.

(2) The Investigator Model

The investigator model presents a very different approach from the hearing model by avoiding any semblance of a trial. Instead, the investigator model is conducted more like an independent investigation utilizing a factfinder who is usually given significant training. Several organizations offer specific training programs for these types of investigations, which include training on issues such as how to understand trauma and how to weigh evidence in a campus proceeding.[15] Accordingly, the advantage to this model is that the investigator is usually well-trained to oversee the process. Additionally, the investigator approach can be less overwhelming and intimidating for victims and alleviates concerns about no show witnesses, as the investigators can connect with student witnesses on their own schedule.

(3) Mediation

Another less frequently used, and more controversial, approach to resolving complaints is mediation. This option can be both useful and dangerous at the same time. The upside to mediation is that, if navigated successfully, the victim can get the most important facets of the protection they need without hinging their future on the outcome of a disciplinary process. The downside, however, is that the internal and external pressures on most victims can lead them to agree to unhealthy terms that do not protect them from the effects of the harassment. If the victim is considering a mediated resolution, they should be encouraged to envision and discuss the future impact of the resolution with their attorney, therapist, or a victim advocate.

---

[15] For example, the National Center for Campus Public Safety provides trauma-informed sexual assault investigation and adjudication trainings. *Trauma-Informed Sexual Assault Investigation and Adjudication Institute*, Nat'l Ctr. for Campus Pub. Safety, https://www.nccpsafety.org/training-technical-assistance/trauma-informed-sexual-assault-investigation-and-adjudication (last visited Apr. 18, 2018).

IV. Intersection of Campus Judicial Proceedings with Criminal and Civil Actions

Historically, the criminal justice system has not been known to be a friendly environment for the victim of trauma.[16] Predictably, victims largely choose not to report to the police and, for the few who do so, the overwhelming majority are met with a decision that the prosecution will not file charges.[17]

As the movement to speak out against domestic violence grows, campuses have developed more robust options for victims in lieu of or in addition to reporting to law enforcement. For many victims, these newer campus processes seem less intimidating and better able to assist in the primary goal of continuing their life and education free from harassment.

The overlap between criminal, civil, and campus proceedings offers a wider range of options for victims of domestic violence, including the ability to report to the police, the school, or no one at all.[18] To help victims navigate this decision-making process, practitioners should be aware that many victims are unaware of basic differences in the criminal, civil, and campus systems and an easily digestible explanation of the differences, and benefits or drawbacks of each may be required.

While campus proceedings offer an alternative avenue for investigating domestic violence, with trained investigators that are at times more skilled than some of their police counterparts, victims and practitioners must be aware that the level of skill and diligence exhibited by school investigators varies greatly.

Where a victim chooses to proceed with both a campus proceeding and a criminal report, there may be some overlap in investigation, or the two entities may pursue entirely different investigation strategies. Though schools should not rely solely on the investigation of law enforcement, one solid practice that has developed more recently is the doubling up of the interview process so that the Title IX office can sit in on the law enforcement interview. This avoids duplication in an already traumatic process, and can be of great benefit particularly where a victim wishes to pursue both processes simultaneously.

---

[16] *A Review of the American Bar Association's Guidelines for Fair Treatment of Crime Victims and Witnesses,* NAT'L CRIME VICTIM L. INST. (2006), *available at* https://law.lclark.edu/live/files/6450-a-review-of-abas-guidelines-for-fair-treatment-of.

[17] *The Criminal Justice System: Statistics,* RAINN, https://www.rainn.org/statistics/criminal-justice-system (last visited Apr. 18, 2018).

[18] Victims may choose to separately or simultaneously file a petition for an order of protection in a civil court.

V. Other Legal Remedies and Relief

For many victims of sexual assault and domestic violence, campus judicial proceedings and/or parallel criminal actions will be sufficient to ensure that a perpetrator is held responsible for his or her actions, and that adequate protections and accommodations are put in place to support the victim in the aftermath of the violence.

In some scenarios, however, the response of a school or university simply is not enough. The school may refuse to acknowledge or address a report of sexual assault or domestic violence by a student, leaving the victim to fend for himself or herself. Or the school may institute a process that is grossly inadequate or even biased against the victim in order to protect the interests of the school or the abuser. This can sometimes happen where the abuser is a high-profile athlete or a prestigious member of the university community. When a school fails to take proper action to remedy known harassment or discrimination that is occurring against its students, it can be said to be acting with deliberate indifference. This deliberate indifference can make the school liable in a potential civil lawsuit in federal court.

Civil liability typically arises from two types of claims: (1) deliberate indifference to a substantial risk of harm to the victim, and (2) deliberate indifference to the victim's report. In the first scenario, a university may have actual knowledge of an abuser on campus who has previously assaulted or abused another student. When a school is deliberately indifferent to this knowledge and fails to take action to stop that abuser from reoffending, this creates a substantial risk of harm to the other students on campus. If a student is later the victim of a sexual assault or gender-based violence at the hands of that same perpetrator, the second victim may be able to sue the school for the damages resulting from that harm.

In the second scenario, a victim may report sexual assault, sexual harassment, or any other form of domestic violence to a university and, although the university has actual knowledge of the report, it fails to take any action to investigate the report or provide support and accommodations to the victim who reported. In this scenario, the school's deliberate indifference did not result in the assault itself, but it does create an ongoing hostile environment for the victim. The victim may then be able to sue for damages resulting from having to face the abuser at school and deal with an unsupportive and hostile educational environment. Especially where the victim felt compelled to leave the school due to that environment, these claims can be sizable.

In either scenario, victims of domestic violence can recover two different types of remedies if they bring a civil lawsuit. First, they can try to recover damages for the harm that they incurred. Second, if they are still at the school, they can seek injunctive relief against the school to change the way that the school is operating.

Damages in a civil lawsuit are wide-ranging. They can include damages for physical harm, damages for mental health and emotional harms, prospective needs for treatment and/or therapy, reimbursement for medical bills, the costs of having to relocate or take other precautionary measures, reimbursement for tuition and school expenses because of time taken off from school, compensation for delayed entry into the workforce, and any other expenses that may be incidental to the deliberate indifference of the school.

Injunctive relief can be personal to the victim himself or herself or broadly applicable to the school as a whole. For many victims, the primary frustration that drives a lawsuit is the feeling that the school failed to do what it was supposed to do and did not support victims on campus. Injunctive relief that requires schools to change their policies and procedures under Title IX, or offer certain support and accommodations to victims, can feel very satisfying and rewarding to plaintiffs, and can help to ensure that future victims do not suffer the same harms that the plaintiff did. Alternatively, for some plaintiffs, injunctive relief that allows them to continue their education and graduate can also be incredibly helpful. This can include requirements that a student be provided an escort, be allowed to move dormitories, or be given the option to take classes online rather than in person.

No matter what route a victim of sexual assault and domestic violence takes, there are important roles that attorneys can take in assisting clients through the process. Attorneys can often assist victims throughout campus judicial proceedings as an advocate or advisor, although the degree to which the attorney can be involved is highly dependent on campus policies, so it is best to consult with the school about what an attorney can and cannot do.

If your client feels that the school's proceedings were biased or extremely inadequate, or no school proceeding is offered at all, the client may elect to file a civil lawsuit in which case attorney representation will be necessary. Title IX lawsuits must be filed in federal court and can be accompanied by additional 42 U.S.C. § 1983 claims for state schools or state law claims, where appropriate. Prevailing plaintiffs can recover their attorneys' fees in a Title IX action.

Finally, attorneys can assist victims of domestic violence in considering the possibility of a civil order of protection, particularly where a school is unwilling to put necessary protections or accommodations in place. Many schools will only enforce orders of protection with strict requirements on how far apart a victim and perpetrator must remain, so attorney representation in an order of protection proceeding may be helpful to ensure a victim gets adequate protection from a judge.

VI. Conclusion

Sexual assault and domestic violence are perpetrated by students on every college campus. As a country, we are learning just how common these assaults are, and Congress has developed policies providing victims with a variety of possible relief. In addition to state law and a school's own policy, federal law provides victims of these crimes with remedies that enable them to continue their education in a safe environment. Attorneys should strive to be aware of local campus policies, as well as the intricacies of state and federal law, to best advocate for clients on campus in a university, civil, or criminal setting.

Intersection of Title IX and the Clery Act

The purpose of this chart is to clarify the reporting requirements of Title IX and the Clery Act in cases of sexual violence and to resolve any concerns about apparent conflicts between the two laws. To date, the Department of Education has not identified any specific conflicts between Title IX and the Clery Act.

Title IX	The Clery Act
What types of incidents must be reported to school officials under Title IX and the Clery Act?	
Overview: Title IX promotes equal opportunity by providing that no person may be subjected to discrimination on the basis of sex under any educational program or activity receiving federal financial assistance. A school must respond promptly and effectively to sexual harassment, including sexual violence, that creates a hostile environment. When responsible employees know or should know about possible sexual harassment or sexual violence they must report it to the Title IX coordinator or other school designee. ➢ **Sexual Harassment:** Sexual harassment is unwelcome conduct of a sexual nature, including unwelcome sexual advances, requests for sexual favors, and other verbal, nonverbal, or physical conduct of a sexual nature. ➢ **Sexual Violence:** Sexual violence is a form of sexual harassment. Sexual violence refers to physical sexual acts perpetrated against a person's will or where a person is incapable of giving consent (*e.g.*, due to the student's age or use of drugs or alcohol or an intellectual or other disability that prevents the student from having the capacity to give consent). Sexual violence includes rape, sexual assault, sexual battery, sexual abuse, and sexual coercion.	**Overview:** The Clery Act promotes campus safety by ensuring that students, employees, parents, and the broader community are well-informed about important public safety and crime prevention matters. Institutions that receive Title IV funds must disclose accurate and complete crime statistics for incidents that are reported to Campus Security Authorities (CSAs) and local law enforcement as having occurred on or near the campus. Schools must also disclose campus safety policies and procedures that specifically address topic such as sexual assault prevention, drug and alcohol abuse prevention, and emergency response and evacuation. The Clery Act also promotes transparency and ongoing communication about campus crimes and other threats to health and safety and empowers members to take a more active role in their own safety and security. **Criminal Offenses:** Criminal homicide; rape and other sexual assaults; robbery; aggravated assault; burglary; motor vehicle theft; and, arson as well as arrests and disciplinary referrals for violations of drug, liquor, and weapons laws. ➢ **Hate Crimes:** Any of the above-mentioned offenses against persons and property and incidents of larceny-theft, simple assault, intimidation or destruction/damage/vandalism of property, in which an individual or group is intentionally targeted because of their actual or perceived race, gender, religion, national origin, sexual orientation, gender identity, ethnicity, or disability. 20 U.S.C. §1092(f)(1)(F)(ii). Use FBI definitions, and the

modifications from the Hate Crime Statistics Act. 20 U.S.C. §1092(f)(7).

➤ **VAWA**: The reauthorization of the Violence Against Women Act of 1994 amended the Clery Act to include disclosure of statistics regarding incidents of dating violence, domestic violence, and stalking as defined in 20 U.S.C. §1092(f)(1)(F)(iii) and 20 U.S.C. §1092(f)(7).

Institutions must disclose crime statistics for Clery-reportable offenses that occur on its so-called "Clery Geography." Clery Geography includes three general categories:

➤ **Campus:** Any building or property that an institution owns or controls within a reasonably contiguous area that directly supports or relates to the institution's educational purposes. On campus also includes residence halls and properties the institution owns and students use for educational purposes that are controlled by another person (such as a food or retail vendor). The definition of "controlled" includes all such properties that are leased or borrowed and used for educational purposes. 20 U.S.C. §1092(f)(6)(ii)

➤ **Non-campus building or property:** Any building or property that is owned or controlled by a recognized student organization. And, any building or property that is owned or controlled by the institution that is used in support of its educational purposes but is not located within a reasonably contiguous area to the campus. 20 U.S.C. §1092(f)(6)(iii).

➤ **Public property:** All public property within the reasonably contiguous geographic area of the institution that is adjacent to or accessible from a facility the institution owns or controls and that is used for educational purposes. Examples include sidewalks, streets, and parking facilities. 20 U.S.C. §1092(f)(6)(iv).

Occurring where? (geography/jurisdiction)

Recipients must respond to sexual violence that occurs:

➤ **In the context of a school's education programs and activities:** This includes academic, educational, extracurricular, athletic, and any other school programs, whether those programs take place in a school's facilities, on a school bus, at a class or training program sponsored by the school at another location, or elsewhere. Additional examples include school-sponsored field trips, school-recognized fraternity or sorority houses, and athletic team travel; and events for school clubs that occur off campus.

➤ **Off-campus:** Even if the sexual violence did not occur in the context of an educational program or activity, a school must process such complaints and consider the effects of the sexual violence when evaluating whether there is a hostile environment on campus or in an off-campus education program or activity.

Who must report details of an incident of sexual violence, including personally identifiable information?

Responsible employees

➢ A responsible employee is any employee who has the authority to take action to redress sexual violence, who has been given the duty to report to appropriate school officials about incidents of sexual violence or any other misconduct by students, or who a student could reasonably believe has this authority or responsibility.

➢ Schools must make clear to all of its employees and students which staff members are responsible employees.

Campus law enforcement officers, non-law enforcement campus safety officers, and local law enforcement officers

➢ These individuals are normally required to fully document all operative facts of an incident that are reported or that are developed throughout the course of a criminal investigation. The information collected during such an investigation will normally include personally-identifiable information (PII).

CSAs other than law enforcement/campus safety officers

➢ Most of these CSAs are not typically required to disclose PII as part of their normal reporting obligations. (see CSA definition below)

Who can provide completely confidential support services to victims of sexual violence?

Professional and pastoral counselors

➢ A professional counselor is a person whose official responsibilities include providing mental health counseling to members of the institution's community and who is functioning within the scope of his or her license or certification. This definition applies even to professional counselors who are not employees of the institution, but are under contract to provide counseling at the institution. This also includes an individual who is not yet licensed or certified as a counselor, but is acting in that role under the supervision of an individual who is licensed or certified. An example is a Ph.D. counselor-trainee acting under the supervision of a professional counselor at the institution.

➢ A pastoral counselor is a person who is associated with a religious order or denomination, is recognized by that religious order or denomination as someone who provides confidential counseling, and is functioning within the scope of that recognition. In this context, a pastor or priest who is functioning as an athletic director or as a student advocate would not be exempt from the reporting obligations.

➢ Professional and pastoral counselors are not required to report any information regarding an incident of alleged sexual violence. The exemption from reporting obligations for professional and pastoral counselors under Title IX is consistent with the Clery Act.

Who can provide services and keep personally identifiable information about incidents of sexual violence confidential?

denomination, is recognized by that religious order or denominations as someone who provides confidential counseling, and is functioning within the scope of that recognition. In this context, a pastor or priest who is functioning as an athletic director or as a student advocate would not be exempt from the reporting obligations.

➢ Crimes reported to a pastoral or professional counselor are not required to be reported by an institution under the Clery Act; however, institutions are strongly encouraged to establish voluntary, confidential reporting processes so that incidents of crime that are reported exclusively to professional and pastoral counselors will be included in the annual crime statistics. 34 C.F.R. §668.46(b)(2)(iii).

Non-professional counselors or advocates

➤ Individuals who are not professional or pastoral counselors, but work or volunteer in on-campus sexual assault centers, victim advocacy offices, women's centers, or health centers, including front desk staff and students, and provide assistance to students who experience sexual violence, should report aggregate data, but are not required to report, without the student's consent, incidents of sexual violence to the school in a way that identifies the student.

Most non-law enforcement/campus safety officers who are CSAs because of they have significant responsibilities for student and campus activities.

➤ The definition of campus security authority includes campus police and/or security personnel; any individual who has responsibility for campus security but is not part of a campus police or security department; an individual or organization specified in an institution's statement of campus security policy as one to which students and employees should report criminal offenses; and an official of an institution who has a significant responsibility for student and campus activities, including, but not limited to, student housing, student discipline, and campus judicial proceedings. Most of these mandatory reporters are specifically not required by the Clery Act to disclose PII. 34 C.F.R. §668.46(a).

➤ Because specific occupational titles, descriptions and statements of duties vary so significantly, each institution must conduct a substantive review of all of its officials, including students with official duties for example, resident assistants, and evaluate whether the Clery Act designates the individual a CSA and thereby confers reporting obligations. CSAs must be identified, notified of their reporting obligations, be properly training, and provided with a mechanism for communicating reported incidents to the appropriate officials. (Handbook, 75).

What should non-professional counselors, advocates, and CSAs report about incidents of sexual violence?

Aggregate Data

➢ In order to identify patterns or systemic problems related to sexual violence, a school should collect aggregate data about sexual violence incidents from non-professional counselors or advocates in their on-campus sexual assault centers, victim advocacy offices, women's centers, or health centers.

➢ Such individuals should report only general information about incidents of sexual violence such as the nature, date, time, and general location of the incident and should take care to avoid reporting information that would personally identify a student. Non-professional counselors and advocates should consult with students regarding what information needs to be withheld to protect their identity.

Aggregate Data

➢ Typically, most non-law enforcement/campus safety officer CSAs must only report the nature, date, time, general location, and the current disposition of the incident, if known.

➢ Most non-law enforcement/campus safety officer CSAs typically are not required to disclose PII or other information that would have the effect of identifying the victim.

What must a school tell the complainant about the outcome of a sexual violence complaint and how does FERPA apply?[1]

Notice of the Outcome

➢ Title IX requires a school to tell the complainant whether or not it found that the sexual violence occurred, any individual remedies offered or provided to the complainant or any sanctions imposed on the perpetrator that directly relate to the complainant, and other steps the school has taken to eliminate the hostile environment, and prevent recurrence.

➢ Sanctions that directly relate to the complainant include, but are not limited to, requiring that the perpetrator stay away from the complainant until both parties graduate, prohibiting the perpetrator from attending

Results of Institutional Disciplinary Proceedings

➢ The Clery Act specifically mandates that "each institution shall develop and distribute procedures for simultaneously notifying the accuser and accused of the outcome of institutional disciplinary proceedings." 20 U.S.C. §485f(1)(J)(8)(B)(iv)(III)(aa).

➢ FERPA includes a provision that specifically allows schools to disclose to alleged victims of any crime of violence or rape and other sexual assaults, the final results of any disciplinary proceedings conducted by the institution against the alleged perpetrator of the offense. 20 U.S.C.

---

[1] This chart also addresses how the Family Educational Rights and Privacy Act (FERPA) applies to Title IX and the Clery Act. Once again, the Department of Education has not identified any specific situations where compliance with Title IX or the Clery Act will cause an institution to violate FERPA.

school for a period of time or transferring the perpetrator to another residence hall, other classes, or another school.

➤ The Department of Education interprets FERPA as not conflicting with the Title IX requirement that the school notify the complainant of the outcome of its investigation, *i.e.*, whether or not the sexual violence was found to have occurred, because this information directly relates to the victim. FERPA also permits the school to notify a complainant of sanctions imposed upon a student who was found to have engaged in sexual violence when the sanction directly relates to the complainant.

➤ The FERPA limits on re-disclosure of information do not apply to information that institutions are required to disclose under the Clery Act. 34 C.F.R. §99.33(c). Institutions may not require a complainant to abide by a nondisclosure agreement, in writing, or otherwise, that would prevent the re-disclosure of this information in any Title IX complaint that involves a Clery Act offense, such as sexual violence.

§1232g(b)(6).

➤ The "final results" of any proceeding are defined as: the name of the student, the findings of the proceeding board/official, any sanctions imposed by the institution, and the rationale for the findings and sanctions (if any). The presence of names of any other student, such as a victim or witnesses, may be included only with the consent of that student. 20 U.S.C. §1232g(c).

➤ The FERPA limits on re-disclosure of information do not apply to information that institutions are required to disclose under the Clery Act. 34 C.F.R. §99.33(c). Institutions may not require a complainant to abide by a nondisclosure agreement, in writing, or otherwise, that would prevent the re-disclosure of this information.

How does FERPA apply to other obligations under Title IX and the Clery Act?

All Other Title IX Obligations

➤ FERPA continues to apply in the context of Title IX enforcement, but if there is a direct conflict between the requirements of FERPA and the requirements of Title IX, such that enforcement of FERPA would interfere with the primary purpose of Title IX to eliminate sex-based discrimination in schools, the requirements of Title IX override any conflicting FERPA provisions.

Timely Warnings

➤ The Clery Act requires institutions to issue timely warnings to the campus community about crimes that have already occurred but may continue to pose a serious or ongoing threat to students and employees. Timely warnings are only required for Clery-reportable crimes that occur on Clery Geography although institutions are encouraged to issue appropriate warnings regarding other criminal activity that may pose a serious threat as well. 20 U.S.C. §485f(1)(J)(3); Handbook, 118.

➤ FERPA does not preclude an institution's compliance with the timely warning provision of the Clery Act. FERPA recognizes that information can, in the case of an emergency, be released without consent when needed to protect the health and safety of others. 34 C.F.R. §99.36(a). Further, if institutions utilize information from the records of campus law enforcement to issue a timely warning, those records are not protected by FERPA. 20 U.S.C. §1232g(a)(4)(B)(ii).

➤ However, timely warning reports must withhold the names and other identifying information about victims as confidential. 34 C.F.R. §668.46(e).

Emergency Response Procedures

➤ The Clery Act requires institutions to have and disclose emergency response and procedures. As part of these procedures, institutions must immediately notify the campus community about *any* significant emergency or dangerous condition that may pose an immediate threat to the health or safety of students or employees occurring on the campus. 20 U.S.C. §485f(1)(J)(1)(i).

➤ An institution that follows its emergency notification procedures is not required to issue a timely warning based on the same circumstances; however, the institution must provide adequate follow-up information to the community as needed. 34 C.F.R. §668.46(e)(3).

➤ FERPA recognizes that information can, in the case of an emergency, be released without consent when needed to protect the health and safety of others. 34 C.F.R. §99.36(a).

Section Three:
Economic Justice

Chapter Ten:
Economic Coercion and Survivor-Centered Economic Advocacy

Katie VonDeLinde and Erika Sussman

Reprinted from Center for Survivor Agency & Justice (CSAJ), Guidebook on Consumer & Economic Civil Legal Advocacy (2017), https://csaj.org/Guidebook.[1]

---

[1] A deeper dive into the case scenario described in this reprinted chapter can be found in CSAJ's Guidebook on Consumer & Economic Civil Legal Advocacy. Katie VonDeLinde & Erika Sussman, *Economic Coercion and Survivor-Centered Economic Advocacy, in* GUIDEBOOK ON CONSUMER & ECONOMIC CIVIL LEGAL ADVOCACY 12 (2017), https://csaj.org/Guidebook.

I. The Link Between Poverty and Violence

There is a reciprocal relationship between domestic violence and economic insecurity.[2] Abuse creates economic instability for survivors. And poverty, in turn, reduces safety options and creates increased vulnerability to future violence. Furthermore, the economic impact of domestic violence has profound consequences that compound across the lifespan. While the domestic violence movement has engaged in important work to enhance economic justice for survivors, current efforts tend to focus on discrete and immediate economic incidents through financial skills development, leaving the depth and breadth of economic harms largely unaddressed.

A. What is Safety?

As advocates and attorneys, we work daily with individuals who struggle with violent relationships and economic hardship, but we rarely pause to examine what safety means to us, personally. Take a moment to close your eyes, ask yourself these questions, and think about your answers:

- What does safety mean to me?

- How do I know when I am safe?

- What is economic safety for me?

---

[2] Complex social problems rooted in oppression challenge us to find language that is both specific enough to describe a phenomenon like domestic violence yet also inclusive enough to describe a wide variety of experiences. We use the term **domestic violence** (DV) to describe relationships in which one individual uses strategies designed to "establish domination in a partner's personal life based on fear, dependence, and deprivation of basic human rights using strategies including intimidation, degradation, isolation and control." EVAN STARK, COERCIVE CONTROL: HOW MEN ENTRAP WOMEN IN PERSONAL LIFE (2007) [hereinafter COERCIVE CONTROL]. *See also* Evan Stark, Rutgers Univ., Keynote Presentation at N.J. Dep't of Children & Families: The Battered Mother's Dilemma: Reframing Child Maltreatment in the Context of Coercive Control (2012), *available at* http://www. cpe.rutgers.edu/njdcf2012/docs/Stark-Keynote-Presentation-Battered-Mothers-Dilemma.pdf. This chapter refers to individuals being controlled in domestic violence relationships as "survivors," and people who perpetrate violence as "abusive partners." While the term "victim" is widely accepted in the legal system and correctly describes someone who has experienced a crime, victim has negative connotations as someone who is passive and can be a harmful representation of those who struggle to survive and thrive in the midst of violence. However, some individuals who experience domestic violence do not like the term survivor and feel that it diminishes the terrible acts of violence perpetrated by their partner. When working with individuals who experience domestic violence, it is important to follow the language used by that individual or to ask what language they would like use to use, especially when describing their abusive partner. While research and practice experience continues to show that a majority of individuals who are impacted by coercive controlling domestic violence are women and that women are disproportionately impacted by the consequences of domestic violence, men do experience domestic violence. Instead of referring to survivors with gendered pronouns, the inclusive term "survivor" is used in this chapter.

Visualizing safety helps us to understand our own perspective about what is safe and asks us to define safety in our own lives. For many of us, it is difficult to imagine being "safe" without economic security. Economic safety ensures that we have adequate housing, reliable transportation, healthy food, and maybe most importantly, financial choices. For example, currently available economic safety nets would give us the financial freedom to leave a job where we were experiencing harassment.

Visioning "Safety"

In a recent webinar hosted by the Center for Survivor Agency and Justice, domestic violence advocates from around the nation defined economic safety as: feeling secure; having choices; being able to act on our own decisions and choices; and financial independence.[3] Life choices for survivors struggling with domestic violence are constrained by their partner's economic abuse *and* by their life circumstances (for example, their access to quality education, childcare, and safe housing as well as their experiences with racism and sexism, etc.).[4]

Sonia's Story

Sonia just got off from her swing shift at a skilled nursing center where she works as a certified nurse assistant, and she is coming to talk to you about her current situation. She is eager to tell you what is going on for her, and behind her tired expression, you see a light in her eyes. Sonia is a 32-year-old woman who describes herself as "a hard worker and dreamer whose life took a turn I wasn't expecting." Sonia's parents are from Puerto Rico, and they raised Sonia in Miami.

Sonia met Robert ten years ago when he was the dental assistant in her dentist's office. Their relationship started out slow and loving, and Sonia was thrilled when they got married a year into their relationship. In the last five years, however, Robert has become increasingly jealous and does not want Sonia going anywhere except for work and her children's school. Sonia and Robert have two kids, Danny, 9 and Samantha, 7. Danny has autism, is non-verbal, and requires a lot of care. Sonia advocates hard to make sure Danny's needs are met at school, and she is relieved that this year, Danny's services are well organized, and he has a loving and smart teacher who seems to "get him."

---

[3] Katie VonDeLinde & Erika Sussman, Webinar Resource: Survivor Centered Economic Advocacy, CTR. FOR SURVIVOR AGENCY & JUST. (Apr. 2, 2015),

[4] JILL DAVIES & ELEANOR LYON, DOMESTIC VIOLENCE ADVOCACY: COMPLEX LIVES, DIFFICULT CHOICES (2d ed. 2014).

Sonia is coming to you because she is at her wit's end. Robert forces Sonia to directly deposit her paycheck into a banking account that she cannot access. She thinks it may be a joint account but is not sure, and Robert has never given her an ATM card or the account number. Sonia is also very upset because she just received notice that a credit card company is suing her. She does not recognize the account, and when she told Robert about it, he just laughed and said, "Yeah, I guess I should have told you I took that out in your name." Sonia has no idea what other accounts he may have opened using her name and information. She also recently found out that Robert has not been paying the mortgage consistently and they have received some kind of notice from the bank, but Robert will not show it to Sonia. Sonia is worried that they could lose their home.

Sonia loves her job and gets a lot of good feedback from her co-workers and supervisor, but lately, Sonia says, "Robert is even trying to ruin that for me." Robert accuses Sonia of sleeping with a co-worker and calls and texts Sonia dozens of times during her shifts. Recently, he showed up at her workplace, loudly yelling her name at the front desk as he came in. Sonia has told her supervisor pieces of what is going on with Robert, and while her supervisor has been tolerant, she is beginning to lose patience.

Sonia tells you that Robert has hit her, but only very occasionally. Sonia says Robert's name-calling hurts a lot worse than the physical abuse, and she misses spending time with her family and friends. She wants to get divorced, but she is worried that Robert, who has access to more of their money and has a better paying job, will get custody of their children, and she does not want to leave her school district due to her son's educational needs.

B. Risks for Survivors of Domestic Violence

Survivors of domestic violence must constantly weigh the risks they face, as they make choices about their daily lives.[5] To understand the complex nature of these choices, we must pay attention to survivors' economic options and risks, their life circumstances, and *our own* reactions and assumptions. Jill Davies and Eleanor Lyon describe the two types of risks that survivors weigh as:

---

[5] *Id.*

(1) Risks Created by the Battering Partner

- Physical injury or illness

- Psychological effects (mental health, substance abuse, suicide)

- Loss or harm to children

- Economic insecurity

- Lost or damaged relationships (family, friends, other social supports)

- Arrest or legal implications (due to legal status, protracted legal case, etc.)[6]

(2) Risks Created by the Survivor's Life Circumstances

- Access to quality education

- Employment options

- Childcare

- Safe housing

- Transportation

- Availability of social or public services

- Experiences of racism, sexism, homophobia, etc.

To advocate effectively for survivors of domestic violence, we need to understand the myriad of risks they face. One of the biggest risks with which survivors contend is economic hardship.

---

[6] Jill Davies, *Safety Planning,* VAW Net (1997), https://vawnet.org/sites/default/files/assets/files/2016-09/DaviesSafetyPlanning.pdf.

As you read Sonia's story, what were some risks that she is weighing?

SONIA'S RISKS

From Her Partner	Inherent in Her Life
Emotional abuse	Gender (sexism)
Isolation	Race/ethnicity (racism)
Physical abuse	Mother of a child with disabilities
Credit abuse	*What else?*
Work interference	
What else?	

What is missing from the chart above? For example, Sonia's story does not tell us this explicitly, but she may also be weighing her risks as a woman (for example, because of her gender, she may make less money than men doing her same job, etc.), and as a Latina (she may have a hard time accessing appropriate resources because of discrimination). Finally, as we take stock of the various risks and choices, we must also consider survivors' strengths: What are some of Sonia's strengths? She is familiar with the educational and health systems and is skilled in navigating them both on behalf of her son; she has a steady job in nursing; and she has strong familial and cultural ties, as well as allies within her employment setting.

C. Poverty Leads to Increased Vulnerability to Violence

For survivors of domestic violence, safety often hinges on access to economic resources. Those who can access and mobilize economic resources have more options for safety. Consequently, although anyone can experience domestic violence, women living in poverty are nearly *twice* as likely to experience domestic violence.[7] The fact that violence can frequently be a factor in the lives of poor women has led some observers to mistakenly conclude that poor people are more violent.[8]

This economic gender gap widens for those further marginalized by race, ability, sexual orientation experience, citizenship status, and other identities.[9] For example, while one in ten white people live at or below the poverty line, at least one in four (and higher) people of all other racial-ethnic groups live in poverty. So, while anyone can experience violence and economic hardship, our unique systems of discrimination restrict those on the social margins from equal options to safety and economic security.

D. Economic Abuse as a Form of Domestic Violence

All forms of abuse create economic instability for survivors in ways that linger, interact, and compound over time. The vast majority of abusive partners use economic tactics to control their partners, stripping them of the material and financial means to access safety and security.[10] In fact, 99 percent of survivors report experiencing some form of economic abuse by their partners.[11] Economic abuse is defined as "controlling a survivors ability to acquire, use and maintain economic resources."[12]

---

[7] *See* Michele C. Black et al., Ctrs. for Disease Control & Prevention, The National Intimate Partner and Sexual Violence Survey: 2010 Summary Report (2010), https://www.cdc.gov/violenceprevention/pdf/nisvs_executive_summary-a.pdf. Joshua R. Vest et al., *Multistate analysis of factors associated with intimate partner violence,* 22 Am. J. Preventive Medicine 156–164 (2002), http://www.ajpmonline.org/article/S0749-3797(01)00431-7/fulltext. Put differently, women with household incomes less than $7500 are seven times more likely to report domestic violence than women in households with incomes over $75,000. *See* Callie Marie Rennison & Sarah Welchans, U.S. Dep't of Just., Off. of Just. Progs., Rep. No. NCJ 178247, Intimate partner violence (2000), http://www.popcenter.org/problems/domestic_violence/PDFs/Rennison%26Welchans_2000.pdf. Similarly, more than half of homeless women report a history of assault by an intimate partner and 70 percent of women receiving public benefits (Temporary Assistance for Needy Families, WIC, Food stamps) report experiencing domestic violence. *See* Eleanor Lyon, Nat'l Resource Ctr. on Domestic Violence, Welfare, Poverty, and Abused Women: New Research and its Implications (2000), http://www.vawnet.org/Assoc_Files_VAWnet/BCS10_POV.pdf.

[8] *See infra* The Role of Poverty.

[9] For a more detailed analysis, see Erika Sussman & Sara Wee, Ctr. for Survivor Agency & Just., Accounting for Survivors' Economic Security Atlas: Mapping the Terrain (2016), https://csaj.org/document-library/CSAJ_Atlas_Mapbook_1_FINAL_TO_POST.pdf.

[10] **Coercive control** is defined by Evan Stark as "a pattern of violent acts and their political framework – the pattern of social, institutional, and interpersonal controls – that usurp a survivor's capacity to determine her destiny." Coercive Control, *supra* note 2.

[11] Adrienne E. Adams et al., *Development of the Scale of Economic Abuse,* 14 Violence Against Women 563–588 (2008), http://doi.org/10.1177/1077801208315529.

[12] *Id.*

Abusive partners frequently control survivors' ability to acquire and keep financial resources by interfering with, obtaining, or maintaining work, education, or community or government benefits. 60 percent of survivors of domestic violence report experiencing work interference (including sabotaging transportation, childcare, destroying uniforms, harassment at work, etc.) from an abusive partner.[13] Survivors also experience financially devastating banking, asset, income, credit and debt coercion from abusive partners. Abusive partners destroy survivor's credit by fraudulently opening accounts in the survivor's name, lying about paying bills in the survivor's name, overcharging credit accounts, or coercing survivors to sign for loans, credit lines, or other expenses. In some abusive relationships, partners also use force or threats to coerce survivors into participating in illegal activity (for example, TANF or SNAP fraud, prostitution, and writing bad checks, etc.). By destroying a survivor's credit or creating a criminal history, perpetrators gain further financial control over survivors' current and future economic choices.[14]

Sonia's options for safety were constrained by Robert's control of their finances, work sabotage, and other forms of abuse. In turn, the economic hardship and risk of poverty or homelessness restricted Sonia from accessing many safety options for her and her children. As seen in Sonia's story, domestic violence has both short- and long-term negative effects that accumulate over a lifetime (CSAJ refers to this as the "Economic Ripple Effect of Intimate Partner Violence (IPV)"). Survivors who struggle with domestic violence experience reduced wages, job experience, job stability, and economic well-being over time.[15]

1. The Role of Poverty: A Slippery Slope

That a woman living in poverty is twice as likely to be a victim of domestic violence may cause some to mistakenly believe that poverty is a cause, or the cause, of domestic violence. On the contrary, poverty functions to restrict survivors' economic options for obtaining safety. An abusive partner can make a survivor's economic instability more intractable by using economic tactics to exert control over the survivor (such as paying for or refusing to pay for items the survivor needs for themselves or their children, e.g., rent, childcare, car payment, or food). Conversely, when abusive partners experience economic problems (lost jobs or chronic unemployment), this can trigger or exacerbate the abusive behavior. For example, the probability of intimate partner homicide increases significantly if an abusive partner is unemployed.[16]

---

[13] Pamela C. Alexander, *Childhood Maltreatment, Intimate Partner Violence, Work Interference and Women's Employment,* 26 J. OF FAM. VIOLENCE 255–261 (2011).

[14] Angela Littwin, *Coerced Debt: The Role of Consumer Credit in Domestic Violence,* 100 CAL. L. REV. 951 (2012).

[15] Melanie M. Hughes & Lisa D. Brush, *The Price of Protection: A Trajectory Analysis of Civil Remedies for Abuse and Women's Earnings,* 80 AM. SOC. REV. 140–165 (2015).

[16] Sussman & Wee, *supra* note 9.

2. The Economic Ripple Effect of IPV

- **During a relationship,** abusive partners engage in behaviors that strip survivors of access to economic and material resources for safety.

- **In seeking safety, or leaving,** survivors literally pay a cost for safety (whether having to rely on credit or losing income or housing). This results in collateral economic damages, which affect survivors in the short term and manifest in various ways throughout the life course.

- **In the short-term,** our systems of support— from housing, to inadequate and expensive legal systems, to enduring employment insecurity, to abusive financial practices (from payday lending to redlining)—fall short in remedying the economic hardships experienced by survivors, and, at worst, lead to increased danger.

- **Across the lifespan,** abuse creates a pathway of economic disadvantage, including lost work and economic opportunities, consumer impacts, and the lingering effects of poor physical and mental health and decreased quality of life.

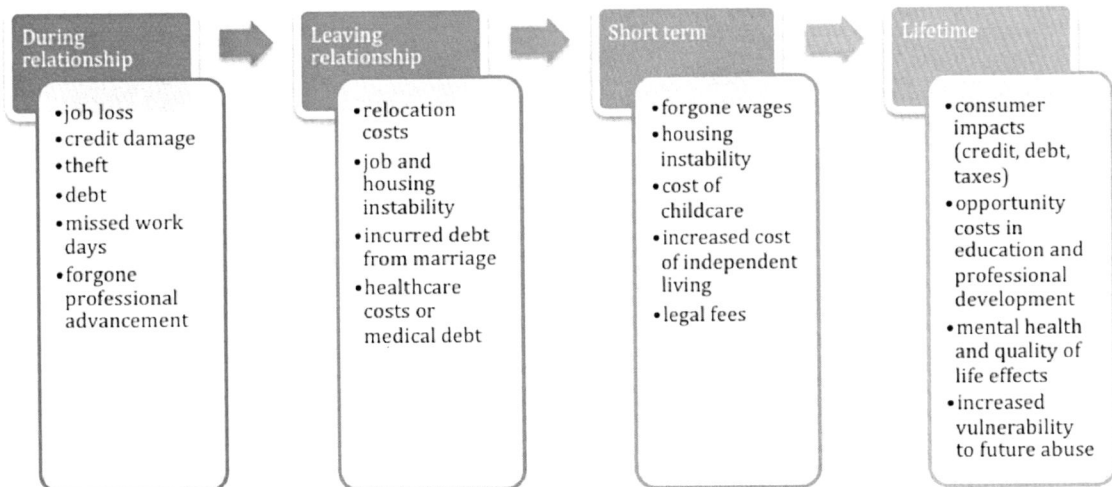

During relationship	Leaving relationship	Short term	Lifetime
• job loss • credit damage • theft • debt • missed work days • forgone professional advancement	• relocation costs • job and housing instability • incurred debt from marriage • healthcare costs or medical debt	• forgone wages • housing instability • cost of childcare • increased cost of independent living • legal fees	• consumer impacts (credit, debt, taxes) • opportunity costs in education and professional development • mental health and quality of life effects • increased vulnerability to future abuse

II. A Legal Ethics Basis for Survivor-Centered Economic Advocacy

What ethical obligations govern lawyers' representation of domestic and sexual violence survivors? Let us begin where lawyers often do: the rules. The Model Code of Professional Responsibility, which provides all lawyers with the baseline standards of legal representation, lends support for survivor-centered advocacy.[17]

Rule 1.1 of the Model Code of Professional Responsibility requires that a lawyer provides ***"competent"*** representation to their client. Competent representation requires, not only knowledge of the law, but also, "skill, thoroughness, and preparation reasonably necessary for the preparation." And, competence includes "inquiry into the analysis of the factual and legal elements of the problem." Therefore, lawyers representing survivors must know not only the legal elements of a remedy, but also the facts. Given the complex nature of domestic violence, it is not enough to be familiar with the limited facts of a particular incident. Rather, lawyers representing survivors must gather a rich understanding of the entire context of coercive control.[18] They must develop a detailed picture of both the batterer-generated risks and the life-generated risks that a particular survivor faces, in order to tailor their representation to consider and be responsive to the complexity of their life circumstances.[19] In addition, even if the lawyer has a limited scope of representation (i.e., protection order representation), he or she should screen for issues related to the survivor's safety and security, and if he or she is not able to represent the client in those matters, for example, consumer and economic civil legal issues, "the lawyer has a duty to refer to the client to competent counsel."[20]

---

[17] *See* A.B.A. Comm'n on Domestic & Sexual Violence, Standards of Practice for Lawyers Representing Victims of Domestic Violence, Sexual Assault and Stalking in Civil Protection Order Cases (2007) (offering helpful guidance). Though the document is focused specifically on representation in civil protection order matters, the concepts are relevant to all areas of practice for attorneys representing survivors. "The purpose of these Standards of Practice is to provide a reference for lawyers representing victims of domestic violence, sexual assault and stalking in civil protection order cases, and to encourage lawyers to provide high-quality legal representation to those clients. These Standards keep the needs of the client at the center of representation and strive to build public confidence in a just and fair legal system by working to promote safety for victims of domestic violence, sexual assault and stalking, and accountability for perpetrators." *Id.*

[18] *Id.* at 1 (indicating that lawyers should "ensure safety planning occur with the client" and that lawyers "be sensitive to the effects of trauma on their clients").

[19] *Id.* at 24 ("In a civil protection order case, the lawyer should have competent knowledge of the dynamics of domestic violence, sexual assault and/or stalking. In particular, the lawyer should understand the potential risk of escalated violence due to litigation, and how the experience of domestic violence, sexual assault and/ or stalking may affect the client-lawyer relationship, including the process of establishing rapport with and gathering information, evidence and case direction from the client.").

[20] *Id.* at 14 ("[E]conomic stability is tantamount to client safety in many cases," the attorney should be knowledgeable about "economic concerns.").

Rule 1.2 of the Model Code of Professional Responsibility, which speaks to the ***"Scope of Representation and Allocation of Authority Between Client and Lawyer,"*** provides: "a lawyer shall abide by a client's decisions concerning the objectives of representation and ... shall consult with the client as to the means by which they are to be pursued." The comment to the Rule further explains that this "confers upon the client the *ultimate authority* to determine the purposes to be served by legal representation." Therefore, lawyers are ethically, if not morally, required to represent domestic violence survivors according to the survivor's own decision-making. The remedies we seek and even our litigation strategies should be crafted in consultation with our clients.[21] The ABA Standards apply this rule to domestic violence representation, noting that representation of domestic violence survivors should be "client-centered," where decision-making authority rests with the survivor.[22] Thus, an advocate's role is to understand the survivor's perspective, provide the survivor with relevant information and the opportunity to make decisions and plans, and then work with the survivor to implement those plans.

"Communication" between lawyer and client is critical. Rule 1.4 of the Model Code of Professional Responsibility provides that a lawyer shall: (1) inform the client of issues where informed consent is required, (2) consult with the client about the *means* by which the client's objectives are to be accomplished. Also, a lawyer shall "explain a matter to the extent reasonably necessary" to enable the client to make "informed decisions regarding the representation." We know that survivors of domestic violence face an array of risks resulting from their abusive partner's behavior—physical, emotional, financial, economic, etc. As a result, when working with a survivor, we must be particularly attuned to the potential consequences of the remedies available, as well as the consequences arising from the legal system that one must navigate to access those remedies. Consideration of both remedies and systems must be done in partnership with the survivor, as the survivor holds all of the information needed to assess the risks and benefits associated with the remedies and systems.[23]

Given the ethical rules laid out, effective legal advocacy for survivors requires, as Jill Davies sets forth in her tool on legal advocacy for survivors: understanding the survivor's perspective, determining whether the legal system may be able to help a survivor meet their goals and address their fears, conveying your

---

[21] The ABA Standards apply this rule to domestic violence representation, noting that representation of domestic violence survivors should be "client-centered," where decision-making authority rests with the survivor.

[22] STANDARDS OF PRACTICE, *supra* note 17, at 35.

[23] The ABA Standards note that effective client communication requires unique skills on the part of attorneys representing survivors, "because their legal concerns are often embedded in very personal, private matters. Effective representation requires that the lawyer earns the trust of a client who has experienced betrayal and/or abuse." STANDARDS OF PRACTICE, *supra* note 17, at 28.

knowledge about the legal remedies to the survivor and analyzing them with them, and helping the survivor to implement their choices.[24]

III. Survivor-Centered Advocacy

Economic coercion combined with poverty and other challenging life circumstances make domestic violence cases very complex for advocates and lawyers. What is the best way to respond to these difficult cases? What can we do to help create meaningful change in the lives of survivors?

A. Survivor-Centered Advocacy is an Evidence-Supported Practice

Survivor-centered advocacy is a practice that accentuates clients' choices and strengths, focuses on the importance of building and supporting a partnership between the survivor and service provider, and pays attention to the context of the survivor's life.[25] Survivor-centered advocacy (also called survivor-defined or women-defined practice) starts with the belief that the survivor's perspective, lived experiences, and knowledge of their own situation are paramount.[26] A survivor-centered advocacy partnership between the lawyer/advocate and the survivor is built through open assessment, non-judgmental active listening and tailored advocacy strategies created jointly through honest and respectful dialogue between the advocate/attorney and the survivor. Through this dialogue, advocates and lawyers build a relationship with the client to: (1) understand the survivor's strengths and the full extent of the survivor's risks and then (2) to honestly and respectfully present information that enhances the survivor's knowledge.

The focus is on *advocacy* as opposed to *service delivery*. While service delivery offers survivors particular services based on an organization's focus, advocacy partners with individual survivors to ensure access to resources and opportunities that are relevant to the individual survivor's needs and life circumstances.[27]

---

[24] Jill Davies, Greater Hartford Legal Aid, *An Approach to Legal Advocacy for Individual Battered Women,* in Family Violence Victim Aid Resource Manual (2d ed. 1997).

[25] Lisa A. Goodman et al., *Survivor Defined Practice in Domestic Violence Work: Measure Development and Preliminary Evidence of Link to Empowerment,* 31 J. Interpersonal Violence 1–23 (2014), *available at* http://journals.sagepub.com/doi/pdf/10.1177/0886260514555131.

[26] Davies & Lyon, *supra* note 4.

[27] Jane Knitzer, Children's Def. Fund, Unclaimed Children: The Failure of Public Responsibility to Children and Adolescents in Need of Mental Health Services (1982).

B. Survivor-Centered Advocacy Requires Full, Open, and Ongoing Assessment

In order to engage fully with a survivor's risks, the advocate/attorney needs a clear understanding of how abuse tactics are impacting the survivor's life and choices without judgment or fear of reprisals from the advocate or attorney. If a survivor feels judgment from an attorney or advocate or senses that an advocate or attorney wants the survivor to choose a certain course of action (for example, file for bankruptcy, obtain new employment, etc.), the survivor may paint a picture that they think will satisfy the advocate or attorney.

When working with Sonia, the advocate/attorney may believe that the best solution for Sonia is to leave her partner. This unspoken desire of the advocate/attorney may influence what services he or she offers (for example, an order of protection) and the focus of the safety plan. As a result, Sonia may not share with the attorney that she has decided to stay with her partner until her children are out of the home, unless things get much worse. This work would not be a partnership, would not meet Sonia's needs in the long term, and may miss key opportunities to increase Sonia's safety while living with her partner. When advocates project their own judgment, they lose trust with their clients, and their advocacy becomes less effective, at best, or dangerous, at worst.

C. Survivor-Centered Advocacy is Built on the Principle of Partnership

Effective partnerships are built on shared power and a willingness to be transparent and learn from one another. Just as survivors assess the ways advocates and attorneys direct them, they can also sense bias (whether due to educational level, race, religion, sexual orientation, etc.). Survivor-centered advocates and attorneys work hard to understand how their own power and/or identities may be influencing the survivor's assessment of their work together. Survivor-centered advocates and attorneys also understand that trust is essential in partnerships and needs to be built over time.

D. Survivor-Centered Advocacy is Flexible and Responds to the Changing Needs of the Survivor

Many of us go into domestic violence or public interest law because we care about making a real difference in the lives of survivors of domestic violence. We see how inequality, violence, and injustice work together to keep people stuck in painful life circumstances, and our impulse is to help. We also have work experience showing what clients have tried and what has and has not worked. We want to protect our clients from going down negative paths. Therefore, at times, we tell our clients what to do or what not to do. When we follow that impulse, we shift from survivor-centered advocacy to provider-defined advocacy. This comes from the best of intentions; we really want to help. And as people who seek services, we can relate to wanting someone else just to tell us what to do. But we also know, from our own life experience, that solutions are most effective when they match our needs, utilize our strengths, and fit into our own lives.

Some survivors fear that they will suffer negative consequences for not following the advice of a lawyer/advocate because they do not have as much institutional power as the advocate or lawyer. Survivors of domestic violence have power and choices taken away from them by their abusive partners. By engaging in provider-directed advocacy, lawyers and advocates mimic this behavior and diminish the agency of survivors at a time when they need it most. Rather than educating or increasing choices for survivors, provider-directed advocacy removes choices, disregards the survivors' expertise, and discounts the survivor's personal and community strengths and assets. All of these things decrease the likelihood that the advocacy we offer will be relevant to the survivor's life, and may, in fact, increase the risks that survivors face.

IV. Survivor-Centered Economic Advocacy

What does survivor-centered advocacy look like when economics are the focus of advocacy? Survivor-centered economic advocacy addresses both the physical and the economic safety needs of survivors. Many advocates or lawyers are well versed in *either* domestic violence or consumer issues; however, survivors' lives are not separated into silos of "financial risks" and "domestic violence risks." Survivors' economic needs are intimately connected with the risks they face within their abusive relationship, and their options for safety have real financial costs, which require access to resources. Sonia will not be fully safe until her financial needs *and* her physical and emotional risks are attended to.

Survivor-centered economic advocacy is holistic. It responds to the wide array of life- and batterer-generated risks and does not decide for the survivor how the risks are prioritized. Rather, survivor-centered economic advocates try to understand the survivor's complex domestic violence and financial situations and use a safety-lens as they partner with survivors to address credit, employment, housing, taxes, budgeting, transportation, childcare, banking, and other economic issues.

A survivor-centered economic advocate asks questions to understand a survivor's priorities, whatever they are, and works with the survivor toward their goals. Without such knowledge, advocates cannot link economic concerns to safety nor can they appreciate the safety implications of different economic decisions. For example, because of our deep insight into Sonia's situation, if she comes to us prioritizing her employment over her physical safety, we understand that her priority may be related to the fact that she enjoys her job and wants to maintain it as a safe place, and she needs a source of income. If she is more concerned about her housing and the mortgage delinquency, we understand that a stable and safe home for her son, given his needs, makes sense to her long-term safety plan.

The conditions of poverty—poor housing, fear of losing housing, limited employment options, health issues, food insecurity, financial stress—feel more oppressive and dangerous than the risk of physical violence. In fact, when low-income domestic violence survivors were asked about the most stressful or upsetting event that they had to cope with in the last month, more than half reported something other than the physical violence.[28]

Furthermore, safety and economic security are inherently linked, so for a survivor, there may be no safety without stable and affordable housing. A survivor-centered economic advocate works to understand these complexities and does not judge a survivor for putting other needs in front of issues with a battering partner.

The goal of survivor-centered economic advocacy is reduction of risk and movement toward long-term safety in its broadest sense—physical, emotional, financial, even spiritual, safety, and human dignity.[29] There is a clear evidence base from research that supports a survivor-centered approach to advocacy.

A. Full and Open Economic Assessment

The first step of survivor-centered consumer advocacy is a full and open assessment of the survivor's financial situation including an understanding of how the abuse is tied into the survivor's financial safety. The assessment asks survivors open-ended questions allowing them to describe and explore their current situation fully. For example, you may ask, "What are your biggest concerns about money right now?" followed by "How does your partner impact your financial concerns?"[30] Financial and safety assessment is an ongoing process that will continue throughout the advocacy relationship.

---

[28] Kimberly K. Eby, *Exploring the Stressors of Low-Income Women with Abusive Partners: Understanding Their Needs and Developing Effective Community Responses*, 19 J. OF FAM. VIOLENCE 221–232 (2004).

[29] This expansive definition of safety is reflected in CSAJ's vision statement, which reads: "The Center for Survivor Agency and Justice envisions a world where all people have equal access to physical safety, economic security, and human dignity." *Our Mission*, CTR. FOR SURVIVOR AGENCY & JUST., https://csaj.org/mission/ (last visited Apr. 30, 2018).

[30] For more assessment questions, see Erika Sussman & Leah Plunkett, *Consumer Rights Screening Tool for Domestic Violence Advocates and Lawyers*, CTR. FOR SURVIVOR AGENCY & JUST. (Nov. 10, 2012), https://csaj.org/library/view/consumer-rights-screening-tool-for-domestic-violence-advocates-and-lawyers.

Evidence Supporting Survivor-Centered Advocacy

This research shows that the relationships built from survivor-centered advocacy, as well as the process of receiving it, are important to survivors in and of themselves *and* lead to outcomes that survivors value.

- Three factors are associated with positive advocacy outcomes: orientation to the whole person, unconditional validation and acceptance, and orientation to information provision and action.[31]
- Survivors with individualized comprehensive community advocates were more effective in acquiring needed community resources than survivors without survivor-centered advocates.[32]
- Survivors who report having greater control over the help-seeking process are more satisfied with services (including legal, criminal justice, and community-based domestic violence advocacy) and much more likely to use those services in the future.[33]
- Survivors who felt that the advocacy they received was responsive to their goals appear to be more optimistic about the support those resources can provide.[34]
- Survivor-centered advocacy is positively related to a survivor's belief in their internal resources (tools/skills) and confidence that they know how to move forward positively in their own lives (agency).[35]

B. Review Economic Plans

As a part of a thorough assessment, survivor-centered advocates and attorneys review the survivor's past, current, and future economic plans. For example, an advocate or attorney working with Sonia will ask, "What do you want to do about your money situation now?" and "What worked well for you in the past with your financial plans? Why? What didn't work for you in the past?" By understanding the survivor's past and current plans, the survivor-centered advocate and attorney builds on the survivor's strengths and respects the work that the client has already accomplished. The survivor's experiences also

---

[31] Nicole E. Allen et al., *Exploring the Core Service Delivery Processes of an Evidence-Based Community Advocacy Program for Women with Abusive Partners,* 41 J. Comm. Psychol. 1–19 (2013).

[32] Cris Sullivan & Deborah Bybee, *Reducing Violence Using Community-Based Advocacy for Women with Abusive Partners,* 67 J. of Consulting & Clinical Psychol. 43 (1999); Allen et al., *supra* note 31.

[33] Goodman et al., *supra* note 25.

[34] *Id.*

[35] *Id.*

frame what hasn't worked well, so that the advocate/attorney understands what strategies have not been a good fit in the client's life and why.

Survivor-centered economic advocacy requires looking at economic situations through the lens of safety while giving clients the right to make decisions in their own lives. We simply cannot predict the future. Even though we may have years of experience with clients and we understand the dynamics of domestic violence, we never know exactly what will happen in survivor's lives. This uncertainty demands that we respond to clients' situations with humility and flexibility. While an advocate/attorney using provider-directed advocacy says, "The best strategy for you seems to be ... ," an advocate/attorney using survivor centered economic advocacy says, "I want to understand ... tell me more about ..."

Flexible advocates/attorneys know that survivors' risks may change and that this change may result in shifting advocacy priorities or strategies. In our example, if Sonia loses her job as a result of Robert's harassment at work, her work with an advocate/attorney may drastically change from looking at banking options to finding new employment.

C. Information Sharing

Survivor-centered economic advocates ask survivors if they would like a piece of information and then explore with the survivor whether and how that information fits their life. For example, when exploring Sonia's desire to find a banking institution you could say, "It sounds like you are weighing your choices regarding a banking institution. I have some information I could provide for you about some of the differences between commercial banks and credit unions. Would it be helpful if I shared that information with you now?" Sonia may say that she is overwhelmed right now and as she gets closer to making that decision she will let you know, but not now. Be sure to validate that feeling and reassure her that you can talk when she is ready. However, Sonia may be ready, and if she agrees, after sharing the information with her you would ask, "How does that information fit with your situation? What questions do you have about what I explained?"

D. Weighing Economic Strategies

After understanding a survivor's economic situation and financial plans and providing financial information, survivor-centered economic advocates work with the survivor to weigh survivor's economic strategies in the light of the client's life and risks generated by an abusive partner.

V. Challenges and Benefits of Survivor Centered Advocacy for Lawyers and Advocates

What does survivor centered economic advocacy look like in practice? This work presents several challenges to lawyers and advocates. However, these challenges can also be reframed as benefits to the work. Below is a description of the challenges and benefits of survivor-centered advocacy, as well sample strategies to help you think of ways to move towards the benefits of survivor centered economic advocacy. Can you think of others?

Challenge: The holistic nature of survivor-centered advocacy may be difficult for attorneys and advocates who work in compartmentalized organizations. If you are tasked to work with clients on domestic violence family law issues solely, it may stretch resources and cut against institutional ideology to expand your advocacy to include both economic and domestic violence needs.

Benefit: By working on both the economic *and* the domestic violence issues at the same time, you can be confident that advocacy efforts will both be safe and sustaining. For example, if you are working on orders of protection with a survivor, by also attending to the economic needs of the survivor, you can work to request financial relief as a piece of the order of protection. This work then becomes more efficient and more effective in creating lasting change in the lives of survivors.

Strategies: Working Toward the Benefits

What economic implications arise in your legal advocacy? What can you ask, generally, to get a sense of safety and/or economic needs? Hold an agency-wide staff meeting where you discuss: How can you better coordinate between departments, expertise, etc.? Train each other on the essentials of assessing for linkages and plan ways to coordinate a case or bring in needed partners or outside expertise.

Challenge: There is no formula to survivor-centered advocacy. It seems like it would take too long.

Benefit: Because there is no formula for survivor-centered advocacy and because the strategies are framed by the survivor's experiences, risks, and strengths, advocates and attorneys have the opportunity to be creative and build new community partnerships. And, while survivor-centered advocacy may take longer upfront, there is an increased likelihood that the tailored intervention will increase the survivor's safety.

Strategies: Working Toward the Benefits

Instead of an advocate or attorney briefly reviewing a case and saying to a client, "X" (organization or action) can help you with "Y" (issue) (for example, "Houses 'R Us can help you find a new apartment."), and instead of wasting time referring a client to an organization that upon further exploration is not a good fit, ongoing assessment helps you devise interventions that truly match the survivor's situation. An attorney or advocate engaged in ongoing assessment would instead ask, "How has Y (issue) impacted your life? What have you done in the past regarding Y that was helpful?" Asking questions in this way creates an assessment of the issue in the context of the survivor's whole reality and evokes responses instead of directing the survivor on what they should do. By partnering with the survivor, you may find that you need "new" partners in the community. You may develop a rich network of relationships with bankers, anti-poverty advocates, mechanics, tenant-rights groups, landlords, etc. that benefit not only the client you have now but many others in the future.

Challenge: Survivor-centered economic advocacy challenges the traditional view of the lawyer or advocate as the expert. By partnering with the survivor, building on the survivor's strengths, understanding what has worked for the survivor and what hasn't worked, advocates and attorneys may wonder: *How can I find my voice as an expert? What if I disagree with a client's assessment of their safety?*

Benefit: Survivor-centered economic advocacy takes the pressure off of the attorney or advocate to be "right" and know what works for everyone. The attorney/advocate does not have to tell anyone what to do or how to do it, but instead builds upon an individual's strengths and assets and lets the survivor guide the advocacy—a true partnership.

> **Strategies: Working Toward the Benefits**
>
> What if you are concerned about the way a survivor is weighing risks and you are afraid for their safety? Survivor-centered economic advocacy is a partnership, so as one partner, you do not have to keep your fears to yourself and you may have some information that is key to the survivor's risk analysis. However, before sharing your fears with the survivor, be slow to react, and do a self-assessment.[36] What about this situation is concerning for me? Do any of my identities (race, gender, sexual orientation, class, education, etc.) or perspectives influence how I am thinking about this situation? If so, how? Is this situation bringing something up for me from another experience (another client, your own life experience, etc.)? After a self-assessment, if you determine that you are still concerned, proceed carefully. State your concern, give evidence of your concern, and ask the survivor how the statement of those fears sounds for them.

Attorneys and advocates that proceed in advocacy with humility, flexibility, partnership, and information sharing can provide effective economic work with survivors.

For example, if Sonia stated that she wanted to open a bank account without telling Robert, and she didn't think he would be too upset about it if he found out, you may say, "It sounds like you do not think Robert will be upset if he finds out that you opened a new bank account, on the other hand, you told me that when you put cash aside last year and hid it from him, and he found it, he was very upset and hurt you pretty badly. I am concerned about how he may respond, but I may be missing something. Tell me how you see this situation as different."

VI. Organizational Readiness: Institutionalizing Survivor-Centered Advocacy

While you, as an advocate or attorney, may embrace survivor-centered economic advocacy, practicing survivor-centered economic advocacy with the full support of your organization is powerful. CSAJ created a readiness/organizational assessment tool to use with your organization. When visualizing and implementing change in your organization, it is helpful to see how other domestic violence or legal organizations have increased organizational survivor-centered advocacy capacity. CSAJ has worked with four groundbreaking demonstration project sites to enhance economic and consumer rights for

---

[36] Davies & Lyon, *supra* note 4.

domestic violence survivors. The Building Partnerships Report offers strategies useful to organizations embarking on survivor-centered economic justice work.[37]

VII. Systems Change and Policy Work

While individual advocacy is necessary to access rights and resources available to survivors, systems and policy changes are critical to ensure that institutions support the economic security of all survivors. Survivor-centered economic advocacy with individual survivors provides lawyers and advocates with rich information regarding the common economic challenges faced by domestic violence survivors. By listening and responding to the needs and priorities of survivors, lawyers and advocates are able to identify systemic barriers and formulate institutional and policy reforms needed to address those barriers and increase their safety. Survivor-centered advocates have the opportunity to use their knowledge to inform policy makers, partner with advocacy groups, and advocate for systemic changes. While individual advocacy is necessary for accessing rights and resources available to survivors, systems and policy changes are critical for transforming the landscape to ensure that institutions support the economic security of all survivors.[38]

Furthermore, an **intersectional approach** to advocacy is required to address the disparate impact that policies and institutions have on survivors who are socially and politically marginalized, restricting their access to the resources needed for their long-term safety. Intersectional IPV approaches address the

---

[37] CTR. FOR SURVIVOR AGENCY & JUST., BUILDING PARTNERSHIPS FOR ECONOMIC JUSTICE: A REPORT ON INNOVATIVE PILOT PROJECTS (2014), *available at* https://csaj.org/document-library/Pilot_Report_Final.pdf.

[38] Examples of CSAJ's systems-level work include:

- CSAJ's systems advocacy efforts with the Department of Education:
  ○ Letter from Erika Sussman, Exec. Dir., Ctr. for Survivor Agency & Just., Jamie Andree & Laura Russell, Women's Resource Ctr., to U.S. Dep't of Educ.; Negotiated Rule Making Comm. re: Testimony for Student Loan Calculations on Behalf of Married Survivors of Domestic Violence (Apr. 28, 2015), *available at* https://csaj.org/document-library/Student_Loan_Testimony_-_for_website.pdf.
  ○ Letter from Erika Sussman, Exec. Dir., Ctr. for Survivor Agency & Just. & Karen Merrill Tjapkes, Expert Advisor, Ctr. for Survivor Agency & Just., to Monica Jackson, Off. of the Exec. Sec'y, Consumer Fin. Prot. Bureau re: Docket No. CFPB-2014-0033 Amendments to the 2013 Mortgage Rules under the Real Estate Settlement Procedures Act (Regulation X) and the Truth in Lending Act (Regulation Z) (Mar. 16, 2015), *available at* https://csaj.org/document-library/CFPB_Regulations-As_Submitted.pdf.
- ERIKA SUSSMAN & SARA WEE, ACCOUNTING FOR ECONOMIC SECURITY: AN ATLAS FOR DIRECT SERVICE PROVIDERS (Feb. 4, 2017), *available at* https://csaj.org/document-library/CSAJ_Atlas_Mapbook_1_FINAL_TO_POST.pdf.
- Catherine Trapani, New Destiny Housing Corp., Webinar Materials: Housing Policy and Systems Advocacy (Sept. 25, 2013), *available at* https://csaj.org/document-library/Housing_Policy_and_Systems_Advocacy_for_Domestic_Violence.pdf.

individual and structural barriers by employing tools that target multiple forms of oppression. CSAJ's Legal Impact for Racial & Economic Equity of Survivors Project (REEP) seeks to remedy the systemic inequalities facing survivors of color that currently impair their access to economic security and safety.[39] In partnership with diverse anti-poverty, race equity, and violence against women practitioners, REEP will shift the current violence against women paradigm by employing impact strategies that engage communities in identifying inequalities, and by employing impact legal and policy strategies that facilitate access to economic opportunity for survivors of color.[40]

VIII. Conclusion

Attorneys and advocates for survivors of domestic violence can meaningfully enhance survivors' access to long-term safety by engaging in survivor-centered economic advocacy. There is a reciprocal relationship between domestic violence and economic hardship; and, domestic violence has an economic ripple effect on survivors' lives. While many domestic violence advocacy programs provide financial literacy skills training, such interventions often fail to address the profound economic harms that survivors face, both as a result of living in poverty and as a result of the economic and physical coercion they have experienced.

Attorneys representing survivors are bound by legal ethics that support survivor-centered practice. Survivor-centered economic advocacy is an evidence-based practice that is based on a partnership between the attorney/advocate and the survivor, which draws upon their combined expertise and is driven by the survivor's priorities and decision-making. Survivor-centered advocacy holds both the economic and the safety needs of the survivor simultaneously, in order to forge complex strategies that address the risks, needs, assets, and opportunities facing an individual survivor.

While there are many challenges in implementing survivor-centered economic practice, strategies exist to overcome those challenges and implement it within differing institutional structures. Indeed, organizations and communities can assess their readiness and implement procedures to create the infrastructure needed to sustain the work. While individual advocacy efforts assist survivors in accessing their rights, systems and policy advocacy is critical to changing the landscape to support the economic security of all survivors better.

---

[39] *Legal Impact for Racial & Economic Equity of Survivors Project (REEP)*, CTR. FOR SURVIVOR AGENCY & JUST., https://us5.campaign-archive com/?u=58f89a02f55fbf512cc8a5f88&id=38b0df8210&e=%5BUNIQID%5D (last visited Apr. 30, 2018).

[40] *CSAJ Project Partners,* CTR. FOR SURVIVOR AGENCY & JUST., https://csaj.org/about/#project-partners (last visited Apr. 30, 2018).

APPENDIX

Resources:

- **Center for Survivor Agency & Justice**
  - Katie VonDeLinde & Erika Sussman, *A Guide to Consumer & Economic Civil Legal Advocacy for Survivors,* CTR. FOR SURVIVOR AGENCY & JUST. (Apr. 30, 2018), https://csaj.org/library/view/building-partnerships-to-enhance-consumer-rights-for-domestic-violence-surv.
  - ERIKA SUSSMAN & SARA WEE, ACCOUNTING FOR ECONOMIC SECURITY: AN ATLAS FOR DIRECT SERVICE PROVIDERS (Feb. 4, 2017), *available at* https://csaj.org/document-library/CSAJ_Atlas_Mapbook_1_FINAL_TO_POST.pdf.

Chapter Eleven:
Credit Discrimination and Predatory Lending

Katie VonDeLinde[1]

Reprinted from Center for Survivor Agency & Justice (CSAJ), Guidebook on Consumer & Economic Civil Legal Advocacy (2017), https://csaj.org/Guidebook.[2]

I. Introduction

Credit discrimination occurs when lenders make unfair credit decisions based on an individual's characteristics, and predatory lending is when creditors impose unfair or abusive terms on loans. Credit discrimination and predatory lending can occur across consumer sectors, from credit cards to short-term loans to home mortgages. Due to the impact of domestic violence on survivors' short and long-term financial needs, survivors face heightened risks related to discriminatory and predatory lending. This chapter will review the practice of credit discrimination and predatory lending in the context of safety for survivors, provide legal remedies and advocacy strategies to address predatory debts, create cost of living plans, and strategize around banking and short-term lending options.

---

[1] With contributions by The Legal Aid Society and the National Consumer Law Center.

[2] A deeper dive into the case scenario described in this reprinted chapter can be found in CSAJ's Guidebook on Consumer & Economic Civil Legal Advocacy. Katie VonDeLinde, *Credit Discrimination & Predatory Lending, in* GUIDEBOOK ON CONSUMER & ECONOMIC CIVIL LEGAL ADVOCACY 50 (2017), https://csaj.org/Guidebook.

II. Domestic Violence, Credit Discrimination and Predatory Lending

While credit discrimination and predatory lending are problems for many Americans, survivors of domestic violence face unique risks due to the impact of domestic violence and economic control. Many survivors of domestic violence are in need of financial assistance or credit in the short-term due to:

- **Physical violence.** Survivors may lose work time or employment due to physical injury.

- **Psychological abuse.** Survivors may experience post-traumatic stress disorder (PTSD) or depression as a result of domestic violence making it difficult to work, pay bills, and be economically safe.

- **Economic abuse.** Abusive partners' denial of access to financial property and destruction of credit makes some survivors financially desperate and unable to rely on more traditional forms of banking.

- **The connection between domestic violence and poverty.** Domestic violence has long and short-term economic impacts that threaten the economic security of survivors. Survivors in poverty are more likely to need money to pay for life's necessities and may be forced to use non-traditional credit services.

Payday lenders typically do not report to CRAs (credit reporting agencies) and these loans will not show up on a survivor's credit report, allowing the survivor to get access to money while reducing the possibility that the abusive partner will find out.[3] Also, short-term lenders do not need as much financial documentation (for example, income stubs, bank account information) to provide a loan as a traditional bank or even most non-profit or governmental organizations would need to provide financial assistance. This is reassuring to survivors who face safety risks when trying to locate financial documentation.

However, short-term lenders often mirror the coercive control of abusive partners when fees stack up, interest rates compound, and survivors get trapped in cycles of debt.[4]

Survivors of domestic violence in need of quick access to money are attractive to predatory and discriminatory creditors looking to capitalize on individuals' desperate situations. And, in fact, because many short-term lenders are not associated with

---

[3] If the debt remains unpaid and goes to a collection agency, the loan will then appear on the credit report. For more information about debt collection, see *Debt, Debt Defense, and Safety Considerations for Survivors* in Section Three of this manual.

[4] See *The Debt Trap for Survivors,* Ctr. for Survivor Agency & Just., https://csaj.org/debttrap (last visited Apr. 30, 2018).

credit reporting agencies, they may be a safer financial resource for survivors who are in danger from abusive partners.

Read the two scenarios below for examples of different ways that survivors can be impacted by financial needs that lead to predatory lending. As you read the scenarios, consider: Why would the survivor make that decision? What are the short-term and long-term consequences of this decision? How would you advocate for the survivor?

Julia's Story

Julia is purchasing a car on her own after leaving an abusive relationship. She has been working on her credit, and her credit score is decent, although she had to close a lot of joint accounts recently due to the separation. At the dealership, the used car salesman is so friendly and such a great listener that Julia finds herself telling him about her abusive situation. She tells him that she desperately needs a car to keep herself and her kids away from her ex-partner, Marcus. She even shares how Marcus used to make fun of her ability to make decisions, how she knows nothing about cars and how nervous she is to be making this transaction by herself. The car salesman comforts her and shows her a car that she falls in love with. He offers her what he says is a great interest rate, at 27 percent with no down payment, and she could walk away with a payment that was within her reach over five years. Julia is in a hurry to get the car, and signs the papers. Two months later, the car needs an expensive repair that Julia cannot afford. She is worried about her safety if she cannot get her car in running order. She comes to you for help.

Sofia's Story

Sofia knows she should ask her grown daughter for some help, some extra money to get by on, but she is so embarrassed, and sharing this need with her daughter would force her to tell so much more. Sofia lives with her partner, Jane, who controls all of the money in the home and gives Sofia an allowance, even though Sofia receives a disability check (SSDI) and should have access to her money. Sofia usually gets enough money from Jane, but with her granddaughter's high school graduation coming up, Sofia needs gas money to drive to visit her in rural Illinois. Sofia has never used a bank on her own and does not know what to do. She is talking with her neighbor who suggests she go to a title loan company down the street. Sofia is comforted that Jane will not find out because the title loan company does not pull credit reports and the salesperson said she could make it work so that Jane did not need to show any evidence of income. The title loan company allows her to get a $300.00 loan that she needs to repay in a month. When Sofia returns from the graduation, Jane is upset that Sofia went on the trip alone. Jane is punishing Sofia by refusing to give her any money for the month and Sofia knows she will not be able to repay the title loan company. Sofia calls you for help.

III. Types of Credit Discrimination and Predatory Lending

Credit discrimination occurs when lenders make unfair credit decisions or offers based on an individual's characteristics, including: race, religion, national origin, sex or marital status, age (as long as you are old enough to enter into a contract), receipt of income from public assistance, familial status, disability or handicap, and alienage. It is illegal for lenders to refuse credit to an individual based on the characteristics listed above, or to discourage individuals from applying for credit, offer credit with less favorable terms that terms offered to someone with similar qualification, or to close an account.

Predatory lending is the practice of "imposing unfair and abusive loan terms on borrowers."[5] Predatory lending exists in many sectors including mortgage, car loans, and short-term loans. Predatory lending includes the practice of charging very high interest rates and fees, but can also include not informing consumers of their ability to negotiate interest rates or failing to clearly disclose the terms, fees, and interest rates in a loan.

Mortgage lending. Predatory lending in mortgages includes charging excessive or hidden fees to get a *mortgage* (loan to purchase a home or property), *prepayment penalties* (charging additional money to consumers who pay off the loan faster than the loan terms), charging fees for the purchase of unnecessary products as part of the loan, structuring the loan to appear affordable at the outset but that is doomed to fail when payment amounts rise, loan flipping, and steering. *Loan flipping* happens when lenders convince borrowers to refinance an existing mortgage, adding fees for the new loan and frequently prepayments on the old loan. *Steering* is the practice of offering higher qualified borrowers *subprime loans* (loans with higher fees and interest rates), even though they could qualify for better loans with better terms.

Steering can occur in other sectors including the car loan business. In Julia's story above, it is likely that she could have qualified for a better loan and could have negotiated the terms of the loan. It appears that the car loan company abused the knowledge that Julia needed the car and that she had not negotiated a loan on her own previously.

Short-term lending occurs when small, short-term loans are provided, frequently with high fees and interest rates. Short-term loans are often used by economically challenged individuals initially to "make ends meet" but can, at times, become a cycle of paying recurring expenses. When lenders are unable to pay back a short-term loan, they are forced to renew the loan creating a long-

---

[5] FDIC, REP. NO. 06-011, CHALLENGES AND FDIC EFFORTS RELATED TO PREDATORY LENDING (2006), https://www.fdicig.gov/reports06/06-011.pdf.

term cycle of debt.[6] This financial desperation can be economically debilitating to borrowers because they end up paying far more in renewal fees than the amount of cash they actually received from the deal. In fact, short-term borrowers are five times more likely to file for bankruptcy than the general population.[7] In the case of title loans, borrowers pledge their cars to secure the loan and can lose them if they do not repay or renew in a timely way.

Short-term lending companies are concentrated in low-resourced communities. In a sample of payday lenders, the lending businesses concentrated in areas where the annual income ranged from $10,000-$40,000, with a median income of $22,476.[8] In that sample, 18 percent of the payday borrowers received government assistance or benefit income.

Many states have laws capping the interest rates on payday and title loans and/or the number of renewals. Some states have passed legislation stopping payday lending altogether.[9] Federal legislation caps payday creditors to an annual percentage rate of 36 percent and prohibits the rolling over loans made to active-duty members of the military and their dependents.

Payday loans (sometimes called cash advances) are high-interest loans usually repaid on the borrower's next payday, usually within two weeks. The borrower secures the loan with a post-dated check or electronic access to the borrower's bank account. Payday loans are offered online and at stores around the country. The average ***principal*** (amount borrowed) is $374.00 plus fees; the median fee is $15.00 per $100.00 borrowed, and the average ***annual percentage rate*** (APR) is 400 percent (APR is the interest rate for the loan over one year that includes most loan fees).[10] Because payday loans are offered as "short-term," generally two weeks, and not regarding how much the interest rate would be annually, borrowers may be misled about the exorbitant annual percentage rates and the impact of the high fees. Instead of offering a periodic interest rate, most payday lenders charge a set fee that is based on the amount borrowed. Much of the payday loan industry profits come from rolled-over loans

---

[6] Consumer Fin. Prot. Bureau, White Paper on pay day loans and deposit advance products (2013), http://www.consumerfinance.gov/data-research/research-reports/white-paper-on-payday-loans-and-deposit-advance-products/; Susanna Montezemolo, Ctr. for Responsible Lending, The State of Lending in America and its Impact on US Households: Car Title Lending Abuses and Predatory Practices (July 11, 2013), http:/www.responsiblelending.org/state-of-lending/car-title-loans/.

[7] Tim Lohrentz, Insight Ctr. for Comm. Econ. Dev., The Net Economic Impact of Payday Lending in the U.S. (2013), http://ww1.insightcced.org/uploads/assets/Net%20Economic%20Impact%20of%20 Payday%20Lending.pdf.

[8] Consumer Fin. Prot. Bureau, *supra* note 6.

[9] For more information about your states' laws, see *Payday Lending State Statutes,* Nat'l Conf. of State Legis. (Jan. 23, 2018), http://www.ncsl.org/research/financial-services-and-commerce/payday-lending-state-statutes.aspx.

[10] Lohrentz, *supra* note 7.

that add additional fees. For example, if a consumer is unable to pay back the payday loan after two weeks, the borrower is able to "roll-over" or extend the loan for two additional weeks, but is charged additional fees.

The average added cost of a loan held (or rolled-over) for five months could range from $172 in Colorado to $701 in Texas.[11] State loan and interest rate regulations matter. More than 50 percent of payday loan recipients have defaulted on their loan. A 2013 study found that two-thirds of payday borrowers had seven or more short-term loans in a year and were in debt to a payday lending company for 40 percent of the year.[12]

Deposit advances are lines of credit offered by banking institutions as a feature of existing checking or savings accounts for consumers who have regular electronic deposits. When a deposit advance is requested, money is deposited into the consumer's account and repaid automatically when the next electronic deposit is made. Deposit advance fees are structured as dollars per amount of money advanced. For example, the banking institution may charge $2.00 in fees for every $20.00 borrowed. However, because there is no set date for the repayment (because the repayment is based on the next incoming electronic deposit), it is impossible to disclose the loan terms as an annual percentage rate. Borrowers often experience additional fees if they overdraft or have insufficient funds in the account. Bank deposit advances are not considered payday loans in most states and are therefore not subject to payday lending laws that states may have restricting fees or rollover periods.

Car title loans are short-term loans given to borrowers that are secured by a title of a vehicle that the borrower owns free and clear. The average title loan is $1000.00. A title loan is a single-payment loan given on one-month terms with an annual interest rate averaging 300 percent without a credit check. Car title loans tend to be renewed multiple times. A typical title loan is ***oversecured***, meaning that an average borrower receives cash equal to 26 percent of the car's resale value. However, if the loan is not paid back, the title loan company can repossess the car and keep the entire profit off reselling the car.[13]

Tax refund anticipation loans (RALS) are loans given to borrowers based on their expected federal income tax refund and are offered January through April. Tax anticipation loans are no longer available through banks but still can be obtained through non-banking financial firms like payday lenders and tax

---

[11] John Kuo, *Need Cash? Personal Loans Cost $446 Less Than Payday Loans,* NERDWALLET (Mar. 17, 2015) (citing a report by Pew Charitable Trust), https://www.nerdwallet.com/blog/loans/personal-loans-less-than-payday-loans/.

[12] CONSUMER FIN. PROT. BUREAU, *supra* note 6; Montezemolo, *supra* note 6.

[13] MONTEZEMOLO, *supra* note 6.

preparers. The effective annual percentage rate for many RALS based on a 10-day loan ranges from 50 percent to nearly 500 percent.

Refund anticipation checks are different from RALS in that they are temporary bank accounts that a bank opens for a consumer to deposit their tax refund from the IRS directly. For consumers who cannot afford to pay for tax preparation upfront, refund anticipation checks allow you to have your taxes prepared. Then, once the tax refund is deposited, the bank takes the tax preparation charge, gives the consumer the remaining refund amount in the form of a check or a prepaid card, and closes the account. Refund anticipation checks come with costs and add-on fees, but are not a loan.

Definition of Terms

Credit discrimination: When lenders make unfair credit decisions or offers based on an individual's characteristics, including: race, religion, national origin, sex or marital status, age, etc.

Predatory lending: The practice of "imposing unfair and abusive loan terms on borrowers."

Mortgage: Loan to purchase a home or property.

Prepayment penalties: Charging additional money to consumers who pay off the loan faster than the loan terms.

Loan flipping: When lenders convince borrowers to refinance an existing mortgage, adding fees for the new loan and frequently prepayments on the old loan.

Steering: The practice of offering higher qualified borrowers loans with higher fees and interest rates (subprime loans) even though they could qualify for better loans with better terms.

Short-term lending: Small, short-term loans that frequently have high fees and interest rates.

Payday loans: Sometimes called cash advances, payday loans are high-interest loans usually repaid on the borrower's next payday (typically within two weeks).

Principal: The amount of money borrowed in a loan.

Annual percentage rate (APR): The interest rate for the loan over one year that includes most loan fees.

Deposit advances: Lines of credit offered by banking institutions as a feature of existing checking or savings accounts for consumers who have regular electronic deposits.

Car title loans: Short-term loans given to borrowers that are secured by a title of a vehicle that the borrower owns free and clear.

Tax refund anticipation loans (RALS): Loans given to borrowers based on their expected federal income tax refund and are offered January through April.

IV. Legal Remedies

A. Federal Law Remedies

Truth in Lending (TILA) was created to guarantee the accurate and meaningful disclosure of the costs of consumer credit. TILA applies to consumer credit transactions (credit obtained primarily for personal, family, or household purposes) that are regularly extended by creditors who charge a finance charge or that are payable by a written agreement in more than four installments. Certain key information must be disclosed in a clear and conspicuous manner, including the APR, the amount financed, the finance charge, and the total of payments.

The APR and finance charge disclosures are the most important required information, and TILA contains detailed rules for determining which fees must be included in the finance charge and reflected in the APR. A violation of these rules entitles the consumer to double the finance charge with a minimum award of $200 and a maximum award of $2,000, plus attorney fees and costs. The consumer must bring an affirmative lawsuit within one year of the violation or may raise the violation as a defense to the lender's collection suit without regard to the one-year period.

Military Lending Act (MLA) caps interest rates to active duty military service members and their dependents at 36 percent. For loans made before October 3, 2016, the MLA effectively banned payday and title loans and restricted tax refund loans. On and after October 3, 2016, the MLA applies to a wider group of non-mortgage loans. Any credit agreement, promissory note, or other contract prohibited by the Act is void and unenforceable from its inception. A person who violates the MLA or regulations is liable for actual damages of not less than $500 for each violation, punitive damages, costs, and attorney fees.

B. State Law Remedies

Unfair and Deceptive Acts and Practices (UDAP) laws: A fairly wide range of unfair or deceptive lender behavior is prohibited under these state laws, provided that the type of lender or transaction is covered. Examples of prohibited behavior include: disguising a payday loan as a sale-leaseback or other sham, and failing to disclosure the interest rate and fees; disclosing a fee but failing to treat it as interest under state law; mispresenting the loan terms. The remedies vary from state to state.

State usury caps: Many states limit the maximum interest rate that lenders can charge a consumer in specific types of loans. These types of claims arise most often when a payday or title lender disguises the loan and charges high fees. Remedies for violations vary from state to state, ranging from voiding the loan at its inception to prohibiting the collection of the excess interest. Note that state usury caps may not apply to federally chartered banks or banks chartered in states with a high cap (or no cap).

Fraud or misrepresentation: Deceit and lies in the course of making a loan are illegal and may provide significant recovery to a consumer. This type of behavior is illegal in all states.

Licensing laws: In many states, lenders are regulated by licensing laws. These laws typically do not apply to lenders that are banks, however. Where they apply, these laws usually specify the permissible terms of the covered loans and often contain significant penalties for lenders who fail to comply. Where obtaining the license is a precondition to lending, failure to do so may give rise to a usury claim in addition to a violation of the licensing law.

V. Strategies for Survivor Defined Advocacy

A. Assessing Credit Discrimination

When beginning advocacy with a survivor surrounding possible credit discrimination or predatory loans, it is helpful to understand the survivor's assessment of the situation before creating an action plan. Because of the complicated experiences and feelings surrounding finances and debt for many survivors, credit advocacy work requires an open, honest, and sensitive assessment. The screening and assessment questions presented here are for issue spotting (often called "intake questions"), are not meant to be prescriptive, and conversations around loans and debt should not be limited to these questions.[14]

Consider asking open-ended, non-judgmental questions about the situation such as:

- How has the experience with the creditor impacted your financial situation? In the short-term? In the long-term?

- What else have you tried when you needed money in the short-term in the past? What has worked? What has not worked?

- How has the experience impacted your safety? How has your partner or ex-partner reacted?

- What do you think could help this situation now?

---

[14] For a fuller description of a survivor centered approach to economic assessment, see *Economic Coercion and Survivor-Centered Economic Advocacy* in Section Three of this manual.

B. Creating Plans to Address Predatory Debt Situations

Based on predatory lending assessment, advocates and lawyers can work with survivors to plan the next best steps for their lives. Because each survivor will have different short- and long-term financial goals, financial obligations, and safety concerns, each plan should be individualized and jointly created with the survivor.

The first step in advocacy is discussing the option of requesting a reduction in fees from a lender. For example, after meeting with her advocate and discussing her car loan, Julia may decide to try and contact the lender to ask for a decrease in the loan amount. What are the pros and cons of this strategy for the survivor? What does the survivor feel comfortable and safe telling the lender? A large, national company may be less likely than a smaller, neighborhood lender in reducing fees. If a lender does agree to reduce fees or extend a due date, make sure to get the agreement in writing.

Advocates should remember that most survivors are in predatory situations because they needed access to money or resources quickly, and that predatory lending was the most accessible source of money and possibly the safest. Because of credit discrimination, some survivors may not have equal access to more traditional, less predatory loans.

Advocacy Tip: As the survivor is paying off debts, be positive and encouraging but be cautious in how much praise is centered on paying off debts. Survivors may be fearful of disappointing their advocates/lawyers. Therefore, if the survivor takes out another payday or other type of predatory loan, they may not want to tell you. Be clear with survivors that you will support them no matter what.

C. Debt Action Planning

When working with the survivor, it is helpful to create a comprehensive, yet flexible debt action plan.[15] A debt plan can be simply a written plan on a piece of paper or can be an excel file. The first step in this process is to discuss with the survivor the benefit of paying off debts with the highest APR (or fees) first.

Advocacy Tip: It is helpful to use a free online debt calculator tool that allows survivors to see how paying off debts with the highest APR first can be financially beneficial.[16] Breaking down predatory loans into pieces can make the debt feel more manageable and can help give hope to survivors.

---

[15] For more information on creating a debt action plan, see *Debt, Debt Defense, and Safety Considerations for Survivors* in Section Three of this manual.

[16] For a free online debt calculator tool, see *When Will I Be Debt Free,* CNN MONEY, http://money. cnn.com/calculator/pf/debt-free/ (last visited May 2, 2018).

Remember that looking at predatory lenders' fees and APRs can be very frustrating to survivors and they may feel angry, cheated, or defeated. It is important to give survivors space to have feelings regarding the situation and work together to create a plan for moving forward.

D. Create Financial Plans to Avoid Needing Predatory Lending in the Future

Long-term plans to reduce the need for predatory lending will require creating a cost of living plan to examine what it costs survivor to live.[17]

Creating a Cost of Living Plan

(1) Ask survivor to track expenses for a month if possible; or at a minimum a week.
  - Discuss safety implications for tracking expenses and safety plan accordingly.
  - Discuss how it may feel psychologically to track expenses and strategies to reduce negative feelings.

(2) Determine fixed, changing, emergency monthly expenses.

(3) Determine income including: benefits, child support, informal and formal income.

(4) If expenses outweigh income reduce expenses:
  - Look through tracked expenses, exploring for strategies to reduce spending that fit with the survivor's safety and values.
  - Most survivors are smart economic planners; they simply do not make enough money to make resources strength.
  - Barter for goods and services if possible.

(5) Increase income
  - What options does the survivor have to increase income? What has worked in the past? What hasn't? Why?
  - Consider increasing education, training, negotiating a raise.

E. Discuss Strategies to Avoid Short-Term Lending in Economic Crises

When working with survivors who are trying to avoid short-term lending, it is important to acknowledge that some strategies (including but not limited to relying on abusive partner or family members, selling drugs or other illegal activity, sex for money) may be less safe for the survivor than short-term lending.

---

[17] For steps to create an effective cost of living plan, see Katie VonDeLinde, *Budgeting & Debt Prioritization,* Ctr. for Survivor Agency & Just. (Nov. 11, 2010), https://csaj.org/document-library/vondelinde2010.pdf.

Be open about discussing risks and tradeoffs with short-term lending with survivors and avoid using your own judgment to decide what is the safest choice for survivors. Discuss the pros and cons of each financial choice.

An alternative strategy for obtaining money or resources in an economic crisis is using local resources that may help with financial needs. For example, your community may have utility, rental or housing, or childcare assistance. Keep in mind that financial assistance is scarce, often requires a lot of documentation that may put the survivor at risk from an abusive partner, and may be difficult for the survivor to pursue (limited hours of operation, transportation to the location, etc.). Additionally, survivors who have experienced racism, homophobia, transphobia, or other discrimination based on their identity, may be concerned about reaching out to a local organization and fear that they will experience discrimination in that setting. Again, just because short-term lending seems like a bad choice for survivors, at times, it may be the best choice out of a lot of bad options.

Advocacy Tip: When making referrals to non-profit or governmental organizations for financial assistance, it is helpful for the advocate/lawyer to: understand how this assistance works, know if the assistance is currently available, be familiar with the organization's practices (policies toward LGBTQ people, for example), and provide a specific contact person or help make the connection.

F. Discuss Alternate Banking Options

Some survivors may not know about other banking options that are available to them for financial needs and services. Because commercial banks have historically avoided some communities (communities of color, low-income communities), some survivors may not be aware of banking opportunities or may not trust banking options. It is important to assess a survivor's relationship to banks.

For example, you may ask:

- Have you ever had experience with a bank before? If so, tell me about it.

- Do you know if you currently owe any money to any banks?

- How do you feel about banks?

- Do you feel like banking is a safe option for you? Why or why not?

If a survivor is interested, it is helpful to explore different banking options. While commercial banks are most accessible regarding locations and variety of services, **credit unions,** which are not-for-profit institutions, generally have lower fees, lower balance requirements, higher annual yield (the amount of interest a consumer receives from a saving account) and lower annual percentage rates for lending. Some credit unions offer short-term lending services with lower fees than typical payday or deposit lending. Recently, anti-poverty and other non-profits have worked together to create credit unions providing short-term loans with fewer predatory fees to their clients. It is helpful to be aware of the banking options in your community.

Advocacy Tip: Consider some systems advocacy, particularly if your client or many clients are confronting banking roadblocks. You may need to advocate with letters or phone calls to the banking institution requesting reduction in fees, waiving balance requirements, or creating a payment plan to pay off old banking debts preventing new accounts. Building relationships with local banks or credit unions can help establish the understanding and willingness to institute special protections, policies, or be willing to work with you on a case-by-case basis. For issues with a banking institution that are not being resolved, another option is to file a complaint with the Consumer Financial Protection Bureau (CFPB). The CFPB will forward the complaint, and the company has 15 days to respond.[18]

G. Alternative Tax Filing Options

For survivors who want to file taxes without the additional cost of tax refund anticipation loans, many communities offer Volunteer Income Tax Assistance (VITA) or Tax Counseling for the Elderly (TCE) services free of charge to help low to moderate income and elderly individuals.[19]

Advocacy Tip: Consider partnering with or bringing VITA/TCE services onsite at your organization for your clients.

VI. Conclusion

While predatory lending options may come at high financial costs for survivors of domestic violence, these options may be the safest alternative for some survivors. Lawyers and advocates should work with survivors to create short, medium, and long-term credit action plans. Open discussion and creative debt action planning are keys to availing survivors of real and flexible options that can adapt to their changing needs and priorities as they seek safety.

---

[18] *Submit a Complaint,* CONSUMER FIN. PROT. BUREAU, http://www.consumerfinance.gov/complaint/ (last visited Apr. 30, 2018) (Ph: (855) 411-2372).

[19] For more information on tax law, see *Tax Law and Domestic Violence* in Section Three of this manual. *See also* Jamie Andree, *Tax Advocacy for Survivors, in* GUIDEBOOK ON CONSUMER & ECONOMIC CIVIL LEGAL ADVOCACY 143 (2017), https://csaj.org/Guidebook.

APPENDIX

Resources:

- **The Center for American Progress**
  - ○ ALYSSA PETERSON, CTR. FOR AM. PROGRESS, PREDATOR PAYDAY LENDING: ITS EFFECTS AND HOW TO STOP IT (2013), https://cdn.americanprogress.org/wp-content/uploads/2013/08/PredatoryLending-brief-1.pdf.

- **The Center for Survivor Agency & Justice**
  - ○ CTR. FOR SURVIVOR AGENCY & JUST., COMMENTS ON PROPOSED RULEMAKING ON PAYDAY, VEHICLE TITLE, AND CERTAIN HIGH-COST INSTALLMENT LOANS (2016), https://docs.google.com/document/d/1Yvoak18hl1fEygAnOZnRHHq1dKi HRn9ZJiD_Fa0XVNA/edit.
  - ○ *The Debt Trap for Survivors,* CTR. FOR SURVIVOR AGENCY & JUST., https://csaj.org/debttrap.
  - ○ Katie VonDeLinde, *Budgeting & Debt Prioritization,* CTR. FOR SURVIVOR AGENCY & JUST. (Nov. 11, 2010), https://csaj.org/document-library/vondelinde2010.pdf.

- **National Association of Consumer Advocates**
  - ○ *Payday, Title, & Lending Loans,* Nat'l Ass'n of Consumer Advoc., https://www.consumeradvocates.org/issues/predatory-lending.

- **Racial & Economic Equity for Survivors Project**
  - ○ ZOE FLOWERS ET AL., SHOWING UP: HOW WE SEE, SPEAK, AND DISRUPT RACIAL INEQUITY FACING SURVIVORS OF DOMESTIC AND SEXUAL VIOLENCE (2018), https://csaj.org/document-library/REEP_Report_Showing_Up_FINAL.pdf.

Chapter Twelve:
Debt, Defense, and Safety Considerations for Survivors

Diane Johnston[1]

Reprinted from Center for Survivor Agency & Justice (CSAJ), Guidebook on Consumer & Economic Civil Legal Advocacy (2017), https://csaj.org/Guidebook.[2]

I. Introduction

Personal income has not kept up with the cost of living, particularly for people with low and average earnings, forcing more people than ever before to rely on credit to pay even their basic needs. Financial institutions have simultaneously increased interest rates and fees for lower income and higher risk consumers, causing individual debt burdens to grow and very often become unmanageable. While frequently associated with credit cards and loans, any unpaid bill can become a problematic debt. About 35 percent of adults, or 77 million of the 220 million Americans with credit files, show debts in collections.[3] Unpaid debts can result in debt collector harassment, lawsuits, garnished wages, and frozen bank accounts, in addition to negatively impacting a consumer's credit report and score.

---

[1] With contributions by Katie VonDeLinde and the National Consumer Law Center.

[2] A deeper dive into the case scenario described in this reprinted chapter can be found in CSAJ's Guidebook on Consumer & Economic Civil Legal Advocacy. Diane Johnston, *Debt, Debt Defense, and Safety Considerations for Survivors*, in GUIDEBOOK ON CONSUMER & ECONOMIC CIVIL LEGAL ADVOCACY 62 (2017), https://csaj.org/Guidebook.

[3] CONSUMER FIN. PROT. BUREAU, ANNUAL REPORT ON THE FAIR DEBT COLLECTION PRACTICES ACT 8 (Mar. 2016), http://files.consumerfinance.gov/f/201603_cfpb-fair-debt-collection-practices-act.pdf.

For survivors of domestic violence, these consequences can be particularly devastating as they jeopardize the survivor's ability to becoming financially self-sufficient. This chapter will explain different types of debt, how debts are treated differently in family law and consumer law, the laws governing debt collection, defenses to a debt collection lawsuit, and safety considerations when dealing with debt.

Maria's Story

Maria is a survivor of domestic violence who finalized her divorce from John over two years ago. She is now in her apartment with her two children, working a minimum wage, part-time job. Funds are extremely tight, and she is struggling to make ends meet. Because her credit was better than John's, during the relationship, they opened all of their credit accounts under her name instead of his. John handled all of the finances for them, so she was not always sure of what accounts were being opened or used. She was allowed use of one of their credit cards and John used the others. She learned the full picture of the debt in her name during her divorce proceedings. Per her divorce, John is supposed to be making payments for a portion of the debt directly to their creditors. She believes that he has been complying with this requirement.

Maria comes to you because she just had her rent check returned to her due to insufficient funds. She knows that she had enough money in her account, but when she speaks with a representative from her bank, they tell her that her account was frozen pursuant to a court judgment against her. Maria is shocked and confused. This is the first time she has learned that a case had been filed against her.

II. Domestic Violence and Debt

Many survivors of domestic violence exit abusive relationships with a high debt load. For some, the process of leaving requires money the survivor does not have, and therefore reliance on credit cards or loans to cover these expenses. Many others have also accrued debt through financial abuse. Experienced by an estimated 99 percent of survivors, financial abuse can include intimate partner identity theft, coerced debt, and an unequal distribution of debts and assets between partners during a relationship.[4] Even after a relationship ends, abusive ex-partners can continue financially harming survivors by accruing additional debt in the survivor's name or by refusing to pay debts as ordered in a divorce.

---

[4] Adrienne E. Adams et al., *Development of the scale of economic abuse,* 14 Violence Against Women 563–588 (2008), http://doi.org/10.1177/1077801208315529. For a more in-depth discussion of identity theft, see Amy Cao, *Identity Theft & Survivors of Domestic Violence: Strategies for Resolution & Protection, in* Guidebook on Consumer & Economic Civil Legal Advocacy 80 (2017), https://csaj.org/Guidebook. Coerced debt is a term coined by scholar Angela Littwin to encompass "all non-consensual, credit-related transactions that occur in a violent relationship." Angela Littwin, *Coerced Debt: The Role of Consumer Credit in Domestic Violence,* 100 Calif. L. Rev. 951, 954 (2012).

In many domestic violence cases, survivors find out the full extent of their debt burden only after they have left the relationship. Dealing with finances often happens once the survivor has been able to get more basic safety and living needs met. Survivors often have fuzzy recollections of what happened and when, especially because of the trauma they have experienced and because the information you will be discussing may be from a long time ago or may have never been entirely clear to the survivor.

You may also have survivors that come to you while they are still in abusive relationships. With these clients, you will want to assess safety risks carefully. Disputing a debt or taking other action related to credit accounts may agitate or tip off the abusive partner that your client is thinking about the future or preparing to leave. You will need to assess whether the client's partner will be able to learn about the action taken and whether the partner is likely to retaliate. In some cases, it may make sense for the survivor to wait until leaving the relationship to start addressing these issues.

A. Screening for Debt Issues

Because of the complicated experiences and feelings surrounding debt for many survivors, debt advocacy work requires an open, honest, and sensitive assessment. The screening and assessment questions presented here are for issue spotting (often called "intake questions"), are not meant to be prescriptive, and conversations around debt should not be limited to these questions.[5]

Attorneys and advocates can set the stage by discussing general feelings about debt and finances, and reassuring survivors that they are not defined by their debt or financial decisions.

When you meet with your client, consider how you can safely pull the survivor's credit report, which you should review along with any debt collection letters received.[6]

Assessment questions could include, but are not limited to:

- Have you ever reviewed your credit report before?

- Have you received any legal papers related to a debt?

- Have you received notice that your wages will be garnished or that your bank account will be frozen?

---

[5] For a fuller description of a survivor centered approach to economic assessment, see *Economic Coercion and Survivor-Centered Economic Advocacy* in Section Three of this manual.

[6] Domestic violence survivors should never use a confidential address to obtain their credit reports. For more information on pulling credit reports safely, see Katie VonDeLinde, *Building & Repairing Credit Reports: Understanding Options and Safety Implications for Survivors, in* Guidebook on Consumer & Economic Civil Legal Advocacy 30 (2017), https://csaj.org/Guidebook.

- Have you had anything of value seized or repossessed?

- Are you receiving phone calls or letters from debt collectors?
  - Are any of those communications threatening or harassing?

- What debts are you aware of?
  - How did you accrue these debts?
  - During your relationship? Before or after?
  - For personal purchases? For your household? For your former partner?

- What were your finances like during the relationship? Who handled the bills?

- Did you have access to shared accounts?

- Do you think your partner has or would ever access your credit report?

Additional assessment questions specific to coerced debt could include:

- Did you ever feel pressure from your partner to make specific financial decisions?

- What do you think would have happened if you had refused?

- What did your partner say or do to convince you?

- If you were in front of another person (like a car salesperson), do you think he or she could have suspected what was going on?

- If the transaction involved opening an account (new credit card, loan, other type of account), do you have any of the contracts?

- Did you get any use or benefit from the transaction (use of a car or credit card, for example)?

B. The Impact of Debt

For many of our clients, talking about and admitting to having a large debt burden is embarrassing or shameful. If the survivor goes to court or does anything to address the debt, they will be required to talk about it; this means they may also be essentially required to talk about their relationship and abuse. For some clients, this may be the first time they are sharing these issues with someone. Dealing with debt collection could mean that your client feels alienated from his or her community or family.

The impacts of debt can be devastating. Dealing with debt collectors—who are often aggressive, may be demeaning, and call incessantly—can be extremely distressing. If your client is sued, the process of going to court is confusing and adds more stress to your client's life, especially if the survivor is already dealing with court dates for other matters related to the abuse, like divorce proceedings, family court cases, and/or a pending criminal case. For survivors like Maria who find out about debts after a default judgment has been entered against them, sudden deprivation of wages or funds in a bank account could be the tipping point that makes it impossible for the survivor to maintain safety, pay rent, or obtain basic necessities. Also, being required to talk about debt related to the abusive relationship can be re-traumatizing for survivors.

Open conversations to prepare survivors for these experiences are critical.

Definition of Terms

Secured debt: Debt from a loan that is connected to something of value, like a house or a car, and the creditor can take back that asset if a consumer fails to pay.

Unsecured debt: Debt that is not tied to any asset, including but not limited to credit card debt, personal loans, medical bills, and utility debt.

Lender: The entity that originates a loan (also called original creditor).

Servicer: Hired by lenders to send account statements or bills to the consumer and to collect payments.

Creditor: The entity that originates accounts that allow the customer to purchase goods or services on credit, and pay back later.

Debt buyers: Companies that purchase defaulted debts in bulk, often for pennies on the dollar.[7]

Account holder: The person liable for the account.

Co-signor or guarantor: A person who signs a credit application together with the primary account holder, and agrees to be held liable for debt if the primary account holder fails to pay.

Authorized user: A person added to an account and granted permission to utilize the credit account, but not as an account holder.

Service of process: The delivering of the initial case paperwork to the person being sued.

Standing: Whether the plaintiff is the proper party to sue on the debt.

Statute of limitations: A time limit set for a creditor to sue for an unpaid debt. It generally starts to run when the first payment is missed.

---

[7] The following website lists many of the common debt buyers you will see, but it is not exhaustive. *Debt Buyers*, Debt Connection, https://debtconnection.com/categories/debt-buyers (last visited May 2, 2018). If your client has store cards, these are often through Department Store National Bank (DSNB), Synchrony, or Comenity. If there is a name that you or your client do not recognize, a quick google search can often point you in the right direction.

III. Starting Principles

A. What Debts are We Talking About?

Almost any money your client owes to someone else can be sent to a debt collection company, reported on his/her credit report, or can result in a debt collection lawsuit against your client and/or your client's partner. This includes debt owed on credit cards, personal loans, medical bills, utilities, rental arrears, student loans, car, a car lease, or any other money owed to another entity.

There are two main types of debt. **Secured debt** is connected to something of value, like a house or a car, and the creditor can take back that asset from your client if he or she fails to pay. **Unsecured debt** includes every other type of debt that is not tied to any asset, including but not limited to credit card debt, personal loans, medical bills, and utility debt.[8]

Advocacy Tip: Instead of asking your client if they have any debt, ask about the specific types of accounts, such as credit cards, and medical and phone bills. Ask your client if he/she has a balance on the account, if he/she is making the required monthly payment, and if he/she makes these payments on time.

B. Who Am I Dealing With?

There are a number of players in the debt collection industry, and sometimes it is difficult to determine who you are dealing with. The entity that originates the account is the **lender,** or the original creditor. When you take out a loan, whether a personal loan, student loan, car loan, or mortgage, you generally borrow from a lender and receive a lump sum of money, a credit card, or the money lent is forwarded to the car or home seller or educational institution. Lenders often hire a **servicer** to send account statements or bills, and to collect payments. Servicers will also negotiate settlements or repayment terms when a borrower defaults, or fails to make payments. **Creditors** are associated with accounts that allow the customer to purchase goods or services on credit and pay back later. The most common type of revolving credit is a credit card. In this chapter, the term creditor will also be used to encompass lenders and servicers.

When a client fails to make timely payments on an account, creditors may hire a **debt collector.** Similar to a loan servicer, these entities will seek payments from the client or ask the client for the partner's location information. The original creditor still owns the debt, but the debt collector is hired to help collect the money on the creditor's behalf. They are often aggressive, calling frequently, and sometimes

---

[8] An important consumer protection for medical debt is that hospital emergency rooms that accept Medicare may not deny life stabilizing and active labor care because of outstanding medical debts. See Nat'l Consumer L. Ctr., Collection Actions § 9.3.3 (3d ed. 2014). National Consumer Law Center (NCLC) manuals are an excellent resource but may not be available without a subscription. If you need to access this information, contact a consumer attorney in your area.

using illegal practices to intimidate your client into making payments. Creditors may change debt collectors after a few weeks or months, or several times over the life of the debt, creating confusion about who is authorized to actually collect on the debt.

After failing to collect a debt, creditors may sell the debt to **debt buyers.** Debt buyers are companies that purchase defaulted debts in bulk, often for pennies on the dollar. They become the legal owner of the debt, with the ability to pursue collection on their own and to sue on the debt. These debts are often sold without guarantees as to the accuracy of the amount owed by the consumer and may limit the debt buyer's right to obtain additional basic information about the debt. A 2013 study by the Federal Trade Commission found that fewer than 50 percent of the debt buyers studied received the name of the original creditor, fewer than 40 percent had information on the account's finance charges and fees, and only 35 percent knew the date of the consumer's alleged default—information basic to identifying who is responsible for the account.[9]

C. What is the Difference between Joint Debt and Separate Debt?

Account holders on credit cards and personal loans are liable for the debt. In consumer law, the named account holder(s) determines whether a debt is joint or separate. A **co-signor** or **guarantor** signs a credit application together with the primary account holder. Just like the primary account holder, the co-signor or guarantor is an account holder and is liable on the account. That means if the primary account holder fails to pay, the financial institution or entity can pursue the co-signor/guarantor for the entire balance of the debt. Similarly, if one of the account holders declares bankruptcy and discharges a particular debt, the other account holder will remain liable for the whole debt.[10] An **authorized user** is added to an account as a person with permission to utilize the credit account, but not as an account holder. This is frequently used between people with familial relationships (intimate partners or parent/child) where one person has better or more established credit than the other. An authorized user may or may not be legally responsible for the debt or even for his or her charges on the account depending on the contract, and state and federal law.[11]

Advocacy Tip: To determine whether your client is an account holder or an authorized user, look at the original agreement documents (which may not be readily available), the billing statements, and/or the client's credit report. The credit report may indicate whether the account is individual, joint, or if the client is an authorized user. Only a few clients will have the credit application and

---

[9] Fed. Trade Comm'n, The Structure and Practices of the Debt Buying Industry 44–49 (2013), http://www.ftc.gov/os/2013/01/debtbuyingreport.pdf.

[10] For more information about bankruptcy, see *Bankruptcy Law and Domestic Violence* in Section Three of this manual. *See also* Karen Merrill Tjapkes, *Bankruptcy & Alternatives for Survivors, in* Guidebook on Consumer & Economic Civil Legal Advocacy 112 (2017), https://csaj.org/Guidebook.

[11] *See* Nat'l Consumer L. Ctr., *supra* note 8.

the contract (the documents that establish your client's legal responsibility) and even the original creditor may have difficulty providing those documents if they are more than three years old. The client's representative's bargaining position may be enhanced with a creditor or debt collector who cannot provide those documents. Such bargaining positions include: this debt is not my client's responsibility; my client cannot pay this debt; my client can only pay a portion of the debt; and/or my client can only pay a specific amount per month.

This is unrelated to how debts are determined to be joint or separate in the family law/divorce context. If your client has had a distribution of debts through a divorce action, this does not change his/her standing with creditors.[12] Creditors will still pursue only the named account holders, and in some states, the authorized users for the debt.

Debt collectors may tell your clients that they can be held liable for their spouse's debt even if they are not an account holder. This is not true in the majority of states that follow **equitable distribution,** and if your client has been told this, he or she likely has a claim for a deceptive or misleading collection practice (see more on these claims below). In **community property** states, both spouses are deemed to equally share all income, assets, and debt acquired during the marriage.[13] This means that both spouses in those states are equally liable for debts, regardless of who is named on the account. Many states have statutes that make spouses responsible for "necessities," like medical care and groceries, provided to their spouse or children.[14] There is some reason to believe that such statutes are seldom used against consumers.[15]

Advocacy Tip: A divorce attorney may be able to prevent this issue from happening by negotiating with opposing counsel or the other party (ex-spouse) to include a provision requiring each party to refinance debt into his/her own name. Many credit cards will allow a new cardholder to transfer a balance from another account for a fee.

IV. Communication with Debt Collectors

As mentioned, debt collectors often call frequently, and sometimes use abusive and other unlawful methods to collect a debt. This can be overwhelming

---

[12] For further discussion on how divorce affects finances, see Laura A. Russell, *Financial Issues in Family Law: Protection Orders, Child & Spousal Support, and Distribution of Assets & Debts*, in GUIDEBOOK ON CONSUMER & ECONOMIC CIVIL LEGAL ADVOCACY 166 (2017), https://csaj.org/Guidebook.

[13] Only a minority of states observe community property instead of equitable distribution: Alaska (by agreement), Arizona, California, Idaho, Louisiana, Nevada, New Mexico, Texas, Washington, and Wisconsin.

[14] *See* NAT'L CONSUMER L. CTR., *supra* note 8.

[15] *See* Ann Britton, *America's Best Kept Secret: An Adult Child's Duty to Support Aged Parents,* 26 CALIF. WESTERN L. REV. 351 (1990).

and stressful for clients. Federal law, the Fair Debt Collection Practices Act (FDCPA), as well as state laws regulate debt collectors.

Within five days of initiating contact, the debt collector must send a written notice with the amount of money owed, the name of the original creditor, and what action the client can take if he/she does not believe the debt is valid.

Advocacy Tip: If your client believes the debt is invalid, he or she should send a dispute and verification request in writing to the debt collector. Once the debt collector receives it, it must obtain verification of the debt from the creditor and send this proof to the client before resuming any collection activities or starting a lawsuit against the client.

A. Timing and Frequency of Phone Calls

Debt collectors can only call your client from 8:00 a.m. and 9:00 p.m. They are not allowed to call repeatedly and frequently. However, repeated calls are allowed if they go unanswered.

If your client does not want to continue receiving phone calls, he or she can write a **Cease Contact Letter** asking the debt collector to stop. Once received, the debt collector cannot contact the client except to confirm that there will be no further contact, or to inform the client that it intends to take specific action to collect the debt, such as bringing a lawsuit.

Advocacy Tip: If your client is overwhelmed with phone calls and has a small number of creditors, encourage him or her to pick up the phone. Your client should verify who they are, get contact information from the debt collector, and state that he or she does not wish to be contacted by phone.

Advocacy Tip: Cease Contact Letters are effective as a hard rule that debt collectors must follow, but sometimes speed up the process in which a creditor files a lawsuit since it is unable to pursue collection over the phone. This may vary regionally and depend on the client's financial position, with judgment proof clients less likely to be sued. Consider whether continued phone calls or a lawsuit in court would be more difficult for your client to handle. If the client seeks freedom from calls, you should counsel your client on how important it is to respond if sued, as people in many states do not get plain language instructions on how to respond to a lawsuit.

B. Who Can a Debt Collector Contact?

Debt collectors cannot contact your client if he/she is known to be represented by an attorney. If your client informs a debt collector that he or she cannot receive calls at work, they must stop calling there. They *can* contact third parties once to obtain your client's contact information, but they cannot share information about the debt in those calls.

If your client is legally married, a debt collector *can* speak with your client's spouse about the debt.[16] This may create safety concerns. For example, if it is an account your client is still using, this may allow the abuser to get information about where your client is shopping or spending money if the collector attempts to confirm charges over the phone. If your client has updated their phone number or mailing address to one that the abuser doesn't know, but has not responded to communications from the debt collector, the collector may try to confirm with the spouse that this contact information is correct.

Advocacy Tip: If your client is still married, or recently divorced, advise him or her not to update a confidential address with any creditors or debt collectors. A debt collector may contact the spouse to verify that the information they have is correct, including a confidential address. Instead, have your client open a P.O. box where he or she can safely receive mail.

The Fair Debt Collection Practices Act (FDCPA)

The FDCPA imposes restrictions on a debt collector's efforts to obtain payment and on where a debt collector can sue a borrower. As a general rule, the FDCPA applies to third-party debt collectors (as opposed to the original lender). The FDCPA establishes general standards of prohibited conduct in order to protect consumers from invasions of privacy, harassment, abuse, false or deceptive representations, and unfair or unconscionable collections methods. The Act also defines and restricts abusive collection actions, such as late night or repetitive phone calls, false threats of legal action or criminal prosecution, and communication with others regarding the debt. The consumer can recover actual damages, statutory damages of up to $1,000, attorney fees, and costs.

C. How Else does the Fair Debt Collection Practices Act (FDCPA) Protect My Client?

Debt collectors are prohibited from making false or misleading statements, threatening or harassing your client. The debt collector cannot *falsely* claim to represent a governmental agency, to be an attorney or a law firm, or to be employed by a credit bureau. Debt collectors may not falsely claim that your client has committed a crime or will be arrested for not paying the debt, or that the collector will take action only permissible after being awarded a judgment in court.

---

[16] 15 U.S.C. § 1692c(d) (2018) ("For the purpose of this section, the term "consumer" includes the consumer's spouse, parent (if the consumer is a minor), guardian, executor, or administrator.").

If a debt collector violates the FDCPA, your client can sue the collector in state or federal court within one year of the violation. Your client can recover their damages plus up to $1,000 and payment of the client's attorney's fees.

Advocacy Tip: Encourage your clients to keep a call log documenting their conversations with creditors and/or debt collectors. This log should include the date and time of the call, the name of the collector, name of the collection company, call back phone number, name of the original creditor and current owner of the debt, alleged amount of the debt, estimate of how long the call lasted, and any other notes about what the collector said. Clients should not give information to debt collectors without knowing that the debt collector is legitimate. The client should get the debt collection company's name, address, and phone number, and check its legitimacy.[17]

Advocacy Tip: In a typical case, your client likely has multiple FDCPA violations, if you can document them. Have your clients keep a call log and retain all documents received from debt collectors and debt collection law firms to build your case.

In the case scenario, Maria tells you she is receiving letters and phone calls from a debt collector regarding an alleged debt to AT&T. Maria does not think she ever had an account with AT&T, so she sends a dispute and verification letter to the debt collector via certified mail, return receipt requested. Although she receives the return receipt and so she knows that the debt collector received the letter, she continues to receive phone calls and letters but not a verification of the debt or response to her dispute. In Maria's call log, you see that the debt collector has told her they will be garnishing her wages if she does not make a payment within a week, even though they have not yet filed a case against her. Maria also tells you that she receives repeated calls at work, even after she has informed the debt collector not to contact her there. This debt collectors has multiple violations of the FDCPA, and Maria can sue the debt collector.

V. Prioritizing Debts

If your client has a budget that allows for payment on debts and would like to do so, review what should take priority. Expenses for essential needs like rent, food, and utilities should always take priority over other debts.[18] If your client has secured debt related to an essential asset, like the home or a car that he/she needs in order to get to work, those debts should also be high on the priority list.

---

[17] The original creditor may verify the debt collector, or the collector may be licensed by the state or listed without its legitimacy being challenged. *Submit a Complaint,* CONSUMER FIN. PROT. BUREAU, https://www.consumerfinance.gov/complaint/ (last visited Apr. 30, 2018).

[18] Note that a utility service provider (phone, electric, gas, internet) can terminate service for nonpayment, usually without a court proceeding.

The next tier of priority should be debts that have more serious consequences. The federal government benefits from additional remedies to collect on debts owed to it, like tax debt and student loans. While other creditors must file a lawsuit and take the debtor to court before being able to collect from anyone, the federal government can garnish a person's income, including income that is protected from other creditors like Social Security, or can seize all or a portion of the person's tax refund. Because these options are available only to the government and not to ordinary creditors, governmental debts should take priority over other types of unsecured debt. Furthermore, programs available through the Department of Education and through the Internal Revenue Service mean that your client may end up with a very affordable settlement or payment.

VI. Affirmative Consumer Litigation Options

In addition to claims brought under the FDCPA, your client may have claims under your state's Unfair and Deceptive Acts and Practices (UDAP) laws or under the Truth in Lending Act (TILA). A consumer lawyer should analyze these claims.

A. Unfair and Deceptive Acts and Practices (UDAP)

UDAP laws are promulgated by each state, and thus can vary tremendously across the country. All UDAP statutes prohibit some combination of unfair, deceptive, and/or unconscionable practices in an effort to protect consumers from predatory business practices. All UDAP laws give state agencies authority to enforce the protections provided therein, and most states also give individual consumers the right to seek remedies on their own. Your client may wish to pursue a UDAP claim depending on your state's laws and remedies.[19]

B. Truth in Lending Act (TILA)

The federal Truth in Lending Act is primarily about disclosure and ensuring that consumers are given the information they need to make informed financial decisions. Many of TILA's disclosure requirements aim to make credit terms understandable and accessible to consumers so that they will understand the cost of the credit they are seeking. TILA contains provisions pertaining to home mortgages, car loans, and credit cards.

Apart from provisions related to mortgages, some important provisions of TILA include:[20]

---

[19] The National Consumer Law Center has more information on each state's UDAP laws. *Unfair & Deceptive Acts & Practices,* Nat'l Consumer L. Ctr., http://www.nclc.org/issues/unfair-a-deceptive-acts-a-practices.html (last visited Apr. 30, 2018).

[20] For more information on mortgages, see *Foreclosure Defense for Survivors* in Section Three of this manual.

(1) The Fair Credit Billing Act (FCBA) provides a process through which consumers can dispute billing errors and unauthorized charges and limits the consumer's liability for these issues. The consumer must send a written dispute within 60 days of learning of the issue, and the creditor then has up to 90 days to investigate and make a determination.

(2) The Credit Card Accountability Responsibility and Disclosure Act (CARD Act) states that credit card issuers must consider a consumer's ability to pay before opening a new account or increasing credit limits. They must give consumers a grace period before charging higher interest rates and between issuing a statement and requiring a payment. They must disclose that making only the minimum payment will result in paying higher interest. The CARD Act also limits fees that credit card issuers may charge.

Advocacy Tip: When creditors decide that there was no billing error or unauthorized use, they will often issue a short statement informing the consumer of this finding. Request additional information about their investigation to determine if the dispute was properly investigated and resolved.

Why Your Client Needs to Establish a Safe Mailing Address

While receiving mail from debt collectors and creditors can be stressful, it is important that your client has a safe mailing address so that they can safely pull and monitor their credit and so that they are kept up to date with what is happening on their accounts. Keeping an old address on file with USPS, the Department of Motor Vehicles, and other entities could result in your client being served at an old address, thus never receiving notice of a lawsuit yet not having a service defense. If your client cannot afford a P.O. box, check into your state's Address Confidentiality Program to help her or him establish a safe address.

VII. Defending a Debt Collection Lawsuit

A. Initiation of a Lawsuit

Generally speaking, your client will not usually benefit from avoiding or refusing service of process. If your client received a court summons signaling a lawsuit against him or her, check for a state bar, law library, or state court website that explains the rules of civil procedure for responding in your state to ensure that your client knows the deadline and method for responding, if they choose to.[21] Also, if possible, speak to a consumer expert to determine the best

---

[21] Speak with an attorney in your state if possible. The Legal Information Institute at Cornell University Law School maintains links to each state's rules of civil procedure. *Civil Procedure – State Laws,* Legal Info. Inst., https://www.law.cornell.edu/wex/table_civil_procedure (last visited Apr. 30, 2018).

course of action. In New York, for example, failure to file a written answer with the court's clerk means that the client will not receive notice of the scheduled court appearance, streamlining the process for a creditor to obtain a default judgment.

Most defenses are asserted in your client's answer. In some states, the answer can be in the form of a checklist and the client does not need to elaborate on any given defense in the answer. If your client has been sued, you should try to find her or him an attorney or another resource for legal assistance. Many courthouses and some state court libraries have a "*pro se*" desk, clerk, or website that can provide basic information to litigants who do not have an attorney.[22]

Few clients can adequately defend themselves against a debt collection suit without a lawyer representing them. Some legal aid and private attorneys represent consumer against debt collectors' lawsuits in some states.

B. Common Debt Collection Defenses

1. Lack of or Improper Service

The debt collection industry is notorious for problems with **service of process** (the delivering of the initial case paperwork to the person being sued), commonly known as "sewer service." By withholding effective service of process, creditors are able to obtain default judgments without ever notifying the consumer of the lawsuit. The client may also have a defense if service was made but was improper. For example, if the law requires personal service (that the defendant receives the paperwork in person), but the plaintiff only mailed the summons and complaint. Domestic violence survivors are more prone to miss even proper service if they have fled to a shelter, a new apartment, or the home of a friend or family member and have not notified creditors or other entities. If service was improper, the court lacks personal jurisdiction, and the client can file a motion to dismiss on that basis.

In the case scenario, a debt collector, LR Credit, sues Maria. The Summons and Complaint are mailed to the address where she lived with John, but she moved about six years ago before filing for divorce. She has since changed her address with USPS and the Department of Motor Vehicles but never updated her address directly with her creditors. This debt was one that Maria was supposed to be responsible for, but she believes her last payment on the underlying debt was more than ten years ago.

Depending on her state's rules of civil procedure, Maria likely has a service defense. In New York, for example, a Summons and Complaint can be served by mail only if it is also affixed to the door of the defendant's actual place

---

[22] *See Self-Representation State Links*, Nat'l Ctr. for State Courts, http://www.ncsc.org/Topics/Access-and-Fairness/Self-Representation/State-Links.aspx (last visited Apr. 30, 2018).

of residence, and this type of service is only permissible after due diligence attempts to serve the defendant in person or via substitute service. Thus, Maria could challenge service both because the Summons and Complaint were sent by mail only and because they were sent to the wrong address. Maria also has a statute of limitations defense under New York law, because consumer debt actions have a maximum statute of limitations of six years. Lastly, Maria should raise the defense of standing, because she is sued by a debt collector and not an original creditor.

2. Standing

If the client does not recognize the entity suing her, or if the entity is a debt buyer, he or she should assert lack of standing as a defense. This challenges whether the plaintiff is the proper party to sue on the debt. The plaintiff must prove that it is the legal owner of the debt and must provide evidence showing that the debt was legally obtained. If a debt has been sold multiple times, this evidence must include proof of each sale of the debt.

Advocacy Tip: You will often first see this evidence in a debt collector plaintiff's Motion for Summary Judgment. Scrutinize these documents carefully. Creditors often include standard credit card agreements without your client's name or account number, or print offs of spreadsheets with account numbers but no names. Check if the documents connect your client to the account number. These documents must be accompanied by an affidavit that lays the proper foundation for admissibility under the business records exception to the hearsay rule. Does the affidavit describe how the writer's job duties provide him or her with personal knowledge of the facts? Are all of the elements for the business records exception established in the affidavit? Is there an affidavit for each sale of the debt, written and signed by someone who works for the entity that sold it?

3. Statute of Limitations

The statute of limitations sets a time limit for a creditor to sue for an unpaid debt. It generally starts to run when the first payment is missed. However, if the consumer subsequently makes a payment, the statute of limitations will start to run again in many states. Confirm how your state applies the statute of limitations on consumer debts. Note that the statute of limitations may differ for a revolving credit account like a credit card, a contract for the sale of goods like a car, or a retail installment agreement.

Advocacy Tip: Debt buyers sometimes purchase debts after the statute of limitations has already run; these debts are sometimes referred to as "zombie debts." In these cases, collectors will often offer extremely affordable payments, like $5 a month, in order to pressure your client to make a payment that will restart the statute of limitations. Clients should resist these offers on old debts, particularly when made outside of court.

4. Client Does Not Owe the Debt

Raise this defense if your client is a victim of identity theft or mistaken identity, or if your client simply does not owe the debt the plaintiff alleges.[23] Many domestic violence survivors may not recognize they are victims of identity theft when their partner opened or utilized an account in their name without their knowledge or permission. Even if the perpetrator was your client's partner or spouse, it is still identity theft if your client did not apply for, receive, or use the account in question.

Advocacy Tip: If your client is the victim of identity theft or mistaken identity, pull his or her credit report to check if the debt appears there as well. You should help your client dispute this debt by using the Federal Trade Commission's online Identity Theft Affidavit and writing dispute letters to the Credit Reporting Agencies to have these lines removed.

5. Unfair Collection Process

Your answer may include a counterclaim for violation of the FDCPA or your state's Unfair and Deceptive Acts and Practices (UDAP) laws. When debt collectors do not obtain default judgments, they may dismiss the case instead of proceeding with insufficient evidence to litigate the case. This is more frequent when the consumer appears in the case, and even more frequent when an attorney appears.[24] Some courts may find this dismissal strategy involves an illegal debt collection practice prohibited by the Fair Debt Collection Practices Act.[25]

C. Judgments

Many consumer defendants do not learn of cases against them until after the creditor has obtained a default judgment against them, and the client's wages are subsequently garnished, or his/her bank account is frozen. You likely have several options to vacate a default judgment under state law. One likely option is to challenge service and vacate for lack of personal jurisdiction. To do so, you should review the plaintiff's affidavit of service with your client for discrepancies. For example, check if the affidavit alleges service at the wrong address. If the affidavit claims to have served your client personally, check if the description matches your client's physical description at the time and if it was at a time when your client would have been home. If the affidavit claims to have served another person (substitute service), check if the name and description of the person match anyone with whom your client is familiar.

Judgments may also appear in cases where your client had notice but lost the case. In these cases, if it appears that your client asserted defenses, your

---

[23] For a further discussion of intimate partner identity theft, see Cao, *supra* note 4.

[24] *See* Mary Spector, *Where the FCRA Meets the FDCPA: The Impact of Unfair Collection Practices on the Credit Report*, 20 Geo. J. on Poverty L. & Pol'y 479, 479 (2012–2013).

[25] *See supra* Section IV.

advocacy strategy may be to try to negotiate a settlement of the judgment at a lower amount. Judgments negatively impact your client's credit score and can often be enforced for many years, depending on your state's laws, so they should be taken seriously. Personal bankruptcy offers important remedies that may help with some types of debts and protect some of the consumer's future income.[26]

D. Enforcement

A creditor may enforce its judgment by garnishing (taking) some of the debtor's wages or funds in a bank account, or by seizing or attaching a lien to assets, like a car or home. If the creditor seeks to garnish wages, the maximum it can obtain under federal law is the lesser of 25 percent of the debtor's disposable earnings for the week, or earnings in excess of the 30 times the federal minimum wage.[27] Disposable earnings are defined as wages remaining after required withholdings.[28] Note that specific debts are excluded from this limitation, including debts for spousal or child support payments and debts for state and federal taxes.[29] Also note that this is the maximum creditors can garnish under federal law, but many states protect higher amounts of income. The federal dollar amount limits are per debtor, not per creditor. Thus, if your client has several creditors seeking to enforce their judgments, the maximum that would be garnished at any one time is 25 percent of disposable earnings.

Under federal and state law, many types of benefits are exempt from enforcement. Exempt federal benefits include Social Security, Veterans', and Supplemental Security Income benefits.[30] Many states also protect child support payments and state benefits, but this varies by state. Generally, state benefits including public assistance, workers compensation, and unemployment insurance are exempt but check with your state.

If the creditor seeks to enforce its judgment against an asset, the process and impact can differ greatly by state and the asset involved. For a car loan, for example, the creditor can usually repossess the vehicle without suing your client. After that, the creditor may sue your client for the deficiency between the amount

---

[26] Deciding whether to file for bankruptcy requires careful, individualized analysis. If your client is considering bankruptcy, help them find a qualified bankruptcy attorney in your area. For more information on bankruptcy, see *Bankruptcy Law and Domestic Violence* in Section Three of this manual. *See also* Tjapkes, *supra* note 10. For information and referrals, see Nat'l Ass'n of Consumer Bankruptcy Att'ys, www.nacba.org (last visited Apr. 30, 2018).

[27] Consumer Credit Protection Act, 15 U.S.C.A. § 1673(a).

[28] *Id.* § 1672(b).

[29] *Id.* § 1673(b).

[30] Other protected benefits include Civil Service and Federal Retirement and Disability benefits; Military Annuities and Survivors' Benefits; Student Assistance; Railroad Retirement Benefits; Merchant Seamen Wages; Longshoremen's and Harbor Workers' Death and Disability benefits; Foreign Service Retirement and Disability benefits.

owed on the loan and the amount that the vehicle sold for at auction. Another common method of enforcement, as we saw in Maria's case, is to freeze or seize funds from a bank account. While many states offer protections for specific types of funds in a bank account or for specific amounts, even a freeze on an account can have serious consequences if scheduled payments for living necessities are bounced. Each state exempts specific types of property from seizure by creditors, but apart from these exemptions, ordinary creditors may be able to go after the debtor's vehicle, home, and less often household goods.[31] If you discover that your client has a judgment, contact an attorney in your area.

VIII. Building Partnership to Enhance Survivors' Consumer Rights[32]

Despite the overlap between the work of domestic violence and consumer lawyers, there is an enormous gap in collaboration between the fields. While domestic violence attorneys typically focus on physical protections and family law matters, consumer lawyers focus on longer-term financial, legal issues. Without proper collaboration between family law and consumer law attorneys, domestic violence advocates and attorneys may not account for the economic or consumer law issues that victims could be facing, or that could enhance their options for safety. Similarly, consumer attorneys may not consider the safety and privacy concerns of survivors in their cases, which could pose enormous risks for the survivor. Thus, enhanced capacity of a partnership between domestic violence and consumer lawyers is critical to achieving the joint goals of physical and economic safety. It requires purposeful cross training, networking, and sustained partnership building.

Some strategies for building partnerships between consumer law and domestic violence attorneys include:

- DV advocates/attorneys can assist the survivors in contacting consumer law attorneys (such as the National Association of Consumer Advocates (NACA) directory) to familiarize them with the survivor's needs and begin conversations around coordinating legal advocacy.[33]

- Develop a process for coordinating legal needs such as: schedule regular "check-in" meetings between family law and consumer lawyers and the survivors; establish a protocol for sharing relevant case information, with the survivor's permission.

---

[31] For more on state exemptions, see CAROLYN CARTER & ROBERT J. HOBBS, NAT'L CONSUMER L. CTR., NO FRESH START (2013), https://www.nclc.org/images/pdf/pr-reports/report-no-fresh-start.pdf.

[32] *See* CTR. FOR SURVIVOR AGENCY & JUST., BUILDING PARTNERSHIPS TO ENHANCE CONSUMER RIGHTS FOR DOMESTIC VIOLENCE SURVIVORS: AN ASSESSMENT AND RESOURCE TOOL FOR ATTORNEYS AND ADVOCATES (2013), https://csaj.org/document-library/Building_Partnerships_Pilot_Report_Webinar_-_HANDOUT.pdf.

[33] NAT'L ASS'N OF CONSUMER ADVOC., https://www.consumeradvocates.org/ (last visited Apr. 30, 2018).

Co-create opportunities to institutionalize partnerships: establish regular meetings to connect the domestic violence and consumer agencies in your area; develop cross-training opportunities; make new contacts (with state consumer bar association or state domestic violence coalition) and cultivate the relationship.

IX. Conclusion

Consumer debt issues can be both intimidating and emotionally difficult for clients and can jeopardize their safety as well as their path toward financial self-sufficiency. Many clients may not realize that taking action on their consumer debt can implicate their safety or put them in contact with their abusive partner again; as an advocate, you can help guide your clients through this process and ensure that they understand all of their options before taking any action.

APPENDIX

Resources:

- **Attorneys**
  - ○ Some legal aid offices and law school clinics provide consumer representation. A local legal aid program may know of other legal resources available to help consumer defendants without cost to the client.

  - ○ To find a free attorney in your area, search on:
    - LawHelp.org, https://www.lawhelp.org/.
    - Legal Servs. Corp., https://www.lsc.gov/.

  - ○ Hundreds of private lawyers who represent consumers against debt collectors for no or low fee are listed at https://www.consumeradvocates.org/. Private attorneys on the NACA list may help or suggest another attorney who handles such cases for a low or no fee.

- **The Center for Survivor Agency & Justice**
  - ○ Katie VonDeLinde, *Budgeting & Debt Prioritization,* Ctr. for Survivor Agency & Just. (Nov. 11, 2010), https://csaj.org/document-library/vondelinde2010.pdf.

  - ○ Adrienne Adams et al., *Debt in the Context of Safety: Coerced Debt & Debt Defenses for Survivors,* Ctr. for Survivor Agency & Just. (Apr. 29, 2016), https://csaj.org/calendar/view/149/.

  - ○ Fred Corbit, *Debt Prioritization and Collection Defense Resources*, Ctr. for Survivor Agency & Just. (Mar. 27, 2013), https://csaj.org/news/view/debt-prioritization-and-collection-defense-resources.

  - ○ *Debt Collection Agent Form Letter,* Ctr. for Survivor Agency & Just. (Mar. 25, 2013), https://csaj.org/library/view/debt-collection-agent-form-letter.

Chapter Thirteen:
Navigating Student Loans for Survivors

Persis Yu[1]

Reprinted from Center for Survivor Agency & Justice (CSAJ), Guidebook on Consumer & Economic Civil Legal Advocacy (2017), https://csaj.org/Guidebook.[2]

I. Introduction

Many survivors find themselves dealing with student loan debt. Currently, in the United States, roughly 43 million people owe around $1.5 trillion on their student loans. This makes student loan debt the second largest source of debt in the United States, just behind mortgages. Unfortunately, federal data show that more than one in four of these borrowers are delinquent or in default on their federal student loans.

There are extraordinary penalties for borrowers who go into default, and survivors of domestic violence may face particular challenges in repaying their loans and further risks to safety and future economic security once in default or when trying to resolve student loan issues. Thus, helping a survivor avoid default or get out of default may be important to their financial security.

---

[1] National Consumer Law Center (NCLC) intern Jessica Park provided substantial work and contributions to this chapter.

[2] A deeper dive into the case scenario described in this reprinted chapter can be found in CSAJ's Guidebook on Consumer & Economic Civil Legal Advocacy. Persis Yu, *Navigating Student Loan Solutions for Survivors*, *in* GUIDEBOOK ON CONSUMER & ECONOMIC CIVIL LEGAL ADVOCACY 96 (2017), https://csaj.org/Guidebook.

This chapter will provide an overview of the student loan system, summarize student loan problems domestic violence survivors may face, and outline factors and steps advocates should consider when guiding clients to the right solution to access, protect, and repay student loans.

Anne's Story

Anne took out a subsidized and an unsubsidized Stafford Loan and a Perkins loan to support her undergraduate education, but dropped out after one year of school when she became pregnant by her then-boyfriend, Ben. They are now married. Ben's abuse started shortly after the birth of their first child. He is their sole source of income, and they now have four children to support. Since leaving school, Anne has not been able to obtain a job due to Ben's abuse and her need to care for the children. After a recent physical assault by Ben, Anne fled to a shelter with her children. While helping her kids adjust she has also begun seeking employment.

Since her student loans came due for repayment, Anne has not been able to make consistent payments. Though she is not exactly sure when she made her last payments, Anne does not believe she is in default yet. Ben controls the finances, makes all the tax filings, keeps records of Anne's personal information (social security number, etc.), and has prevented Anne's access to such information in the past. Anne is unfamiliar with her financial or tax information and does not know how to access that information readily. She comes to you, hoping for help in getting a handle on all her finances. To make ends meet, she knows she may need to return to school in the future and so is worried about how to pay for her current loans.

Consider Anne's story as you think about the connection between abuse and student loans.

II. Domestic Violence and Student Loan Debt

Student loan debt is one of the largest sources of debt in the U.S. Survivors face unique risks of default, as well as challenges in resolving, paying off, and/or accessing new student loans.

Survivors trying to resolve student loan issues may face unique difficulties because of their abusive partners or because of their vulnerability as survivors. For example, survivors may have trouble accessing income-driven repayment plans not only due to lack of information about the plans, but also due to difficulty obtaining personal information, income information, or necessary documentation from or because of an abusive partner. Partners may also take out loans in survivors' name without their knowledge; when this happens, the survivor may not even know about the loans until they are in default. Survivors who have defaulted on their student loans face further financial hardship because the lender may seek repayment through involuntary collection.

Additionally, survivors may face extra challenges in repaying their loans. Survivors may be targets of predatory for-profit schools that recruit individuals who are vulnerable, unemployed, and/or low-income and that leave students with heavy debts and little improvement in economic mobility. A survivor who did not complete school may have extra difficulty in repaying these loans without a degree. A survivor may also be unable to repay these loans because the abusive partner withholds financial support and any income must pay for necessities (e.g., housing, food, supporting children).

Survivors may also find that they need to go back to school to support themselves and/or their families, or to escape a dangerous situation. However, borrowers in default on federal student loans are ineligible for federal financial aid, so survivors who want to go back to school may need help avoiding or getting out of default.

In-depth screening questions are provided later in this chapter to help determine the available solutions for a student loan borrower. However, before determining the solution, it is important to find out how the debt is currently impacting the survivor. For example, if the survivor is currently making payments, it is helpful to know whether those payments are affordable. If the survivor is not making payments, have there been any consequences such as harassing phone calls or garnished wages? Finally, what is the survivor's long-term goal? It might be to go back to school. If the borrower is the victim of identity theft, it might be to eliminate the loan. Or the borrower's main goal may be to resolve credit reporting problems caused by a defaulted student loan. The solution will vary depending on the borrower's goal.

A. The Impact of Student Loan Debt

The impact of student loan debt cuts across many domains of a survivor's financial and physical wellbeing. In a recent study, employment instability (reduced hours, changing jobs, trouble finding a job) lasted up to three years after an abusive relationship ended. Advancing educational attainment is often key to securing jobs or promotions that can provide for a family. Having a delinquent or defaulted loan can severely limit the options available to survivors. For example, borrowers in default are not eligible for federal financial aid, and are often targeted for predatory, high-cost lending.

Also, defaulted loans can impact a survivor's credit history. A negative credit history can make a survivor's life more difficult in many ways, negatively impacting applications for an apartment, car, or even a job.[3]

In the face of economic abuse and other debts, student loan debt presents a tough challenge to survivors' long-term options, with profound implications for their economic security and continued safety.

III. Key Terms and Concepts

A. Types of Federal Loans

Student loan law is riddled with terminology, and it is important to understand the basics. There are a number of types of federal student loans, which, with the exception of Perkins loans, may be either a Direct or Federal Family Education Loan (FFEL) loan. As the name indicates, a **Direct Loan** is a federal loan in which the federal government directly provides the funds. Direct Loans can take the form of a **Stafford**, Direct **PLUS**, or Direct **Consolidation** loan.

Stafford loans are available to undergraduate and graduate students and are subsidized or unsubsidized. Subsidized Stafford loans are awarded based on financial need, and borrowers are not charged interest before the repayment period begins. Unsubsidized Stafford loans are not awarded based on need, and interest is charged at the time the loan is disbursed. PLUS loans can be Parent or Grad PLUS loans, but the student must first be determined to be eligible for a Stafford loan. Parent PLUS loans allow parents to borrow for dependent undergraduate children, while grad PLUS loans allow graduate or professional students to borrow. In both cases, a credit check must be completed, and the borrower cannot have adverse credit history. A consolidation loan is created when a borrower consolidates all, some, or one of their existing student loans. Consolidation loans will be discussed later in the chapter.

One type of student loan, the **FFEL loan,** is no longer offered, but many borrowers took them out in the past and are still repaying them. With FFEL loans, the federal government guaranteed the loan but did not directly provide funding for the loan. Instead, the funds came from a non-governmental financial institution. FFEL loans also took the form of a Stafford, PLUS, or consolidation loan.

A **Perkins loan** is originated and serviced by the participating school, but the federal government provides money to the school to help fund the loans.

---

[3] For more information on the intersection of domestic violence and debt, see *Debt, Debt Defense, and Safety Considerations for Survivors* in Section Three of this manual; Katie VonDeLinde, *Building & Repairing Credit Reports: Understanding Options and Safety Implications for Survivors*, in Guidebook on Consumer & Economic Civil Legal Advocacy 30 (2017), https://csaj.org/Guidebook.

B. Repayment Options

Federal loan borrowers have many different repayment options as well as routes to postpone payment temporarily. **Income-driven repayment plans** are useful options for borrowers to reduce unsustainable monthly payments. These plans calculate monthly payments based on income and family size and forgive any outstanding balances after 20 to 25 years of repayment. There are several different income-driven repayment plans, often referred to by their acronyms: **IBR** (Income-Based Repayment), **PAYE** (Pay As You Earn), **REPAYE** (Revised Pay As You Earn), and **ICR** (Income-Contingent Repayment). Each has different terms and eligibility requirements, as discussed below.

Forbearance and **deferment** are options allowing a borrower to postpone or reduce monthly payments. When a subsidized loan is in a deferment, the borrower is not charged interest.

Generally, the most complete remedy a borrower can obtain on a student loan is **discharge** or **loan cancellation,** which forgives outstanding principal and interest amounts and in some cases, allows for refunds of amounts already paid by the borrower. The federal loan program includes several statutory loan cancellation programs, but it is difficult to qualify for a loan discharge.

In contrast to federal student loans, *private student loans* are ones made by banks and other financial institutions without federal guaranty. Private loans provide fewer protections and are not required to provide income-driven repayment plans, deferments, or discharges.

Borrowers will need to know the different entities responsible for their loans. The *loan holder* or *lender* is the entity or person holding the promissory note and has the right to collect on the loan. A *loan servicer* is a company responsible for collecting payments, responding to customer inquiries, and performing administrative tasks to maintain the loan on behalf of the lender. *Guaranty agencies* are state or private agencies that administer the federal guaranteed loan program. A *debt collector* is a third party who pursues a borrower in an attempt to collect on a defaulted loan.

Definition of Terms

Direct loan: A loan in which the federal government directly provides the funds. Common forms of Direct Loans are a Stafford, Direct PLUS, or Direct Consolidation loan.

FFEL loan: Loans that the federal government guaranteed but did not directly provide funding for the loan. They are no longer offered, but many borrowers took them out in the past and are still repaying them.

Income-driven repayment plans: Loan repayment plans that calculate monthly payments based on income and family size and forgive any outstanding balances after 20 to 25 years of repayment. Common plans include: IBR (Income-Based Repayment), PAYE (Pay As You Earn), REPAYE (Revised Pay As You Earn), and ICR (Income-Contingent Repayment).

Forbearance and deferment: Postponing or reducing monthly payments on a loan. When a subsidized loan is in a deferment, the borrower is not charged interest.

Discharge or loan cancellation: When the outstanding principal and interest amounts of loans are forgiven, and in some cases allows for refunds of amounts already paid by the borrower.

Private student loans: Loans made by banks and other financial institutions without federal guaranty.

Loan holder or lender: The entity or person holding the promissory note and has the right to collect on the loan.

Loan servicer: The company responsible for collecting payments, responding to customer inquiries, and performing administrative tasks to maintain the loan on behalf of the lender.

Guaranty agencies: State or private agencies that administer the federal guaranteed loan program.

Debt collector: A third party who pursues a borrower in an attempt to collect on a defaulted loan.

Delinquent or in default: When a borrower has missed payments on a student loan.

Collection: Methods to collect past due (delinquent) payments on loans, and may include involuntary methods such as seizing tax refunds, garnishing wages, and offsetting social security benefits, to recover unpaid loan amounts.

Consolidation: The process by which federal student loans can be combined or converted into a Direct Consolidation loan.

Rehabilitation: Taking a loan out of default by making nine on-time payments in agreed-upon amounts within 10 consecutive months.

IV. Key Legal Concepts

Student loan law can seem complicated, but understanding some of the key legal concepts can help advocates familiarize themselves with the system and better advise clients.

A. Loan Type and Related Protections

Figuring out the type(s) of student loan(s) the survivor has is the most important piece of information to obtain. Student loans for higher education can come in the form of federal or private loans, but federal loans are the most common. The most common types of federal loans are Stafford loans (which may be either subsidized or unsubsidized), PLUS loans (grad and parent), Perkins loans, and consolidation loans. Except for Perkins loans, these loans can be Direct Loans (made directly by the federal government) or FFEL Program loans (made by private lenders but guaranteed by the federal government). FFEL origination was eliminated as of July 1, 2010, but FFEL regulations continue to apply to outstanding FFEL loans, many of which are still serviced and held by FFEL lenders or guaranty agencies. Private loans are often made by banks or other financial institutions without financial backing by the federal government, and often require a co-signer.

Federal loans come with important protections for borrowers, including programs to repay the loans based on a percentage of the borrower's income, programs allowing the borrower to delay payment temporarily, and, in limited circumstances, programs to discharge the loans. These protections are crucial and generally make federal loans safer for borrowers than private loans. Unfortunately, federal loans are hard to escape. If a borrower defaults, the government may then utilize extraordinary powers to collect. The options for a federal loan borrower who is unable to repay differ based on both the type of loans and whether it is in default.

Since private loans are not subject to the rules governing federal loans, private loans provide fewer protections to borrowers. Additionally, private loans may have higher interest rates than federal loans, and the rates may be variable. Financially distressed borrowers are generally at the mercy of the creditor, and private lenders are generally inflexible in accommodating borrowers. Private lenders do not have the same range of collection tools as the government and will usually hire third-party debt collectors to pressure borrowers for repayment.

B. Loan Status and Consequences of Default

A key to understanding the borrower's options is to know the status of the loans. As will be discussed in this chapter, survivors in good standing on their loans should consider various repayment options. If a borrower has missed payments on a student loan, the loan may be either delinquent or in default.

A borrower is delinquent after missing the scheduled loan payments by the stipulated due dates. Once the borrower is delinquent for a certain period of time, the loan will be in default, and the entire loan balance becomes due at that time. For most federal loans, the period between delinquency and default is 270 days. For private loans, default will be determined by the terms of the promissory note.

Becoming delinquent on a student loan will negatively impact the borrower's credit history. Defaulting on a federal loan, however, has more serious consequences, and avoiding or getting out of default should be a top priority. Once a borrower defaults on a federal loan, the loan will likely be transferred to a private debt collection agency, at which point the borrower may be subjected to aggressive and sometimes illegal collection tactics. The government is also able to use involuntary collection methods, such as seizing tax refunds, garnishing wages, and offsetting social security benefits, to recover unpaid loan amounts. Furthermore, the borrower is ineligible for additional financial aid while in default, which is a problem for borrowers who need financial aid to continue their education. As will be discussed in further detail, some borrowers may be eligible to get out of default and into an affordable repayment plan.

C. Joint Consolidation Loans

Joint consolidation loans were created when married borrowers consolidated their loans with their spouses' loans, leaving both spouses jointly and severally liable for repayment of the total. The ability to jointly consolidate loans was eliminated in July 2006, but some borrowers still have joint consolidation loans. These loans pose special difficulties for domestic violence survivors because both spouses must cooperate to obtain relief—even if they have divorced and maintain separate finances and tax filings. For example, borrowers may repay joint consolidation loans under income-driven repayment plans, but both spouses must qualify for and request the same plan. Further, the loan servicer will determine eligibility and monthly payment amounts based on both spouses' combined income and eligible federal loans—again, even if they have divorced. A survivor who successfully discharges the portion of the joint consolidation loan they incurred for their education will still be liable for the remaining balance, incurred by a spouse. Unfortunately, there is no way to split a joint consolidation loan, but the Department of Education has encouraged borrowers facing domestic violence issues to contact the FSA Ombudsman to explore options in confidence.[4]

---

[4] *Frequently Asked Questions for Consumer Advocates and Counselors*, FED. STUDENT AID, https://ifap.ed.gov/eannouncements/attachments/ConsumerAdvocateFAQs.pdf (last updated Oct., 2015).

V. Understanding the Client's Situation

Though many student loan borrowers face similar issues, it is important to take an individualized approach to understanding the client's situation to find the best solution that weighs both physical and economic safety risks.

A. Assessing Student Loan Debt

Because of the complicated experiences and feelings surrounding debt for many survivors, advocacy to address student loan debt requires an open, honest, and sensitive assessment. The screening and assessment questions presented here are for issue spotting (often called, intake questions), are not meant to be prescriptive, and conversations around student loans should not be limited to these questions.[5]

The following information can help guide interactions with the survivor:

- Do you know what kind of loan(s) you have (and use the National Student Loan Data System (NSLDS) to confirm)?[6]

- What is the status of your loans (e.g., current, delinquent, default, in forbearance or deferment)? If the loan is a federal loan, the NSDLS will show its current status.

- How much do you still owe? What are the monthly payments? Do you remember the date of the last payment?

- [If the survivor is married]: Do or did you and your spouse file taxes jointly or separately? Who controls the household finances, tax filings, etc.?

- What is your current income, family size, and financial ability?

- Has the lender tried to seek repayment from you?

- Where and when did you go to school? Did you finish or have problems with the school?

---

[5] For a fuller description of a survivor centered approach to economic assessment, see *Economic Coercion and Survivor-Centered Economic Advocacy* in Section Three of this manual.

[6] The National Student Loan Data System (NSDLS) is a database run by the U.S. Department of Education compiling data from schools and various loan programs and can help identify what kind of federal loan a borrower has. Borrowers can access their federal student loan information online at *NSLDS Student Access: National Student Loan Data System,* Fed. Student Aid, https://www.nslds.ed.gov/nslds/nslds_SA/ (last visited May 2, 2018).
Note: The difference between federal and private loans is not always clear because the same lender may make both kinds of loans. Since the NSLDS only lists federal loans, determining that a loan is listed in the NSLDS is a way of verifying that it is a federal loan. The borrower's promissory note will also state the federal loan program under which the loan was extended if it is a federal loan.

- Are you trying to go back to school? Would you need more loans to do so? (If so, then avoiding or getting out of default is critical.)

- Have you ever filed for bankruptcy?

- Are you a veteran or do you have a disability?

Because private loans operate on the terms of their individual promissory notes, some of these general considerations may not be relevant, and advocates should closely read the loan agreement to determine next steps. Private loans will not show up on the borrower's NSLDS report. Though there is no official database of private loans, many will appear on the borrower's credit report.

Advocacy Tip: For survivors who have changed their name, especially those who have not engaged with their loans since being in school, many loan documents will be in the name used when the survivor was in school. Depending on the reason for the name change, this can be a sensitive issue for survivors.

VI. Remedies and Solutions for Federal Loans

A. Loan Discharge or Cancellation

Regardless of whether the borrower is in default, loan discharge should be considered first because it is the best option and provides the most complete remedy for borrowers. The primary discharge programs are related to school closure and certain school conduct, disability or death, profession, or repayment plans. School-related discharges are available in some limited circumstances, such as if the borrower was unable to complete an educational program because the school closed, or if the school falsely certified the borrower's eligibility for federal aid.

Additionally, a borrower may be able to raise a borrower defense to repayment premised on misconduct by the school that harmed the borrower—for example, if the school breached a contract with the borrower, or misrepresented job placement rates and the borrower relied on those placement rates when deciding to attend. A successful borrower defense may result in full or partial cancellation of the loan. As of this writing, the Department of Education is developing new rules governing borrower defenses, so this area is in flux.[7]

Applying for a federal loan discharge or borrower defense is free, and application forms are available through the Department of Education website or the borrower's loan servicer.

---

[7] For more information, see *Borrower Defenses,* Student Loan Borrower Assistance, http://www.studentloanborrowerassistance.org/loan-cancellation/school-related/borrower-defenses/ (last visited Apr. 17, 2018).

Advocacy Tip: The borrower may also consider seeking a discharge through bankruptcy. Declaring bankruptcy can protect borrower against collection actions on all debt for a period of time, but bankruptcy can have additional costs and remain part of the borrower's credit history. Furthermore, discharging student loans through bankruptcy is much more difficult than discharging other debt.[8]

B. Pre-Default Repayment

If the client is not yet in default, the next step is to consider pre-default repayment options, including income-driven repayment plans, which are often a desirable alternative to standard, graduated, or extended repayment plans for borrowers facing difficulty with their payments. Borrowers may also want to consider forbearance or deferment.

C. Standard, Graduated, and Extended Repayment Plans

Under the standard repayment plan, monthly payments will be the same amount for each installment period and will only change if there is a variable interest rate. Standard plans carry the highest monthly payments, and generally, borrowers must pay within five to ten years. Borrowers who do not select a different repayment plan within the allotted time period will be automatically assigned the standard repayment plan. Under the graduated repayment plan, monthly payments start out low and increase over the course of the repayment period. For most borrowers, income-driven repayment plans are a safer option because they base payments on actual income, rather than an expectation of reliable raises, and they reduce payments if income drops. The extended repayment plan applies to borrowers with a loan exceeding $30,000. Under this plan, the borrower may repay on either a fixed or graduated scale for longer than 10 years, but no more than 30 years.

Advocacy Tip: Beware of "Student Loan Relief" companies. Predatory companies have targeted borrowers, particularly low-income and vulnerable borrowers, by claiming to provide a service to aid borrowers in applying for reduced loan payments. These companies often charge excessive fees and may falsely hold themselves out to be authorized agents of the federal government. Applying for reduced loan payments on a federal student loan is free, and can be done online using the Department of Education's website or with help from the borrower's loan servicer. Similarly, applying for a federal loan discharge is free. Be wary of any company your client may have paid to aid in applying for relief.

---

[8] For more information on discharging loans under bankruptcy, see DEANNE LOONIN ET AL., NAT'L CONSUMER L. CTR., *Discharging Student Loans in Bankruptcy, in* STUDENT LOAN LAW 191 (5th ed. 2015); Karen Merrill Tjapkes & Sarah Bolling Mancini, *Bankruptcy & Alternatives for Survivors, in* GUIDEBOOK ON CONSUMER & ECONOMIC CIVIL LEGAL ADVOCACY 112 (2017), https://csaj.org/Guidebook.

D. Income-Driven Repayment Plans

Income-driven repayment plans calculate the borrower's monthly loan repayment using income and family size. The Department of Education's income-driven repayment plan selection form includes the option to place the borrower on the plan with the lowest monthly payment of the income-driven plans for which the borrower qualifies. Though lower payments under income-driven repayment plans mean borrowers may take longer to pay off loans, this is preferable to the consequences of default. There are currently four main income-driven repayment options:

- Income Based Repayment (IBR);

- Pay As You Earn (PAYE);

- Revised Pay As You Earn (REPAYE); and

- Income Contingent Repayment (ICR) plans.

IBR, PAYE, and REPAYE are the three newest and most generous plans for borrowers. All three plans calculate payments at 10 or 15 percent of the borrower's discretionary income (see table below). For these repayment plans, discretionary income is defined as adjusted gross income in excess of 150 percent of the poverty guidelines. After 20 or 25 years of repayment, any remaining balance will be forgiven. (These forgiven amounts are currently treated as taxable income.) Under each of the three plans, the borrower's calculated monthly payment will be $0 if the borrower's adjusted gross income is below 150 percent of the poverty guideline. In our case scenario, since Anne is not currently working and does not appear to have any taxable income, she is likely to qualify for a $0 monthly payment. This means that although she will not be making payments on her loans, her failure to pay will not be considered default, and she will accrue time in the repayment plan that will count toward forgiveness.

Subtle differences may influence which of these three plans is likely to be best for a given borrower.[9]

---

[9] For more details on the comparison of REPAYE, PAYE, and IBR, see DEANNE LOONIN ET AL., NAT'L CONSUMER L. CTR., § 3.3.3.9 *Considerations for Borrowers Eligible for Multiple Income-Driven Plans, in* STUDENT LOAN LAW 49 (5th ed. 2015).

Plan	Repayment Calculation
Pre-July 2014 IBR	Lesser of 15 percent of discretionary income or monthly payments the borrower would have made under the standard repayment plan as of the date the borrower entered plan.
PAYE	Lesser of 10 percent of discretionary income or monthly payments the borrower would have made under the standard repayment plan as of the date the borrower entered plan.
REPAYE	10 percent of discretionary income.

ICR plans are primarily useful for borrowers who had parent PLUS loans and consolidated them into Direct consolidation loans. Monthly payments on ICR are usually higher than the other income-driven repayment plans. Balances are forgiven after 25 years of repayment.

Eligibility for income-driven repayment plans varies and is based on (1) the type of loan, (2) when the loan was originated, and (3) whether the borrower has partial financial hardship. Importantly, parent PLUS loans are not eligible for any of these plans.[10]

For all income-driven repayment plans, borrowers must annually recertify their income and family size so the monthly payment amount can be readjusted as necessary each year. Borrowers may also request their loan servicer to recalculate the monthly payment amount at any time based on a loss of income or increase in family size. Failing to recertify on time annually may lead to negative consequences, including an abrupt increase in monthly payments and capitalization of accrued interest.

Advocacy Tip: It is important for survivors, especially those who are in a shelter or otherwise in an unstable housing situation, to understand these consequences and to have a plan in place to ensure that they can receive their loan notices. In some circumstances, a survivor's inability to receive loan notices may mean that an income-driven repayment plan is not a viable option.

Borrowers may apply for income-driven repayment plans on the StudentLoans.gov website or by sending in a paper form that can be obtained from the borrower's loan servicer. Unfortunately, applying for an income-driven repayment plan can be complicated for survivors, especially for survivors like

---

[10] The Institute for College Access and Success created a summary chart to help borrowers understand the various income-driven repayment plans. *Summary of Income-Driven Repayment Plans*, Inst. for Coll. Access & Success, https://ticas.org/sites/default/files/pub_files/existing_idr_options.pdf (last updated Dec. 17, 2015).

Anne who do not have access to important financial documents. Survivors who are separated from their spouses or file taxes separately should take note of some differences in the repayment plans. For married borrowers who file taxes separately from their spouses, under IBR and PAYE, only the borrower's own individual income is be considered. REPAYE generally considers both the borrower's and spouse's income and eligible student debt, although the Department of Education allows individualized treatment for borrowers who certify that they are either separated from their spouses or are unable to reasonably access their spouses' income information—a common circumstance in domestic violence situations. A borrower whose sole source of income is public assistance can certify that they have no taxable income and will have a $0 monthly payment.[11]

Public Comments to U.S. Department of Education on Student Loans for Married Borrowers

CSAJ and the National Consumer Law Center (NCLC) partnered to provide comments to the U.S. Department of Education (DOE) regarding married survivors' experiences with student loan debt when the DOE was formulating the REPAYE plan. This resulted in the exception for survivors to continue filing taxes as "married filing separately" and qualify for the income-based repayment plan.[12]

---

[11] For more detailed information on the various income-driven repayment plans and how to apply, see DEANNE LOONIN ET AL., NAT'L CONSUMER L. CTR., *Pre-Default Repayment Options, in* STUDENT LOAN LAW 39 (5th ed. 2015); *Income-Driven Repayment Options*, STUDENT LOAN BORROWER ASSISTANCE, http://www.studentloanborrowerassistance.org/repayment/federal-loans/payment-plans/income-based-options/ (last visited Apr. 17, 2018). The Department of Education also maintains helpful information about federal student loan repayment options. *See generally* FED. STUDENT AID, https://studentloans.gov (last visited Apr. 17, 2018); *Income-Driven Repayment Plans*, FED. STUDENT AID, https://studentaid.ed.gov/sa/sites/default/files/income-driven-repayment-q-and-a.pdf (last updated Feb., 2016). The Department of Education online repayment estimator is a tool allowing borrowers to estimate their monthly payments under different payment plans using their FSA ID (or estimates of their loan balances and rates) and income. *Repayment Estimator*, FED. STUDENT AID, https://studentloans.gov/myDirectLoan/mobile/repayment/repaymentEstimator.action (last visited Apr. 17, 2018). Borrowers must use their Federal Student Aid (FSA) ID to access the Department of Education's FSA online systems, including NSLDS and online applications for income-driven repayment plans and loan consolidation. Borrowers can create or recover their FSA ID online. *Create a New FSA ID*, FED. STUDENT AID, https://fsaid.ed.gov/npas/index.htm (last visited Apr. 17, 2018).

[12] ZOE FLOWERS ET AL., SHOWING UP: HOW WE SEE, SPEAK, AND DISRUPT RACIAL INEQUITY FACING SURVIVORS OF DOMESTIC AND SEXUAL VIOLENCE (2018), https://csaj.org/document-library/REEP_Report_Showing_Up_FINAL.pdf.

Advocacy Tip: When discussing the repayment options, note the implications of the survivor's tax filing and discuss the option of certifying the survivor's separation or inability to obtain information.[13]

E. Postponement Options

As in Anne's case, a borrower who is not yet in default may also consider postponing repayment as an alternative to a repayment plan. Deferments or forbearances are postponement options, and both carry qualification requirements and different implications for accruing interest.

Deferments, which allow the borrower to postpone loan repayments, are available in limited circumstances. The grounds for deferment that are most likely to be relevant to survivors are that the borrower is currently in school, is unemployed, or faces economic hardship. Deferment is an option only for borrowers not yet in default. Deferment can be particularly useful because interest will not accrue on subsidized loans or Perkins loans during the deferment period. However, interest will still accrue on all other federal loans.

If Anne was to apply and qualify for deferments, her subsidized and Perkins loans would not accrue interest, but her unsubsidized loan would.

Each deferment can be granted for up to six months, and the borrower must reapply to extend the deferment after the deferment period expires. Deferments generally carry maximum time limits. For example, a borrower may not obtain more than three years' worth of economic hardship deferments.[14]

If Anne does not qualify for deferment, she may need to consider forbearance instead. Forbearance is a tool for borrowers to postpone or reduce payments if financial distress is not likely to last long.[15] During forbearance, interest will continue to accrue on all loans. Similar to deferment, forbearance is a method of postponing payment, but can also be a means of gaining an extension on payments or making smaller payments. For borrowers not yet in default, forbearance can delay going into default. Forbearance is also available to borrowers even if the 270-day default threshold has been passed, as long as the loan has not been transferred to a guaranty agency or collector. A borrower who was on an income-driven

---

[13] For more on tax filing status and tax related issues, see Jamie Andree, *Tax Advocacy for Survivors, in* Guidebook on Consumer & Economic Civil Legal Advocacy 143 (2017), https://csaj.org/Guidebook.

[14] The borrower may reach out to the loan servicer to obtain a deferment form or access most of the forms on NCLC's Student Loan Borrower Assistance. *Forms,* Student Loan Borrower Assistance, http://www.studentloanborrowerassistance.org/resources/referral-resource/important-forms/ (last visited Apr. 17, 2018).

[15] For more information on repayment postponement options, see Deanne Loonin et al., Nat'l Consumer L. Ctr., *Postponing Repayment on Federal Student Loans, in* Student Loan Law 53 (5th ed. 2015).

repayment plan but did not recertify in time may be able to obtain a forbearance that will prevent the loan from going into default during the gap while the monthly payment is recalculated based on the late recertification. A forbearance can also be backdated to cure a delinquency.

Advocacy Tip: Advocates should be aware that borrowers may be steered into a deferment or forbearance. These can be administratively easier for servicers to complete. On the surface, a deferment or forbearance may seem more relevant to the borrower's circumstances. For example, Anne may be tempted to apply for an economic hardship forbearance or an unemployment forbearance. But in many cases, an income-driven repayment plan will be more favorable, especially in the long-term. For low-income borrowers, monthly payments may be $0, and thus will provide the same benefit as a deferment or forbearance, while also allowing the borrower to accrue time toward the 20 or 25 year forgiveness period.

F. Getting Out of Default

Assume Anne is not eligible for loan discharge, and she is unable to resolve her student loan issues. More than 270 days pass from Anne's last payment, and she is now in default. The next step is to consider Anne's options to get out of default—specifically, **consolidation** or **rehabilitation**. Once Anne is out of default, she may access the various repayment plan options discussed above.

Consolidation is the process by which federal student loans can be combined or converted into a Direct Consolidation loan.[16] The newly consolidated loan is considered a new loan and offers a fresh start by getting the borrower out of default. The borrower must also elect to either (1) make three consecutive reasonable and affordable payments (which will be based on the borrower's total financial circumstances), or (2) agree to select an income-driven repayment plan for repayment of the new consolidation loan. Most borrowers will select an income-driven repayment plan and will thus be eligible for a prompt consolidation. If the loans the borrower wishes to consolidate are subject to judgment or wage garnishment, the judgment or garnishment must be vacated or lifted, respectively, before the borrower can pursue consolidation.

A borrower can also **rehabilitate** a loan out of default by making nine on-time payments in agreed-upon amounts within 10 consecutive months. The borrower will generally need to provide income information to the loan holder to determine the payment amount, generally set at 15 percent of discretionary income (the pre-2014 IBR formula), subject to a minimum payment of $5 per month. If the payment amount using the 15 percent formula is not affordable, borrowers can request that the amount be based upon their income and expenses. However, the borrowers should be aware that the monthly payment amount after getting out of default will

---

[16] Most forms are available in both English and Spanish. However, consolidation applications are currently only available in English.

likely be 10 or 15 percent of discretionary income. Notably, loans rehabilitated on or after August 14, 2008 cannot be rehabilitated again. Therefore, before choosing rehabilitation, the borrower should ensure that the repayment plan after getting out of default will be affordable. As with consolidation, loans that are subject to a judgment are not eligible to be rehabilitated.

If a borrower's wages are being garnished while also making monthly payments on that same loan under a loan rehabilitation agreement, the loan holder must continue collecting the loan by garnishment until the borrower makes five qualifying payments under the rehabilitation agreement. In our scenario, if Anne is experiencing a wage garnishment but also wants to rehabilitate her loans, she may not be able to afford to pay 15 percent of her discretionary income. To resolve this problem, Anne can request that her rehabilitation payment be based upon her income and expenses. This calculation would consider the garnishment in the calculation of her expenses.

Consolidation and rehabilitation both offer benefits and drawbacks that borrowers should carefully weigh in light of their circumstances. Consolidation tends to be a faster and more reliable means of getting out of default than rehabilitation. However, some borrowers will be ineligible to consolidate out of default, for example, if they have already consolidated all of their federal loans into a Direct Consolidation loan. Some borrowers may prefer rehabilitation because, unlike consolidation, rehabilitation removes the loan default from the borrower's credit history (though it does not remove missed payments or other negative history associated with the defaulted loans).[17]

Additionally, borrowers with parent PLUS loans should be careful when consolidating because if the borrower consolidates a parent PLUS loan with other federal student loans, the PLUS loan "taints" the entire consolidation loan and renders it ineligible for IBR, PAYE, or REPAYE.

With both consolidation and rehabilitation, collection fees may be added to the principal balance. However, currently, loans held by the government are not charged collection fees for rehabilitation.[18]

---

[17] For a comparison of rehabilitation and consolidation, see *Should I Consolidate or Rehabilitate My Federal Student Loan?*, STUDENT LOAN BORROWER ASSISTANCE, http://www. studentloanborrowerassistance.org/wp-content/uploads/2013/05/information-sheet.pdf (last visited May 7, 2018).

[18] For more information on consolidation and rehabilitation, see DEANNE LOONIN ET AL., NAT'L CONSUMER L. CTR., *Repayment Strategies for Getting Out of Federal Student Loan Default, in* STUDENT LOAN LAW 79 (5th ed. 2015); *Getting out of Default*, STUDENT LOAN BORROWER ASSISTANCE, http://www.studentloanborrowerassistance.org/collections/federal-loans/getting-out-of-default-federal/ (last visited Apr. 17, 2018).

G. Collections

As previously mentioned, the federal government has extraordinary powers to collect on student loans. For example, the government may use administrative wage garnishment or seize tax refunds to collect defaulted federal student loans. Borrowers can challenge these collection actions, but timing is critical. Borrowers should check all notices to determine whether it is possible to request a hearing in time to prevent a collection action. Borrowers can request a hearing at any time, but if the request is made after the deadline on the notice, the collection action will occur until the resolution of the hearing.

A borrower who does not have any money or property that can be legally taken to pay the debt is collection-proof. However, the federal government has such extraordinary collection powers—including interception of tax refunds and offset of certain government benefits—that it is rare for a student loan debtor to be completely collection-proof.

Advocacy Tip: Note, there is no statute of limitations on the government collecting on defaulted federal loans. Therefore, even if a client is collection-proof, circumstances could change so that they may not be collection proof in the future. If Anne receives a notice indicating that her tax refund is subject to offset, she may be tempted to ignore this notice because Ben claimed the kids on his return and she is not expecting a refund this year. However, next year, she is expecting to work and have custody of the kids and will likely have a sizable refund that includes the Earned Income Tax Credit. The notice for tax offsets applies to future tax years as well, so ignoring the notice will jeopardize that future refund.

The federal government and FFEL loan guarantee agencies rely heavily on private collection agencies, which may also employ more "traditional" collection efforts, including making collection calls and sending collection letters. The involvement of private collection agencies may confuse borrowers as to who to contact regarding their loans and has also been found to foster abusive debt collection practices. Information about which private collection agency is collecting on a federal student loan can be obtained from the Department of Education's Default Resolution Group (DRG) for loans held by the Department or, for FFEL loans, the guaranty agency identified on NSLDS. Borrowers can find contact information for DRG or their guaranty agency on the NSLDS report. When seeking to get out of default on a loan being collected by a private collection agency, borrowers or their advocates will generally need to deal with that agency to enter a rehabilitation agreement. If consolidating out of default, borrowers can apply directly online.[19]

H. Private Loans

Private loans can go into default as soon as a borrower misses a payment. The borrower should check what, if any, default conditions and grace periods are specified in the loan contract. Options for the borrower will differ based on the terms of the loan agreement. For example, some lenders may offer forbearance, deferment, or discharge options. However, borrowers should be aware that private lenders may charge fees if the borrower calls upon any such option.[20]

Advocacy Tips:

- If the borrower is in default, the next step is to try and negotiate with the lender, unless the borrower has a legal claim or defense against the lender or entity collecting on the loan.

- Private loans may not be consolidated into a Direct Consolidation loan.

- The borrower may have claims or defenses against the lender or collector, including claims that the statute of limitations has expired, the entity collecting on the loan has no authority to do so, or the lender is liable for school misconduct. Importantly, making a payment on a loan will reset the statute of limitations in many states.

- If a private collection agency is used, borrowers may have claims under the Fair Debt Collections Practices Act.

VII. Additional and Unique Considerations for Survivors

Domestic violence survivors may face unique complications when trying to address student loan issues. Because abusive partners may have controlled the finances and tax filings, survivors may have limited understanding or knowledge of income information. This can impede or slow the process for a survivor trying to apply for available remedies. Survivors may also face real barriers to

---

[19] *See generally* FED. STUDENT AID, https://studentloans.gov (last visited Apr. 17, 2018). For more information on the collection process, the major collection players, possible defenses to student loan collection lawsuits, and possible fair debt collection claims, see DEANNE LOONIN ET AL., NAT'L CONSUMER L. CTR., STUDENT LOAN LAW 93–190, 245–322 (5th ed. 2015) (Chapters 8, 9, 12, and 13). For additional debt collection and defense strategies, see *Debt, Debt Defense, and Safety Considerations for Survivors* in Section Three of this manual.

[20] For more on private student loan relief, see DEANNE LOONIN ET AL., NAT'L CONSUMER L. CTR., *Private Student Loans, in* STUDENT LOAN LAW 245 (5th ed. 2015). The Consumer Financial Protection Bureau also provides a student loan assistance tool to help guide analysis of private loans *Repay Student Debt*, CONSUMER FIN. PROT. BUREAU, https://www.consumerfinance.gov/paying-for-college/repay-student-debt/ (last visited Apr. 18, 2018).

accessing documentation or information. A survivor who is still married to the abusive partner and files taxes jointly may encounter difficulty getting spousal information or signatures for income-driven repayment plan applications or accessing money for payments.

A survivor experiencing housing instability may also have issues receiving critical information or notifications. Since all the income-driven repayment plans, deferments, and forbearances need to be annually renewed or recertified, it is important for the survivor to stay in contact with the lender. For federal loans, the survivor should contact the loan servicer with updated address information and should consider signing up for electronic communications if appropriate. Some survivors may opt to have their mail sent to friends and family. Borrowers should always assess the risks of putting their current address on any document.[21]

Survivors who are in repayment or are delinquent should work hard to stay out of default. Survivors in default, however, need to be realistic about their capacity, especially if they are collection-proof. While there are many options available to borrowers, many of the affordable repayment plans require a borrower to be proactive for several years in order to stay in good standing on the loan. Failing to follow through can result in re-defaulting. Unfortunately, re-defaulting can be worse than staying in default because consolidation and rehabilitation are only available one time.

VIII. Conclusion

Because the student loan system can be difficult to understand and navigate, student loan issues can become another burden and keep survivors from moving forward. By helping survivors understand and address the situation, advocates can help survivors tackle the problem and move on.

---

[21] For tips on setting up confidential mailing addresses for survivors, see *Debt, Debt Defense, and Safety Considerations for Survivors* in Section Three of this manual.

APPENDIX

Resources:

- **The Center for Survivor Agency and Justice**
  - *Public Comments to U.S. Department of Education on Student Loans for Married Borrowers*, CTR. FOR SURVIVOR AGENCY AND JUSTICE, https://csaj.org/library/view/testimony-to-u.s.-department-of-education-on-student-loans-for-married-borr.

- **The Consumer Financial Protection Bureau**
  - *Repay Student Debt*, CONSUMER FIN. PROT. BUREAU, http://www.consumerfinance.gov/paying-for-college/repay-student-debt.

- **Federal Student Aid, The U.S. Department of Education,** https://studentloans.gov
  - *Consumer Advocate FAQs*, FED. STUDENT AID, U.S. DEP'T OF EDUC., http://ifap.ed.gov/eannouncements/attachments/ConsumerAdvocateFAQs.pdf.
  - *Glossary*, FED. STUDENT AID, U.S. DEP'T OF EDUC., https://studentaid.ed.gov/sa/glossary#Federal_Student_Aid_Programs.
  - *Income-Driven Repayment Plans: Questions and Answers* (Feb. 2016), FED. STUDENT AID, U.S. DEP'T OF EDUC., https://studentaid.ed.gov/sa/sites/default/files/income-driven-repayment-q-and-a.pdf.
  - *National Student Loan Data System*, FED. STUDENT AID, U.S. DEP'T OF EDUC., https://www.nslds.ed.gov/.
  - *Repayment Estimator*, FED. STUDENT AID, U.S. DEP'T OF EDUC., https://studentloans.gov/myDirectLoan/mobile/repayment/repaymentEstimator.action.

- **The Institute for College Access & Success**
  - *Summary of Income-Driven Repayment Plans*, INST. FOR COLL. ACCESS & SUCCESS, http://ticas.org/sites/default/files/pub_files/existing_idr_options.pdf.

- **The National Consumer Law Center**
  - NAT'L CONSUMER L. CTR., STUDENT LOAN LAW (5th ed. 2015), https://library.nclc.org.
  - *Student Loan Borrower Assistance*, NAT'L CONSUMER L. CTR., http://www.studentloanborrowerassistance.org/.

For more referral resources, see NCLC's Student Loan Borrower Assistance referral page (http://www.studentloanborrowerassistance.org/resources/referral-resource/important-forms/), or reference the contact list (https://ifap.ed.gov/docs/CallQRef.pdf) maintained by the Department of Education for various service centers. If the client has difficulty understanding English, language assistance services for public information can be reached by emailing Ed.Language.Assistance@ed.gov or by calling 1-800-872-5327.

Chapter Fourteen:
Bankruptcy Law and Domestic Violence

I. Introduction

Economic abuse can take many forms. Frequently, victims are prevented from working, or from keeping or controlling their own earnings. Economic abuse may involve the abuser preventing the victim from obtaining immigration status and thus work authorization. The abuser may also impede education or training, or interfere with the victim's employment by stalking them at work or causing the victim to miss work. Abusers use numerous tactics designed to prevent their victims from realizing their full earning potential. Additionally, abusers often withhold information about the household finances and do not allow victims to participate equally in financial decision-making. Many abusers place all the household assets in their own name (or in the names of their family members or friends), while amassing debts under the victim's name. This leaves the victim with few resources, in addition to a poor credit rating. There are also many cases in which an abuser has coerced a victim into co-signing a loan or putting charges on a credit card in the victim's name. The economic abuse experienced by domestic violence victims can have a devastating long-term impact on their ability to free themselves from abuse and gain economic self-sufficiency.[1]

Economic security is a crucial component of ensuring victim safety. In order for a victim to separate from their abuser, the long-term consequences of economic abuse must be addressed and resolved. Attorneys working with

---

[1] *See* Off. of Manhattan Borough President Scott M. Stringer, Sakhi for South Asian Women & The Worker Inst. at Cornell, Economic Abuse: The Untold Cost of Domestic Violence (Oct. 2012), *available at* https://www.ilr.cornell.edu/sites/ilr.cornell.edu/files/Economic-Abuse-Untold-Cost-of-DV. pdf.

victims of domestic violence should recognize the importance of undertaking an economic needs assessment with their clients. One major area to address is both your client's and the abuser's debts.[2] Bankruptcy can affect victims either if they need to file for bankruptcy to address the crippling debt accumulated due to economic abuse, of if their abusers file for bankruptcy. This chapter will discuss both scenarios.

Filing bankruptcy can help a person by discarding debt or making a debt repayment plan. A bankruptcy case normally begins when the debtor files a petition with the bankruptcy court. A petition may be filed by an individual, by spouses together, or by a corporation or other entity. All bankruptcy cases are handled in federal courts under rules outlined in the U.S. Bankruptcy Code.

There are different types of bankruptcies, which are usually referred to by their chapter in the U.S. Bankruptcy Code. The types that most frequently arise for DV victims are those involving individuals, and sometimes those involving businesses.

Different Types of Bankruptcy

The Bankruptcy Code provides two types of individual bankruptcy proceedings: Chapter 7 and Chapter 13. Under Chapter 7, a debtor can seek an immediate discharge of debts by relinquishing non-exempt assets to creditors. In Chapter 13 bankruptcy proceedings, a payment plan is created by which the debtor retains assets but makes payments to creditors for a period of years, and the debts remaining after compliance with the payment plan are discharged. There are also special bankruptcy processes for family farmers and fishermen (Chapter 12) and for business reorganization (Chapter 11).

II. Bankruptcy as a Tool to Assist Victims

If the abuser and victim were married at the time the debts were accrued, the victim may ask the court to hold the abuser accountable for the repayment of the debts as part of a divorce action. However, there are cases in which victims cannot recoup the money to pay their debts from their abusers. One example is when an abuser fails to compensate the victim, even though there is a court order requiring the abuser to do so. If the abuser does not have any assets that can easily be seized to satisfy the debt, the debt will continue to accrue interest, harming the victim's credit rating. In addition, a savvy abuser is likely to avoid

---

[2] *See* Leah A. Plunkett & Erika A. Sussman, *Consumer Rights Screening Tool for Domestic Violence Advocates and Lawyers,* 45 Clearinghouse Rev. 488, 489 (2012), *available at* https://scholars.unh.edu/cgi/viewcontent.cgi?article=1087&context=law_facpub; Wider Opportunities for Women, Getting Started: A Handbook to Address Economic Security for Survivors (2012), *available at* https://iwpr.org/wp-content/uploads/2017/01/Getting-Started-A-Handbook-to-Address-Economic-Security-for-Survivors.pdf.

having their bank accounts frozen by placing their money in an account under a third party's name. Victims who are seeking to achieve financial independence may have their efforts thwarted when their new accounts are frozen by creditors.

If the abuser and victim were not married at the time the debts were accrued, it is unlikely that the victim will be able to recover money from the abuser to cover the victim's debts. Civil suits against the abuser are possible, but proof that the abuser is responsible for the debt can be difficult to obtain.

Victims who have a great number of debts in their name and insufficient means to pay off those debts find themselves in a vicious cycle in which interest continues to pile up, and getting out of debt becomes more and more an impossibility. Their vehicles may be repossessed, their homes foreclosed upon, and their wages garnished. Bad credit can prevent victims from obtaining necessary educational and home loans, and may even disqualify them from obtaining a lease to rent an apartment. Already traumatized because of the domestic violence, victims who owe money to creditors then suffer additional harassment from debt collectors. For many victims, the only way to curb the ballooning debt and stop the collection calls is to file for bankruptcy.

Advocacy Tip: Domestic violence attorneys can screen their clients to determine whether filing bankruptcy is a viable and appropriate option.[3] You should review your client's income and expenses, debts, the nature of the debts (to determine whether they are debts that may not be dischargeable), and assets. You may then be able to assist the victim to determine whether their property or income is subject to collection efforts by creditors. Your client will need help evaluating whether bankruptcy will provide the relief they need. Your client must also consider the timing of the bankruptcy. There are some cases in which immediate filing is advantageous, such as staying a foreclosure action or to recover property that was seized by a creditor. In other cases where there is no reason to file immediately, and your client is likely to continue amassing more debt, it may be strategically advantageous to delay filing until a later date.

Clients who then want to proceed with filing for bankruptcy should be referred to a legal services agency that handles bankruptcy cases or *pro bono* attorney from a private law firm that handles bankruptcy cases.

A. Joint Bankruptcy Filings

11 U.S.C. § 302(a) gives married couples the right to file a joint bankruptcy petition. This is based upon the family law premise that married couples are in an economic partnership, meaning that they are jointly liable for their debts, and

---

[3]   *See* Karen Merrill Tjapkes & Sarah Bolling Mancini, *Bankruptcy & Alternatives for Survivors, in* Guidebook on Consumer & Economic Civil Legal Advocacy 98 (2017), https://csaj.org/Guidebook.

own most of their property together.[4] Filing a joint petition saves on legal fees and time spent in court, as one spouse can attend court without the other. Unmarried couples who are economically linked are unable to take advantage of filing a joint petition.[5] One result of marriage equality was the right for same-sex couples to jointly file for bankruptcy.[6] In cases in which a parent and child or other unrelated individuals have attempted to file jointly, the courts either dismissed the petition of one individual, required that one party remove herself or himself from the petition, or bifurcated the case into two separate cases.[7]

B. Individual Filings

If parties are unmarried, they must file as individuals. Some married debtors may also choose to file individually rather than jointly with their spouse. For example, if one spouse owns valuable property that would have to be sold in a chapter 7 bankruptcy, it may be desirable for that spouse to not file bankruptcy, thus avoiding the loss of that asset to creditors. In the case of parties filing individually, parties must determine which debts are in their name as they are individually liable only for debts in their own name, and not those in their spouse's name only.

To file jointly, both spouses need to consent to the filing. In cases in which cooperation between the spouses is not feasible, such as cases where domestic violence is involved, filing individually may be the only feasible option. It is important to note that one spouse's individually filed bankruptcy does not discharge the other spouse's liability for a joint debt. The non-filing joint borrower remains responsible for the debt after it has been discharged as to the borrower who filed for bankruptcy.

---

[4] *See* A. Mechele Dickerson, *Family Values and the Bankruptcy Code: A Proposal to Eliminate Bankruptcy Benefits Awarded on the Basis of Marital Status*, 67 FORDHAM L. REV. 69 (1998) (critiquing the requirement that a couple be married to file a joint bankruptcy petition).

[5] Courts have allowed cases filed separately by unmarried couples with shared living expenses to be jointly administered after they were filed. *See* In re Malone, 50 B.R. 2, 3 (Bankr. E.D. Mich. 1985); In re Coles, 14 B.R. 5, 6 (Bankr. E.D. Pa. 1981).

[6] The Defense of Marriage Act (DOMA) prohibited the federal government from recognizing same-sex marriage, irrespective of whether state law allowed same-sex marriage. The Supreme Court overturned Section 3 of DOMA on June 26, 2013 in United States v. Windsor, 133 S. Ct. 2675 (2013), allowing same-sex couples to enjoy many federal benefits allowed for married couples, including the right to file a joint bankruptcy petition.

[7] *See, e.g.*, In re Stancil, 473 B.R. 478, 480–485 (D.C. 2012) (treating an attempted joint filing by debtor with his mother as two separate bankruptcy cases and dismissing the mother's due to ineligibility); *see also* In re Lam, 98 B.R. 965, 966 (W.D. Mo. 1988) (finding that joint filings can only be done by spouses and requiring one filer to remove herself as a party where a mother and her minor daughter jointly filed to discharge medical debt which creditors were attempted to collect from both of them); *see also* In re Lucero, 408 B.R. 348, 349 (C.D. Cal. 2009); *see also* In re Wilkerson, 2006 Bankr. LEXIS 3392 (M.D. Ga. 2006).

States have differing laws regarding whether individual creditors can reach property held as tenants by the entirety.[8] If a state recognizes tenants by the entirety, when one spouse is sued for an unpaid debt that was contracted solely in the name of that spouse, the creditor cannot force the sale of the property or place a lien against it, because it is also owned by the other spouse. The Bankruptcy Code incorporates the states' definition of tenancy by the entirety to shield such property from creditors. Therefore, in most states, creditors cannot take a property unless they have a claim against both spouses.

III. Bankruptcy Used by Abusers

One way in which a victim may be negatively affected by bankruptcy is when the abuser files for bankruptcy without any notification to the victim. If the abuser's debts that are jointly held with the victim are discharged in bankruptcy, creditors will still be able to collect the debt against the victim co-borrower to satisfy the outstanding debt. If the parties are married, the victim may be able to obtain relief in a divorce action to address the resulting inequity. For example, if the abusive spouse has discharged the debts in bankruptcy, the victim may still be able to get the family law court in which the divorce case is pending to take the debt remaining in the victim's name into account when determining the appropriate distribution of assets and debts.

In addition, abusers frequently threaten to file for bankruptcy to avoid paying money owed to their victims in maintenance, child support, or equitable distribution of marital property in the context of a divorce action, even when the debts are non-dischargeable. Such threats can take a serious emotional toll upon victims in need of these funds to rebuild their lives after separating from their abusers.

The filing of a bankruptcy petition stays the commencement or continuation of any state or federal litigation.[9] While the application of the stay in bankruptcy proceedings to family law actions is subject to a specific state's statutory and case law, many states have adopted certain exceptions to the stay of family law proceedings, such as divorces. For example, even if the stay applies to distribution of assets that might be in dispute in a divorce action, it may not prevent the court from awarding certain *pendente lite* relief such as temporary maintenance, child support, and custody. In addition, criminal contempt proceedings and civil contempt for nonpayment of support also may not be

---

[8] When married couples hold title to property together, each spouse individually owns the entire property as a "tenant by the entirety." The spouses are treated as a single legal entity. Some states reserve this type of ownership to real estate only (with one limiting it to the "homestead" and not investment real estate), while others apply it to all types of property.

[9] U.S. Bankr. Code, 11 U.S.C. § 362(a).

estopped by the automatic stay in a bankruptcy action.[10] Therefore, bankruptcy cannot be used by an abuser to avoid actions to enforce support orders.

Section 523(a)(5) of the Bankruptcy Code and the case law interpreting it establish an exception to a discharge of debts in bankruptcy proceedings when the debt is to a spouse, former spouse, or child of the debtor when the debt relates to alimony, maintenance, or support.

The bankruptcy court determines whether financial awards in divorce actions are debts subject to dischargeability. The analysis of the bankruptcy court generally hinges upon whether the award is "in the nature of support" to the debtor's spouse or former spouse. However, bankruptcy courts have not limited the protections of section 523(a)(5) to "alimony," "maintenance," or "child/spousal support" awards. For example, attorney's fees have sometimes been found to be support, and therefore not dischargeable (although at other times, they have been found dischargeable).[11] The bankruptcy court looks beyond how the payment to the former spouse is labeled when determining whether it is appropriate to be discharged. Payment of debts in the other spouse's name that are part of a divorce settlement or judgment can be considered to be in the nature of support, and therefore non-dischargeable, even though they do not qualify as alimony or support under state law.[12] In addition, distributive awards that may seem on their face to be dischargeable as a property settlement may be determined to be in the nature of support where "one of the primary functions to be served by the property settlement was to section the source and means to generate support."[13] An award of a portion of the debtor's pension was found not dischargeable in bankruptcy as it had already become the former spouse's separate property.[14] Some bankruptcy courts have established a

---

[10] *See* In re Maloney, 204 B.R. 671,673–675 (Bankr. E.D.N.Y. 1996); In re Newman, 196 B.R. 700, 703 (S.D.N.Y. 1996); In re Kearns, 168 B.R. 423, 425 (D. Kan. 1994); In re Tipton, 257 B.R. 865, 875 (E.D. Tenn. 2000).

[11] *See* In re Bieluch, 2000 U.S. App. LEXIS 15793 (2d Cir. 2000) (holding that the award of counsel fees could be bifurcated into a "core award" that was equated with alimony because it was payable to the spouse prior to her death or remarriage and, therefore, was not dischargeable and "Survival Terms," consisting of payments that would continue after her death or remarriage, which were considered punitive in nature and thus dischargeable).

[12] *See* In re Gianakas, 917 F.2d 759, 763–764 (3d Cir. 1990) (holding that the debtor's obligation for a second mortgage on a former marital residence pursuant to a separation agreement incorporated into a divorce decree could be found to be in the nature of support so as to be nondischargeable); In re Yeates, 807 F.2d 874, 879 (10th Cir. 1986) (holding that where the wife waived her right to alimony in consideration of the husband assuming a marital debt, the obligation was in the nature of support and was nondischargeable).

[13] In re Brody, 120 B.R. 696, 698 (E.D.N.Y. 1990); In re Azia, 159 B.R. 71, 73 (D. Mass. 1993).

[14] *See* In re Potter, 159 B.R. 672, 675 (N.D.N.Y. 1993); In re Chandler, 805 F.2d 555, 557–558 (5th Cir. 1986).

factor test to determine whether the debt is in the nature of support, while other bankruptcy courts examine the totality of the circumstances in each case.[15]

Advocacy Tip: Family law attorneys who are concerned about having some components of a divorce settlement discharged in a subsequent bankruptcy proceeding may be able to include language in their settlements to attempt to protect their clients. A provision to guard against subsequent bankruptcy filings seeking to absolve themselves of their obligations under the agreement should be included in divorce stipulations where this is a concern.[16]

IV. Special Bankruptcy Considerations

A. Bankruptcy for Persons Under Guardianship

Rule 1004.1 of the Federal Rules of Bankruptcy Procedure states that "[i]f an infant or incompetent person has a representative, including a general guardian, committee, conservator, or similar fiduciary, the representative may file a voluntary petition on behalf of the infant or incompetent person." Rule 7017 of the Federal Rules of Bankruptcy Procedure makes Rule 17 of the Federal Rules of Civil Procedure applicable in bankruptcy matters. Rule 17 permits a guardian or conservator to sue without joining the person for whose benefit the action is brought.

There is a high incidence of domestic violence perpetrated against persons with disabilities and the elderly, which includes economic abuse by a caregiver,

---

[15] *See* In re Gianakas, 917 F.2d at 762–63 (identifying and examining three principal indicators of intent: (1) the language and substance of the state court's order; (2) the parties' financial circumstances at the time of the order; and (3) the function served by the obligation at the time of the order); *see* In re Smith, 398 B.R. 715, 718 (1st Cir. 20080 (acknowledged that the court had not "adopted a specific multi-factor test" and that the "the critical factors depend[ed] on the totality of circumstances . . .").

[16] Sample language may include: It is the intent of the parties that the obligations assumed by each in this Agreement, including any and all indemnifications and money judgments, shall not be dischargeable in any future bankruptcy proceeding. The parties recognize that the support and equitable distribution provisions are interrelated; in the event one party is called upon to make payment on a debt, or fails to make payment to the other of an asset, as provided herein, such a circumstance would be considered a significant change in circumstance, warranting an application for a modification of the support provisions provided for herein, as well as a redistribution of assets and liabilities in order to effectuate the overall intent of this Agreement. As a result of the interrelationship between the support and equitable distribution provisions of this agreement, it is the intent of the parties to consider the payment of debts and transfer of assets, including indemnifications, to be in the nature of alimony, support, or maintenance for purpose of interpretation under the Bankruptcy Code. Moreover, the parties acknowledge that the benefit to the defaulting party of discharge of any obligations hereunder in any future bankruptcy proceeding will not outweigh the detrimental consequences to the non-defaulting party. As a result, it is the intent of the parties that the obligations assumed hereunder shall not be dischargeable in any future bankruptcy proceeding.

including a spouse, partner, or other relative. Guardianship can be problematic in these cases because what is meant to offer protection to the incapacitated person can be an instrument of abuse. Court oversight of the actions of a guardian is required or recommended for some legal actions taken on behalf of the incapacitated person, but court oversight is not always consistent and the rules regarding obtaining court approval for such actions are not concrete.[17] Some bankruptcy courts have recognized that parties in interest in the case who lack capacity may also be entitled to representation by a guardian *ad litem* under Rule 17(c).

Advocacy Tip: If a victim is under a guardianship or a temporary guardianship, it is best practice to obtain the permission of the guardianship court to do a bankruptcy filing on their behalf. It is important for attorneys who are appointed as guardian *ad litem* to attempt to ascertain whether there is an abusive relationship between the incapacitated person and the person seeking to be named their guardian or conservator.

B. Bankruptcy for Undocumented Immigrants

Undocumented victims are likely to be subjected to some of the same forms of economic abuse as those with citizenship. Abusers with legal status may withhold immigration filings to obtain lawful residency in order to maintain power and control over their victims. The financial consequences to them, however, can be compounded by their lack of immigration status.

While many lenders do not offer mortgages or other loans to individuals without Social Security Numbers (SSNs), some banks offer mortgages and credit cards to people with Individual Taxpayer Identification Numbers (ITINs). In addition, they may purchase consumer goods such as vehicles with dealership financing that does not require them to submit SSNs. Many undocumented immigrants are reluctant to apply for bank loans or mortgages because of the threat of deportation if they come to the attention of the government. Therefore, payday lenders with extremely high interest rates are sometimes utilized. Moreover, many undocumented adults lack health insurance, leading to significant medical debt.[18]

---

[17] The Uniform Law Commission created a Uniform Guardianship, Conservatorship, and Other Protective Arrangements Act in 2017 ("the Uniform Guardianship Act"). It has not been adopted in its entirety by all states, and each state has its own separate guardianship system with differing terminology. Section 117 of the Uniform Guardianship Act requires that before accepting appointment as a guardian or conservator, they must disclose to the court their bankruptcy or criminal history, if any. Even the Uniform Guardianship Act does not require court approval for the guardian to file for bankruptcy on behalf of the incapacitated person.

[18] *See* Chrystin Ondersma, *Debt Without Relief: An Empirical Study of Undocumented Immigrants,* 68 Rutgers L. Rev. 1801, 1803 (2016).

The Bankruptcy Code does not require the debtor to prove lawful immigration status.[19] However, undocumented immigrants face many barriers to obtaining the relief from financial distress that bankruptcy can provide. Lack of information about bankruptcy leads some undocumented immigrants to believe that they would automatically lose their homes and all of their possessions by filing for bankruptcy.[20] In addition, undocumented immigrants may have a legitimate fear that Immigration and Customs Enforcement (ICE) will apprehend and deport them if they seek relief through the court system.

V. Conclusion

As a result of economic abuse, many victims are unable to attain economic freedom and leave their abusers. One way in which the effects of economic abuse may be alleviated is by filing a petition on the victim's behalf in bankruptcy court. Domestic violence attorneys should be aware that while bankruptcy may be helpful to a victim of domestic violence, it may also be used by an abuser as a means of further harassment. Family law attorneys who do not have expertise in bankruptcy may assist clients by screening them for appropriateness of bankruptcy as a viable avenue; advising clients about the dischargeability of the abuser's financial obligations in bankruptcy; and when it is a concern, incorporating language regarding future bankruptcy filings in the divorce settlement.

---

[19] Federal Rules of Bankruptcy Procedure 1007(f) requires an individual debtor to submit a verified statement of their SSN or state that the debtor does not have a SSN. Debtors can file using their ITIN if they do not have a SSN. There is also a form for debtors who have neither a SSN nor an ITIN. They must, however, be able to verify their identity.

[20] *See* Ondersma, *supra* note 18, at 1833.

APPENDIX

Organizations:

Center for Survivor Agency and Justice
https://csaj.org/

National Association of Consumer Advocates
https://www.consumeradvocates.org/

National Consumer Law Center
https://www.nclc.org/

Resources:

Economic Abuse: The Untold Cost of Domestic Violence, CORNELL U. (Oct.2012), https://www.ilr.cornell.edu/sites/ilr.cornell.edu/files/Economic-Abuse-Untold-Cost-of-DV.pdf.

Karen Merrill Tjapkes & Sarah Bolling Mancini, *Bankruptcy & Alternatives for Survivors, in* GUIDEBOOK ON CONSUMER & ECONOMIC CIVIL LEGAL ADVOCACY FOR SURVIVORS 98 (Ctr. for Survivor Agency & Just. ed., 2017), *available at* https://csaj.org/Guidebook_form. Nolo Bankruptcy, https://www.nolo.com/legal-encyclopedia/bankruptcy.

HENRY SOMMER, NAT'L CONSUMER L. CTR., CONSUMER BANKRUPTCY LAW AND PRACTICE (John Rao ed., 11th ed. 2016):

- HENRY SOMMER, NAT'L CONSUMER L. CTR., *Answers to Common Bankruptcy Questions, in* CONSUMER BANKRUPTCY LAW AND PRACTICE 1414 (John Rao ed., 11th ed. 2016), *available at* https://www.nclc.org/images/pdf/older_consumers/cib_common_bankruptcy_ques.pdf.

- HENRY SOMMER, NAT'L CONSUMER L. CTR., *Using Credit Wisely After Bankruptcy, in* CONSUMER BANKRUPTCY LAW AND PRACTICE 1422 (John Rao ed., 11th ed. 2016), *available at* https://www.nclc.org/images/pdf/older_consumers/cib_common_bankruptcy_ques.pdf.

- HENRY SOMMER, NAT'L CONSUMER L. CTR., *Your Legal Rights During and After Bankruptcy, in* CONSUMER BANKRUPTCY LAW AND PRACTICE 1419 (John Rao ed., 11th ed. 2016), *available at* https://www.nclc.org/images/pdf/older_consumers/cib_bankruptcy_legal_rights.pdf.

Consumer Rights Screening Tool:

Leah A. Plunkett & Erika A. Sussman, *Consumer Rights Screening Tool for Domestic Violence Advocates and Lawyers* (2011), *available at* https://csaj.org/document-library/consumerrightsscreeningtool-9-11.pdf.

Chapter Fifteen:
Tax Law and Domestic Violence

I. Introduction

Tax lawyers are in a unique position to aid victims of domestic violence. Since financial control is a significant component of domestic violence, lawyers dealing with financial matters—including tax attorneys—are certain to encounter cases where domestic violence is present. This chapter is written at a time of tax policy and statutory transition, and presents some tax issues both as the provisions existed prior to the passage of the Tax Cut and Jobs Act of 2017 (the 2017 Tax Act), as well as how those provisions will change post-2017. Because regulations and cases under the 2017 Tax Act will largely not be available at the time of publication, the practitioner reading this chapter is guided, as always, to thoroughly research any tax provisions addressed on behalf of a client.

The tax issues addressed in this chapter do not exclusively impact domestic violence victims, but they are the provisions victims will most likely encounter.[1] This chapter is intended to alert the non-tax lawyer to the basic issues that may arise in tax law and tax issues that may arise in family law cases.[2]

---

[1]   Alternate tax treatment due to community property status is not addressed.

[2]   IRS Publication 504 contains tax information for divorced or separated individuals. INT. REVENUE SERV., PUB. 504, DIVORCED OR SEPARATED INDIVIDUALS 18 (2017). One caution on IRS publications: the publications cannot be relied upon in the event of an error. The Internal Revenue Code, memoranda, and tax cases are suitable authority that can be relied upon in defending a taxpayer or in giving tax advice. For a comprehensive volume, see MELVYN B. FRUMKES & BRIAN C. VERTZ, DIVORCE TAXATION (James Publ'g 16th ed. 2017). The U.S. MASTER TAX GUIDE is a yearly publication that briefly addresses tax provisions. U.S. MASTER TAX GUIDE (Wolters Kluwer 2018).

II. Preliminary Issues

A. Important Preliminary Actions for the Client

The Internal Revenue Service (IRS) sends all communications to the last address on file for the taxpayer. Typically, this is the address on the taxpayer's most recently filed income tax return. If your client relocates, the client should send a certified notice to the IRS informing them of the new address.[3] Maintaining the record of receipt is important in the event the IRS begins any actions against the taxpayer and the client does not receive notice. Prompt notification from the IRS will ensure that the client has notice of any audits, tax assessments, and other concerns. The client will also have notice of any favorable determinations, such as additional tax refunds. The client should repeat the address notification process each time the client moves.[4]

Advocacy Tip: Some victims need to keep their new address confidential for safety reasons. In those cases, write across the top of each form: "This is a domestic violence case. Keep [the taxpayer's name]'s address confidential." While electronic filing is convenient, typically there is no way to write this warning on the electronic form. Consider writing the warning in red ink, making the information more visible. Also, consider writing the warning on each page filed, and not only on the first page of each filing.

B. Important Preliminary Tax Concerns for the Practitioner

Failure to consider income tax consequences of a divorce or separation agreement can lead to malpractice for family law attorneys. A practitioner who does not have access to competent tax advice should alert the client to this in their retainer agreement. Judges are obliged to report tax fraud.[5] As discussed later in this chapter, tax fraud is not unusual in domestic violence cases. You must prepare your client for possible consequences of either failing to file or filing inaccurate income tax returns.

C. Considerations for Immigrant Clients

Certain tax advantages are available only to those who meet certain immigration status qualifications. For example, the child tax credit is limited to those children who are U.S. citizens, resident aliens, children of U.S. citizens

---

[3] If electronic filing is preferred, be sure to keep a record of date, time, record number for the filing and any other pertinent information. Consider backing up the electronic notice with a hard copy, certified mailing.

[4] Form 8822, Change of Address, may be used to notify the IRS of the new address. Int. Revenue Serv., Form 8822, Change of Address, https://www.irs.gov/pub/irs-pdf/f8822.pdf.

[5] *See generally* Hon. Richard Dollinger, *Judicial Ethics: The Obligation to Report Tax Evasion in Support Cases,* 27 J. Am. Acad. Matrimonial L. 1 (2015), http://aaml.org/sites/default/files/MAT107_6. pdf.

living abroad, and other classifications.[6] At each stage of tax planning, the practitioner should check to see if immigration status alters the tax advice.

An undocumented immigrant, who is not eligible for a social security number, may apply for an Individual Tax Identification Number (ITIN) in order to file income tax returns. Each individual named on the return must have a separate ITIN.[7]

D. Obtaining Guidance on Tax Law Issues

If an attorney does not have expertise in tax law, but has a case where tax advice is needed, the practitioner could contact law firm *pro bono* offices or bar associations for assistance. Transactional lawyers generally are willing to assist by offering their expertise either as expert witnesses, or in providing support services, such as tax planning or other tax assistance. When it comes to federal tax advice, there is no reason to restrict your search for *pro bono* tax counsel to your local area. While federal tax can have local tax consequences, for the major tax issues that victims face, federal law will control.

III. Identifying Domestic Violence and Conflicts of Interest

A. Dynamics of Domestic Violence

Critical to the tax law practitioner's competency is the ability to understand and recognize domestic violence. Because of the pervasiveness of domestic violence in the United States, lawyers, paralegals, and other staff would all benefit from training in the dynamics of abuse. Local shelter advocates and other domestic violence practitioners may be available to provide this type of training.

There are some fundamental precepts of domestic violence that the tax lawyer should understand. Educational, professional, and economic status are irrelevant in assessing whether there is domestic violence in a relationship. Additionally, physical violence is only one control technique used by abusers. While some victims experience continuing physical abuse, many others do not experience physical abuse at all. Approximately 25 percent of women who die at the hands of a current or former partner had no reported history of prior physical abuse.[8] Therefore, lawyers should not disbelieve or diminish a client who is concerned for safety even though the physical abuse is minimal or has not occurred. The

---

[6] *Is My Child a Qualifying Child for the Child Tax Credit?,* IRS, https://www.irs.gov/help/ita/is-my-child-a-qualifying-child-for-the-child-tax-credit (last updated Dec. 23, 2017). The term "resident alien" is used by the IRS. *See U.S. Tax Guide for Aliens,* Int. Revenue Serv. after *Is My Child a Qualifying Child for the Child Tax Credit?* and before (Feb. 28, 2018), https://www.irs.gov/pub/irs-pdf/p519.pdf.

[7] See I.R.C. § 6109 (2018).

[8] Jacquelyn C. Campbell et al., *Risk Factors for Femicide in Abusive Relationships: Results from a Multisite Case Control Study,* 93 Am. J. of Pub. Health 1089, 1094 (2003).

abuser has likely used other tactics to control the victim.[9] These methods include financial control, isolation of the victim from family and friends, stalking, and jealousy.[10]

B. Conflicts of Interest

Because couples often seek joint representation for financial matters, such as will preparation, tax planning, and tax audits where a joint income return was filed, tax lawyers are likely to encounter clients that are intimate partners. Lawyers commonly begin with a presumption that a married, or otherwise committed, couple seeking assistance for a joint legal problem does not present a conflict of interest. This presumption is faulty, and practitioners must determine on a case-by-case basis whether a conflict exists or is likely to arise. For both your own professional protection, as well as the protection of your clients, you must take adequate steps to determine whether a conflict of interest exists and if so, whether the conflict is waivable.

Lawyers can begin assessing their ethical obligations in joint representation by reviewing the ABA Model Rules of Professional Conduct, or local rules applicable in their jurisdiction.[11] ABA Model Rule of Professional Conduct 1.7 Conflict of Interest addresses conflicts of interest with current clients.[12] ABA Model Rule 1.7 requires that a lawyer not "represent a client if the representation involves a concurrent conflict of interest."[13] The rule sets out specific, yet broad, definitions of when a conflict of interest exists. A conflict exists if "the representation of one client will be directly adverse to another client; or there is a significant risk that the representation of one or more clients will be materially limited by the lawyer's responsibility to the other client … ."[14]

1. Conducting Individual Interviews with Clients

In determining whether a conflict exists, best practices dictate that each client be interviewed separately. While in a non-abusive situation, a joint interview may be sufficient, a lawyer cannot assume that the couple sitting in their office is in

---

[9] Mary Ann Dutton & Lisa Goodman, *Coercive in Intimate Partner Violence: Toward a New Conceptualization,* 52 Sex Roles 743, 743 (2005).

[10] Mary M. Lovik, *If My Spouse Ever Hit Me I'd Just Leave,* 90 Mich. B.J. 24, 26 (2011).

[11] Model Rules of Prof'l Conduct (Am. Bar Ass'n 2016). All U.S. jurisdictions base their professional rules, at least in part, upon the American Bar Association's Model Rules of Professional Conduct.

[12] Model Rules of Prof'l Conduct r. 1.7 (Am. Bar Ass'n 2016) ("Conflicts of Interest: Current Clients").

[13] *Id.*

[14] *Id.*

a non-abusive relationship.[15] In addition to assessing whether there is a conflict, individual meetings provide the practitioner with the opportunity to inform a victim of the available resources that may assist in remaining safe, or in developing an exit strategy.

The process leading to separate interviews can be complicated. Due to the dynamics of domestic violence, a lawyer should expect resistance to any plan to separate the clients. The lawyer should explain to the clients that determining whether a conflict exists is an obligation in all joint representation cases. It may be helpful to provide the clients with a copy of ABA Model Rule 1.7 or the state equivalent. The lawyer can then explain that parties will be required to sign a waiver of any identified conflict, and an acknowledgment of what happens if an insurmountable conflict arises during representation. The lawyer should not rely upon responses in a joint meeting as to whether there are any objections to both clients being represented. Again, the victim-client is unlikely to voice objection in the presence of the abuser.

During the separate meetings with each client, the victim's interview should not last longer than the abuser's interview. One technique is to separate not only the prospective clients but the interviewers, as well. A lawyer or paralegal trained in domestic violence dynamics can interview the suspected victim, while the primary lawyer conducts the interview with the suspected abuser. Both interviewers can explain that the clients have ongoing control over whether joint representation continues, and each client may terminate the joint representation at any time. Should an interviewer have any reason to suspect that a client is a victim of domestic violence, the interviewer can explain that the law firm maintains a list of resources for assistance should the victim-client ever need it. Should the victim disclose domestic violence, the interviewer must be prepared with referrals for the client. If the suspected victim either does not disclose, or discloses and does not want assistance with the situation, the interviewer should at least inform the client that assistance is available. At some point, the client must be asked if there is any objection to the law firm's representing both parties, and it would be unusual for the victim to object to joint representation.

If the victim does object to joint representation, the interviewer must be ready to discuss safety planning with the client, including the possibility of either transporting the client to a domestic violence advocacy program or bringing an advocate to the attorney's office in person, by phone, or by other electronic means.

---

[15] Of course, even without the presence of abuse, disagreements can occur between partners over disposition of assets and other financial decisions. Sometimes it is only in a separate interview that these differing interests become apparent.

In either instance, before closing the separate interview, the lawyer must agree with the victim-client what will be presented to the other party.[16] If the victim-client does not agree to the joint representation, then the client will need to direct whether it is safe for them to return to the joint interview, and how the abuser will be informed of the decision not to proceed.[17] Otherwise, the parties will proceed with signing conflict of interest waivers, either as a separate document or as a term of the retainer agreement. Signing the waiver may be the safest option for the victim. Even if the victim has disclosed domestic violence, the victim's safety decisions must be respected.

Should the lawyer will recognize signs of abuse during the course of representation, after having signed a joint retainer, it is still best practice to initiate separate interviews. A good time to do so is when the estate or tax plan is ready for client review. The lawyer may present separate meetings to review document drafts as being a routine matter, and follow suggestions made above for conducting separate interviews.

2. Best Interests of the Client

To successfully represent a victim of domestic violence in a joint client context, the lawyer must broaden the definition of "best interests" of the client. Tax lawyers may be accustomed to thinking of "best interests" in terms of minimizing financial repercussions for the client. But for domestic violence victims, maximizing safety may be the primary interest of the client, even if the tax or estate plan is not financially beneficial to the victim. If the victim-client determines that safety is the priority, the lawyer must be mindful of that goal in drafting documents.

Joint representation where only one partner appears for the interview, and the other client is otherwise unavailable, should not be undertaken except in the most extraordinary of circumstances.[18] The lawyer's obligation to obtain waivers for joint representation is paramount to ethical practice.

One area where tax lawyers are likely to see an unresolvable conflict between married clients is when the victim has a valid innocent spouse claim to a tax

---

[16] MODEL RULES OF PROF'L CONDUCT r. 1.7(a)(2) (AM. BAR ASS'N 2016) (Joint clients have the right to know of all communications between the lawyer and the other client. The lawyer should keep in mind that the individuals seeking representation at this point are not clients. Indeed, the information gleaned through the interviews may determine whether the lawyer wishes to proceed with representation).

[17] For a discussion of Ethics of Joint Representation, see Lucian T. Pera, *The Ethics of Joint Representation,* 40 Litig. 1 (2013), https://www.americanbar.org/content/dam/aba/publications/litigation_journal/fall2013/ethics-joint-representation.authcheckdam.pdf.

[18] For example, a person with a disability may have executed a power of attorney specifically directing the drafting of estate documents as presented by the visiting client. Even this can be risky, however, as the POA may have been executed under duress. The attorney should make every effort to meet both parties under those and similar circumstances.

assessment resulting from a joint return filed with the abuser. In that instance, ABA Model Rule 1.7 is implicated because representation would involve the "assertion of a claim by one client against another client in the same litigation or other proceeding before a tribunal."[19] Innocent spouse relief will be discussed later in this chapter.

IV. Tax Issues in Family Law Cases[20]

A. Alimony/Spousal Support

The 2017 Tax Act will dramatically change the tax consequences of paying or receiving alimony beginning in 2019.[21] Until then, alimony payers will continue to be able to deduct alimony payment, and the alimony recipients will report the payments as income. This tax policy has encouraged former spouses to comply with alimony/spousal support orders.

Beginning in 2019, alimony will no longer be tax deductible to the payer, and will not be taxable income to the recipient. The tax treatment of alimony will be determined according to the date of the judgment of divorce or settlement agreement. For example, a divorce agreement executed on December 31, 2018 will result in alimony payments made under that agreement to be tax deductible to the payer and taxable income to the payee. An agreement entered into on January 1, 2019 will cause any alimony payments to be a tax-free transaction.

This change represents a shift in tax policy. The non-deductibility will likely result in the government raising additional revenue. The presumption that the payer is a higher earner than the recipient will result in higher income tax payments by the payer, as tax will be paid on the payer's original income without reduction for alimony paid. Victims whose alimony agreements or judgments are dated January 1, 2019 or later may encounter more difficulty with collection because of the additional tax burden on the payer.

For pre-2019 agreements that are modified, the agreement or judgment of the court must include a term that the modification specifically incorporates the changed tax provisions of the 2017 Tax Act for the payments to be no longer tax deductible to the payer, and to not be taxable to the payee. The revised

---

[19] MODEL RULES OF PROF'L CONDUCT r. 1.7(b)(3) (AM. BAR ASS'N 2016).

[20] Contemporary language in family law agreements and court judgments is more appropriately descriptive of parents' circumstances than it once was. For example, the term "custody" is archaic and implies possession, and all the negative property implications that attaches to custody. Consequently, many jurisdictions today use the term "primary residential parent" in lieu of "custodial parent." Rather than "visitation," the term "parenting time" is generally preferred. Likewise, the word "alimony" is often replaced by "spousal support" or "separate maintenance" by courts today. The Internal Revenue Code (IRC) has not made these language adjustments; therefore, throughout this chapter, you will encounter older family law terminology.

[21] The tax treatment of alimony is covered in I.R.C. § 71 (2018).

tax provisions are silent on whether the pre-2019 tax treatment provisions can be likewise incorporated into post-2018 agreements or judgments, but the presumption is that there is no authority do so. To continue the deductibility of alimony payments would be against current tax policy, and defeat the intention of the change. The reason that the 2017 Tax Act permits incorporation of the post-2018 change in tax treatment of alimony is because the change favors the government.

Because the change in the tax treatment of alimony is specifically not intended to apply to agreements and judgments entered before January 1, 2019, there is a strong argument that the change in tax treatment will be insufficient in and of itself to establish a substantial change in circumstances sufficient to trigger the application of the changed income tax treatment established by the 2017 Tax Act. The moving party (usually the payer) must prove that the impact on the payer is substantial or otherwise meets the jurisdiction's standard for a successful modification.

Nevertheless, attorneys should be prepared for alimony payer arguments that alimony awards should be reduced due to the non-deductibility of payments. One way to deflate this argument is to obtain a copy of the payer's most recent income tax return, and add in the amount of actual alimony paid during that tax year and calculate the income tax due. The attorney may then negotiate how much of that income tax increase should be returned to the payer in the form an alimony reduction. The practitioner must be armed with the information of how much income tax the victim-client will save if payments are no longer taxable income to the victim. If the victim has incurred no income tax due to the alimony, the lawyer may have a strong argument that due to the client's low-income status, any reduction in alimony will create unwarranted hardship. Remember, the fact that the tax treatment of alimony has changed under the 2017 Tax Act is insufficient in and of itself to trigger a modification.

Sometimes, pre-2019 alimony payments were negotiated to qualify for tax deductibility when in reality, the payments are in lieu of property division. The IRS Code has addressed this problem through "recapture." Essentially, if alimony payments in the third post-divorce or separation year are $15,000.00 (or more) less than the alimony paid in the first or second year, the rule might cause a retroactive disqualification of the payments as alimony for income tax purpose.[22] The same rule will apply for payments that have excessive fluctuations in amounts paid during the first three years without regard to the $15,000.00 condition. Post-2018, this provision will be irrelevant because first-time alimony payments ordered or agreed upon will no longer be deductible by the payer. If alimony payments are disqualified as alimony due to the recapture rule, the

---

[22] Other irregularities in payments may initiate the rule as well.

alimony recipient should amend income tax returns to remove the reported alimony from taxable income.

Tax Treatment of Attorneys' Fees

Attorneys' fees paid to obtain taxable income are generally tax deductible. For alimony recipients whose alimony is taxable (under judgments or agreements prior to January 1, 2019), that portion of attorneys' fees paid to obtain alimony are deductible.[23]

Attorneys' fees incurred to obtain property, such as a home or investment property, are not immediately deductible, but are added to the basis of the property. Basis is the amount that is returned to the owner, tax free, upon sale of the taxable or potentially taxable asset.

B. Qualified Domestic Relations Orders

"A qualified domestic relations order (QRDO) is a judgment, decree or court order (including an approved property settlement agreement) issued under a state's domestic relations law" that awards one spouse a property interest in a pension or other retirement account that is attached to the employment of the other spouse.[24] The spouse whose employment triggered accrual of the account is referred to as "the participant." The account is often divided based on the number of years during the marriage that the participating spouse worked at the job where the retirement asset accrued. For example, if a couple was married for twenty years, and the participating spouse began working for the employer through which the retirement account developed for the last ten years, the account is likely to be divided equally. However, if the participant worked at the position for twenty years, and the parties were married for ten years, then most likely the non-participating spouse would receive only 25 percent of the retirement account.

Most attorneys do not draft QDROs. Technical requirements often make drafting QDROs time consuming and beyond the expertise of most practitioners. There are lawyers and other pension specialists who draft these documents. For this reason, most divorce agreements specify how payment of the QDRO specialist will be paid. Ordinarily, the non-participant spouse will have the same tax consequences as the participant at the time that benefits are distributed. For example, a client may not have worked throughout the marriage and be awarded 50 percent of the spouse's pension; when that client begins receiving

---

[23] I.R.C. § 212(1) (2018).

[24] Int. Revenue Serv., Pub. 504, Divorced or Separated Individuals 18 (2017); I.R.C. § 414 (2018). In some instances, the account may be used for the benefit of the participant's child or other dependent.

benefits, the non-working spouse will have the same income tax obligations as the working spouse.

Advocacy Tip: If your client is the non-participating spouse, be sure to include survivor's benefits in the negotiations and subsequent court order. Read the plan documents in advance of negotiations so you understand the particular requirements of the plan, as well as what your client will receive if the participating spouse dies. There may also be life insurance tied to the participating spouse's benefits that you will want maintained for the benefit of the victim-client.

V. Exemptions and Tax Credits

A. Exemptions

Claiming exemptions can be complicated for parents who are separated or divorced.[25] Exemptions will be temporarily eliminated as of 2018, but will be reinstated for tax year 2026 (or sooner). During 2017, the amount of each exemption was $4,050.00. There is a personal exemption for each taxpayer, and an exemption for each dependent. The exemptions reduce the amount of taxable income for the taxpayer. For higher earning parents, the value of claiming the dependency exemption phases out.

Exemptions are particularly important for low-income taxpayers. The number of exemptions a parent claims can determine whether the client has sufficient income to support the family. One important factor in determining tax exemptions is with whom the child resides. If the child lives with one of the parents for more than six months of the year, then that parent is entitled to claim the child as a dependent. However, parents can agree in their divorce or separation instrument to allocate the right to claim the child as they wish. A lawyer should check that the jurisdiction of practice permits the family court to allocate the dependency exemptions, which most do.[26] As of this writing, South Dakota, Georgia, Texas, and Virginia do not.[27]

Advocacy Tip: If the parent awarded the dependency exemption is subject to a child support order, often the parent's ability to claim the child exemption may be tied to all child support being paid in full at the close of the calendar (tax) year.[28] This provision helps victims to receive timely payment of support. One tip is to

---

[25] Dependency exemptions are addressed under I.R.C. § 152(e).

[26] *See, e.g.,* Iv v. Hang, 988 N.E.2d 1 (Mass. App. Ct. 2013) (affirming the lower court's authority to assign the child dependency exemptions and remanded for consideration of an order compelling the parent who was not assigned the exemptions to sign the waiver form 8332).

[27] FRUMKES & VERTZ, *supra* note 2.

[28] *See* Funderberg v. Molstad, 390 N.W.2d 19 (Minn. Ct. App. 1986).

suggest that the custodial parent's execution of Form 8332 can be contingent upon timely payment of child support.[29]

Post-2017, all personal exemptions will be suspended, but the standard deduction will increase to $12,000.00 per tax filer. This amount benefits both parents, each of whom may claim a $12,000.00 standard deduction. This change will end the lengthy negotiations over which parent is to be awarded the dependency exemption. This is typically a contentious point in family law cases involving domestic violence.[30]

By 2026, exemptions will be reinstated. Practitioners should follow any changes in the treatment of exemptions when they are reinstated and determine if 2017 protocols will remain in place. Congress has seven years to make changes in reimplementation or to extend the time for suspension of personal exemptions.

B. Child Tax Credit

As of tax year 2018, the amount of the child tax credit is $2,000.00 per qualifying child. Only one parent may claim the child as a qualifying tax credit. The primary criteria for a child to qualify are:

- The child must be a son, daughter, stepchild, foster child, brother, sister, half-brother, half-sister, stepbrother, stepsister, or a descendant of either parent;

- The child must be under age 19 at the end of the year, and younger than the taxpayer (or the taxpayer's spouse if filing jointly);

- The child must be under age 24 at the end of the year, a student, and younger than the taxpayer (or the taxpayer's spouse if filing jointly), or any age, if permanently and totally disabled;

- The child must have lived with the taxpayer for more than half of the year;

- The child must not have provided more than half of his or her own support for the year; and

- The child isn't filing a joint return for the year (unless that joint return is filed only to claim a refund of withheld income tax or estimated tax paid).[31]

Special rules apply for children of divorced or separated parents. Because the child must have lived with the parent for more than half the year, the primary

---

[29] *Id.*

[30] Because the abuser looks to keep the victim financially impoverished, tax benefits typically are an area of intense negotiations.

[31] *See* I.R.C. § 24 (2018).

residential parent will customarily claim the qualifying child, but this presumption can be altered. Under 2017 rules, the non-primary custodial parent may claim the qualifying child when the other parent waives the right to claim the child as a dependent for exemption purposes. This is accomplished by the primary custodial parent signing Form 8332.[32] The same form provides for revocation of the allocation of the dependency exemption should circumstances warrant it.

Because dependency exemptions will disappear from 2018 through 2025, the practitioner should inquire as to whether and what form a waiver will take, if the parents will be shifting eligibility for claiming a qualifying child.

Advocacy Tip: If the child stays with the parents for exactly equal time during the calendar year, the qualifying child is claimed by the parent with the higher adjusted gross income. Attorneys who represent domestic violence victims should be mindful of this rule and argue against its application where the client is the lower earning parent.

Pre-2018, the child tax credit was tied to the dependency exemption so that only parents claiming the exemption would be permitted to claim the credit. Because the dependency exemption is being suspended through 2025, the practitioner will need to explore whether any regulations change on which parent may claim the child tax credit. Also, the practitioner should explore whether parties can agree to allocate the credit or whether courts can order an allocation. This allocation may begin following the same path as the dependency exemption allocation followed.

C. Child Care Tax Credit

Unlike the child tax credit, the child care tax credit is not limited to the parent who claims the child as a dependent.[33] The tax credit may be claimed for a child under the age of 13. If the child has a disability, the child might qualify even when older than 13. The suspension of the dependency tax exemption will not impact the ability to claim this credit, because the provision was never tied to claiming the child as a dependent for exemption purposes. Like other provisions regarding children, the child for whom the exemption is claimed must meet the requirements of a "qualifying child." The practitioner must review each applicable code section for the definition of a "qualifying child" as the requirements are not always uniform.

---

[32] Int. Revenue Serv., Form 8332, Release/Revocation of Release of Claim to Exemption for Child by Custodial Parent, https://www.irs.gov/pub/irs-pdf/f8822.pdf.

[33] I.R.C. § 21 (2018).

D. Earned Income Tax Credit

The earned income tax credit is available for low to moderate taxpayers.[34] The amount received can be several thousand dollars, and can make a significant difference to low-income parents. In 2017, the credit may be pursued by those with or without claiming "qualifying children" as dependents. As with other tax code provisions, the definition of "qualifying children" varies, and should be examined within the applicable code section. If a child is claimed by the other parent in any given tax year, the parent not claiming the child as a dependent may still qualify for the earned income tax credit. Post-2017, claiming the child as a dependent will be irrelevant until 2026. The practitioner should check any change in tax policy and implementation of the earned income tax credit under the 2017 Tax Act provisions. This credit is available only for those U.S. citizens or resident aliens with valid social security numbers.[35]

VI. Tax Relief for Victims for Joint Returns

A. Joint and Several Liability

Married individuals are permitted to file their taxes jointly. In many instances, filing jointly will result in less tax liability than filing separate returns. Married individuals may not file as "single" but may file as "head of household," if the taxpayer qualifies.

Joint filing has significant consequences. By filing jointly, each partner may be held responsible for all tax liability that arises out of the joint return, even if an individual taxpayer was not responsible for any omissions, errors, or fraud.

Since financial control is common in domestic violence situations, the lawyer should not be surprised to learn that jointly filed returns have irregularities that could result in serious financial consequences for the victim-client. If the return is deemed to be fraudulent, federal and state criminal consequences could result. More typically, the consequences are financial. The victim may find paychecks attached, liens on properties, and other actions taken by the IRS or local taxing authorities in order to satisfy a tax debt.

Possible pathways for relief from liability are discussed in the next section. Again, keeping the IRS informed of the client's current address is vital so that timely defenses can be raised, should audit or collection actions be commenced post-separation.

---

[34] I.R.C. § 32 (2018).

[35] *EITC, Earned Income Tax Credit, Questions and Answers,* IRS, https://www.irs.gov/credits-deductions/individuals/earned-income-tax-credit/eitc-earned-income-tax-credit-questions-and-answers (last updated Aug. 27, 2017).

B. Innocent Spouse Relief

Commonly, we refer to tax relief for victims as "innocent spouse" relief. Innocent spouse is a form of relief for victims who find themselves in a tax liability situation after filing joint returns with their abuser. There are three pathways to relief.[36]

1. Innocent Spouse

This is the traditional form of relief available to domestic violence victims. One problem with this approach is that the spouse claiming "innocence" must have had no knowledge of the tax evasion. This relief is found in IRC § 6015(b) and applies to both understatements of income and to deficiencies. This form of relief may be elected even if the spouse claiming innocence is living with the abuser. In addition, the return's understatement of tax must be attributable only to one spouse. The decision whether to grant relief under this provision will be based upon all facts and circumstances.

2. Adjustment of Liability

Relief by adjustment of liability is found in IRC § 6015(c). This form of relief permits the grievant to separate out the victim's tax liability from that of the abuser. The victim would then be responsible only for their own tax. This relief is available to those who have been divorced, legally separated, widowed, or living apart for 12 months prior to making the election. The victim must not have participated in any tax fraud scheme through fraudulent transfers or otherwise. This form of relief is often the most appropriate for victims. This relief does not have the stricter "innocence" qualifications that "innocent spouse" relief requires.

3. Equitable Relief

This form of relief is found in IRC § 6015(e), and is available to the victim only if relief under IRC §§ 6015(b) or (c) is unavailable. This relief does not have the stricter "innocence" qualifications that the "innocent spouse" relief requires. While 6015(b) and (c) require varying levels of non-participation for the client seeking relief, the only requirement of (e) is that the non-fraudulent spouse relied upon the other spouse to pay any tax liability.

Often the victim-client had sufficient information to know or suspect that tax returns might not be accurate. Sometimes, the victim may be the one who has not reported cash earnings, at the insistence of the abuser. Or, more commonly, the victim is coerced into signing the joint return. The equitable relief defense was created to accommodate this category of victim. That said, there are some cautions the practitioner must understand. Marital status of the victim is but one factor in determining whether relief will be granted. Often, stereotypes of victims

---

[36] All may be found in I.R.C. § 6015 (2018).

must be confronted. For example, if the parties are separated, the client will fare better if the client does not file any further joint returns with the abuser. Family courts may not understand the victim's resistance to joint filing when there is a clear financial advantage in doing so, but victim's counsel must explain to the victim the hazards of agreeing to joint filing. The lawyer may advise the client to file separately, as a joint return can be filed later when the accuracy of the information has been assessed.

The level of understanding of domestic violence will vary among IRS employees. The same will be true of Tax Court judges. All depends on the level of training and education on the topic the individual has experienced. For this reason, should the matter proceed to Tax Court, the practitioner should consider having an expert witness testify in order to explain why the victim would have knowingly or otherwise signed fraudulent income tax returns. This need is particularly acute when the victim is not physically abused prior to signing. Some judges will be sufficiently experienced with equitable defense claimants to understand that all abuse is not physical. A review of that judge's IRC § 6015(e) decisions might shed some light on the level of the judge's understanding.

All of the above defenses must be timely raised.[37] Defenses may be raised at both the administrative and the judicial levels, and it is important to do so as soon as possible. The mechanics of filing for relief are not complicated, but the timing can be. A practitioner not familiar with tax procedure should consult with an expert as early as possible.

4. Injured Spouse Relief

Injured spouses are those who have filed joint income tax returns but the refunds have been withheld to apply to the debt of the spouse. This situation arises most commonly in two situations: (1) one spouse may owe child support and the IRS takes the refund for payment toward the child support debt, and (2) when one spouse has student loan debt. Of course, the same will happen for any income tax debt owed. The IRS has a means for the non-debtor spouse (the injured spouse) to receive the amount of refund attributable to the income of the injured spouse.[38]

---

[37] The defenses are raised by filing Form 8857. INT. REVENUE SERV., FORM 8857, REQUEST FOR INNOCENT SPOUSE RELIEF, https://www.irs.gov/pub/irs-pdf/f8857.pdf.

[38] Form 8379 is used to claim the injured spouse's share of the refund. INT. REVENUE SERV., FORM 8379, INJURED SPOUSE ALLOCATION, https://www.irs.gov/pub/irs-pdf/f8379.pdf.

APPENDIX

Resources:

- **Internal Revenue Service**
  - ○ *Contact Your Local IRS Office,* IRS, https://www.irs.gov/help/contact-your-local-irs-office (last updated Apr. 17, 2018).
  - ○ *Where's My Refund,* IRS, https://www.irs.gov/refunds (last updated Mar. 29, 2018).

- **National Women's Law Center**
  - ○ *Tax & Budget,* NAT'L WOMEN'S L. CTR., https://nwlc.org/issue/tax-budget.

- **Taxation: A Section of the American Bar Association**
  - ○ A.B.A. SEC. OF TAXATION, https://www.americanbar.org/groups/taxation.html.
  - ○ *Low Income Taxpayer Clinics (LITCs),* A.B.A. SEC. OF TAXATION, https://www.americanbar.org/groups/taxation/tax_pro_bono/Low_Income_Taxpayer_Clinics.html.

- **Taxpayer Advocate Service**
  - ○ Contact Us, TAXPAYER ADVOCATE SERV., https://taxpayeradvocate.irs.gov/contact-us.

Tax Preparation Resources:

- **AARP Foundation**
  - ○ *AARP Foundation Tax-Aide Locator,* AARP, https://secure.aarp.org/applications/VMISLocator/searchTaxAideLocations.action.

- **Internal Revenue Service**
  - ○ *Free File: Do Your Federal Taxes for Free,* IRS, https://www.irs.gov/filing/free-file-do-your-federal-taxes-for-free (last updated Apr. 23, 2018).
  - ○ *Free Tax Return Preparation for Qualifying Taxpayers,* IRS, https://www.irs.gov/individuals/free-tax-return-preparation-for-you-by-volunteers (last updated Dec. 12, 2017).
  - ○ PUBL'N 3676-B, IRS CERTIFIED VOLUNTEERS PROVIDING FREE TAX PREPARATION, https://www.irs.gov/pub/irs-pdf/p3676bsp.pdf.
  - ○ *The Volunteer Income Tax Assistance (VITA) Program and The Tax Counseling for the Elderly (TCE) Program Locator Tool,* https://irs.treasury.gov/freetaxprep.

- **Military OneSource Tax Services**
  - ○ *Tax Services,* MILITARY ONESOURCE, http://www.militaryonesource.mil/web/mos/tax-services.

IRS Forms and Publications:

- **Application for IRS Individual Taxpayer Identification Number**
  - PUBL'N 1915, UNDERSTANDING YOUR IRS INDIVIDUAL TAXPAYER IDENTIFICATION NUMBER ITIN (2018), https://www.irs.gov/pub/irs-pdf/p1915.pdf.
  - FORM W-7, APPLICATION FOR IRS INDIVIDUAL TAXPAYER IDENTIFICATION NUMBER (2016), https://www.irs.gov/pub/irs-pdf/fw7.pdf.

- **Change of Address**
  - FORM 8822, CHANGE OF ADDRESS (2015), https://www.irs.gov/pub/irs-pdf/f8822.pdf.

- **Child Tax Credit**
  - PUBL'N 972, CHILD TAX CREDIT (2017), https://www.irs.gov/pub/irs-pdf/p972.pdf.
  - SCHEDULE 8812 FORM, CHILD TAX CREDIT (2017), https://www.irs.gov/pub/irs-pdf/f1040s8.pdf.

- **Child Care Tax Credit**
  - PUBL'N 503, CHILD AND DEPENDENT CARE EXPENSES (2017), https://www.irs.gov/pub/irs-pdf/p503.pdf.
  - FORM 2441, CHILD AND DEPENDENT CARE EXPENSES (2017), https://www.irs.gov/pub/irs-pdf/f2441.pdf.

- **Dependency Exemption Release and Revocation Form for Custodial Parent**
  - PUBL'N 501, EXEMPTIONS, STANDARD DEDUCTION, AND FILING INFORMATION (2017), https://www.irs.gov/pub/irs-pdf/p501.pdf.
  - FORM 8332, RELEASE/REVOCATION OF RELEASE OF CLAIM TO EXEMPTION FOR CHILD BY CUSTODIAL PARENT (2010), https://www.irs.gov/pub/irs-pdf/f8332.pdf.

- **Earned Income Tax Credit**
  - PUBL'N 596, EARNED INCOME CREDIT (EIC) (2017), https://www.irs.gov/pub/irs-pdf/p596.pdf.
  - *Using the EITC Assistant,* IRS, https://www.irs.gov/credits-deductions/individuals/earned-income-tax-credit/use-the-eitc-assistant (last updated Jan. 5, 2018).
  - SCHEDULE EIC FORM, EARNED INCOME CREDIT QUALIFYING CHILD INFORMATION (2017), https://www.irs.gov/pub/irs-pdf/f1040sei.pdf.

- **Injured Spouse Relief**
  - FORM 8379, INJURED SPOUSE ALLOCATION (2016), https://www.irs.gov/pub/irs-pdf/f8379.pdf.

- **Innocent Spouse Relief**
  - Publ'n 971, Innocent Spouse Relief (2014), https://www.irs.gov/pub/irs-pdf/p971.pdf.
  - Form 8857, Request for Innocent Spouse Relief (2014), https://www.irs.gov/pub/irs-pdf/f8857.pdf.

- **Tax Information for Divorced and Separated Parents**
  - Publ'n 504, Divorced or Separated Individuals (2017), https://www.irs.gov/pub/irs-pdf/p504.pdf.

Chapter Sixteen:
Domestic Violence Issues in Wills, Trusts, and Estates

I. Introduction

This chapter describes how the laws related to wills, trusts, and estates may be used to the benefit or detriment of victims of domestic violence and their families. This area of law has developed to protect and effectuate decisions made by individuals, but is also reflective of societal values and norms about individual freedom, familial relationships, and obligations.[1] The laws relating to wills, trusts, and estates developed in the context of United States property law in which individuals claimed ownership of land previously occupied by Native Americans, and individuals claimed ownership of enslaved people. U.S. property laws reflected the interests of those who held power and their desire to preserve the socioeconomic status quo for their heirs.

Free white women were also excluded from property ownership, as they were considered an extension of their male relatives: under the control and supervision of their fathers until marriage, and their husbands thereafter. When white women gained the right to inherit and own property, implicit bias influenced probate courts' analysis of wills made by them, as well as those in which women were the beneficiaries.[2]

---

[1] For an in-depth discussion of how the law of wills, trusts, and estates could benefit from consideration of its development and impact on people of color, women, LGBT individuals, low-income individuals, individuals with disabilities, and nontraditional families, see Bridget J. Crawford & Anthony C. Infanti, *A Critical Research Agenda for Wills, Trusts and Estates,* 49 REAL PROP. TR. & EST. L.J. 317, 317 (2014), *available at* http://digitalcommons.pace.edu/lawfaculty/1008/.

[2] *See id.* at 329. There are numerous cases in which courts have determined the undue influence doctrine to set aside wills in which gender stereotypes formed a basis for setting aside a will. For example, a female may be viewed as submissive and weak-minded, and thus more susceptible to undue influence over the creation of her will. *Id.* A younger female beneficiary inheriting from an older male may be viewed as someone who tricked the testator into putting her in his will. *Id.*

In addition, wills, trusts, and estates laws have developed under an assumption about a traditional family structure comprised of a married heterosexual couple with their biological or adopted children. Nontraditional families—such as those in which partners are not legally married, or blended families with children who are not legally adopted—are disadvantaged in that they may require more complex estate planning to ensure their inheritance rights.[3] The same can be said of people who change their names and identification documents to reflect their gender identities.[4] Thus, racism, classism, sexism, and heteronormativity were built into property and inheritance laws from the inception of this country, and have long-term and continuing consequences for American society.

The intersectional critique of wills, trusts, and estates law also applies in terms of its historical failure to recognize issues that arise for victims of domestic violence. Therefore, it is of critical importance that attorneys serving victims of domestic violence are aware of the legal challenges, as well as the potential benefits, of estate planning for their clients.

II. Overview of Wills, Trusts, and Estates

A will, sometimes called a "last will and testament," is a document that states the decedent's final wishes, usually regarding distribution of their estate. "Estate" is the term used to refer to the interest a person has in any kind of property, including but not limited to real estate, bank accounts, stocks, cash, vehicles, intellectual property, or personal property.

If a person dies without a will or without leaving evidence of their wishes with respect to the disposal of their property after their death, they are said to have died "intestate," and the intestacy law will apply. The court will use the intestacy laws to determine which surviving relatives will inherit the decedent's estate. Each jurisdiction sets its own rules of succession regarding who will inherit when a person dies intestate, so the laws vary from state to state.[5] Generally, an administrator of the estate is chosen by the court and has the responsibility of distributing the decedent's property, and the surviving spouse is the first person (and the only non-blood, non-adoptive relative) to inherit, if the spouse dies intestate. This is the case even if the parties are informally separated, but not if they are divorced or legally separated. The remainder typically goes to the

---

[3] *See* Wendy S. Goff, *Planning for Nontraditional Families,* 46TH ANN. ADVANCED ALI-ABA SUMMER PROGRAM (June 16, 2011), https://papers.ssrn.com/sol3/papers.cfm?abstract_id=1867304; A. Spencer Bergstedt, *Estate Planning and the Transgender Client,* 30 W. NEW ENGLAND L. REV. 675, 699–702 (2008), *available at* http://digitalcommons.law.wne.edu/cgi/viewcontent.cgi?article=1054&context=lawreview.

[4] Bergstedt, *supra* note 3.

[5] Some states have adopted the Uniform Probate Code, but often with variations.

children, grandchildren, or great-grandchildren of the decedent, if the decedent had children. Otherwise, the assets may go to the decedent's parents, if they are still living.

A will is a legally-binding document used to direct how the decedent's assets are to be distributed according to the decedent's wishes. A will can direct who will take care of the decedent's minor children after their death, if the children have no other living legal parent. Having a will can speed up the probate process, a court procedure by which the decedent's estate is divided. The will includes appointment of a person to entrust with the responsibility of acting as executor of the estate. Executors put all of the decedent's financial affairs in order, such as paying outstanding bills, canceling credit cards, and notifying banks and business institutions that the account-holder is deceased. A will can be used to disinherit individuals who would otherwise inherit from the decedent under the rules of intestacy. A will can be changed at any time so long as the maker of the will is alive, including to account for life changes such as births, deaths, and divorces. An individual under guardianship pursuant to a court order may be able to make or update a will if they can prove that they have testamentary capacity.[6] A guardian or conservator does not have to the right to create or change a will for another individual.

Assets can be passed directly to one's heirs or held in trust for their benefit. A trust is created by a person known as the "grantor," who determines the rules governing the operation of the trust. The rules include a designation of the "beneficiary," who will receive the income and, ultimately, the principal of the assets in the trust. A trust can be revocable or irrevocable. The grantor appoints a "trustee," whose job is to manage the trust and its assets, according to the rules set by the grantor. The trust receives gifts from a "donor," which forms the principal or "corpus" of the trust, and later the trust will also have interest, dividends, and profits (if any) from any increases in value to the principal ("capital gains").

III. Wills Issues for Victims of Domestic Violence

When domestic violence is involved, victims may have been excluded from equal participation in decision-making about the family's finances, and the same may hold true for preparation of their wills. Victims may be unaware of what is in their abusive partner's will. Victims may also not be aware of what is in their own

---

[6] The standard for capacity to make a new will is different from the determination of whether the person needs a guardian or conservator. While being placed under a court-ordered guardianship creates a presumption that the person lacks capacity, the presumption can be rebutted by evidence that they had testamentary capacity at the time the will was made by showing that they understood they were making a will, understood its purpose, had a general understanding of the property owned, knew who the heirs were, and had formed a reasonable judgment about the terms of the will.

will if the abuser engaged an attorney to prepare the wills together, but made all the decisions on behalf of both wills. Attorneys preparing wills may not realize that spouses or intimate partners engaging their services together have adverse interests in terms of estate planning. Attorneys should educate themselves on the ethical implications of joint representation in these kinds of cases and assess whether the interests of both parties may be met.[7]

It is important for victims of domestic violence to consider making a will (or revising an existing will) with a separate attorney, if possible. If a victim dies without a will, an abusive spouse will certainly inherit a share of the victim's estate. Depending upon the intestacy laws of the jurisdiction, and whether the victim has any living children, the abuser may be poised to inherit all of the victim's estate. However, wills may also be created in the context of coercive control, if the victim has not separated from their abuser.

Divorce or disinheriting will divest an abusive spouse of rights in the estate of their victim. If the victim is not yet divorced from the abuser, executing a will can be a way for a victim to try to disinherit the abusive spouse. However, wills divesting abusive spouses may still meet challenges, and could be overturned based upon the public policy of providing support to a surviving spouse. An elective share is a portion of the decedent's estate that can be claimed by the surviving spouse in place of their inheritance. It is also called a statutory share, a widow's share, or a forced share. The purpose of permitting an elective share is to prevent disinheritance of a spouse. The elective share is usually a fraction of the estate that is fixed by law. When spouses divorce, they generally waive their future interest in the elective share in each other's estates. In cases in which a domestic violence victim has not completed a divorce from their abuser at the time of death, the abuser, as the surviving spouse, may still be able to claim an elective share of the estate rather than what was left to them (or denied them) in the will.

The Uniform Probate Code does not address domestic violence.[8] Many states have laws barring inheritance by people convicted of child and elder abuse, but no such laws address inheritance by those who commit domestic violence.[9] Thus, abusers are able to inherit from their victims either under the rules of intestacy, or as a result of provisions made in a victim's will.

The common bases used to contest a will are lack of capacity of the testator; fraud; undue influence; insane delusion; and duress. In some cases, a victim's

---

[7] Goff, *supra* note 3, at 3–6.

[8] *See* Thomas H. Shepherd, *It's the 21st Century … Time for Probate Codes to Address Family Violence: A Proposal That Deals with the Realities of the Problem*, 20 St. Louis U. Pub. L. Rev. 449, 473 (2001).

[9] Carla Spivak, *Spousal Abuse Should Bar Inheritance*, 90 Or. L. Rev. 247, 250 (2011).

family members may be able to challenge wills created under duress or undue influence by the abuser, but it is a high bar to prove the elements necessary to invalidate a will. Some jurisdictions allow the presumption of undue influence to arise where there was a "confidential relationship" between the parties and "suspicious circumstances" surrounding the creation of the will.[10]

Some states, but not all, have enacted statutory provisions to address the issue of inheritance rights of abusers who are convicted of murder or manslaughter of their spouse. However, in general, neither spouse can terminate a tenancy by the entirety, or sell or transfer their ownership interest without the consent and permission of the other. A tenancy by the entirety treats both spouses as a single legal entity. Therefore, without a specific provision of the law addressing this issue, an abuser who kills their spouse may still be entitled to a share of property held with the victim as tenants by the entirety.

Joint Tenants vs. Tenants by the Entirety

When there are assets that are jointly owned by the decedent and another person, the manner in which they can be passed on by a will depends upon the nature of the joint ownership. Where land or property is owned by two or more people, the owners are said to have **joint tenancy.** If the two people who own the property are married to each other, some states recognize the property owners as **tenants by the entirety.** Tenants by the entirety have rights of survivorship, which means that when one spouse dies, the surviving spouse immediately becomes the sole owner of the property. In other words, property passes to their spouse outside probate rather than according to the terms of the deceased spouse's last will and testament, or in trust to their heirs.

In some states, inheritance may be barred or limited when spouses have been living apart for a prolonged period prior to the decedent's death such that they are spouses "in name only." In such cases, the surviving spouse is disqualified from taking their intestate share of the decedent's estate. These provisions may specifically refer to cases in which the separation resulted from domestic violence.

A client may ask that their will designate someone other than the abusive surviving parent to have custody of their children if they die, but, unfortunately, they will not be able to supersede the surviving parent's rights to the children in this manner. However, such a declaration could be useful in the event of the abuser's death, or to help bolster a custody or visitation claim against the abuser by the victim's relatives.[11]

---

[10] RESTATEMENT (THIRD) OF PROP.: WILLS & OTHER DONATIVE TRANSFER § 8.3(b) (2003).

[11] State laws vary, but there are many states that recognize the rights of grandparents and other relatives to seek custody or visitation of children upon the death of a parent.

IV. Powers of Attorney

A power of attorney (POA) is a legal document by which an individual can authorize another person to act on their behalf. The person who is giving the authority is called the principal and the person who takes on the authority to act for the principal is the "agent" or "attorney-in-fact."

A. Durable Powers of Attorney for Health Care

A health care proxy, also known as a "durable power of attorney for health care," "medical power of attorney," or "appointment of a healthcare agent," is a document that appoints another person (a proxy or agent) to make health care decisions on behalf of an incapacitated person. A health care proxy or durable power of attorney is often executed in conjunction with a living will. A health care proxy is an important way to ensure that a person's wishes, contained in a living will or other medical directive, are actually carried out. The person named to carry out those responsibilities may be called the "agent," "healthcare proxy," or "attorney-in-fact" of the person who executes the durable power of attorney.

Living Wills

Different from a last will and testament, a living will is a directive to physicians and other health care providers to ensure that the wishes of the patient are known in the event the patient becomes incapacitated. It has no application after death. Doctors and family members are not left guessing what the seriously ill person would want regarding end-of-life medical care.

Each state has its own legal requirements for creating a valid living will. They typically include directions regarding administration of "palliative care" and "extraordinary measures."[12] A living will can either become effective at the time it is signed, or only when the person is no longer able to express their wishes.

B. Financial Powers of Attorney

A financial power of attorney is a specific type of POA by which someone gives another person the authority to act on financial matters. Many states have a form that must be used in order for a POA to be considered legally valid.

When a financial POA is executed, the agent can conduct a wide range of financial transactions on behalf of the principal, regardless of the capacity of the principal, and without limiting the principal's ability to act on their own behalf.

---

[12] Palliative care includes medical interventions aimed at decreasing pain and suffering. Extraordinary measures include cardiopulmonary resuscitation (CPR) and other attempts to prolong life.

A few examples include presenting the POA to a third party, such as a bank, to withdraw money from the principal's accounts; operating the principal's business; handling insurance or retirement benefits transactions; or signing papers on the principal's behalf to buy or sell real estate. The actions taken by the agent are legally binding upon the principal.

Some financial POAs are effective immediately and others come into effect upon the occurrence of a future event. A POA ends upon the death of the principal. It can also end upon the principal becoming incapacitated, unless the POA is set up as a durable POA. The authority of the agent can also end if the principal revokes it or a court invalidates it. In some states, it automatically ends if the agent was the principal's spouse, and they divorce.

Victims may be coerced into signing over authority to handle their financial affairs to their abuser or to another family member who will act against their interests. There are also cases in which abusers have used forged POAs to transfer or sell the victim's assets. In addition, victims of domestic violence, particularly those with a low level of literacy or lack of English proficiency, are vulnerable to having their abuser coerce or threaten them to get them to sign documents without knowing or understanding what they are signing. Even victims who are educated and fluent in English may sign papers placed in front of them by their abuser in order to avoid making the abuser angry.

Victims may lack financial literacy. They may also have internalized a negative view of their own capacity to independently handle their financial affairs without help from others. In these circumstances, they may transfer control of their finances from their abuser to another individual rather than undertake the role themselves. This abdication of independent financial control can have disastrous results for victims who entrust their finances to the wrong person.

Advocacy Tip: Victims who are capable of acting on their own behalf should be counseled about the dangers of signing over POAs to other people. Referrals to financial literacy programs to help build victims' confidence in handling their own finances can be extremely beneficial. If a client has a disability, or is concerned about becoming incapacitated due to a medical issue, you should engage with them in a serious discussion of who can be entrusted with a POA to act on their behalf.

V. Special Considerations for Victims with Disabilities

A. Living Wills and Durable Powers of Attorney for Health Care

A common tactic abusers use is controlling as many aspects of the victim's life as possible. For victims with a disability, or chronic or terminal illness, abusers have opportunities to exercise power and control that can seriously impact the victim's quality of life and may even have life or death consequences. When a victim is married to their abuser and becomes incapacitated, the abuser can control the victim's access to medical care, including pain relief as well as life-saving measures by medical professionals.

Victims who are still legally married to their abusers can execute living wills or health care proxies to ensure that the abusive spouse does not make medical decisions that are against the victim's wishes if the victim is incapacitated, and unable to express their wishes. They may designate someone other than their abuser to make end-of-life decisions on their behalf. Victims should make sure their medical providers have a copy of any living will or health care proxy they have executed in order to ensure that their abuser does not have the opportunity to overrule their wishes by keeping the doctors ignorant of the existence of a legally-binding statement of their patient's wishes. Copies of these legal documents should be kept with other trusted individuals in a location where the abuser does not have the ability to destroy them.

Advocacy Tip: If your client is legally married to their abuser, especially if they have a serious medical condition, discuss with your client what their wishes are with respect to medical treatment and who they trust to make their medical decisions in the event they become incapacitated. Explain their rights with respect to executing a living will, health care proxy, or durable power of attorney.

B. Special Needs Trusts

Victims with disabilities need long-term financial stability to remain free from violence. In cases in which the victim has disabilities that prevent them from working, they often must rely on government benefits such as Supplemental Security Income (SSI), Social Security Disability Insurance (SSDI), or public assistance to pay for basic necessities.[13] Attorneys representing these survivors in civil actions (including torts, family law actions, and probate matters) must understand how financial gains awarded in those cases could affect their clients' eligibility for government benefits.

---

[13] SSI is a federal income supplement program designed to help aged, blind, and disabled people who have little or no income and few resources. It provides cash assistance to meet basic needs for food, clothing, and shelter. U.S. citizens and a few specific categories of immigrants are eligible to apply for SSI. Applicants must reside in one of the 50 states, the District of Columbia, or the Northern Mariana Islands (Note: Residents of Puerto Rico and other U.S. territories cannot collect SSI). SSDI is a federal benefit for individuals who are deemed completely disabled by the Social Security Administration's (SSA) definition of total disability. Applicants must have worked and paid Federal Insurance Contributions Act (FICA) premiums while working for at least five of the past ten years, with the work requirement varying by the age of the applicant. Public assistance (or public benefits) refers to a range of federal and state welfare programs, including Temporary Assistance for Needy Families (TANF), Supplemental Nutrition Assistance Program (SNAP), and Medicaid benefits. For more information on public benefits, see *Public Benefits and Domestic Violence in Section* Four of this manual.

First, the attorney must ascertain what type of government benefits their client is receiving. If a client is unsure, the attorney will need to examine the client's documents from the Social Security Administration (SSA) or the local department of social services. Some types of government benefits are "means-tested," which means that they have resource and income caps that can affect the client's eligibility for continued receipt of those funds. Many income caps are extremely low, such that a one-time deposit of a lump sum settlement or inheritance into the bank account would cause the client to lose their benefits.

A Special Needs Trust or Supplemental Needs Trust (SNT) is a way of utilizing funds given to a person with a disability that does not jeopardize any government support payments. There are federal statutory requirements for a SNT.[14] SNTs may be used to help victims receive their inheritance or the award they won in litigation without losing their eligibility for critically important government benefits. These trusts are designed to preserve the beneficiary's eligibility for "means-tested" government benefit programs.[15] Funds in SNTs are not considered for purposes of most "means-tested" government benefits, meaning they do not count against the amount of resources the recipient of the benefit is allowed to have without becoming ineligible for the benefits. Particular types of distributions can be made from a SNT without adversely affecting the beneficiary's eligibility.[16]

Advocacy Tip: Review the potential effect of a divorce settlement or a tort settlement, etc. on the government benefits your client is receiving or for which they have applied. Have a conversation with your client early in the litigation process about a Special Needs Trust, and who could administer the trust on behalf of the client. Your client should also be advised to speak with a trusts and estates attorney about how the type of trust established will affect what happens to any funds left in the trust upon their death, and whether the funds can be left to beneficiaries designated by the client.

VI. Conclusion

Attorneys working with victims of domestic violence should be aware of the impact that wills, trusts, and estates law can have on their clients, and what

---

[14] 42 U.S.C. § 1396(d)(4)(A); *see also Program Operations Manual System (POMS),* Social Security Administration, http://policy.ssa.gov (last visited May 1, 2018).

[15] For an in-depth discussion of Special Needs Trusts, see Kristen M. Lewis, *Planning for Beneficiaries with Special Needs* (American L. Inst., CLE Materials, 2017).

[16] Examples of permissible distributions include payments for services for the sole benefit of the beneficiary such as utilities, cable, internet service, home security systems, accountants and investment advisors, housekeepers, special education advocates, personal care services, laundry services, hair stylists, massage therapists, counselors; for goods such as medical equipment and supplies, household appliances, furniture, clothing; for transportation such as taxis and public transportation; and for non-food grocery items such as hygiene items and over-the-counter medications.

may take place if the client becomes incapacitated or passes away. Victims of domestic violence may come to you with questions ranging from how to best protect their assets to how to designate someone to make important health care or financial decisions on their behalf. They may also come to you with the common but mistaken belief that they can prevent an abusive co-parent from gaining custody of the children by designating a caregiver for their children in their will. Attorneys should also be conscious of the conflict issues that may arise in representation involving estates, and be advised of concerns that may arise if the client has disabilities, and the impact an inheritance will have on a client's government benefits.

APPENDIX

Resources:

- *Estate Planning FAQs,* A.B.A. Real Prop., Trust & Estate L., https://www.americanbar.org/groups/real_property_trust_estate/resources/estate_planning/estate_planning_faq.html.

- *Introduction to Wills,* A.B.A. Real Prop., Trust & Estate L., https://www.americanbar.org/groups/real_property_trust_estate/resources/estate_planning/an_introduction_to_wills.html.

- Wendy S. Goff, *Planning for Nontraditional Families,* 46th Annual Advanced Ali-Aba Summer Program (June 16, 2011), *available at* https://papers.ssrn.com/sol3/papers.cfm?abstract_id=1867304.

- Kristen M. Lewis, *Planning for Beneficiaries with Special Needs* (Am. L. Inst., CLE Materials, 2017).

- *Living Wills and Advance Directives for Medical Decisions,* Mayo Clinic, https://www.mayoclinic.org/healthy-lifestyle/consumer-health/in-depth/living-wills/art-20046303.

- *Fact Sheet: 2017 Social Security Changes,* Soc. Security Admin. (2017), https://www.ssa.gov/news/press/factsheets/colafacts2017.pdf.

Chapter Seventeen:
Tort Law And Domestic Violence

I. Introduction

Historically, courts upheld doctrines that made it nearly impossible for victims of domestic violence to hold their abusers accountable in civil court. For example, the doctrine of chastisement granted men permission to engage in violent conduct toward their wives that today would constitute the essential elements of a domestic violence tort.[1] The doctrine of coverture made it such that, upon marriage, a woman's legal rights and obligations were subsumed by those of her husband because a husband and wife were considered to be one person. Therefore, if a wife sued her husband, whatever she recovered from her husband would legally belong to him. Until it began to lose hold in the 1970s, the vast majority of states recognized the doctrine of spousal immunity.[2] These tools of the patriarchy are generally outdated, but vestiges of them remain today. For example, a number of states still do not allow spouses to sue each other for intentional infliction of emotional distress.[3]

Many insurance companies have policies that appear to sustain the doctrine of spousal immunity, barring coverage for cases between spouses, family members,

---

[1] The United States stopped recognizing this doctrine in the 1870s.

[2] Thanks to the Women's Property Acts enacted in the 1840s, courts generally allowed wives to finally sue their husbands for torts arising from property interests. However, most courts refused to interpret the new Acts as allowing a married woman to sue her husband for torts arising from injury to the person.

[3] *See, e.g.,* Henry v. Henry, 534 N.W.2d 844, 847 (S.D. 1995) (holding that intentional infliction of emotional distress claims are only allowed based on conduct after divorce, but not based on conduct during marriage).

and those involving intentional acts. For this reason, traditional contingency-fee personal injury attorneys, who typically rely on collecting a judgment from insurance companies, might avoid taking on domestic violence tort claims, especially because of a widely-held assumption that batterers are judgment-proof. Meanwhile, family law attorneys privy to an abuser's income and assets might feel unqualified to litigate torts. Finally, lawyers who work at nonprofit legal aid organizations are prohibited from litigating domestic violence tort claims if they are federally funded by the Legal Assistance for Victims Grant Program.[4]

There is a serious lack of awareness, even in the domestic violence advocacy community, that a civil remedy for domestic violence even exists. But awareness is growing. There are several law review articles on the subject.[5] Some scholars are pushing for inclusion of domestic violence sections in first-year tort textbooks and courses.[6] A growing number of attorneys across the country, including Alipato Project, the first and only nonprofit organization to obtain financial justice for domestic violence victims by suing their abusers in civil court, have successfully litigated domestic violence tort cases, holding abusers accountable, providing resources to victims, and sending a strong message to the community that domestic violence will not be tolerated.[7]

II. Anatomy of a Tort Case

A. Intake and Decision to Litigate

It is important for an attorney to seriously consider whether filing a domestic violence tort case is in the client's best interest. The attorney should advise their client that litigating a domestic violence tort case can be a long and arduous process. In addition, the attorney should consider that filing a civil suit may escalate the violence against the victim, or even give the abuser the idea of counter-suing. Other times, a victim might choose not to go forward with a civil suit because their abuser is judgment-proof. However, nonfinancial benefits may also motivate victims. For example, the act of filing a complaint might bring a victim empowerment, therapeutic benefits, closure, and/or deterrence. A sample intake form can be found in the appendix to this chapter.

---

[4] U.S. DEP'T OF JUST. OFF. OF VIOLENCE AGAINST WOMEN, OFFICE OF VIOLENCE AGAINST WOMEN, OMB No. 1122-0020, OVW FISCAL YEAR 2013 LEGAL ASSISTANCE FOR VICTIMS GRANT PROGRAM 10–11 (2013), *available at* http://www.ovw.usdoj.gov/docs/2013-lav-solicitation.pdf.

[5] *See, e.g.,* Camille Carey, *Domestic Violence Torts: Righting a Civil Wrong,* 62 U. KAN. L. REV. 695 (2014); Rhonda L. Kohler, *The Battered Woman and Tort Law: A New Approach to Fighting Domestic Violence,* 25 LOY. L.A. L. REV. 1025 (1992).

[6] *See, e.g.,* Jennifer B. Wriggins, *Domestic Violence in the First-Year Torts Curriculum,* 54 J. OF L. EDUC. 511 (2004).

[7] Scott Morris, *Tia Katrina Taruc Canlas Holds Domestic Abusers Accountable,* EAST BAY EXPRESS (Sept. 13, 2017), https://www.eastbayexpress.com/oakland/spreading-the-fire/Content?oid=9073668.

Client Safety

Work closely with victim advocates, shelters, or other service providers to create a safety plan for your client before filing a lawsuit.

Lawyers are not trained to respond to an emergency and your client should know this. Instead of being your client's emergency contact, you can help your client choose their first responder.

B. Proving Liability

In civil actions, the general standard of proof is by a "preponderance of the evidence." This requires the trier of fact to believe that more likely than not (more than 50 percent probability), the abuser assaulted/battered/stalked/etc. the victim. However, if punitive damages are sought, a victim plaintiff must prove by a "clear and convincing evidence" standard that the abuser acted with oppression, fraud, or malice.

C. Common Law Claims

Assault	An abuser is liable for assault if they act intending to cause a harmful or offensive contact with the victim or acts intending to cause an imminent apprehension of such a contact, and the victim is put in imminent apprehension of such a contact.[8]
Battery	An abuser is liable for battery if they act intending to make harmful or offensive bodily contact with the victim, the victim does not consent to the contact, and harmful or offensive contact results.[9]
Intentional Infliction of Emotional Distress (IIED)	An abuser is liable for IIED if they intentionally or recklessly cause severe emotional harm to the victim through extreme and outrageous conduct.[10]

---

[8] *See* RESTATEMENT (SECOND) OF TORTS § 21.

[9] *Id.* §§ 13, 18.

[10] *See* RESTATEMENT (THIRD) OF TORTS § 46.

Invasion of Privacy	The right of privacy is invaded by: (a) unreasonable intrusion upon the seclusion of another … or (b) appropriation of the other's name or likeness … ; or (c) unreasonable publicity given to the other's private life … ; or (d) publicity that unreasonably places the other in a false light before the public.[11]
Negligent Infliction of Emotional Distress (NIED)	An abuser is liable for NIED if they negligently cause a victim to suffer serious emotional distress. (a) Direct victims: occurs when a victim suffers emotional distress as a result of fearing for their own safety.[12] (b) Bystander victims: occurs when a person who is not directly abused, but who witnesses a family member being abused may sue. For example, children who suffer serious emotional harm as a result of contemporaneously perceiving an event caused by the negligence of the abuser which results in sudden serious bodily injury to a close family member.[13] However, many jurisdictions still recognize immunity for tort suits filed by a child against a parent.[14]
False Imprisonment	An abuser is liable for false imprisonment if they act intending to confine the victim within boundaries fixed by the abuser, the abuser's act directly or indirectly results in confinement of the victim, and the victim is conscious of the confinement or is harmed by it.[15]

---

[11] *See* RESTATEMENT (SECOND) OF TORTS § 652(A)(2).

[12] *See* RESTATEMENT (THIRD) OF TORTS § 47.

[13] *See id.* § 48.

[14] Carey, *supra* note 5.

[15] *See* RESTATEMENT (SECOND) OF TORTS § 35.

Nonconsensual Pornography

Abusers might be liable for IIED and invasion of privacy torts for subjecting their victims to **nonconsensual pornography**, commonly and erroneously referred to as "revenge porn."[16] A California jury in 2014 awarded a woman $250,000 after an ex-boyfriend posted nude photographs of her on Facebook in violation of privacy laws.[17] Similarly, **cyberstalking,** or online harassment, can also give rise to these common law causes of action.

Tort of Domestic Violence

Some states have developed a specific tort claim for domestic violence, including a Battered Woman's Syndrome tort in Washington and New Jersey, and a Domestic Violence Tort statute in California. Some jurisdictions recognize torts arising from gender-motivated violence or hate crimes. For example, Illinois and New York City acknowledge gender-motivated violence claims, while Minnesota, Nebraska, New Jersey, and D.C. have hate crime statutes that create civil liability for gender-based domestic violence and sexual assault. Other relevant torts include non-consensual pornography and cyberstalking.

Examples of these specific tort claims and other relevant torts are discussed below, but it is important to recognize that statutes and remedies will vary by jurisdiction.

- Washington

In 1993, the Spokane County Superior Court created a new tort of Battered Woman's Syndrome. The Court enumerated the elements of the tort of battered woman's syndrome as follows: "(1) a pattern of volitional acts, which include physical acts and gestures, as well as statements, threats, or verbal utterances; (2) which is reasonably calculated to create fear or anxiety or to establish perceptions of fear or anxiety for the victim's self or family; (3) that is continuous in nature, and occurs over a period of time; (4) that could reasonably have been foreseen to, and that in fact did cause; (5) physical injury, emotional distress, or a state of emotional dependency that renders a victim unable to effectively maintain an action against her abuser."[18]

---

[16] Calling nonconsensual pornography "revenge porn" suggests the victim has done something to deserve being sexually exploited.

[17] Liamsithisack v. Bruce, Case No. 1-12-CV-233490 (Santa Clara Super. Ct. 2014) (plaintiff sued for invasion of privacy).

[18] Order Denying Defendant's Motion to Dismiss Petition for Battered Women's Syndrome Pursuant to CR 12(b)(6) at 143, Jewett v. Jewett, No. 93-2-01846-5 (Wash. Super. Ct. Spokane Cnty. 1993).

- New Jersey

In *Cusseaux v. Pickett*, the New Jersey Superior Court, Law Division articulated the essential elements of the tort of battered woman's syndrome: "(1) involvement in a marital or marital-like relationship; and (2) physical or psychological abuse perpetrated by the dominant partner to the relationship over an extended period of time; and (3) the aforestated abuse has caused recurring physical or psychological injury over the course of the relationship; and (4) a past or present inability to take any action to improve or alter the situation unilaterally."[19]

- California

In 2002, the California Legislature established a new cause of action specifically for the intentional tort of domestic violence. This statute enhanced the civil remedies available to domestic violence victims to "underscore society's condemnation of these acts, to ensure complete recovery to victims, and to impose significant financial consequences upon perpetrators."[20]

California Civil Code Section 1708.6 provides that a victim can sue for the tort of domestic violence if they suffered an injury resulting from "abuse" committed by a "spouse, cohabitant, former cohabitant, or person with whom the suspect has had a child or is having or has had a dating or engagement relationship."[21] "Abuse" is defined as it is defined in the California Penal Code: to "intentionally or recklessly causing or attempting to cause bodily injury, or placing another person in reasonable apprehension of imminent serious bodily injury to himself or herself, or another."[22]

Under Civil Code Section 1708.6, a victim may recover general damages, special damages, punitive damages, costs, reasonable attorney's fees, and any other relief that the court deems proper.[23]

- Illinois

In 2004, the Illinois State Legislature enacted the Illinois Gender Violence Act, which provides that victims of "gender-related violence" may seek actual damages, damages for emotional distress, punitive damages, attorney's fees, costs, and other appropriate relief.[24] "Gender-related violence" means any of the following:

(1) One or more acts of violence or physical aggression satisfying the elements of battery . . . that are committed, at least in part, on the basis of a person's sex . . .

---

[19] Cusseaux v. Pickett Jr., 652 A.2d 789, 793–794 (N.J. Super. Ct. Law Div. 1995).

[20] CAL. CIV. CODE § 1708.6, added by Stats. 2002, ch. 193, § 2.

[21] CAL. PENAL CODE § 13700(b).

[22] *Id.* § 13700(a).

[23] CAL. CIV. CODE § 1708.6(b)–(c).

[24] 740 ILL. COMP. STAT. 82/15.

(2) A physical intrusion or physical invasion of a sexual nature under coercive conditions satisfying the elements of battery . . .

(3) A threat of an act described in item (1) or (2) [above] causing a realistic apprehension that the originator of the threat will commit the act.[25]

• Minnesota's Civil Damages for Bias Offenses

Minnesota provides that victims of "bias offenses" have a civil cause of action and is entitled to recover the greater of $500 or actual general and special damages, punitive damages, or other appropriate relief.[26] "Bias offense" means conduct that would constitute a crime that was committed because of the victim's or another's actual or perceived sex, race, color, religion, sexual orientation, disability, age, or national origin.[27]

D. Damages

A victim of domestic violence is entitled to compensatory, special, and punitive damages. Compensatory damages are intended to compensate a plaintiff for all the detriment proximately caused by the wrongdoing. These damages include general damages, those that necessarily or usually result from particular wrongful acts, and are implied by law to have occurred. General damages can include pain and suffering, mental suffering, loss of consortium, and other noneconomic damages. Special damages are those that do not arise from a wrongful act but depend on the circumstances peculiar to the infliction of each respective injury. They generally correspond to economic damages and include loss of earnings, medical expenses, and are pecuniarily measurable. Punitive damages are intended not to compensate the victim, but to punish the abuser and deter future misconduct.

A sample complaint containing causes of action and damages sought can be found in the appendix to this chapter.

III. Additional Considerations

A. Statute of Limitations (SOL)

It is important to familiarize yourself with remedies unique to your jurisdiction because sometimes domestic violence victims benefit from a more generous statute of limitations.

---

[25] 740 ILL. COMP. STAT. 82/5.

[26] MINN. STAT. § 611A.79(1)–(2).

[27] *Id.* subd. (1).

- For example, in Illinois, the SOL for assault and battery is two years.[28] However, the SOL for certain acts of gender-related violence is seven years.[29]

- Similarly, in Minnesota, the SOL for assault, battery, and false imprisonment is two years, unless "the conduct that gives rise to the cause of action also constitutes domestic abuse," in which case the SOL is six years.[30]

- In California, the SOL is three years from the date of the last act of domestic violence by the abuser against the victim.[31]

B. Venue

Generally, venue is proper where the defendant lives, or where the abuse took place. Often, when choosing a venue, you may find that venue is proper in more than one court. The abuser might live in one county, while the abuse occurred in another county.

Advocacy Tip: Common considerations when choosing a venue include:

- Whether potential jurors in one area may view your case more favorably

- Attorney's proximity to the court

- Witnesses' proximity to the court

- Whether a particular court seems biased against domestic violence claims

To ensure the victim can take advantage of the best venue available, be sure to know your jurisdiction's venue rules:

- For example, in Texas, venue is proper where "a substantial part of the events . . . giving rise to the claim occurred," or "in the county of defendant's residence at the time the cause of action accrued."[32]

- In Arizona, if "there exists in the county where the action is pending so great a prejudice against the party requesting a change of venue that he cannot obtain a fair and impartial trial," then the court may change the venue.[33]

---

[28] 735 ILL. COMP. STAT. 5/13-202.

[29] 740 ILL. COMP. STAT. 82/20.

[30] MINN. STAT. § 541.07(1); Minn. Stat. § 541.05, subd. (9).

[31] CAL. CODE. CIV. PROC. § 340.15(a)(1).

[32] TEX. CIV. PRAC. & REM. § 15.002(a).

[33] ARIZ. REV. STAT. § 12-406 (2016).

C. Family Court, Joinder, *Res Judicata*, and Collateral Estoppel

Depending on your state, joinder of tort and divorce cases may be prohibited, required, or permitted.[34] The abuser might also plead claim preclusion or issue preclusion as a defense to the tort case on the grounds that domestic violence claims and/or issues were already raised and litigated in the dissolution proceedings.[35]

Advocacy Tip: If a dissolution proceeding is pending, you should work closely with the victim's family attorney. If a dissolution proceeding has been finalized, go over the family court case file to spot issues that may affect your tort case. In addition to the issues of joinder, *res judicata*, and collateral estoppel, boilerplate divorce settlements often have release clauses that might prohibit a victim from bringing a subsequent tort case.

D. Bankruptcy Court

An abuser's bankruptcy should have no impact or effect on the enforceability of a domestic violence tort judgment because the bankruptcy rules do not discharge an individual debtor from any debt resulting from "willful and malicious injury by the debtor."[36]

E. Persons with Disabilities

Women with disabilities have a 40 percent greater chance of experiencing domestic violence than women without disabilities.[37] People with disabilities may experience unique forms of abuse that are difficult to issue-spot, but are nevertheless tortious. For example, an abuser might remove or destroy a victim's mobility devices, deny access to prescribed medication, or abuse a victim's service animal.

---

[34] Joinder of tort and divorce cases may be prohibited. *See, e.g.,* Simmons v. Simmons, 773 P.2d 602, 605 (Colo. Ct. App. 1988) (holding that "sound policy considerations preclude either permissive or compulsory joinder of interspousal tort claims … with dissolution of marriage proceedings"). Joinder of tort and divorce cases may be required. *See, e.g.,* Brown v. Brown, 506 A.2d 29, 33–35 (N.J. Super. Ct. App. Div. 1986) (concluding that the "entire controversy doctrine" ordinarily requires joinder but that exceptional cases render that doctrine unfair). Joinder of tort and divorce cases may be permitted. *See, e.g.,* Boblitt v. Boblitt, 190 Cal. App. 4th 603, 606 (2010) (recognizing that remedies sought in a marital dissolution proceeding "is not based on the same primary right as a tort action based on domestic violence and therefore a party is not necessarily precluded from seeking damages for alleged acts of domestic violence and also asking a family law court to consider those same acts of domestic violence …").

[35] Claim preclusion, or *res judicata,* prevents re-litigation of the same cause of action in a second suit between the same parties. Issue preclusion, or collateral estoppel, precludes re-litigation of issues argued and decided in prior proceedings.

[36] 11 U.S.C. § 523(a)(6).

[37] *Facts and Resources: Abuse of Women with Disabilities,* Am. Psychological Ass'n, http://www.apa.org/topics/violence/women-disabilities.aspx (last visited Apr. 18, 2018).

Abusers and their attorneys might try to argue that the damages your client seeks are a result of a preexisting condition. For example, if your client seeks emotional damages for depression, the defense might argue that your client had depression even before the parties met. When such an argument is made, it is important to remember that all American jurisdictions award what are commonly called "eggshell damages."[38] Under the "eggshell plaintiff," "special sensitivity," or "thin-skull" rule, a defendant is liable for a plaintiff's unforeseeable and uncommon reactions to the defendant's tortious act.[39]

F. Undocumented Immigrants and Evidence Rules

Abusers often use their victim's immigration status to exert power and control over their victims. Abusers might convince their victims to stay by saying "nobody will believe an undocumented immigrant." As such, you may want to consider what disclosures regarding immigrant status of your client or their witnesses to make to the jury.

The California Legislature agrees. In 2016, it ended a decades-long norm allowing a person's immigration status to be considered with tort suits claiming loss of future wages. Until recently, an award for the loss of future wages included consideration of what an undocumented immigrant would earn in their country of origin, and not in the United States. However, the California Legislature has now declared that "evidence of a person's immigration status shall not be admitted into evidence, nor shall discovery into a person's immigration status be permitted."[40] Washington adopted a similar rule the following year.[41]

Advocacy Tip: If your state allows the admission of a victim's immigration status into evidence, file a motion *in limine* arguing that the probative value of one's immigration status is outweighed by the danger of unfair prejudice or confusion of the issues.

For example, the Washington Supreme Court ruled in *Salas v. Hi Tech Erectors,* that "the probative value of a plaintiff's undocumented status … is substantially outweighed by the danger of unfair prejudice."[42] The case involved a scaffolding company that was found liable for using ladders that violated safety codes. The first jury found the company negligent, but did not award the plaintiff any damages, having heard evidence of his immigration status. After the Washington Supreme

---

[38] RESTATEMENT (THIRD) OF TORTS: Liab. for Physical & Emotional Harm § 31 cmt. B, reporters' note (2005) ("Every United States jurisdiction adheres to the thin-skull rule; more precisely, extensive research has failed to identify a single United States case disavowing the rule.").

[39] BLACK'S LAW DICTIONARY 593 (9th ed. 2009).

[40] Cal. Evid. Code §351.2(a).

[41] In the Matter of the Proposed New Rule of Evidence 413 – Immigration Status, No. 25700-A-1201 (Wash.) (will become effective September 1, 2018).

[42] Salas v. Hi Tech Erectors, 230 P. 3d 583, 587 (2010).

Court granted the plaintiff another trial in which evidence of his immigration status was inadmissible, the jury awarded him $2.6 million in damages.

G. LGBTQ Plaintiffs and Privacy Torts

The prevalence of domestic violence may be as high or even higher among LGBTQ individuals than the general population.[43] LGBTQ victims face unique forms of control that may give rise to unique tort claims.[44]

For example, abusers in the LGBTQ community might use the threat of "outing" as a way to control their victim. In some cases, "outing" may be actionable. A Colorado appellate court held that disclosing another person's sexual orientation can give rise to civil liability.[45] In California, a jury awarded a transgender woman $250,000 in compensatory damages, and $525,000 in punitive damages, for an invasion of privacy action against a newspaper that "outed" her.[46] The California appellate court reviewing that case noted that a transgender person's gender assigned at birth is a private matter.[47]

IV. Conclusion

While domestic violence tort claims may be one of the rarest and most challenging areas of tort law, they constitute another pathway in which victims may be helped by the law. Through these cases, victims can be financially compensated; additionally, filing a lawsuit against their abuser might be empowering to a victim. Tort law is another area of law that attorneys should consider when representing victims of domestic violence.

---

[43] Taylor N.T. Brown & Jody L. Herman, Williams Inst., *Intimate Partner Violence and Sexual Abuse Among LGBT People: A Review of Existing Research* (Nov. 2015), *available at* https://williamsinstitute.law.ucla.edu/wp-content/uploads/Intimate-Partner-Violence-and-Sexual-Abuse-among-LGBT-People.pdf.

[44] Some scholars have noted that while invasion of privacy torts are promising in theory, they have proved to be disappointing in practice. *See, e.g.,* Anita L. Allen, *Privacy Torts: Unreliable Remedies for LGBT Plaintiffs,* 98 Cal. L. Rev. 1711 (2010).

[45] Borquez v. Ozer, 923 P.2d 166, 172 (Colo. App. 1995).

[46] Diaz v. Oakland Tribune, Inc., 188 Cal. Rptr. 762, 762 (1983).

[47] *Id.*

APPENDIX

Resources:

- **Alipato Project**- DV Tort Lawyers
  - Contact Tia Katrina Taruc-Myers
  - (510) 393-2723

Alipato Project is the first and only nonprofit organization to provide direct legal representation to victims of domestic violence in tort actions against their batterers. Alipato Project hosts MCLE classes and can provide training materials to lawyers interested in pursuing DV torts.

- **Cyber Civil Rights Legal Project (CCRLP)**- Nonconsensual Pornography Lawyers
  - Contact David A. Bateman, K&L Gates
  - (206) 270-6682

The Cyber Civil Rights Legal Project was founded to help victims of nonconsensual pornography by providing them legal assistance on a *pro bono* basis.

Articles:

Camille Carey, *Domestic Violence Torts: Righting a Civil Wrong*, 62 U. KAN. L. REV. 695 (2014).

Jennifer Wriggins, *Domestic Violence Torts*, 75 S. CAL. L. REV. 121 (2001).

Rhonda L. Kohler, *The Battered Woman and Tort Law: A New Approach to Fighting Domestic Violence*, 25 LOY. L.A. L. REV. 1025 (1992).

Sarah M. Buel, *Access to Meaningful Remedy: Overcoming Doctrinal Obstacles in Tort Litigation Against Domestic Violence Offenders*, 83 OR. L. REV. 945 (2004).

ALIPATO PROJECT
Together, we can hold batterers financially accountable.

Sample Intake Form

Date: _____ Interviewer: _____

Name: _____ Phone Number: _____

Message? Y / N [48]

Name of DV Advocate/Counselor:[49] _____

Ethnicity/Nationality: _____ Preferred Gender Pronoun: _____

Place of Birth: _____ Immigration Status: _____

Disabilities/Diagnoses: _____ [50]

Witnesses (Name and Contact Info): _____

Evidence (Circle): Medical Records/Police Reports/Counseling Records/ Harassing E-mails/Text Messages/Photos/Journals/Other:_____

Reason for pursuing civil case: _____ [51]

Information about Perpetrator

Name: _____ County of Residence:[52] _____

DOB: _____ Perpetrator's Attorney:_____

Monthly Income: _____ Assets:_____

Home Owner's Insurance: Y / N Children in common: Y/N

Family Law Case:[53] No/ In progress/ Complete_____

First and last instances of DV, Date(s):[54]_____

Your Proudest Accomplishments:[55] _____

---

[48] Sometimes it is unsafe to leave voice mails for the client.

[49] If the client does not have a domestic violence advocate or counselor, you may want to refer them to one.

[50] Knowing whether your client is a member of a marginalized community will help you better serve them.

[51] This question will help you and the client get on the same page with regard to goals and tactics.

[52] Consider venue options to help your client decide whether to pursue the case.

[53] Make sure that a previous family law court or criminal court order does not preclude your client from seeking damages.

[54] Check the statutes of limitation in your jurisdiction.

[55] End the intake on a positive note. Seeking help is often difficult for victims. Remind them that they are not defined by domestic violence.

ATTORNEY NAME
LAW FIRM
YOUR ADDRESS
CITY, STATE ZIP CODE
PHONE
EMAIL

ATTORNEY FOR _____

IN THE SUPERIOR COURT OF THE STATE OF CALIFORNIA

FOR THE COUNTY OF ALAMEDA COUNTY

PLAINTIFF'S NAME,
 	
                Plaintiff,
        vs.
 	
DEFENDANT's NAME
 	
        Defendants.
	Case No.
	
	Complaint for Damages For:
	
	1) **SEXUAL BATTERY;**
	2) **DOMESTIC VIOLENCE;**
	3) **INTENTIONAL INFLICTION OF EMOTIONAL DISTRESS;**
	4) **NEGLIGENCE;**
	5) **STALKING**
	
	JURY TRIAL DEMANDED

NATURE OF ACTION

1. This is a complaint seeking to make PLAINTIFF whole from the injuries she suffered at the hands of DEFENDANT. PLAINTIFF brings claims against DEFENDANT for sexual battery, for domestic violence (as a continuing tort) under California Civil Code §1708.6, for intentional infliction of emotional distress, for negligence, and for stalking under California Civil Code §1708.7.

THE PARTIES

2. PLAINTIFF is an individual living in _____ County.

3. DEFENDANT is an individual living in _____ County.

COMPLAINT

1

FACTUAL ALLEGATIONS

4. PLAINTIFF and DEFENDANT were married on: [DATE].

5. During the course of their relationship, DEFENDANT engaged in a pattern of emotional and physical abuse over PLAINTIFF.

6. DEFENDANT subjected PLAINTIFF to emotional abuse on an almost daily basis. Examples of this include DEFENDANT calling PLAINTIFF names like [LIST DEROGATORY NAMES].

7. PLAINTIFF is unable to remember the details of every single incident of emotional and physical abuse that occurred between [YEAR] and [YEAR]. However, she documented some of those incidents, some of which are summarized as follows:

8. On DATE, shortly after DEFENDANT and PLAINTIFF were arguing about their relationship, DEFENDANT approached PLAINTIFF and kicked PLAINTIFF's leg.

9. LIST ALL EXAMPLES

FIRST CAUSE OF ACTION
(Sexual Battery)

10. PLAINTIFF incorporates and re-alleges each of the allegations set forth above as though fully set forth herein.

11. On numerous occasions, beginning in or about YEAR and continuing until DATE, DEFENDANT acted with the intent to cause a harmful contact with PLAINTIFF's breasts, buttocks, and genitals.

12. At no time did PLAINTIFF consent to any of the acts of DEFENDANT as alleged above.

13. As a direct and legal result of DEFENDANT's wrongful conduct, PLAINTIFF suffered a sexually offensive contact. As a result of that sexually offensive contact, PLAINTIFF suffered general and special damages.

14. In committing the acts alleged above DEFENDANT acted with malice, oppression, and in reckless disregard of PLAINTIFF's rights and safety. DEFENDANT's conduct warrants an assessment of punitive damages in an amount sufficient to deter such conduct in the future and in an amount to be determined according to proof at trial.

WHEREFORE, PLAINTIFF prays for relief as set forth below.

//

//

COMPLAINT

2

SECOND CAUSE OF ACTION
(Domestic Violence)

15. PLAINTIFF incorporates and re-alleges each of the allegations set forth above as though fully set forth herein.

16. On numerous occasions, beginning in or about YEAR and continuing until DATE, DEFENDANT intentionally or recklessly caused or attempted to cause bodily injury on PLAINTIFF.

17. On numerous occasions during the parties' relationship, DEFENDANT placed PLAINTIFF in reasonable apprehension of imminent serious bodily injury to herself, or another.

18. At no time did PLAINTIFF consent to any of the acts of DEFENDANT as alleged above.

19. As a direct and legal result of DEFENDANT's wrongful conduct, PLAINTIFF sustained injuries. As a result of these injuries, PLAINTIFF suffered general and special damages.

20. Pursuant to Civil Code §1708.6(c), PLAINTIFF is entitled to recover her reasonable attorney's fees in having to prosecute this action as a result of DEFENDANT's wrongful conduct.

21. In committing the acts alleged above, DEFENDANT acted with malice, oppression, and in reckless disregard of PLAINTIFF's rights and safety. DEFENDANT's conduct warrants an assessment of punitive damages in an amount sufficient to deter such conduct in the future and in an amount to be determined according to proof at trial.

WHEREFORE, PLAINTIFF prays for relief as set forth below.

THIRD CAUSE OF ACTION
(Intentional Infliction of Emotional Distress)

22. PLAINTIFF incorporates and re-alleges each of the allegations set forth above as though fully set forth herein.

23. DEFENDANT's conduct, as set forth above, was outrageous.

24. DEFENDANT intended and/or acted with reckless disregard to cause PLAINTIFF emotional distress.

25. As a direct and legal result of DEFENDANT's wrongful conduct, PLAINTIFF suffered severe emotional distress.

26. In committing the acts alleged above, DEFENDANT acted with malice, oppression, and in reckless disregard of PLAINTIFF's rights and safety. DEFENDANT's conduct warrants an

COMPLAINT

3

assessment of punitive damages in an amount sufficient to deter such conduct in the future and in an amount to be determined according to proof at trial.

WHEREFORE, PLAINTIFF prays for relief as set forth below.

FOURTH CAUSE OF ACTION
(Negligence)

27. PLAINTIFF incorporates and re-alleges each of the allegations set forth above as though fully set forth herein.

28. DEFENDANT was negligent.

29. As a direct and legal result of DEFENDANT's wrongful conduct, PLAINTIFF sustained injuries. As a result of these injuries, PLAINTIFF suffered general and special damages.

WHEREFORE, PLAINTIFF prays for relief as set forth below.

FIFTH CAUSE OF ACTION
(Stalking)

30. PLAINTIFF incorporates and re-alleges each of the allegations set forth above as though fully set forth herein.

31. On numerous occasions between DATE and DATE, DEFENDANT engaged in a pattern of conduct the intent of which was to follow, alarm, place under surveillance, or harass PLAINTIFF.

32. On DATE, DEFENDANT violated a restraining order protecting PLAINTIFF from him.

33. On DATE, DEFENDANT called PLAINTIFF"s cell phone __ times in a row.

34. LIST ALL EXAMPLES.

35. As a result of the pattern of conduct described above, PLAINTIFF reasonably feared for her safety, or the safety of an immediate family member.

36. On numerous occasions, between DATE and DATE, DEFENDANT made a credible threat with the intent to place PLAINTIFF in reasonable fear for her safety, or the safety of an immediate family member.

37. DEFENDANT's course of conduct caused PLAINTIFF to suffer substantial emotional distress.

38. On at least one occasion, PLAINTIFF clearly and definitively demanded that DEFENDANT cease and abate his pattern of conduct. However, DEFENDANT persisted in said conduct.

COMPLAINT

4

39. A reasonable person in PLAINTIFF's situation would have feared for her safety, or the safety of an immediate family member.

40. A reasonable person in PLAINTIFF's situation would suffer substantial emotional distress.

41. As a direct and legal result of DEFENDANT's wrongful conduct, PLAINTIFF sustained injuries, causing her general and special damages.

42. In committing the acts above, DEFENDANT acted with malice, oppression, and in reckless disregard of PLAINTIFF's rights and safety. DEFENDANT's conduct warrants an assessment of punitive damages in an amount sufficient to deter such conduct in the future and in an amount to be determined according to proof at trial.

WHEREFORE, PLAINTIFF prays for relief as set forth below.

PRAYER FOR RELIEF

WHEREFORE, PLAINTIFF prays that this Court enter judgment in her favor on every claim for relief set forth above and award her relief including, but not limited to, the following:

For compensatory and general damages in an amount to be proven at trial;

For past and future medical, incidental, and services expenses according to proof;

For prejudgment and post judgment interest as provided by law;

For punitive damages in an amount according to proof or taking some measure to ensure that an example is made of DEFENDANT to deter similar future conduct;

For costs of suit incurred herein;

For reasonable attorney's fees pursuant to Civil Code §1708.6(c); and

For such other relief as the Court deems just and proper.

JURY DEMAND

PLAINTIFF demands trial by jury on all issues so triable.

DATE

_____
NAME
ATTORNEY FOR PLAINTIFF

COMPLAINT

5

Section Four:
Benefits

Chapter Eighteen:
Public Benefits And Domestic Violence

I. Introduction

Victims face many significant barriers to leaving their abusers, but perhaps the greatest obstacle for victims is financial dependence. Therefore, it is important for attorneys who represent victims to acquire familiarity with the many means-tested public benefit programs available to their clients, as well as have a basic understanding of the application and appeal processes.

It is important to note that this chapter will not cover every type of public benefit that may be available to your client. You should also keep in mind that the public benefit programs described in this chapter are distinguishable from other benefit programs which may be available to your client (including Title II Social Security, unemployment insurance, workers compensation, etc.) because they are means-tested.[1] In most cases, the financial, immigration status, and other program eligibility parameters vary from state to state.

II. Federal Rules on Immigrant Eligibility for Public Benefits

A. Overview of the 1996 Welfare Reform Act

Prior to the passage of the Personal Responsibility and Work Opportunity Reconciliation Act of 1996 (PRWORA or 1996 Welfare Reform Act), restrictions on eligibility for public benefits based on an applicant's immigration status were few. With the exception of immigrants who were undocumented or

---

[1] For more information on worker's compensation, see *Employer Responsibilities to Victims of Domestic Violence* in Section Five of this manual. For more information on unemployment insurance, see *Unemployment Insurance and Domestic Violence* in Section Four of this manual.

living in the United States on temporary visas, immigration status was not a barrier to eligibility. Prior to 1996, immigrants with legal status, such as Lawful Permanent Residents (LPRs), were eligible for public benefits in the same way as U.S. citizens.[2] However, since the passage of the 1996 Welfare Reform Act, immigrants other than U.S. citizens and a group of immigrants newly designated as "qualified aliens" are generally excluded from eligibility for public benefit programs for a period of five years.[3]

PRWORA created two categories of immigrants: "qualified alien" immigrants, and all others. The term "qualified alien" is misleading because, in most cases, "qualified" immigrants do not qualify for means-tested public benefits. The term "qualified alien" is defined in the Act as an immigrant who falls into one of the following eight categories: (1) LPR, (2) Refugee, (3) Asylee, (4) Person granted withholding of removal/deportation, (5) Conditional entrant, (6) Person paroled for at least one year, (7) Cuban or Haitian immigrant, (8) Certain battered spouses and children.[4]

The Five-Year Bar is a restriction contained in PRWORA that applies to most (but not all) "qualified aliens" based on how long the immigrant has held his or her designated immigration status (LPR, Cuban or Haitian immigrant, etc.).[5] The Five-Year Bar is the biggest single obstacle to public benefit eligibility for lawfully residing immigrants Although exceptions exist, the Five-Year Bar generally disqualifies "qualified aliens" for "federal means-tested public benefits" for the first five years the immigrant falls within the relevant immigration status.[6] "Qualified aliens" specifically exempt from the Five-Year Bar under the 1996 law are: refugees, asylees, immigrants whose deportation is being withheld, Cuban and Haitian immigrants, and veterans and active duty military and their spouses and dependent children.[7]

States have the authority to determine the eligibility of "qualified aliens" for TANF, Medicaid, and CHIP once the Five-Year Bar has been completed.[8]

---

[2] Lawful permanent residents (LPRs), also known as "green card" holders, are non-citizens "lawfully accorded the privilege of residing permanently in the United States." 8 U.S.C. § 1101(a)(20).

[3] *See* 8 U.S.C. § 1613(a).

[4] 8 U.S.C. § 1641(b)–(c).

[5] 8 U.S.C. § 1613(a).

[6] *See* 8 U.S.C. § 1613(b) (setting forth a list of immigrants exempt from the Five-Year Bar). But see 8 U.S.C. § 1613(c) (setting forth exceptions to the definition of "federal means-tested public benefits."). *See also* 8 U.S.C. § 1613(b),(d).

[7] *See Id.*

[8] 8 U.S.C. § 1612(b). States are not permitted to exclude immigrants from these programs if they fall into the following categories: refugees, asylees, persons whose deportation is being withheld, and LPRs who have or can be credited with 40 quarters of coverage under Social Security. 8 U.S.C. § 1612(b)(2)(B).

However certain classes of immigrants are always exempt from the Five-Year Bar relative to TANF, Medicaid, and CHIP.[9] Although most immigrants lost SNAP eligibility in 1996 as a result of PROWRA, in 2002 Congress restored SNAP eligibility to most legal immigrants who (1) are children, regardless of the date they entered the U.S., (2) have lived in the U.S. for five years, or (3) are receiving disability-related assistance or benefits, regardless of date of entry into the U.S.[10]

The following public benefits are available to everyone, regardless of immigration status:

- WIC
- Emergency Medicaid
- The School Lunch Program
- The Summer Meal Program
- Public Health
- Disaster Relief

B. Victims of Human Trafficking

In 2000, Congress created an exception to restrictions contained in the 1996 Welfare Reform Act for survivors of human trafficking.[11] As a result, human trafficking victims are now eligible for public benefits to the same degree as refugees and asylees.

C. Public Charge Concerns

Sadly, the 1996 Welfare Reform Act's immigration restrictions caused widespread fear and confusion among immigrant families, resulting in decreased participation in the major public benefit programs. Part of the law's chilling effect was due to immigrant applicants' concerns that receiving public benefits would result in being deemed a "public charge." Public charge is a term used to refer to a person considered primarily dependent on government funds for subsistence. Under Section 212(a)(4) of the Immigration and Nationality Act, a client seeking to immigrate to the U.S. or seeking to adjust status to that of an LPR is inadmissible if the individual, "at the time of application for admission or

---

[9] Refugees, people granted asylum or withholding of deportation/removal, Cuban/Haitian entrants, certain Amerasian immigrants, Iraqi and Afghan Special Immigrants, victims of human trafficking, qualified alien veterans and active duty military and their spouses and dependent children are exempt from the Five-Year Bar relative to TANF, Medicaid, and CHIP. Tanya Broder et al., Nat'l Immigr. L. Ctr., Overview of Immigrant Eligibility for Federal Programs (Dec. 2015), *available at* https://www.nilc.org/wp-content/uploads/2015/12/overview-immeligfedprograms-2015-12-09.pdf.

[10] *See* Supplemental Nutrition Assistance Program Guidance on Non-Citizen Eligibility, U.S. Dep't. of Agric. (Sept. 27, 2011), *available at* https://fns-prod.azureedge.net/sites/default/files/Non-Citizen_Guidance_Presentation_Webinar_092711.pdf.

[11] *See* Victims of Trafficking and Violence Protection Act, 22 U.S.C. § 7105(b)(1)(A)–(B) (2000).

adjustment of status, is likely at any time to become a public charge."[12] The public benefits programs that could result in a finding of public charge are those that provide cash assistance (SSI, TANF, and state-funded General Assistance) and institutional Medicaid (Medicaid for long-term care).[13] Though the Public Charge doctrine currently applies to only a fraction of immigrants, due to the serious immigration implications of your client being deemed a public charge, it is crucial to be aware of and able to spot this issue.[14]

Advocacy Tip: Use of cash benefit programs and Medicaid for long-term care can impact the finding of public charge, but other non-cash programs will not.

Advocacy Tip: So long as they are applying for benefits on behalf of their children only, applicants are never required to provide their own Social Security numbers or those of other household members.

The federal law governing the intersection of immigration law and public benefits is challenging, even for the experienced advocate. Further, since the federal laws grant a certain amount of discretion to individual states, in some cases, benefits eligibility for immigrants varies from state to state. Fortunately, there are web-based resources available to help advocates navigate this area of the law.[15]

III. Due Process and Public Benefits

Since the landmark U.S. Supreme Court case of *Goldberg v. Kelly*, public benefits applicants and recipients have had a legally recognized right to fundamental fairness in the context of public benefit administration.[16] *Goldberg v. Kelly* established the procedural due process right to notice of adverse action and a full and fair hearing before the social services agency's tribunal prior to termination of benefits.[17] As a result, state agencies administering public benefit programs must provide a notice detailing the reasons for the proposed termination and a pre-termination hearing, including the following procedural safeguards: an opportunity to confront and cross-examine witnesses at the hearing, the right to present an oral argument, the right to representation, and the

---

[12] 8 U.S.C. § 1182.

[13] *See* Public Charge Fact Sheet, U.S. Citizenship & Immigr. Services, https://www.uscis.gov/news/fact-sheets/public-charge-fact-sheet (last visited Apr. 23, 2018).

[14] *See* Public Charge, U.S. Citizenship & Immigr. Services, https://www.uscis.gov/greencard/public-charge (last visited Mar. 9, 2018); *see* Public Charge, Nat'l Immigr. L. Ctr., https://www.nilc.org/get-involved/community-education-resources/pubcharge/ (last visited Apr. 23, 2018).

[15] *See, e.g.,* Overview of Immigrant Eligibility for Federal Programs, Nat'l Immigr. L. Ctr. (Dec. 2015), https://www.nilc.org/wp-content/uploads/2015/12/overview-immeligfedprograms-2015-12-09.pdf.

[16] Goldberg v. Kelly, 397 U.S. 254, 254 (1970).

[17] In most cases, applicants also have the right to at least one appeal of the administrative tribunal's final agency decision in state or tribal court.

right to adjudication by an impartial decisionmaker whose final, written decision explains its reasoning and cites supporting evidence.[18] Administrative hearings are often conducted via telephone, but in-person hearings are also available, especially if requested as an accommodation for a disability.

Clients should be urged to request an administrative hearing under the following circumstances: the agency has failed to process the application for benefits within the mandated timeframe; the client's benefits have been reduced or cut off; the client's application for benefits was denied; or the agency has made another change to the client's benefits that the client does not agree with.

Since state agencies now use sophisticated technology to administer public benefit programs, errors such as automatic case closures are common. Unfortunately, in many cases, the first time the agency's caseworker takes a hard look at your client's case is after an appeal has been requested. This is why requesting an administrative appeal, even when you and your client are not sure of the underlying merit of the case, is never a bad idea. After all, the client or client's advocate can always drop the appeal if it later becomes apparent that the agency's action was lawful.

Advocacy Tip: Although administrative hearings may be requested via telephone, clients should be advised to request a hearing in writing whenever possible.

Advocacy Tip: Public Benefit applicants cannot legally be required to "prove a negative," such as that they lost a job or are no longer receiving child support.

IV. Public Benefits

The benefits that will be discussed in the remainder of this chapter include SNAP, TANF, WIC, Medicaid, CHIP, LIHEAP, Emergency Medicaid for Aliens, Childcare Assistance, SSI, and General Assistance.

A. SNAP

1. Introduction

SNAP stands for Supplemental Nutritional Assistance Program. SNAP is the federally funded benefit program formerly known as Food Stamps. SNAP benefits are issued electronically via a debit card called an Electronic Benefits Transfer (EBT) card. SNAP applicants are subject to income and asset thresholds and, in the case of able-bodied adults without dependent children, may be required to participate in work activities as a condition of receipt.

---

[18] *See, e.g.,* 45 C.F.R. § 431.200 (setting forth minimum due process rights in context of state-administered Medicaid programs).

2. Income

The gross income threshold for SNAP eligibility is 130 percent of the federal poverty level (FPL), and the net income threshold is 100 percent of the FPL. Most SNAP households must meet both the gross and net income tests, but households that include an elderly member or member with a disability need only meet the net income test.[19] Households in which all members receive either SSI or TANF are called "categorically eligible" households, and such households are exempt from the gross and net income thresholds.

3. Resources

SNAP households may have up to $2250 in "countable" resources. For households containing an elderly member or member with a disability, the countable resource limit is $3500. Certain resources, such as a retirement account, the house in which the SNAP applicant resides or, in most cases, the household's primary vehicle, are excluded from the resource computation.[20]

4. The SNAP Household

SNAP benefits are available regardless of whether the applicant's household contains minor children, and multiple SNAP "households" (benefit units) may exist within a single dwelling unit if the members of the SNAP household eat, buy, and prepare food as a unit, separate from other members of the dwelling unit. For example, a client who is diabetic might adhere to a diet meant to control blood sugar. In that case, so long as the client eats, prepares, and buys food separately from the rest of the people in the home, the client will be considered a one-person SNAP household.[21] If so, only the client's income and assets are considered when determining the SNAP benefit award.

5. Work Requirement for ABAWDs

Unlike TANF, there is no limit to how many months recipients can receive SNAP during their lifetimes; however, there is a time limit on receipt of SNAP by persons designated able-bodied adults without dependents (ABAWDs) who fail to comply with SNAP work program requirements. An ABAWD is someone between the ages of 18 and 49 who has no dependents, and does not have a disability. ABAWDs can

---

[19] *See* SUPPLEMENTAL NUTRITION ASSISTANCE PROGRAM: ELIGIBILITY, U.S. DEP'T. OF AGRIC., https://www.fns.usda.gov/snap/eligibility (last visited Apr. 23, 2018).

[20] *See* SUPPLEMENTAL NUTRITION ASSISTANCE PROGRAM: RESOURCES, U.S. DEP'T. OF AGRIC., https://www.fns.usda.gov/snap/resources-rules-resource-limits (last visited Apr. 23, 2018).

[21] 7 C.F.R. § 273.1(a); *but see* 7 C.F.R. § 273.1(b) (outlining "required household combinations").

get SNAP for only three months in a three-year period if they do not meet certain work requirements.[22]

The SNAP rules require ABAWDs to either (1) work 80 hours per month, (2) participate in qualifying education and training activities at least 80 hours per month, or (3) comply with a workfare program. The ABAWD work requirements to not apply in every jurisdiction, however; state agencies may apply for waiver of the SNAP work rules for a group of persons within the state, and such a waiver will be granted if USDA's Food and Nutrition Service determines that the area in which the individuals reside has (1) a greater than 10 percent unemployment rate, or (2) does not have a sufficient number of jobs for the persons for whom the waiver is requested.[23]

6. Exceptions to the SNAP Work Requirement

Although there are no SNAP rules expressly geared toward addressing the needs of victims of domestic violence, exceptions to the work requirements and time limit for SNAP receipt are available to some able-bodied adult SNAP participants, such as: those responsible for the care of a child or incapacitated household member, those medically certified as physically or mentally unfit for employment, and pregnant women.[24]

7. Immigrant Eligibility

Although most immigrants lost eligibility for SNAP in 1996 as a result of PRWORA, the 2002 Farm Bill restored eligibility to most legal immigrants who (1) are children, regardless of the date they entered the U.S., (2) have lived in the U.S. for five years, or (3) are receiving disability-related assistance or benefits, regardless of date of entry into the U.S.[25]

Advocacy Tip: Undocumented immigrants and others ineligible for SNAP due to immigration status should be urged to apply on behalf of their eligible children.

---

[22] *See* Time Limit for Able-Bodied Adults, 7 C.F.R. § 273.24. For additional guidance on ABAWD work rules/time limits, see Supplemental Nutrition Assistance Program (SNAP): Able-Bodied Adults Without Dependents (ABAWDS), U.S. Dep't. of Agric., https://www.fns.usda.gov/snap/able-bodied-adults-without-dependents-abawds (last visited Apr. 23, 2018).

[23] 7 C.F.R. § 273.24(f).

[24] *See* Supplemental Nutrition Assistance Program: Able-Bodied Adults Without Dependents, *supra* note 22.

[25] *See* Supplemental Nutrition Assistance Program Guidance on Non-Citizen Eligibility, *supra* note 10.

8. Eligibility Screening

Although SNAP applications must be made through individual state social services agencies, the USDA's Food and Nutrition Service has an online pre-screening tool that can help determine whether your client is likely to be found eligible for SNAP.[26]

9. Emergency/Expedited SNAP

Applicants whose needs are especially dire are eligible for "expedited" or "emergency" SNAP benefits. Those eligible for expedited SNAP are entitled to have their applications processed and benefits delivered within seven days.[27] To be eligible for expedited SNAP, your client must fall into one of the following categories: (1) monthly income and money in the bank add up to less than your monthly housing expenses (including utility bills), (2) monthly income is less than $150 and money in the bank is less than $100, or (3) your client or someone in your client's household is a migrant worker with less than $100 in the bank.[28]

B. TANF

1. Introduction

When Congress passed PRWORA in 1996, the cash assistance program known as Aid for Families with Dependent Children (AFDC) was abolished, and a federal block-grant program called Temporary Assistance to Needy Families (TANF) took its place. TANF is the federally funded benefit program that provides cash assistance to indigent families. TANF benefit groups must be composed of families including at least one minor child, or else a pregnant woman.[29] When applying for TANF on behalf of a dependent child, the parent-applicant may have to provide the state with identifying information about the absent parent so that the state may seek reimbursement from the absent parent (i.e., through the state's child support enforcement agency).[30]

Advocacy Tip: You should warn your clients that they will likely be required to cooperate with their state's child support enforcement agency as a condition of receiving TANF.

---

[26] *See* SUPPLEMENTAL NUTRITION ASSISTANCE PROGRAM, PRE-SCREENING ELIGIBILITY TOOL, U.S. DEP'T OF AGRIC., https://www.snap-step1.usda.gov/fns/ (last visited Apr. 23, 2018).

[27] 7 C.F.R. § 274.2(b).

[28] 7 C.F.R. § 273.2(i)(1).

[29] 42 U.S.C. § 608(a)(1).

[30] 42 U.S.C. § 608(a)(2)–(3). *But see* 42 U.S.C. § 602(a)(7)(A)(iii) (pursuant to a determination of good cause, states may waive TANF program requirements including child support cooperation requirements).

2. Policy Behind TANF

Like SNAP and most other benefit programs described herein, TANF is a benefit program enacted under the cooperative federalism model, whereby the federal government, through the Department of Health and Human Services, provides funding and guidelines to the individual states, tribal bodies, and territories (hereinafter "states"), and grants the states broad flexibility to implement their own individual TANF programs so long as they meet the legislative goals of TANF. The express purposes of the TANF program are: (1) to provide assistance to needy families so that children can receive care at home, (2) to reduce dependency by promoting job preparation, work, and marriage, (3) to prevent extramarital pregnancies, and (4) to encourage the formation and maintenance of two-parent families.[31] Under the law, states have broad flexibility to create programs that best serve their individual communities, and may use TANF funds in any manner "reasonably calculated to accomplish the purposes of TANF."[32] Because of the broad discretion given to the states, TANF income and asset qualification rules and maximum benefit allotments vary from state to state.

3. Lifetime Limit

As a general rule, TANF rules prohibit the grant of benefits to applicants who have already received 60 months of TANF benefits within their lifetimes.[33] This restriction is known as the TANF "lifetime limit." Waivers to the "lifetime limit" are available to recipients who face hardships that make it difficult or impossible for them to transition to the workforce.[34] Participants eligible for an extension of the 60-month lifetime limit may include those who: (1) suffer from a mental or physical condition which prevents them from working, (2) are required to stay home to care for an ill or incapacitated person, (3) cannot be gainfully employed due to domestic violence, or (4) have been battered or subject to extreme cruelty.[35] While 60 months is the lifetime limit contemplated in the federal law, states are granted discretion to create TANF programs with shorter lifetime limits. For example, in 2016, Arizona adopted a 12-month lifetime limit, the shortest in the nation.[36]

---

[31] 42 U.S.C. § 601(a).

[32] 42 U.S.C. § 604(a).

[33] 42 U.S.C. § 608(a)(7).

[34] 42 U.S.C. § 608(a)(7)(C).

[35] *See, e.g.,* Social Services, 8.102.410.17 (D)–(F) NMAC (New Mexico regulation re: hardship exception to TANF lifetime limit).

[36] *See* Mary Jo Pitzl, *Arizona Limits Poverty Aid to 1 Year; Strictest in U.S.,* AZ CENTRAL (July 1, 2010), https://www.azcentral.com/story/news/politics/arizona/2016/07/01/arizona-limits-poverty-aid-1-year-strictest-us/86499262/.

4. The Family Violence Option

TANF is likely the only federally funded major public benefit program whose enacting legislation expressly addresses the needs of victims. Federal TANF guidelines encourage the states to adopt TANF programs incorporating something called the Family Violence Option (FVO). The FVO is designed to give states flexibility to waive TANF requirements, i.e., work requirements, and to provide services to victims of domestic violence.[37] Adoption of the FVO by states is optional, and, of those states that have adopted some form of the FVO, policies vary widely. Pursuant to a determination of good cause, states adopting the FVO may waive "program requirements such as time limits (for as long as necessary) for individuals receiving assistance, residency requirements, child support cooperation requirements, and family cap provisions."[38] In states that have adopted the FVO, program time limits (such as the lifetime limit), work activities, and cooperation with child support enforcement agencies are the requirements most commonly waived by the state through the FVO.[39]

5. TANF Work Rules

Although there are some exceptions, adult TANF participants generally must participate in work activities as a condition of receipt of cash benefits. Under federal law, each state must engage at least 50 percent of its TANF families with one work-eligible adult and at least 90 percent of its TANF families with two work-eligible adults in work or "work-related activities" for a minimum number of hours per month. Under the FVO, however, a state may waive its TANF program requirements, including work program rules, for a client affected by domestic violence if complying with those requirements would make it more difficult for the client to escape domestic violence, or would act as a penalty to the individual.[40]

Advocacy Tip: Clients should be advised of their right to waiver of certain TANF program requirements due to hardship stemming from active domestic violence or, in some cases, the long-term effects of domestic violence.

6. Immigration Status and TANF

The children in a TANF household must be U.S. citizens or "qualified aliens."[41] Depending on the state, "qualified alien" applicants may be subject to eligibility restrictions.[42] However, refugees and asylees, aliens whose deportation is being

---

[37] 42 U.S.C. § 602(a)(7); 45 CF.R. § 260.50 *et seq.*

[38] 42 U.S.C. § 602(a)(7)(A)(iii).

[39] *See* Legal Momentum, Family Violence Option: State by State Summary, http://www.ncdsv.org/ images/LM_FamilyViolenceOptionStateByStateSummary_updated-7-2004.pdf (last updated July 2004).

[40] *See* 45 C.F.R. §§ 260.52, 260.54, 260.55.

[41] *See* 8 U.S.C. § 1641(b) (defining "qualified alien").

[42] *See* 8 U.S.C. § 1612(b)(1).

withheld, and LPRs with 40 quarters of coverage are always eligible for TANF.[43] Immigrant clients, such as undocumented immigrants who are not expected to qualify for TANF themselves due to their immigration status, should be urged to apply on behalf of their qualifying (i.e., U.S. citizen) children. Only the Social Security numbers of the household members for whom benefits are requested must be provided.

C. WIC

WIC, short for Special Supplemental Nutrition Program for Women, Infants & Children, is a federal program that provides healthcare referrals, nutritional counseling, and free WIC-approved supplemental foods (such as breakfast cereal, whole grain bread, milk, cheese, yogurt and tofu) to pregnant, postpartum and breastfeeding women, and children up to age five.[44] The WIC income threshold for household eligibility in the 48 contiguous states is approximately 185 percent of the FPL.[45] The WIC program is one of the very few federally funded public benefit programs with no restrictions on eligibility based on immigration status—even undocumented immigrants are eligible for WIC.[46] The USDA's Food and Nutrition Service has an online pre-screening tool that can be used to screen for WIC eligibility.[47]

D. MEDICAID

Medicaid is a federal and state-funded health insurance program for low-income persons with and without disabilities. It is the single largest health insurer of U.S. children. Individual states oversee numerous and various Medicaid programs for different low-income groups, including: children, the elderly, blind persons, persons with disabilities, pregnant women, persons in need of coverage for family planning services, and others. Individual state Medicaid programs vary widely, both in terms of the types of benefits covered, and categorical and other eligibility parameters. However, all states have programs designed to provide the following for those with limited incomes and assets: (1) cover the cost of nursing home care for those who need institutional care, (2) provide home and

---

[43] 8 U.S.C. § 1612(b)(2).

[44] *See* 42 C.F.R. § 1786.

[45] *See* Income Eligibility Guidelines, U.S. Dep't. of Agric. (2017), https://fns-prod.azureedge.net/sites/default/files/wic/WIC-IEGS-2017.pdf.

[46] Others include Emergency Medicaid for Aliens, public health programs that provide immunizations and/or treatment of communicable disease symptoms, the School Lunch Program, and the Summer Meal Program. *See* 8 U.S.C. § 1611(b).

[47] *Special Supplemental Nutrition Program for Women, Infants and Children,* U.S. Dep't of Agric., https://wic.fns.usda.gov/wps/pages/start.jsf (last visited Apr. 23, 2018).

community-based care for those in need of long-term care services, and (3) cover home health care for those who need it.[48]

Historically, work participation requirements have never been associated with Medicaid, however this area of the law is currently in flux. In January 2018, states were encouraged to apply for waivers under Section 1115 of the Social Security Act which would allow the implementation of weekly work requirements for able-bodied adults receiving Medicaid.[49] One such Section 1115 waiver request has been approved (for Kentucky) and, as of the time of writing, applications from 10 other states are pending.[50] Section 1115 of the Social Security Act allows HHS to waive some federal Medicaid requirements if the waivers (1) have an experimental purpose, and (2) promote the objectives of Medicaid (i.e., to provide health services) for so long as needed for the experiment. Health law advocates filed suit challenging the use of the 1115 waiver application process on January 24, 2018 in the U.S. District Court for the district of Kentucky. The suit, brought on behalf of fifteen Kentucky Medicaid recipients, alleges that, in approving the Kentucky Waivers, the Department of Health and Human Services exceeded its authority under Section 1115, since the waivers: (1) are not experiments, and (2) reduce access to health services. It also asserts the administration violated the Administrative Procedure Act's notice and comment requirement when it told state Medicaid directors it would support work requirements. As of the time of writing, the suit is currently pending.[51]

1. Immigration Status and Medicaid

Low-income U.S. citizens are eligible for Medicaid, and "qualified aliens" are often eligible as well, though some are subject to the Five-Year Bar. Depending on the state, "qualified alien" applicants may be subject to other eligibility

---

[48] *Medicaid Overview,* Medicare Interactive, https://www.medicareinteractive.org/get-answers/programs-for-people-with-limited-income/medicaid-and-medicare/what-is-medicaid (last visited Apr. 24, 2018).

[49] Section 1115 of the Social Security Act gives the Secretary of Health and Human Services authority to approve experimental, pilot, or demonstration projects that are found to be likely to assist in promoting the objectives of the Medicaid program.

[50] *See* Sarah Grusin, *Sec. 1155 Waiver Tracking Chart,* Nat'l Health L. Program (Mar. 05, 2018), *available at* http://www.healthlaw.org/issues/medicaid/waivers/1115-waiver-tracking-chart#.WmvksK6nEdU.

[51] The KY suit was brought by the National Health Law Program, Southern Poverty Law Center, and the Kentucky Equal Justice Center. *See* Jane Perkins et al., *Summary of Lawsuit Filed Against HHS Approval of Kentucky Waivers,* Nat'l Health L. Program (Jan. 24, 2018), *available at* https://nationaldisabilitynavigator.org/wp-content/uploads/news-items/NHeLP_Summary-Lawsuit-Kentucky-Waivers_Jan-2018.pdf.

restrictions.[52] Refugees, asylees, aliens whose deportation is being withheld, and LPRs with 40 quarters of coverage are eligible for Medicaid in every state.[53]

As is the case for TANF, when applying for Medicaid on behalf of a dependent child, the parent may have to provide identifying information about the absent parent so that the state may seek reimbursement from that party.

E. CHIP

The Children's Health Insurance Program (CHIP) is a low-cost health insurance program for children whose families' earnings puts them slightly over the income threshold for their state's Children's Medicaid program. CHIP is jointly funded by state and federal monies. Each state has its own CHIP program which is closely linked to its state Medicaid program, and state Medicaid agencies are required to screen child Medicaid applicants for CHIP eligibility. Applications for CHIP can either be submitted through your state Medicaid agency or through your state's Health Insurance Exchange. There is no special enrollment period for CHIP—applicants can apply year-round.

CHIP benefits vary somewhat from state to state; however, all states are required to provide comprehensive coverage, including: routine check-ups, immunizations, doctor's visits, prescriptions, dental/vision care, hospital care (both inpatient and outpatient), lab and x-ray services, and emergency services. Although federal CHIP funding was in jeopardy during the January 2018 congressional budget negotiations, Congress eventually passed a bill authorizing CHIP funding for the next six years.[54]

F. LIHEAP

A federally funded energy assistance program known as the Low Income Home Energy Assistance Program (LIHEAP) provides a lump sum subsidy once annually to cover heating (or, in rare cases, cooling) costs for those at less than 150 percent of the federal poverty level.[55] The subsidy is paid directly to the provider (i.e., electric or gas utility company, propane vendor, firewood/wood pellet vendor, etc.). LIHEAP benefits may also include weatherization. To establish eligibility, at least one member of the LIHEAP household must be either a U.S. citizen or "qualified alien." In many states, LIHEAP households who are current on their utility bill prior to the start of the heating season are guaranteed

---

[52] *See* 8 U.S.C. § 1612(b)(1).

[53] 8 U.S.C. § 1612(b)(2).

[54] *See* Julie Rovner, *CHIP Renewed for Six Years as Congress Votes to Reopen Federal Government*, Kaiser Health News (Jan. 22, 2018), https://khn.org/news/chip-renewed-for-six-years-as-congress-votes-to-reopen-federal-government/.

[55] *See* 42 U.S.C. § 8621 *et seq.*

a moratorium on utility disconnection during the winter months.[56] LIHEAP is available to households regardless of whether they include a child. The process of determining eligibility for LIHEAP is established by each individual state. U.S. citizens and all categories of "qualified aliens" may be found eligible for LIHEAP. The Five-Year Bar does not apply to this program.

G. Childcare Assistance

Childcare assistance is a program which provides financial subsidies for childcare. It is usually administered by state child protective services agencies. This subsidy is made available to families through funds that are paid directly to childcare providers. Participating families must pay a co-pay for the services, and the participating childcare provider must have been approved by the agency providing the benefit. Undocumented parents can apply for the childcare assistance program for their U.S. citizen children or "qualified alien" children. The childcare assistance subsidy program is, like many other benefit programs described herein, a federal-state cooperative program effectuated through block grant funding. States are granted the discretion to define income eligibility policies and many other specifics of their state program; however, they are required to establish a benefit certification period lasting at least 12 months, so that the recipient's compliance burden is minimized.[57]

H. SSI

The Supplemental Security Income program (SSI) is a federally funded welfare program for persons with disabilities. In order to qualify, applicants must meet income and asset qualifications, and must demonstrate that they suffer from a disabling condition or conditions expected to last at least 12 months or to result in death, and which prevents them from being able to perform a "substantial" amount of work.[58] Also known as Title XVI, the SSI program provides monthly disability payments to those who have not contributed sufficient earnings into the Social Security Trust Fund to allow them to qualify for Social Security Disability Insurance (aka Title II or RSDI). Like Social Security Disability and Retirement, the SSI program is administered primarily by the Social Security Administration; however, unlike those benefit programs created under Title II of the Social Security Act, the SSI program is funded entirely by U.S. Treasury funds.

SSI recipients receive a set cash benefit amount each month ($750 per eligible individual/$1125 per eligible couple in 2018), with small adjustments for cost-

---

[56] *See State Disconnection Policies,* U.S. Dep't of Health & Hum. Services, https://liheapch.acf.hhs.gov/Disconnect/disconnect.htm (last visited Apr. 24, 2018) (outlining the terms of each state's LIHEAP program relative to winter moratorium on heating utility disconnects).

[57] *See Fact Sheet,* U.S. Dep't of Health & Hum. Services, https://www.acf.hhs.gov/occ/fact-sheet-occ (last visited Apr. 24, 2018).

[58] 42 U.S.C. § 1382(c)(a)(3).

of-living (COLA) annually.[59] The SSI benefit award for a given year is known as the SSI Standard of Need. Some states supplement the federal SSI benefit with additional payments, resulting in the SSI benefit award being higher in those states.

Although the SSI beneficiary's award is lower than that of a person with a disability who qualifies for SSDI, SSI recipients are entitled to receive a comprehensive category of Medicaid health insurance (SSI Medicaid) with their SSI cash benefit. Even individuals who only receive a small monthly amount of SSI (i.e., $1) as a supplement to their monthly SSDI or Social Security Retirement award receive this comprehensive type of Medicaid with the SSI.

Because the SSI recipient's financial situation is so precarious, it is crucial for clients on SSI to be familiar with the financial eligibility factors and other SSI rules lest they run afoul of them and lose benefits. The SSI resource limits are $2000 for a single person, and $3000 for a married couple who are both on SSI. If your client's resources (i.e., bank account balance) exceeds these limits, the client may be found ineligible and lose SSI benefits. The income rules are more complex, however. After income disregards, a recipient's SSI benefits are offset by other income at the rate of 50 cents for each dollar of income.[60] Finally, SSI recipients will be deemed no longer disabled and face benefit cessation if they return to the workforce and accrue gross monthly earnings in excess of the Substantial Gainful Activity (SGA) level for a given year. In 2018, the SGA for a non-blind individual is $1180, and $1970 for a blind individual.[61]

If your client is just beginning the SSI application/appeal process, make sure your client understands that it is very common to be denied at the application stage and first level of appeal (Request for Reconsideration). At the second appeal level, however, your client will have the opportunity to present his or her disability claim at a hearing before an Administrative Law Judge of the Social Security Administration. At this level of appeal (ALJ Hearing), your client's odds of approval increase dramatically.[62]

---

[59] *Cost of Living Adjustment,* Soc. Sec. Admin., https://www.ssa.gov/news/cola/ (last visited Apr. 24, 2018).

[60] The first $20 in unearned income and the first $65 of earned income per month are disregarded under SSI rules. *See Income Exclusions for SSI Program,* Soc. Sec. Admin., https://www.ssa.gov/oact/cola/incomexcluded.html (last visited Apr. 24, 2018).

[61] *See 2018 Social Security Changes Fact Sheet,* Soc. Sec. Admin. (2018), https://www.ssa.gov/news/press/factsheets/colafacts2018.pdf.

[62] *See, e.g.,* Javier Meseguer, *Outcome Variation in the Social Security Disability Insurance Program: The Role of Primary Diagnoses,* 73 Soc. Sec. Bull. (2013), *available at* https://www.ssa.gov/policy/docs/ssb/v73n2/v73n2p39.html.

Advocacy Tip: Advise your client of the availability of private attorney representation on contingency fee basis (25 percent of lump sum for retroactive benefits or $6000, whichever is less) in SSI disability appeals.

I. Emergency Medicaid for Aliens

Immigrants, including undocumented immigrants, who are ineligible for all other types of Medicaid due to their immigration status and find themselves in an emergency medical situation can receive a limited type of medical insurance coverage designated for medical emergencies.[63] This type of Medicaid program, which goes by different names depending on the state, covers emergency medical bills, including labor and delivery.[64] This limited type of Medicaid covers emergency services for persons who do not meet the qualifying immigration criteria specified in their state's Medicaid regulations but otherwise meet the eligibility requirements of their state's Medicaid plan.[65] An applicant who is eligible for Medicaid under this category is eligible for emergency services coverage only for the duration of the emergency.

J. State-Funded Cash Assistance Programs

The unfortunate truth is that there is no federally supported safety net program for poor childless adults not on SSI. "General Assistance," a program which goes by different names in different states, is state or locality-funded cash assistance designed to provide a safety net of support to indigent recipients (usually adults) who are very poor and not covered by any other assistance programs. The maximum benefit award for this type of cash assistance is quite low—in nearly all states, the maximum benefit is below 50 percent of the poverty line for a one-person household. Despite the great need for this sort of safety-net program, the number of states that have a "General Assistance" type of public assistance program decreased dramatically between 1989 and 2015—from 38 states to only 26.[66]

---

[63] *See* 42 C.F.R. § 435.139.

[64] *See* Sarah Andrews et al., *Emergency Medicaid for Non-Qualified Immigrants – Medical Coverage and Services for Immigrants*, Am. U. (Dec. 7, 2016), *available at* http://library.niwap.org/wp-content/uploads/2015/pdf/PB-Man-Ch17.1-EmergencyMedicaid.pdf (specifically, Emergency Medicaid for Aliens (NM); Emergency Treatment for Aliens (AK); Emergency Medicaid (CT), Emergency Medical for Ineligible Non-citizens (IL)); *see* 42 C.F.R. § 440.255.

[65] *See* 42 C.F.R. § 435.406(b).

[66] *See* Liz Schott & Misha Hill, *State General Assistance Programs Are Weakening Despite Increased Need,* Ctr. on Budget & Policy Priorities (July 9, 2015), https://www.cbpp.org/research/family-income-support/state-general-assistance-programs-are-weakening-despite-increased.

V. Conclusion

Economic hardship and domestic violence often go hand-in-hand. Thus, when representing a low-income victim, it is imperative to screen that client for eligibility for the various public benefits programs available in your jurisdiction. Even in the case of an undocumented immigrant or a childless able-bodied adult, a thorough screening will almost always reveal eligibility for one or more means-tested benefit programs that can help ease the financial burdens associated with domestic violence and facilitate your client's transition to financial independence.

APPENDIX

Public Benefit Eligibility Websites:

- SNAP Eligibility Requirements
  - https://www.fns.usda.gov/snap/eligibility

- SNAP Resource Limits
  - https://www.fns.usda.gov/snap/resources-rules-resource-limits

- SNAP Pre-Screening Tool
  - https://www.snap-step1.usda.gov/fns/

- WIC Eligibility Requirements
  - https://www.fns.usda.gov/wic/wic-eligibility-requirements

- WIC Pre-Screening Tool
  - https://wic.fns.usda.gov/wps/pages/start.jsf

Other Resources:

- Federal Poverty Level Calculator
  - http://www.safetyweb.org/fpl.php

- USDA's Food and Nutrition Services' State SNAP Office Locator
  - https://www.fns.usda.gov/snap/snap-application-and-local-office-locators

- SNAP Special Rules for the Elderly or Disabled
  - https://www.fns.usda.gov/snap/snap-special-rules-elderly-or-disabled

- SSA's SNAP Fact Sheet
  - https://www.ssa.gov/pubs/EN-05-10101.pdf

- USDA's Food and Nutrition Services' Guidance on SNAP Work Rules
  - https://www.fns.usda.gov/snap/able-bodied-adults-without-dependents-abawds

- USDA's Food and Nutrition Services' SNAP Guidance on Non-Citizen Eligibility
  - https://fns-prod.azureedge.net/sites/default/files/Non-Citizen_Guidance_Presentation_Webinar_092711.pdf

- Center on Budget and Policy Priorities, "Policy Basics: An Introduction to TANF" (updated June 15, 2015)
  - https://www.cbpp.org/research/policy-basics-an-introduction-to-tanf

- TANF Overview and Links to Information on Individual State Programs
  - https://www.benefits.gov/benefits/benefit-details/613

- Information on Medicaid and CHIP Programs in Each State
  - https://www.medicaid.gov/medicaid/by-state/by-state.html

- SSI Frequently Asked Questions
  - https://faq.ssa.gov/link/portal/34011/34019/ArticleFolder/422/Supplemental-Security-Income-SSI

Chapter Nineteen:
Unemployment Insurance and Domestic Violence

I. Introduction

Victims of domestic violence are at an increased risk of job loss when compared to employees who are not experiencing abuse. An abuser's interference with the victim's employment can take many forms. For example, abusers may stalk their victims during work hours through unwanted visits, calls, or texts. An abuser may hide a victim's keys and wallet, destroy work uniforms, or threaten injury to prevent the victim from attending work on time or at all.

Victims often adopt a variety of coping mechanisms to try and minimize the impact of the abuse, some of which interfere with work. Victims may avoid coworkers or customers when emotionally distraught or injured. They may break workplace rules in order to appease the abuser or attempt to avoid a disruptive confrontation at their workplace. Further, the victim's family members may experience adverse consequences of domestic violence themselves, by missing work or being late in order to assist the victim. All these issues interfere with the victim or victim's family members' ability to maintain steady employment. They may face discipline, including termination, or quit a job due to domestic violence.

Unemployment insurance benefits allow victims to reduce or eliminate their economic dependence on an abuser after a job loss. Benefits may even provide the resources needed to leave an abusive relationship.

II. Unemployment Insurance System

Unemployment insurance offers temporary, partial wage-replacement benefits to workers who lose their jobs through no fault of their own. Benefits are administered by each state in accordance with federal and state laws.[1] Employers pay an unemployment tax to the state on a portion of each employee's wages. The employer's tax rate increases with the number of claims successfully filed against the employer, incentivizing employers to challenge claims.

Claimants apply for benefits in the state where they were last employed. If the claimant worked in several states in the past 12–18 months, the state where they file should compile wages from the other jurisdictions before calculating benefits. Benefit amounts vary state to state, but are based on past wages.

Claimants must meet initial eligibility requirements. They must have earned sufficient wages during the period of time specified by state law. These wages must have come from a common law employer-employee relationship, and not contractor status. The employer may not be a religious institution or federal job-training program. Unlike the Federal Wage and House Law, undocumented immigrants are not eligible for unemployment insurance.

Further, claimants must have lost their most recent job in a manner that does not disqualify them from benefits. As a safety net system, claimants are presumed to be qualified for benefits unless proven otherwise by their own admission or evidence provided by an employer. While state laws vary, generally, in order to qualify, a claimant must have either voluntarily quit their job for good cause or been terminated for reasons other than gross misconduct.

If a claimant was terminated for misconduct that is deemed to be less severe than gross misconduct (often called "simple misconduct" or "other than gross misconduct" in state statues), they are often eligible for partial benefits after a disqualifying period. Even claimants who have been terminated for intentional wrongdoing should apply for unemployment insurance or consider appealing denials of initial claims to seek partial benefits.

III. Eligibility for Victims of Domestic Violence

Thirty-six states and the District of Columbia have amended their unemployment insurance statues to include protections for claimants who lose

---

[1] *See* Federal Unemployment Tax Act (FUTA), 26 U.S.C. § 3301 *et seq.* (1999) and Title III of the Social Security Act, 42 U.S.C. § 501 *et seq.* A partial list of state unemployment compensation statutes can be found at *Unemployment – State Laws,* Cornell L. Sch. Legal Info. Inst., https://www.law.cornell.edu/wex/table_unemployment (last visited Apr. 18, 2018).

their jobs because of domestic violence.[2] Many states adopted these protections, or amended existing protections, in 2009 and 2010 after Congress offered federal incentive payments to states that expanded their unemployment compensation rules. Among the options available, states could begin offering benefits for "any compelling family reason," defined to include domestic violence against the claimant or a member of the claimant's family.[3]

State courts have begun interpreting these domestic violence protections.[4] In order to assess possible arguments for benefits, claimants must first assess the standard of causation in their state and how tightly or loosely the domestic violence must be related to the job loss.[5]

However, even in states without a domestic violence statutory provision, victims may still be eligible for unemployment benefits under existing rules. For example, good cause for voluntarily quitting may exist where an abuser has threatened the victim in the workplace, creating an unsafe work environment for the victim and victim's coworkers.[6] Good cause may also exist when a victim

---

[2] Alaska Admin. Code tit. 8, § 85.095; Ariz. Rev. Stat. Ann. § 23-771; Ark. Code Ann. § 11-10-513; Cal. Unemp. Ins. Code §§ 1030, 1032, 1256; Colo. Rev. Stat. § 8-73-108; Conn. Gen. Stat. § 31-236(a)(2)(A)(iv); Del. Code Ann. tit. 19, § 3314; D.C. Code § 51-131–136; Ga. Code Ann. § 34-8-194(1)(B)(ii); Haw. Rev. Stat. § 383-7.6; 820 Ill. Comp. Stat. 405/601; Ind. Code §§ 22-4-15-1(1)(c)(8), 22-4-15-1(1)(e), 22-4-15-2(e), 5-26.5-2-2; Kan. Stat. Ann. § 44-706(a)(12), (c)(4); Me. Stat. tit. 26, §§ 1193(1)(A)(4) and 1043(7-B), (23)(B)(3); Md. Code Ann., Lab. & Emp. § 8-1001(b)(3); Mass. Gen. Laws ch. 151A, §§ 1(g 1/2), 14(d)(3), 25(c), 25(e), 30(c); Minn. Stat. § 268.095(1)(9), (6)(b)(10); Mo. Rev. Stat. § 288.501(2)(c); Mont. Code Ann. § 39-51-2111; Neb. Rev. Stat. § 48-628.13(1); N.H. Rev. Stat. Ann. § 282-A:32(I)(a)(3); N.J. Stat. Ann. § 43:21-5; N.M. Stat. Ann. § 51-1-7(A)(1)(b), (F)(1); N.Y. Lab. Law § 593(1)(b)(i); N.C. Gen. Stat. § 96-14.8(2); N.D. Cent. Code § 52-06-02(1)(j); Okla. Stat. tit. 40, § 2-210; Or. Rev. Stat. § 657.176(12); 28 R.I. Gen. Laws § 44-17.1; S.C. Code Ann. §§ 41-35-125, 41-35-130(K); S.D. Codified Laws § 61-6-9.1; Tex. Lab. Code Ann. §§ 204.022(a)(11), (d)(4) and 207.046(a)(2), (c)(4); Vt. Stat. Ann. tit. 21, §§ 1251–1255; V.I. Code Ann. tit. 24, § 304(b)(12)(A); Wash. Rev. Code §§ 50.20.050(1)(b)(iv), (2)(b)(iv), 50.20.100(4), 50.20.240(b), 50.29.020(3)(d), (3)(e); Wis. Stat. § 108.04(7)(s); Wyo. Stat. Ann. § 27-3-311(a)(i)(C).

[3] The American Recovery and Reinvestment Act (ARRA), Pub. L. No. 111-5, 123 Stat. 115 (codified at 42 U.S.C. § 1103).

[4] *See* L.C. v. Bd. of Review, Dep't of Labor, 110 A.3d 949, 949 (N.J. Super. Ct. App. Div. 2015); E.C. v. RCM of Washington, Inc., 92 A.3d 305, 305 (D.C. 2014); Matter of Loney, 731 N.Y.S.2d 279, 279 (N.Y. App. Div. 2001); Constantine v. Employment Dep't, 117 P.3d 279, 280 (Or. Ct. App. 2005).

[5] For example, some states, like Maryland, require proof that domestic violence is "directly attributable" to the job loss (in this state, voluntary quit). Md. Code Ann., Lab. & Emp. § 8-1001(b)(3) (allowing benefits where claimants voluntarily quit for a cause "directly attributable" to being a victim of domestic violence). *See also* Del. Code Ann. tit. 19, ch 33, § 3314(1) (requiring proof that the claimant leaves work "due to circumstances directly resulting from the individual's experience of domestic violence"). Other states require proof that separation was "due to" domestic violence, D.C. Code § 51-131, with "due to" being defined as domestic violence being a "substantial factor," but not necessarily the sole factor, in the job loss, see E.C. v. RCM of Wash., Inc., 92 A.3d 305, 321 (D.C. 2014).

[6] *See* Scott v. Butler, 759 S.E.2d 545, 545 (Ga. Ct. App. 2014).

quits in order to relocate to another state to escape the abuser.[7] Even claimants who are terminated for alleged misconduct may demonstrate that the actions that led to their termination do not rise to the level of either gross or simple misconduct in their state. For example, a claimant who is repeatedly absent due to injuries may demonstrate that the absences were due to no fault of their own and thus not within the common law definition of misconduct in their state.

Many states require that claimants submit written proof of domestic violence. Claimants should check state law to determine what forms of proof are acceptable. Strict requirements limit proof of domestic violence to court orders and police records.[8] More liberal requirements also allow a statement from a wide range of professionals who assist victims, including shelter employees, counselors, attorneys, medical doctors, or clergy members.[9] Victims who cannot provide documentary proof as required by state law should still file for unemployment insurance, as they may be able to obtain benefits under the standard rules for separation (i.e., proving good cause for a voluntary quit or defending against accusations of misconduct if terminated).

Confidentiality Protections for Domestic Violence Victims

Many victims are hesitant to share information about domestic violence with their employer because of internalized shame or fear of damage to their professional reputation. Some states have enacted confidentiality provisions requiring unemployment agencies to safeguard information that claimants reveal about domestic violence in their claims, including the District of Columbia, Hawaii, Illinois, Indiana, Missouri, New Hampshire, New York, Oklahoma, Rhode Island, and South Carolina.[10] However, state agency employees may not be knowledgeable about the confidentiality programs and, unfortunately, these provisions do not include remedies for disclosure of protected information. Victims should seek legal advice if they are concerned about disclosing certain information related to domestic violence.

IV. Obtaining Unemployment Insurance

Victims seeking unemployment insurance benefits must apply in the state where they worked. This is also true if the claimant's states of residence and work differ.

---

[7] *See* Brown v. Div. of Emp. Sec., 320 S.W.3d 748, 748 (Mo. Ct. App. 2010).

[8] Md. Code Ann., Lab. & Emp. § 8-1001(b)(3)(ii) (requiring "active or recently issued" temporary order of protection, order of protection, or other court order documenting domestic violence, or police record documenting "recent" domestic violence).

[9] *See* D.C. Code § 51-132.

[10] *See, e.g.,* D.C. Code § 51-136.

If claimants have worked several jobs in the past 18 months in different states, the state where the victim files should contact all the other states to ensure that the victim receives proper credit for wages in the other jurisdictions.[11] If claimants have a choice of where to file, advocates should compare the benefit rates—including the benefit calculation, maximum amount of benefits, and duration of benefits—to see where the claimant will receive the highest benefit amount. Refer to local rules for these requirements.

Advocacy Tip: If a victim is worried about the impact of domestic violence on his or her job stability, the victim should seek legal advice from an unemployment expert *before* the job loss, whenever possible. Rules on separation vary significantly by state.

V. Appealing Denials of Unemployment Insurance[12]

If a victim's initial claim for unemployment benefits is denied, they have the right to a fair hearing before an impartial tribunal.[13] In most states, the arbiter is an administrative law judge. Deadlines to appeal are short—often 10 to 15 days—with limited opportunities to appeal past the deadline.[14] Claimants should provide the unemployment agency with a reliable address and check their mail regularly to monitor for possible appeals deadlines. This may be challenging for victims living in a shelter or staying with friends and family, or victims living with an abuser who controls the influx of mail.

VI. Continued Eligibility for Unemployment Insurance

Unemployment insurance benefits require the claimant to be attached to the labor market. Thus, once awarded benefits, claimants must meet the ongoing eligibility requirements in their state. Claimants must file periodic claim cards, usually weekly or biweekly. Claimants must be able to work, available for work, and actively search for work during any week in which they claim unemployment benefits.[15] These requirements are difficult for some victims who are actively engaged with medical treatment or transitioning their housing. Some states have relaxed these standards for domestic violence victims and the U.S. Department

---

[11] Information about how to file for unemployment insurance benefits can be found at local American Job Centers funded by the federal government. To find the American Job Center in your local area, see *American Job Center Finder,* CAREERONESTOP, https://www.careeronestop.org/LocalHelp/AmericanJobCenters/find-american-job-centers.aspx (last visited Apr. 18, 2018).

[12] Victims should seek free legal advice or representation to assist with the appeal. See the Appendix to this chapter for resources.

[13] 42 U.S.C. § 503(a)(3).

[14] *See, e.g.,* D.C. Code § 51-111(b) (extending the 15-day appeal deadline in the District of Columbia for excusable neglect or good cause).

[15] 42 U.S.C. § 503(a)(12).

of Labor has indicated that other states can adopt similar legislation.[16] Claimants must further participate in reemployment services and accept suitable work.[17]

To prevent improper payments that could result in being overpaid, as well as potential fraud penalties, claimants should promptly report earned income and any changes in the certification requirements. For example, if a claimant enters a domestic violence shelter or loses access to childcare, they may no longer be considered "available for work."

VII. Conclusion

Domestic violence has the potential to affect victims' jobs in very negative ways. Victims may lose their jobs due to the direct actions of their abusers, or from indirect consequences of domestic violence, such as coming into work late, or having to take time off for medical treatment and legal proceedings. Victims who are worried about losing their jobs because of domestic violence should be directed to attorneys specializing in unemployment insurance. Victims should be advised that they may still be eligible for unemployment insurance even if they were terminated for misconduct, and that partial benefits are a possibility. Receiving unemployment benefits may be crucial to victims who would otherwise become financially dependent on their abusers, and may also enable a victim to leave an abusive relationship.

---

[16] REBECCA SMITH, RICK McHUGH, ANDREW STETTNER & NANCY SEGAL, NAT'L EMP. PROJECT, BETWEEN A ROCK AND A HARD PLACE: CONFRONTING THE FAILURE OF STATE UNEMPLOYMENT INSURANCE SYSTEMS TO SERVE WOMEN AND WORKING FAMILIES 24 (2003), *available at* http://www.nelp.org/content/uploads/2015/03/Between-a-Rock-and-a-Hard-Place-070103.pdf.

[17] 42 U.S.C. § 503(a)(10).

APPENDIX

Resources:

- **Legal Momentum's State Law Guide to Domestic Violence Provisions in Unemployment Insurance Codes**
  - *State Law Guide: Unemployment Insurance Benefits for Domestic & Sexual Violence Survivors*, LEGAL MOMENTUM, https://www.legalmomentum.org/sites/default/files/reports/State%20Law%20Guide-Unemp%20Ins%20for%20Victims%20of%20DV%20%26%20SA-7-14.pdf (last updated July 2014).

- An **Unemployment Benefits Finder** is available online and contains state-specific information on how to file an unemployment insurance claim and find assistance for claimants.
  - *Find Unemployment Benefits*, CAREERONESTOP, https://www.careeronestop.org/localhelp/unemploymentbenefits/unemployment-benefits.aspx.

- **State Unemployment Law List from the Legal Information Institute**
  - *Unemployment – State Laws*, CORNELL L. SCH. LEGAL INFO. INST., https://www.law.cornell.edu/wex/table_unemployment.

- Jennifer Mezey & Drake Hagner, *Expanding Access to Unemployment Benefits for Survivors of Domestic Violence*, CLEARINGHOUSE COMMUNITY (Nov. 2014), http://povertylaw.org/clearinghouse/stories/mezey.

- To search for free unemployment insurance representatives to assist claimants with appeals, visit https://www.lawhelp.org/.

Section Five:
Domestic Violence and the Workplace

Chapter Twenty:
Employment Protections
For Victims Of Domestic Violence[1]

I. Introduction

Domestic violence is widespread in the United States and has significant and long-lasting negative physical, emotional, psychological, health, educational, social, and financial impacts on victims.[2] Given the prevalence, it is likely that many workers are either victims of domestic violence or abusers. This has significant consequences for victims' employment and employment opportunities, as well as for workplaces' bottom lines and security. Abusers often harass, stalk, or harm their victims in workplaces, because they know the victim will be in a specific location during a particular time period. Indeed, homicide is the leading cause of fatal injury to women on the job, and a family member or domestic partner was the perpetrator in 40 percent of work-related homicides involving

---

[1] Material in portions of this chapter previously appeared in Lisalyn R. Jacobs & Maya Raghu, *The Need for a Uniform Federal Response to the Workplace Impact of Interpersonal Violence,* 11 Geo. J. Gender & L. 593 (2010). Such material appears here with the permission of the authors.

[2] *See* Michele C. Black et al., Ctrs. For Disease Control & Prevention, The Nat'l Intimate Partner and Sexual Violence Survey (2011), *available at* http://www.cdc.gov/violenceprevention/pdf/nisvs_report2010-a.pdf. Women of color experience disproportionately high rates of violence. *Id.* at 39.

women in 2016.[3] Accordingly, before taking any action to secure a client's employment or challenge an employment action, it is important to assess the consequences for the client's safety.

A. Workplace Impact on Victims

Economic stability and opportunity are critical to victims being able to take steps to separate from violence and maintain their health and safety while supporting their families. Employment is a key element of this stability, but victims of domestic violence face significant barriers in obtaining and maintaining employment and suffer adverse financial consequences that limit their future economic security.

Victims may be forced to miss work, leave their jobs, or be fired due to stalking, harassment, or an employer's concerns over potential liability. A 2009 study found that more than half of stalking victims lost five or more days of work.[4] Each year, victims of domestic violence are forced to miss nearly eight million days of paid work.[5] Approximately 130,000 victims of stalking in a 12-month period from 2005 to 2006 reported that they were fired or asked to leave their jobs as a result of the stalking.[6] Almost 50 percent of sexual assault survivors lose their jobs or are forced to quit in the aftermath of the assaults.[7] Moreover, a

---

[3] U.S. Bureau of Labor Stat., Census of Fatal Occupational Injuries 2016 (2017), https://www. bls.gov/iif/oshwc/cfoi/cfch0015.pdf. A 2012 study found that nearly 33 percent of women killed in U.S. workplaces between 2003-2008 were killed by a current or former intimate partner. Hope M. Tiesman, Kelly K. Gurka, Srinivas Konda, Jeffrey H. Coben & Harlan E. Amandus, *Workplace Homicides Among U.S. Women: The Role of Intimate Partner Violence,* 22 Ann. Epidemiology 277–284. *See also* Emiko Petrosky, Janet M. Blair, Carter J. Betz, Katherine A. Fowler, Shane P.D. Jack & Bridget H. Lyons, *Racial and Ethnic Differences in Homicides of Adult Women and the Role of Intimate Partner Violence — United States, 2003–2014,* 66 Ctrs. for Disease Control & Prevention, Morbidity & Mortality Weekly Report 741, 741–746 (July 21, 2017), *available at* https://www.cdc. gov/mmwr/volumes/66/wr/mm6628a1.htm#contribAff ("Nearly half of female victims are killed by a current or former male intimate partner.").

[4] Off. of Just. Programs Bureau of Just. Stats., National Crime Victimization Survey: Personal and Property Crimes, 2000 (Aug. 2002); Katrina Baum, Shanna Catalano, Michael Rand & Kristina Rose, Off. of Just. Programs, Bureau of Just. Stats., Stalking Victimization in the United States (2009), *available at* https://www.justice.gov/sites/default/files/ovw/legacy/2012/08/15/bjs-stalking-rpt.pdf [hereinafter Stalking Victimization].

[5] Nat'l Ctr. for Injury Prevention & Control, Costs of Intimate Partner Violence Against Women in the United States (2003), *available at* http://www.cdc.gov/violenceprevention/pdf/IPVBook-a.pdf [hereinafter Costs of Intimate Partner Violence].

[6] Stalking Victimization, *supra* note 4.

[7] U.S. Gen. Acct. Office, Domestic Violence Prevalence and Implications for Employment Among Welfare Recipients 19 (Nov. 1998); S. Rep. No. 138, 103rd Cong., 2d Sess. 54, n. 69 (citing E. Ellis, B. Atkeson & K. Calhoun, *An Assessment of the Long-Term Reaction to Rape,* 50 J. Abnormal Psychol. 264 (1981)).

2005 study of female employees in Maine who were victims of domestic violence found that 60 percent lost their jobs due to the violence.[8]

In addition to missing work and losing jobs, victims also lose income and suffer from other adverse financial impacts. One study found that three in ten stalking victims accrued significant out-of-pocket costs, such as attorney fees, replacing or repairing damage to property, childcare costs, moving expenses, or changing phone numbers.[9] Furthermore, abusers may ruin the victim's credit score and rental history, making it more difficult for victims to find new jobs and housing; sabotage transport and child care arrangements; and steal or control assets, including bank accounts and credit cards.[10]

Victims may require changes in the workplace to improve safety and performance or accommodations for disabilities related to the violence. For instance, victims may have performance issues related to the violence, possibly due to fear, trauma, or a medical condition, requiring workplace changes or intermittent absences. Victims may be absent from or late to work due to stalking, harassment, or violence by an abuser, occurring either away from work or at work. One of the most common accommodations needed by victims is time off to meet with the police, appear in court for an order of protection or criminal hearing, obtain medical attention for injuries caused by the violence, relocate, or to meet with an advocate to engage in lifesaving safety planning for themselves or a family member who is a victim of violence. However, many victims do not have access to leave or sick days, either paid or unpaid, or cannot afford to take unpaid leave, and risk losing a job if they do so. Unfortunately, many victims are unable to secure these accommodations or supports, and are often forced into the untenable position of having to choose between getting paid or taking these critical steps toward securing their health and safety.

B. Costs of Domestic Violence to the Workplace

Domestic violence, sexual assault, and stalking have significant economic impacts for employers, including lost productivity, absenteeism, and safety concerns. The Centers for Disease Control and Prevention (CDC) estimated that in 2003, the cost of intimate partner rape, physical assault, and stalking totaled $5.8 billion each year for direct medical and mental health care services

---

[8] ELLEN RIDLEY, JOHN RIOUX, KIM C. LIM, DESIRAE MASON, KATE FARAGHER HOUGHTON, FAYE LUPPI & TRACEY MELODY, ME. DEP'T OF LABOR & FAMILY CRISIS SERV., DOMESTIC VIOLENCE SURVIVORS AT WORK: HOW PERPETRATORS IMPACT EMPLOYMENT (2005), *available at* http://www.maine.gov/labor/labor_stats/publications/dvreports/survivorstudy.pdf.

[9] STALKING VICTIMIZATION, *supra* note 4; INST. FOR WOMEN'S POL'Y RES., THE ECONOMIC COST OF INTIMATE PARTNER VIOLENCE, SEXUAL ASSAULT, AND STALKING (Aug. 2017), *available at* https://iwpr.org/wp-content/uploads/2017/08/B367_Economic-Impacts-of-IPV-08.14.17.pdf [hereinafter THE ECONOMIC COST].

[10] *See* THE ECONOMIC COST, *supra* note 9, at 4.

and lost productivity from paid work and household chores.[11] Converted to 2017 dollars, the cost in the United States would be $9.3 billion.[12] The annual cost of lost productivity due to domestic violence was estimated to be $727.8 million (in 1995 dollars), with more than 7.9 million paid workdays—the equivalent of more than 32,000 full time jobs—lost each year.[13] The CDC reported the costs of direct medical and mental health care services related to intimate partner violence to be nearly $4.1 billion a year.[14]

Domestic violence and stalking also pose significant financial and security risks for the workplace. In a 2007 national survey, 43 percent of CEOs and 91 percent of employees said domestic violence negatively impacts the bottom line.[15] In addition, stalking poses risks to the safety of victims, coworkers, and customers or clients, and often results in property damage.

C. Impact of Abusers on Workplaces

Employees can be abusers as well, and a abuser's behavior can also impact their employer's bottom line. Abusers often use their employers' property, including company cars, devices, computers, and sometimes fellow employees, to keep track of their victim's whereabouts. In one study, 78 percent of domestic violence abusers reported that they had used their employer's workplace resources at least once to express remorse or anger, check up on, pressure, or threaten the victim.[16]

Abusers' own work performance and ability to concentrate—and thus, their employers' financial health—are negatively impacted by the violence as well. In a 2004 study of domestic violence abusers, 48 percent reported having difficulty concentrating at work, and 42 percent reported being late to work.[17] A 2012 study in Vermont found that 80 percent of abusers said their own job performance was negatively affected by their perpetration of domestic violence; 19 percent caused or almost caused an accident at work.[18] Participants in the study had lost a total

---

[11] COSTS OF INTIMATE PARTNER VIOLENCE, *supra* note 5.

[12] *See* THE ECONOMIC COST, *supra* note 9, at 4.

[13] COSTS OF INTIMATE PARTNER VIOLENCE, *supra* note 5.

[14] *Id.*

[15] *2007 CEO and Employee Survey,* CORP. ALL. TO END PARTNER VIOLENCE (2007), http://www.caepv.org/about/program_detail.php?refID=34.

[16] LOIS GALGAY RECKITT & LAURA A. FORTMAN, ME. DEP'T OF LABOR, IMPACT OF DOMESTIC OFFENDERS ON OCCUPATIONAL SAFETY & HEALTH: A PILOT STUDY 1 (2004), *available at* http://www.maine.gov/labor/labor_stats/publications/dvreports/domesticoffendersreport.pdf.

[17] *Id.*

[18] MICHELE CRANWELL SCHMIDT & AUTUMN BARNETT, VT. COUNCIL ON DOMESTIC VIOLENCE, EFFECTS OF DOMESTIC VIOLENCE ON THE WORKPLACE: A VERMONT SURVEY OF MALE OFFENDERS ENROLLED IN BATTERER INTERVENTION PROGRAMS (Jan. 2012), *available at* http://www.uvm.edu/crs/reports/2012/VTDV_WorkplaceStudy2012.pdf.

of 52,731 days of work—equivalent to 27 years of fulltime employment and $5.4 million in estimated lost wages—because of consequences related to domestic violence.[19] Significantly, these surveys found that in many cases, a supervisor was aware of the abuser's behavior but failed to confront or admonish the employee about it.[20]

II. Victims' Rights and Remedies in the Workplace

Victims have several legal rights in the workplace, including protections from employment discrimination and access to critical supports, like workplace accommodations and paid or unpaid leave. However, availability of those rights and supports depends on the jurisdiction in which the victim lives, the type of violence they have experienced, and the victim's particular needs. Currently, federal law does not provide workplace antidiscrimination protection specifically for domestic violence victims, nor does it provide access to workplace accommodations or job-protected paid leave. Some victims have pursued sex discrimination or sex stereotyping claims, with varying degrees of success, under Title VII of the Civil Rights Act of 1964 (Title VII), or state or local antidiscrimination statutes. Victims with disabilities may be able to obtain antidiscrimination protections and reasonable accommodations pursuant to the federal Americans with Disabilities Act and its amendments (ADA), or under state and local antidiscrimination laws.

In the absence of a federal mandate, states and localities have enacted a variety of reforms over the last 15 years to address the workplace impact of domestic violence, whether providing protection from employment discrimination, or providing access to accommodations, leave, or unemployment insurance benefits.[21] While providing crucial supports for some victims, this local and incremental approach has yielded a patchwork of laws that means that victims' employment security and personal safety is largely dependent on where they live.

A. Anti-discrimination Protections

Victims of domestic violence often fear that telling their current or prospective employers about the violence will jeopardize their employment or employment prospects, and with good reason. The belief that domestic violence is a "private" or "personal" matter often underlies employers' discomfort and reactive behavior when confronted with the workplace impacts of violence. When an employee discloses the violence, or asks for assistance in dealing with it, a common response from employers is to fire them. Victims may also be denied jobs or

---

[19] *Id.*

[20] *Id.;* RECKITT & FORTMAN, *supra* note 16.

[21] For more information on unemployment insurance, see *Unemployment Insurance and Domestic Violence* in Section Four of this manual.

suffer demotions, transfers, or denials of promotions. In some cases, victims lose their jobs because they need workplace accommodations or require changes an employer deems too costly. They may also lose their jobs because their abusers disrupt the workplace, or because of gendered stereotypes about victims. And all too often, employers impose their own beliefs or expectations about what the "correct" course of action is for a victim (i.e., file a police report or obtain an order of protection), and penalize victims for failing to do so, without taking into account the needs and concerns of victims who may not choose that same course of action because it would jeopardize their own safety or wellbeing, or that of their families.

Currently, no federal law specifically prohibits employment discrimination against victims of domestic or sexual violence or stalking. The Security and Financial Empowerment (SAFE) Act, which would prohibit such discrimination, has been introduced in several sessions of Congress, but not enacted.[22] The Obama Administration recognized the impact of domestic and sexual violence on workers and workplaces through an April 2012 memorandum directing all federal agencies to establish and implement policies addressing the workplace impact of domestic violence, sexual assault, stalking and the workplace, and to provide assistance to employees who are victims.[23] In 2012, the U.S. Equal Employment Opportunity Commission (EEOC) issued a fact sheet explaining how Title VII and the ADA could provide protection for victims of domestic and sexual violence.[24] In the absence of specific federal workplace protection, some victims have pursued and obtained redress under Title VII, the ADA, and state and local antidiscrimination laws. Courts have recognized Title VII sex discrimination claims, including sexual harassment, by plaintiffs who were victims of domestic

---

[22] *See* Security and Financial Empowerment Act, S. 2208, 114th Cong. (2015); Security and Financial Empowerment Act, H.R. 3841, 114th Cong. (2015); Security and Financial Empowerment Act, H.R. 1229, 113th Cong. (2013); Security and Financial Empowerment Act, H.R. 3271, 112th Cong. (2011); Security and Financial Empowerment Act, S. 1740, 111th Cong. (2009); Security and Financial Empowerment Act, H.R. 739, 111th Cong. (2009); Victims' Empowerment and Economic Security Act (SEES Act), S.1136, 110th Cong. (2007); Security and Financial Empowerment Act (SAFE Act), H.R. 2395, 110th Cong. (2007).

[23] Memorandum from President Barack Obama on Establishing Policies for Addressing Domestic Violence in the Federal Workforce to the Heads of Executive Dep'ts & Agencies (Apr. 18, 2012), *available at* https://www.gpo.gov/fdsys/pkg/CFR-2013-title3-vol1/pdf/CFR-2013-title3-vol1-other-id225.pdf; U.S. Off. of Personnel Mgmt., Guidance for Agency-Specific Domestic Violence, Sexual Assault, and Stalking Policies (Feb. 2013), *available at* https://www.opm.gov/policy-data-oversight/worklife/reference-materials/guidance-for-agency-specific-dvsas-policies.pdf.

[24] *Questions and Answers: The Application of Title VII and the ADA to Applicants or Employees Who Experience Domestic or Dating Violence, Sexual Assault, or Stalking,* U.S. Equal Emp. Opportunity Comm'n, http://www.eeoc.gov/eeoc/publications/qa_domestic_violence.cfm (last visited Apr. 20, 2018) [hereinafter EEOC, Questions and Answers].

violence and/or sexual assault.[25] Some victims have also been able to challenge discriminatory actions through tort-based claims that their terminations were in violation of public policy.[26]

Alternatively, victims can pursue sex stereotyping claims under Title VII or state or local antidiscrimination laws.[27] *Price Waterhouse v. Hopkins* affirmed that sex discrimination includes discrimination based on sex stereotypes (social norms and expectations about appropriate behavior, roles, and appearance for men and women).[28] Although both women and men can be victims of domestic violence, and such violence occurs in opposite and same-sex relationships, the majority of victims of domestic violence are women and the majority of abusers are men. This has led to the creation of gendered stereotypes about victims and perpetrators of violence.

Female victims are often blamed—by employers, courts, and community members—for the violence perpetrated against them. They are presumed to have provoked the violent or controlling behavior, or seen to be "hysterical" or untruthful in order to deliberately cause problems for the abuser. When an abuser appears at the workplace and disrupts it or threatens the victim, the victim may be blamed for failing to control the abuser's behavior and be penalized with discipline or termination. Employers may believe that if the victim is fired, the victim will leave with the "problem," and the violence will no longer the

---

[25] *See, e.g.,* Meritor Savings Bank v. Vinson, 477 U.S. 57, 62 (1986) (finding hostile work environment claim where plaintiff had been sexually assaulted by her co-worker); Crowley v. LL Bean, Inc., 303 F.3d 387, 392–394 (1st Cir. 2002) (upholding jury verdict on hostile work environment claim and systemic sex discrimination claim where plaintiff was stalked and harassed by co-worker who was fired only after she obtained an order of protection); Excel Corp. v. Bosley, 265 F.3d 365, 367 (9th Cir. 1999) (affirming jury's award on sexual harassment and disparate treatment claims where husband sexually harassed wife, a co-worker, after they separated); Fuller v. City of Oakland, 41 F.3d 1522, 1530 (9th Cir. 1995) (finding successful hostile work environment sexual harassment claim where police officer who ended romantic relationship with fellow officer was stalked and harassed by him, and employer failed to adequately address the situation); Rohde v. K.O. Steel Castings Inc., 649 F.2d 317, 318 (5th Cir. Unit A 1981) (finding Title VII disparate treatment claim successful where plaintiff, who was physically assaulted by co-worker with whom she was in a relationship, was fired where the male employee who assaulted her was not); Valdez v. Truss Components, Inc., No. CV98-1310-RE, 1999 U.S. Dist. LEXIS. 22957 (D. Or. 1999) (denying summary judgment on disparate treatment claim where plaintiff who dated co-worker and was stalked and threatened by him was fired).

[26] *See, e.g.,* Apessos v. Memorial Press Group, No. 01-1474-A, 2002 Mass. Super. LEXIS 404. (Mass. Super. Ct. 2002); Imes v. City of Asheville, 594 S.E.2d 397, 398 (N.C. 2004).

[27] *See* EEOC, QUESTIONS AND ANSWERS, *supra* note 24.

[28] Price Waterhouse v. Hopkins, 490 U.S. 228 (1989).

workplace.[29] Conversely, an abuser may be perceived by the community and the employer as stable, credible, and rational. In situations where the victim and abuser are co-workers, it is often the victim who bears the employment consequences of the violence (firing, transfer, resignation) when the abuse is discovered. Additionally, employers may retaliate against victims who need workplace accommodations, including leave or a modified schedule, which employers may deem too costly or complicated.[30]

Victims with physical or mental conditions related to domestic violence may be able to obtain protection from workplace discrimination and access reasonable accommodations through the ADA.[31] This federal law protects employees with qualifying disabilities who work for employers with at least 15 employees. Most states and many localities have civil rights laws that provide the same or greater protection to individuals with qualifying disabilities, and often cover small employers. Pursuant to the ADA, an employee must have a physical or mental impairment that substantially limits, or severely interferes with, the ability to engage in major life activities. For example, a victim of domestic or sexual violence may suffer from post-traumatic stress disorder (PTSD), which has been found to be a qualifying disability under the ADA.[32] In addition to protection from employment discrimination, victims of domestic violence may be able to obtain "reasonable accommodations"—workplace changes or adjustments that enable people to perform the essential functions of their jobs without creating an "undue hardship" for the employer.[33]

In the absence of a specific federal mandate, several states have enacted laws that specifically prohibit employment discrimination against actual or perceived victims of domestic violence. For instance, California, Connecticut, Delaware, Hawaii, Illinois, New York, and Oregon have added domestic violence victims

---

[29] Employers may take affirmative steps to protect the workplace, such as reporting harassment to the police, obtaining a nuisance or trespass order against the perpetrator, or, in states that authorize it, seeking a workplace restraining order to address harassing or disruptive conduct, rather than firing the victim of the violence. *See* State Law Guide: Domestic and Sexual Violence Workplace Policies, Legal Momentum (Sept. 22, 2015), https://www.legalmomentum.org/sites/default/files/reports/SLG-Domestic%20and%20Sexual%20Violence%20Workplace%20Policies%20-%20rev%209-15.pdf.

[30] *See* Complaint at 5-11, Greer v. Beck's Pub & Grille, Civ. No. C03-2070LRR (N.D. Iowa 2006) (plaintiff who obtained an order of protection against coworker boyfriend was fired); Sereno-Morales v. Cascade Food Inc., 819 F. Supp. 2d 1148, 1149 (D. Ore. 2011) (plaintiff was fired for refusing to withdraw an order of protection she obtained against her co-worker and former boyfriend who assaulted her).

[31] *See* EEOC, Questions and Answers, *supra* note 24.

[32] *See* Job Accommodation Network, Accommodation and Compliance Series: Employees with *Post Traumatic Stress Disorder (PTSD)*, Job Accommodation Network, https://askjan.org/media/ptsd.html (last updated Oct. 8, 2015).

[33] *See* 42 U.S.C. §§ 12111 (9), (10).

(and in some states, sexual assault and stalking victims as well) to the classes of individuals protected from employment discrimination.[34] New York City's law, enacted in 2001, also specifies that discrimination "includes taking actions against a victim based solely on the acts of a person who has perpetrated acts or threats of violence against the victim," addressing the fact that employers often blame victims for the acts of abusers.[35]

B. Reasonable Accommodations

Most employed victims want to keep working. However, they are often unable to do so because of an abuser's harassment or stalking, or an abuser's sabotage of the victim's education and employment, housing, and childcare arrangements. In some cases, with a few key workplace accommodations or changes, victims can continue to work and be safe, which also helps the workplace maintain safety and productivity. For example, a victim may need time off to meet with an attorney or receive counseling, a schedule change to accommodate new childcare arrangements, or a temporary change in work location to evade a stalker.

A few jurisdictions, including Illinois and New York City, provide victims with the right to request and receive reasonable accommodations to address the violence, and protection from retaliation for doing so.[36] Employers in those jurisdictions are required to make reasonable accommodations for victims, such as a modified schedule, to permit her or him to perform their essential job duties, unless doing so would create an undue hardship for the employer. Generally, the reasonable accommodation laws permit employers to request certification that the employee is a victim, typically in the form of a police or court record; documentation from a victim services agency, attorney, clergy member, medical or other professional services provider; or in some cases, the victim's self-certification.

Advocacy Tip: Even if a jurisdiction does not provide victims with a right to request and receive reasonable accommodations, the client may nevertheless request them with the risk of retaliation. In many instances, accommodations may be simple or low-cost. For example, for a victim of stalking, a temporary schedule change, change of work location, or change of entrance or exit to the worksite can help protect both the victim and workplace from the abuser. An employer can provide a victim of phone harassment with a new phone number, or route all calls through the main line. An employer could provide a stalking victim with an escort

---

[34] *See* Cal. Lab. Code §§ 230, 230.1; Conn. Gen. Stat. § 31-51ss; Del. Code Ann. tit. 19 § 711(h); Haw. Rev. Stat. § 378-2; 820 Ill. Comp. Stat. 180/30; N.Y. Exec. L. § 296-1(a); Ore. Rev. Stat. §659A.290(2).

[35] N.Y.C. Admin. Code § 8-107.1.

[36] For the details of these laws, see State Law Guide: Employment Rights for Victims of Domestic or Sexual Violence, Legal Momentum (2015), https://www.legalmomentum.org/sites/default/files/reports/employment-rights.pdf [hereinafter Employment Rights].

to and from the parking lot or public transportation stop to the worksite. Working with your client to create an array of options, including low-cost alternatives, may help persuade your client's employer to provide an accommodation.

C. Leave

Victims often need job-protected leave to address the violence in their lives. As with antidiscrimination protections, the availability of job-protected leave, and the purpose for which it may be used, varies significantly among states and localities.

Federal law does not specifically provide victims of domestic or sexual violence with job-protected leave, whether paid or unpaid. Some victims may have qualifying medical or family situations that entitle them to leave under the federal Family and Medical Leave Act (FMLA). The FMLA provides up to 12 weeks of unpaid, job-protected leave to employees working nearly fulltime for employers with 50 or more employees. Although the statute does not expressly discuss domestic or sexual violence, victims may be able to take time off from work to address their own or a family member's "serious health condition."[37] However, the FMLA does not provide leave for victims' non-medical needs, including obtaining an order of protection, attending court, or securing new housing. Moreover, few individuals, especially those in low-wage jobs, can afford to take 12 weeks of unpaid leave.

Fifteen states, including California, Florida, and Illinois, now provide some form of job-protected unpaid leave specifically for victims of domestic violence, and in some cases sexual assault and stalking as well.[38] Although the details of the laws vary regarding the size of the employer covered, the approved reasons for leave, and the required notice of leave and certification, generally the laws allow victims to take time off from work to obtain an order of protection; participate in a court proceeding; obtain medical attention, legal advice, counseling, or victim services; or relocate.

Victims who have reported the violence to law enforcement also may be able to take job-protected unpaid leave from work under their state's crime victim leave laws. More than 30 states prohibit an employer from firing individuals who take time off from work to participate in a court proceeding.[39] Some laws only apply if the individual is the crime victim; others provide protection where the individual takes leave for a proceeding where a family member is the crime victim. Some laws are only triggered if the victim is subpoenaed or involved in a criminal proceeding.

---

[37] *See* Municipality of Anchorage v. Gregg, 101 P. 3d 181, 184 (Alaska 2004) (holding that a woman's condition resulting from domestic violence, a car accident, and pregnancy constituted a "serious health condition" within the meaning of the FMLA).

[38] For the details of these laws, see EMPLOYMENT RIGHTS, *supra* note 36.

[39] *Id.*

The United States is one of only a few countries that does not guarantee workers any paid sick leave. In 2016, Executive Order 13706 required businesses contracting with the federal government to provide their employees with up to 56 hours of paid sick leave annually, including use of paid leave for family care, and to address domestic violence.[40] An increasing number of states and localities now provide workers with access to earned paid sick time, which in some jurisdictions can also be used by victims of domestic violence to address needs related to the violence.[41] The details regarding the accrual of the time and the circumstances in which the leave can be used vary; some jurisdictions allow the worker to use paid sick time only when the worker is the victim.

Considering the substantial variation among states and localities in terms of the availability of antidiscrimination protections, access to reasonable accommodations and paid or unpaid leave, it is critical for victims' attorneys to review the laws of the relevant jurisdiction(s) carefully.

III. Enforcement and Remedies

If a victim wishes to pursue a claim of discrimination, retaliation, or denial of accommodations or leave, first review the employer's personnel policies and complaint reporting procedure, if one exists. The client may want to make use of that process in the first instance.[42] If the client has an employment contract, check whether the contract includes a provision subjecting all employment-related claims to mandatory arbitration. If the client is a member of a union, review the collective bargaining agreement; he or she may be required to file a grievance.

A client who wishes to bring a discrimination or retaliation lawsuit under Title VII or the ADA must first file an administrative complaint with the EEOC or the appropriate state or local agency. State and local laws may also require administrative exhaustion as a prerequisite to a lawsuit. If a victim proceeds with a Title VII or ADA suit and wins, they may recover monetary damages

---

[40] Establishing Paid Sick Leave for Federal Contractors, 81 Fed. Reg. 67598 (Sept. 30, 2016).

[41] Currently eight states (Arizona, California, Connecticut, Massachusetts, Oregon, Rhode Island, Vermont, and Washington), and a number of cities and localities, including New York City, San Francisco, and Washington, DC, allow victims to use accrued paid sick time to take time off from work to address issues related to the violence. For details of these laws, see *Overview of Paid Sick Time Laws in the United States*, A BETTER BALANCE, https://www.abetterbalance.org/resources/paid-sick-time-legislative-successes/ (last updated Mar. 15, 2018).

[42] In harassment cases, an employer may assert an affirmative defense to vicarious liability if it had a procedure for preventing and redressing harassment and the employee unreasonably failed to take advantage of that procedure. *See* Burlington Indus., Inc. v. Ellerth, 524 U.S. 742, 744 (1998); Faragher v. City of Boca Raton, 524 U.S. 775, 780 (1998).

including back pay, front pay, and compensatory and punitive damages.[43] However, federal law caps total compensatory and punitive damages awards at $50,000 to $300,000, depending on the size of the employer.[44] Uncapped damages are sometimes available under state and local law. Compensatory and punitive damages are not available in ADA reasonable accommodation cases where the employer made a good faith, but unsuccessful, attempt to reasonably accommodate an employee with a qualifying disability.[45]

A client who wishes to pursue a lawsuit for violation of the FMLA can do so without first filing a complaint with the Department of Labor's Wage and Hour Division. For claims under state and local laws involving a denial of a victim's request for reasonable accommodations, or for issues related to different types of leave, the complaint procedure and available remedies vary widely.

Finally, antidiscrimination laws, and state and local victim-specific laws, generally protect employed undocumented victims. However, victims who are undocumented may not be entitled to the full range of remedies available under these protections, particularly with federal laws like Title VII and the ADA. This is a complex and evolving area of the law requiring careful analysis and expert advice.[46]

IV. *Advocacy Tips*

- Check the employer's personnel manuals for any policies addressing how to report discrimination (including sexual harassment) and retaliation; accrual and use of paid and unpaid leave, including sick time, FMLA leave, and leaves of absence; and provision of accommodations, including for individuals with disabilities.

- If your client is a member of a union, check the collective bargaining agreement. Be sure to consult the shop steward and determine whether the client needs to file a grievance. If the abuser is a member of the same union, ensure that the union provides fair advocacy and representation for your client.

---

[43] For a detailed discussion of available damages under federal civil rights statutes, see Barbara L. Johnson, *Types of Damages Available in Employment Cases* (A.B.A. Sec. of Labor & Emp. L., 2011 Annual Conf., Aug. 4–7, 2011), https://www.americanbar.org/content/dam/aba/administrative/labor_law/meetings/2011/annualmeeting/004.authcheckdam.pdf.

[44] 42 U.S.C. §§ 1981(a), (b).

[45] 42 U.S.C. § 12117(a); 42 U.S.C. § 1981(a)(3).

[46] For more information on addressing the needs of immigrant victims of violence, see *Immigration Law and Domestic Violence* in Section Two of this manual.

- If the abuser is the client's coworker or fellow union member, assess whether the abuser has been missing work, (mis)using work resources, or is being treated more favorably than the victim. Collect all such evidence to counter employer or union resistance to assisting the client or to support a discrimination claim.

- If your client has not done so, be prepared to explain to employers, judges, and civil rights agencies why the client did not report to law enforcement or seek an order of protection. This is especially important for clients who are LGBTQ victims or immigrant victims, who have traditionally faced distrust and hostility from law enforcement.

- When appropriate, ask the court to include the workplace in a civil or criminal order of protection sought by the client.

- If your client seeks an order of protection, considering asking the court to require the abuser to provide rent/mortgage payments or support for alternate child care arrangements.

- If your client requests reasonable accommodations, do not allow the employer to merely assert, without proof, that providing the accommodation would impose an undue hardship.

- Counter employer assumptions and stereotypes about the client and victims by developing a relationship with a local service provider or coalition who can provide a helpful letter or an expert affidavit/testimony in a legal proceeding. A letter or testimony from a service provider or advocate can help explain why the client made particular choices (such as not reporting to law enforcement or seeking an order of protection), or needs certain assistance, or requests reasonable accommodations from an employer even when they are not available under the law. This is particularly important to bolster credibility in cases involving LGBTQ and immigrant victims.

- Many state civil rights agencies and EEOC field and district offices will be unfamiliar with charges that allege sex discrimination based on an employer's treatment of victims. Be prepared to educate the agencies and advocate for your client to prevent them from dismissing the charge.

- Ask law enforcement, the prosecutor's office, or court personnel to provide a letter or evidence of the client's appearances in court to support the need for time off.

- Ensure that the employer consults with your client before taking any actions to promote workplace safety, or providing your client with accommodations. For example, in some states employers can seek trespass/nuisance or workplace restraining orders to protect the workplace from a perpetrator. It is critical that the employer consults your client first to address any safety implications for the victim before doing so.

- If a client quits or separates from employment due to domestic violence, encourage them to apply for unemployment insurance benefits. Make sure that you can provide evidence that violence was the reason for the separation, and be prepared to respond to the employer's contestation of benefits.

APPENDIX

Resources:

- KNOW YOUR RIGHTS: DOMESTIC VIOLENCE OR SEXUAL ASSAULT AT WORK, LEGAL MOMENTUM (2005), https://www.legalmomentum.org/sites/default/files/reports/injuries.pdf.

- Lisalyn R. Jacobs & Maya Raghu, *The Need for a Uniform Federal Response to the Workplace Impact of Interpersonal Violence*, 11 GEO. J. GENDER & L. 593 (2010).

- Lisalyn R. Jacobs & Maya Raghu, *Workplace Violence Revisited: Progress and Updates Five Years Post, "The Need for a Uniform Federal Response to the Workplace Impact of Interpersonal Violence"* (A.B.A. Sec. of Labor & Employment L. 9th Annual Labor and Employment Law Conf., Philadelphia, PA, November 4–7, 2015), https://www.americanbar.org/content/dam/aba/events/labor_law/2015/november/annual/papers/20b.authcheckdam.pdf.

- STATE LAW GUIDE: EMPLOYMENT RIGHTS FOR VICTIMS OF DOMESTIC OR SEXUAL VIOLENCE, LEGAL MOMENTUM (2015), https://www.legalmomentum.org/sites/default/files/reports/employment-rights.pdf.

- STATE LAW GUIDE: WORKPLACE RESTRAINING ORDERS, LEGAL MOMENTUM (2015), https://www.legalmomentum.org/sites/default/files/reports/Guide%20on%20Workplace%20Restraining%20Orders%20rev%209-15.pdf.

- *Questions and Answers: The Application of Title VII and the ADA to Applicants or Employees Who Experience Domestic or Dating Violence, Sexual Assault, or Stalking,* U.S. EQUAL EMP. OPPORTUNITY COMMISSION, http://www.eeoc.gov/eeoc/publications/qa_domestic_violence.cfm.

- WORKPLACES RESPOND TO DOMESTIC & SEXUAL VIOLENCE, https://www.workplacesrespond.org/.

Chapter Twenty-one: Employer Responsibilities To Victims Of Domestic Violence

I. Introduction

Domestic violence is often thought of as a private matter that takes place at home. However, domestic violence unavoidably permeates all aspects of a victim's daily life, including in the workplace. According to the Centers for Disease Control and Prevention (CDC), "[a]pproximately 27% of women and 11% of men in the U.S. have experienced contact sexual violence, physical violence, or stalking by an intimate partner."[1] The high rates of victimization make it clear that employers need to address the issue of domestic violence due to its potential to affect so many employees and their coworkers.

Domestic violence in the work place impacts performance and productivity.[2] Up to half of employed victims of domestic violence report that they lost their jobs due at least in part to the domestic violence.[3] In addition to its impact on victims, perpetrators' abusive behavior may also have a dramatic, negative effect on their own workplaces. For example, a 2003 study by the Maine Department of Labor found that "78% of offenders used workplace resources at least once

---

[1] *Intimate Partner Violence: Consequences,* CTRS. FOR DISEASE CONTROL & PREVENTION, https://www.cdc.gov/violenceprevention/intimatepartnerviolence/consequences.html (last updated Aug. 22, 2017).

[2] *7 Reasons Employers Should Address Domestic Violence,* FUTURES WITHOUT VIOLENCE, https://www.futureswithoutviolence.org/seven-reasons-employers-should-address-domestic-violence/ (last visited Apr. 19, 2018).

[3] U.S. GEN. ACCOUNTING OFFICE, *GAO/HHES-99-12: Domestic Violence: Prevalence and Implications for Employment Among Welfare Recipients* 19 (1998), *available at* http://www.gao.gov/archive/1999/he99012.pdf (collecting studies).

to express remorse or anger, check up on, pressure, or threaten their victims."[4] The total annual cost of lost productivity from employment and household chores is $858.6 million; $727.8 million of this total represents the lost productivity from employment.[5]

Domestic violence can also lead to a liability concern for companies.[6] 74 percent of victims are harassed by their abusers at work.[7] When employers do not take steps that adequately protect their employees from violence at work, they may be held legally liable. "Jury awards for inadequate security suits average $1.2 million nationwide and settlements average $600,000."[8]

For these reasons and more, employers have an incentive and responsibility to address domestic violence within their companies. This chapter will describe the ways in which employers may be held liable for disregarding its obligations to address domestic violence in the workplace, and discuss how employers can mitigate their risk of civil liability by implementing clear policies and procedures, developing a comprehensive safety plan, and taking other steps to ensure the workplace is a safe environment.

II. Developing Workplace Policies and Procedures

Employers are responding to the effects of domestic violence on their employees and workplaces. A 2007 study of corporate leaders commissioned by Safe Horizon, the Corporate Alliance to End Domestic Violence, and Liz Claiborne Inc. found that 63 percent of corporate leaders considered domestic violence a major problem; 55 percent cited its harmful effect on productivity; 70 percent believed it has a harmful effect on employee attendance; and 43 percent said their company's bottom line performance had been damaged as a result.[9] In the same survey, 98 percent of employees surveyed believe that domestic violence impacts victims at their workplaces; and 90 percent stated that it is appropriate for workplaces to offer programs and other support related to domestic violence.[10]

---

[4] Lois Galgay Reckitt & Laura A. Fortman, Impact of Domestic Offenders on Occupational Safety & Health: A Pilot Study 1 (Me. Dep't of Labor, 2004), *available at* http://www.maine.gov/labor/labor_stats/publications/dvreports/domesticoffendersreport.pdf.

[5] Nat'l Ctr. for Injury Prevention & Control, Costs of Intimate Partner Violence Against Women in the United States 31 (2003), *available at* https://www.cdc.gov/violenceprevention/pdf/ipvbook-a.pdf.

[6] Futures without Violence, *supra* note 2.

[7] *Workplace Statistics,* Corp. All. to End Partner Violence (citing Victim Services of New York, Report on Costs of Domestic Violence *(1987))*, http://www.caepv.org/getinfo/facts_stats.php?factsec=3 (last visited Apr. 19, 2018).

[8] Futures without Violence, *supra* note 2 (citing P. Perry, *Assault in the workplace,* 23(8) Folio: The Mag. for Mgmt. 4 (1994)).

[9] *See CEO & Employee Survey 2007,* Corp. All. to End Partner Violence, http://www.caepv.org/about/program_detail.php?refID=34 (last visited Apr. 19, 2018).

[10] *Id.*

Recognizing the problem and its accompanying liability concerns, employers have developed a range of responsive policies and procedures. For example, some employers have adopted procedures that permit an employee to use accrued paid or unpaid sick time, vacation time, personal time, or disability leave to address the effect of violence on their lives. Leave provisions in collective bargaining agreements similarly have been invoked to authorize domestic violence-related leave.

Attorneys for employers can and should take an active role in developing and implementing workplace policies and procedures that address the possibility that domestic violence will affect the workplace. Commitment from the highest levels of the organization is critical to send the message that domestic violence is a serious workplace concern. Human resources and security managers charged with developing overall employer policies and procedures should ensure that the issue is addressed not only in written policies but in employee training and in emergency response protocols. An employer's failure to prepare for and to respond quickly and appropriately to domestic violence in the workplace can lead to a plethora of potential areas of liability, as described later in this chapter.

III. Developing a Comprehensive Safety Plan

When an employer becomes concerned that domestic violence may impact the workplace, the prudent employer should develop a comprehensive safety plan designed to provide maximum protection to both the employee who is the target of the violence and the employee's coworkers. Effective employer responses include developing a multi-disciplinary task force or committee with representatives from all levels and relevant departments, such as human resources and security, that is charged with developing workplace modifications designed to prevent the perpetrator from harming the intended victim or any other employee. These policies should include an immediate review of current security arrangements for any necessary enhancements. Those enhancements may include installing or changing locks or key cards; increasing overall security measures, including the temporary hiring of additional security personnel; making the identity of the perpetrator known to security personnel; and providing instructions to preclude the entrance of the perpetrator onto the employer's premises. Depending upon the seriousness of the problem, the police may be called to patrol; a private investigative firm may be engaged; and, in some cases, a psychologist with expertise in dealing with the particular problems posed by the perpetrator may be folded into the response team. Employers should strive to protect victim confidentiality to the maximum extent possible. In some cases, there may be a tension between the goal of confidentiality and the need to protect the safety of everyone in the workplace. Victims should be informed about this limitation, and the employer should develop a communication plan for the victim and the victim's coworkers that furthers the goal of keeping all employees safe without unnecessarily publicizing the victim's personal information.

When assessing safety risks resulting from domestic violence, employers should keep in mind that generally, victims are in the best position to judge whether abusers pose a safety risk. Consequently, victims should be consulted whenever possible as part of the employer's efforts to determine what plans or interventions will make the victim and their coworkers most safe. An employer and the victim together can strategize to determine whether steps such as a transfer to another city, state, or worksite, if available, or a change in working hours, are likely to increase workplace safety. The employee who is experiencing abuse may be referred to a local domestic violence program. If the employer has an employee assistance program (EAP), its counselors should be trained in dealing with domestic violence; the EAP also may be a valuable resource for the victim.

Employers should be prepared to respond with appropriate discipline, up to and including termination, when their own employees are perpetrators of domestic violence, particularly when they use employer resources or commit these acts while on company time. Almost every employer forbids the use of company time and resources in the commission of crimes and acts of domestic violence. Like "drug-free workplace" policies, domestic violence workplace policies may require employees to report acts of domestic violence (such as an arrest for domestic violence or the issuance of a domestic violence protection order against an employee) even if they are committed outside the workplace. In some states, taking action against an employee based on an arrest alone may infringe the employee's rights and could subject an employer to tort liability, particularly if the underlying allegations later are determined to be unfounded. Attorneys should be aware of the potential legal issues and the applicable law in their jurisdictions and should counsel the employer in accordance with those legal requirements.

While the employers' obligations and the applicable legal requirements are generally very similar in the public and private sectors, some additional policy concerns may apply to public employers. For example, a public sector employer might deem acts of domestic violence "conduct unbecoming a public employee" and determine that taxpayer dollars should not be spent on an employee who commits abusive acts or that the commission of those acts renders the employee unfit for public service. A public employer's policy might require a perpetrator to be disciplined for domestic violence, up to and including termination.

States have taken a variety of approaches to respond to the impact of domestic violence on the workplace. Some states have policies that require or encourage employers to proactively address domestic violence, to disseminate information on available resources, or to train human resource professionals and other staff on the effects of domestic violence on the workplace.[11] Other states require state agencies to adopt model workplace safety policies that spell out recommended responses if certain violent behaviors or threats are perceived in the workplace.[12]

There are potentially serious implications of an employer's failure to be proactive when faced with the risk that domestic violence will impact the workplace. The prudent employer will consider and adopt such modifications as are appropriate.

IV. Restraining Orders

Employers may face exposure for failing to take adequate measures to keep the workplace safe from domestic violence. This may lead to tort claims or liability under workers' compensation statutes as discussed later in this chapter. Measures that employers may take in some states include filing for a workplace restraining order and assisting with the enforcement of an employee's civil protective order.

A. Workplace Restraining Orders

Several states have enacted laws that enable employers to apply for restraining orders to prevent violence, harassment, or stalking of their employees.[13] These laws vary significantly in the terms under which an employer may seek a restraining order and with respect to whether the employee who is the victim of such violence must be consulted prior to the employer seeking a restraining order.[14] The victim should be consulted whenever possible before

---

[11] *See, e.g.*, STATE LAW GUIDE: DOMESTIC AND SEXUAL VIOLENCE WORKPLACE POLICIES, LEGAL MOMENTUM (Sept. 22, 2015), https://www.legalmomentum.org/sites/default/files/reports/SLG-Domestic%20 and%20Sexual%20Violence%20Workplace%20Policies%20-%20rev%209-15.pdf.

[12] *See, e.g.*, N.Y. Exec. Order No. 19 (Oct. 22, 2007) (requiring state agencies to develop domestic violence workplace policies in consultation with the state Office for the Prevention of Domestic Violence).

[13] STATE LAW GUIDE: WORKPLACE RESTRAINING ORDERS, LEGAL MOMENTUM (June 20, 2013), https://www. legalmomentum.org/sites/default/files/reports/Guide%20on%20Workplace%20Restraining%20 Orders%20rev%209-15.pdf. These states include Arizona (Ariz. Rev. Stat. § 12-810); Arkansas (Ark. Code § 11-5-115); California (Cal. Civ. Proc. Code § 527.8 & § 527.85); Colorado (Colo. Rev. Stat. § 13-14-104.5 (7)(b)); Georgia (Ga. Code Ann. § 34-1-7); Indiana (Ind. Code § 34-26-6); Nevada (Nev. Rev. Stat. § 33.200-.360); North Carolina (N.C. Gen. Stat. § 95-261); Rhode Island (R.I. Gen. Laws § 28-52-2); and Tennessee (Tenn. Code §§ 20-14-101 to -109). *Id.*

[14] *See, e.g.*, Ark. Code Ann. § 11-5-115 (2009); N.C. Gen. Stat. § 95-261 (2009) (allowing an employer to seek a civil no-contact order on behalf of an employee who has been subject to unlawful conduct at the workplace, such as physical injury or threats of violence). The North Carolina law requires the employer to consult the employee who is the target of the violence to determine whether the employee's safety would be jeopardized. *Id.*

such an order is obtained, since obtaining a protective order sometimes places the employee at greater risk by angering the abuser.

The availability of employer-sought temporary restraining orders may implicate legal issues such as standing and employee privacy. Nevertheless, in some circumstances, events may cause the employer to conclude that a restraining order is necessary to protect others in the workplace.

B. Enforcing Employee Civil Protective Orders

A 2003 study by the Maine Department of Labor found that 21 percent of abusers reported that they contacted their victims at the workplace in violation of a no-contact order.[15] Some states have adopted policies addressing the enforcement of civil protective orders in the workplace in the context of the employer's duty to keep the workplace safe. For example, Indiana requires management employees to make good faith efforts to maintain and enforce a protective order if an employee chooses to notify management about it.[16] Attorneys should be mindful of their own states' requirements, if any, with respect to protection order enforcement laws.

V. Negligence Claims

In some cases, employers may face liability when abusers commit abusive acts at the victim's place of employment. In situations where workers' compensation laws do not apply, employees who are victims of sexual or domestic violence that occurred at work may allege that their employer was negligent by failing to take reasonable steps after knowing or having reason to know of the risk of abuse at work or by intentionally exposing the employee to emotional distress. Common claims include negligence; negligent failure to warn; negligent hiring, retention, and supervision; and intentional infliction of emotional distress.[17]

For example, in *Yunker v. Honeywell, Inc.*, the employer had rehired the abuser-employee after he finished serving a prison term for the strangulation death of a female coworker. During his second period of work with the company, he murdered another female coworker who had spurned his advances.[18] The

---

[15] Reckitt & Fortman, *supra* note 4, at 1.

[16] Ind. Exec. Order No. 99-6 (2009).

[17] *See* Stephanie L. Perin, *Employers May Have to Pay When Domestic Violence Goes to Work*, 18 Rev. Litig. 365, 371 (1999); John E. Matejkovic, *Which Suit Would You Like? The Employer's Dilemma in Dealing with Domestic Violence*, 33 Cap. U. L. Rev. 209 (2004). *See also* Nesheba M. Kittling, Negligent Hiring and Negligent Retention: A State by State Analysis (Nov. 6, 2010), *available at* https://www.americanbar.org/content/dam/aba/administrative/labor_law/meetings/2010/annualconference/087.authcheckdam.pdf.

[18] Yunker v. Honeywell, Inc., 496 N.W.2d 419, 421 (Minn. Ct. App. 1993).

appeals court allowed the victim's representative to maintain a cause of action of negligent retention against the employer.[19]

In *Jerner v. Allstate Insurance Company,* an Allstate employee was terminated for bringing a gun to work in his briefcase.[20] Though he had previously made death threats to his coworkers, Allstate gave the employee a neutral reference.[21] He was then hired at a different company, and upon his termination there, he shot five of his supervisors, killing three of them.[22] The appeals court held there could be a cause of action against Allstate for negligent misrepresentation.[23]

Generally, whether an employer may be held liable to employees who suffer injury by an abuser depends on whether the employer knew of or should have foreseen the risk of violence and took appropriate responsive actions. The risk of violence at work may be more foreseeable when the abuser is an employee, particularly if they have a known history of abuse. For example, in *Crapp v. Elberta Crate & Box Co.,* the appeals court overturned a grant of summary judgment in favor of the employer after an employee shot his female coworker at work.[24] The court determined that the employer may have breached its duty of ordinary care to the victim-employee when it arranged for the perpetrator to return to work to pick up his final check after he had beaten the woman at work. In that case, the employer knew the employee-abuser had a history of violence against women and failed to warn the female employee that the abuser would be returning.[25] On the other hand, the employer in *Clark v. Carla Gay Dress Co.,* was not liable for an abusive husband's shooting of the victim at her workplace.[26]

A victim-employee may succeed in bringing a claim for intentional infliction of emotional distress against an employer if the employer's reckless or intentional behavior exposed the victim to severe emotional distress. For example, in *Gantt v. Security U.S.A. Inc.,* the court upheld an employee's claim of intentional infliction of emotional distress after determining that the employer deliberately allowed the abuser to access and contact the victim at work and insisted that

---

[19] *Id.* at 424.

[20] PLC Labor & Emp't, *Workplace Violence, Practical Law Practice Note* (2014), *available at* https://www.americanbar.org/content/dam/aba/events/labor_law/am/2014/1g_workplace_violence2.authcheckdam.pdf.

[21] *Id.*

[22] *Id.*

[23] *Id.*

[24] Crapp v. Elberta Crate & Box Co., 479 S.E.2d 101, 102-03 (Ga. Ct. App. 1996).

[25] *Id.; accord* Yunker, 496 N.W.2d at 424 (upholding negligent retention claim after employee strangled and killed coworker, when the murderer's post-imprisonment employment demonstrated a propensity for abuse and violence against the employee he eventually killed).

[26] Clark v. Carla Gay Dress Co., Inc., 342 S.E.2d 468, 472 (Ga. Ct. App. 1986).

she have contact with him, despite the employer's knowledge of both the victim's protective order against him and of her fear for her life.[27]

Public Policy Exception for At-Will Employment

Most states recognize a public policy exception to the general rule that employers may dismiss employees at will.[28] Some states recognize that a decision to terminate an employee because of their status as a victim of domestic violence falls within this exception.[29] However, other courts have found that terminating a domestic violence survivor violates public policy only if the state maintains a specific statutory or constitutional provision or an explicitly expressed policy.[30] This may be an area of increasing litigation as more states issue policy mandates specifically addressing domestic violence.

VI. Workers' Compensation

When employees are injured while on the job, they may be entitled to compensation through the workers' compensation system rather than through a negligence claim. In many states, workers' compensation is the presumptive remedy for workplace injuries. The employee does not have to prove that the employer was at fault to receive workers' compensation benefits.[31] Workers' compensation is a state-run system of workplace insurance that each employer is required to carry, and generally covers "medical bills, lost wages, and rehabilitation costs" derived from injuries sustained in the workplace.[32] State laws generally permit employees to pursue a worker's compensation claim or a tort claim, but not both types of remedies.

Employers are not liable for every kind of injury sustained by an employee on the job.[33] To be eligible for workers' compensation in the domestic violence

---

[27] Gantt v. Security, USA, Inc., 356 F.3d 547, 553-57 (4th Cir. 2004).

[28] *See, e.g.,* Mark Rothstein et al., Employment Law 174 (3d ed. 2005).

[29] *See, e.g.,* Apessos v. Memorial Press Group, 15 Mass. L. Rptr. 322 (Mass. Super. Ct. 2002); *see also, e.g.,* Sandra S. Park, *Working Towards Freedom from Abuse: Recognizing a "Public Policy" Exception to Employment-at-Will for Domestic Violence Victims,* 59 N.Y.U. Ann. Surv. Am. L. 121 (2003).

[30] *See, e.g.,* Imes v. City of Asheville, 594 S.E.2d 397, 397-398 (N.C. Ct. App. 2004), *aff'd* 606 S.E.2d 117 (N.C. 2004).

[31] Know Your Rights: Domestic Violence or Sexual Assault at Work, Legal Momentum (2005), https://www.legalmomentum.org/sites/default/files/reports/injuries.pdf.

[32] Jill C. Robertson, *Addressing Domestic Violence in the Workplace: An Employer's Responsibility,* 16 Law & Ineq., 633, 638 (1998), *available at* https://scholarship.law.umn.edu/cgi/viewcontent.cgi?referer=https://www.google.com/&httpsredir=1&article=1554&context=lawineq.

[33] Lenora M. Lapidus, Emily J. Martin & Namita Luthra, The Rights of Women: The Authoritative ACLU Guide to Women's Rights 173 (4th ed. 2009).

context, the victim must have been subjected to domestic violence within the scope of his or her employment, meaning that the injuries "must arise out of employment," "in the course of employment."[34] In this context, courts have been reluctant to classify domestic violence injuries as compensable injuries, instead deeming them as derived from a purely personal issue or "personal animus."[35] For example, in *Epperson v. Industrial Commission*, a husband came to his wife's workplace, and after disarming the security guard, shot his wife.[36] The court in that case found that the assault was of a "purely private origin," and did not find that it had been exacerbated by the circumstances of her employment, and was therefore not a compensable injury.[37]

Conversely, in *Hall v. New England Business Service, Inc.*, an employee was attacked in the parking lot after work by another employee, whom she had been dating and had received a protective order against.[38] The victim employee argued that because she was not working at the time of the attack, the injuries she sustained were not connected to her employment. The Court sided with the employer and held that the victim employee's injuries were compensable because the "injuries resulted from a risk created by her employment, and because they occurred within the "boundaries of time and space" created by the terms of her employment, those injuries "arose out of her employment.""[39]

If an employee's injuries are not compensable under workers' compensation, an employer may still be held liable under another negligence theory.

VII. Conclusion

Domestic violence has a substantial impact on the workplace. Any attorney representing employees, employers, or unions should be aware of the intersection between domestic violence and the workplace, and of the emerging legislative responses. Employers' attorneys should be especially proactive in advising their clients about how to respond to a workplace problem that involves domestic violence to ensure a safe environment for employees, while recognizing the various liability theories.

---

[34] KNOW YOUR RIGHTS: DOMESTIC VIOLENCE OR SEXUAL ASSAULT AT WORK, *supra* note 31; *see* Royall v. Indus. Comm'n of Ariz., 476 P.2d 156, 159 (Ariz. App.1970).

[35] LAPIDUS, MARTIN & LUTHRA, *supra* note 33, at 173.

[36] Epperson v. Industrial Comm'n, 549 P.2d 247, 249 (Ariz. App.1976).

[37] *Id.*

[38] Hall v. New England Bus. Serv. Inc., No. CIV 03-83-M, 2003 WL 2004375, at *1 (D.N.H. Apr. 29, 2003).

[39] *Id.*

APPENDIX

Websites:

- **Legal Momentum**
  - https://www.legalmomentum.org/

- **Corporate Alliance to End Partner Violence**
  - http://www.caepv.org/

- **Safe at Work Coalition**
  - http://safeatworkcoalition.org/

- **Work Places Respond to Domestic & Sexual Violence**
  - https://www.workplacesrespond.org/

Articles:

Corporate Alliance to End Partner Violence: National Benchmark Telephone Survey on Domestic Violence in the Workplace, Corp. All. to End Partner Violence (2005), http://www.ncdsv.org/images/CAEPVSurvey.WorkPlace.pdf.

State Law Guide: Domestic and Sexual Violence Workplace Policies, Legal Momentum (Sept. 22, 2015), https://www.legalmomentum.org/sites/default/files/reports/SLG-Domestic%20and%20Sexual%20Violence%20Workplace%20Policies%20-%20rev%209-15.pdf.

Work Places Respond to Domestic & Sexual Violence:

- Futures Without Violence, *Confidentiality is Critical,* Workplaces Respond to Domestic & Sexual Violence (2017), https://www.workplacesrespond.org/wp-content/uploads/2017/01/Confidentiality-is-Critical.pdf.

- Futures Without Violence, *Guide for Supervisors,* Workplaces Respond to Domestic & Sexual Violence (2017), https://www.workplacesrespond.org/wp-content/uploads/2017/01/Guide-for-Supervisors.pdf.

- Futures Without Violence, *Protection Order Guide,* Workplaces Respond to Domestic & Sexual Violence (2017), https://www.workplacesrespond.org/wp-content/uploads/2017/01/Protection-Order-Guide.pdf.

Model Workplace Policies:

American Bar Association

Comm'n on Domestic & Sexual Violence & Section of Individual Rights & Responsibilities, *Model Workplace Policy on Employer Responses to Domestic Violence, Sexual Violence, Dating Violence, and Stalking*, https://www. americanbar.org/content/dam/aba/administrative/domestic_violence1/Workplace/ Updated%20112a.authcheckdam.pdf.

Work Places Respond to Domestic & Sexual Violence

Futures Without Violence, *Model Workplace Policy on Domestic Violence, Sexual Violence, and Stalking*, WORKPLACES RESPOND TO DOMESTIC & SEXUAL VIOLENCE, https://www.workplacesrespond.org/wp-content/uploads/2017/01/Model-Policy. pdf.

Section Six:
Health Law

Chapter Twenty-two:
The Health Care System and Domestic Violence

I. Introduction

During the past two decades, there has been growing recognition among health care professionals that domestic violence is a highly prevalent public health problem with devastating effects on individuals, families, and communities. In addition to injuries sustained during violent episodes, physical and psychological abuse are linked to numerous adverse medical health effects including arthritis, chronic neck or back pain, migraine or other types of headache, sexually transmitted infections (including HIV/AIDS), and chronic pelvic pain. Six percent of all pregnant women are battered, and pregnancy complications are significantly higher for abused women, as are maternal rates of depression, suicide attempts, and substance abuse. Annually, more than one million women and men seek medical treatment for injuries deliberately inflicted upon them by their current or former intimate partners. In addition, it is estimated that between 20 and 30 percent of patients in ambulatory care settings are victims of domestic violence.

Health care providers have begun to conduct routine inquiry and assessment to identify victims within the health care system and provide information, intervention, and referral. However, not all providers have the awareness to assess or respond to domestic violence effectively. In some states, health care providers are required to receive continuing education on domestic violence. In a few states, health care clinics and/or hospitals are required by state law to have protocols addressing domestic violence or family violence. Hospitals that are accredited by the Joint Commission on the Accreditation of Health Care Organizations are also required to have in place policies and procedures that address the identification and treatment of family violence.

II. Mandatory Reporting[1]

Most states have enacted mandatory reporting laws, which require the reporting of specified injuries and wounds, and suspected abuse or domestic violence for individuals being treated by a health care professional. Mandatory reporting laws are distinct from elder abuse or vulnerable adult abuse and child abuse reporting laws, in that the individuals to be protected are not limited to a specific group, but pertain to all individuals to whom specific health care professionals provide treatment or medical care, or those individuals who come before the health care facility.

The laws vary from state to state but generally fall into four categories: (1) states that require reporting of injuries caused by weapons; (2) states that mandate reporting for injuries caused in violation of criminal laws, as a result of violence, or through non-accidental means; (3) states that specifically address reporting in domestic violence cases; and (4) states that have no general mandatory reporting laws.[2]

A. Implications for Victims of Domestic Violence

With the increasing awareness about domestic violence as a health care issue, attention has turned to how health care providers can best assist their patients through routine assessment, documentation, intervention, and referral. Unfortunately, applying mandatory criminal injury reporting laws to domestic violence cases is most often not helpful to victims. Research indicates that the most critical elements of providing victims with quality health care responses include offering ongoing and supportive access to medical care, addressing safety issues, and guiding patients through available options.

The goals potentially served by mandatory reporting include enhancing patient safety, improving health care providers' response to domestic violence, holding abusers accountable, and improving domestic violence data collection and documentation. However, upon closer examination, it becomes apparent that mandatory reporting does not necessarily accomplish these goals.

There are a number of risks and consequences associated with mandatory reporting, as well as ethical concerns raised by such a policy. Some of these include:

- *Deterrent to Seeking Care.* Many victims, including those in the LGBTQ community, believe that calling the police is not a safe or preferred option,

---

[1] This section is taken in large part from Ariella Hyman, Family Violence Prevention Fund, Mandatory Reporting of Domestic Violence by Health Care Providers: A Policy Paper (1997).

[2] Four states have exceptions for reporting injuries due to domestic violence: New Hampshire, Oklahoma, Pennsylvania, and Colorado. For more details about these exceptions, see *Compendium of State and U.S. Territory Statutes and Policies on Domestic Violence and Health Care, infra* note 3.

and will place them and their children in greater danger. Undocumented immigrant victims may fear that such action may result in deportation. The increased anxiety when seeking care and decreased candor with the provider may prevent them from obtaining necessary care and information.

- *Risk of retaliation.* Mandatory reporting can place victims at risk of retaliation by their abusers.

- *Limited Response to Reports.* Mandatory reporting by health care providers may create expectations of services and protections that cannot be met by the criminal justice system and, thereby, decrease patient trust in the provider and system.

- *Documentation.* Documentation of domestic violence is critical. Although mandatory reporting has the potential of achieving useful documentation, it is not a preferred means of accomplishing this goal. Documentation of abuse in the medical record serves the goal of documentation while better preserving privacy and confidentiality. In addition, it is a more reliable source of evidence for legal cases than a reporting form submitted to law enforcement or a state agency. A medical record can provide more thorough, detailed information on the abuse. The record may include patient statements and provider observations regarding the abuse, body maps, pictures, and a history of the abuse.

- *Ethical issues.* In the health care system, competent and informed patients determine the course of action that is in their best interest. Mandatory reporting negates patients' ability to make critical life decisions and raises ethical medical issues, including patient autonomy, confidentiality, and informed consent. For many victims isolated by their abuser from their friends, family, and social services, health care providers may be the only professionals to whom they have safe access. Mandatory reporting of domestic violence related injuries interferes with the confidential nature of the provider-patient relationship and can undermine victims' trust in health care providers.

III. Advising Victims About Seeking Medical Care

- Encourage your client to seek medical care for any injuries or chronic health problems due to or that could be attributed to domestic violence. Encourage the client to talk to their clinician about how domestic violence is affecting their life, if the client can do so safely.

- If the client is reluctant to seek care because of your state's mandatory reporting law, you should emphasize the importance of their getting treatment for any possible injuries. Advise the client on how to minimize harm. The client may:

(1) Ask the health care provider, when making the required report, to inform the law enforcement or state agency that the client is not interested in any further intervention by law enforcement.

(2) Ask to be present when the provider is making the police report or state agency report.

(3) Talk directly to the police or state agency representative from the private office, clinic, or hospital.

- If the client wants law enforcement intervention, the most effective way to initiate action by the police is to make a report directly to their local law enforcement agency.

It is important that legal professionals understand their state's domestic violence reporting laws. In order to maximize the client's input regarding law enforcement action, legal professionals should also familiarize themselves with how local law enforcement agencies respond to such reports. Becoming familiar with these procedures will allow you to better aid your clients in safety planning and advising them on what to expect.

Mandated reporting responsibilities should always be discussed with clients seeking medical care.[3]

IV. Health Insurance Portability and Accountability Act

The Health Insurance Portability and Accountability Act (HIPAA) permits health care providers to disclose protected health information about a victim of abuse, neglect, or domestic violence to an authorized government authority if: (1) the individual agrees, or (2) the disclosure is: (a) required by state law (mandatory reporting laws) or (b) expressly authorized by statute or regulation. In most instances, HIPAA requires that the provider must promptly inform the victim (either orally or in writing) that a report has been made or will be made.

Under HIPAA, health care providers do not have to inform the victim if: (1) they believe informing the individual would place the individual at serious risk of harm, or (2) the entity would be informing a personal representative (such as

---

[3] NANCY DURBOROW ET AL., FUTURES WITHOUT VIOLENCE, COMPENDIUM OF STATE AND U.S. TERRITORY STATUTES AND POLICIES ON DOMESTIC VIOLENCE AND HEALTH CARE (2013), *available at* https://www.futureswithoutviolence.org/userfiles/file/HealthCare/Compendium%20Final%202013.pdf (providing updated information on state laws and regulations including mandated reporting). The *Compendium* lists each state and U.S. territory with its corresponding mandatory reporting law, and brief summaries of the laws. However, it is important to review the text of the entire law to understand things such as the specific health care providers required to report, under what conditions, and definitions and penalties.

the abusive partner), and the entity reasonably believes the representative is responsible for the abuse.[4]

Under the HIPAA "Privacy Rule," covered entities must obtain the individual's written authorization for any use or disclosure of protected health information that is not for treatment, payment, or health care operations.[5]

V. *Advocacy Tips*

- Analyze your state's mandatory reporting laws to determine if health care providers are required to report to law enforcement or other state agencies domestic violence or other "crimes" that may include domestic violence.[6] Inform your client of any health care provider mandatory reporting laws in your state.

- Obtain information about whether your client has ever sought medical treatment for a domestic violence related injury or health condition. Discuss whether your client would like you to read the records of that treatment; if so, the client should complete an "Authorization for Release of Medical Records".

- Discuss with your client the benefits of seeking medical treatment for injuries related to domestic violence.

- In order to better assist the client in safety planning and knowing what to expect, familiarize yourself with how local law enforcement or state agencies respond to mandated reporting by health care providers.

---

[4] For more specific information on domestic violence and HIPAA, see Futures Without Violence, Health Insurance Portability and Accountability Act: Summary of Federal Medical Privacy Protections for Victims of Domestic Violence, https://www.futureswithoutviolence.org/health-insurance-portability-and-accountability-act-hippa-summary-of-federal-medical-privacy-protections-for-victims-of-domestic-violence/ (last visited Mar. 12, 2018).

[5] 45 CFR § 164.508. The HIPAA "Privacy Rule" applies to HIPAA-covered entities and business associates of the HIPAA-covered entity. 45 CFR § 160.103. "Covered entity means (1) A health plan. (2) A health care clearinghouse. (3) A health care provider who transmits any health information in electronic form in connection with a transaction covered by this subchapter." *Id.*

[6] For state laws, see Durborow et al., *supra* note 3. Contact your local domestic violence agency or state coalition to determine if there have been any legislative changes to the law. Contact information for state coalitions can be found at *Resources for Victims & Survivors,* The Nat'l Domestic Violence Hotline, http://www.thehotline.org/resources/victims-and-survivors/ (last visited May 11, 2018). Many state coalitions list local program contact information on their websites.

APPENDIX

Resources:

- FAMILY VIOLENCE PREVENTION FUND, NATIONAL CONSENSUS GUIDELINES ON IDENTIFYING AND RESPONDING TO DOMESTIC VIOLENCE VICTIMIZATION IN HEALTH CARE SETTINGS (2004), *available at* https://www.futureswithoutviolence.org/userfiles/file/Consensus.pdf.

- RODNEY HUDSON, FAMILY VIOLENCE PREVENTION FUND, SUMMARY OF NEW FEDERAL MEDICAL PRIVACY PROTECTIONS FOR VICTIMS OF DOMESTIC VIOLENCE (2003).

- Ariella Hyman et al., *Laws Mandating Reporting of Domestic Violence: Do They Promote Patient Well-Being?*, 273 J. AM. MED. ASS'N 1781 (1995).

- ANNE L. GANLEY, FAMILY VIOLENCE PREVENTION FUND, IMPROVING THE HEALTH CARE RESPONSE TO DOMESTIC VIOLENCE; A RESOURCE AND TRAINING MANUAL FOR HEALTH CARE PROVIDERS (1998).

- Jane Stoever, *Domestic Violence Victims Shouldn't Have to Choose Between Deportation and Medical Care,* L.A. TIMES (July 17, 2017), http://www.latimes.com/opinion/op-ed/la-oe-stoever-mandatory-reporting-domestic-violence-20170717-story.html.

- Isaac Thomas, *Against the Mandatory Reporting of Intimate Partner Violence, Virtual Mentor,* 11 AM. MED. ASS'N. J. OF ETHICS 137, 137–140 (Feb. 2009).

- Laura Iavicoli, *Mandatory Reporting of Domestic Violence: The Law, Friend or Foe?*, 72 MT. SINAI J. MED. 228 (2005).

- Cris M. Sullivan & Leslie A. Hagen, *Survivors' Opinions About Mandatory Reporting of Domestic Violence and Sexual Assault by Medical Professionals*, 20 AFFILIA (2005).

- Alisa Smith & Kristin Parsons Winokur, *What Doctors and Policymakers Should Know: Battered Women's Views About Mandatory Medical Reporting Laws*, 32 J. OF CRIM. JUST. 207 (2004).

Chapter Twenty-three:
Insurance Discrimination Against
Victims of Domestic Violence

Some insurance companies use domestic violence history to deny or limit access to insurance coverage.[1] Based on current or past domestic violence, insurers have refused to issue and renew insurance, canceled policies, restricted coverage provided, charged higher rates, written policies that exclude coverage for injuries resulting from domestic violence, and denied claims arising out of domestic violence. Such practices have occurred in every line of insurance—life, health, disability, and property and casualty—and affect individuals, families, and organizations that provide services to victims of domestic violence.[2]

For example, in 1993, a Pennsylvania woman was denied life, health, and mortgage disability insurance by State Farm Insurance, and life insurance by First Colony Life Insurance Company.[3] The insurance companies based their denials on information in the victim's medical records relating to an incident of domestic violence: she had been pushed into a piece of furniture with a pointed corner, resulting in a gash in her hip, and bruises on her body.[4] This information was in her medical records because she did what advocates often advise victims of domestic violence to do—she specifically asked her doctor to record the nature

---

[1] Terry L. Fromson & Nancy Durborow, Insurance Discrimination Against Victims of Domestic Violence (2014), *available at* http://www.womenslawproject.org/wp-content/uploads/2016/04/Insurance_discrim_domestic_violence-1.pdf.

[2] *Id.*; Nat'l Ass'n of Ins. Comm'rs, *Discriminatory Practices Working Group of the Accident and Health Insurance Committee*, Transcript of Public Hearing (Mar. 14, 1995).

[3] Katherine Q. Seelye, *Insurability for Battered Women*, N.Y. Times (May 12, 1994), http://www.nytimes.com/1994/05/12/us/insurability-for-battered-women.html.

[4] Deborah L. Shelton, *Twice a Victim*, 23 Hum. Rts. 26, 26 (1996).

and cause of her injuries in case she needed evidence to protect herself and her daughter in the future.[5]

Insurers have denied life insurance and disability insurance to victims in Iowa, Nebraska, and Washington because of histories of domestic violence related medical treatment.[6]

Insurers have denied claims for property damage under homeowner's policies in Pennsylvania and Washington, after abusers set fire to the victims' homes or otherwise perpetrated property damage after the victims separated from the abusers.[7]

In addition, domestic violence shelters in Minnesota were denied health insurance for their staff because their programs were considered too risky by the insurer.[8] Shelters in Washington, New Hampshire, Colorado, Wisconsin, Vermont, and Nebraska reported difficulties obtaining property insurance or auto insurance due to the nature of their organizations.[9] Similarly, the homeowner's insurance of a woman who volunteered her home as a safe home for victims was cancelled.[10]

Insurers justified their actions on the preposterous basis that victims of domestic violence voluntarily assume the risk of abuse, analogizing a victim of domestic violence to someone who makes a voluntary lifestyle choice such as skydiving or riding a motorcycle. Failing to recognize the nature of domestic violence, and the danger a victim faces upon leaving an abusive relationship, some insurers stated they could not insure a victim of domestic violence as long as they remained with the abuser. Life insurers claimed insuring a victim of domestic violence would create an incentive for the beneficiary to commit murder in order to collect proceeds, despite insurance laws and policy provisions that prohibit recovery for intentional acts.[11]

Insurers obtain information about the domestic violence history of an applicant or insured from documentation of victims' efforts to obtain help with domestic violence, including medical, police, and court records.[12] Such practices discourage victims of domestic violence from seeking help by placing those who seek help in the untenable position of risking loss of insurance coverage necessary for healthcare, housing, and replacement income in the event of

---

[5] *Id.*

[6] *See* FROMSON & DURBOROW, *supra* note 1, at 11–12.

[7] *Id.* at 14–15.

[8] *Id.* at 11.

[9] *Id.* at 13–14.

[10] *Id.* at 10–16.

[11] *Id.* at 17–20.

[12] *Id.* at 3–4.

disability or death for themselves and their children. Insurance discrimination thus jeopardizes the safety and welfare of victims and their families.

When it was first realized that insurers were using domestic violence as a basis to determine whom to cover and how much to charge, no laws outlawed such practices. Efforts were immediately pursued with significant success. Since 1994, 45 states and the District of Columbia have passed laws restricting insurance actions based on domestic violence.[13] Federal legislation has been introduced for many years with some success.[14] The Health Insurance Portability and Accountability Act of 1996 (HIPAA) prohibits group health plans and insurers offering group coverage from discriminating in eligibility, benefits, and premiums on the basis of a number of health factors which include "conditions arising out of domestic violence."[15] The Final Privacy Rule, adopted pursuant to HIPAA, provides individuals the right to request that health plans restrict uses and disclosures of individually identifiable information.[16] This provision is important to domestic violence victims who have an interest in preventing an abuser from accessing their personal information. The Financial Services Modernization Act of 1999 prohibits banks that sell insurance from considering status as a domestic violence victim or provider of services as a basis for decisions about pricing, renewal, coverage, and claims payment in health and life insurance.[17] The Patient Protection and Affordable Care Act (ACA) prohibits preexisting condition exclusions and premium rate discrimination and guarantees availability and renewability of insurance, protecting victims of domestic violence from many of the adverse actions to which health insurers have subjected them.[18] The Security and Financial Empowerment Act of 2017 is the most recent legislation introduced in Congress, and provides uniform protection from insurer discrimination on a national basis.[19]

Advocacy Tip: Evaluate your client's insurance coverage.

---

[13] These jurisdictions include Alabama, Alaska, Arizona, Arkansas, California, Colorado, Connecticut, Delaware, District of Columbia, Florida, Georgia, Hawaii, Illinois, Indiana, Iowa, Kansas, Kentucky, Louisiana, Maine, Maryland, Massachusetts, Michigan, Minnesota, Mississippi, Missouri, Montana, Nebraska, Nevada, New Hampshire, New Jersey, New Mexico, New York, North Dakota, Ohio, Oklahoma, Oregon, Pennsylvania, Rhode Island, Tennessee, Texas, Utah, Virginia, Washington, West Virginia, and Wisconsin.

[14] *See, e.g.,* Security and Financial Empowerment Act (S.A.F.E.), H.R. 3420, 108th Cong., Title IV (2003); S. 1740, 111th Cong. (2009), H.R. 739, 111th Cong. Title IV (2009).

[15] 29 U.S.C. § 1182(a)(1)(G); H.R. 3103, 104th Cong. (1996), P.L. 104-191, 110 Stat. 1936.

[16] 45 C.F.R. § 164.522.

[17] 12 U.S.C. § 1831x(e).

[18] H.R. 3590, 111th Cong. (2010), Pub. L. No. 111-148, 124 Stat. 119.

[19] S. 2043, 115th Cong. (2017); H.R. 4198, 115th Cong. (2017). At the time of this printing, the Security and Financial Empowerment Act has been introduced, but not passed.

- Review your client's health insurance coverage. If your client is covered by a group health policy provided through their spouse's employer, include in any domestic relations petition a request that the spouse be ordered to continue to provide your client and any dependent children with continuing coverage under the employer sponsored plan during pendency of the proceedings. By continuing to receive group health insurance, your client will not have to apply for insurance in the individual health insurance market where insurers typically engage in underwriting—the process of risk assessment by which insurers obtain medical and other records to determine whether to provide insurance coverage and thereby uncover information about abuse. Once a divorce a finalized, however, the client would no longer be able to stay on their spouse's employer sponsored health care plan.[20] The client could have an option to retain coverage under the spouse's health insurance plan by electing COBRA insurance.[21]

- Review your client's homeowners insurance. Only 27 states and the District of Columbia have laws that prohibit property insurers from discriminating against victims of domestic violence.[22] Some homeowners policies exclude coverage for intentional or criminal acts. If your state law does not require severability of interests of co-insureds, such exclusions will operate to exclude the first party claims by innocent victims whose injuries arise out of the intentional or criminal act of the co-insured spouse. For example, if an abuser returns to the home and destroys property, a victim will be unable to recover under a joint insurance policy. While some state courts have outlawed the application of intentional act exclusions to co-insureds, others have not.[23] Family or household exclusions may preclude recovery for bodily injury to members of the insured's family or household. Consider having the property and the insurance placed solely in your client's name, either by agreement or court order. If your client is no longer co-insured with the abuser, insurers will be unable to deny coverage on the basis of intentional criminal acts or family exclusions.

---

[20] Barbara Marquand, *5 Crucial Insurance Changes After Divorce*, FORBES (May 25, 2016, 7:53 PM), https://www.forbes.com/sites/barbaramarquand/2016/05/25/5-crucial-insurance-changes-after-divorce/#767874d4c986.

[21] *Id.* COBRA stands for the Consolidated Omnibus Budget Reconciliation Act, and "require[s] group health plans to provide a temporary continuation of group health coverage that otherwise might be terminated." *FAQs on COBRA Continuation Health Coverage*, U.S. DEP'T OF LABOR (Nov. 2015), https://www.dol.gov/sites/default/files/ebsa/about-ebsa/our-activities/resource-center/faqs/cobra-continuation-health-coverage-consumer.pdf.

[22] These jurisdictions include Alabama, Alaska, Arizona, Arkansas, California, Colorado, Delaware, District of Columbia, Florida, Georgia, Hawaii, Illinois, Iowa, Kentucky, Massachusetts, Missouri, Montana, Nebraska, New Hampshire, New Jersey, New Mexico, New York, Oregon, Pennsylvania, Rhode Island, Virginia, Washington, and Wisconsin.

[23] *See, e.g.,* Krupp v. Aetna Life & Cas., 479 N.Y.S. 2d 992, 994 (App. Div. 1984) (holding the wrongful act of a spouse should not be attributed to the innocent co-insured); Hosey v. Siebels Bruce Group, S.C. Ins. Co., 363 So. 2d 751, 752 (Ala. 1978).

- If you think your client is being overcharged for insurance of any kind and that the insurer may have uncovered information about a history of domestic violence, request an explanation for the amount of the premium. If domestic violence was a factor in setting the premium, assist your client in pursuing remedies under state or federal law. If you are not experienced in insurance law, you may wish to identify a referral with appropriate expertise.

Advocacy Tip: Protect your client's confidentiality.

- When your clients apply for insurance, advise them not to authorize further disclosure of information to the insurer. Insurers often seek to have applicants authorize release of information to databases that serve as shared repositories of risk profiles on prospective insureds.

- Your client may want to find out if they have been entered into the Medical Information Bureau's (MIB) database as a "high risk" individual associated with violence.[24]

- Notify insurers not to disclose any information about your client to the abuser. Insurers are in possession of information that may endanger your client's safety. This includes your client's whereabouts, as well as claims-related information. In at least one instance, an insurance company told an abuser that he was the prime suspect in causing the property damage claimed by the policyholder, and the abuser retaliated by beating the victim.[25]

Advocacy Tip: Challenge adverse insurance actions against victims of domestic violence.

- Demand a written explanation for any adverse action by an insurance company.

- Determine whether domestic violence is the motivation behind the insurer's adverse action.

- Find out if your state has statutory or regulatory provisions to address insurance discrimination against victims of domestic violence and assist your client in pursuing remedies that exist. If you are not experienced in insurance law, you may wish to identify a referral with appropriate expertise.

---

[24] MIB will provide a copy of a consumer file upon request made in writing to MIB, Inc., 50 Braintree Hill Park, Suite 400, Braintree, MA 02184-8734, emailing infoline@mib, or using MIB's online request form at https://www.mib.com/request_your_record.html. Individuals may also request correction of incorrect information found in MIB's records through MIB's dispute process described on its website at How to Dispute Your MIB Consumer File, https://www.mib.com/how_to_dispute_your_consumer_file.html (last visited Apr. 24, 2018).

[25] L. H. Otis, *Abuse Victim Claims Raise New Risks,* Nat'l Underwriter 1 (Feb. 12, 1996).

- If your state has no such statutory protection, explore other insurance laws relating to gender discrimination, unfair trade practices, bad faith claims, and confidentiality, which may offer a remedy.

- If an insurer takes action based on your client's medical condition, determine whether any federal or state laws restricting preexisting condition exclusions or requiring guaranteed issue of health insurance prohibit such action.

Support Advocacy Efforts to Stop Domestic Violence Based Insurance Discrimination

With your client's permission, please share with the Women's Law Project (215-928-9801) any domestic violence related discriminatory practices you uncover. The Women's Law Project may have information about or contacts with the company, which can help solve your client's problem. In addition, anecdotal evidence will assist in advocacy efforts to stop this particular type of insurance discrimination.

APPENDIX

Websites:

- **Women's Law Project**
  - http://www.womenslawproject.org/

- **The National Health Resource Center on Domestic Violence, a project of Futures Without Violence**
  - https://www.futureswithoutviolence.org/health/national-health-resource-center-on-domestic-violence/

- **Futures Without Violence**
  - http://www.futureswithoutviolence.org/health

- **National Women's Law Center**
  - https://nwlc.org/?s=insurance+discrimination+domestic+violence

Publication:

Terry L. Fromson & Nancy Durborow, Insurance Discrimination Against Victims of Domestic Violence (2014), *available at* http://www.womenslawproject.org/wp-content/uploads/2016/04/Insurance_discrim_domestic_violence-1.pdf.

Articles:

Brent R. Lindal, *Comment: Insurance Coverage for an Innocent Co-Insured Spouse*, 23 Wm. Mitchell L. Rev. 433 (1997).

Michelle J. Mandel, *Review of Selected 1997 California Legislation: Ensuring that Victims of Domestic Abuse are Not Discriminated Against in the Insurance Industry*, 29 McGeorge L. Rev. 677 (1998).

Sheri A. Millikin, *A Cost Analysis Approach to Determining the Reasonableness of Using Domestic Violence as an Insurance* Classification, 25 J. Legis. 195 (1999).

Ellen J. Morrison, *Insurance Discrimination Against Battered Women: Proposed Legislative Protections*, 72 Ind. L. J. 259 (1996).

Emily C. Wilson, *Stop Re-Victimizing the Victims: A Call for Stronger State Laws Prohibiting Insurance Discrimination Against Victims of Domestic Violence*, Am U.J. Gender Soc. Pol'y & L. 413 (2015).

Section Seven: Housing Law

Chapter Twenty-four:
Homelessness, Housing, and Domestic Violence

I. Introduction

Victims often face discrimination by housing providers with evictions or removals from housing due to domestic violence, jeopardizing their safety and placing them at risk of becoming homeless. Victims also experience a myriad of barriers when seeking housing, including the lack of affordable housing, long waitlists (or closed waitlists) for some federal subsidized housing, and limited or no shelter. These obstacles to access are exacerbated by discrimination by housing providers because of a victim's race, immigration status, and/or lack of English proficiency.[1] As a result, 38 percent of all domestic violence victims become homeless at some point in their lives.[2] Fortunately, there are federal housing protections and, in some jurisdictions, state and local protections that extend to private housing as well. For lawyers, understanding victims' rights can be the difference between helping them access or maintain safe housing and becoming homeless, or in many cases, returning to the violent situation.

This chapter will describe the challenges facing victims seeking housing, maintaining housing, and leaving unsafe housing. It will introduce types of federally subsidized housing, as well as federal, state, and local housing protections to address some of the challenges. Lastly, it will provide some advocacy tips for lawyers representing victims in housing cases.

---

[1] Nat'l All. for Safe Housing, Safe Housing Needs Assessment Highlights (2017).

[2] Charlene K. Baker, Sarah L. Cooker & Fran H. Norris, *Domestic Violence and Housing Problems; A Contextual Analysis of Women's Help-Seeking, Received Informal Support, and Formal System Response*, 9 Violence Against Women 754, 766 (2003).

II. Challenges for Victims: Seeking Safe Housing

A. Housing Denials on the Basis of Domestic Violence

Housing providers discriminate against victims based on their actual or perceived status as a victim of domestic violence. An example of this kind of discrimination is if a former landlord discloses to a prospective housing provider that the applicant has experienced or is fleeing domestic violence, and the prospective housing provider then denies the applicant housing. Housing providers may discriminate for several different reasons, including fear of property damage, or a belief that the tenant may be more likely to break the lease; however, these reasons are not lawful and often based on misperceptions of domestic violence, as well as victim blaming. Victims of domestic violence, like any other tenant, should be able to apply and receive housing if they qualify and it is available.

Housing providers also deny housing to applicants who experienced domestic violence due to poor rental or credit history. Victims sometimes have issues with credit or rental history due to financial abuse. An abuser may control financial decisions, even taking out credit in the victim's name without the victim knowing.[3] This impacts the victim's credit score, which could lead to the denial of housing. Furthermore, victims may have a spotty rental history due to a prior eviction or unpaid property damage. This rental history may come up during the application process, leading to denial of housing.

Housing may also be denied because of a victim's criminal record. Some applicants may have criminal records directly connected to domestic violence. For example, an abuser may force a victim to take or deal illegal drugs, resulting in a criminal record that causes a denial of housing.

Scenarios like these make finding housing especially challenging for victims, because housing providers typically complete credit/rental history or criminal record checks, particularly in the private market. When the housing provider performs these checks, these issues come up, likely resulting in denials of housing.

B. Marginalized Statuses

In addition to facing discrimination due to domestic violence, victims are also discriminated against based on race, national origin, disability, sexual orientation, or gender identity. In other words, there may be more than one reason a housing provider is discriminating against a victim. A study conducted in 2009 found that in 79 percent of test cases, Latinos seeking housing were

---

[3] *Financial Abuse*, Womenslaw.org, https://www.womenslaw.org/about-abuse/forms-abuse/financial-abuse (last updated June 19, 2017).

subject to discriminatory treatment.[4] According to another study, African American renters who contacted providers about housing units learned about more than 11 percent fewer available units than equally qualified white renters.[5] Discrimination based on race can overlap with discrimination based on the applicant's actual or perceived status as a victim of domestic violence status, causing additional barriers for victims seeking housing or keeping safe housing.

Housing providers also discriminate against victims who are immigrants or have limited English proficiency. For instance, an applicant seeking housing who has an accent or does not speak English may be denied the opportunity to even apply for available housing. Victims with disabilities face discrimination as well. For example, an applicant who has a mental health issue may be perceived as being physically combative and denied housing access even though there is an available unit.[6]

In addition to race, national origin, and disability, housing providers discriminate based on gender identity or sexual orientation, resulting in housing instability and possible homelessness.[7] For example, discrimination may occur when a housing provider asks an applicant what their gender identity is, and denies access based on the answer, even if a unit is available.

For victims, the layering of discrimination upon discrimination compounds the challenges they already face to accessing safe housing.

III. Challenges for Victims: Maintaining Safe Housing

A. Evictions and Assistance Terminations

When housing providers evict or terminate assistance to victims of domestic violence, the housing provider generally does not state that the adverse action is taking place due to domestic violence. The housing provider may use another reason to evict the victim, such as the victim called the police too many times. For instance, a victim could be evicted or have their assistance terminated, or threatened with eviction, for contacting first responders, including police or emergency medical care. In fact, some jurisdictions have nuisance ordinances

---

4 Dep't of Housing & Cmty. Dev., Fair Housing for All: The Disparate Response to Latino Housing Needs in Frederick County, MD (2010), https://frederickcountymd.gov/DocumentCenter/View/254494.

5 U.S. Dep't of Housing & Urban Dev., Housing Discrimination Against Racial and Ethnic Minorities (2013), https://www.hud.gov/sites/documents/discriminatoryeffectrule.pdf.

6 Nat'l Housing L. Project, Maintaining Safe and Stable Housing for Domestic Violence Victims (2012), http://www.nhlp.org/files/NHLP%20Domestic%20Violence%20and%20Housing%20Manual%202.pdf.

7 U.S. Dep't of Housing & Urban Dev., An Estimate of Housing Discrimination Against Same-Sex Couples (2013), https://www.huduser.gov/portal/Publications/pdf/Hsg_Disc_against_SameSexCpls_v3.pdf.

that penalize housing providers and tenants with fines or even criminal penalties for calling the police too many times. In jurisdictions with nuisance ordinances, housing providers sometimes evict domestic violence victims to avoid these penalties.[8] Another all too common issue is if an incident of domestic violence occurs in the unit, resulting in the housing provider evicting them or terminating their assistance or threatening the victim with eviction.

B. Removing the Abuser from the Lease (Lease Bifurcation)

Some victims would feel safe or safer staying in their current housing, where they may be connected to community resources or supportive social networks. If your client would feel safe residing in the current housing if the abuser were no longer able to access the unit, the abuser would need to be removed from the lease. It is likely that the victim may not know this is an option, so it is important to speak with your client about whether this is something that would be appealing to them. If a victim must leave a housing situation that could be safe because a housing provider does not remove the abuser from the lease, the victim's housing and community supports, and safety, could be jeopardized. Furthermore, it could result in homelessness.

C. Early Lease Termination and Security Deposit

A victim may need to leave a current housing situation to seek safe housing because of fear and safety concerns; however, that is not always easy to do. This is critical for lawyers representing victims to understand because it is extremely important to help victims be safe and avoid homelessness. Understanding that early lease termination could be an option and that victims may not be liable for damages caused by domestic violence are critical avenues to helping victims find safety. However, some housing providers keep a security deposit if a victim leaves a unit early or for property damage caused by the abuser. For instance, if an abuser makes repeated visits to a victim's apartment building, and the victim no longer feels safe living there, the victim may be liable for rent through the duration of the lease or until another tenant occupies the unit.

IV. Federally Subsidized Housing[9]

Federally subsidized housing is often the only affordable housing option for low-income victims. The most common federally subsidized housing includes: public housing, Section 8 Housing Choice Vouchers (often referred to as Section 8), Project-based Section 8, and the Low-Income Housing Tax Credit programs.

---

[8] *I am Not a Nuisance: Local Ordinances Punish Victims of Crime*, AM. CIV. LIBERTIES UNION, https://www.aclu.org/other/i-am-not-nuisance-local-ordinances-punish-victims-crime (last visited Apr. 29, 2018).

[9] These federally subsidized programs and homeless service assistance programs are covered under VAWA.

In addition, the federal government funds programs that support homeless individuals and families (authorized under the McKinney/Vento Homeless Assistance Act), and other homeless assistance programs.

A. U.S. Department of Housing and Urban Development (HUD)

For public housing, Section 8 Housing Choice Vouchers, and Project-based Section 8, HUD provides funding to local housing authorities known as public housing authorities, or sometimes referred to as public housing agencies (PHAs). PHAs administer public housing and Section 8 voucher programs in jurisdictions to low-income individuals and families. To be eligible, applicants must meet specific programmatic requirements based on income, immigration status, and other criteria.[10] Unfortunately, there are often long waitlists for these programs, and the waitlists can even be closed. It can take years to gain access to this type of housing. In some jurisdictions, PHAs have established an admissions preference for domestic violence victims that places them closer to the top of the list.

- **Public Housing**[11]
  Public Housing was developed to provide housing for low-income individuals and families, the elderly, and persons with disabilities.[12] PHAs collect rent and maintain the units, which come in all sizes and types.[13] There are approximately 3,300 PHAs managing these public housing units in the United States.[14]

- **Section 8 Housing Choice Vouchers (HCVs)**[15]
  HCVs allow low-income recipients to find their own housing in the private market so long as the housing meets program requirements. The local PHA administers the voucher, and a housing subsidy is paid to the housing provider. The recipient pays the difference between the subsidized amount and the actual rent for the housing unit. HCV recipients may not pay more

---

[10] U.S. Dep't of Housing & Urban Dev., Rental Assistance (2017), https://www.hud.gov/topics/rental_assistance. HUD has developed income limits used by PHAs to determine income eligibility. *See Income Limits*, U.S. Dep't of Housing & Urban Dev. (Apr. 1, 2018), https://www.huduser.gov/portal/datasets/il.html.

[11] *Id.*

[12] *HUD's Public Housing Program*, U.S. Dep't of Housing & Urban Dev., https://www.hud.gov/topics/rental_assistance/phprog (last visited Mar. 9, 2018).

[13] *Public Housing,* U.S. Dep't of Housing & Urban Dev., https://www.hud.gov/program_offices/public_indian_housing/programs/ph (last visited Mar. 9, 2018).

[14] *Id.* For contact information, see *PHA Contact Information*, U.S. Dep't of Housing & Urban Dev., https://www.hud.gov/program_offices/public_indian_housing/pha/contacts (last visited Apr. 29, 2018).

[15] *Housing Choice Voucher Fact Sheet*, U.S. Dep't of Housing & Urban Dev., https://www.hud.gov/topics/housing_choice_voucher_program_section_8 (last visited Apr. 29, 2018).

than 40 percent of their adjusted monthly income for rent. A good way to think about these vouchers is that they belong to the recipient, rather than the housing provider, meaning that they are also portable. For victims, the portability of HCVs is a significant benefit, because a victim can take the voucher anywhere in the country so long as another PHA accepts it.

- **Section 8 Project Based Vouchers**[16]
Under Project Based Vouchers, PHAs contract with housing providers who set aside a certain number of units in a building specifically for individuals with vouchers. When a unit becomes available, the PHA uses the waitlist to determine placement. If a recipient moves out of the unit, the voucher stays with the unit/housing provider. The recipient can move and might be eligible for an HCV, but would likely need to go back on the waitlist.

- **Homeless Assistance Programs**
Homeless Assistance Programs are intended for homeless individuals and families. They include homeless shelters and housing programs that are part of the Continuum of Care (CoC) as well. To qualify for a Homeless Assistance Program, the definition of homeless must be met.[17] CoC and Emergency Shelter Grant (ESG) programs are generally open to immigrants without restrictions.[18]

B. U.S. Department of Agriculture (USDA)

- **Multi-Family Housing (MFH)**[19]
Rural Development, an agency within USDA, provides affordable rental housing for low-income rural residents through MFH.[20] The program "provide[s] grants to sponsoring organizations to repair or rehabilitate housing for needy families" and "subsidize[s] rents for low-income tenants

---

[16] U.S. Dep't of Housing & Urban Dev., Project Based Vouchers – Frequently Asked Questions (2017), https://www.hud.gov/sites/documents/DOC_9157.pdf.

[17] HUD defines a homeless individual or family as: "Any individual or family who is fleeing, or is attempting to flee, domestic violence; has no other residence; and lacks the resources or support networks to obtain other permanent housing." U.S. Dep't of Housing & Urban Dev., Coordinated Entry and Victim Service Providers (2015), https://www.hudexchange.info/resources/documents/Coordinated-Entry-and-Victim-Service-Providers-FAQs.pdf. HUD defines fleeing or attempting to flee to include: "domestic violence, dating violence, sexual assault, stalking, or other dangerous life-threatening conditions (including human trafficking) that relate to violence against the individual or a family member, including a child, that has either taken place within the individual's or family's primary nighttime residence or has made the individual or family afraid to return to their primary nighttime residence." *Id.*

[18] Miguel Morales & Leslye E. Orloff, HUD Programs and Immigrant Eligibility (2017), http://library.niwap.org/wp-content/uploads/2015/pdf/PB-Man-Ch16.2-HUDProgramsImmEligibility-7.10.13.pdf.

[19] U.S. Dep't of Agric., Rural Housing Services (2017), https://www.rd.usda.gov/about-rd/agencies/rural-housing-service.

[20] Rural Development also offers assistance for low-income ownership and owners.

in [their] projects who cannot afford to pay their full rent."[21] The Rural Development website has a list of properties by state.[22]

C. U.S. Department of Treasury

- **Low Income Housing Tax Credit Program (LIHTC)**[23]
  The Low-Income Housing Tax Credit Program gives state and local finance agencies the ability to issue tax credits to build or rehabilitate rental units for low-income households. LIHTC housing may also be subsidized through other state, local, or federal funding. HUD maintains a database that provides information on where this type of housing is located.[24]

V. Federal Housing Protections

A. Fair Housing Act (FHA)[25]

The federal Fair Housing Act (FHA) applies to most private housing and federally subsidized housing, and most shelters. The federal FHA prohibits discrimination on the basis of sex, race, color, religion, national origin, familial status, and disability. Domestic violence claims under federal FHA can be brought based on sex, but some claims can be brought under race, national origin, or disability as well.[26] While federal FHA does not include sexual orientation or gender identity as protected classes, claims may also be brought under sex discrimination.[27]

---

[21] *Multi-Family Housing Programs*, U.S. Dep't of Agric. Rural Dev., https://www.rd.usda.gov/programs-services/all-programs/multi-family-housing-programs (last visited Mar. 9, 2018).

[22] *Multi-Family Housing Rentals*, U.S. Dep't of Agric. Rural Dev., https://rdmfhrentals.sc.egov.usda.gov/RDMFHRentals/select_state.jsp (last visited Mar. 9, 2018).

[23] Nat'l Housing L. Project, Working with State Housing Agencies to Improve Victims' Access to and Retention of LIHTC Housing (2013), http://nhlp.org/files/Combined%20LIHTC%20QAP%20Packet.pdf.

[24] *LIHTC Database Access*, U.S. Dep't of Housing & Urban Dev., https://lihtc.huduser.gov/ (last visited Apr. 30, 2018).

[25] 42 U.S.C. § 3604 (2018).

[26] Memorandum from Sara K. Pratt on Assessing Claims of Housing Discrimination Against Victims of Domestic Violence Under the Fair Housing Act and Violence Against Women Act (Feb. 2011).

[27] *Ending Housing Discrimination Against Lesbian, Gay, Bisexual and Transgender Individuals and Their Families*, U.S. Dep't of Housing & Urban Dev., https://www.hud.gov/program_offices/fair_housing_equal_opp/LGBT_Housing_Discrimination (last visited Apr. 30, 2018). Note that if a lawyer brings an administrative claim it will likely be recognized; however, if an affirmative law suit was brought under federal or state court, sexual orientation and sexual identity may not be recognized because they are not protected classes under federal FHA.

Under federal FHA, victims have the right to be:

- Protected from discrimination when seeking housing to buy or rent;

- Protected from eviction;

- Treated the same as other tenant/occupants by a housing provider; and

- Reasonably accommodated, to ensure someone with a disability equal opportunity to use and enjoy housing.

Although domestic violence victims do not constitute a protected class under federal FHA, claims can be brought under two sex discrimination theories: disparate treatment and disparate impact. Lawyers can make the claims simultaneously, and they can be used both as defense claims or affirmatively.[28] Disparate treatment can arise when housing providers treat female tenants differently from male tenants. This is also known as intentional sex discrimination. Disparate treatment claims have also been brought based on sex-based stereotypes against domestic violence victims.[29]

Disparate impact, on the other hand, can be used in cases where there is no direct evidence of unequal treatment, but a policy or practice disproportionately affects victims of domestic violence.[30] It is important to note, however, that disparate impact claims have become more challenging due to the U.S. Supreme Court holding in *Texas Dept. of Hous. and Cmty. Affairs v. Inclusive Communities Project, Inc.*[31]

B. Violence Against Women Act (VAWA)[32]

Under the Violence Against Women Act of 2013 (VAWA), someone who is a victim, or a threatened victim of domestic violence, accessing or maintaining

---

[28] Nat'l Housing L. Project, *supra* note 6.

[29] *Id.*

[30] Pratt, *supra* note 26. Lawyers interested in learning more about these claims in domestic violence cases should seek the assistance of the National Housing Law Project (NHLP) or American Civil Liberties Union, Women's Rights Project (see the Appendix to this chapter for more information).

[31] 135 S.Ct. 2507 (2016).

[32] 42 U.S.C.A. § 14043e-11.

certain federally subsidized or homeless service assistance programs, is entitled to VAWA protections.[33]

VAWA applies to victims regardless of sex, gender identity, sexual orientation, disability, or age. It provides housing protection to victims of domestic violence, dating violence, sexual assault, and stalking, and applies to the affiliated individuals of the victim (including individuals who are not on the lease but are in the victim's immediate family or individuals living in the household). However, the affiliated individuals must be either tenants or applicants.[34]

Under VAWA, victims have the right to:

- Be accepted into shelter/housing. For example, a housing provider cannot deny an applicant housing/assistance because of domestic violence, including a victim's criminal history or poor credit history connected with domestic violence;

- Remove the abuser from the public housing lease or Section 8 Housing Choice Voucher and stay in the unit;

- Ensure that the PHA and Section 8 landlords honor an order of protection,

- especially if it addresses the abuser's access to where the victim lives;

- Port (move to another location), if the victim has a Section 8 Housing Choice Voucher;

- Seek an emergency transfer;

- Remain in the unit, even if there is (or has been) criminal activity at the unit that is directly related to the domestic violence; and

- Confidentiality of information about domestic violence, dating violence, sexual assault, or stalking. This information can be shared only if requested by the victim in writing, is required for use in an eviction proceeding, or is otherwise required by law.

---

[33] Under HUD: Public housing, Housing Choice Voucher program (Section 8), Project-based Section 8, Section 202 supportive housing for the elderly, Section 811 supportive housing for persons with disabilities, Section 236 multifamily rental housing, Section 221(d)(3) Below Market Interest Rate housing (BMIR), HOME, Housing Trust Fund, Housing Opportunities for Persons with AIDS (HOPWA), McKinney-Vento Act programs (including Emergency Solutions Grants and Continuum of Care). Under USDA, Rural Development (RD) multifamily housing programs (MFH) and USDT, Low-Income Housing Tax Credit program (LIHTC).

[34] 24 C.F.R. §§ 5, 91, 92, 93, 200, 247, 574, 576, 578, 880, 882, 883, 884, 886, 891, 905, 960, 966, 982, 983 (2018).

Limitations to VAWA. Housing providers:

- May authorize a lease bifurcation (though they are not required to);

- Can evict or terminate assistance on non-VAWA violations;

- Can evict or terminate assistance for victims if they can demonstrate an "actual and imminent threat" which consists of a physical danger that is real, would occur within an immediate time frame, and could result in death or serious bodily harm;

- Can request documentation from the victim as proof of domestic violence.

While housing providers are not required to request documentation of the domestic violence, they may. The request must be in writing. The victim has 14 business days to provide documentation, though the deadline can be extended by the housing provider. The victim can self-certify using the HUD designated form (Form HUD-5382, which comes in 15 different languages); provide a signed letter from a victim service provider (including domestic violence organizations), attorney, or a medical/mental health professional; or provide a police report, court order (i.e., order of protection) or administrative record.[35]

The victim, not the housing provider, gets to determine which form of documentation will be provided. If there are conflicting accounts/evidence, the housing provider may ask for documentation from a third party (i.e., signed letter from a victim advocate or police report).

C. Section 504 of the Rehabilitation Act (Section 504)[36]

Section 504 prohibits discrimination against victims of domestic violence with disabilities by housing providers that receive federal funding.

---

[35] For Form HUD-5382, see *HUD Forms 5 through 5974*, U.S. DEP'T OF HOUSING & URBAN DEV., https://www.hud.gov/program_offices/administration/hudclips/forms/hud5a (last visited Apr. 30, 2018).

[36] 29 U.S.C. §§ 701 et seq. (2012).

Under Section 504, victims with a disability have the right to:

- Be protected from discrimination. For example, if a victim of domestic violence is deaf or hard of hearing, the housing provider should find ways to make sure services and support are received as needed;

- Confidentiality; and

- Reasonable accommodations. For example, allowing a guide dog to stay with a program participant/tenant.

D. Americans with Disabilities Act (ADA)[37]

Victims with a disability are entitled to protections under the ADA. Essentially, the ADA extends the protection under Section 504 to non-federally assisted entities. It prohibits discrimination against individuals with disabilities in public accommodations. The ADA also applies to all shelters operated by the government and to private shelters.

VI. Additional State and/or Local Housing Protections

Many jurisdictions on the state and local level have statutory housing protections for victims of domestic violence that extend to private landlords. Those protections may include but are not limited to: discrimination laws that offer additional protection, eviction defense, early lease termination (breaking a lease), lock changes, reasonable accommodations for safety, imposing liability on the abuser for damages, and protections allowing the victim to contact first responders.[38] Lawyers who are representing domestic violence victims in housing cases need to remember that VAWA only applies to federal housing (as noted above). State and local housing protections are critical for victims of domestic violence because they often provide more comprehensive rights and remedies and fill the protection gaps.

A. Fair Housing

There are some state and local jurisdictions that include status as a domestic violence victim, sexual orientation, and gender identity as protected classes. It is important for lawyers to familiarize themselves with their state and/or local fair housing statutes because they may be more extensive.

---

[37] 42 U.S.C. § 12101 et seq.

[38] Nat'l. Housing L. Project, Housing Rights of Domestic Violence Victims: A State and Local Law Compendium (2016), http://nhlp.org/files/Domestic%20violence%20housing%20compendium%20 FINAL7.pdf.

B. Eviction Defense

Twenty-four state and local jurisdictions have eviction defense statutes.[39] The statutes vary, but generally provide a defense to an eviction if the eviction is based on domestic violence (for example, if a victim is evicted due to noise complaints that arose from domestic violence). Some statutes extend to lease renewal as well. For instance, if a housing provider does not want to renew the tenancy of a victim because the police have been called several times, if the police were called in response to domestic violence, this may be protected by some state and local statutes. Many eviction defense statutes require documentation from a qualified third party. The definition of a qualified third party varies, but often includes victim service provides and members of law enforcement. Eviction defense statutes are critical to helping victims maintain housing, providing them with the chance to avoid housing instability or homelessness.

C. Early Lease Termination

Twenty-seven state and local jurisdictions have early lease termination statutes.[40] Early lease termination statutes provide victims with the opportunity to request to be released from the lease prior to the end of the original lease terms. Some of the statutes require the victim to make the request in writing or provide documentation from a qualified third party. Again, the definition of qualified third party differs, but may include victim service providers and law enforcement. Some statutes provide a timeframe in which the request must be made. For example, a statute may require that a victim make the request within 90 days of the domestic violence incident. Early lease termination gives victims the opportunity to leave an unsafe situation, and not be penalized monetarily or with a poor rental history.

D. Damages

Sometimes there is damage to the housing unit connected to the domestic violence, and housing providers may try to hold the victim responsible for damage caused by the abuser. Fortunately, in eleven states, the abuser is held liable for damages to the unit, lock changes, and moving expenses.[41] There may also be a fair housing violation if the victim is charged for damages resulting from domestic violence, while other tenants who are crime victims are not.

---

[39] *Id.*

[40] *Id.*

[41] *Id.*

E. Lock Changes

There are eighteen state and local statutes that explicitly give domestic violence victims the right to request and receive lock changes.[42] Generally, under these statutes, if victims must pay for the lock change cost, they cannot be charged differently than any other tenant who receives a lock change. Additionally, these statutes often give a timeframe by which the locks must be changed once the request is made (i.e., 24-48 hours). The ability to have locks changed is a safety measure that is critical to a victim, especially if the abuser once had access to the unit.

F. Lease Bifurcation

Removing an abuser from a lease can be an important way to help victims feel and stay safe at home. This is known as lease bifurcation. Eight states allow lease bifurcations in cases of domestic violence.[43] Many of these statutes require an order of protection as documentation for the housing provider to move forward.

VII. *Advocacy Tips*

Advocacy Tip: Understand the federal, as well as state and local protections that apply in your jurisdiction. When discussing options related to housing, prioritize your client's safety and provide information on safety planning.

It is important for all attorneys, including housing attorneys, to learn about the dynamics of domestic violence. Your state or local domestic violence program may offer trainings for attorneys or community members. While you do not have to be an expert, understanding the basics of domestic violence may help you recognize the safety issues your client is facing. Your client knows best what the safety concerns are, including those related to housing. Your client may not understand the range of protections available, and assume the only option is to leave their current housing situation or become homeless. Be sure to share with your client as much information as possible regarding the federal, state and local protections that may apply.

With your legal knowledge, you may provide your client with options that will enable them to feel safer, and may even prevent them from becoming homeless. For example, letting your client know that seeking early lease termination or lease bifurcation is possible would provide the client with the chance to weigh the safety options regarding their current housing. For clients who fear leaving their current housing situation, informing them that

---

[42] *Id.*

[43] *Id.*

they cannot be discriminated against based on the domestic violence when seeking new housing, or that they are not responsible for damages caused by the abuser, will better equip them to seek new housing if appropriate. If your client is homeless, knowing that shelters cannot deny access because of your client's status as a domestic violence victim can help increase emergency shelter options.

Additionally, because safety is extremely important, you should provide your client with information about safety planning. Your state or local domestic violence service provider may be able to provide resources on safety planning to you and your client. Safety planning can directly impact your client's safety, especially if they are currently in a dangerous living situation.[44]

Advocacy Tip: Educate housing providers/landlords and public housing authorities.

You may not be surprised to learn that housing providers are often unfamiliar with the housing protections that exist. In addition to educating housing providers on federal, state, and local housing laws, you can educate them about domestic violence and the benefits of taking certain actions, even if they are not required by law. For example, letting a victim out of the lease early can certainly benefit the housing provider if the abuser is threatening the tenant and even other residents. Not only are there liability issues, but many housing providers do not want to further fuel violence. Forcing a victim to be liable for rent, essentially making it impossible for the victim to afford to leave and find safer housing, is an argument that is persuasive with some housing providers.

There are many benefits to outreach and education targeted at housing providers. State or local domestic violence service providers, as well as national technical assistance and training organizations with expertise on safe housing issues, can provide you with ideas and support around outreach and education.[45]

Advocacy Tip: Use national, state, and local resources.

Representing domestic violence victims in housing cases does not require you to know all the answers. This chapter is meant to give you an overview of the challenges victims face and different federal, state, and local housing protections. Contact the organizations in the appendix to this chapter for

---

[44] For more information on safety planning, see *Client Counseling, Intake, and Referral, in* A Lawyer's Handbook: Volume 1, The Domestic Violence Civil Law Manual: Protection Orders and Family Law Cases 10–18 (4th ed. 2016).

[45] See the organizations listed in the Appendix to this chapter.

support, and use your legal peer networks; connect with lawyers in your community who have handled domestic violence and housing cases before.

It is also critical to educate yourself on the available flexible funding and crime victims compensation resources in the community to which your client may have access.[46] These funding sources can support a range of expenses, including installing home security features or covering costs associated with relocating to a safer location.

---

[46] For more information on crime victims' compensation, see *Crime Victims Compensation* in Section Eight of this manual.

APPENDIX

Resources:

- **American Civil Liberties Union, Women's Rights Project**
  - *Safe at Home*, Am. Civ. Liberties Union, https://www.aclu.org/other/safe-home (last visited Apr. 30, 2018).
  - This website provides valuable resources, fact sheets, blog posts, and policy advocacy as well as case law specific to housing issues impacting victims. Lawyers can also find information regarding nuisance ordinances and domestic violence.

- **National Alliance for Safe Housing (NASH)**
  - *National Alliance for Safe Housing*, Safe Housing Partnerships, https://safehousingpartnerships.org/taxonomy/term/205 (last visited Apr. 30, 2018).
  - NASH is a project of the District Alliance for Safe Housing, and provides programs and communities with the tools, strategies, and support necessary to improve coordination between domestic and sexual violence services and homeless and housing providers. NASH also provides Training and Technical Assistance on federal, state, and local housing protections.

- **National Housing Law Project (NHLP)**
  - Nat'l Housing L. Project, https://www.nhlp.org/OVWgrantees (last visited June 5, 2018).
  - NHLP provides technical assistance, training, and support to victim advocates, housing advocates, legal services attorneys, and housing providers across the country on a variety of matters impacting the housing rights of domestic violence victims. NHLP has an extensive online library of resources that includes webinars, manuals, toolkits, and fact sheets on critical issues that affect victims accessing and maintaining safe and affordable housing.

- **National Law Center on Homelessness and Poverty (NLCHP)**
  - Nat'l L. Ctr. on Homelessness & Poverty, https://www.nlchp.org/ (last visited Apr. 30, 2018).
  - NLCHP advocates for families and individuals that need access to housing. Lawyers can access resources and materials specific to domestic violence and homelessness.
  - Nat'l L. Ctr. on Homelessness & Poverty, There's No Place Like Home: State Laws that Protect Housing Rights for Survivors of Domestic and Sexual Violence (2012), https://www.nlchp.org/documents/Theres_No_Place_Like_Home.

- **Safe Housing Partnerships**
  - ○ SAFE HOUSING PARTNERSHIPS, http://safehousingpartnerships.org/ (last visited Apr. 30, 2018).
  - ○ Safe Housing Partnerships is new website for the Domestic Violence and Housing Technical Assistance Consortium, and provides useful resources and tools on the critical intersection of domestic violence, sexual assault, homelessness, and housing. Lawyers can find a range of resources on this website, including but not limited to toolkits, policies, and laws and regulations.

- **U.S. Department of Housing and Urban Development (HUD)**
  - ○ U.S. DEP'T OF HOUSING & URBAN DEV., https://www.hud.gov/ (last visited Apr. 30, 2018).
  - ○ Lawyers can find information on the HUD website regarding HUD federally subsidized housing, CoC and Homeless Assistance Programs, the federal FHA and VAWA final rule, and forms. Federal FHA complaints and Section 504 complaints can be filed through the HUD portal, and by phone as well.

- **WomensLaw.org**
  - ○ *Housing Laws*, WOMENSLAW.ORG, https://www.womenslaw.org/laws/general/housing-laws.
  - ○ WomensLaw.org is a project of the National Network to End Domestic Violence, and provides state-specific plain-language legal information and resources for survivors of domestic violence.

Chapter Twenty-five:
Foreclosure Defense for Survivors:
Process, Defenses, and Alternatives

Karen Merrill Tjapkes and Sarah Bolling Mancini

Reprinted from Center for Survivor Agency & Justice (CSAJ), Guidebook on Consumer & Economic Civil Legal Advocacy (2017), https://csaj.org/Guidebook.[1]

I. Introduction

Foreclosure is the means by which a mortgage creditor takes the property securing the mortgage loan when a borrower is not able to make the payments. In recent years, a significant percent of homeowners have struggled to make their mortgage payments at one time or another, and faced the risk of foreclosure. Survivors of domestic violence who own a home and have separated from an abusive partner face particular risks due to the reduction in household income, job insecurity, and grappling with other debts or financial needs that typically follow a separation. More often than not, a recently separated survivor will attempt to make ends meet with reduced monthly income, which may cause them to fall behind on mortgage payments. Avoiding foreclosure involves specific challenges when a survivor remains in a home that was (fully or partly) owned by an abusive partner who has now left, especially if the abusive partner was the sole borrower on the mortgage. Survivors who are still in the home with an abusive partner may also be struggling to make a mortgage payment if the household is under financial strain.

---

[1] A deeper dive into the case scenario described in this reprinted chapter can be found in the chapter originally published by the Center for Survivor Agency & Justice. Karen Merrill Tjapkes & Sarah Bolling Mancini, *Foreclosure Defense for Survivors: Process, Defenses & Alternatives, in* Guidebook on Consumer & Economic Civil Legal Advocacy 126 (2017), https://csaj.org/Guidebook.

This chapter covers the players involved in the mortgage market, how foreclosures take place, and the critical information advocates need to advise a survivor about options to avoid foreclosure. We will also address different foreclosure avoidance, or "loss mitigation," options, issues that arise when the survivor is not the original borrower on the loan, and ways that the family law court can help keep foreclosure at bay.

Patricia's Story

Patricia's story is intended to demonstrate the way a survivor might deal with the risk of foreclosure.

Patricia, a 39-year-old woman, has a mobility disability. After an attack by her ex-husband, she was hospitalized and later diagnosed with partial paralysis. She now uses a wheelchair.

After the attack, Patricia left and filed for divorce. The Court awarded Patricia the house, but the divorce process was financially exhausting. Even though she has a full-time job at a call center, she can no longer rely on her ex-husband for transportation, running errands, or assisting with her health needs, so now much of her income is consumed by these new expenses. She relies solely on her personal employment income, which is much less than the joint income they once had as a married couple. To make matters worse, her ex-husband is not paying the child support he was ordered to pay for their two children. Patricia has not been able to make mortgage payments in months and is getting letters that say that her loan is about to be referred for foreclosure.

Patricia has tried to ask her mortgage company for help or a way to get caught up on the payments, but they have been giving her the run-around and will not tell her anything. The last time she called, they told Patricia that they could not talk to her without her ex-husband's permission because he was the only borrower on the loan. Patricia comes to you, confused and scared at the prospect of losing her home. She tells you that she knows that when they bought the house ten years ago, she went to the closing and had to sign certain documents. Patricia's name is on the deed, along with her ex-husband's name. "No one is telling me anything. What if they take my home?" she asks you.

As you try to help Patricia calm herself, you make a note of the issues you need to unpack to advise her. How far behind is the mortgage? How long is the foreclosure timeline in your state? Is her income alone enough to afford a loan modification on the mortgage? And is it safe for Patricia to stay in the house? These are a few of the facts you will need to explore as you help Patricia decide on her next steps.

II. Foreclosure and Domestic Violence

Unfortunately, often domestic violence and foreclosure go hand in hand. The domestic violence may initiate the foreclosure problem as the abusive partner cuts off financial support, the division into two households may dramatically reduce the income available to make the mortgage payments, or other debts created by the abusive partner may come into the light. Conversely, a pending foreclosure may escalate an abusive situation with this additional, significant financial stressor.

The intersection of foreclosure and domestic violence brings additional issues to the forefront: Is there a way to require the abusive partner to make payments? Is there a way to make the situation affordable for the survivor to sustain the mortgage on their own? Is there a way for the survivor to communicate with a mortgage servicer that insists they must have the abusive partner's cooperation and consent?

A. Assessing Foreclosure Options

Because of the complicated experiences and feelings surrounding homeownership for many survivors, foreclosure advocacy requires an open, honest, and sensitive assessment. The screening and assessment questions presented here are for issue spotting (often called "intake questions"), are not meant to be prescriptive, and conversations around foreclosure should not be limited to these questions.[2]

Foreclosures additionally present the problem of long-term, protracted financial negotiation, dissolution of assets, strain on changing income, communication and cooperation with an abusive partner, each posing unique privacy and safety risks. To begin a discussion with survivors about their housing and foreclosure concerns, some screening questions may include, but are not limited to:

- What is your goal—to stay in the home or to transition safely to another housing option? What factors are important to you in making that decision?

- What concerns do you have about safety and stability that might impact your decision about whether to stay in the house?

- What is your current monthly income? Is there any way to increase your income, such as by enforcing a child support order?

- Are you facing a permanent reduction in income or a temporary hardship?

- What information do you have about the mortgage, such as monthly payment amount and how far behind are the payments?

---

[2] For a fuller description of a survivor centered approach to economic assessment, see *Economic Coercion and Survivor-Centered Economic Advocacy* in Section Three of this manual.

- What have been the most recent communications from the mortgage servicer?

B. The Impact of Foreclosure

Maintaining stable housing is extremely critical for survivors of domestic violence recovering from trauma and abuse. For survivors who own a home, the risk of foreclosure jeopardizes their financial wellbeing as well as their ability to stay in a neighborhood where they may have networks of support, a job, and their children's school. Finding affordable housing after a foreclosure can be tremendously difficult due to the impact on a survivor's credit. Therefore, it can make a huge difference when an advocate helps a survivor find options to avoid foreclosure and obtain an affordable mortgage payment.

III. Key Legal Concepts and Players

A. What are the key legal concepts involved in foreclosure?

An individual obtaining a mortgage loan to buy a home or refinance their existing loan signs two critical documents for the financing: a **note** and a **mortgage** (or **deed of trust**). A **note** is a borrower's legally binding written promise to repay a debt to a lender by a certain date and under certain terms. A **mortgage** (or deed of trust—the term and precise nature of the transaction may vary depending on state law) gives an interest in a property to secure an obligation, usually the repayment of a loan evidenced by a note. Many times, the mortgage or deed of trust imposes other responsibilities on the homeowner, in addition to making payments on the note, such as paying real estate taxes and maintaining homeowner's insurance.

If the party giving the mortgage, **the mortgagor**, defaults on the obligation, then the party given the interest, **the mortgagee**, can proceed with foreclosure. **Foreclosure** is the process by which a mortgagee forces the sale of the property because of a default, usually a failure to make payments but it may also be an inability to perform other requirements. Depending on the state law, the foreclosure process can require judicial action or be a non-judicial sale by advertisement without any significant court oversight. In states that use a deed of trust, the sale may be conducted by a trustee.

Homeowners who are having problems paying their mortgage loan may want to try to have their loan modified to lower their payment or sell the house through a short sale to avoid foreclosure. These options to avoid foreclosure are often referred to as **loss mitigation** because they mitigate the potential loss to the mortgage investor from a foreclosure.

B. Who are the players in a mortgage foreclosure situation?

Survivors may find there are multiple people or entities involved in their mortgage loan—some they may be very familiar with, others they may not. It is important to get familiar with the different players to best understand the survivor's legal position and options moving forward. For example, in Patricia's story above, she knows she signed documents with Bank of America, but then a few years ago she started getting monthly statements from Nationstar Mortgage. How can you help her begin sorting out who is who and what is their role?

Most individuals begin the mortgage loan process by taking a loan from a financial institution, the **originating lender**. Some individuals may work directly with the originating lender to set up the mortgage loan; other times individuals work with a mortgage broker who chooses the originating lender (often based upon the loan terms and the commissions offered to the mortgage broker). While the originating lender may loan the initial funds, rarely does the homeowner repay the originating lender. Instead, the originating lender nearly always sells the mortgage loan to an **investor**.[3] The investor may be one of the two mortgage giants, Freddie Mac or Fannie Mae, or (as was commonplace during the subprime mortgage explosion in the 2000s) the loan may be sold to a trustee as a part of a securitization process.[4] Many of these mortgage transfers are tracked through a computer database known as the Mortgage Electronic Registration System, or MERS. In many states, MERS is appointed as the "nominee" or the mortgagee and may pursue foreclosure in its own name. Homeowners have some access to the MERS database and can use it to learn more about their mortgage loan if they have a MERS mortgage.[5]

The player that all homeowners know is their **mortgage servicer**—this is the financial institution to whom the homeowner makes their payments and with whom the homeowner communicates, especially if there are problems with payments. Often, the mortgage servicer does not own the mortgage loan but collects the payments on behalf of that owner, which may be Fannie Mae, Freddie Mac, a private trust or another bank. Servicers include large national banks as well as non-bank financial institutions.

Some mortgage loans may also have **mortgage insurance**. Distinct from homeowner's insurance (which most homeowners will also have), mortgage insurance is designed to cover any shortfall if there is a default and foreclosure of

---

[3]   Federal law requires that the homeowner be notified when their mortgage loan is sold to a new investor. *See* 15 U.S.C. § 1641(g) (2018).

[4]   Fannie Mae and Freddie Mac both have websites that a homeowner can use to find out if Fannie or Freddie (respectively) owns their loan. *Fannie Mae Loan Lookup*, FANNIE MAE, https://www.knowyouroptions.com/loanlookup (last visited Apr. 30, 2018); *Loan Lookup Tool*, FREDDIE MAC, https://ww3.freddiemac.com/loanlookup/ (last visited Apr. 30, 2018).

[5]   MERS SERVICER ID, https://www.mers-servicerid.org/sis/index.jsp (last visited Apr. 30, 2018).

the loan. The most popular mortgage insurance program is through the Federal Housing Administration, FHA (run by the Department of Housing and Urban Development, HUD)[6]. Other government programs include VA insurance program and the direct and guaranteed mortgage loan programs through the United States Department of Agriculture. There is also private mortgage insurance, often identified as PMI for short. It is important to identify if there is mortgage insurance involved in the mortgage loan as the insurance program may have its own requirements and guidelines for servicing, loss mitigation, and foreclosure.

Advocacy Tip: Homeowners may find that their mortgage servicer will change throughout their repayment term. Under federal law, mortgage services are supposed to notify the homeowner regarding such a servicing transfer, including providing information regarding where to make payments.[7] Talk with survivors about whether they have received these notices, or if they have not, the servicer's name and contact information should be on the monthly mortgage statement. For survivors who have been denied basic information about the mortgage loan by an abusive partner, and may not have access to the mortgage statements or other letters about the mortgage, they should be able to ask the servicer for basic information by phone if they at least know the servicer's name.[8]

---

[6] The HUD FHA insurance program includes both traditional mortgages as well as a special product for senior citizens, the Home Equity Conversion Mortgage (HECM) program, commonly referred to as a "reverse mortgage."

[7] *See* 12 U.S.C. § 2605(b)–(d); 12 C.F.R. § 1024.33 (b)–(c).

[8] This should be the case if the survivor is a borrower on the mortgage loan. If the survivor is not an original borrower on the loan, communicating with the servicer may prove difficult. We discuss strategies for dealing with this problem later in this chapter.

Definition of Terms

Note: A borrower's legally binding written promise to repay a debt to a lender by a certain date and under certain terms.

Mortgage: Gives an interest in a property to secure an obligation, usually the repayment of a loan evidenced by a note (also called a deed of trust).

The mortgagor: The party giving the mortgage.

The mortgagee: The party given the interest.

Foreclosure: The process by which a mortgagee forces the sale of the property because of a default, usually a failure to make payments.

Originating lender: The entity providing the loan (usually a financial institution).

Mortgage servicer: The financial institution to whom the homeowner makes their payments and with whom the homeowner communicates, especially if there are problems with payments.

Investor: The entity to whom the originating lender sold the mortgage loan to. The investor may be the mortgage giants, Freddie Mac or Fannie Mae, or the loan may be sold to a trustee as a part of a securitization process.

Mortgage insurance: Different than homeowner insurance, it is designed to cover any shortfall if there is a default and foreclosure of the loan.

Judicial foreclosure: A lawsuit must be filed to initiate a foreclosure.

Non-judicial foreclosure: States where a foreclosure can occur without court oversight. In those states, the mortgage or deed of trust will contain a power of sale clause that permits a non-judicial foreclosure.

Successor in interest: Someone who became the owner of a home after a transfer, such as a divorce or death.

IV. Foreclosure Basics

A. What is foreclosure and how does a foreclosure happen?

As discussed above, foreclosure is the process by which a mortgagee (creditor) forces the sale of the property because of a default, usually a failure to make payments, although it may also be a failure to perform other obligations. Depending on the state law, the foreclosure process can require **judicial action** or allow a **nonjudicial sale** process.

In states that require foreclosure be by judicial action, a lawsuit must be filed. The investor or current owner of the mortgage loan usually files the lawsuit, although some states allow the mortgage servicer or MERS to file the court action. If the court finds that the mortgage loan is in default, the court will enter a judgment for the amount owed plus the court costs and, often, attorneys' fees. The court will then order that the house be sold, and the proceeds of the sale will be applied to the judgment amount. If there is still a balance due, some states will permit a deficiency judgment to be entered against the individual, and some will not.

In non-judicial foreclosure states, a foreclosure can occur without court oversight. In those states, the mortgage or deed of trust will contain a power of sale clause that permits a non-judicial foreclosure. Some states use a trustee to handle the sale process; in other states, the foreclosure attorneys conduct the foreclosure sale. In these states, the lender may be required to record a notice of default or mail a notice to the borrower before conducting the sale. If the homeowner does not cure the default, then the trustee or foreclosure attorneys may initiate the sale of the home; in most states, this requires the publication of notices advertising the sale and a public auction where the home is sold to the highest bidder. It is common for the servicer or owner of the mortgage to be the highest (and only) bidder and end up with the house. If the sale of the house does not satisfy the amount owed, the lender may or may not be able to seek a deficiency against the borrower, depending on state law.

Most states, whether the foreclosure process is judicial or non-judicial, require an eviction action after the foreclosure whereby the foreclosure sale purchaser evicts the person(s) residing in the home. In some states, the eviction may not take place until the end of a redemption period, during which the homeowner can try to buy back the house by tendering the full loan amount. The eviction process and timeline will vary depending on state law; the process is the same as that used to evict a tenant since the former owner is now a tenant without a lease.

Advocacy Tip: If the survivor knows a foreclosure will take place and intends to move out rather than fighting to save the home, the survivor may want to sign a lease for an apartment before the foreclosure is completed. The survivor may also want to negotiate a move-out agreement (sometimes called a "cash for keys" agreement) in order to prevent an eviction lawsuit from being filed. Foreclosure and eviction are typically reported on the borrower's credit report, and can make finding a new apartment more difficult.[9]

Advocacy Tip: Because there are such stark differences in the foreclosure process from state to state, it is important that domestic violence advocates learn the

---

[9] For more information on credit reporting, see Katie VonDeLinde, *Building & Repairing Survivors' Credit Reports: Understanding Options and Safety Implications for Survivors, in* Guidebook on Consumer & Economic Civil Legal Advocacy 30 (2017), https://csaj.org/Guidebook.

foreclosure process in their own area. To do so, you should check with a local attorney who practices in this area of law or consult the National Consumer Law Center's *Foreclosures and Mortgage Servicing* manual, which contains the citations to every state's foreclosure statute.[10] Attorneys with expertise in foreclosure matters may be found at local legal services offices or by using the attorney search function at the National Association of Consumer Advocates website.[11]

B. What is the critical information advocates and survivors need to understand the options in a mortgage foreclosure situation?

One of the most important things that an advocate can help a survivor do is gather the information necessary to assess the options. Some of the information may be difficult to access, especially if the abusive partner is controlling the situation. However, there may be some tools that the survivor can use to help gather that information.

First, the survivor will need to gather information regarding the mortgage loan itself.[12] This information is found in the following documents:

- The original documents from when they first took out the mortgage loan, sometimes called the closing packet;

- Current monthly statements; and

- Any other notices from the mortgage servicer.

The survivor will also need to know the amount of the monthly payment, how much is owed if the loan is in default, and whether the loan has been referred to foreclosure. The monthly mortgage statement should contain most of this information. This is important because once a mortgage is at least 120 days past due, the lender may begin the foreclosure process.[13]

If the survivor does not have this information, they can send the mortgage servicer a "**request for information**." Under federal law, the mortgage servicer is required to acknowledge a request for information within five days and provide a full response within 30 business days.[14] The period may be lengthened by an additional 15 days in some situations, but a request only for the identity of the loan owner be answered within 10 business days. However, if the survivor did not

---

[10] Nat'l Consumer L. Ctr., Foreclosures and Mortgage Servicing (5th ed. 2014).

[11] *Find an Attorney*, Nat'l Ass'n of Consumer Advoc., https://www.consumeradvocates.org/find-an-attorney (last visited Apr. 30, 2018).

[12] Some of this information, such as the mortgage itself, may be available from the local land records office. It may also be possible to contact the title office that helped process or "close" the loan to see if they still have copies of documents available.

[13] 12 C.F.R. § 1024.41(f).

[14] *Id.* § 1024.36.

sign the note, they may be unable to access information about the loan through a request for information, at least initially. This is discussed later in the chapter.

Second, it is important to gather the information regarding the survivor's current financial status. This should include evaluating their current sources of income, potential changes in income, and expenses.

With this information, the survivor can begin to review the various options and begin to formulate a plan for how to proceed. Some questions to consider include:

- Does the survivor want to remain in the house?

- Does the survivor feel they can remain in the house safely?

- What is survivor's short-term, as well as long-term, financial capacity to afford the home (the mortgage loan as well as other costs of homeownership and utilities)?

- What other options are available to prevent foreclosure?

- What other housing options are available?

Advocacy Tip: It is important to work with the survivor to evaluate their full financial situation. Due to the social value placed on homeownership, many homeowners perceive losing or giving up a home as a failure. It is important to explain to the survivor that they are not their foreclosure, that they have options after a foreclosure, and it is important to discuss what their other financial priorities are, and how they may influence choices about their home.

V. Alternatives to Foreclosure

Reviewed below are many of the options for preventing the foreclosure of a mortgage loan.

A. What is loss mitigation, what are the loss mitigation options, and how does that process work?

Loss mitigation is the process by which a mortgage servicer (often using the guidelines established by and with the approval of the investor and/or insurer of the loan) reviews a mortgage loan for possible options to avoid a foreclosure, thereby mitigating the loss to the mortgage investor. There are several loss mitigation options available to homeowners, and federal law sets forth a process that nearly all mortgage servicers must follow regarding how the servicer must handle a request for assistance with a mortgage loan.

There are loss mitigation options that allow a homeowner to keep the home and loss mitigation options that require the homeowner to leave the home, but still avoid foreclosure. Avoiding foreclosure may be important to some homeowners, especially those who are concerned about their credit score and ability to get a new mortgage loan in the future.

In evaluating loss mitigation options, the mortgage company will want to evaluate the survivor's "hardship," or reason why the homeowner fell behind or is about to fall behind on their payments. Additionally, the mortgage company will want to know whether the hardship is a short-term or long-term hardship. For example, one short-term hardship would be a pregnancy where a homeowner is off work for several months but will be able to return to their prior income. A long-term hardship, for example, would include when a homeowner becomes disabled and is unable to return to full-time work or has permanently lost a spouse's income due to divorce or separation.

Loss mitigation options vary somewhat depending on the type of loan and the players involved, for example, if Fannie Mae or Freddie Mac owns the loan or if there is FHA insurance. Fannie Mae, Freddie Mac, and FHA have their servicing and loss mitigation instructions easily available on their web pages. Possible options include the following:

Forbearance: Allows for a suspension or reduction of payments for a set period so the homeowner may recover from a short-term crisis. The delinquent amount is not forgiven, so the borrower must make arrangements to become current on the mortgage loan when the forbearance ends (usually after 6 or 12 months), often through a repayment plan or a loan modification.

Repayment plan: The amount that the homeowner is delinquent is spread out over a set period of time (usually 3–12 months) and added to the regular monthly payment. This may be a good option for someone who suffered a temporary loss or reduction in income, but whose income has now reached a level where they can afford the regular payment plus a little extra.

Loan modification:[15] Involves adjusting the terms of the note so that the borrower will start fresh, typically by adding the missed payments to the balance owed on the loan, and usually making the monthly payment more affordable. Adjustments may include lowering the interest rate or reamortizing the loan over a longer period, such as a new 30 or 40 years from the date of the modification. Most loan modification programs seek to target a modified mortgage payment somewhere between 31 percent and 40 percent of the borrower's gross monthly income. Loan modification evaluations also typically consider whether the investor will lose more money by foreclosing or by offering the loan modification; if the modification is financially beneficial to the investor, it should be offered.

---

[15] There are online calculators to check eligibility for a loan modification. *See, e.g., CheckMyNPV,* Making Home Affordable.gov, www.checkmynpv.com (last visited Apr. 30, 2018).

Advocacy Tip: When you are helping a homeowner apply for a loan modification to reduce the principal and interest payment on the mortgage, it is a good idea to help the homeowner investigate whether the portion of the payment going to pay property taxes and homeowner's insurance (called the "**escrow payment**," because these monthly amounts are held in escrow until costs come due once a year) can be reduced. For example, does the survivor need to apply for the basic property tax **homestead exemption** (allowed for an owner-occupant) or a special property tax exemption? In the case scenario, because Patricia has a disability, she may qualify for an additional exemption for elderly homeowners or homeowners with disabilities in some states. Or, can the survivor find cheaper homeowner's insurance? If the escrow payment can be reduced, it will help with the overall affordability of the mortgage.

Short sale: Option to sell the home for less than the amount owed on the mortgage loan with the approval of the mortgage service and other parties. This is most likely to be available if the home is "underwater," meaning the borrower owes more than the house is worth.

Deed in lieu of foreclosure: The homeowner executes a deed conveying the home to the mortgage lender or servicer without a foreclosure sale. When sustained efforts to market the property for sale or short sale have failed, this option is the last resort. Typically, the home is worth less than the amount owed on the mortgage, and it will be important to ensure that the lender is waiving any deficiency (and to get advice about the tax consequences).

Advocacy Tip: It is important in a short sale or deed in lieu to make sure that the lender is waiving the deficiency (the difference between the sale price and the amount owed) and advise the survivor that this may have income tax consequences, and they should seek advice from a tax professional.

State hardest hit funds program: The federal government designated eighteen states (and the District of Columbia) as "hardest hit" by the foreclosure and unemployment crises. Survivors in these states may be able to qualify for special assistance from their state Hardest Hit Funds program, particularly if they have experienced a hardship arising from job loss, divorce, medical problem, or disability. These programs may provide temporary payment assistance, money to bring the loan current, or a large payment to reduce the principal balance on the loan.[16] Most Hardest Hit Fund programs are set to expire in 2020.

To apply for a loss mitigation option such as a loan modification, the homeowner must submit a financial packet for review to the servicer. Often, the homeowner can begin the process with a telephone call to the mortgage

---

[16] For a map of the states designated as hardest hit, and links to each state's program, see *Hardest Hit Fund*, U.S. Dep't of Treasury, https://www.treasury.gov/initiatives/financial-stability/TARP-Programs/housing/hhf/Pages/default.aspx (last updated Apr. 26, 2018).

servicer, who will then send the necessary application and a list of required documents. The required documents to submit in the financial packet will typically include proof of income, bank account statements, and a hardship letter outlining the reasons why the homeowner is having financial difficulty with the mortgage payments.

Federal regulations promulgated by the Consumer Financial Protection Bureau (CFPB) under the Real Estate Settlement Procedures Act (RESPA) outline the process by which mortgage servicers must process loss mitigation requests. When a mortgage loan becomes past due, the mortgage servicer must make a good faith effort to establish contact with the borrower and inform the borrower of their loss mitigation options.[17] The servicer must also send a written notice to the borrower with the servicer's contact information, information regarding loss mitigation options, and HUD approved housing counselor information for assistance.[18]

If a borrower submits a loss mitigation application, and if the packet is submitted more than 45 days before a foreclosure sale, the servicer must review the packet within five business days and either notify the borrower that the packet is complete or inform the borrower what information is required to complete the application.[19] Once the application is complete, if the complete application is submitted at least 37 days before a foreclosure sale, then the servicer must evaluate the application for all available loss mitigation options and provide a written decision to the borrower within 30 days of the date the complete application was received by the servicer.[20] Importantly, if the application is submitted and completed more than 37 days before the foreclosure sale, the mortgage servicer may not proceed with the sale until they have fully evaluated the loss mitigation application for all options.[21]

Depending on when the complete application was received, the borrower may have the option to appeal a denial for a loss mitigation option.[22]

Advocacy Tip: Make sure to explain to survivors that although federal regulations appear to require a quick consideration process, the reality is that most mortgage servicers take far longer to evaluate a loss mitigation request. Supporting documents "expire" after a certain number of days and will need to be updated on a regular basis. Survivors may want to consider contacting a HUD-

---

[17] 12 C.F.R. § 1024.39(a)

[18] *Id.* § 1024.39(b).

[19] *Id.* § 1024.41(b).

[20] *Id.* § 1024.41(c).

[21] *Id.* § 1024.41(g).

[22] *Id.* § 1024.41(c), (e).

certified housing counselor to assist them with this process as it can be quite overwhelming for homeowners to handle themselves.[23]

Advocacy Tip: In their attempts to find qualified assistance, survivors should be wary of private companies offering to help. While some of these companies may be legitimate, many are scams that will just take the homeowner's money without providing any actual assistance. Even those companies that may be helpful will charge a fee, which a survivor, who is already in financial distress, can ill afford to spend. Because there is a network of free housing counselors available in most areas, survivors do not need to hire a private company to assist them in most situations.

VI. Assuming the Mortgage: Issues in Loan Servicer Communication

A. What do you do if the mortgage servicer will not talk to the survivor without the abusive partner's permission because they claim the survivor is not the borrower?

In assisting survivors of domestic violence, you may come across quite a few survivors who are living in the home and have (or likely will) become the sole owner of the home through a divorce decree, property settlement agreement, or separation agreement, but who were not the original borrower on the mortgage loan. It is possible that the ex-spouse was the only borrower on the note, even if the survivor jointly owned the home and had to sign certain documents at closing. This can lead to a very difficult situation where the mortgage servicer refuses to let the survivor apply for a loan modification or refuses even to provide any information about the mortgage.[24]

In general, if a survivor needs a modification to make the mortgage payment affordable, they will likely need to "assume" the debt. An **assumption** is a legal agreement by which someone takes on personal liability and becomes obligated on the debt. By assuming the loan, the survivor steps into the shoes of the borrower, and should then be entitled to loan information and modification options, just like the original borrower. The question, then, is whether a survivor can assume the mortgage.

---

[23] Homeowners can find certified, non-profit housing counselors through HUD. *HUD Approved Housing Counseling Agencies*, U.S. Dep't of Housing & Urban Dev., http://www.hud.gov/offices/hsg/sfh/hcc/hcs.cfm (last visited Apr. 30, 2018).

[24] *See* Sarah Bolling Mancini & Alys Cohen, *Surviving the Borrower: Assumption, Modification, and Access to Mortgage Information after a Death or Divorce*, 43 Pepp. L. Rev. 345, 349 (2016). For additional background on these issues, see *Saving the Family Home After Death or Divorce*, Nat'l Consumer L. Ctr. (Dec. 12, 2014), https://www.nclc.org/other-webinars/saving-the-family-home-after-death-or-divorce.html; *Snapshots of the Struggle: Saving the Family Home After Death or Divorce*, Nat'l Consumer L. Ctr. (Mar. 2016), http://www.nclc.org/issues/snapshots-of-struggle.html.

Most survivors in this situation will have acquired their ownership interest in the home because of a transfer. That transfer of the home could have been effectuated through a quitclaim deed signed by the ex-spouse, or through a divorce decree or separation agreement awarding the house to the survivor. Even if a survivor owned a half-interest in the home since it was purchased, they may have received a transfer of the other one-half interest through a divorce decree.

Most mortgage contracts are drafted to restrict transfers; they contain a clause called a "due-on-sale" or "due-on-transfer" clause that says that if the borrower transfers the home without the lender's approval, the lender may accelerate the loan and foreclose. Due-on-sale clauses allow the servicer to accelerate the mortgage loan, and then to foreclose, after an unauthorized transfer. In 1982, Congress passed the Garn-St Germain Act, which pre-empted state laws limiting the enforcement of due-on-sale clauses, but also carved out important exceptions for certain kinds of transfers. If a transfer falls within a Garn-St Germain exception, the mortgagee may **not** enforce the due-on-sale clause.[25] Successors who receive an interest through this kind of transfer are sometimes referred to as Garn-exempt or Garn-protected transferees.

Garn-St Germain carves out several kinds of protected transfers wherein a creditor may not enforce a due-on-sale clause, including:

- A transfer to a relative resulting from the death of a borrower;

- A transfer to a spouse or child of the borrower; or

- A transfer resulting from a decree of a dissolution of marriage, legal separation agreement, or from an incidental property settlement agreement, by which the spouse of the borrower becomes an owner of the property.[26]

Because the due-on-sale clause is the only mechanism a servicer has to block an assumption of the mortgage by a new owner, servicers must allow a survivor to assume the loan if he or she falls within one of the Garn exceptions, even if there is an otherwise valid due-on-sale clause in the loan contract.[27] Without an

---

[25] 12 U.S.C. § 1701j-3(d).

[26] *Id.* §§ 1701j-3(d)(3), (5), (6), (7).

[27] *See, e.g.,* FANNIE MAE, SINGLE FAMILY SERVICING GUIDE § 408.02 (2003) ("Generally, the servicer must process these exempt transactions without reviewing or approving the terms of the transfer.").

enforceable due-on-sale clause, contracts are freely assumable and assignable under state contract law.[28]

New Regulations Effective 2018 Protect Non-Borrower Homeowners

The CFPB issued a new regulation under RESPA in August 2016, which took effect on April 19, 2018, giving much broader protections to successors in interest. This regulation requires servicers to communicate with all successors covered by the Garn-St Germain Act and allows a potential successor to send a request for information for the purpose of asking how to prove his or her successor status. The regulation requires servicers to respond to this kind of request in the manner required for other "requests for information," discussed above. In addition, once it has been confirmed that a homeowner is a successor protected by the Garn-St Germain Act, the new rule makes the confirmed successor a borrower under RESPA, meaning that all of the protections of RESPA discussed in the prior section—the right to send requests for information and notices of error, specific loss mitigation procedures and timelines, and restrictions on foreclosing when a complete loan modification application has been submitted—now apply.

If the borrower has died or if a divorce has taken place, a survivor can point to the regulation issued by CFPB under RESPA, which took effect April 19, 2018. Under this regulation, servicers are required to have policies and procedures reasonably designed to "[u]pon notification of the death of a borrower or of any transfer of the property securing the mortgage loan, promptly facilitate communication with any potential or confirmed successor in interest regarding the property."[29] The servicer is also required to promptly provide any potential successor in interest with a list of the documents the servicer reasonably requires in order to confirm successor status, and upon receipt of such documents, promptly inform the potential successor whether he or she has been confirmed as a successor, has been determined not to be a successor, or needs to provide additional information.[30] The Official Interpretation to the regulation discusses several examples of what would be reasonable documentation for a servicer to require. In a situation where

---

[28] *See* Restatement (Second) of Contracts § 323 cmt. a (Am. L. Inst. 1981) ("The assent of the obligor is not ordinarily necessary to make an assignment valid."); Brush v. Wells Fargo Bank, N.A., 911 F.Supp.2d 445, 460 (S.D. Tex. 2012) (finding daughter, who inherited property from her father, had right to assume the mortgage despite existence of due-on-sale clause); Olson v. Etheridge, 686 N.E.2d 563 (Ill. 1997) (finding that contracting parties can modify who has primary responsibility for payment of a debt, without reference to the wishes of the creditor of that debt); Andrews v. Holloway, 231 S.E.2d 548, 549 (Ga. Ct. App. 1976) (holding that lender's consent to assumption was not required where mortgage contract provided it was binding on the borrower's "assigns").

[29] 12 C.F.R. § 1024.38(b)(i)(vi).

[30] *Id.*

a property settlement agreement in connection with a divorce set forth the transfer of ownership of the home to the successor, the Bureau noted that it would not be reasonable for a servicer to also demand a quitclaim deed executed by the ex-spouse.[31]

Also, if Fannie Mae or Freddie Mac owns the loan, or if the loan is FHA insured, there are specific rules that require the servicer to evaluate a successor in interest for a simultaneous loan modification and assumption.[32] If you find out that the survivor's loan falls into one of these categories, it is important to cite to the appropriate guidebook and, if necessary, to escalate the case to Fannie, Freddie, or the FHA National Servicing Center.[33]

Advocacy Tips:

Here are a few practice tips for helping a survivor who was not the original borrower on the mortgage loan:

- Send the servicer a letter explaining that the survivor became the owner of a home through a transfer covered by the Garn-St. Germain Act. Attach proof of the survivor's ownership of the house, such as a divorce decree or legal separation agreement conveying the house to your client or a quitclaim deed from the borrower to your client.[34]

- You can opt to send this letter and proof of ownership before sending a loan modification application or along with the loan modification package. As always, keep a copy of what you send and proof that the documents were received.

- If the loan is owned by Fannie Mae or Freddie Mac or insured by the FHA, cite to the appropriate handbook or guidance requiring the servicer to evaluate the survivor for a simultaneous modification and assumption.

VII. Safety Planning and Privacy Concerns

While working with a survivor, it is especially important to develop an appropriate safety plan and address privacy concerns. The mortgage

---

[31] Official Interpretation 1024.38(b)(1)(vi)-3(iii); 81 Fed. Reg. 72160, 72380 (Oct. 19, 2016).

[32] *See* Fannie Mae, Lender Letter LL-2013-04, Fannie Mae Servicing Guide Announcement SVC-2013-17 (2013); Fannie Mae, Single Family Servicing Guide § D1-4.1-02; Freddie Mac, Bull. 2013-3 (Feb. 15, 2013); Freddie Mac, Single Family Servicing Guide § 9207.2; FHA Servicing Handbook § III. A. 2. j. ii (B) (4) (search for "non-borrowers who acquired title through an exempted transfer").

[33] To escalate a wrongful denial by a servicer, you can contact resource_center@fanniemae.com, FMBH@freddiemac.com, or for FHA loans, call the National Servicing Center at 1-877-622-8525.

[34] Remember that if the divorce decree or separation agreement does not clearly award ownership of the house, you will likely also need a quitclaim deed signed by the non-resident ex-spouse.

foreclosure context is no different, and these factors need to be addressed with the survivor.

First, it is important to partner with the survivor to understand the abusive partner and identify potential risks, especially the potential for retaliation. The survivor is the expert in gauging how the abusive ex-partner may react to their intentions regarding the home and foreclosure. For example, how will the former abusive partner react to a request to assist with the loss mitigation process; will they be willing to sign required documents? Some abusive former partners may place conditions on their participation in the loss mitigation process, such as requiring in-person meetings that may place the survivor at risk.

Second, plans for how to proceed with the foreclosure and potential loss mitigation options should be based upon that risk assessment. In some cases, the safety risks may be so great that the survivor should not attempt to keep the home because they need to keep their location secret. In those situations, and other situations where keeping the home is not appropriate or possible, advocates should discuss with the survivor that it is ok to leave the house and that a foreclosure may be preferable to a course of action that may compromise their safety.

It is also important to remember that, while financial institutions do have obligations to protect personal information, this obligation may not stop the disclosure of the survivor's information. This is especially true if the abusive partner is also on the mortgage loan. Accordingly, if the survivor has concerns regarding the release of their information they may want to weigh the benefits of loss mitigation versus the potential risks.

VIII. Using the Family Court Proceeding to Address Mortgage Foreclosure

It may be possible to use the family court to better position survivors in the mortgage foreclosure context, especially to address some of the roadblocks that the abusive partner may attempt to construct for the survivor.

A. Family Court Strategies for Keeping the Property

Possible family court strategies for keeping the property may include:[35]

---

[35] For strategies to enhance economic security or provide financial relief through family law cases, see Laura A. Russell, *Financial Issues in Family Law: Protection Orders, Child & Spousal Support, and Distribution of Assets & Debts, in* Guidebook on Consumer & Economic Civil Legal Advocacy 166 (2017), https://csaj.org/Guidebook.

- Obtain orders requiring the payment of child support and/or alimony, to increase the survivor's financial resources to make payments or use as a base for loss mitigation options.

- Consider requiring the family court to order mortgage payments by the abusive partner as a part of or in lieu of spousal support if that is appropriate for the circumstance. Among other factors, the motivation to preserve the asset and a credit history may be more effective than the motivation to pay support.

- See if the court will provide that the survivor remain in the home and pay the mortgage (perhaps with a modification) for several years until the children are adults and/or real estate markets improve to allow a more profitable sale. It may be appropriate to require the abusive partner to assist with maintaining the payments. While some states permit the transfer of real property by a judgment or decree or divorce, the title insurance and mortgage industries do not always recognize the transfer. Many mortgage servicers will require this to work with the survivor but not the abusive partner for loss mitigation purposes. Accordingly, it is always best to have a deed signed when there is a property transfer in a domestic relations case.

B. Family Law Strategies for Selling the Property

Possible strategies to review for selling the property or permitting the foreclosure to go through may include:

- Requesting a court order to permit the sale of the property without the abusive partner's consent or involvement, if he will not cooperate with the survivor to sell the property.

- If the sale or foreclosure does not pay the balance due on the mortgage, using the family court to allocate responsibility for the deficiency. Whether the abusive partner was cooperative with efforts to modify the loan or sell the house may be a factor the family court judge can consider in deciding how to allocate the responsibility for the deficiency.[36] To the extent the survivor is required to pay something, then work with the survivor to develop strategies for how the deficiency will be paid.

---

[36] *See, e.g.,* Lawson v. Lawson, 228 S.W.3d 18 (Ky Ct. App. 2007) (assigning deficiency after mortgage foreclosure to husband where his own misconduct caused him to cease making payments); Porath v. Porath, 855 N.E.2d 511 (Oh. Ct. App. 2006) (finding equal distribution of assets inequitable where wife thwarted husband's attempts to avoid foreclosure of marital home); In re Marriage of Cook, 453 N.E.2d 1357 (Ill. App. Ct. 1983) (awarding substantial marital assets to wife where husband failed to keep up the mortgage payments on the family home).

C. Other Strategies

There are also other creative strategies that advocates may consider using the family court proceedings to assist the survivor with the mortgage loan and possible foreclosure. These options may include:

- **Motion for Joinder of Third Parties.** In some states, the family court may be willing to assert jurisdiction over the property and make determinations that would then bind third parties related to the property.[37]

- **Consolidation of foreclosure proceedings and divorce proceedings.** In states where foreclosures are judicial, it may be possible to request that the cases be consolidated. This may allow the family court to be informed by the foreclosure court and vice versa and make better decisions regarding the disposition of the property.[38]

- **Motions to compel signatures or other cooperation with the mortgage servicer and loss mitigation process.** May be considered at times when the mortgage servicer is requiring the abusive partner to cooperate with the process, such as providing documentation or sign applications. Additionally, may be necessary to have such an order to move forward with the sale of a property if the abusive partner refuses to participate in the sale process. The survivor may consider a motion requiring the abusive partner to sign an authorization allowing the mortgage servicer to release information to the survivor if efforts to require the mortgage servicer to do so without the authorization have failed.

IX. Conclusion

All too often, survivors of domestic violence must grapple with the risk of foreclosure, either while living with abusive partner under financial strain or after leaving, while attempting to save a home with a reduced household income. Advocates can help survivors feel empowered to address the problem, rather than shutting down when faced with the prospect of a foreclosure. With the tools discussed in this chapter, advocates and survivors can work together to find alternatives to foreclosure, understand the legal protections available, and make a plan that protects the survivor's safety and pursues their goals.

---

[37] *See, e.g.,* Glade v. Glade, 45 Cal. Reptr. 2d 695 (Cal. Ct. App. 1995) (family law court acquired jurisdiction over community property in the hands of third parties and cold properly order their joinder).

[38] In re Marriage of Schweihs, 584 N.E.2d 472 (Ill. App. Ct. 1991); In re Marriage of Elliott, 638 N.E.2d 1172 (Ill. App. Ct. 1994).

APPENDIX

Resources:

- **Center for Survivor Agency & Justice**
  - Karen Tjapkes, *Domestic Violence in Foreclosure: The Foreclosure Process, Defenses & Alternatives for Survivors*, Ctr. for Survivor Agency & Just. (June 22, 2016), https://csaj.org/calendar/view/146/.
  - *Comments to CFPB on Amendments to the 2013 Mortgage Rules*, Ctr. for Survivor & Agency Just. (Mar. 16, 2015), https://csaj.org/document-library/CFPB_Regulations-As_Submitted.pdf.

- **National Consumer Law Center**
  - Nat'l Consumer L. Ctr., Foreclosures and Mortgage Servicing (5th ed. 2014), *updated at* www.nclc.org/library.
  - *Foreclosures & Mortgages*, Nat'l Consumer L. Ctr. http://www.nclc.org/issues/foreclosures-and-mortgages.html.

- **U.S. Department of Housing & Urban Development**
  - Find HUD-certified nonprofit housing counselors. *HUD Approved Housing Counseling Agencies*, U.S. Dep't of Housing & Urban Dev., http://www.hud.gov/offices/hsg/sfh/hcc/hcs.cfm.

- **U.S. Department of Treasury**
  - *Hardest Hit Fund*, U.S. Dep't of Treasury, https://www.treasury.gov/initiatives/financial-stability/TARP-Programs/housing/hhf/Pages/default.aspx.
  - Sarah Bolling Mancini & Alys Cohen, *Surviving the Borrower: Assumption, Modification, and Access to Mortgage Information after a Death or Divorce*, 43 Pepp. L. Rev. 345, 349 (2016).

Additional Information on Successors in Interest:

- **National Consumer Law Center**
  - *Saving the Family Home After Death or Divorce*, Nat'l Consumer L. Ctr. (Dec. 12, 2014), https://www.nclc.org/other-webinars/saving-the-family-home-after-death-or-divorce.html.
  - *Snapshots of the Struggle: Saving the Family Home After Death or Divorce*, Nat'l Consumer L. Ctr. (Mar. 2016), http://www.nclc.org/issues/snapshots-of-struggle.html.

Section Eight:
Criminal Matters

Chapter Twenty-six:
Domestic Violence:
The Intersection of Criminal Law and Civil Law

I. Introduction

In the criminal law system, domestic violence cases often begin with a 911 call.[1] The caller may be a victim asking for help, an abuser trying to head off a victim's call, a child in the home, a witness who saw or heard some portion of the incident, or hospital staff providing treatment to a victim. Once the report is made, the victim no longer has the ability to prevent the state from conducting an investigation, filing charges, and prosecuting the abuser. Though every state has passed a Victims' Rights Act that affords various rights and protections to victims of crime, none of those rights confer any control over prosecution.[2]

Domestic violence is a unique crime in that it is often the subject of simultaneous proceedings. While a criminal case is working its way through the local district attorney's office, the victim may be requesting a civil order of protection or filing for custody of children in common. These proceedings will be heard by different judges, each with distinct authority, but will nonetheless lead to the issuance of overlapping orders addressing contact between the victim and abuser.

---

[1] This heartbreaking 911 call, made by 6-year-old Lisa Floyd on November 21, 1990, has been used to educate people on the effects domestic violence has on children. *Little Girl Calls 911 As Her Mother Is Being Beaten By Her Stepfather,* S.F. GLOBE, Feb. 11, 2018, http://sfglobe. com/2014/12/06/little-girl-calls-911-as-her-mother-is-being-beaten-by-her-stepfather/. The entire call, with subtitles, can be found at *Lisa's 911 Phone Call (Full Version) Part 1,* YOUTUBE (Nov. 3, 2015), https://www.youtube.com/watch?v=u-7J5akhSA8.

[2] *Victim's Rights,* NAT'L CTR. FOR VICTIMS OF CRIME, http://victimsofcrime.org/help-for-crime-victims/get-help-bulletins-for-crime-victims/victims%27-rights (last visited Apr. 16, 2018).

The biggest hurdle for your domestic violence practice in these situations will be helping your clients navigate the complicated web created by the intersection of their family court cases with criminal litigation. Though you may only be the attorney of record in one of your client's multiple cases, it is important for you to understand enough of the process to address key issues that will arise during the representation of your client. This chapter is going to lay out the basic groundwork for how civil attorneys can utilize concurrent civil and criminal litigation to best advocate for their clients.

II. Prosecuting Domestic Abuse

A. Criminal Domestic Violence

Crimes of domestic violence are first identified by the relationship between the victim and abuser, rather than the act itself. Spouses, former spouses, and co-parents of children fall into this category in every jurisdiction in the United States. Each state takes a different view on expanding protections beyond these key associations.[3] Before domestic violence charges can be filed, there must be evidence the victim is in one of the delineated relationships with the abuser. Some states extend domestic abuse statutes to cover romantic partners—even when there are no children in common—and other family members.[4]

After establishing the necessary relationship, the next step for responding officers is determining whether the reported conduct is considered criminal in your jurisdiction.[5] States may codify specific crimes of domestic violence, or simply prosecute general criminal offenses that have been committed in the context of an abusive relationship.

Advocacy Tip: Not all acts of domestic violence are considered crimes of domestic violence. Your clients may be confused or offended about what conduct the state chooses to prosecute, particularly if they feel the more serious offenses have gone unpunished. Remember, it is not that the prosecutor does not consider such conduct egregious, but it may be non-criminal under the law.

---

[3] *Domestic Violence/Domestic Abuse Definitions and Relationships,* NAT'L CONF. OF STATE LEGISLATURES, http://www.ncsl.org/research/human-services/domestic-violence-domestic-abuse-definitions-and-relationships.aspx (last updated Jan. 8, 2015).

[4] Of course, crimes such as assault and battery still exist outside of the context of domestic or family relationships. Where no such relationship exists but you have a client who has been assaulted, refer to your local assault and battery laws.

[5] *See id.*

What About My Relationship?

Statutes that narrowly define family or interpersonal relationships for purposes of domestic violence prosecution can unintentionally leave many vulnerable groups unprotected. Jurisdictions that require a sexual or cohabitation component to a dating relationship leave teenage victims of domestic violence without standing to request domestic violence orders of protection, simply because they may reside with their parents, may not be sexually active, or may be unwilling to admit to having engaged in sexual activity with their abuser for fear of reprisals from their family or communities.

For example, Nikolas Cruz, the young man responsible for the mass shooting at Marjory Stoneman Douglas High School in Parkland, Florida on February 14, 2018, sent numerous threatening messages to an ex-girlfriend, her friends, and her new boyfriend.[6] On one occasion, he attacked the new boyfriend at school.[7] Under Florida's statutory definition of "family or household member," none of these incidents constituted criminal acts of domestic violence.

B. The Criminal Process

Many people incorrectly believe that a victim has the power to "press charges" against their abuser, and to later "drop the charges." All crimes are considered offenses against the People. Criminal complaints are prosecuted on behalf of the state, not the individual who made the report, or even those who were personally harmed. This means that only the state (through law enforcement officers such as police and prosecutors) can initiate or dismiss criminal charges.[8]

---

[6] Victor Oquendo, Nery Ynclan & Morgan Winsor, *Student Says Nikolas Cruz Threatened to 'Kill' Him, Sent Photo of Guns Months Before School Shooting,* ABC NEWS (Feb. 22, 2018, 5:46 PM), http://abcnews.go.com/US/student-nikolas-cruz-threatened-kill-photo-guns-months/story?id=53280687.

[7] *Id.*

[8] The exact procedure for charging domestic violence crimes varies state by state, with some states enacting "mandatory arrest" policies that limit an officer's charging discretion when responding to a domestic disturbance. *See* A.B.A. COMM'N ON DOMESTIC & SEXUAL VIOLENCE, DOMESTIC VIOLENCE ARREST POLICIES BY STATE, https://www.americanbar.org/content/dam/aba/images/domestic_violence/Domestic%20Violence%20Arrest%20Policies%20by%20State%202011%20(complete).pdf (last updated June 2011).

The Sequence of Events in the Criminal Justice System

CRIME

Reported Crime

Investigation → Unsolved or Not Arrested

Arrest → Released without Prosecution

Booking → Released without Prosecution

Petty Offenses ← Initial Appearance → Charges Dropped or Dismissed

Preliminary Hearing → Charges Dropped or Dismissed

Misdemeanors ← Bail or Detention → **Felonies**

Pretrial Activities → Charge Dismissed ← Pretrial Activities

Reduction of Charge

Guilty Plea | Trial → Acquitted   Guilty Plea | Trial → Acquitted

Sentencing   Appeal ← Sentencing

Fine | Probation   Probation

Nonpayment | Revocation   Revocation

Jail   Habeas Corpus ← Penitentiary

Revocation

Parole   Pardon and Clemency   Pardon and Clemency

Capital Punishment

Out of the System   **Out of the System**

Entry into the System

Prosecution and Pretrial Services

Adjudication

Sentencing and Sanctions

Corrections

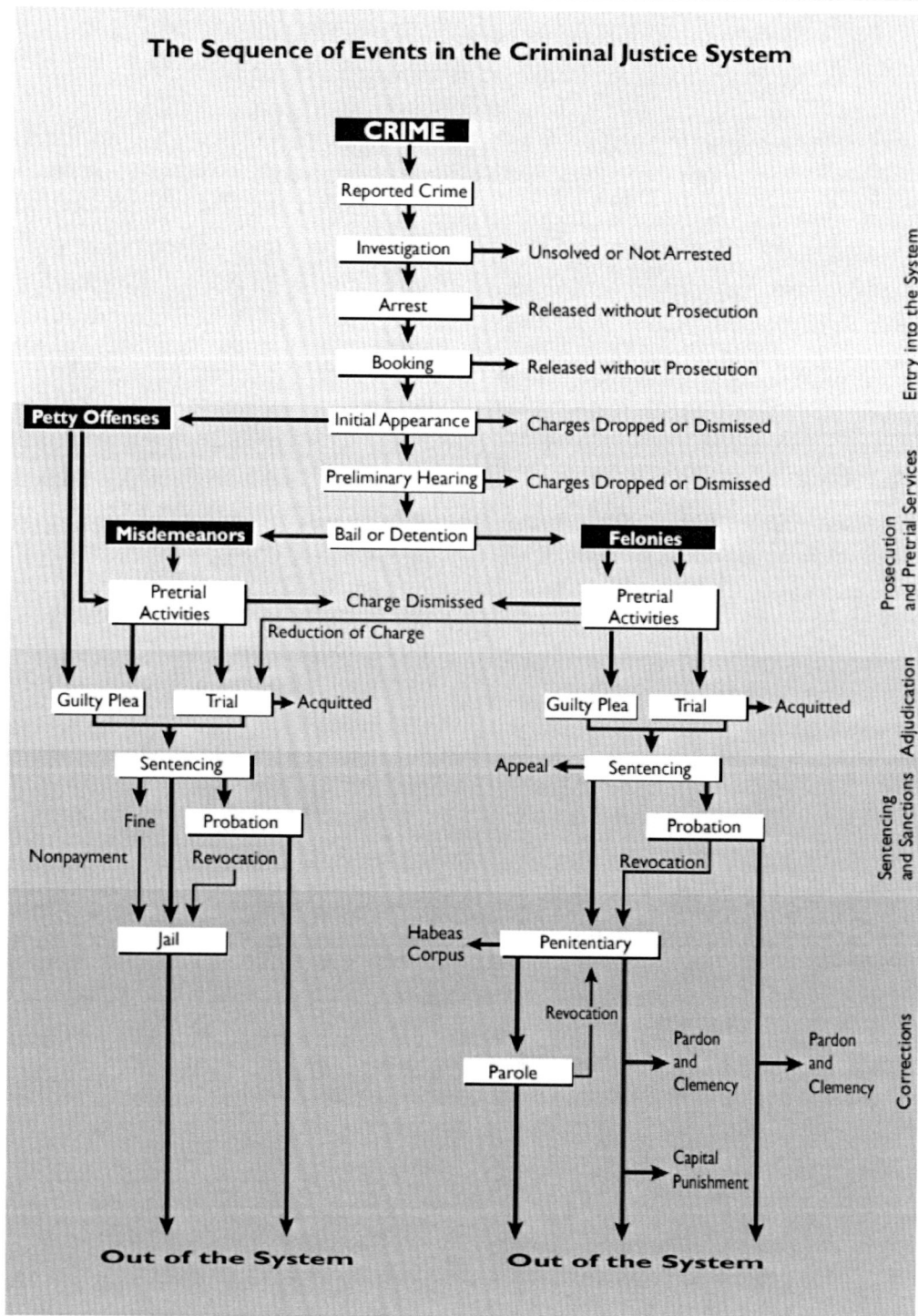

[9] A.B.A. Division for Pub. Educ., Steps in a Trial, https://www.americanbar.org/groups/public_education/resources/law_related_education_network/how_courts_work/casediagram.html (last visited Apr. 16, 2018).

Victims and other witnesses will be asked to give statements multiple times as the case works its way through the criminal justice system. The initial statement is given to the police. If the defendant is entitled to, and does not waive, a preliminary hearing, the victim may be subpoenaed to testify at this probable cause hearing shortly after charges are filed. If there is not a preliminary hearing, the defense attorney may be entitled to pre-trial interviews or depositions with all potential witnesses. Finally, assuming the defendant does not enter a plea agreement, there will be a trial. It is imperative that the prosecutor's office always has current contact information for the victim, so they may advise and prepare them for their role throughout this process.

Advocacy Tip: Criminal trials can take a year or more to resolve. One of the goals of the defense lawyer is to mine these multiple statements for inconsistencies so they can attack the credibility of the witness at trial. Remind your client that it is better to admit a lapse in memory than to guess. A victim can always ask to review a written statement, police report, or recording of a prior statement to refresh their recollection.

C. Barriers to Successful Prosecution

It is common in domestic violence criminal cases for victims to be reluctant or unwilling to participate in prosecution. The victim may refuse to provide a statement to police, refuse to talk with prosecutors, or recant. Research shows that abuse continues after arrest as defendants continue "to use abusive strategies … along with other sophisticated emotional manipulation (e.g. sympathy appeals) to erode victim's agency and achieve their goal of getting out of [the charge, jail]."[10]

Prosecutors and advocates have known for years that witness tampering and intimidation are significant problems in domestic violence cases, and that victims may recant or refuse to participate in prosecution due, in part, to perpetrators' manipulation and threats. As recognized by the U.S. Supreme Court, "[t]his particular type of crime is notoriously susceptible to intimidation or coercion of the victim to ensure she does not testify at trial."[11]

---

[10] Amy E. Bonomi et al., *"Meet Me at the Hill Where We Used to Park": Interpersonal Processes Associated with Victim Recantation,* 73 Social Sci. & Med. 1054 (2011).

[11] Davis v. Washington, 547 U.S. 813 (2006).

When Victims Recant or Minimize Domestic Violence

The prevalence and impact of domestic violence, stalking, and sexual assault on victims and their children is significant.[12] Some victims stay with their abusers because the alternatives are bleaker and more precarious than the current conditions of their relationships.[13] Victims may recant or minimize the abuse to avoid further violence, often denying that it happened, blaming themselves by insisting they did something to provoke the abuser, or inventing various accidents that are responsible for injuries (e.g. "I walked into a doorknob" or "the dog did it."). There are a variety of valid reasons why a victim may recant or minimize domestic violence because recanting is a survival skill victims utilize to protect themselves and their families.

To address these barriers to prosecution, many District Attorney's Offices have adopted "no-drop" or "evidence-based prosecution" policies, wherein they will take domestic violence cases to trial regardless of victim cooperation.[14] The successful prosecution of such cases requires a thorough investigation and sufficient evidence to prove the case beyond a reasonable doubt.

As a civil attorney, you may have access to discovery or evidence that would increase the chances of a guilty verdict in the criminal case. If your client is unable or unwilling to testify at trial, discuss the benefits of conviction with them, and discuss the option of assisting the prosecution in other ways besides testifying, such as disclosing incriminating evidence. Remember that the prosecutor has a duty to disclose all evidence they receive to the defense attorney. Do not share anything with the prosecutor you are not ready to share with the defense.

Advocacy Tip: Injuries appear worse over time, particularly bruising. Suggest that your clients take daily photos throughout their healing process, and provide these to the prosecution. Make sure the camera date and time settings are correct, and that your client includes at least one full body shot each day they take pictures,

---

[12] According to a 2010 survey on domestic violence, 24 people per minute are victims of rape, physical violence, or stalking by an intimate partner in the United States. Over the course of a year, that equals more than 12 million women and men. Those numbers only tell part of the story—more than one million women are raped in a year, and more than six million women and men are victims of stalking in a year. These findings emphasize that sexual violence, stalking, and intimate partner violence are widespread public health problems in the United States. Press Release, Ctrs. for Disease Control & Prevention, Sexual Violence, Stalking, and Intimate Partner Violence Widespread in the US (Dec. 14, 2011), *available at* https://www.cdc.gov/media/releases/2011/p1214_sexual_violence.html.

[13] Linell A. Letendre, *Beating Again and Again and Again: Why Washington Needs a New Rule of Evidence Admitting Prior Acts of Domestic Violence*, 75 Wash. L. Rev. 973, 979–80 (2000).

[14] Heather J. Davies, Robert C. Davis & Barbara E. Smith, *Effects of No-Drop Prosecution of Domestic Violence Upon Conviction Rates*, 3(2) Just. Res. & Pol'y 1 (Fall 2001).

so that there are no barriers to admissibility. Photographs should be taken in natural light with no flash, as flash reduces the visibility of bruising.

III. Concurrent Civil and Criminal Proceedings

A. Civil Orders of Protection vs. Criminal Protection Orders

A standard condition of pre-trial release is that the defendant have no contact with any victims or possible witnesses in the state's case. These orders are referred to as no contact orders, restraining orders, or criminal protection orders, and are issued upon a defendant's release from custody pending trial.

Such orders are distinct from the domestic violence order of protection (DVOP) that is issued by a civil court. DVOPs are issued on a temporary basis following the filing of a petition, and on a long-term or permanent basis only after the abuser has been served and had the opportunity to contest the order at a hearing. Each violation of a DVOP can lead to a new criminal charge.

A criminal "no contact" order is not an order of protection as the civil attorney understands it. No contact orders are not entered into the National Crime Information Center (NCIC), which means they are not in a centralized database, and cannot be enforced by police. Rather, they are a *pro forma* order issued by judges at the request of the state. These orders are routinely issued without a substantive hearing as courts are disinclined to allow contact between a defendant and victim due to the high risk of witness intimidation.[15] No contact orders are issued commonly during pending criminal litigation, even when a victim is requesting contact.[16] Violations are treated akin to contempt of court. Upon learning of a violation, even if initiated by the victim, the prosecutor must file a motion with the court requesting that the defendant's bond be revoked pending trial. Depending on local practices and caseloads, it can take weeks or even months for a hearing to be held. The no contact order dissolves immediately upon resolution of a criminal case, regardless of whether that resolution comes through a dismissal, plea, or verdict.

Advocacy Tip: The criminal justice system does not retain indefinite jurisdiction over abusers. Eventually they will leave the system, removing any possible sanctions for contacting their victim. DVOPs provide long-term protection that is easily enforceable across multiple jurisdictions. Do not rely on criminal no-contact orders to protect your clients.

---

[15] For additional information on witness intimidation, see AEQUITAS: THE PROSECUTORS' RESOURCE ON VIOLENCE AGAINST WOMEN, WITNESS INTIMIDATION: MEETING THE CHALLENGE (2013), *available at* http://www.aequitasresource.org/Witness-Intimidation-Meeting-the-Challenge.pdf.

[16] Jeannie Suk, *Criminal Law Comes Home,* 116 YALE L.J. 2, 8 (2006).

B. Other Orders Addressing Contact

In addition to DVOPs and pre-trial no contact orders, contact between a victim and abuser may be restricted by various other enforceable orders.

1. Probation

Victims often believe they have a "criminal protection order" because their abuser pled guilty to a past crime of domestic violence. These orders are most likely codified as a no contact provision in the defendant's probation. Similar to the pre-trial no-contact orders, these orders, though part of a criminal case, are not entered into NCIC or any other law enforcement databases. Violations must be reported to probation officers, not law enforcement. The probation officer can then take steps to violate the abuser's probation, but may choose to do so at any time before probation expires.

2. Criminal Trespass Orders

Many victims request that law enforcement "trespass" an abuser who will not stop coming over to their home. These criminal trespass orders ("CTO") are not filed with the courts or registered in NCIC. They are, however, maintained by local law enforcement, who notify the targeted individual that if they come back to the protected address, they will be arrested and charged with trespassing. A CTO works as a no trespassing sign directed only at one person.

Advocacy Tip: Stalkers often attempt to contact their victims at work, at a friend's home, or at family gatherings. CTOs prevent an abuser from setting foot on private property, even when the victim is not present. This can alleviate some of the burden on friends, family members, and coworkers when a victim is dealing with a stalker, or trying to leave an abusive relationship. CTOs can be issued for any privately-owned property. If you need to protect a residence, the owner or tenant must request the order. When an abuser harasses or stalks a victim at a privately-owned company to the point the business would prefer the abuser be banned, management or another authorized employee must request the CTO.

3. Family Court

Family court judges routinely issue orders that address appropriate contact between former spouses or co-parents regarding joint assets and shared children. Most orders require a certain degree of open communication. However, if the judge is aware of a history of substance abuse or domestic violence, there may be varying levels of restrictions regarding the means and manner through which any contact can be made. For example, a custody order may prohibit an abuser from communicating with their victim in any form other than email or an online tool such as "Our Family Wizard," so that the court can, if necessary, review the manner and tone of all contact.

Similarly, if child protective services or juvenile probation officers are involved with a family, there may be orders coming out of juvenile court regarding contact between parents for the sake of the children, such as mandatory attendance at joint counseling sessions or therapeutic team meetings.

4. Military Restraining Orders

If either the victim or abuser is in the military, they may be subject to a military restraining order, which is a written order from their commanding officer to refrain from contacting the other party. Though such orders are not enforceable in civilian courts, violations can have serious consequences for an individual's military career.

C. Contradiction between Civil and Criminal Court Orders

Contradicting orders regarding contact are inevitable when the same family appears in front of multiple judges. It is imperative that the civil attorney discuss and strategize the interplay between existing or imminent criminal court orders during a civil case, particularly when children are involved. For example, if the family court judge orders shared legal custody, thus requiring that joint decisions be made regarding welfare and wellbeing of the children, it could potentially conflict with a criminal order that prohibits any contact between parties.

Your clients will come to you for advice as to how to untangle conflicting orders regarding contact. They will want to know which order to adhere to, and the consequences for failure to do so. The interplay in enforcement between conflicting orders is often very jurisdiction-specific, so make sure you are aware of your local practices before advising your clients on following contradiction provisions.

Advocacy Tip: A criminal no-contact order can be an effective way of temporarily ensuring the safety of the children pending a motion to modify custody. You do not need to rush the custody hearing if the criminal order is in place providing your client a justifiable means of cancelling visits pending a full hearing on the best interests of the children or resolution of the criminal case.

D. Issues of Double Jeopardy

When a DVOP is violated, the victim has two options for enforcement. They may report the violation to law enforcement, resulting in a new criminal charge against the defendant, or ask the judge to hold the abuser in contempt for violating the court's order by filing a motion and request for a hearing in the civil case.

If the violation is for non-criminal conduct that was prohibited by the DVOP, such as text messaging or phone calls, the victim generally cannot ask the state to press charges while simultaneously requesting sanctions from the presiding judge. This is due to the prohibition against double jeopardy; a defendant cannot be punished twice for the same conduct. Thus, the victim must choose to allow the state to prosecute, or proceed on their own in the civil case.

Double jeopardy does not apply if the underlying violation of the DVOP is an act that is criminal on its own, such as battery. In that situation, criminal charges can be filed for the battery while the victim requests civil sanctions for the violation of the court's order against contact. The state, however, would be prohibited from pursuing charges for violation of the DVOP in conjunction with the battery charge. The key is to ensure that the elements of the crimes charged are distinct from the elements of the violation addressed by the civil court.

Advocacy Tip: When deciding whether to report to police or file for a civil violation, consider what the ultimate goal is. If you want something to prompt an action, such as payment of restitution or return of property, a civil violation is the more appropriate remedy. If you want the abuser to stop calling, texting, or following the victim, then criminal sanctions are more appropriate, and the violations need to be reported to law enforcement.

E. Undocumented Victims

Undocumented victims often endure violence without seeking assistance for fear that their undocumented status will be a barrier to obtaining help. If charges are pending, undocumented victims dodge law enforcement's attempts to interview them in an effort to protect themselves from deportation.

Keep in mind that domestic violence coupled with the fear of law enforcement and the court system is a lethal combination that requires a culturally sensitive approach. Practitioners should also be aware that victims may come from "mixed status families," where there are some family members, most often minor children, who are documented. This increases a victim's fear of law enforcement and the courts, as there is a legitimate concern that the victim-parent will not only be deported, but also separated from the children they are trying to protect.[17]

Advocacy Tip: At the outset, clarify with the client that your consultation and help is confidential. Make sure they are aware that cooperation with the police or the prosecution may make them eligible for a U visa.[18] Even if the police and the prosecutor decide not to pursue charges, making the report may qualify the client to apply for a U visa. In essence, reporting the domestic violence they have

---

[17] *Frequently Asked Questions "What is a mixed-status family?",* Nat'l Immigr. L. Ctr., https://www.nilc.org/issues/health-care/aca_mixedstatusfams/ (last updated Dec. 2014).

[18] For more information on the U visa and other humanitarian benefits available to victims of domestic violence, see *Immigration Law and Domestic Violence* in Section Two of this manual.

endured can protect them from future deportation, regardless of the ultimate outcome of the criminal case.[19]

F. Firearms[20]

Federal law prohibits certain abusers subject to DVOPs from possessing firearms.[21] Unfortunately, federal authorities do not typically enforce these laws, which cannot be enforced by state officials. Certain states do prohibit persons subject to DVOPs from possessing firearms, but only a handful of those states mandate the surrender of firearms in the abuser's possession.[22]

Even if your state does not statutorily prohibit the possession of firearms during the term of a DVOP, the court can still include a provision in the DVOP itself that prevents an individual abuser from owning or possessing firearms. The victim needs to express a basis for the request, such as a history of gun violence, death threats, or negligent use of firearms when intoxicated. A gun-related concern is key when requesting a firearm restriction in order to avoid second amendment challenges to the DVOP itself. The Court of Appeals in Ohio struck down such a challenge when there was a "sufficient nexus between the restriction on access to firearms and the conduct to be prevented."[23]

Advocacy Tip: If an abuser fails to surrender their guns as required by a DVOP, do not file an affidavit of violation or ask for a status hearing. Report him to law enforcement immediately so the state can file charges for violation of a DVOP (and any other gun-possession statute that may apply). When a gun is subject to a criminal charge, law enforcement takes it immediately into evidence, ensuring the abuser no longer has access to that particular weapon.

IV. Conclusion

As an attorney, you are the expert from the legal system that your clients rely on to understand and navigate the complex web that they must work within. They will seek your guidance in every case they are involved in, even when it is not

---

[19] *See Victims of Criminal Activity: U Nonimmigrant Status,* U.S. CITIZENSHIP & IMMIGR. SERVS., https://www.uscis.gov/humanitarian/victims-human-trafficking-other-crimes/victims-criminal-activity-u-nonimmigrant-status/victims-criminal-activity-u-nonimmigrant-status (last updated Aug. 25, 2017).

[20] For more information regarding domestic violence and firearms, see *Domestic Violence and Firearms: A Lethal Connection* in Section One of this manual.

[21] *Protection Orders and Federal Firearms Prohibitions,* BUREAU OF ALCOHOL, TOBACCO, FIREARMS & EXPLOSIVES, *available at* http://www.pcadv.org/Resources/atf-i-3310-2.pdf (last updated Sept. 2011).

[22] Following the Sandy Hook shooting, the Office of Legislative Research in Connecticut began researching the loopholes throughout the U.S. that enabled abusers to legally obtain guns. *See* VERONICA ROSE, FIREARM POSSESSION AND DOMESTIC VIOLENCE RESTRAINING OR PROTECTIVE ORDERS AND CONVICTIONS, OFF. OF LEGIS. RES. REP. NO. 2014-R-0181 (July 31, 2014), *available at* https://www.cga.ct.gov/2014/rpt/pdf/2014-R-0181.pdf.

[23] Cee v. Stone, 2017-Ohio-8687.

your area of expertise. Your support on these matters will ensure your client is able to participate in criminal justice system without further trauma, harassment, or re-victimization.

APPENDIX

Resources:

- SHARON G. SMITH ET AL., NAT'L CTR. FOR INJURY PREVENTION & CTRS. FOR DISEASE CONTROL & PREVENTION, THE NATIONAL INTIMATE PARTNER AND SEXUAL VIOLENCE SURVEY (NISVS): 2010-2012 STATE REPORT (2017), *available at* https://www.cdc.gov/violenceprevention/pdf/NISVS-StateReportBook.pdf.

- MIKEL L. WALTERS, JIERU CHEN & MATTHEW J. BREIDING, NAT'L CTR. FOR INJURY PREVENTION & CTRS. FOR DISEASE CONTROL & PREVENTION, THE NATIONAL INTIMATE PARTNER AND SEXUAL VIOLENCE SURVEY (NISVS): 2010 FINDINGS ON VICTIMIZATION BY SEXUAL ORIENTATION (2013), *available at* https://www.cdc.gov/violenceprevention/pdf/nisvs_sofindings.pdf.

- NAT'L COALITION OF ANTI-VIOLENCE PROGRAMS, N.Y.C. GAY & LESBIAN ANTI-VIOLENCE PROJECT, LESBIAN, GAY, BISEXUAL, TRANSGENDER, QUEER, AND HIV-AFFECTED INTIMATE PARTNER VIOLENCE IN 2015 (2016), *available at* https://avp.org/wp-content/uploads/2017/04/2015_ncavp_lgbtqipvreport.pdf.

- JANINE M. ZWEIG ET AL., URB. INST., TECHNOLOGY, TEEN DATING VIOLENCE AND ABUSE, AND BULLYING (2013), *available at* https://www.ncjrs.gov/pdffiles1/nij/grants/243296.pdf.

- U.S. DEP'T OF JUST., OFF. OF CMTY. ORIENTED POLICING SERVS., IDENTIFYING AND PREVENTING GENDER BIAS IN LAW ENFORCEMENT RESPONSE TO SEXUAL ASSAULT AND DOMESTIC VIOLENCE (2016), *available at* https://ric-zai-inc.com/Publications/cops-w0796-pub.pdf.

- CHRISTOPHER WILSON ET AL., UNDERSTANDING THE NEUROBIOLOGY OF TRAUMA AND IMPLICATIONS FOR INTERVIEWING VICTIMS (Nov. 2016), *available at* http://www.evawintl.org/Library/DocumentLibraryHandler.ashx?id=842.

- SUBSTANCE ABUSE & MENTAL HEALTH SERVS. ADMINISTRATION (SAMHSA) TRAUMA & JUST. STRATEGIC INITIATIVE, SAMHSA'S CONCEPT OF TRAUMA AND GUIDANCE FOR A TRAUMA-INFORMED APPROACH (July 2014), *available at* https://store.samhsa.gov/product/SAMHSA-s-Concept-of-Trauma-and-Guidance-for-a-Trauma-Informed-Approach/SMA14-4884.

- Viktoria Kristiansson & Charlene Whitman-Barr, *Integrating a Trauma-Informed Response in Violence Against Women and Human Trafficking Prosecutions*, 13 STRATEGIES: THE PROSECUTORS' NEWSLETTER ON VIOLENCE AGAINST WOMEN (Aequitas), Feb. 2015, *available at* http://www.aequitasresource.org/Integrating-A-Trauma-Informed-Response-In-VAW-and-HT-Strategies.pdf.

- T.K. LOGAN & ROB VALENTE, WHO WILL HELP ME? DOMESTIC VIOLENCE SURVIVORS SPEAK OUT ABOUT LAW ENFORCEMENT RESPONSES (Nat'l Domestic Violence

Hotline, 2015), *available at* http://www.thehotline.org/wp-content/uploads/sites/3/2015/09/NDVH-2015-Law-Enforcement-Survey-Report.pdf.

- NAT'L CRIME VICTIM L. INST., *Victims' Rights Compel Action to Counteract Judges' and Juries' Common Misperceptions About Domestic Violence Victims' Behaviors*, VIOLENCE AGAINST WOMEN BULL., Sept. 2014, *available at* https://law.lclark.edu/live/files/18123-bulletincountering-common-misperceptions-of-dv.

Law Review Articles:

- Hadar Aviram & Annick M. Persinger, *Perceiving and Reporting Domestic Violence Incidents in Unconventional Settings: A Vignette Survey Study*, 23 HASTINGS WOMEN'S L.J. 159 (2012).

- Leigh Goodmark, *Transgender People, Intimate Partner Abuse, and the Legal System*, 48 HARV. C.R.-C.L. L. REV. 51 (2003).

- Kae Greenberg, *Still Hidden in the Closet: Trans Women and Domestic Violence*, 27 BERKELEY J. GENDER L. & JUST. 198 (2012).

- Jason Palmer, *Eleventh Annual Review of Gender and Sexuality Law: Criminal Law Chapter: Domestic Violence*, 11 GEO. J. GENDER & L. 97 (2010).

- Leonard Pertnoy, *Same Violence, Same Sex, Different Standard: An Examination of Same-Sex Domestic Violence and the Use of Expert Testimony on Battered Woman's Syndrome in Same-Sex Domestic Violence Cases,* 24 ST. THOMAS L. REV. 544 (2012).

Tools:

- **Power and Control Wheel**
  - https://www.theduluthmodel.org/wheels/

- **Immigrant Power and Control Wheel**
  - http://endingviolence.org/files/uploads/ImmigrantWomenPCwheel.pdf

- **LGBTQ Power and Control Wheel**
  - http://tcfv.org/pdf/Updated_wheels/LGBT.pdf

- **Danger Assessment**
  - https://www.dangerassessment.org

Note: The danger assessment has only been validated for women in heterosexual relationships. Studies are underway to adapt the tool for male victims and victims in same-sex relationships.

- **Domestic Violence Arrest Policies**
  - https://www.americanbar.org/content/dam/aba/administrative/domestic_violence1/Resources/statutorysummarycharts/2014%20Domestic%20Violence%20Arrest%20Policy%20Chart.authcheckdam.pdf

Chapter Twenty-seven:
Immigration Consequences of Domestic Violence

I. Introduction

Domestic violence victims face numerous negative consequences as a result of being arrested, charged, and/or convicted of a crime. For noncitizen victims, the consequences of contact with the criminal law system and a conviction can be even more devastating, because it can result in serious immigration consequences including deportation. Early and effective intervention is needed to prevent or mitigate these possible negative consequences.

This chapter will assist legal advocates expand their capacity and skills to work with immigrant victims of domestic violence who are facing criminal charges or already have a criminal record. The information in these materials is not intended to make advocates experts in the complex and ever-changing areas of immigration law, policy, and procedure. Rather, the information contained here is designed to provide legal advocates with a working understanding of some of the key concepts and issues they will encounter when working with immigrant domestic violence victims, and to offer some basic advocacy strategies and tools.

II. Understanding the Federal Immigration Enforcement Framework

Prioritizing the enforcement of immigration laws against those who have been involved in the criminal justice system has increasingly been a federal priority over the last decade. In 2017, the focus was broadened even further to allow for targeting of all undocumented immigrants, including those who have never had contact with the criminal justice system, and are victims.

While Congress makes the immigration laws, the Executive Branch has wide latitude in setting immigration policy. Specifically, the Executive Branch has the leeway to determine the extent to which it will implement the laws, and also sets other immigration policy, particularly where Congress has not spoken. One such area is immigration enforcement, where the federal government sets priorities for who it will prioritize for deportation. Every Administration generally issues memoranda setting forth their immigration enforcement priorities and tactics.

Immigration law is federal law and therefore, the same laws apply to all the states. However, the implementation of certain federal immigration laws and policies, and in particular immigration enforcement, may differ from state to state based on various factors, including state immigration-related laws and local law enforcement policies pertaining to immigration enforcement. For example, in California, due to various laws, local law enforcement has limited cooperation with the federal government. On the other hand, in Texas, because of SB 4, a state law that went into partial effect on September 2, 2017, local law enforcement is required to cooperate with immigration authorities. Also affecting the implementation of immigration laws in certain regions are federal Circuit Court decisions which can interpret immigration laws differently, including the immigration consequences of state criminal convictions.

A. Who is a Target for Immigration Enforcement?

Beginning January 2017, the White House issued multiple immigration-related executive orders that revamped and broadly expanded the ways in which the federal government targeted undocumented immigrants for deportation.[1] Under an Executive Order and Department of Homeland Security ("DHS") Memorandum focused on immigration enforcement in the interior of the United States ("DHS Memo on Interior Enforcement"), DHS was directed to expand its priorities for immigration enforcement.[2] While DHS previously focused its resources on deporting people with certain criminal convictions, now DHS could deport anyone it considered to have violated immigration laws, including anyone that they labeled as a "removable alien."[3] The Administration's priorities included, but are not limited to, people with *any* criminal conviction(s), as well as those charged

---

[1] Laura Jarrett, *Trump Signs Three New Executive Orders on Crime Reduction,* CNN (Feb. 10, 2017), http://www.cnn.com/2017/02/09/politics/trump-executive-orders-crime-reduction/index.html.

[2] Memorandum from John Kelly, U.S. Sec'y of Homeland Security on Enforcement of the Immigration Laws to Serve the National Interest, to Kevin McAleenan, Acting Comm'r, U.S. Customs & Border Protection et al. (Feb. 20, 2017), *available at* https://www.dhs.gov/sites/default/files/publications/17_0220_S1_Enforcement-of-the-Immigration-Laws-to-Serve-the-National-Interest.pdf [hereinafter DHS Memo on Interior Enforcement].

[3] Marcelo Rochabrun, *An ICE Memo Tells Officers to Go After All Undocumented Immigrants Encountered While on Duty,* BUSINESS INSIDER (July 7, 2017, 12:27 PM), http://www.businessinsider.com/memo-tells-ice-to-go-after-all-undocumented-immigrants-immigration-deportation-news-2017-7.

with a criminal offense(s), or who have committed an act(s) that could potentially be charged as a criminal offense.[4]

The DHS Memo on Interior Enforcement also provided that "the Department will no longer exempt classes or categories of removable aliens from potential enforcement."[5] This meant that all undocumented people living in the United States, including victims of crimes, those with U.S. citizen children, and those without any prior criminal history, were at risk of deportation.

B. Immigration Enforcement Tactics

Tactics for enforcing immigration laws include relying on increased cooperation with state and local law enforcement and conducting home and workplace raids. As described in the prior section, the extent of enforcement may depend upon the jurisdiction because some local law enforcement agencies (police and sheriff departments) have contracted or expanded their cooperation with federal immigration enforcement efforts. In many places, there is a significant presence of Immigration & Customs Enforcement ("ICE") (immigration authorities charged with interior enforcement) agents, and in border states, a significant presence of Customs and Border Patrol ("CBP") (immigration authorities charged with enforcement at the border and ports of entry) agents in state and local jails.[6]

In places where there is cooperation with immigration authorities, individuals who are arrested can expect they will likely have contact with ICE or CBP agents either at the time of or soon after initial contact with local law enforcement or after being arrested and booked into jail.[7] Advocates should be aware that there are some limits to this enforcement. Absent some authority conferred by federal authorities, local and state law enforcement officers do not have legal authority under the Constitution to stop or arrest someone solely based on their immigration status.[8] Also, per the U.S. Supreme Court's decision in *Arizona v. U.S.*, local law enforcement cannot legally prolong someone's detention to investigate their immigration status or wait for ICE or CBP to show up to arrest the person.[9]

---

[4] DHS Memo on Interior Enforcement, *supra* note 2, at 2.

[5] *Id.*

[6] To check your local jail cooperation with ICE, see *National Map of Local Entanglement with ICE*, IMMIGRANT LEGAL RESOURCE CTR. (Jan. 25, 2018), https://www.ilrc.org/local-enforcement-map.

[7] To learn more about the immigration enforcement programs that are used in tandem with local law enforcement authorities, see *Enforcement*, IMMIGRANT LEGAL RESOURCE CTR., www.ilrc.org/enforcement (last visited Apr. 18, 2018).

[8] Arizona v. U.S., 567 U.S. 387, 388 (2012).

[9] *Id.*

III. How Convictions Impact Immigrants Involved in Domestic Violence

Involvement in the criminal justice system not only flags and prioritizes an individual for immigration enforcement action, but the outcome of a criminal case may cause serious immigration consequences including detention (sometimes mandatory), denial of immigration benefits such as a work or student visa or application for lawful permanent residence (also called a green card), and deportation.

Noncitizens who are residing in the U.S. with lawful immigration status may become deportable when they obtain certain criminal convictions. In fact, criminal convictions are a primary way noncitizens with lawful status (green card holders, refugees/asylees, visa holders) lose their status and get deported. Both domestic violence victims and abusers with legal status can be detained and deported if they have certain convictions, including domestic violence. A noncitizen who has been lawfully admitted is subject to the *grounds of deportability* under federal immigration law.[10]

Individuals who are present in the U.S. without lawful immigration status may be removable/deportable on that basis alone.[11] However, these individuals, especially victims of domestic violence and other serious crimes, may remain eligible for some relief against removal, unless they are convicted of certain crimes, including some minor misdemeanors. For example, a domestic violence victim who was married to a U.S. citizen abuser would be eligible to "self-petition" for their green card (also called lawful permanent residence). However, if they are convicted for even a minor misdemeanor offense, for example, possession of a small amount of illegal drugs or for shoplifting, it can close the door to them obtaining lawful status and result in their deportation from the U.S. An undocumented abuser with a domestic violence conviction will likely face greater obstacles in obtaining legal status than a victim and may have fewer avenues to obtaining legal status. In addition to undocumented immigrants, immigrants who have a work or student visa or refugee/asylee status still need to apply for lawful permanent resident (LPR) status and therefore, may be prevented from doing so based on a criminal conviction, including domestic violence. A noncitizen who has

---

[10] 8 U.S.C. § 1227(a)(2). A noncitizen who has been admitted to the United States but is convicted of an offense that makes her or him deportable can lose lawful status and be "removed" (deported), unless she or he can apply for some relief from removal.

[11] In immigration cases begun before April 1, 1997, persons were placed in deportation or exclusion proceedings. Beginning on April 1, 1997, persons were placed instead in removal proceedings. The words removal and deportable are used interchangeably throughout this article and are meant to convey the same meaning.

not been lawfully admitted to the U.S. or is applying for an immigration benefit (e.g., LPR status) is subject to the *grounds of inadmissibility*.[12]

If a noncitizen with legal status, or a noncitizen who is undocumented, is arrested by immigration authorities and placed into removal proceedings before an Immigration Judge, there are two key legal questions that must be answered. The first question is whether the noncitizen is removable as charged by DHS. If not, removal proceedings must be terminated. If the person is removable, the second question becomes whether the removable noncitizen is nevertheless eligible for relief (or a defense) against removal. Within this second inquiry, the Court must determine both statutory eligibility for the relief sought, and whether the case warrants a grant of such relief. Therefore, a finding of removability means that a person *can* be removed, but does not necessarily mean that a person *will* be removed.

In determining removability, a court will need to analyze the immigration consequences of a criminal conviction. This analysis is complex as the law is constantly evolving in this area as the courts frequently make significant changes in the law and/or new interpretations of the law.[13] In addition, each state has its own criminal laws; therefore, an individual analysis of how federal law applies to each state criminal law must be conducted. In many instances, there is no case precedent on the immigration consequences of specific state crimes. Moreover, specific case facts must be considered in the immigration consequences analysis, which includes, for example, the person's individual immigration status, immigration history, and prior criminal history. Since all these factors will vary heavily from case to case, it is important to note that blanket application of general immigration law concepts to any given case often leads to inaccurate analysis.

Criminal convictions lead to specific grounds of removability, which can fall under the grounds of deportability and/or inadmissibility. Domestic violence convictions can fall within any of the following grounds of removability:

- "Domestic Violence" deportation ground (*see* 8 U.S.C. § 1227(a)(2)(E)(i));

- "A crime of child abuse, neglect or abandonment" deportation ground (*see* 8 U.S.C. § 1227(a)(2)(E)(i));

---

[12] 8 U.S.C. § 1182(a)(2). A noncitizen who is inadmissible due to crimes may be unable to get any *new* status, admission to the U.S., waiver of a crime, or other new benefit you apply for from the government. However, being inadmissible will not take away the lawful status that one already has. The only exception is if the person with lawful status *leaves* the U.S. after becoming inadmissible for crimes. In that case, the person can be denied admission back into the U.S. for being inadmissible.

[13] Criminal removal grounds and their application to state specific crimes are defined (and redefined) by constantly changing case law coming out of the Board of Immigration Appeals (which provides administrative review of decisions by Immigration Judges and falls under the Department of Justice's Executive Office for Immigration Review), as well as the U.S. Circuit Court of Appeals.

- "Stalking" deportation ground (*see* 8 U.S.C. § 1227(a)(2)(E)(i));

- "If found in civil or criminal court to have violated certain sections of a domestic violence protective order" deportation ground (*see* 8 U.S.C. § 1227(a)(2)(E)(ii));

- "Aggravated Felony" deportation ground (*see* 8 U.S.C. § 1101(a)(43)(F));[14] and

- "Crime Involving Moral Turpitude" deportation and inadmissibility grounds (*see* 8 U.S.C. § 1182(a)(2)(A)(i)(I) and 8 U.S.C. § 1227(a)(2)(A)(i)).

There are additional removability grounds for other offenses that may relate to domestic violence, such as theft or drug use and possession. These have separate and additional consequences under immigration law.

To illustrate the complexity of conducting an immigration consequences analysis, consider a "crime of domestic violence." The state crime label does not determine whether the crime is one of domestic violence under immigration law, nor does the type of sentence imposed (e.g., domestic violence counseling sentence). Rather, federal law defines a deportable "crime of domestic violence" as 1) a conviction of a crime of violence, defined at 18 U.S.C. § 16, 2) that is committed against a person with whom the defendant has or had a certain domestic relationship, and 3) occurred after September 30, 1996. When analyzing a specific state domestic violence conviction, one will have to determine all of the following elements: 1) whether the individual is even subject to the domestic violence ground of deportability and if not, whether the conviction nonetheless triggers other immigration consequences, 2) whether the elements of the state conviction meets the definition of a crime of violence at 18 U.S.C. § 16, and 3) whether the crime was committed against a person who had a certain relationship to the abuser as defined under federal immigration law (including those protected under state laws).[15] In conducting this analysis, practitioners employ the "categorical analysis," a tool used by the courts to

---

[14] Aggravated felonies are defined at 8 U.S.C. § 1101(a)(43), which lists dozens of common law terms and references to federal statutes. They can include non-violent misdemeanors. They are the most damaging type of conviction for a noncitizen, as they can lead to mandatory deportation and detention, as well as other severe consequences.

[15] 8 U.S.C. § 1227(a)(2)(E)(i) provides that "any crime of violence [as defined in 18 U.S.C. § 16] against a person committed by a current or former spouse of the person, by an individual with whom the person shares a child in common, by an individual who is cohabiting with or has cohabited with the person as a spouse, by an individual similarly situated to a spouse of the person under the domestic violence or family violence laws of the jurisdiction where the offense occurs, or by any other individual against a person who is protected from the individual's acts under the domestic or family violence laws of the United States or any State, Indian Tribal government, or unit of local government."

compare and contrast the elements of the federal immigration definition to a state conviction.[16]

The analysis of whether a particular conviction meets the definition of removability ground is just one piece of the puzzle when assessing immigration consequences of a criminal conviction. One may also have to apply specific facts from the person's immigration history to the analysis. For example, in considering whether a particular conviction triggers deportation as a Crime Involving Moral Turpitude (CIMT), a green card holder who is convicted of committing a first CIMT, for which a sentence of one year *may* be imposed, six years after receiving the green card is not removable; however, a green card holder who is convicted of the same offense within five years of receiving the green card is not only removable but ineligible for discretionary relief, which for many people means automatic deportation.

Because a single conviction can fit within multiple removal grounds, prompting several and possibly different immigration consequences, analysis must be conducted under each applicable removal ground. Sometimes a person may not have a domestic violence conviction under immigration law, but may still be removable from the U.S. because the conviction causes another removal ground.

Once an individual is determined to be removable, the next step is analyzing whether the person is eligible for relief from removal. Various criminal convictions can make a person ineligible for immigration relief. Some of these forms of relief and their criminal bars to eligibility are discussed in the next section.

IV. Legal Remedies and Other Relief Available to Domestic Violence Victims with Criminal Convictions

If an individual is removable based on a criminal conviction, there are various types of discretionary relief for qualifying undocumented persons and persons with legal status to defend against deportation. Also, even if someone is not in deportation proceedings, there are affirmative ways to obtain lawful status and preempt deportation, including for immigrant crime victims. Some forms of relief are available only when a person is in deportation proceedings, and other forms of relief are available both defensively and affirmatively. Each avenue of relief has its own legal requirements including different bars based on criminal convictions/acts.

---

[16] Moncrieffe v. Holder, 569 U.S.184, 186 (2013). To read more about the categorical analysis, see *How to use the Categorical Approach Now*, Immigrant Legal Resource Ctr. (Apr. 10, 2017), https://www.ilrc.org/how-use-categorical-approach-now.

Some common forms of relief against deportation and for obtaining legal status, particularly for domestic violence victims, include the following:[17]

A. Violence Against Women Act ("VAWA") Cancellation of Removal

This form of relief is only available in removal proceedings and allows an immigration judge to cancel removal and grant lawful permanent residence to certain undocumented victims of domestic violence.[18] There are many criminal bars to this relief. The person must be of "good moral character" for three years.[19] This term is defined in the negative, and includes many criminal acts and criminal convictions such as crimes involving moral turpitude and controlled substance offenses. The person must also not be inadmissible under grounds relating to crimes or terrorism/national security,[20] and must not be deportable under grounds relating to crimes and other grounds.[21] However, a client who receives a waiver of the domestic violence deportation ground is not barred.[22] A noncitizen convicted of an aggravated felony is not eligible for VAWA cancellation of removal.[23]

B. VAWA Self-Petitioning & Adjustment of Status for DV Victims

A domestic violence victim spouse, child, or parent can apply on their own (without reliance on their abuser) for lawful immigration status through a process called "VAWA self-petitioning."[24] Like VAWA Cancellation, the person must be a person of "good moral character." If a bar to good moral character is an offense that also could be waived under 8 U.S.C. § 212(h)—for example, if it is one or more convictions of a crime involving moral turpitude—and the offense was connected to the abuse, the bar may be forgiven.[25] Once the self-petition is granted and it is time for the self-petitioner to adjust status to lawful permanent

---

[17] For a more thorough overview of avenues of discretionary relief available to undocumented immigrants to avoid removal/deportation and obtain lawful status to remain in the U.S., and avenues available to persons with lawful status (lawful permanent residents, refugees, and asylees), see § N.17 Immigration Relief Toolkit For Criminal Defenders: *How to Quickly Spot Possible Immigration Relief for Noncitizen Defendants*, IMMIGRANT LEGAL RESOURCE CTR. (Jan. 2016), https://www.ilrc.org/sites/default/files/resources/n.17_questionnaire_jan_2016_final.pdf.

[18] 8 U.S.C. § 1229b(2)(a).

[19] 8 C.F.R. § 316.10.

[20] 8 U.S.C. §§ 1182(a)(2) or (3).

[21] 8 U.S.C. §§ 1227(a)(1)(G), (2), (3), or (4).

[22] 8 U.S.C. § 1227(a)(7)(A).

[23] 8 U.S.C. § 1229b(b)(2)(A)(iv).

[24] 8 U.S.C. § 1154(a)(1)(A)(iii).

[25] 8 U.S.C. § 1154(a)(1)(C). *See also* Memorandum from Paul E. Novak, Dir., Vt. Service Ctr. on Determinations of Good Moral Character in VAWA-Based Self-Petitions to William R. Yates, Assoc. Dir. for Operations, U.S. Citizenship & Immigr. Services (Mar. 30, 2004), *available at* https://www.uscis.gov/sites/default/files/USCIS/Laws/Memoranda/Static_Files_Memoranda/Archives%201998-2008/2005/gmc_011905.pdf.

residence, your client must not be inadmissible under the crimes-based grounds, or if inadmissible, must obtain a waiver.

C. Crime Victims "U visa"

U nonimmigrant status, commonly referred to as the "U visa," provides an avenue to obtain lawful status for noncitizens who are victims of serious crimes, including domestic violence, and who are helpful or likely to be helpful to police, prosecutors, and others in the course of investigating and prosecuting certain qualifying crimes.[26] If your client is a victim of domestic violence, but is not eligible for VAWA relief, either because of a criminal record or because the abuser is not a U.S. citizen or permanent resident, or the client is not married to her abuser, they may still qualify to apply for a U visa. This is a more generous form of relief than VAWA cancellation or VAWA self-petitioning, especially for those with criminal convictions. U visa applicants who would be found ineligible due to legal grounds of inadmissibility under the immigration laws, including as a result of criminal acts and convictions, can apply for a special waiver of all of these grounds of inadmissibility that would permit approval of their U visa application.[27] However, in the case of U visa applicants inadmissible on criminal grounds, the regulation states that discretionary waivers for those convicted of "violent and dangerous crimes" will only be granted "in extraordinary circumstances," and that waiver denials are both revocable and administratively unappealable.[28] Three years after approval of the U visa (during which time the person can live and work legally in the U.S.), the U visa holder can apply to become an LPR. Any criminal convictions that occur during this three-year time can have a negative impact on the application for LPR status, and there is a risk of deportation.

There is cap limiting the number of U visas to 10,000 per fiscal year, and the number of people eligible for this protection has exceeded the cap for several years; therefore, there is a significant backlog for these petitions.[29] As a result, U visa petitioners must wait several years before receiving a final decision on their case. However, U.S. Citizenship and Immigration Services will issue preliminary determinations on cases in the queue, which can allow petitioners to be granted deferred action (temporary protection against deportation) and be eligible for work authorization.[30] Given the volume of cases, however, it is currently taking two years or more to get even this preliminary determination.

---

[26] 8 U.S.C. § 1101(a)(15)(U).

[27] 8 U.S.C. § 1182(d)(14).

[28] 8 C.F.R. §§ 212.17(b), (c).

[29] INA § 214(p)(2)(A).

[30] 8 C.F.R. § 214.14(d)(3).

D. Victims of Trafficking "T visa"

T nonimmigrant status, commonly referred to as the "T visa," provides an avenue to obtain lawful status for noncitizens who are victims of "a severe form of trafficking in persons,"[31] are in the U.S. on account of the trafficking, and who would suffer "extreme hardship involving unusual and severe harm" if removed from the U.S.[32] T visa applicants who would be found otherwise inadmissible (including as a result of criminal acts and convictions) can apply for a special waiver as long as the activities to be waived were caused by or incidental to the trafficking victimization, in addition to any other waiver for which they are eligible.[33] If the person cannot show that their criminal act was related to the victimization, the federal government will only grant the waiver in exceptional circumstances. Three years after approval of the T visa (during which time the person can live and work legally in the U.S.), they can then apply to adjust their status to become an LPR. Any criminal convictions that occur during this three-year time will lead to ineligibility for LPR status and risk of deportation.

E. Asylum

Asylum is a form of relief granted to noncitizens who have faced past persecution or have a "well-founded fear" of future persecution on account of race, nationality, religion, political opinion, or membership in a particular social group if returned to their home country. Domestic violence has been recognized as a viable claim for asylum.[34] In order to be eligible, the applicant cannot have been convicted of a "particularly serious crime" (e.g., robbery, rape, serious assaults, drug trafficking) or a crime that constitutes an "aggravated felony" under immigration law (which includes some non-violent misdemeanors). An aggravated felony is automatically considered a particularly serious crime for purposes of asylum. Other than the aggravated felony bars, determining whether an offense is a particularly serious crime is done on a case-by-case basis. The adjudicator may look beyond the record of conviction to factors including whether the offense involved violence against people, the extent of injury, and the length of sentence.[35] Generally, a misdemeanor that is not an aggravated felony is not

---

[31] Severe trafficking includes sex trafficking of persons, and recruiting or obtaining persons for labor or services through the use of force, fraud, or coercion "for the purpose of subjection to involuntary servitude, peonage, debt bondage, or slavery" (in other words, labor trafficking).

[32] 8 U.S.C. § 1101(a)(15)(T).

[33] 8 C.F.R. § 212.16(b)(2).

[34] Matter of A-R-C-G-, 26 I. & N. Dec. 388 (B.I.A. 2014). **Immediately prior to this printing (June 2018), *Matter of A-R-C-G-* was overturned by *Matter of A-B-*, impacting this area of asylum law. Matter of A-B-, 27 I. & N. Dec. 316 (A.G. 2018).**

[35] *See* Matter of N-A-M-, 24 I. & N. Dec. 336, 342 (B.I.A. 2007); *see also* Matter of Frentescu, 18 I. & N. Dec. 244, 247 (B.I.A. 1982).

a particularly serious crime.[36] Once granted asylum, an asylee can then apply for LPR status after one year, but will be subject to the grounds of inadmissibility.

F. Cancellation of Removal for Lawful Permanent Residents

The overwhelming majority of lawful permanent residents (LPRs) who end up in removal proceedings end up there due to criminal convictions. The primary form of discretionary relief from removal available to LPRs with criminal convictions is known as "LPR Cancellation."[37] In addition to other requirements, the criminal conviction(s) cannot be classified as an "aggravated felony" under immigration law and the person must show they have been "rehabilitated" from their criminal activity.

Determining the options for discretionary relief that are available to a noncitizen can be a complex process. Unless you are an experienced advocate, you may not be able to make definitive determinations about whether your client qualifies for a particular type of discretionary relief. If you identify that your client may be eligible to pursue an application for discretionary relief to avoid removal/deportation and/or obtain lawful status, you should consult with an experienced immigration attorney.

In some cases, your client will be removable and ineligible for immigration relief based on a prior criminal conviction. In these cases, post-conviction relief may be the only avenue to alleviate the immigration consequences of your client's criminal record. Immigrant post-conviction relief is a broad term that covers any effort to erase or mitigate the immigration consequences of an existing conviction. Post-conviction relief can refer to expungements, sentence modifications (like felony to misdemeanor reductions), or substantive motions to vacate based claims of legal or constitutional invalidity. A skilled immigrant post-conviction relief practitioner will be able to select the appropriate form of post-conviction relief that will help eliminate the grounds of removability or open new pathways to immigration relief.

The best preventative measure to avoid immigration consequences of a criminal conviction, however, is addressing these consequences at the front end when a noncitizen is facing criminal charges. It is critical that every noncitizen client be represented by a competent criminal defense attorney who can assist them in determining the immigration consequences of entering a plea or being convicted, even in misdemeanor cases. The U.S. Supreme Court in *Padilla v. Kentucky* held that the Sixth Amendment of the U.S. Constitution requires that effective assistance of counsel be given to noncitizens.[38] This means that

---

[36] Matter of Juarez, 19 I. & N. Dec. 664, 665 (B.I.A. 1988).

[37] 8 U.S.C. § 1229b(a).

[38] Padilla v. Kentucky, 559 U.S. 356 (2010).

criminal defense counsel is required to affirmatively provide accurate advice to a defendant about the immigration consequences of being convicted of the criminal charges against them, as well as the immigration consequences of any pleas to alternative criminal charges offered by the prosecutor.

V. Strategies and Tips for Legal Advocates Working with Immigrant Victims

While immigration law is complex, and especially so at the intersection of immigration and criminal law, there are many things that legal advocates can do to help protect noncitizen domestic violence victims from the immigration consequences of criminal convictions and other contact with the criminal justice system. Your role as a legal advocate is particularly important as you may be able to flag and mitigate the potential devastating consequences resulting from a criminal record.

Advocacy Tip: Ensure that your client is working with a criminal defense attorney.

- If your client is currently facing criminal charges, you should ensure that they are working with a criminal defense attorney, and if they cannot afford to hire an attorney, that the court appoints a public defender to represent them in the criminal proceedings. Your client can tell the court that there *may* be immigration consequences if they plead guilty or are convicted after a trial; they have a right to have a criminal defense attorney representing them to determine what these criminal consequences are, and explore how the criminal proceedings may be resolved so as to not to lead to adverse immigration actions.[39]

- Once your client has defense counsel, you should explain that immigration consequences are both an issue and a priority for your client. You should also help gather and share the relevant information about the client including their immigration status, immigration history, prior criminal history, and potential avenues to relief. A sample intake form can be found in the appendix following this chapter.

Advocacy Tip: Inform your client of their legal rights.

- You should inform your client of their rights against immigration enforcement. Your client may be targeted by local law enforcement on the street, in jail, or with probation officers. If they are no longer in the criminal justice system, they may be targeted by immigration authorities at their home, their place of work, or at other public places including courthouses.

---

[39] A non-citizen client, however, has a Fifth Amendment Constitutional right not to disclose their specific immigration status in the criminal proceedings, and in consultation with their attorney may choose to respectfully inform the court that they do not need or wish to do so.

- You should make sure your client knows what to do if they are approached by local law enforcement or immigration authorities about immigration matters. They should know that they have a right to remain silent and they should not answer any questions, especially about their birth place, immigration status, or how they entered the U.S. They should assert their right to speak with a lawyer. They should also know that they have the right to demand a warrant before letting anyone into their home, to make a phone call once arrested, and to refuse to sign anything or show any documents before they talk to a lawyer. An information sheet on immigrant rights can be found in the appendix following this chapter.

Advocacy Tip: Help your client prepare safety plans.

- You should also help your client prepare in advance safety plans in the event they are arrested and detained. This includes making child care plans; parents should ensure that all information and emergency contacts are up to date at their children's school(s), including who can and cannot pick up their children. They should also complete a caregiver's authorization affidavit so another adult can care for their children temporarily.

- They should create a sheet of emergency contact information and a file of important documents so that they, their family, or their emergency contact person can easily access them.[40]

Finally, you should help gather relevant information about your client to assess or to obtain assistance to assess your client's immigration case. This information includes their immigration status, immigration history, and criminal history. If you have some immigration expertise, you can conduct an initial assessment of your client's immigration options and the potential impact of their criminal record on these options. Otherwise, you should refer your client to a local immigration legal services provider who has expertise in the immigration consequences of crimes.[41]

VI. Conclusion

Immigrant victims of domestic violence with criminal records face significant risks and challenges. Although they are exposed to immigration enforcement and must likely overcome obstacles to stabilize or protect their immigration

---

[40] Other ideas for safety planning can be found at *Family Preparedness Plan*, IMMIGRANT LEGAL RESOURCE CTR. (Mar. 1, 2017), https://www.ilrc.org/family-preparedness-plan; *see also Protecting Assets and Child Custody in the Face of Deportation: A Guide for Practitioners Assisting Immigrant Families*, APPLESEED (2017), http://www.appleseednetwork.org/deportationmanual/.

[41] You can find immigration legal help on the Immigration Advocates Network's national directory of free or low-cost nonprofit immigration legal services providers at https://www.immigrationlawhelp.org.

status, with the assistance of an informed legal advocate there are a variety of preventative measures and interventions that can be taken to protect them and mitigate the immigration consequences of their individual cases.

APPENDIX

Resources:

- **Immigrant Legal Resource Center**
  - https://www.ilrc.org/crimes

Along with publishing DEFENDING IMMIGRANTS IN THE NINTH CIRCUIT, the Immigrant Legal Resource Center creates extensive online materials for criminal defense attorneys and advocates on the immigration consequences of criminal convictions.

- **Law Offices of Norton Tooby**
  - http://www.nortontooby.com/
  - Phone: (510) 601-1300, Fax: (510) 595-6772

A criminal practitioner for more than thirty years who has become a national expert in immigration law as well, Norton Tooby has written several books that are national in scope. CRIMINAL DEFENSE OF NON-CITIZENS includes an in-depth analysis of immigration consequences and moves chronologically through a criminal case. SAFE HAVENS, AGGRAVATED FELONIES, and TOOBY'S CRIMES OF MORAL TURPITUDE provide general discussion of these areas, and also discuss and digest in chart form all federal and administrative immigration opinions relating to these categories. Other books include studies of means of obtaining post-conviction relief under California law, and nationally. The website of the Law Offices of Norton Tooby offers a very valuable collection of archived articles and a free newsletter. Other services, including constant updating of Mr. Tooby's books, are offered for a small fee.

- **National Immigration Project of the National Lawyers Guild.**
  - https://www.nationalimmigrationproject.org/

The National Immigration Project publishes the comprehensive and encyclopedic national book: DAN KESSELBRENNER, LORY D. ROSENBERG & MARIA BALDINI-POTERMIN, IMMIGRATION LAW AND CRIMES (Nat'l Immigr. Project of the Nat'l Law. Guild, Winter 2017).

- **Executive Order: Enhancing Public Safety in the Interior of the United States**
  - Exec. Order No. 13,768, 82 Fed. Reg. 8799 (Jan. 25, 2017), *available at* https://www.whitehouse.gov/presidential-actions/executive-order-enhancing-public-safety-interior-united-states/.

- **Immigration Relief for Immigrant Survivors of Abuse: Comparative Quick Reference Chart**
  - *Immigration Relief for Immigrant Survivors of Abuse: Comparative Quick Reference Chart*, IMMIGRANT LEGAL RESOURCE CTR. (July 5, 2017),

https://www.ilrc.org/sites/default/files/resources/comparative_chart_7.5.17_finalv2.pdf.

- **Immigration Relief Toolkit for Criminal Defenders**
  - ○ *§ N.17 Immigration Relief Toolkit for Criminal Defenders: How to Quickly Spot Possible Immigration Relief for Noncitizen Defendants*, Immigrant Legal Resource Ctr. (Jan. 2016), https://www.ilrc.org/sites/default/files/resources/n.17_questionnaire_jan_2016_final.pdf.

Websites:

- Board of Immigration Appeals (BIA) decisions can be accessed from a government website. Go to **http://www.justice.gov/eoir/**, click on "Virtual Law Library," and look for "BIA/AG administrative decisions."

- Memoranda, policy statements, and forms can be accessed from two government websites: **https://www.uscis.gov/** (adjudicating applications) and **https://www.ice.gov/** (enforcement).

- The website of the **Immigrant Legal Resource Center** offers material on a range of immigration issues, including a free downloadable manual on immigration law affecting children in delinquency, dependency and family court, and extensive information about forms of relief such as DACA (Deferred Entry of Childhood Arrivals), the U visa for victims of crimes, applications for persons abused by U.S. citizen parent or spouse under the Violence Against Women Act (VAWA).
  - ○ https://www.ilrc.org/
  - ○ For immigrant community resources relating to recent developments, visit: https://www.ilrc.org/community-resources.

- The **National Immigration Project of the National Lawyers Guild** offers practice guides and updates on various issues that can affect criminal defendants. The National Immigration Project provides information and a brief bank on immigration and criminal issues, on VAWA applications for persons abused by citizen or permanent resident spouse or parent, and applications under the former § 212(c) relief.
  - ○ https://www.nationalimmigrationproject.org/

- The **Immigrant Defense Project in New York** has excellent practice guides as well as a chart of immigration consequences of New York offenses.
  - ○ https://www.immigrantdefenseproject.org/

Immigrant Rights

What Immigrant Families Can Do Now

⤷ Talk to an immigration services provider about your immigration options

Find immigration legal help on the Immigration Advocates Network's national directory of free or low-cost nonprofit immigration legal services providers at https://www.immigrationlawhelp.org

- If you have a green card, find out if you can become a U.S. citizen.
- If you are here on a visa, find out if you can get a green card.
- If you do not have immigration status, find out if you may be eligible to get a visa or work permit.
- If you have a criminal arrest or conviction, find out how it might affect your case, or if there is a way to erase it from your record.

⤷ Make a child care and family preparedness plan (https://www.ilrc.org/family-preparedness-plan)

- Make sure all information and emergency contacts are up to date at your children's school(s) including who can and cannot pick up your children.
- Create a sheet of emergency numbers and contact information and a file of important documents so that you, your family or your emergency contact person can easily access them.
- Complete a caregiver's authorization affidavit so another adult can care for your children temporarily (available in California).
- Register your child's birth with your country's government (for example, with your country's consulate) if your child was born in the United States.

⤷ Figure out which documents you should and should not carry with you

- If you have a valid work permit or green card, carry it with you at all times. If you do not have one, generally it is advisable to carry a municipal ID, state ID or driver's license if it was issued in the United States and contains *no information at all* about your immigration status or your country of origin. Ask a local immigration advocate about what kind of documents are safe to carry in your area.
- Do not carry any documentation about your country of origin.
- Do not carry any false identity documents or false immigration documents.
- At all times, carry a red card (https://www.ilrc.org/red-cards) to exercise your right to remain silent in case you are stopped or interrogated by ICE or police officers.

Everyone's Rights During an Immigration (ICE) Raid

Everyone – both documented and undocumented persons – have rights in this country.

⟳ Make sure you and others know what to do if approached by ICE officers.

Inform your family members (even children), housemates, neighbors and co-workers, regardless of their immigration status, of their right to remain silent and all of these rights if ICE or the police comes to your home, neighborhood or workplace.

⟳ You have the right to remain silent.

You can refuse to speak to an ICE agent. Do not answer any questions, especially about your birth place, immigration status or how you entered the United States. Say that you want to remain silent until you speak with a lawyer.

⟳ You have the right to demand a warrant before letting anyone into your home.

Do not open your door to authorities without a warrant. You do not need to open the door unless an ICE agent shows you a warrant signed by a judge with your specific and correct name and address on it. If they say they have one, do not open the door for them to show it to you. Ask them to slip it under the door or through a window.

⟳ You have the right to speak to a lawyer and the right to make a phone call.

⟳ You have the right to refuse to sign anything before you talk to a lawyer.

Do not sign anything. That could eliminate your right to speak with a lawyer or have a hearing in front of an immigration judge. This may result in you being deported immediately without a hearing.

⟳ You have the right to refuse to show any documents before speaking with a lawyer.

> **Remain calm and do not try to run away.**
> **If you do, ICE or the police may use that against you.**

What Allies Can Do During an Immigration Raid

⟳ If you can do so safely, take photos of, video record, document and report raids and arrests.

- Obtain the names and phone numbers of any witnesses.
- Share information about the raid with your co-workers. If there is a union in your workplace, contact a union official.
- If ICE agents or police officers enter without a proper warrant, ask for their names and/or write down their badge numbers.

⟳ To report a raid, contact United We Dream's hotline 1-844-363-1423 or text 877877.

- Report any incidents of raids or abuses/mistreatment by ICE, police or border patrol.

Immigrant Legal Resource Center, www.ilrc.org   *Immigrant Defendant Questionnaire*
January 2017

IMMIGRANT DEFENDANT QUESTIONNAIRE

Your name	Defendant's case number (from your office, court, etc.)	Defendant's A# (if possible)

Def's Country of Birth	Def's Date of Birth	ICE Detainer/Hold/Notification ☐Yes ☐No ☐ Don't Know

1. ENTRY:

Date first entered U.S.	Visa Type (or 'none')	Departures from U.S. (approximate OK; append list)
		Date/s: Length of departure/s:

2. IMMIGRATION STATUS:

Lawful permanent resident ("green card")	Other Current Immigration status
☐ Yes ☐ No Date Obtained?____ On what basis (e.g. family visa, refugee): ☐ Check one. To obtain LPR status, D: --Went to an interview in the home country ☐ --Processed ("adjusted status") here in U.S. ☐	☐ Undocumented ☐ Doesn't know ☐ Has work permit but unsure of status ☐ Refugee ☐ Asylee ☐ Temporary Protected Status ☐ Deferred Action Childhood Arrivals (DACA) Other:
Screen for possible US citizenship:	
☐ Grandparent or parents were US citizen at time of D's birth; OR ☐ Parent/s were USCs while D was under age 18; (Mark even if parents or grandparents now are deceased. Stepparents do not qualify here) ☐ Neither of the above	**USC or LPR Parent, Spouse, Child** List each relative and whether the person is an LPR or a USC. Include age of each child.

3. PRIOR REMOVAL/DEPORTATION/VOLUNTARY DEPARTURE:

Was D ever deported or got "voluntary" departure?	Describe what happened, to extent possible (e.g., Saw immigration judge? Just signed form before leaving U.S.? Caught at the border?)	Where? When? For each deport/voluntary departure
☐Yes ☐No ☐ Don't know		

Immigrant Legal Resource Center, www.ilrc.org
January 2017

Immigrant Defendant Questionnaire

Immigrant Defendant Questionnaire, p. 2

Your name: Client case number:

Information on Prior Conviction/s from any jurisdiction:

Include additional page if needed				
Code section, F/M	Offense Date	Conviction Date	Sentence	Post-Con relief (PC 17 etc)

Information on Current Charges

Include additional page if needed			
Code sec.	F/M, strike, etc.	Date committed	Other info

Current Plea Offer/s if any

Include additional page if needed			
Code sec	F/M, strike, etc	Sentence	Other info: DA flexibility, priorities; Your comments

Immigrant Legal Resource Center, www.ilrc.org
January 2017

Immigrant Defendant Questionnaire

Immigrant Defendant Questionnaire, p. 3
Your name: Client case number:

Eligible to Apply for Lawful Status or Relief from Deportation

If the answer to any question is "yes," the client might be eligible for the relief indicated. References are to the *Relief Toolkit for Defenders*, available free online at www.ilrc.org/chart.

"USC" stands for U.S. Citizen and "LPR" stands for lawful permanent resident (green card-holder)

Questions for <u>LPR</u> Clients (green card-holders) Only:

*1. **Has your LPR client lived in the U.S. for at least seven years?**   ☐ Yes ☐ No*
To apply for this waiver in deportation proceedings, client must be an LPR who (a) is not convicted of an aggravated felony; (b) has been a LPR for at least five years; and (c) has lived in the U.S. for at least seven years since being admitted in any status (e.g. as a tourist, LPR, etc.). *See §17.5 LPR Cancellation.*

*2. **Can your LPR client apply for U.S. Citizenship?**   ☐ Yes ☐ No*
An LPR can apply for U.S. citizenship after five years LPR status, or three years of marriage to a USC while an LPR; must establish good moral character and should not be deportable. More beneficial rules apply to some current and former military personnel. *See §17.4 Naturalization*

Questions for <u>All</u> Immigrant Clients, Including Undocumented Persons and LPRS

*3. **Has your client been abused by a USC or LPR relative?**   ☐ Yes ☐ No*
Your client, or certain family member/s, have been abused (including emotional abuse) by a USC or LPR spouse, parent, or adult child. What relative and what immigration status? _ _
See §17.8 VAWA. (If abuser does not fit this profile, consider U Visa, below.)

*4. **Is your client a juvenile and a victim of abuse, neglect, or abandonment?**   ☐ Yes ☐ No*
Client can't be returned to at least one parent, due to abuse, neglect or abandonment. *See §17.9 Special Immigrant Juvenile.*

*5. **Is your client a victim of abuse who also was convicted of domestic violence?**   ☐ Yes ☐ No*
Client was convicted of a deportable DV or stalking offense, but in fact client is the primary victim in the relationship. A waiver of the DV deportation ground, or the DV bar to non-LPR cancellation, might be available. *See §17.11 Domestic Violence Waiver.*

*6. **Did your client enter the U.S. before his or her 16th birthday?**   ☐ Yes ☐ No*
Client entered U.S. before turning 16 and before 6/15/2007. *See §17.12 DACA.*

*7. **Has your client lived in the U.S. for at least ten years?**   ☐ Yes ☐ No*
To be eligible for this defense in removal proceedings, client must have lived in U.S. at least ten years and have a USC or LPR parent, spouse or child (see *§17.14 Non-LPR Cancellation of Removal)* or lived here at least ten years and all deportable convictions occurred before April 1, 1997 (see *§ 17.15 Suspension of Deportation, available in Ninth Circuit states).*

Immigrant Legal Resource Center, www.ilrc.org
January 2017

Immigrant Defendant Questionnaire

Immigrant Defendant Questionnaire – p. 4
Your name: Client case number:

8. Has your client been a victim of a crime?   ☐ **Yes** ☐ **No**
Client must have been a victim of a crime such as DV, assault, false imprisonment, extortion, stalking, or sexual abuse, and be or have been willing to cooperate in investigation or prosecution of the crime. *See §17.16 The "U" Visa.*

9. Has your client been a victim of human trafficking?   ☐ **Yes** ☐ **No**
Client must have been victim of (a) sex trafficking of persons (if under age 18, could have been consensual), or (b) labor trafficking, including being made to work by force, fraud, etc. *See §17.17 "T" Visa.*

10. Is your client afraid to return to his or her home country for any reason?   ☐ **Yes** ☐ **No**
Mark "yes" if (a) Client fears persecution or even torture if returned to the home country, *see §§ 17.19 Asylum and Withholding* and *17.20. Convention Against Torture*; or (b) Client already is an asylee or refugee, *see §17.21 Refugees and Asylees*; or (c) Client is from a country that the U.S. designated for TPS status, based on natural disaster, civil war, or the like, *see §17.22 Temporary Protected Status (TPS).*

11. Is your client from the former Soviet Bloc, El Salvador, Guatemala, or Haiti?   ☐ **Yes** ☐ **No**
Your client might be eligible for a program if he/she from these areas *and* applied for asylum or similar relief in the 1990's -- or is a dependent of such a person. *See §17.23 NACARA for Central Americans,* and see *§17.24 HRIFA for Haitians and Dependents.*

12. Does your client, or parent or spouse, have an imm case from 1980's "amnesty"? ☐ **Yes** ☐ **No**
The application still might be pending and viable. *See §17.25.*

Chapter Twenty-eight:
Sex Trafficking and Domestic Violence

I. Introduction

Sex trafficking generates approximately $99 billion U.S. dollars annually by selling human beings for commercial sex acts.[1] Setting aside legal definitions, sex trafficking is encapsulated by the straightforward theory of supply and demand.[2] A high demand for commercial sex acts creates a lucrative market for vulnerable individuals, mostly women and girls, to be exploited for sex.[3]

---

[1] Int'l Labour Off., Profits and Poverty: The Economics of Forced Labour 5 (2014), *available at* http://www.ilo.org/wcmsp5/groups/public/@ed_norm/@declaration/documents/publication/wcms_243027.pdf.

[2] *Sex Trafficking*, Nat'l Hum. Trafficking Hotline, https://humantraffickinghotline.org/type-trafficking/sex-trafficking (last visited Apr. 29, 2018) ("Sex trafficking is a market-driven criminal industry that is based on the principles of supply and demand. Therefore, people who purchase commercial sex increase the demand for commercial sex and likewise provide a profit incentive for traffickers, who seek to maximize profits by exploiting trafficking victims.")

[3] Int'l Labour Off., Global Estimates of Modern Slavery: Forced Labour and Forced Marriage 10 (2017), *available at* http://www.ilo.org/wcmsp5/groups/public/---dgreports/---dcomm/documents/publication/wcms_575479.pdf ("Women and girls are disproportionately affected by modern slavery, accounting for 28.7 million, or 71 per cent of the overall total [world-wide]. More precisely, women and girls represent 99 per cent of victims of forced labour in the commercial sex industry and 58 per cent in other sectors, 40 per cent of victims of forced labour imposed by state authorities, and 84 per cent of victims of forced marriages.").

Where does Sex Trafficking Happen?

Sex trafficking occurs in large cities and rural towns across all 50 states. Traffickers exploit victims for a range of commercial sex acts, including, but not limited to, prostitution, pornography, stripping, live-sex shows, mail-order brides, and sex tourism. This exploitation occurs in a range of settings including fake massage businesses, escort services, brothels, residential homes, on public streets, truck stops, strip clubs, hotels, farms, legitimate places of business, large sporting events, political conventions, and elsewhere.

The Trafficking Victims Protection Act of 2000 (TVPA) introduced the most universal definition of human trafficking in the United States.[4] The TVPA has since been reauthorized four times with strong bipartisan support.[5] The TVPA's definition of sex trafficking includes three components, which experts have distilled into a framework known as the Act-Means-Purpose model.[6] First, the perpetrator, or "trafficker," takes any one of seven enumerated actions, including "recruitment, harboring, transportation, provision, obtaining, patronizing, or soliciting."[7] Then, the trafficker employs the *means* of "force, fraud or coercion," for the *purpose* of compelling the victims to provide a commercial sex act.[8] When the victim is under the age of 18 and induced to perform a commercial sex act, human trafficking is proven without evidence of force, fraud, or coercion.[9] Contrary to common misconception, trafficking in persons does *not* require movement across international or state borders.[10] At its essence, human trafficking is the exploitation of vulnerabilities in order to extract labor or sex.[11]

---

[4] 22 U.S.C. § 7102(10) (2000).

[5] Saba Baig & Kathryn Liss, *How Do Foreign National Victims of Trafficking Fare Under the Trump Administration?*, A.B.A. Young Law. Division Tyl (2017), https://www.americanbar.org/groups/young_lawyers/publications/tyl/topics/immigration-law/how-do-foreign-national-victims-trafficking-fare-under-trump-administration.html.

[6] Nat'l Hum. Trafficking Res. Ctr., Understanding the Definition of Human Trafficking: The Action Means Purpose (Amp) Model (2012), https://humantraffickinghotline.org/sites/default/files/AMP%20 Model.pdf.

[7] 22 U.S.C. § 7102(10).

[8] 22 U.S.C. §§ 7102(9)(A), 7102(10).

[9] 22 U.S.C. § 7102(9)(A).

[10] *Myths and Misconceptions*, Nat'l Hum. Trafficking Hotline, https://humantraffickinghotline.org/ what-human-trafficking/myths-misconceptions (last visited Mar. 2, 2018).

[11] Dorchen A. Leidholdt & Katherine P. Scully, *Defining and Identifying Human Trafficking, in* Lawyer's Manual on Human Trafficking: Pursuing Justice for Victims 27, 28 (Jill Laurie Goodman & Dorchen A. Leidholdt, eds. 2011), *available at* https://www.nycourts.gov/ip/womeninthecourts/pdfs/ lmht.pdf. For more information about labor trafficking and domestic violence, see *Labor Trafficking and Domestic Violence in Section Eight* of this manual.

Acts + Means + Purpose = Human Trafficking		
Adapted from the National Human Trafficking Resource Center (NHTRC)		
Act	***Means***	***Purpose***
Recruitment, Harboring, Transportation, Provision, Obtaining, Patronizing, or Soliciting	Force, Fraud, or Coercion	Commercial Sex Act (Sex Trafficking) or Labor/Services (Labor Trafficking)
* If a victim under 18 years old is induced to perform a commercial sex act, human trafficking occurs, irrespective of force, fraud, or coercion.		

II. Similarities Between Sex Trafficking and Domestic Violence

Sex trafficking and domestic violence, while distinct crimes, have considerable similarities in (1) the perpetrators, (2) the victims, and (3) the tactics used to control victims. The greatest distinction between sex trafficking and domestic violence is that domestic violence lacks the commercial element of sex trafficking. In addition, trafficking victims face greater barriers to self-identification, and therefore are much less likely to receive help. After decades of advocacy, domestic violence has become a more familiar concept, which allows victims to increasingly advocate for themselves. However, human trafficking continues to present a particular challenge for advocates and victims alike, in part because of its highly variable fact patterns and dehumanizing effect, making it difficult to recognize.

Sex traffickers target vulnerable victims to generate the greatest profit with the lowest risk. Individuals who have experienced inequality or previous trauma are traffickers' greatest targets, because they may be more easily manipulated and less likely to report to law enforcement.[12] Examples of these vulnerability factors

---

[12] Leidholdt & Scully, *supra* note 11, at 28 ("[H]uman traffickers often exploit political, social, and economic conditions of dire inequality—especially poverty; gender, racial, and ethnic discrimination; gender, racial and ethnic violence; civil unrest and armed conflict; and natural disasters—to recruit and maintain power and control over trafficking victims.").

include youth, homelessness,[13] lack of immigration status, unemployment, history of mental health issues, LGBTQ individuals,[14] gender, and domestic violence.

Who is Involved in Sex Trafficking?

Sex trafficking schemes involve perpetrators (the "traffickers"), victims (compelled to provide commercial sex acts), and the buyer/consumer ("John"). The trafficker(s) can be a gang member(s), a family member(s) (such as parents, aunts, uncles, cousins), a friend, romantic partner, or spouse. They can operate individually or as part of a network of pimps and traffickers. However, the business structure is often concealed from the victim, who may only interact with one pimp/trafficker.

Sex traffickers have found that the best way to recruit victims is by feigning genuine relationships and posing as their boyfriends, spouses, or "sugar daddies."[15] These traffickers are indistinguishable from batterers in domestic violence situations; indeed, they are one and the same. In these situations, where a pimp poses as an intimate partner, individuals are simultaneously victims of domestic violence and sex trafficking.[16] The role the pimp plays as a romantic partner, who can provide for someone's every need, exploits the vulnerabilities

---

[13] LAURA T. MURPHY, LABOR AND SEX TRAFFICKING AMONG HOMELESS YOUTH: A TEN-CITY STUDY EXECUTIVE SUMMARY 4 (2017), https://www.covenanthousestudy.org/landing/trafficking/docs/Loyola-Research-Results.pdf?_ga=2.205197206.764329831.1512326431-1924367502.1512326431 (finding that of the 641 youth interviewed at Covenant House homeless shelters throughout the United States and Canada, "nearly one in five (19% or 124) were identified as victims of some form of human trafficking…More than 14% (92) of the total population had been trafficked for sex, while 8% (52) had been trafficked for other forced labor. 3% (22) were trafficked for both sex and labor."); *see also Tariro Mzezewa, Homeless Youth at High Risk of Human Trafficking,* N.Y. TIMES (Apr. 17, 2017), https://kristof.blogs.nytimes.com/2017/04/17/homeless-youth-at-high-risk-of-human-trafficking/?_r=0).

[14] Kevin M. Ryan, *One in Five Homeless Youth Trafficking, New Research Reveals,* HUFFINGTON POST (Apr. 17, 2017), https://www.huffingtonpost.com/entry/one-in-five-homeless-youth-trafficked-new-research_us_58f5032ee4b015669722517d (Between the dual studies by researchers at the University of Pennsylvania and Loyola University, of the 911 homeless youth across 13 cities in the United States and Canada, "nearly 34 percent of lesbian, gay, bisexual, transgender and questioning (LGBTQ) homeless youth had survived human trafficking, although they accounted for only 19 percent of the interview pool. Twenty-seven percent of LGBTQ youth—more than one in four—had been trafficked for sex").

[15] Dorchen A. Leidholdt, *Human Trafficking and Domestic Violence: A Primer for Judges, in* 52 THE JUDGES' J. (A.B.A., ed., 2013). ("All over the world pimps, a subset of traffickers, have learned that the best way to recruit vulnerable women and girls into prostitution is through love and romance.")

[16] Amy Barasch & Barbara C. Kryszko, *The Nexus Between Domestic Violence and Trafficking for Commercial Sexual Exploitation, in* LAWYER'S MANUAL ON HUMAN TRAFFICKING: PURSUING JUSTICE FOR VICTIMS 83, 87 (Jill Laurie Goodman & Dorchen Leidholdt, eds. 2011), *available at* https://www.nycourts.gov/ip/womeninthecourts/pdfs/lmht.pdf.

of many intersecting oppressive dynamics.[17] Given their past trauma, victims of domestic violence[18] and sexual assault[19] are frequently targeted by sex traffickers as the ideal victim.

Sex traffickers and batterers use the very similar tactics of power and control against their victims.[20] The Power and Control Wheel, used by domestic violence advocates to identify the methods batterers use to control their victims,[21] has been adapted to describe the tactics used by traffickers.[22] The distinction between the tactics used by traffickers as opposed to domestic violence abusers is better understood as a difference in degree rather than type. While domestic violence abusers seek to exploit the victim for their personal benefit, sex traffickers exploit their victims to "the demands of the countless men who will buy the victims for sex and turn this continuous abuse into a lucrative profit."[23]

---

[17] Kimberlé Crenshaw, *Why Intersectionality Can't Wait*, Wash. Post (Sept. 24, 2015), https://www.washingtonpost.com/news/in-theory/wp/2015/09/24/why-intersectionality-cant-wait/?noredirect=on&utm_term=.228ed32ec815.

[18] Leidholdt, *supra* note 15 ("Human-trafficking experts often talk about push and pull forces: conditions that propel or lure vulnerable people into situations of prostitution or forced labor. Domestic violence often serves as a push or pull force. People at risk, usually women and girls, often fall under the control of traffickers while attempting to escape intimate-partner abuse. Conversely, they frequently inadvertently become ensnared in abusive intimate-partner relationships trying to escape sex or labor trafficking. Usually lacking economic resources and family support, victims are easy marks for intimate-partner predators. Desperate to leave intolerable conditions, they fail to see that the person offering refuge and protection is himself an abuser.").

[19] The Field Ctr. for Children's Pol'y, Prac. & Res., Field Center Completes Multi-City Study on Child Trafficking Among Homeless Youth; Identifies Risk And Resilience Factors 1 (2017) (A sex trafficked youth stated in an interview, "When I was younger I was raped and molested so it was like I always thought it was okay to go out and have sex with different people because this happened."); *see also* Asian Pacific Inst. on Gender-Based Violence, Intersections of Human Trafficking, Domestic Violence, and Sexual Assault: National Organizational Advocacy Roundtable 7 (2016) ("[Commercial Sexual Exploitation of Children] victims, particularly those who have experienced childhood sexual abuse may be socialized into believing that having sex with, or purchasing sex from minors is acceptable, even normal. Hence, difficulties in establishing and maintaining boundaries from a young age can be one of multiple developmental traumas that increase vulnerability.").

[20] Dorchen A. Leidholdt, *Prostitution and Trafficking in Women: An Intimate Relationship*, 174 Trafficking & Traumatic Stress 160, 167–183 (Melissa Farley ed., 2003) ("Domestic violence has come to be understood not as a discrete series of violent acts but as a system of power and control the batterer institutes and maintains over his victim through the use of an array of interconnected strategies: isolation, intimidation, emotional abuse, economic abuse, sexual abuse, and threats (Power and Control Wheel, Domestic Abuse Intervention Project, Duluth, Minnesota).").

[21] Save: Stop Abusive and Violent Environments, Gender-Inclusive Power and Control Wheel, http://saveservices.org/pdf/PowerandControlWheel.pdf (adaption of the original power and control wheel developed by the Domestic Abuse Intervention Project in Duluth, Minnesota).

[22] Nat'l Hum. Trafficking Res. Ctr., Human Trafficking Power and Control Wheel (Jan. 2010), https://humantraffickinghotline.org/sites/default/files/HT%20Power%26Control%20Wheel%20NEW.pdf (adaption of the original power and control wheel developed by the Domestic Abuse Intervention Project in Duluth, Minnesota).

[23] Barasch & Kryszko, *supra* note 16, at 86.

Sex traffickers often seek to repackage a victim's identity through a new name or nickname, revealing clothing, and tattoos.[24] Isolation is also often greater with trafficking victims, frequently moving a victim from one place to another, and surveillance is often increased, ensuring that the victim is always being watched by the trafficker or another agent.[25] Another factor unique to sex trafficking is the ability of the trafficker to benefit from the criminal justice system's tendency to penalize sex trafficking victims.

Advocacy Tip: If a client describes only one individual as the perpetrator of domestic violence, seek to learn more about how this perpetrator might be connected to a larger network of exploiters, whether familial, cultural, or otherwise. Drawing a map or family tree connecting everyone in your client's story can assist your client to make these connections. Developing this fact pattern can assist adjudicators to conceive of the crime as sex trafficking in addition to intimate partner violence.

III. Criminalization of Sex Trafficking Victims

Despite universal agreement that sex traffickers, and not their victims, should be punished for this crime, many victims are arrested and prosecuted for conduct they were forced to engage in.[26] Cultural misconceptions about prostituted persons contribute to the harmful assumption that a person in prostitution is a law breaker, rather than a possible victim of crime.[27] Despite the reality that the vast majority of individuals in prostitution have no other viable option for survival and many are under the control of a pimp, police often mistake trafficking victims as

---

[24] *Id.*

[25] *Id.*

[26] Kate Mogulescu, *The Public Defender as Anti-Trafficking Advocate, An Unlikely Role: How Current New York City Arrest and Prosecution Policies Systematically Criminalize Victims of Sex Trafficking*, 15 CUNY L. Rev. 471, 474 (2012).

[27] Despite a common misconception that prostitution is a sanitized and straightforward exchange of money for sex by consenting adults, it is agreed upon by opposing political groups that prostitution brings with it alarming rates of physical, sexual and emotional violence, discrimination, including exclusion from health and housing services, as well as risk of unwanted pregnancy and sexually transmitted infections. *See* Catherine Murphy, *Sex Workers' Rights Are Human Rights*, Amnesty Int'l (Aug. 14, 2015), https://www.amnesty.org/en/latest/news/2015/08/sex-workers-rights-are-human-rights/; *Q&A: Policy to Protect The Human Rights of Sex Workers*, Amnesty Int'l, https://www.amnesty.org/en/qa-policy-to-protect-the-human-rights-of-sex-workers/ (last visited Mar. 2, 2018); Kari Lerum et al., *Reducing the Violence Against Sex Workers: What are the Policy Options?*, Hum. Rights For All (Feb. 28, 2011), http://faculty.washington.edu/lerum/Policy%20Brief%20FINAL.pdf; Richard Warnica, *Barely Illegal: New Prostitution Laws May Drive Sex Work Underground—But Can it Stop it?*, Nat'l Post (May 7, 2015), http://news.nationalpost.com/news/canada/barely-illegal-new-prostitution-laws-may-drive-sex-work-underground-but-can-it-stop-it; Mary Sullivan, *What Happens When Prostitution Becomes Work? An Update on Legalization of Prostitution, in* Coal. Against Trafficking in Women 21 (2005), http://www.catwinternational.org/Home/Article/93-what-happens-when-prostitution-becomes-work.

"prostitutes" willfully breaking the law.[28] At the point of arrest, law enforcement officials are often not trained to assess whether the individual is a victim.[29] At the same time, a victim's fear of punishment often keeps them from affirmatively disclosing the abuse they have suffered at the hands of their trafficker.[30] Once the victim is arraigned in court, the criminal justice system, which is designed to process high-volume cases, often fails to adequately screen for trafficking.[31] When the trafficking victim must endure the public shame of being arrested, placed in jail, and convicted in a formal setting, this creates an additional barrier to reaching out for help. This implementation of the criminal justice system works in favor of traffickers, and reinforces the threats of arrest and/or deportation they make toward their victims.

IV. Civil Legal Remedies for Victims of Sex Trafficking

Civil attorneys who represent domestic violence victims are poised to identify indicators of sex trafficking. With experience in recognizing dynamics of power and control and training in trauma-informed lawyering, these attorneys have cultivated skills to effectively assist these clients.[32] With the assistance of reliable tools, attorneys can screen for human trafficking rather than rely on traumatized clients to self-identify.[33] Perhaps most importantly, attorneys who establish a judgment-free space will create an environment in which trafficking victims feel safe to disclose their trauma without fear of negative consequences.

---

[28] Melissa Farley et al., *Prostitution and Trafficking in Nine Countries An Update on Violence and Posttraumatic Stress Disorder*, 2 J. Trauma Prac. 34, 213 (2004) (finding that in a survey of 854 people currently or recently in prostitution across nine countries, 89% wanted to "escape prostitution, but did not have other options for survival").

[29] Michelle Madden Dempsey, *Decriminalizing Victims of Sex Trafficking*, 52 Am. Crim. L. Rev. 207, 211 (2015) (citing Polaris Project, 2013 Analysis of State Human Trafficking Laws 1 (2013), http://www.polarisproject.org/sites/default/files/2013-State-Ratings-Analysis.pdf).

[30] Barasch & Kryszko, *supra* note 16, at 86.

[31] With the exception of ten counties in Nevada, prostitution is a criminally punishable offense across the United States that is frequently the target of arrests. Catharine A. MacKinnon, *Trafficking, Prostitution and Inequality*, 46 Harv. C.R.-C.L. L. Rev. 271, 274 (2011).

[32] Polaris Project, Understanding Victim Mindsets (2014), https://humantraffickinghotline.org/sites/default/files/Understanding%20Victim%20Mindsets.pdf (outlining 19 common barriers sex or trafficking survivors face to leaving a trafficking situation).

[33] *See* Vera Inst. of Just., Out Of The Shadows: A Tool for the Identification of Victims of Human Trafficking (2014), https://www.vera.org/publications/out-of-the-shadows-identification-of-victims-of-human-trafficking (providing human trafficking screening tools in English and Spanish, as well as user guidelines); *see also* Nat'l Hum. Trafficking Res. Ctr., Comprehensive Human Trafficking Assessment Tool (2011), https://humantraffickinghotline.org/sites/default/files/Comprehensive%20Trafficking%20Assessment.pdf.

Advocacy Tip: Given the high levels of trauma that sex trafficking victims endure, it is imperative to refer clients to social service professionals as soon as they are identified as a victim of trafficking. If the client's non-legal needs are not addressed, it will be more challenging for the client to focus on the legal issue and divert the attorney's resources from legal to non-legal needs.

Once a civil attorney has identified a victim of sex trafficking, they can assist victims navigate the legal remedies designed to protect them. The following list is illustrative of the available remedies and not exhaustive:

A. Immigration Relief

For many undocumented victims of trafficking with no immigration status, T Nonimmigrant Status ("T visa") is the most transformative form of relief.[34] The T visa provides four years of legal immigration status, work authorization, and access to the same federal benefits as refugees.[35] Some states, like California and Illinois, also provide benefits to T visa applicants in the process of applying for this status, recognizing that victims are most vulnerable before they secure immigration status.[36] T visa holders can apply for legal permanent residence after three years in status, or after the Department of Justice has confirmed that the investigation or prosecution of their crime has ended.

Even survivors with grounds of inadmissibility, such as criminal convictions, that would make them ineligible for other forms of legal status, are not categorically disqualified from the T visa. A waiver of inadmissibility was designed to assist T visa applicants who can prove their ground of inadmissibility was related to their victimization, and it is in the national interest to waive these grounds.[37] Given the difficulty of identifying victims, the T visa is highly

---

[34] Immigration & Nationality Act, 8 U.S.C. § 1101(a)(15)(T) (2018) [hereinafter INA]; *see also* 8 C.F.R. § 214.11 (2018) (federal regulations for T Nonimmigrant Status).

[35] *Id.*

[36] Letter from Alice Mak, Acting Chief Medi-Cal Eligibility Division, State of California Department of Health Care Services, to All County Welfare Directors (Jul. 22, 2015), *available at* http://www.dhcs.ca.gov/services/medi-cal/eligibility/Documents/ACWDL2015/ACWDL15-25.pdf (clarifying the California state-funded benefits for noncitizen victims of human trafficking, domestic violence, and other serious crimes.); ILL. DEP'T OF HUM. SERVS., MR No. 17.19: MEDICAL BENEFITS FOR NON-CITIZEN VICTIMS OF TRAFFICKING, TORTURE OR OTHER SERIOUS CRIMES (2017), http://www.dhs.state.il.us/page.aspx?item=97367.

[37] 8 C.F.R. § 212.16.

underutilized.[38] While this lack of identification is troubling, the surplus of this remedy makes it a more efficient option than some other forms of immigration relief.[39]

In addition to the T visa, your client may be eligible for additional forms of relief including U Nonimmigrant status, asylum, and the VAWA self-petition.[40] Therefore, referring your client to an immigration attorney with expertise in humanitarian forms of relief, in addition to experience assisting victims of trafficking, is essential.

B. Post-Conviction Relief

Survivors of sex trafficking who are compelled to commit crimes on behalf of their trafficker often have criminal records that impede their recovery. For example, a criminal conviction can prevent survivors from getting a job, receiving medical care, education, housing assistance, and may disqualify them from applying for a loan or obtaining immigration relief.[41] In addition, the stigma of a criminal record can cause a victim shame and embarrassment. In 2010, New York became the first state to pass a law that allows survivors of trafficking to vacate criminal convictions based on their victimization.[42] Since then, more than 30 states have followed New York's lead and passed laws that help seal, expunge, or vacate arrest and/or conviction records for prostitution or related

---

[38] U.S. CITIZEN & IMMIGR. SERVS, NUMBER OF FORM I-914, APPLICATION FOR T NONIMMIGRANT STATUS BY FISCAL YEAR, QUARTER, AND CASE STATUS 2008-2017 (2017), https://www.uscis.gov/sites/default/files/USCIS/Resources/Reports%20and%20Studies/Immigration%20Forms%20Data/Victims/I914t_visastatistics_fy2017_qtr3.pdf (showing that between fiscal years 2008 to 2016, USCIS has never granted more than 17 percent of the available T-1 Nonimmigrant Status applications in a single fiscal year. In fiscal year 2017, only 672 of the available 5,000 T-1 Principal Applications were approved, which amounts to 87 percent of the available T-1 Nonimmigrant Status grants as unused. Generally, these numbers are not explained by unduly restrictive adjudicators, but instead a national problem of ineffective identification of trafficking victims).

[39] U.S. CITIZENSHIP & IMMIGR. SERVS., USCIS PROCESSING TIME INFORMATION FOR THE VERMONT SERVICE CTR., https://egov.uscis.gov/cris/processTimesDisplayInit.do (showing T visa processing time as approximately 11 months and U visa processing time as over three years).

[40] INA §§ 101(a)(15)(U), 204(a)(1)(A)–(B), 208; 8 C.F.R. § 208. For more information on these various forms of immigration relief, see *Immigration Law and Domestic Violence* in Section Two of this manual

[41] JESSICA EMERSON ET AL., OBTAINING POST-CONVICTION RELIEF FOR SURVIVORS OF HUMAN TRAFFICKING 1, 5 (2014), https://www.americanbar.org/content/dam/aba/directories/pro_bono_clearinghouse/ejc_2014_182.authcheckdam.pdf.

[42] *Id.*

crimes.[43] It is important to check your state's vacatur laws to determine the scope of convictions that may be able to be sealed, expunged, or vacated.[44] Doing so may greatly improve your client's ability to move forward with their life.

C. Civil Litigation/Damages

Congress created the right for trafficking victims to sue their traffickers for damages in federal court through the Trafficking Victims Reauthorization Act of 2003. This created an opportunity for victims to pursue justice without relying on state or federal actors to prosecute their trafficker. Strategic litigation can secure large monetary damages for victims, punish perpetrators, and help deter others from engaging in this crime.[45] However, this process can be resource intensive and take several years. Therefore, it is essential to advise the client on a realistic time frame and expectations before the client decides to pursue civil litigation. The Human Trafficking Legal Center is the leader in strategic litigation for human trafficking, and provides resources and technical assistance for pro bono attorneys representing trafficking victims in federal court.[46]

D. Crime Victim Advocacy in Criminal Prosecution

Sex trafficking victims who are cooperating in law enforcement's investigation and/or prosecution of the trafficker(s) will likely benefit from representation by a civil or immigration attorney. While assisting local police, FBI investigators, and/or state and federal prosecutors, a victim might incorrectly assume that the prosecutor is their own attorney. However, because cooperating witnesses do not benefit from attorney-client privilege, and the information they provide to law enforcement may be turned over to immigration authorities or the opposing counsel without their consent, it is important that the victim have their own attorney throughout this cooperation.

---

[43] Rudy Costillo, *Vacatur Laws: Decriminalizing Sex Trafficking Survivors,* AM. U. J. GENDER & SOC. POL'Y & L., http://www.jgspl.org/vacatur-laws-decriminalizing-sex-trafficking-survivors/#_ftn11; *see Vacatur & Expungement Database,* THE HUM. TRAFFICKING PRO BONO LEGAL CTR., https://sites.google.com/a/htprobono.org/vsdatabase/home (last visited Mar. 2, 2018). As of this printing, 33 states have passed vacatur laws. *Laws by State,* A.B.A. COMM'N ON DOMESTIC & SEXUAL VIOLENCE, THE SURVIVOR REENTRY PROJECT, https://www.americanbar.org/groups/domestic_violence/survivor-reentry-project.html (last visited May 16, 2018).

[44] *See* Fifty-State Survey: Safe Harbor Laws and Expungement, Sealing, and Vacatur Provisions, with Related Statutes, Pertaining to Trafficked Persons, Advocating Opportunity (2015), https://docs.google.com/viewer?a=v&pid=sites&srcid=aHRwcm9ib25vLm9yZ3x2c2RhdGFiYXNlfGd4OjlxMGI4OGM0ZDQwOTBkOWM.

[45] HUM. TRAFFICKING PRO BONO LEGAL CTR. & THE FREEDOM FUND, ENDING IMPUNITY, SECURING JUSTICE: USING STRATEGIC LITIGATION TO COMBAT MODERN-DAY SLAVERY AND HUMAN TRAFFICKING (2015), http://www.htprobono.org/wp-content/uploads/2015/12/FF_SL_AW02_WEB.pdf.

[46] HUM. TRAFFICKING LEGAL CTR., http://www.htlegalcenter.org/ (last visited Jan. 15, 2018).

In addition, victims who choose to provide a victim impact statement at the trafficker's sentencing often benefit from assistance in preparing this statement, and calculating damages. Given the often traumatic experience of testifying in front of their own trafficker, it is recommended that the client's social service worker be informed of this process to identify potential difficulties or hurdles and provide emotional support.

E. Orders of Protection

For sex trafficking victims whose traffickers are intimate partners or family members, a civil order of protection may benefit the victim.[47] Although these orders of protection were designed for domestic violence victims, they can be effective as part of the safety planning process for trafficking victims. If your client is interested in seeking an order of protection against their trafficker, a referral to an experienced family law attorney is recommended.

F. Family Law/Divorce/Custody

If the sex trafficking victim was married to their trafficker, filing for a divorce may improve safety and provide distance from the perpetrator. If the victim had children with their trafficker, filing for sole custody of the children may be in their best interest. In either case, referring your client to an experienced family law attorney is recommended.

Advocacy Tip: Many cities across the country have human trafficking task forces that combine interdisciplinary teams to address the crime in their region. Joining a human trafficking task force may provide connections to social service providers and law enforcement officials, which may greatly benefit your client.

V. Conclusion

The overlap between domestic violence and sex trafficking is considerable, yet too many trafficking victims go unrecognized and are unable to access the legal remedies designed to protect them. Given the great barriers to disclosing the trafficking, the attorney, rather than the victim, may have the greatest opportunity to identify the situation and intervene. Attorneys working with populations that are especially vulnerable to trafficking (including victims of domestic violence and sexual assault, youth, homeless persons, LGBTQ identifying individuals, women, immigrants, those with addiction,[48] and clients with intersecting identities) should screen for trafficking and learn about the different forms of civil legal remedies available to victims of sex trafficking.[49]

---

[47] Barasch & Kryszko, *supra* note 16, at 89.

[48] EMERSON ET AL., *supra* note 41.

[49] *See* VERA INST. OF JUST., *supra* note 33; NAT'L HUM. TRAFFICKING RES. CTR., *supra* note 22.

APPENDIX

Human Trafficking Screening Tools:

- **National Human Trafficking Resource Center**
  - Nat'l Hum. Trafficking Res. Ctr., Comprehensive Human Trafficking Assessment Tool (2011), https://humantraffickinghotline.org/sites/default/files/Comprehensive%20Trafficking%20Assessment.pdf.

- **National Human Trafficking Training and Assistance Center**
  - Nat'l Hum. Trafficking Training & Assistance Ctr., Adult Human Trafficking Screening Tool (2018), https://www.acf.hhs.gov/sites/default/files/otip/adult_human_trafficking_screening_tool_and_guide.pdf.

- **Vera Institute of Justice**
  - Vera Inst. of Just., Out of The Shadows: A Tool For The Identification of Victims of Human Trafficking (2014), https://www.vera.org/publications/out-of-the-shadows-identification-of-victims-of-human-trafficking.

Human Trafficking Power & Control Wheel:

- **National Human Trafficking Resource Center**
  - Nat'l Hum. Trafficking Res. Ctr., Human Trafficking Power and Control Wheel (2010), https://humantraffickinghotline.org/resources/human-trafficking-power-and-control-wheel.

Practice Manuals:

- Exposing and Responding to Human Trafficking in 2014 (Practising L. Inst. 2014).

- Lawyer's Manual on Human Trafficking: Pursuing Justice for Victims (Jill Laurie Goodman & Dorchen A. Leidholdt, eds. 2011), *available at* https://www.nycourts.gov/ip/womeninthecourts/pdfs/lmht.pdf.

- A.B.A. Comm'n on Domestic & Sexual Violence, The Survivor Reentry Project, Post-Conviction Advocacy for Survivors of Human Trafficking; A Guide For Attorneys, *available at* https://www.americanbar.org/content/dam/aba/administrative/domestic_violence1/SRP/practice-guide.authcheckdam.pdf.

Websites:

- **Coalition to Abolish Slavery & Trafficking**
  - http://www.castla.org/

- **National Human Trafficking Hotline**
  - https://humantraffickinghotline.org
  - Phone: 1-888-373-7888
  - Text: 233733

- **Polaris Project**
  - https://polarisproject.org

- **The Human Trafficking Pro Bono Legal Center**
  - http://www.htlegalcenter.org/

Chapter Twenty-nine:
Labor Trafficking and Domestic Violence

I. Introduction

Characterized as one of the world's fastest growing criminal enterprises, trafficking in persons has been estimated to generate worldwide profits of $150 billion per year.[1] Because human trafficking is clandestine by nature, the identification and protection of victims and the prosecution of the criminals who exploit them remains a challenge. However, attorneys and victim advocates can play key roles in helping victims obtain protections through both the criminal justice and civil litigation arenas. This chapter will focus specifically on the intersection of domestic violence and labor trafficking, a less widely discussed but still significant area of victimization. Part one of this chapter will provide a general overview of labor trafficking that focuses on key terms, vulnerability factors, and victim identification. Part two will apply the framework to three unique case examples: intimate partner violence, forced marriage with child exploitation, and domestic worker abuse. Finally, part three of this chapter will highlight critical litigation strategies, tips, and remedies to assist attorneys. Overall, this chapter is meant to introduce manifestations of labor trafficking. In consideration of this fact, the appendix following this chapter lists resources with more detailed information for attorneys representing victims of labor trafficking.

A. Key Legal Concepts, Terms, and Definitions

The Trafficking Victims Protection Act (TVPA) and its subsequent reauthorizations provide the federal statutory framework for the crime of human

---

[1] *Human Trafficking by the Numbers*, HUM. RIGHTS FIRST (Jan. 7, 2017), https://www.humanrightsfirst.org/resource/human-trafficking-numbers.

trafficking and victim protections in the United States.[2] While all fifty states have specific legislation on human trafficking, for the purposes of this chapter, all definitions and legal standards will comport with those used in the TVPA.

Human trafficking has been commonly described as "modern day slavery," and generally involves the use of force, fraud, or coercion to exploit human beings for some type of labor or commercial sex purpose.[3] This chapter will focus on the dynamics between domestic violence and one form of human trafficking: labor trafficking.

Labor trafficking is a "severe form of trafficking in persons," defined as "the recruitment, harboring, transportation, provision, or obtaining of a person for labor or services, through the use of *force, fraud, or coercion* for the purpose of subjection to *involuntary servitude, peonage, debt bondage*, or slavery" (emphasis added).[4] Prior consent by an employee to work for an employer is not legally relevant once the employee's labor has been exploited, using any of the methods articulated in the TVPA.[5]

Coercion includes the following acts: "threats of serious harm to or physical restraints against any person; any scheme, plan, or pattern intended to cause a person to believe that failure to perform an act would result in serious harm to or physical restraint against any person or the abuse or threatened abuse of the legal process."[6]

Debt bondage is "the status or condition of a debtor arising from a pledge by the debtor of his or her personal services or of those of a person under his or her control as a security for debt, if the value of those services as reasonably assessed is not applied toward the liquidation of the debt or the length and nature of those services are not respectively limited and defined."[7] A common scenario of debt bondage arises when the trafficker confiscates a victim's wages to repay the cost of transportation to the United States and subsequent costs such as housing and food.

Involuntary servitude is defined as occurring in one of two ways. First, it can occur through a "scheme, plan or pattern intended to cause a person to

---

[2] Trafficking Victims Protection Act of 2000, 22 U.S.C. § 7101, *amended by* Trafficking Victims Protection Reauthorization Acts of 2003, 2005, 2008, and 2013.

[3] Minors induced into commercial sex do not need to demonstrate force, fraud, or coercion. 22 U.S.C. § 7102(9)(A) (2012).

[4] 22 U.S.C. § 7102(9)(B) (2012).

[5] *See* U.N. Protocol to Prevent, Suppress and Punish Trafficking in Persons, Especially Women and Children (Palermo Protocol), U.N. Doc. A/RES/55/25 (2000). The United States signed the Palermo Protocol on December 13, 2000, and the Senate ratified it on October 7, 2005.

[6] Trafficking Victims Protection Act, 22 U.S.C. § 7102(3) (2000).

[7] 22 U.S.C. § 7102(5) (2012).

believe that, if the person did not enter into or continue such condition, that person or another person would suffer serious harm or physical restraint."[8] The most common pattern includes threats of physical harm or death to loved ones. Second, involuntary servitude may be triggered by the abuse or threatened abuse of the legal process "in any manner or for any purpose for which the law was not designed, in order to exert pressure on another person to cause that person to take some action or refrain from taking some action."[9] For example, traffickers often threaten to report a victim's undocumented status to authorities or threaten to revoke green card/visa applications submitted on behalf of the victim. Traffickers may also force victims to commit crimes and use knowledge of such acts to perpetuate involuntary servitude.

> Advocates representing trafficking victims frequently employ an Action/ Means/Purpose analysis that looks at the **action** of the trafficker (induces, recruits, harbors, transports, provides or obtains), the **means** by which the victim is trafficked (through force, fraud or coercion) for a **purpose** (labor/ services or commercial sex).[10]

The broad definition of labor trafficking anticipates the myriad ways in which individuals may be exploited for labor or services. Consequently, knowledgeable practitioners can obtain protections for their clients under the TVPA even as the means of exploitation continue to evolve.

B. Victims: Vulnerability Factors and Identification

Despite national anti-trafficking awareness campaigns, victim identification remains a challenge, with both the crime and the exploited individuals frequently described as "hidden in plain sight".[11] Identification is the first of many hurdles the legal community faces in assisting victims and prosecuting traffickers.

Adults and children of all genders, ages, races, and socio-economic backgrounds may be labor trafficked, but certain factors may compound a vulnerability to victimization. Common risk factors include recent migration,

---

[8] *Id.* § 7102(6).

[9] *Id.* § 7102(1).

[10] For a sample diagram of the Action-Means-Purpose analysis, see *What is Human Trafficking?*, Nat'l Hum. Trafficking Hotline, https://humantraffickinghotline.org/what-human-trafficking (last visited Apr. 19, 2018).

[11] John Morton, *Hidden in Plain Sight: ICE's Work to Combat Human Trafficking*, Dep't of Homeland Sec. (Jan. 11, 2013), https://www.dhs.gov/blog/2013/01/11/hidden-plain-sight; *Blue Campaign Initiatives*, U.S. Immigr. & Customs Enforcement (June 6, 2013), https://www.ice.gov/factsheets/dhs-blue-campaign#wcm-survey-target-id (last updated Nov. 10, 2015).

substance abuse, mental health issues, disabilities, unstable housing, and youths experiencing homelessness.[12]

Research indicates that gender influences the manner in which victims are abused. Women and girls are primarily targeted for sexual exploitation, whereas men are targeted largely for labor exploitation. Although data indicates an overall decrease in the percentage of female victims and, conversely, an overall increase in the percentage of male victims, researchers have estimated that women and girls account for roughly 75 percent of all victims.[13]

A subset of labor trafficking victims in the United States involves migrants who initially enter the country without legal documentation or with a legal status that eventually lapses during victimization. This lack of lawful immigration status is a vulnerability that traffickers exploit to perpetuate victimization.[14]

Advocacy Tip: In many cases, victims who are non-citizens are threatened with adverse immigration consequences should they attempt to escape. Absent overt threats, coercion can also be shown through a trafficker's confiscation or "safeguarding" a victim's legal documentation. Similarly, multiple ignored requests for the return of documentation can satisfy the coercion element.[15] However, as courts have demonstrated in their decisions, there is a fine line between pointing out adverse immigration consequences and abusing the immigration process to ensure continued labor.[16]

---

[12] Nat'l Hum. Trafficking Hotline, *More Assistance. More Action. 2016 Statistics from the National Human Trafficking Hotline and BeFree Textline*, Polaris (2016), http://polarisproject.org/sites/default/files/2016-Statistics.pdf.

[13] The percentage of female victims decreased from 84 percent in 2004 to 71 percent in 2014. *Global Report on Trafficking in Persons 2016*, U.N. Off. on Drugs & Crime (2016), https://www.unodc.org/documents/data-and-analysis/glotip/2016_Global_Report_on_Trafficking_in_Persons.pdf. As of 2016, "women and girls are disproportionately affected by modern slavery, accounting for 28.7 million, or 71% of the total." 2016 *Global Estimate of Modern Slavery: Frequent Asked Questions*, Int'l Labor Org. (2016), http://www.ilo.org/wcmsp5/groups/public/---ed_norm/---declaration/documents/publication/wcms_575605.pdf. *But see More Assistance. More Action, supra* note 12 (explaining that 83 percent of survivors identified through the National Human Trafficking Hotline are female).

[14] Colleen Owens et al., Understanding the Organization, Operation, and Victimization Process of Labor Trafficking in the United States (Urb. Inst., Oct. 21, 2014), *available at* https://www.urban.org/research/publication/understanding-organization-operation-and-victimization-process-labor-trafficking-united-states/view/full_report.

[15] Ramos v. Hoyle & Perales, 08-cv-21809 (S.D. Fla. 2008) (coercion found where defendants took plaintiffs' passports and refused requests to return them); In re Applicant, 2007 WL 5360868 (no coercion found where applicant did not indicate that he requested his passport and was refused); In re Applicant, 2007 WL 5360664, at 13 ("The applicant has not asserted that she attempted to recover her passport.").

[16] *Compare* United States v. Afolabi, 508 Fed.Appx. 111, 118–119 (3d Cir. 2013) in which the court found an abuse of the immigration process, *with* In Re Applicant, 2007 WL 5360664 (DHS Nov. 21, 2007) where a court found no coercion.

Individuals with disabilities, particularly those who are deaf or who have cognitive impairments, are at high risk for victimization largely due to a pattern of discrimination, marginalization, and barriers to communication that make the power and control dynamic much easier to establish and enforce.[17] Victims who are physically, cognitively, or emotionally unable to advocate for themselves are more prone to manipulation and less likely to seek help.[18] Despite these challenges, anti-trafficking prosecutions or civil litigation may successfully ensure protection of individuals with disabilities.[19]

The above risk factors, coupled with certain recurring behaviors, may provide clues to identifying victimization. Several organizations and government agencies have created guidelines highlighting indicia of trafficking.[20] While neither the risk factors above nor activities below are dispositive, some combination of the following is common among victims:

- Loss of freedom of movement

- Low pay with excessively long work hours and unusual restrictions

- Debt to employer

- Fearful, anxious, or paranoid behavior

- Malnourishment

- Signs of physical or sexual abuse

---

[17] These categories are not mutually exclusive, and multiple vulnerabilities compound barriers for victims in obtaining assistance. Mellissa Withers, *The Underrecognized Victims of Trafficking: Deaf Women*, PSYCHOL. TODAY (Sept. 21, 2017), https://www.psychologytoday.com/blog/modern-day-slavery/201709/the-underrecognized-victims-trafficking-deaf-women. *See also Trafficking of Persons with Disabilities in the United States*, HUM. TRAFFICKING PRO BONO LEGAL CTR. (Apr. 2016), http://www.ndrn.org/images/webcasts/2016/Trafficking-of-Persons-With-Disabilities-in-the-United-States-04.12.2016.pdf.

[18] Off. for Victims of Crime, *Victims with Physical, Cognitive, or Emotional Disabilities*, OFF. OF JUST. PROGRAMS, https://www.ovcttac.gov/taskforceguide/eguide/4-supporting-victims/45-victim-populations/victims-with-physical-cognitive-or-emotional-disabilities/ (last visited Apr. 19, 2018).

[19] United States v. Kaufman, 546 F.3d 1242, 1263 (10th Cir. 2008) (compelled labor or services could include actions such as coerced sexual acts or coerced sexual performances for videotaping); United States v. Paoletti-Lemus, et al., No. 1:97-cr-00768 (E.D.N.Y. 1998) (case in which 55 deaf Mexican nationals were brought to the U.S. to sell trinkets in subway stations); *see also* Joseph P. Fried, *2 Sentenced in Mexican Peddling Ring*, N.Y. TIMES (May 8, 1998), http://www.nytimes.com/1998/05/08/nyregion/2-sentenced-in-mexican-peddling-ring.html?src=pm, (defendants ordered to pay $1.5 million in restitution); *Ashland Woman Sentenced to 32 Years in Prison for Labor Trafficking and Related Crimes Involving Disabled Women*, U.S. DEP'T. OF JUST. (July 24, 2014), https://www.justice.gov/usao-ndoh/pr/ashland-woman-sentenced-32-years-prison-labor-trafficking-and-relate-crimes-involving (last updated Mar. 12, 2015).

[20] See the Appendix to this chapter for a list of organizations and government sites that have thorough guidelines for victim identification.

- Lacks control of their money and identification documents

- Drug or alcohol addictions

- Trauma bonding with trafficker or signs of PTSD

- For children, a lack of school attendance

- Third party to whom the potential victim defers, or presence of third party who seems to be in control of the situation

- Recruited for work different from that which the individual is doing

- Required to live in employer provided housing

- Unaware of their location, the current date, or time

The next section examines three cases that demonstrate the overlap between labor trafficking and domestic violence. While considering each case study, it is important to identify the risk factors and characteristics discussed above.

II. Labor Trafficking and Domestic Violence

While not all labor trafficking involves domestic violence, both forms of abuse rely upon a dynamic of "power and control" over victims. Power and control is maintained using coercion and threats, intimidation, emotional and economic abuse, isolation from systems of support, and victim blaming.[21] The power and control wheel that is traditionally employed by domestic violence advocates when working with victims is equally relevant to trafficking.[22]

The fact patterns below were drawn from narratives of real clients, with some modifications to protect client identity. The first hypothetical involves the intersection between labor trafficking and intimate partner violence, where the dynamics of power and control found in domestic violence situations escalate to include labor exploitation. The second hypothetical explores the intersection of servile marriage and trafficking of minors, where the abuse is inflicted by a purported spouse, and may involve the complicity of family. The final scenario investigates domestic worker abuse, where employees live with their employer, work predominantly in the home, and fall subject to employment abuse and domestic violence.

---

[21] Courts have found that compelled labor or services, including coerced sexual acts, provided in the context of a familial or romantic relationship potentially could satisfy the definition of labor trafficking. United States v. Marcus, 487 F.Supp.2d 289 (E.D.N.Y. 2007), *vacated on other grounds*, 538 F.3d 97 (2d Cir. 2008).

[22] *See* Lawyer's Manual on Human Trafficking: Pursuing Justice for Victims 313–314 (Jill Laurie Goodman & Dorchen A. Leidholdt, eds. 2011), *available at* https://www.nycourts.gov/ip/womeninthecourts/pdfs/lmht.pdf.

A. Case Study: Intimate Partner Violence

Historically known as "domestic violence," the term "intimate partner violence" describes physical violence, sexual violence, stalking, and psychological aggression (including coercive acts) by a current or former intimate partner.[23] An intimate partner is a person with whom one has a "close personal relationship" that may include emotional connectedness, regular contact, ongoing physical contact and sexual behavior, identity as a couple, and/or familiarity and knowledge about each other's lives. Intimate partner violence can occur between current or former partners of any sexual orientation and does not require cohabitation.[24] While intimate partner abuse has frequently been linked to sex trafficking, a current or former intimate partner can similarly exert force, fraud, or coercion to obtain labor or services.[25]

Advocacy Tip: While domestic partners may share household duties, chores such as cooking, cleaning, and laundry can be activities that qualify for a finding of labor trafficking when the relationship is not consensual.

Dora's Story

Dora was raised in Hungary. While vacationing in Los Angeles on a visa waiver program, Dora met and fell in love with a charming man named John. John told Dora that he wanted to start a livery car business with her and encouraged Dora to move in with him so that they could be partners "in life and in business." When she hesitated, John proposed marriage, promising they would wed as soon as the business earned enough to support them.

Dora moved in with John, who told her that he would register the business under her name "for her protection," and asked her to pay the startup costs because his own funds were tied up in another business venture. Dora, believing this was an investment for their life together, depleted her savings. After a few weeks, when Dora asked John to see the ledger, he threw it at her head, screaming at her. The ledger hit her in the eye, and John immediately apologized, sobbing that he loved her and had not meant to hurt her. As the days and weeks passed, Dora's doubts grew. John told Dora that she had to serve as the call dispatcher until they could afford to hire someone else. Dora found herself taking phone calls 24 hours per day, 7 days per week, while John disappeared without explanation. Oftentimes, John would stand over Dora's shoulder, screaming at

---

[23] Nat'l Inst. of Just., *Intimate Partner Violence*, Off. of Just. Programs, https://www.nij.gov/topics/crime/intimate-partner-violence/Pages/welcome.aspx (last updated Mar. 30, 2017).

[24] Matthew J. Breiding, Kathleen C. Basile, Sharon G. Smith, Michele C. Black & Reshma Mahendra, Intimate Partner Violence Surveillance Uniform Definitions and Recommended Data Elements 11 (Ctrs. for Disease Control, 2015), *available at* https://www.cdc.gov/violenceprevention/pdf/intimatepartnerviolence.pdf.

[25] *See More Assistance. More Action, supra* note 12, at 5.

her that she didn't speak English well enough for the customers and calling her a "stupid immigrant." Despite the high call volume, Dora never saw any profits, and one time, after she asked John where the money went, he beat her for "not believing in him."

Dora grew afraid to ask further questions. She was also fearful of leaving John—he punched her in the face during one argument when she said that she wanted to break up with him, shouting that she would get "much worse" if she tried. John also swore that he would call "immigration" to have Dora arrested and deported for working illegally, and hinted that he had connections with "tough guys" in Hungary if she ever tried to escape.

When Dora learned that John had another girlfriend, whose name was registered for several of the livery cars, she realized that their relationship was built on lies. She contacted a domestic violence organization that she had seen advertised on a poster, and one night, when John was out, fled to its shelter for help.

> Applying an Action-Means-Purpose analysis: Dora was subjected to the **actions** of being induced and recruited into the livery car business through the **means** of *fraud* (and later, force and coercion) for the **purpose** of providing *labor/services* as an unpaid call dispatcher. Dora's situation highlights the convergence of domestic violence with labor trafficking, such that it becomes difficult to distinguish one from another. Often, domestic violence advocates focus more on physical and emotional abuse, without specifically identifying the workplace exploitation as trafficking. However, identification of labor trafficking in a domestic violence situation can be critically important to understanding what remedies are available to a victim, particularly if the victim is an immigrant.

B. Case Study: Forced Marriage

Forced marriage is a marriage that is executed without the full, free, and informed consent of *both* parties. A marriage entered into with mutual consent can transition into a forced marriage if one or both parties are stripped of the right to leave the marriage.[26] While often discussed as a form of domestic violence, forced marriages can include labor trafficking, commonly manifested as involuntary servitude. Individuals may be labor trafficking victims if forced to enter a marriage during which they experience physical and sexual violence, or are fearful of ending the relationship because of actual or perceived threats of serious harm.

---

[26] *About Arranged/Forced Marriage*, UNCHAINED AT LAST, http://www.unchainedatlast.org/about-arranged-forced-marriage/ (last visited Apr. 19, 2018).

Victims of forced marriages may come from a variety of backgrounds but gender and age are common risk factors. Marriage license data suggests that more than 200,000 children were married in the United States between 2000 and 2015.[27] Forced marriages are a particular concern for underage girls forced to marry adult men, who are in some cases decades older than them.[28] While the legal age of consent for marriage is 18, underage marriage is permitted by law in all fifty states either through judicial approval or parental consent.[29] With respect to judicially approved marriages, dozens of states do not have a minimum age of marriage resulting in girls as young as 11 forced to marry significantly older men.[30] A dynamic that would otherwise be considered statutory rape is legalized with a marriage license. The Tenth Circuit clarified that involuntary servitude applies to coerced acts other than work in the strictly economic sense, such as compelled sexual activity.[31]

Alea's Story

Alea and her family came to Michigan from Yemen when she was 11 years old. Alea adjusted quickly to her new school, but her parents struggled financially because they did not have work permits. A "gift" seemed to appear in the form of the family's 30-year old neighbor, who originally came from a village not far from theirs, and who had become a naturalized U.S. citizen. The neighbor offered to marry Alea, now 15 and a high school freshman, in exchange for sponsoring her and her family for green cards. Her own parents had married through an arranged marriage when they were her age. Believing that it was the best way to ensure that all family members would receive legal status, they agreed on the condition that Alea be permitted to graduate high school. Alea cried and said that she did not want to marry the neighbor, but after a religious ceremony, the new husband took Alea to his home and raped her on their wedding night. He continued to rape Alea regularly, and ordered her to cook for him and clean the apartment, beating her when she protested. Alea, bruised and terrified, tearfully confided in her favorite teacher, who notified the authorities. Alea's husband was arrested and Alea and her siblings were placed in the custody of Children's Protective Services.

---

[27] Nurith Aizenman, *The Loopholes That Allow Child Marriage in the U.S.*, NPR (Aug. 30, 2017), https://www.npr.org/sections/goatsandsoda/2017/08/30/547072368/a-look-at-the-loopholes-that-allow-child-marriage-in-the-u-s.

[28] Tahirih Just. Ctr., Child Marriage in the United States: A Serious Problem with a Simple First-Step Solution (Oct. 23, 2017), *available at* http://www.tahirih.org/wp-content/uploads/2016/11/Tahirih-Child-Marriage-Backgrounder-2.pdf.

[29] *Child Marriage – Legal in Every State*, Unchained at Last, http://www.unchainedatlast.org/child-marriage-legal-in-every-state/ (last visited Apr. 19, 2018).

[30] Nicholas Kristof, *11 Years Old, a Mom, and Pushed to Marry Her Rapist in Florida*, N.Y. Times (May 26, 2017), https://www.nytimes.com/2017/05/26/opinion/sunday/it-was-forced-on-me-child-marriage-in-the-us.html.

[31] United States v. Kaufman, 546 F.3d 1242, 1263 (10th Cir. 2008).

Applying an Action-Means-Purpose analysis: Alea was subjected to the **actions** of being *harbored, transported, provided, or obtained* through the **means** of *fraud* (and later, force and coercion) for the **purpose** of providing *labor/services* in the form of both household labor and sexual services.[32]

Alea's story illustrates the challenges labor trafficking victims may experience in disclosing their abuse. While violence and threats by her husband established control over Alea, abuse can also occur in forms that are less visibly apparent but often more powerful. Traditional norms such as obedience to parents or other authority figures and a willingness to put the interests of the group ahead of the individual are all manipulated by traffickers to dominate their victims. For Alea, the risk of jeopardizing her family's immigration status and their hope for a better life served as a powerful deterrent to seeking help.

Advocacy Tip: Advocates should be vigilant of both risk factors and warning signs to identify victims of forced marriage. Cultural influences and a sense of family obligation can deter a victim from seeking help. Youth are particularly vulnerable, as they are often isolated from the outside world, unaware of laws that protect children, and fearful of threats of harm to their parents or siblings. Compounded with physical, emotional, and sexual abuse, as well as financial dependence, it is particularly challenging for children to escape victimization.

C. Case Study: Domestic Worker Abuse

Labor trafficking and domestic violence also co-occur in the exploitation of domestic workers. While some domestic workers are recruited without the requisite employment authorization, each year, thousands of other individuals enter the country on nonimmigrant visas to provide domestic care for families.[33] Many of these domestic workers are employed by diplomats, employees of international organizations, or as au pairs. There is generally an extensive, and often expensive, recruitment process involved, leaving workers vulnerable to debt bondage. Fees vary and have been documented to be as high as $40,000,

---

[32] While the focus of this article is on labor trafficking, an argument can be made that the abuse Alea suffered also qualifies as sex trafficking, as the family received something of value (promise of legal status) in exchange for a "sex act," here the repeated rape of a child. Labor and sex trafficking claims are not mutually exclusive, and individuals may simultaneously be victims of both forms of abuse. Such a strategy would be particularly persuasive in this example, as sex trafficking does not require a showing of "force, fraud or coercion" when the victim is a minor.

[33] Sameera Hafiz & Michael Paarlberg, Nat'l Domestic Workers All. & Inst. for Pol'y Stud., The Human Trafficking of Domestic Workers in the United States (Narbada Chhetri et al. eds., 2017), *available at* http://www.ips-dc.org/wp-content/uploads/2017/03/Beyond-Survival-2017-Report_FINAL_PROOF-1-1.pdf; Press Release, U.S. Dep't of Just., *Woodbury Woman Pleads Guilty in Labor Trafficking Case* (May 31, 2017), *available at* https://www.justice.gov/usao-mn/pr/woodbury-woman-pleads-guilty-labor-trafficking-case.

forcing many immigrants to work for free to repay the debt.[34] The repayment of the debt, however, is generally irrelevant, as it exceeds what can be repaid through the labor required, and is often subject to usurious interest rates and "surcharges" for lodging, food, and other necessities. Many domestic workers are trafficked for an average of 5 years—some as long as 25 years—before escape.[35]

Attorneys advocating for victims of debt bondage/domestic worker abuse have an array of legal remedies at their disposal. In addition to exploring forms of relief for victims of labor trafficking, advocates should also be cognizant of potential domestic violence remedies when the victim and employer share a domicile. Just as domestic violence advocates should consider trafficking remedies, so should employment attorneys investigate whether domestic worker abuse can also qualify as domestic violence, thereby providing additional avenues for relief. This analysis is state specific, as some states such as Arizona, Florida, and Pennsylvania require an intimate partner or familial relationship. Others, such as California, New Jersey, and New York permit cohabitants or current/former members of the same household to petition for orders of protection.[36]

Constance's Story

Twenty-year old Constance helped her mother run a small restaurant in their village in Nigeria but dreamed of becoming a nurse. One day, Constance's relative, Linda, who had emigrated to America, visited the restaurant, looking for "a girl" to help care for her children in Maryland. When Linda added that the job would include support to attend university, Constance jumped at the opportunity.

Linda offered to "arrange everything" for her—not only the airfare, but the passport, and even the visa application. Constance felt blessed, but was confused when she received a passport containing her photo and visa, but in another person's name. After they boarded the airplane, Linda took Constance's passport for "safekeeping," and advised her not to speak with anyone upon arrival. Linda and Constance cleared U.S. immigration without incident, and Samuel, Linda's husband, welcomed Constance with a tight embrace.

Upon her arrival, Constance learned that she would be sleeping on the floor of the baby's room so she could feed him during the night. Additionally, Constance was forced to wake up at 6:00 a.m. to make breakfast and get the other children ready for school, since Linda had to leave early for her job. Samuel explained

---

[34] Hafiz & Paarlberg, *supra* note 33, at 22.

[35] *Id.* at 19.

[36] For a full list of state-by-state requirements for orders of protection, see A.B.A. Comm'n on Domestic & Sexual Violence, *Domestic Violence Civil Protection Orders* (Aug. 2016), https://www.americanbar.org/content/dam/aba/administrative/domestic_violence1/Charts/2016%20CPO%20Availability%20Chart.authcheckdam.pdf.

that he would drive the children to school in the morning, and that Constance should not leave the house under any circumstances. When Constance asked when she could register for college, the couple replied that it would take a while because they had to "straighten out the problem with the passport issue" if she wanted a degree in her own name.

After two weeks of cleaning, cooking, and doing the laundry, with no mention of college, Constance asked Linda when she would get paid. The two had not discussed salary in Nigeria, in part because Linda was family, and in part because Constance had focused on attending school, but Constance's mother needed her income to support her other children. To Constance's shock, Linda slapped her hard, calling her "ungrateful." Linda said she had spent a great deal of money to bring Constance to America, and now she and Samuel were providing Constance with free room and board plus the chance to attend school. When Constance began to sob, Linda kicked her and sent her to the kitchen to prepare dinner.

Months passed, and as the abuse worsened, Constance's only respite was permission to attend church on Sunday, if she completed all her chores before the noon service. She relished the peace, but was terrified to speak with the other parishioners, since Linda warned that she would be arrested if anyone found out that her true name was not what appeared on the passport. One parishioner, a kind woman originally from Ghana, handed Constance a slip of paper with her number on it, in case she "ever needed a friend."

One morning, when Constance was cleaning, Samuel raped her. He warned Constance never to tell Linda about "their relationship" because she would have Constance arrested. The following Sunday, Constance approached the Ghanaian parishioner, and haltingly confided that she needed a friend. The woman brought Constance to her home, and after hearing of Constance's abuse, offered to let her sleep on her sofa until they could find her assistance.

> Applying an Action-Means-Purpose analysis, Constance was subjected to the **actions** of being *recruited, harbored, transported, or obtained* through the **means** of *force, fraud and coercion* for the **purpose** of providing labor/ services as a domestic worker.

These three case studies illustrate some of the challenges inherent in victim identification. While some industries may be more readily associated with labor trafficking (agriculture, food processing, and restaurants), when trafficking occurs in a domestic violence context, it is often more difficult to detect. However, with proper training across all sectors—law enforcement, attorneys, social workers, school officials, hospitals, and nonprofit organizations—improved identification can lead to a range of remedies for the victim, as well as prosecution and civil penalties for the abusers. The next section of this chapter will briefly discuss litigation strategies. The appendix to this chapter contains a list of resources for individuals seeking more detailed information.

Advocacy Tip: The loss of freedom of movement is a red flag when identifying victims. Many victims experience restricted or supervised movement. While different circumstances will inform how advocates utilize such facts, it is important to note that "opportunities to escape mean nothing" if the defendant gives reasons to fear leaving.[37]

III. Legal Remedies

Trafficking cases intersect with multiple areas of law, including criminal law, immigration, and civil litigation. Strategic legal interventions for all possible claims can: (1) ensure that victims access multiple remedies, ranging from immigration relief to monetary compensation; (2) lead to prosecution of traffickers; and (3) help build a more robust body of case law that can serve as a deterrent to would-be traffickers.

A. Criminal Liability

Human trafficking is a crime under both state and federal law, and while a victim may choose to report trafficking under state law, this discussion will be limited to the federal framework under the TVPA. Forced labor and involuntary servitude are crimes under 18 U.S.C. § 1589 and 1584 respectively.[38] Additionally, federal courts have found that rape and other forms of sexual abuse are "force" that would support a conviction for labor trafficking.[39]

While law enforcement and prosecutors are responsible for the decision to investigate or prosecute a trafficking case, victim advocates nonetheless have a role in ensuring that their clients receive the protections and resources to which they are entitled. For example, the federal anti-trafficking statutes explicitly provide for mandatory restitution.[40] The purpose of mandatory restitution is to make victims whole, and it has resulted in significant awards against traffickers.[41] The mandatory criminal restitution provision can be invoked absent a criminal

---

[37] *See* United States v. Djoumessi, 538 F.3d 547 (6th Cir. 2010).

[38] *See* United States v. Sabhnani, 599 F.3d 215 (2nd Cir. 2010) (upholding convictions under forced labor statute in connection with Indonesian domestic servants); United States v. Djoumessi, 538 F.3d 547 (6th Cir. 2010) (upholding conviction for violation of involuntary servitude statute in connection with Cameroonian domestic servant).

[39] Sexual abuse in an employment context has been found to constitute force against a victim of involuntary servitude. United States v. Udeozor, 515 F.3d 260, 265 (4th Cir. 2008).

[40] 18 U.S.C. § 1593 ("[C]ourt[s] shall order restitution for any offense" committed in violation of the TVPA, and require recovery of "the full amount of the victim's losses.").

[41] *See* United States v. Sabhnani, 599 F.3d 215, 224 (2d Cir. 2010); United States v. Lewis, No. 1:09-CR-00213 (D.D.C. 2009).

conviction under the TVPA.[42] Invoking the Fair Labor Standards Act (FLSA), a formula is applied to calculate criminal restitution: "The greater of the gross income or value to the defendant of the victim's services or labor, or the value of the victim's labor as guaranteed under the minimum wage and overtime guarantees."[43] Under FLSA, a victim of trafficking is entitled to recover minimum wage for hours worked and sets overtime pay at 150 percent of the regular wage.[44] While live-in domestic workers are exempted from the overtime pay provision, they are still entitled to pay for every hour worked.[45]

Advocacy Tip: Despite the "mandatory" provision of restitution to trafficking victims, one study revealed that it was only awarded in approximately one-third of trafficking cases.[46] Attorneys representing victims must advocate vigorously to ensure that their clients are awarded the restitution to which they are entitled by law.

B. Immigration Relief

This section will briefly identify some immigration remedies that a practitioner may wish to explore on behalf of a client who is a survivor of labor trafficking. Reference material that offers more detailed guidance on these remedies is cited in the appendix to this chapter.[47]

Advocacy Tip: Many immigration remedies are not mutually exclusive from one another, and a practitioner may want to consider a combination of them when seeking relief for a client.

1. Continued Presence

Federal law enforcement officials who encounter an immigrant trafficking victim may request the Continued Presence of that immigrant in the United States. While Continued Presence allows the victim to remain lawfully and obtain

---

[42] For example, in U.S. v. Edwards, defendants pled to non-trafficking offenses, but prosecutors successfully argued for restitution under 18 U.S.C. § 1593. Through expert testimony and detailed documentation evidencing total hours worked by the victims, prosecutors were able to secure $369,580.80 in restitution, including liquidated damages and back wages. United States v. Edwards, No. 8:11-CR-00316 (D. Md. 2011). *See* Alexandra F. Levy, Martina E. Vandenburg & Lyric Chen, When Mandatory Restitution Does Not Mean Mandatory: A Failure to Obtain Criminal Restitution in Federal Prosecution of Human Trafficking Cases in the United States 1 (Michelle D. Miller ed., 2014), *available at* http://www.htlegalcenter.org/wp-content/uploads/mandatory.pdf.

[43] Levy, Vandenburg & Chen, *supra* note 42, at 1 (citing 18 U.S.C. § 1593 (b)(3)).

[44] Minimum wage is currently set at $7.25. 29 U.S.C. § 201 (2012).

[45] U.S. Dep't of Labor Wage & Hour Division, Paying Minimum Wage and Overtime to Home Care Workers 24, *available at* https://www.dol.gov/whd/homecare/homecare_guide.pdf.

[46] Levy, Vandenburg & Chen, *supra* note 42, at 3.

[47] For additional information about the immigration remedies available to victims of domestic violence, see *Immigration Law and Domestic Violence in Section Two* of this manual.

employment authorization in the United States temporarily during an investigation or prosecution of the criminal activity, it does not convey any additional immigration benefit.[48] However, the grant of Continued Presence can be useful evidence for other immigration applications, particularly for T Nonimmigrant Status.[49]

2. T Nonimmigrant Status[50]

Immigrant victims of labor trafficking may qualify for T Nonimmigrant Status (commonly referred to as a "T visa"), which provides them with employment authorization for four years, as well as opportunities for reunification with and derivative status for certain family members, access to public assistance, and a path to permanent resident status. And, unlike the application for U Nonimmigrant Status, discussed below, some victims are exempted from the requirement to report their abuse to law enforcement.[51]

Despite the extensive benefits provided by the T visa, it is sadly underutilized: the 5,000 per year cap on T visas has never been met, with the most recent USCIS report showing that just over 1,000 applicants received T visas in 2017.[52] In the hypothetical case studies discussed earlier in this chapter, each of the immigrant victims could potentially qualify for a T visa.

3. U Nonimmigrant Status[53]

U Nonimmigrant Status (U visa) can provide immigration relief to victims of an array of crimes, and while it is most commonly associated with domestic violence offenses, trafficking is also a "U eligible" crime.[54] While there may be some strategic reasons that a practitioner would want to seek a U visa instead of a T visa, it is currently disfavored: applicants face a lengthy wait before receiving

---

[48] 28 C.F.R. § 1100.35 (2017).

[49] 8 C.F.R. §§ 214.11(f), (g)(4)(ii) (2018).

[50] Immigration and Nationality Act § 101(a)(15)(T), 8 U.S.C. § 1101(a)(15)(T) (2012).

[51] Immigration and Nationality Act §§ 101(a)(15)(T)(III)(bb)–(cc), 8 U.S.C. §§ 1101(a)(15)(T)(III)(bb)–(cc) (2012).

[52] *Number of Service-wide Forms by Fiscal Year to-date Quarter and Form Status*, U.S. CITIZENSHIP & IMMIGR. SERVS. (2017), https://www.uscis.gov/sites/default/files/USCIS/Resources/Reports%20 and%20Studies/Immigration%20Forms%20Data/All%20Form%20Types/Quarterly_All_Forms_ FY17Q4.pdf.

[53] Immigration and Nationality Act § 101(a)(15)(U), 8 U.S.C. § 1101(a)(15)(U) (2012).

[54] Immigration and Nationality Act § 101(a)(15)(U)(iii), 8 U.S.C. § 1101(a)(15)(U)(iii) (2012).

a final adjudication on their U visa petition due to a cap of 10,000 approvals per year.[55]

In the hypothetical examples discussed earlier in this chapter, all three victims could potentially qualify for a U visa if they reported their victimization to law enforcement in accordance with procedures set forth in immigration statutes and regulations.[56]

4. VAWA Self-Petition

The Violence Against Women Act (VAWA) provides immigrants who are legally married to a U.S. citizen or lawful permanent resident the opportunity to "self-petition" for legal status.[57] This remedy offers the distinct benefit of providing a direct path to lawful permanent residence, rather than a path through a nonimmigrant visa. However, because it relies on both the immigration status of the abuser as well as the relationship between the abuser and victim, and because it offers more limited waivers of inadmissibility, the VAWA self-petition is available to a smaller pool of potential victims. In the hypothetical examples provided, none of the victims appear to have the requisite marriage to a U.S. citizen or lawful permanent resident. Although child marriage may be legally permissible in some states, in Alea's example, a religious ceremony that was not legally recognized under state law would not give her the necessary status to seek a VAWA self-petition. [58]

---

[55] Despite the current backlog a practitioner may consider seeking a U visa instead of a T visa because the U visa has broader grounds for waivers of inadmissibility. *Practice Advisory: The U Visa Inadmissibility Waiver After L.D.G. v. Holder*, Nat'l Immigr. Just. Ctr. (January 2016), http://immigrantjustice.org/sites/immigrantjustice.org/files/LDG%20v%20%20Holder%20Practice%20Advisory%202016.01.pdf. As of FY 2017, 110,511 principal petitions for U nonimmigrant status are pending. *Number of Form I-918, Petition for U Nonimmigrant Status, by Fiscal Year, Quarter, and Case Status 2009–2017*, U.S. Citizenship & Immigr. Servs. (2017), https://www.uscis.gov/sites/default/files/USCIS/Resources/Reports%20and%20Studies/Immigration%20Forms%20Data/Victims/I918u_visastatistics_fy2017_qtr4.pdf.

[56] U.S. Dep't of Homeland Sec., U Visa Law Enforcement Certification Resource Guide, *available at* https://www.dhs.gov/xlibrary/assets/dhs_u_visa_certification_guide.pdf.

[57] Immigration and Nationality Act § 204(a)(1), 8 USC § 1154(a)(1). For USCIS instructions on eligibility and the application process, see *Battered Spouse, Children & Parents*, U.S. Citizenship & Immigr. Servs., https://www.uscis.gov/humanitarian/battered-spouse-children-parents (last updated Feb. 16, 2016).

[58] The VAWA self-petition statute does allow for a self-petition when the petitioner believes that she was legally married but where the ceremony was invalid because of bigamy. Immigration and Nationality Act §§ 204(a)(1)(A)(iii)(II)(aa)(BB), (B)(ii)(II)(aa)(BB), 8 U.S.C. §§ 1154(a)(1)(A)(iii)(II)(aa)(BB), (B)(ii)(II)(aa)(BB) (2012).

5. Asylum[59]

Asylum, commonly associated with individuals fleeing persecution in their home country, is a remedy that can also provide relief to certain immigrant victims of human trafficking. Where the client's trafficker is a powerful figure associated with the government (such as a diplomat), or where the client's status as a trafficking victim may cause them to face persecution in their country of origin, an attorney may wish to investigate asylum eligibility. However, asylum applicants typically face filing deadlines that should be evaluated by an experienced immigration attorney. Unlike the previous forms of immigration relief, failure to receive asylum affirmatively will result in the applicant being referred into removal proceedings.

To determine whether the three individuals in the hypothetical examples discussed above might qualify for asylum, more information about the ability of the trafficker to retaliate against the victim in the victim's home country would be required, as well as more research about the status of formerly trafficked people in each home country.

6. Special Immigrant Juvenile Status[60]

As the name indicates, Special Immigrant Juvenile Status (SIJS) relief is available to certain undocumented immigrants under the age of 21 who have been abused, neglected, or abandoned by one or more parents. A child who qualifies for SIJS may receive employment authorization and ultimately, permanent resident status. The process involves both a family court petition and immigration filings, and currently, SIJS applicants are experiencing considerable waiting periods before receiving legal status. Advocates should consult carefully with an immigration attorney experienced in SIJS applications, particularly as visas for SIJS applicants from certain countries are experiencing backlogs.[61] In the hypothetical examples above, Alea could qualify for status under a SIJS application; a practitioner may want to obtain more information to determine whether Constance could qualify for SIJS status.

C. Civil Remedies

In addition to mandatory restitution through the criminal provisions of the TVPA, trafficking victims are also eligible for civil damages under the Trafficking Victims Protection Reauthorization Act of 2003.[62] While practitioners should

---

[59] Immigration and Nationality Act § 208, 8 U.S.C. § 1158; 8 C.F.R. § 208 (2018).

[60] Immigration and Nationality Act, § 101(a)(27)(J) (2015), 8 U.S.C. § 1101(a)(27)(J) (2015).

[61] *Update on Special Immigrant Juvenile Status: What is Visa Availability?*, Immigrant Legal Res. Ctr. (Feb. 2017), *available at* https://www.ilrc.org/sites/default/files/resources/update_on_sijs_visa_availability_2.28.17.pdf.

[62] 22 U.S.C. § 7101 (2004); 15 U.S.C. § 1595 (2012).

research the applicable statute of limitations requirements to ensure timely filing, the Department of Justice will typically seek a stay of any civil proceedings while the federal criminal case is litigated.[63]

Upon completion of the prosecution of your client's trafficker, attorneys should pursue civil remedies. Attorneys can explore claims under the TVPA, Fair Labor Standards Act, as well as intentional torts, negligence, and breach of contract claims. The comprehensive guide produced by the Human Trafficking Legal Center and the Freedom Fund contains detailed information on civil litigation of human trafficking cases.[64] A brief overview of some of the most common claims follows.

1. Racketeer Influenced and Corrupt Organizations Act (RICO)

RICO, passed in 1970, was aimed at targeting organized crime. Civil claims using RICO must be based on a pattern of racketeering, which includes peonage, slavery, and trafficking in persons.65 RICO claims offer plaintiffs the benefit of treble damages and reasonable attorney's fees and costs. Defendants in RICO actions are individuals who engage in any of the predicate offenses through an "enterprise" defined as "any individual, partnership, corporation, association or other legal entity, and any union or group of individuals associated in fact although not a legal entity."[66]

2. Fair Labor Standards Act (FLSA)

FLSA, which applies to most occupations and industries including live-in domestic workers, provides compensatory and liquidated damages to trafficked workers who are paid below minimum wage for their services. Immigration status is irrelevant under the statute and has no bearing on the existence of an employment relationship. All eligible workers, whether legally present in the United States or not, are protected under FLSA, and any willful wage and hour violations are actionable.[67] Calculating hours worked to ascertain wages lost is highly specific under FLSA. Rest and meal breaks, sleep time, and other

---

[63] 18 U.S.C. § 1595.

[64] MARTINA E. VANDENBERG, THE HUM. TRAFFICKING LEGAL CTR., ENDING IMPUNITY, SECURING JUSTICE, *available at* http://www.htlegalcenter.org/wp-content/uploads/Ending-impunity-securing-justice.pdf (last visited May 2, 2018).

[65] 18 U.S.C. § 1961(1) (2012); *see also Civil Litigation on Behalf of Victims of Human Trafficking*, SOUTHERN POVERTY L. CTR. (Nov. 30, 2008), https://www.splcenter.org/20081130/civil-litigation-behalf-victims-human-trafficking#PROCEDURE. Other predicate acts that can be used in trafficking cases are: fraud in connection with identification documents, forgery or false use of passport, fraud and misuse of visas, importation for an alien for immoral use or extortion.

[66] 18 U.S.C. § 1961(4).

[67] *Fact Sheet: Retaliation Based on Exercise of Workplace Rights Is Unlawful*, U.S. DEP'T OF LABOR (Dec. 10, 2015), https://www.dol.gov/dol/fact-sheet/immigration/ RetaliationBasedExerciseWorkplaceRightsUnlawful.htm.

free time are considered.[68] Therefore, if the defendant fails to provide detailed records of hours worked, victim-plaintiffs can provide a reasonable estimation corroborated by task lists, children's daily schedules, and other witnesses.[69]

3. Tort Claims

Torts are an additional avenue to explore, but with some urgency, since the statute of limitations for common law torts is generally one year.[70] Tort claims open up the possibility of not only compensatory damages, but also punitive damages. Torts that may apply in trafficking situations include, but are not limited to, intentional infliction of emotional distress, false imprisonment, assault, battery, fraudulent misrepresentation, negligence, and negligent infliction of emotional distress.[71]

Advocacy Tip: The number of civil suits litigated successfully on behalf of trafficking victims is growing, and many cases contain multiple causes of action. In one case, the defendant was convicted of TVPA violations for forced labor and involuntary servitude, violation of the FLSA, breach of contract, fraud, and false imprisonment.[72]

Advocacy Tip: The statute of limitations for civil and criminal causes of action will vary. For example, most torts have a short statute of limitations, whereas the statute of limitations for civil actions under 18 U.S.C. § 1595 is ten years. Advocates should quickly assess the various statutes of limitations that may apply and initiate cases accordingly.

IV. Conclusion

These very broad tips are meant to act as a starting point for attorneys delving into human trafficking litigation. The most critical factor for successful intervention, however, is to always maintain a client-centered approach. These cases are as much about justice for the clients as they are about punishment for the traffickers. While no remedy can erase the harm suffered by victims, a client-centered relationship can rebuild trust not only in others but also in our justice

---

[68] Wage & Hour Division, *Fact Sheet #22: Hours Worked Under the Fair Labor Standards Act (FLSA)*, U.S. DEP'T OF LABOR, https://www.dol.gov/whd/regs/compliance/whdfs22.pdf (last updated July 2008).

[69] "An employer that has violated the recordkeeping provisions of the FLSA cannot complain that the resulting calculation of the number of hours worked or back pay owed is too uncertain or approximate." Ellen C. Kearns, *The Fair Labor Standards Act* (2003), http://apps.americanbar.org/labor/lel-aba-annual/papers/2003/kearns.pdf.

[70] Tort laws vary greatly between jurisdictions so always check the applicable jurisdiction for guidance on statute of limitations.

[71] *Civil Litigation on Behalf of Victims of Human Trafficking*, *supra* note 65.

[72] Lagasan v. Al-Ghasel, 92 F.Supp.3d 445 (E.D. Va. 2015).

system. Increased prevalence of human trafficking cases in our courts will lead to further exposure of the scope of the problem in our communities. Ultimately, greater awareness in the public forum will encourage victims to emerge from the shadows, shed light on their abuse and exploitation, and obtain justice.

APPENDIX

General Resources:

- **Polaris Project**
  - Polaris Project is a national anti-trafficking organization that operates the National Human Trafficking Hotline, provides reports on trafficking matters.

  - https://polarisproject.org

- **National Human Trafficking Resource Center**
  - The National Human Trafficking Resource Center is a national anti-trafficking hotline serving victims and survivors of human trafficking and the anti-trafficking community in the United States. It contains statistical information and range of resources, including information on safety planning and prevention.

  - http://www.traffickingresourcecenter.org

- **Tahirih Justice Center**
  - The Tahirih Justice Center provides information and advocacy tools on forms of gender-based violence, including trafficking and child/forced marriage.

  - http://www.tahirih.org

Resources for Attorneys:

- **Coalition to Abolish Slavery and Trafficking (CAST)**
  - CAST is a Los Angeles-based anti-trafficking organization that provides training and resources for attorneys and advocates.

  - http://www.castla.org

- **The Human Trafficking Legal Center**
  - Contains extensive information on civil remedies for victims of human trafficking, as well as a range of resources and a federal civil trafficking case database for pro bono attorneys.

  - http://www.htlegalcenter.org/

- **The Southern Poverty Law Center**
  - Civil Litigation on Behalf of Victims of Trafficking

  - https://www.splcenter.org/20081130/civil-litigation-behalf-victims-human-trafficking

- LAWYER'S MANUAL ON HUMAN TRAFFICKING: PURSUING JUSTICE FOR VICTIMS (Jill Laurie Goodman & Dorchen A. Leidholdt, eds. 2011), *available at* https://www.nycourts.gov/ip/womeninthecourts/pdfs/lmht.pdf.

  This manual offers a broad overview on trafficking representation, including identification, trauma-informed attorneys, immigration remedies, and the convergence of labor trafficking and domestic violence. A trafficking specific Power and Control Wheel can be found on page 313 of this manual.

- LAURA SIMICH, LUCIA GOYEN, ANDREW POWELL & KAREN BERBERICH, VERA INST. OF JUST., OUT OF THE SHADOWS: A TOOL FOR THE IDENTIFICATION OF VICTIMS OF HUMAN TRAFFICKING (June 2014), https://www.vera.org/publications/out-of-the-shadows-identification-of-victims-of-human-trafficking.

Chapter Thirty:
Crime Victims Compensation

I. Introduction

The Victims of Crime Act (VOCA), passed in 1984 and amended in 1988, established the crime victims compensation fund (hereinafter referred to as "the fund"), as well as the office of Victims of Crime (OVC).[1] VOCA provided states with a framework for setting up and distributing funds to victims of violent crime seeking compensation, different and separate from restitution.[2]

It is best practice to advise your client about the option of filing for crime victims compensation as part of your case planning meeting. It is important to note that a crime victim does not need to have a lawyer to file for crime victims compensation, and may file on their own.

Additionally, familiarity as a practitioner with the crime victim compensation fund may also help the client with safety planning, including relocation services for clients who cannot afford to move and leave an abusive situation. Finally, legal services lawyers often have cases where the criminal defendant, the opposing party in most cases, is also likely to be low income, reducing the chance of receiving restitution in a criminal case, leaving the fund as the only viable option for crime victims to be able to achieve financial compensation for losses suffered.

---

[1] 34 U.S.C. § 201 (2018).

[2] For a deep dive, see generally Doug Rendleman, *Measurement of Restitution: coordinating Restitution with Compensatory Damages and Punitive Damages*, 68 Wash. & Lee L. Rev. 973 (2011).

Definitions of Terms

Defendant: A person accused of committing a crime.

Reparation: Compensation for an injury or wrong—to fix it or make amends.

Restitution (Criminal): Payment by defendant to the victims to compensate victim, in full or part, for financial losses caused by the defendant.

Conviction: A court order or decision that the defendant is guilty of committing an offense beyond reasonable doubt.

Acquittal: A decision or court order that the defendant is not guilty of the crime they were charged with.

Impact Statement: A statement made by a victim of crime in court either in writing or delivered orally to tell the court how a crime affected them, what damages, if any, they suffered, and sometimes even specifics relating to how they want the defendant to be sentenced or punished.

II. Victims Compensation Benefits Overview

Crime victims compensation is a fund of last resort—one that should be investigated as an option when every other avenue (including support or compensation from the defendant, the criminal justice system, and/or any sort of insurance) has been pursued and exhausted.[3] If an abuser is not apprehended, a criminal case is dismissed, or the defendant is acquitted, crime victims compensation funds are key to helping restore losses, both tangible and intangible.[4]

Based on your state's crime victim compensation laws, a victim of crime can receive compensation not just for visible physical injuries, damage to property, and/or actual eligible expenses resulting directly from the crime, but also costs involved with recovery from trauma, safety planning, and lost income. The programs are designed to allow for the victims to identify the gaps that require covering, and not just provide fixed sets of items that the compensation program are allowed to cover. For example, most programs cover mental health services that are associated with recovering from being victimized, which is especially

---

[3] "It's also important to remember that crime victim compensation programs are payers of last resort, which means that other insurance benefits or government programs, like Medicaid or Social Security, must be accessed first, and these collateral resources will be deducted from any victim compensation award." *Id.*

[4] The origin of the funds for crime victims dates back to 1975, with the purpose of helping victims on the road to recovery, when the criminal justice system is unable to help clients. Nat'l Ctr. for Victims of Crime, Landmarks in Victims' Rights & Services (2013), https://victimsofcrime.org/docs/ncvrw2013/2013ncvrw_5_landmarks.pdf?sfvrsn=0.

applicable to people who have suffered from crimes like domestic violence, sexual assault, trafficking, and stalking.[5]

Advocacy Tip: Your client may not have discussed with you the possibility of seeking mental health services, which means you will have to proactively counsel them about both availability of services and the means to pay for them, if your client chooses to receive these services.

Attorneys representing victims should have, and be able to provide, information that will help their clients access mental health care, medical accommodations, and economic security, among other things. While each state has its own policies regarding what can and cannot be covered, there are some common items that are covered regardless of specific state laws. Specific states have enacted additional benefits, and practitioners must familiarize themselves the specific benefits available in their jurisdictions to best plan with their clients.[6]

Generally, most state compensation programs will provide funds for the following:

- Medical and medical related expenses, including dental services and care;

- Mental health treatment;

- Funeral and burial expenses;

- Lost income or wages (check your state laws for limits);

- Cost of replacing medically necessary devices like eyeglasses, wheelchairs, and any retrofitting required to accommodate medical needs resulting from the crime (for example, a ramp and wheelchair for a disability resulting from the crime);

- Relocation for safety, which includes, in some jurisdictions, paying for alarms or security systems and/or lock changes.[7]

---

[5] "Crime victim compensation programs will generally pay for … counseling costs." *Benefits*, Nat'l Ctr. for Victims of Crime, http://victimsofcrime.org/help-for-crime-victims/get-help-bulletins-for-crime-victims/crime-victim-compensation (last visited Apr. 30, 2018).

[6] *Crime Victim Compensation*, RAINN, https://www.rainn.org/articles/crime-victim-compensation (last visited Apr. 30, 2018).

[7] *Victim Compensation*, OFF. FOR VICTIMS OF CRIME, https://www.ovc.gov/pubs/crimevictimsfundfs/intro.html#VictimComp (last visited Apr. 30, 2018); *see, e.g.*, CAL. GOV'T CODE § 13957 (providing for relocation, lock change, and alarm systems).

Where Does the Money Come From?

The fund is made up of criminal fines, forfeited bail bonds, penalties, and special assessments collected by the federal criminal justice system.[8] The fund is managed at the federal level and then disbursed locally to state compensation programs—which are either boards or commissions who are eligible to receive the monies from the federal fund.[9]

At the state level, the monies are disbursed based on state laws that govern the board or commission in each state.[10] Apart from directly granting monetary compensation to eligible victims, the funds can also be allocated to victim service agencies, to legal service agencies, as well as to community-based organizations providing direct services like shelter, transportation, court accompaniment, crisis interventions, etc.

Existing federal rules require that states match federal dollars up to 20 percent from their local fund, which obtains funds through methods similar to the collection of federal funds.[11] Each state decides during its legislative budget sessions each year on the exact amount of restitution, fines, and fees that are to be deposited into the state funds. The federal dollars, along with local state dollars together, are available as one state fund for clients to apply to. Each applicant applies to the state fund, and not to any federal body.

Generally, the rules for compensation allow victims to rebuild their lives, but not to replace items or repair damages.[12] For example, if a victim had their car vandalized during a robbery, they cannot seek payment to repair the damage to the car. However, if the vehicle needs to be retrofitted to accommodate a victim who became disabled as a result of a crime, the victim can seek compensation from the fund for the necessary modifications. This stems from the idea that the fund is meant to help a victim get back on track after a crime takes place, not replace items that are lost because of the crime.

---

[8] *Primary Sources of Revenue,* Off. For Victims Of Crime, https://www.ovc.gov/pubs/crimevictimsfundfs/intro.html#PrimarySources (last visited Apr. 30, 2018).

[9] *Fund Support for Victim Services,* Off. for Victims of Crime, https://www.ovc.gov/pubs/crimevictimsfundfs/intro.html#FundSupport (last visited Apr. 30, 2018).

[10] For a list of commissions and boards, see Nat'l Ass'n of Crime Victim Compensation Boards, http://www.nacvcb.org/index.asp?sid=6 (last visited Apr. 30, 2018).

[11] 28 C.F.R. §§ 94.101–94.122.

[12] "Reimbursing crime victims for expenses incurred as a result of a crime such as . . . replacement of stolen property … is not allowed." *Final Program Guidelines*, Off. for Victims of Crime, https://www.ovc.gov/voca/vaguide.htm (last visited Apr. 30, 2018).

Advocacy Tip: Domestic violence victims can usually seek repair costs if the crime they suffered was not a property crime.[13] For your client to be able to replace damaged items, you will have to determine if the damage was a result of a property crime, in which case the client is ineligible for replacement or repair, or a result of being a victim of domestic violence, in which case there is a possibility to seek reimbursement.

A. Lost Wages

Each state has its own unique rules regarding the replacement of lost wages. The general rule is that the victim must apply with specific information about the days they missed work, connected directly to the crime, for example, if a victim needed mental health services before being able to return to work, or had to take care of court proceedings, including filing for an order of protection, or had to stay with a minor victim of crime.[14]

It is important to remember that your client will have to provide proof of income earned and/or employment information to claim compensation. If your client does not want to disclose to their employer that they were a victim of crime, especially if they are reluctant to disclose experiencing domestic or sexual violence, then they should reconsider applying for this relief because most funds require substantiation for lost wages and pay from the victim's employer.[15]

B. Special Consideration: Funds from Bail Paid by the Victim

Bail is a deposit that is made by some criminal defendants to guarantee that they will return to court to complete their criminal proceedings as an alternative to waiting in jail while the case is pending. Bail is akin to paying a security deposit, in the sense that when the criminal case has ended, the person who paid the amount can get the deposit back. However, if the defendant does not appear to follow-up court dates, the bail money is forfeited, which means that the court/county where the case is filed gets to keep the money. However, some states allow for restitution monies, if any, to be distributed from the bail money if there is a conviction entered.[16] Again, this occurs only if the case has concluded.

---

[13] Repairs may be allowable if the repairs "contribute to maintaining a healthy and/or safe environment for crime victims." *Id.*

[14] *See, e.g.,* Cal. Code Regs. tit. 2, § 649.32 (2018) (providing for replacement of up to 30 days of lost wages for the legal guardian or parent of a crime victim who misses work to attend to a minor victim of crime who was hospitalized or who dies).

[15] *See, e.g., Claim Application & Instructions,* N.Y. State Off. of Victim Servs. (Sept. 2015), https://ovs.ny.gov/sites/default/files/general-form/ovs-claim-application-9-2015.pdf. ("If you do not want us to contact your employer, you cannot ask to be reimbursed for Lost Wages.").

[16] Nat'l Ctr. for Victims of Crime, Use of Bail/Bonds Funds for Restitution (2011), https://victimsofcrime.org/docs/restitution-toolkit/b4_bail-bond-funds-for-restitution.pdf?sfvrsn=2.

If a victim paid for the abuser's bail, you must counsel the victim to seek restitution during the criminal proceedings, which is where a court can order return of the bail monies to the victim. If a victim paid for the abuser's bail, which is then forfeited/kept by the court or county, losing that money is akin to loss of property, which victims' compensation funds do not usually cover. However, if your client can connect the payment of the bail to the domestic violence, some states allow for the return of the amount paid.

C. Other Remedies for Victims

Advocates must counsel their clients on the different types of remedies available to them based on the nature of proceedings that they are involved in. The remedies available vary depending on the nature of the proceeding, whether criminal, family, or in civil court.

1. Restitution

Most crime victims who file a report with law enforcement and then cooperate with law enforcement can have the opportunity to seek restitution from the defendant. Restitution covers loss of tangible property, actual medical bills, replacement of stolen monies or items, etc.[17]

2. Civil Lawsuits

Some crime victims file civil lawsuits for damages, over and above the amount they receive from restitution, or if they do not receive any restitution monies (i.e., the case was dismissed or the defendant was acquitted), which helps them recover monetary sums for losses they suffered.[18]

III. Victims Compensation Eligibility Overview

Most program funds provide compensation related to the physical, emotional, financial, and safety needs of a victim of violent crime. As a practitioner working with victims, you should familiarize yourself with the eligibility requirements in your state, both in terms of coverage but also in terms of proof required for eligibility to apply for funds. This may be accomplished by visiting your state's victims compensation program website.[19] The board or commission in your state may also be willing to provide you and your office training on compensation.

---

[17] *See, e.g.,* 18 U.S.C. § 3663A. For more information on restitution, see *Restitution Law for Victims of Crime*, NOLO, https://www.nolo.com/legal-encyclopedia/restitution-law-victims-crime.html (last visited Apr. 30, 2018).

[18] For information on filing a civil suit against an abuser, see *Tort Law and Domestic Violence* in Section Three of this manual.

[19] Nat'l Ass'n of Crime Victim Compensation Boards, *supra* note 10.

A. Cooperation with Law Enforcement

The key to being able to claim compensation from your state's victim compensation fund is that under most circumstances, the victim must cooperate in reporting a crime to law enforcement. State law varies on when the reporting must occur or whether reporting must occur at all.

For example, California Government Code § 13956 provides for eligibility for compensation to victims of domestic violence, sexual assault, and/or trafficking even if the crime was unreported.[20] Additionally, some states do not require reporting if the crime involved a child victim.[21]

Eligibility for victims compensation funds is not tied directly to criminal proceedings. Most states have specific rules, but there is no requirement a criminal proceeding must result from a victim's report to be eligible for compensation.[22] Also, crime victims applying for compensation need to demonstrate cooperation with reporting the crime (unless exempt from reporting), but this cooperation can be demonstrated in other ways aside from participating in criminal proceedings.

One important consideration for all practitioners is advising their clients that reporting the crime, and cooperating in the investigation of the crime, may be conditions of receiving compensation. Attorneys should recognize, however, that the client may not feel safe reporting the crime or cooperating with law enforcement. Attorneys should advise their clients that while reporting is required for most crimes, there is no requirement for a criminal proceeding to have resulted from the reporting for a victim of crime to apply for compensation. Another important aspect is that there does not even have to be an arrest for the purposes of filing for compensation. In fact, the reason the fund was created was primarily to act as a fund of last resort when victims have suffered as a result of a crime, but are unable to receive compensatory assistance from the criminal justice system.

---

[20] *See, e.g.*, CAL. GOV'T CODE § 13956(b)(2) ("An application for a claim based on domestic violence shall not be denied solely because a police report was not made by the victim.").

[21] "Most state compensation program require that victims: report the crime promptly to the police (the reporting time varies between states and *nearly all states have good exceptions for child victims*, incapacitated victims, and other special circumstances." *Eligibility*, NAT'L CTR. FOR VICTIMS OF CRIME (emphasis added), http://victimsofcrime.org/help-for-crime-victims/get-help-bulletins-for-crime-victims/crime-victim-compensation (last visited Apr. 30, 2018); *see, e.g.*, Tex. Code Crim. Proc. Ann, art. 56.46 (West 2017).

[22] "Generally, the victim must cooperate with police and prosecutors in any investigation and prosecution, but compensation eligibility does not depend on apprehension or conviction of an offender." *Eligibility Requirements*, NAT'L ASS'N OF CRIME VICTIMS COMPENSATION BOARDS, http://www.nacvcb.org/index.asp?bid=6 (last visited Apr. 30, 2018).

Advocacy Tip: Keep in mind that cooperating with law enforcement for the sake of obtaining compensation will disqualify most applicants in most states.[23] The purpose is not to report for the sake of reporting, but rather to encourage crime victims to seek help, which is the core of why victims' compensation programs exist.

B. Substantiation of Costs

For most medical expenses, applicants will have to provide substantiation of costs incurred, or anticipated costs. Applicants will also need to substantiate that those medical costs will not be covered through other means, such as insurance, restitution, or other safety net programs. If your client must take measures to secure her/his safety after reporting the crime, like a lock change, or in some states, even relocation, there are funds that reimburse moving expenses but many have limits. Also, rules can differ if your client has applied for compensation in the past, based on how recently the application was filed, as well as the type of crime suffered.

One important distinction is that the fund does not cover or pay for pain and suffering from a violent crime. However, this is different from obtaining compensation for therapy or mental health treatment that result from a crime of domestic or sexual violence. The fund compensates for emotional and psychological effects of suffering a crime, so long as your client is claiming compensation for the effects of suffering a crime, and the claims relate directly to the crime committed (e.g., counseling for victims of sexual assault; relocation for safety reasons for a victim of violent crime, etc.).

Crime victims can seek compensation for a crime they suffered where the perpetrator of the crime is an intimate partner or a former/current spouse. There is no prohibition from household members seeking compensation from the fund. However, most funds require that the applicant/victim agree that the fund can recover any amounts paid out to the applicant from the perpetrator. For parties who are married and live in a state that follows community property laws for married couples, practitioners will have to advise clients on whether the community funds could be impacted if the state fund sues the perpetrator for reimbursements for amounts paid.[24] Practitioners can look to their state's restitution laws for guidance on what funds are tapped for reimbursements. Typically, the rules provide for perpetrators to first use their separate property to pay restitution, keeping community property immune from being depleted.

---

[23] *See generally* MARLENE A. YOUNG, THE ROLE OF VICTIM COMPENSAITON IN REBUILDING VICTIMS' LIVES (2009), http://www.iovahelp.org/About/MarleneAYoung/RoleOfVictComp.pdf.

[24] The nine community property states are Alaska, Arizona, California, Idaho, Louisiana, Nevada, New Mexico, Texas, Washington, and Wisconsin. *Marriage & Property Ownership: Who Owns What?*, NOLO, https://www.nolo.com/legal-encyclopedia/marriage-property-ownership-who-owns-what-29841.html (last visited Apr. 30, 2018).

Additionally, if your client files a civil lawsuit against the perpetrator and seeks funds at the same time, most state funds require applicants to reimburse the fund if they get a payout from civil lawsuits.

IV. Applying for Victims Compensation Funds

For practitioners with clients who do not have the ability to navigate the system or are hearing for the first time about the relief available under the fund, it is best to begin by connecting your client to the Office of Victims of Crime at your local District Attorney's office. Some states have detailed information on their websites about the state's victim compensation fund that attorneys can direct their clients to visit.

If your client has limited English proficiency, you might be able to find applications in a language other than English to better advise your client. However, it is best to advise these clients in person rather than send them to a website, because the breadth of information may be overwhelming.

Practitioners working with undocumented victims must clarify that there is no requirement for survivor to have legal status in order to be eligible for compensation from the fund. However, it is extremely important to verify how the payment will be made, because your client may not have a bank account. Another important item to remember is that your undocumented client may not have a social security number. In this case, you will have to discuss safety planning with your client when the client submits their application without an SSN.[25] Finally, the ability of your client to report a crime may be compromised if they are undocumented, so you might have to first counsel them about the benefits of reporting, the possibilities of immigration relief by reporting, as well as eligibility for compensation if they report.

Like child support and some federal benefits, IRS rules provide that compensation received from the fund is not taxable income.[26] When applying for eligibility for programs that are income-based, check with the program whether non-taxable income such as crime victims compensation is considered to be earned income.

When helping clients file for the fund, a critical element is collecting supporting documents that your client needs to provide to the fund for a successful claim. Remember that all documents that are confidential and covered by disclosure laws apply, so find out if your client can file supporting documents under

---

[25] For more information on safety planning with and representing immigrant victims of domestic violence, see *Immigration Law and Domestic Violence* in Section Two of this manual.

[26] *Taxes: Do Victims Have to Report Compensation as Income*, CRIME VICTIM COMPENSATION Q., 2012, at 5, http://www.nacvcb.org/NACVCB/files/ccLibraryFiles/Filename/000000000151/newsletter.2012-2final.pdf.

confidential cover sheets. Bear in mind that there could be a lag time between your client deciding about filing and collecting all the documents necessary. You must make sure that the delay in collecting supporting documents does not impact the timeline for your client's eligibility to apply for the fund. Just as you can supplement court filings, most funds allow applicants to supplement their filings with additional supporting documents.

Again, the fund only pays as a last resort, and if your client is seeking advice on applying for funds for a crime that has already been adjudicated, the question to ask your client is whether they sought restitution at the time of adjudication. The fund can only be tapped for payments once all other avenues, including collecting restitution money, have been exhausted. It would be prudent for practitioners with clients seeking advice on older cases to retrieve criminal proceeding documents and gain understanding of the trajectory of the case before sending the client to submit an application for compensation.

V. Conclusion

Applicants can file for victims compensation on their own without a lawyer. However, if you have a client who could be eligible to claim compensation, it is best practice to include advice about their eligibility, and availability and access to the funds as part of your case plan.

Crime victims compensation is an area that all attorneys should familiarize themselves with. The money a victim obtains from the funds could potentially allow a victim to seek additional help from other avenues, and play a major role in her or his ability to recover from violence.

APPENDIX

Resources:

- **National Association of Crime Victims Compensation Boards**
  - ○ NAT'L ASS'N OF CRIME VICTIM COMPENSATION BOARDS, http://www.nacvcb.org/index.asp?sid=1.

- **The National Center for Victims of Crime**
  - ○ NAT'L CTR. FOR VICTIMS OF CRIME, http://victimsofcrime.org/home.

- **Office for Victims of Crime**
  - ○ *Help for Crime Victims: Toll-Free and Online Hotlines*, OFF. FOR VICTIMS OF CRIME, https://www.ovc.gov/help/tollfree.html.

  - ○ *Online Directory of Crime Victim Services*, OFF. FOR VICTIMS OF CRIME, https://ovc.ncjrs.gov/findvictimservices.

  - ○ *U.S. Resource Map of Crime Victim Services & Information*, OFF. FOR VICTIMS OF CRIME, https://www.ovc.gov/map.html.

State and U.S. Territorial Bar Associations

Alabama State Bar
P.O. Box 671
Montgomery, AL 36101
(334) 269-1515
(334) 261-6310 Fax
http://www.alabar.org/

Alaska Bar Association
P.O. Box 100279
Anchorage, AK 99510-0279
(907) 272-7469
(907) 272-2932 Fax
http://www.alaskabar.org/

State Bar of Arizona
4201 N. 24th St.
Ste. 100
Phoenix, AZ 85016-6266
(602) 252-4804
(602) 271-4930 Fax
http://www.azbar.org/

Arkansas Bar Association*
2224 Cottondale Ln.
Little Rock, AR 72202
(501) 375-4606
(501) 375-4901
http://www.arkbar.com/

State Bar of California
180 Howard St.
San Francisco, CA 94105
(415) 538-2000
(415) 538-2212 Fax
http://www.calbar.ca.gov

Colorado Bar Association*
1900 Grant St., Ste. 900
Denver, CO 80203
(303) 860-1115
(303) 894-0821 Fax
http://www.cobar.org/

Connecticut Bar Association*
30 Bank St.
New Britain, CT 06050-0350
(860) 223-4400
(860) 223-4488 Fax
http://www.ctbar.org/

Delaware State Bar Association*
405 North King St.
Ste. 100
Wilmington, DE 19801
(302) 658-5279
(302) 658-5212 Fax
http://www.dsba.org/

Bar Association of the District of Columbia*
1016 16th St. NW
Washington, DC 20036
(202) 223-6600
(202) 293-3388 Fax
http://www.badc.org/

District of Columbia Bar
1101 K St., NW
Ste. 200
Washington, DC 20005-5937
(202) 737-4700
(202) 626-3471 Fax
http://www.dcbar.org/

The Florida Bar
651 E. Jefferson St.
Tallahassee, FL 32399-2300
(850) 561-5600
(850) 561-9429 Fax
http://www.flabar.org/

*Denotes voluntary bar association

Please note that all information listed here is accurate as of Spring 2017

State Bar of Georgia
104 Marietta St. NW
Ste. 100
Atlanta, GA 30303
(404) 527-8700
(404) 527-8717 Fax
http://www.gabar.org/

Guam Bar Association
120 West O'Brian Dr.
Hagatna, Guam 96910
(671) 475-3396
(671) 475-3400 Fax
http://www.guambar.org/

Hawaii State Bar Association
Alakea Corporate Tower
1100 Alakea St.
Ste. 1000
Honolulu, HI 96813
(808) 537-1868
(808) 521-7936 Fax
http://www.hsba.org/

Idaho State Bar
P.O. Box 895
Boise, ID 83701
(208) 334-4500
(208) 334-4515 Fax
http://www.isb.idaho.gov

Illinois State Bar Association*
Illinois Bar Center
424 S. Second Street
Springfield, IL 62701
(217) 525-1760
(217) 525-0712 Fax
http://www.isba.org/

Indiana State Bar Association*
One Indiana Square
Ste. 530
Indianapolis, IN 46204-2199
(317) 639-5465
(317) 266-2588 Fax
http://www.inbar.org/

Iowa State Bar Association*
625 East Court Ave.
Des Moines, IA 50309-1939
(515) 243-3179
(515) 243-2511 Fax
http://www.iowabar.org

Kansas Bar Association*
1200 SW Harrison
Topeka, KS 66612-1806
(785) 234-5696
(785) 234-3813 Fax
http://www.ksbar.org/

Kentucky Bar Association
514 W. Main St.
Frankfort, KY 40601-1883
(502) 564-3795
(502) 564-3225 Fax
http://www.kybar.org/

Louisiana State Bar Association
601 St. Charles Ave.
New Orleans, LA 70130-3404
(504) 566-1600
(504) 566-0930 Fax
http://www.lsba.org/

Maine State Bar Association*
P.O. Box 788
Augusta, ME 04332-0788
(207) 622-7523
(207) 623-0083 Fax
http://www.mainebar.org/

*Denotes voluntary bar association
Please note that all information listed here is accurate as of Spring 2017

Maryland State Bar Association*
520 W. Fayette St.
Baltimore, MD 21201
(410) 685-7878
(410) 685-1016 Fax
http://www.msba.org/

Massachusetts Bar Association*
20 West St.
Boston, MA 02111-1204
(617) 338-0500
(617) 542-7947 Fax
http://www.massbar.org/

State Bar of Michigan
306 Townsend St.
Lansing, MI 48933-2083
(517) 346-6300
(517) 482-6248 Fax
http://www.michbar.org/

Minnesota State Bar Association*
600 Nicollet Mall
Ste. 380
Minneapolis, MN 55402
(612) 333-1183
(612) 333-4927 Fax
http://www.mnbar.org/

The Mississippi Bar
643 North State St.
Jackson, MS 39202
(601) 948-4471
(601) 355-8635 Fax
http://www.msbar.org/

The Missouri Bar
326 Monroe St.
P.O. Box 119
Jefferson City, MO 65102
(573) 635-4128
(573) 635-2811 Fax
http://www.mobar.org/

State Bar of Montana
7 W. 6th Ave., Ste. 2B
P.O. Box 577
Helena, MT 59624
(406) 442-7660
(406) 442-7763 Fax
http://www.montanabar.org/

Nebraska State Bar Association
635 S. 14th St.
Ste. 200
Lincoln, NE 68508
(402) 475-7091
(402) 475-7098 Fax
http://www.nebar.com/

State Bar of Nevada
3100 W. Charleston Blvd.
Ste. 100
Las Vegas, NV 89102
(702) 382-2200
(702) 385-2878 Fax
http://www.nvbar.org/

New Hampshire Bar Association
2 Pillsbury St.
Ste. 300
Concord, NH 03301
(603) 224-6942
(603) 224-2910 Fax
http://www.nhbar.org/

New Jersey State Bar Association*
One Constitution Center
New Brunswick, NJ 08901-1520
(732) 249-5000
(732) 249-2815 Fax
http://www.njsba.com/

*Denotes voluntary bar association
Please note that all information listed here is accurate as of Spring 2017

State Bar of New Mexico
5121 Masthead St. NE
Albuquerque, NM 87109
(505) 797-6000
(505) 797-6098 Fax
http://www.nmbar.org/

New York State Bar Association*
One Elk St.
Albany, NY 12207
(518) 463-3200
(518) 463-5993 Fax
http://www.nysba.org/

North Carolina Bar Association*
8000 Weston Pkwy.
Cary, NC 27513
(919) 677-0561
(919) 677-0761 Fax
http://www.ncbar.org

North Carolina State Bar
217 East Edenton St.
Raleigh, NC 27601
(919) 828-4620
(919) 821-9165 Fax
http://www.ncbar.gov

State Bar Association of North Dakota
1661 Capitol Way
Ste. 104LL
Bismarck, ND 58501
(701) 255-1404
(701) 224-1621 Fax
http://www.sband.org/

Ohio State Bar Association*
1700 Lake Shore Dr.
Columbus, OH 43204
(614) 487-2050
(614) 487-1008 Fax
http://www.ohiobar.org/

Oklahoma Bar Association
1901 North Lincoln Blvd.
Oklahoma City, OK 73152
(405) 416-7000
(405) 416-7001 Fax
http://www.okbar.org/

Oregon State Bar
16037 SW Upper Boones Ferry Rd.
Tigard, OR 97224
(503) 620-0222
(503) 684-1366 Fax
http://www.osbar.org/

Pennsylvania State Bar*
100 South St.
Harrisburg, PA 17101
(717) 238-6715
(717) 238-1204 Fax
http://www.pabar.org/

Puerto Rico Bar Association
Ave. Ponce de Leon 808
Miramar, PR 00902
(787) 721-3358
(787) 725-0330 Fax
http://www.capr.org/

Rhode Island Bar Association
41 Sharpe Dr.
Cranston, RI 02920
(401) 421-5740
(401) 421-2703 Fax
http://www.ribar.com/

South Carolina Bar
950 Taylor St.
Columbia, SC 29201
(803) 799-6653
(803) 799-4118 Fax
http://www.scbar.org/

*Denotes voluntary bar association

Please note that all information listed here is accurate as of Spring 2017

State Bar of South Dakota
222 E. Capitol Ave. #3
Pierre, SD 57501
(605) 224-7554
(605) 224-0282 Fax
http://www.statebarofsouthdakota.com/

Tennessee Bar Association*
221 4th Ave. N.
Ste. 400
Nashville, TN 37219-2198
(615) 383-7421
(615) 297-8058 Fax
http://www.tba.org/

State Bar of Texas
1414 Colorado St.
Austin, TX 78701
(512) 427-1463
(512) 427-4103 Fax
http://www.texasbar.com/

Utah State Bar
645 S. 200 East
Salt Lake City, UT 84111
(801) 531-9077
(801) 531-0660 Fax
http://www.utahbar.org/

Vermont Bar Association*
P.O. Box 100
Montpelier, VT 05601-0100
(802) 223-2020
(802) 223-1573 Fax
http://www.vtbar.org/

The Virginia Bar Association
701 E. Franklin St.
Ste. 1120
Richmond, VA 23219
(804) 644-0041
(804) 644-0052 Fax
http://www.vba.org/

Virginia State Bar
1111 E. Main St.
Ste. 700
Richmond, VA 23219-0026
(804) 775-0500
(804) 775-0501 Fax
http://www.vsb.org/

Virgin Islands Bar Association2155
King Cross St.
Ste. 2
Christiansted, VI 00822
(340) 778-7497
(340) 773-5060 Fax
www.vibar.org

Washington State Bar Association
1325 Fourth Ave.
Ste. 600
Seattle, WA 98101-2539
(206) 443-9722
(206) 727-8316 Fax
http://www.wsba.org/

The West Virginia Bar Association*
P.O. Box 2162
Huntington, WV 25722
(304) 522-2652
(304) 522-2795 Fax
http://www.wvbarassociation.org/

West Virginia State Bar
2000 Deitrick Blvd.
Charleston, WV 25311-1231
(304) 533-7220
(304) 558-2467 Fax
http://www.wvbar.org/

State Bar of Wisconsin
5302 Eastpark Blvd.
Madison, WI 53718-2101
(608) 257-3838
(608) 257-5502 Fax
http://www.wisbar.org/

*Denotes voluntary bar association
Please note that all information listed here is accurate as of Spring 2017

Wyoming State Bar Association
4124 Laramie St.
Cheyenne, WY 82003
(307) 632-9061
(307) 632-3737 Fax
http://www.wyomingbar.org

*Denotes voluntary bar association
Please note that all information listed here is accurate as of Spring 2017

State and U.S. Territory Domestic Violence Coalitions

Alabama Coalition Against
Domestic Violence
P.O. Box 4762
Montgomery, AL 36101
(334) 832-4842
(800) 650-6522

Alaska Network on Domestic Violence
and Sexual Assault
130 Seward St., Ste. 214
Juneau, AK 99801
(907) 586-3650

Arizona Coalition Against
Domestic Violence
2800 N. Central Ave., Ste. 1570
Phoenix, AZ 85004
(602) 279-2900
(602) 279-7270 TTY
(800) 782-6400

Arkansas Coalition Against
Domestic Violence
1401 West Capitol Ave., Ste. 170
Little Rock, AR 72201
(501) 907-5612
(800) 269-4668

California Partnership to End
Domestic Violence
1107 9th St., Ste. 910
Sacramento, CA 95814
(916) 422-2111
(800) 524-4765

Statewide California Coalition for
Battered Women
P.O. Box 19005
Long Beach, CA 90807-9005
(562) 981-1202
(562) 981-1202 TTY
(888) 722-2952

Colorado Coalition Against
Domestic Violence
P.O. Box 40328
Denver, CO 80204
(303) 831-9632
(888) 778-7091

Connecticut Coalition Against
Domestic Violence
912 Silas Deane Hwy., Lower Level
Wethersfield, CT 06109
(860) 282-7899
(800) 281-1481

DC Coalition Against Domestic Violence
5 Thomas Cir. NW
Washington, DC 20005
(202) 299-1181

Delaware Coalition Against Domestic
Violence
100 W. 10th St., Ste. 903
Wilmington, DE 19801
(302) 658-2958

Florida Coalition Against
Domestic Violence
425 Office Plaza Dr.
Tallahassee, FL 32301
(850) 425-2749

Georgia Coalition Against
Domestic Violence
114 New St., Ste. B
Decatur, GA 30030
(404) 209-0280

Hawaii State Coalition Against
Domestic Violence
1164 Bishop St., Ste. 1609
Honolulu, HI 96813
(808) 832-9316

Please note that all information listed here is accurate as of Spring 2017

Idaho Coalition Against Sexual
and Domestic Violence
Linen Building
1402 W. Grive St.
Boise, ID 83702
(208) 384-0419

Illinois Coalition Against
Domestic Violence
806 South College St.
Springfield, IL 62704
(217) 789-2830

Indiana Coalition Against
Domestic Violence
1915 West 18th St., Ste. B
Indianapolis, IN 46202
(317) 917-3685
(800) 538-3393

Iowa Coalition Against
Domestic Violence
6200 Aurora Ave., Ste. 405E
Urbandale, IA 50322
(515) 244-8028

Kansas Coalition Against Sexual
and Domestic Violence
634 SW Harrison
Topeka, KS 66603
(785) 232-9784

Kentucky Coalition Against
Domestic Violence
111 Darby Shire Cir.
Frankfort, KY 40601
(502) 209-5382

Louisiana Coalition Against
Domestic Violence
P.O. Box 77308
Baton Rouge, LA 70879-7308
(225) 752-1296

Maine Coalition to End
Domestic Violence
One Weston Ct., Box #2
Augusta, ME 04330
(207) 430-8334

Maryland Network Against
Domestic Violence
4601 Presidents Dr., Ste. 370
Lanham, MD 20706
(301) 429-3601-4574
(800) 634-3577

Massachusetts Coalition Against Sexual
Assault and Domestic Violence/Jane
Doe, Inc.
14 Beacon St., Ste. 507
Boston, MA 02108
(617) 248-0922
(617) 263-2200 TTY

Michigan Coalition to End Domestic
and Sexual Violence
3893 Okemos Rd., Ste. B2
Okemos, MI 48864
(517) 347-7000
(517) 381-8470 TTY

Minnesota Coalition for
Battered Women
60 East Plato Blvd., Ste. 130
St. Paul, MN 55107
(651) 646-6177
(651) 646-6177 TTY
(800) 289-6177

Mississippi Coalition Against
Domestic Violence
P.O. Box 4703
Jackson, MS 39296-4703
(601) 981-9196
(800) 898-3234

Please note that all information listed here is accurate as of Spring 2017

Missouri Coalition Against Domestic
& Sexual Violence
217 Oscar Dr., Ste. A
Jefferson City, MO 65101
(573) 634-4161

Montana Coalition Against Domestic
and Sexual Violence
P.O. Box 818
Helena, MT 59624
(406) 443-7794
(888) 404-7794

Nebraska Domestic Violence
Sexual Assault Coalition
245 South 84th St., Ste. 200
Lincoln, NE 68510
(402) 476-6256

Nevada Network Against
Domestic Violence
250 Rock Blvd., Ste. 116
Reno, NV 89502
(775) 828-1115

New Hampshire Coalition Against
Domestic and Sexual Violence
P.O. Box 353
Concord, NH 03302
(603) 224-8893

New Jersey Coalition to End
Domestic Violence
1670 Whitehorse-Hamilton Square Rd.
Trenton, NJ 08690
(609) 584-8107

New Mexico Coalition Against
Domestic Violence
1000 Cordova Pl. #52
Santa Fe, NM 87505
(505) 246-9240

New York State Coalition Against
Domestic Violence
119 Washington Ave.
Albany, NY 12210
(518) 482-5465

North Carolina Coalition Against
Domestic Violence
3710 University Dr., Ste. 140
Durham, NC 27707
(919) 956-9124
(888) 997-9124

CAWS North Dakota
525 N. 4th St.
Bismark, ND 58501
(701) 255-6240

Ohio Domestic Violence Network
1855 E. Dublin-Granville
Columbus, OH 43229
(800) 934-9840

ACTION OHIO Coalition for
Battered Women
5900 Roche Dr., Ste. 445
Columbus, OH 43229
(614) 825-0551
(888) 622-9315

Oklahoma Coalition Against Domestic
Violence and Sexual Assault
3815 N. Santa Fe
Oklahoma City, OK 73118
(405) 524-0700

Oregon Coalition Against Domestic
and Sexual Violence
9570 SW Barbur Blvd., Ste. 214
Portland, OR 97219
(503) 230-1951

Please note that all information listed here is accurate as of Spring 2017

Pennsylvania Coalition Against
Domestic Violence
3605 Vartan Way, Ste. 101
Harrisburg, PA 17110
(717) 545-6400
(800) 932-4632
(800) 553-2508 TTY

Comision Para Los Asuntos
De La Mujer
Apartado 193008
San Juan, Puerto Rico 00919-3008
(787) 281-7579

Rhode Island Coalition Against
Domestic Violence
422 Post Rd.
Warwick, RI 02888-1524
(401) 467-9940

South Carolina Coalition Against
Domestic Violence and Sexual Assault
P.O. Box 7776
Columbia, SC 29202
(803) 256-2900

South Dakota Coalition Ending
Domestic and Sexual Violence
P.O. Box 141
Pierre, SD 57501
(605) 945-0869
(800) 572-9196

Tennessee Coalition to End Domestic
and Sexual Violence
2 International Plaza Dr., Ste. 425
Nashville, TN 37217
(615) 386-9406
(800) 289-9018

Texas Council on Family Violence
P.O. Box 163865
Austin, TX 78716
(512) 794-1133

Utah Domestic Violence Council
124 South 400 East, Ste. 300
Salt Lake City, UT 84111
(801) 521-5544

Vermont Network Against Domestic
Violence and Sexual Assault
P.O. Box 405
Montpelier, VT 05601
(802) 223-1302
(802) 223-1115 TTY

Virginia Sexual & Domestic Violence
Action Alliance
5008 Monument Ave., Ste. A
Richmond, VA 23230
(804) 377-0335

Washington State Coalition Against
Domestic Violence
500 Union St., Ste. 200
Seattle, WA 98101
(206) 389-2515

West Virginia Coalition Against
Domestic Violence
5004 Elk River Rd. South
Elkview, WV 25071
(304) 965-3552
(304) 965-3552 TTY

End Domestic Abuse Wisconsin:
The Wisconsin Coalition Against
Domestic Violence
1245 East Washington Ave., Ste. 150
Madison, WI 53703
(608) 255-0539
(608) 255-3560 TTY

Wyoming Coalition Against Domestic
Violence and Sexual Assault
710 Garfield St., Ste. 218, P.O. Box 236
Laramie, WY 82073
(307) 755-5481

Please note that all information listed here is accurate as of Spring 2017

Family Resource Center, Inc.,
Virgin Islands
2317 Commandant Gade
Charlotte Amalie, St. Thomas 00802
(340) 776-3966

Women's Coalition of St. Croix,
Virgin Islands
P.O. Box 222734
Christiansted, VI 00822-2734
(340) 773-9272

Please note that all information listed here is accurate as of Spring 2017

Biographical Information and Acknowledgments

The American Bar Association Commission on Domestic & Sexual Violence thanks all the authors for their contributions (see biographies below); and also thanks Bonnie Carlson, Rebecca Henry, Vivian Huelgo, Anya Lynn-Alesker, and Jane Zhi for their editorial guidance; Sara Wee, Director of Research and Programs with the Center for Survivor Agency and Justice, for her valuable input; Alicia Aiken, Michelle Duarte, Kristen Galles, Rosie Hidalgo, Sally Kinoshita, Atiya Mosley, Kate Mogulescu, Karlo Ng, Stacey Platt, Beth Posner, Lauren Ruvo, Kat Schaal, Komal Shah, Erika Sussman, and Erica Wood for their assistance with this publication; and Robert Horowitz for his guidance and support. Special thanks to Mark Schickman, Chair of the Commission on Domestic & Sexual Violence, for his dedication and leadership.

AUTHORS

Alicia Aiken has been the Director of Confidentiality Institute, a national organization empowering people to protect privacy for crime victims, since 2011. Ms. Aiken specializes in delivering targeted, entertaining, and interactive training. In 2014, Ms. Aiken and Confidentiality Institute launched the Protecting Privacy to Enhance Safety Subpoena Defense Pro Bono Project for the American Bar Association. In 2015, Ms. Aiken & Practising Law Institute's ground-breaking web course "Effective Communication with the Legal Services Client" was honored for Outstanding Achievement in Technology by the Association for Continuing Legal Education. In 2016, she became the inaugural Faculty Fellow for PLI's Interactive Learning Center.

Ms. Aiken graduated from the University of Michigan (A.B. 1992, J.D. 1995), and then spent 15 years with LAF (Legal Assistance Foundation), the largest legal services program in Illinois, where she represented victims of domestic violence and people living in poverty in a wide variety of complex legal matters. While at LAF, Ms. Aiken rose to the position of Director of Training, Pro Bono and Client Support Services, and served on the Executive Committee of the 13 million dollar non-profit organization.

She has also been privileged to teach for and consult with the University of Michigan, DePaul College of Law, Loyola University Chicago School of Law, the University of Oregon, the American Bar Association, the Office on Violence Against Women, National Council of Juvenile and Family Court Judges, Allstate Foundation, Break the Cycle, the National Network to End Domestic Violence, and state-based domestic and sexual violence organizations across the U.S.

Sara Block is the Domestic Violence Project Attorney at the Family Defense Center. Sara received her J.D., *magna cum laude*, from Loyola University Chicago School of Law in 2007, where she was a Child Law Fellow and the Features Editor of the *Children's Legal Rights Journal*. Sara was a Skadden Fellow at LAF (Legal Assistance Foundation) with a fellowship focusing on the intersection of domestic violence and child welfare. As a three-time Skadden Flom Incubator Grant recipient, Sara has been advocating to improve the way the Illinois Department of Children and Family Services intervenes into the lives of families experiencing domestic violence, and co-founded the Domestic Violence Child Welfare Resource Coalition.

Sara is an Adjunct Professor in the Masters of Jurisprudence in Child Law program at Loyola University Chicago School of Law, in which she teaches Child Welfare Law and Policy, and Juvenile Justice Law Policy. In 2014, Sara was awarded the Family Defense Center's Major Litigation Award for her involvement in *Julie Q. v. DCFS,* and the Jewish United Fund's "36 Under 36" award. Sara also received the 2017 Outstanding Partner Award from the Chicago Metropolitan Battered Women's Network.

Sara is currently the President of the Board of Directors of SHALVA, a domestic violence agency serving the Jewish community in the Chicagoland area. Sara received her Bachelor of Arts degree with honors in American Studies from Northwestern University. Sara has two daughters and feels honored to be their mother.

Sarah Bolling Mancini is Of Counsel to the National Consumer Law Center (NCLC), focusing on foreclosures and mortgage lending, and works as a Senior Attorney in the Home Defense Program of Atlanta Legal Aid. She represents homeowners in bankruptcy cases as well as mortgage litigating in state, federal, and bankruptcy courts.

Sarah received her B.A. in public policy from Princeton University and her J.D. from Harvard Law School. She joined the Home Defense Program of the

Atlanta Legal Aid Society as a Skadden Fellow in 2007. In 2010, Sarah moved to Durham, North Carolina, where she worked at the Land Loss Prevention Project representing farmers and landowners facing debt, foreclosure, and real property issues. Beginning in 2011, Sarah served as a judicial clerk for the Honorable Amy Totenberg of the U.S. District Court, Northern District of Georgia. She returned to Atlanta Legal Aid's Home Defense Program in October 2012 at the conclusion of her judicial clerkship.

Sarah complements her individual client representation with media outreach and policy advocacy. In her role with NCLC, she trains consumer attorneys around the country, comments on proposed legislation and regulations, and writes chapters in several of NCLC's publications, including *Mortgage Lending, Foreclosure and Mortgage Servicing, Truth in Lending*, and *Fair Credit Reporting*. Sarah is also a co-author of *Georgia Real Estate Finance and Foreclosure* and a contributing author of *Collier on Bankruptcy*. She is a frequent presenter on foreclosure and bankruptcy issues at NCLC's Consumer Rights Litigation Conference and Summer Mortgage Conference. Sarah was selected to participate in the Next Generation Bankruptcy Judges program of the National Conference of Bankruptcy Judges in 2013. She became a member of the Board of Directors of the Southeastern Bankruptcy Law Institute in 2017.

Cassandra Brulotte is a Domestic Violence Prosecutor with the Third Judicial District Attorney's Office in New Mexico, where she has implemented an evidence-based prosecution policy for crimes of domestic violence.

Cassandra's career representing victims of domestic violence began as a staff attorney for Alaska Legal Services Corporation when a woman walked into her office to ask for help because the ex-boyfriend that had shot her in the chest in front of their son was seeking custody. From that day on, Cassandra focused on representing victims of domestic violence and sexual assault in family, civil, and administrative matters throughout south-central Alaska. She eventually moved to New Mexico, becoming a Managing Attorney for New Mexico Legal Aid where she coordinated the legal helpline for victims of domestic violence, stalking, and sexual assault.

Cassandra has presented at CLEs in both Alaska and New Mexico on the unique issues facing LGBTQ victims, and has regularly conducted legal education seminars for community groups on a variety of domestic violence topics.

Hilary Chadwick is an Equal Justice Works Fellow at the National Immigrant Justice Center's (NIJC) Counter-Trafficking Project. Hilary leads an initiative to increase identification and protection of immigrant survivors of human trafficking. She represents detained and non-detained survivors in their immigration cases, and trains *pro bono* attorneys to represent survivors in their T visa applications. Hilary educates social, medical, and faith-based service providers to recognize indicators of human trafficking and ensure earlier access to legal counsel.

Prior to joining NIJC, Hilary worked with survivors of gender-based violence at the Tahirih Justice Center, and contributed to federal sex trafficking prosecutions as an intern at the United States Attorney's Office for the Northern District of Illinois. Prior to law school, Hilary was the *Pro Bono* Coordinator at Simpson Thacher & Bartlett, where she worked with the firm's *Pro Bono* Counsel to manage over 500 *pro bono* cases across 11 offices worldwide. She received the Above & Beyond Pro Bono Achievement Award for her contribution to Simpson Thacher's *pro bono* team, which secured legal status for a sex trafficking survivor, and represented her throughout two criminal investigations of an international trafficking ring.

Hilary became involved in anti-trafficking advocacy in 2010, while working for the Coalition Against Trafficking in Women in Mexico City. Since then, Hilary has served trafficking survivors in New York City, Washington, D.C., Boston and Chicago. Hilary holds a J.D. from the Boston University School of Law, where she received the Warren S. Gilford Humanity and Law Prize.

Alicia Clark received her J.D. from Vermont Law School in 2007 and has been a legal services attorney with New Mexico Legal Aid, Inc., ever since. Her specialty is public benefits. She loves representing indigent clients and humbly suggests that anyone unhappy in his or her current job should seriously consider becoming a civil legal services attorney.

Prior to law school, Alicia worked in the medical fields, first as a Certified Nurse's Aide and later as a Certified Veterinary Technician. She holds a B.S. in Sociology from the University of Oregon and an A.A.S. in Veterinary Technology from Portland Community College.

Alicia lives in Albuquerque, New Mexico with her wonderful dog, Penelope, and her equally wonderful boyfriend, Ray. Her favorite things include animals (of all kinds), nature, skateboarding, and learning. She wishes to dedicate her contribution to this publication to her mother, Elaine Phelas Taylor.

John Clune joined Hutchinson Black and Cook LLC in 2013, continuing his practice in civil rights litigation and plaintiff's personal injury.

John started his career as a criminal prosecutor in the mountains of Colorado and served as Chief Deputy District Attorney for Eagle County. While in the District Attorney's office, John served as trial counsel for the landmark skier homicide conviction of *People v. Nathan Hall*. After leaving the prosecutors' office, John spent several years in a litigation based practice primarily focused on felony criminal defense and family law matters.

In recent years John has focused a substantial amount of his practice on representation of students and families on campus rape/Title IX matters. John has additionally represented clients in a number of high-profile cases including the sexual assault civil matter against Kobe Bryant, the civil lawsuit against Major League Baseball player Johan Santana, and several actions against schools for Title IX violations. John's cases have been featured on many national news outlets including 60 Minutes, Good Morning America, the Wall Street Journal, ESPN, and the New York Times and he is a regular speaker on navigating media coverage of high profile litigation.

In 2009, John co-founded and served as the first legal director for the Rocky Mountain Victim Law Center (RMvlc), a *pro bono* non-profit organization dedicated to the enforcement of the rights of crime victims and currently serves on the Board of RMvlc.

Lori Cohen is Director of the Anti-Trafficking Initiative at Sanctuary for Families, Center for Battered Women's Legal Services in New York, where she represents immigrant and domestic victims of human trafficking and conducts training sessions for the judiciary, law enforcement, legal and health care professionals, social service providers, and community based organizations. Ms. Cohen has lectured on trafficking and other forms of gender-based violence across the U.S. and internationally. Her work on behalf of trafficking victims has been reported widely in the media. Additionally, Ms. Cohen has served as a lecturer at Yale University's Jackson Institute for Global Affairs and at the University of Michigan Law School. Ms. Cohen is a contributing author to "The Lawyers' Manual on Human Trafficking" and "The Lawyers' Manual on Domestic Violence," both published by the New York State Judicial Committee on Women in the Courts.

Juanita Davis is a Program Manager for the National Clearinghouse on Abuse in Later Life (NCALL), a project of End Domestic Abuse Wisconsin (End Abuse). In her role at NCALL, she provides nationwide leadership, technical assistance, and training to professionals across the country on various topics related to abuse in later life. She leads NCALL's work on the Office for Victims of Crime's National Resource Center on Reaching Underserved Victims. She also assists in the development of various training resources, materials, and publications related to abuse in later life.

In her past work, Davis represented survivors of domestic violence in family law cases and coordinated leadership development opportunities for survivors and advocates of color in Wisconsin. She has also assisted domestic violence programs enhance their outreach and services to marginalized populations.

She received her law degree from the University of Wisconsin Law School. Davis has a Master of Arts in Special Education from San Francisco State University.

Sarah Deer (Muscogee (Creek) Nation) has worked to end violence against women for over 25 years and was named a MacArthur Fellow in 2014. Her scholarship focuses on the intersection of federal Indian law and victims' rights. Professor Deer is a co-author of four textbooks on tribal law. Her latest book is

The Beginning and End of Rape: Confronting Sexual Violence in Native America, which has received several awards. Her work on violence against Native women has received national recognition from the American Bar Association and the Department of Justice. She currently teaches at the University of Kansas. Professor Deer is also the Chief Justice for the Prairie Island Indian Community Court of Appeals.

Radha Desai is an associate at Coffinas & Lusthaus, P.C., a boutique firm in Brooklyn dedicated to all aspects of family law. Before joining private practice, Ms. Desai was a judicial law clerk for the Hon. Mark A. Baber at the Hudson County Courthouse in Jersey City, New Jersey focusing predominantly on domestic violence cases. Her passion for fighting injustice led her to addressing human trafficking from judicial, policy and direct advocacy positions: first with the Hon. Toko Serita at the Queens Human Trafficking Intervention Courts assisting with and observing the implementation of the nation's first statewide court initiative designed specifically to address human trafficking; then with Human Rights First's Anti-Trafficking Campaign publishing several online articles on human trafficking; and lastly, with Sanctuary for Families assisting survivors obtain legal immigration status.

An immigrant from Zambia, Ms. Desai earned her law degree from the City University of New York in 2016 where she served as a staff member on the Executive Articles editing team of CUNY Law Review. She received her B.A. from Fordham University in 2011.

Margaret Drew teaches the Human Rights at Home Clinic (HRAH) at the University of Massachusetts School of Law. Students represent survivors of intimate partner abuse in a variety of needs including family law, credit matters, appeals, and other matters. HRAH students also work for several national organizations that work on behalf of survivors of intimate partner abuse. Prior to entering academia full-time in 2005, Professor Drew practiced law in Massachusetts for 25 years. She represented clients in the District, Probate and Family and Appellate Courts of Massachusetts. Professor Drew's practice focused on family, probate and residential real estate. She handled numerous appeals, primarily in domestic violence matters.

Professor Drew is a member of several bar associations including the American Bar Association, having served with its Commission of Domestic & Sexual Violence since its founding. Professor Drew is a past chair of the Commission. She is a member and vice-chair of the ABA AIDS Coordinating Committee. Professor Drew is a member and past chair of the *amicus* committee of the National Association of Women Lawyers (NAWL) and is NAWL's liaison to the Commission.

Prior to coming to UMass Law, Professor Drew taught domestic violence clinics at the University of Alabama Law School, Northeastern University School of Law, and the University of Cincinnati College of Law. Professor Drew is co-founder and editor of Human Rights at Home Blog.

Nancy Durborow is the former State Coalition Technical Assistance Specialist with the National Network to End Domestic Violence (NNEDV). Prior to her work with NNEDV, she worked for 23 years as the Health Projects Manager for the Pennsylvania Coalition Against Domestic Violence. In that capacity, she created, developed, and oversaw the Coalition's medical advocacy projects (collaborative partnerships between domestic violence programs and health care systems) that provided direct services to battered women in more than 85 Pennsylvania hospitals and other health care settings, as well as extensive training to health care professionals. She also worked at the state and national level to stop insurance discrimination against victims of domestic violence. She has been a consultant for Futures Without Violence for more than 20 years. She holds a Master's Degree in Counseling from Shippensburg University.

Cecelia Friedman Levin serves as Senior Policy Counsel at ASISTA Immigration Assistance, where she focuses on policy, technical assistance, and trainings related to immigration remedies for survivors of crime.

Before joining ASISTA in 2012, Cecelia worked as a supervising attorney at Women Empowered Against Violence in Washington, DC, representing survivors of domestic violence and sexual assault in civil and immigration cases. Cecelia also acted as the domestic violence staff attorney at the National Law Center for Homelessness and Poverty where she worked on federal and local housing protections for survivors of domestic violence. She has also provided legal representation in a variety of defensive and affirmative immigration applications as a staff attorney at Ayuda in Washington, DC. Prior to law school, Cecelia was a Fulbright Research Scholar in Santiago, Chile assessing community responses to domestic violence. Cecelia received her B.A. in International Studies and Women & Gender studies from American University, and her J.D. from American University-Washington College of Law.

Terry Fromson is the Managing Attorney of the Women's Law Project (WLP), a Pennsylvania-based legal advocacy organization whose mission is to create a more just and equitable society by advancing the rights and status of women and girls. Since joining the WLP in 1994, Terry has brought high-impact litigation and pursued significant policy initiatives at the local, state, and national levels on a wide variety of issues. Terry's priorities include eliminating inequities in women's economic status, improving the criminal justice response to sexual and domestic violence, and enforcing legal obligations of educational institutions to address sex discrimination and sexual harassment.

Terry has had extensive litigation experience seeking redress for sex discrimination under Title VII, Title IX, and the Pennsylvania Equal Rights Amendment. Notable public policy achievements include leading a national effort to stop insurance companies from discriminating against victims of domestic violence, co-leading an innovative collaboration to improve police response to sexual assault in Philadelphia, which led to the FBI's expansion of the definition of rape, participating in a collaboration to implement the Family Violence Option in Pennsylvania, and helping change Pennsylvania law to provide victims of domestic violence a safe and confidential process to change their names.

Terry is a principal author on several WLP publications relating to elimination of institutional bias, insurance discrimination against victims of domestic violence, and access to justice for *pro se* litigants in Philadelphia Family Court. Terry received her law degree from NYU School of Law.

Lauren Groth joined Hutchinson Black and Cook LLC in 2014 after completing a clerkship with the Honorable Richard A. Paez on the United States Court of Appeals for the Ninth Circuit. Prior to the clerkship, Lauren worked for an international law firm in Washington, D.C., where she was involved in civil litigation and white collar matters, as well as advising clients on issues related to the Foreign Corrupt Practices Act.

Lauren's current practice focuses on general civil litigation matters, including Title IX litigation and immigration matters.

Before attending law school, Lauren lived and worked in Durban, South Africa where she obtained her master's degree in International Development Studies and worked as a consultant to the South African Government and international NGOs on a variety of policy matters.

Drake Hagner, formerly a Senior Staff Attorney at the Legal Aid Society of the District of Columbia, represented low-income workers in unemployment insurance matters, as well as recipients of state and federal public benefits. She also engaged in policy advocacy and court and agency reform efforts to improve the District's unemployment insurance system.

Drake initially joined Legal Aid in September 2011, as an Equal Justice Works Fellow providing direct representation and advocacy to low-wage workers who had been wrongfully denied unemployment insurance. Along with her colleagues at Legal Aid, Drake represented Ms. E.C., a victim of domestic violence, in her evidentiary hearing and appeal to the D.C. Court of Appeals, in *E.C. v. RCM of Washington, Inc.*, 92 A.3d 305 (D.C. 2014), one of the first cases to interpret a domestic violence provision in an unemployment insurance statute.

Drake graduated with a B.A. from Vassar College. She received her J.D., *cum laude*, from Georgetown University Law Center, where she served as Editor-in-Chief of the Georgetown Journal of Gender and the Law. Upon graduation, Drake clerked for Magistrate Judge Alan Kay of the U.S. District Court for the District of

Columbia. Drake has contributed to two treatises on unemployment insurance law, including the DC Bar Practice Manual and the Employment Justice Center's Workers Rights Manual.

Lisa James is Director of Health at Futures Without Violence. As part of a National Health Initiative on Domestic Violence, Ms. James has collaborated with health care providers, domestic violence experts, and health policy makers in over 25 states across the U.S. to develop statewide health care responses to domestic and sexual violence and human trafficking through training, health policy reform, and public education. She collaborates with national medical and nursing associations to enact effective health policy and programmatic health care responses to abuse and was the recipient of the American Medical Association's Citation for Distinguished Service for her efforts to train health care providers on violence and abuse.

During her over 20 years with Futures without Violence, Ms. James has also worked with the international program, collaborating with leaders from non-governmental and health care organizations in Russia, Mexico, India, and China to build the capacity of health systems, providers, and community members to identify and help victims in reproductive health settings.

Diane Johnston is a staff attorney with the Legal Aid Society's Domestic Violence Consumer Advocacy Project, a new initiative she spearheaded as a Kirkland & Ellis Fellow. Her practice focuses on unwinding the consequences of financial abuse for domestic violence survivors through consumer debt and personal bankruptcy representation, community education, and systemic advocacy. Diane is a 2015 graduate of NYU School of Law, where she was a Root-Tilden-Kern scholar.

The Legal Aid Society is the oldest and largest legal services provider for low-income families and individuals in the United States. Annually, the Society handles some 300,000 individual cases and legal matters for low-income New Yorkers with civil, criminal, and juvenile rights issues. Through a network of 16 neighborhood and courthouse-based offices in all five boroughs and 23 city-wide and special projects, the Society's Civil Practice provides direct legal assistance to low-income New Yorkers, helping them to obtain or maintain the basic necessities of life—housing, healthcare, food, public benefits, safety, employment, and means of self-sufficiency.

As part of its Civil Practice, the Legal Aid Society's Domestic Violence Project provides legal representation to hundreds of domestic violence survivors each year on a range of family law matters as well as immigration and economic justice issues. Through its Consumer Law Project, the Legal Aid Society also represents defendants in consumer debt and related actions in New York City's civil, supreme and federal courts, including cases brought by landlords seeking rental arrears. Diane's practice was started in recognition of the intersection of these two areas and the unique financial issues domestic violence survivors face, particularly in the aftermath of financial abuse.

Angie Junck is the Supervising Attorney at the Immigrant Legal Resource Center (ILRC) based in San Francisco. With more than a decade of nonprofit experience, Angie manages several of ILRC's program areas, including immigration consequences of crime, immigration enforcement, and immigrant youth.

Angie has co-authored a number of publications including *Defending Immigrants in the Ninth Circuit: The Impact of Crimes under California and Other State Laws (ILRC); Remedies and Strategies for Permanent Resident Clients (ILRC); Motions to Suppress: Protecting the Constitutional Rights of Immigrants in Removal Proceedings (ILRC); Special Immigrant Juvenile Status and Other Immigration Options for Children & Youth (ILRC); Immigration Benchbook for Juvenile and Family Court Judges (ILRC);* and *Guide to Juvenile Detention Reform: Noncitizen Youth in the Juvenile Justice System (Juvenile Detention Alternatives Initiative, Annie E. Casey Foundation).*

Prior to joining the ILRC, Angie worked on post-conviction relief for immigrants at the Law Office of Norton Tooby and advocated on behalf of incarcerated survivors of domestic violence as the co-coordinator of Free Battered Women and a member of the Habeas Project. Angie is a Commissioner with the American Bar Association's (ABA) Immigration Commission and is the co-chair of the Immigration Committee of the ABA's Criminal Justice Section. She is also an advisory board member and attorney consultant with the California Coalition for Women Prisoners.

Larisa Kofman is the Director of the National Alliance for Safe Housing (NASH), a project of the District Alliance for Safe Housing. NASH provides programs and communities with the tools, strategies and support necessary to improve coordination between domestic and sexual violence services and homeless and housing providers, so that survivors and their children can avoid homelessness as the only means of living free from abuse.

Ms. Kofman has over twenty years of experience in the domestic violence and public policy fields. Her legal and policy work spans the national, state and local level. She has worked on issues including: domestic violence, housing, employment, disability, civil rights, criminal justice, custody, child welfare, budget and appropriations. Ms. Kofman led legislative advocacy efforts resulting in the passage of several pieces of legislation that enhanced the legal rights of underserved populations in the District of Columbia. She spearheaded a campaign resulting in the passage of an innovative law providing eviction and discrimination protections for victims of domestic violence. She served on the Georgetown Journal on Gender and the Law, Georgetown University Law Center, Board of Advisors. She also served on the Board of Directors for several local nonprofit organizations. She currently also serves as an adjunct Associate Professor at the University of Maryland University College. Ms. Kofman holds a law degree from the University of Maryland School of Law and a Master of Arts in Teaching from the University of Southern California.

Debbie Lee has been with Futures Without Violence, formerly, Family Violence Prevention Fund (FVPF), since 1980. She is currently a Senior Vice President. She led the Start Strong: Building Healthy Teen Relationships initiative (funded by the Robert Wood Johnson Foundation), an initiative funding 11 comprehensive community-based models of prevention that can lead to decreases in relationship violence and increases in positive, protective relationship skills over time, with a focus on 11–14 year olds.

She directed the U.S. Dept. of Health and Human Services' funded National Health Resource Center on Domestic Violence (HRC) from 1993 to 2008, which seeks to strengthen the health care response to domestic violence. She led partnerships in 27 states, working with public health departments and domestic violence programs, as well as an initiative with 25 health centers in Tribal communities across the country. Over the years, she has worked in state and federal policy and issues impacting immigrant and refugee women.

Ms. Lee was appointed to the Department of Justice & Office on Violence Against Women National Advisory Council on Violence Against Women serving from 2010-2012. She was a founding board member of the San Francisco-based Asian Women's Shelter, the Asian and Pacific Island Institute on Gender-Based Violence, the National Network on Behalf of Immigrant and Refugee Women, two California state coalitions on domestic violence, and The Women's Foundation. Ms. Lee was the recipient of the first annual California Office of Women's Health Helen Rodriguez-Trias 2002 Award for Excellence in Community-Based Women's Health Leadership. She is currently a selected fellow of *MOVE to END VIOLENCE*, a program of the NoVo Foundation.

David Martin is a Senior Deputy Prosecutor for the King County Prosecuting Attorney's Office (KCPAO) in Seattle, Washington. He serves as supervisor of the KCPAO Domestic Violence (DV) Unit and co-manager of the Regional Domestic Violence Firearms Enforcement Unit. Most of his 20 year career as a prosecutor has been spent in the Domestic Violence Unit. He serves on several DV task forces and work groups, is co-chair of the national Association of Prosecuting Attorney's Domestic Violence Committee, and is a current liaison and former commissioner for the American Bar Association Commission on Domestic & Sexual Violence.

David has authored several of Washington's new criminal DV laws including removal of the marital rape exception, stalking reform, batterer treatment, felony DV sentencing reform, strangulation, and repeat DV assault. He is coauthor of Washington's statewide DV prosecution manual, articles on strangulation, and recantation. David has served on the board of multiple community based domestic violence groups including New Beginnings and LifeWire. He provides training on DV locally, nationally, and internationally.

David is the recipient of the Prosecuting Attorney's Outstanding Trial Advocacy award, LifeWire Norm Maleng award, Consejo Founder's Award, and the Coalition Ending Gender-Based Violence System Change award.

Amanda Norejko is the Director of the Matrimonial and Economic Justice Project and Victoria J. Mastrobuono Economic Justice Fellow at the Center for Battered Women's Legal Services at Sanctuary for Families. She specializes in representation of domestic violence and trafficking survivors. Ms. Norejko supervises a team of staff and *pro bono* attorneys in family law, matrimonial, housing, and public benefits matters. She engages in legislative and policy advocacy aimed at combating violence against women and promoting women's economic empowerment on the local, state, national, and international levels.

She serves on the Board of Directors of the New York State Coalition Against Domestic Violence and Vice President of the New York Women's Bar Association. She is a Co-Chair of the Domestic Violence Committee of the Women's Bar Association of the State of New York (WBASNY) and has been an active participant in the New York State Anti-Trafficking Coalition, the New York City Bar Association, and the Lawyers Committee Against Domestic Violence, which awarded her with the *In the Trenches Award* in 2014. In 2016, City & State recognized Ms. Norejko's work with its *Above & Beyond* award Honoring Women of Public and Civic Mind. She is a 2001 graduate of New York University School of Law, which presented her with an Alumni Association award in 2011.

Protima Pandey is the Director for Office of Women's Policy in Santa Clara County, California. As part of the County Executive, her office works to bring a gender lens to policy decision-making, building a pipeline to leadership, and creating equity in governance. Prior to that, she was the Managing Attorney and Regional Counsel for Immigration at Bay Area Legal Aid (BayLegal), beginning her career there as a staff attorney litigating on family law and immigration cases for survivors of domestic violence, as well as allied legal relief in areas of public benefits, housing preservation, and economic justice. Most recently she won a precedent setting case in California, *Kumar v. Kumar*, a complex immigration and family law cross-over case. She also led the firm-wide post-graduate fellowship program to shepherd and develop fellowship proposals through the national selection process.

She is also one of 17 lawyers nationwide appointed as a Commissioner to the American Bar Association Commission on Domestic & Sexual Violence to work on issues impacting delivery of legal services to survivors, where she is also a litigation skills faculty. She also serves as faculty for Practising Law Institute in San Francisco, training on issues relating to housing rights for immigrants and representation of domestic violence survivors in family courts as well as on understanding personal bias, working with diverse populations, and on domestic violence awareness.

Prior to joining BayLegal, Protima was the Public Policy specialist for California Partnership to End Domestic Violence in Sacramento, California where she worked on legislation and policy advocacy on behalf of agencies serving survivors and their families.

Maya Raghu is Director of Workplace Equality and Senior Counsel at the National Women's Law Center in Washington, D.C. She leads federal and state policy development and advocacy, litigation, education, and stakeholder engagement focused on women's economic security and employment opportunity, including equal pay, pregnancy discrimination, and sexual harassment.

Prior to joining the Center, she was a senior attorney at Futures Without Violence and a senior staff attorney at Legal Momentum (formerly NOW Legal Defense and Education Fund), focusing on economic security, gender discrimination, and gender-based violence, with an emphasis on immigrant and low-income women. Her work encompassed litigation, legislative and policy advocacy, public education and training, multi-sector initiatives, and cross-movement collaboration.

Maya was also previously an associate at Simpson Thacher & Bartlett LLP and a law clerk to the Honorable Vanessa D. Gilmore of the Southern District of Texas. She is a graduate of Trinity University and Georgetown University Law Center. She has been quoted in a number of media outlets, including PBS Newshour and *The New York Times.*

Robin Runge is the Senior Gender Specialist in the Equality and Inclusion Department at the Solidarity Center and a professorial lecturer in law at The George Washington University Law School where she has taught Public Interest Lawyering and Domestic Violence Law since 2004, including in the clinical education program. Robin is one of the pioneers in the field of gender-based violence and the workplace. She is an expert on the development of policies and laws domestically and internationally to address the impact of domestic violence, sexual violence, dating violence and stalking on women and the workplace. Since 2003, she has consulted with non-profit organizations domestically and internationally to prevent and address gender-based violence including development of programs and policies to address domestic violence, sexual harassment, and sexual violence in the workplace and on campus.

Prior to joining the staff of the Solidarity Center, Robin was the Director of Enforcement Policy and Procedures in the Wage and Hour Division and a Senior Policy Advisor in the Civil Rights Center at the U.S. Department of Labor. From 2009–2013, Robin was an assistant professor at the University of North

Dakota School of Law where she taught in the Housing and Employment Law Clinic and Domestic Violence Law. In 2012–2013, she lived in Beijing, China as a Fulbright Senior Research Scholar studying the legal system response to domestic violence in China. From 2003 to 2009, Robin directed the American Bar Association Commission on Domestic Violence (now known as the American Bar Association Commission on Domestic & Sexual Violence), where she led efforts to expand civil legal assistance for victims of domestic violence nationally. Previously, she was Deputy Director and Coordinator of the Program on Women's Employment Rights (POWER) at the D.C. Employment Justice Center. Upon graduation from law school, Robin was awarded an Equal Justice Works Fellowship and created the Domestic Violence and Employment Project at the Legal Aid Society of San Francisco, one of the first programs in the country devoted exclusively to advocating for the employment rights of domestic violence victims. She is a graduate of The George Washington University Law School and Wellesley College.

Erika Sussman is the Founder and Executive Director of the Center for Survivor Agency and Justice (CSAJ), a national organization that promotes advocacy approaches that remove systemic barriers, enhance organizational responses, and improve professional practices to meet the self-defined needs of domestic and sexual violence survivors. During her tenure, CSAJ has launched the Consumer Rights for Domestic and Sexual Assault Survivors Initiative, the Safe Economic Security Atlas Project, the Legal Impact for Racial and Economic Equity of Survivors Project, and engaged in other work focused on survivor-centered advocacy and economic security for survivors living at the margins.

Prior to her work with CSAJ, Ms. Sussman served as the Senior Attorney of the Legal Assistance Providers' Technical Outreach Project, a national project of the Pennsylvania Coalition Against Domestic Violence, which offered technical assistance to civil attorneys and advocates funded by the Office on Violence Against Women. For several years, Ms. Sussman served as an adjunct professor at Cornell Law School, where she taught a seminar course on Law and Violence Against Women. She also taught law students and litigated in Georgetown University Law Center's Domestic Violence Clinic. As a litigation associate at Swidler Berlin Sherreff Friedman, LLP, she provided *pro bono* representation to domestic violence survivors and co-counseled, with the ACLU, a class action lawsuit against the State of Maryland for the practice of racial profiling by law enforcement. Immediately following law school, she served as a Law Clerk to Justice Gregory Hobbs of the Colorado Supreme Court.

Ms. Sussman earned her J.D. from Cornell Law School and her LL.M. in Advocacy from Georgetown University Law Center. She has published numerous articles and chapters and served as faculty for various academic and practitioner workshops related to violence against women, with a particular emphasis on survivor-centered advocacy and economic justice.

Tia Katrina Taruc-Myers founded the Alipato Project, the first and only nonprofit organization to represent resisters of domestic violence in tort actions against their batterers. Tia has presented on the topic of DV torts at Yale Law School's RebLaw Conference, Berkeley Law's Domestic Violence Law Seminar, and the San Quentin State Prison's Restorative Justice Roundtable Symposium. Her work in DV Tort Law has been featured in the East Bay Express, Ozy Magazine, Feministing, and others. When she is not suing batterers, she plays chess at Alchemy Collective Cafe, reads radical picture books to a preschool class, and co-directs a campaign to bring a People's Budget to Oakland.

Karen Merrill Tjapkes is a supervising attorney and Director of Strategic Litigation at Legal Aid of Western Michigan (LAWM) in Grand Rapids. Her practice is concentrated primarily on consumer and bankruptcy law, housing law and mortgage litigation, as well as supervising the Homeownership Preservation Project and the West Michigan Low Income Taxpayer Clinic at LAWM. She is also an Expert Advisor with the Center for Survivor Agency and Justice concerning consumer law rights for domestic violence survivors.

In addition, Ms. Tjapkes sits on the Steering Council and is past chair of the Grand Rapids Area Coalition to End Homelessness. She is a current member and past chair of the Consumer Law Section Council of the State Bar of Michigan, sits on the State Bar of Michigan's Steering Committee for Innovation and Implementation, and has presented on housing, bankruptcy, and mortgage lending issues for many audiences including the Michigan Foreclosure Prevention Project, the Michigan Poverty Law Program, the Debtor's Bar of West Michigan, the Michigan Conference on Affordable Housing, and the National Consumer Law Center's Consumer Rights Litigation Conference. Ms. Tjapkes has taught Consumer Law as an adjunct professor and is a frequent guest lecturer in the clinical program at Cooley Law School in Grand Rapids. She earned her B.A., with honors, from James Madison College at Michigan State University in 1997, and her J.D., *cum laude*, from Loyola University Chicago School of Law in 2000.

Rob Valente is a consultant to the National Coalition Against Domestic Violence and the Battered Women's Justice Project, with specialized interests in firearms, federal domestic violence laws and interventions, and tribal issues relating to domestic violence. Ms. Valente has served as the Chief Officer for Government Affairs for the National Domestic Violence Hotline, working on their policy, data, and evaluation projects. She works with the National Task Force to End Sexual and Domestic Violence to advocate for federal laws and funding to protect survivors of sexual and domestic violence, serving as one of the coordinators of legislative work to reauthorize the Violence Against Women Act in 2013 and in 2018. Ms. Valente has served as a consultant on civil legal issues regarding domestic violence for various organizations, including the National Network to End Domestic Violence, the Alaska Native Women's Coalition, the National Congress of American Indians, and the Domestic Violence Resource Network. She also served as Attorney Advisor to the U.S. Department of Justice Office on Violence Against Women and as the founding Director of the American Bar Association Commission on Domestic Violence (now known as the American Bar Association Commission on Domestic & Sexual Violence).

Ms. Valente is grateful to have received the American Bar Association Commission on Domestic & Sexual Violence's 2011 Sharon L. Corbitt Award. In 2009, the National Congress of American Indians presented Ms. Valente with the NCAI Public Sector Leadership Award for her work to obtain the legislative authority necessary to bring safety and justice to Native communities.

Katie VonDeLinde energetically and creatively educates domestic violence advocates, social workers, and educators on economic justice and survivor-defined advocacy to increase holistic safety for those impacted by intimate partner violence (IPV). After serving as Assistant Director of a DV program in rural Iowa and confronting a myriad of economic barriers impacting survivors, Ms. VonDeLinde searched for innovative economic advocacy strategies at Comprehensive Solutions to Domestic Violence Initiative. Ms. VonDeLinde directed Redevelopment Opportunities for Women's Economic Action Program, providing financial advocacy, developing curricula, and educating domestic violence advocates across the nation on economic advocacy.

Ms. VonDeLinde has been advocating, writing, thinking, and teaching on issues of IPV for more than 20 years and is currently an adjunct faculty member at University of Missouri- St. Louis and Washington University, where she has won teaching and advising awards. Ms. VonDeLinde co-directs KMCV Consulting, LLC and has served as an expert advisor to the Center for Survivor Agency and Justice since 2008.

Lydia Watts is the CEO of the Service Women's Action Network (SWAN), a role she assumed in June 2017. SWAN was started by women veterans to assume "a seat at the table" regarding laws and policies that directly affect active duty and veteran women. SWAN quickly became a leading voice and advocate for the issue of Military Sexual Trauma (MST). SWAN's mission is to connect, support and advocate for women in the military—past, present and future (active duty, guard, reserve, retire and veteran).

Lydia has spent the past 28 years working with survivors of intimate partner and sexual violence. After doing so as a volunteer for a number of years, assisting in the implementation of one of the first lay court advocacy programs in Massachusetts, she decided to go to law school. While in her third year of law school, Lydia, along with three fellow clinical students, founded Women

Empowered Against Violence (WEAVE), where she served as Executive Director from 1995–2005. WEAVE was a multi-disciplinary agency that provided teen and adult victims of domestic violence in Washington, DC an innovative range of services including legal services, counseling, clinical case management, economic literacy and empowerment, outreach and education. Lydia is the founding board chair of the Network for Victim Recovery (NVRDC) in DC, and was on the board from March 2012 to August 2015. Other positions include: Executive Director of the Massachusetts Alliance on Teen Pregnancy and the Victim Rights Law Center, both based in Boston; the Director of Quality and Program Enhancement of the Civil Programs of the National Legal Aid and Defender Association (NLADA); Deputy Director of the DC Access to Justice Commission; Supervising Attorney at the DC Volunteer Lawyers Project; and is the Principal of a consulting firm she started in September 2005 called Greater Good Consulting.

Lydia is also the proud mother of her two-year-old, Sifa Saupaulor Gborkorquellie, who she is raising with her partner, Maoti.

Persis Yu is a staff attorney at the National Consumer Law Center (NCLC) and the director of NCLC's Student Loan Borrower Assistance Project. She is a contributing author to NCLC's *Fair Credit Reporting and Student Loan Law*. She has also authored several reports including: *Voices of Despair: Student Borrowers Trapped in Poverty When Government Seizes Their Earned Income Tax Credit* and *Pushed into Poverty: How Student Loan Collections Threaten the Financial Security of Older Americans*.

The National Consumer Law Center is America's leading consumer law organization, helping consumers, their advocates, and public policy makers use powerful consumer laws to build financial security and assure marketplace justice. NCLC's Student Loan Borrower Assistance Project provides information about student loan rights and responsibilities for borrowers and advocates. It also seeks to increase public understanding of student lending issues and to identify policy solutions to promote access to education, lessen student debt burdens, and make loan repayment more manageable.

Jane Zhi joined the American Bar Association Commission on Domestic & Sexual Violence as a staff attorney in March 2017. Between 2013 and 2017, she worked as a staff attorney at New Mexico Legal Aid (NMLA) in their Albuquerque office. At NMLA, she coordinated *pro bono* efforts through the Volunteer Attorney Program and Justice for Families Project, oversaw the Domestic Violence Legal Helpline, and provided direct representation to victims of domestic violence in family court. Prior to that, she coordinated outreach at LAF (Legal Assistance Foundation) in Chicago, Illinois. Jane is a graduate of the University of Iowa College of Law and received her Bachelor of Arts from the University of California, Berkeley.

Y0-DCV-049

SYSTEM OF OPHTHALMOLOGY

The scheme for the "System of Ophthalmology" is as follows, but its division into different volumes is liable to alteration.

SYSTEM OF OPHTHALMOLOGY

EDITED BY

SIR STEWART DUKE-ELDER

VOL. V

OPHTHALMIC OPTICS

AND

REFRACTION

By

Sir Stewart Duke-Elder
G.C.V.O., F.R.S.

and

David Abrams
D.M., F.R.C.S.

Consulting Ophthalmic Surgeon, the Royal Free Hospital, London
and the Central Middlesex Hospital

WITH 882 ILLUSTRATIONS AND 9 COLOURED PLATES

LONDON

HENRY KIMPTON

1970

Standard Book Number 85313 758 7

Published in the United States of America
by The C. V. Mosby Company, St. Louis.

——

MADE AND PRINTED IN GREAT BRITAIN

PREFACE

THIS is not a text-book on Optics; such a book would require many
volumes to do justice to a subject so comprehensive, the story of which
extends from prehistoric times and today covers many aspects of life from
television from Mars to looking at an invisibly small object at an optically
increased diameter of over 1,000,000 times. The present volume is limited
to those parts of the subject which concern ophthalmology; although thus
restricted, this is itself a many-sided study.

It is unfortunately the case that many clinical ophthalmologists look
upon optics with a feeling approaching horror. Their feeling towards
mathematics is often worse, but it (not necessarily Euclid's) is the most
elastic and satisfying discipline in the world; Pythagoras was not far from
the truth—"numbers sit at the heart of the universe"—and he saw in mathematical relationships the foundation of everything that exists. This feeling
of antipathy is indeed a pity for, apart from the inherent interest of the
subject, most ophthalmologists (if we exclude those who live in their peculiar
super-specialties above the clouds) spend much of their time on the prescription of spectacles or contact lenses. Indeed, of all aspects of medicine this
practice gives to more people more comfort and increased efficiency than any
other medical technique. Surely these should not be advised as a routine by
one who is acquainted only with the technology of the subject, but by someone
who also understands the theory and philosophy underlying his activities;
and with its long history and beautifully logical reasoning, optics is fascinating, and in this volume it is strictly confined to matters of clinical utility.

This present volume represents in some degree the two sections of
theoretical and clinical optics which appeared in the first and fourth volumes
of the *Text-Book of Ophthalmology*. They are, however, much expanded. The
history of the subject has received a special chapter since it lends human
interest to a factual science, a chapter on malingering has been added to the
section dealing with refractive errors since the inconsistencies between
objective findings and subjective responses are liable to cause difficulties and
anxieties, while large additions have been made to the chapter on visual aids
and particularly to that on contact lenses, a subject now developing not from
year to year but from week to week with such rapidity that to keep abreast
of it is difficult; a new chapter is added on the optics of the more common
diagnostic clinical instruments.

As a result I can only hope that the book gives a little of the pleasure to
the reader that it has already given to the writers.

STEWART DUKE-ELDER.

INSTITUTE OF OPHTHALMOLOGY,
UNIVERSITY OF LONDON,
1970.

ACKNOWLEDGEMENTS

I must gratefully acknowledge the help given to us by Mr. Ian Mackie for his critical advice on the chapter on contact lenses and also for the preparation of the coloured plates illustrating the significance of fluorescein patterns in their fitting, as well as some other figures. In a subject changing so rapidly and technically so complex, the advice of a specialist is essential and this has been freely given. For the preparation of many of the illustrations we are indebted to Mr. T. R. Tarrant of the Institute of Ophthalmology; those borrowed from other sources are duly acknowledged as they occur, but as usual Dr. F. N. L. Poynter of the Wellcome Institute of the History of Medicine has provided many of the historical portraits of those who have contributed to our subject.

Once again Mr. A. J. B. Goldsmith and Miss Mina H. T. Yuille have read the proofs and thus eased some of our anxieties. We are also indebted to Miss Carolyn Phillips, Mr. Abrams's secretary, for her assistance, and above all—as has been the case in all these volumes—to Miss Rosamund Soley for her indispensable help in preparing the manuscript and the figures for publication, vetting the multitude of references to the literature, and compiling the Index.

One thing has been sad in writing this book. Mr George Deed, the publisher who had reached the age of 91 has died; since I started writing these books about 40 years ago he has guided my footsteps and helped me in every way. This I shall miss; but his son, Mr. Ronald Deed, has fully and ably taken his place.

STEWART DUKE-ELDER

CONTENTS

INTRODUCTION

SECTION I

OPTICS

Chapter II

Geometrical Optics

CHAPTER III

THE DIOPTRIC IMAGERY OF THE EYE

CHAPTER IV

ADJUSTMENTS TO THE OPTICAL SYSTEM

SECTION II

ANOMALIES OF REFRACTION AND ACCOMMODATION

CHAPTER V

ANOMALIES OF THE OPTICAL SYSTEM

CHAPTER VI

SIMPLE REFRACTIVE ERRORS

CONTENTS

CHAPTER VII

PATHOLOGICAL REFRACTIVE ERRORS

CHAPTER VIII

APHAKIA

CHAPTER IX

CLINICAL METHODS OF ESTIMATING THE REFRACTION

CHAPTER X

ANOMALIES OF ACCOMMODATION

CHAPTER XI

MALINGERING

SECTION III

BINOCULAR FACTORS IN REFRACTION

CHAPTER XII

ANISOMETROPIA

CHAPTER XIII

ANISEIKONIA

CONTENTS

SECTION V

OPTICAL APPLIANCES

CHAPTER XVII

SPECTACLES

CHAPTER XVIII

CONTACT LENSES

Chapter XIX

Visual Aids

Chapter XX

The Prescription of Spectacles

CONTENTS

CHAPTER XXI

THE OPTICS OF CLINICAL OPHTHALMIC INSTRUMENTS

FIG. 1.—KEPLER'S ESCUTCHEON.

Above, a figure symbolizing the sun as the centre of Copernicus's system and the earth as a mirror reflecting its rays. Below, the sun in a divided field indicating that the sun shines equally during day and night—eternally (Courtesy of Josef Klepesta, Prague).

INTRODUCTION

CHAPTER I

THE HISTORY OF OPHTHALMIC OPTICS

AMONG the ancient Chinese there was a considerable knowledge of optics. Thus in the Chou Dynasty, MO TI [*c*. 479–381 B.C.], who lived between the times of Confucius and Mencius and inspired the philosophy of the Mohists with their dualistic doctrine of non-pacific universal love, discussed many problems of physics and optics in those fragments of his " Canons " which are available. The camera obscura was a " locked treasure-room " and the inversion of the image created therein was correctly explained, while the reflection of light from plane, convex and concave mirrors was studied and empirical rules deduced for the forms of the varying images thus obtained. Unfortunately, the vigorously creative thought characteristic of this period was never to be repeated in the disturbed and chequered history of that country, and in mediæval times such optical works as *Than Chhiao's Book of Transformations* (*c*. 940) contained little new.

Although there is evidence that some vague knowledge of the laws of optics existed in the Hindu, the Babylonian and the Egyptian civilizations, it would seem likely that it was limited to deductions from ordinary observable phenomena. It was in classical Greece that the first extant records of an emergent science are to be found; nevertheless, it was limited to the simplest features. The first substantial treatise which survives is the *Optics* of EUCLID of Athens [330–280 B.C.], wherein propositions and proofs from widely different sources were gathered. This was followed in Alexandria by the work of ARISTARCHUS of Samos [310–230 B.C.], the *Catoptrics* of HERON [1st century A.D.], and ultimately by the *Optics* of CLAUDIUS PTOLEMY [*c*. 90–160], the greatest astronomer of antiquity, fragments of whose writings have come down to us through a later Latin translation by Eugenius of Palermo derived from mutilated Arabic manuscripts.

All these classical writers accepted that light travelled in straight lines at a speed so great that the stars could be seen immediately the eyes were opened, but their detailed knowledge was limited to catoptrics wherein the reflection of light from mirrors of various shapes was studied. In this their interpretation was correct; thus the incident and reflected rays were found to lie in the same plane and the angles subtended by each were equal. Their knowledge of dioptrics, however, was more limited. It is true that POSIDONIUS of Apamea [*c*. 135–50 B.C.] discovered atmospheric refraction, a subject more fully explored by Ptolemy who pointed out the observational

3

errors to which it might give rise as, for example, that the sun and the stars could be seen before they had arisen or after they had set. Ptolemy also claimed that the incident and refracted rays lay in the same plane and that the angles they subtended were not equal but proportional, and he published tables of refraction when a ray passed from air to water or glass, or from water to glass; these conclusions, however, may have been partly derived from Babylonian sources. On the other hand, that a practical knowledge of dioptrics existed among the Assyrians and the Greeks which was passed on to the Romans seems indicated by the lenses of glass, crystal or transparent stone found in Nimrud by Layard perhaps dating from 1000 B.C., or in other ancient sites in Italy, particularly Pompeii (destroyed in A.D. 79), Germany and England, which may have been used as an aid to vision in making the exquisitely cut miniature engravings that are still extant; this was paralleled by the use of bottles filled with water for their magnifying and heat-collecting power as burning glasses used by Aristophanes (c. 424 B.C.) to destroy the writing on wax tablets and by surgeons in Greece and Rome. Although the surgeon Heliodoros of Larissa (2nd century A.D.), explained this as a refractive phenomenon, their nature was not understood. The Roman philosopher, Seneca, interpreted the magnifying power as a property of water; this Roman writer also knew but could not adequately explain such refractive effects as the apparent rising of a coin at the bottom of an empty vessel when regarded at an angle so that it is seen when the bowl is filled with water, while Lucretius similarly noted the apparent break in a rod or an oar when it was partially submerged in the sea.

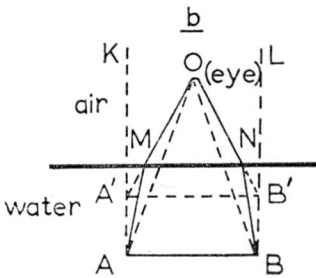

FIG. 2.—PTOLEMY'S INTERPRETATION OF REFRACTION.

In viewing an object under water (see text).

While Ptolemy's understanding of reflection was correct, his interpretation of refraction was not so accurate. His construction of an object, AB, seen under water is drawn in Fig. 2. The rays from the eye, OM and ON, are refracted at the surface of the water and reach the object along the paths MA and NB. Ptolemy knew that a ray of normal incidence is not refracted, and concluded that the virtual image, A′B′, is located by protracting the rays, OM and ON, until they reached the perpendiculars, AK and BL; it was magnified because the visual angle, A′OB′, was greater than the angle AOB, through which it would have been seen if in air. This construction was copied by such subsequent scholars as Al-Hazen, Grosseteste, Bacon and John of Peckham, and remained the standard explanation until it was corrected by Isaac Barrow in 1674.[1]

The optical system of the eye, however, could not be understood in classical Greece or Rome partly because of the primitive knowledge of refraction and partly because of erroneous views of the processes of vision.

[1] *Lectiones opticæ et geometricæ*, London (1674).

In a previous Volume[1] we have seen that the popular belief was the emanation hypothesis of vision, advanced by Pythagoras (c. 600 B.C.) and accepted by such classical writers as Euclid, Hipparchos and Ptolemy and after them by Galen. In this hypothesis the visual spirit originating in the brain emanated from the lens (the essential organ of vision) forming a cone of linear rays; in the perfect and geometrically symmetrical universe of the Greeks, light travelled in straight lines because these were the shortest and, according to Heliodorus, the visual cone (and therefore the visual field) formed a perfect circle subtending an angle of 90° because this angle was unique. It is true that an alternative view was propounded by Democritos (5th century B.C.) and modified by Aristotle [384–322 B.C.] that light emanated from external luminous or illuminated bodies taking the form of an ethereal substance but, although Plato [c. 429–327 B.C.] attempted to combine both theories, in neither scheme was there any place for ophthalmic optics.

The writers of the Arabian period of learning[2] which bridged the gap between the fall of Rome and the beginning of the Renaissance in Europe, served to keep the philosophy of Greece alive. The scholars in the many centres of the widespread empire of the Arabs occupied themselves essentially in the organization and systemization of the classical works—a gift of untold value to posterity—but added little that was fundamentally new. To this, however, there were two remarkable exceptions in optics. AL-HAZEN (IBN AL-HAITHAM) [965–?1043] (Fig. 3), who was born in Basra and lived in Cairo, among his many varied writings transformed this science in *The Book of Optics (Opticæ Thesaurus)* and *De Luce*. He was very familiar with the phenomena of reflection, making experiments with plane, spherical, cylindrical and parabolic mirrors; moreover, he showed that Ptolemy's law that the angle of incidence is proportional to the angle of refraction was true only for small angles, while his studies of magnifying glasses brought him close to a rational theory of convex lenses. Of more importance, however, was the philosophical theory he presented on the nature of light; he discarded the sterile and fanciful emanation hypothesis and adopted the Aristotelian view that rays of light travelled from external objects into the eye, a theory subsequently widely accepted in the Arabic world by such writers as IBN SINA (AVICENNA) [980–1038] of Bokhara, and IBN RUSHD (AVERROËS) [1126–98], the Arabian-Spaniard. The inspired deduction of the latter, the greatest of all Arabic Aristotelian commentators, was the suggestion that the retina and not the lens was the photoreceptor in the eye, a revolutionary hypothesis that was not revived until the time of Platter and Kepler.

These two contributors to Arabic thought were of great ultimate significance but they stimulated no immediate revolution in ophthalmic optics. Like the Greeks, the Arabic scholars knew the laws of reflection but their scant understanding of dioptrics precluded a correct explanation of the refractive system of the eye. For this reason the crude diagrams they

[1] Vol. IV, p. 435.   [2] Vol. II, p. 20.

FIG. 3.—IBN-AL-HAITHAM (AL-HAZEN).
[965–?1043]
A modern reproduction of his likeness.

Apart from first pointing out that the retina was the visual receptor, Al-Hazen made many original investigations on the reflection of light by spherical and parabolic mirrors, and the optics of the pin-hole camera. His historical book, *Kitab-ul-Manazir*, was an outstanding treatise on optics (translated into Latin by Risner, Basle, 1572); while other widely different scientific studies interested him, including the first plan for building a dam on the river Nile. (Courtesy of Hakim Mohammed Said, Hamdard National Foundation, Karachi.)

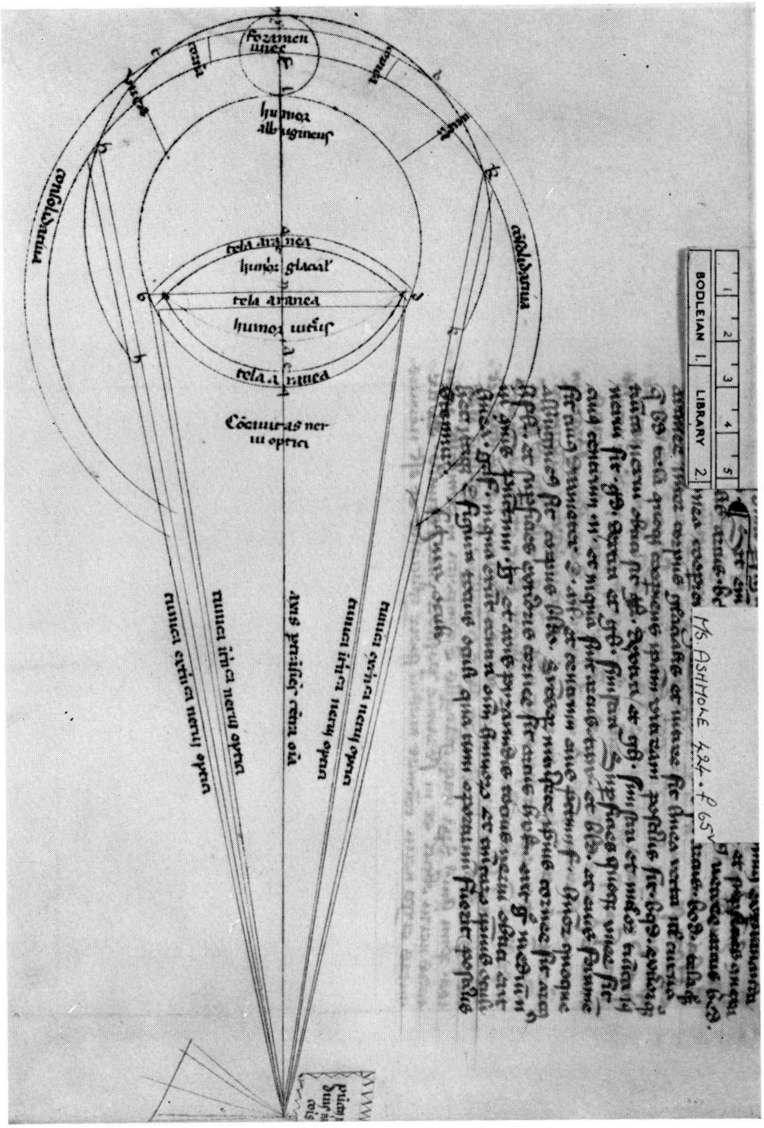

FIG. 4.—VITELLO'S OPTICS OF THE EYE.

In a Latin manuscript of *Perspectiva* (*c.* 1270) (from the Bodleian Library, Oxford).

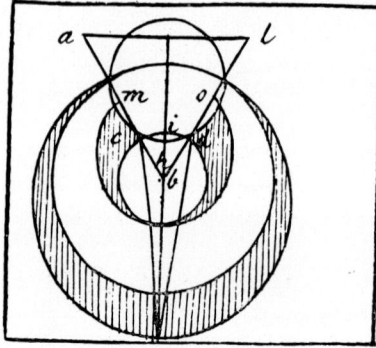

FIG. 5.—ROGER BACON'S DRAWING OF THE EYE.
Showing the light from " the visual pyramid " (a, b, l) traversing the " foramen uveae " (m, o) (pupil), to enter the anterior part of the " humor glacialis " (c, i, d) (from *Opus Majus*, c. 1268, taken from the first folio edition, London, 1733).

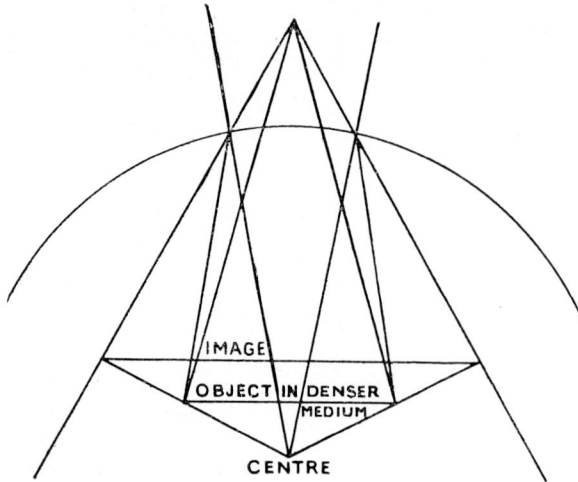

FIG. 6.—ROGER BACON'S DIAGRAM OF THE EFFECT OF A PLANO-CONVEX LENS.
The diagram is wrong, but the idea is there.

evolved dealt only with perpendicular rays when the eye was compared to a camera obscura, then a well-known phenomenon wherein no refraction occurred. When Greek thought as amended by the Arab scholars began to filter into Western Europe towards the end of the 11th and during the 12th centuries, these simple and inaccurate concepts were retained and slavishly copied in the early treatises on optics, debased by the translators who had transcribed them from Arabic scripts. The diagrams found in the optical writings of the late Middle Ages were thus jumbles of lines and circles with no optical and little anatomical reality. One such treatise, the *Perspectiva* or *Ten Books of Optics* by VITELLO [c. 1220–1270], of Silesia, then part of Poland, written about 1270, was essentially a commentary on Al-Hazen's *Thesaurus* (Fig. 4), but its importance was surpassed by the three contemporaneous English writers of the school of Oxford: Robert Grosseteste, Roger Bacon and John of Peckham. In their time the classical Greek and Arabic texts were becoming available in Western Europe and these served as a stimulus for their studies and speculations. Of the three, the greatest was Bacon who advocated experiments as well as being an original observer. An Arabic scholar, he profited by the works of Al-Hazen and discussed reflection and refraction and, in his *Perspectiva*, he gave details of a scheme of the optical system of the eye (Fig. 5). He taught that the difficulty experienced by the aged in seeing near objects was due to an increase of moisture in the eye and a wrinkling of the cornea resembling the wrinkling in the aged skin, and suggested as a remedy the magnification given by the lesser segment of a sphere of glass or crystal when laid upon the letters to be read (Fig. 6); by such means, he said, the smallest particles of sand or dust could be seen.[1] On account of this, historians have accredited him with inventing spectacles and telescopes; this he did not do, but he certainly pointed out the way for their realization and the principles for their construction.

This triad of Franciscans who founded English optics and spread knowledge of it throughout Europe deserves a short note.

ROBERT GROSSETESTE [1175—1253], a scholar of Oxford who ultimately became Bishop of Lincoln where he created as big a revolution in ecclesiastical discipline as he did in optics, was essentially a deductive metaphysician and mathematician and not an experimentalist, but for the first time he introduced formal lectures on optics to the West, wherein he treated of reflection and refraction.[2]

His pupil at Oxford, ROGER BACON [1214–?1294] (Fig. 7), had a more chequered career. Born into a wealthy family of wool merchants who were ruined during the civil wars of Henry III, he studied in Paris and Oxford where he joined the Franciscan Order, founded some 40 years previously. Arrogant and contemptuous of the doctrines of the Franciscan Order, he was twice incarcerated in prison by the Church for his views against accepted theological dogma, first in Paris in an institution where he was forbidden books and writing material. Writing to the Pope pleading that an encyclopædia of all knowledge should be written, he obtained permission and between 1266 and 1267 he wrote his *Opus majus*, *Opus minus* and *Opus tertium*. Thereafter in 1278 he was sent to Ancona on the Adriatic coast of Italy where he was subjected to solitary confinement in chains and was incarcerated for thirteen years without communication with anyone. Immediately on his release, however, with unquenchable spirit in the cause of intellectual freedom, he commenced to write his *Compendium studii theologiæ* which began with a disquisition on the sources of error, " the first among which is undue reliance on authority ". He died two years after his liberation before this work was finished. During his chequered life he wrote widely over the whole field of philosophy, for which he was known as *Doctor mirabilis*.

Of the three Franciscans, JOHN OF PECKHAM [c. 1228–1294], who eventually became Archbishop of Canterbury, probably had the most widespread influence on the development of optics since his concise *Perspectiva communis*, so-called because of its

---

[1] p. 610. [2] *De iride seu de iride et specula.*

Fig. 7.—Roger Bacon.
[c. 1214–1294].

Jos Archiepiscopi Cantuariensis Perspectiua communis

FIG. 8.—FRONTISPIECE OF JOHN OF PECKHAM'S
Perspectiva Communis, Venice (1504).

widespread use, served as the standard text throughout Europe during the Middle Ages until the beginning of the 17th century (Fig. 8). In it he discussed reflection, refraction by concave and convex lenses, and also the optical system of the eye, but the book contained less originality than Bacon's treatise.

To all those three English pioneers, however, the essential source of knowledge was the *Thesaurus* of Ptolemy. All considered the lens to be the photoreceptor, and therefore their concepts of the optical system of the eye were completely unrealistic. Even the great Florentine genius, LEONARDO DA VINCI [1452–1519], in spite of the beauty and accuracy of most of his art, produced absurd diagrams of the optical system of the eye, reflecting the same Arabic influence with all its virtues and its faults (Fig. 9).

In the 16th century, small advances in optics were made by two scholars of the Italian Renaissance. The brilliant mathematician, FRANCESCO MAUROLICO [1494–1575] of Messina, in his *Photismi de lumine et umbra* (1554), a work, however, not published until 1575 in Venice, made a systematic study of prisms, mirrors, lenses and the dioptric system of the human eye and was the first to establish that rays from a luminous point were collected together by a convex lens to a point-focus, and suggested that the optical principle of the eye was of the same nature. Shortly thereafter, GIOVANNI BATTISTA DELLA PORTA [1536–1615] of Naples (Fig. 10), in his *Magiæ naturalis* (1598), the first systematic treatise on lenses to be written, and in his *De refractione* (1593), added a convex lens to the pin-hole of the camera obscura, thus making it resemble more closely the optical system of the eye.

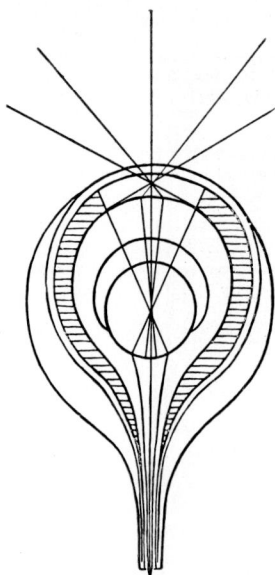

FIG. 9.—LEONARDO DA VINCI'S DRAWING OF THE EYE.

Showing the double refraction of light as the rays pass through the pupil and again on their path through the central, round lens; they finally impinge on the optic nerve.

To all those, however, an adequate understanding of ocular dioptrics was impossible, for the old belief that the lens was the photoreceptor was still prevalent and the laws of dioptrics were still obscure; indeed, the action of lenses was neglected for these were generally considered as conjurors' tricks. We have seen in a previous Volume[1] that the first error was corrected by FELIX PLATTER [1536–1614], the anatomist of Basle, in his *De corporis humani structura*; he revived the concept of Ibn Rushd and maintained that light entered the eye to be focused by the crystalline lens upon the retina where the image was formed, a view proved experimentally by the Bavarian Jesuit experimentalist, CHRISTOPHER SCHEINER [1575–1650],[2] by the

---

[1] Vol. IV, p. 436, Fig. 121.   [2] Vol. II, Fig. 37.

FIG. 10.—GIOVANNI BATTISTA DELLA PORTA
[1536–1615].

simple expedient of observing its formation after the sclera and choroid had been removed. It is also important that Scheiner introduced the use of chemical fixatives in the preparation of the globe for anatomical study and thus was able in his book, *Oculus* (1619), to correct several errors in previous descriptions, particularly that the radius of curvature of the cornea was less than that of the sclera (a point noted by Galen) and that the lens was situated immediately behind the iris and was not centrally placed. The second blank in knowledge was filled with astonishing success and completeness by Kepler who gave a detailed account of the phenomena of refraction and of the dioptric system of the eye in his classical works, *Ad vitellionem paralipomena* (Frankfurt, 1604) and *Dioptrice* (1611). Therein he showed that the rays of light did not intercross as they traverse the pupil as in a camera obscura but were refracted by the cornea and the lens to be " painted " upon the retina as an inverted image comprised of an aggregation of as many " image-points " as there were distinguishable " object-points " in the object. Thus were the fundamental scientific principles of the dioptrics of the eye for the first time established as well as the laws governing refraction by convex and concave lenses.

While Ptolemy may be regarded as the father of optical science and particularly of catoptrics, JOHANNES KEPLER [1571–1630] (Fig. 11) must be acclaimed as the founder of dioptrics. The foremost mathematician and astronomer of his age, he had a curious and interesting history. The son of a soldier-of-fortune who became an inn-keeper in Württemberg, and a delicate premature child whose sight was permanently impaired by smallpox at the age of four, he was sent to study to become a Protestant pastor at the University of Tübingen (1588). Here he absorbed the views of Nicholas Copernicus, the Polish-German scholar who had propounded a new theory of astronomy wherein the earth and the other planets circled round the central sun, thus opposing Ptolemy's theory with its tradition of 2,000 years that the immovable earth was the centre of the universe around which the sun and the planets revolved. Kepler's advocacy of the Copernican theory while occupying the Chair of Astronomy at Gratz (1594–1601) attracted the attention of Tycho Brahe, the celebrated astronomer of Prague, who invited him in 1600 to be his assistant ; after Brahe's death a few months later, Kepler became the astronomer and astrologer of the Emperor Rudolph II, an apparently curious mixture but only by being the court astrologer could an astronomer live. In Prague he entered upon a series of astronomical observations of great accuracy and outlined the course of the planetary orbits as ellipses, thus placing heliocentric astronomy on a firm basis. His escutcheon is seen in Fig. 1, showing the sun as the centre of the universe and the earth merely as a mirror reflecting its rays. He was also the first to calculate correctly latitude and longitude, he designed several new telescopes, formulated the law of inverse squares expressing the diminution of the intensity of light with distance and, just as his contemporaries, Galileo Galilei [1564–1642] and William Gilbert [1540–1603] may be said respectively to have founded experimental mechanics and the science of magnetism, so Kepler founded modern experimental optics. Unfortunately, his later years were clouded by financial and family worries, rendered worse by the political and religious disputes of the period; in 1628 he migrated to Silesia where he continued his studies until he died in Ratisbon in 1630.

Kepler's pioneering and revolutionary discoveries stimulated a host of subsequent advances which have been maintained to our own generation.

Fig. 11.—Johannes Kepler
[1571–1630].
A gravure probably made after a painting during Kepler's employment at the court of Rudolf II or his successor, Mathias (courtesy of Josef Klepesta, Prague).

He thought that the refractive power of a medium was proportional to its density, but the English mathematician, THOMAS HARRIOT [1560–1621], who mapped out the colony of Virginia with Sir Walter Raleigh, pointed out that oil is more refractive than water but less dense. In the year of Harriot's death, the Dutchman, WILLEBRORD SNELL [1591–1626] (Fig. 14), professor of mathematics at Leiden, determined the correct law for the refraction of light, a law approximately deduced by Kepler—that the sines of the angles of incidence and refraction bear a constant relation (the refractive index) for a given interface between two media. The first work on optics to utilize Snell's law was *La Dioptrique* (Leyden, 1637), by the great French philosopher, RENÉ DESCARTES [1596–1650],[1] who conceived light as consisting of small particles rebounding from an elastic surface according to the laws of reflection, and being reduced in speed and bent in their paths towards the interface as they passed from one medium to another much as a ball would behave on breaking through a thin cloth.

Descartes's theoretical deduction that light travelled faster in a dense than in a sparse medium was questioned by PIERRE DE FERMAT [1608–1665] of Toulouse in his " principle of natural economy," who reasoned that the laws of refraction followed as a necessary deduction if it were presumed that light travelled more slowly in denser media. This view was confirmed by the Danish astronomer, OLAUS ROMER [1644–1710], who showed between 1672 and 1676 that light travelled with a constant velocity through the " luminiferous ether " of space, but that it was slowed down while passing through a denser medium since it had to make detours around the particles of the transparent body and thus become refracted. Finally, the great English scientist, ISAAC NEWTON [1642–1727] (Fig. 12), by the beautiful experiments which seemed to flow spontaneously from his genius, all described in his *Opticks* (London, 1704) with an affectionate wealth of detail, consolidated the entire system of optics, reflection, refraction, the formation of images and the dioptric system of the eye, as well as the first elements of a scientific theory of colours.

After Newton there were no great advances in ophthalmic optics for a century, although the advances in observational science stimulated the study of the optics of lens-systems. About the beginning of the 17th century, however, compound microscopes and telescopes had been produced by the Dutch craftsmen of Middelburg and the theoretical principles of their optical action were studied by such scholars as Galileo, Kepler and Harriot, while Newton, believing that lenses would always produce images distorted by chromatic and spherical aberration, introduced the reflecting telescope wherein light was concentrated by a concave mirror; for this invention he was admitted as a Fellow into the Royal Society in 1672. Some years previously, in 1663, JAMES GREGORY [1638–1675], professor of mathematics at Edinburgh, had designed but had not constructed a similar instru-

[1] Vol. II, Fig. 50.

Isaac Newton.

FIG. 12.—ISAAC NEWTON
[1642–1727].

ment, but his nephew, DAVID GREGORY [1661–1708], professor of mathematics at Edinburgh and then at Oxford, challenged Newton's scepticism that lenses could not be constructed without aberration on the basis of the apparent absence of such distortions in the human eye. The construction of a telescope producing images devoid of coloured fringes was eventually achieved in 1733 by an amateur English scientist, CHESTER MOORE HALL, while the London instrument maker, JOHN DOLLAND [1706–61] made the production of achromatic lenses a practical possibility in 1758. The eventual development of the compound microscope with aplanatic and achromatic lenses was attained by GIOVANNI BATTISTA AMICI [1786–1863][1] of Bologna in 1820.

During all this period and for some time thereafter, however, little progress was made in the study of the optics of the eye. It is true that in his *Dioptrice*, Kepler (1611) had established the rationale of myopia and a century later Isaac Newton (1704)[2] had theoretically demonstrated the possibility of long sight, while in 1793 the great English scientist, THOMAS YOUNG [1773–1829][3] proved the existence of astigmatism in his own eyes by observing a difference in focus between vertical and horizontal lines; this defect was corrected by a cylindrical lens in 1827 by SIR GEORGE BIDDELL AIRY [1801–1892] (Fig. 610), the Astronomer Royal and director of the Greenwich Observatory, and the mathematics of the problems involved was clarified by JACQUES CHARLES FRANÇOIS STURM [1803–1855], professor of mathematics first at the École Polytechnique in Paris and then of mechanics in the Faculté des Sciences.[4] Among his many other contributions to physiological optics, including particularly the mechanism of accommodation and the enunciation of the wave-theory of light, Thomas Young formulated remarkably accurate measurements of the optical constants of the eye.

The difficulty of resolving the principles of a compound optical system of this type, however, remained insuperable until a simplified theory was evolved whereby a complex optical system need not be regarded as a series of its constituent elements considered in isolation but could be understood and treated as a unity. A preliminary trial at this formidable task was offered by ROBERT SMITH [1689–1768], the English mathematician and professor of astronomy at Cambridge[5] and more elaborate assays to derive general laws were evolved by Leonard Euler in 1771[6] and Joseph Louis Lagrange,[7] but it was due to K. F. Gauss (1841)[8] that an elegant solution was eventually produced. This revolutionary work of Gauss has stood the test

---

[1] Vol. II, Fig. 41.   [2] *Opticks*, London (1704).
[3] *Phil. Trans.*, **91**, 23 (1801). For a portrait of Thomas Young, see Vol. IV, Fig. 252.
[4] Sturm. Mémoire sur la théorie de la vision. *C.R. Acad. Sci.* (Paris), **20**, 554, 761, 1238 (1845).
[5] *A Compleat System of Opticks*, Camb. (1738).
[6] *Dioptrica*, Berlin (1771).
[7] *Mécanique analytique*, Paris (1788).
[8] *Dioptrische Untersuchungen*, Göttingen (1841).

of time and is accepted in its essentials today although further simplifications have been suggested such as the use of matrix algebra as a notation for the analysis.[1]

These three Continental mathematicians deserve a special note. LEONARD EULER [1707–1783], a Swiss from Basle, must be considered as one of the founders of pure analytical mathematics. Trained also in theology, oriental languages and medicine, he was a man of the widest culture. At the invitation of Catherine I he went to St. Petersburg in 1727 where he became professor of physics and then of mathematics, and in 1741, at the command of Frederick the Great, he went to Berlin, returning to Russia in 1766. Unfortunately in his later years he became blind but worked unceasingly, evolving his elaborate computations in his head.

JOSEPH LOUIS LAGRANGE [1736–1813], probably the greatest mathematician France has produced, was born at Turin, and followed Euler at the Academy of Berlin at the invitation of Frederick the Great who wished " the greatest king in Europe " to have " the greatest mathematician " at his Court; at the death of Frederick 20 years later, he returned to Paris to live greatly honoured at the Louvre where he happily survived the revolution, eventually to be buried in the Pantheon.

KARL FRIEDRICH GAUSS [1777–1855] (Fig. 13) was one of the greatest mathematicians of history, ranking in stature with Archimedes and Newton. Born at Brunswick, the son of a small contractor, he detected an error in his father's pay-sheet before the age of three and such was his precocious arithmetical insight that the Duke of Brunswick paid for his education at school and at the University of Göttingen, a university incidentally founded by King George III of England. In addition to his work on optics he made revolutionary contributions to many aspects of science, making the first marked advances in Euclidean geometry for 2,000 years and introducing non-Euclidean geometry, the fundamental theory of algebra, the theory of numbers including quadratic residues and reciprocity and Gaussian integers, the Gaussian distribution of probability and the measurement of magnetic flux density of which the " gauss " is still the standard unit. In all these his ideas were original. His *Werke* published in Göttingen in 14 volumes from 1870 to 1929 are a unique exposition of creative ability and accuracy of computation applied with the highest logical rigour in reasoning.

The work of Gauss stimulated a further intensive study of the optical system of the eye, first by L. MOSER [1844][2] who, however, took a mean value (1·384) for the total refractive index of the lens and thus placed the image behind the retina. Greater accuracy was attained in 1845 by BENEDIKT LISTING [1808–1882] who had the advantage of studying mathematics and optics with Gauss and eventually became professor of mathematical physics and optics at Göttingen.[3] In 1853 he calculated the optics of a very accurate theoretical schematic eye[4] which, with some modifications, was adopted by HERMANN VON HELMHOLTZ [1821–1894] (Fig. 130) of Berlin in his extremely accurate and extensive studies on which all subsequent work has been based.[5] The immense labours of von Helmholtz

[1] T. Smith. The primordial co-efficients of asymmetrical lenses. *Trans. opt. Soc. Lond.*, **29**, 170 (1928).

[2] Ueber das Auge, in Dove's *Repert. d. Physik*, p. 337 (1844).

[3] *Beitrage zur physiologischen Optik*, Göttingen (1845).

[4] Dioptrik des Auges, in Wagner's *Handwörterbuch der Physiologie*, Braunschweig, **4**, 451 (1853).

[5] *Hb. d. physiologischen Optik*, Leipzig (1856–66).

FIG. 13.—KARL FRIEDRICH GAUSS
[1777–1855].
A painting by Albrecht Jensen (courtesy of Prof. W. Hallermann, Göttingen).

allowed FRANS CORNELIS DONDERS [1818–1889] (Fig. 191) of Utrecht to advocate and popularize the routine correction of optical defects with spectacles in his *On the Anomalies of Accommodation and Refraction of the Eye* (London, 1864). This pioneer work was consolidated and advanced by many others, particularly by MARIUS HANS ERIK TSCHERNING [1854–1939][1] (Fig. 191), the Danish ophthalmologist who became the successor to Louis Emile Javal as director of the Laboratory of Ophthalmology at the Sorbonne in Paris, when he became blind from glaucoma and by ALLVAR GULLSTRAND [1862–1930] (Fig. 131),[2] for which he received a Nobel Prize in 1911.

At the same time progress was continually being made in the optics of lenses. Since the 17th century these had been annotated according to the radius of curvature of their two surfaces, a clumsy and complicated technique varying in its units in different centres such as London and Paris; in 1872 FELIX MONOYER [1836–1912] of Lyons contributed a considerable advance by introducing a simple system based on the metric power of vergence, the dioptre.[3] This distinguished French oculist, incidentally, introduced the decimal system of measuring visual acuity.[4] Monoyer's suggestion was warmly advocated by Donders at the International Congress at Heidelberg in 1875 and thereafter was generally accepted. Finally, as we shall see later, the design of lenses was continually improved by a succession of workers dating from W. H. Wollaston of Cambridge, F. Ostwald and M. H. E. Tscherning of Paris, A. S. Percival of Newcastle-upon-Tyne, and Allvar Gullstrand of Uppsala, but most notably by the remarkable team at Jena—Ernst Abbé, Moritz von Rohr, H. Boegehold and H. Hartinger.

The history of the special aspects of our subject such as the mechanism of accommodation and the use of spectacles and contact lenses will be dealt with in the appropriate chapters.

On the Nature of Light

In the previous Volume[5] the story of the development of our ideas on the nature of light was briefly told and the appropriate literature quoted. We have seen that the classical theory advanced by DEMOCRITOS in the 5th century B.C. and modified by ARISTOTLE in the 4th century B.C. held that light was an activity of an ethereal substance originating from luminous bodies. This corpuscular theory was probably originally derived from India where materialistic doctrines existed before the birth of Brahmanism. In general, Aristotle's views were accepted by the Arabs and throughout mediæval Europe, except that with the growth of Christianity specific theories were eclipsed by the revealed belief that light was created and directly given by

[1] *Optique physiologique*, Paris (1898).
[2] *Einfuhrung in die Methoden d. Dioptrik d. Auges d. Menschen*, Leipzig (1911).
[3] *Ann. Oculist.* (Paris), **68**, 101 (1872).
[4] *Gaz. méd. Paris*, **21**, 258 (1875).
[5] Vol. IV, Chapter X.

God. It was not until the 17th century that this implicit acceptance of divinity began to be questioned and more definite kinetic theories were tentatively suggested. LEONARDO DA VINCI [1452–1519] knew that sound was due to an agitation of the air and suspected that light might have an analogous origin, while GALILEO [1564–1642] concluded that it involved the motion of an unknown medium but he could not decide whether this was due to the collision of particles or to waves. The first attempt to introduce a definite theory since the inspired guesses of the Classical Greeks was that of RENÉ DESCARTES [1596–1650] in whose world of corpuscular vortices of different degrees of subtlety, light was a rhythmic variation of pressure.

In the second half of the 17th century, however, a series of advances demonstrated the inadequacy of the Cartesian theories. In 1665 the discovery of the dispersion of light of FRANCESCO GRIMALDI [1618–1663], the Jesuit mathematician of Bologna, was posthumously published wherein he postulated that it was produced by the rhythmic agitation of a medium. In 1664 the English experimentalist, ROBERT HOOKE [1635–1703], studied the iridescent colours in thin films of mica; in 1670 ERASMUS BARTHOLIN [1625–1698] of Denmark discovered double refraction; in 1675 the Danish astronomer, OLAUS ROMER [1644–1710], proved that light travelled with a finite and constant velocity, on the basis of which in 1678 the Dutch physicist, CHRISTIAAN HUYGENS [1629–1695] suggested that light was a wave-motion propagated longitudinally through a stationary ether. Thus matters stood until the appearance of the *Opticks* of ISAAC NEWTON in 1704 (Fig. 12), who found that the phenomena he elucidated were best explained by a corpuscular theory of light, retaining, however, elements of a wave-theory by supposing that the particles of light excited vibratory movements in the surrounding ether.

The undisputed authority of Newton precluded speculation on the nature of light for a century until in 1801 THOMAS YOUNG[1] who, while " venerating the name of Newton ", claimed that he was " not therefore obliged to believe that he was infallible. I see with regret that he was liable to err and that his authority has, perhaps, sometimes even retarded the progress of Science ". Reasoning largely from the phenomena of interference, he suggested that light was best described as waves through the ether with a vibration orientated transversely to its path, at the same time calculating the wavelengths of the vibrations. The revival of the wave-theory provoked discussions on the merits of the two hypotheses for over half a century until a further series of still more dramatic events eventually reconciled the two schools of thought.

The first of these discoveries was the demonstration of JAMES CLERK MAXWELL [1831–1879][2] in 1862 that electromagnetic phenomena were oscillatory disturbances which behaved in the same way as light and he

[1] Vol. IV, Fig. 252.   [2] Vol. IV, Fig. 128.

therefore advanced an electromagnetic theory of light, a dramatic and revolutionary concept suggesting that light was not a specific entity but a form of radiational energy. This concept was consolidated by the equally brilliant researches of MICHAEL FARADAY [1791–1867] who studied photo-electric effects. The second dramatic advance was the classical experiment of the American astronomers, A. MICHELSON and E. W. MORLEY in 1887, whereby they showed that there was no reason to assume that an all-pervading ether existed. There followed the discovery, initiated between 1888 and 1894 by HEINRICH HERTZ [1857–1894] that light was a small octave in the universe of the continuous energy spectrum, the evolution of ideas on the electron-structure of matter by such scientists as LORD KELVIN [1824–1907], LORD RUTHERFORD [1871–1937] and J. J. THOMSON [1856–1940], and the discovery by MAX PLANCK [1858–1937][1] in 1900 that energy was propagated not continuously but in minute indivisible quanta.

This opened the way for the development of the Theory of Relativity by ALBERT EINSTEIN [1879–1955][2] between 1905 and 1924 whereby all these divergences were unified in a concept wherein matter and energy were identical, the form of which could be expressed mathematically either as particles or waves[3]; the quantum determines the passage of energy, the surrounding electromagnetic field where the laws of wave-motion are observed determines where the quantum shall go. In the previous Volume of this *System* we dealt essentially with the quantal properties of light in its action upon the retina to excite the visual process; in this Volume, discussing the paths taken by light, we shall be concerned with light as a wave-motion.

[1] Vol. IV, Fig. 129.
[2] Vol. IV, Fig. 133.
[3] For a fuller discussion, see Vol. IV, Chap. X.

SECTION I

OPTICS

WILLEBRORDUS SNELLIUS
PROFESSOR MATHESEOS.

Fig. 14.—Willebrord Snell
[1591–1626].
(Courtesy of Prof. M. C. Colenbrander, Leiden.)

CHAPTER II

GEOMETRICAL OPTICS

THE laws of reflection are simple and easily observed and consequently, as we have seen in the previous Chapter, were well known to the classical mathematicians and astronomers such as Euclid, Ptolemy and Al-Hazen. The laws of refraction, however, were a more difficult proposition. The fact of atmospheric refraction was discovered by Posidonius in the first century B.C. and was more fully explored by Ptolemy who claimed that the angles of incidence and refraction were proportional, a relation shown by Al-Hazen to apply only for small angles. These phenomena were more fully elucidated by Kepler who demonstrated that atmospheric refraction was not restricted to stars of low altitude as was thought by the classical astronomers, but was a continuous effect decreasing from a maximum at the horizon to a minimum at the zenith; he also first pointed out the determining importance of refraction in the dioptric system of the eye. He made his calculations, however, by an empirical rule and failed to enunciate a general law of refraction. This was first accomplished by the Dutch mathematician, WILLEBRORD SNELL [1591–1626] (Fig. 14), who succeeded his father, Rudolph Snell, in 1613 as professor of mathematics at Leyden. He did not publish his generalization before his early death, and this was first done by Isaac Voss, and in his *La Dioptrique*, published as an appendix to the *Discours de la méthode* in 1637, René Descartes gave it wide publicity without acknowledging its source. Snell's other achievements were outstanding, particularly in the emergent technique of trigonometry, in his original method of measuring the earth and in determining the positions of the fixed stars and the motions of the planets.

Most ophthalmologists probably tend to think of optics as an assembly of geometrical figures and mathematical formulæ learnt in youth and now largely forgotten. While a knowledge of these figures and formulæ plays little part in the day-to-day practice of ophthalmology, there is not the slightest doubt that a complete understanding of the basic principles of the optics of the eye, of our instruments and of therapeutic optical devices is impossible without it.

It may be argued that many highly competent ophthalmologists make use of what is merely empirical optical knowledge. Their distaste for mathematics may perhaps be personal and it must be admitted that optics is an inherently devious subject. However precise the figures and formulæ may be, they often conceal a basic approximation or inaccuracy. In many instances such approximations are close enough to reality to be justified, the inaccuracies small enough to be ignored. Nevertheless, much of the exposition of geometrical optics, particularly in its application to the optics of the eye, is concerned with just these approximations and inaccuracies. There is small wonder, therefore, at the slight feeling of exasperation the clinician may experience in attempting to digest the subject.

In the following account mathematics has been kept to a minimum. Proofs of some formulæ are not given and may be obtained, if desired, from larger works devoted to the whole field of optics. Only those parts of the subject of relevance to the clinician are presented.

The scope of geometrical optics includes the properties of light travelling in a single uniform medium and the effects of the introduction of a change of medium in its path, particularly in relation to the geometry of the boundary between the media.

THE PROPAGATION OF LIGHT IN A UNIFORM MEDIUM

A basic principle of geometrical optics as first enunciated by Euclid is that of the *rectilinear propagation of light*—light travels in straight lines; rays of sunlight coming through a gap in the curtains or the beam of a searchlight are well-known illustrations of this. An important condition for rectilinear propagation is that the medium through which the light passes should be uniform, and because of this its velocity is constant.

In order to understand how the principle arises from the concept of light as waves, we may imagine a very small source emitting light, the wave-fronts

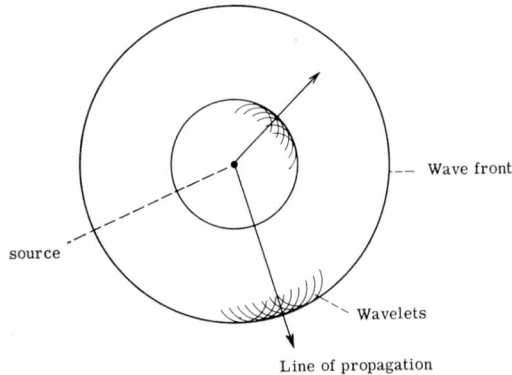

FIG. 15.—THE WAVE FRONTS FROM A SOURCE OF LIGHT.
Propagated outwards as an expanding sphere.

of which are moving outwards as an expanding sphere (Fig. 15). The direction of propagation in these circumstances is along any radius of the sphere so that it is always at right angles to the wave-front; a line drawn to represent the line of propagation is called a RAY; a small bundle of rays a PENCIL.

Since the same quantity of light falls on the inner sphere as on the outer, its intensity in any area must vary as the square of the radius of the sphere. This rapid diminution of the intensity as the distance from the source increases is expressed in Kepler's fundamental LAW OF INVERSE SQUARES: *the intensity at any point is inversely proportional to the square of the distance of the point from the source.*

In the propagation of light through a homogeneous medium, it is of interest to consider its behaviour in passing through a minute aperture (or pin-hole) in an opaque screen, or past the edges of an opaque body when shadows are cast.

PIN-HOLES AND SHADOWS

The PIN HOLE CAMERA (the *camera obscura* of Ptolemy and Al-Hazen) produces an image of an object (AB, Fig. 16) by means of an opaque screen (EF) which interrupts the light-rays to such an extent that only the narrowest pencil for each point on the object can pass through the tiny hole in it. It is obvious that rays from the top of the object fall on the lower part of the screen and, since the hole is small, only a minute quantity of light traverses it; a faint inverted image is thus formed (CD).

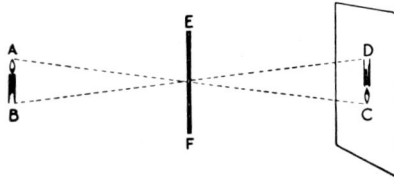

FIG. 16.—PIN-HOLE CAMERA.

If the hole is large the bundle of rays passing through it is too wide to produce a recognizable image on the screen. If several small holes are made, many overlapping images are found. This process of increasing the number of holes can be carried out until no screen is left; at this point we are in the same situation as having one large hole and therefore no clear image is formed, the surface being merely diffusely illuminated.

SHADOWS, from the optical aspect, may be thought of as the converse of the pin-hole camera. In Fig. 16 the portion of the surface which does not have an image upon it is, of course, the shadow of the screen, EF. Shadows vary with the shape and size of the source of light and of the interrupting

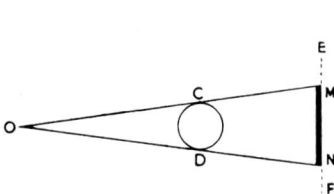

FIG. 17.

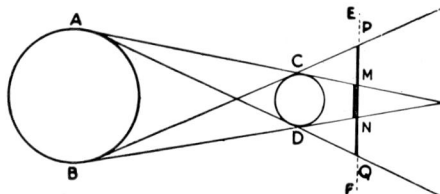

FIG. 18.

FIGS. 17 and 18.—SHADOWS.

body. With a point-source (O, Fig. 17), a clearly-cut shadow (MN) of an opaque body (CD) is formed on a screen (EF). With an extended source (AB, Fig. 18) there is a central dense shadow, the *umbra* (MN), surrounded by a less dense area, the *penumbra* (PM, QN), the latter becoming progressively brighter as we pass from the umbra towards the fully illuminated surface. The application of these facts to eclipses of the sun by the moon is well known ; the earth travelling in the umbra of the moon will experience a total eclipse and in the penumbra, a partial eclipse.

The pin-hole aperture and shadows play a valuable part in clinical optics. The former can be used as a kind of universal focusing device, and the latter is of importance in retinoscopy. They both clearly illustrate the rectilinear propagation of light. We might end this section, however, by pointing out that this principle is one of those many approximations in geometrical optics to which we have already referred. In reality, opaque obstacles which partially obstruct the path of light invariably cause some bending of the rays out of their straight path. Suffice it to say here that this phenomenon, *diffraction*,[1] while of some physiological importance, may be ignored in the present discussion of geometrical optics.

THE EFFECTS OF THE INTERPOSITION OF A SECOND MEDIUM

If a ray of light meets a second medium in its pathway three things may happen: REFLECTION, whereby the light is thrown back at the surface of the second medium roughly in the direction from which it came; TRANSMISSION, whereby the light passes onwards into the new medium; or ABSORPTION, whereby the light changes into some other form of energy, usually heat. It is important to remember that all three phenomena always occur to some extent when there is a change of the medium through which the light passes, although one effect is often found to be the most marked depending upon the properties of the media concerned.

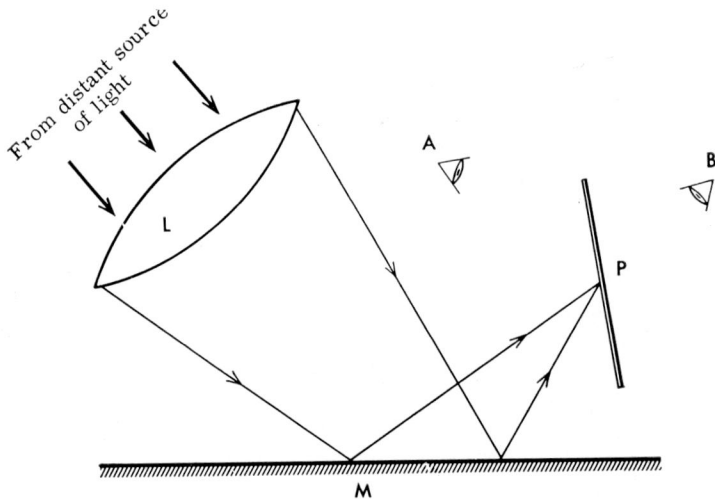

FIG. 19.

An imaginary " burning " glass experiment will illustrate this point (Fig. 19). Light from a very bright source reaches a glass lens (L) which focuses it onto a piece of paper (P) after it has been reflected by a mirror (M). The lens predominantly transmits, the mirror predominantly reflects, and the paper, to a much greater extent than the

[1] p. 78.

others, absorbs the light-energy until it becomes hot and charred. The paper, of course, also reflects light to some extent as it likewise transmits the remainder, but the way it does this illustrates further the effects of changing the medium through which light is travelling. An observer (A) looking at the spot becoming charred from the side of the incident light sees a very bright area; this is a region of reflection. But this is *diffuse reflection* which is different from the *specular reflection* produced by the highly polished mirror: the mirror gives a clearly cut picture by its regularly reflective properties but diffuse reflection by the paper does not.

Again, if an observer (B) looks at the paper from the side opposite that of the incident light, the area about to become charred will look bright because some light is transmitted through the paper. But if we compare this transmission with that through the glass of the lens we notice that the uniformity of the glass allows a clear picture to be seen through it, whereas the light coming through the irregular substance of the paper will be diffused.

As far as transmission is concerned, a medium which is uniform and allows a high proportion of light to pass onwards is called *transparent*; if it is not uniform but transmits a proportion of light it is called *translucent*. A medium which largely absorbs light is called *opaque*. It is to be remembered that a medium which allows light to pass through it, and is therefore transparent, may appear to be opaque because it does not have the same optical properties at all points; it consequently acts as many different media, and the entering light is reflected and transmitted many times in passing through until it may be completely scattered or *diffused*. Such a medium is spoken of as being *optically heterogeneous* (or *anisotropic*) as opposed to *homogeneous* (or *isotropic*); the most obvious example of a heterogeneous medium is ground glass.

When light strikes the surface of a reflecting surface or passes from one medium to another, its path of propagation is deflected from its original direction. Such an alteration from its rectilinear path may offer the opportunity for the rays to meet; in this event, if a pencil of rays (or their prolongations) meet at a point, such a point is called a FOCUS, and a collection of foci, corresponding to all the luminous points of an object, forms an IMAGE. If the rays actually meet at this point the image is *real*; if the point is imaginary, formed not by the reunion of the rays themselves but of their prolongations, it is termed *virtual*. A real image can be received on a screen but a virtual image cannot, although it can be perceived by an eye which is in the path of the rays since the optical system of the eye forms a real image of it on the retina. It may be noted that since the path of light is always reversible the positions of a source and its image can always be interchanged; their relative positions are therefore spoken of as *conjugate points*.

THE REFLECTION OF LIGHT

THE LAWS OF REFLECTION

When a ray of light meets the surface of a medium through which it cannot pass, its direction of propagation is altered according to well-defined laws; the *laws of reflection*, which date from Euclid, may be simply summarized by saying that when light strikes a reflecting surface it rebounds in exactly the same way as a ball does from a hard tennis court. The directions of the rays are defined with reference to the normal at the point of incidence. The *normal* is a line perpendicular to the tangent at a point on a surface; if the surface, as in AB, Fig. 20, is perfectly flat (plane), the tangent lies in the plane of the surface. The angles which the incident and reflected rays make with the normal at the point of incidence are called respectively the ANGLE OF INCIDENCE and the ANGLE OF REFLECTION. Thus in Fig. 20, if PM meets the surface AB at M and is reflected along MR, PMN is the angle of incidence (*i*) and RMN is the angle of reflection (*r*). The direction of the reflected ray, MR, is determined by two laws:

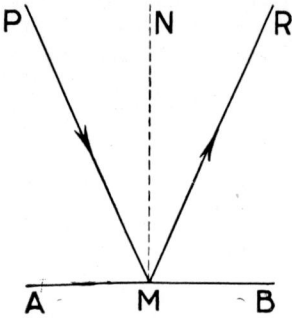

FIG. 20.—REFLECTION FROM A REGULAR SURFACE.

1. The incident ray, the normal to the surface at the point of incidence, and the reflected ray lie in one plane.

2. The incident and reflected rays are equally inclined to the normal, and lie on opposite sides of it: that is, the angle of reflection is equal to the angle of incidence.

REFLECTION AT IRREGULAR SURFACES

In a previous example (Fig. 19) we have already compared specular and diffuse reflection, the former from a regular, brightly polished surface, the latter from an irregular one. In the latter case the reason for the lack of the formation of a precise image is seen in Fig. 21. The downward prolongations of the reflected rays do not meet at a single focus but are scattered over many points; at each of these is a feeble image of the point-source (I)

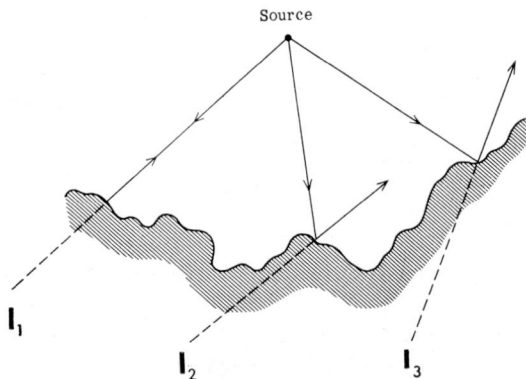

FIG. 21.—REFLECTION FROM AN IRREGULAR POLISHED SURFACE.

but there are so many of them that only a vague and diffuse blur of light is seen.

Diffuse reflection is of no great importance in geometrical optics. It should, however, be remembered that it is by diffuse reflection that most objects are seen. However brightly polished a surface may be, there is always some diffuse reflection for a perfect specular reflector does not in fact exist ; if it did, we would see not the reflector but merely objects reflected in it. Apart from their diffuse reflection, of course, objects may become visible because they are self-luminous, for example, the sun or electric light filaments.

REFLECTION AT PLANE SURFACES : PLANE MIRRORS

As we have seen, we refer here to specular reflection from a highly polished plane surface. In Fig. 22, let us imagine an observer at point X

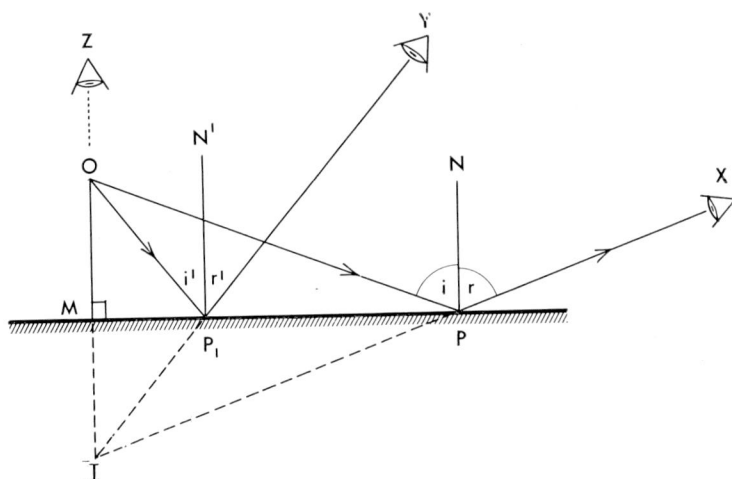

FIG. 22.—REFLECTION BY A PLANE MIRROR.

looking at the reflection of a point-source of light O. If his eye is at X the light reflected into his eye will come from P, which is a point on the surface of the mirror such that the laws of reflection are obeyed whereby the angle of incidence (i) = the angle of reflection (r) and the line NP is the normal to the surface.

Suppose the observer now moves to Y. Again, the ray from O which is reflected at P_1 to Y obeys the laws of reflection whereby $i' = r'$ and $N'P_1$ is the normal at the surface. If the observer moved to Z, the special case arises of the ray from the object striking the mirror at right angles and therefore (by the laws of reflection) being reflected back along its own path.

The observer gets his idea of where an image appears to be by " imagining " it to be along the line of the reflected ray (prolonged downwards in the figure). When a point-image of a point-source is formed by a plane mirror, *all* the reflected rays prolonged downwards must meet at a point in a specific position. Rays OM and XP meet at a point I. The triangles OMP and IMP are congruent because they have a common side, PM, and two identical angles, OPM ($90° - i$) and IPM ($90° - r$), and since $i = r$ by the law of reflection, this also equals ($90° - i$). Because of this congruence, OM = IM.

Similarly, if we consider rays OM and YP_1, the point of intersection of their downward prolongations is a point the distance of which from M is equal to OM, in other words, it is the same point I. It is clear, therefore, that the downward prolongation of any reflected ray will strike the prolongation

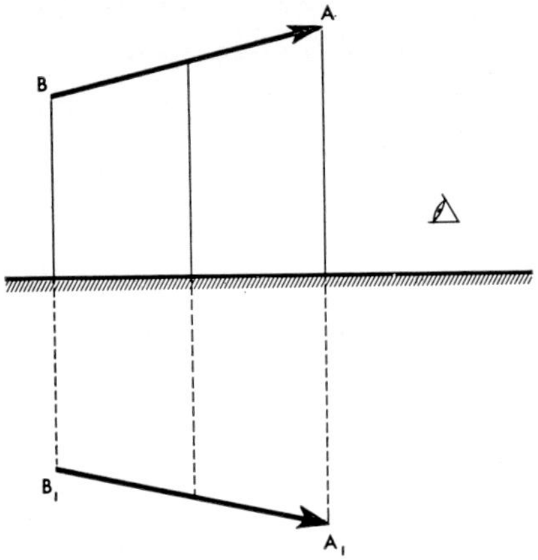

FIG. 23.

of the ray, OM, at the same point. In other words, *a virtual point-image is formed and it is as far behind the mirror as the object is in front.*

If, instead of a point-source, we consider an object of some size, the position of its image can be found from our knowledge of the position of point-images. This is shown in Fig. 23 wherein each point in the object, AB, can be regarded as a point-source. If A_1 is the point-image of A, and B_1 is similarly the point-image of B, it is obvious that the virtual image of the whole of AB is on the line joining the two points, A_1 and B_1. An observer looking at AB directly will see A to his right; while the image of A in the mirror appears to be to the left. This well-known phenomenon is called *lateral inversion or perversion of the image;* it has, of course, become a common-place to refer to the "mirror-image" of an object. In spite of this change of appearance, however, reflection in a plane mirror produces an image which is *unchanged in size,* as is clear from Fig. 23.

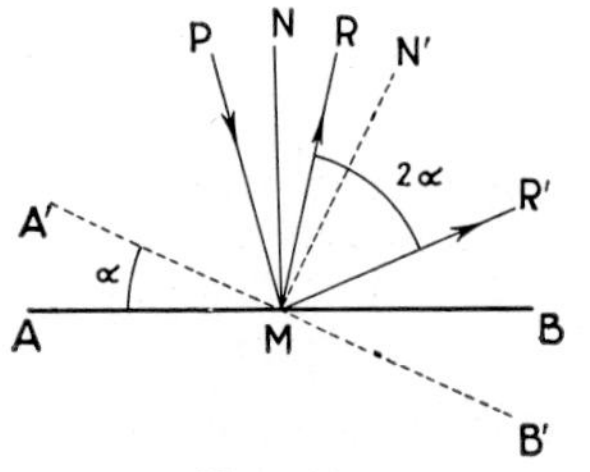

FIG. 24.

The Rotation of a Mirror. It follows from our

discussion that if the mirror is rotated in the plane of incidence of the light, the angle traversed by the reflected ray is twice that through which the mirror is turned.

Thus in Fig. 24, where PM is the incident ray, MR the reflected ray, and NM the normal, if α is the angle through which the mirror (AB) is turned, then the angle through which the reflected ray is turned $= \angle RMR' = \angle PMR' - \angle PMR = 2\angle PMN' - 2\angle PMN = 2\angle NMN' = 2\alpha$.

REFLECTION AT UNIFORMLY CURVED SURFACES :
SPHERICAL MIRRORS

The most important uniformly curved reflecting surface to be considered forms part of a sphere—the SPHERICAL MIRROR. Figure 25a illustrates the form of a concave mirror; a convex mirror may be similarly envisaged (Fig. 25b) if the reflecting surface is on the outside of the sphere while the light falls upon it from the opposite direction; in this case the same definitions apply. Before proceeding further, a system must be agreed for naming and measuring the various elements of optical systems in which spherical mirrors take part.

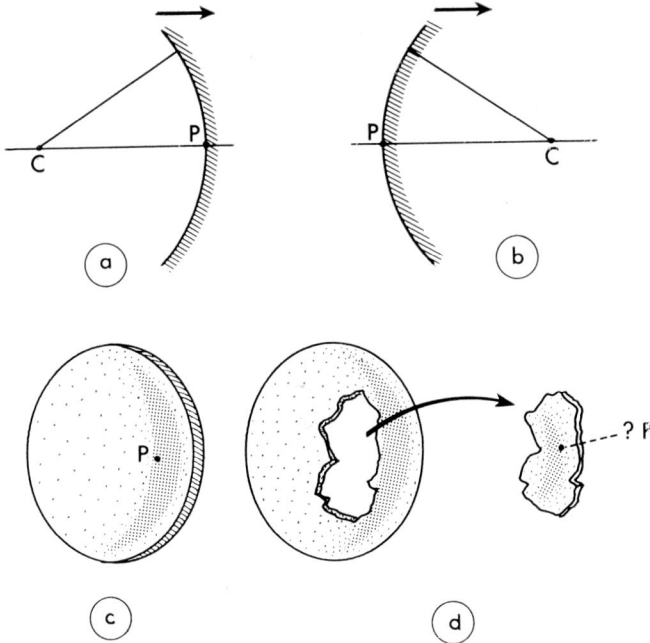

FIG. 25.—THE POLE OF A MIRROR (see text).

The *centre of curvature* (C, Fig. 25) is the centre of the sphere of which the mirror is part; the radius of the sphere is called the *radius of curvature* and being perpendicular to the tangent at any point on the surface, it becomes the normal ray at that point. The *pole* (P) (or *vertex*) of the mirror is the central point of the reflecting surface, but it may have an uncertain location. This point is readily identifiable if the *aperture* of the mirror, that is, the part of the mirror upon which the light is allowed to fall, is circular and regular (Fig. 25c), but if the aperture of a spherical mirror is irregular, the pole is necessarily at another site (Fig. 25d). In our drawings we shall consider simple cross-sections of spherical surfaces which appear as arcs of circles and in them the pole is the mid-point of the arc.

An *axis* is any line passing through the centre of curvature and striking the mirror. That passing through the pole of the mirror is called the *principal axis*; any other is a *subsidiary axis*. If the aperture is irregular and the position of the pole therefore in doubt, it may be impossible to say which is the principal and which is the subsidiary axis; indeed, drawing the image may be made easier by ignoring the distinction altogether since any line through the centre of curvature may be used as a frame of reference.

In most instances the object and image are at different distances from the mirror and they may both be on the same side or one on each side of it. It is thus necessary to decide how to measure these distances and define their direction. This is a matter of choice and even the physicists themselves disagree as to the best method, but it is important to retain one system of nomenclature. The convention most widely used today is that all distances are measured from the pole of the mirror, those in the direction of the incident light being called *positive* and those against the incident light *negative*.

THE SIGNIFICANCE OF PARAXIAL RAYS

We may begin the geometrical optics of spherical mirrors by examining the reflection at a spherical curved surface of a bundle of rays parallel to the principal axis (Fig. 26); such a bundle of rays travels as if from a source which

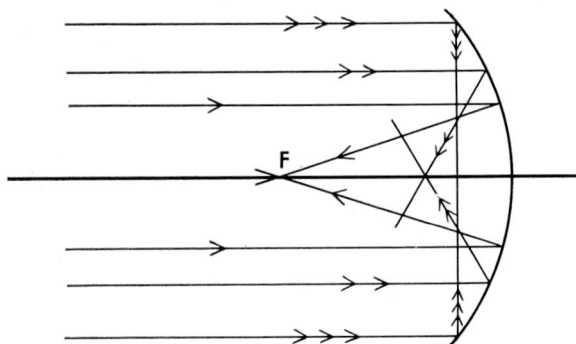

FIG. 26.—REFLECTION OF PARALLEL RAYS BY A SPHERICAL CURVED MIRROR.
F is the paraxial principal focus.

is a great ('infinite') distance away. On striking the mirror all the rays obey the law of reflection, that is, they are reflected so that the angle of reflection (between it and the radius of curvature at that point) is equal to the angle of incidence (Fig. 26). It follows that the rays further from the axis are focused closer to the pole of the mirror than those near the axis. Now the very fact that there is a difference between the focus of the peripheral (*marginal*) rays and those close to the axis (*paraxial*) implies that a spherical mirror never forms a true point-image of an object which is a great distance away. By confining our attention to a small pencil of light consisting only of the paraxial rays and ignoring the marginal rays, however, with a little geometrical juggling it is possible to indicate where the majority of the rays are focused, giving a reasonable approximation to a point image, the PRINCIPAL FOCUS.

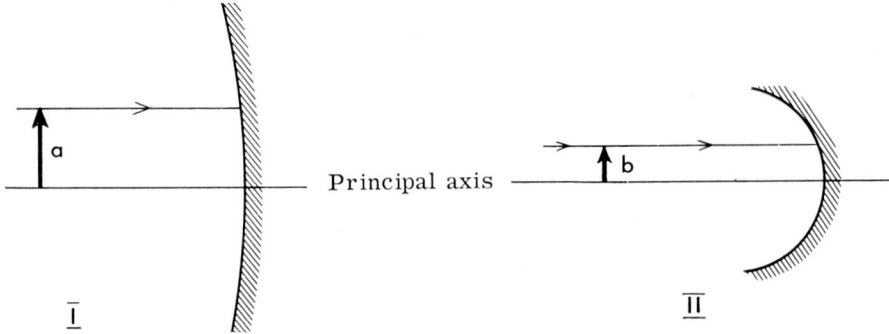

FIG. 27.—THE LIMITS OF PARAXIAL RAYS IN MIRRORS OF DIFFERENT CURVATURE.

The limits of the paraxial rays depend on the degree of curvature of the mirror, and upon its aperture. For example, we can consider a and b in Fig. 27 to be the limits of the truly paraxial rays, b being nearer to the axis than a because of the greater curvature of the mirror in II; the more curved the mirror, the smaller will be the aperture which can legitimately be considered to reflect paraxial rays.

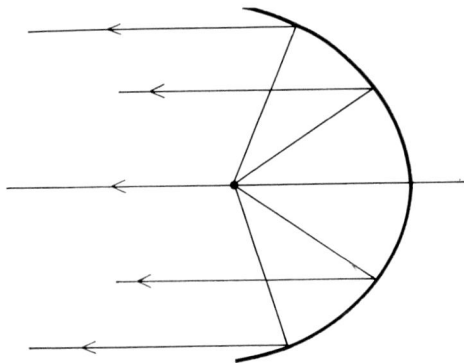

FIG. 28.—REFLECTION FROM A LARGE PARABOLOIDAL MIRROR.

Although there is thus no true focus for spherical mirrors of large aperture, a large-aperture mirror curved in the shape of a paraboloid focuses a beam of parallel rays from infinity (Fig. 28). Motor car headlights, for example, are designed with reflectors of this shape and, since the filament is at the focus of the mirror, a parallel beam emerges.

Protracted geometrical proof of the formula relating the distances of the object and its image for a spherical mirror is possible but a simpler method is to use the well-known approximation from trigonometry that the tangent of an angle approximately equals the angle itself (expressed in radians, not degrees) if the angle is *small*. This approximation can be applied to paraxial optics for we are dealing only with the reflection of small pencils of light reflected by spherical mirrors of small aperture.

Consider a point object, O, on the principal axis of a spherical concave mirror, at a distance, u, from the pole, P (Fig. 29). After reflection the paraxial ray from this point (OS) will form a point-image, I, at a distance, v,

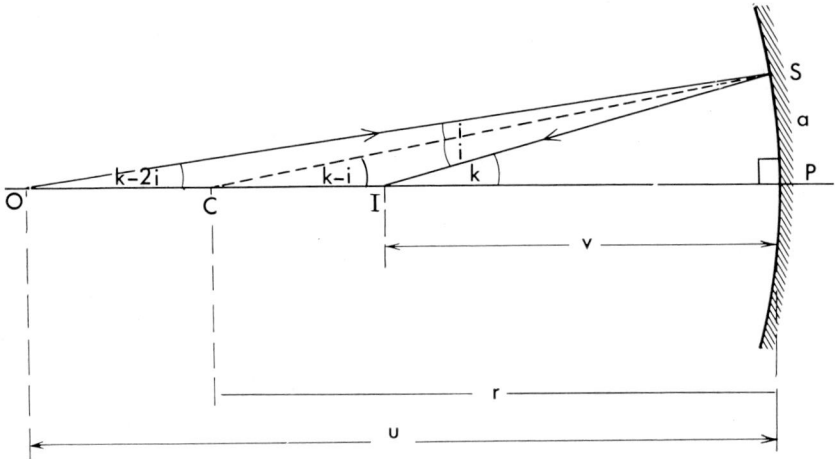

FIG. 29.

from the pole such that, according to the law of reflection, OS and SI make equal angles with the normal CS, C being the centre of curvature. Let us call this angle i, and the angle between the reflected ray SI and the axis we shall refer to as k. SCP is therefore $k - i$, and SOP is $k - 2i$ (the external angle of a triangle is equal to the sum of the two opposite angles). If we consider only rays close to the axis, the arc SP, of length a, can be regarded as a straight line and SPI will be virtually a right angle. We have therefore :

$$\tan k \simeq k = a/v$$
$$\tan k - i \simeq k - i = a/r$$
$$\tan k - 2i \simeq k - 2i = a/u$$

If we eliminate k, i and a from these equations we get :

$$2/r = 1/u + 1/v$$

It can easily be shown that the same formula applies to convex mirrors.

A further simple calculation enables us to work out the position of the (paraxial) PRINCIPAL FOCUS which, as we have seen in Fig. 26, is the point where parallel rays—as if coming from a very distant object—are focused after reflection. If the factor u is infinity in the above formula, it therefore becomes $2/r = 1/v$.

In this instance, v is known as the FOCAL LENGTH of the mirror and is equal to half its radius of curvature. The mirror formula therefore becomes:

$$\frac{1}{u} + \frac{1}{v} = \frac{1}{f}$$

The power of spherical mirrors is usually expressed numerically as the reciprocal of the focal length in metres. The sign of the power is conventionally agreed to be positive for concave mirrors and negative for convex mirrors. Thus the power is expressed as $(-\frac{1}{f})$.

CONSTRUCTION OF THE IMAGE

In order to construct the image of an extended object, XY (Fig. 30), given by a concave mirror we can simplify matters by considering the point X

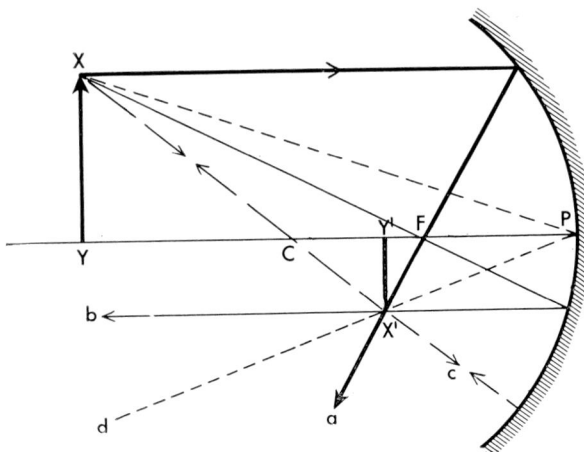

FIG. 30. THE IMAGE FORMED BY A CONCAVE MIRROR.

on it which is furthest away from the axis. We can assume—as it is reasonable to do for mirrors of small aperture—that each point on the object will form an appropriate point-image. The position of the image of X may be found by choosing any two of four rays: (a) the ray parallel to the axis which must be reflected (by definition) through the principal focus; (b) the ray passing through the principal focus which after reflection must be parallel to the axis (this is another example of the principle of *reversibility of light paths*); (c) the ray through the centre of curvature which by definition must go back along the same path since it strikes the reflecting surface at right angles; and (d) the ray from X to P, the pole of the mirror, which can always be constructed by applying the law of equality of the angles of incidence and reflection to it and the principal axis.

The intersection of any two of these four rays—and they all intersect at one point—gives the position X' where the image of the point X is formed. It follows that the image of the object XY is in the region of X'Y' in the figure.

A similar construction illustrates the formation of the image of a convex mirror.

MAGNIFICATION

We shall now define the relationship of the size of the image to that of the object. Consider once more the ray (d) from the extreme end of the object in Fig. 30; its path after reflection is indicated for a concave mirror in

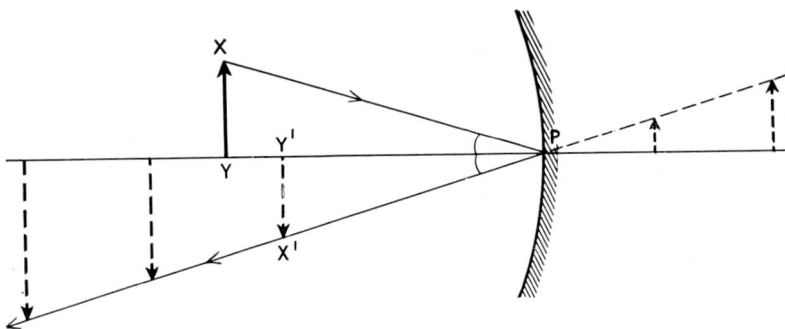

FIG. 31. MAGNIFICATION OF THE IMAGE.

Fig. 31. The image must lie somewhere along this path. We have seen that its exact position can be found by choosing another ray a, b or c. But wherever it is, XYP and X'Y'P are similar triangles so that XY (object-size) bears the same ratio to X'Y' (image-size) as YP does to Y'P. In other words, *object-size and image-size are related in the same way as their distances from the mirror*. The geometry still holds true even if (as the dotted lines of the figure show) the image is virtual, on the opposite side of the mirror to the object. It also applies similarly to convex mirrors.

Magnification is thus expressed as the size of the image divided by that of the object and numerically this, as we have seen, equals v divided by u, when v is the distance of the image and u that of the object. There is a little difficulty connected with signs; if objects and images above the principal axis are considered positive and those below negative, the formula then becomes:

$$M(\text{magnification}) = i/o = -v/u.$$

It follows that we can now determine not only the magnification for any

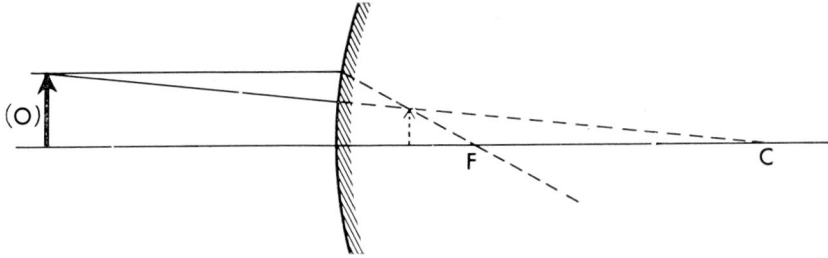

Fig. 32.

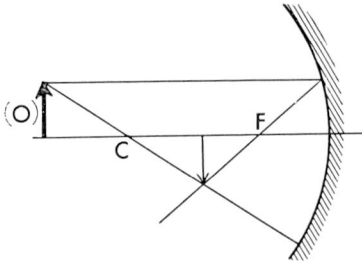

Fig. 33.

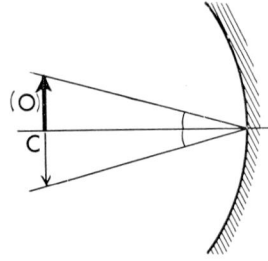

Fig. 34.

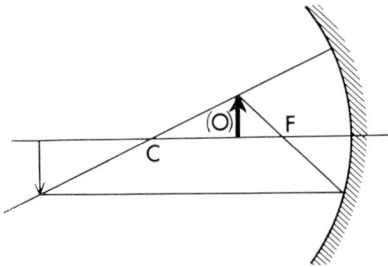

Fig. 35.

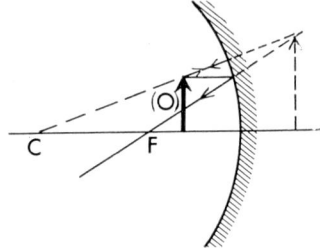

Fig. 36.

Figs. 32 to 36.—The Type and Position of the Images formed by Extended Objects at Spherical Surfaces of small Aperture in Convex (Fig. 32) and Concave Mirrors (Figs. 33–36).

object but also whether the image is erect or inverted, the former giving a positive figure for magnification and the latter a negative.

The type and position of the images formed by extended objects at spherical mirrors of small aperture can now be constructed. In the case of a convex mirror this is simple for the image is erect, virtual and diminished, and this holds for every real object (Fig. 32). In the case of a concave mirror, however, the position varies according to the relationship of the object to the centre of curvature and the principal focus.

If it is more distant than the centre of curvature the image is inverted, real and diminished (Fig. 33). As we approach the centre of curvature the image increases in size (remaining real and inverted) until at the centre of curvature it is inverted, real and of the same size as the object (Fig. 34).

Between the centre of curvature and the focus the image is larger than the object and remains inverted and real; it is situated outside C (Fig. 35). At the principal focus the image is at infinity, but once inside the principal focus it becomes erect, virtual and magnified (Fig. 36).

Note that from the formula $M = -v/u$, if v and u are of the same sign (that is, object and image are both real), M will be negative and therefore the image will be inverted. It follows that *all real images are inverted*; conversely, *all virtual images are erect*.

THE REFRACTION OF LIGHT

We have seen that light travels through an isotropic medium in straight lines at a constant velocity. The velocity depends upon the amount of resistance offered by the medium to the passage of light, a property known as OPTICAL DENSITY. Consequently, if a beam leaves one medium and enters a second isotropic medium of greater optical density, its progress will be retarded: if it enters perpendicularly the wave-fronts will travel in the same straight line but at a slower rate; but if the beam strikes the body obliquely one edge of an advancing wave-front will enter the body before the other, and consequently will be retarded earlier. The resultant change of direction or bending of the wave-front due to a change in its velocity is known as REFRACTION.

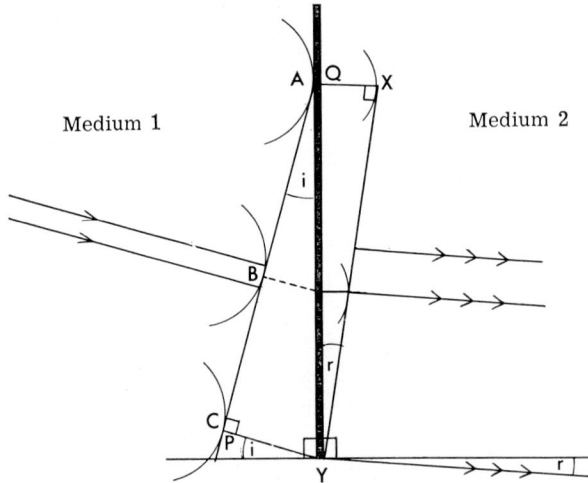

FIG. 37.—THE REFRACTION OF LIGHT.

The rationale of this phenomenon is seen in Fig. 37. Consider the wavelets A, B and C of the wave-front. A enters the denser medium which is bounded by a plane surface and expands onwards while C just reaches the new medium. During this period the distance travelled by the top wavelet in the second medium will be less than that travelled by the bottom wavelet in reaching the boundary between the two media, that is, AX is less than PY. The alteration of direction of the rays will therefore depend on the change in the speed of transmission of the light; in this change of direction $\angle$ PQY is the angle of incidence (i) and $\angle$ XYQ the angle of refraction (r), both being measured in relation to the normal.

If the speeds of light in the two media are referred to as V_1 and V_2, then the time taken for wavelet C to reach the new medium is PY/V_1 and this is the same as the time during which wavelet A travels from Q to X, that time being QX/V_2. It therefore follows that $PY/V_1 = QX/V_2$, whence $V_2/V_1 = QX/PY$.

The ratio, PY/QX, is also the same as that between the sines of the angle of incidence and the angle of refraction (from triangles PQY and QXY). If we now eliminate QX and PY from consideration, we find that $V_1/V_2 = \sin i/\sin r$.

It follows that the ratio of the speeds of light in the two media are related as the sines of the angles of incidence and of refraction. If the media are isotropic, these velocities are constant and the ratio between the two must be constant. This ratio is known as the INDEX OF REFRACTION between the two media concerned. If the first medium is a vacuum, $\sin i/\sin r$ is an absolute value for the second medium and is known as its REFRACTIVE INDEX (n). The refractive index of air (1·0003) may be conveniently accepted as unity. If two media have refractive indices n_1 and n_2, the passage of light from the first to the second is governed by the law:

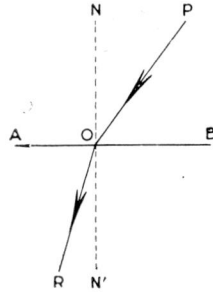

FIG. 38.

$$\sin i/\sin r = n_2/n_1 = {}_1n_2 \text{ (a constant).}$$

We are now able to generalize this equation by stating the LAWS OF REFRACTION first formulated by Willebrord Snell in 1621.[1]

1. The incident ray, the normal to the surface at the point of incidence, and the refracted ray lie in one plane.

2. The sine of the angle of refraction bears a constant relation to the sine of the angle of incidence, the value of the ratio depending on the nature of the two media and on the nature of the incident light.

These are illustrated simply in Fig. 38, where NOP is the angle of incidence and N'OR the angle of refraction.

Some interesting consequences follow from these laws and the factors which define indices of refraction. If we call the index of refraction for medium 1 to medium 2, ${}_1n_2$, the *principle of reversibility* of light paths applies and we find that ${}_1n_2 = 1/{}_2n_1$. In passing from a less dense to a more dense medium, the light is therefore bent towards the normal (Fig. 39); in passing in the reverse direction it is bent away from the normal (Fig. 40). Another important feature can be appreciated when we consider larger angles of incidence; with the light travelling into an optically denser medium, i must

[1] p. 27.

always be greater than r and when i is $90°$ (tangential to the surface) $\sin i$ becomes unity, so that $\sin r$ must be somewhat less than unity.

If the light is going in the opposite direction, when the angle of incidence (now r) is small the rays can still emerge into the less optically dense medium but they become flatter and flatter towards the surface as r increases (Fig. 41). Eventually the emerging ray will just creep out tangential to the surface. With a still greater angle r, it is obviously impossible for it to emerge. At one angle, the sine of which is equal to the refractive index, the refracted ray runs parallel to the surface between the two media (R_1, Fig. 42). This is called the CRITICAL ANGLE of incidence (δ) and is defined by the formula:

$$\sin \delta = 1/_1n_2, \text{ or } _1n_2 = 1/\sin \delta$$

It is noteworthy that measurement of this angle is a convenient way of determining the index of refraction between two media.

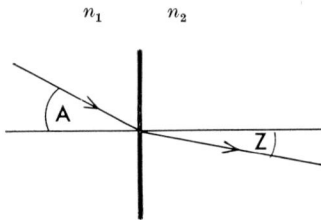

$$_1n_2 = \frac{n_2}{n_1} = \frac{\sin A}{\sin Z}$$

Fig. 39.

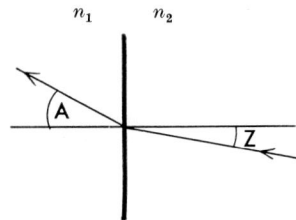

$$_2n_1 = \frac{n_1}{n_2} = \frac{\sin Z}{\sin A}$$

Fig. 40.

Figs. 39 and 40.—The Principle of Reversibility in Refraction.

If the angle of incidence is still further increased, the incident ray cannot pass out of the denser medium to enter the second medium but is reflected at the surface between the two, a phenomenon known as a TOTAL INTERNAL REFLECTION (R_2, Fig. 42). Such total internal reflection is possible only when light is travelling from a more optically dense medium (with a greater refractive index) into one less so. Reflection of this type is the most effective known and use of it is made in numerous optical devices, for example, prism binoculars and fibre optics. It is also, of course, partly responsible for the rainbow. The total internal reflection of light emerging from the angle of the anterior chamber prevents its observation; by abolishing this, a gonioscope allows the angle to be seen.

Let us now turn to some common optical phenomena associated with refraction. We shall first consider refraction at plane surfaces and then at curved surfaces, examining in either case the effects of single and multiple surfaces.

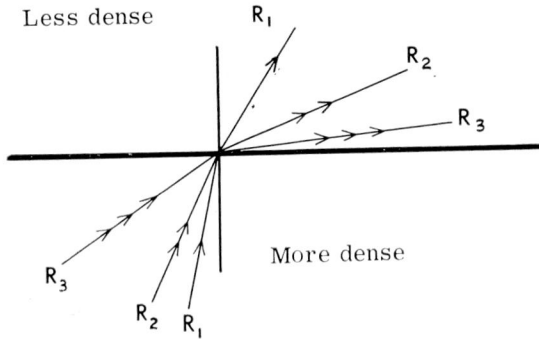

FIG. 41.

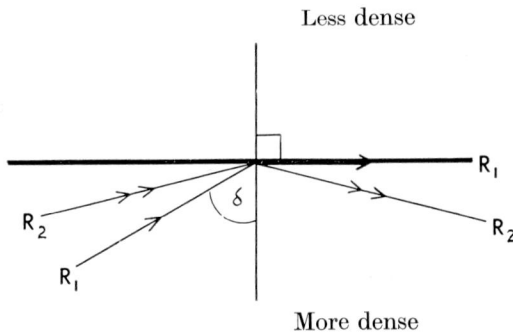

$$\frac{\sin \delta}{\sin 90°} = {}_2n_1 \qquad \therefore \quad \sin \delta = {}_2n_1 = \frac{1}{{}_1n_2}$$

FIG. 42.

FIGS. 41 and 42.—THE CRITICAL ANGLE AND TOTAL INTERNAL REFLECTION.

REFRACTION AT A SINGLE PLANE SURFACE

This has already been examined in the general discussion of refraction. A well-known example of it is the phenomenon of apparent depth. Suppose an observer looks at a penny (P) lying at the bottom of a tank of water (Fig. 43); the rays from the penny destined to strike his eye reach the surface of the water at S and are then bent outwards (away from the normal) because air is less optically dense than the water. Now the observer imagines the path of

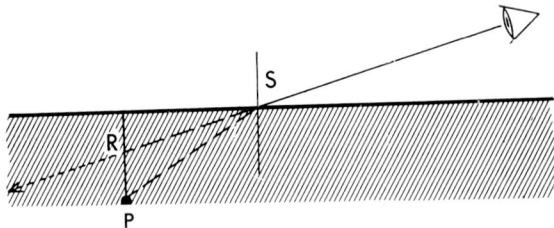

FIG. 43.

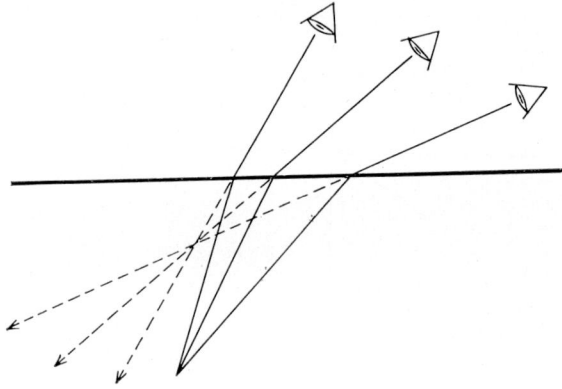

FIG. 44.

the rays in the air to give the clue to the direction of the penny and he mentally " imagines " it at R. This gives him the impression that the penny is lying on the bottom of a much shallower tank than is actually the case. From Fig. 44 it can also be appreciated that the more obliquely the observer views the penny the shallower the tank appears to be.

REFRACTION BY A PARALLEL-SIDED BLOCK OF GLASS

Let us consider a point-object (P) looked at through a block of glass with parallel sides, AB and CD (Fig. 45). The paths of the rays of light are shown in the figure. As AB and CD are parallel, it is easy to show that the ray emerging from the block is parallel to the ray entering the block, provided the medium on one side of it is the same as on the other. But an observer will actually see the object displaced from its natural position, the degree of displacement of the image varying with the obliquity of the observer's view. It is least when close to the normal direction, but as the observer moves outwards the object will also appear to move; in fact, there is no one point which is the image for all the possible positions of view. We do not get this sensation on looking through windows which are essentially similar because

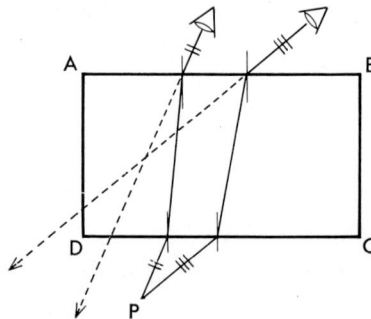

FIG. 45. REFRACTION THROUGH A MEDIUM WITH PARALLEL PLANE SIDES.

the thickness of the glass is so small that the displacement of the object is minimal and is not noticeable unless an extremely oblique sighting is taken.

There is an interesting property of glass blocks with parallel sides which depends upon the displacement of the image. Suppose as in the diagram (Fig. 46) that someone looks at a pencil through the glass block. For a particular point of observation one end, H, of the pencil will be displaced to the left to H_1 and the other end, B, will be imaged further out to the right at B_1, so that H_1B_1 is larger than HB. The effect of this is to give the impression of magnification. Use of this can be made in designing the so-called size-lenses[1] in which magnification is obtained without focal power. In practice

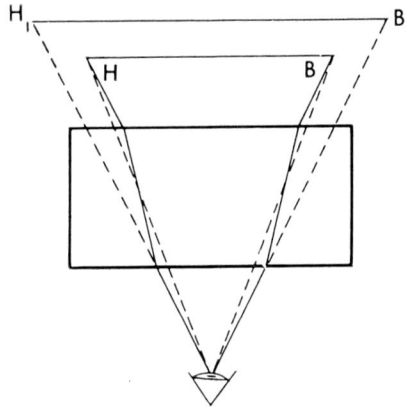

FIG. 46.

their two surfaces are not strictly " parallel " to one another but the principle is the same. The magnification depends on the distance between the surfaces, in other words, on the thickness of the " lens ".

REFRACTION THROUGH TWO PLANE SURFACES INCLINED AT AN ANGLE—THE PRISM

We have seen that the ray emerging from a parallel-sided glass block is parallel to the entrant ray; we now consider the effect when such a glass medium has sides which are not parallel to one another. Such a refracting device is called a PRISM. The geometric definition of a prism is a portion of a refracting medium bordered by two plane surfaces which are inclined at a finite angle. Some new terms must be introduced before we discuss its optical properties.

The angle between the two plane surfaces is called the *apical* or *refracting angle* of the prism (a) (Fig. 47). A line bisecting the angle is called the *axis* of the prism and the surface which is opposite the refracting angle is referred to as the *base*. In most cases the axis cuts the base at right angles. Even if this should not be so, the base is always the thickest part of the prism.

We also denote *angles of incidence* (i) and of *emergence* (e) which relate to

[1] p. 682.

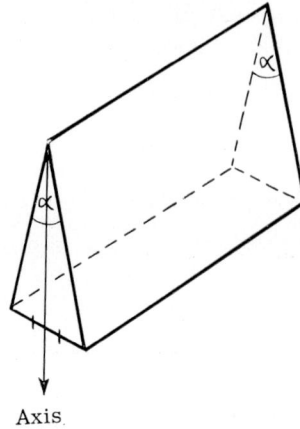

Axis

FIG. 47. THE APICAL ANGLE OF A PRISM.

rays striking the first plane surface and emerging from the second (Fig. 48).
The actual net change in direction of a ray produced after refraction by both
surfaces of a prism is called the *total deviation* (D); it is seen that the *deviation
increases as the apical angle of the prism increases*, and that the *total deviation
equals the sum of the angles of incidence and emergence, minus the apical angle
of the prism.* The direction of the deviation is therefore away from the apex

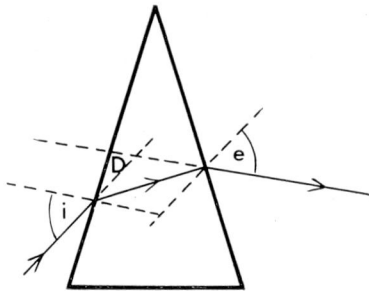

FIG. 48.

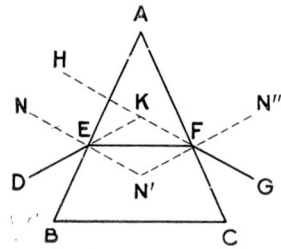

FIG. 49.

of the prism and to an observer looking at an object through the prism from
G (Fig. 49) its direction will appear to be displaced towards the apex. Thus
while *the light is deviated towards the base, the image is displaced towards the
apex of the prism.*

The actual amount of deviation can be calculated as follows :

If DEFG (Fig. 49) is a ray passing through a prism ABC with a refracting angle α,
and if the angles of incidence at the two faces, DEN $= i$, EFN$' = i'$, and the angles of
refraction FEN$' = e'$, and GFN$'' = e$;

but $\angle$ AEF $= 90° - e'$ and $\angle$ AFE $= 90° - i'$

hence $\quad \alpha + (90° - e') + (90° - i') = 180°$

$\quad\quad \therefore \alpha = i' + e'.$

The deviation at AB is measured by $(i - e')$ and at AC by $(e - i')$.

Therefore the total deviation $D = i - e' + e - i'$

$$= i + e - (e' + i')$$

$\quad\quad$ *i.e.* $\quad D = i + e - \alpha.$

In ophthalmology the prisms used are comparatively thin and in the majority of cases the rays pass through *symmetrically;* this is the condition in which the angle of the incidence is the same as the angle of emergence. In this instance the total deviation is the smallest possible for that particular prism; any different angle of incidence (and therefore angle of emergence) leads to a larger deviation.

For symmetrical rays, therefore, the relationship between the refracting angle (α), the total deviation (D) and the angles of incidence (i) and of emergence (e) can be simplified:

$$\text{since } D = i + e - \alpha, D = 2i - \alpha, \text{ and } i = \frac{D + \alpha}{2}.$$

From Fig. 50 it is seen that in $\varDelta BCD$, $\angle BCD = 180° - 2r$. In the quadrilateral ABCD, $\angle BAD + \angle BCD = 180°$. Therefore $\alpha + 180° - 2r = 180$: whence $\alpha = 2r$.

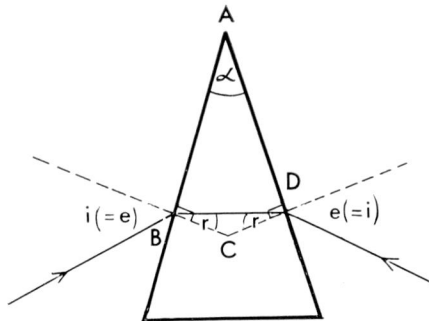

Fig. 50.—Symmetrical Refraction.

Now, $\sin i = n \sin r$, and therefore $i \simeq nr$, if both angles are small (their sines being equal to the angles themselves):

$$\therefore \frac{D + \alpha}{2} = \frac{n\alpha}{2}$$

and $D = (n - 1)\alpha.$

For glass with a refractive index of $1 \cdot 5$, $n - 1$ will be $0 \cdot 5$.

$$D = \alpha/2.$$

In ophthalmic practice, therefore, we may assume that for all practical purposes the total deviation is equal to half the refracting angle of the prism.

THE DISTORTION PRODUCED BY PRISMS

In these calculations we have made several approximations but in some circumstances these are inapplicable and some interesting optical effects occur. In the first place, we agreed to consider the angle of incidence as small, as it usually is in ophthalmology, but if an observer looks through the prism so that the angle of incidence is not small, strangely distorted images occur: a point-source of light, for example, does not appear as a point-image. Indeed, the apparent direction of the rays emerging from the prism and striking the observer's eyes varies so much from one ray to the next that they do not appear to emanate from a single point (Fig. 51). In the second place, a further distortion occurs due to the rays undergoing refraction in a plane at right angles to that we have just considered (Fig. 52). If we also take into

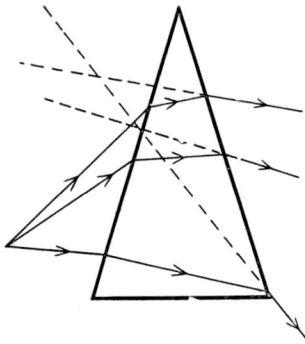
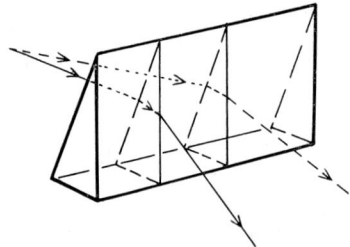

Fig. 51.　　　　　　　　　　Fig. 52.

Figs. 51 and 52.—Distortion by Prisms.

account the fact that the two eyes of an observer may experience different degrees of these various effects, it is clear that the wearers of prismatic spectacle corrections sometimes suffer a marked distortion of the shape of the image as well as anomalies of their spatial sense; straight lines appear curved and flat surfaces appear to slope (Fig. 51). Nevertheless, if the angles of incidence are small and the prisms are thin, such distortions are small and may pass unnoticed. Avoidance of the defects of a thick prism is one reason why a prismatic correction should be equally divided between the two eyes.

In our calculation to prove that $D = a/2$, we assumed that n was a constant. But white light is made up of many radiations, each with a characteristic wavelength and therefore a particular refractive index. When white light is passed through a prism we must therefore be careful to apply the original formula, $D = (n - 1)a$, remembering that n will be slightly different for each particular wavelength. As n varies, so also will D, thus leading to the phenomenon of DISPERSION. In this connection Newton's famous experiment in which by means of a prism he split up white light into its spectral components is well known.[1] Dispersion does not have an effect of great importance with ophthalmic prisms as such, but becomes more important when ophthalmic lenses are discussed.

THE NOMENCLATURE OF PRISMS

Many systems for categorizing prisms used to be employed, but in ophthalmology only one of these is in general use which is adequate in the circumstances. The unit is the PRISM DIOPTRE (Δ) and is defined as *the strength of a prism which will produce a linear apparent displacement*

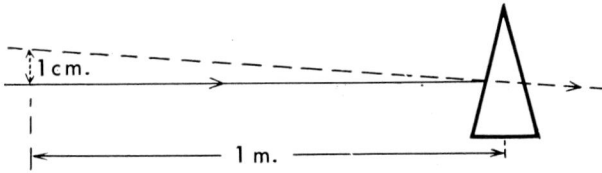

FIG. 53.—THE PRISM DIOPTRE.

of 1 cm. of an object situated 1 metre away (Fig. 53). All other methods of denoting prisms, such as the arc centune, the angle of minimum deviation or the refracting angle of the prism have specific advantages in certain circumstances but in ophthalmological work they can be considered collectively as obsolete. The strength of a prism in prism dioptres numerically approximates the refracting angle in degrees, each being twice the angle of minimum deviation.

The use of prisms in ophthalmology takes advantage of their power to deviate rays with little distortion or change in the size of the image, provided their thickness is not too great, but they may be incorporated in spectacle lenses to allow binocularity to be maintained in the presence of a manifest or latent squint. They are used in many optical instruments and here advantage may also be taken of a further effect depending upon the total internal refraction of light. Figure 54 shows how prisms effect such an action. Light entering a right-angled prism normally through one of the sides bounding the right angle strikes the hypotenuse at an angle of incidence greater than the critical angle; it is therefore totally internally reflected and emerges deviated at a right angle from its initial direction.

Rotating prisms are sometimes used in ophthalmology. If two equal prisms are placed base to apex, there is no prismatic effect since they act as a plate with parallel sides;

[1] Vol. IV, p. 617.

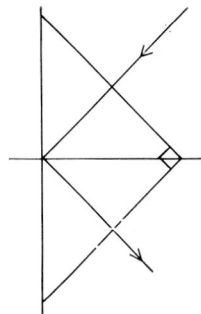

FIG. 54.—TOTAL INTERNAL REFLECTION.

if these are rotated upon each other in reverse directions they produce the effect of a single prism of gradually increasing strength, until eventually when they are apex to apex a maximum effect is obtained equal to the sum of the single prisms.

REFRACTION AT A SINGLE SPHERICAL SURFACE

Most of the curved surfaces dealt with in physiological optics are of this nature and we must be clear about refraction at such a single surface before we can proceed to discuss the optical effects of combinations of these.   The

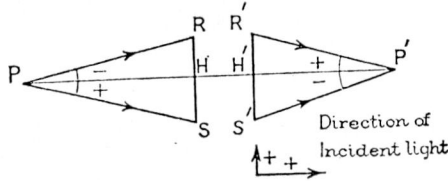

FIG. 55.—THE SIGN CONVENTION.

The sign of an angle between the ray and the axis is found by completing the triangle, PRH. The angle is positive if its tangent is positive, lengths being measured from the corner where the right angle is situated. Thus HR is positive and HP negative, so that RPH is negative and other angles are as marked. The light is always incident from the left, and signs both for horizontal and for vertical directions are the same as in the Cartesian coordinate system (R. W. Ditchburn).

convention adopted about distances and signs applies here as with mirrors; distances are measured from the centre of the refracting surface; they are positive when in the direction of the incident light and *vice versa* (Fig. 55). The principal axis is the line joining the centre of curvature to the centre of the refracting surface.

A simple formula can be worked out relating the object and image distances (u and v respectively), the radius of curvature of the surface (r) and the refractive index of the medium (n). The object is considered to be in a vacuum.

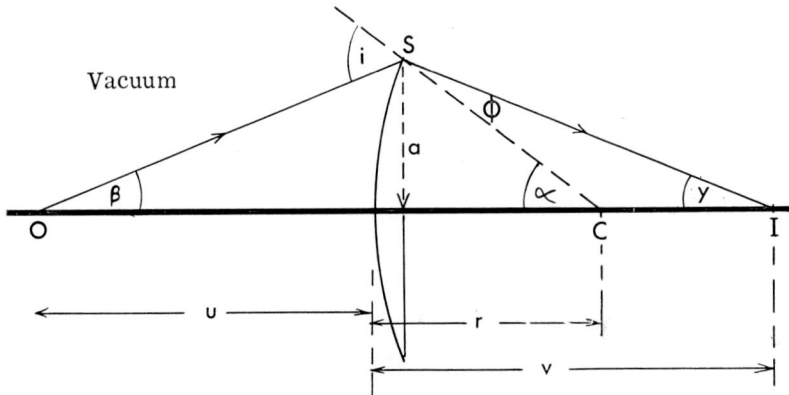

FIG. 56.

In Fig. 56, consider a ray from the object (O), which after striking the refracting surface (S) situated at a distance a from the principal axis, forms an image I. If ι and ϕ are respectively the angles of incidence and refraction at S, $\sin \iota = n \sin \phi$. For paraxial rays, $\sin \iota \simeq \iota$ and $\sin \phi \simeq \phi$; whence $\iota = n\phi$.

$$\text{From } \varDelta SOC, \iota = \alpha + \beta$$

$$\text{From } \varDelta SCI, \alpha = \gamma + \phi$$

Eliminating ι and ϕ we have $n(\alpha - \gamma) = \alpha + \beta$

For paraxial rays (retaining the sign convention), we have, where u and v are the object- and image-distances and r the radius of curvature of the surface,

$$\alpha \simeq \tan \alpha \simeq a/r$$

$$\beta \simeq \tan \beta \simeq - a/u$$

$$\gamma \simeq \tan \gamma \simeq a/v$$

$$n\left(\frac{a}{r} - \frac{a}{v}\right) = \frac{a}{r} - \frac{a}{u}.$$

$$\therefore \frac{n}{v} - \frac{1}{u} = \frac{n-1}{r}.$$

Two special positions of the object and the image can be derived from this formula. When the object is at infinity, in other words, when the rays striking the surface are parallel, $\frac{1}{u} = 0$, so that $\frac{n}{v} = \frac{n-1}{r}$. The position of the point-image of the rays parallel to the principal axis is called the *second focal point* (or *second principal focus*), F_2, and the *second focal length* (f_2) is given by v in the formula, therefore $f_2 = \frac{nr}{n-1}$ (Fig. 57). The *first focal length* (f_1) is the distance of an object from the surface such that after refraction the rays are parallel to the axis. This object is at the *first principal point* or *first principal focus*, F_1 (Fig. 58). From the above equation it follows that $f_1 = \frac{-r}{n-1}$. The relation between the principal foci is given by the formula :

$$f_2/f_1 = -n$$

provided the medium the light leaves (to the left in the figure) is air. When neither of the two media is air, the formula must be modified according to the refractive indices of the two media. If these are n_1 and n_2 for the first and second media, the formula becomes :

$$\frac{n_2}{v} - \frac{n_1}{u} = \frac{(n_2 - n_1)}{r}$$

$$\text{also,} \quad f_1 = n_1 r/(n_1 - n_2)$$

$$f_2 = n_2 r/(n_2 - n_1)$$

$$\text{and} \quad f_1/f_2 = -n_1/n_2.$$

That is, *the principal focal distances are to one another directly as the refractive indices of the corresponding media.*

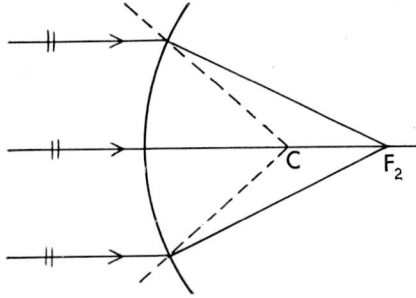

FIG. 57.

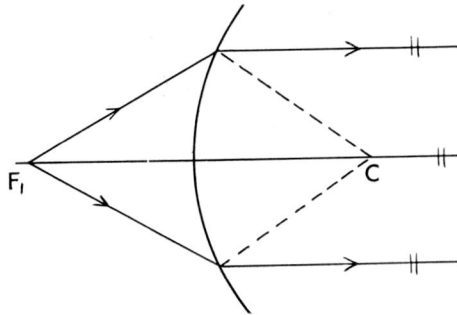

FIG. 58.

CONSTRUCTION OF THE IMAGE OF AN EXTENDED OBJECT

In order to construct the images of extended objects we choose rays with properties that we know (Fig. 59). One of these (1) will be the ray from the extremity of the object parallel to the principal axis which after refraction must pass through the second focal point. Another (2) runs from this point through the centre of curvature; this will pass undeviated through the surface because it strikes it at right angles. A third ray (3) which it is always possible to draw is that through the first focal point which emerges parallel to the principal axis.

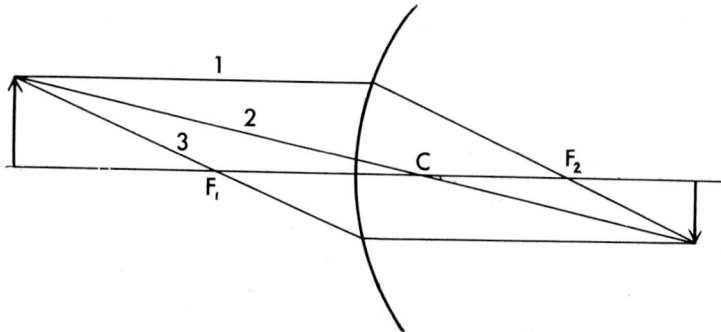

FIG. 59.—THE CONSTRUCTION OF THE IMAGE OF AN EXTENDED OBJECT.

The cornea is a refracting surface of great importance in visual optics; the magnifying properties of such a surface are therefore important and can be illustrated by constructing the image of the pupil (Fig. 60) according to the method we have just explained. P P₁ is the actual pupil; its image as seen from the air is found by taking lines through its extremities (as seen in cross section), firstly through C, the centre of curvature, and secondly parallel to the axis. Rays along the first line will continue undeviated. The second rays will emerge to pass through the first principal focus. A A₁ is therefore the image of the pupil which is seen to be larger than the actual size of the pupil.

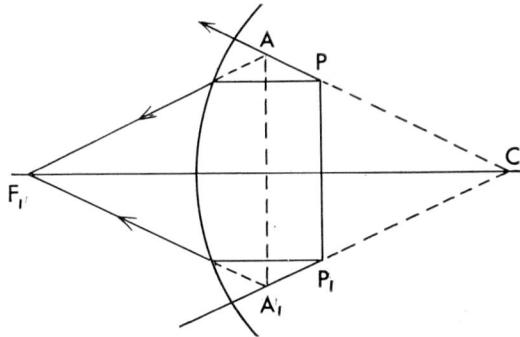

Fig. 60.—The Image of the Pupil seen through the Cornea (see p. 106).

In general terms the MAGNIFICATION of an object in a medium of refractive index n_1 separated by a spherical surface from a medium of refractive index n_2 is given by

$$\frac{n_1}{n_2} \times \frac{v}{u}$$

where u and v are the distances of the object and the image.

REFRACTION AT TWO SPHERICAL SURFACES—
THE SPHERICAL LENS

Although a single spherical refracting surface is of basic importance in visual optics, much of its practice is concerned with two such surfaces having a common axis. A refracting medium bordered by two coaxial surfaces of revolution is called a LENS. When the surfaces are spherical we have a *spherical lens*. Various forms of spherical lens are possible. In some of these one of the two surfaces may be plane. This does not contradict our definition if we regard the plane surface as part of a sphere of " infinite " radius. The following combinations are therefore possible :

I. Convex : (*a*) bi-convex (Fig. 61), (*b*) plano-convex (Fig. 62), (*c*) concavo-convex meniscus (Fig. 63).

II. Concave : (*a*) bi-concave (Fig. 64), (*b*) plano-concave (Fig. 65), (*c*) convexo-concave meniscus (Fig. 66).

FIGS. 61 to 66.—TYPES OF LENSES.

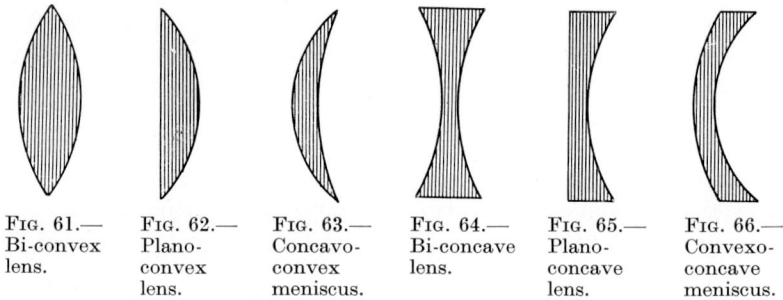

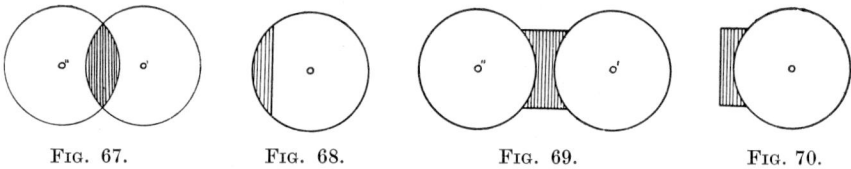

| FIG. 61.—Bi-convex lens. | FIG. 62.—Plano-convex lens. | FIG. 63.—Concavo-convex meniscus. | FIG. 64.—Bi-concave lens. | FIG. 65.—Plano-concave lens. | FIG. 66.—Convexo-concave meniscus. |

FIG. 67.   FIG. 68.   FIG. 69.   FIG. 70.

FIGS. 67 to 70.—THE FORMATION OF LENSES.

A bi-convex lens (Fig. 67) may be considered as formed by the intersection of two spheres, the centres of which are o′ and o″; a plano-convex lens (Fig. 68) by the intersection of a sphere by a plane surface. A bi-concave lens (Fig. 69) may be considered to be formed by the approximation of two spheres the centres of which are o′ and o″; a plano-concave lens (Fig. 70) by the approximation of a sphere and a plane surface.

The constitution of these from the surfaces of revolution is evident from Figs. 67—70.

A lens may be considered to be made up of a series of prisms. If two prisms are placed base to base, it is evident that the rays which were originally parallel can be brought to focus, since each is deviated towards the common base (Fig. 71). An infinite series of prisms arranged in this way will produce a curved surface, which will focus parallel rays of light at a point

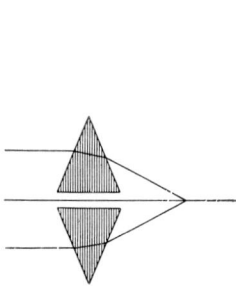

FIG. 71.—REFRACTION TO A FOCUS BY TWO PRISMS.

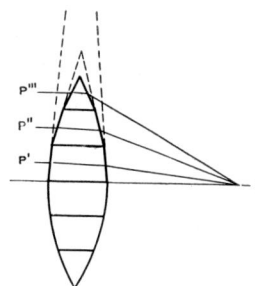

FIG. 72.—REFRACTION TO A FOCUS BY A SYSTEM OF PRISMS.

A series of prisms, base to base, constitutes a convex lens.

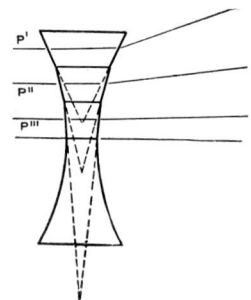

FIG. 73.—REFRACTION BY A SYSTEM OF PRISMS.

A series of prisms, apex to apex, constitutes a concave lens.

(Fig. 72): this arrangement of prism-elements becomes a bi-convex lens. Conversely, if the prism-elements are arranged apex to apex a bi-concave lens will be produced which diverges parallel rays of light, bringing them to a virtual focus in front of the lens (Fig. 73). A convex lens is therefore a converging lens and a concave lens a diverging lens.

The common axis of the two surfaces of revolution is the PRINCIPAL AXIS of the lens; on it must therefore be the centres of curvature of the two surfaces. A ray passing along the principal axis, being normal to both surfaces, does not suffer refraction (C'OC, Fig. 74). If the beam does not strike the lens normally but obliquely, there is again one central ray which is not converged. PQRS represents such a ray, since from the figure it will be seen that parallel tangents can be drawn at the points where it meets the two surfaces, Q and R, thus reducing this element of the lens to a plate with

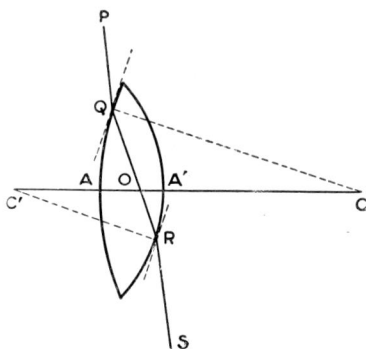

FIG. 74.

parallel sides. Such a ray, therefore, although slightly refracted, leaves the lens parallel to its original direction; and if the lens is thin, this slight refraction may be neglected so that the ray may be considered to proceed in a direction continuous with that of the incident ray. Such a ray is spoken of as occupying a SECONDARY AXIS, and the point (O) which forms the centre of the optical system of the lens, where all the secondary axes meet the principal axis, is called the OPTICAL CENTRE; all rays which pass through it may thus be considered to be undeviated.

THE OPTICAL CENTRE OF A LENS. In Fig. 74, let CQ and C'R be parallel radii (r_1 and r_2) of the two spherical surfaces of the lens.

Since triangles QOC and ROC' are similar,

$$OC/OC' = CQ/C'R = r_1/r_2$$

$$\text{Hence } \frac{r_1}{r_2} = \frac{OC}{OC'} = \frac{r_1 - OA}{r_2 - OA''}$$

which reduces to $OA/OA' = r_1/r_2$.

It follows that the position of the optical centre of a lens depends only upon the radii of curvature of the spherical surfaces. Hence in a bi-convex or bi-concave lens the optical centre lies within the lens, its distances from the two surfaces being directly as their radii ; in a plano-convex or plano-concave lens it lies upon the curved surface ; and in a meniscus it lies outside the lens.

PRINCIPAL FOCI. The points on the principal axis related to rays of light parallel to this axis are the principal foci. They are defined as follows :

The *first principal focus* (F_1) is that point on the principal axis which sends out rays such that after refraction by the lens these are parallel to that axis (Figs. 75–8). The *second principal focus* (F_2) is that point on the

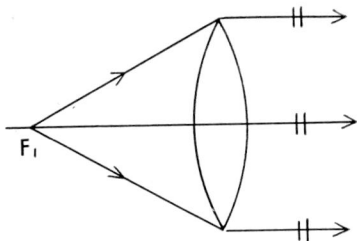

FIG. 75.

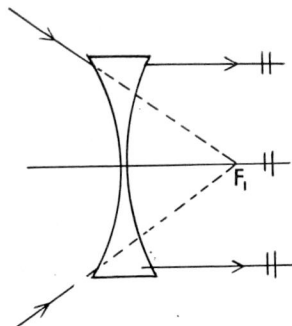

FIG. 76.

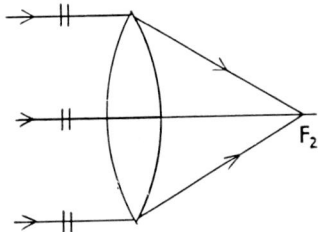

FIG. 77.

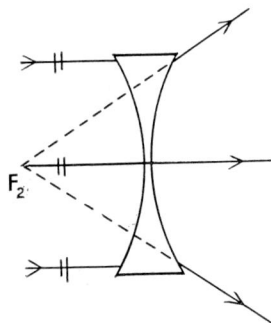

FIG. 78.

FIGS. 75 TO 78.—THE PRINCIPAL FOCI OF LENSES.

principal axis on which rays are focused which, before refraction, were parallel to that axis.

The distances of the principal foci from the optical centre of the lens are called the *focal lengths*, first and second. When the lens has the same medium on both sides of it (such as air), the two focal lengths have the same value but, obeying our sign convention, they are of opposite sign to one another, *i.e.*, $f_1 = -f_2$.

It is possible to determine the focal lengths of a lens in air provided we know the curvature of the surfaces and the refractive index of the material of which it is made. The thickness of the lens is assumed to be negligible; many of the lenses we deal with in ophthalmic optics come into this category, the lens of the eye being a notable exception.

Image-formation by spherical lenses in air: the lens-formula

In the sections on spherical mirrors and single refracting surfaces we have considered the formation of images of point-objects on the principal axis; from this the appropriate formula has been derived. Subsequently, we

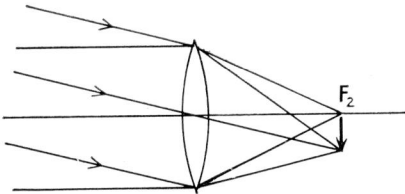

FIG. 79.

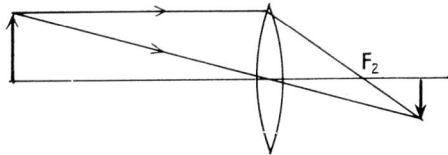

FIG. 80.

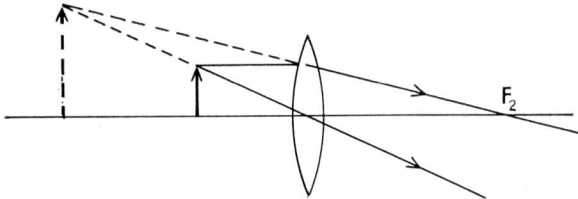

FIG. 81.

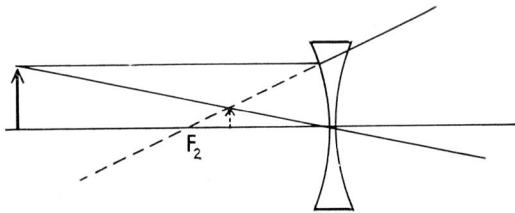

FIG. 82.

FIGS. 79 to 82.—THE POSITION AND CHARACTER OF THE IMAGE PRODUCED BY CONVEX AND CONCAVE LENSES.

have seen how to construct the image of extended objects. It is possible to proceed in the same way with thin lenses. We can in fact derive the lens-formula by regarding them as combinations of two spherical refracting surfaces very close together, and by applying to each of these the formula previously determined.[1] It is simpler, however, to consider first the formation by thin lenses of images of extended objects.

The image can be constructed as for spherical mirrors by taking into

[1] p. 53.

consideration the same three particular rays from the extremities of the object: first, the ray through the optical centre of the lens, which passes straight on undeviated; second, the ray parallel to the axis, which after refraction of the lens passes, by definition, through the second principal focus; third, the ray which, after refraction, emerges parallel to the axis and by definition must pass through the first principal focus on its way to the lens.

We can now draw the image for some of the positions of the object produced by convex and concave lenses; these are shown in Figs. 79–82 and are summarized in Table I.

TABLE I

THE IMAGES FORMED BY LENSES

POSITION OF OBJECT	POSITION OF IMAGE	CHARACTER OF IMAGE
CONVEX LENS		
At infinity	At second principal focus	Real.
Between ∞ and $-2f$	Between $+f$ and $+2f$	Real, inverted, diminished.
At $-2f$	At $+2f$	Real, inverted, same size.
Between $-2f$ and $-f$	Between $+2f$ and $+\infty$	Real, inverted, magnified.
At $-f$	At $+\infty$	
Between $-f$ and lens	Between $-\infty$ and lens	Virtual, erect, magnified.
CONCAVE LENS		
At infinity	At second principal focus	Virtual.
Between ∞ and lens.	Between second principal focus and lens	Virtual, erect, diminished.

This provides an easy method of identifying whether a spherical lens is convex or concave. If we look at an object through the lens at any distance and the object appears to be upside down, the lens is convex. If it appears to be the right way up its size should be noted: if it appears enlarged the lens is convex, if it is diminished it is concave. This rough test is adequate only for predominantly spherical (not cylindrical) lenses.

A formula relating object- and image-distance to the focal length is relatively easily derived and from this the *magnification of the image* can be determined.

In Fig. 83 Δs ABC and GCD are similar

$$\therefore \text{AB/AC} = \text{DG/DC} \tag{1}$$

Also, Δs ECF and GDF are similar

$$\text{GD/DF} = \text{EC/CF} \tag{2}$$

In formula (1), AB is equal to the size of the object (o), AC is the distance of the object ($-u$, to fit in with our sign convention), DG is the size of the image which, being inverted, is $-i$. DC is equal to v, the distance of the image. Formula (1) therefore becomes:

$$o/-u = -i/v \tag{3}$$

Transposing, $i/o = v/u$, it follows that the magnification is the ratio of the image- and object-distances.

Since BA and EC are equal, formula (2) can be shown to be the same as

$$\frac{-i}{v - f_2} = \frac{o}{f_2} \tag{4}$$

Transposing, $\dfrac{i}{o} = \dfrac{f_2 - v}{f_2}$

Equating (3) and (4), $v/u = 1 - v/f_2$.

Dividing by v and transposing, $1/v - 1/u = 1/f_2$.

This is the standard formula relating the distances of the object and image for a thin lens in air.

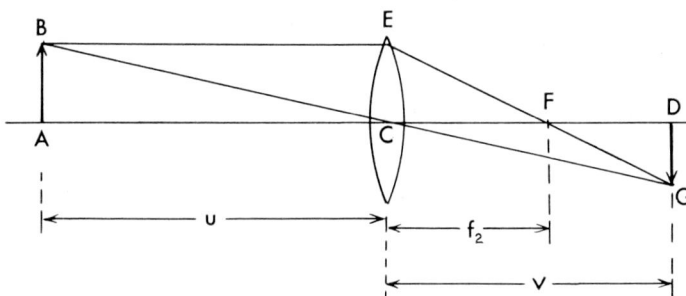

FIG. 83.—THE RELATION OF THE OBJECT- AND IMAGE-DISTANCES TO THE FOCAL LENGTH.

As long as we observe the sign convention, the formula for the magnification i/o will also give an indication as to whether the image is upright or inverted; it will be positive in the first case and negative in the second.

A convenient formula for calculating the distances of the object and the image from the *principal focal points* was employed by Newton. If x is the distance of the object from the first principal focus and y the distance of the image from the second principal focus, then Newton's formula becomes

$$xy = f_1 f_2 = -f_2{}^2$$

and the magnification

$$M = -f_1/x = -y/f_2$$

It may be realized that we have glossed over an important aspect of the optics of lenses. In defining the second principal focus as a point at which parallel rays meet after refraction by the lens, we assumed that such a point exists. Although a true point-focus does not really exist, a sufficiently close approximation can be found provided we consider only the paraxial rays (Fig. 84). The situation thus resembles that arising in the optics of spherical mirrors.[1] In the case of lenses, however, the convention to consider only paraxial rays is not adequate for some of the circumstances that arise in visual optics; we shall therefore have to re-examine the effects caused by the peripheral rays in a later section.[2]

[1] p. 35. [2] p. 83.

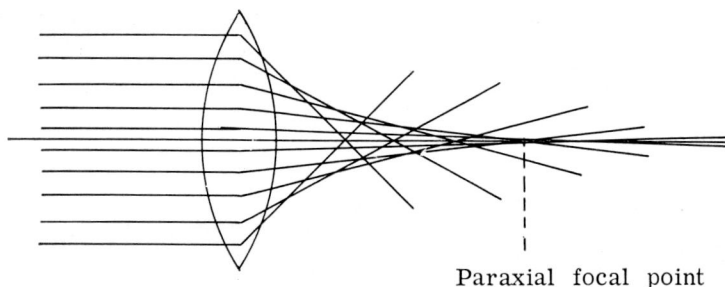

Paraxial focal point

Fig. 84.

THE ASTIGMATIC LENS

We have seen that in a spherical lens when all the meridians of each surface have the same curvature, an image can at least theoretically be formed at a point. When all the meridians do not have the same curvature this is not possible; such a case is called an ASTIGMATIC LENS ($\overset{'}{a}$, privative; $\sigma\tau\acute{\iota}\gamma\mu a$, a point). Such lenses may be of two types, *cylindrical* and *toric*.

CYLINDRICAL LENSES. The simplest astigmatic lens is that in which one of the surfaces forms part of a cylinder while the other is plane: such a lens is called a cylindrical lens. It may be regarded as formed by the inter-section of a solid cylinder, ABDC (Figs. 85–6), by a vertical plane, EFGH, in

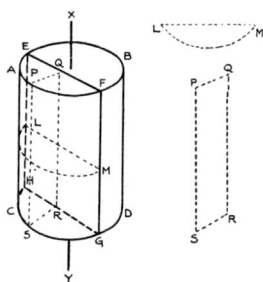

Fig. 85.

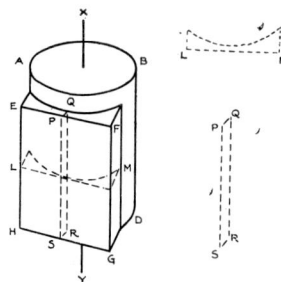

Fig. 86.

the line of the axis, XY. It is thus curved in the horizontal meridian (LM), in which it acts as a spherical lens, and not in the vertical (PS), in which it acts as a plate with parallel sides; this latter meridian is called the axis. Consequently, the cylinder does not refract light falling perpendicularly upon it in the plane corresponding to the line of the axis. Since, as we have seen, a lens can be considered to act optically as a series of prisms, a cylinder can be considered as acting as if it were composed of many series of prisms arranged in superimposed rows.

The action of a convex cylinder is demonstrated in Fig. 87. Rays falling upon such a lens in a direction at right angles to the axis are refracted just as in the case of a convex spherical lens; thus one section of parallel rays will be brought to a principal focus at F', while rays which are in the plane of the axis of the cylinder will proceed undeviated. This will occur down the entire length of the cylinder, and thus in place of a point of convergence we shall have a line of convergence running in the same direction as the axis of the cylinder; in the figure, where the incident rays are parallel, each component segment of which the cylinder may be regarded as being composed will have a principal focus at a corresponding point, and the line F'F'', which is made up of the sum of these individual foci, will be the FOCAL LINE. Consequently, if a point of light is placed in front of the cylinder, no sharp image

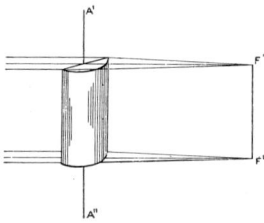

FIG. 87.

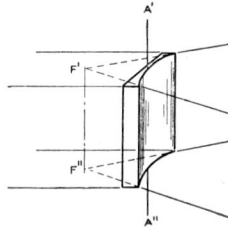

FIG. 88.

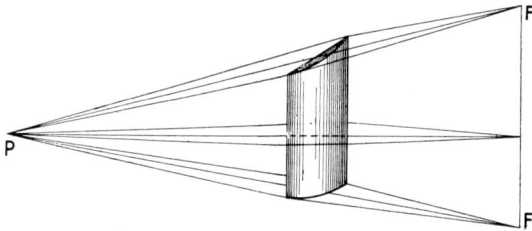

FIG. 89.

as a point can be formed on a screen, but a bright line may be obtained (Fig. 89). Conversely, in the case of a concave cylinder, rays falling perpendicular to the axis are diverged, according to the same principles as we have discussed when considering the refractive properties of concave lenses (Fig. 88).

TORIC LENSES. A lens wherein both meridians are curved, but to a different degree, forms a more complex system: such an astigmatic surface is exemplified in the bowl of a spoon, the curve from side to side being greater than that from handle to tip: a TORIC LENS. Where the two meridians in question are at right angles to each other, the condition is termed *regular astigmatism*; with this alone we need concern ourselves here. Geometrically the surface of such a lens is formed by the revolution of a circle above a line parallel to a diameter. The refractive properties of such a complicated lens may be gathered from a consideration of Fig. 90, where a lens is represented as having different curvatures in two meridians, the vertical meridian (VV) being more curved than the horizontal (HH). It is evident that the more curved meridian will refract the rays incident upon it to a greater degree than the less curved, so that if parallel rays fall upon it the vertical rays will come to a focus before the horizontal. There are thus two foci, the distance between which (BF) is termed the FOCAL INTERVAL. No definite image of a point source is therefore ever formed as a point of light, but merely the blurred effect produced by a diffused bundle of rays.

The appearance of the bundle of rays at different points is illustrated in the figure, the construction being known as *Sturm's conoid*.[1] At A, where the vertical rays are converging more rapidly than the horizontal, a section of the bundle will be in the form of a horizontal oval ellipse. At B, the

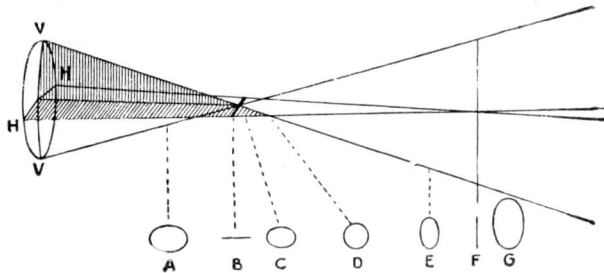

FIG. 90.—STURM'S CONOID (see text).

vertical rays have now come to a focus while the horizontal are still converging; here the section will be a horizontal straight line. Beyond B the vertical rays are now diverging while the horizontal are still converging; at first the section (C) of the bundle will be a horizontal oval ellipse, but when the point D is reached, where the two opposing tendencies are equal and opposite, the section becomes a circle: since the least amount of distortion takes place here, this is called the CIRCLE OF LEAST CONFUSION. Beyond this point the divergence of the vertical rays preponderates, and an ellipse is again formed, this time with its long axis vertical (E), until at F, where the horizontal rays come to a focus, the section will become a vertical straight line. Beyond this point, as at G, where both sets of rays are always diverging, the section will take the form of a gradually increasing vertical oval.

Just as is the case with spherical lenses, it is possible to calculate the position of the foci and the focal interval from the various curvatures of the surface and the refractive index of the lens material, provided we ignore the thickness of the lens.

[1] p. 18.

THE POWER AND NOTATION OF LENSES: VERGENCE

THE VERGENCE OF SPHERICAL LENSES

The lens-formula $1/v - 1/u = 1/f_2$ is somewhat inconvenient for rapid use composed as it is of a worrying collection of reciprocals, each term consisting of a measured quantity (object-distance, for example) divided into one. It is more convenient to consider the reciprocals so that optical formulæ are converted into simple additions or subtractions. Since a spherical lens is characterized by its second focal length, the reciprocal of this ($1/f_2$) is thus called the VERGING POWER, and the unit introduced by Felix Monoyer[1] in 1872 of a DIOPTRE (D) is the verging power of a lens with a focal length of 1 metre. It follows that a convex lens of a second focal length of + 10 cm. has a +10 D of power, while a concave lens of second focal length − 50 cm. has a power of −2 D.

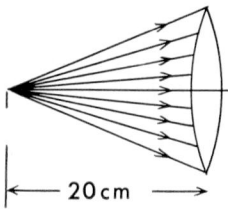

FIG. 91.—If the object is 20 cm. away from the lens, $\dfrac{1}{0\cdot2} = 5$ D of divergence at the lens.

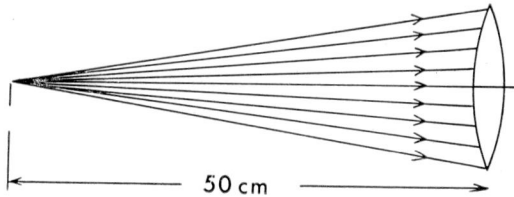

FIG. 92.—If the object is 50 cm. away from the lens, $\dfrac{1}{0\cdot5} = 2$ D of divergence at the lens.

If we now look at the other terms of the lens equation we can see that it is possible to think of the object- and image-distances also in terms of their reciprocals. Supposing we have an object 20 cm. away from the lens of power +10 D; the distance of this object can be said to have a dioptric value of 100/20, or 5. The reciprocal of object-distance in metres is thus the *dioptric value of the object-distance* which is thus a measure of the vergence of the rays and indicates how " rapidly " they are approaching or departing from one another. The vergence of the rays, of course, relates only to a specific position of the object in relation to a lens since, if we move the lens or the object, the dioptric value of the object-distance clearly changes as also does the vergence (Figs. 91–2).

The concept of the vergence of rays (convergence and divergence) and of dioptric distance allows us to re-state the lens-formula in a simpler way : *the dioptric power of the lens added to the dioptric value of the object-distance gives the dioptric value of the image-distance.* Thus an object 25 cm. away from a +6 D lens will give the following formula :

[1] p. 21.

Dioptric value of the object-distance $= -100/25 = -4$ D.

Adding $+6$ D, we get $+2$ D.

$\therefore$ Image-distance $= 100/2 = +50$ cm.

Since a plus lens (convex) will increase the positive vergence or convergence, it is therefore known as a *converging lens*. A concave or *diverging lens* does the opposite, increasing the negative vergence or divergence.

REDUCED VERGENCE. The concept of vergence was extended in a more general sense by Gullstrand. Hitherto we have considered the simple case of a lens with air on each side, but we can also use expressions for vergence in the media on the two sides of a single refracting surface. The dioptric value of the object- and image-distances are then not simply the reciprocals of the relevant distances but the reciprocals multiplied by the appropriate refractive index.

Thus we can write a formula for refraction at a single spherical surface separating (say) water (refractive index n_1) from glass (refractive index n_2) as $n_2/v - n_1/u = n_2/f_2$, or $(n_2 - n_1)/r$. Now n_1/u is the reduced vergence of the incident pencil; n_2/v is the reduced vergence of the rays after refraction; n_2/f_2 is the power of the surface. The formula can now be stated in a general form—the reduced vergence of the emergent pencil is equal to that of the incident pencil added to the power of the surface. It is to be noted that the use of the term "reduced" is etymologically misleading; reduced vergence is, of course, numerically equal to or greater than simple vergence because no medium has a refractive index smaller than unity.

The concept of surface power $(n_2/f_2 = -n_1/f_1 = (n_2 - n_1)/r)$ is of considerable importance in the optics of many of the intra-ocular interfaces and also particularly in keratometry.

THE VERGENCE OF ASTIGMATIC LENSES

The power of a spherical lens to alter the vergence of incident rays is the same in all its meridians but, as we have seen, this is not true of the astigmatic lens. In ophthalmology most astigmatic lenses have the two axes of refraction at right angles to one another. We can therefore regard every astigmatic lens as a combination of a spherical with a cylindrical lens, while a cylindrical lens may be considered as an astigmatic lens with a spherical element of zero power, so that the vergence of rays is altered *only* in a direction at right angles to its axis. The power of the combination is given as the power of the sphere added to the power of the cylinder (Fig. 93). Its exact effect will largely depend on the axis of the cylindrical element in relation to any optical system of which it is part. As far as visual optics and spectacle lenses are concerned, the standard convention is seen in Fig. 94 wherein the observer is facing the subject, a similar notation being used for each eye.

This notation was adopted by the Optical Society in 1904; a representative committee in Germany (*Technischer Ausschuss für Brillenoptik*—whence the Continental

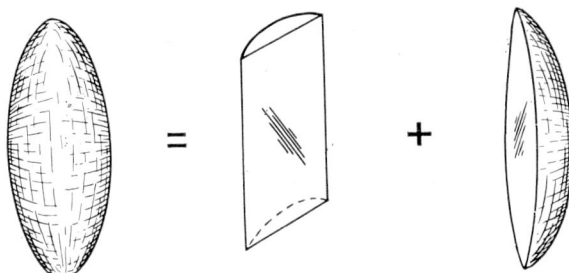

FIG. 93.

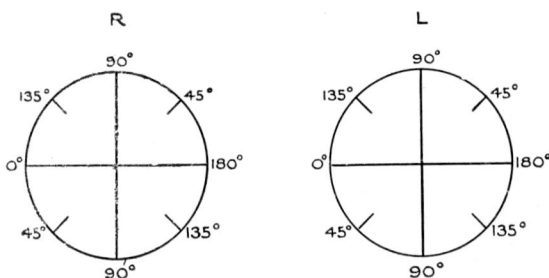

FIG. 94.

name T.A.B.O.) confirmed it in 1917; and the Council of British Ophthalmologists endorsed it in 1921. It is the notation adopted by every mathematical science in which all optical and mathematical instruments are graduated and it is the standard notation of all opticians in all countries.

THE DETECTION AND MEASUREMENT OF LENSES AND PRISMS

In order to find out the nature and strength of a lens it is necessary to discover the position of its principal focus, a procedure which may be carried out on an optical bench. In practice, however, it is easier to neutralize its effect by superimposing upon it a series of lenses of known strengths in succession until one is obtained which is equal and opposite; in this case the image looked at through the combination will be of normal size and will not be displaced, but will appear as if looked at merely through a glass plate with parallel sides. The effect is seen in Fig. 95.

Thus if a convex lens is held up before the eye and a distant object is regarded through it, when the lens is moved a little from side to side the image is seen to move in the opposite direction (Fig. 96). With a concave lens, on the other hand, the image moves in the same direction, as is seen in Fig. 97. From the direction of this movement we can tell the nature of the lens with which we are dealing. A lens of known refractive power and of the opposite kind is now placed in apposition to the first, and by a process of trial and error a combination is found which gives no displacement in which case the strength of this lens is equal and opposite to that of the unknown lens.

By a similar method the presence of a cylinder may be detected. When such a lens is moved in front of the eye, an object looked at through it appears to be unequally displaced in different directions. When the cylinder is moved in the line of its axis, no displacement is produced since there is no refraction in this plane, but when the cylinder is moved in any other plane, a gradually increasing degree of displacement is evident, which reaches its maximum when the plane at right angles to the first is

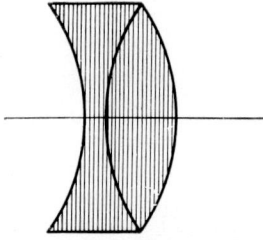 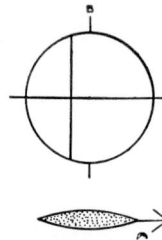 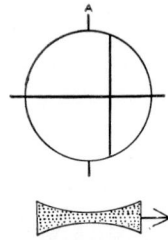

FIG. 95.   FIG. 96.   FIG. 97.

reached. This gives us the direction of the axis of the cylinder. The direction of the displacement, whether in the same or the opposite sense, gives us information as to the nature of the cylinder, whether concave or convex; and by neutralizing the displacement by combining it with another cylinder of the opposite kind, the refractive power of which is already known, we can determine its strength. It is important to remember that in such a test the lenses should be held closely together and their optical centres should be in contact as nearly as possible.

To detect the presence of a prism in an optical system we make similar use of the fact that it displaces an image towards its apex. It is held up between the eye and an

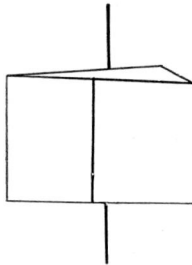 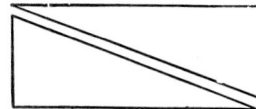

FIG. 98.   FIG. 99.

object which forms a straight line, and if the continuity of the line is broken, as in Fig. 98, a prism is present. The direction in which the line appears to be deviated is the direction of the apex, and the amount of deviation produced is an index of the strength of the prism. In practice this may be measured by neutralizing the unknown prism by placing it in contact with other prisms of known strengths facing the opposite direction until the linear object appears once more as a straight line, in which case the prism used must be of the same strength as that in the optical system but with its apex in the opposite direction (Fig. 99).

It is sometimes necessary to identify a spherical cylindrical lens in which a prism is incorporated. Here we usually neutralize first the sphero-cylindrical element so that no movement of a distant object occurs. The displacement of the object is then neutralized by a prism in the appropriate (opposite) direction.

The Optics of Homocentric Systems of Refracting Surfaces

Since the normal eye is compounded of more than one refracting element, it is necessary to study the law governing refraction through a system of refracting surfaces which are centred upon the same axis (a HOMOCENTRIC or COAXIAL SYSTEM). The most obvious method of treating such a system is to take the image formed by the first refracting element as the object, the rays from which are to be refracted by the second, and so on.

In the case of a simple system of thin lenses such a course is practicable. When two lenses are placed in apposition to one another, the effect of the combination is additive provided they are infinitely thin, are infinitely near and are accurately centred, the total refracting power of the system being equal to the algebraic summation of the refracting power of each component lens.

The power of such a simple combination may be calculated as follows:

Consider two convex lenses, A and B, of focal distance f_1 and f_2 (Fig. 100).

In the case of A, $1/v_1 - 1/u = 1/f_1$

and in the case of B, $1/v - 1/u_2 = 1/f_2$.

If the lenses are in contact and thin, $u_2 = v_1$

whence $$1/v - 1/v_1 = 1/f_2$$

Also, if the object is at infinity $v_1 = f_1$

hence $$1/v = 1/f_1 + 1/f_2.$$

If F is the focal distance of a lens equivalent to the combination, then $F = v$

hence $$1/F = 1/f_1 + 1/f_2.$$

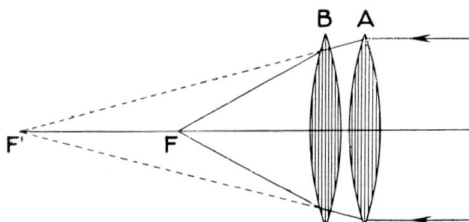

FIG. 100.

These formulæ can be extended to any number of lenses provided their total thickness can be neglected. *The reciprocal of the equivalent focal length of a number of thin lenses in contact is therefore equal to the sum of the reciprocals of the focal lengths of the individual lenses.* It follows that *the power of the combination is equal to the sum of the individual powers of the lenses.*

A similar result will be obtained by combining cylindrical lenses: if they are in contact with their axes parallel, their combined power will be the sum of the power of each. If, however, they are held with their axes at right angles, there will be two focal lines perpendicular to one another, and since all rays must pass through both of these, they must meet at the point where these lines intersect; it follows that if the component lenses are of the same strength the combination thus acts as a spherical lens the refracting power of which is equal to the refracting power of the cylinders. In the same way, combinations of spheres and cylinders are additive. Thus if a $+2$ D sphere is combined with a -2 D cyl. axis horizontal, the two curvatures in the vertical meridian will neutralize each other, leaving those elements of the sphere the curvatures of which are horizontal to act as a cylinder with a vertical axis, and so on.

COMPLEX OPTICAL SYSTEMS

The procedure just outlined may, however, become very tedious, and in the case of thin lenses separated from each other or thick lenses it becomes a task of great difficulty and complexity. A much more simple method was introduced by the German mathematician and physicist, Gauss[1] in 1840, who showed that any homocentric system could be treated as a unity.

Part of the stumbling block to easy acceptance of the theory set out below arises from the fact that the understanding of complex optical systems demands more physical knowledge than is available to the average ophthalmologist. In view of this, it seems pointless to include complicated proofs based on unproven premises; such proofs are really superfluous to a text of ophthalmic optics but are available in comprehensive textbooks on optics. We shall therefore simply enumerate the premises of the theory and describe how it is applied.

CARDINAL POINTS

The theory of Gauss, as modified by Listing, is based on the fact that a compound lens-system can be treated as a whole if the object- and image-distances are measured from two theoretical planes called PRINCIPAL PLANES. It is impossible to find a single lens which, placed in any position, will act in the same way as the system. Its action can, however, be reconstructed if a thin lens is placed in the first principal plane to receive the rays of light, and is then placed at the second principal plane to discharge the rays of light.

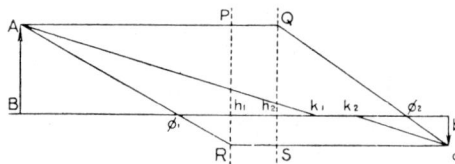

FIG. 101.—CARDINAL POINTS.

The coordinates (or *cardinal points*) upon which the system is based are as follows (Fig. 101):

1. TWO PRINCIPAL FOCI (f_1 and f_2), which correspond in the complex system to the two principal foci of a simple lens. The first or anterior (f_1) is therefore the point on the principal axis such that any ray passing through it will emerge from the system parallel to the principal axis; the second or

[1] p. 19.

posterior (f_2) is the point on this axis at which parallel rays entering the system will be brought to a focus. The planes passing through these points are called FOCAL PLANES.

2. TWO PRINCIPAL POINTS (h_1 and h_2) which are where two PRINCIPAL PLANES strike the principal axis of the system. The principal planes are sometimes called UNIT PLANES because an object thought of as placed at one plane would produce an image in the second plane of the same size, that is, the magnification is unity. Complicated ideas about imaginary objects need not concern us here, but the two planes have an important property because of the unit magnification. A ray parallel to the principal axis striking the first principal plane leaves the system on its way to the second principal focus as if originating from the second principal plane *at the same vertical distance from the axis*. All distances relating to the system are measured from the principal points or planes.

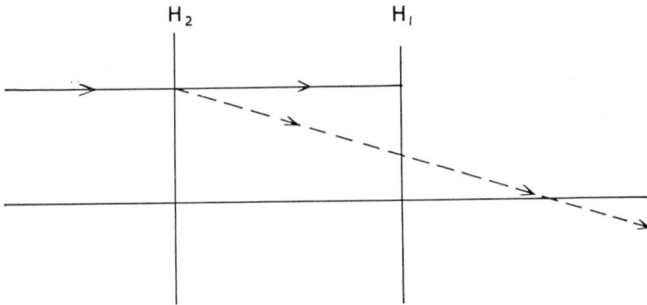

FIG. 102.

3. TWO NODAL POINTS (k_1 and k_2) which correspond to the single optical centre of a simple lens. Consequently (as will be seen from Fig. 101), an incident ray directed to the first nodal point (k_1) will emerge from the system in the same direction along a line which comes from the second nodal point (k_2). The planes passing through these points are called NODAL PLANES. Important relationships of the nodal points arise out of their symmetrical position with respect to the other cardinal points: the distance of one nodal point from the corresponding focal point is the same as that between the other principal and focal points. Thus the posterior nodal distance equals the anterior focal distance and *vice versa*.

It must be realized that this theory of cardinal points is merely a means of representing in a simple form the complex optics of many successive coaxial surfaces of revolution. To emphasize this schematic nature we may take an example of the application of theory that is at first slightly illogical. Although we have agreed to call the principal planes first and second, these may appear in a diagram based on Gaussian principles as if crossed. In the accompanying figure the rays are travelling left to right (Fig. 102) yet in some optical systems we have to put h_1 to the right of h_2. Even so, we adhere to the rules about the properties of the principal planes.

No matter how many lenses constitute the coaxial system and whatever media the rays may have to traverse, the position and magnification of the image can be deduced given a knowledge of its cardinal points; with this information to hand, the position and curvature of the surfaces and the refractive indices may be neglected. Strictly speaking, however, the properties of these points hold only when images are formed of small objects by rays inclined at a small angle to the axis. The formulæ for rays incident obliquely to the principal axis must be worked out by more laborious methods. Since, however, we see an object clearly only when we are looking directly at it, we need not consider the eccentric refraction of the eye in this study.

THE CONSTRUCTION OF THE IMAGE

We are now in a position to construct images formed by such complex systems. All we have to know is the properties of the six cardinal points (two principal foci, two principal points, and two nodal points) and their

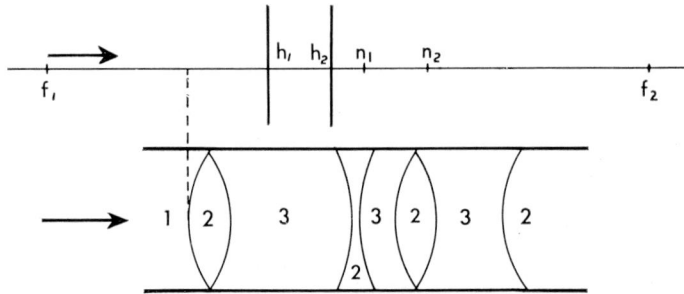

FIG. 103.—A REAL REFRACTING SYSTEM (BELOW) IN RELATION TO ITS CARDINAL POINTS (ABOVE).

Notice that the anterior focal distance $(f_1 h_1)$ is equal to the posterior nodal distance $(f_2 n_2)$ and vice versa. n_1 and n_2 are the nodal points.

position in relation to any particular fixed point of the actual optical system (usually the centre of its front or back refracting surface). An example of how this is applied is shown in Fig. 103.

In succeeding Chapters we shall examine the optics of the eye, which is a complex system such as the theory of cardinal points was designed to simplify. In this case we shall refer the position of the theoretical cardinal points to an actual anatomical site, usually the apex of the cornea.

An extended object is treated as a series of points, the two main points being the extremities of the object. From any point we draw in two of three rays (Fig. 101). The first is the ray (AP) parallel to the principal axis, which will strike the first principal plane and emerges as from the same height on the second principal plane to pass through the second principal focus. The second is the ray through the first nodal point (Ak_1) which emerges as from the second nodal point in the same direction as it strikes the first. The third is the ray (AR) through the anterior principal focus which strikes the first principal plane and emerges as from the second principal plane parallel to the principal axis.

We can also apply in modified form some of the formulæ which we derived for thin lenses, their proof being essentially the same. The best known of these is the formula for deriving the image-distance, $1/v - 1/u = 1/f_2$. The condition must be observed, however, that v, u and f_2 are measured, not from any true point in the optical system but from the respective principal planes; in other words, u is measured from the first principal plane, v and f_2 from the second.

These relationships apply *only* if the media on the extreme sides of the actual optical system are the same, as for a system of lenses in air. In these circumstances the anterior and posterior focal lengths are numerically equal but of opposite signs. It can be shown in this case that the first nodal and the first principal points are in the same place, as also are the second nodal and second principal points. Moreover, the magnification is given by the ratio of the image- to the object-distance, again as measured from the principal planes. If, however, the first and last media are not the same, we find, as with a single refracting surface, that the two focal lengths are different. They are then in the same numerical ratio to one another as the refractive indices of the first and last media.

$$f_1/f_2 = -n_a/n_z$$

Because of the unequal focal lengths, such combinations of refracting surfaces placed in media that differ on the two sides are called *unequifocal systems*. The eye is such a system, the differing media being air anterior to the cornea, and the vitreous posterior to the lens.

The relationship between the distances of object and image in such systems is then expressed as $n_z/v - n_a/u = (n_z - n_a/f_2$. The Newtonian relationship also applies and from it a useful extension can be derived:

$$f_1/u + f_2/v = 1.$$

Magnification can be expressed as $n_a/u \times v/n_z$. The concept of reduced vergences of the positions of the object and the image is clearly of great value in the optics of unequifocal systems.

EQUIVALENT AND VERTEX POWERS

We also speak of the *equivalent power* of these optical systems. In the case of identical media on either side of the complex we know that the anterior and posterior focal lengths are equal. When the medium is air, the power in dioptres is therefore the reciprocal of the second focal length in metres (as with a thin lens).

If the two media are not identical, the equivalent power of the system depends not only on the focal lengths but also on the refractive indices of the media on either side. Taking these as n_a and n_z, we have seen that $f_1/f_2 = -n_a/n_z$, and the equivalent power is obtained by transposing this to $-n_a/f_1 = n_z/f_2$.

Of great practical utility are the concepts of vertex focal lengths and powers. The front and back vertices are the centres of the first and last refracting surfaces of an optical system. The *vertex focal lengths*, anterior and posterior, are the distances between these points and the respective focal points. The vertex powers, front and back, can be worked out simply from the vertex focal lengths. Thus the *front vertex power* is the negative reciprocal of the anterior vertex focal length multiplied by the refractive index of the medium from which light enters the optical system. Similarly, the *back vertex power*, a parameter of great importance in spectacle optics, is the reciprocal of the posterior vertex focal length multiplied by the refractive index of the medium which the light enters on leaving the system. In calculating powers, lengths are considered in metres, as with thin lenses.

SPECIAL APPLICATIONS OF THE THEORY OF CARDINAL POINTS

A SINGLE SPHERICAL REFRACTING SURFACE

Although it is hardly ever necessary to think of it as such, even a single spherical surface can be thought of in terms of cardinal points. Here we have these special conditions: there are two focal points; the first and second principal points are the same as one another and coincide with the centre of the refracting surface. The first and second nodal points also coincide, being the single point which is the centre of curvature of the refracting surface.

THE THIN LENS

It may also seem absurd to reconsider the simple optics of the thin lens in the complicated framework of cardinal points. We may mention, however, that the more advanced theory is equally applicable to the thin lens, which consists of two (coaxial) surfaces with a similar medium on each side, the surfaces being a negligible distance apart. In the thin lens the two nodal points and the two principal points (of the Gaussian system) are all the same, being at the centre of the lens, and the two principal foci are equivalent to the anterior and posterior focal points.

COMBINATIONS OF THIN LENSES

We have already noted that the power of two thin lenses in contact is the sum of their separate powers, their common optical centre being the combined nodal and principal points of the combination.[1] When two thin lenses in air are separated by a finite distance, the situation is not so simple

[1] p. 69.

(Fig. 104). Consider the two lenses A_1 and A_2, the light being incident from the left. The incident parallel light is convergent after passing through A_1 and would be brought to a focus were it not for the lens A_2. When the light reaches A_2 its convergence is still further increased and a focus is formed at F′.

If BD_1 and $F'D_2$ are produced to intersect at H′, it can be seen that a single thin lens placed at this point, P′H′, with a focal length P′F′, would have the same effect as the two lenses A_1 and A_2, *i.e.*, the parallel rays would still be brought to a focus at F′. This lens at P′ is called the EQUIVALENT THIN LENS, the distance P′F′ is the *equivalent focal length*, and its reciprocal, THE EQUIVALENT POWER. The point P′ and the plane P′H′ are the

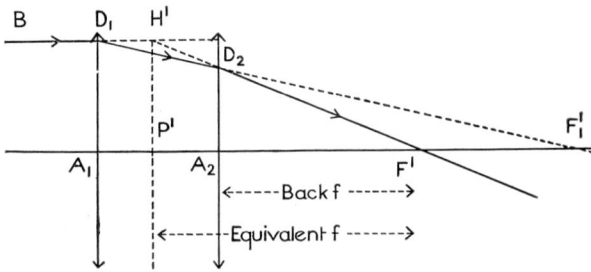

FIG. 104.—THE EQUIVALENT AND VERTEX POWERS OF TWO THIN LENSES.

second principal point and the *second principal plane* respectively of the combination. The back vertex distance is that between lens A_2 and F′, and its reciprocal is the back vertex power. The first principal point and plane (not shown in the figure) relate to light proceeding from right to left.

This can be generalized as follows:

If d is the separation of the two lenses in metres, and F_1 and F_2 the powers of the two lenses, then the convergence of the light reaching the second lens

$$= \frac{1}{f'_1 - d} = \frac{1}{1/F_1 - d}$$

The convergence of the light leaving the second lens $= \dfrac{1}{1/F_1 - d} + F_2$

that is, the *back vertex power* $(F'_v) = \dfrac{F_1 + F_2 - dF_1 F_2}{1 - dF_1}$.

Assume that $A_1D_1 = 1$ cm., then

$$A_2D_2 = \frac{f'_1 - d}{f'_1} = 1 - \frac{d}{f'_1} = 1 - dF_1$$

$$\frac{P'F'}{A_2F'} = \frac{1}{1 - dF_1}$$

therefore the equivalent focal length,

$$P'F' = \frac{1}{F'_v} \times \frac{1}{1 - dF_1} = \frac{1 - dF_1}{F_1 + F_2 - dF_1F_2} \times \frac{1}{1 - dF_1} = \frac{1}{F_1 + F_2 - dF_1F_2}.$$

The *equivalent power* of the combined system (F) is the reciprocal of this:

$$F = F_1 + F_2 - dF_1F_2$$

It also follows that the *back vertex power*

$$F'_v = \frac{F_1 + F_2 - dF_1F_2}{1 - dF_1} = \frac{F}{1 - dF_1}$$

and the *front vertex power*

$$F_v = \frac{1}{1/F_2 - d} + F_1 = \frac{F}{1 - dF_2}$$

Thus for two thin lenses of $+5$ D and $+10$ D separated by 5 cm., the equivalent power is 12·5 D, the back vertex power is 16·67 D, and the front vertex power is 25 D.

THE THICK LENS

Here we cannot ignore the distance separating two coaxial spherical refracting surfaces, but the limitation of the surfaces to two, and the similarity of the media on each side, allow us once again to make a simplification in the Gaussian theory. In this case we reduce the cardinal points to four: two principal foci and two principal or nodal points, the principal points being the same as the nodal points for a thick lens in air.

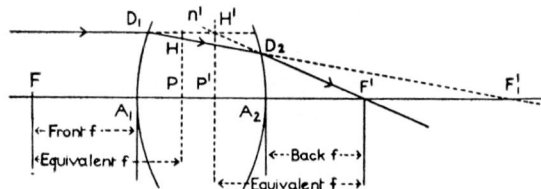

FIG. 105.—THE EQUIVALENT AND VERTEX POWERS OF A THICK LENS.

The treatment of a thick lens as regards calculation is similar to that of two separated lenses except that the medium between the lenses is now glass and not air. Thus a thick lens has a back vertex power, front vertex power, and equivalent power depending upon the thickness of the glass, the powers of the surfaces and the refractive index of the glass. In Fig. 105, if D_1 and D_2 are the front and back surfaces of the lens, let PH and P'H' represent the first and second principal planes, PF and P'F' the first and second equivalent focal lengths which are identical since the lens is surrounded by air. A_1F and A_2F' are the front and back vertex focal lengths. If we consider a thick lens as being two thin lenses separated by glass of refractive index n, then d will be substituted by d/n which is the " *reduced* " distance between the lenses.

When F_1 and F_2 are the surface powers, front and back, of the thick lens, the equivalent power $F = F_1 + F_2 - \dfrac{d}{n} F_1 F_2$

the back vertex power (B.V.P.) $F'_v = \dfrac{F}{1 - \dfrac{d}{n} F_1}$

and the front vertex power (F.V.P.) $F_v = \dfrac{F}{1 - \dfrac{d}{n} F_2}$.

It follows that $F_1 = \dfrac{F'_v - F_2}{1 + \dfrac{d}{n}(F'_v - F_2)}$

and $F'_v = \dfrac{F_1 + F_2\left(1 - \dfrac{d}{n} F_1\right)}{1 - \dfrac{d}{n} F_1}$

$= F_1\left(\dfrac{1}{1 - \dfrac{d}{n} F_1}\right) + F_2$

$\simeq F_1 + F_2 + F_1{}^2\, d/n$

The factor $\dfrac{1}{1 - \dfrac{d}{n} F_1}$ is sometimes known as the *shape factor* and $F_1{}^2\, d/n$ is referred to as the *allowance factor*. The latter is of some importance in spectacle optics where the back vertex power is widely employed. This, as we have just seen, is the sum of the surface powers plus the allowance factor.

If a lens has surface powers of $+\ 10 \cdot 00$ D and $-\ 6 \cdot 00$ D (meniscus), a centre thickness of 3 cm. and is made of glass of $1 \cdot 523$ refractive index.

The equivalent power is $F_1 + F_2 - \dfrac{d}{n} F_1 F_2$

$$= 10 + (-6) - \frac{0 \cdot 03}{1 \cdot 523} \times 10(-6) = +\ 5 \cdot 18 \text{ D.}$$

The back vertex power is $\dfrac{F}{1 - \dfrac{d}{n} F_1} = \dfrac{5 \cdot 18}{1 - \dfrac{0 \cdot 03}{1 \cdot 523} \times 10} = +\ 6 \cdot 48$ D.

The front vertex power is $\dfrac{F}{1 - \dfrac{d}{n} F_2} = \dfrac{5 \cdot 18}{1 - \dfrac{0 \cdot 03}{1 \cdot 523} \times (-6)} = +\ 4 \cdot 39$ D.

The effect of the form of a thick lens on the position of the principal planes is of some importance and is illustrated in Figs. 106 and 107.

COMBINATIONS OF SYSTEMS

If many coaxial systems of refracting surfaces are acting in combination (*i.e.*, they each have a common axis), then the Gaussian theory allows us to simplify the optics. Such a combination occurs when we deal with the placing of optical devices such as spectacles in front of the eye. In these cases, instead of several sets of cardinal points, one for each system, the combination as a whole can be treated by reference to one series of cardinal points, the position of which can be worked out by reference to those of the components of the combination.

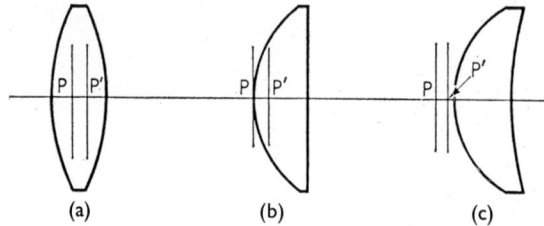

FIG. 106.—THE EFFECT OF FORM ON THE POSITION OF THE PRINCIPAL POINTS IN POSITIVE LENSES.

(a) equiconvex; (b) plano-convex; (c) meniscus.

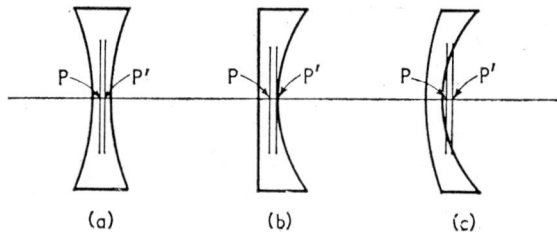

FIG. 107.—THE EFFECT OF FORM ON THE POSITION OF THE PRINCIPAL POINTS IN NEGATIVE LENSES.

(a) equiconcave; (b) plano-concave; (c) meniscus.

THE DEFECTS OF OPTICAL IMAGES

Hitherto in our consideration of geometrical optics we have assumed that light is homogeneous, that it travels in rectilinear paths and that optical media are bounded by theoretically perfect surfaces upon which rays fall near the axial zone at a slight inclination. None of these assumptions is true, and it is necessary to bring geometrical theory into line with practical physics. The defects which consequently appear in the image may be divided into two main classes: those depending on the nature of light, and those depending on the optical instrument. The most important from the ophthalmological point of view are listed in Table II.

Aberrations Depending on the Nature of Light

1. DIFFRACTION OF LIGHT

We have seen that in general terms light travels in straight lines. This, however, concerns only the inner portions of the wave-front, for here

TABLE II

A. ABERRATIONS DEPENDING ON THE NATURE OF LIGHT

1. DIFFRACTION	
2. CHROMATIC ABERRATION	Longitudinal—Chromatic difference of focus.
	Transverse—Chromatic difference of magnification.

B. MONOCHROMATIC ABERRATIONS—THE FIVE SEIDEL ABERRATIONS

Type	Direction of Aberration	Type of objects with which it occurs
1. SPHERICAL ABERRATION	Longitudinal	Point objects on and off the principal axis.
2. COMA	Transverse	Point objects off the principal axis.
3. ASTIGMATISM OF OBLIQUE PENCILS	Longitudinal	Point objects off the principal axis.
4. CURVATURE	Longitudinal	Extended objects.
5. DISTORTION	Transverse	Extended objects.

any single wave is prevented from deviating out of the straight path (so to say) by the equal and opposite tendency of its neighbours on either side. But at the edges of the wave-front this support is lacking, and here the waves tend to spread out from the main body. As the waves spread they eventually interfere with each other so that at the edge of the wave-front a series of maxima and minima of intensity is produced, representing zones where the waves reinforce and neutralize each other. The edges of an image are therefore never sharp, and on the outside of a shadow there is a series of alternating maxima and minima of gradually fading intensity (Fig. 108). We have seen[1] that this phenomenon, which is known as diffraction, was discovered in the latter part of the 17th century by Grimaldi, and was mathematically stated by Fresnel (1816).

It is obvious that the amount of diffraction will increase with the distance which the beam has to travel; and, moreover, since any distance will seem greater to a short wavelength than to a long one, it will also vary with the wavelength of the light. It is also obvious that the narrower the beam of light the greater will be the proportion diffracted. Thus if a slit is many wave-

[1] p. 22.

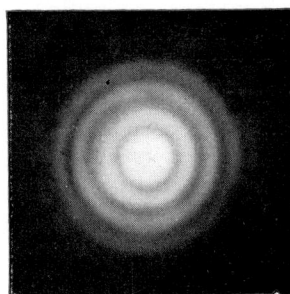

FIG. 108.—THE AIRY DISC.

Showing the diffraction rings of several light and dark bands when sodium light is brought to a focus (W. H. A. Fincham).

lengths wide it can be regarded as two straight edges; but if it is only a small fraction of a single wavelength there will be no shadow at all, for rays will diffuse in all directions, giving a uniform illumination. Such a condition is readily obtained with the much larger waves of sound: the wavelength of middle C on the piano is about 120 cm. and the minimum diameter of a slit which would allow diffuse spread is as great as 109·4 cm. For the same reason when light emanates from a point on a luminous object, it cannot be brought to a point-focus but actually gives rise to a blurred disc of light and dark bands with a bright spot in the centre. This is called the Airy disc (Fig. 108); the central spot receives about 84% of the incident light, the first ring has 1/57 and the second 1/240 of the intensity of the central area.

It follows that none of the conclusions of geometrical optics is absolutely true, and that, from the nature of light itself, *no point-image can be formed but only a diffraction pattern*; and from the above reasoning we can deduce that the diffraction pattern formed by any system of lenses varies directly as the focal length of the system and the wavelength of light, and inversely as the aperture (or pupil) through which the light passes.

The dependence of the diffraction pattern on these factors is shown in the formula for the radius (r) of the first dark ring formed round the image of a point. The formula is $r = 1 \cdot 22 f \lambda / d$, where f is the focal length of the system, λ the wavelength of the light and d the diameter of the aperture through which the light travels. It can be immediately appreciated that the effects of diffraction become important particularly when the wavelength is large in relation to the size of the aperture.

RESOLVING POWER

Since owing to the wave-nature of light diffraction cannot be overcome, and since the elements of an image are therefore made up of blurred circles of light surrounded by diffraction rings, a limit of magnification can be reached beyond which no fresh detail can be attained. The closest distance at which two separate luminous points can be recognized is when the centre of the diffraction disc of one falls on the innermost dark ring of the other, and we have seen that this occurs when the distance between the images on the focal plane of the system is $1 \cdot 22 f \lambda / d$, or when the angle between the object-points is $1 \cdot 22 \lambda / d$. This angle, representing the limits of practical utility, is the RESOLVING POWER of the system. No matter to what extent the system may be optically perfected and no matter to what extent the image in the focal plane be magnified, the limit of efficiency is determined by the resolving power.

2. CHROMATIC ABERRATION

We have seen that the white light is composed of rays of different wavelengths which, when separated or *dispersed*, form the various colours of the spectrum. As we would expect, the short waves are retarded most in passing through a refractive medium, and hence on their way through a prism or a lens they are more acutely bent so that they come to a focus in front of the longer waves. In the case of a prism they are more acutely bent towards the base than the longer rays, a phenomenon which allowed Newton in his famous experiment to show that white light was compounded of a mixture of the spectral colours. Again, if a convex lens forms a real image of a source of white light, it actually forms a series of coloured images at different distances from the lens, the violet image being nearest the lens and the red farthest away (Fig. 109). This phenomenon is termed CHROMATIC DIFFERENCE OF FOCUS. Since the yellow is the brightest part of the spectrum this is naturally focused, but superimposed upon the yellow image are all the other colour images slightly out of focus, the effect being to give a blurred white image.

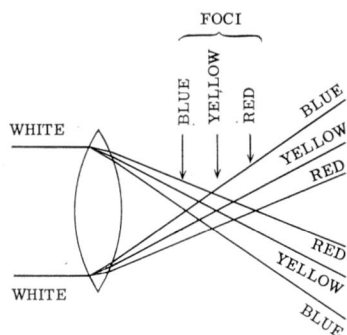

FIG. 109.—CHROMATIC ABERRATION.

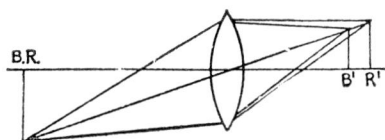

FIG. 110.—CHROMATIC DIFFERENCE IN MAGNIFICATION.

The longer red rays (R′) form a larger image than the shorter blue rays (B′) in oblique pencils.

It is obvious that if a screen is moved out of focus towards the lens, the edge of the image becomes tinged with red; if away from the lens, the edge becomes tinged with blue. The difference in size of the various coloured images is called CHROMATIC DIFFERENCE IN MAGNIFICATION (Fig. 110) which, however, does not become marked unless a lens with a wide aperture allows the passage of peripheral rays.

DISPERSIVE POWER. Chromatic aberration is measured by the standard of the wavelengths corresponding to the " Fraunhofer lines ", a series of dark lines in the solar spectrum caused by the absorption of bands of wavelengths by the sun's and the earth's atmospheres. Some of them are :

$$C = \text{Red} \quad = 6.563 \times 10^{-5} \, \text{cm.} \quad F = \text{Blue} \quad = 4.862 \times 10^{-5} \, \text{cm.}$$
$$D = \text{Yellow} = 5.893 \times 10^{-5} \, \text{cm.} \quad G = \text{Violet} = 4.308 \times 10^{-5} \, \text{cm.}$$

For each individual wavelength, a lens of a particular material will have a certain focal length and a corresponding refractive index. The C and F lines for red and blue are taken as standards and the chromatic aberration is measured by the difference between the focal length of the red and blue divided by the " average " focal length (the average is worked out as the square root of the product of the red and blue focal lengths). This spread or *dispersive power* of a lens is usually called δ and can be calculated from the three refractive indices—that for red, that for blue, and the average of these two. The formula is:

$$\delta = \frac{n_F - n_C}{n - 1}.$$

The value for δ for hard crown glass is 0·01654, and for dense flint glass is 0·02771.

ACHROMATIC SYSTEMS

Fortunately, contrary to Newton's conclusion,[1] the dispersive powers of different materials are not necessarily related to their differing refractivities; one material may have a high dispersive power and low refractivity, another the reverse. Thus if we combine a convex lens of low dispersive power with a concave lens of high dispersive power but of a lower refractive power, the dispersion can be neutralized while a considerable proportion of the refractivity of the former will remain available. Such a lens, called an ACHROMATIC LENS, was first constructed by the London optician, Dolland, by combining crown and flint glass.

In such a combination of two lenses, the condition for achromatism is that their focal lengths should be opposite in sign (one lens being convex and the other concave), and the ratios of the focal lengths are equal to the ratio of the dispersive powers of the materials of which the lenses are composed. It follows that if $f_1 f$ are the two focal lengths of the " achromatic pair ", as the components of the combination are sometimes called, then

$$f_1/f = \delta_1/\delta.$$

By a simple mathematical extension, three thin lenses of glass of different dispersive powers may be combined into a single lens so that the images of three different colours coalesce, and so on.

Monochromatic Aberrations

We have already considered some of the optical systems wherein point-sources do not form point-images. The first was in relation to reflection by spherical mirrors. There it was pointed out that we have to confine our attention only to the paraxial rays if we are to retain the simple concept of a point-image. The marginal rays form an image or images in different positions and the combined marginal and paraxial images therefore appear blurred; this is the condition known as SPHERICAL ABERRATION. Thus in Fig. 111, if we consider a plane pencil of rays meeting a spherical mirror, while PM_1 is reflected to P_1, a ray such as PM_3 will meet the axis at P_3. A line tangential to all the reflected rays (EP_1) is called a CAUSTIC CURVE, and since the reflected rays are most closely packed here it will appear on a screen as a bright line. The point where the central cusp of the caustic cuts the axis (P_1) is the image formed by the central part of the mirror. If instead of a plane pencil of rays we have a solid conical pencil diverging from P, the figure may be considered to be rotated around OP as axis and the caustic curve traces out a caustic surface.

[1] p. 18.

The *form of aberration* is represented graphically in Fig. 112, where MM_1 represents a small portion of the mirror, P_1 the image formed by the rays inclined at a small angle to the axis, and P_2 the point to which two marginal rays are reflected from M and M_1. The curved dotted line represents the caustic curve. Now a screen at LL_1 will be illuminated by a large circular patch with a bright edge. As the screen approaches P_2 the patch contracts, and at P_2 a bright spot appears at the centre. At KK_1 the patch reaches its smallest diameter; thereafter it enlarges, a dim zone increasing round the outside and a bright patch appearing in the centre until at EE_1 we have a brilliant point P_1 surrounded by a dim disc EE_1.

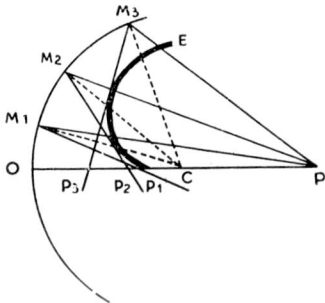

FIG. 111.

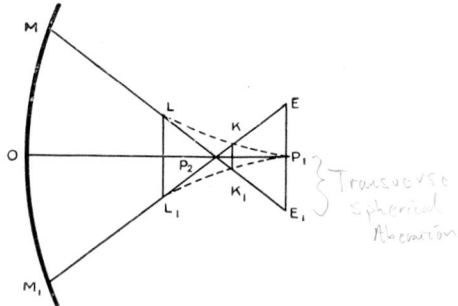

FIG. 112.

FIGS. 111 and 112.—SPHERICAL ABERRATION.

The circle KK_1, which is the nearest approach to an undistorted image, is called the CIRCLE OF LEAST CONFUSION; P_1 is the PARAXIAL FOCUS, P_2 the MARGINAL FOCUS, the distance P_1P_2 is called the LONGITUDINAL SPHERICAL ABERRATION, and P_1E the LATERAL SPHERICAL ABERRATION. We have also noted that a non-spherical reflecting surface can be designed so that aberration-free images can be formed[1]; such surfaces, for example a parabolic reflector focusing parallel rays, are referred to as APLANATIC.

Of greater importance in ophthalmology are the aberrations which occur in refraction. Some of the effects produced by refraction at plane surfaces have already been discussed. Through a single surface we saw that no single point could be represented as the site of the image of a point-source; the position of the image depends entirely on the angle of emergence of the rays at that plane surface. An envelope of all these possible lines of emergence is called a caustic curve (CP_1, Fig. 113), and consequently to an eye which is in a position to receive them the image appears at the points where they meet this curve. Thus an eye at R_3 would see the image of P at the point where the line R_3P cuts the caustic.

[1] p. 18.

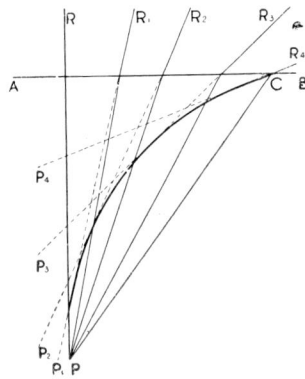

FIG. 113.

The distortion produced by a prism should perhaps also be considered as a defect of images produced through plane surfaces. We may recall how the simple theory was applicable to thin prisms producing minimum deviation; the oblique passage of rays through a thick prism inevitably leads to failure of point-image formation.[1]

The most important aberrations associated with refraction are those relating to spherical lenses.

ABERRATIONS OF SPHERICAL LENSES

SPHERICAL ABERRATION

The image formed of a point-object by a spherical lens is never a single point because the paraxial rays form images which differ from those formed by the marginal rays. It is usually the case that the foci of the peripheral rays are closer to the lens than the central (*positive* or *undercorrected*

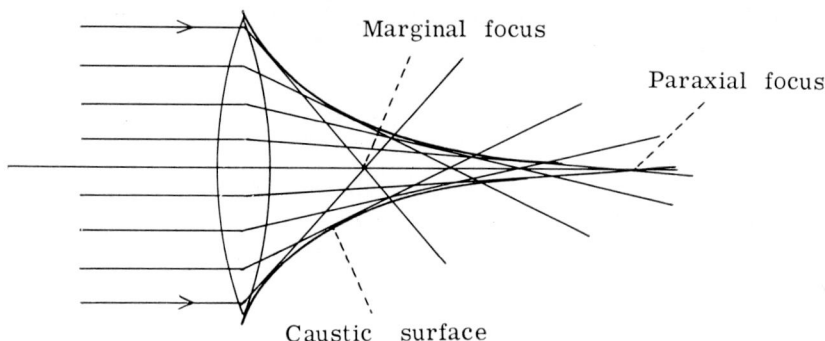

Fig. 114.—Spherical Aberration.

aberration). We can often identify reasonably distinct point-foci for paraxial and for marginal rays, although, as with spherical mirrors, the zone where these foci are found forms a caustic surface (Fig. 114). The point on which the peripheral rays converge is called the MARGINAL FOCUS, and that upon which the central rays converge is called the PARAXIAL FOCUS (Fig. 115).

Spherical aberration can be measured in several ways. The simplest is the distance between the marginal focus and the paraxial focus. Alternatively, it can be expressed as the difference between marginal and paraxial image vergences.

From the geometrical point of view, the circle of least confusion will occur at one quarter of the distance from the marginal to the paraxial focus, and the diameter of the disc of least confusion will be $0.5 \ P_1P_2 \tan u$, when P_1P_2 is the longitudinal spherical aberration and u is the marginal angle of convergence. When, however, the phenomena of diffraction are taken into

[1] p. 50.

account the issue becomes more complicated. Lord Rayleigh found in 1879 that the image does not deteriorate appreciably so long as the maximum difference in equivalent optical path at the best focus does not exceed a quarter of a wavelength of light (*the Rayleigh limit*), and it has been shown that within this limit the best image (so far as primary spherical aberration is concerned) will be located *midway between the paraxial and marginal foci;* around this there is a considerable " focal range " within which the image will

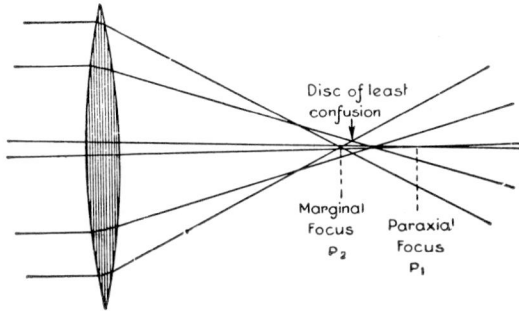

Fig. 115.—Spherical Aberration.

appear equally good. Beyond the Rayleigh limit much of the marginal light is scattered widely over the field.

In any particular optical system several factors determine the magnitude of the spherical aberration. Clearly, the aperture of the system is of great importance, for it will be considerably diminished by a confinement of the rays to the paraxial group. A further important factor is the precise form of the lens or lenses used. Huygens [1629–95], the Dutch physicist who

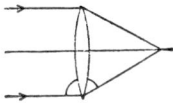
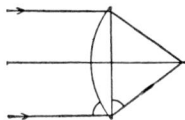
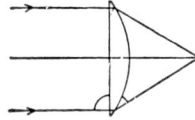

Fig. 116.   Fig. 117.   Fig. 118.

Figs. 116 to 118.—The Variation of Spherical Aberration with the Curvature of the Surfaces of the Lens.

was responsible for the wave-theory of light,[1] first suggested that lenses should be corrected in some such manner as to correct the defect: such lenses are called APLANATIC. Since the degree of deviation produced by a lens depends upon the ratio of the curvature of its surfaces, the error can be diminished by making the curvature of the anterior surface greater than that of the posterior; it is for this reason that the objectives of optical instruments are bulged in front. This can be deduced from elementary principles. The degree of aberration depends upon the degree of deviation of

[1] p. 22.

the rays of light, and this is reduced to a minimum when the deviation produced at each surface of the lens is the same. A consideration of Figs. 116 to 118 will show that this also is best attained when the more convex surface faces the incident rays (Fig. 117). The peculiar condition of the eye makes the problem of an ideal spectacle lens difficult, a matter which will be discussed at a later stage; but for general optical instruments Huygens proposed a ratio of the curvatures of the surfaces of 6 to 1. We can, of course, abandon spherical surfaces and grind the lenses so that their peripheral curvature is less than in the axial region : these are known as *aplanatic surfaces*.

The design of lenses and optical systems having the minimal spherical aberration is an elaborate procedure but, apart from the components of the system themselves, certain conjugate foci may be found for which this aberration is absent or very small. Such foci are called *aplanatic points*. In general terms, an aplanatic optical system is one from which two of the Seidel aberrations are absent, these being spherical aberration and coma.

COMA

Strictly speaking, we should use the term spherical aberration only for points on the principal axis; *coma* is an aberration of the image formed of a point-source off the principal axis. It consists of a spreading out of the image in a plane roughly at right angles to the optic axis, producing a comet-like tail (κομή, a head of flowing hair), and is always associated with more distortion due to a type of spherical aberration along the secondary axis (Fig. 119).

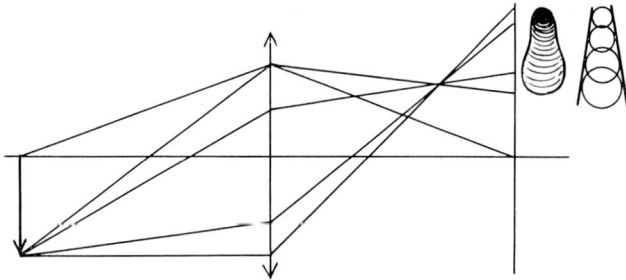

FIG. 119.—COMA.

It is due to unequal magnification of different zones of the lens and can be eliminated by stops or by particular arrangements of lenses in the system as well as of the surface curvatures. As we have noted, for some particular object- and image-positions of the lens system, the so-called *aplanatic points*, coma and spherical aberration, will both be absent.

THE SINE CONDITION. For an optical system to be free from both coma and spherical aberration the magnification of each zone of the system must be the same as for paraxial rays. This principle was discovered by Abbé,[1] and

[1] Vol. II, p. 43.

when θ and θ' represent the slope-angles of the rays from the object and to the image, and θ_p and θ'_p the corresponding angles for paraxial rays, it is expressed mathematically as follows (Fig. 120):

$$\frac{\sin \theta}{\sin \theta'} = \frac{\theta_p}{\theta'_p} = \text{a constant for all values of } \theta.$$

This relationship is known as the SINE CONDITION. The principle can be derived from the geometrical optics of paraxial and marginal rays passing through a single refracting surface. For the former, Lagrange's theorem[1] holds:

$$ny\theta_p = n'y'\theta'_p$$

where n and n' are the refractive indices, y and y' object- and image-size. This is a special case of the sine theorem, $ny \sin \theta = n'y' \sin \theta'$, for all rays.

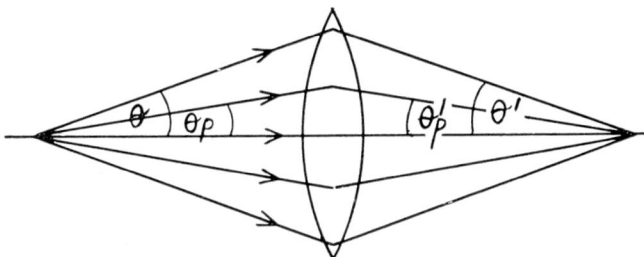

FIG. 120.—THE SINE CONDITION.

In summary, therefore, coma and spherical aberration go together and elimination or reduction of one will similarly affect the other. They are the only two aberrations affected significantly by the bending of lenses.

ASTIGMATISM OF OBLIQUE PENCILS

If a point-object is not on the axis of a lens, the light-pencils from it will strike the lens in such a way as to produce the comatic image we have just described. But even if coma is eliminated we may meet another distortion because of astigmatism. This defect is independent of coma and its origin can be appreciated by considering how the refraction varies in different planes.

It will be remembered that when a pencil of light traverses an astigmatic lens, the light is converged upon two focal lines, one in the plane containing the principal ray and the centre of curvature and the other perpendicular to this plane (Fig. 90). Point-sources will therefore form elongated images, sharp in one meridian and fuzzy in the other, or equally confused but undistorted in a mean meridian at the circle of least confusion. When the lens is traversed by an oblique pencil of light the same effect is produced. The

[1] p. 19.

astigmatism thus suffered is seen in Fig. 121 when the pencil of light runs at an obliquity to the axis of the lens.

It is evident that two focal lines are formed, the *meridional* (*tangential* or *peripheral*) *focal line* (F'_m) and the *sagittal* (or *radial*) *focal line* (F'_s). If the obliquity (σ) of the principal ray (the central ray, PB, passing through the centre of the stop) is finite, the *astigmatic difference* (the distance $F'_mF'_s$) is also finite and, growing directly as the square of the aperture and the square of the field, it increases rapidly with the angle of obliquity. The *astigmatic difference* is therefore an expression of the astigmatism of the surface for that particular obliquity.

The effective curvature of the refracting surface will be different for the rays in the plane of the paper (the *tangential plane*) from that acting on rays at

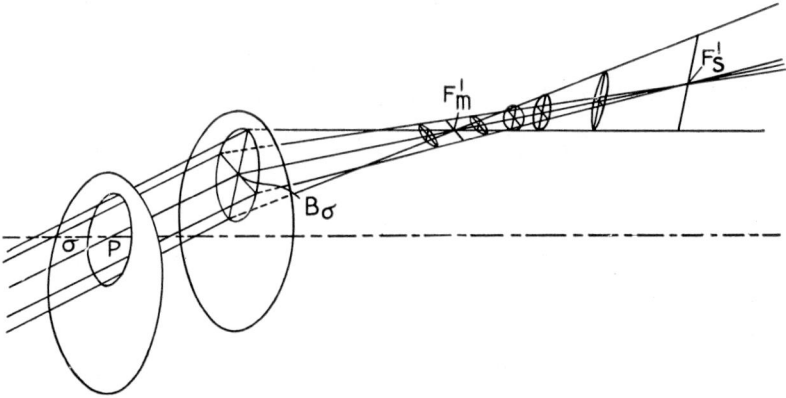

FIG. 121.—THE ASTIGMATISM OF OBLIQUE PENCILS.

The two focal lines, F'_m (the meridional or tangential focal line) and F'_s (the sagittal or radial focal line) are separated by the *astigmatic difference* ($F'_mF'_s$) (compare Fig. 90).

right angles to the plane of the paper (the *sagittal plane*). Two focal lines are thus formed corresponding to each of these planes and a circle of least confusion emerges about half-way between them. Generally speaking, the more oblique the point-object, the worse is the resulting astigmatism (Fig. 121).

This aberration is also considerably affected by the exact form of the lens used and the employment or otherwise of stops to reduce the effective aperture. The position of the stops will be of vital importance in determining the kind and degree of oblique astigmatism which results. The importance of this in the design of spectacle lenses will be discussed at a later stage.

Two types of aberration which apply to the images of extended objects must also be considered : *curvature* and *distortion*.

CURVATURE

If it becomes possible by the suitable design of an optical system to produce undistorted point-images (stigmatic) of point-objects, there is unfortunately no guarantee that the images of a series of such points from an extended object will bear the same relationship to each other as that of the object-points. A straight extended object in one plane, a pin for example, may appear bent or curved, while a flat object the plane of which is at right angles to the principal axis may have an image on a curved surface (Fig. 122). This lack of spatial correspondence is called CURVATURE. How much the image is curved has been shown to depend on the refractive indices of the material of the lenses as well as on the degree of curvature of the lens-surfaces; this applies when spherical aberration, coma and oblique astigmatism have already been eliminated.

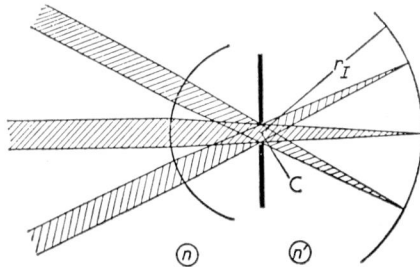

FIG. 122.—THE PETZVAL SURFACE.

The curvature of an image by a convex refracting surface, a diaphragm with a small aperture being placed at the centre of curvature, C, to eliminate oblique astigmatism. Each image-forming pencil gives rise to an image-point, the sum of which will construct a spherical image-surface concentric with C, of radius r_I. n, the refractive index of the first medium, and n' the refractive index of the second.

It is possible, however, to obviate this defect and obtain point-focal imagery on a surface which is appropriately curved and is usually paraboloidal. It is concave towards the lens with a radius of curvature equal to the focal length of the lens × its refractive index. Such a surface is generally called a *Petzval surface*.[1]

The great English mathematician, Sir George Biddell Airy (Fig. 610), however, published this fact some years previously (1830),[2] enunciating the basic theorems determining the conditions of the requirements of point-focal imagery in a most eloquent paper. The paper, however, was published in a journal which had not a wide circulation and was essentially on the aberration of the eye-pieces of telescopes, although Airy pointed out specifically that the same deductions applied to spectacle and other lenses. This probably accounts for the designation of Petzval's surface which, however,

[1] JOSEPH M. PETZVAL, a professor at Vienna, was the first to make photographic objectives from calculated formulæ rather than by trial and error; his conditions for this were published in 1843.

[2] Airy's papers were first read to the Cambridge Philosophical Society in May, 1827, and published in *Trans. Camb. phil. Soc.*, **3**, 1 (1830).

should properly be *Airy's surface*. A somewhat similar fate befell the work of Henry Coddington, also of Cambridge, who became vicar of Ware, and published his treatise in 1829.

Curvature and astigmatism are defects which may both be minimized by employing aperture-stops or a suitable separation of the lenses of a system. Two lenses in combination, one convex, the other concave, may be used. In a favourable arrangement the *Petzval condition* may be attained wherein $n_1 f_1 + n_2 f_2 = 0$, where f_1 and f_2 are their focal lengths and n_1 and n_2 their refractive indices. In this condition curvature and astigmatism are at their lowest values.

FIGS. 123 to 125.—THE DISTORTION OF IMAGES.

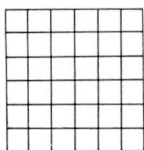

FIG. 123.—The shape of the object.

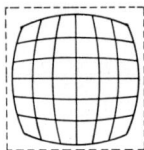

FIG. 124.—Barrel distortion.

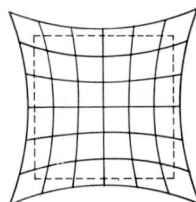

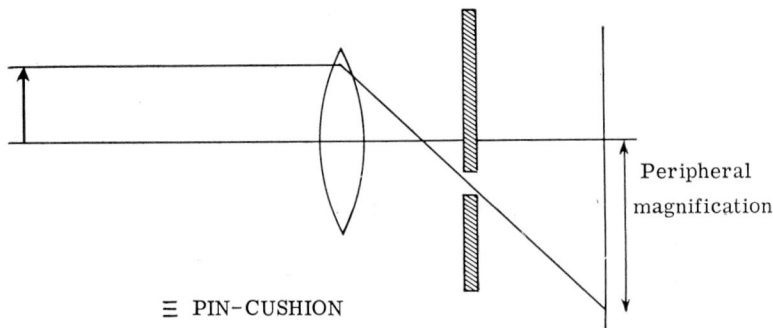

FIG. 125.—Pin-cushion distortion.

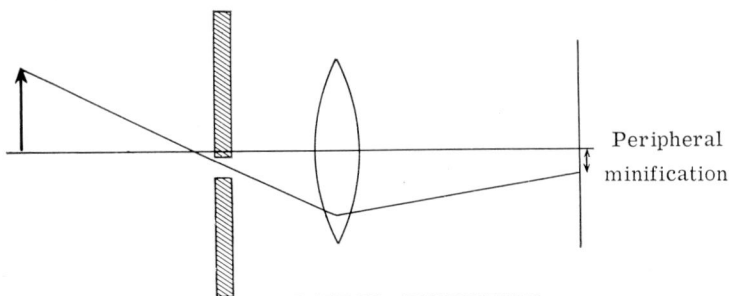

Peripheral minification

≡ BARREL DISTORTION
FIG. 126.

Peripheral magnification

≡ PIN-CUSHION DISTORTION
FIG. 127.

FIGS. 126 and 127.—THE EFFECT OF A STOP.

DISTORTION

Even if the relationship of a series of points is reproduced in their images with regard to their plane, their relation one to another within that plane may be untrue. This leads to the condition of *distortion* of images. Thus the magnification of the peripheral parts of an object viewed through a lens is different from that of the central area. This difference may occur in either direction; thus we get " pin-cushion " distortion when the peripheral magnification is greater than the central, and " barrel distortion " in the reverse condition (Figs. 123–5).

The condition of distortion is markedly influenced by the presence of stops in optical systems and by their exact position. Moving a stop may completely alter the nature of the distortion, especially if its situation is changed from the image- to the object-side of the system (Figs. 126–7).

FIG. 128.

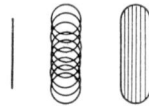

FIG. 129.

It is obvious that these aberrations which we have considered, which are partly inherent in the nature of light and partly necessary concomitants of any optical system, preclude the formation of any ideally clear image. Apart from extended objects, a point of light cannot therefore be brought to a point-focus, but appears as a circle of confusion involving a certain amount of blurring (Fig. 128). Similarly, the image of a line, which is a number of points, may be construed as a number of such circles superimposed the one upon the other so as to overlap to a large extent; a narrow line therefore becomes converted into a broad band (Fig. 129). The smaller these circles are, the greater will be the efficiency of the optical system.

LITERATURE

Bennett. *Graphical Methods of Solving Optical Problems*, London (1948).
Bennett and Francis. Davson's *The Eye*, London, **4**, 3 (1962).
Ditchburn. *Light*, 2nd ed., London (1963).
Fincham. *Optics*, 6th ed., London (1959).
Jenkins and White. *Fundamentals of Optics*, 3rd ed., N.Y. (1957).
Linksz. *Physiology of the Eye*, Vol. I, *Optics*, N.Y. (1950).
Martin. *Technical Optics*, London (1948).

FIG. 130.—HERMANN VON HELMHOLTZ
[1821–1894].

CHAPTER III

THE DIOPTRIC IMAGERY OF THE EYE

THE essential interest in the subject of physiological optics is the study of the transmission of rays of light through the ocular media so that clear images of external objects are produced on the sentient layer of the retina. In the eye, three types of imagery are encountered—DIOPTRIC, CATOPTRIC and ENTOPTIC. Here we are primarily concerned with dioptric images; catoptric images are those formed by reflection at the ocular interfaces; entoptic images are formed on the retina by objects inside the eye or on its surface. This last type of imagery is of great interest and of some diagnostic significance; for this reason it is fully considered elsewhere,[1] but is of no importance in our present subject. Catoptric imagery, however, is of interest to us in the measurement of the optical components of the eye and will be discussed presently in this connection.

In the first Chapter we have already traced the history of our knowledge of the dioptric system of the eye and have shown how the classical concept of a camera obscura wherein refraction does not occur was replaced by the revolutionary concept of Johannes Kepler (Fig. 11) who outlined the correct refractive scheme. Among the great figures who more recently elaborated our knowledge by the extent and accuracy of their studies, three names stand out—von Helmholtz, Tscherning and Gullstrand; Tscherning's photograph introduces the Chapter on accommodation; those of the other two are a suitable introduction to this Chapter.

HERMANN VON HELMHOLTZ [1821–1894] (Fig. 130) was one of the greatest physicists and physiologists of all time. His father, a professor of philology and philosophy in Berlin, could not afford a university education for him, so he was educated at the expense of the state in return for serving for eight years in the Prussian army. During his military service he published eight papers, including his classical work on the universal application of the first law of thermodynamics. When his military service was completed he became professor of physiology successively at Königsberg, Bonn and Heidelberg, and of physics in Berlin. Apart from his fundamental work on vision and hearing, his paper on the doctrine of energy (1847) ranks among the greatest physical papers of the 19th century, while his work on electro- and thermo-dynamics, nerve conduction and many other subjects was equally fundamental and brilliant. His standard work on vision with which we are concerned here, *Handbuch der physiologischen Optik*, appeared from 1856–67, a second edition was published in 1885, and a third edition was brought out (1909–10) by Gullstrand, von Knies and Nagel, and was translated into English by the Optical Society of America in 1924. In it were established for the first time the dioptrics of the eye as founded on experiment and observation. His photograph appears elsewhere in this *System*[2] in connection with his invention of the ophthalmoscope, an instrument which introduced a new era into ophthalmology; but the revolution he created in the accurate assessment of the dioptrics of the eye merits this further tribute.

[1] Vol. VII, p. 445.   [2] Vol. VII, Fig. 217.

FIG. 131.—ALLVAR GULLSTRAND
[1862–1930].
(Courtesy of Prof. G. von Bahr, Uppsala.)

ALLVAR GULLSTRAND [1862–1930] (Fig. 131) was first a lecturer in clinical ophthalmology at the Caroline Institute in Stockholm (1890–94) and later became professor of ophthalmology at Uppsala (1894) and then research professor of physiological and physical optics at this university (1914–27). This Swedish ophthalmologist was one of the most ingenious and accurate experimental workers in optical physics who ever lived and contributed more to a mathematical understanding of the eye as an optical instrument than anyone except von Helmholtz. He may be said to have founded the science of the dioptrics of heterogeneous media. He thus transformed the simple theory of von Helmholtz wherein the eye was regarded as a schematic collinear optical instrument into its complicated reality. Applying the methods of mathematical physics propounded by the eminent Irish astronomer Sir William Rowan Hamilton in 1828, he treated this problem as comprising widely diffused bundles of rays refracted through a system of continually curving planes, and differentiated the actual ocular image from its theoretical optical projection. In the eye, for example, the course of the rays in astigmatism is not represented by Sturm's conoid. Apart from his classical work on astigmatism, his main contributions to our subject were his general theory of monochromatic aberrations, his study of the dioptrics of the crystalline lens and his discovery of the intracapsular mechanism of accommodation, his introduction of a method of estimating corneal astigmatism and a micrometric technique of obtaining the exact form of a normal and diseased cornea by photographing its reflex. His genius also provided us with ophthalmic instruments of great value and precision such as the slit-lamp (1902) and the reflexless ophthalmoscope (1912), while he designed aspherical lenses for eyes with high refractive errors providing a clearer image and a wider field than hitherto. For " work on the diffraction of light by lenses as applied to the eye " he was deservedly awarded a Nobel Prize in 1911 and was ophthalmologically honoured with the von Graefe Medal in 1928.[1]

The formation of the images of external objects upon the retina may be regarded from two standpoints, qualitative and quantitative. The first offers no difficulty. On entering the eye rays of light are refracted to the greatest extent by the outer surface of the cornea, which has a considerable power of convergence. Little, if any, refraction occurs at the interface between the posterior surface of the cornea and the aqueous humour since both these media have approximately identical refractive indices. A more significant refraction occurs at the two surfaces of the lens which is of appreciably higher optical density than the media on its two sides, while further converging power is contributed by the interior of the lens which does not have a uniform refractive power. Having passed through the lens into the vitreous body, the rays travel to the retina without further refraction.

A more precise quantitative evaluation of the refractive properties of the eye and its components is best made initially in terms of simple geometrical optics. We shall therefore first consider the eye as a system of coaxial spherical refracting surfaces bounding media of uniform refractive indices. Such a description is necessarily inadequate, partly because the eye does not correspond to a system of this simple nature and partly because all the approximations which we have seen to be inherent in geometrical optics must be taken into account. This simplified version will therefore be followed by a

[1] See also another portrait in Vol. VII, Fig. 164.

description of the departures of the dioptric system of the eye from this
concept.

THE EYE AS A SYSTEM OF COAXIAL SPHERICAL REFRACTING SURFACES

The most convenient approach to this subject is, in the first place, the
analytical study of the individual refracting surfaces and media treated
seriatim; thereafter a synthesis can be made of the optical properties of the
individual tissues, the cornea and the lens, and finally of the eye as a whole.
In this connection the optics of the eye provides an excellent example of the
application of the Gaussian theory of cardinal points.[1]

The Optical Constants of the Eye

The eye has four refracting interfaces: the two surfaces of the cornea
and the two surfaces of the lens. The important optical features of these are
their curvature, their separation and the refractive indices of the media
between them and bounding them.

Methods of Measurement

In the measurement of the optical constants of the eye extensive use is
made of the catoptric images formed by reflection at the interfaces; these act
as spherical mirrors and, as we have seen in the previous Chapter, such
images provide a means of measuring the curvature of the reflecting surfaces.

These CATOPTRIC IMAGES formed by the optical surfaces were first described by
Johannes E. Purkinje (1823)[2] and were re-described by the Parisian ophthalmologist
Louis Joseph Sanson (1838) who first used them for diagnostic purposes: hence their
usual name, the PURKINJE-SANSON IMAGES (Fig. 132). Holding a lighted candle
in front of the eye somewhat eccentric from the visual axis, Purkinje described four
images: the bright erect image formed by reflection at the anterior corneal surface (I),
(a reflection, incidentally, known in classical times), the dim erect images at the posterior
corneal surface (II) and the anterior surface of the lens (III), and the dim image at the
posterior surface of the lens (IV) which, being formed by a concave mirror, is inverted.
The indistinct posterior corneal image was lost sight of until re-discovered by Blix (1880)
and Tscherning (1890). To these, Demicheri (1895) added
another two equally indistinct images reflected by the
anterior and posterior surfaces of the nucleus of the lens;
while further images within the lens were added by Hess
(1911). In subsequent years the use of the slit-lamp has
greatly increased our knowledge of these images; but at
the same time, since it has rendered the surfaces themselves evident, it has detracted from their clinical
(although not their optical) importance.

It may be of interest to note other catoptric images
formed by reflection in the eye. The images of Purkinje
are of " the first order " since they are formed by a
single reflection at an ocular interface; others " of the

FIG. 132.—THE PURKINJE-
SANSON IMAGES (H. von
Helmholtz).

[1] p. 70.   [2] Vol. VII, Fig. 355.

second order '' are formed by multiple reflections (Fig. 133). Theoretically the process is capable of extension to a very complicated construction, but for all practical purposes two secondary images merit consideration (Tscherning, 1890)—one produced by a first reflection at the anterior surface of the lens and a second reflection at the anterior surface of the cornea, and the other due to a first reflection at the posterior surface of the lens and a second at the anterior surface of the cornea. It will be noted that these rays return to the retina, and therefore can theoretically be perceived subjectively. The focus of the first system is near the posterior surface of the lens, and consequently the rays are so dispersed on reaching the retina as to be invisible ; the focus of the second, however, is very near the retina in the emmetrope, and can more easily be observed.

By this process a considerable amount of light is deflected from the main dioptric path. Reflections of the first order, forming the images of Purkinje, travel out of the eye and therefore constitute *lost rays;* while those of the second order, reaching the

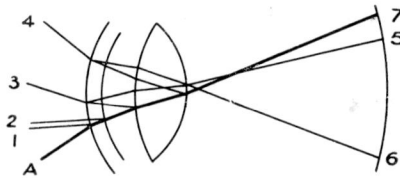

FIG. 133.—CATOPTRIC IMAGES OF THE EYE.

The thick line, A7, is the main ray. Reflections of the first order are shown occurring at the anterior surface of the cornea (1), the posterior surface of the cornea (2), the anterior (3) and posterior (4) surfaces of the lens. (3) and (4) are partially reflected back to the retina, forming images of the second order (5) and (6).

retina, constitute *harmful rays* which diminish the optical efficiency of the eye, although to a very small extent. The eye, however, sets a higher standard in this respect than most optical instruments, for the whole of the light thus lost does not equal 2%.

The optical constants of the eye cannot be measured directly in the living eye, and in the dead eye the conditions are altered ; consequently an indirect optical method is employed. The standard method of measurement using the Purkinje images is to employ as the '' object '' two widely separated illuminated sources. Each gives its own set of catoptric images and the distance between the sources and between corresponding images gives object- and image-sizes for each of the surfaces to be measured. Apart from that of the anterior corneal surface, the calculation of the true curvature of the surface is somewhat complex since the images II, III and IV are formed by refraction as well as by reflection. In addition, use may be made of these images in a calculation of the apparent separation of the refractive surfaces. The characteristics of these images are summarized in Table III.

THE CURVATURE OF THE OCULAR INTERFACES

THE ANTERIOR SURFACE OF THE CORNEA

For our present purposes we are concerned only with the axial area of the cornea—about 4 mm. in diameter—and for the moment we shall assume this

Table III

The Purkinje-Sanson Images

Image	Source	Mode	Nature	Relative Brightness	Utility
I	Anterior Corneal Surface	Reflection	Virtual—just behind anterior surface of the lens. Erect. Diminished.	$+ + + + +$	Keratometry. Measurement of the thickness of the cornea. Measurement of angle alpha and general diagnosis of strabismus.
II	Posterior Corneal Surface	Reflection. Refraction via the corneal stroma	Virtual (close to I). Erect. Diminished (slightly smaller than I).	$+ +$	Unimportant. Determination of curvature of posterior corneal surface and thickness of cornea.
III	Anterior Lens Surface	Reflection through aqueous humour; refraction by cornea	Virtual in the vitreous (in the unaccommodated eye). Erect. Diminished but larger than I (in the unaccommodated eye).	$+$	Curvature of anterior lens capsule. Accommodation. Measurement of anterior chamber depth.
IV	Posterior Lens Surface	Reflection through lens substance. Refraction into aqueous and through cornea	Real—close to I. Inverted. Diminished.	$+$	Curvature of posterior lens surface. Accommodation.

to be spherical. The radius of curvature of the anterior surface of this area has an average value in an adult emmetropic eye of about 7·8 mm. Since the pupil restricts the rays entering the posterior half of the eye to those which pass through the axial region of the cornea this region is sometimes referred to as the OPTICAL or APICAL ZONE.

The first measurement of the curvature of the anterior surface of the cornea was made by Christopher Scheiner (1619) who sat the subject in front of a window and compared the corneal reflex thus obtained with the image of the cross-bars on a series of graduated marbles. The more accurate technique of *keratometry* makes use of the first Purkinje image (von Helmholtz, 1856). This surface acts as a convex mirror so that the size of the image produced varies with the curvature—the greater the curvature of the mirror, the smaller the image.[1] A luminous body is therefore held up before the cornea, and the image as seen therein is measured; hence, knowing the size of the object and its distance from the eye, the radius of curvature of the cornea can be deduced.

[1] p. 35.

The radius of curvature can be calculated from Fig. 134. Consider an object AB of size O from which an image ED of size I is formed by reflection at the front surface of the cornea.

Ray BC passing towards the centre of curvature, C, of the cornea is reflected back on itself. Ray BF in the direction of the focal point of the mirror strikes it at S and is then reflected back parallel to the axis, AC. D and F are very close together, so near, in fact, that we can consider EDS to be a triangle. This being similar to ABF, we can write:

$$I/O = ES/AF \simeq f/AF$$

The distance AF is kept constant for any instrument by using a short-focus telescope in order to view the reflected image. If AF is denoted b, and substituting $r/2$ for f, we get:

$$I/O = r/2b, \text{ therefore } r = 2b\,I/O$$

From this it is clear that for a known object-size, measurements of the image-size will allow us to determine r, the radius of curvature.

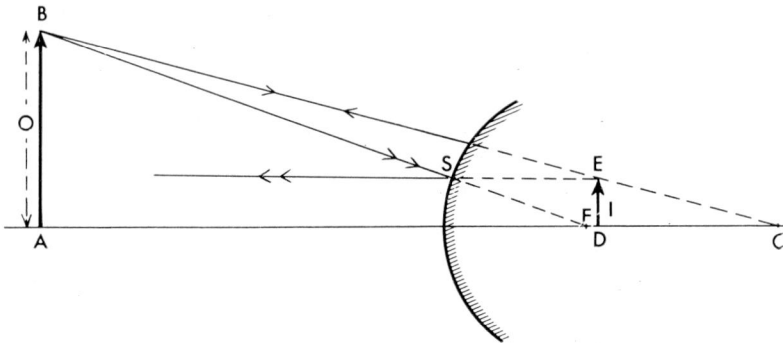

FIG. 134.

The accurate measurement of such an image, however, raises a problem, since it is impossible to immobilize the living eye completely while the image is under observation. This has been overcome by the use of a device, the *principle of visible doubling*, which was originally introduced by Servington Savery (1753) in the heliometer, was adopted in the ophthalmometer devised by Jesse Ramsden, the instrument-maker to Sir Everard Home (1796), and was perfected by von Helmholtz (1856). The image is doubled by refraction through two rotating glass plates, which are then adjusted so that the lower edge of one image coincides with the upper edge of the other; if the eye moves during the process, both images move together, and therefore difficulties in adjustment are avoided. From the amount of rotation of the glass plate necessary just to double the image, its size can be calculated.

The principle of von Helmholtz's instrument is as follows:

Two glass laminæ (D,E, Fig. 135), which can be inclined to each other at known and variable angles, are placed side by side so that each covers half of the objective of a short-distance telescope (L), the axis of which coincides with the plane of separation of the glass plates. Rays from a point O appear to undergo lateral displacement on refraction through D and E, so that, as viewed through L, the two objects appear at A and B. Two real images of A and B are thus formed by L at A′ and B′; and if the eye-piece of the telescope (M) is so arranged that its principal focus coincides with the plane of A′B′, the eye receives parallel rays which come to a focus without accommodation on the retina at a and b. If the position of the plates is such that the two images A and B just touch at O, then each plate has displaced the image through half its length, and the total displacement gives the size of the images (Fig. 136).

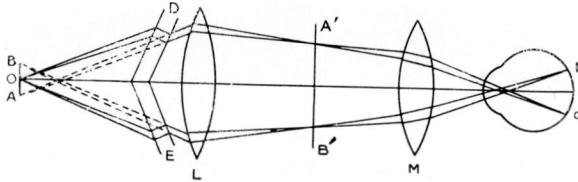 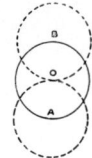

Fig. 135.   Fig. 136.

FIGS. 135 and 136.—THE OPHTHALMOMETER OF VON HELMHOLTZ.

The ophthalmometer of von Helmholtz (1856) is undoubtedly accurate for scientific work, but several modifications have been introduced to facilitate its use as a clinical instrument for measuring corneal astigmatism. Landolt (1877) introduced prisms to replace the glass plates, and Javal and Schiøtz (1881) employed a Wollaston's prism, which consists of two rectangular quartz prisms cut in the opposite axes of a quartz crystal and cemented together so as to form a thick plate. The combination is doubly refracting and symmetrical with regard to the incident ray, so that two complete cones of light are produced instead of a single cone being divided into halves. Moreover, in place of the original flames as objects, these observers employed diffused light reflected from white surfaces ("mires") disposed on a circular arc which could be rotated round the axis of the instrument (Fig. 137); this makes the investigation of any normal section of the cornea as easy as the horizontal meridian.

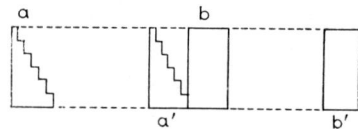

Fig. 138.

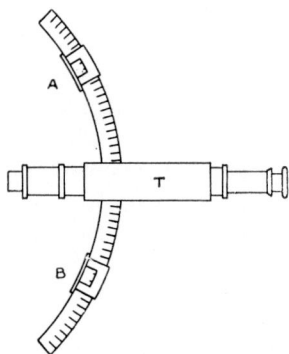

Fig. 137.   Fig. 139.

FIGS. 137 to 139.—THE OPHTHALMOMETER OF JAVAL AND SCHIØTZ.

The mires are shaped as *a* and *b* in Fig. 138, and are considered as the ends of a linear object, AB (Fig. 137) which appears upon the cornea in duplicate as *ab* and *a'b'* (Fig. 138). The length of the object, AB, is then adjusted by moving A and B on the arc so that the two images *a'* and *b* touch each other as in Fig. 138. The arc is now rotated through 90° and a similar reading taken. If the curvature in this meridian is the same, the mires will again approximate, but if the second meridian has a greater curvature the sizes of *ab* and *a'b'* will diminish and the mires will overlap (Fig. 139). One mire (A) is so constructed that each step of the image *a'* corresponds to a dioptre of difference of refractive power, so that the difference in refractive power between the two meridians is readily read off by counting the degrees of overlap. In the Haag-Streit keratometer (Fig. 140) based on the Javal-Schiøtz design the mires are red and green objects and are internally illuminated.

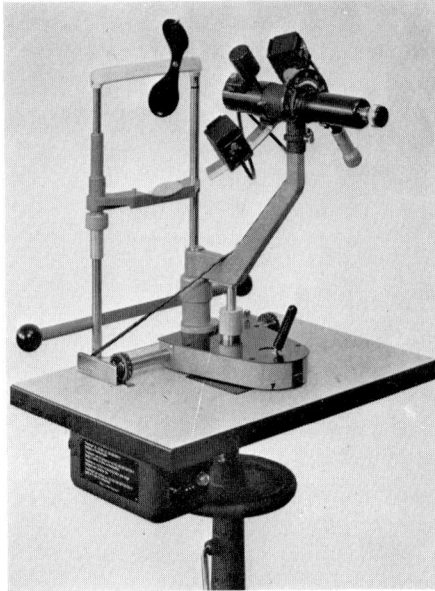

FIG. 140.—THE HAAG-STREIT KERATOMETER.

The principle used in the Javal-Schiøtz type of instrument is thus seen to be slightly different from that in the Helmholtz ophthalmometer. In the latter, the size of the image is determined by varying the doubling produced by the plates; in the Javal-Schiøtz instrument the amount of doubling is fixed and the size of the object is made to vary. Both the " fixed doubling " type of instrument such as the Haag-Streit and the modern " variable doubling " type such as that of Bausch and Lomb, are calibrated so as to read directly the radius of curvature of the cornea as well as the dioptric power. The latter figure is usually calculated on the basis of a deliberately chosen low value for the refractive index of the corneal substance, thus taking into account the slight refractive effect of its posterior surface; the reading is therefore a net dioptric value for the central part of the cornea as a whole.

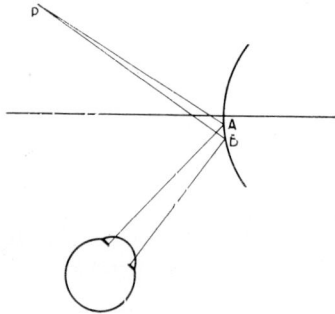

Fig. 141.

It can be shown that the usual types of keratometer measure the curvature of an area roughly 3 mm. in diameter. This fortunately is slightly less than the size of the assumed spherical region of the cornea. It is evident from Fig. 141 that at any one time light from a small portion only of the cornea (AB) can enter the observer's eye; with the ophthalmometer two small points of the cornea 1·2 mm. from the visual line are utilized, and when the arc is rotated a concentric ring of this radius is investigated without reference to the curvature of the parts outside or inside this ring.

It may be noted that Westheimer (1965) introduced an ingenious *photo-electric keratometer* wherein a series of photo-electric cells received the light reflected from the cornea as a beam formed by a narrow slit moved across its surface.

THE POSTERIOR SURFACE OF THE CORNEA

The optical effect of the posterior surface of the cornea depends on the refractive index of the cornea, the refractive index of the aqueous humour and the curvature of the surface itself. The measurement of this last depends on simple optical concepts but is somewhat difficult because of the dimness of the second Purkinje image formed by reflection by this surface. The principle used in measurement is to compare the size of an image reflected by the anterior surface with that reflected by the posterior surface; the calculation, however, must take into account the fact that the latter image is produced by refraction through the corneal substance as well as by reflection at its posterior surface.

A typical value for the radius of curvature of the posterior surface of the cornea can be taken as 6·7 mm. (Gullstrand, 1911).

While the figures we have quoted may be taken as average values for the radii of curvature of both corneal surfaces, it is obvious that considerable variations will be found in different individuals, some of which will be considered at a later stage.

THE SURFACES OF THE LENS

As with the posterior surface of the cornea, the principle of measurement of the curvatures of the surfaces of the lens is to compare the sizes of the third and fourth Purkinje images with that of the first. The apparent radius of curvature of any internal surface bears the same relationship to the radius of curvature of the anterior corneal surface as does the apparent size of its Purkinje image to that of the first Purkinje image.

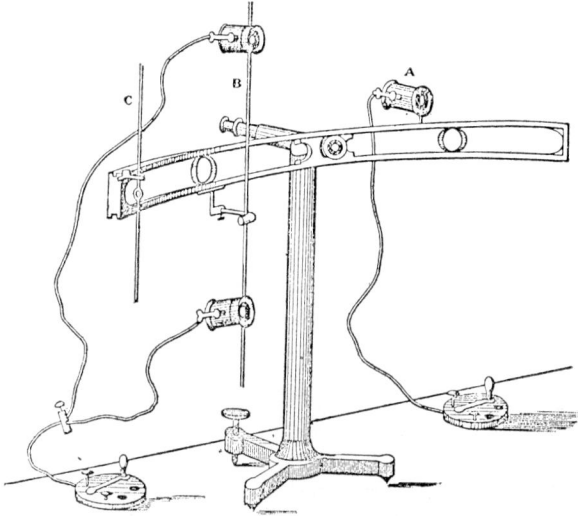

FIG. 142.—TSCHERNING'S OPHTHALMOPHAKOMETER.

A is the cursor which carries a lamp; B the cursor which carries two lamps placed on the same vertical rod; and C the third cursor which carries the rod on which moves a small bright ball which serves as the point of fixation. In the centre is an observing telescope. Each lamp is enclosed in a tube carrying a plano-convex lens which concentrates the light on the observed eye.

The *ophthalmophakometer* of Tscherning was one of the first instruments to make use of this principle (Fig. 142). Two pairs of lamps are used, one brighter pair gives the third Purkinje image from the anterior surface of the lens and the other more feeble pair gives rise to the corneal reflections. The separation of the images of the latter pair is adjusted to be the same as that between the images of the brighter pair. The curvature of the posterior surface of the lens can be measured by the same technique.

Modern methods of investigation of the curvature of the surfaces of the lens make similar use of the Purkinje images by a photographic technique first introduced by Fincham (1925) (Fig. 143). At the time of Fincham's early experiments satisfactory results could be obtained in only a few subjects, since the images are faint and the photographic emulsions then available were slow, but subsequent improvements in the speed of emulsions have made it possible to obtain measurable results from about 90% of eyes, while the use of an electronic flash obviates the effect of any movement of the eye during the period of measurement.

Photography of the third Purkinje images has also been employed by Nakajima

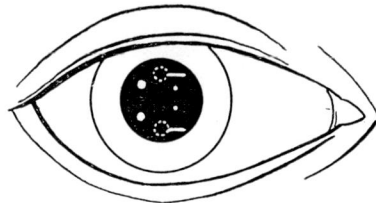

FIG. 143.—THE CATOPTRIC IMAGES IN THE EYE.

The large white circles to the left represent the reflections from the anterior corneal surface; the dotted circles, those from the anterior lens surface; the small white circles to the right the posterior lens surface; and the horizontal white lines the corneal images of the comparison lamps (E. F. Fincham).

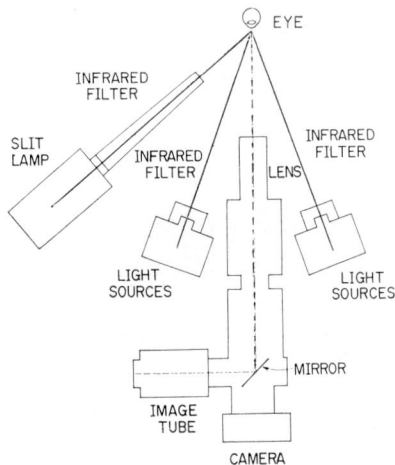

FIG. 144.—THE INFRA-RED PHAKOMETER (S. KABE).

FIGS. 145 and 146.—THE PURKINJE-SANSON IMAGES WITH THE
INFRA-RED PHAKOMETER (S. Kabe).

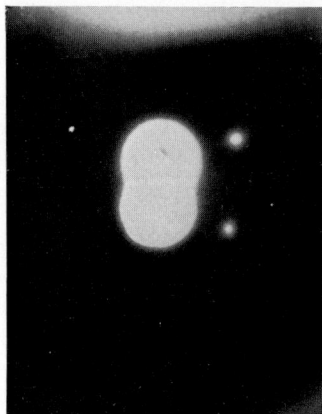

FIG. 145.—The third Purkinje-
Sanson images.

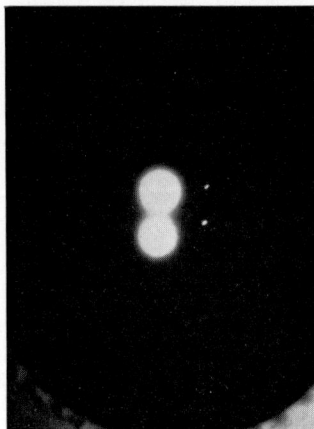

FIG. 146.—The fourth Purkinje-
Sanson images.

(1955) and Sorsby and his colleagues (1961) for phakometry and used by Kirchhof (1940) and Allen (1949) to study the speed of accommodation, by Le Grand and Marandon (1949) to assess the effect of drugs on accommodation, by Otero (1951), Campbell and Primrose (1953), Koomen and his co-workers (1953) and Mellerio (1966) in the study of night myopia, and by Whiteside (1957) for studying space myopia. Moreover, Ludlam and his colleagues (1965) found that the dim third and fourth Purkinje images could be improved with the use of monochromatic light, while Wulfeck (1955), Otsuka and his co-workers (1965) and Kabe (1968) have described techniques of photographing these images by infra-red radiation (Figs. 144–6); this is particularly useful in studying the changes in the lens on accommodation since in the dark mydriasis is obtained without cycloplegia.

The shape of the lens is subject not only to individual variations but also to alterations and adjustments in the same individual at various times. It is, therefore, even more difficult to give average values for the curvature of its surfaces, but representative figures may be taken as 10 mm. for the radius of curvature of the anterior surface and 6 mm. for the posterior in the adult emmetropic unaccommodated eye.

THE POSITION OF THE OCULAR INTERFACES

In this section we must consider not only the relative positions of the refracting surfaces but also the relationship of all these to the plane in which the dioptric images are focused. It is convenient to consider these optical features under four headings: the thickness of the cornea, the depth of the anterior chamber, the thickness of the lens, and finally, the axial length of the eyeball.

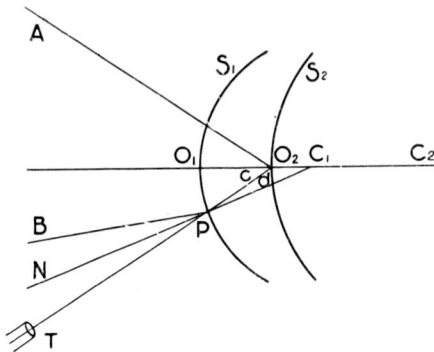

FIG. 147.

The apparent position of any ocular interface can be found by Tscherning's (1898) method of ophthalmophakometry. One light forms an image from the anterior corneal surface and this is moved until, as seen in a viewing telescope, it appears to be in the same direction as the image of a second brighter light formed by the surface in question. From the angular separations of the two lights the apparent depth of the surface can be calculated. The apparent depth can be corrected to a true value by taking into account the refractive power of the media between the anterior surface of the cornea and the surface in question.[1] This technique has been used to calculate the thickness of the cornea, the depth of the anterior chamber and the thickness of the lens.

The principle of Tscherning's method is seen in Fig. 147. Let S_1 be the anterior surface of the cornea and S_2 any other surface. A lamp of sufficient power (A) to produce an image on the surface in question is placed so that the optic axis bisects its angular distance from the telescope (T). A second source (B), sufficiently feeble to give

[1] p. 42.

an image only on the anterior surface of the cornea, is so placed that the image of A on S_2 is in line with that of B on S_1. Then, since c is half the angular distance of AT, and d is half the angular distance of BT, we can calculate the apparent depth of the surface S_2 provided that the radius of curvature of the cornea (r) is known.

This gives the *apparent position* of the surface. It must be remembered, however, that owing to the refraction by the corneal surface and the ocular media, any point in the anterior part of the eye is seen as a virtual erect and magnified image displaced towards the corneal surface[1]; the optical system thus corresponds to that wherein an object is placed between a lens and its principal focus and will be evident from Fig. 81.

The actual construction is seen in Fig. 148. Here, AB is the real position of an intra-ocular structure: one ray parallel to the axis (AO) passes after refraction through F_1, a second passing through F_2 leaves the system parallel to the axis (AQP), and consequently the image, or the apparent position of A, is at A′ where the prolongations of these two rays meet.

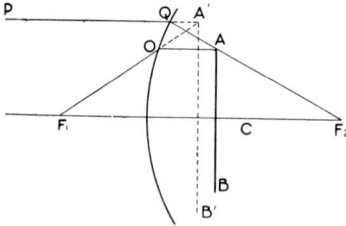

FIG. 148.

The image of the posterior surface of the cornea, therefore, appears to be nearer the anterior surface than it actually is, appearing at A′B′ instead of at AB in Fig. 148; but knowing the apparent position, the real position can be calculated from the general formula, $f_1/u + f_2/v = 1$.[2]

Simple microscopy has also been extensively used, the various ocular interfaces being focused in turn, and the movement of the microscope being measured. Since any movement of the subject's eye or an alteration in the observer's accommodation vitiates the accuracy of this method, special optical devices have been invented to allow the simultaneous inspection of the two surfaces the distance between which is to be measured ; some of these will be described at a later stage.

THE THICKNESS OF THE CORNEA

The axial thickness of the cornea is approximately half a millimetre. The precise measurement is by no means easy, however, owing to the faintness of the second Purkinje image. This difficulty was first overcome by Blix (1880) who employed a microscope of high magnification to observe the image cast by a brightly illuminated diaphragm which was set in place of the ocular of a second microscope. The reflex image on the anterior surface is accurately focused, and then the image on the posterior surface, the displacement of the instrument being equal to the apparent thickness. Koby (1928) used the Gullstrand slit-lamp and corneal microscope, the ocular of which was fitted with a micrometer, in much the same manner ; while Gullstrand (1911) used the ophthalmometric Nernst slit-lamp.

[1] p. 45.   [2] p. 73.

In more modern methods the principle of doubling used in the keratometer was initially employed by von Bahr (1948) who inserted two glass plates,
the angle of inclination of which to the optical system of the slit-lamp could
be varied; one of the glass plates covered the lower half of the illuminating
beam and the other covered the lower part of the objective of the viewing

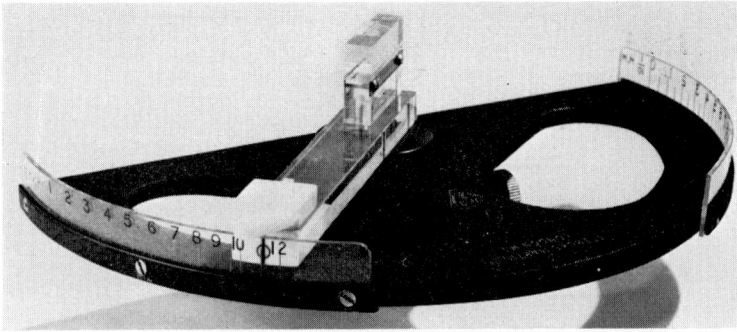

FIG. 149.—THE PACHOMETER OF MAURICE.

The instrument is fixed on the lamp arm of the Haag-Streit slit-lamp. The
beam is divided in two parts which may be moved relatively to each other on
rotatory movements of the Perspex plate. It is suitable for measuring the thickness
of the cornea or the depth of the anterior chamber.

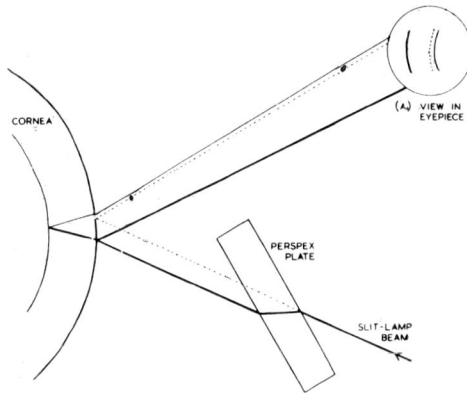

FIG. 150.—THE CORNEAL THICKNESS.

A simplified diagram of the determination of the corneal thickness by the
rotation of a Perspex plate (D. M. Maurice and A. Giardini).

microscope. Maurice and Giardini (1951) devised an elegant attachment to
the Haag-Streit slit-lamp whereby doubling is achieved by using a cut-out
area in a Perspex plate covered by coloured celluloid; on rotation of the
plate, light passing through the cut-out remains undeviated but that through
the plate is shifted (Figs. 149–50). It is possible thereby to align the reflexes
from the epithelial and endothelial surfaces so that the angle of rotation gives
a mea ure of the corneal thickness, the apparatus being calibrated against

Perspex shells of known thickness. A somewhat similar instrument was devised by Mishima and Hedbys (1968).

Some calculations by various workers for the thickness of the cornea in the optical zone or thinnest region are given in Table IV.

TABLE IV

THE THICKNESS OF THE CORNEA

in mm.

The figures in brackets give the number of eyes tested.

Blix (1880)	0·482–0·576 (10)
Tscherning (1898)	1·15 (1)
Gullstrand (1909)	0·46 and 0·51 (2)
Koby (1928–30)	0·46–0·703 (20) (average 0·583)
Fincham (1930)	0·48–0·59 (12) (average 0·538)
Sobański (1934)	0·40–0·67 (20) (average 0·53)
von Bahr (1948)	0·46–0·67 (224) (average 0·565)
Maurice and Giardini (1951)	0·507±0·0042 (88)
Santoni (1952)	0·524±0·0041 (80)
Cook and Langham (1953)	0·536±0·04 (10)
Donaldson (1966)	0·522±0·041 (268)
Martola and Baum (1968)	0·523±0·039 (209)
Mishima and Hedbys (1968)	0·518±0·02 (40)

THE DEPTH OF THE ANTERIOR CHAMBER

Numerous methods have been devised for measuring the depth of the anterior chamber. von Helmholtz (1856) first made accurate measurements, adapting his ophthalmometer for this purpose, and Tscherning's (1898) method of ophthalmophakometry is also applicable. Donders (1872), on the other hand, employed a corneal microscope with which the anterior surface of the cornea and then the edge of the pupil were focused. The method can be used clinically with the slit-lamp by means of Ulbrich's (1914) drum mounted upon the microscope.

Several other special techniques have been employed.[1] The principle of von Helmholtz's instrument has been modified by inserting one or two

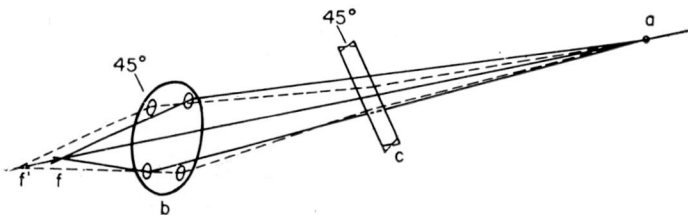

FIG. 151.—THE MEASUREMENT OF THE DEPTH OF THE ANTERIOR CHAMBER.

The optics of Stenström's modification of Lindstedt's device.

Light from an illuminated diaphragm (*a*) is projected by means of a sphero-cylindrical lens system provided with 4 diaphragm openings (*b*), 2 in the 45° meridian and 2 in the 135° meridian. Bundles of rays passing through the diaphragm of the 135° meridian produce a focal point at a constant distance (*f*) which is focused on the first surface to be measured (the corneal vertex). In the 45° meridian a negative lens (*c*) is inserted which is moved along the axis of the apparatus until it is focused on the posterior surface to be measured (*f′*) (the anterior lens vertex).

[1] See also Vol. VII, p. 263.

rotatable glass plates into the beam of the slit-lamp as in the instruments of von Bahr (1948), Maurice and Giardini (1951) and Jaeger (1952). By the use of totally refracting prisms, Raeder (1922) simultaneously focused the pupillary margin in one ocular of the corneal microscope and the corneal surface in the other; the adjustment of the ocular required to do this allowed a calculation of the depth of the anterior chamber. By using a sphero-cylindrical optical system, Lindstedt (1916), Rosengren (1930–31) and Stenström (1953) could focus the anterior focal line on the proximal surface and the posterior on the more distant surface, the interfocal distance giving the depth of the anterior chamber (Fig. 151) (Törnquist, 1953; Snydacker, 1956; and others).

FIGS. 152 and 153.—MEASUREMENT OF THE DEPTH OF THE
ANTERIOR CHAMBER (G. M. Bleeker).

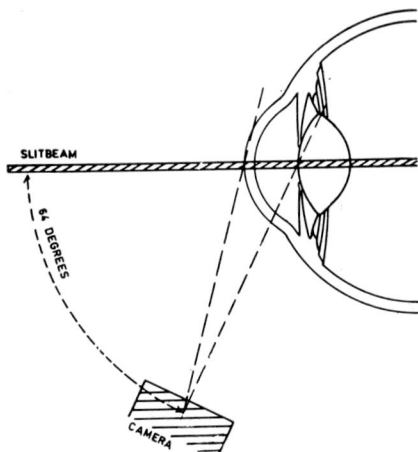

FIG. 152.—The camera provides life-size negatives of the distance between the anterior surfaces of the cornea and the lens, as seen from an angle of 64°, the relative depth of the anterior chamber.

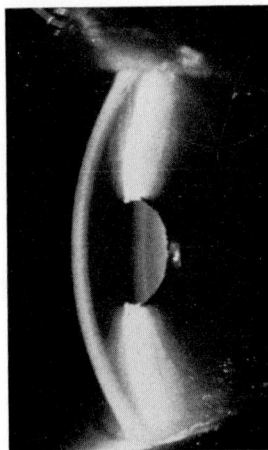

FIG. 153.—Photograph of the slit-lamp image taken from an angle of 64°. The distance between the anterior surface of the cornea and of the lens can be measured.

A further method, which avoids errors due to movements of the subject, makes use of the photography of an optical section of the eye as seen by the slit-lamp (Heim, 1941; Goldmann, 1941; Bleeker, 1960–61; Jones and Maurice, 1963) (Figs. 152–3).

Many of the original estimates were distances from the anterior surface of the cornea to the anterior surface of the lens in the axial region from which it was necessary to subtract the estimated or measured corneal thickness. The true depth of the anterior chamber is usually about 3 mm. in an adult emmetrope but, as we shall see later, this is one of the parameters in optical measurement which is subject to considerable variation.

THE THICKNESS OF THE LENS

The methods employed to estimate the thickness of the lens are based on the principles we have already discussed. They involve the determination of the position of the posterior surface of the lens and require complicated calculations. Light reaching and reflected from this surface traverses three different ocular media, the cornea, the aqueous humour and the lens; the refractive indices of these media must therefore be taken into account. As we shall see, there is some uncertainty about the true refractive index of the lens so that the calculation by optical means of the position of its posterior surface must, therefore, be equally uncertain.

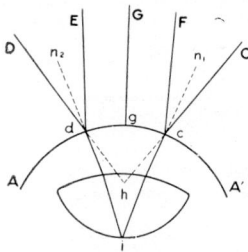

FIG. 154.

von Helmholtz used the method of super-imposition of the corneal and lenticular reflections of an illuminated object. Tscherning's ophthalmo-phakometer is similarly applicable.

The thickness of the lens was calculated by von Helmholtz on the same principle as that employed for the position of the anterior surface; lacking, however, the orientation of the edge of the iris, he had recourse to the device of reduplicating his observations (Fig. 154). A source of light was made to produce an image on the anterior surface of the cornea (CcF) and the posterior surface of the lens (CcidD): the positions of the object and observing eye were then reversed (DdicC). If the image reflected by the lens is covered in each case by a corneal image, the apparent position of the former will be at the point of intersection (h) of the observer's visual lines passing through the two corneal images. From measurements which can be taken this can be calculated, and the real position deduced.

Measurement of the slit-lamp section through the lens using the Ulbrich drum is also possible, and Fincham (1924–25) adapted a similar method in combination with photography. Ultrasonic techniques[1] have been applied to the measurement of intra-ocular distances and the thickness of the lens is certainly a parameter which can be estimated by their use (Figs. 158–9).[2]

Accommodation, of course, markedly influences the distance between the surfaces of the lens, but in the adult unaccommodated eye an average figure for the thickness of the lens is about 4 mm.

THE AXIAL LENGTH OF THE GLOBE

We have so far concerned ourselves with the separation of these interfaces from one another. The optical part they play in the dioptrics of the eye depends on a knowledge of the axial length of the globe since this determines the plane on which rays of light parallel to the axis are focused in emmetropia.

The methods of measurement may be either optical or direct. The optical or indirect methods make use of one of the techniques just described,

[1] Vol. VII, p. 325.   [2] p. 113.

such as ophthalmophakometry. Having measured the curvature and separation of the interfaces and assuming certain values for the refractive indices of the media, we are in a position to determine the effect of each interface on the vergence of rays passing through; the vergence of these rays emerging into the vitreous from the lens which are subsequently focused on the retina can be calculated. From this the distance between the posterior surface of the lens and the back of the eye is easily calculated and, adding to this the distances between the other interfaces, we obtain the axial length of the eye.

Here we are considering the unaccommodated emmetropic eye but the method can also be used for ametropic eyes. In the emmetropic eye we assume that the vergence of rays reaching the cornea is nil; in ametropia the appropriate vergence can be calculated from the measured refractive error.

A further method for deducing the axial length of the eye depends on chromatic aberration. Schoute (1940) and Colenbrander (1940) pointed out that the position of circles of diffusion in the fovea depends on the axial length of the eye, a measure which is proportional to the difference in the apparent distance between objects of different colour. By the use of monochromatic red and blue light it is possible to measure exactly the chromatic aberration of the eye and deduce therefrom reliable values for this defect in the lens; moreover, assuming that the specific chromatic aberration in all human eyes is identical, the refractive power of the lens and the axial length of the eye can be deduced therefrom.

Direct methods make use of non-optical techniques and the two most widely practised are by means of x-rays and ultrasonic vibrations.

The first to measure the axial length of the eye by x-rays was Rushton (1938) of London; his technique depends on the sensitivity of the dark-adapted eye to these radiations, a fact known to the pioneers of radiology (Edison, 1896; Röntgen, 1897; Dorn, 1898) but almost forgotten until it was re-discovered by Pirie (1932) and Taft (1932) and used clinically by Gifford and Barth (1934) to test retinal function in eyes with opaque media and for the subjective localization of intra-ocular foreign bodies. Rushton's apparatus is seen in Fig. 155. An x-ray beam, screened to a ribbon shape, is thrown across the eye at right angles to the optic axis. If it cuts the eye near the equator a narrow bluish circle is seen corresponding to the circle of retina stimulated (Fig. 156). As the beam is moved backwards this circle becomes smaller until, when it cuts the " retinal posterior pole ", the circle becomes a minute spot at the fixation point. The position of the beam at that moment gives the plane of the posterior pole; the plane of the vertex of the cornea is determined by visual measurement under microscopical control, using a ribbon of light passing tangentially to the cornea and running parallel to the x-ray beam.

Any diameter of the globe can be measured by the same technique. All that is required is to throw an x-ray beam across the eye at right angles to

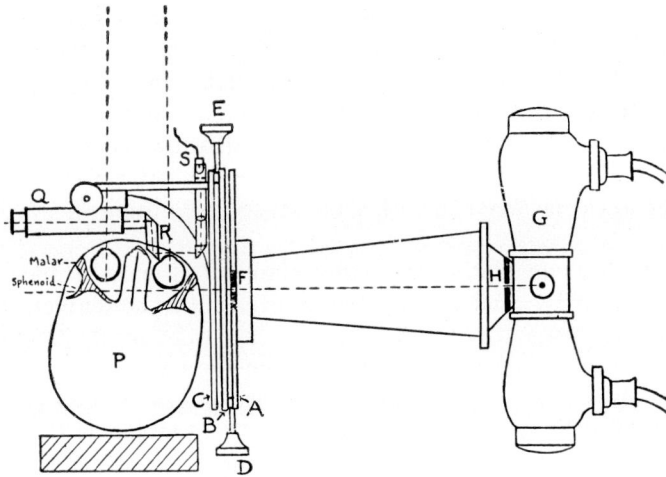

FIG. 155.—RUSHTON'S APPARATUS FOR MEASURING THE AXIAL LENGTH
OF THE EYE.

The patient's head, seen in horizontal section at P, is anchored to the frame B
by suitable clamps (not shown); the whole apparatus is pivoted about the centre of
the x-ray tube (G) so that all independent movements are shared.

Two frames (A, C) slide on a third frame (B), the movement of A being controlled
by the milled knob D, and of C by E. A scale and vernier indicate the position of A
with respect to C. In A there is a slit between lead plates at F, and arrangements
are made so that rays passing through the small holes H and F are perpendicular
to all three frames.

A microscope (Q) is mounted on C so that its axis is parallel to the x-ray beam
and a cross-wire in the eye-piece is parallel to the x-ray slit. A prism (R) enables
the apex of the cornea to be observed tangentially. The microscope is illuminated
by a faint pencil of light from a lamp S attached to the frame C, the light being
arranged so as to come to a line-focus at the position occupied by the cornea.

The zero error is found by moving the microscope frame until a beam of light
sent along the track of the x-ray beam is superimposed on the cross-wire. When
the patient is fixed, dark-adapted and fixing a suitable luminous spot, the microscope
frame is adjusted so that the cross-wire touches the corneal image tangentially, and
simultaneously the x-ray frame is adjusted to the position whereat the patient sees
the luminous circle dwindle into a central spot. The reading of the scale, less the
zero error, then gives the axial length of the eye from the cornea to the retina (see
Fig. 156).

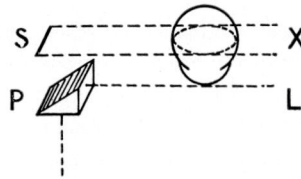

FIG. 156.—To show the paths of the x-ray beam (X) issuing from the slit (S) and
the beam of light (L) controlled by the prism (P) to cut the apex of the cornea
tangentially. When X cuts the posterior pole of the eye, LX is the axial length.

the diameter to be measured, and then to discover the two points at opposite poles at which the circles become spots. These two points can be marked by exposures on an x-ray film, the diameter being thus obtained by direct measurement. The error is $\pm$ 0·5 mm., corresponding to the width of the slit.

This apparatus has been modified by Goldmann and Hagen (1942) and Sorsby and O'Connor (1945), and has been most extensively used by Stenström (1946) and Deller and his colleagues (1947); with its aid it has been conclusively demonstrated that the axial length varies independently of the total refraction of the eye (Fig. 157). Although a subjective method unsuitable for young subjects, it is generally considered to be reasonably reliable and is often used as a standard for the accuracy of other methods of measurement (Sorsby et al., 1957; Jansson, 1963).

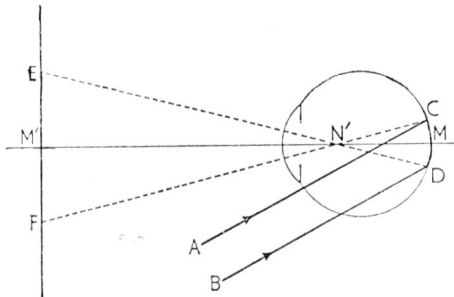

FIG. 157.—THE METHOD OF GOLDMANN AND HAGEN FOR DETERMINING THE POSTERIOR NODAL DISTANCE, N'M.

ULTRASONOGRAPHY, a tehnique pioneered in America by Mundt and Hughes (1956), has been extensively investigated in recent years[1] and is of accepted value in the measurement of intra-ocular distances, particularly the axial length of the eye. The technique used is the " time-amplitude recording " of the echoes received from various ocular interfaces (Figs. 158–9). In theory the method is ideal : the time taken for ultrasonic energy to travel from a transducer through the eye to the reflecting interfaces and then back again to a transducer is measured. The peaks in the figure represent reflections from the various ocular interfaces; their linear separation is a measurement of the time taken for the ultrasonic vibrations to pass between them. The determination of intra-ocular distances depends on the speed of the ultrasonic vibrations in the various media of the eye. The following values for the velocity of ultrasound in the various media at 22°C were given by Oksala and Lehtinen (1958) : cornea 1550 metres per sec., aqueous and

---

[1] For the clinical application of ultrasonography, see Vol. VII, p. 325. See also Oksala and Lehtinen (1957–61), Oksala (1958–65), Yamamoto (1960–61), Franken (1962), Jansson and Sundmark (1961), Jansson (1963), Itin (1963), Otsuka et al. (1961), Sorsby et al. (1963), Ricci (1964), Franceschetti and Gernet (1965), Gernet (1965), Kimura (1965), Nover and Grote (1965,) R. Weekers et al. (1967), Coleman and Carlin (1967), Gernet and Franceschetti (1967), and many others.

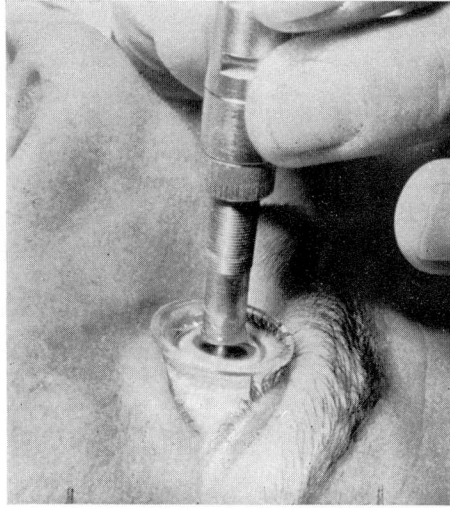

FIG. 158.

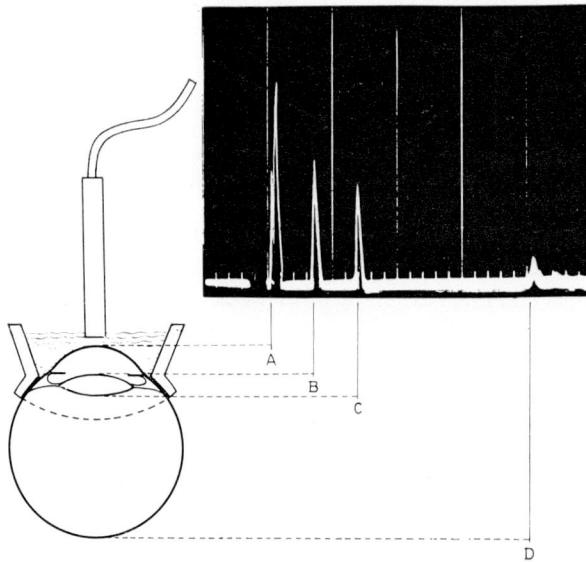

FIG. 159.

FIGS. 158 and 159.—ULTRASONIC MEASUREMENT OF INTRA-OCULAR DISTANCES (A. Franceschetti).

The ultrasonic probe is inserted into a ring-shaped contact glass filled with water (Fig. 158). The peaks in the echogram represent reflections at the anterior surface of the cornea (A), the anterior and posterior surfaces of the lens (B, C), and at the surface of the retina (D). AD is the axial length.

vitreous 1495, lens 1650, sclera 1630. It will be noted that the speed is some 10% greater in the lens than in the aqueous and vitreous. It is interesting that the actual calculation of intra-ocular distances from the ultrasonic echogram involves the assumption of these particular data, a situation which finds a parallel in optical methods such as phakometry wherein values for the refractive indices of the ocular media must be assumed.

Comparisons between the results of ultrasonic measurements show good agreement with those obtained by other methods such as phakometry and by x-rays (Otsuka *et al.*, 1961; Jansson and Kock, 1962; Sorsby *et al.*, 1963). Moreover, it is a simpler technique than the optical methods and, being objective, can be used in young children. It is true that the necessity to couple the probe and the eye with fluid owing to the fact that high-frequency ultrasonic energy is dissipated in air after travelling a very short distance makes the technique somewhat complicated, but this slight inconvenience is offset by the rapidity of the examination. For this purpose the small probe designed by Ricci (1964) which dips into a ring-shaped scleral contact lens filled with water is suitable (Fig. 158). Alternatively, a combination of the optical and ultrasonographic methods may be employed: thus Gernet (1963) measured the distance between the vertex of the cornea and the anterior surface of the lens optically (by Jaeger's 1952 technique[1]) and the remainder of the distances ultrasonographically.

TABLE V

THE AXIAL LENGTH OF THE EYE

Indirect method	Gullstrand (1909)		24·0 mm.
Radiographic method	Goldmann and Hagen (1942)		23·4 mm.
	Stenström (1946)		23·92 mm.
Ultrasonic method	Yamamoto *et al.* (1961)		23·1 mm.
	Franken (1961)		25·0 mm.
	Jansson (1963)	males	24·0 mm.
		females	23·14 mm.
Opto-ultrasonic method	Gernet (1963–64)	males	23·3 mm. ± 0·7
		females	22·7 mm. ± 0·9

The axial length of the emmetropic human eye as determined by these various techniques is shown in Table V. As would be expected there is some physiological variation, but average values are between 23 and 24 mm., while the eye of females is somewhat shorter than that of males, indicating a higher refractive power in female emmetropes.

THE REFRACTIVE INDICES OF THE OCULAR MEDIA

The determination of the refractive indices of the cornea, the aqueous and the vitreous is a comparatively simple procedure; these media are uniform and any individual measurement of their refractive indices is of significance. Gullstrand (1911) gave the values 1·376 for the cornea and 1·336 for the aqueous and vitreous.

---

[1] p. 109.

This, however, is not true of the substance of the lens, the determination of the refractive index of which presents difficulties, partly because the investigation must be carried out on the excised lens, and also because the substance of the lens is not optically uniform so that direct methods of measurement are not applicable. The most reliable figures are perhaps those of Freytag (1907) who found the index of the cortex at the anterior and posterior poles to be 1·387 and 1·385, while that of the centre was 1·406.

It is no simple matter, however, to take into account the complex architecture of the lens. If a single lamination is considered, the form of the lens may be constructed as a central bi-convex core (the nucleus, A) surrounded by two meniscus lenses (the cortical layers, B,C) (Fig. 160); the image formed by B is therefore focused by A, and this in turn is focused by C. As a result the lens has a greater refracting power than it would have if it were homogeneous with a refractive index equal even to that of the core; moreover, this arrangement diminishes the spherical aberration and, as we shall see, considerably increases the accommodative range. The older observers (von Helmholtz, 1856) overcame the difficulty presented by this varying complexity by postulating a *hypothetical homogeneous lens* which, while retaining the same shape and focal length as the actual lens, was composed of a material of greater refractivity. The imaginary refractive index of such a lens was taken by von Helmholtz to be 1·44, and by Tscherning (1898) 1·42. An imaginary lens, however, of the true shape and a hypothetical total refractive index, cannot be reconciled with the Gaussian theory of cardinal points applied to the eye; to overcome this disadvantage, Gullstrand (1911) treated the lens as if it were composed of a cortex and a core. He calculated the total refractive power of the lens from the loss of refraction which is suffered by the eye when the lens is extracted. He accepted Freytag's measurements of the refractive indices at the poles and in the centre and postulated a *hypothetical equivalent core-lens* of imaginary shape but of the same index of refraction as the central area, which was suspended in a medium of the index of refraction of the cortex at the poles. Calculation showed that such a hypothetical core-lens would require to have anterior and posterior radii of 7·9108 and 5·7605 mm. and a thickness of 2·4187 mm. This method has the advantage that such a lens-system has the same optical characteristics as the actual lens if the anterior surface of the core-lens is 0·5460 mm. from the anterior pole of the lens; there is no doubt that this is the preferable approach.

The data upon which the optical system of the eye can be constructed may now be summarized in Table VI. It is always to be remembered, however, that with the exception of the curvature of the anterior surface of the cornea, none of the measurements is of mathematical accuracy. The

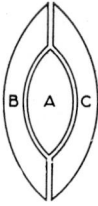

FIG. 160.

measurements of Tscherning and Gullstrand are in substantial agreement. They show, however, some discrepancies; and since Tscherning's measurements were based on the observation of one eye (that of a tall man), we shall rely on the calculations of Gullstrand which are more representative and are certainly more accurate than the earlier (but excellent) data of von Helmholtz.

TABLE VI

THE OPTICAL SYSTEM OF THE EYE

(*in mm.*)

	von Helmholtz	Tscherning	Gullstrand
POSITION OF SURFACES			
Cornea, ant. surf.	0	0	0
Cornea, post. surf.	—	1·15	0·5
Lens, ant. surf.	3·6	3·54	3·6
Lens, post. surf.	7·2	7·60	7·2
Lens, core, ant. surf.	—	—	4·146*
Lens, core, post. surf.	—	—	6·565*
RADII OF CURVATURE			
Cornea, ant. surf.	8·0	7·98	7·7
Cornea, post. surf.	—	6·22	6·8
Lens, ant. surf.	10·0	10·20	10·0
Lens, post. surf.	−6·0	−6·17	−6·0
Lens, core, ant. surf.	—	—	7·911*
Lens, core, post. surf.	—	—	−5·76*
REFRACTIVE INDICES			
Cornea	—	1·377	1·376
Aqueous and vitreous	1·336	1·3365	1·336
Lens	1·44*	1·42 (total)*	{ 1·386 (cortex) 1·406 (core)

* Calculated values.

The Combination of the Optical Components of the Eye

We shall now examine how the various interfaces and media of the eye combine to form an effective focusing device. For this purpose we shall proceed from the geometry of the individual components and investigate the optical properties of the two important and well-defined anatomical entities, the cornea and the lens.

THE OPTICS OF THE CORNEA

The thickness of the peripheral part of the cornea is greater than that of the axial region: thus in 209 eyes Martola and Baum (1968) found the former to average 0·660 mm. and the latter 0·523 mm. It follows that the curvature of the posterior corneal surface is a little greater than that of the anterior; this structure may therefore be considered as a weak concave lens. In isolation it would in fact have a slight diverging power, but in the eye it acts in a very powerful converging fashion because the aqueous humour has a refractive index differing only slightly from that of the corneal substance.

The powers of both surfaces of the cornea can be calculated from their curvatures and the various refractive indices, according to the formula previously given.[1] The anterior surface of a cornea of average curvature has nearly 49 D of convergence, the posterior nearly 6 D of divergence; the total refractive power of the cornea is therefore about 43 D in an average subject.

It is also possible to express the refraction of the cornea-aqueous system in terms of the cardinal points of Gauss; Gullstrand's figures for this are given in Table VII.

TABLE VII

THE OPTICS OF THE CORNEA

(Cardinal points measured from ant. corneal surface; distances in mm.)

First principal point	-0.0496
Second principal point	-0.0506
First nodal point	(7.754)*
Second nodal point	(7.753)*
First focal point	-23.277
Second focal point	30.981
Anterior focal length	-23.227
Posterior focal length	31.031
Refractive power	$+43.05$ D

* Calculated by Percival (1928)

THE OPTICS OF THE LENS

Measurement of the power of the isolated lens has until recently been unsatisfactory because of the alteration in its shape when removed from the eye. The investigation of subjects who have had their lenses removed, however, allows the alteration in the refractive power of the eye to be calculated, and from this it has been deduced that the power of the lens *in situ* is about 19 D.

The theoretical calculation of the power of the lens from the known surface curvatures and refractive indices leads to difficulties since, as we have seen, there is no uniform refractive index throughout this tissue and the assumption of a theoretical value, such as that of von Helmholtz (1.44), brings with it other discrepancies. The equivalent core-lens of Gullstrand is the most satisfactory simplification of what is a very complicated optical situation, but it must be remembered that the dimensions and refractive index of this core-lens, as in Table VI, relate merely to a purely hypothetical structure and are calculated so as to agree with the known power of the lens. We have seen that the Gaussian theory of cardinal points cannot be legitimately applied to the lens since it should be applied only to a system in which the media between the interfaces are of uniform refractive index, but it may be regarded as applicable if we consider each lamina of the lens to be of uniform optical density. Thus the lens as a whole can be considered to be a

[1] p. 99.

system of coaxial refracting surfaces. On this basis, Gullstrand's figures for the lens are given in Table VIII.

TABLE VIII

THE OPTICS OF THE LENS

(*Principal points measured from ant. corneal surface*)

First principal point	5·678 mm.
Second principal point	5·808 mm.
Anterior and posterior focal lengths	69·908 mm.
Refractive power	+19·11 D

THE EYE AS A WHOLE

THE OPTICAL POWER OF THE EYE

The total optical power of the eye can be derived from the known powers of the corneal and lenticular systems. A simple addition of these, however, is inaccurate since the two systems are separated from one another, thereby increasing the total effective power. It emerges that the power of the normal eye is slightly less than 60 D (see Table IX).

An interesting and rather beautiful technique for *measuring the total refraction of the eye* has been elaborated by Goldmann and Hagen (1942). The total refraction can be calculated when the size of the object, the size of the image and the distance between the two are known; but the absolute size of the image cannot normally be measured independently of optical distortion. The non-refrangibility of x-rays by the optical media of the eye allows this difficulty to be overcome (Fig. 157). The method consists of traversing the eye in the sagittal plane with two parallel and vertical x-ray beams (AC and BD) a known distance apart (5·2 mm.); these are seen by the dark-adapted subject as two vertical lines in space. Arrangements are made so that the subject, with his head fixed, projects these symmetrically on either side of a red fixation light on a wall a known distance away (M'). Two lines of light are then projected on the wall and manipulated so that they coincide exactly with and overlie the röntgen images (E and F). It follows that the lines of light must form images on the retina at the points cut by the x-ray beams. The distance between the lines of light on the wall (which is measured on a scale) and the known distance between the x-ray beams can be considered as conjugate object- and image-sizes. In Fig. 157, CD and M'N' are predetermined, EF is measured and N'M is therefore easily calculated. In an emmetropic eye M is the posterior focal point and N'M is the posterior nodal distance. Since this equals the anterior focal length[1] the latter is known and its reciprocal gives the equivalent power. By this technique the total refraction can be calculated to an experimental error of ±0·5 D.

THE CARDINAL POINTS OF THE EYE

As the refractive indices of the corneal substance, the aqueous humour and the vitreous are all much the same, we are able to consider these as a common medium. The *optical system thus reduces itself into two elements: (1) the corneal surface separating air from the common medium*, and (2) *the lens immersed in the common medium*. Refraction by each of these can be expressed in terms of the Gaussian system of cardinal points. The two systems

[1] p. 58.

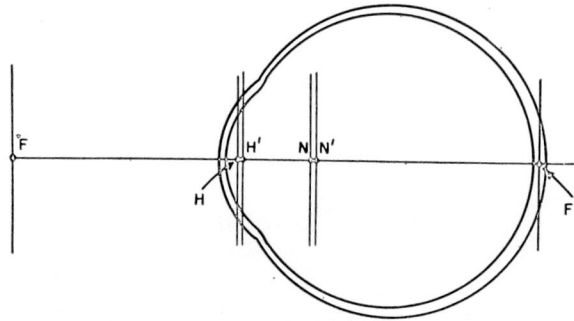

FIG. 161.—THE CARDINAL POINTS OF THE GULLSTRAND SCHEMATIC EYE.

In this eye the secondary focus, F', falls 0·387 mm. behind the retinal photo-sensitive elements. The principal points, H and H', are located 1·348 mm. and 1·602 mm. from the front surface of the cornea respectively. $FH - N'F' = 17·055$ mm., and $H'F' = FN = 22·785$ mm. The ratio $H'F'/HF$ is equal to the index of the vitreous (after G. A. Fry).

can thus be combined to give a single system of cardinal points for the eye as a whole.

J. B. Listing (1853), who studied with Gauss at Göttingen, was the first to propose that the eye could be considered in such a simple fashion, and from his work the concept of the SCHEMATIC EYE has been derived. The cardinal points of this dioptric system as calculated by Tscherning and Gullstrand are given in Table IX and illustrated in Fig. 161. Incidentally, the data for the corneal system seen in Table VII provide the data for the aphakic eye.

TABLE IX

THE OPTICS OF THE COMPLETE SCHEMATIC EYE

(*Distances in mm.*)

	Tscherning	Gullstrand
First principal point	1·54	1·348
Second principal point	1·86	1·602
First nodal point	7·30	(7·079)*
Second nodal point	7·62	(7·333)*
First focal point	−15·59	−15·707
Second focal point	24·75	24·387
Anterior focal length	−17·13	−17·055†
Posterior focal length	22·89	22·785
Refractive power	+58·38 D	+58·64 D

* Calculated by Percival (1928).
† Percival (1928) pointed out that the value given by Gullstrand (1911), 17·055, is probably a misprint for 17·054.

THE REDUCED EYE

On examining these data it is obvious that the two principal points are very close (0·254 mm. apart in the normal and 0·010 in the aphakic eye), as also are the two nodal points (0·254 in the normal and 0·001 in the aphakic)

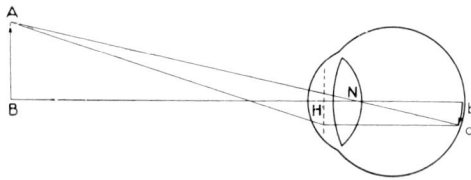

FIG. 162.—THE REDUCED EYE.

(Fig. 161). So near, indeed, are they that no great inaccuracy will arise if we substitute for each pair an intermediate point and consider them as one (Fig. 162). Without introducing any appreciable error, we can thus treat the optical system of the eye as if it were a single ideal refracting surface. This concept of a REDUCED EYE was introduced by Listing (1853), whose figures were further simplified by Donders (1864). Their values are expressed in mm., compared in Table X with the values calculated from the data of Gullstrand.

TABLE X

THE REDUCED EYE

(*Distances in mm.*)

	Listing	Donders	Gullstrand	
	Phakic eye	Phakic eye	Phakic eye	Aphakic eye
Principal point	2·3448	2	1·35	1·35
Radius of curvature	5·1248	5	5·73	7·8
Anterior focal length	−15·1774	−15	−17·05	−23·23
Posterior focal length	20·4742	20	22·78	31·03

From the Table it is evident that the reduced eye is *an ideal spherical surface, the radius of curvature of which is 5·73 mm., which separates two media of refractive indices 1 and 1·336. It lies 1·35 mm. behind the anterior surface of the cornea, that is, in the anterior chamber. Its nodal point (optical centre) is therefore 7·08 mm. behind the anterior corneal surface, that is, in the posterior part of the lens. Its anterior focal distance is 17·054 mm. (or 15·7 mm. in front of the cornea), and its posterior focal distance is 22·78 mm. (or 24·13 mm. behind the anterior surface of the cornea), that is, in a normal eye, upon the retina; its power is 58·6 D.*

THE CONSTRUCTION OF THE RETINAL IMAGE

The construction of the retinal image can be made from the cardinal points of the dioptric system of the eye as in Fig. 161. In the reduced eye, however, this is simpler, as in Fig. 163, and is represented by drawing straight lines from the extremities of the object (AB) through the nodal point (N) and producing them until they reach the retina (*ab*). It is evident that *the*

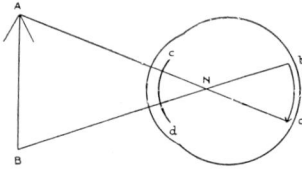

FIG. 163.

image thus obtained is real, inverted, and diminished; it is re-inverted psychologically in the cerebral cortex.

THE VISUAL ANGLE. These two lines will enclose an angle at the nodal point of the eye; this, the angle ANB, is known as the VISUAL ANGLE, and is defined as *the angle subtended by the object at the nodal point.* It is, of course, equal to the angle *a*N*b* which is subtended by the retinal image at the nodal point. An early and delightful representation of the visual angle is seen in Fig. 164.

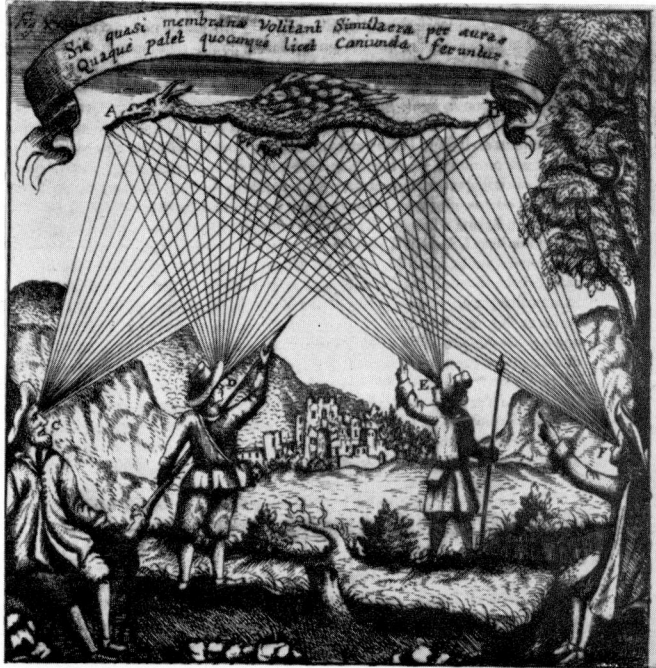

FIG. 164.—THE VISUAL ANGLE.

The view of an object (a dragon flying in the air, AB) as seen by four observers, C, D, E and F. " Different eyes or the same eye in different places can always see multitudinous points in the same object." From *Oculus artificialis teledioptricus sive telescopium* by Johann Zahn (1685) (courtesy of the Library of the British Optical Association).

THE DISTANCE OF THE RETINAL IMAGE is given by the formula :

$$f_1/u + f_2/v = 1 \quad \text{or} \quad xy = f_1f_2$$

where u and v are the distances of the object and its image from the principal plane, and x and y are the distances of the object and the image from their respective focal points.

THE SIZE OF THE RETINAL IMAGE is given by the formula:

$$\frac{o}{i} = -\frac{x}{f_1} = -\frac{f_2}{y}$$

$$= \frac{f_1 - u}{f_1} = \frac{f_2}{f_2 - v}$$

In the reduced eye the size of the image can be calculated simply from the construction of Fig. 165. Let AB be the object and ab the image, then since $\triangle$s ABN and abN are similar,

$$ab : AB = bN : BN$$
$$ab = AB \times bN/BN$$

Since the posterior nodal distance is equal to the anterior focal distance,

$$bN = 17 \cdot 054 \text{ mm.}$$
$$i = 17 \cdot 05 \times o/D$$

when o is the size of the object and D its distance from the (nodal point of the) eye. *The size of the retinal image of any external object depends on the visual angle*, which is approximately equal to o/D.

The value of the concepts of the schematic and reduced eye must not be exaggerated; it is true that they offer a simple means of comprehending the total refraction of the eye and provide a convenient method whereby the processes and formulæ of geometrical optics may be applied. We shall see shortly, how-

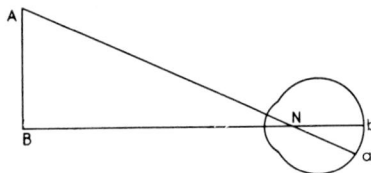

FIG. 165.

ever, that not only are these simplifications subject to the limitations of geometrical optics as such, but the concept of a " normal " eye is untenable. For example, it has become meaningless to give particular values to the anterior or posterior focal length of the eye, and it is certainly pointless to give the " optical constants " values to several places of decimals. In due course when we study the range of variations of the optical constants of the eye it will become obvious that it is possible to define an optically normal eye only in statistical terms.

In the first place, however, we must re-examine the presuppositions we have made regarding the optical system of the eye in order to describe it in terms of geometrical optics, and how the defects inherent in geometrical optics are relevant to its dioptric imagery.

Allen. *Amer. J. Optom.*, **26**, 279 (1949).
von Bahr. *Acta ophthal.* (Kbh.), **26**, 247 (1948).
   Trans. ophthal. Soc. U.K., **68**, 515 (1948).
Bleeker. *Arch. Ophthal.*, **63**, 821 (1960); **65**, 369 (1961).
Blix. *Oftalmometriska studier*, Upsala, **15**, 349 (1880).

Campbell and Primrose. *Trans. ophthal. Soc. U.K.*, **73**, 353 (1953).
Coleman and Carlin. *Ultrasonics in Ophthal.* (Symposium, Münster, 1966), Basel, 207 (1967).
Colenbrander. *Ophthalmologica*, **99**, 402 (1940).

Cook and Langham. *Brit. J. Ophthal.*, **37**, 301 (1953).

Deller, O'Connor and Sorsby. *Proc. roy. Soc. B*, **134**, 456 (1947).

Demicheri. *Ann. Oculist.* (Paris), **113**, 93 (1895).

Donaldson. *Arch. Ophthal.*, **76**, 25 (1966).

Donders. *On the Anomalies of Accommodation and Refraction of the Eye*, London (1864).
IV int. Cong. Ophthal., London, 184 (1872).

Dorn. *Arch. roent. Ray*, **2**, 69 (1898).

Edison. *Elect. Engineer*, **22**, 601 (1896).

Fincham. *Trans. opt. Soc. Lond.*, **26**, 239 (1924–5).
(1930). *See* Koby (1930).
Trans. ophthal. Soc. U.K., **55**, 145 (1935).
The Mechanism of Accommodation (B.J.O. Monog. Suppl. VIII), London (1937).

Franceschetti and Gernet. *Trans. Amer. Acad. Ophthal.*, **69**, 465 (1965).

Franken. *Metingen aan het levende menselijke oog met behulp van de echo van ultrasone trillingen*, Utrecht (1961).
Ophthalmologica, **143**, 82 (1962).

Freytag. *Vergl. Untersuch. ü. d. Brechungs-indices d. Linse*, Wiesbaden (1907).

Gernet. *v. Graefes Arch. Ophthal.*, **166**, 402, 424, 530 (1963–4).
Ophthalmologica, **147**, 235 (1964).
Bull. Soc. franç. Ophtal., **77**, 644 (1964).
Klin. Mbl. Augenheilk., **146**, 863 (1965).

Gernet and Franceschetti. *Ultrasonics in Ophthal.* (Symposium, Münster, 1966), Basel, 175 (1967).

Gifford and Barth. *Arch. Ophthal.*, **11**, 81 (1934).

Goldmann. *Ophthalmologica*, **102**, 7 (1941).

Goldmann and Hagen. *Ophthalmologica*, **104**, 15 (1942).

Gullstrand. *Hb. d. physiologischen Optik von H. v. Helmholtz*, 3rd ed., Hamburg, **1** (1909).
Einführung in d. Methoden d. Dioptrik d. Auges d. Menschen, Leipzig (1911).

Heim. *Ophthalmologica*, **102**, 193 (1941).

von Helmholtz. *Hb. d. physiologischen Optik*, Leipzig, **1** (1856).

Hess. *Graefe-Saemisch Hb. d. ges. Augenheilk*, 3rd ed., Leipzig, Kap. IX, *Path. u. Ther. d. Linsen-Systems* (1911).

Home. *Phil. Trans.*, **86**, 1 (1796).

Itin. *Ann. Oculist.* (Paris), **198**, 465 (1963).

Jaeger. *v. Graefes Arch. Ophthal.*, **153**, 120 (1952).

Jansson. *Acta ophthal.* (Kbh.), **41**, 25, 236; Suppl. 74 (1963).

Jansson and Kock. *Acta ophthal.* (Kbh.), **40**, 420 (1962).

Jansson and Sundmark. *Acta ophthal.* (Kbh.), **39**, 899 (1961).

Javal and Schiøtz. *Ann. Oculist.* (Paris), **86**, 5 (1881).

Jones and Maurice. *Exp. Eye Res.*, **2**, 233 (1963).

Kabe. *Jap. J. Ophthal.*, **12**, 146 (1968).

Kimura. *Acta Soc. ophthal. jap.*, **69**, 963 (1965).

Kirchhof. *Z. Biol.*, **100**, 408 (1940).

Koby. *Rev. gén. Ophtal.*, **42**, 292 (1928); **43**, 57 (1929); **44**, 222 (1930).

Koomen, Scolnik and Tousey. *J. opt. Soc. Amer.*, **43**, 27 (1953).

Landolt. *Cong. périod. int. Sci. méd.*, 5th Sess., Geneva, 1877, p. 772 (1878).

Le Grand and Marandon. *C.R. Acad. Sci.* (Paris), **228**, 1381 (1949).

Lindstedt. *Arch. Augenheilk.*, **80**, 104 (1916).

Listing. *Zur Dioptrik d. Auges*, in Wagner's *Handwörterbuch d. Physiologie*, Braun-schweig, **4**, 451 (1853).

Ludlam, Wittenberg and Rosenthal. *Amer. J. Optom.*, **42**, 394 (1965).

Martola and Baum. *Arch. Ophthal.*, **79**, 28 (1968).

Maurice and Giardini. *Brit. J. Ophthal.*, **35**, 169 (1951).

Mellerio. *Vision Res.*, **6**, 217 (1966).

Mishima and Hedbys. *Arch. Ophthal.*, **80**, 710 (1968).

Mundt and Hughes. *Amer. J. Ophthal.*, **41**, 488 (1956).

Nakajima. *Acta Soc. ophthal. jap.*, **59**, 783 (1955).

Nover and Grote. *v. Graefes Arch. Ophthal.*, **168**, 388, 405 (1965).

Oksala. *Nord. Med.*, **59**, 721 (1958).
Klin. Mbl. Augenheilk., **137**, 72 (1960).
J. pediat. Ophthal., **2**, 45 (1965).

Oksala and Lehtinen. *Ophthalmologica*, **134**, 387 (1957).
Acta ophthal. (Kbh.), **36**, 633 (1958); **38**, 599 (1960); **39**, 50 (1961).

Otero. *J. opt. Soc. Amer.*, **41**, 942 (1951).

Otsuka, Tokoro and Araki. *Acta Soc. ophthal. jap.*, **65**, 1777 (1961).

Otsuka, Tokoro and Kabe. *Acta Soc. ophthal. jap.*, **69**, 970 (1965).

Percival. *The Prescribing of Spectacles*, Bristol (1928).

Pirie. *Canad. med. Ass. J.*, **27**, 488 (1932).

Purkinje. *Commentatio de examine physio-logico organi visus*, Breslau (1823).

Raeder. *v. Graefes Arch. Ophthal.*, **110**, 73 (1922).

Ricci. *Bull. Soc. franç. Ophtal.*, **77**, 652 (1964).

Röntgen. *S. B. Akad. Wiss. Wien*, **1**, 576 (1897).

Rosengren. *Acta ophthal.* (Kbh.), **8**, 99 (1930); **9**, 103 (1931).

Rushton. *Trans. ophthal. Soc. U.K.*, **58**, 136 (1938).

Sanson. *Leçons sur les maladies des yeux*, Paris (1838).

Santoni. *Rass. ital. Ottal.*, **21**, 219 (1952).

Savery. *Phil. Trans.*, **48**, 167 (1753).

Scheiner. *Oculus hoc est: fundamentum opticum*, Oeniponti, 13 (1619).

Schoute. *Ophthalmologica*, **99**, 282 (1940).

Snydacker. *Trans. Amer. ophthal. Soc.*, **54**, 675 (1956).

Sobański. *Klin. oczna*, **12**, 317 (1934).

Sorsby, Benjamin, Davey *et al.* *Emmetropia and its Aberrations* (M.R.C. Spec. Rep. Series, No. 293), London (1957).

Sorsby, Benjamin and Sheridan. *Refraction and its Components during the Growth of the Eye from the Age of Three* (M.R.C. Spec. Rep. Series, No. 301), London (1961).

Sorsby, Leary, Richards and Chaston. *Vision Res.*, **3**, 499 (1963).

Sorsby and O'Connor. *Nature* (Lond.), **156**, 779 (1945).

Stenström. *Acta ophthal.* (Kbh.), Suppl. 26 (1946); **31**, 265 (1953).

Taft. *Amer. J. Roentgenol.*, **28**, 245 (1932).

Törnquist. *Acta ophthal.* (Kbh.), Suppl. 39 (1953).

Tscherning. *Arch. physiol.* (Paris), **3**, 96 (1890).

Optique physiologique, Paris (1898).

Ulbrich. *Klin. Mbl. Augenheilk.*, **53**, 244 (1914).

Weekers, R., Luyckx-Bacus and Weekers, J. *Ultrasonics in Ophthal.* (Symposium, Münster, 1966), Basel, 215 (1967).

Westheimer. *Amer. J. Optom.*, **42**, 315 (1965).

Whiteside. *Problems of Vision in Flight at High Altitude*, London (1957).

Wulfeck. *J. opt. Soc. Amer.*, **45**, 928 (1955).

Yamamoto, Namiki, Baba and Kato. *Acta Soc. ophthal. jap.*, **64**, 1333 (1960).

Jap. J. Ophthal., **5**, 134 (1961).

THE OPTICAL DEFECTS OF THE EYE

It is obvious that no biological system could hope to attain the accuracy demanded by a perfect Gaussian system of coaxial spherical refracting surfaces. The assumption whereon the first section of this Chapter is based must therefore be re-examined by a discussion of the departures of the eye from such theoretical perfection.

" Wenn mit nun ein Optiker ein Instrument verkaufen wollte, welches die letzt-genannten Fehler hätte, so ist es nicht zuviel gesagt, dass ich mich vollkommen berech-tigt glauben würde, die härtesten Ausdrücke über die Nachlässigkeit seiner Arbeit zu gebrauchen, und ihm sein Instrument mit Protest zurückzugeben. In Bezug auf meine Augen werde ich freilich letzteres nicht thun, sondern im Gegentheil froh sein, sie mit ihren Fehlern möglichst lange behalten zu dürfen. Aber der Umstand, dass sie mir trotz ihrer Fehler unersetzlich sind, verringert doch, wenn wir uns einmal auf den zwar einseitigen, aber berechtigten Standpunkt des Optikers stellen, die Grösse dieser Fehler nicht " (von Helmholtz, *Vorträge und Reden*, Braunschweig, 1, 286 (1903)).

A free translation runs as follows. " If an optician should try to sell me an instru-ment possessing the faults mentioned above, it seems to me without overstressing the matter that I should think myself wholly justified in using the most severe language with regard to the carelessness of his work and returning the instrument under protest. With regard to my eyes, however, I shall do no such thing but, on the contrary, I shall be glad to keep them as long as possible notwithstanding their shortcomings. But the fact that they, in spite of their faults, are irreplaceable to me does not lessen the size of the faults when looked at from the one-sided but justified standpoint of the optician."

The Approximate Nature of the Optical Constants

THE SHAPE OF THE CORNEA

The cornea is not really spherical in shape. The PARAXIAL (OPTICAL) AREA is nearly spherical but even in this region keratometry shows that the curvature may vary in different meridians; indeed, this corneal *astigmatism* is found to some degree in so high a proportion of the population that it should be regarded as the normal state of affairs. It is, therefore, more strictly accurate to refer to the paraxial area of the cornea as being a *toric* rather than a spherical surface. We shall see that the surfaces of the lens are probably also astigmatic so that the refractive system of the eye as a whole has some " built in " physiological astigmatism. This, however, is not usually marked and we shall consider it further when discussing astigmatism as a clinical refractive error.

The shape of the PERIPHERAL PART OF THE CORNEA has fascinated students of optics for many years and it has recently become important in relation to the fitting of corneal contact lenses. It is well to realize at the outset that the shape of the cornea is irregular and cannot be described in terms of a simple geometrical construction. It has long been known from anatomical studies that the periphery of the cornea is flatter than the axial area, an observation confirmed by early ophthalmometric studies. von Helmholtz (1856), following Senff (1846), believed that the shape of the entire cornea was that of a paraboloid of revolution, but Blix (1880) found that this was not so. It has therefore become customary to consider the cornea as having a central (*optical* or *apical*) zone (or *corneal cap*) and a peripheral (*basilar*) zone, a concept we owe to Aubert (1876–85). We have seen[1] that in standard keratometry the curvature of the optical zone is measured and there is wide agreement that this curvature is spherical or, more exactly, toroidal (Aubert, 1876; Matthiessen, 1891; Sulzer, 1892; Eriksen, 1893; and others).

A curious feature of the subject of corneal topography is the difficulty of deciding which point to take as the apex. Gullstrand (1911) used the term *ophthalmometric pole*, that is, the position of the corneal reflection of an object held very close to the eye when the subject looks directly at it. This point is rarely the same as the centre of the apical zone which has usually been said to be slightly below and temporal to the ophthalmometric pole—a view, however, which may no longer be tenable.[2] The centre of the apical zone is not easily defined as the zone itself may be of uncertain shape and extent. If the apex is defined as the point of maximum curvature of the cornea, this may not coincide with the line of sight which presumably strikes the cornea at the ophthalmometric pole (Girard, 1964; Ludlam and Wittenberg, 1966; Mandell and St. Helen, 1969). It has also been suggested that the toroidal form of the cornea may be less marked at the apex than as measured on the line of sight; measurement at this latter situation may be a combination of true toroidicity with, in addition, an effect due to tilt of an aspherical surface.

A further difficulty arises in attempting to define the size of the apical zone and to determine where the apical zone ends and the peripheral zone begins. Much depends on the criteria adopted and the technique used in measurement in deciding whether the corneal curvature is uniform or decreasing outwards from the apex. The classical criterion defined the apical zone as all those areas varying in power by not more than 1 dioptre, but when individual variations are taken into account it is not surprising that very

[1] p. 100.   [2] p. 128.

different areas have been quoted. An average figure of 4 mm. or slightly more is usually given for its diameter.[1]

The difficulties arising in attempting to define the apical zone are exceeded in the study of the corneal periphery. The measurement of the curvature of this region is a complicated task for which many methods have been devised.

Keratometry, as we have seen, is applicable only to strictly spherical surfaces; the corneal periphery is aspherical and the use of modified standard keratometers in this region is not only inaccurate but difficult because of the irregularity of the images. The keratometer as ordinarily employed makes use of reflections from two corneal areas about 3 mm. apart from one another; this is clearly much too large for determining the curvature of the periphery where we cannot assume that any small area is spherical. Nevertheless, attempts have been made to adapt the keratometer for measurement of the non-axial areas by asking the subject to look slightly eccentrically instead of at the standard fixation object (Bayshore, 1959; Grosvenor, 1961; Soper *et al.*, 1962; Ruben,

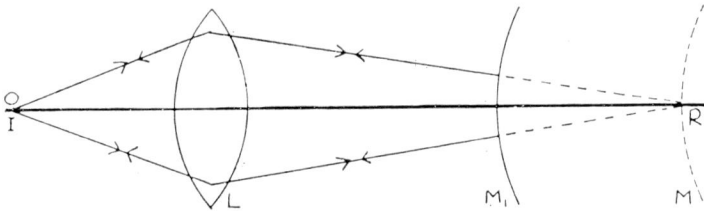

FIG. 166.—JENKINS'S ONE-ZONE KERATOMETER.

The principle of the keratometer is that of measuring the radius of curvature of a convex mirror. O is the object, L a convex lens, M the mirror to be measured. Adjustments are made until a sharp image of the object is formed on the surface of the mirror (M) at R. The mirror is then moved towards the lens to the position M_1, where the image of the object, I, is formed in the plane of the object, the light returning along its own path to the centre of curvature, R. The distance between the two positions of the mirror is its radius of curvature (T. C. A. Jenkins).

1967). Inaccuracies obviously arise because of the uncertainties about the centre of rotation of the eyes but empirically the method seems satisfactory. For this purpose Mandell (1965) used a special small-mire version of the Bausch and Lomb keratometer, while the instrument devised by Bonnet and Cochet (1960) is said to be capable of measuring the curvature of areas as small at 0·5 mm. or less. The Drysdale (1900) principle was employed by Fincham (1925), Jenkins (1963) and Bennett (1964) (Fig. 166): a convex lens is placed between a point-source and the reflecting surface to be measured, initially focusing an image at the surface itself. If a constant distance is maintained between the source and the lens and both are approached to the reflecting surface, at a certain distance the reflected image will be formed very close to the source. The distance which the lens and source are moved inwards to this point is equal to the radius of curvature of the surface.

The determination of the curvature of all parts of the cornea by *keratoscopy* may be said to have originated in the observation of the variations in and distortions of the image of a candle-flame by David Brewster (1827). A more sophisticated instrument

[1] Reynolds (1959) 2 to 3 mm., Jenkins (1963) 4 mm., Girard (1964) 3·8 to 9 mm., Bonnet (1964) 5 mm., Mandell (1965) 4·5 mm.

consisting of a luminous square was used by Henry Goode (1847–48) who viewed the image from the side. A further improvement was introduced by the Portuguese oculist, Antonio Placido (1880–82) who devised the keratoscope now generally employed consisting of a series of black and white rings on a circular disc, the observation of the reflex being made through a central perforation.[1] In its subsequent applications many techniques have been devised. These include photo-keratoscopy, a technique first initiated by Placido (1882), Javal (1882) and Nordenson (1883), which was given a high degree of accuracy by Gullstrand (1896) who used a keratoscopic disc of concentric circles, the images of which become elongated along the meridian of least refraction (Fig. 167). The subject first looked centrally and then in such a direction in each principal meridian that the most peripheral surface elements of the central image coincided with the most central element of the peripheral image, the photographs being subsequently measured microscopically. This technique was subsequently used in modified form by Berg (1929), Dekking (1930), Knoll and his colleagues (1957), and Reynolds and Kratt (1959) who employed a photo-electronic technique. Other photo-reflective methods have made use of different objects such as an illuminated source at " infinity " or a series of lamps on the arc of a circle centred on the cornea (Lenoble and Salomon, 1953; Cochet and Amiard, 1966); an elegant version of this technique has been devised by Westheimer (1965). Photo-keratoscopy has also been used by Ludlam and his associates (1965–67) to determine the position of the corneal apex making use of the moiré fringe-pattern. In this an analyser which is a transparency of concentric rings is placed over a photograph of similar rings formed by reflection from the cornea; the shift of the moiré pattern is said to indicate the direction of the corneal apex. The validity of this method has, however, been questioned (Mandell and St. Helen, 1969).

FIG. 167.—THE KERATOSCOPIC DISC OF GULLSTRAND.

Other diverse methods of estimating the corneal shape have been employed, such as *shadowgraphs* of the cornea either from the eye itself or from a mould, which give some information about the corneal contour, but not with any great accuracy (Figs. 168–70) (Mandell, 1961; Stone, 1962; Hamilton, 1963; Ruben, 1964). Further information regarding the shape of the corneal periphery can be obtained from templates applied to moulds of the eye or the fit of standard corneal lenses. A modified technique for photographing the contour of the living cornea was introduced by Collignon-Brach and her associates (1966).

An entirely different photographic technique is that of *stereophotogrammetry* such as employed by Erggelet (1922) and more recently by R. Bonnet (1959), who took stereophotographs of the cornea after it had been powdered with talcum of Venice. These grains form reflective points, allowing the correct reconstitution of a plaster image, and from this image the contours of the corneal periphery can be measured. Such photographic methods record the shape of the entire cornea both in the optical zone and the periphery.

A second difficulty in the study of the corneal periphery is that of finding a means of expressing the results. In general terms, we know that the cornea becomes flatter the further we are from the axial area. Gullstrand's

[1] A similar instrument was employed by Louis Emile Javal (*VI int. Cong. Ophthal.*, Milan, 1880) who used such a disc pasted onto an ophthalmoscopic mirror or on the Javal-Schiøtz ophthalmometer (*Int. med. Cong.*, London, 1881).

FIG. 168.   FIG. 169.

FIGS. 168 and 169.—To show the relationship of a centred curve to a cornea in different meridians; it is obvious that the contours of the cornea are not regular curves. Fig. 168, 90° axis; Fig. 169, 180° axis.

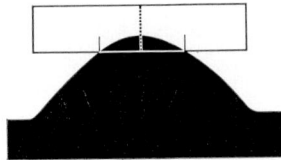

FIG. 170.—Shadowgram with a sag measuring rule to measure the asymmetry of the peripheral corneal curves.

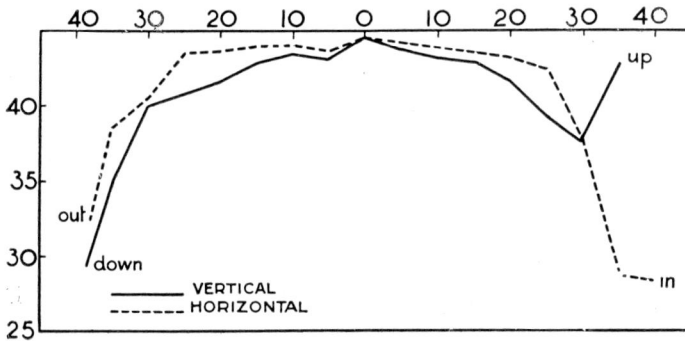

FIG. 171.—THE CURVATURE OF THE CORNEA IN THE VERTICAL AND HORIZONTAL MERIDIANS.

Abscissa, distances from the visual line in degrees; ordinate, corneal refraction in dioptres ($n = 1.3375$) (from the data of Gullstrand).

classical data are summarized in Fig. 171 wherein the corneal power is plotted against eccentricity from the visual line. A more modern series based on his technique of small-mire keratometry is that of Mandell (1965) (Fig. 172).

From these results the magnitude of the individual variations in the form of the cornea can be appreciated, and the high proportion of subjects with no definite spherical zone is particularly noticeable; in fact Mandell believed that the curvature at the corneal apex is more often elliptical than spherical. Moreover, individual corneæ also differ in the direction and degree of eccentricity of the point of maximum curvature in relation to the ophthalmometric pole. It is obvious that the classical view that the centre of the spherical zone is decentred outwards and a little downwards is by no means

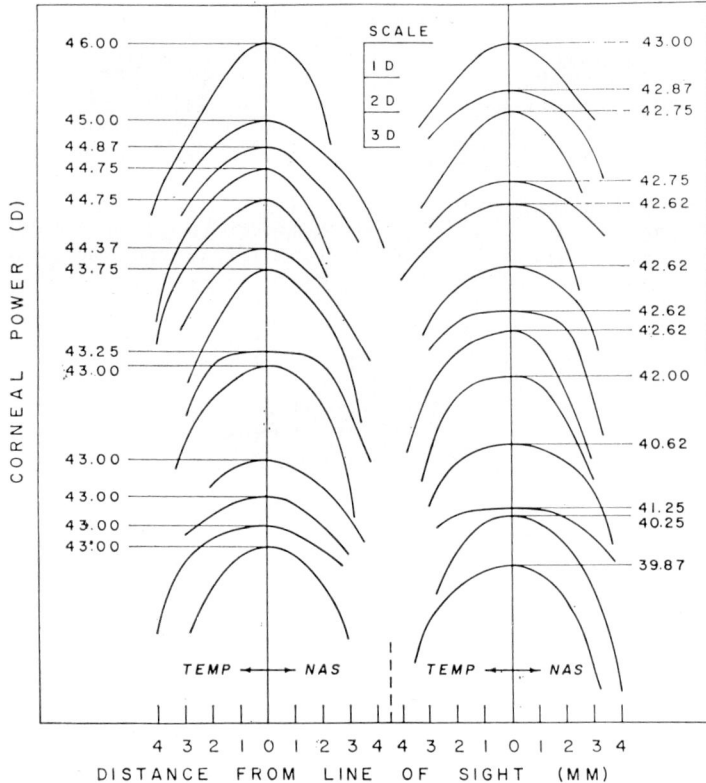

FIG. 172.—CORNEAL CONTOURS AS MEASURED BY SMALL-MIRE KERATOMETRY (R. Mandell).

universally true; and although in this series the nasal cornea tends to be flatter than the temporal, this also is not invariably so.

When we attempt to be more specific and to give a mathematical formulation of the shape of the corneal periphery, we find that none is completely successful.

To define the radius of curvature of the peripheral zone under consideration (r), Berg (1929) suggested the formula:

$$r = \frac{r_o}{1 - \tan^4 \phi}$$

where r_o is the radius of curvature of the apical zone, and ϕ is the angle between the normal at the peripheral point and the normal at the ophthalmometric pole (Fig. 173).

Bonnet and Cochet (1960) evolved a slightly different formula:

$$r/r_o - 1 = a \sin^2 \phi + b \sin^2 \phi,$$

a and b being coefficients related to the deviation of the actual shape of the cornea from the sphere of which the apical zone is a part.

A further generalization was subsequently proposed by Bonnet and Cochet (1960).

The coefficients a and b in the above formula depend on an agreed axis of reference, but in any formula attempting to describe the entire cornea (including the apical zone as well as the periphery) it is obviously begging the question to assume that any particular axis of reference is suitable. Bonnet and Cochet therefore proposed the equation:

$$\log \beta = k\,\alpha + b$$

where β is the normal deviation of any point on the cornea from the sphere of which the optical zone is part, k is a flattening coefficient, b a factor defining the extent of the optical zone, and α an angle related to the movement of the eye so as to bring the point of the cornea under consideration into the field of view of the special topographic ophthalmometer devised by Bonnet. Ten measurements of the radius of curvature were taken, two being the classical readings in the optical zone and two taken in each of the principal demi-meridians of the cornea.

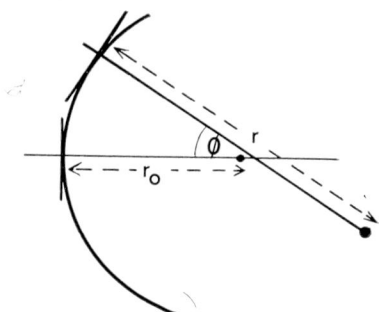

FIG. 173.—THE SHAPE OF THE CORNEAL PERIPHERY (see text) (after F. Berg).

These workers found that corneæ with large spherical zones flatten rapidly at the periphery; those with smaller spherical zones flatten more slowly. The determination of b in the various meridians indicates how the ophthalmometric pole is decentred in relation to the spherical zone. The comparative values of b for these quadrants thus permit the determination of the decentration of the ophthalmometric pole in relation to the regular spherical zone. The following values were found:

For 4% of the subjects, there is no decentration.
For 60% of the subjects, there is temporal decentration.
For 30% of the subjects, there is nasal decentration.
For 47% of the subjects, there is inferior decentration.
For 43% of the subjects, there is superior decentration.
For 10% of the subjects, the decentration is undetermined because of difficulties in measurement.
65% of subjects obey the logarithmic law of Bonnet and Cochet.

The technique used by these authors also indicates the form of the cornea in cases wherein the law does not apply. These are of three main types. The " umbrella " shape (20% of subjects) in which beyond the spherical zone there is a flattened zone followed by a further spherical zone and finally the logarithmic peripheral flattening; the " ring-cushion " shape (11% of subjects) in which outside the spherical zone there are two zones, first a rapid flattening and then more peripherally a more gentle flattening; finally, there is the " cowl " shape (4% of subjects) in which a non-axial region has a greater curvature than that of the axial spherical zone and beyond this non-axial region is a zone wherein the normal peripheral flattening occurs.

It has been suggested by Bier (1956) that there might be a negative zone in the corneal periphery, that is to say, it may be actually concave in one region, a deduction, however, denied by others (Bonnet and Cochet, 1960; Knoll, 1961; Mandell, 1965).

To add to the complexities of the subject of the shape of the cornea, it apparently may vary with time. Either the optical zone or the periphery may alter during the course of the day, relative flattening of the cornea being the rule in the early morning (Reynolds and Kratt, 1959); a diurnal variation in corneal astigmatism has also been reported (Le Grand, 1961; Matsuo, 1964). The state of the pupil, the temperature of the environment, the menstrual cycle and the activity of the extrinsic ocular muscles, especially during convergence, are all said to influence the shape of the cornea. Moreover, during each pulse-beat its radius of curvature is slightly increased so that with the volumetric change in the eye the cornea becomes flatter (Suzuki, 1962). Lastly, the wearing of contact lenses may cause marked irregular alterations of the shape of the cornea.

Of these factors the most important is muscular action, particularly the effect of the pull of the medial rectus on convergence. With the ophthalmometer, Fairmaid (1959) showed that during convergence and accommodation the refractive power of the cornea decreases up to 1·5 D in the horizontal and 0·5 D in the vertical meridian, and Löpping and Weale (1965), with a photo-keratometer, proved that the increase in the horizontal radius of curvature was due to convergence and not accommodation by finding that no alteration occurred if the near object were placed directly in front of one eye so that it remained in its primary position while the other converged strongly, but did when the object was in the sagittal plane so that both eyes converged.[1] The definite diurnal variation in curvature in the same sense found by Le Grand (1961) might also be due to the increase of the activity of the medial rectus during the day compared with the night. It has also been reported that significant alterations in corneal curvature occur as a result of the action of the lids, digital pressure and rubbing the eye (Mandell and St. Helen, 1968). Finally, the usual alteration in astigmatism with age whereby the meridian of maximum curvature tends to change from the vertical to the horizontal, found by such observers as Steiger (1894), Fischer (1948), Marin-Amat (1956) and Hirsch (1959), may be partly due to a loss of tonicity of the orbicularis muscle with age as well as to the long-continued effect of the medial rectus over many years.

In conclusion we may say that, while realizing how complex the true shape of the cornea appears to be, the important part of the corneal surface is the optical area opposite the pupil, and this appears to have a spherical or toric curvature in the majority of subjects. The shape of the peripheral part of the cornea, in so far as it has any influence on the optics of the eye, may

---

[1] This finding, incidentally, seems to question the validity of Hering's law whereby the innervation of the ocular motor muscles of both eyes is said to be equal, but the medial rectus, although apparently quiescent, shows some activity. See Vol. VI.

play a part in reducing spherical aberration.[1] The importance of the peripheral cornea in fitting corneal lenses is obvious, but it is premature to consider our present knowledge of this problem as anything more than empirical.

THE SHAPE AND REFRACTIVE INDEX OF THE LENS

As with the cornea, the surfaces of the lens are not truly spherical but show a definite flattening towards the periphery. This problem is not easy to investigate in the living eye and is even less easy to express in simple mathematical terms. An attempt, however, was made by Besio (1901) with the ophthalmometer and somewhat similar results were obtained by Dalén (1906) in the dead lens. The former author found that the anterior surface had a radius of curvature of 10·2 mm. at the pole, which increased to 14 mm. at a distance of 2 mm. from the axis and to 18 at 3 mm. The precise form of the surfaces of the lens has, of course, been extensively considered in relation to the changes they undergo on accommodation, in which context we shall examine this problem in greater detail. In the meantime it should be noted that there is considerable experimental evidence from the work of Fisher (1969) to the effect that the form of the surfaces of the lens is ellipsoidal.

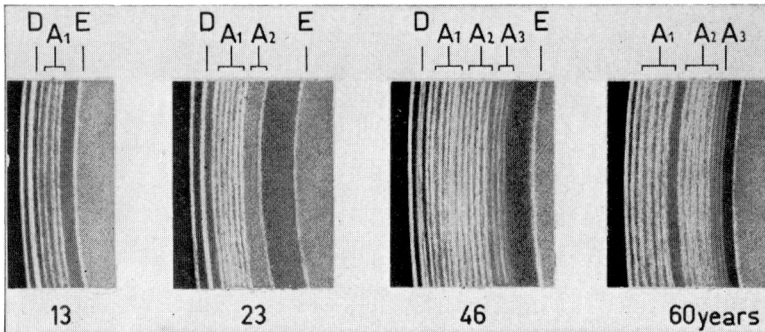

FIG. 174.—THE ELEMENTARY ZONES OF THE NUCLEUS OF THE LENS.

The elementary zones in the adult nucleus in people of the ages given below the figures. A_1, formed in childhood; A_2, added after puberty; A_3, added after the 40th year of life; D, zone of disjunction; E, infantile nucleus (H. Goldmann).

There is also possibly some true lenticular astigmatism but this may be due to a combination of factors; not only may the curvature of each surface differ in various meridians but the whole lens may be tilted in relation to the optic axis of the eye. According to Tscherning (1898) its deviation is made up of two components: a rotation of 3 to 7° round a vertical axis so that the temporal border lies behind the nasal, and 0 to 3° round the horizontal axis so that its upper border is in front of the lower.

[1] p. 82.

Moreover, internal variations in the refractive index may contribute further to lenticular astigmatism. These have already been noted in our attempt to simplify ocular dioptrics, but the " equivalent core-lens " is an artificial although useful concept. There are in fact many zones of optical discontinuity within the lens and these vary both in refractive index and in radius of curvature (Fig. 174). About these, however, very little accurate information is available. It has been established that the refractive index of the cortex of the lens varies with its distance from the axis, being about 1·375 near the equator and from 1·385 to 1·388 close to the pole ; the higher figures apply to the area near the anterior pole. At the centre of the fœtal nucleus the index is higher still, between 1·40 and 1·41. All that is known about the curvatures of these zones of discontinuity is that they increase the further we proceed from the pole into the substance of the lens. Their number increases with age. It should be realized that because of the shutter-like activity of the pupillary aperture the curvature and refraction of the peripheral part of the lens are in fact of minor importance in visual optics, although they are of importance in the study of the anatomy of the eye, both normal and pathological.

Defects in the Optical Synthesis

THE COAXIAL POSITION OF THE OPTICAL ELEMENTS

THE CONCEPT OF THE OPTIC AXIS

We have so far taken it for granted that the refractive elements of the eye are all coaxial and our study in terms of geometrical optics assumes that the components of such a refractive system are symmetrical about the principal axis. Strictly speaking, none of the refracting surfaces of the eye obeys this condition (Ivanoff, 1950 ; Biot, 1960). It is, indeed, difficult to be sure of the optic axis of any single element, and when the relationship of these various ill-defined axes one to another is examined, it is hardly surprising that the definition of an optic axis of the eye as a whole is impossible ; this is therefore a theoretical concept. Only if all the refractive surfaces of the eye were optically symmetrical about axes through their optical centres and if these surfaces were related to one another so that each of these axes passed through the same common axis, would such an optic axis exist. That it does not is best illustrated by the fact that the Purkinje images of an object at which the eye looks directly can never be accurately superimposed on one another as they would be if there were a true optic axis (Figs. 175–6).

Some of the deviations of the eye for this ideal state have already been mentioned such as the lack of a true optical centre of the cornea and the tilting of the lens, but it is perhaps more surprising that the best optic axis that can be conceived, assuming that the refractive elements are coaxial, does not usually strike the fovea. It follows that the theoretically desirable focal point of the dioptric system of the eye is not on the optic axis. Nevertheless, it must be said that the concept is not altogether unreasonable because the departures of the real from the theoretical eye are small. Moreover, it seems that these departures are probably physiologically valuable; the astigmatism produced by tilt of the lens, for example, may tend to cancel out that of the cornea.

Bearing in mind these reservations we can, therefore, accept the concept of an optic axis; it is the theoretical axis upon which lie the optical centres

FIGS. 175 and 176.—THE ANGLE ALPHA.

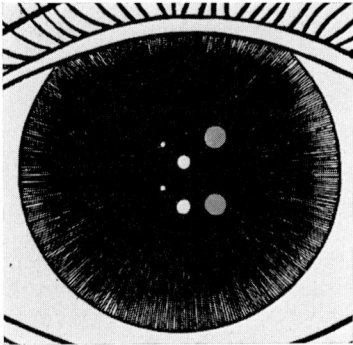 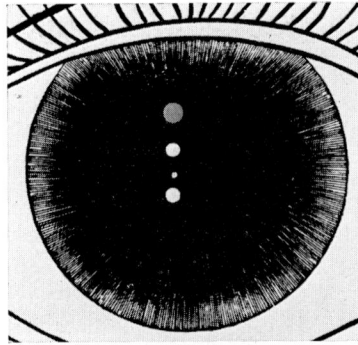

FIG. 175.   FIG. 176.

FIG. 175.—The position of the Purkinje images when a subject looks directly into the telescope of Tscherning's phakometer. In the middle the image of the cornea; on the right those of the anterior surface of the lens; on the left those of the posterior surface of the lens.

FIG. 176.—The Purkinje images aligned when the subject looks at an angle corresponding to the angle alpha towards the nasal side. The optic axis of the eye now coincides with the axis of the telescope (M. Tscherning).

of the refractive surfaces of the eye and is the common optic axis of all of them. By this definition the optic axis passes through the nodal point of the eye (ANB, Fig. 177).

THE VISUAL AXIS—THE ANGLE ALPHA

Since the eye is not a truly centred system it is necessary to take into account other axes of importance in vision. When an object is fixated, the eye is moved in such a way that the image falls upon the fovea, the fixation point and the fovea being thus conjugate foci. The VISUAL AXIS is most simply defined as *the line joining the fixation point and the fovea* and, like the optic axis, it must pass through the nodal point of the eye (FNM, Fig. 177).

We have already noted that the optic axis rarely passes through the fovea; it therefore follows that

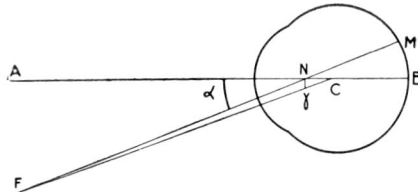

FIG. 177.—THE ANGLES ALPHA AND GAMMA.
(Their size is much exaggerated.)

between the optic and the visual axes there is in most instances a small angle where the two cross at the nodal point: this is called the *angle alpha* (ANF, Fig. 177). In the commonest optical situation the optic axis strikes the retina about 1 mm. above and to the nasal side of the fovea; correspondingly the visual axis passes through the cornea above and nasal to its centre. In this situation the angle alpha amounts to nearly 5° and is said to be *positive*.[1] Should the visual axis cut the cornea temporal to its centre, the angle alpha is said to be *negative*, a circumstance rarely found save in highly myopic eyes.

The estimation of the angle alpha is most easily made by the ophthalmophakometer of Tscherning (Fig. 142). The subject first looks down the axis of the telescope and then, while the telescope remains still, the eye is moved so that the various Purkinje images of the light sources directly above and below it appear aligned. Strictly speaking, this is not possible, but the closest approximation will give the position of the optic axis and the degree of rotation of the eye will indicate the size of the angle alpha.

There has been considerable confusion over terminology here. Considering that the corneal curvature was an ellipsoid, von Helmholtz (1856) defined the angle α as that between the visual line and the major axis of the corneal ellipse, a view adopted by Snellen and Landolt (1874). Since, however, as we have seen, the cornea has no true axis of symmetry, such a definition is strictly without meaning. Donders (1864) assumed that the major axis of the cornea coincided with the optic axis so that his angle corresponds to the above definition. Tscherning (1898) maintained its use as denoting the angle between the visual and optic axes.

It follows that, however defined, the angle alpha must be a fictitious entity. We know that there can be no true nodal point or points of the eye because its optical system is not truly Gaussian. The concept of the visual axis is feasible if defined as above, but to insist that it passes through a non-existent point and to define an angle it makes at this point is clearly of limited value.

THE FIXATION AXIS—THE ANGLE GAMMA

We may try to rationalize this complex situation by invoking the FIXATION AXIS as defined by von Helmholtz (1856) (see Fig. 177). This is *the line joining the fixation point to the centre of rotation of the eye;* the angle formed between this axis and the optic axis at the centre of rotation is known as the *angle gamma*. As can be appreciated from the figure, the angle gamma is always less than the angle alpha but the two are approximately the same for a distant object; in this situation the visual and fixation axes are almost parallel.

We have seen that the nodal point is a theoretical concept, but the centre of rotation of the eye, while not arising in pure theory, is in practical terms very difficult to locate. Methods of measurement which involve ocular

---

[1] If MB in Fig. 177 is 1·25 mm. and if we accept NM = 15 mm., as in Donders's reduced eye, sin a = 1·25/15 = 0·083, whence a = 5.

movements such as the ophthalmophakometric technique just described must, however, assume that there is a reasonably well-defined centre of rotation. Nevertheless, many authorities hold that the movements of the eye occur in a manner which suggests that there is no such single well-defined point. It follows that from the practical point of view the decentration of the eye can best be assessed if we avoid reference to axes through points which are either purely theoretical or difficult to locate with certainty.

AXES THROUGH THE CENTRE OF THE ENTRANCE PUPIL—THE ANGLE KAPPA AND THE ANGLE OF INCIDENCE

The centre of the visible pupil is an easily identified landmark and this point may be taken as the reference for two axes which are very similar to the optic and visual axes. The first is the PUPILLARY AXIS or CENTRAL PUPILLARY LINE which is *perpendicular to the corneal surface and passes through the mid-point of the entrance pupil*—the image of the real pupil seen through the dioptric system in front of the iris.[1] This axis may be taken as the counterpart of the optic axis. The visual axis may best be represented by the PRINCIPAL LINE

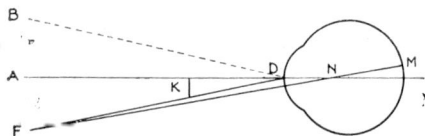

FIG. 178.—THE ANGLE KAPPA.

OF VISION (FD, Fig. 178) which passes *from the centre of the entrance pupil to the point of fixation;* for a distant object the visual axis and the principal line of vision are parallel.

The *angle kappa* is defined as the angle between the central pupillary line and the principal line of vision (ADF, Fig. 178) (Snellen and Landolt, 1874). It is somewhat smaller than the angle alpha when, as is usually the case, there is a slight nasal decentration of the pupil. It is interesting that the central pupillary line cuts the cornea roughly at the centre of the optical zone when the diameter of the pupil is of the order of 4 mm. In some subjects the angle kappa will vary with the size of the pupil if there is a tendency for the eccentricity of the pupil to alter with its change in diameter.

A simple method of estimating the angle kappa is for the subject to fix a perforated white disc over the objective of a telescope; he then moves his fixation point until the disc appears to the observer to be concentric with the pupil. The degree of rotation of the eye will give the value of the angle kappa.

It can be appreciated from Fig. 178 that the principal line of vision does not strike the cornea at right angles. The angle it makes with the normal at this point is known as the ANGLE OF INCIDENCE (ι) which is somewhat less than the angle kappa.

As an example of the confusion which still persists in the terminology of these angles and axes, we may refer to the use of the term *sighting line (line of sight)* by Lancaster (1943) which he defined as the line from the point of fixation to the centre of the apparent pupil. As we have just seen, this is also known as the *principal line of*

----

[1] p. 106.

vision. Lancaster also defined the angle at the centre of the apparent pupil between the pupillary axis and the line of sight as the *angle lambda.* If, however, the line of sight and the principal line of vision are identical, the angle lambda as defined by Lancaster would be the same as the angle kappa as we have just defined it. It should be added that Lancaster used the term angle kappa for the angle between the pupillary axis and the visual line, the latter being the line from the point of fixation to the anterior nodal point and from the posterior nodal point to the fovea (therefore a broken line). It is difficult to agree with this definition since it attempts to bring together a purely theoretical with a clinically verifiable axis. In the present account we are following the definitions originally suggested by Gullstrand (1911) and accepted more recently by Le Grand (1952).

The decentration of the eye, slight though it is, constitutes an important optical feature which we shall consider in the next section and also in relation to the aberrations of its optical system.

Aubert.   *Graefe-Saemisch Hb. d. ges. Augen-heilk.*, 1st ed., Leipzig, **2**, 393 (1876).

Pflügers Arch. ges. Physiol., **35**, 597 (1885).

Bayshore.   *Contacto*, **3**, 188 (1959).

Bennett.   *Brit. J. physiol. Opt.*, **21**, 234 (1964).

Berg. *Acta ophthal.* (Kbh.), **7**, 225, 386 (1929).

Besio.   *J. Physiol. path. gén.*, **3**, 547, 761, 783 (1901).

Bier. *Amer. J. Optom.*, **33**, 291 (1956).

Biot.   *Ann. Soc. Sci. Brux.*, **75**, 175 (1960).

Blix.   *Upsala Läk. Förh.*, **15**, 349 (1880).

Bonnet, R.   *Rev. opt.* (Paris), **38**, 447 (1959). *La topographie cornéene et l'adaptation des lentilles de cornée*, Paris (1964).

Bonnet, R. and Cochet.   *Bull. Soc. franç. Ophtal.*, **73**, 688 (1960).

Brewster.   *Edinb. J. Sci.*, **7**, 326 (1827).

Cochet and Amiard.   *Arch. Ophtal.*, **26**, 387 (1966).

Collignon-Brach, Papritz and Prijot.   *Bull. Soc. belge Ophtal.*, No. 144, 971 (1966).

Dalén.   *Mitt. Augenklin. Carol. med.-chir. Inst.*, Stockholm, **8**, 45 (1906).

Dekking.   *v. Graefes Arch. Ophthal.*, **124**, 708 (1930).

Donders. *On the Anomalies of Accommodation and Refraction of the Eye*, London (1864).

Drysdale.   *Trans. opt. Soc. Lond.*, **2**, 1 (1900).

Erggelet.   *Bes. dtsch. ophthal. Ges.*, **43**, 106, 115 (1922).

Eriksen. *Hornhindemaalingen*, Aarhus (1893).

Fairmaid.   *Brit. J. physiol. Opt.*, **16**, 2 (1959).

Fincham.   *Trans. opt. Soc. Lond.*, **26**, 239 (1925).

Fischer. Sorsby's *Modern Trends in Ophthal.*, London, **2**, 54 (1948).

Fisher.   *J. Physiol.*, **201**, 1, 21 (1969).

Girard.   *Corneal Contact Lenses*, St. Louis (1964).

Goode.   *Trans. Camb. phil. Soc.*, **8**, 493 (1847). *Edinb. mthly. J. med. Sci.*, **8**, 711 (1848).

Grosvenor.   *Amer. J. Optom.*, **38**, 237 (1961).

Gullstrand.   *Kongl. Svenska Veterskaps.-Akad. Hdl.*, **28**, 7 (1896).

Einführung in d. Methoden d. Dioptrik d. Auges d. Menschen, Leipzig (1911).

Hamilton.   *Contacto*, **7** (3), 9 (1963).

von Helmholtz.   *Hb. d. physiologischen Optik*, Leipzig (1856).

Hirsch.   *Amer. J. Optom.*, **36**, 395 (1959).

Ivanoff.   *C.R. Acad. Sci.* (Paris), **231**, 526 (1950).

Javal.   *Zbl. prakt. Augenheilk.*, **6**, 122 (1882).

Jenkins.   *Brit. J. physiol. Opt.*, **20**, 59, 161 (1963).

Knoll.   *Amer. J. Optom.*, **38**, 389 (1961).

Knoll, Stimson and Weeks.   *J. opt. Soc. Amer.*, **47**, 221 (1957).

Lancaster.   *Amer. J. Ophthal.*, **26**, 122 (1943).

Le Grand.   *Optique physiologique*, Paris (1952).

Trans. int. ophthal. Opt. Cong., London, 67 (1961).

Lenoble and Salomon.   *Ann. Opt. oculaire*, **2**, 19 (1953).

Löpping and Weale.   *Vision Res.*, **5**, 207 (1965).

Ludlam and Wittenberg.   *Brit. J. physiol. Opt.*, **23**, 178, 249 (1966).

Ludlam, Wittenberg and Rosenthal.   *Amer. J. Optom.*, **42**, 394 (1965).

Ludlam, Wittenberg, Rosenthal and Harris. *Amer. J. Optom.*, **44**, 276 (1967).

Mandell.   *J. Amer. optom. Ass.*, **32**, 627; **33**, 137 (1961).

Contact Lens Practice, Springfield, Ill. (1965).

Mandell and St. Helen.   *Amer. J. Optom.*, **45**, 797 (1968); **46**, 25 (1969).

Marin-Amat.   *Bull. Soc. belge Ophtal.*, No. 113, 251 (1956).

Matsuo.   *Acta Soc., ophthal. jap.*, **68**, 1841, (1964).

Matthiessen.   *Beitr. Psychol. Physiol. Sinnes.* (Festschr. v. Arthur König), Hamburg, 49 (1891).

Nordenson.   *Ann. Oculist.* (Paris), **89**, 110 (1883).

Placido. *Periodico ophthal. prat.*, Lisbon, **2** (2), 27; (5–6), 44 (1880).

Zbl. prakt. Augenheilk., **30**, 157 (1882).

Reynolds. *Contacto*, **3**, 229 (1959).

Reynolds and Kratt. *Contacto*, **3**, 53 (1959).

Ruben. *Trans. ophthal. Soc. U.K.*, **84**, 15 (1964); **87**, 661 (1967).

Senff. Wagner's *Handwörterbuch d. Physiologie*, Braunschweig, **3** (1), 271 (1846).

Snellen and Landolt. *Graefe-Saemisch Hb. d. ges. Augenheilk.*, 1st ed., Leipzig, **3** (1), 210 (1874).

Soper, Sampson and Girard. *Arch. Ophthal.*, **67**, 753 (1962).

Steiger. *Arch. Augenheilk.*, **29**, 98 (1894).

Stone. *Brit. J. physiol. Opt.*, **19**, 205 (1962).

Sulzer. *Arch. Ophtal.*, **11**, 419 (1891); **12**, 32 (1892).

Suzuki. *Jap. J. Ophthal.*, **6**, 190 (1962).

Tscherning. *Optique physiologique*, Paris (1898).

Westheimer. *Amer. J. Optom.*, **42**, 315 (1965).

The Paraxiality of the Incident Rays

THE APERTURE OF THE SYSTEM

The theory of Gauss demands that the optical system be limited to a small aperture so that the rays are limited to the axial region: this is not fulfilled in the eye. In optical instruments an aperture of 10° is generally considered the maximum compatible with efficiency; and the pupil of the eye averages approximately 4 mm. in diameter, which corresponds to an

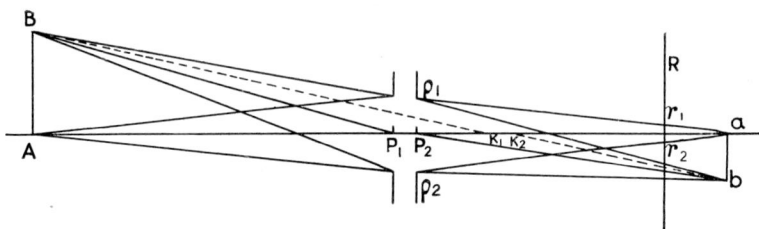

Fig. 179.—The Entrance and Exit Pupils.

AB is the object and *ab* its image. r_1 and r_2, diffusion circles on the retina, R. P_1 and P_2, the pupils of entrance and exit. The centre of the diffusion circle on the retina is determined by the pupillary line joining the centre of the exit pupil, P_2, with the image *ab*, not by the line joining the posterior nodal point with the image K_2b.

aperture of 20° at the cornea. The size of the pupil determines the size of the circles of diffusion on the retina. The incident rays, however, are refracted by the cornea before they reach the pupil and the emergent rays are refracted by the lens before they reach the retina. The base of the cone of incident light is thus the image of the pupil formed by the cornea (the APPARENT PUPIL or the ENTRANCE PUPIL of Abbé), and the base of the cone of emergent light is the image of the pupil formed by the lens when the pupil is regarded from the vitreous (the EXIT PUPIL of Abbé) (P_1, P_2, Fig. 179). It is seen that the centre of a diffusion circle on the retina (R) is determined by the line joining the centre of the exit pupil with the posterior focus (P_2b), that is, the *pupillary line*, and not by the line joining the posterior nodal point with the posterior focus (K_2b) (the *visual line*).

It was pointed out[1] that the apparent (or entrance) pupil is the virtual, erect and magnified image of the true pupil, so that the aperture appears larger and nearer to the cornea than it actually is. The position of the entrance pupil is calculated from the formula $f_1/u + f_2/v = 1$. Taking the data of the simplified eye, $f_1 = 24$, $f_2 = 32$, and with v, the distance of the real pupil, as 3·6 mm., we find that u, the apparent distance, is 3·04 mm.

Similarly, from the formula $i/o = f_2/(f_2 - v)$, taking the size of the real pupil $(o) = 4$ mm., we obtain a value for i, the size of the apparent pupil, of 4·5 mm. The pupil thus appears *enlarged by 0·5 mm. and displaced forwards by the same amount*. The position and size of the exit pupil are given by the same formulæ for, since the pupil is in contact with the anterior surface of the lens, only refraction at the posterior surface need be considered. It is found to be *displaced about 0·1 mm. backwards, and to be enlarged about 0·2 mm.*

The diameter of the circles of diffusion can be approximately calculated if we know the diameter of the entrance pupil, the distance of the object from the eye and the dioptric power of the eye. To make this estimate, however, Gaussian optics must be employed and in doing this it is assumed that the

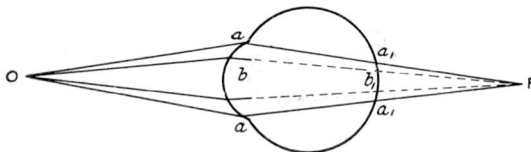

FIG. 180.—DIFFUSION CIRCLES.

When an object, O, is regarded through a large pupil, aa, the converging pencil covers a large area in the macular region, $a_1 a_1$. With a small pupil, b, the area b_1 is smaller.

rays are paraxial; with large pupillary apertures this does not hold good. In the case of smaller pupillary apertures it is fair to assume that the circles of diffusion would be proportionately smaller, and such is indeed the case as witness the clinical use of the stenopæic disc which is, in effect, an artificially small pupil (Fig. 180). Similarly, a hypermetrope prefers to read in brilliant illumination, so that the pupil is contracted down to a minimal size, and a myope gets into the habit of looking at objects through the half-closed lids, gaining thereby the advantages of a stenopæic slit. Such a procedure, however, carries with it disadvantages, for when the pupil contracts the amount of light entering the eye is correspondingly reduced and the object is rendered less bright but more distinct.

Whatever the practical value of a small aperture of the optical system of the eye, theoretical calculations of the size of the circles of diffusion are vitiated by the effects of diffraction. These preclude the use of Gaussian optics which applies to *a coaxial system of small aperture made up of homogeneous media bounded by perfectly spherical surfaces*, and only *if monochromatic light meets the dioptric surfaces almost at right angles*. It is therefore

[1] p. 106.

obvious that the clarity of the retinal image cannot be accurately expressed in terms of geometrical optics. The size of the pupil is a critical factor. If it is small diffraction cannot be ignored; if it is large the condition of paraxiality of the rays no longer holds and aberrations of the refraction occur. These we must now consider.

Aberrations of the Optical System of the Eye

MONOCHROMATIC ABERRATIONS

SPHERICAL ABERRATION

When the normal eye looks at a distant object the marginal rays come to a focus slightly in front of the paraxial. This is easily demonstrated by passing a slit across the pupil: near the edge of the pupil objects appear to an emmetropic observer to move in the same direction as the slit (Fig. 181). The optical system of the eye therefore shows spherical aberration.

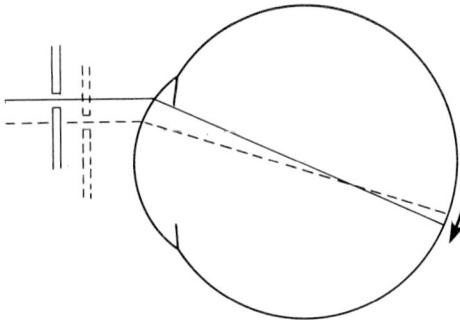

FIG. 181.—SPHERICAL ABERRATION.

When a slit is passed across the pupil near its edge, objects appear to move in the same direction as the slit.

From the historical point of view, this phenomenon was investigated and measured among others by Young (1801) with his optometer, by Tscherning (1898) with his aberroscope, and in greater detail by Gullstrand (1911) by " subjective " and " objective " *stigmatoscopy*. By the former method a small luminous point is regarded and different sections of the caustic curve are thrown upon the retina by changing the focusing of the eye by spectacle lenses. The constitution of the bundle of rays refracted in the eye is thus analysed and a complete exploration of the caustic curve obtained by the subject himself. In objective stigmatoscopy, a method which can be applied clinically (Jackson, 1896), the subject is made emmetropic and a luminous point of light is seen in the pupil (the cusp of the caustic curve) giving off star-shaped rays surrounded by a dark zone, while the borders of the pupil show a luminous red reflex. The observer then approaches the subject until the ring disappears, and the distance traversed gives the amount of aberration ; thus if it disappears at 25 cm. the aberration is $+ 4$ D. If the dark ring is not seen, the subject is made myopic until it does appear, and the degree of aberration is measured by the extent of artificial myopia necessary to make it disappear again. Thus if it disappears with a myopia of -4 D, the aberration is -2 D (2 D being deducted since the observer is at 0·5 metre distance).[1]

[1] This will be explained when the theory of retinoscopy is discussed, p. 391.

More recently, the spherical aberration has been estimated with several different techniques by Ames and Proctor (1921), Pi (1925), Stine (1930), Granström (1943), von Bahr (1945), Ivanoff (1947–52), Arnulf and his colleagues (1948), van den Brink (1962), Jenkins (1963) and Schober and his colleagues (1968).

So far as the cornea is concerned, although the peripheral flattening tends to render the surface aplanatic, there is still a considerable amount of positive spherical aberration in the mid-periphery (Gullstrand, 1911) (Fig. 182). If, however, the pupil is dilated, the flat periphery over-corrects the condition and induces negative aberration. Taking ophthalmometric measurements of the corneal aberration, von Brudzewski (1900) found it usually positive, the average variation lying between $+ 3 \cdot 0$ D and $- 1 \cdot 5$ D; it was negative most frequently on the nasal side.

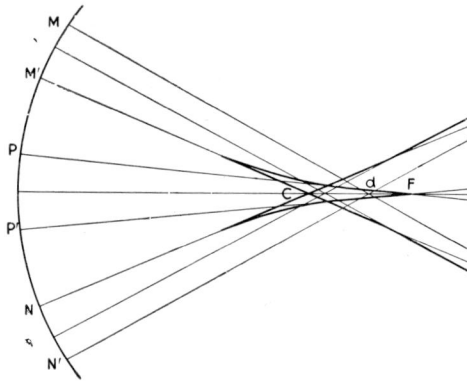

FIG. 182.—THE ABERRATION OF THE CORNEA.
Compare Fig. 115 (A. Gullstrand).

It is possible to predict the theoretical depth of spherical aberration which should be present in eyes with presumed spherical surfaces. Ivanoff (1952), however, found that the actual value is very different from that predicted; towards the centre of the pupil it is slightly greater than the compensated value for an unaccommodated eye, but further out it is considerably less than the estimated degree. In Fig. 183, taken from Ivanoff (1952), the values are compared to those found at various distances from the centre of the pupil. The investigations of many observers indicate that the under-corrected type of spherical aberration, that is, wherein the marginal rays converge more rapidly than the paraxial, exists in the unaccommodated human eye to the extent of 0·5 to 3 D. Its magnitude depends on the size of the pupil but this dependence is less than might be expected if all the media of the eye had truly spherical refracting surfaces.

It is therefore clear that although the eye does not constitute an aplanatic system the effects of spherical aberration are small—much smaller than the effects of either diffraction or chromatic aberration (Krauskopf, 1964).

This is due partly to the fact that the cornea is flatter in the periphery than in the centre, but more largely to the fact that the core of the lens is more highly refractive than the periphery. Both these circumstances cause the axial rays to be refracted more strongly than the peripheral, a tendency which, it will be remembered,[1] counteracts the effects of spherical aberration.

The slight degree of spherical aberration that is present in the human eye is found to vary between individuals; some show over-corrected aberration even in the unaccommodated state. There is also some variation in the value of the spherical aberration in the different meridians of the eye. It also

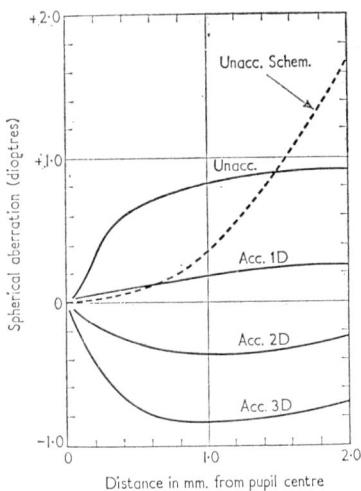

FIG. 183.—SPHERICAL ABERRATION OF THE EYE.

Plotted in dioptres against height of incidence in mm. from the pupillary centre. The unbroken curves, each marked with the stimulus to accommodation, show the mean results for 10 subjects. The dotted line shows the theoretical spherical aberration, computed by ray-tracing methods, of the unaccommodated schematic eye (after A. Ivanoff).

shows a variation with age; while the under-corrected type of spherical aberration is the rule in later life, in young children the over-corrected type is not uncommon (Jenkins, 1963).

As we have mentioned, the high refractive index of the core of the lens is a minimizing influence on spherical aberration. It might be expected, therefore, that accommodation would influence the spherical aberration. That this is so can be easily demonstrated to oneself by the slit-method referred to above. Figure 183 illustrates this effect quantitatively. It is seen that the type of spherical aberration changes to become over-corrected, that is, wherein the marginal rays are focused behind the paraxial, and that the aberration is least when 1 to 2 D of accommodation is exerted.

[1] p. 86.

OTHER MONOCHROMATIC ABERRATIONS

We have already recognized that some degree of obliquity of the rays striking the eye is present even in those which reach the fovea, a circumstance which depends on the lack of coincidence of the optic with the visual axis. Nevertheless, the angle between them is usually very small and as far as central vision is concerned the effects of OBLIQUE ASTIGMATISM, LATERAL SPHERICAL ABERRATION and COMA—the main aberrations relevant to points off the axis—are negligibly small.

The formation of images in the retinal periphery must, of course, involve a considerable obliquity of incidence of the relevant rays, but two factors lessen the significance of the resulting aberrations. In the first place, the

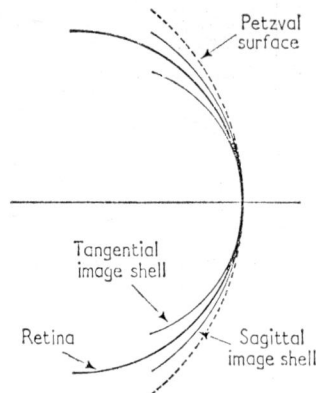

FIG. 184.—THE RELATION OF THE CURVATURE OF THE RETINA TO THE
IMAGE-SHELLS AND THE PETZVAL SURFACE.

Tangential and sagittal image-shells, conjugate to an object plane at infinity, for the unaccommodated schematic eye. The diagram also shows the position of the retina and of the Petzval surface (A. Bennett and J. Francis).

retina itself is curved and it can be shown in the case of oblique astigmatism that the tangential and sagittal image-shells both approximate to the true shape of the retina (Fig. 184). Secondly, the degree of clarity required for an image formed in the retinal periphery is less than in the foveal region because of the great difference in the neuro-retinal organization of the two areas ; the fovea is " geared " to a high degree of perceptive ability, while the retinal periphery is not.

CURVATURE OF THE FIELD and DISTORTION may also be present to a slight degree. The former may be accounted for by the retinal curvature. Distortion should theoretically be found because of the presence of a stop, the pupil, but it is almost certainly negligible.

Some other defects of the eye should be mentioned which are found in all optical instruments ; these are scattered light, halation and flare which together are probably best known compositely as " parasitic light ".

Fig. 185.—Nevil Maskelyne
[1732–1811].
(Courtesy of the Royal Society.)

SCATTERED LIGHT. There is a considerable amount of light reflected from the retina[1] —it is by this the fundus is seen—but very little of it is allowed to confuse the retinal image. The shape of the fundus causes the light reflected from the back of the retina to travel out of the pupil or to strike the insensitive anterior parts of the retina. Light which falls upon the peripheral retina could be reflected to the visually important posterior region, but this amount is small since the eye is protected from oblique illumination by the eyebrows and nose. Moreover, such light as is scattered is largely absorbed by the retinal pigment.

HALATION would appear to be of negligible amount. The term applies to the reflection of light back to the sensitive surface from other surfaces immediately close to it; but the reflecting layer of the retina is so near to the rods and cones that this disturbance can be of little moment.

FLARE is also negligible in quantity. This refers to light reflected at the boundary surfaces between media in its course through the optical system; but the refractive indices of the ocular media are so closely related, the lens being immersed in a medium of approximately the same index as itself, that the reflected light is minimal.

CHROMATIC ABERRATION

The eye is not achromatic as was at one time believed. The first estimate of the magnitude of the chromatic aberration of the eye was made by the Astronomer Royal, the Reverend Nevil Maskelyne (1789) (Fig. 185)

[1] Vol. VII p. 286.

whose primary aims were the furtherance of the science of navigation and the determination of the density of the earth; in the eye he found that the difference in focal length for the violet and red rays was 0·025 in. (0·535 mm.)—a computation which agrees well with modern averages. The extent of this aberration was also demonstrated by Wollaston (1801) who, on looking at a luminous point through a prism, noted that the red end of the spectrum was in accurate focus while the blue end was diffuse when the source of light was at a great distance but, when it was brought nearer to the eye, the blue end came into focus and the conditions were reversed. The aberration is most readily demonstrated by observing a light through cobalt glass, which allows only the blue and red of the spectrum to pass. Beyond the far point of distinct vision a red centre surrounded with a blue halo is seen; within the near point of distinct vision it appears as a blue spot surrounded by red (Fig. 186).

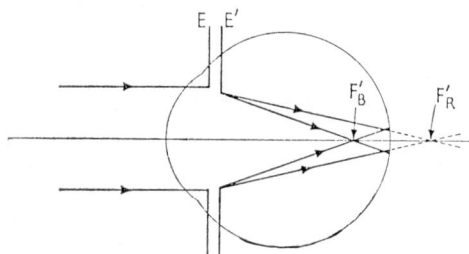

FIG. 186.—CHROMATIC ABERRATION OF THE EYE.

An incident parallel pencil of white light is dispersed on refraction, the " blue " rays focusing at F'_B and the " red " rays at F'_R. A blur-patch of overlapping diffusion circles is formed on the retina. E is the entrance pupil, E' the exit pupil (A. Bennett and J. Francis).

Although this aberration is not considerable it must be remembered that the Gaussian theory applies only to monochromatic light; indeed, for the schematic eye there should perhaps be a set of cardinal points to correspond to each wavelength of visible light but this is unnecessarily detailed. Nevertheless, the various spectral components form different foci in the normal eye, the violet rays focusing in front of the retina, the red behind. Thomas Young (1801) estimated the extent of this aberration as 1·3 D. Fraunhofer (1814) obtained more accurate measurements by determining the distance at which a spider's thread could be distinctly seen in the blue and red ends of the spectrum respectively (1·5 to 3·0 D); von Helmholtz (1856) found 1·8 D. More recent investigations have been made by several workers[1]; Ivanoff (1946–52) found a difference of 0·9 D between the C line (red-orange) of the spectrum and the F line (blue).

[1] Nutting (1914), Ames and Proctor (1921), Polack (1923), Sheard (1926), Pinegin (1941), Biot (1946), Ivanoff (1946), Wald and Griffin (1947), Bedford and Wyszecki (1957).

We have noted that one effect of chromatic aberration is to produce a *chromatic difference of magnification* for points which are off the axis (Einthoven, 1885) (Figs. 187–8). The decentration of the optical system of the eye leads to the production of blur circles for different colours which are not exactly concentric and hence to the phenomena of colour stereoscopy. In the ordinary course of events, however, if the eye is focused for yellow light, the error introduced is small and, such as it is, since the image of blue owing to its greater refrangibility is smaller than that for red, it tends to correct the error of chromatic difference of focus. Although the eye

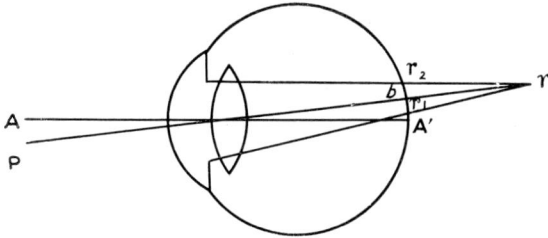

Fig. 187.

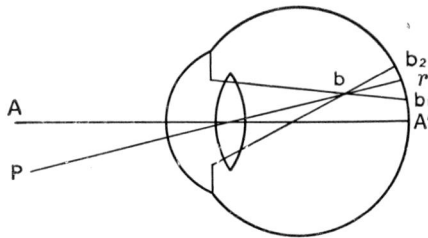

Fig. 188.

Figs. 187 and 188.—Chromatic Difference in Magnification.

usually focuses for yellow light (Hartridge, 1918), Ivanoff (1952) found that the wavelength focused depended on the accommodative state and shifted from the longer to the shorter waves as accommodation became active.

In general, therefore, the defect due to the chromatic aberration of the eye is not of great consequence. The composite focus made up of the foci of several colours sounds much worse than it actually is. With a 2 mm. diameter pupil, 70% of the incident light falls on an area of 0·005 mm. diameter; chromatic aberration therefore falls within the same order of magnitude as diffraction and its effects are too slight to be perceived in the ordinary course of events. It is to be noted that the effects of chromatic aberration increase as the pupil widens, but as this is accompanied by a decrease in diffraction, the two changes acting together leave the actual definition of the image practically unchanged with alterations of the pupil.

DIFFRACTION AND RESOLVING POWER

It is generally accepted that the foveal cones are the end-organs of vision in the central area of the retina. It was said that if two luminous points were to be distinguished separately two cones must be stimulated while an intermediate one remains unstimulated, so that the smallest resolvable image must have a diameter just greater than that of a macular cone. Anatomical measurements show that this distance on the retina is about 0·002 mm. Consequently, from Fig. 165 the *minimal visual angle* optically possible is determined by

$$\tan aNb = \frac{ab}{bN} = \frac{0\cdot002}{17\cdot054} = \tan 24\cdot14 \sec.$$

The inadequacy of such a simple geometrical concept becomes obvious, however, when we recall that in any optical system with an aperture of definite size such as the pupil, a point-image is never formed from a point-object. We have seen[1] that the effect of diffraction at such a circular aperture is to produce, instead of a point-image, a series of alternate dark and light circular bands surrounding a central bright disc, the Airy disc (1835) (Fig. 108). The size of this disc is usually expressed as the angular radius of the first dark ring. Lord Rayleigh suggested that in order to distinguish visually between two points, a separation of their diffraction patterns of this order was necessary ; this limit to the differentiation of two images, that is, the limit of practical utility of the eye, is known as its RESOLVING POWER. It follows that the resolution of very small angular subtenses by the dioptric system of the eye is impossible, no matter how good the visual acuity may be (see Westheimer, 1960 ; Röhler, 1962).

The resolving power of the eye as determined by diffraction can be calculated from the formula for the angular size of the Airy disc (1835) (Fig. 108). This is determined by the formula $\phi = 1\cdot22\lambda/d$, where λ is the wavelength and d the diameter of the pupil (to be strictly accurate, the entrance pupil). For yellow light and a pupillary diameter of 6·0 mm., the limit of capacity would be a visual angle of 0·3 minute of angle ; for a pupil of 3 mm. it would be 0·82 minute, and only for a pupil of 2·0 mm. is the angle for yellow light 1·22 minutes, while for blue-green light it is 1·05 minutes.

The resolving power of an optical system[2] is the classical method of estimating one aspect of its efficiency, but a more modern and sophisticated approach to the same problem is given by the OPTICAL TRANSFER FUNCTION. This concept arises from analogies between optical and electrical systems.

A signal entering an electrical system can be considered as a series of sinusoidal wave-forms by means of Fourier analysis. The emerging response can be treated in the same way, but the sinusoidal elements will differ among themselves in the degree to which they have been attenuated during transmission. The curve of attenuation against frequency is called the " frequency response function ".

[1] p. 79.   [2] p. 80.

The optical analogue of such electrical systems derives from consideration of the light in the object-plane as a series of spatial frequencies, each the representation of an imaginary grating. The curve of amplitude of these frequencies by an optical system against the spatial frequency is the optical transfer function. Above a certain critical frequency the response is nil and such light is diffracted out of the system; this frequency is dependent upon the aperture. Westheimer (1960) applied these concepts to the efficiency of the eye as an optical instrument and found satisfactory agreement with theory. Interference fringes developed on the retina and allowed the determination of a retinal modulation sensitivity curve. This agreed with theoretical calculations of the optical transfer function based on a system similar to that of the eye but without aberration and with a 2 mm. entrance pupil. For 100% modulation, the absolute sensitivity corresponded to a little over a half-a-minute of arc. According to Röhler (1962), light scattered inside the eye may account for the transfer function found by photographing the retinal image.

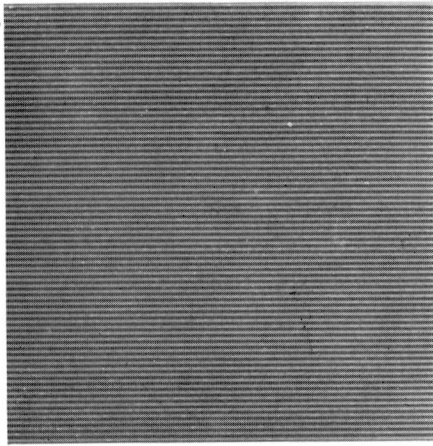

FIG. 189.—A SINUSOIDAL GRATING.

Recent experimental investigation of the resolving power of the human eye, based on the optical transfer function, consists in presenting as test-object a sinusoidal grating developed on the screen of a cathode-ray oscilloscope (Campbell and Green, 1965). The contrast at which the grating can just be resolved is determined by the subject (Fig. 189) and from the results of such experiments it is possible to estimate the contrast-sensitivity of the whole apparatus of vision, in other words, the dioptric mechanism—retina—brain.

It is also possible to evaluate the contribution of the dioptric apparatus to this combination by using the interference fringes produced on the retina since these are to a large extent unaffected by the focusing mechanism of the eye. The laser offers an elegant method of producing such fringes and the contrast-sensitivity of the retina itself can be measured independently of the dioptric apparatus. The relationship between this contrast-sensitivity and that of the visual apparatus as a whole gives the transfer function of the dioptric apparatus.

This work is now being extended to several problems in physiological optics. A loss of visual acuity occurs if an artificial pupil is used to decentre the entrant rays (Campbell, 1958). It was postulated that such an effect might be due to the optical properties of the foveal cones imparted by their long thin shape. Campbell and

Gregory (1960), using Fraunhofer diffraction images, showed that much of this effect was due to optical aberrations and little if any to a directional acuity of the photoreceptors. More recently, Green (1967), using the techniques described above, has shown clearly that practically all the effect is due to aberrations; the optical transfer function of the off-axis aberration resembled that which would be produced by a small amount of coma in the system. Chromatic aberration can be similarly investigated (Campbell and Gubisch, 1967).

DEPTH OF FOCUS

The DEPTH OF FOCUS of an optical instrument is *the greatest distance through which an object-point can be moved while a clear image is produced.* In the case of the eye, as the object is moved its image may be theoretically blurred but the depth of focus is taken to connote a degree of clarity not recognizably different to the observer. In any optical instrument the amount of elasticity permissible depends principally on two factors, the distance of the object—for it is obvious that the greater the distance the greater the depth of focus—and the aperture of the system—the smaller the aperture the greater the depth of focus. Other less important considerations are the visual acuity—the better this is, the greater the depth of focus (Ogle and Schwartz, 1959)—and an increase in background illumination which also has a beneficial effect (Campbell, 1959). As we have seen, the optical aberrations of the eye also have a varying influence.

TABLE XI

THE DEPTH OF FOCUS

Pupillary diameter	Depth at Infinity	Depth at 1 metre
1 mm.	From infinity to 1·25 m.	5.0 m. to 56 cm.
2 mm.	From infinity to 2·33 m.	1·8 m. to 70 cm.
3 mm.	From infinity to 2·94 m.	1·5 m. to 75 cm.
4 mm.	From infinity to 3·57 m.	1·4 m. to 78 cm.

Of these variables, the distance of the object and the diameter of the pupil are the most potent factors (Fig. 190). Campbell's (1957) figures are given in Table XI. From this it is seen that if the eyes are focused for an object at a distance of 1 metre, when the diameters of the pupils are 1 mm., objects 5 metres and 56 cm. away are seen clearly, but when the pupils are of 4 mm. diameter the depth of focus is restricted to distances of 1·4 metres and 78 cm.

A summary of the influence of the pupil in physiological optics may not be out of place here. It controls the resolving power of the eye and the amount of light reaching the retina. A small pupil is advantageous in that it lessens the influence of spherical and chromatic aberration and increases the depth of focus; it has the disadvantage of increasing the influence of diffraction and reducing the brightness of the retinal image. The visual acuity always improves as the retinal luminance is increased. Even with a pupillary diameter of 5 mm., however, chromatic aberration is negligible (Bedford and

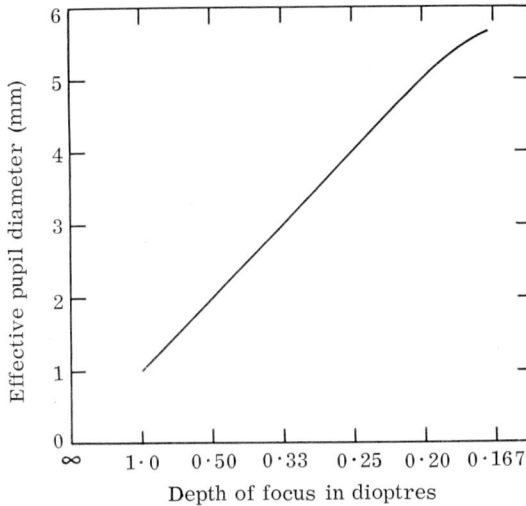

FIG. 190.—THE DEPTH OF FOCUS OF THE EYE AS A FUNCTION OF THE
EFFECTIVE PUPILLARY DIAMETER (after F. W. Campbell).

Wyszecki, 1957) and spherical aberration has only a limited effect (Krauskopf, 1964). If visual acuity is measured as a function of the pupillary diameter, however, with a constant retinal illumination and making experimental allowance for the Stiles-Crawford effect,[1] it has been found that as a small pupil is enlarged the acuity increases rapidly at first and then more slowly until a maximum is reached when its diameter is between 3 and 4 mm., whereafter a lowering of acuity occurs (Leibowitz, 1952). It is interesting that Campbell and Gregory (1960) have shown that the human pupillary light reflex so adjusts the aperture of the eye as to allow the retina to utilize the maximum visual acuity over a large range of luminances.

Airy. *Trans. Camb. phil. Soc.*, **5**, 283 (1835).

Ames and Proctor. *J. opt. Soc. Amer.*, **5**, 22 (1921).

Arnulf, Flamant and Françon. *Rev. opt.* (Paris), **27**, 741 (1948).

von Bahr. *Acta ophthal.* (Kbh.), **23**, 1 (1945).

Bedford and Wyszecki. *J. opt. Soc. Amer.*, **47**, 564 (1957).

Biot. *Ann. Soc. Sci. Brux.*, **60**, 138 (1946).

van den Brink. *Vision Res.*, **2**, 233 (1962).

von Brudzewski. *Arch. Augenheilk.*, **40**, 296 (1900).

Campbell. *Optica Acta*, **4**, 157 (1957).
J. Physiol., **144**, 25P (1958).
Brit. J. physiol. Opt., **16**, 188 (1959).

Campbell and Green. *J. Physiol.*, **181**, 576 (1965).

Campbell and Gregory. *Nature* (Lond.), **187**, 1121 (1960).

Campbell and Gubisch. *J. Physiol.*, **192**, 345 (1967).

Einthoven. *v. Graefes Arch. Ophthal.*, **31** (3), 211 (1885).

Fraunhofer. *Ann. Phys.* (Lpz.), **56**, 304 (1814).

Granström. *Nord. Med.*, **20**, 2449 (1943).

Green. *J. Physiol.*, **190**, 583 (1967).

Gullstrand. *Einführung in d. Methoden d. Dioptrik d. Auges d. Menschen*, Leipzig (1911).

Hartridge. *J. Physiol.*, **52**, 175 (1918).

von Helmoltz. *Hb. d. physiol. Optik*, Leipzig (1856).

Ivanoff. *C.R. Acad. Sci.* (Paris), **223**, 170 (1946).
J. opt. Soc. Amer., **37**, 730 (1947).
Lcs aberrations de l'oeil, Paris (1952).

Jackson. *Skiascopy*, Phila., 58 (1896).

Jenkins. *Brit. J. physiol. Opt.*, **20**, 59, 161 (1963).

Krauskopf. *J. opt. Soc. Amer.*, **54**, 715 (1964).

Leibowitz. *J. opt. Soc. Amer.*, **42**, 416 (1952).

Maskelyne. *Phil. Trans.*, **79**, 256 (1789).

[1] Vol. IV, p. 577.

Nutting. *J. Wash. Acad. Sci.*, **4,** 385 (1914).

Ogle and Schwartz. *J. opt. Soc. Amer.*, **49,** 273 (1959).

Pi. *Trans. ophthal. Soc. U.K.*, **45,** 393 (1925).

Pinegin. *C.R. Acad. Sci.* (URSS), **30,** 206 (1941).

Polack. *Bull. Soc. Ophtal. Paris*, 401 (1923).

Röhler. *Vision Res.*, **2,** 391 (1962).

Schober, Munker and Zolleis. *Optica Acta*, **15,** 47 (1968).

Sheard. *J. opt. Soc. Amer.*, **12,** 79 (1926).

Stine. *Amer. J. Ophthal.*, **13,** 101 (1930).

Tscherning. *Optique physiologique*, Paris, (1898).

Wald and Griffin. *J. opt. Soc. Amer.*, **37,** 321 (1947).

Westheimer. *J. Physiol.*, **152,** 67 (1960).

Wollaston. See Young (1801).

Young. *Phil. Trans.*, **91,** 23 (1801).

CHAPTER IV

ADJUSTMENTS TO THE OPTICAL SYSTEM
ACCOMMODATION

WE have seen that the dioptric system of the emmetropic eye brings parallel rays of light to a focus upon the retina without effort. We have also seen that the depth of focus of the eye allows a certain amount of latitude if the distance of the object from the eye is moved and that this diminishes as the object approaches the eye. It is obvious that if the eye is to function adequately, it must be able to vary its focus to allow objects which are near at hand to be seen clearly. Thus in Fig. 191 parallel rays coming from an object (theoretically) infinitely far away are focused upon the retina; if the object is brought nearer (to A), the image will be formed at the conjugate focus (A′) behind the retina, and the large diffusion circles at the level of the retina

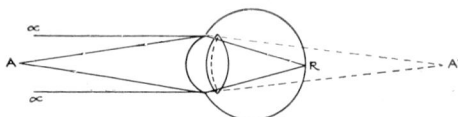

FIG. 191.

will allow only a blurred image to be seen. The mechanism whereby the converging power of the eye is increased so that a distinct image is still retained (the focus being brought from A′ to R) is called ACCOMMODATION.

The word *accommodation* is of comparatively recent origin and was introduced by C. A. Burow in 1841.[1] Standard textbooks before that time, such as Johannes Müller's *Handbuch der Physiologie des Menschen für Vorlesungen*, (Coblenz 1835–40), used the term *adaptation*, now accepted as connoting the changes in the sensitivity of the retina to varying intensities of light, while others used circumlocutary descriptive phrases.

HISTORY

There are few subjects upon which so many diverse opinions have been entertained as the mechanism of accommodation; nor is everyone by any means agreed upon it today. It was suggested by the great French physiologist, François Magendie (1816), on finding that the image on the sclera of an albino rabbit did not change with the distance of the object from the eye, that no mechanism of accommodation existed, the eye differing from other optical systems in possessing the faculty of bringing objects situated at different distances to a single focus-plane. Others, such as Phillippe de la

---

[1] *Beiträge zur Physiologie und Physik des menschlichen Auges*, Berlin, p. 212 (1841).

FIG. 192.—MARIUS HANS ERIC TSCHERNING
[1854–1939].

Hire (1685), held that this was approximately true, for he thought that objects were perceived for what they are in spite of inadequacies in the sensory excitation. Similarly, the anatomist Treviranus (1828) believed that the lens with its many layers had a universal focus. Jacques Charles François Sturm (1845), reasoning from the astigmatic nature of the ocular refractive surfaces, considered that clear vision was possible in the absence of any mechanism of adjustment so long as the retina lay between the two focal planes.

The existence of an accommodative mechanism had been proved, however, by the classical but unappreciated experiment of Scheiner (1619). Two pin-holes are made in a card at a distance apart less than the diameter of the pupil, and the eye, looking through them, is focused on a needle held at right angles to a line joining the two holes: the needle appears single. If, however, the eye is focused on some other object nearer or further away, the needle appears double. If three holes are made, three needles are seen, and so on. The explanation is clear from Fig. 193. If the card is perforated at *e* and *e*, the object, *o*, is brought to a focus on a screen, R, at I, where one image

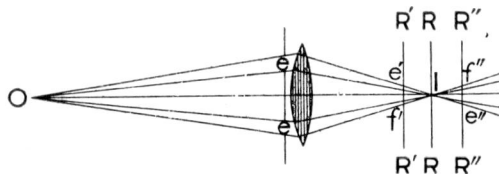

Fig. 193.—Scheiner's Experiment.

will appear. If the screen is held at R′ or R″, however, two images appear (*e′f′* and *e″f″*). The experiment therefore proves that in the eye there is a mechanism controlling the adjustment of focus. The true explanation of this classical experiment was offered by William Porterfield (1759) who suggested that accommodation was effected by a change in the lens.

Every possible hypothesis has been put forward to explain the rationale of accommodation. The great German physiologist, Albrecht von Haller (1763), considered that the contraction of the pupil diminished the blur-circles sufficiently to account for the phenomenon, a mechanism resembling a camera obscura which is present in some animals but is refuted in the case of man by the fact that a stenopæic opening smaller than the pupil itself does not render near objects distinct when the eye is looking into the distance (von Helmholtz, 1856). Others suggested that an elongation of the eyeball caused by the contraction of the extra-ocular muscles was responsible, a view advanced by J. Chr. Sturm (1697) and supported by such authorities as Hosack (1794) and Listing (1853); this is the old method adopted to alter the focus of a camera in which the photographic plate is moved, and a somewhat similar arrangement is seen in the eye of the mollusc, *Pecten*. For a century and a half this was the most popular explanation, but its occurrence in man was disproved by Thomas Young (1801). This great experimentalist who contributed so much to visual science presented his first paper on this subject to the Royal Society of London in 1793 and thereby was elected to the Fellowship of that body a few days before his 21st birthday, and his principal contribution appeared in 1801. Having prominent eyes[1] he was able on looking strongly inwards to place a ring at the inner angle of the orbit pressing against the globe, and a second at the outer pressing on the sclera over the macular region. The pressure of the latter stimulates the retina and produces a bright spot in the field of vision due to a mechanical phosphene,[2] but on strong accommodation neither of the rings was displaced nor did the pressure-image alter, showing that no axial elongation of the eye could have occurred. The theory of Lobé (1742), vigorously supported by Home (1795), that the corneal curvature altered by bulging forwards with near vision was also disproved by Young (1801) who showed that the power of accommodation remained unimpaired if the corneal refraction were eliminated by attaching a glass lens (virtually a contact lens) to his cornea and filling the space between them with water; it is to be noted that although these observers were correct in showing that the radius of curvature does change slightly on accommodation, it would have to change from 8 to 6·8 mm. to produce the desired effect.

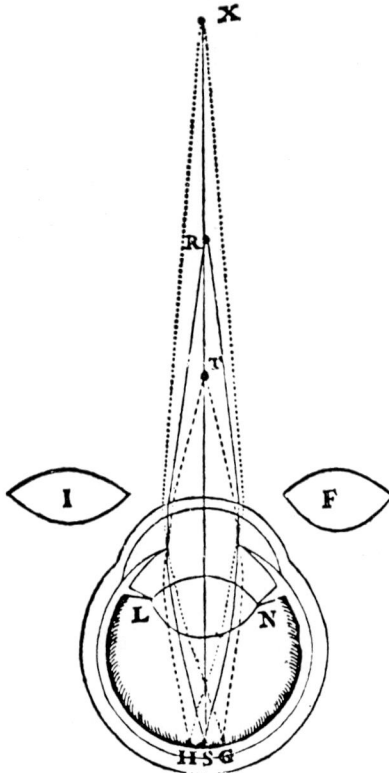

FIG. 194.—DESCARTES'S CONCEPT OF ACCOMMODATION.

" In order to represent the point X distinctly it is necessary that the whole shape of the humour NL be changed and that it becomes a little flatter as that which is marked I, and to represent the point T it is necessary to become a little more convex like that which is marked F."

There thus remained only the lens. The original theory of Kepler (1611) that changes in focus were attained by forward and backward movements of the lens (as occurs in some fishes) received support by such authorities as Scheiner (1619), Johannes Müller (1826) and Burow (1841), until it was demonstrated that an impossible excursion would require to be executed in order to obtain the requisite change in focus: it would, indeed, require to

[1] See Vol. IV, Fig. 252.   [2] Vol. IV, p. 465.

move forwards by 10 mm. The remaining possibility—that accommodation was accomplished by a change in the shape of the lens—was suggested (but not proved) at a very early date by Descartes (1677) (Fig. 194); it was shown to occur by Porterfield (1759), and would have been strongly supported by the great English surgeon and experimentalist, John Hunter, in the Croonian Lecture he was to have given to the Royal Society in 1794, had he not died in 1793 (see Home, 1794–95). It is interesting that, since the ciliary muscle had not yet been discovered, Hunter considered the lens itself to be muscular, largely from his studies on the lenses of cuttlefish, a view also adopted by Thomas Young (1801) (the "musculus crystallinus" of Leeuwenhoek). That a change in the shape of the lens was the probable explanation was demonstrated by Young (1801) in his observations on the aberration of light at the periphery of the pupil, a conclusion supported by his corroboration of

Porterfield's finding that accommodation was absent in aphakic patients. This suggestion, however, did not receive general credence until Langenbeck (1849) showed that the reflex images originally described by Purkinje (1823) formed at the surfaces of the lens altered on accommodation. Indeed, by the electrical stimulation of the eyes of animals, Cramer (1851) was able to show that the changes in the lens were the result of muscular activity; he thought that the ciliary muscle pulled the choroid forwards so that the vitreous pressed on

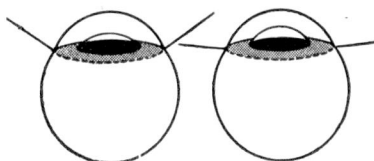

FIG. 195.   FIG. 196.

FIGS. 195 and 196.—HENSEN AND VÖLCKERS'S EXPERIMENT.

Two needles are inserted into the ciliary muscle at rest (Fig. 195); on stimulation of the muscle (Fig. 196) the points of the needles are carried forward.

the back of the lens, the periphery of which was retained in place by the contracted pupil while the central area bulged forwards. This forward pull of the contracted ciliary muscle was proved by Hensen and Völckers (1873) who, in their classical experiments on cats, apes and man, showed that if two needles were inserted through the sclera into the ciliary body, stimulation of the ciliary muscle resulted in a backward movement of their free ends, indicating a forward movement of their buried points (Figs. 195–6); but the restraining action of the pupil was disproved by von Graefe (1860) who demonstrated the presence of a full amplitude of accommodation in a case of aniridia.

Shortly thereafter, von Helmholtz (1853–56) devised a technique for the scientific analysis of the change in shape of the lens and propounded a simple mechanical theory to account for its occurrence. It will be remembered that the size of the image in a curved mirror of an object varies as the radius of curvature of the mirror; and by means of the phakoscope,[1] using two luminous squares as an object, von Helmholtz was able to show that the action of accommodation was accompanied by an increase in curvature of both

[1] p. 158.

surfaces of the lens and an increase in its thickness (Figs. 197–8). Although
the images showed that the corneal convexity increases slightly in accommodation, the changes were not sufficient to account for the alteration in
focus and they have since been shown to be due to convergence.[1] He considered that the lens was elastic and under tension from the ciliary muscle,
the relaxation of which allowed the lens to become more convex. As we
shall show presently, this simple mechanism, although supported enthusiastically by Carl von Hess (1896–1904), was opposed by Tscherning (1894–
1908) who thought that on its contraction the ciliary muscle would increase
the tension on the zonule. He concluded that the lens on accommodation
became flattened in its periphery and bulged forwards conoidally in the
region of its axis and, accepting the
suggestion of Cramer, now supported
by von Pflugk (1906), he postulated
that this was due to the pressure of
the vitreous which was counteracted
in the periphery of the lens by the
tension of the zonule. In its day this
theory, the opposite of that of von
Helmholtz, excited a storm of controversy. The conoidal shape of the
axial region on accommodation was
corroborated by Gullstrand (1911) in
his study of the mechanism of the
intracapsular accommodation of the
lens. In the first microscopic examination of the lens, van Leeuwenhoek
(1684), indeed, had suggested that the capsule had muscular qualities which
could change the shape of this organ, and variations in its thickness and its
elasticity were remarked by Winslow (1732), Wintringham (1740), Thomas
Young (1793) and Bowman (1849). At a later date Gullstrand (1911) denied
von Helmholtz's view that the lens itself was elastic but considered that
the force opposing the ciliary muscle was the elasticity of the capsule, and the
characteristic shape of the accommodated lens was explained by Fincham
(1925) by the moulding capacity of this membrane determined by its peculiar
configuration. That this is the entire explanation is somewhat difficult to
accept and more recently Kikkawa and Sato (1963) and Fisher (1969) have
shown that the lens substance itself has some inherent elasticity which,
opposed to that of the capsule, determines the change in its shape on the
relief of tension by a balance between the two.

Figs. 197 and 198.—von Helmholtz's
Diagram of the Purkinje Images on
Accommodation.

Using two luminous squares as an object.

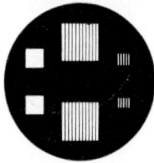   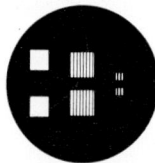

Fig. 197.   Fig. 198.

Fig. 197.—In the unaccommodated eye.
Fig. 198.—In the accommodated eye (the
difference being greatly exaggerated). The
bright corneal images remain practically
stationary while those due to the lens approximate and become smaller.

Of the great figures in this short historical sketch, the portrait of CHRISTOPHER
SCHEINER [1575–1650], who proved the existence of accommodation, appears elsewhere in this *System*.[2] This Jesuit friar who was born at Wald in Bavaria and died in

---

[1] p. 132.   [2] Vol. II, Fig. 37.

Niesse in Silesia made great advances in our knowledge of the anatomy of the eye by the introduction of chemical fixatives for the examination of the globe, thus allowing him for the first time to locate the crystalline lens and the optic nerve-head in their correct positions, and also in ocular physiology by experimentally proving Platter's suggestion that the visual image was formed on the retina.[1] He also discovered that the pupil contracted on accommodating for near vision.

Unfortunately, a portrait of WILLIAM PORTERFIELD [?1700–1771], who interpreted Scheiner's experiment to show that accommodation was a function of the lens, does not appear to exist. This somewhat peculiar Scottish ophthalmologist, born in Ayrshire at an unknown date, died at Sancerre in France. In 1724 he was appointed professor of medicine to Edinburgh University but, failing to deliver any lectures, he resigned after 18 months; nevertheless, he became President of the Royal College of Physicians of Edinburgh in 1748. In 1759 he wrote a remarkable *Treatise on the Eye* in two volumes. A joy to read, it was speculative rather than practical, and therein appeared his work on accommodation together with the invention of the first optometer and the claim that the retina was the visual receptor. When Mariotte discovered the blind-spot the view that the optic nerve fibres were the visual receptors was abandoned and he and others claimed that this was a function of the choroid in view of its absence at the disc; Porterfield showed that the retina was the essential organ.

The story and photograph of Thomas Young are in the Volume dealing with Physiology.[2]

Of the more modern investigators the photographs of von Helmholtz (Fig. 130) and Gullstrand (Fig. 131) appear elsewhere, but this is a suitable place to introduce those of Tscherning and Fincham.

MARIUS HANS ERIC TSCHERNING [1854–1939] (Fig. 192) was born in Aestrup, a small Danish village, and studied medicine in Copenhagen where, stimulated by Edmund Hansen Grut, the father of modern Danish ophthalmology, he interested himself in this subject. Going to Paris on a visit, he remained there for 26 years, first as the assistant of Louis E. Javal, whose small two-roomed laboratory founded in 1876 was the most famous in Europe for physiological optics, and then as Javal's successor as director of a new laboratory at the Sorbonne. Here, a remarkable and enthusiastic experimentalist with a genius for constructing apparatus out of small resources, he greatly enriched our science, apart from his classical contributions to the mechanism of accommodation. He first studied the ocular movements (1887) with the aid of a beautiful assistant, he standing on a central stove, she running up and down a ladder placed at different angles to fix the various positions of gaze—with the result that he married her. He made classical advances in our knowledge of colour vision and colour blindness, of adaptation for which he devised his photometric lenses (1922), of the catoptric images in the eye in which connection he evolved his ophthalmophako-meter, and of the optical aberrations of the eye for which he introduced best-form lenses. Resigning from his laboratory, he returned to Copenhagen to follow Bjerrum in the university Chair of that city, and continued his researches after his retirement in 1925 to the ripe age of 85. With his untidy hair, his vast black cravat and his laughing grey eyes he attracted not only his first assistant but everyone he encountered.

A note on EDGAR FRANK FINCHAM [1893–1963] (Fig. 199) is a suitable ending to this historical résumé, for he did much to consolidate our knowledge on this subject. Trained in optics, he served in the RAMC throughout the Macedonian campaign in the First World War where he acquired unusual expertise in the histological study of the retina, and thereafter became lecturer in applied optics in the Northampton Poly-technic in London (1919–50). During this period he produced his classical papers on accommodation, culminating in a monograph (1937), and also devised his coincidence

[1] Vol. IV, p. 437.   [2] Vol. IV, p. 617, Fig. 252.

FIG. 199.—EDGAR FRANK FINCHAM
[1893–1963].

optometer.[1]   From 1950 to 1961 he headed the research department of ophthalmic optics at the Institute of Ophthalmology in London and on his retirement pursued further research at the Polytechnic, the latter period being mainly concerned with the reciprocal actions of accommodation and convergence.   Fincham was a delightful person; diffident and shy and a skilful etcher, a superb photographer, an inveterate traveller and a lover of old books, he supplemented his scientific activities with a host of hobbies.

The Mechanism of Accommodation

An adequate theory of the mechanism of accommodation in man must be capable of accounting for the changes observable in the human eye during accommodation, and providing a reasonable explanation of the decline in this function with age.

The Changes in the Human Eye during Accommodation

OBSERVATIONS ON THE LIVING EYE

CHANGES IN THE LENS.   In his classical theory to explain the mechanism of accommodation, von Helmholtz (1855) considered that the lens assumed a more spherical form; in a general sense this is true.   All are agreed that the

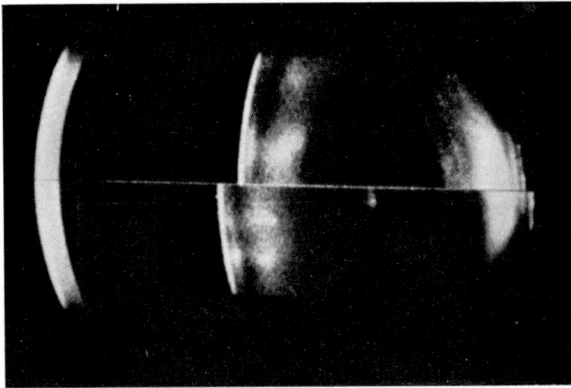

Fig. 200.—The Shape of the Lens in Accommodation.

A comparison of the slit-lamp photographs of the same lens without (above) and with (below) accommodation.   Note the change in thickness of the lens and in the depth of the anterior chamber.   The smaller strip of lens photographed in the accommodated eye is due to the associated miosis (B. Patnaik).

lens increases in thickness during accommodation; it can readily be observed that its anterior surface approaches the cornea, making the anterior chamber shallower, while its posterior surface remains comparatively stationary, a change observed photographically with the slit-lamp (Patnaik, 1967) (Fig. 200) and gonioscopically (Burian and Allen, 1955) (Figs. 201–2). Fincham's (1937) measurements of these changes are seen in Tables XII and

[1] p. 412.

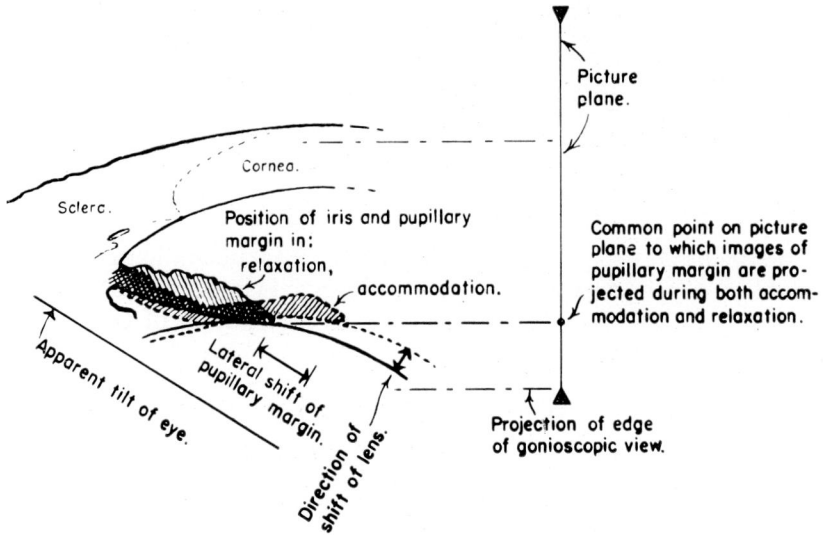

Fig. 201.—The Changes during Accommodation.

Schematic cross-section of the region of the angle of the anterior chamber showing shifting of the iris and pupillary margin and the direction of movement of the anterior surface of the lens (with no indication to show its extent) during accommodation (H. M. Burian and L. Allen).

TABLE XII

THE CHANGE IN THICKNESS OF THE LENS

(Fincham)

	Accommodation in dioptres	Central thickness of lens in mm.	Increase of thickness of lens in mm.
Case 1	1	3·66	0·58
	9	4·24	
Case 2	1	3·84	0·36
	9	4·20	

TABLE XIII

THE CHANGE IN DEPTH OF THE ANTERIOR CHAMBER

(Fincham)

	Case 1			Case 2		
Accommodation in dioptres	Depth of anterior chamber in mm.	Movement of anterior pole of lens in mm.	Accommodation in dioptres	Depth of anterior chamber in mm.	Movement of anterior pole of lens in mm.
1	3·68	—	1	3·33	—
4	3·55	0·13	4	3·22	0·11
6	3·50	0·18	6	3·17	0·16
9	3·34	0·34	9	3·06	0·27

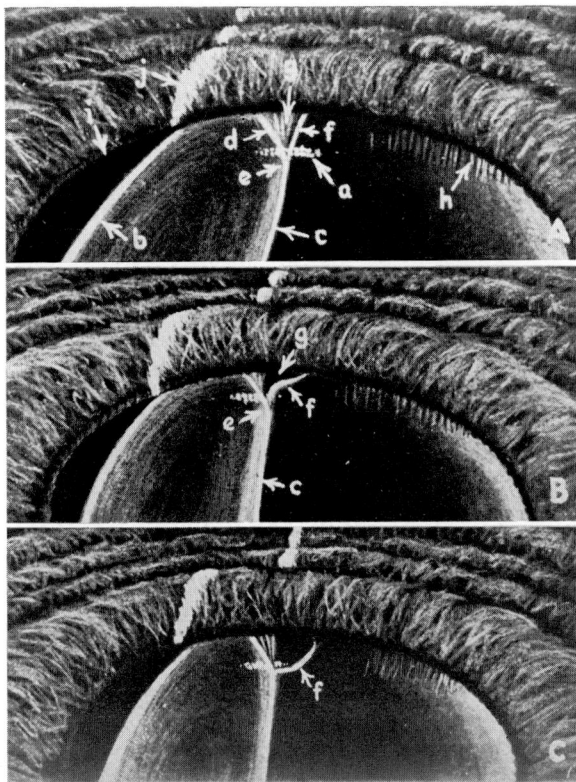

FIG. 202.—CHANGES IN THE PERIPHERY OF THE POSTERIOR SURFACE OF
THE LENS ON ACCOMMODATION.

A, during relaxation of accommodation. *a*, specular reflection of points of
insertion of the posterior zonular fibres. *b*, slit-lamp beam on the anterior surface
of the lens. *c*, the posterior surface of the lens centrally to the hyaloideo-capsular
ligament. *d*, the posterior surface of the lens between this ligament and the equator.
e, the point of angulation of the lens surface. *f*, the anterior surface of the vitreous.
g and *h*, zonular fibres. *i*, the pupillary margin. *j*, the beam of the slit-lamp on
the iris.

B, during active accommodation. The peripheral posterior surface of the lens (*c*)
is flattened and its angulation increased (*e*). The anterior surface of the vitreous is
relaxed and bowed forward (*f*), and there is an optically empty space in front of the
vitreous (*g*).

C, an exceptional appearance in active accommodation when the surface of
the vitreous (*f*) is bowed backward (H. M. Burian and L. Allen).

XIII. Moreover, its equatorial diameter diminishes at the same time, as was
demonstrated by Grossmann (1904), Story (1924) and Fincham (1937) in
cases of aniridia, and by Libby (1910) in a case of albinism. Thus Grossmann
found that the apparent diameter of a lens which was 11·5 mm. at rest
became 12·25 with homatropine and 10·25 with eserine, Libby estimated
that with eserine the diameter was 9 mm. while with atropine it was 10 mm.,

FIGS. 203 to 205.—THE CHANGES IN THE LENS ON ACCOMMODATION
SEEN IN ANIRIDIA (E. F. Fincham).

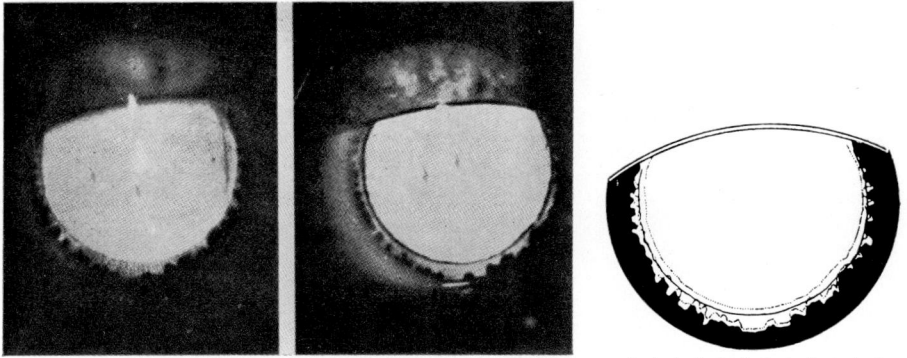

FIGS. 203 to 205.—THE CHANGES IN THE LENS ON ACCOMMODATION
SEEN IN ANIRIDIA (E. F. Fincham).

FIG. 203.   FIG. 204.   FIG. 205.

FIG. 203.—In the unaccommodated eye.
FIG. 204.—In the accommodated eye.
FIG. 205.—Comparison of the photographs of the lens in the two states.

and Fincham found a diminution of 0·4 to 0·45 mm. in the visually accommodated eye (Figs. 203–5).

The increase in thickness, however, has not usually been held to consist merely of a simple increase in spherical curvature. Young, as early as 1801, had demonstrated that the spherical aberration of the lens diminishes during accommodation, and the reverse should happen if it became more spherical. This observation was verified by Tscherning (1898) and with considerable accuracy by Koomen and his colleagues (1949) and Ivanoff (1956). In general, the light passing through the edge of the pupil is focused in front of

FIGS. 206 and 207.—THE PURKINJE-SANSON IMAGES TAKEN IN ORDINARY
LIGHT (E. F. Fincham).

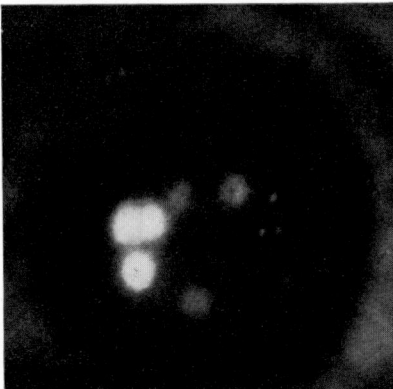

FIG. 206.—In the unaccommodated eye.   FIG. 207.—In the accommodated eye.

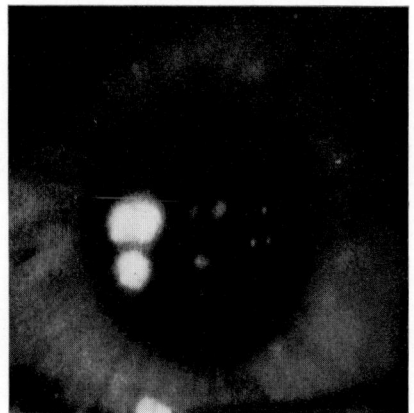

the axial rays (positive spherical aberration); as the eye accommodates this becomes less until the aberration disappears and eventually becomes negative, the axial rays being now focused in front of the peripheral. By a study of the reflex images, Tscherning attributed this to the assumption by the anterior cortical area of the lens of a hyperbolic shape in the axial region. The flattening of the periphery and bulging of the centre of the accommodated lens was verified histologically by von Pflugk (1906), and optically by several investigators, notably by Fincham (1925–37), who deduced with

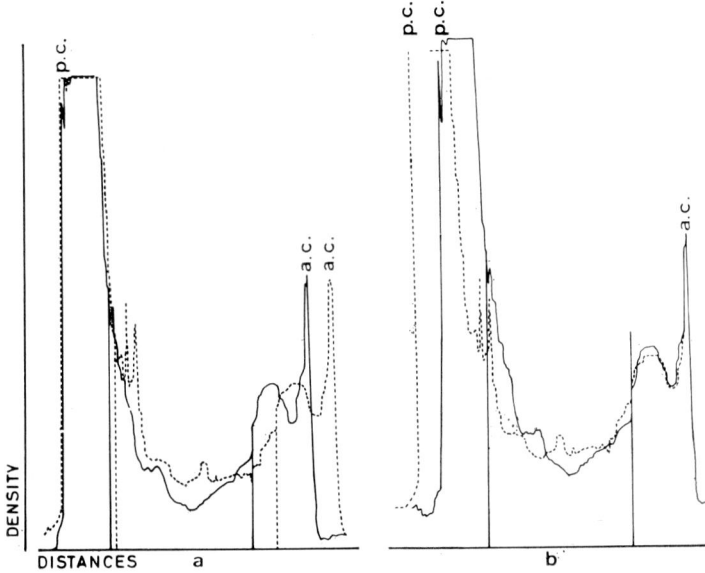

FIG. 208.—LENTICULAR CHANGES IN ACCOMMODATION.

The densitograms of the two photographs seen in Fig. 200 superimposed. The solid line indicates no accommodation and the dotted line full accommodation. a, the posterior capsules (p.c.) coinciding; b, the anterior capsules (a.c.) coinciding. While the change in thickness of the anterior cortex is negligible and that in the posterior cortex is minimal, the intercortical zone undergoes a remarkable change (B. Patnaik).

the aid of the slit-lamp and an ingenious device for recording photographically the images produced by reflection at the surface of the lens that the pupillary portion of the anterior surface assumed a conoidal curve on accommodation (Figs. 206–7). At the same time it should be noted that, taking into account the influence of corneal refraction on the apparent changes of the images on the surface of the lens, Nordenson (1917–43) convinced himself that the anterior surface of the lens maintained an ellipsoidal shape with the radius of curvature of the central area smaller than in the periphery, but without assuming the conoidal form described by Tscherning and Fincham, a view recently corroborated by the ellipsoidal shape assumed by the anterior surface of the excised lens in which state it is generally accepted to have taken its accommodated form (Fisher, 1969).[1]

In either case, it is obvious that there must be an axial displacement of the substance of the lens during accommodation, a phenomenon which can be demonstrated clinically with the slit-lamp when the axial shifting of a small subcapsular opacity can be observed (Vogt, 1924). The extent of the shifting theoretically necessary was estimated mathematically by Gullstrand (1909–12) by postulating the existence of iso-indicial[2] zones of greater refractive index the nearer they were to the centre of the lens, and from his work emerged the fact that in this *internal mechanism of accommodation* there was a shifting of the individual parts in the direction of the axis during the increase in the thickness of the lens (Fig. 223). This, indeed, is what one would expect from the development, the anatomical shape and arrangement of the lenticular fibres. It was originally thought, however, that only these cortical zones of the lens were appreciably altered in refractivity (Koch and Fischer, 1933), but changes in the central nuclear region also appear to occur, perhaps greater than in the cortex (Fig. 208) (Fincham, 1937; Huggert, 1946–64; Patnaik, 1967). By serial cinephotography of the third Purkinje image, Kabe (1967) concluded that when accommodation is increasing the change in the apparent curvature of the anterior surface of the lens is slow and continuous, but when accommodation is decreasing this change involves a prompt followed by a slow phase.

It seems, therefore, that in the act of accommodation there is *an increase of thickness and a decrease in diameter of the lens;* its anterior surface becomes more convex axially; the posterior surface also becomes more convex but only slightly so; the anterior pole approximates the cornea while the posterior pole moves only to a small extent.

CHANGES IN THE CILIARY BODY. That accommodation is brought about by a contraction of the ciliary muscle is universally accepted; and we have already discussed[3] the mechanism whereby on its contraction the choroid is pulled bodily forwards, while the ciliary processes are bulged towards the equator of the lens, thus approximating the two and releasing the tension on the zonule. Confirmation of this has come from the observation of the ciliary processes in cases of aniridia or in patients who have had an iridectomy performed or in albinotic subjects; this has been photographically verified by Fincham (1949) in a case of iridodialysis (Figs. 209–10), and the change as interpreted through gonioscopic observations by Busacca (1945–55) (Figs. 211–13) and Burian and Allen (1955) is seen in Figs. 202, 214. Any precise individual action of the various anatomical fibre-groups of this complex muscle in bringing this about is not yet understood, but it would seem likely that the entire muscle acts as a single individual entity.

[1] p. 170.
[2] Iso-indicial zones mean those having the same index of refraction.
[3] Vol. II, p. 156.

FIGS. 209 and 210.—THE MOVEMENTS OF THE CILIARY PROCESSES IN THE
NON-ACCOMMODATED AND ACCOMMODATED EYE

In a case of traumatic iridodialysis (the remains of the iris are seen lying across
the area of the fundus glow) (photographed by E. F. Fincham).

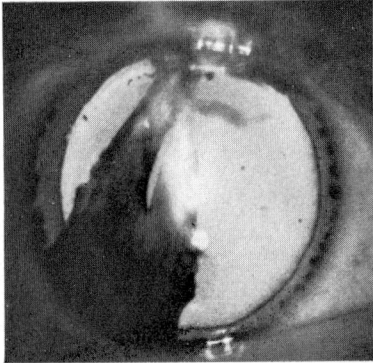

FIG. 209.—In the non-accommodated
eye the ciliary processes are seen
around the periphery as small dark
projections.

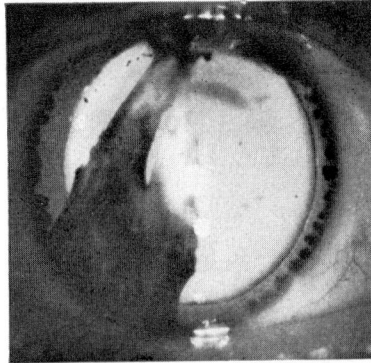

FIG. 210.—In the accommodated eye
these processes become much larger
and become displaced axipetally towards the lens.

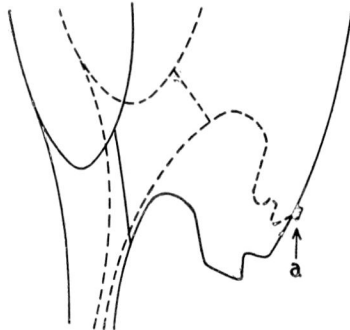

FIG. 211.—THE ACTION OF THE CILIARY MUSCLE.

To show the displacement of the ciliary body and the lens under the influence of
atropine (continuous line) and of eserine (broken line). a, is the position of ciliary
anchorage at the scleral spur (after A. Busacca).

FIGS. 212 and 213.—The gonioscopic appearance of the ciliary body in an eye
with a basal iridectomy.

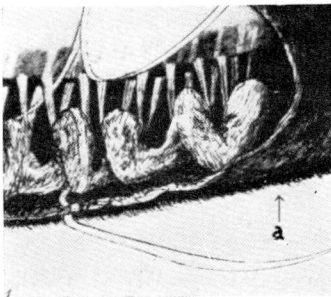

FIG. 212.—The appearance of the ciliary
processes in the accommodated position after
the administration of eserine.

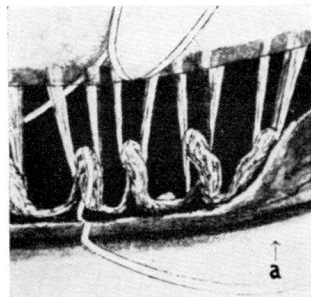

FIG. 213.—The appearance of the ciliary
processes in the non-accommodated position
after the administration of atropine.

a, the line of the scleral spur (A. Busacca).

There has been a very great deal written, dating from the time of Dobrowolsky (1885), about the so-called *dynamic lenticular astigmatism* or *astigmatic accommodation*. There is, however, no scientific foundation for the claim that the accommodative effort of the ciliary muscle deforms the lens unequally in different meridians. The idea was based upon the experimental work of Hensen and Völckers (1868–78), who showed that when a filament of the ciliary nerve was divided, a local contraction of that part of the ciliary muscle supplied by the filament can be induced on its stimulation. But this will occur if the local nerve supply of any muscle is separately stimulated, and such an isolated contraction under experimental conditions bears no relation to the normal action of the muscle in life. A localized or sectional action, however, is possible. Thus contraction may be produced by drugs rendered " heavy " with sucrose such as pilocarpine or relaxation by atropine injected intracamerally so as to reach preferentially one portion of the muscle (Bárány, 1966). On the other hand, all the evidence goes to show that in ordinary circumstances if any part of the ciliary muscle contracts in life it contracts equally all round. Moreover, as was pointed out by Donders (1864),

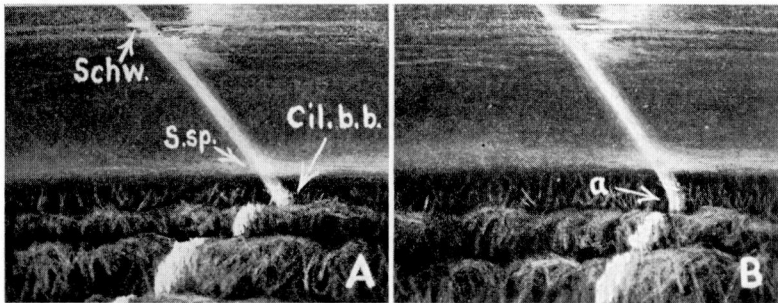

FIG. 214.—THE ANGLE OF THE ANTERIOR CHAMBER IN ACCOMMODATION.

A, during relaxation of accommodation. There is a limited exposure of the band of the ciliary body (*cil.b.b.*) and the root of the iris. *S.sp.*, scleral spur; *Schw.*, Schwalbe's ring.

B, during active accommodation. There is increased exposure of the band of the ciliary body and the root of the iris and a change in contour (*a*) of the ciliary body (H. M. Burian and L. Allen).

if one muscle contracts the muscle in the other eye acts equally and simultaneously in all ordinary conditions. Hess and Neumann (1892), for example, found that in the normal individual it was possible to compensate for a difference in refraction between the two eyes of only 0·12 D.

As an incidental result of the contraction of the ciliary muscle, the intra-ocular pressure tends to fall, due presumably to an increase in the facility of the outflow of aqueous by some 30 to 60% following the widening of the angle of the anterior chamber (Armaly and Burian, 1958 ; Armaly and Rubin, 1961 ; Armaly and Jepson, 1962).

CHANGES IN THE ZONULE. A relaxation of the zonule has been amply shown to occur during accommodation. Indeed, on forced accommodation the lens is displaced in the direction of gravity by some 0·3 to 0·35 mm. (Coccius, 1888; Tscherning, 1895; von Hess, 1896–1901) and may even become tremulous (von Hess, 1904); this downward movement was verified by von Hess who observed the upward displacement of the entoptic image of an opacity in his own lens when he accommodated. It can also be readily confirmed in cases (iridectomy, etc.) wherein the periphery of the lens is visible, for slit-lamp observation in the unaccommodated state (or after atropine) shows that the insertions of the " fibres " of the zonule into the equator of the lens are marked by fine crenations in the capsule—obviously caused by a considerable amount of traction—which disappear on the act of accommodation (or after eserine), allowing the outline of the equator of the lens to become smooth—evidently the effect of a decrease in the tension of the fibres (Brown, 1928; Duke-Elder, 1929). The relaxation of the capsule was dramatically shown by Graves (1926) who observed by the slit-lamp the action of voluntary accommodation, miotics and mydriatics in a case wherein

Figs. 215 to 217.—The Lens Capsule in Accommodation (B. Graves).

Fig. 215.—The normal state of the capsule at rest. The posterior capsule (P) is more mobile than the anterior (A), and sometimes floats forwards almost to touch the anterior capsule (a), at other times backwards (b).

Fig. 216.—The capsule in active accommodation. Both parts, but especially the posterior (P), become slack.

Fig. 217.—The capsule under the influence of eserine. It has now become very lax.

the entire lens had become absorbed after trauma, leaving only the empty and transparent capsule *in situ*. In the normal state the capsule was almost taut (Figs. 215–17); on complete relaxation it became quite taut; and in the act of accommodation or on the instillation of eserine, it became lax and folded upon itself, movements of the eye causing it to tremble (Figs. 216–7).

EXPERIMENTAL OBSERVATIONS

The isolated intact lens of primates assumes the form of the accommodated state and the demonstration by Fincham (1937) that in the enucleated eye of a child severance of the zonular attachment resulted in the assumption of this shape by the lens confirms the fact that the zonule is under tension when the lens is unaccommodated. The shape assumed by the whole lens was studied by Fisher (1970) by examining its profiles, using the ingenious centrifugal forces acting in a radial direction. This technique of spinning is unique in so far as forces are impressed upon the lens without seriously disturbing its structure. This is made clear by Figs. 218 and 219 wherein the shape of the lens before and after spinning is depicted, while the regional changes are seen in Fig. 220. The interesting thing is that after spinning the structure of the lens is virtually unchanged except for the alterations determined by the internal mechanism of accommodation (Fig. 223), whereas after deformation by previous methods the arrangement of the fibres is highly disorganized (Fig. 225); the optical confirmation of this is seen in Figs. 222, 224 and 226 wherein the image of a spot of light by the spun lens is as defined as that of the normal lens while the image of the compressed lens is completely distorted.

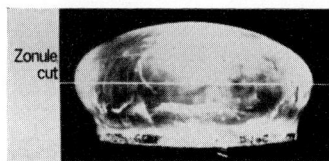

FIG. 218.

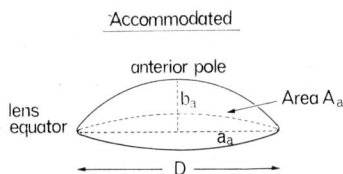

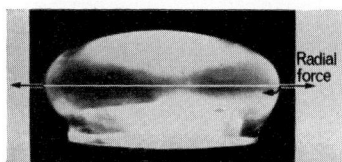

FIG. 219.

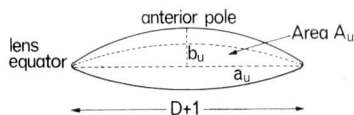

FIG. 220.

FIGS. 218 TO 220.—CHANGES IN THE SHAPE OF THE LENS IN ACCOMMODATION.
By the spinning technique of R. F. Fisher.
FIG. 218.—The stationary lens.
FIG. 219.—The spinning lens.
FIG. 220.—Areal changes in shape. Area A_a is the area during accommodation; area A_u in the unaccommodated lens. D, diameter; b_a and b_u, the distance of the anterior pole of the lens from its equator. Posterior to the equator, a_a and a_u, there is little change.

The forces exerted on the lens *in vivo* by zonular tension are probably comparable to the centrifugal forces imposed on the spinning lens, since under radial stress the lens behaves as a simple elastic body. It is interesting that on placing extracted lenses in hypotonic solutions, Odqvist (1937) found that when they swelled osmotically and stretched the capsule they assumed a more spherical form without a lenticonus. Moreover, values for the changes in dioptric power do not necessitate the assumption of a conoidal shape in its axial area.

The influence of the capsule in determining the shape of the lens is undoubted. Decapsulation of the young human lens leads to a change from the accommodated to the unaccommodated form. The most significant

FIGS. 221 to 226.—CHANGES IN THE STRUCTURE OF THE LENS IN ACCOMMODATION.
By the spinning technique of R. F. Fisher.

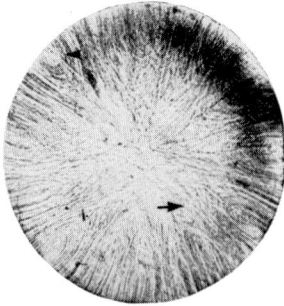

FIG. 221.   FIG. 222.

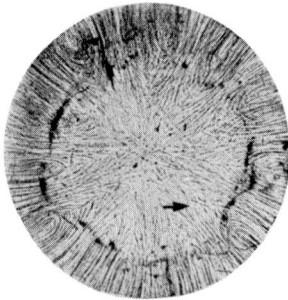
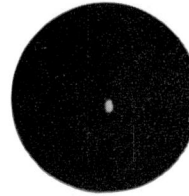

FIG. 223.   FIG. 224.

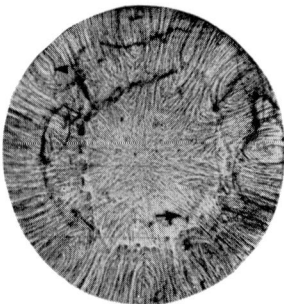
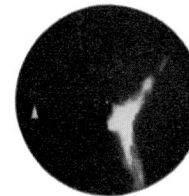

FIG. 225.   FIG. 226.

FIG. 221.—The unspun lens.
FIG. 222.—The optical image of a point of light.
FIG. 223.—The spun lens, showing the internal mechanism of accommodation.
FIG. 224.—The optical image is good.
FIG. 225.—The compressed lens.
FIG. 226.—The optical image is distorted.

The black arrows on the top left side of Figs. 221, 223 and 225 point to the anterior commencement of the equatorial fibres, while the lower arrows point to the apical fibres.

physical property of the capsule is its elasticity, a property, as we have seen, long recognized by observers such as Gullstrand (1908), and confirmed by a number of experimenters.[1] It was measured by Fisher (1969) who determined the relation between volume and pressure when it was distended and found its modulus of elasticity to be 6×10^7 dynes per cm.^{2} at birth, decreasing to 3×10^7 dynes per cm.^{2} at the age of 60, and $1 \cdot 5 \times 10^7$ dynes in extreme old age, an elasticity comparable to lightly vulcanized rubber

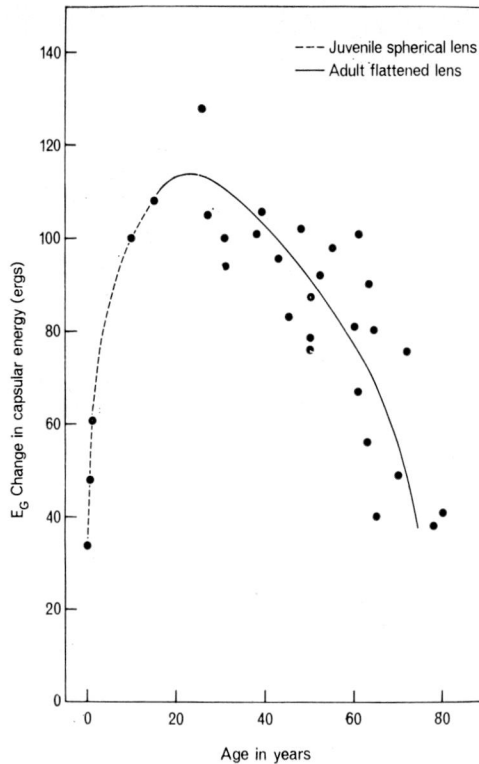

FIG. 227.—THE VARIATION OF THE ENERGY STORED IN THE ANTERIOR HUMAN CAPSULE WITH AGE.

Average of 30 human lenses (R. F. Fisher).

allowing a linear elongation of 29% independent of age (Fig. 227). The energy thus stored in the capsule to change the shape of the lens in accommodation varies with its elasticity and its thickness and is more effective the flatter the lens and the smaller the volume of its anterior segment. Since the anterior capsule is some 5 to 6 times thicker than the posterior, most of this energy is exerted by the anterior surface, and since the lenses of such animals

[1] von Pflugk (1932), Vogelsang (1934), Jäger and Vogelsang (1935), Fincham (1937), Pau (1951), Kikkawa and Sato (1963), Fisher (1969).

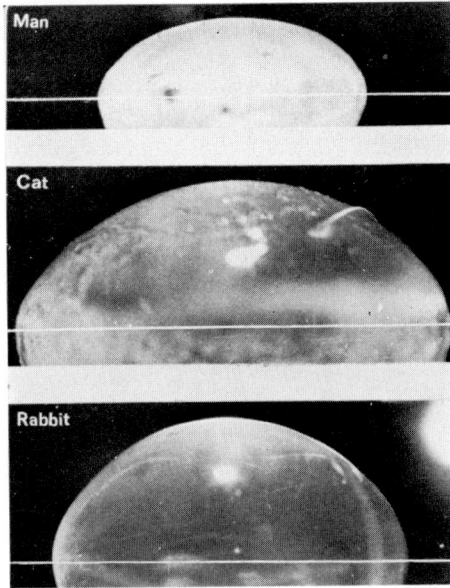

FIG. 228.—The white line is drawn through the equator of the lens. The amplitude of accommodation in man is 12 D, in the cat 2 D, and in the rabbit 1 D.

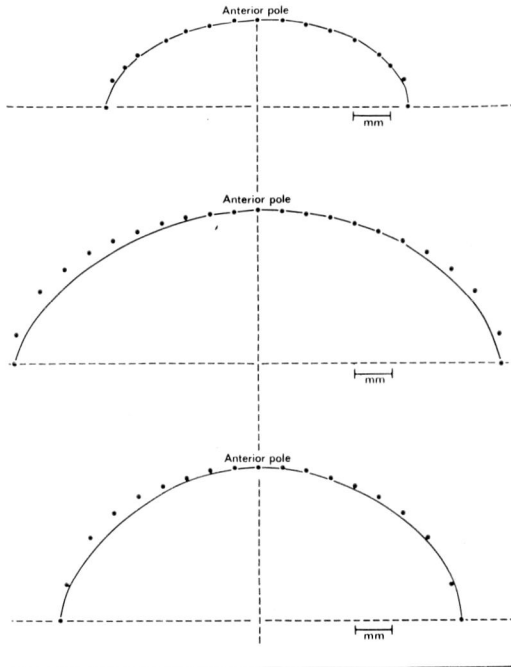

FIG. 229.—The profiles of the lenses seen in Fig. 228; superimposed on each are points plotted at 0·5 mm. increment in the radius of the lens.

as the cat or the rabbit are more spherical than that of man, the capsular energy is less effective in moulding the lens (Figs. 228–9).

In Fincham's (1937) view, as in Gullstrand's (1908), the substance of the lens is plastic, tending to take the shape imparted to it by the capsule. As Weale (1962) pointed out, however, Fincham's observation that decapsulation of a young human lens leads to a change from the accommodated to the unaccommodated form strongly suggests that the lenticular substance has an elasticity of its own; that such is, indeed, the case has been established by Kikkawa and Sato (1963) who showed that the deformation of the lens

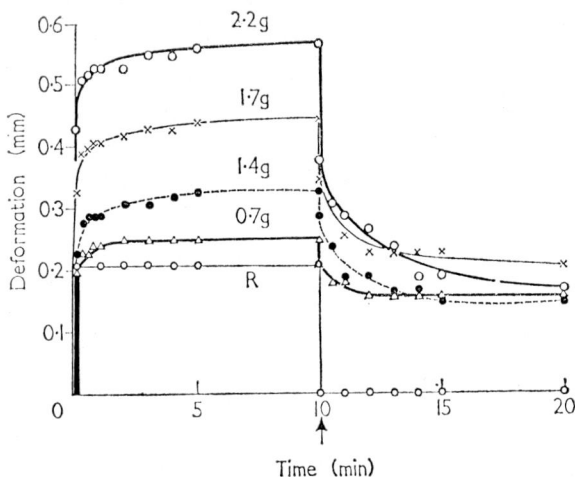

FIG. 230.—THE ELASTICITY OF THE LENS.

To show the deformation and recovery of the normal lens when compressed with various forces, given in grams over each curve. The compressive force was released at the point indicated by the arrow. Each curve represents an individual experiment. R, the ideal plot obtained from a rubber ballon (Y. Kikkawa and T. Sato).

produced by the application of an external force was restored to a considerable extent, at first rapidly and then gradually, and was approximately the same with or without the capsule (Fig. 230). This assumption of the unaccommodated shape when the elastic capsule is removed suggests that the lens matrix is not plastic (in the sense that putty is) but naturally returns to its unaccommodated form when external stresses are removed, a change which necessitates the possession by the lens itself of some degree of inherent elasticity. The origin of this property is at present unknown, but presumably it lies in the fibres, for the contractility of which there is some evidence (Gillessen, 1938). An indication of their contractile properties seems to be shown by the experiments of Kleifeld (1956) who found on electrical stimulation with small direct currents (2·0 mA) that they varied in thickness and moved towards one another; moreover, he found that during accommodation the content of sugar and lactic acid decreased and the oxygen consumption increased, suggesting that the change in shape involved the expenditure of energy rather than being entirely a passive deformation impressed upon the lens by the capsule. The effect, however, of the many lenticular laminæ in any such activity, their compressibility and their adherence to each other and that of the cortical layers to the capsule are as yet unexplored.

As with the capsule, the zonule is also elastic; this was demonstrated by von Pflugk (1932) who observed the wide gape that resulted when it was incised in the freshly enucleated eye, and was measured by Fincham (1937) who recorded its excursion when an iron wire was placed behind the posterior surface of the lens and was temporarily attracted by a magnet.

THE OPTICAL CHANGES IN ACCOMMODATION

It is obviously advisable to have some means of assessing the optical changes which occur on accommodation.

THE RANGE AND AMPLITUDE OF ACCOMMODATION

The furthest distance away at which an object can be seen clearly is called the FAR POINT (PUNCTUM REMOTUM). In order to see such an object the emmetropic eye is in a state of rest, the ciliary muscle is relaxed, and the refractivity is at a minimum. When maximum accommodation is in force, the nearest point which the eye can see clearly is called the NEAR POINT (PUNCTUM PROXIMUM). The distance between the far point and the near point, that is, the distance over which accommodation is effective, is called the RANGE OF ACCOMMODATION. The difference between the refractivity of the eye in the two conditions—when at rest with a minimal refraction and when fully accommodated with a maximal refraction—is called the AMPLI-TUDE OF ACCOMMODATION. The range is therefore an indication of the availability of accommodation and the amplitude is an expression of the work done. In the first case, where no effort is involved, we call the refraction of the eye *static*; when the refraction is altered by the exercise of accom-modation it is spoken of as *dynamic*.

Mathematically, the amplitude of accommodation (A) is expressed by Donders's formula, $A = P - R$, where P is the dioptric value of the near-point distance and R is the dioptric value of the far-point distance. For an emmetropic subject R is nil (the reciprocal of infinity) and with a near point of 10 cm. P would be 10 D and A would also be 10 D. When the eye focuses a point between the far and near points the amount of accommodation is given by the formula $A = V - R$, where V is the dioptric value of the point in question. There is some dispute regarding the origin from which these distances should be measured; for this the apex of the cornea is usually taken, which differs little from other perhaps more theoretically acceptable points such as the first principal point or the centre of the entrance pupil.

THE OPTICS OF THE ACCOMMODATED EYE

It is possible to calculate the increase in dioptric power of the lens from the observation of the change in curvature of its surfaces during accom-modation. The radius of curvature of the axial part of the anterior surface may decrease from 10 to 5 mm. Some of Fincham's (1937) measurements are given in Table XIV. An interesting feature emerges in that the estimated increase of power of the lens, based solely on a change of curvature of its surfaces, is insufficient to account for the observed increase in optical power of the eye as a whole, a fact which led Gullstrand to postulate largely on theoretical grounds the "intracapsular mechanism of accommodation" whereby alterations in the substance of the lens occur, leading to an effective increase in its refractivity.[1]

TABLE XIV

RADIUS OF THE ANTERIOR SURFACE OF THE LENS

Case 1, male aged 19, R.E. hyp. 1 D		Case 2, male aged 19, R.E. hyp. 1 D	
Radius ant. surface of cornea 7·74 mm.		Radius ant. surface of cornea 7·6 mm.	
Apparent depth of A.C. 3.15 mm.		Apparent depth of A.C. 2·8 mm.	
True depth of A.C. 3·68 mm.		True depth of A.C. 3·3 mm.	
Accommodation in dioptres	Radius of lens surface in mm.	Accommodation in dioptres	Radius of lens surface in mm.
1	11·62	1	12·0
2	10·58	3	10·06
2·5	9·90	4	9·2
3·5	9·19	5	8·5
5·0	8·50	6	7·6
6·0	7·80	8	6·2
7·0	7·55	9	5·5
9·0	6·90	10	5·0

Reverting to the schematic eye and the theory of cardinal points, it is clear that because of the alterations in the curvature of the surfaces of the lens and of its refractive index, any optical simplification of the accommodated eye will differ significantly from that of the unaccommodated. The differences between the two are seen in Table XV, from which it will be seen that the principal points become shifted towards the retina during accommodation. There is necessarily a shortening of the focal lengths to correspond to the increase in power of the eye, which in a young emmetropic adult may rise from approximately 60 D in the unaccommodated state to approximately 70 D in maximal accommodation; this increase is due to an increase in the power of the lens from under 20 D to more than 30 D.

Other optical changes occur on accommodation. Since the size of the retinal image is related to the distance of the second nodal point from the retina, the visual angle subtended by the object at the nodal point increases because the nodal point(s) move away from the retina. During accommodation the size of the retinal image ought therefore to increase but, in fact, if its size in the accommodated eye is compared with that of the blurred image of the relaxed eye looking at (but not focusing) the object at the same distance, no significant difference is noticed.

[1] p. 166.

TABLE XV

	V. HELMHOLTZ		GULLSTRAND	
	Accom. Relaxed	Max. Accom.	Accom. Relaxed	Max. Accom.
Position behind ant. surf. cornea (mm.)				
Ant. surf. lens	3·6	5·6	3·6	3·2
Post. surf. lens	7·2	7·2	7·2	7·2
Ant. surf. equiv. core lens			4·146	3·8725
Post. surf. equiv. core lens			6·565	6·5275
Radius of Curvature (mm.)				
Ant. surf. lens	10·0	6·0	10·0	5·33
Post. surf. lens	−6·0	−5·5	−6·0	−5·33
Ant. surf. equiv. core lens			7·911	2·655
Post. surf. equiv. core lens			−5·76	−2·655
Refracting Power (D)				
Ant. surf. lens			5·0	9·375
Post. surf. lens			8·33	9·375
Equiv. core lens			5·985	14·96
Lens System				
Refracting power			+19·11 D	+33·06 D
Position of 1st principal pt. (mm.)			5·678	5·145
Position of 2nd principal pt.			5·808	5·255
Focal length	43·707	33·785	69·908	40·416
Complete Optical System of Eye				
Refracting power			+58·64 D	+70·57 D
Position of 1st principal pt. (mm.)	1·9403	2·0330	1·348	1·772
Position of 2nd principal pt.	2·3563	2·4919	1·602	2·086
Position of 1st focal pt.	−12·918	−11·241	−15·707	−12·397
Position of 2nd focal pt.	22·231	20·248	24·387	21·016
1st focal dist.	−14·858	−13·274	−17·055	−14·169
2nd focal dist.	19·857	17·756	22·785	18·930
Position of near point				−102·3

We have seen that the lens drops slightly during accommodation. Minor alterations are therefore to be expected in the optical axes such as a slight decrease of the angle kappa. The small nasal shift of the pupil, which occurs during the concomitant miosis, also affects the axes of the eye so that in compensation a minute temporal movement may be observed during accommodation (Auricchio, 1952). A small increase in astigmatism may also occur with a change in its axis (Hughes, 1941); cyclotorsion of the eyes during the act of accommodation might be cited as a reason for this, but O'Brien and Bannon (1947) concluded that this was insufficient to cause it and suggested that asymmetrical changes in the lens were the causal factor.

AGE CHANGES

Any theory of accommodation must account for the known decline in the ability of the eye to alter its focus as age advances—the condition known as PRESBYOPIA ($\pi\rho\acute{e}\sigma\beta\upsilon\varsigma$, old; $\overset{\circ}{\omega}\psi$, eye). We shall deal later with the optical and clinical phenomena associated with presbyopia[1]; here we must review those changes within the eye due to ageing which are relevant to the mechanism of accommodation. The lens increases in size throughout life[2]; this is due to the continuous formation of fresh fibres in the equatorial region so that a series of elementary zones is laid down in the cortex while the most aged fibres remain in the nuclear zone (Goldmann, 1937). Gullstrand's (1908) view is generally accepted that the older the lens fibres, the more rigid

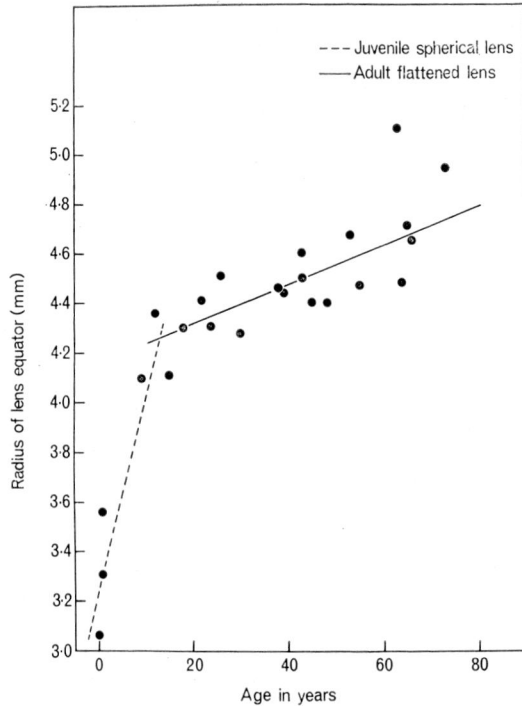

FIG. 231.—THE VARIATION OF THE RADIUS OF THE LENS AT ITS EQUATOR WITH AGE.
Average of 24 human lenses. The interrupted line indicates the rapid growth of the lens and the increase of its equatorial radius until the age of 10, thereafter the continuous line shows the slow increase throughout life (R. F. Fisher).

they become. Fisher (1969) has provided strong corroborative evidence that a considerable degree of the loss of accommodative power of the lens with increasing age is due to a decrease in the elasticity of its capsule (Fig. 231). His assessment of these changes is seen in Figs. 232–3; and in view of its decrease and the change in the shape of the lens with age, he concluded that the influence of these two factors on the effective capsular energy could account for 55% of the loss of accommodation between the ages of 16 and 60,

[1] p. 458.   [2] Vol. II, p. 320.

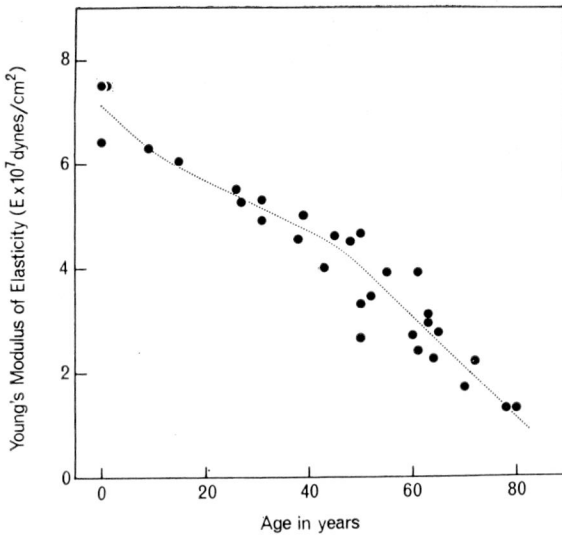

Fig. 232.—The Variation in the Elasticity of the Anterior Human Lens Capsule with Age.

Averaged for 30 human lens capsules. The ordinate indicates Young's modulus of elasticity of the central portion of the capsule, 4.0 mm. in diameter, reacting against a pressure of distension between 0 and 120 mm. Hg (R. F. Fisher).

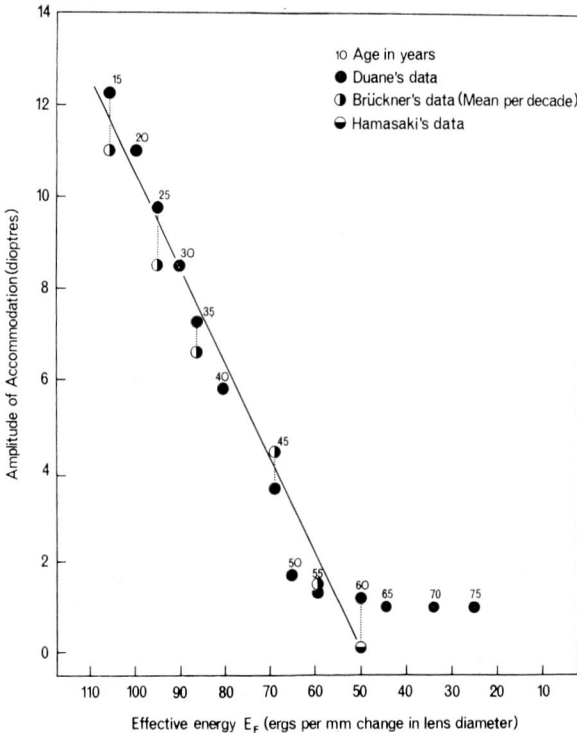

Fig. 233.—The Change of the Amplitude of Accommodation and the Effective Energy of the Lens Capsule with Age (R. F. Fisher).

assuming that the power of the ciliary muscle and the resistance of the lens itself to deformation remained constant.

The ciliary body and the ciliary muscle are also known to alter with age owing to a gradual increase in size due to the slow accumulation of fibrous tissue; this, together with the growth of the lens while the volume of the eye remains the same, may be of some significance, leading to a reduction in the circumlental space (Stieve, 1949). Little is known about the mechanical changes in the zonule with ageing, but it is reasonable to presume that the tension imparted to it by its supports, the ciliary body and the lens, must be influenced by the gradual approximation of these structures with their continual growth resulting in a relaxation of its tension. The changes in the zonule and ciliary body are, however, probably less significant than those in the lens itself, but it is obvious that these several factors add up to diminish the effectivity of accommodation in the second half of adult life.

The Theory of Accommodation

The consensus of opinion on the mechanism of accommodation derives from the theory of von Helmholtz (1855). He considered that the suspensory ligament was normally in a state of tension, and that when the ciliary muscle contracted during accommodation the ligament was relaxed, allowing the lens to assume a more spherical form by virtue of the elasticity of the capsule. This simple theory cannot stand in its original form, since it does not explain the form assumed by the anterior surface. Gullstrand (1908) therefore concluded that the intracapsular mechanism is controlled by a balance

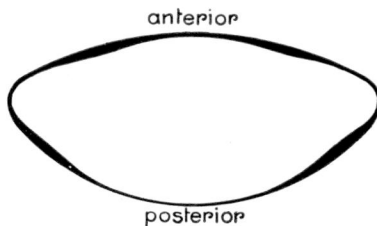

FIG. 234.—The lens capsule reconstructed from post-mortem specimens.

Relative thickness magnified 100 times (E. F. Fincham).

between the elasticity of the capsule on the one hand and the elastic pull of the suspensory ligament on the other: when the suspensory ligament relaxes, the elastic capsule, now allowed free play, moulds the cortical parts of the lens into a more spherical shape. At a later date, as we have seen, Fincham (1925) suggested that the peculiar form taken in this moulding might be due to the structure of the capsule (Fig. 234). The variations of its thickness in different parts suggest that on the application of tension a flattening of the lens would occur, preferentially in the periphery where the capsule is thickest and strongest, and a bulging in the axial region where it is weakest; O'Neill and Doyle (1968) showed that this is theoretically possible, but the tension required to produce this change was shown by Fisher (1969) to be greater than the breaking strain of the capsule. At the posterior pole the capsule is very thin, and here the maximal curvature of the lens occurs even in the unaccommodated state. Moreover, the zonular fibres running towards the posterior pole are probably little affected by the contraction of the ciliary muscle (Stuhlman, 1943) while the pull of the anterior fibres (which varies inversely as the cube of the cosine of the angle of slope) on the flatter anterior surface will be greater (Alpern, 1962).

The theory of accommodation, therefore, as elaborated by von Helmholtz, Hess, Gullstrand, and Fincham, is that on the contraction of the ciliary muscle the zonule is relaxed; this diminishes the tension on the capsule which, by virtue of its elasticity and its peculiar structure, moulds the softer cortical portions of the lens in an axipetal direction. Although the elasticity

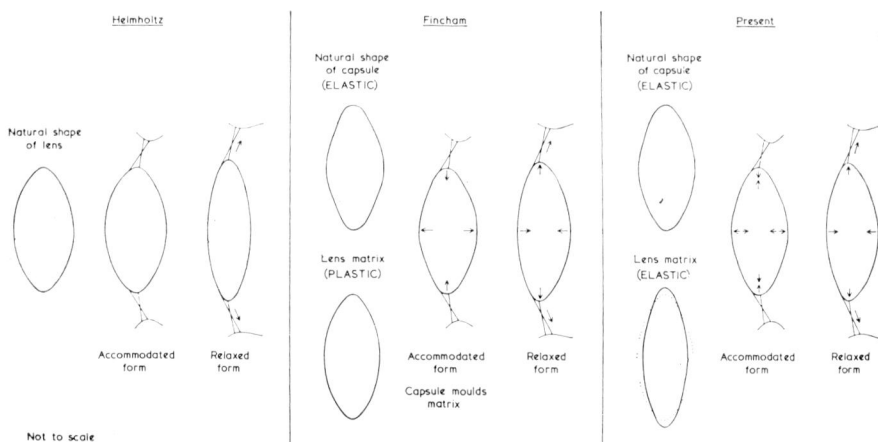

FIG. 235.—CHANGES IN THE LENS IN ACCOMMODATION.

In von Helmholtz's theory (1855) the accommodated eye assumes its natural form and in the relaxed condition it flattens owing to the pull of the suspensory ligament.

In Fincham's theory (1925) the elastic capsule imposes its natural conoidal shape on the plastic lens substance during accommodation.

In the present-day theory of Weale (1962) the elastic capsule imposes its natural conoidal shape on the lens substance which resists the elastic forces of the capsule.

of the capsule in the mechanism of accommodation is unquestioned, the crucial influence of the form of the capsule in determining the shape of the accommodated lens is less convincing. If, on the other hand, the lens is assumed to have some inherent elasticity tending to revert it to its " natural " unaccommodated state, in the act of accommodation the relief of tension on the capsule allows its elasticity to overcome that of the lens matrix so that it is moulded into the accommodated form. In the classical view of von Helmholtz, the unaccommodated lens was pulled out of its normal shape and was constantly under tension. The work of Fisher has suggested that the substance of the lens in its relaxed state assumes the form determined by its own natural elasticity, while during accommodation this is overcome by the greater elasticity of the capsule which moulds it into its accommodated form

(Fig. 235).   It is thus the accommodated lens which is under greater strain. In presbyopia the configuration of the structures of the eye, with the increase in size both of the lens and the ciliary body, lessens the effect of any pull by the zonule, while with the loss of elasticity both of the lens substance and the capsule the balance between the two is upset and the lens retains its natural (unaccommodated) form.

Two other theories should be briefly noted here.   That enthusiastically sponsored by Tscherning (1895–1907), already adumbrated by Cramer (1851), Mannhardt (1858) and Schoen (1885), relying largely on the conoidal configuration assumed by the anterior pole, claimed that contraction of the ciliary muscle tightened the zonule and compressed the vitreous against the lens, pushing forwards its anterior pole.   We have seen, however, that the evidence that the zonule slackens during accommodation is irrefutable ; moreover, there is no evidence of a rise in pressure in the vitreous and the gonioscopic observations of Burian and Allen (1955) suggest that its anterior surface becomes more relaxed (Fig. 202).

The only other theory advanced to explain the mechanism of accommodation was the bizarre *hydraulic theory* suggested by Leonard Hill (1920), Lindsay Johnson (1924) and Noiszewski (1925) ; it need be mentioned only for reasons of historical completeness. The contracting ciliary muscle was said to raise the pressure of the aqueous in the posterior chamber confined by the iris on contraction of the pupil ; this resulted in compression of the periphery of the lens and a bulging forward of its axial region.

Alpern.   Davson's *The Eye*, London, **3**, 204 (1962).

Armaly and Burian.   *Arch. Ophthal.*, **60**, 60 (1958).

Armaly and Jepson.   *Invest. Ophthal.*, **1**, 480 (1962).

Armaly and Rubin.   *Arch. Ophthal.*, **65**, 415 (1961).

Auricchio. *Boll. Oculist.*, **31**, 721 (1952).

Bárány.   *Trans. ophthal. Soc. U.K.*, **86**, 539 (1966).

Bowman.   *Lectures on the Parts concerned in the Operations on the Eye*, London, 62 (1849).

Brown.   *Amer. J. Ophthal.*, **11**, 383 (1928).

Burian and Allen.   *Arch. Ophthal.*, **54**, 66 (1955).

Burow.   *Beitr. z. Physiologie u. Physik d. mensch. Auges*, Berlin, 94 (1841).

Busacca.   *Eléments de gonioscopie*, Sao Paulo (1945).
   Ann. Oculist. (Paris), **188**, 1 (1955).

Coccius.   *VII int. Cong. Ophthal.*, Heidelberg, 197 (1888).

Cramer.   *Ned. Lancet*, **1**, 529 (1851).
   Het accommodatie-vermogen, physiologisch toegelicht, Haarlem (1853).

Descartes.   *Traité de l'homme*, Paris (1677).

Dobrowolsky.   *Klin. Mbl. Augenheilk.*, **23**, 157 (1885).

Donders.   *On the Anomalies of Accommodation and Refraction of the Eye*, London (1864).

Duke-Elder.   *Recent Adv. in Ophthal.*, 2nd ed., London, 69 (1929).

Fincham.   *Trans. opt. Soc. Lond.*, **26**, 239 (1925).

The Mechanism of Accommodation (B.J.O. Monog. No. 8), London (1937).
   Proc. roy. Soc. Med., **42**, 451 (1949).

Fisher.   *J. Physiol.*, **201**, 1, 21 (1969); in press 1970.

Gillessen.   *v. Graefes Arch. Ophthal.*, **138**, 598 (1938).

Goldmann.   *Arch. Augenheilk.*, **110**, 405 (1937).

von Graefe.   *v. Graefes Arch. Ophthal.*, **7** (2), 150 (1860).

Graves.   *Brit. med. J.*, **1**, 46 (1926).

Grossmann.   *Ophthal. Rev.*, **23**, 1 (1904).

Gullstrand.   *Kongl. svenska Vetensk. Akad. Hdl.*, **43** (2), 1 (1908).
   Hb. d. physiologischen Optik von H. v. Helmholtz, 3rd ed., Hamburg, 1 (1909).
   Einführung in d. Methoden d. Dioptrik d. Auges d. Menschen, Leipzig (1911).
   Arch. Augenheilk., **72**, 169 (1912).

von Haller.   *Elementa physiologiæ corporis humani*, Lausanne, **5**, 516 (1763).

von Helmholtz.   *Monatsber. preuss. Akad. Wiss.*, Berlin, 137 (1853).
   v. Graefes Arch. Ophthal., **1** (2), 1 (1855).
   Hb. d. physiologischen Optik, Leipzig (1856).

Hensen and Völckers.   *Exper. Untersuch. ü d. Mechanismus d. Akkommodation*, Kiel (1868).
   v. Graefes Arch. Ophthal., **19** (1), 156 (1873) ; **24** (1), 1 (1878).

Hess.   *Ber. dtsch. ophthal. Ges.*, **25**, 41 (1896).
   v. Graefes Arch. Ophthal., **42** (1), 288 ; (3), 249 (1896) ; **52**, 143 (1901).
   Klin. Mbl. Augenheilk., **42** (1), 309 (1904).

Hess and Neumann. *v. Graefes Arch. Ophthal.*, **38** (3), 184 (1892).

Hill. *Lancet*, **1**, 359 (1920).

de la Hire. *J. d. Sçavants*, Paris, 196, 219, 398 (1685).

Home. *Phil. Trans.*, **84**, 25 (1794); **85**, 1 (1795).

Hosack. *Phil. Trans.*, **84**, 196 (1794).

Huggert, *Acta ophthal.* (Kbh.). **24**, 43 (1946); **25**, 425 (1947); Suppl. 30 (1948); **42**, 389 (1964).

Hughes. *Arch. Ophthal.*, **26**, 742 (1941).

Hunter. *Roy. Soc. Letters and Papers, No.* 52, M5 (1793).
Phil. Trans., **84**, 21 (1794).

Ivanoff. *Optica Acta*, **3**, 47 (1956).

Jäger and Vogelsang. *Arch. Augenheilk.*, **109**, 103 (1935).

Johnson. *Arch. Ophtal.*, **41**, 746 (1924).

Kabe. *Rinsho Ganka*, **21**, 341 (1967).

Kepler. *Dioptrice*, Augsburg (1611).

Kikkawa and Sato. *Exp. Eye Res.*, **2**, 210 (1963).

Kleifeld. *Docum. ophthal.*, **10**, 132 (1956).

Koch and Fisher. *Arch. Augenheilk.*, **107**, 434 (1933).

Koomen, Tousey and Scolnik. *J. opt. Soc. Amer.*, **39**, 370 (1949).

Langenbeck. *Klin. Beitr. a. d. Gebiete d. Chirurgie u. Ophthal.*, Göttingen (1849).

van Leeuwenhoek. *Phil. Trans.*, **14**, 791 (1684).

Libby. *Ann. Ophthal.*, **19**, 245 (1910).

Listing. Wagner's *Handwörterbuch d. Physiologie*, Braunschweig, **4**, 498 (1853).

Lobé. *Dissertatio de oculo humano, Lugd. Batav.*, 119 (1742).

Magendie. *Précis élémentaire d. physiologie*, Paris, **1**, 73 (1816).

Mannhardt. *v. Graefes Arch. Ophthal.*, **4** (1), 269 (1858).

Müller, J. *Zur vergl. Physiologie d. Gesichtssinnes d. Menschen u. Thiere*, Leipzig, 212 (1826).

Noiszewski. *Arch. Ophtal.*, **42**, 477 (1925).

Nordenson. *Skand. Arch. Physiol.*, **35**, 101 (1917).
Brit. J. Ophthal., **27**, 127 (1943).

O'Brien and Bannon. *Amer. J. Ophthal.*, **30**, 289 (1947).

Odqvist. *Acta ophthal.* (Kbh.), **15**, 521 (1937). *Svenska Läk.-Sällsk. Handl.*, **63**, 321 (1937).

O'Neill and Doyle. *Vision Res.*, **8**, 193 (1968).

Patnaik. *Invest. Ophthal.*, **6**, 601 (1967).

Pau. *v. Graefes Arch. Ophthal.*, **151**, 565 (1951).

von Pflugk. *Ueber d. Akkommodation d. Auges d. Taube*, Wiesbaden (1906).
v. Graefes Arch. Ophthal., **128**, 179 (1932).
Münch. med. Wschr., **79**, 2036 (1932).

Porterfield. *Treatise on the Eye, the Manner and Phenomena of Vision*, Edinb. (1759).

Purkinje. *Beobachtungen u. Versuche z. Physiologie d. Sinne*, Prague, **2**, 128 (1823).

Scheiner. *Oculus hoc est: fundamentum opticum*, Oeniponti, 13 (1619).

Schoen. *v. Graefes Arch. Ophthal.*, **31** (4), 1 (1885).

Stieve. *Anat. Anz.*, **97**, 69 (1949).

Story. *Trans. ophthal. Soc. U.K.*, **44**, 413 (1924).

Stuhlman. *Introduction to Biophysics*, N.Y., 107 (1943).

Sturm, J. C. *Dissertatio de presbyopia et myopia*, Altdorfii (1697).

Sturm, J. C. F. *C.R. Acad. Sci.* (Paris), **20** 554, 761, 1238 (1845).

Treviranus. *Beitr z. Anatomie u. Physiologie d. Sinneswerkzeuge d. Menschen u. d. Thiere*, Bremen, **1**, 46 (1828).

Tscherning. *Arch. Physiol. norm. path.*, **4**, 158 (1892); **6**, 40 (1894); **7**, 181 (1895). *Optique physiologique*, Paris (1898). *J. Physiol.* (Paris), **1**, 312 (1899). *Trans. opt. Soc. Lond.* **9**, 1 (1907).

Vogelsang. *Arch. Augenheilk.*, **108**, 565 (1934).

Vogt. *Klin. Mbl. Augenheilk.*, **72**, 412 (1924).

Weale. *Brit. J. Ophthal.*, **46**, 660 (1962).

Winslow. *Exposition anatomique de la structure du corps humain*, Paris (1732).

Wintringham. *An Experimental Enquiry on some Parts of the Animal Structure*, London, 256 (1740).

Young. *Phil. Trans.*, **83**, 169 (1793); **91**, 23 (1801).

The Neurophysiology of Accommodation

An alteration in the state of accommodation of the eye may be considered as a reflex response to a particular visual situation; it cannot be induced except indirectly when it is stimulated by a voluntary act of convergence. In this, as in other reflex arcs, we find a sensory element, a central neuronal organization and a motor or effector limb. In addition to this, motor activity of other kinds is associated with accommodation involving changes in the pupil and in the extra-ocular muscles. We shall now consider the reflex arc and the interrelationship of accommodation and these other motor phenomena.

THE STIMULUS TO ACCOMMODATION

In viewing a near object the stimulus to accommodate is produced by the interplay of several factors. Among these are the changes in the retinal image, the movement of the object of regard, its apparent size and apparent distance as well as binocular influences; clearly, the higher cerebral functions must be implicated, particularly the mechanism of attention.

The mechanism and interrelation of these have not yet been completely clarified but some analysis has been experimentally attempted. Blurring of the retinal image when the focal point recedes behind the retina is certainly of importance. This can be observed with the optometer, an instrument which allows the observer to view the image on the subject's retina. When a young emmetropic subject regards a distant object the retinal image is seen to be accurately focused; if a convergent lens is introduced into the system so that the image is focused in front of the retina, no reaction results, but on the introduction of a divergent lens the focal point recedes behind the retina and within a fraction of a second an accommodative effort brings it again into focus on the retina, to be as quickly relaxed when the lens is removed. It is interesting that it is the defocusing of the image in a particular direction that is important, not the blurring of the image by itself, for a blurring of the target which was not defocused was found by Fincham (1951) to have no such effect. Moreover, only a moderate degree of blurring acts as an effective stimulus; thus Fincham (1951) found that a degree of out-of-focus blurring greater than 1·25 D failed to produce a response.

The fact that some 60% of his subjects did not respond to this reaction when monochromatic light was used led Fincham to suggest that chromatic aberration might play a part in determining the response; we have already seen that in a hypermetropic refraction a white point-image is surrounded by a red circle and it is possible that the eye distinguishes the aberration pattern in this way. That it is not the only stimulus is seen in the facts that the response is not invariable and the defect resulting from absence of chromatic aberration can be readily compensated by teaching the subject to rely on other things (Campbell and Westheimer, 1959). Fincham (1951) also found that cessation of the scanning movements of the eyes abolished the reflex; this requirement that the image constantly traverses the central area of the retina ensures that the blur circles of the out-of-focus image fall with different degrees of obliquity on the foveal cones and suggests that their directional sensitivity in the Stiles-Crawford effect[1] is an important necessity for accommodation in achromatic conditions. As we shall see presently, the proprioceptive mechanism of convergence also shares in the stimulus. When these stimuli are reduced accommodation diminishes and in their absence it fails; thus the amplitude of accommodation diminishes with a lowering of the luminance of the background (Ferree and Rand, 1933; Alpern and David,

[1] Vol. IV, p. 577.

1958).   Indeed, the light minimum required to elicit the accommodative response is only slightly (0·25 log unit) greater than the threshold of visibility (Campbell, 1954).

PSYCHICAL STIMULI can also excite accommodation, such as apparent size, apparent distance or stereopsis.   The effect of apparent distance is well exemplified in the Pulfrich stereo-effect[1] wherein, when fusion is exercised, the bob of a swinging pendulum appears not to obey an approximately rectilinear motion but to follow an elliptical path; during the illusory approach of the bob accommodation, miosis and convergence are exercised (Fig. 236).

THE STATE OF ACCOMMODATION IN THE ABSENCE
    OF STIMULI

In the absence of the stimulus to obtain a clear retinal image a certain amount of accommodation develops in non-presbyopic eyes; this occurs in darkness when such an eye becomes myopic by about 0·5 to 1·5 D (NIGHT MYOPIA) or when no contours are imaged on the retina as in the empty space encountered in flying at high altitudes (SPACE MYOPIA).

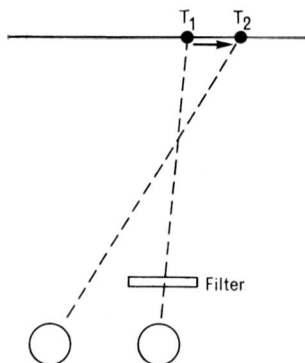

FIG.   236.—THE   PULFRICH
EFFECT.

T$_1$, a point in time when the right (occluded) eye "sees" the pendulum; T$_2$ the same for the free (left) eye. As T$_1$ precedes T$_2$, and both messages arrive at the brain simultaneously, the latter resolves the dilemma by projecting the cyclopic image to the point of intersection of the visual axes. In this manner the trajectory assumes the shape of a circle or ellipses, the horizontal axes of which are displaced beyond the objective trajectory of the pendulum (R. A. Weale).

The history of night myopia dates back to the astronomers who observed that they could not readily see small stars in the dark.   While this phenomenon must have been noticed by many observers its discovery has usually been ascribed to Lord Rayleigh but, as Levene (1965) pointed out, the first record was made by Nevil Maskelyne (1789) (Fig. 380) who found that his normal myopic correction had to be increased by 1·0 D when working at night. This fact was corroborated by William Kitchener (1824), a wealthy eccentric whose hobbies were optics, cookery and music, and was paralleled by the observations of Sir William Herschel (1800) in England and E. S. Holden (1881) in America on the ability of telescopes to penetrate into space at night.   The phenomenon was investigated by Lord Rayleigh (1883-85) who, independently of Maskelyne's discovery, described how he became short-sighted when in a dark room.   Thereafter several observers studied the problem, such as Jackson (1888), the first to introduce it into ophthalmic literature, and Schoute (1903), but it was not until and after the second World War when the problems of flying by night became important that general interest was aroused.[2]

At the same time, similar difficulties became evident to aviators flying at high altitudes during the day and it was realized that night myopia was merely a special

[1] Vol. IV, p. 704.

[2] Otero and Duran (1941), Palacios (1944), Wald and Griffin (1947), Ivanoff (1947), Schoen (1950), Bouman and van den Brink (1952), Márquez (1952), Knoll (1952), Koomen et al. (1953), Campbell (1953), Chin and Horn (1956), Williamson-Noble (1956), Alpern and David (1958), Jenkins (1963), Arriaga and Cantullera (1967), and others.

instance of the increase in accommodation which resulted when no contours were imaged on the retina (space myopia) (Whiteside, 1952; Whiteside and Campbell, 1953; Westheimer, 1957). A myopia of the same type, averaging from $-1\cdot4$ to $-2\cdot5$ D, may be induced when looking into a microscope (*instrument myopia*) (Shimojima *et al.*, 1967; Schober, 1967).

The change in curvature of the lens in night myopia was shown by Campbell (1954) to be due to the act of accommodation by photographing the Purkinje images in total darkness, but its occurrence is not due entirely to this. Of the other factors which contribute to the total effect, mention should be made of the influence of chromatic aberration (as was first suggested by Maskelyne, 1789) associated with the Purkinje shift in spectral sensitivity due to the change from cone to rod vision,[1] spherical aberration resulting from the increased size of the pupil, and the Stiles-Crawford effect concerning the directional sensitivity of the retinal cones.[2] It is interesting that, as with other accommodative efforts, night myopia is associated with convergence although the two changes are not strictly correlated in complete darkness (Ivanoff, 1946) and with miosis (Weale, 1960; Mellerio, 1966), together with a disintegration of the near reflex (Fincham, 1962). In general, however, the amplitude of accommodation is considerably reduced in the dark[3]; not only is there an approach of the far point but also a recession of the near point, thus inducing a *night presbyopia*. Finally, as suggested by Weale (1960), in the dark or in an environment without contours as in a mist, vision is naturally centred at about arm's length.

The phenomenon of night myopia is to be distinguished from NIGHT ASTIGMATISM which is attributable to the use of the paramacular region of the retina with its high capacity for adaptation, so that with this angle of view the visual axis makes a larger angle with the optic axis than in foveal photopic vision (Aguilar and Yunta, 1952).

THE TEMPORAL CHARACTERISTICS OF THE RESPONSE

When the stimulus to accommodate has been received by the retina the time-reactions of the response during which the retinal stimulus is analyzed and the response initiated are remarkably short, although not as short as other visual reflexes (Robertson, 1937; Kirchhof, 1940; Allen, 1956). When the object of regard is approximated to the eye, Campbell and Westheimer (1960), using an optometric method, found that the latent period was $0\cdot36 \pm 0\cdot089$ sec. (Fig. 237); the reaction-time for a change from a near to a far stimulus is somewhat longer, averaging $0\cdot38 \pm 0\cdot08$. According to these measurements the reaction-time for accommodation is thus considerably longer than the miotic response to a near target ($0\cdot26$ sec., Kawahata, 1954), twice as long as that for a fusional vergence movement ($0\cdot20$ sec., Westheimer

[1] Vol. IV, p. 524.
[2] Palacios (1944), Otero (1951), Koomen *et al.* (1951), Knoll (1952), Irving (1957), Mellerio (1966), and others.
[3] Otero and Duran (1941), Cabello (1945), Ivanoff (1946), Campbell (1954), Alpern and Larson (1960).

and Mitchell, 1956) and three times as long as that for a saccadic lateral movement (Westheimer, 1954). On the other hand, taking cinephotographs of the Purkinje images, Bleichert and his associates (1960) found a slightly shorter latent period of 0·2 to 0·25 second. When a single response is measured the velocity of the response to a change of 2 D is about 10 D per sec. and the time which elapses between the onset of the stimulus and the attainment of a reasonably steady level of accommodation is about 1 second (Campbell and Westheimer, 1960) or 1·7 sec. (Bleichert et al., 1960). When the target is moved slowly so that the process of defocusing is gradual, the

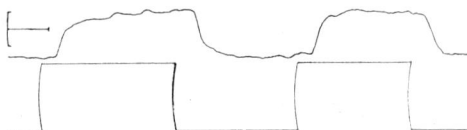

FIG. 237.—SINGLE-SWEEP ACCOMMODATIVE RESPONSES.

Record of accommodative responses to a 2 D step stimulus and return to zero level of accommodation. Allowance should be made for the arc of the pen. Top line, accommodation (length of horizontal line, 1 sec.; height of arc, 1 D); upward movement represents far-to-near accommodation. Bottom line, stimulus signal, same scale (F. W. Campbell and G. Westheimer).

accommodation does not change continuously but in oscillatory fluctuations so that the extent of the response is not always correct and may even temporarily err in the wrong direction (Kirchhof, 1940; Westheimer, 1954).

OSCILLATIONS IN ACCOMMODATION

As was pointed out by Collins (1937), using an electronic refractometer, micro-fluctuations constantly occur in the degree of accommodation of the non-presbyopic eye. This phenomenon was extensively investigated by Arnulf and his associates (1951–55) using an elaborate ophthalmoscopic technique, by Glezer and Zagorul'ko (1955) by measuring the changes in curvature of the anterior surface of the lens, by Whiteside (1957) by cine-photography of the variations in the third Purkinje image formed by this face of the lens, and by Campbell and his co-workers (1958–59) using an infra-red photometer. The magnitude of these fluctuations is small, varying between 0·04 and 0·14 D, and they have dominant frequency components in the region of 0·5 cycle/sec. and with a large pupil about 2 cycles/sec. (Fig. 238). Campbell and his associates (1959) considered that they occurred only during accommodation and disappeared on looking at infinity or during cycloplegia, but Arnulf and his co-workers found that they were present although only to a minute degree when the accommodation was relaxed, a finding corroborated by Millodot (1968) who suggested that Campbell's negative results were due to the inherent " noise " in the apparatus. The phenomenon can be appreciated by gazing at the ring-target of von Helmholtz (1896) (Fig. 239); when the head and target are rigidly fixed a

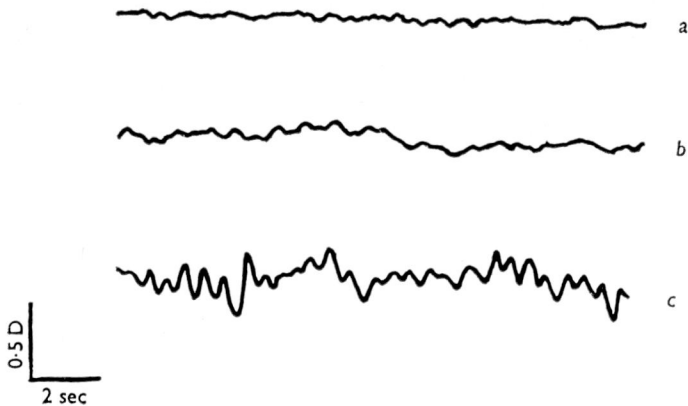

FIG. 238.—THE ACCOMMODATIVE RESPONSE.

a, the noise generated by the optometer with no subject in position. *b*, the subject viewed a small test-object placed at his optical infinity. *c*, the subject viewed a target placed at an optical distance of 1 D with a pupil of 7 mm. diameter (F. W. Campbell).

system of moving sectors is seen by a subject with reasonably active accommodation, the time-course of the oscillations corresponding to the variations in accommodation (Campbell and Robson, 1959). The phenomenon has little effect on visual acuity; only when chromatic aberration is compensated is this improved or when the micro-fluctuations are eliminated by a cycloplegic agent (Millodot, 1968).

The fluctuations in accommodation seem obviously due to the normal activity of the ciliary muscle and are comparable to the motor tremor seen in all muscles; this is seen in the eye in the constant variations in the diameter of the pupil and the movements of the globe (between saccadic movements) which prevent absolute fixation (Fig. 240). They have been electrically recorded by Swegmark (1968) with electrodes mounted on the perilimbal surface of a suction cup. In the three associated features in the act of accommodation—contraction of the ciliary muscles, miosis and convergence —similar oscillations occur. In the muscular system generally these tremors are due to the feed-back by the muscle-spindles to the central motor control in order to maintain a desired tension. In the accommodative mechanism the sensory information comes from the retina, depending on the conditions of focusing and the presence of a blurred image, although other factors are probably implicated such as the scanning movements of the eyes and the directional sensitivity of the retinal cones.

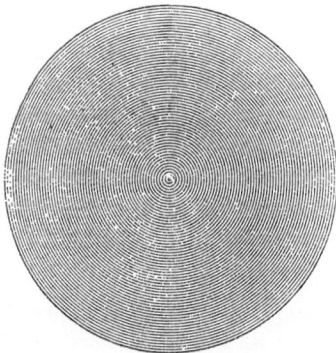

FIG. 239.—THE RING TARGET OF VON HELMHOLTZ.

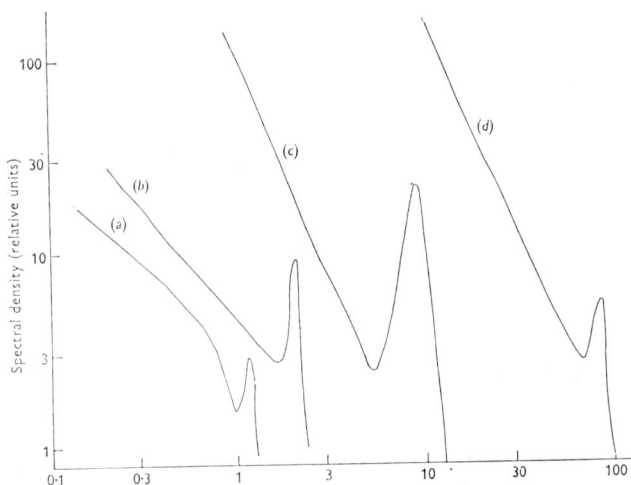

FIG. 240.—FLUCTUATIONS IN THE RANGE OF FREQUENCY OF VARIOUS
MOTOR SYSTEMS.

Cycles per sec., logarithmic co-ordinates.

(a) Pupillary diameter during steady illumination of the retina; (b) accommodation during steady viewing of a near target; (c) finger displacement during steady pointing; (d) eye-ball position during steady fixation (between saccadic movements) (F. W. Campbell).

THE NERVOUS PATHWAY

As with all autonomic activities it seems probable that accommodation is subserved by each of the two antagonistic constituents of this system, the sympathetic and the parasympathetic, the fibres of both of which are distributed over all the muscle fibres in a syncytial network; other nerve fibres travelling along the first division of the trigeminal nerve from the semilunar ganglion end as sensory bulbs in the connective tissue without contact with the muscle cells themselves.[1]

The *parasympathetic supply* is the main effector and its peripheral course has long been well known. The medullated fibres start in the paired Edinger-Westphal nuclei, lying in the central grey matter of the tegmentum immediately dorsal to the corresponding oculomotor nuclei in its rostral two-thirds[2]; this serves as the essential parasympathetic component of the oculomotor complex. By electrical stimulation of the mid-brain of the monkey in the region of the antero-median nuclear complex, Jampel and Mindel (1967) obtained accommodative changes up to 12 D, and Chin and his associates (1968) up to 28 D, changes which were diminished by the ocular instillation of homatropine and phenylephrine and enhanced by echothiopate.

The peripheral cell-station is the ciliary ganglion and perhaps in the accessory scleral ganglion of Axenfeld[3] (Morgan and Harrigan, 1951), whence

[1] Vol. II, p. 155. Agababow (1893–97), Matteucci (1947), Corrado (1948), Wolter (1953), Genís Gálvez (1957), Conrads (1959), Mawas (1959).
[2] Vol. II, p. 708.
[3] Vol. II, p. 863.

the fibres enter the globe along the short ciliary nerves. It has been generally agreed that stimulation of these fibres results in contraction of the ciliary muscle. In monkeys Törnquist (1967) found that the maximal effect was obtained by stimuli varying from 20 to 50 per second, when a change from 6 to 11 D resulted, that is, a less effective response than is obtained by pharmacological agents such as pilocarpine in the monkey (Törnquist, 1964) or in man (Fincham, 1955). The site or sites of the supranuclear connections of this pathway are unknown; but Jampel (1959) obtained a bilateral increase in accommodation, miosis and convergence on faradic stimulation of area 19 of the occipital cortex in monkeys.

The *sympathetic supply* travels with the other sympathetic fibres to the head in the cervical sympathetic trunk through a synapse at the superior cervical ganglion, along the internal carotid plexus and to the eye mainly by the long ciliary nerves (Morgan, 1944) with perhaps a subsidiary route along the short ciliary nerves through the ciliary ganglion (Wolff, 1933; Morgan, 1944). The role it plays in accommodation, however, was not recognized by the classical writers, although an action of relaxing accommodation was suggested by Jessop (1888) and Morat and Doyon (1891) as a result of their observations on the stimulation of the cervical sympathetic nerve. For half a century controversy continued, but experimental and clinical observations eventually clarified the matter.

It has been shown in the cat, the rabbit and the dog that stimulation of the peripheral end of the cut sympathetic nerve or the superior cervical ganglion gives a marked flattening of the lens and an increase in hypermetropia as measured by retinoscopy and photography of the Purkinje images, whether the eye is atropinized or not, whether the IIIrd nerve is cut or intact, and when the effects of pressure on the globe are eliminated by cutting the extrinsic ocular muscles. In these lower animals the sympathetic stimulation has a greater effect than in monkeys (Olmsted, 1944; Törnquist, 1967), a difference possibly due to the greater α-adrenergic innervation[1] in the former (van Alphen *et al.*, 1965). Removal of the superior cervical sympathetic ganglion in the cat involves a permanent decrease in hypermetropia, and stimulation of the oculomotor nerve causes myopia whether the sympathetic is cut or not (Morgan and Olmsted, 1939; Olmsted and Morgan, 1939–41; Morgan *et al.*, 1940). A sudden hypermetropic change has also been found to follow a sensory excitatory stimulus in the eye of the rabbit and of man (Olmsted and Morgan, 1941).

From the pharmacological point of view, Graves (1926) showed that in a patient in whom the lens was absorbed after an injury but in whom the capsule remained intact,[2] the latter became relatively taut on looking in the distance and quite taut after the instillation of cocaine. Moreover, Poos (1928) found that the instillation of adrenaline had no reaction in the normal eye but decreased the accommodation when the sympathetic was paralyzed; this is an action exactly comparable with the paradoxical dilatation of the pupil with adrenaline. He noted that cocaine affected the normal iris and ciliary body equally. Heath (1936), Cogan (1937), Siebeck (1953) and Biggs and his associates (1959) also found that sympathomimetic drugs opposed accommodation for near vision.

From the clinical point of view, it has been shown that in Horner's syndrome wherein the sympathetic is paralyzed the accommodation becomes unequal, the near-

[1] Vol. IV, p. 67. [2] p. 169.

point being from 1 to 4 cm. closer on the affected side than on the normal (Cobb and
Scarlett, 1920; Cogan, 1937). A similar effect was found after blockade of the superior
cervical ganglion by procaine in man (Dybicka, 1963). Conversely, there is evidence
that irritation of the sympathetic (Cogan, 1937), or its over-activity in hyperthyroidism
(Grancher, 1880), tends to make the near-point recede and renders close work difficult to
sustain without strain.

The mechanism of the sympathetic influence has given rise to controversy.
It was thought at one time that the parasympathetic determined accommodation for near vision by causing contraction of the circular fibres of the
ciliary muscle (Müller's muscle), while the sympathetic contracted the
meridional fibres (Brücke's muscle) so that an active accommodation for
distant vision was effected. On the other hand, Morgan (1946) suggested
that the sympathetic, which is also a vasoconstrictor, acted by decreasing
the blood-content of the ciliary body and therefore its volume so that the
tension on the zonule was increased. Although some corroborative experimental evidence was provided by Fleming (1957–59) and White and Wood
(1962) that on sympathetic stimulation the changes in refraction ran parallel
with the vascularity both of the ciliary body and the ear, the fact that in the
enucleated eye sympathomimetic drugs (Meesmann, 1952) or the direct
stimulation of the long ciliary nerves (Melton *et al.*, 1955) induces accommodative changes, proves that the effect is not entirely circulatory. Moreover, the distribution of both types of nerve to all the fibres of the muscle
suggests that, as in other autonomic activities, there is an overall mutually
antagonistic neural activity comprised of a dominant parasympathetic
mechanism focusing for near vision and a subsidiary sympathetic mechanism
focusing for distant vision.

The extent of the role played by the sympathetic, however, should not be
exaggerated. The evidence in favour of such a role in man and certain other
species is reasonably convincing, but the experiments on the monkey by
Törnquist (1966–67) which showed that stimulation of the sympathetic
against a background of parasympathetic activity produced only a slight and
tardy effect indicate that the sympathetic plays only a minor part in the
control of accommodation.

Agababow. *Anat. Anz.*, **8**, 555 (1893).
  Int. Mschr. Anat. Physiol., **14**, 53 (1897).
Aguilar and Yunta. *An. Fis. Quim. A*, **48**,
  244 (1952).
Allen. *Amer. J. Optom.*, **33**, 201 (1956).
Alpern and David. *Industr. Med. Surg.*, **27**,
  551 (1958).
Alpern and Larson. *Amer. J. Ophthal.*, **49**,
  1140 (1960).
van Alphen, Kern and Robinette. *Arch.
  Ophthal.*, **74**, 253 (1965).
Arnulf and Dupuy. *Rev. Opt.* (Paris), **39**,
  195 (1960).
Arnulf, Dupuy and Flamant. *C.R. Acad.
  Sci.* (Paris), **232**, 349, 438 (1951).
  Ann. Opt. Ocul., **3**, 109 (1955).

Arriaga Cantullera. *Arch. Soc. oftal. hisp-
  amer.*, **27**, 927 (1967).
Biggs, Alpern and Bennett. *Amer. J.
  Ophthal.*, **48** (2), 169 (1959).
Bleichert, Wagner and Kobor. *Pflügers
  Arch. ges. Physiol.*, **272**, 22 (1960).
Bouman and van den Brink. *Ophthalmo-
  logica*, **123**, 100 (1952).
Cabello. *An. Fis. Quim. A*, **41**, 439, 449
  (1945).
Campbell. *J. opt. Soc. Amer.*, **43**, 925 (1953);
  50, 738 (1960).
  Brit. orthop. J., **11**, 13 (1954).
  J. Physiol., **123**, 357 (1954).
  Brit. J. physiol. Opt., **16**, 188 (1959).

Campbell and Robson. *J. opt. Soc. Amer.*, **49**, 268 (1959).

Campbell, Robson and Westheimer. *J. Physiol.*, **145**, 579 (1959).

Campbell and Westheimer. *J. opt. Soc. Amer.*, **49**, 568 (1959).
J. Physiol., **151**, 285 (1960).

Campbell, Westheimer and Robson. *J. opt. Soc. Amer.*, **48**, 669 (1958).

Chin and Horn. *J. opt. Soc. Amer.*, **46**, 60 (1956).

Chin, Ishikawa, Lappin *et al. Invest. Ophthal.*, **7**, 386 (1968).

Cobb and Scarlett. *Arch. Neurol. Psychiat.* (Chic.), **3**, 636 (1920).

Cogan. *Arch. Ophthal.*, **18**, 739 (1937).

Collins. *Brit. J. physiol. Opt.*, **1**, 30 (1937).

Conrads. *v. Graefes Arch. Ophthal.*, **161**, 214 (1959).

Corrado. *Ann. Ottal.*, **74**, 148 (1948).

Dybicka. *Klin. oczna*, **33**, 141 (1963).

Ferree and Rand. *Trans. illum. Engng. Soc.*, **58**, 590 (1933).

Fincham. *Brit. J. Ophthal.*, **35**, 381 (1951).
J. Physiol., **128**, 99 (1955).
Vision Res., **1**, 425 (1962).

Fleming. *Amer. J. Ophthal.*, **43**, 789 (1957); **47**, 585 (1959).

Genís Gálvez. *Anat. Rec.*, **127**, 219 (1957).

Glezer and Zagorul'ko. *Fiziol. Zh.*, **41**, 830 (1955).

Grancher. *Gaz. Hôp. Paris*, **53**, 1060 (1880).

Graves. *Brit. med. J.*, **1**, 46 (1926).

Heath. *Arch. Ophthal.*, **16**, 839 (1936).

von Helmholtz. *Hb. d. physiol. Optik.*, Leipzig, **1** (1856); 2nd ed., Hamburg, 175 (1896).

Herschel. *Phil. Trans.*, **90**, 67 (1800).

Holden. *Amer. J. Sci.*, **22**, 129 (1881).

Irving. *Ametropia at Low Illuminations* (Thesis), Manchester (1957).

Ivanoff. *C.R. Acad. Sci.* (Paris), **223**, 1027 (1946).
J. opt. Soc. Amer., **37**, 730 (1947).

Jackson. *Trans. Amer. ophthal. Soc.*, **5**, 141 (1888).

Jampel. *Amer. J. Ophthal.*, **48** (2), 573 (1959).

Jampel and Mindel. *Invest. Ophthal.*, **6**, 40 (1967).

Jenkins. *Brit. J. physiol. Opt.*, **20**, 188 (1963).

Jessop. *VII int. Cong. Ophthal.*, Heidelberg, 188 (1888).

Kawahata. *Acta Soc. ophthal. jap.*, **58**, 841 (1954).

Kirchhof. *Z. Biol.*, **100**, 408 (1940).

Kitchener. *Economy of the Eyes. . . .*, London, 101 (1824).

Knoll. *Amer. J. Optom.*, Monog. 131 (1952).

Koomen, Scolnik and Tousey. *J. opt. Soc. Amer.*, **41**, 80 (1951); **43**, 27 (1953).

Levene. *Notes and Records, Roy. Soc.*, London, **20**, 100 (1965).

Márquez. *IV Cong. Pan-Amer. Oftal.*, **2**, 1020 (1952).

Maskelyne. *Phil. Trans.*, **79**, 258 (1789).

Matteucci. *Ophthalmologica*, **114**, 377 (1947).

Mawas. *Bull. Soc. franç. Ophtal.*, **72**, 45 (1959).

Meesmann. *v. Graefes Arch. Ophthal.*, **152**, 335 (1952).

Mellerio. *Vision Res.*, **6**, 217 (1966).

Melton, Purnell and Brecher. *Amer. J. Ophthal.*, **40** (2), 155 (1955).

Millodot. *Vision Res.*, **8**, 73 (1968).

Morat and Doyon. *Arch. Physiol.* (Paris), **3**, 507 (1891).

Morgan. *Amer. J. Optom.*, **21**, 87 (1944); **23**, 99 (1946).

Morgan and Harrigan. *Amer. J. Optom.*, **28**, 242 (1951).

Morgan and Olmsted. *Proc. Soc. exp. Biol.* (N.Y.), **41**, 303; **42**, 612 (1939).

Morgan, Olmsted and Watrous. *Amer. J. Physiol.*, **128**, 588 (1940).

Olmsted. *J. nerv. ment. Dis.*, **99**, 794 (1944).

Olmsted and Morgan. *Amer. J. Physiol.*, **127**, 602 (1939); **133**, 720 (1941).

Otero. *J. opt. Soc. Amer.*, **41**, 942 (1951)

Otero and Duran. *An. Fis. Quim. A*, **37**, 459 (1941).

Palacios. *Port. phys.*, **1–2**, 47 (1944).

Poos. *Klin. Mbl. Augenheilk.*, **80**, 749 (1928).

Rayleigh. *Proc. Camb. phil. Soc.*, **4**, 324 (1883).
Nature (Lond.), **31**, 340 (1885).

Robertson. *Arch. Ophthal.*, **17**, 859 (1937).

Schober, Dehler and Kassel. *Ber. dtsch. ophthal.*, **68**, 299 (1967).

Schoen. *Amer. J. Optom.*, **27**, 88 (1950).

Schoute. *Ann. Oculist.* (Paris), **129**, 276 (1903).

Shimojima. *Rinsho Ganka*, **21**, 985 (1967).

Shimojima, Yamashita and Nishi. *Rinsho Ganka*, **21**, 991 (1967).

Siebeck. *v. Graefes Arch. Ophthal.*, **153**, 425, 438 (1953).

Swegmark. *Acta. ophthal.* (Kbh.) **46**, 580 (1968).

Törnquist. *Invest. Ophthal.*, **3**, 388 (1964); **6**, 612 (1967).
Acta physiol. scand., **67**, 363 (1966).

Wald and Griffin. *J. opt. Soc. Amer.*, **37**, 321 (1947).

Weale. *The Eye and its Function*, London, 144 (1960).

Westheimer. *Arch. Ophthal.*, **52**, 710, 932 (1954).
J. opt. Soc. Amer., **47**, 714 (1957).

Westheimer and Mitchell. *Arch. Ophthal.*, **55**, 848 (1956).

White and Wood. *Amer. J. Physiol.*, **202**, 495 (1962).

Whiteside. *J. Physiol.*, **118**, 65P (1952).
Problems of Vision in Flight at High Altitudes, London, 153 (1957).

Whiteside and Campbell. *Gt. Brit. Flying Pers. Res. Comm.*, F.R.R.C. 821 (1953).

Williamson-Noble. *Trans. ophthal. Soc. U.K.*, **76**, 633 (1956).

Wolff. *Anatomy of the Eye and Orbit*, London, 173 (1933).

Wolter. *Ber. dtsch. ophthal. Ges.*, **58**, 327 (1953).

THE EFFECTOR MECHANISM

We have seen that the essential factor in accommodation is a contraction of the ciliary muscle which determines a change in shape of the lens; this is a reflex act carried out without conscious effort. With it, however, two phenomena are associated which, although not necessarily accompanying it on all occasions or to the same degree, usually act in concert with it—a contraction of the pupil and convergence. Such an associated action has been called a *synkinesis* (σύν, with; κίνησις, movement), and together the three factors constitute the *near reaction*. We have also shown that the stimulus to accommodation is a change in the vergence of the light; if, however, an object approaches the eyes in the mid-line the images must move temporally from each fovea; this provides the stimulus for convergence in binocular accommodation. The contraction of the pupil in the near reflex is also a reflex act and the configuration of the oculomotor nucleus suggests that all three functions are closely related, although the association of the three is not so intimate as to constitute a single reflex. Some authorities have suggested that there is a fixed relationship between convergence and accommodation[1] but, although the relationship between them is intimate, a certain degree of elasticity exists; this is probably determined largely by accommodation which admits a considerable degree of adjustment for the attainment of clear vision so that, for example, the hypermetrope can exert a higher degree of accommodation than convergence in order to see a near object clearly and at the same time direct his visual axes onto the object. Even so, an innate relationship exists to some extent for such a hypermetrope may develop a convergent (accommodative) squint, and it is the conditioned correction in mutual adjustment that the orthoptist hopes to improve by fusional exercises. Of the two functions, clear vision and binocularity, the former and older is of more practical significance and therefore takes precedence over the later acquired and more plastic function of convergence.

CILIARY CONTRACTION

Although contraction of the ciliary muscle primarily determines the physical act of accommodation, it is obvious that its attainment involves two factors—the ease with which the lens can change its shape and the power of the ciliary muscle to bring this about[2]. If the shape of the lens cannot alter, accommodation cannot be effected by the muscle no matter how strong it is and, conversely, the contraction of a weak or paralysed muscle will not be able to induce effective changes in the lens however normal its physical properties. E. Fuchs (1922) drew attention to this double consideration, and differentiated the two influences as PHYSICAL and PHYSIOLOGICAL ACCOMMODATION. Physical accommodation is measured in dioptres; Flieringa

[1] Maddox (1886), Ames and Gliddon (1928), Ogle and Prangen (1951), Morgan (1952), and others.
[2] See Vol. II, p. 149 for the anatomy of the ciliary muscle.

(1923) introduced the convenient term MYODIOPTRE as a unit of the physiological component and suggested that it should express the contractile power
of the ciliary muscle necessary to raise the refractive power of the lens by one
dioptre. A decrease in the physical accommodation is evident in presbyopia ;
a diminution in the physiological power of the muscle may come on in states
of debility at any age and, in the opinion of Fuchs (1922) and Jackson (1922),
since an attempt is made to overcome its deficiencies by a sustained and
exaggerated ciliary effort, such a weakness may be responsible for the
illusion of micropsia, delay in optical adjustment, and the distressing
symptoms of asthenopia and eye-strain.

The distinction between the contraction of the ciliary muscle and the
actual response of the lens becomes especially important in consideration of
presbyopia because of the alteration in the physical properties of the lens.
The accurate measurement of these physical properties of the lens at various
ages is obviously necessary before we are able to evaluate the relative
importance in presbyopia of the lens itself and of the muscular contraction.
The assessment of the degree of shortening of the ciliary muscle is far from
being a straightforward matter because it must depend either on the response
of the lens or on some phenomenon associated with accommodation. As far
as the first factor is concerned, difficulties have arisen for two reasons. While
a contraction of the ciliary muscle and the alteration in the shape of the lens
are closely related, an experiment which uses one as the index of the other
may give equivocal results. Secondly, in many experiments the assessment
of the degree of accommodation in man has depended upon subjective
responses which may be unreliable either because of binocular influences[1]
or because of the depth of focus of the eye ; indeed, objective measurements
of the degree of accommodation obtained by optometry or stigmatoscopy
indicate the unreliability of some subjective responses.

Again, in assessing the activity of the ciliary muscle, the phenomena
associated with accommodation, convergence and miosis, have been assumed
to parallel closely the events in the ciliary body. But even if the innervational stimuli to the ciliary muscle and to those associated muscular structures are parallel, there is no guarantee that the response of the ciliary muscle
or of the ciliary body will always be the same. For example, the nature of the
relationship between accommodation and convergence is extremely complex
because, although these two functions are interconnected, each is subject to
other influences. Convergence is only one of a multiplicity of factors which
make up the stimulus to accommodation and, conversely, the stimulus to
convergence does not derive entirely from accommodation even although it is
probable that the response of the former to a change in accommodation is the
more stable interrelationship between these two functions (Flom, 1960).

We have already noted that by the electrical stimulation of the eyes of
animals, Cramer (1851) showed that the lenticular response was due to

[1] p. 197.

muscular action.   The recording of the muscular contraction is, however, difficult to interpret.   By incorporating electrodes into the shell of a contact lens posterior to the limbus, Schubert (1955), Bornschein and Schubert (1957) and Alpern and his colleagues (1958) showed that there is a shift of potential on accommodating from far to near or in the reverse direction.   The last experimenters eliminated the movements of the musculature of the iris in their experiments and the movements of the eye, but that the effect was entirely due to the activity of the ciliary muscle has not yet been proved.

MIOSIS

The contraction of the pupil on accommodation, the *near reflex* first observed by Scheiner (1619), serves several functions.   The diminution of the aperture of the system lessens optical aberrations and eliminates those

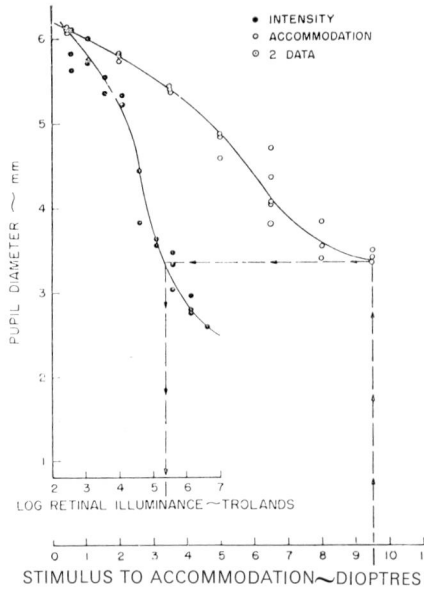

FIG. 241.—Diameter of the pupil under various stimulus intensities of light exposed to the contralateral eye and under various stimuli to accommodation. The intensity of the light required to give the same degree of pupillary constriction as the maximum change in the stimulus to accommodation is recorded by the pattern of the dotted line. It is equal to 4×10^5 trolands of retinal illuminance (after M. Alpern *et al.*).

associated with the periphery, cuts down the relative increase of light entering the eye from near objects and increases the depth of focus; in fact, before the invention of spectacles this contraction of the pupil afforded the only relief against the disadvantages of presbyopia.   The stimulus for pupillary contraction is associated with the increased innervation for accommodation and does not necessarily parallel the physical accomplishment of accommodation; thus Alpern and his associates (1958) found that in a subject whose maximal accommodation-response was 6 D, the pupil still diminished in size when the accommodation-stimulus was increased to 9·5 D (Fig. 241). The miosis thus induced, however, is not the total contraction available; these workers found that the smallest pupil thus obtainable can be still further contracted by shining a bright light into the contralateral eye, while the degree of miosis varies with the luminance even although the change in the stimulus for accommodation remains constant (Roth, 1969).

The near reflex is elicited in the macaque by stimulation of Brodmann's cortical areas 19 and 22 (Jampel, 1959)[1]; but Schubert and Burian's (1936) claim that a *fusion reaction* occurs whereby miosis accompanies fusion of the two retinal images was not confirmed by Marg and Morgan (1950) using a well-controlled haploscopic technique.

CONVERGENCE

When the eyes regard a near object the visual axes must be directed upon it if single binocular vision is to be retained. The unit of convergence is conventionally taken as the *metre angle* (m.a.), the amount normally required to converge upon an object 1 metre away. It therefore follows, since the amount of accommodation normally required for vision at a distance of 1 metre is 1 D, that the amount of accommodation expressed in dioptres is equal to the amount of convergence expressed in metre angles.

It is obvious that accommodation and convergence should work, if not exactly hand in hand, at least in harmony. It follows that when the visual axes are stimulated to converge, accommodation is induced; this is called CONVERGENT ACCOMMODATION, and it can occur as a reflex without the stimulus of a change in the vergence of the light (Fincham and Walton, 1957). Conversely, if one eye is made to accommodate, convergence occurs; this is referred to as ACCOMMODATIVE CONVERGENCE.

Although the two functions of accommodation and convergence are normally closely but elastically related, either can be exercised separately. Thus an object can be seen distinctly by an emmetrope if either the accommodation or the convergence is altered by placing weak spherical lenses or prisms respectively before the eyes, thus disturbing the balance between the two functions. Again, convergence continues although the accommodation has failed in the presbyope or if the ciliary muscle has been paralysed by atropine; moreover, we shall see[2] that the hypermetrope has continually to use his accommodation in excess of his convergence and the myope his convergence in excess of his accommodation. The amount of dissociation which is possible is not, however, unlimited, and the effort to dissociate the two may give rise to considerable distress and, indeed, the necessary amount of dissociation may on occasion be impossible to attain. The amount of accommodation which it is possible to exert while the convergence remains fixed is called the RELATIVE ACCOMMODATION; the amount in excess

[1] Vol. II, p. 872.　　　[2] p. 258.

of the convergence is called *positive*, that below, *negative*. The relation between these will be made clear from Fig. 242.

The subject is emmetropic, and has his far point (R) at infinity and his near point (P) at 10 cm. Suppose he looks at an object (A) situated 33 cm. away, he will then be exercising 3 D of accommodation and 3 m.a. of convergence. Concave lenses are now placed in front of his eyes until the object begins to be blurred; if this occurs with − 3 D lenses he has augmented his accommodation from 3 to 6 D, and his relative near point (P′) is at a distance equivalent to 6 D, that is, at 17 cm. Convex lenses are now substituted for the concave, and it is found that the image begins to be blurred when lenses of 2 D are presented. He has thus relaxed his accommodation by 2 D, that is, from 3 to 1 D, and his relative far point (R′) is at a distance from the eye equivalent to 1 D, that is, 1 metre. For 3 m.a. of convergence, therefore, the relative far point is at 1 metre, the relative near point is at 17 cm., the relative range of accommodation is 83 cm. (R′P′), of which 67 cm. (R′A) are negative and 16 cm. (AP′) positive, and the relative amplitude is 5 D (*i.e.* 6 D − 1 D), of which 2 D are negative and 3 D are positive.

It is obvious that the nearer the object is to the eye, the smaller will be the positive and the larger the negative range of accommodation. In the ultimate, if the eyes are emmetropic and the object of fixation is at infinity, there will be no negative accommodation; and conversely, if the object is at the near point, the positive moiety will have become nil. Thus *while there is one absolute far point, one absolute near point, and one absolute range of accommodation, there is a different relative far point, near point, and range for every degree of convergence.*

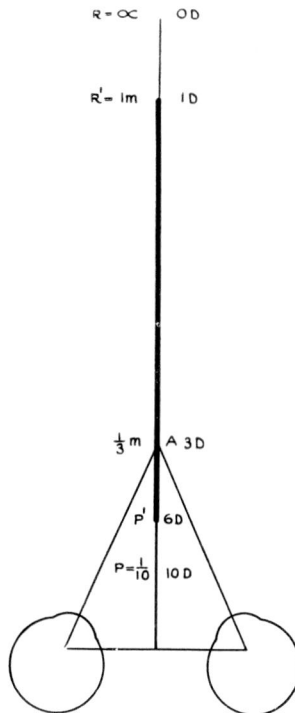

FIG. 242.—RELATIVE ACCOMMODATION.

In a similar manner, if the accommodation be kept constant, the convergence may be made to vary. The amount of convergence which can thus be exerted or relaxed is called the RELATIVE CONVERGENCE. This can be measured by accommodating for a fixed object and varying the convergence by prisms (Fig. 243). The strongest prism, base outwards, which can be tolerated without producing diplopia is a measure of the *positive* portion (B*a*) of the relative convergence (*ab*), or the amount by which the normal convergence can be augmented. Similarly, the strongest prism, base inwards, which can be borne is a measure of the *negative* portion (B*b*) of the relative convergence, and is the amount by which the convergence can be relaxed.

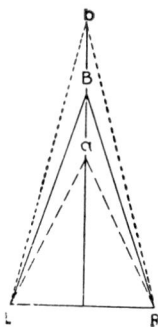

FIG. 243.—RELATIVE CONVERGENCE

Binocular Accommodation. Not only are convergence

and accommodation closely related, they also have a mutual effect. This is seen in the excess of binocular over uniocular accommodation which averages about 0·5 dioptre, and may be as high as 1·5 D.

Duane (1925) gave the following figures:

Below 17 years, excess averages				0·6 D
18 to 31	,,	,,	,,	0·5 D
32 to 53	,,	,,	,,	0·4 D
Above 52	,,	,,	,,	0·3 D

It appears to be established that this additional accommodative efficiency is due to the stimulus derived from convergence. It is not a result of the accompanying pupillary contraction, for it occurs independently of this; nor is it due to an increase in visual acuity depending upon the fusion of

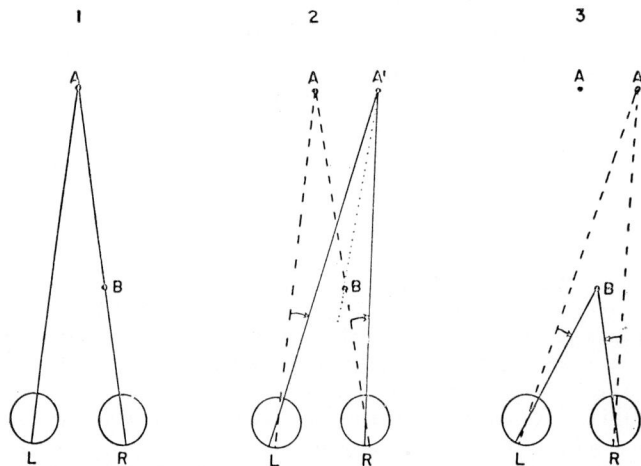

FIG. 244.—THE SEQUENCE OF MOVEMENTS IN CHANGING FIXATION.

1, binocular fixation of A; 2, conjugate lateral movement without change of convergence to A′ so that the bisector of the angle of convergence passes through B; 3, convergence movement from A′ to B.
Steps 2 and 3 are to some extent superimposed, but in view of their time-characteristics they are easily distinguished (G. Westheimer and A. Mitchell).

the images from both eyes, for the increase is as notable in patients in whom one eye is amblyopic or who have a divergent squint which allows an effort of convergence but does not permit a fusion of the two images. The two functions are closely interwoven physiologically, and it appears that their maximal efficiency can be attained only if, by working with and supplementing each other, their synkinetic action is retained.

Binocular convergence occurs if one eye is occluded or if the object is placed asymmetrically. Thus if a relatively far object (A, Fig. 244, No. 1) is placed in the midline between the two eyes and it is proposed to fixate a second object (B) in front of and nearer to the right eye, both eyes are directed to the right (A′) until the bisector of the angle of convergence includes the new fixation point (No. 2); thereafter, convergence to the new fixation point occurs (No. 3). This, however, is not a simple movement, but while convergence of the left eye towards the object occurs, the right eye takes a rapid saccadic slip outwards in association with its fellow and then turns inwards to its original position as a response to binocular convergence for B (Fig. 245) (Alpern and Wolter, 1956; Westheimer and Mitchell, 1956). If in the same circumstances the left (non-fixing) eye is occluded, no movement of the fixing eye is observed but the occluded eye converges (Alpern and Ellen, 1956).

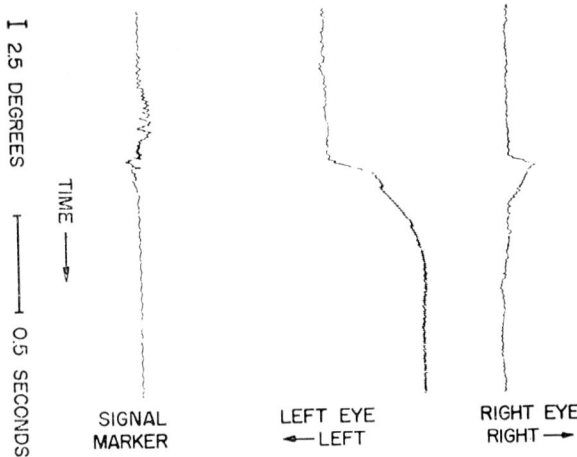

FIG. 245.—Binocular re-fixation from a far (3.4 metre) to a near (0.186 metre) vertical black line on a white background. The near vertical line was carefully aligned on the line of sight of the right eye while it fixated the far vertical line uniocularly. At the mark on the signal the near line was fixated; the movements of the two eyes were recorded by electro-oculography. While the left (covered) eye describes a movement of convergence, the right (fixing) eye makes a rapid saccadic slip outwards, as does the left, and then turns inwards to its original position (M. Alpern and J. L. Wolter).

It is to be remembered, however, that accommodation is not the only factor which may stimulate convergence. Maddox (1886–1907) differentiated three of these (Fig. 246):

(1) basic tonus, maintaining the eyes in the primary position instead of the (divergent) position of rest,

(2) accommodative convergence, demanded by accommodation,

(3) fusional convergence which maintains the position of the eye in accommodation; and to these should be added

(4) proximal convergence, induced by the sense of nearness of an object.

It is to be noted that fusional convergence need not maintain the object of regard exactly on the fovea for some positional slip is allowed with which binocular fusion can be maintained; indeed, at the fovea the corresponding areas of Panum (which have the same direction in space)[1] measure about 6 mins of arc. The difference thus allowed is called the *angle of disparity* (Ogle *et al.*, 1949–67; Ogle, 1950) which in normal

[1] Vol. IV, p. 682.

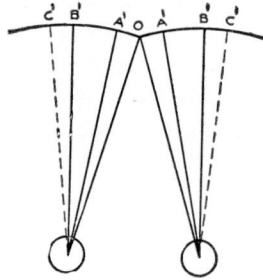

FIG. 246.—INVOLUNTARY CONVERGENCE.

The object (0) is at the near-point of convergence. At C′ the eyes are in the position of rest (usually slight divergence). At B′ they are directed straight forwards. In the total convergence to O, C′B′ is the tonic convergence, B′A′ the accommodative convergence, and A′O the fusional convergence.

people is small but is sufficient to cater for the constant micro-movements of the eye, and may be enlarged considerably if fusion is maintained in heterophoria.

Of the factors stimulating accommodation, we are concerned here only with the accommodative convergence; the other constituents are discussed in the subsequent Volume on ocular motility. Our essential interest lies in the effect an increase in accommodation has on convergence; expressed as the magnitude of the change in convergence in prism dioptres caused by an increase in accommodation expressed in dioptres, the relationship is known as the *accommodative convergence/accommodation ratio* (AC/A). In the same individual this ratio is usually remarkably constant, so that in general terms the accommodative convergence varies with the accommodative stimulus (Fincham, 1955), averaging 3·5 △/D and varying only within 0·25△ as a function of time (Flom, 1960) (Fig. 247), but in some 10% of people the relationship is not linear (Martens and Ogle, 1959; Flom, 1960). It is to be remembered, however, that a small pupillary diameter is of some importance since the consequent greater depth of focus destroys the linear relationship; only when the diameter of the pupil exceeds 1·4 mm. is the AC/A ratio independent of it (Ripps *et al.*, 1962). Conversely, the normal link between accommodation and convergence can be broken by some people in the act of voluntary convergence, an accomplishment which can be increased by training.

The ratio, however, is upset if the tone of the ciliary muscle is changed or in presbyopia. Thus cycloplegic drugs increase the ratio and miotic drugs decrease it (Christoferson and Ogle, 1956; Alpern and Larson, 1960) but in every case the reduction of accommodation relative to convergence is accompanied by a corresponding reduction in the maximal accommodation (Figs. 247–50) (Fincham, 1955). On the other hand, there is no obvious increase in the ratio with age (Alpern *et al.*, 1959).

The failure of accommodation with age has a considerable bearing on the

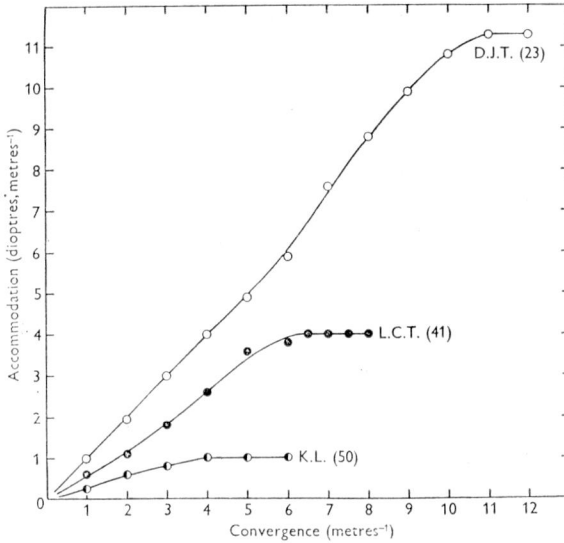

FIG. 247.—ACCOMMODATION INDUCED BY CONVERGENCE.

Results on three subjects of different ages (in brackets). Both the maximum and the rate of increase of accommodation relative to convergence become less with age. Convergence is shown in the units metres^{-1}, as comparable with dioptres of accommodation (after E. F. Fincham).

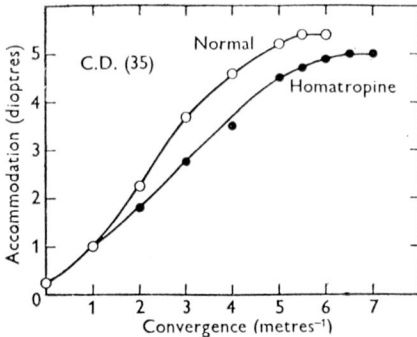

FIG. 248.

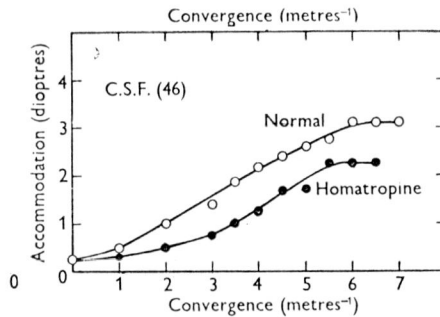

FIG. 249.

FIGS. 248 and 249.—THE EFFECT OF SLIGHT PARESIS OF THE CILIARY MUSCLE UPON CONVERGENCE-ACCOMMODATION.

In each case the accommodation and convergence in a normal individual before and after the instillation of homatropine are given (E. F. Fincham).

mode of action of the ciliary muscle and the nature of presbyopia. Two opposing views have been expressed on this subject but no consensus of opinion has yet been reached as to the validity of either. On the one hand, it has been argued that the degree of shortening of the ciliary muscle required to produce a unit-change of accommodation increases with age, the assumption being that each fraction of the range of accommodation corresponds to an equal fraction of the contractility of the muscle. A decline in the power of the ciliary muscle could thus be a factor in the decline in accommodation. Alternatively, it has been said that the same degree of shortening of the muscle is necessary to produce a unit-change in accommodation provided the lens is able to accommodate effectively, the assumption being that much of the accommodative power lies latent in presbyopia because of the sclerosis of the lens. In the first view, the amount of shortening of the ciliary muscle required to produce a change of accommodation of 1 D increases with age; a young person possessing 14 D of accommodation has only to use a small fraction of his available ciliary power to increase his refraction by 1 D, whereas a person who has reached an age at which only 1 D of accommodation remains has to use all his ciliary power to produce this effect. In the

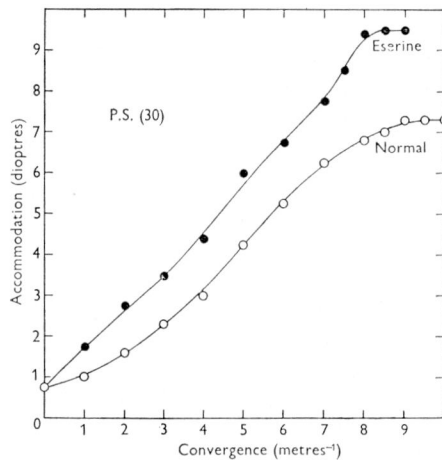

FIG. 250.—THE EFFECT OF ESERINE ON CONVERGENCE-ACCOMMODATION.
The reaction is the reverse of that seen in Figs. 248 and 249 (E. F. Fincham).

second, the amount of shortening of the ciliary muscle required to produce a change of accommodation of 1 D is the same at all ages.

The first hypothesis was advocated by Donders (1864) whose views were supported by Landolt (1903), Clarke (1920), Duane (1925) and Fincham (1932–55). The earlier authors relied in their reasoning largely on the action of drugs on the ciliary muscle, while Fincham argued on the effects of the convergence-stimulus for accommodation which diminish with age; if the innervation stimulated by a given change in convergence-stimulus remains constant throughout life, a given shortening of the ciliary muscle produces a smaller dioptric change in presbyopia. Moreover, when homatropine is instilled the amount of accommodation induced by convergence becomes smaller, while with eserine it becomes larger. This increase with eserine suggests that the lens itself is not the only limiting factor. At the same time, it must be remembered that the degree of accommodation obtainable with a convergence-stimulus is considerably less than that resulting from optimal stimulation (Balsam and Fry, 1959). Other investigations have not been conclusive. Goldmann and Aschmann (1946), partially paralysing one eye with homatropine, found that the physiological amplitude of accommodation was always greater than the physical but that the difference between them became smaller with age, whereas if sclerosis of the lens were the determining factor it would presumably become larger, a result corroborated by Morgan and Harrigan (1951) in a patient with unilateral paralysis of accommodation, and by the use of partially paralysing drugs by Morgan (1954) and Van Hoven (1959).

The second hypothesis that the defect of accommodation depended on lenticular sclerosis was advanced by von Helmholtz (1856) and supported by Hess (1901), Gullstrand (1908), Fuchs (1922), Flieringa and van der Hoeve (1924) and van der Hoeve and Flieringa (1924). The effect of age on the AC/A ratio was investigated by Alpern (1950) and Alpern and Larson (1960), who found that as the accommodative stimulus increased the accommodative convergence increased without any dioptric change, a result which suggested the existence of an inflexible relationship between the two and that the increased innervation resulted in an increase in vergence but not in accommodation because of the sclerosis of the lens.

None of these experiments is crucially conclusive and, in addition, many of the results are influenced by the training of the subject. In addition to this purely practical factor, the theoretical basis for the " degree of shortening of the ciliary muscle " must be called into question if attempts are made to define this at various ages. The changes with age in the muscle and the ciliary body which have been stressed by Stieve (1949), Kornzweig (1951) and Weale (1963) make it difficult to compare the degree of shortening which occurs in youth and at a later period of life. In other words, even if the innervational stimuli to the ciliary muscle are the same at two periods of life, the responses of the muscle and the consequent changes in the configuration of the ciliary body at these ages may differ. It must be admitted that the dispute is still unresolved. Nevertheless, although age may have an effect on the function of the ciliary muscle, the mechanics of the lens itself appears to be the most important factor in the determination of presbyopia.

Alpern. *Amer. J. Optom.*, **27**, 491 (1950).

Alpern and Ellen. *Amer. J. Ophthal.*, **42** (2), 296 (1956).

Alpern, Ellen and Goldsmith. *Arch. Ophthal.*, **60**, 592 (1958).

Alpern, Kincaid and Lubeck. *Amer. J. Ophthal.*, **48** (2), 141 (1959).

Alpern and Larson. *Amer. J. Ophthal.*, **49**, 1140 (1960).

Alpern and Wolter. *Arch. Ophthal.*, **56**, 685 (1956).

Ames and Gliddon. *Trans. Sect. Ophthal., Amer. med. Ass.*, 102 (1928).

Balsam and Fry. *Amer. J. Optom.*, **36**, 567 (1959).

Bornschein and Schubert. *v. Graefes Arch. Ophthal.*, **159**, 45 (1957).

Christoferson and Ogle. *Arch. Ophthal.*, **55**, 779 (1956).

Clarke. *Trans. ophthal. Soc. U.K.*, **40**, 260 (1920).

Cramer. *Ned. Lancet*, **1**, 529 (1851).

Donders. *On the Anomalies of Accommodation and Refraction of the Eye*, London (1864).

Duane. *Amer. J. Ophthal.*, **8**, 196 (1925).

Fincham. *Rep. Physiol. and Opt. Socs. Jt. Discussion on Vision*, London (1932).
J. Physiol., **128**, 105 (1955).

Fincham and Walton. *J. Physiol.*, **137**, 488 (1957).

Flieringa. *Untersuch. auf dem Gebiete d. relativen Akkommodationsbreite (Diss.)*, Leiden (1923).

Flieringa and van der Hoeve. *v. Graefes Arch. Ophthal.*, **114**, 1 (1924).

Flom. *Amer. J. Optom.*, **37**, 517, 524 (1960).

Fuchs, E. *Arch. Ophthal.*, **51**, 21 (1922).

Goldmann and Aschmann. *Ophthalmologica*, **111**, 182 (1946).

Gullstrand. *K. svenska Vetensk. Acad. Handl.*, **43** (2), 1 (1908).

von Helmholtz. *Hb. d. physiol. Optik*, Hamburg, **1** (1856).

Hess. *v. Graefes Arch. Ophthal.*, **52**, 143 (1901).

van der Hoeve and Flieringa. *Brit. J. Ophthal.*, **8**, 97 (1924).

Jackson. *Amer. J. Ophthal.*, **5**, 837 (1922).

Jampel. *Amer. J. Ophthal.*, **48** (2), 573 (1959).

Kornzweig. *Trans. Amer. Acad. Ophthal.*, **55**, 261 (1951).

Landolt. *Graefe-Saemisch Hb. d. ges. Augenheilk.*, 2nd ed., Leipzig, **4** (1903).

Maddox. *J. Anat. Physiol.*, **20**, 475, 565 (1886).
The Clinical Use of Prisms and the Decentring of Lenses, 5th ed., Bristol (1907).

Marg and Morgan. *Arch. Ophthal.*, **43**, 871 (1950).

Martens and Ogle. *Amer. J. Ophthal.*, **47** (2), 455 (1959).

Morgan. *Arch. Ophthal.*, **47**, 745 (1952).
Amer. J. Optom., **31**, 219 (1954).

Morgan and Harrigan. *Amer. J. Optom.*, **28**, 242 (1951).

Ogle. *Researches in Binocular Vision*, Phila. (1950).

Ogle, Martens and Dyer. *Oculomotor Imbalance in Binocular Vision and Fixation Disparity*, Phila. (1967).

Ogle, Mussey and Prangen. *Amer. J. Ophthal.*, **32**, 1069 (1949).

Ogle and Prangen. *Amer. J. Ophthal.*, **34** (2), 57 (1951).

Ripps, Chin, Siegel and Breinin. *Invest. Ophthal.*, **1**, 127 (1962).

Roth. *Vis. Res.*, **9**, 1259 (1969).

Scheiner. *Oculus hoc est: fundamentum opticum*, Oeniponti (1619).

Schubert. *v. Graefes Arch. Ophthal.*, **157**, 116 (1955).

Schubert and Burian. *Pflügers Arch. ges. Physiol.*, **238**, 184 (1936).

Stieve. *Anat. Anz.*, **97**, 69 (1949).

Van Hoven. *Amer. J. Optom.*, **36**, 22 (1959).

Weale. *The Aging Eye*, London, 60 (1963).

Westheimer and Mitchell. *Arch. Ophthal.*, **55**, 848 (1956).

SECTION II

ANOMALIES OF REFRACTION AND ACCOMMODATION

Fig. 251.—James Ware

[1756–1815]

(From an engraving in the Wellcome Institute of the History of Medicine, by courtesy of the Wellcome Trustees.)

CHAPTER V

ANOMALIES OF THE OPTICAL SYSTEM

ALTHOUGH anomalies of the dioptric system of the eye have excited attention from early times, their optical clarification was long delayed. In the Aristotelian writings the very obvious condition of short-sight was appreciated; animals, it was said, with prominent eyes do not see as well at a distance as do those with small eyes. To Galen the myope possessed a clear " visual spirit " but in too small a quantity to reach a distant object. Myopia was contrasted by Aristotle with presbyopia, the long-sight of old age, long known and corrected in mediæval times by Roger Bacon[1] ; this contrast persisted for many centuries in the literature. The optics of myopia, however, was first elucidated by Johannes Kepler (1604) (Fig. 11) in his initial clarification of ophthalmic dioptrics when he correctly assumed that the incident light was brought to a focus in front of the retina, a view accepted by Isaac Newton (1704). Both of these pioneers in optics also considered myopia and presbyopia to be antitheses. The reason for the displacement of the focus in myopic eyes excited much attention. Francesco Maurolico (1575) of Messina looked upon it as due to abnormal convexity of the lens. Vopiscus Fortunatus Plempius (1632), professor of therapeutics at Loewen in Holland, described anatomically the unusual distance between the lens and the retina, a view confirmed by Georg Albert Hamberger (1696), professor of mathematics at Jena, while Hermann Boerhaave (1708) of Leyden attributed the defect either to an increased convexity of the cornea or to the undue length of the globe. This latter cause was factually confirmed by Giovanni Battista Morgagni (1761) of Padua, Pierre Guérin (1769) of Lyon, Louis Florentin Dehais-Gendron (1770) of Paris, A. G. Richter (1790) of Göttingen, and finally by Antonio Scarpa (1801) of Padua.

Hypermetropia has a shorter history. It is true that Daza de Valdés (1623) (Fig. 383) prescribed convex lenses for distant vision as well as for near vision in the aged, and the first optical appreciation of the anomaly was made by Hamberger (1696). The story, however, is confused, largely because long-sight was considered identical with presbyopia. The latter was thus explained by Newton (1704) : " If the Humours of the Eye by old Age decay, so as by shrinking to make the Cornea and the Coat of the Crystalline Humour grow flatter than before, the Light will not be refracted enough, and for want of a sufficient Refraction will not converge to the bottom of the Eye but to some place beyond it. . . . This is the reason for the decay of sight in old Men and shews why their Sight is mended by Spectacles. For their Convex glasses supply the defect of plumpness in the Eye, and by increasing the Refraction make the Rays converge sooner, so as to convene at the bottom of the Eye if the Glass have a due degree of convexity. And the contrary happens in short-sighted Men whose Eyes are too plump. For the Refraction being now too great, the Rays converge and convene in the Eyes before they come to the bottom . . . unless the Object be brought so near to the Eye as that the place where the converging Rays convene may be removed to the bottom . . . or the Refraction is diminished by a Concave-glass of a due degree of concavity." The same theme was described and illustrated by the great mathematician of Cambridge, Robert Smith (1738), and transcribed by Abraham Gotthelf Kästner (1755), professor of mathematics at Leipzig, who in his annotated translation of Smith's book called the optical state in long-sighted individuals *hyperpresbytas*; the general

[1] p. 9.

outline of the optics of long-sight, still described as presbyopia, was also understood by Porterfield (1759) and Thomas Young (1807).[1] From the clinical point of view, Jean Janin (1772), the ophthalmologist of Montpellier and Avignon, distinguished three types of sight—normal, short-sight and long-sight, " the first two occurring naturally and the third fortuitous and occurring only in old people ".

It is curious that the teaching of Hamberger (1696) that presbyopia could occur in the young and even congenitally was forgotten. It is interesting that William Charles Wells (1811), who was born in America of Scottish parents and spent his working life in London, noted that at the age of 55 he required abnormally strong convex glasses to see clearly in the distance. But the first person in the 19th century to make it clear that long-sight was not necessarily associated with presbyopia was the English ophthalmologist, James Ware (1813); he described " young persons who have so disproportionate a convexity of the cornea or crystalline, or of both, to the distance of these parts of the retina, that a glass of considerable convexity is required to enable them to see distinctly, not only near objects, but also those that are distant ". Such an idea, however, was not understood and even the astute William Mackenzie (1830) ascribed such a visual defect to asthenopia. Thereafter several writers noted but failed completely to understand a defect of sight occurring in the young or even as a congenital anomaly which could be improved by convex glasses (Weller, 1821; Ritterich, 1843; Böhm, 1845; Sichel, 1845; White Cooper, 1853; Ruete, 1853; Smee, 1854; and others), until Stellwag von Carion (1855) gave a relatively clear account with an optical explanation, still to a certain extent retaining the old concepts by calling the condition *hyperpresbyopia*. It was left to Franz Donders (1858–64) to establish fully the optical nature and frequent occurrence of hypermetropia and point out its differentiation from presbyopia.

The history of our knowledge of astigmatism is shorter still. It was first recognized as a defect in his own eye by the great English scientist, Thomas Young (1801), by practising Scheiner's experiment[2] and finding that he had 3·94 D of myopia in the vertical meridian and 5·62 D in the horizontal. His observation was verified by the Astronomer Royal, George Biddell Airy (1827) (Fig. 610) who followed out the astigmatic change that had occurred in his eyes 22 years later (1849), and to correct it designed an astigmatic lens made by an optician, Fuller, in Ipswich, in 1827. The name " astigmatism " was suggested to Airy in 1849 by the Rev. Dr. Whewall, professor of mathematics and philosophy at Cambridge. Several other cases were reported by Sir William Hamilton (1847) of Dublin, visually characterized by the distinctness of horizontal and the indistinctness of vertical lines, and also by Henry Goode (1847–48); one case was reported from Europe by Pastor Schnyder (1849) of Lucerne, who corrected the error in his own eyes by astigmatic lenses, and three by J. Hays (1854) of Philadelphia in the American edition of Lawrence's *A Treatise on Diseases of the Eye*. Again, the optics and the importance of the defect were first clearly defined by Donders (1864).

From among these pioneers whose photographs have not appeared in this *System*, as an introduction to this Chapter we are choosing those of James Ware who first clearly differentiated hypermetropia from presbyopia, and Stellwag von Carion who considerably clarified the optical condition in such eyes.

JAMES WARE [1756–1815] (Fig. 251) was born at Portsmouth and studied medicine at St. Thomas's Hospital in London and was one of the first to raise British ophthalmology from the degradation of quackery to the status of medicine. With a sole and obsessional interest in ophthalmology in a country wherein ophthalmic surgery

---

[1] Moritz von Rohr (1915) drew attention to the optics of hypermetropia as described by Johann George Leutmann (1728) and J. Bischoff (1772).

[2] p. 155.

FIG. 252.—KARL STELLWAG VON CARION
[1823–1904].

was merely an incidental activity of the general surgeon, he devoted himself to private practice and writing to such good purpose that he was elected a Fellow of the Royal Society in 1801 for his pioneering work on the discission of congenital cataract, the first " bare oculist " to acquire that distinction. The second paper he contributed to that Society in 1813 was " Observations on the near and distant vision in different persons ", the subject of our present study.

KARL STELLWAG VON CARION [1823–1904] (Fig. 252), was a Moravian who went to the University of Prague in 1841 and studied medicine in Vienna, where he graduated in 1848. Here he worked with A. von Rosas, Ferdinand Arlt and Eduard Jaeger and directed the First Eye Clinic until 1894. He was an excellent surgeon and his contributions to the literature on a multitude of ophthalmic subjects were manifold. Among them his work on refractive anomalies and accommodation appeared in 1855, a subject hitherto almost completely neglected in central Europe; his textbook on the practice of ophthalmology (1861–2) was a landmark as an assessment of the new ophthalmology that was emerging at that period pioneered at Vienna, and his name is eponymously remembered in " Stellwag's sign ", the infrequency and incompleteness of the movement of blinking in Graves's disease (1869). Retiring in 1894, he gave himself up to his hobbies of botany, history and playing the violin. He was Vice-President of the first International Congress of Ophthalmology in Brussels in 1857 but, somewhat austere in manner with a lack of urbanity, he mixed uneasily with his ophthalmic colleagues but was loved by his hospital patients, particularly children. In 1903, on his 80th birthday, he was visited by a group of his old students; in the following year he died of a gangrenous hernia.

The Types of Ametropia

We have seen that in the physiologically normal eye parallel rays converge upon the retina to form a circle of least diffusion; when these ideal optical conditions occur with the eye in a state of rest the condition is termed EMMETROPIA ($\dot{\epsilon}\nu$, within; $\mu\dot{\epsilon}\tau\rho o\nu$, measure; $\ddot{\omega}\psi$, the eye). It would be

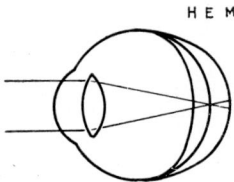

FIG. 253.

strange if this were a common state of affairs, for its attainment depends on an exactitude to within a fraction of a millimetre of such measurements as the length of the eye and the shape of the cornea and the lens; and such regularity and conformity to type as optical perfection would necessitate, demand a mathematical accuracy which is nowhere realized in the constitution of living organisms. Emmetropia may be optically normal, but it is no more biologically normal than would be the universal attainment of a uniform height of 5 feet 6 inches. The opposite condition of AMETROPIA ($\dot{a}$, privative; $\mu\dot{\epsilon}\tau\rho o\nu$, measure; $\ddot{\omega}\psi$, the eye), when parallel rays of light are not focused exactly upon the retina with the eye in a state of rest, is therefore much the more common.

Ametropia may be of three main types: a principal focus may be formed by the refractive system of the eye, but instead of its being situated on the retina (as in emmetropia, E, Fig. 253), it may be situated either behind it or in front of it. In the first case, the eye is relatively too short, and the condition is then called HYPERMETROPIA ($\dot{v}\pi\epsilon\rho$, in excess) (HYPEROPIA by von Helmholtz) (H, Fig. 253); in the second it is relatively too long, when the term MYOPIA is used ($\mu\dot{v}\omega$ I close[1]; $\ddot{\omega}\psi$, the eye) (*brachyopia* was suggested but not adopted by Donders) (M, Fig. 253). Alternatively, the refractive elements may not be spherical so that no single focus is formed, in which case ASTIGMATISM is present.

These refractive anomalies may be caused by varying conditions.

I. *The Position of the Elements of the System*

(*a*) The antero-posterior diameter of the eye is too short: *axial hypermetropia.*

(*b*) The antero-posterior diameter of the eye is too long and the retina is too far away from the optical system: *axial myopia.*

(*c*) Lenticular displacement. If the crystalline lens is dislocated forwards, myopia will exist; if backwards, hypermetropia.

II. *Anomalies of the Refractive Surfaces*

The curvature of the cornea or of the lens may be too small, giving a *curvature hypermetropia;* or too great, giving a *curvature myopia;* or be irregular, varying in different meridians, giving *astigmatism.*

In hypermetropic astigmatism, the curvatures of both axes are unequal and too small; in myopic astigmatism they are both unequal and too great; when the two conditions are combined so that one axis is hypermetropic and the other myopic, the condition is termed *mixed astigmatism.*

(i) If the axes showing the greatest difference in curvature are at right angles, the condition is called *regular* astigmatism.

(ii) If they are not so related, the astigmatism may be called *bi-oblique.*[2]

(iii) If there is no symmetry about the refraction and different groups of rays form foci at different positions, as occurs in the cornea after corneal ulceration or in the lens in developing cataract, the astigmatism is called *irregular.*

III. *Obliquity of the Elements of the System*

(*a*) *Lenticular Obliquity.* If the lens is placed obliquely or subluxated, astigmatism will result.

(*b*) *Retinal Obliquity.* The posterior pole of the eye may be placed obliquely, as when it bulges backwards in a staphyloma in high myopia, and if the summit of the staphyloma does not correspond to the fovea the rays do not fall upon this region perpendicularly. If the focus were a point this would be without effect, but since it is a diffusion circle of measur-

---

[1] From the habit short-sighted people develop of half-closing the lids to gain the advantage of a stenopæic aperture, p. 29.   [2] See, however p. 274.

able diameter the obliquity will deform and increase it, thus diminishing visual acuity.

IV. *Anomalies of the Refractive Index*

(*a*) If the refractive index of the aqueous humour is too low, or that of the vitreous humour is too high, there will be an *index hypermetropia*. Conversely, if the index of refraction of the aqueous is too high or that of the vitreous too low, there will be an *index myopia*.

(*b*) If the refractive index of the lens as a whole is too low, there will be *index hypermetropia*. If the index of the cortex increases relatively and approximates that of the nucleus, as it does normally with age, the lens tends to act as a single refractive element, and consequently has less converging power than normal ; the eye therefore becomes hypermetropic. Conversely, if the refractive power of the nucleus increases, as frequently occurs in early cataract, *index myopia* is produced. If the increase in the refractive index of the nucleus is very marked a false lenticonus may be produced wherein the central part of the pupil is myopic and the periphery hypermetropic. If the index of any part varies irregularly in different localities, as in developing cataract, an *index astigmatism* is produced.

V. *Absence of an Element of the System*

The absence of the lens, a condition known as *aphakia* (ἀ, privative ; φακός, lens), produces hypermetropia.

As we shall see shortly, many of the definitions just given in this classification of refractive anomalies are illegitimately simple and require qualification. The concept of an eye which is too long or too curved or has

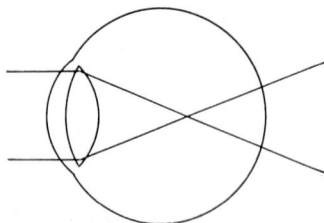

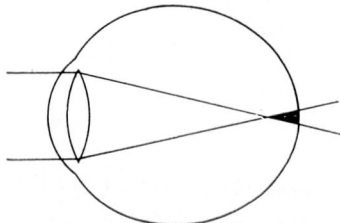

FIG. 254.—REFRACTIVE AMETROPIA.   FIG. 255.—AXIAL AMETROPIA.

any other physical or geometrical abnormality of optical significance leads by implication to the notion that normal values can be established. This is not so. Nevertheless, it is useful to retain the distinction between *axial ametropia* wherein an alteration in axial length is the main factor, and *refractive ametropia* wherein the anomaly lies principally in the curvature or indices of the refracting media (Figs. 254–5).

THE DIOPTRIC SYSTEM OF THE AMETROPIC EYE

In the emmetropic eye parallel rays of light are brought to a focus upon the retina (Fig. 256); but in the hypermetropic eye parallel rays come to a focus behind the retina, and the diffusion circles which are formed result in a blurred and indistinct image (Fig. 257). In those cases wherein the axis of the eye is shorter and the retina is nearer the nodal point, it necessarily follows, as is obvious from Fig. 264, that the image is smaller than in emmetropia. Conversely, rays coming from a point on the retina of the emmetropic eye will emerge parallel, while in the hypermetropic eye they will be divergent. In the first case they will meet at infinity, in the second they will meet behind the eye (Fig. 259). It follows that with the emmetropic eye objects theoretically at infinity are seen distinctly when the eye is at rest, while in hypermetropia the formation of a clear image of any kind is impossible unless the converging power of the optical system is increased either by placing a convex lens in front of the eye (Fig. 261) or by an effort of accommodation (Fig. 263). In myopia, on the other hand, parallel rays of light come to a focus in front of the retina, and the image is therefore made up of the circles of diffusion formed by the diverging beam (Fig. 258). In axial cases, since the distance of the retina from the nodal point is greater, the image, neglecting diffusion circles, is larger than in the emmetropic eye (Fig. 264). Conversely, rays coming from a point on the retina will be convergent, and will therefore meet at a point in front of the eye (Fig. 260). If they are to be brought to a focus, parallel rays coming from distant objects must be rendered more divergent, and this can only be done by placing a concave lens in front of the eye (Fig. 262). It follows that distant objects cannot be seen clearly without artificial aid; only divergent rays will meet at the retina, and thus, in order to be seen clearly, an object must be brought close to the eye, so that the rays coming from it are rendered sufficiently divergent (Fig. 260). This point, the furthest at which objects can be seen distinctly, is called the *far point* (punctum remotum). In the emmetrope it is at infinity; in the hypermetrope it is behind the eye and therefore virtual; and in the myope it is a finite distance in front of the eye and therefore real, and the higher the myopia, the shorter is the distance.

THE MEASUREMENT OF AMETROPIA

The far point offers a convenient method of expressing the degree and type of ametropia which an eye possesses. The refraction of any eye is the *dioptric value of the far-point distance*. This distance is usually taken as that between the corneal vertex and the far point; strictly speaking, the anterior principal point is the more optically correct, but the corneal vertex is for all practical purposes sufficiently close. The refraction of an eye is also the same as the power in dioptres of a correcting lens placed at the cornea.

FIGS. 256 to 264.—THE OPTICAL CONDITIONS IN AMETROPIA.

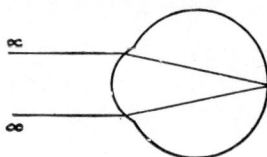

FIG. 256.—The optics of emmetropia.

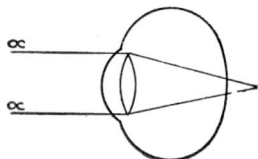

FIG. 257.—In hypermetropia the focus is behind the retina.

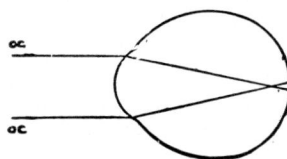

FIG. 258.—In myopia the focus is in front of the retina.

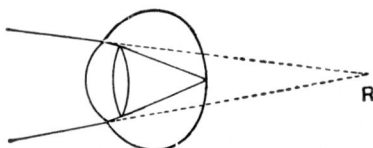

FIG. 259.—In hypermetropia convergent rays come to a focus on the retina.

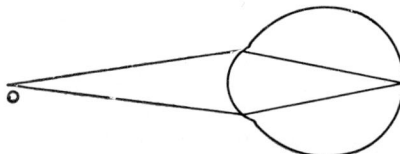

FIG. 260.—In myopia divergent rays from a near object are focused on the retina.

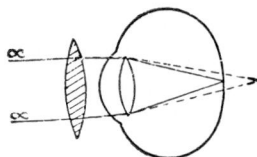

FIG. 261.—In hypermetropia a convex lens increases the converging power.

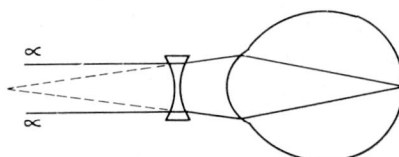

FIG. 262.—In myopia a concave lens focuses parallel rays on the retina.

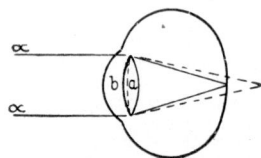

FIG. 263.—In hypermetropia accommodation increases the converging power (continuous line).

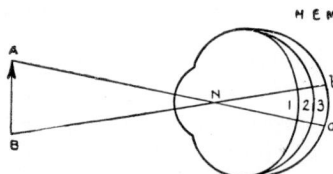

FIG. 264.—The size of the image in hypermetropia, emmetropia and myopia.

It would seem at first sight reasonable to apply to the ametropic eye the same methods for constructing the image as for the emmetropic eye; in other words, we might make use of the schematic or reduced eye and the system of cardinal points. The value of the schematic and reduced eyes in physiological optics has already been fully assessed, but in attempting to extend these useful optical concepts to the ametropic eye we must be careful to make a distinction between those ametropias due principally to a change in axial length and those due to refractive alterations in the dioptric elements. Since the cardinal points of an eye with refractive ametropia are certain to differ from those of the (emmetropic) schematic eye, it is a doubtful exercise to compare any ametropic eye with the schematic or reduced eye unless its optical defect is known to be solely axial in nature. Even among emmetropic eyes, as we shall see later, there may be variations which cast doubt upon the practical significance of this simplification.

The Gaussian system of cardinal points should theoretically allow the construction of the image formed by any eye, whether emmetropic or ametropic, and whether the ametropia is axial or refractive. We shall, indeed, make extensive use of this system in discussing and illustrating the optics of the ametropic eye, but we must not delude ourselves into believing that we have any definite knowledge of the position of the cardinal points of a particular ametropic eye, or of how these positions differ from those in the hypothetical " normal " eye. Nevertheless, it remains a useful simplification to consider the optics of the ametropic eye as if the optical defect were axial, and we shall draw attention to those instances wherein the distinction between axial and refractive ametropia is of particular importance.

THE ACCOMMODATION IN AMETROPIA

The relation between the range and the amplitude of accommodation in different refractive states can be gathered from Figs. 265–7. We have seen[1] that the amplitude is an expression of the work done, while the range is an indication of the availability of accommodation in that it indicates the distance at which clear vision is possible. Thus a hypermetrope will require to employ a greater amount of accommodation to see distinctly at a distance of 10 cm. than an emmetrope, and a myope may be able to see at this distance without effort. Again, an emmetrope or a low hypermetrope with active accommodation is able to see distinctly over all ranges which may be considered to exist in practical life; in both the range is infinite, but a high hypermetrope whose near point is some considerable distance away may be incapacitated for near work without the artificial aid of spectacles. A myope, on the other hand, may have his far point so close to his eye that without spectacles his vision is extremely limited, and the range at his disposal so small

---

[1] p. 175.

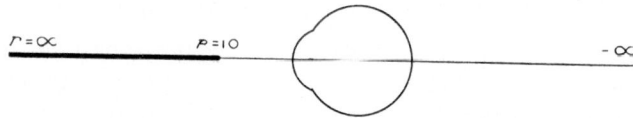

FIG. 265.—ACCOMMODATION IN EMMETROPIA.

$r = \alpha$; $p = 10$. The amplitude of accommodation (10–0) is therefore 10 D, and the range is infinite.

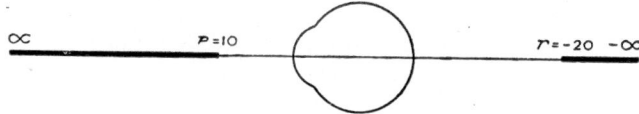

FIG. 266.—ACCOMMODATION IN HYPERMETROPIA.

In a hypermetrope of + 5 D, $r = - 1/5$ metre, the far point being behind the eye; $p = 10$. The amplitude of accommodation is therefore 15 D [10—(—5)], and the range is again infinite.

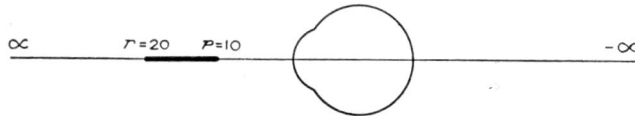

FIG. 267.—ACCOMMODATION IN MYOPIA.

In a myope of —5 D, $r = 20$, $p = 10$. The amplitude of accommodation is therefore 5 D (10—5) and the range 10 cm.

as to render his accommodation practically useless. The fact that part of the refractive error of a hypermetrope is correctable by his accommodation is of clinical importance, since the constant attempt at correction may tend to induce a condition of strain and fatigue.

THE DIOPTRIC SYSTEM OF THE CORRECTED EYE

THE POSITION OF THE IMAGE

The imagery of a system composed of the eye and a lens placed in front of it is of practical importance since such a lens may be employed to alter the direction of the rays entering an ametropic eye so that the image falls upon the retina instead of in front of or behind it. In any type of ametropia a correcting lens (for distance) is such that, when placed in a suitable position, it has its second principal focus at the remote point of the eye; the image of the remote point is brought to the retina by the dioptric system of the eye, and the correcting lens is such that incident parallel rays, after refraction by it, will appear to come from the remote point; the combination will therefore focus incident parallel rays upon the retina. The value of the lens required to bring about the desired alteration will depend upon two circumstances: the actual strength of the lens, and the distance it is placed from the eye. For a distant object this relationship is seen in Figs. 268–9.

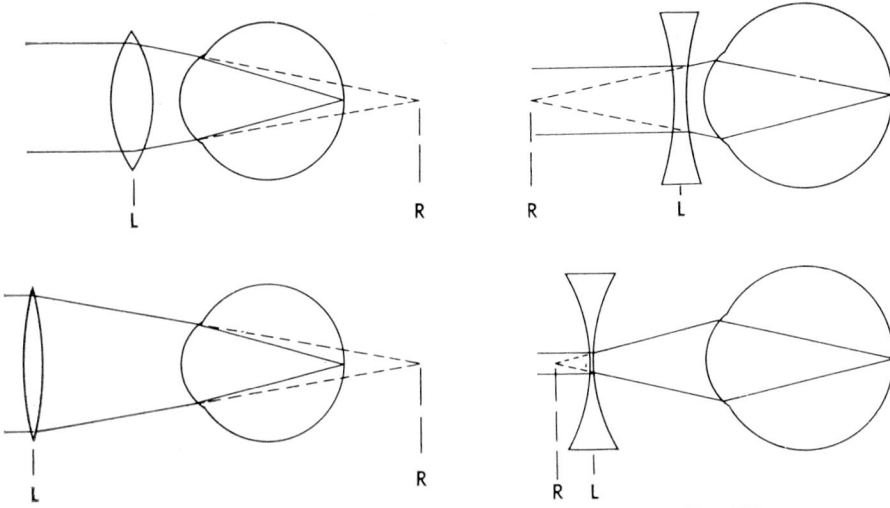

FIG. 268.   FIG. 269.

FIGS. 268 and 269.—THE POSITION OF THE LENS IN THE CORRECTION OF
THE AMETROPIC EYE.

The position of the image depends on the strength of the correcting lens (L) and the distance it is placed from the eye. R is the remote point of the eye.

In hypermetropia the same optical effect is given by a strong convex lens close to the eye or a weaker convex lens some distance away (Fig. 268). In myopia the reverse applies with a concave lens (Fig. 269).

We shall consider first the case when the optical centre of the lens is placed in the anterior focal plane of the eye, the principal planes of which are represented by P_1P_2 (Fig. 270). In the absence of the lens the image of AB is formed at ab, the meeting place of a ray which enters the system in a parallel direction and passes through the posterior principal focus (F_2) and another ray which passes through the anterior principal focus (F_1) and proceeds parallel to the optic axis. If a convex lens is placed at F_1 the image of AB is formed at A_1B_1; the ray from B leaving the lens in a parallel

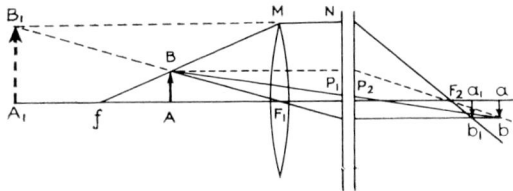

FIG. 270.

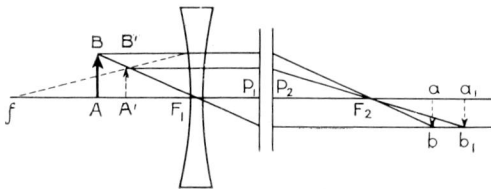

FIG. 271.

direction (MN) must come from the principal focus of the lens (f). Entering the optical system of the eye parallel to the optic axis it must pass through F_2. The ray BF_1, passing through the optical centre of the lens and being therefore unaffected by it, will proceed as before. The image of A_1B_1 is therefore situated at a_1b_1.

If a concave lens is placed at F_1, a similar construction (Fig. 271) shows that the image of AB is changed from the position ab to a_1b_1.

It is thus seen that *a convex correcting lens in front of the eye causes the image to move forwards, thus correcting hypermetropia, while a concave lens moves it backwards, thus correcting myopia.*

The displacement of the image can be calculated thus. In Fig. 272 let $\phi_1\phi_2$, h_1h_2, k_1k_2 denote the cardinal points of an axially myopic eye, the retina of which is at M; the eye is therefore too long by ϕ_2M, a distance which we shall call x.

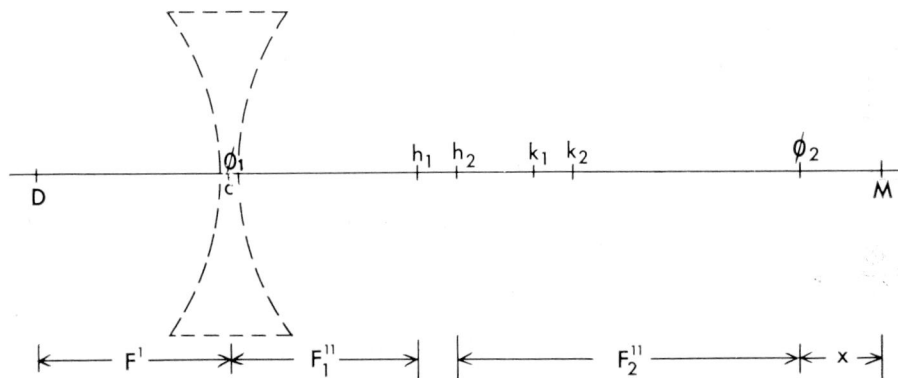

Fig. 272.

Let $F_1''F_2''$ be the focal lengths of the eye, and let D be its remote point. In the absence of a correcting lens, D and M are conjugate points. Consider a concave lens of focal length F', placed with its optical centre, c, at the anterior principal focus of the eye.

$$\text{Then} \quad -x = h_2M - h_2\phi_2 = h_2M - F_2''$$
$$\text{and} \quad F' = Dh_1 - \phi_1h_1 = Dh_1 - F_1''$$

The Newtonian formula for the coordinate distances of object and image is $l_1l_2 = F_1F_2$, where l is the distance of object from the anterior principal focus, l_2 the distance of the image from the posterior principal focus, F_1 and F_2 the first and second focal lengths.

Therefore
$$(Dh_1 - \phi_1h_1)(h_2M - h_2\phi_2) = F_1''F_2''$$
or
$$F'(-x) = F_1''F_2''$$
whence
$$-x = \frac{F_1''F_2''}{F'} \simeq \frac{(17)(-22{\cdot}8)}{F'}$$
whence
$$F' \simeq \frac{388}{x} \text{ in mm.}$$

The formula gives the focal length in mm. of the lens necessary to correct the axial error x, when its optical centre is placed in the anterior focal plane of the eye (15·706 mm. in front of the cornea). *A lens of $\pm$ 1 D, the optical* *centre of which is placed in this position, therefore corrects an axial displacement of approximately* ± 0·39 mm. (or a lens of ± 3 D a displacement of ± 1·17 or approximately 1 mm.). Similarly, *a displacement of* ± 1 mm. *is corrected by a lens of* ± 2·57 D.

In the aphakic eye, of course, the conditions alter. Here the anterior focal plane is 23·27 mm. in front of the cornea, and $F_1''F_2''$ are respectively 23·227 mm. and − 31·031 mm. It follows that in this case, when the lens is placed so that its optical centre is 23·27 mm. in front of the cornea, each dioptre brings about a difference in level of the image of 0·72 mm. (or 3 D corresponds to 2·16 mm.), while a displacement of the image of 1 mm. is corrected by a lens of 1·3874 D.

THE POSITION OF THE CORRECTION

In practice a lens which corrects ametropia is rarely placed at the anterior focal point of the eye. It is usually somewhat closer, the commonest form being a spectacle lens worn about 12 mm. from the cornea (the *spectacle distance*); in the case of contact lenses, however, the optical correction is virtually at the cornea.

The position at which the correction for ametropia is worn has three important aspects, the effectivity for distant and for near vision and its influence upon the size of the retinal image.

EFFECTIVITY

When either of two lenses brings light from the same source to the same focus each is said to have the same EFFECTIVITY *as the other.* In Fig. 273 let a lens of power D converge parallel rays to a focus, F, and a lens of power D_1 converge to the same focus; and let the focal length of D be LF, that of D_1 be L_1F, and let the difference between these (LL_1) be n, all measurements being expressed in metres.

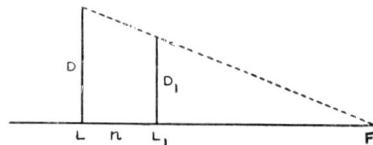

FIG. 273.

Then $\qquad L_1F = LF - LL_1$ and $LF = L_1F + LL_1$

whence $\qquad \dfrac{1}{D_1} = \dfrac{1}{D} - n$ and $\dfrac{1}{D} = \dfrac{1}{D_1} + n$

or $\qquad D_1 = \dfrac{D}{1 - nD}$ and $D = \dfrac{D_1}{1 + nD_1}$

THE EFFECTIVE POWER FOR DISTANT VISION. The application of this to the correction of ametropia for distant vision is shown in Fig. 274. A thin lens placed at A corrects the optical error of a hypermetropic eye, the far point of which is at F'. If the correcting lens were placed at B, its focal length would necessarily require to be reduced by an amount d' if it were to have the same optical effect. It follows that the two lenses to be equally effective must be of different powers, the focal length of the convex lens being decreased and that of the concave lens increased, since in myopia the far point lies in front of the eye (see Figs. 268–9). Consequently (for parallel rays of light) the further a correcting lens is removed from the eye the weaker it must be in hypermetropia and the stronger in myopia. Conversely, the effective power of a positive lens increases as it is moved from the eye while that of a negative lens decreases. (See Tables XXXVI–VII.)

The importance of effectivity is strikingly seen in the prescription of contact lenses after the clinical estimation of the spectacle refraction. For example, if a myope wears his correction of − 20 D at 12·5 mm. in front of the cornea, the power required in a contact lens which is virtually the true ocular refraction, K, is only − 16 D.

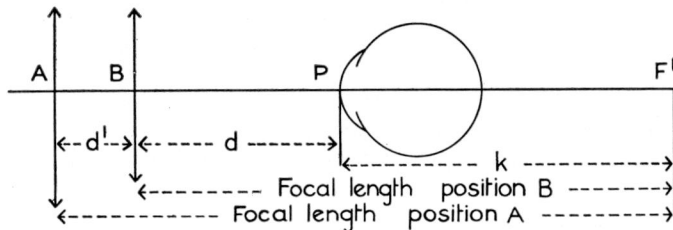

FIG. 274.—THE EFFECTIVE POWER OF A LENS.

THE EFFECTIVITY FOR NEAR VISION. When divergent rays enter the system, that is, when the eyes are used for near vision, all lenses, both convex and concave, are less effective than when parallel rays are in question. If the same lenses are used for distant and near vision, therefore, a correction for this should theoretically be made.

Thus with a + 10 D lens, if the fixation point is 33·3 cm. away from the correcting lens, the light reaching the lens is diverging by − 3 D; that leaving it is converging by − 3 + 10 = + 7 D. The effectivity at the surface of the (reduced) eye is therefore + 7·76 D. Since the effective power for distant vision of such a lens is + 11·63 D, an addition of 11·63 − 7·76 = 3·87 D of refractivity is required, or + 0·87 D if the normal accommodative effort of + 3·0 for this distance is to be expended. In myopia this under-correction for near work may be an advantage; in hypermetropia it may necessitate the prescription of a presbyopic correction at an earlier age than usual; but in high astigmatism a considerable moiety of the astigmatism remains un-corrected for near vision and the comfort of the patient may demand a higher correction.

Percival (1928) devised a simplified formula to allow for this correction. The strength of the lens, Fn, which, when used for near work, has the same effect as the lens $F\infty$ when used for distance, is represented by:

$$Fn = \frac{p_1{}^2}{\dfrac{p^2}{F\infty} + n^2 p}$$

when p_1 is the distance of the near fixation point from the cornea, p its distance from the correcting lens, and n the distance of the correcting lens from the cornea. A series of calculated values is given in Table XXXII in the Appendix.

We have already seen[1] that in presbyopes with an extra spherical element for reading, the additional convexity makes the incident light more nearly parallel so that a smaller correction factor is required.

Some further consideration must be given to the effect of the position of the spectacle lens on the accommodative requirement. This arises because of the difference between *spectacle accommodation* which is conventionally expressed as the vergence of rays from a near object at the spectacle plane and the true *ocular accommodation* which is the actual change in focusing made by the eye. Thus if a myope changes his distance correction from spectacles to contact lenses, the accommodative advantage given by his concave lenses a certain distance from the eye is lost. Indeed, the greater accommodative requirement when wearing contact lenses may be an inconvenience to myopes who commence to use them when their accommodation is reaching presbyopic restrictions. Conversely, the accommodative requirement of a hypermetrope is greater wearing spectacles than contact lenses.

THE SIZE OF THE IMAGE

From Figs. 270 and 271, since the lines aa_1 and bb_1 are parallel, it is at once evident that when a lens is placed in the anterior focal plane of the eye the size of the image is the same as that of one formed by the dioptric apparatus of the eye by itself; this image is, of course, not on the retina. Lenses forming an image of the same size are said to be EQUIVALENT; it follows that *all lenses in the anterior focal plane of the eye are equivalent.*

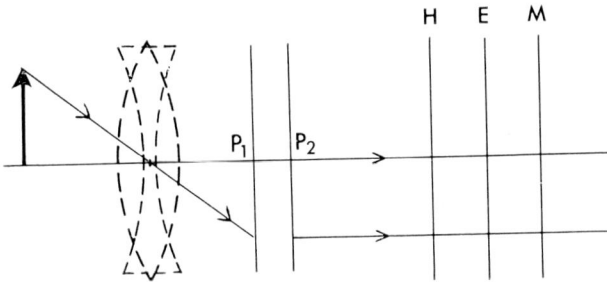

FIG. 275.

In the case of an eye with axial ametropia, the anterior principal focus and the principal points are the same as those of an emmetropic eye (Fig. 275). If, therefore, a correcting lens is placed at the anterior principal focus, the ray from an extremity of an object which passes through this point will not be deviated. As it is this ray by which the size of the retinal image is determined, it follows that *in an axially ametropic eye corrected by a lens situated in the anterior focal plane, the size of the image is the same as that*

[1] p. 218.

formed by an emmetropic eye; an eye corrected by a lens in this position is thus equivalent to a normal eye.

The concept of equivalence is, however, of limited applicability in the optics of the corrected ametropic eye. In the first place there is the practical question of the position in which most corrections are worn, which is usually closer to the eye than the anterior focal plane. A second consideration is the difficulty of comparison with the size of the image in the emmetropic eye, the optics of which is itself subject to considerable variation.

When the correcting lens is not in the anterior focal plane, several situations arise. It is evident that a virtual image of an object AB will be

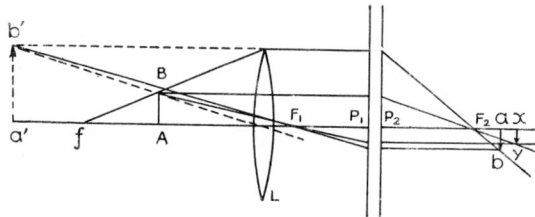

Fig. 276.—The Effect of a Convex Lens placed in Front of the Anterior Focus.

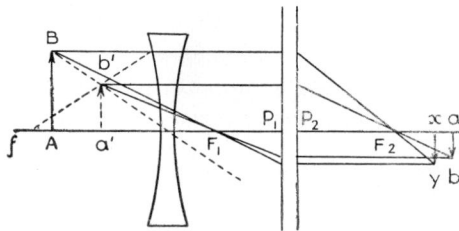

Fig. 277.—The Effect of a Concave Lens placed in Front of the Anterior Focus.

formed at $a'b'$, and this, by the construction shown in Fig. 276, will form an image at ab. It is seen that this is larger than xy, the image which would be formed by the refractive system of the eye alone. Similarly, if a concave lens is placed in front of the anterior focal plane the size of the image is reduced (Fig. 277), and converse constructions will show the opposite changes if the lens is placed between the anterior focal plane and the cornea.

It follows that while all lenses placed in the anterior focal plane are equivalent, *if a convex lens is moved away from the anterior focal plane of the eye* within limits, *the image increases in size and moves forwards, while it diminishes and moves backwards if the lens is moved towards the eye. If a concave lens is moved away from the anterior focal plane of the eye the image diminishes and moves backwards, while it increases and moves forwards if the lens is moved towards the eye.*

Wherever the correction is placed, two comparative aspects of its effect on the size of the retinal image require consideration. First, how does it compare with the size of the image in the uncorrected eye?—this is the *spectacle magnification*; secondly, how does it compare with the size of the image of the emmetropic eye?—the concept of *relative spectacle magnification*.

SPECTACLE MAGNIFICATION can be estimated only by deciding upon a method for denoting the size of the blurred retinal image in the uncorrected ametropic eye. This has obvious difficulties but the most satisfactory solution is to consider the centre of the blur-circle formed by the image of the extremity of the object in question; this point is taken as the extremity of the image to be considered. In order to determine the position of this point, we have recourse to the consideration of the entrance and exit pupils[1]. In Fig. 278 the ray from the extremity of the object to the centre of the entrance pupil (E) will emerge from the centre of the exit pupil (E′) and where

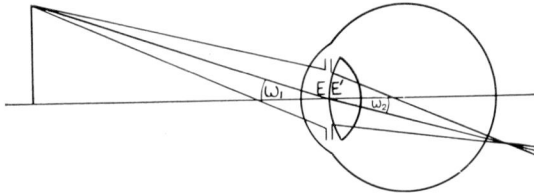

FIG. 278.—The determination of the size of the blurred image by the ray passing through the centres of the entrance (E) and exit (E′) pupils (A. G. Bennett).

this ray strikes the retina is considered to be the point in question. The angle which these rays make with the axis before striking the entrance pupil and on leaving the exit pupil, ω_1 and ω_2 respectively, may be assumed to bear a constant relationship with one another, and any alteration in the angle subtended at the entrance pupil will thus proportionately affect the angle subtended at the exit pupil. Since the change in the latter produced by interposing a correcting lens represents the change in size of the retinal image before and after correction, the alteration in the angle subtended at the entrance pupil can be used to define spectacle magnification.

Spectacle magnification (SM) may therefore be defined as the ratio between the angles subtended by this ray at the centre of the entrance pupil with and without the optical correction. The angle without the correction is that subtended by the extremity of the object itself, the angle with the correction in place is that subtended by the extremity of the image which the correcting lens forms of the object. This can be expressed as follows:

$$\text{SM} = \frac{\text{Angle subtended by image at the centre of the entrance pupil}}{\text{Angle subtended by object situated at infinity at centre of entrance pupil}}$$

$$= \omega_c/\omega_s \text{ in Fig. 279.}$$

[1] p. 137.

In Fig. 279, let h be the height of the virtual image formed by a myopic correcting lens of an object at infinity.

$$\text{Tan } \omega_c = \frac{h}{-f + d} \qquad\qquad \text{Tan } \omega_s = \frac{h}{-f}$$

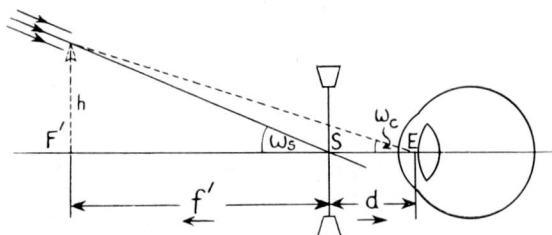

FIG. 279.—SPECTACLE MAGNIFICATION (A. G. Bennett).

If the angles are small their tangents are equal to the angles themselves, therefore:

$$\text{SM} = \frac{\omega_c}{\omega_s} \simeq \frac{\text{Tan } \omega_c}{\text{Tan } \omega_s} \quad \text{and} \quad \text{SM} = \frac{1}{1 - dF} \; (\simeq 1 + dF \text{ if the factor } dF \text{ is small})$$

where F is the power of the lens and d the distance between the plane of the correction and the entrance pupil.

From this it is seen that unless a correcting lens is placed at the entrance pupil it always alters the size of the retinal image, diminishing it in myopia and increasing it in hypermetropia. Furthermore, the closer the correction is placed to the entrance pupil the less the effect it has on the size of the retinal image.

Thus the blurred retinal image of an uncorrected eye is altered considerably less in size by a contact lens than by orthodox spectacles (Fig. 280). It is worth noting that the term spectacle magnification applies both to contact lenses and to spectacle lenses; in fact, as we have just seen, the spectacle magnification produced by contact lenses is almost unity.

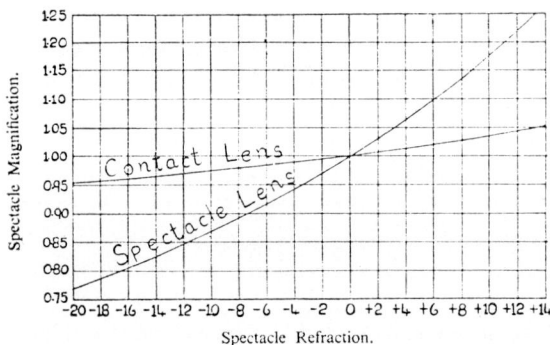

FIG. 280.—SPECTACLE MAGNIFICATION OF ORTHODOX SPECTACLES
AND CONTACT LENSES.

The graph shows the magnification computed for thin lenses placed 12 mm. in front of the corneal vertex (15 mm. from the entrance pupil) and the corresponding graph for contact lenses (assumed thin) positioned 3 mm. from the entrance pupil. The figures make allowance for effectivity so that both sets of the results are plotted in terms of the spectacle refraction (A. G. Bennett).

(RSM) is the ratio of the size of the retinal image of a distant object in the corrected ametropic eye to that in the emmetropic eye. For the purpose of this definition the latter should be specified as the schematic emmetropic eye.

The sizes of the images of an object at infinity formed by two refracting systems are in inverse proportion to their equivalent power; therefore, if

F_E is the power of the schematic emmetropic eye and
F_A the power of an (uncorrected) ametropic eye,
F_s the spectacle refraction,
d the distance from the spectacle plane to the first principal point of the eye, and
F the equivalent power of the corrected ametropic eye,

$$\text{RSM} = \frac{F_E}{F} = \frac{F_E}{F_A + F_s - dF_A F_s}$$

In purely axial ametropia this can be shown to be

$$\frac{1}{1 - (f + d)F_s}$$

where f = the anterior focal length of an uncorrected ametropic eye, which in this instance is identical with that of the schematic emmetropic eye.

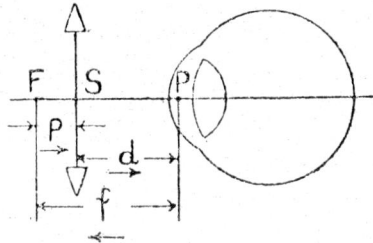

FIG. 281.—RELATIVE SPECTACLE MAGNIFICATION.

F, 1st principal focus; P, corneal vertex; S, spectacle point; d, distance from S to P; f, 1st focal length; p, distance from anterior focal point of eye to spectacle point. $p = -(f + d)$ (after A. G. Bennett).

The factor $(f + d)$ may be denoted by the letter p, and this, if the sign convention is observed, is the distance between the correcting lens and the anterior focal plane of the eye. When p is zero the relative spectacle magnification becomes unity, and therefore the size of the retinal image in an axial ametropic eye is the same as that in a schematic emmetropic eye (Fig. 281).

$$\text{RSM is therefore } \frac{1}{1 + pF_s} \simeq 1 - pF_s$$

In refractive ametropia the position differs. If K is the ocular refraction as measured at the principal point, then $F_A = F_E - K$. Using this expression in the formula for relative spectacle magnification we get:

$$\frac{F_A + K}{F_s + F_A - dF_s F_A}$$

and since K is $\dfrac{F_s}{1 - dF_s}$, it can easily be shown that

$$\text{RSM} = \frac{1}{1 - dF_s} \simeq 1 + dF_s$$

Figure 282 shows a comparison of relative spectacle magnification for various spectacle refractions on the assumption of purely refractive or purely axial ametropias, calculated for a spectacle distance of 12 mm.

Since we cannot at present easily determine whether or to what degree an ametropia is axial or refractive, and since the schematic emmetropic eye is somewhat of a myth, the whole question of relative spectacle magnification is an academic matter.

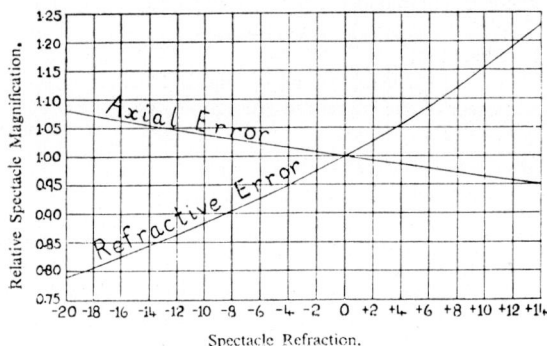

FIG. 282.—The relative spectacle magnification of orthodox spectacles on the assumption of a purely axial and of a purely refractive error (A. G. Bennett).

The importance of the size of the retinal image in relation to the position of the correction is seen when the refractive errors of the two eyes differ (anisometropia). If the ametropia is purely axial in nature, retinal images of similar sizes will be produced by spectacle lenses in the anterior focal plane of each eye. The size-difference between the blurred images of the uncorrected eyes, however, would be present in the same degree as between the clear images of the eyes corrected by contact lenses.

Airy. *Trans. Camb. phil. Soc.*, **2,** 267 (1827); **8,** 361 (1849).

Bennett. *Optics of Contact Lenses*, 4th. ed., London (1966).

Bischoff (1772). Cited by von Rohr (1915).

Böhm. *Das Schielen und der Sehnenschnitt*, Berlin (1845).

Boerhaave. *Prælectiones publicæ, de morbis oculorum* (1708); edited by Haller, publ. Göttingen (1750).

Cooper, White. *On Near Sight, Aged Sight and Impaired Vision*, London, 97 (1853).

Daza de Valdés. *Uso de los antojos para todo genero de vistas*, Seville (1623).

Dehais-Gendron. *Traité des maladies des yeux*, Paris (1770).

Donders. *v. Graefes Arch. Ophthal.*, **4** (1), 301, (1858); **6** (1), 62; (2), 210 (1860). *On the Anomalies of Accommodation and Refraction of the Eye*, London (1864).

Goode. *Trans. Camb. phil. Soc.*, **8,** 493 (1847). *Edin. Monthly J. med. Sci.*, **8,** 711 (1848).

Guérin. *Traité sur les maladies des yeux*, Lyons (1769).

Hamberger. *Optica oculorum*, Jena (1696).

Hamilton. *Edin. Monthly J. med. Sci.*, **7,** 891 (1847).

Hays. Lawrence's *A Treatise on the Diseases of the Eye*, Phila., 669 (1854).

Janin. *Mémoires et observations anatomiques, physiologiques et physiques sur l'oeil*, Paris, 429 (1772).

Kästner. *Vollständiger Lehrbegriff d. Optik*, Altenburg (1755).

Kepler. *Ad vitellionem paralipomena*, Frankfurt (1604).

Leutmann. *Neue Anmerckungen vom Glasschleiffen*, 1st ed., Wittenberg (1728); 2nd ed., Halle (1738).

Mackenzie. *A Practical Treatise on the Diseases of the Eye*, London, 718 (1830).

Maurolico. *Photismi de lumine et umbra*, Venice (1575).

Morgagni. *De sedibus et causis morborum per anatomen indigatis*, Venice (1761).

Newton. *Opticks*, London (1704).

Percival. *The Prescribing of Spectacles*, Bristol (1928).

Plempius.   *Ophthalmographia*, Amsterdam (1632).
Porterfield. *A Treatise on the Eye*, Edinb., **2**, 36, 57 (1759).
Richter.   *Anfangsgründe   der   Wundarznei-kunst*, Göttingen, **3** (1790).
Ritterich.   *Das Schielen und seine Heilung*, Leipzig, 73 (1843).
von Rohr. *Z. ophthal. Opt.*, **3**, 111 (1915).
Ruete. *Lhb. der Ophthalmologie für Aerzte u. Studirende*, Braunschweig, **1**, 234 (1853).
Scarpa. *Saggio di osservazioni e d'esperienze sulle principali malattie degli occhi*, Pavia, 211 (1801).
Schnyder.   *Ann.   Oculist.* (Paris), **21**, 222 (1849).

Sichel. *Ann. Oculist.* (Paris), **13**, 5, 49, 109, 169; **14**, 14, 193 (1845).
Smee.   *The Eye in Health and Disease*, London, 33 (1854).
Smith.   *A Compleat System of Opticks*, Camb. (1738).
Stellwag von Carion. *S.B. Akad. Wiss. Wien, Math. Klasse*, **16**, 187 (1855).
Ware. *Phil. Trans.*, **103**, 43 (1813).
Weller. *Diätetik für gesunde und schwache Augen*, Berlin (1821).
Wells. *Phil. Trans.*, **101**, 378 (1811).
Young. *Phil. Trans.*, **91**, 23 (1801).
  A Course of Lectures on Natural Philosophy and the Mechanical Arts, London, **1**, 447 (1807).

The Developmental Evolution of the Refractive State

CHANGES IN THE REFRACTIVE STATE IN CHILDHOOD

It is an extraordinary fact that an approximation to emmetropia is maintained throughout infancy and childhood in spite of great alterations in the constituents of the refractive system. Measurements of the axial length of the eyes of new-born infants have been made by many workers.[1] The investigations of Sorsby and Sheridan (1960) indicate that the neonatal eye is about 18 mm. in length; ultrasonic determinations by Gernet (1964) gave a slightly smaller value. An axial growth of about 6 mm. to the average adult length of approximately 24 mm. would lead to the development of some 15 or more dioptres of myopia were this growth not accompanied by compensatory changes in the other components of the refractive system.

The changes with age in the axial length of the eye are obviously difficult to investigate in the first years of life and the earlier studies inaugurated by von Jaeger (1861) produced too few data to provide conclusive evidence, but from the work of Weiss (1897) it was deduced that the growth of the globe was complete by the age of seven. The evidence for this conclusion, however, was not substantial and the recent studies of Sorsby and his associates (1961) indicated otherwise; their investigations showed that at the age of three the eye attains almost its adult length and that between the ages of 3 and 13 the additional elongation averaged only 1 mm. It would seem, indeed, that the greatest increase in the axial length occurs in the early months of the first year, particularly in premature infants (Grignolo and Rivara, 1968).

The cornea probably reaches its adult proportions as quickly if not more so than the rest of the globe, practically all its post-natal growth occurring in the second six months of life.[2] Priestley Smith (1879) found little corneal growth between the ages of 5 and 19, and there is considerable evidence to show that the corneal diameter is of adult size well before the age of five,

---

[1] Vol. III, p. 311.   [2] Vol. III, p. 306.

possibly not much later than the first year (Holm, 1925; Kaiser, 1926; A. and S. Druault, 1946).

More important in consideration of the ocular refraction is the change in the corneal curvature during the period of growth, and here the evidence, again difficult to obtain in the early years, is less conclusive. Tscherning (1886) believed that the corneal radius of curvature remained at one-third of the axial length throughout life. von Reuss (1881) claimed that a progressive increase in the radius of curvature occurred, but other observers found fluctuations with age without evidence of a progressive increase in radius (Nordenson, 1883; Schiøtz, 1886). It would seem probable, however, that it is somewhat less in the new-born than in the adult (Donders, 1864, 6·67 mm.; de Vries, 1901, 7·2–6·6 mm.), but at which age it assumes its adult proportions is unknown. Holm (1925) found that the cornea gained only 4 D in refractive power during childhood, and Sorsby and his colleagues (1961) found little alteration between the ages of 3 and 13. This factor can therefore compensate only slightly for the change in axial elongation of the globe during this period.

The gradual deepening of the anterior chamber with development counteracts the optical effect of axial elongation to some extent; but the greatest compensating influence is the changes in the lens.

The alterations in the lens which occur during the growth of the eyeball are profound; indeed, many years ago Priestley Smith (1879) established the fact that the lens continues to grow throughout life. Its radii of curvature are considerably smaller in the new-born than in the adult[1]; thus von Pflugk's (1909) figures for the former are 5 mm. for the anterior and 4 mm. for the posterior surface, the corresponding adult figures being 11 and 6 mm. At birth the equatorial diameter averages about 6 to 6·5 mm. (von Jaeger, 1861; Merkel and Orr, 1891–92; Seefelder, 1908; Alajmo and Sala, 1932), some 3 mm. less than in an adult. The thickness of the lens in the new-born has been estimated at approximately 3 to 4 mm. (Heine, 1898; Stadfeldt, 1898; von Pflugk, 1909), but higher values have been suggested and the precise alteration during growth is not definitely known. It is, however, most probable that there is a steady increase during the first few years of life (Collins, 1890; Weale, 1963). How, if at all, the refractive index of the lens alters during growth is uncertain. We have already noted that the refractive index of its substance is not uniform and there is some suggestion that the general refractivity increases slightly in the first few years of life; the evidence, however, is contradictory (Woinow, 1874; Freytag, 1908; Huggert, 1948).

During growth, therefore, the lens increases its equatorial diameter and probably its thickness but its radii of curvature decrease, and this last factor is perhaps the most important in the decline of its optical power during early life. How these changes are related in time to other alterations in the optical

[1] Vol. III, p. 307.

components of the eye is not certain; there is some evidence that they take place to a large extent, although not wholly, within the first three years of life and possibly during a shorter period.

The change in total ocular refraction during the growth of the eyeball has been extensively studied. We have already remarked on the close approximation to emmetropia which exists in most subjects in early life, but the evidence suggests that a hypermetropia of +2 to +3 D is the usual refractive state in infants.[1] In the first six or seven years of life Brown and Kronfeld (1929) found that in 50% and Bothman (1932) in 75% of children no change or a slight increase of hypermetropia occurred (see Brown, 1936–42). In adolescence, however, the hypermetropia tends to lessen or gives way to myopia (Fig. 283). This trend of decreasing hypermetropia in the

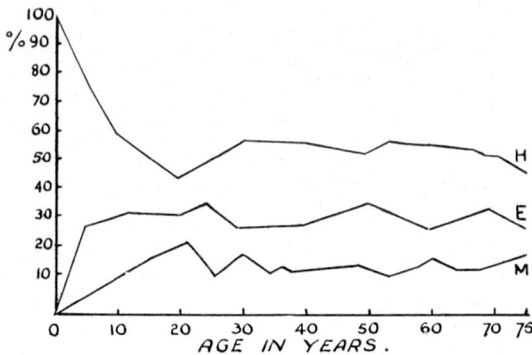

FIG. 283.—REFRACTIVE VARIATIONS WITH AGE.

The variation of the three types of refraction (H, hypermetropia; E, emmetropia; M, myopia) in the half-decades of life (after Herrnheiser).

years of rapid growth had been established at an early date (Germann, 1885; Herrnheiser, 1892; de Vries, 1901; and others) and has been observed in schoolchildren and college students in representative countries all over the world.[2]

That a slight increase in hypermetropia was the rule during the first seven years of life was found by Brown (1936–38) in a study of 8,820 refractive changes in 1,203 people aged from infancy to 51 years. This rather surprising finding was confirmed by Slataper (1950), but his figures for refraction in the early years of life were restricted and he included Brown's figures in his own series. On the other hand, the longitudinal studies of Hirsch (1964) on a

[1] Horstmann (1880), Ely (1880), Königstein (1881), Germann (1885), Merkel and Orr (1892) Herrnheiser (1892), de Vries (1901), Wibaut (1925), Franceschetti (1935), Cook and Glasscock (1951), Molnár (1961), Graham and Gray (1963), Gotoh and Kitazawa (1968), and others.

[2] In England, Dunstan (1932), Sorsby (1935); in the United States, Tenner (1915), Brown and Kronfeld (1929), Bothman (1932), Jackson (1932); in Germany, Cohn (1867–92), Randall (1888), Hess and Diederichs (1894), Bücklers (1953); in Austria, von Reuss (1881); in Holland, de Vries (1901), van der Meer (1901); in Scandinavia, Holm (1925), Goldschmidt (1968); in Russia, Popov (1931), Litvinova et al. (1964); in Japan, Miyashita (1931); and many others.

FIGS. 284 and 285.—THE OCULAR REFRACTION IN RELATION TO AGE
(A. SORSBY *et al.*).

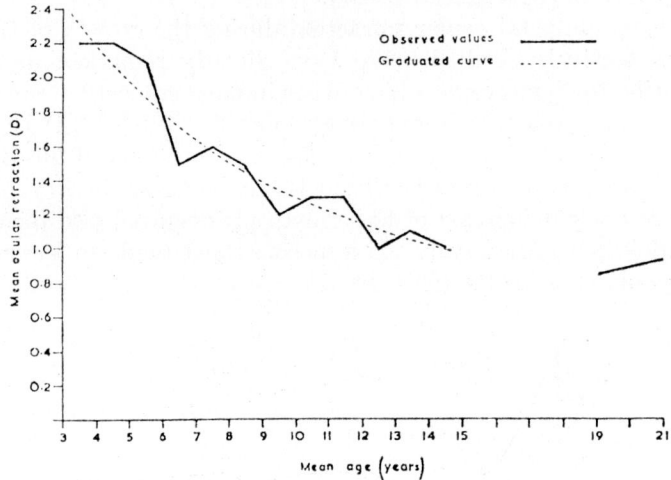

FIG. 284.—IN BOYS AND ARMY RECRUITS.

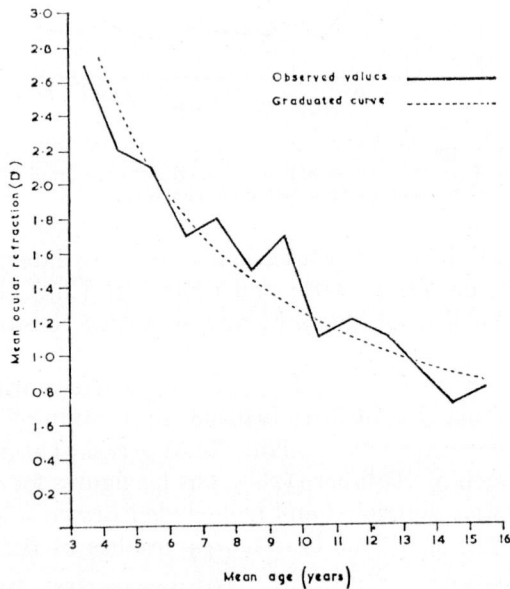

FIG. 285.—IN GIRLS.

It will be seen that the refraction in the vertical meridian declines with increasing age at first rapidly and then more slowly.

slightly older age-group appear to indicate that, while an increase of hyper-metropia is found in a small proportion of children, a decrease is the rule. The work of Sorsby and his colleagues (1961) who investigated the ocular refraction in children aged between 3 and 13 appears to confirm the traditional view that in general there is a steady decrease in refraction over these years, after which it remains fairly constant (Figs. 284–5).

It appears, therefore, that during the growth of the globe the 2 to 3 dioptres of hypermetropia present at birth largely disappear before puberty. This comparatively slight alteration in refraction is accompanied by the marked changes in the dimensions of the globe which occur very early, certainly under the age of three and most probably in the first year of life. It is true that our knowledge of physiological optics in the infant and in children up to the age of three is scanty ; between this age and thirteen, Sorsby and his colleagues (1961) found that a cross-section of their subjects showed a slight increase in axial length (but only by an average of 1·0 mm.) compared with an estimated growth of 4 to 5 mm. before the age of three, while the corneal power was little altered. These findings thus agree well with the widely held view that a decrease in power of the lens during growth is the principal factor counterbalancing the optical effect of an increase in the axial length. During this second slower phase of growth there is an average decline in the power of the lens by 1·5 D, associated with a decrease in the average total refraction of about 2 D.

These findings were based principally on a cross-sectional study but longitudinal studies show a more variable picture, and it should be emphasized that much is to be learnt from the behaviour of individual subjects in relation to the results of the survey. Thus, in some individuals the rates of change of the ocular components investigated during the period of slow growth differed markedly from the average. Some children have a relatively stationary axial length and in these it seems that the alterations in power of lens and cornea are similarly slight. Most of the children with marked axial elongation appear to be adequately compensated by more pronounced changes in the lens and cornea. It follows that the growth of the eye is a co-ordinated process. If it were not so in a particular individual, for example, when axial elongation is not fully compensated by a decline in the power of the optical components, then a significant myopic refractive error would result. How this co-ordinated growth is achieved is uncertain. Sorsby and his associates (1961) invoked embryonic organization as the factor responsible for the negative correlation between the power of the lens and the axial length. Simple mechanical factors, however, may provide a partial explanation ; thus the ring into which the outer extremity of the suspensory ligament is inserted increases in diameter with the growth of the globe and so will tend to flatten the lens (Collins, 1890 ; Weale, 1963), and it has been suggested that the tone of the ciliary muscle may affect the axial length of the globe (van Alphen, 1961).

The development of the refractive state has an obvious bearing on the definitive optical condition in adult life if such can be said to exist. This subject will therefore be discussed further when considering the nature of refractive errors.

CHANGES IN THE REFRACTIVE STATE IN THE ADULT

We have seen that it is probable that significant growth of the eye proceeds only until early puberty; thereafter in the majority of subjects the axial length of the globe remains practically unaltered. Nevertheless, after the stage when ocular growth has ceased, the evidence indicates that refractive changes occur with age. Thus Slataper (1950) found that there was a slight but steady increase in hypermetropia from the third to the seventh decade, and it is generally recognized that this process, although mild in degree, is the rule after the age of 40 (Hirsch, 1958; Exford, 1965). Thus an eye which was emmetropic at 30 years of age will show 0·25 dioptre of hypermetropia at 55, an addition of 0·75 may be evident at 60, of 1 dioptre at 70, and at 80 years this may increase to about 2·5 dioptres. Hypermetropia of this origin is frequently designated ACQUIRED HYPERMETROPIA (SENILE HYPERMETROPIA of Straub, 1899–1901; Dubois, 1907). On the other hand, in extreme old age a trend towards myopia may develop but this change may be due to the presence of incipient cataract; indeed, of 1,404 subjects in the eighth decade examined by Slataper (1950), only 18% had clear lenses.

The precise cause of these variations in refraction is not certain but it is not disputed that they originate from changes in the lens. In this connection the decreasing curvature of its surfaces as it continues to grow throughout life is probably of importance, while it has been suggested that changes in the refractive index involving an increase in optical density of the cortex, thus making the lens more uniformly refractive, could also contribute to a decrease of its optical power (Parsons, 1906). As we have noted, however, it is by no means certain that the refractive index of the nucleus of the normal lens or cortex alters with age. Possibly the relative or absolute size of the nucleus may decrease with advancing years, thereby reducing the lenticular power (Huggert, 1946; Weale, 1963).

This increase of hypermetropia with age is real; an *apparent increase* due to the progressive failure of accommodation also occurs with advancing years. In early life, unless the error is unusually large, the accommodative power can correct all the hypermetropia; in later life a progressively smaller proportion of the error can be overcome in this way. In this respect, although the hypermetropia does not, in fact, increase, it increases functionally with great rapidity[1]. On the other hand, longitudinal studies have shown that this increase of hypermetropia is by no means invariable; myopia may similarly increase progressively in an unexplained way from the third to the ninth decade (− 6·5 to − 20·0 D, Bücklers, 1953).

[1] p. 177.

Alajmo and Sala. *Boll. Oculist*, **11**, 130 (1932).
van Alphen. *Ophthalmologica*, **142**, Suppl. (1961).
Bothman. *Arch. Ophthal.*, **7**, 294 (1932).
Bourgeois and Tscherning. *Ann. Oculist.* (Paris), **96**, 203 (1886).
Brown. *Amer. J. Ophthal.*, **19**, 1106 (1936). *Arch. Ophthal.*, **19**, 719 (1938); **28**, 845 (1942).
Brown and Kronfeld. *XIII int. Cong. Ophthal.*, Amsterdam, **1**, 87 (1929).
Bücklers. *Brit. J. Ophthal.*, **37**, 587 (1953).
Cohn. *Untersuch. d. Augen d. 10,060 Schulkindern*, Leipzig (1867). *v. Graefes Arch. Ophthal.*, **17** (2), 305 (1871). *Die Hygiene d. Auges in den Schulen*, Leipzig (1883). *Lhb. d. Hygiene d. Auges*, Leipzig (1892).
Collins. *Roy. Lond. ophthal. Hosp. Rep.*, **13**, 81 (1890).
Cook and Glasscock. *Amer. J. Ophthal.*, **34**, 1407 (1951).
Donders. *On the Anomalies of Accommodation and Refraction of the Eye*, London (1864).
Druault, A. and S. *Ann. Oculist.* (Paris), **179**, 375 (1946).
Dubois. *Over de verandering der refractie gedurende den loop van het leven* (Diss.), Utrecht (1907).
Dunstan. *Med. Officer*, London, **48**, 111 (1932).
Ely. *Arch. Augenheilk.*, **9**, 431 (1880).
Exford. *Amer. J. Optom.*, **42**, 685 (1965).
Francheschetti. *Klin. Mbl. Augenheilk.*, **95**, 98 (1935).
Freytag. *Die Brechungsindices d. Linse*, Wiesbaden (1908).
Gernet. *v. Graefes Arch. Ophthal.*, **166**, 530 (1964).
Germann. *v. Graefes Arch. Ophthal.*, **31** (2), 121 (1885).
Goldschmidt. *Acta ophthal.* (Kbh.), Suppl. 98 (1968).
Gotoh and Kitazawa. *Jap. J. Ophthal.*, **12**, 203 (1968).
Graham and Gray. *Brit. med. J.*, **1**, 1452 (1963).
Grignolo and Rivara. *Ann. Oculist.* (Paris), **201**, 817 (1968).
Heine. *v. Graefes Arch. Ophthal.*, **46**, 525 (1898).
Herrnheiser. *Z. Heilk.*, **13**, 342 (1892).
Hess and Diederichs. *Arch. Augenheilk.*, **29**, 1 (1894).
Hirsch. *Amer. J. Optom.*, **35**, 229 (1958); **41**, 137 (1964).
Holm. *Acta ophthal.* (Kbh.), **3**, 121, 335 (1925).

Horstmann. *Klin. Mbl. Augenheilk.*, **18**, 495 (1880).
Huggert. *Acta ophthal.* (Kbh.), **24**, 43 (1946); Suppl. 30 (1948).
Jackson. *J. Amer. med. Ass.*, **98**, 132 (1932).
von Jaeger. *Ueber die Einstellungen des dioptrischen Apparates in menschlichen Auge*, Vienna (1861).
Kaiser. *v. Graefes Arch. Ophthal.*, **116**, 288 (1926).
Königstein. *Med. Jb.*, Wien, 47 (1881).
Litvinova, Volokitenko and Pikolova. *Oftal. Zh.*, No. 2, 87 (1964).
van der Meer. *Onderzoek der oogen var de leerlingen van het stedelijk gymnasium en van de middelbare scholen te Amsterdam gedurende 1898* (Diss.), Amsterdam (1901).
Merkel and Orr. *Anat. Hefte*, **1**, 271 (1891–2).
Miyashita. *Acta Soc. ophthal. jap.*, **35**, 934 (1931).
Molnár. *v. Graefes Arch. Ophthal.*, **163**, 518 (1961).
Nordenson. *Ann. Oculist.* (Paris), **89**, 110 (1883).
Parsons. *The Pathology of the Eye*, London, **3**, 929 (1906).
von Pflugk. *Klin. Mbl. Augenheilk.*, **47** (2), 1 (1909).
Popov. *Russ. oftal. Z.*, **14**, 88 (1931).
Randall. *VII int. Cong. Ophthal.*, Heidelberg, 511 (1888).
von Reuss. *v. Graefes Arch. Ophthal.*, **27** (1), 27 (1881).
Schiøtz. *Arch. Augenheilk.*, **16**, 37 (1886).
Seefelder. *v. Graefes Arch. Ophthal.*, **68**, 275 (1908).
Slataper. *Arch. Ophthal.*, **43**, 466 (1950).
Smith, Priestley. *Glaucoma*, London (1879).
Sorsby. *Lond. Cnty. Cncl. Ann. Rep. (1933)*, **4** (3), 55 (1935).
Sorsby, Benjamin and Sheridan. *Refraction and its Components during the Growth of the Eye from the Age of Three* (MRC Spec. Rep. Series, No. 301), London (1961).
Sorsby and Sheridan. *J. Anat.*, **94**, 193 (1960).
Stadfeldt. *Den menneskelige linses optiske konstaner*, Copenhagen (1898).
Straub. *Ned. T. Geneesk.*, **35**, 570 (1899). *Z. Psychol. Physiol. Sinnes.*, **25**, 78 (1901).
Tenner. *N.Y. med. J.*, **102**, 611 (1915).
Tscherning. *Hospitalstidende*, **4**, 1129 (1886).
de Vries. *Ned. T. Geneesk.*, **37**, 325 (1901).
Weale. *The Aging Eye*, London (1963).
Weiss. *Anat. Hefte*, **8**, 191 (1897).
Wibaut. *v. Graefes Arch. Ophthal.*, **116**, 596 (1925).
Woinow. *Klin. Mbl. Augenheilk.*, **12**, 407 (1874).

Variations of the Refractive State

THE INCIDENCE OF REFRACTIVE ERRORS

The relative incidence of refractive errors has naturally excited a great deal of interest and many statistical studies are available. With exact clinical measurements (up to 0·12 D), emmetropia is found to be very rare indeed, since the usual refractive condition includes some degree of astigmatism. When, however, small refractive errors are neglected, it is found that most people are emmetropic or practically so. While mathematical emmetropia does not therefore exist, clinical emmetropia is the most common condition found in the adult. The relative incidence of refractive errors as

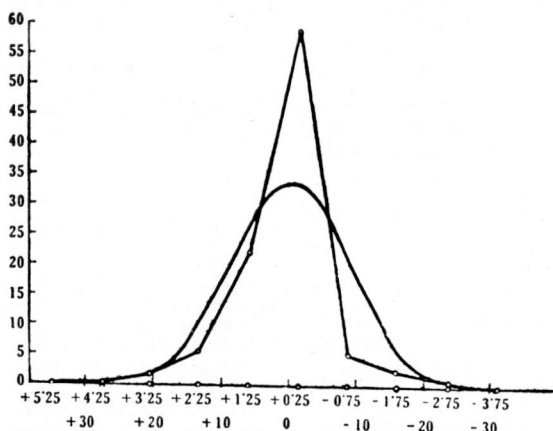

FIG. 286.—THE RELATIVE INCIDENCE OF REFRACTIVE ERRORS.

The refraction curves of Scheerer and Betsch compared with the theoretically derived binomial variation curve. The refractions were measured without cycloplegia (after A. Franceschetti).

observed over large numbers of individuals shows that, with two reservations, the significance of which will be discussed presently—namely, that the emmetropic cases are greater than theoretical expectation and the myopic include a disproportionate excess—the incidence of the various conditions can be regarded as physiological variations around a common mean such as would occur in any large group of people with reference to many biological characteristics such as height and so on.[1] The combined curve of Scheerer and Betsch, compiled from the examination of 12,000 eyes, is shown in Fig. 286, where it is compared with a theoretically derived binomial curve indicating variations determined by chance. Strömberg (1936) collected figures indicating that 98% of all refractions fell between + 4 and − 4 D;

[1] Steiger (1913), Wibaut (1925), Scheerer (1928), Kempf *et al.* (1928–29), Betsch (1929), Brown and Kronfeld (1929), Kronfeld and Devney (1931), Jackson (1932), Strömberg (1936), McLaren (1961), and others.

a graphic representation of this produced by Sorsby and his colleagues (1957) is given in Fig. 287.

We have already seen that there is a significant *variation with age*, but the relative incidence remains approximately the same. Wibaut (1925) analysed the refractive data of 2,398 newborn infants under cycloplegia from several German observers and found a distribution wherein the mode of the refraction curve is at 2 D of hypermetropia. The figures obtained by Cook and Glasscock (1951) for 1,000 eyes of newborn American infants, also examined

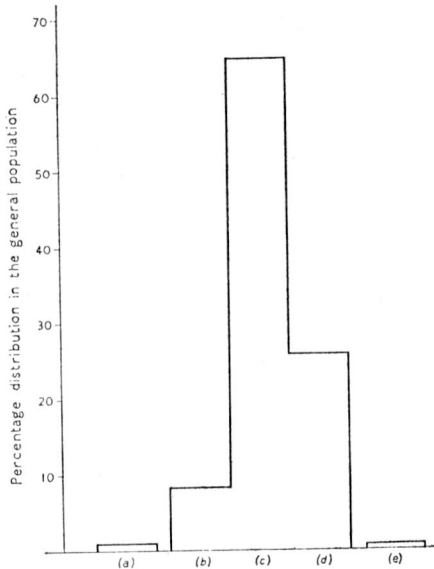

FIG. 287.—THE PERCENTAGE OF AMETROPIA IN THE GENERAL POPULATION (AFTER STRÖMBERG, 1936).

(a) Axial myopia (−4.25 D and over).
(b) Myopic aberrations (− 0.25 to 4.0 D).
(c) Emmetropia (0.0 to + 0.75 D).
(d) Hypermetropic aberrations (+ 1.0 to 3.75 D).
(e) Axial hypermetropia (+ 4.0 D and over).

under cycloplegia, are seen in Table XVI. Similar observations on London children between the ages of 4 and 8 (Sorsby, 1934) and 4 and 15 (Dunstan, 1932) gave comparable results; Sorsby's curve showed a peak at 2·3 D of hypermetropia (Fig. 288). Measuring 10,000 American eyes under cycloplegia and separating adolescents below 25 years of age from adults above that age, Brown and Kronfeld (1929) found both curves approximately symmetrical with the apex at + 1·0 dioptre (Fig. 289). The statistics of Scheerer (1928) and Betsch (1929) in adults without cycloplegia showed a norm of + 0·5 D (Fig. 286). In general terms, the relative distribution of refractive errors is thus approximately the same at all ages, but there is a shift of the whole

TABLE XVI

CLASSIFICATION OF TYPES OF REFRACTIVE ERRORS IN INFANTS

(Cook and Glasscock, 1951)

Type of error	White	Negro	Total	%
Simple hypermetropia	168	271	439	43·9
Hypermetropia with astigmatism	126	165	291	29·1
Simple myopia	49	118	167	16·7
Myopia with astigmatism	15	49	64	6·4
Mixed astigmatism	7	22	29	2·9
Plano	3	5	8	0·8
Cataracts	2	0	2	0·2
Totals	370	630	1,000	100·0

curve from hypermetropia towards myopia occurring rapidly in early life and then more slowly until maturity is reached.

Race undoubtedly exerts an influence upon refraction, a factor determined in the main by hereditary influences. Most of the statistics have been worked out on schoolchildren and young adults, but these, particularly the latter, are representative. In Britain the most instructive statistics are those of Harman (1936) covering 30,000 subjects over 16 years of age drawn from the general population who presented themselves for ocular examination: emmetropia and smaller errors are therefore generally absent. The distribution of refractive errors was:

Simple myopia, 4·5%; myopia over 5 D, 3·0%; myopia with astigmatism or myopic astigmatism, 19·5%. Total myopia, 27%.

Hypermetropia, 14%; hypermetropia with astigmatism or hypermetropic astigmatism, 42%. Total hypermetropia, 56%.

Mixed astigmatism, 2·25% (presbyopia, 39%).

Clarke (1924), in London, found among 5,000 eyes of patients presenting themselves for visual examination, 4·5% myopic and 8·5% hypermetropic; 86·0% were astigmatic with hypermetropic astigmatism approximately four times more common than myopic. Among Scottish children Thomson (1919) found 18·8% myopic.

In the United States of America the variation is somewhat comparable although myopia appears to be less frequent (Brown and Kronfeld, 1929); Jackson (1932), among 1,482 patients between 20 and 30 years of age, found 13·7% emmetropic, 66·7% hypermetropic and 19·6% myopic. Downing (1945), in an examination of 60,000 men of military age, found that 3·16% had vision below 20/200 owing to myopia (approximately − 2·5 D and over).

There would seem to be a regional distribution, for several statistics point to a lower incidence of myopia in the West than obtains in the Eastern States: thus, Derby (1880) found 35% of myopia, 15% hypermetropia and 49% emmetropia among Boston students, while Burnett (1911) found that among students of the University of California, 15% were myopic (over 0·25 D)—a very low figure. If, however, the native

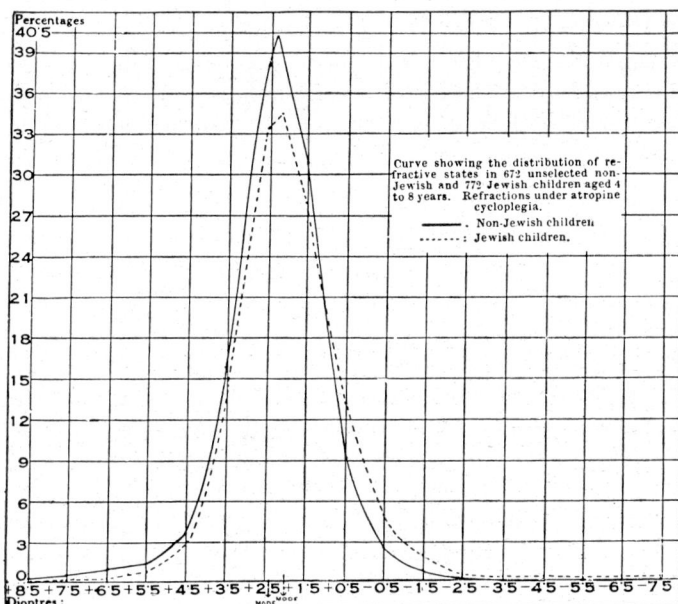

Fig. 288.—The relative incidence of refractive errors in children from 4 to 8 years of age (A. Sorsby).

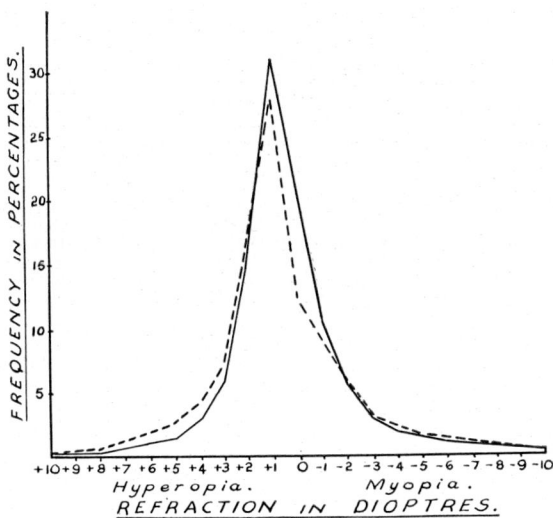

Fig. 289.—The relative incidence and refractive errors in adolescents (under 25 years)—broken line, and adults (above 25 years)—unbroken line (E. V. L. Brown and P. C. Kronfeld).

students alone were considered the figure fell to 12% (6% with myopia and 6% with myopic astigmatism).

In Central Europe the proportion compares with British figures. Witte (1923) found an incidence of myopia among the general population in Germany of 13·8% and Hess and Diederichs (1894) in schoolchildren aged 10 to 14 found :

emmetropia 35% ; hypermetropia up to 1 D, 22·4%, and above, 15·7% ; myopia up to 1 D, 11·1%, and above, 15·7%.

In Vienna, von Reuss (1881) found 51% emmetropic, 33·9% hypermetropic and 14·5% myopic. Russian figures approximate the German (Erismann, 1871) as also do Armenian and Georgian (Reich, 1878); among Russian children (8 to 10) Popov (1931) found 23% emmetropic, 57% hypermetropic and 2·4% myopic. Somewhat similar figures have been found in Holland (v. d. Meer, 1901; Straub, 1909), but a less tendency to myopia is seen in Scandinavia (Ask, 1910, in Sweden; Heinonen, 1923–29, in Finland; and Holm, 1925, Blegvad, 1927, 5% and Goldschmidt, 1986, who found 9·5% in children and 14·5%, in conscripts in Denmark). A considerably greater incidence of myopia occurs in Japan (Miyashita, 1931 ; Majima *et al.*, 1960) and also in China : Li (1920) found 53% of Chinese students myopic—about four times the incidence in a British or American college. Rasmussen (1936), analysing 120,000 cases presenting themselves for visual correction in China, found the proportions to be 70% myopia and myopic astigmatism, 20% hypermetropia with or without astigmatism and 10% presbyopia. In the Caucasian lands Dzen (1921) found 52·4% of myopia among the Chinese and 21·81% among the native Caucasians. In the West Indies myopia is as common as in Europe (van Trotsenburg, 1908) ; so also is it in Egypt, but the Nubians and Sudanese are almost free of short-sight (Meyerhof, 1910–14). Among Arabs myopia, sometimes of high degree, is common (Butler, 1916). Negroes as a race are more prone to hypermetropia than myopia (Druault-Toufesco, 1922 ; Holm, 1937), and among the Jews the opposite relationship occurs.

The Jews, indeed, are notoriously short-sighted and although comparable figures have been cited for Jews and Gentiles in Germany (Weiss, 1885 ; Kirchner, 1889), most authors find the incidence of myopia in the former unusually high (Gallus, 1922). That this tendency is racial rather than environmental is suggested by the fact that in various countries, Jews show a considerable excess of myopia, particularly of the higher types, compared with the indigenous population—in London (10·6% short-sighted Jewish children compared with 1·2% native in the London schools, Pearson and Moul, 1927; Sorsby, 1934), and similarly in New York (Tenner, 1915) (Fig. 288).

There seems to be no correlation with *sex*.

Wild animals are usually emmetropic or hypermetropic, while domesticated animals such as horses or cattle, while usually hypermetropic (Lang and Barrett,

1886), show a considerable percentage of myopes (some 30% of horses myopic from 1 to 5 D, and higher figures in cattle: Sørensen, 1920; Wiedemann, 1926; Dubar and Thieulin, 1927; and others). Cats and dogs are usually emmetropic (Lang and Barrett, 1886; Vogt, 1936); rats and mice hypermetropic (Lang and Barrett, 1886); but monkeys, independently of their age or their term of captivity, show a large proportion of myopes, sometimes of very high degree (up to − 20 D) (Behr, 1919; Jablonski, 1926, from the Berlin Zoo; Tamura, 1932, in Japan).

Ask. *III int. Cong. School Hyg.*, Paris (1910).
   See Nagel's *Jber. Ophthal.*, **42,** 762 (1911).
Behr. *Klin. Mbl. Augenheilk.*, **62,** 412 (1919).
Betsch. *Klin. Mbl. Augenheilk.*, **82,** 365 (1929).
Blegvad. *Acta ophthal.* (Kbh.), **5,** 49 (1927).
Brown and Kronfeld. *XIII int. Cong. Ophthal.*, Amsterdam, **1,** 87 (1929).
Burnett. *Univ. Calif. Publ. Physiol.*, **4,** 75 (1911).
Butler. *Ophthalmoscope*, **14,** 60 (1916).
Clarke. *The Errors of Accommodation and Refraction of the Eye*, 5th ed., London (1924).
Cook and Glasscock. *Amer. J. Ophthal.*, **34,** 1407 (1951).
Derby. *Boston med. surg. J.*, **102,** 620 (1880).
Downing. *Arch. Ophthal.*, **33,** 137 (1945).
Druault-Toufesco. *Ann. Oculist.* (Paris), **159,** 321, 493, 709, 865 (1922).
Dubar and Thieulin. *Reg. gén. Méd. vétérin.*, **36,** 561 (1927).
Dunstan. *Med. Officer*, London, **48,** 111 (1932).
   Brit. J. Ophthal., **18,** 404 (1934).
Dzen. *Nat. med. J. China*, **7,** 206 (1921).
Erismann. *v. Graefes Arch. Ophthal.*, **17** (1), 1 (1871).
Gallus. *Z. Augenheilk.*, **48,** 215 (1922).
Goldschmidt. *Acta ophthal.* (Kbh.), Suppl. 98 (1968).
Harman. *Brit. med. J.*, **2,** Suppl., 214 (1936).
Heinonen. *Finska Läk.-Sällsk. Handl.*, **65,** 172 (1923).
   Acta ophthal. (Kbh.), **2,** 35 (1924); **6,** 238 (1928); **7,** 301 (1929).
Hess and Diederichs. *Arch. Augenheilk.*, **29,** 1 (1894).
Holm. *Acta ophthal.* (Kbh.), **3,** 121 (1925); Suppl. 13 (1937).
Jablonski. *Arch. Augenheilk.*, **97,** 369 (1926).
Jackson. *J. Amer. med. Ass.*, **98,** 132 (1932).
Kempf, Jarman and Collins. *Publ. Hlth Rep.*, Wash., **43,** 1713 (1928).
   Refractive Errors in the Eyes of Children (Bull. 82, U.S. Publ. Hlth. Serv.) (1929).
Kirchner. *Z. Hyg.*, **7,** 3, 397 (1889).
Kronfeld and Devney. *Arch. Ophthal.*, **4,** 873 (1930).
   v. Graefes Arch. Ophthal., **126,** 487 (1931).
Lang and Barrett. *Roy. Lond. ophthal. Hosp. Rep.*, **11,** 103 (1886).
Li. *Nat. med. J. China*, **6,** 108 (1920).
McLaren. *Brit. J. Ophthal.*, **45,** 604 (1961).
Majima, Nakajima, Ichikawa and Watanabe. *Amer. J. Ophthal.*, **50,** 139 (1960).

van der Meer. *Onderzoek der oogen var de leerlingen van het stedelijk gymnasium en van de middelbare scholen te Amsterdam gedurende 1898* (*Diss.*), Amsterdam (1901).
Meyerhof. *Zbl. prakt. Augenheilk.*, **34,** 193 (1910).
   Klin. Mbl. Augenheilk., **48** (2), 220 (1910).
   Ann. Oculist. (Paris), **151,** 257 (1914).
Miyashita. *Acta Soc. ophthal. jap.*, **35,** 934 (1931).
Pearson and Moul. *Ann. Eugen.*, **2,** 111, 290; **3,** 1 (1927).
Popov. *Russ. oftal. J.*, **14,** 88 (1931).
Rasmussen. *Brit. J. Ophthal.*, **20,** 350 (1936).
Reich. *v. Graefes Arch. Ophthal.*, **24** (3), 231 (1878).
von Reuss. *Wien. med. Presse*, **22,** 200, 234 (1881).
   v. Graefes Arch. Ophthal., **27** (1), 27 (1881).
Scheerer. *Ber. dtsch. ophthal. Ges.*, **47,** 118 (1928).
Sørensen. *Mschr. prakt. Tierheilk.*, **31,** 341 (1920).
Sorsby. *Trans. ophthal. Soc. U.K.*, **54,** 459 (1934).
Sorsby, Benjamin, Davey *et al. Emmetropia and its Aberrations* (*MRC Spec. Rep. Series No. 293*), London (1957).
Steiger. *Die Entstehung d. sphärischen Refraktionen d. menschlichen Auges*, Berlin (1913).
Straub. *v. Graefes Arch. Ophthal.*, **70,** 130 (1909).
Strömberg. *Acta ophthal.* (Kbh.), **14,** 281 (1936).
Tamura. *Acta Soc. ophthal. jap.*, **36,** 193 (1932).
Tenner. *N.Y. med. J.*, **102,** 611 (1915).
Thomson. *Brit. J. Ophthal.*, **3,** 303 (1919).
von Tratsenburg. *Ned. T. Geneesk.*, **44,** 1222 (1908).
Vogt. *Die Kurzsichtigkeit*, 3rd ed., Zürich (1936).
Weiss. *v. Graefes Arch. Ophthal.*, **31** (3), 239 (1885).
Wibaut. *v. Graefes Arch. Ophthal.*, **116,** 596 (1925).
Wiedemann. *Z. Veterinärkunde*, **38,** 257 (1926).
Witte. *Z. Augenheilk.*, **51,** 163 (1923).

THE NATURE OF REFRACTIVE ERRORS

The story of the evolution of thought on the genesis and nature of refractive errors is a perfect example of the way in which an orthodox theory founded on apparently unimpeachable but inadequate evidence can dominate the ideas and practice of successive generations to the exclusion of everything else, even although the logical application of the theory has involved the most far-reaching and frequently unfortunate social results. The view that the myopic eye was too long and the hypermetropic too short was based on the work of two mathematicians—Kepler (1611) who showed that in the former parallel rays of light came to a focus in front of the retina, and Newton (1704) who suggested that in the latter such rays were focused some

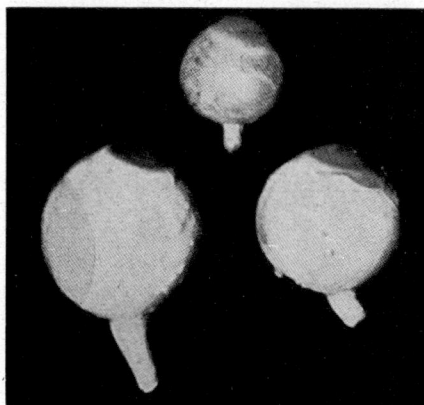 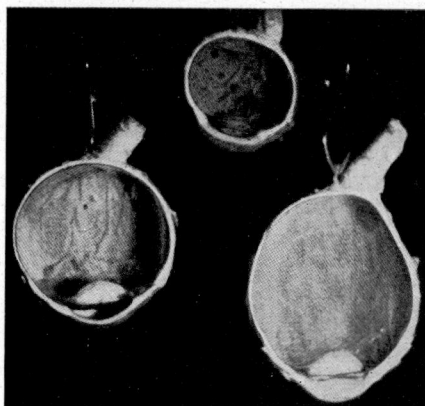

Fig. 290. Fig. 291.

FIGS. 290 and 291.—THE RELATIVE SIZES OF TYPICAL HUMAN EYES.

The globes (Fig. 290) of a newborn infant (on top), an emmetropic young adult (below right) and a myope of 12 D (below left); their sections are seen in Fig. 291 with the myopic eye to the right (A. Elschnig).

distance behind it. Confirmation of these views was rapidly received by the anatomical demonstration of the length of the myopic eye (Plempius, 1632; Boerhaave, 1708; and others), but little interest was taken until attention was drawn to the problem by Arlt (1856) who established the generalization that enucleated myopic eyes were long and pear-shaped, showing thinning of the posterior segment of the sclera (Figs. 290–1). The atrophic retinal changes in the central area and the occurrence of crescents at the disc were thus interpreted as traction phenomena due to weakness of the globe. The views of Arlt seemed to be confirmed by Donders's (1858) observation, using the Helmholtz keratometer, that the corneal refraction did not usually vary directly with the refractive state. A further elaboration was made by Schnabel and Herrnheiser (1895) who found the axial lengths of emmetropic and slightly myopic eyes to be of the same order, but significantly increased in myopia over 10 D. They concluded that while the length of the eye was not the only determinant in causing refractive errors, it was the essential cause of high myopia. For long, however, it was tacitly assumed that the refraction of the lens was practically constant and the theory of axial length remained generally unquestioned—the hypermetropic eye was an un-developed eye which had not fully grown and the myopic eye was overgrown, stretched and weak. The natural corollary, advocated by the extremist teachings of such enthusiasts as Cohn (1867–92), was that innumerable adolescents, unfortunately myopic, have for decades been condemned to educational handicap or even inactivity.

It was clearly stated by Donders (1864) in his classical work on refraction, that the dioptric power of the eye is the result of the convexity of the cornea, of the position and focal distance of the lens and of the length of the visual axis, each of which may in itself differ considerably in the appar-ently normal emmetropic eye so that they mutually compensate each other. A new era, however, was introduced in 1913 when the Swiss ophthalmologist ADOLF STEIGER [1868–1920] (Fig. 292), first approached the subject broadly from the bio-mathematical aspect in a study of the variability of the optical elements of the eye. Although the importance of his pioneer work was not fully appreciated for some 20 years, it is obvious that a statistical approach provides the only rational solution of a problem of this type. Using the Javal-Schiøtz ophthalmometer[1] he measured the refracting power of the corneæ of the eyes of 5,000 children and found variations over a con-siderably wider range than had ever been suspected (from 39 to 47 D) which he concluded occurred according to the laws of normal variability. As was the habit of the time, however, he neglected the lens and deduced the axial length by subtracting the corneal from the total refraction. He decided that the corneal refraction and axial length were unrelated, freely variable quantities, the chance union of which could produce all types of refractive error. He assumed that these components were determined by heredity and enunciated the quite unorthodox view that refractive errors were simply physiological variations, and that individuals were hypermetropic or myopic by the same chance that they were small or tall. Although his views cannot be unreservedly accepted, he must receive the credit for introducing a completely novel and revolutionary idea which had in it more of the elements of truth than the orthodox opinion of the previous half century.

In the meantime some attention had been given to the lens and its influence on the total refraction. von Reuss (1877–80), measuring 31 eyes painstakingly with the Helmholtz ophthalmometer, had found considerable variations in the curvature of the surfaces of this tissue and, collecting some 70 measurements from the literature, Awerbach (1900) had substantiated this conclusion. Subsequently, Zeeman (1911), Czellitzer (1927) and Tron (1929), with the more efficient aid of Tscherning's ophthalmophakometer,[2]

[1] p. 100.   [2] p. 103.

FIG. 292.—ADOLF STEIGER
[1868–1920]
(Courtesy of Prof. A. Huber, Zürich.)

FIG. 293.—EUGENE JANOVITCH TRON
[1892–1967]

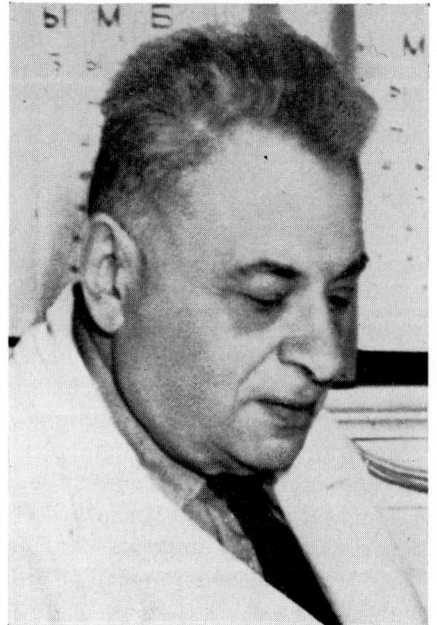

showed that the variation in the refractive power of the lens was of the order
of 14 D. Finally, E. J. TRON [1892–1967] (Fig. 293), who spent his professional
life in the Research Institute of Neurosurgery in Leningrad, in his two
classical papers discussing an analysis of 275 eyes (1934–35), established
conclusively the great variability of all the optical constants of the eye.
Tron's results showing these variations are given in Table XVII, the axial
length of the eye being determined by the difference between the total
refraction and its other optical constituents.

TABLE XVII

VARIABILITY OF THE OPTICAL CONSTANTS

(E. J. Tron)

	Limiting values	Mean square deviation	Average value
Radius of curvature of cornea (mm.)	6·85– 9·02	±0·34	7·77
„ „ „ ant. lens surface (mm.)	7·52–16·90	±0·78	11·00
„ „ „ post. „ „ (mm.)	3·51– 9·04	±0·87	5·78
Depth of anterior chamber (mm.)	2·16– 5·05	±0·41	3·27
Thickness of lens (mm.)	2·13– 5·37	±0·58	3·62
Refractive power of cornea (D)	37·10–48·98	±1·84	43·41
„ „ „ lens (D)	14·95–28·88	±2·20	20·44
„ „ „ entire eye (D)	52·59–66·88	±2·75	59·80
Deduced length of axis (mm.)	20·75–38·18	±3·13	25·15

Since Tron's investigations the gap in clinical methods has been filled
by the introduction of techniques which allow measurement of the length of
the axis of the eye by radiography and ultrasonography. These methods
have only comparatively recently been applied on a sufficiently large scale
to provide statistical results of significant value ; but their exploitation is of
unusual interest, for practical clinical methods are now available for obtaining
all the necessary information regarding the different constituents of the
optical system.

The variability of the optical elements of the eye is very striking.
Deller and his colleagues (1947), for example, found in a case of marked
anisometropia that the axial length of a highly myopic eye was more nearly
within " normal " limits than that of its emmetropic fellow. Analysis of
Tron's material shows that in emmetropia the refractive power of the eye
can vary between 52·59 and 64·21 D and the axial length between 22·42 and
27·30 mm. Within these very wide limits *different combinations of refractive
power and axial length can produce a " normal " refraction;* a hypermetrope
frequently has an abnormally long eye and the globe of a myope is often
abnormally short. Tron, indeed, found two emmetropic cases with axial
lengths of 21·19 and 30·39 mm. respectively ; and he established that in
ametropia only 30·2% of cases have an axial length outside the limits for
emmetropia, a percentage which is greatly reduced if eyes only within the

limits of $+ 4.0$ D and $- 6.0$ D are considered (Fig. 294). It would appear, therefore, that the refractive condition is determined by many variable components and that the *axial length is of no specific determining consequence in the incidence of low and medium errors of refraction* but only in the higher degrees of hypermetropia and myopia—a very different conclusion from the orthodox conception of a refractive state conditioned essentially by the combination of a number of optical constants with a variable axial length.

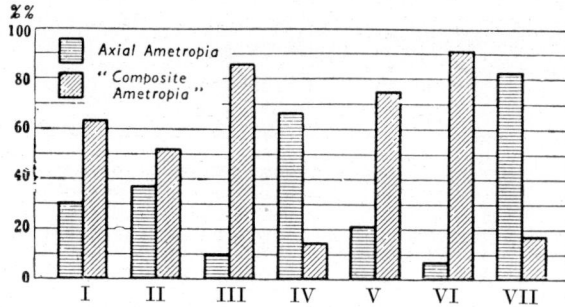

FIG. 294.—THE SIGNIFICANCE OF AXIAL LENGTH IN AMETROPIA.

I. Ametropic cases generally (215 eyes).
II. Myopia generally (120 eyes).
III. Myopia up to –6 D (62 eyes). The influence of axial length is insignificant.
IV. High myopia over –6 D (58 eyes). The influence of axial length is preponderant.
V. Hypermetropia generally (95 eyes).
VI. Hypermetropia up to $+ 4$ D (77 eyes). The influence of axial length is insignificant.
VII. High hypermetropia over $+ 4$ D (18 eyes). The influence of axial length is preponderant.

It is seen that the specific influence of axial length in determining the total refraction is marked only outside the limits of $+ 4$ and $- 6$ D (E. J. Tron).

The significance of these variations in the optical elements of the eye as pointed out by Tron (1934–35) is of considerable importance. He showed that the variations in the different elements follow approximately the chance distribution of the regular binomial curve with the single exception of the length of the axis (Figs. 295 to 302). If, however, myopic eyes of greater than $- 6.0$ D were excluded, he found that a symmetrical curve is again obtained (Fig. 303), a finding which can also be deduced from the statistics of Scheerer (1928) and Betsch (1929) by eliminating all cases which showed abnormal changes in the fundus (Fig. 304). These findings have been verified by Stenström (1946) who measured the total refraction, the curvature of the anterior surface of the cornea, the depth of the anterior chamber and the antero-posterior axis radiologically in 1,000 individuals. He found that all the elements of the refractive system showed a variation which did not noticeably diverge from the statistically normal with the exception of the antero-posterior axis. The conclusion therefore seems legitimate that, *with this exception, the variability of the constituent elements of the total refraction is a matter of chance.*

The continuous lines indicate the theoretical binomial curve, the broken lines indicate Tron's statistical results.

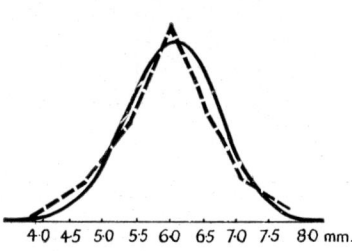

4·0 4·5 5·0 5·5 6·0 6·5 7·0 7·5 8·0 mm.

Fig. 295.—Depth of the anterior chamber.

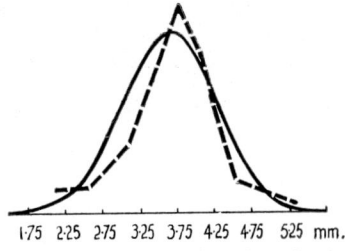

1·75 2·25 2·75 3·25 3·75 4·25 4·75 5·25 mm.

Fig. 296.—Thickness of the lens.

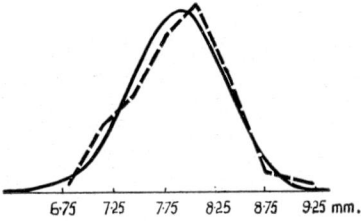

6·75   7·25   7·75   8·25   8·75   9·25 mm.

Fig. 297.—Radius of the cornea.

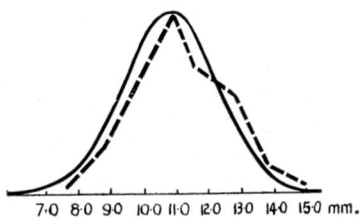

7·0 8·0 9·0 10·0 11·0 12·0 13·0 14·0 15·0 mm.

Fig. 298.—Radius of anterior surface of the lens.

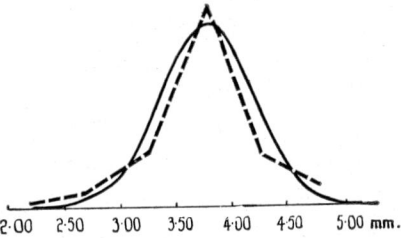

2·00   2·50   3·00   3·50   4·00   4·50   5·00 mm.

Fig. 299.—Radius of posterior surface of the lens.

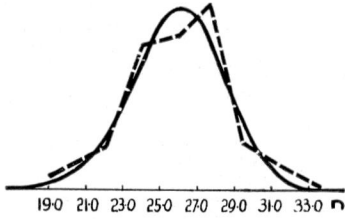

19·0 21·0 23·0 25·0 27·0 29·0 31·0 33·0 D.

Fig. 300.—Refractive power of the lens.

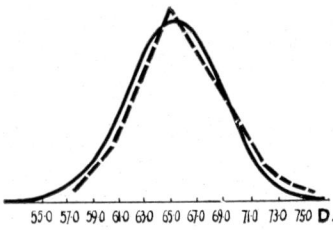

55·0 57·0 59·0 61·0 63·0 65·0 67·0 69·0 71·0 73·0 75·0 D.

Fig. 301.—Refractive power of the eye.

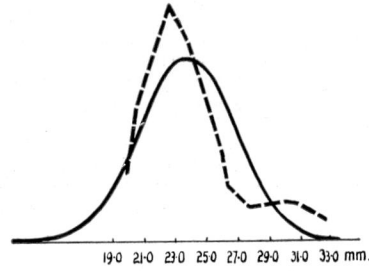

19·0 21·0 23·0 25·0 27·0 29·0 31·0 33·0 mm.

Fig. 302.—Axial length of all eyes.

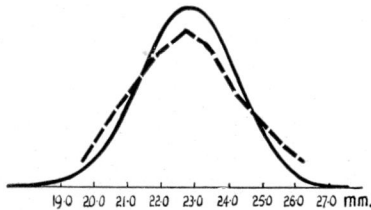

19·0 20·0 21·0 22·0 23·0 24·0 25·0 26·0 27·0 mm.

Fig. 303.—Axial length excluding eyes with a myopia greater than—6 D.

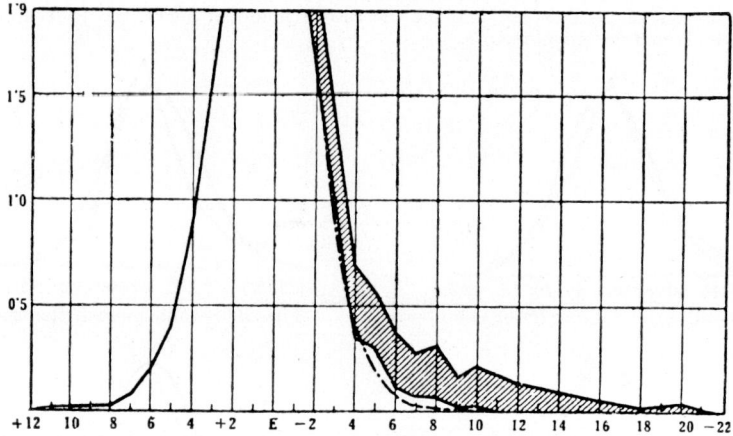

FIG. 304.—THE REFRACTION CURVE ELIMINATING CASES OF DEGENERATIVE CHANGES
IN THE FUNDUS.

Scheerer's frequency curve of refraction as seen in Fig. 286. The shaded area
covers the cases of myopia with degenerative fundus changes. The broken line shows
the theoretically derived binomial curve on the myopic side.

Stenström's (1946) statistical findings given in Table XVIII show the
small divergence of all the components of the refractive system except the
antero-posterior axis. The variation of this component diverges by showing
a considerable positive skewness and a pronounced positive excess. The
results indicate that the axis of the globe is a very important but not the
only element in determining the refraction.

TABLE XVIII

Elements	Arithmetic mean	Dispersion	Skewness	Excess
Radius of cornea (mm.)	7·86 ± 0·008	± 0·26 ± 0·006	—	—
Depth of anterior chamber (mm.)	3·68 ± 0·009	± 0·29 ± 0·006	—	—
Internal axial length (mm.)	24·00 ± 0·035	± 1·09 ± 0·024	+ 0·81 ± 0·077	+ 3·35 ± 0·154
Refractive power of cornea (D)	42·84 ± 0·044	± 1·40 ± 0·031	—	—
Refractive power of lens (D)	17·35 ± 0·044	± 1·38 ± 0·031	—	—
Total refractive power of the eye (D)	58·13 ± 0·056	± 1·78 ± 0·040	—	—

When we consider the variations in the total refraction of the eye,
however, in addition to the weighted variation occurring in the higher
degrees of ametropia, a second signficant divergence from chance variation
occurs—the excessive number of approximately emmetropic eyes as seen in
the high peak in Fig. 287. It would seem, indeed, as if, superimposed on
chance incidence, there is some regulating process which seeks to reproduce

the theoretically perfect eye, by which an excess in one constituent is balanced by moderation in another. This tendency was called EMMETROPIZATION by Falkenburg and Straub (1893). We shall see presently that the dominance of the emmetropic condition is further emphasized by the fact that astigmatism is rarer in this than in association with any other refractive state.[1]

In order to explain this preponderance and determine the relationship of the various elements in the dioptric system with each other, a study of the combinations in which they are usually found should provide information as to whether there is a tendency for a variation in one value to be balanced by an opposite variation in another. This question is of interest not only from the point of view of physiological optics, but also of the relative importance of genetic and environmental influences in determining the ultimate refraction of the eye; moreover, it raises wider issues on problems of growth and the inheritance of multiple characteristics. The earlier workers on this problem suffered from lack of adequate understanding of the variations of the optical components of the system,[2] although observations on the refractive differences found in twins provided a field for study less crowded with variables.[3] Accumulating data have given more significance to the work of Wibaut (1925–29), Berg (1931), Tron (1934–35), Stenström (1946), and more recently Sorsby and his colleagues (1957–62) and Dashevsky (1962).

The study of Sorsby and his colleagues of 94 emmetropes largely confirmed Tron's conclusions that a normal refraction may result from many different associations of optical components; axial lengths of 21 to 26 mm., corneal powers of 38 to 48 D and lens powers of 17 to 26 D were found. In a total series of 341 eyes, emmetropic and ametropic, it was again demonstrated that in the lower degrees of ametropia ($+ 4$ to $- 4$ D), a range which takes in about 98% of refractions, all the components including the axial length had a normal distribution.

As in the case of the series previously reported, the number of emmetropes exceeded that expected on purely statistical grounds and an analysis of how this arose showed that the corneal power, the lens power and the axial length were closely correlated in the emmetropic subjects. The correlation of lens power and axial length is close and holds even for the commonest refractive anomalies which appear to arise from a breakdown in correlation between the corneal power and the axial length. Emmetropization is presumably also partly determined by the combination of a greater axial length with a flatter cornea; at the same time, many emmetropes with similar corneal curvatures show a marked variation in axial length, for which the power of the lens must clearly compensate (Gernet, 1964). We have already seen that the organizing function of the growing retina is possibly a factor in

[1] p. 280.

[2] Barrington and Pearson (1909), Zeeman (1911), Streiff (1915), Wessely (1920), Pearson and Moul (1927).

[3] Jablonski (1922–26), Heinonen (1924), Beckershaus (1926), Schmidt (1928), Waardenburg (1930).

determining the decrease of the power of the lens which is associated with an increased axial length (Sorsby et al., 1961), but that simple physical changes such as an increase in the equatorial diameter of the globe or the tonus of the ciliary muscle may have some influence.

That the various tissues of the eye have a mutual relationship which tends towards emmetropization is, of course, a well-established phenomenon. The process of developmental induction under the influence of chemical organizers has been discussed in a previous Volume[1] and has recently been summarized by Coulombre (1965). Thus the development of the neural retina depends on the pigmentary epithelium, the induction of the lens as well as its orientation relative to the optic axis depends on the retina, while the lens to some extent controls the development of the cornea.

Whereas the lower degrees of ametropia may be determined by a faulty correlation between axial length and corneal power, there is little doubt that in the higher ranges, beyond $+ 4$ and $- 6$ D, an abnormal axial length is the greatest single determinant; indeed, Stenström's work (1946) seems to indicate that this is of the most importance in all refractive states.

The interrelationship of the various factors contributing to the ocular refraction is far from simple and is, indeed, impossible to describe other than mathematically. It is inevitable that some of the conclusions of such work cannot be expressed verbally but only as a series of correlation coefficients.

When two components of a system vary, if an increase in the value of one is accompanied by a simultaneous increase in the other the correlation is *positive*; if by a compensatory decrease in the other the correlation is *negative*. The degree to which any such interrelation occurs is expressed by the *coefficient of correlation*. When no relationship exists between the variations of the two components, the coefficient is 0; when the interrelationship is maximal so that each change in one is compensated exactly by a change in the other, the coefficient is 1.

Wibaut, Tron and Stenström found a negative correlation between the total refractive power and the axial length ($- 0.5$, $- 0.76$, $- 0.76 \pm 0.014$), which indicates that, although there is a compensating relation between them, all combinations between the two are not equally frequent.

van Alphen (1961) has subjected the methods and results of Stenström (1946) and Sorsby and his colleagues (1957) to rigorous examination along these lines. In Table XIX the correlation coefficients for various combinations of the optical elements are compared. In some there is a marked discrepancy between the two sources, as, for example, in that between the axial length and the power of the lens. His own extended analysis of the correlations between the optical elements based on partial and multiple correlation coefficients and factor analysis has led him to postulate three factors in the genesis of the refractive state.

The S factor operates in corneal power and axial length and does not contribute to the variability of refraction, anterior chamber depth and lens-power. Steiger had, in fact, realized that corneal curvature and axial length were correlated, the larger eye having the flatter cornea, but he paid little attention to this. van Alphen's P factor represents an underlying influence leading to deeper anterior chambers and flatter lenses in larger eyes. In this connection he provided some experimental evidence in the cat to suggest that the tone of the ciliary muscle could engender a tension in the choroid. This would counteract the tendency of the intra-ocular pressure to stretch the

[1] Vol. III, p. 51 *et seq.*

sclera during development. The third factor, R, relates to the shape of the eye. An eye of any basic size (factor S) stretches (factor P) during growth to become emmetropic from its initial hypermetropic state; the degree of adjustment (factor R) determines the final refraction and shape of the globe. He suggested that the possible influence of higher centres and psychological factors on the ciliary tonus might play a role in what he described as the " eye's self-focusing mechanism ".

TABLE XIX

CORRELATION COEFFICIENTS CALCULATED FROM THE DATA OF STENSTRÖM (1946) AND SORSBY
et al. (1957) (COMPUTER DATA)
(van Alphen)

The correlations are between 5 essential elements: 1, refraction (D), 2, axial length (mm.), 3, chamber depth (mm.), 4, corneal power (D) and 5, lens power (D).
Col. I and II, correlation coefficients between the optical elements for all eyes.
Col. III and IV, correlation coefficients for the 90% of eyes between ± 3 D.

Correlations	Stenström ± 10 dioptres I	Sorsby ± 8 dioptres II	Stenström ± 3 dioptres III	Sorsby ± 3 dioptres IV
12	−0·75	−0·77	−0·45	−0·59
13	−0·34	−0·46	−0·40	−0·50
14	−0·19	−0·30	−0·21	−0·26
15	−0·02	+0·28	+0·13	+0·42
23	+0·44	+0·46	+0·45	+0·39
24	−0·31	−0·28	−0·52	−0·51
25	−0·39	−0·49	−0·60	−0·60
34	+0·09	+0·19	+0·09	+0·14
35	−0·26	−0·46	−0·32	−0·44
45	−0·10	−0·10	−0·09	−0·09
Number of right eyes	1000	96	886	78

Of crucial significance is the validity of the methods used for determining the axial length of the eye. As we have noted, Stenström used the radiographic technique while Sorsby's group employed an optical method, claiming reasonably good correspondence to the radiographic method in a series of cases in which the two techniques were compared. van Alphen (1961), however, found significant differences in the correlation coefficients between two components as calculated from axial lengths based on phakometry and on the radiological method. Validation of the optical method has been claimed using ultrasonic techniques (Sorsby *et al.*, 1963; Leary *et al.*, 1963); the latter has itself been compared to radiography (Jansson, 1963). There is, nevertheless, some doubt whether any of the presently available techniques are sufficiently accurate to substantiate conclusions so far reaching as the relationship of the axial length to other ocular components. An appraisal of the ultrasonic technique by Gernet (1967) indicated that an accuracy not greater than 0·3 mm. can be expected: this is equivalent to a whole dioptre of refractive change. Moreover, both van Alphen (1961) and Ludlam and his associates (1965) have cautiously criticised any conclusions regarding the interrelationship of axial length as computed by optical methods and the powers of the cornea and of the lens; since the two latter factors are used in the calculations of axial length they are not independent variables, thus casting some doubt on any conclusion drawn from the relationship. It is therefore reasonable to conclude that the nature of the correlation responsible for the high proportion of emmetropes in spite of the apparently random variation of the optical components is perhaps not yet clearly defined; but of the outstanding significance of the axial length in determining high refractive errors there can be no doubt. As a reminder of the incompleteness of our studies we may perhaps recall the paucity of our knowledge of the multiple hereditary factors in the transmission of the components of the ocular refraction. Again, in this respect the most important element is the axial length, particularly in relation to any retinal complications that may accompany its extreme variations.

Meanwhile, however, it must be accepted that the old idea that emmetropia represents the perfect and normal and that any aberration therefrom is to be regarded as pathological, is indefensible; and as a working hypothesis we shall conclude that *anomalies of refraction can be classified into two types—* SIMPLE REFRACTIVE ERRORS, *made up of the chance combinations of essentially normal elements of the refractive system of the eye (variational refractive errors; " combination ametropia ",* Tron, 1934–35; *" correlation ametropia ",* Sorsby, *et al.,* 1962) *and* PATHOLOGICAL REFRACTIVE ERRORS *determined by abnormal developmental or acquired variations in its optical components ("component ametropia ",* Sorsby *et al.,* 1962).

THE INHERITANCE OF REFRACTIVE ERRORS

It is a matter of common observation that refractive errors are frequently inherited, but in view of the complexity and variability of the components which together form the total refraction and our ignorance of their share in determining the final optical condition in any particular case, it is not surprising that the mechanism of inheritance is by no means clear. It is to be remembered that when the transmission of a hereditary characteristic is determined by multiple factors the simple numerical laws of inheritance do not hold, and if these constituent factors behave differently the ultimate result may be difficult to predict, particularly in a condition so widespread among the population that clear transmission factors are difficult to trace. It is obvious, therefore, that any definitive knowledge of the laws of the inheritance of refractive errors must await the full elucidation of the factors determining the refraction and their hereditary behaviour. In the meantime, however, several principles are clear—that refractive states are frequently hereditarily transmitted not only within a family but in races and species; that the mode of their transmission in monozygotic and dizygotic twins proves the occurrence of hereditary characteristics; that the lower errors are transmitted differently from the higher; and that, particularly so far as the latter are concerned, it would seem likely that it is not the refractive condition alone which is transmitted but frequently associated ocular conditions, such as microphthalmos, pigmentary retinal dystrophy, nystagmus, nyctalopia and so on, as well as environmental factors which may determine the refractive state. It is not surprising, therefore, that mere statistical evidence may be most misleading. The evidence, however, suggests that the refractive properties of the eye are determined more by genetic than by environmental factors and that the inheritance of the refraction and its components in the general population as a rule follows the pattern set by a number of genes with additive effects (Sorsby et al., 1962–66).

Much of the earlier work on the heredity of the refractive state derived from the study of the total ocular refraction in twins. Concordance to a high degree is generally found in monozygotic twins[1]; dizygotic twins, on the other hand, show no more concordance than between otherwise similar pairs of the population and the refractive differences may be very marked.[2] An important feature is that the concordance found in monozygotic twins extends also to the individual components of the refraction, the corneal power, the depth of the anterior chamber, the curvature and thickness of the lens and the axial length. Discordant ocular refractions, however, are occasionally found, even in monozygotic twins (Orth, 1954), particularly if one of them had pathological changes at an early age (retrolental fibroplasia, Vidal, 1959).

The findings of Sorsby and his colleagues (1962) in the investigation of 78 pairs of monozygotic twins are important; on the whole the distribution of their refractive errors was similar to that found in the general population. There was 71·8% of concordance in corneal power, 67% for the depth of the anterior chamber, 70% for the thickness of the lens, 86% and 54% for the powers of the anterior and posterior surfaces of the lens, and 83% for the axial length. These values were approximately true both in emmetropia and in ametropia. In contrast, in 40 pairs of dizygotic twins of like sex and 48 unrelated control pairs, the concordance for the ocular refraction and its ocular components was negligible. These conclusions have been further confirmed in a statistical analysis of these twins and the controls by Sorsby and Fraser (1964), and have been largely corroborated by Kimura (1965), particularly in regard to the curvature of the cornea, the posterior surface of the lens and the axial length. The deduction seems inescapable that refractive errors are not due to faulty optical components as much as to faulty correlation between them determined largely by heredity.

Apart from the studies of twins, there have been relatively few investigations of the refraction and its components in several members of the same family. Sorsby and his associates (1957) studied 21 families in this way, but their results were inconclusive; as Waardenburg (1963) suggested, a study of the optical components in emmetropic families would be valuable. The difficulties, however, which beset such a project are obvious; we may recall

[1] Jablonski (1926), Beckershaus (1926), Schmidt (1928), Waardenburg (1930), Jancke (1941), Weber (1941), Hofmann and Carey (1942), Burns (1949), Vogel and Balthaser (1956), Weekers et al. (1956), Sorsby et al. (1962), Goldschmidt (1968).
[2] Glatzel (1931), Krüger (1937), Lisch (1941), Weekers et al. (1956), and others.

that the very definition of emmetropia is somewhat elastic and that in any event the refractive state of the subject to be investigated in such a survey is liable to all the variations we have already discussed which occur with age.

The inheritance of emmetropia, in fact, remains the core of the problem because of the tendency in all generations for this to exist in excess of what would be expected from a normal distribution of ocular components and their random combinations. It is perhaps the coordinating mechanism itself which is transmissible; if, as Sorsby and his colleagues (1957) suggested, the retina acts as the organizer, it is to this organ that we must look for further elucidation of the inheritance of the refractive state.

In various ametropias, several different types of hereditary transmission occur. These will be dealt with individually when we are discussing each particular condition in the subsequent pages.

van Alphen. *Ophthalmologica*, **142,** Suppl. (1961).

Arlt. *Die Krankheiten d. Auges*, Prague, **3** (1856).

Awerbach. *The Dioptrics of Eyes with varying Refraction* (Diss., in Russian), Moscow (1900).

Barrington and Pearson. *Eugen. Lab. Mem.,* **5** (1909).

Beckershaus. *Z. Augenheilk.,* **59,** 264 (1926).

Berg. *v. Graefes Arch. Ophthal.,* **127,** 606 (1931).

Betsch. *Klin. Mbl. Augenheilk.,* **82,** 365 (1929).

Boerhaave. *De morbis oculorum,* 211 (1708), published Göttingen (1750).

Burns. *Brit. J. Ophthal.,* **33,** 491 (1949).

Cohn. *Untersuch. d. Augen d. 10,060 Schulkindern,* Leipzig (1867).

  v. Graefes Arch. Ophthal., **17** (2), 305 (1871).

  Die Hygiene d. Auges in den Schulen, Leipzig (1883).

  Lhb. d. Hygiene d. Auges, Leipzig (1892).

Coulombre. *Invest. Ophthal.,* **4,** 411 (1965).

Czellitzer. *Klin. Mbl. Augenheilk.,* **79,** 301 (1927).

Dashevsky. *Helmholtz ophthal. Inst., Sci. Notes,* **7,** 253 (1962).

Deller, O'Connor and Sorsby. *Proc. roy. Soc.* B, **134,** 456 (1947).

Donders. *v. Graefes Arch. Ophthal.,* **4** (1), 301 (1858).

  On the Anomalies of Accommodation and Refraction of the Eye, London (1864).

Falkenburg and Straub. *Arch. Augenheilk.,* **26,** 336 (1893).

Gernet. *Ophthalmologica,* **147,** 235 (1964).

  Ultrasonics in Ophthalmology (ed. Oksala and Gernet), Basel (1967).

Glatzel. *Z. klin. Med.,* **116,** 632 (1931).

Goldschmidt. *Acta ophthal.* (Kbh.), Suppl. 98 (1968).

Heinonen. *Acta ophthal.* (Kbh.), **2,** 35 (1924).

Hofmann and Carey. *Amer. J. Ophthal.,* **25,** 1495 (1942).

Jablonski. *Arch. Augenheilk.,* **91,** 308 (1922); **97,** 369 (1926).

  Schw. med. Wschr., **53,** 846 (1923).

  Klin. Mbl. Augenheilk., **73,** 302 (1924).

Jancke. *Klin. Mbl. Augenheilk.,* **106,** 264 (1941).

Jansson. *Acta ophthal.* (Kbh.), **41,** 25; Suppl. 74 (1963).

Kepler. *Dioptrice,* Augsburg (1611).

Kimura. *Acta Soc. ophthal. jap.,* **69,** 963 (1965).

Krüger. *Zwillingsbefunde im gau Mecklenburg* (Diss.), Leipzig (1937).

Leary, Sorsby, Richards and Chaston. *Vision Res.,* **3,** 487 (1963).

Lisch. *Klin. Mbl. Augenheilk.,* **106,** 695 (1941).

Ludlam, Wittenberg and Rosenthal. *Amer. J. Optom.,* **42,** 394 (1965).

Newton. *Opticks,* London (1704).

Orth. *Klin. Mbl. Augenheilk.,* **124,** 304 (1954).

Pearson and Moul. *Ann. Eugen.,* **2,** 111, 290; **3,** 1 (1927).

Plempius. *Ophthalmographia,* Amsterdam (1632).

von Reuss. *v. Graefes Arch. Ophthal.,* **23** (4), 183 (1877); **26** (3), 1 (1880).

Scheerer. *Ber. dtsch. ophthal. Ges.,* **47,** 118 (1928).

Schmidt. *Klin. Mbl. Augenheilk.,* **80,** 553 (1928).

Schnabel and Herrnheiser. *Z. Heilk.,* **16,** 1 (1895).

Sorsby, Benjamin, Davey *et al. Emmetropia and its Aberrations* (*MRC Spec. Rep. Series, No. 293*), London (1957).

Sorsby, Benjamin and Sheridan. *Refraction and its Components during the Growth of the Eye from the Age of Three* (*MRC Spec. Rep. Series, No. 301*), London (1961).

Sorsby and Fraser. *J. med. Genet.,* **1,** 47 (1964).

Sorsby, Leary and Fraser. *J. med. Genet.,* **3,** 269 (1966).

Sorsby, Leary and Richards. *Vision Res.*, **2**, 309 (1962).

Sorsby, Leary, Richards and Chaston. *Vision Res.*, **3**, 499 (1963).

Sorsby, Sheridan and Leary. *Refraction and its Components in Twins* (*MRC Spec. Rep. Series, No. 303*), London (1962).

Steiger. *Die Entstehung d. sphärischen Refraktionen d. menschlichen Auges*, Berlin (1913).

Stenström. *Acta ophthal.* (Kbh.), Suppl. 26 (1946).

Streiff. *Klin. Mbl. Augenheilk.*, **55**, 1 (1915).

Tron. *v. Graefes Arch. Ophthal.*, **122**, 1 (1929); **126**, 454 (1931); **132**, 182 (1934); **133**, 211 (1935).

Vidal. *Arch. chil. Oftal.*, **16**, 11 (1959).

Vogel and Balthaser. *Klin. Mbl. Augenheilk.*, **128**, 456 (1956).

Waardenburg. *Klin. Mbl. Augenheilk.*, **84**, 598, 788, 795; **85**, 169 (1930).

Genetics and Ophthalmology, Oxon., **2**, 1232 (1963).

Weber. *Klin. Mbl. Augenheilk.*, **106**, 78 (1941).

Weekers, Moureau, Hacourt and André. *Bull. Soc. belge Ophtal.*, No. 112, 146 (1956).

Wessely. *Z. Augenheilk.*, **43**, 654 (1920).

Wibaut. *v. Graefes Arch. Ophthal.*, **116**, 596 (1925).

Klin. Mbl. Augenheilk., **82**, 684 (1929).

Zeeman. *v. Graefes Arch. Ophthal.*, **78**, 93 (1911).

FIG. 305.—FRANS CORNELIS DONDERS
[1818–1889]

CHAPTER VI

SIMPLE REFRACTIVE ERRORS

FRANS CORNELIS DONDERS [1818–1889] (Fig. 305) was one of the greatest ophthalmologists of all time and was undoubtedly the first to analyse the various types of refractive error and to point out their great clinical significance. Before his time, little importance was given to them by the medical profession and only spherical corrections were generally prescribed, usually chosen by the patient himself by trial and error. In 1856, however, von Helmholtz's *Physiological Optics* was published which laid the groundwork for all future progress, and Donders at once took up the subject. In 1858 he published a paper on the use and selection of spectacles, in 1860 an essay on *Ametropia and its Results*, in 1862 a monograph on astigmatism and cylindrical glasses, and finally, in 1864, his classical work *On the Anomalies of Accommodation and Refraction of the Eye*, written at the request of the New Sydenham Society of London, for the first time put the theory and practice of optical visual errors and their correction on a sound basis. Fortunately, Donders was self-admittedly " no mathematician ", and he wrote in clear and simple language so that his book at once became popular. It is one of the few classics that have caused a revolution in ophthalmology, and at once removed the study of refraction and the prescription of spectacles out of the atmosphere of prejudice and introduced it into medical practice.

Donders was born in Tilburg in Holland and his father died the year after he was born, leaving his mother to look after Frans and his eight sisters in poor circumstances so that at the age of 11 he became an assistant teacher at his school in order to subsidize himself. Studying medicine at Utrecht and graduating at Leiden (1840), he entered military service and then returned to Utrecht where his career was a continuous academic success. At an early age he was appointed an extra professor in the Faculty of Medicine where he lectured on biology, physiology and ophthalmology but, meeting Sir William Bowman and Albrecht von Graefe on a visit to the Great Exhibition in London in 1851, he determined to make the latter subject his life's work. This trio may be said to have founded modern ophthalmology. He became professor of ophthalmology at Utrecht in 1852, established an ophthalmic hospital (1858) which was later chartered as the Donders Foundation (1888), and founded his physiological laboratory in 1866. Loved and acclaimed by his contemporaries as few men had ever been, and heaped with honours from all over the civilized world, President of the Royal Netherlands Academy of Sciences, of two International Ophthalmological Congresses and a Foreign Member of the Royal Society of London, his international position was unique. His statue in Utrecht and the institution of the Donders Medal by the Dutch Ophthalmological Society are material evidence of the enormous esteem in which he was held in his own country. A century after the establishment of the hospital, the Queen and the Government of the Netherlands celebrated its founding when it was called the Royal Eye Hospital of Utrecht.

Although our knowledge of the subject is not adequate to allow us to be dogmatic, it is obvious from the clinical point of view that some refractive errors are not pathological while others are. We shall define SIMPLE REFRACTIVE ERRORS as those *due to the chance combination of essentially normal elements of the optical system of the eye* (VARIATIONAL REFRACTIVE ERRORS; COMBINATION AMETROPIA, Tron, 1934–35).[1] We have already seen how great is the range of the variability of the components of this system, but we do not yet know the limits of normal variability. Small errors of total refraction may be associated with extreme variations of the constituent elements—indeed, with much greater deviations from the normal than occur in many refractive states which must be considered pathological. The axial length of a static emmetropic eye may be greater than that of a progressively myopic eye; a typical case of the latter with progressive changes in the fundus may have an axial length shorter than the normal (22·39 mm., Tron, 1935) and the same axial length may be a component of a refraction of + 6·0 D and − 9·0 D (Tron). It is impossible, therefore, to define simple refractive errors in terms of the total refraction between limits as from ± 6·0 D or, alternatively, from the point of view of the stability of the optical condition. It is true that hypermetropia and astigmatism are essentially static and myopia is often more labile, but it is to be remembered that all of these tend to shift in the direction of increased refractivity in the normal course of development. And among " simple " myopes there is a large percentage of non-progressive cases —almost as large, indeed, as among hypermetropes. Thus, observing London children of school age, Sorsby (1935) found that while 66% of hypermetropes remained stationary over this period, 35% of myopes behaved similarly and 15% showed only slight progression. Taking an over-all view, such progression is small. In his assessment of refractive changes from birth to the age of 51, involving 8,820 computations in 1,203 persons with all types of refractive error, Brown (1938) found an average increase in total refractivity of only 0·09 D. The vast majority of refractive errors of all types is therefore " simple " and it is to stress this fact—that they, *including the majority of myopes*, present no medical problem and need give rise to no anxiety—that this classification has been adopted.

Such a classification of course, involves the very serious practical defect that in the present state of our knowledge it is impossible to classify any single eye from its refraction alone; *the problem is biological* and not optical, to be solved by the ophthalmologist, not the refractionist; and the decision must be made from a study of the clinical appearance of the eye, particularly with regard to the state of the fundus and the presence of degenerations or affections of the dioptric elements, a consideration of the heredity, and from repeated observations of its behaviour over a period of time. From the clinical point of view, however, it may be said that *simple refractive anomalies are primarily hereditarily determined, of chance incidence, are not progressive beyond the amount included within normal development, are associated (potentially) with good vision and require no treatment apart from their optical correction.* The possible secondary influence of environmental factors will be discussed at a later stage.

[1] p. 244.

Simple Hypermetropia

HYPERMETROPIA (Donders, 1858), HYPEROPIA (von Helmholtz, 1856) or FAR-SIGHT, is that form of refractive error in which *parallel rays of light are brought to a focus some distance behind the sentient layer of the retina when the eye is at rest;* the image formed here is therefore made up of circles of diffusion and is consequently blurred. In simple hypermetropia this is brought about by the variations in the optical components we have already studied—a flattening of the cornea or of the lens, a deep anterior chamber, a low effective refractivity of the lens, or a small axial length of the eye. In so far as it is determined by smallness of the globe, a hypermetropic may be considered an underdeveloped eye; in so far as it is due to flattening of the lens it is over-developed. We have seen that it is the normal optical condition in infants and persists throughout life in some 50% of the population in most countries of the world. The 2 to 3 D of hypermetropia present in infants usually decreases steadily in the early years of life and has largely disappeared in most subjects at about puberty, although in some hypermetropes it may increase between the ages of 5 and 14 (Hirsch, 1964). Any residual hypermetropia tends to remain stationary until mid-life, whereafter, owing to lenticular changes, it tends again to increase (the *senile hypermetropia* of Straub, 1899).

The degree of simple hypermetropia occurring without malformations of the globe or other pathological evidences varies considerably, but in the vast majority of cases is under 3 D although very high values occur, occasionally above 20 D.

Broekema (1909), in 1,976 hypermetropic eyes, found 1,175 between 1 and 2 D, 438 between 3 and 4, 277 between 5 and 6, and 86 between 7 and 10 D. Leber (1906), in 80,000 cases, found only 6 between 8 and 16 D, and among 16,092 eyes Jackson (1932) found the highest degree of hypermetropia to be 10 D. Instances of extreme variations are : Dodd (1901) 15 D in both eyes, with a son with 14 D in both eyes; Harman (1909) 16 and 17 D; Tirelli (1947) 18·5 D; Clausen (1911) R. 17, L. 18 D; Seabrook (1889) 24 D; Gellzuhn (1893) 24 D.

THE INHERITANCE OF SIMPLE HYPERMETROPIA

As is the case with other minor refractive errors, a dominant inheritance seems to operate in simple hypermetropia (Waardenburg, 1963) (Fig. 306); the dominance, however, may be irregular. Sometimes the parents are emmetropic and uncles and aunts are hypermetropic (Czellitzer, 1910–12). As a rule there is concordance between monozygotic twins which usually extends to the precise degree of hypermetropia (Waardenburg, 1930; E. Weber, 1941; Jancke and Holste, 1941). This, together with the transmission of low degrees of the defect in families, indicates the probable transmission of a single unusual optical component, presumably short axial length, which the natural tendency towards emmetropia is unable to counteract (Waardenburg, 1963). It must, of course, be remembered that in family

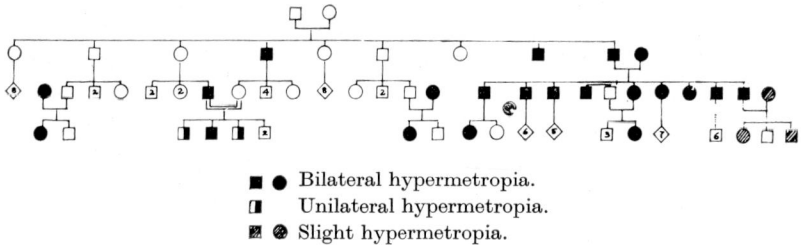

■ ● Bilateral hypermetropia.
◨ Unilateral hypermetropia.
▨ ◉ Slight hypermetropia.

FIG. 306.—MODERATE HYPERMETROPIA
Dominant heredity (after P. J. Waardenburg, 1913–32).

studies the various ages of different generations make a direct comparison of
the degree of the anomaly difficult, not only because of the changes in total
refraction throughout life but also because of the influence of the available
accommodation.

THE OPTICAL CONDITION IN HYPERMETROPIA

The optical condition of the hypermetropic eye has already been
described.[1] Whether the hypermetropia is due to a decrease in the length
of the eye, a decrease of curvature, or to a change in refractive index, the
optical effect is the same: parallel rays come to a focus behind the retina
(Fig. 257) and, since when the anomaly is axial the retina is nearer the nodal
point, it necessarily follows that the image is smaller than in emmetropia
(Fig. 264). Conversely, rays coming from a point on the retina will be divergent
and will meet (theoretically) behind the eye (Fig. 259). It follows that the
formation of a clear image of any kind is impossible unless the converging
power of the optical system is increased either by the eye itself by an effort
of accommodation, or by artificial means with a convex lens (Figs. 261, 263).

ACCOMMODATION IN HYPERMETROPIA

The influence of accommodation in hypermetropia is of considerable
significance. So long as accommodation is active, a certain amount of the
optical error is corrected by the normal physiological tone of the ciliary
muscle; Donders (1864) called the moiety which is thus normally corrected
LATENT HYPERMETROPIA (H*l*). In contradistinction, the remaining portion
which in normal circumstances is uncorrected, is termed MANIFEST HYPER-
METROPIA (H*m*); and the two added together equal the TOTAL HYPERMETRO-
PIA (H*t*). The proportion of the total hypermetropia which is manifest
increases gradually with age as the lens becomes less labile until after the
onset of presbyopia all the hypermetropia becomes manifest. This gradual
progress throughout life is shown in Table XX (Schroeder, 1882; Daniel,
1883).

[1] p. 213.

So long as accommodation for near vision is available, however, the hypermetrope will try so far as he can to accommodate actively in order to see distinctly and supplement the tone of the ciliary muscle by an effort of contraction; he may correct part of his error in this way, or he may be able to correct the entire error. In either case the amount which can be corrected is spoken of as FACULTATIVE HYPERMETROPIA (H*f*). If the error is large and by no effort of accommodation can he see objects clearly, the amount of hypermetropia still remaining uncorrected which cannot be overcome by accommodation is called ABSOLUTE HYPERMETROPIA (H*a*). It will be obvious that in old age when accommodation fails, all hypermetropia tends to become absolute.

TABLE XX

THE VARIATION OF MANIFEST
HYPERMETROPIA WITH AGE

Age	Proportion of Hm
6–15	$\frac{1}{3}$ in 80% of cases
16–25	$\frac{1}{2}$,, 72% ,, ,,
25–36	$\frac{2}{3}$—$\frac{3}{4}$,, 75% ,, ,,
36–45	1 ,, 80% ,, ,,
Over 46	1 ,, 100% ,, ,,

Total hypermetropia may therefore be divided into:

1. Latent hypermetropia, overcome physiologically by the tone of the ciliary muscle.

2. Manifest hypermetropia, made up of

(*a*) Facultative hypermetropia, overcome by an effort of accommodation;

(*b*) Absolute hypermetropia, which cannot be overcome by accommodation.

These different types may be tested clinically as follows: If a hypermetrope cannot see a distant object clearly, convex lenses of gradually increasing strength are placed in front of his eyes until he can; the lens and his total accommodation are both acting, so that with the combination of them both a distinct image is seen. The amount of hypermetropia corrected by the lens, that is, the amount which his efforts of accommodation cannot correct, is the absolute hypermetropia; and it is *measured by the weakest convex lens with which maximal visual acuity can be obtained.* Stronger lenses are now added until clear vision can just no longer be maintained, thus substituting the converging power of accommodation by the lenses and measuring the amount of hypermetropia he can correct in this way by his own efforts. This is the facultative hypermetropia; it is determined by *the difference between the strongest and the weakest convex lens with which maximal visual acuity is obtained.* The limit reached, that is, *the strongest lens with which maximal visual acuity can be obtained,* is the measure of the manifest hypermetropia. Under complete cycloplegia the strongest lens with which maximum visual acuity can be obtained gives the total hypermetropia; it will be found to be more than before by an amount which represents the latent hypermetropia.

It thus appears that a high hypermetrope, or a low hypermetrope with no accommodative power, can see nothing distinctly unless the accommodation is active and the error lies within his facultative limits. To a certain extent this may be an advantage, and the variability of focusing of which he is capable has been aptly compared to the position of an observer looking down a microscope with his finger on the fine adjustment. On the other hand, the constant accommodative effort which is made automatically in the instinctive attempt to obtain distinct vision frequently leads to fatigue and distress, to a disorientation between accommodation and convergence, and to other troubles which we shall consider later.[1] All these symptoms are, of course, considerably more marked when close work is undertaken.

THE STRUCTURE OF THE HYPERMETROPIC EYE

The hypermetropic eye is typically small, not only in its antero-posterior diameter but also in all meridians. The cornea is small, and since the lens varies little in shape but may, if anything, be larger than in emmetropes (Raeder, 1922; Gallati, 1923), this structure is relatively large, thus making the anterior chamber shallow (Zeeman, 1911). The eye is therefore of the type which is predisposed to closed-angle glaucoma, a point which should be remembered in the administration of mydriatics (Priestley Smith, 1890). Its smallness is usually easily recognized, and if it is rotated strongly inwards and the lids drawn backwards, the marked curve in the equatorial region forms a striking contrast to the long curve of the myopic eye. The circular fibres of the ciliary muscle may be hypertrophied from over-use (Iwanoff, 1869), but this is by no means a constant microscopic finding, nor is it confined to hypermetropic eyes.

Ophthalmoscopically the fundus may have a characteristic appearance, which although not solely confined to the hypermetropic eye, occurs much more commonly in the higher degrees of this refractive condition than in any other. The retina appears to have a peculiar sheen—a reflex effect—the so-called SHOT-SILK RETINA (Benson, 1882; Nettleship, 1882). This is often associated with accentuated reflexes on the vessels, which may in some cases suggest changes resembling arteriosclerosis. The vessels themselves may show congenital aberrations, for undue tortuosity and abnormal branchings are not uncommon (Nettleship, 1882; Mackenzie, 1884).

The optic disc sometimes has a characteristic appearance which may resemble an optic neuritis (PSEUDO-PAPILLITIS) (Figs. 307–8). This appearance, first described by de Wecker and Jaeger (1870) and rapidly confirmed by several observers (Mackenzie, 1884; Marcus Gunn, 1895; Holmes Spicer, 1896; Nottbeck, 1897; and others), is not peculiar to, but occurs preferentially in, hypermetropes (34 cases out of 37, Nottbeck, 1897) and bears no relation to the degree of the hypermetropic defect. The disc assumes a dark

[1] p. 461.

greyish-red colour with indistinct and sometimes irregular margins, the haziness of which may be accentuated by a grey areola around it, or by grey radial striations emanating from it. The condition is congenital, and its appearance is largely accentuated by reflex disturbances; it involves no appreciable diminution of vision. It can be distinguished from a true optic neuritis by the absence of venous congestion and of any leak of the dye on fluorescence angiography.

The macula is generally situated farther from the disc than is usual in the emmetropic eye, and the cornea is more decidedly decentred; the visual axis consequently cuts the cornea considerably to the inside of the optic axis, thus making a large positive angle alpha (Fig. 177). This in its most marked degrees frequently gives rise to an apparent divergent squint, a

FIGS. 307 and 308.—PSEUDO-NEURITIS IN HYPERMETROPIA (A. Huber).

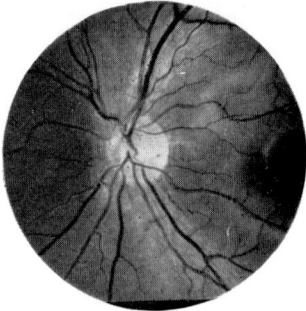

FIG. 307.—The right eye is emmetropic with a normal optic disc.

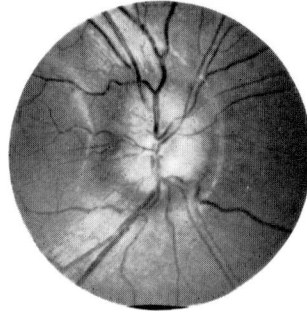

FIG. 308.—The left eye has a hypermetropia of 5 D with a picture similar to papillœdema.

condition the opposite of that found in myopia. As we have noted, there is an association between hypermetropia and closed-angle glaucoma; but there is no evidence that the hypermetropic is more susceptible than the emmetropic eye to other ocular diseases as, for example, cataract (despite its constant accommodative efforts).

VISUAL ACUITY IN HYPERMETROPIA

The *uncorrected visual acuity* in hypermetropes varies with the degree of optical error and the proportion which cannot be overcome by accommodation; visual symptoms in the higher degrees of the error are marked, for nothing is seen clearly, but in the lower degrees, when the accommodation is active and is able to overcome the defect, as usually occurs in youth, they may be entirely absent. Facultative hypermetropia does not by itself involve any decrease in the acuity, but absolute hypermetropia affects distant vision much in the same proportion as myopia. Eggers (1945) found that the uncorrected (Snellen) visual acuity for the proportion of hypermetropia which cannot be overcome by accommodation declined as follows, a proportion which affects an increasing amount of the hypermetropia as age advances until eventually it involves it all:

0·5 D absolute Hm.	— V.A.	20/30 or 6/9
0·75 D „	„ —	„ 20/40 or 6/12
1·0 D „	„ —	„ 20/50
1·5 D „	„ —	„ 20/100
2·0 D „	„ —	„ 20/150
2·5 D „	„ —	„ 20/200 or 6/60
3·5 D „	„ —	„ 20/300
4·5 D „	„ —	„ 20/400 or 3/60

with proportional increases upwards.

The *corrected visual acuity* frequently does not come up to standard, particularly in the higher degrees of the defect. Broekema's (1909) figures are instructive in this respect: he found that normal acuity was obtained in 82% of hypermetropes with an error of 1 to 2 D, in 63·5% of those with an error of 3 to 4 D, in 44% from 5 to 6 D, and in only 15% when the error was from 7 to 10 D. Poor visual acuity (1/6 normal) he found to be rare in the smaller errors (0·8%) and six times more common in the higher (4·6%). This visual deficiency may be due in some degree to a lack of retinal development, particularly in the case of high errors, but perceptual factors probably pay a considerable part in its ætiology. When the subnormal vision is bilateral, as is usually the case when the refractive error was not corrected in early childhood (the *amblyopia of uncorrected ametropia*), the acuity usually improves to some extent after wearing correcting spectacles for some months. On the other hand, probably because of the difficulty of acquiring and maintaining good binocular vision, inequality of the vision in the two eyes is common and unilateral amblyopia no rare event, even in the absence of squint; the same difficulties favour the development of a convergent accommodative squint. These tendencies towards amblyopia and squint are increased when an inequality of the hypermetropia in the two eyes makes their mutual association more difficult. Such uniocular amblyopia is unfortunately only amenable to treatment by occlusion in early life[1]; it is not ordinarily improved by correcting lenses. It is to be remembered, of course, that hypermetropes who do not wear correcting spectacles or only wear them intermittently see better without them than those who have become habituated to them (Jablonski, 1939)—an effect again due to factors operating at the perceptual level.

It is important that uniocular amblyopia is a common condition with serious social effects. Downing (1945), studying 60,000 military selectees in the United States, found a uniocular amblyopia ex anopsia of 6/12 (20/40) or over in 3·2%: in 855 cases the amblyopia was without strabismus, in 770 it was associated with convergent and in 295 with divergent squint. Among 9,000 adult males between the ages of 17 and 25 in

[1] Vol. VI.

Minnesota in 1962–3, Helveston (1965) found 89 (1%) with a similar degree of ambly-opia, and Flom and Neumaier (1966) found 1% among 2,762 American schoolchildren and 1·7% in 7,017 subjects aged between 10 and 50 years. Similarly, in Belgium Vereecken and his colleagues (1966) found the corrected vision less than 5/6 (0·8) in one eye in 42 out of 1,215 children (3·5%) between the ages of 6 and 10, and Evens and Kuypers (1967) found 867 cases (1·52%) with a uniocular amblyopia with vision less than 6/18 (0·3) in 56,879 Army recruits averaging 20 years of age. The commonest cause of such a condition is hypermetropic refractive errors, obviously a source of considerable social and economic disability which could have been prevented in most cases if the visual examination and appropriate therapeutic measures had been adopted at an early age.

CLINICAL SYMPTOMS

In the lower degrees of hypermetropia, particularly in the young in whom accommodation is active, symptoms of hypermetropia, both visual and clinical, are usually entirely absent; in the higher degrees they are marked, for nothing is seen clearly unless with the expenditure of much effort. When the error is large the accommodative power may be insufficient to attain clear vision and the object must be held farther away. Alternatively the tendency develops to make up for its indistinctness by an enlargement of the image and a narrowing of the pupil; both these ends may be attained by holding the book very close to the eyes and employing maximum accom-modation and convergence, an attitude which involves considerable strain and may suggest myopia (the *apparent myopia of hypermetropes*). Even when the error is small there may come a time when accommodation finds itself unequal to its task, a failure which may be physiological owing to advancing age, or may come on in states of physical or nervous debility. In these cases visual troubles usually occur after long-continued application to close work when the vision becomes blurred and indistinct and only recovers if the patient temporarily rests his ciliary muscles.

Symptoms of eye-strain are frequent in these conditions. The head-aches, the general physical disturbances and mental unhappiness to which this may give rise will be subsequently described[1]; essentially the syndrome is due to excessive accommodation and to the forced dissociation between it and convergence (the *accommodative* or *muscular asthenopia* of Donders, 1864). When, despite these difficulties, near work must be done, the strain thrown on the ciliary muscle is comparable to that imposed upon the leg muscles in a correspondingly long and forced march; and it is not surprising in those equipped with little physical or nervous reserves, or whose surround-ings, from bad ventilation or other causes, are not conducive to rapid recovery from muscular fatigue, that the symptoms of distress may be real.

If this state of affairs persists, results of a more concrete type may ensue. Temporary failure of the ciliary muscle may result in obscurations of vision, or the opposite condition of spasm of the ciliary muscle may produce a condition of artificial myopia. The necessity to use accommoda-

[1] p. 559.

tion in excess of convergence leads to a dissociation of muscle balance, and the struggle to maintain binocular vision in these circumstances leads to further strain. Frequently in young people, if binocular fusion is defective or ill-developed, the advantages of binocular vision are abandoned in favour of the more obvious advantages of clear vision, one eye only—usually the better eye—is used to the neglect of the other, and a convergent squint is produced.[1]

TREATMENT

It may be taken as a general rule that if the error is small, the visual acuity and binocular vision are normal and the patient is in good health, complaining of no symptoms of accommodative asthenopia and showing no significant anomalies of muscle balance, treatment of hypermetropia is unnecessary; but if any of these conditions is violated, spectacles should be prescribed.

In young children below the age of 6 or 7 some degree of hypermetropia is physiological, and a correction need be given only if the error is high, binocular vision poor, or if strabismus is present. In those between 6 and 16, especially when they are working strenuously at school, smaller errors may require correction, particularly if complaint is made of definite symptoms of ocular fatigue. If a suspicion of strain is suggested by more indefinite signs— an irritable appearance of the eyes, a complaint of headache, a dislike of work and an early tiring after it is begun, rubbing the eyes and complaints of their itching, twitching of the lids, or a combination of these—an examination should be made. If the error is greater than 3 dioptres, it is probably wise in the presence of symptoms to advise that correcting spectacles be worn constantly; if below, it may suffice that they be used for near work alone.

In all these cases the examination should be conducted initially under cycloplegia. As a general rule, in ordering spectacles, 1 dioptre is deducted from the objective findings to allow for the tone of the ciliary muscle, an amount which may be diminished in cases of strabismus but should be increased in younger children below the age of 6, especially if the error is high, when 1·5 or 2 dioptres can well be deducted. In older children it should be remembered that if the spectacles make a child's vision worse, it is difficult to make him wear them conscientiously. It is usually safest to prescribe the fullest correction consistent with good vision which he will accept, as determined at a post-cycloplegic test if such is possible. A child will frequently tolerate his normal correction with ease, but this is not always so and a considerably weaker convex lens may be the maximum acceptable. In these circumstances, if the symptoms indicate that a determined attempt should be made to reduce his refraction as nearly as possible to emmetropia, as, for example, in cases of squint, weak atropine may be given every second

[1] Vol. VI.

day for a week or two until the ciliary muscle becomes accustomed to its new conditions of work.

It is important to remember that in children more than 7 years old hypermetropia tends normally to diminish with growth. Children should thus be examined once a year and their correction weakened if necessary, until finally in some cases spectacles may safely be discarded. If the conditions determining the wearing of spectacles have passed and the child is comfortable and sees well without them, the advisability of the progressive weakening and ultimate cessation of spectacles should always be borne in mind; their use in such cases to attain a biological optical perfection is unjustifiable.

In older people the advisability of wearing spectacles depends upon the degree of vision and the symptoms experienced—a very variable and individualistic factor. Young adults with a small error who have normal vision and are without symptoms require no correction, for spectacles of any kind carry with them physical and optical disadvantages which make their unnecessary use inadvisable. Conversely, as is the case with children, the decline of accommodative power in middle and later life makes optical correction increasingly necessary. An adult with 3 dioptres of hypermetropia may be comfortable at 25, but at 35 the additional accommodation required for near work will begin to tax his declining power and he may require correcting spectacles for reading; in later life, when his accommodation has gone and all the hypermetropia has become absolute, distance spectacles also will be necessary.

The need to re-examine adult subjects with hypermetropia depends on several factors. If a full correction is being worn and the patient is not yet of presbyopic age, re-testing is hardly necessary except when fresh symptoms arise or when the spectacles themselves, the frame or lenses, are damaged. In this age-group an under-corrected hypermetrope will clearly need more regular supervision, particularly in the fourth decade. Once presbyopia is added to the hypermetropia more frequent re-examinations are indicated and this is particularly so in later life when there is an increase of hypermetropia due to a decrease in the facultative portion or to an increase in the total hypermetropia or to both factors.

If visual symptoms alone are complained of and the refraction is not done under a cycloplegic, it is usually sufficient, after refraction, to order the strongest lenses with which maximal visual acuity can be obtained with both eyes: this will be found to be slightly higher (about 0·25 D) than the correction which each eye will tolerate separately. If circumstances indicate that a cycloplegic should be used, there is some difference of opinion as to the amount of the total hypermetropia which should be corrected. It might be thought that it would be advisable to correct the whole of the hypermetropia and thus place the patient in the position of an emmetrope; but it must be remembered that in these subjects the ciliary muscle has been accustomed to maintain a considerable amount of accommodative tone, which can be renounced only with difficulty; a full optical correction will render such an eye myopic, distant vision may become indistinct, and the spectacles, giving rise to a fresh crop of troubles, may not be tolerated. Moreover, such a course, if persisted in until the accommodation has become tuned down to the requirements of emmetropia, would carry with it the inconvenience that such a patient would be unable to see efficiently whenever he removed or was deprived of his spectacles. It is usually advisable, therefore, to under-correct the total hypermetropia. On the other hand, the headaches and symptoms of asthenopia may persist if a part of the hypermetropia remains uncorrected; we are thus faced with a dilemma the solution of which frequently calls for no little judgment.

In such cases hard and fast rules are inadequate for guidance. Donders (1864) advised that the lens ordered should correspond to the manifest hypermetropia plus one-quarter of the latent, a suggestion which has received general acceptance. The most practical method is to consider each case on its own merits, to determine the manifest hypermetropia and order lenses on this basis, correcting the patient as nearly to his total hypermetropia as possible while remaining within the limits consistent with comfort and good vision, at the same time paying regard to his age, to the state of his accommodation, his symptoms, his muscle balance, his general physical and nervous state, and his vocation. The younger the patient and the greater the latent hypermetropia, the greater the legitimate under-correction. On the other hand, if symptoms of eye-strain are marked it is well to relieve the accommodation by correcting as much of the total hypermetropia as possible. When there is a spasm of accommodation the whole of the error requires correction, as also when there is a tendency to latent convergent squint, in order in the first case to rest the ciliary muscle, and in the second to relieve convergence indirectly by relieving accommodation. In both these cases the spectacles should be constantly worn. Conversely, in the presence of a latent divergent squint, an under-correction, by stimulating accommodation, may stimulate convergence.

Generally, in the presence of asthenopic symptoms, the more fully corrected the error, the better the clinical result, always provided that the lenses are compatible with good vision. As a compromise in a difficult case, it may be well to under-correct considerably at first, and to strengthen the lenses at intervals of a few months until the full correction is comfortably borne; or it may help to advise weaker lenses for distance and the full correction for close work. But in those cases wherein adequate correction is necessary, as in spasm of accommodation and in excessive convergence, every endeavour should be made to induce the patient to wear the spectacles even at the cost of some discomfort; sometimes, where it is not contra-indicated and economic conditions do not preclude it, the instillation of weak solutions of atropine may help in tiding over the difficult initial period.

The form of the lenses to be prescribed may present some problems in the higher degrees of error. The imperfections of highly convex spectacle lenses will be dealt with subsequently in the Section relating to the correction of aphakia.[1]

Finally, it is to be remembered that the symptoms of accommodative asthenopia frequently have a significance deeper than their superficial consideration would indicate. The capacity of the ocular musculature for work serves as an index of the general constitutional state, and the onset of fatigue here should suggest its imminence elsewhere: the eye-strain is a symptom of general strain. Treatment, if it is to be adequate, should not be confined to the optical correction alone, but should include an inquiry into the general physical and nervous state and, if necessary, should involve a re-organization of the habits and activities of the individual so that he lives within the limits of his capabilities. Thus typical symptoms come on in the child starting school, in the youth studying for an examination, in the girl leaving the comparative ease of life at home and setting out in business, in the adult in periods of overwork and anxiety, and in them all in states of physical debility and mental depression. Interpreted in this light, the development of failure to compensate for hypermetropia may be the means of calling attention to the existence of a more deeply seated trouble before it would otherwise have achieved recognition—it is an " early symptom "; and if its true significance is neglected and treatment is confined to the ocular condition alone, sufficient relief and encouragement may be given to the patient to make it possible for him to carry on until a breakdown of a more serious nature may be unavoidable.

Simple Myopia

MYOPIA (SHORT-SIGHT) is that form of refractive error *wherein parallel rays of light come to a focus in front of the sentient layer of the retina when the eye is at rest*. In simple myopia this is brought about by variations within normal limits of the optical system—an increased curvature of the corneal or the lens surfaces, a shallow anterior chamber, a high refractive effectivity of the lens, or a great axial length of the globe. According to Sorsby and his colleagues (1957), in most cases the lower degrees of myopia are produced when the flattening of the cornea and the surfaces of the lens is insufficient to counteract the effect of an increasing axial length during growth. In so far as it is due to an increased length of the globe, the myopic may be con-sidered an over-developed eye in which the processes of growth have exceeded the normal limit; in so far as it is due to a persistence of the high curvature of the surfaces of the lens, the myopic eye may be considered under-developed.

Occasionally a congenital myopia occurs—sometimes of high degree (Harman, 1913–14; Jackson, 1932; Hofmann and Carey, 1942; and others)[2] —and may not increase materially thereafter; as we have seen,[3] however, in the great majority of cases myopia first appears between the ages of 5

[1] p. 378. [2] p. 304. [3] p. 231.

and puberty and may progress during the growing age until adolescence is
passed when the eye stabilizes. Such progress, however, is by no means
constant: thus in a series of children followed over many years, Sorsby
(1935) found that 35% of myopes remained stationary while 15% showed
only slight progress. All the time, however, whether or not progression
occurs, in the majority of myopic cases the eye remains healthy and visual
acuity can be corrected to expected standards with the appropriate lenses.
There is no reason for assuming that such variants in the normal biological
distribution of refractive errors are more abnormal than the corresponding
variants in the direction of hypermetropia; nor that the myopic eye is
unsound or diseased.

THE INHERITANCE OF SIMPLE MYOPIA

The influence of heredity in myopia is particularly difficult to assess
since the borderline between the simple and degenerative types is ill-defined.
Confining our attention to the lower degrees of myopia, less than -4 D,
there is little doubt that this influence is probably autosomally dominant
(Holm, 1926; Wölfflin, 1949; Wold, 1949; Waardenburg, 1963) (Fig. 309);

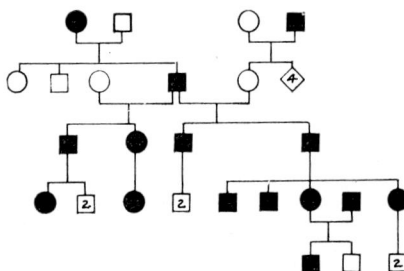

Fig. 309.—Simple Myopia.
Dominant heredity (after K.C. Wold, 1949).

thus, studying four generations including 170 subjects in Finland, Voipio and
his associates (1966) noted that the mother had a myopia of -5 D, in the
next generation 3 out of 14 children, in the next 6 out of 42, and in the next
15 out of 50 over 15 years of age had a slight degree of myopia. On this,
however, there is no general agreement, and other observers believe that the
recessive mode is the commonest form of inheritance (Jablonski, 1922;
Jaensch, 1939). Data derived from studies of twins indicate a high concordance in monozygotic twins (Jablonski, 1922; and many others) but exceptions
occur, one twin being myopic and the other emmetropic (Jancke, 1941).
The importance of the hereditary influence in the incidence of low myopia is
shown by the fact that the high degree of concordance usually seen in
monozygotic twins of all refractions is most marked in those of myopic
refraction (Waardenburg, 1963, Goldschmidt, 1968). At the same time it
would seem likely that genetic transmission is not wholly responsible; thus in

an elaborate investigation involving 9,243 children and 3,651 young adults in Denmark, Goldschmidt (1968) concluded that a moderate degree of myopia (up to 6 or 9 D) developed either before or about puberty in which case its incidence was largely hereditarily determined, or after the period of growth when the type of occupation seemed to exert an influence, suggesting that in these cases environmental factors were important.

THE OPTICAL CONDITION IN MYOPIA

The optical condition in myopia, wherein the dioptric power of the eye is too great for its length or the eye is too long for its dioptric power so that parallel rays of light come to a focus in front of the retina, is described elsewhere.[1] The image on the retina is made up of the circles of diffusion formed by the diverging beam so that distant objects cannot be seen clearly (Fig. 258); only divergent incident rays will focus on the retina and thus, in order to be seen clearly, an object must be brought close to the eye so that the rays coming from it are rendered sufficiently divergent (Fig. 260). The far-point (punctum remotum) is, therefore, a finite distance away, and the higher the myopia the shorter the distance.

Alternatively, parallel rays coming from distant objects must be rendered more divergent by placing a diverging lens in front of the eye (Fig. 262). To some small extent the axial myope compensates for his poor visual acuity for, since the nodal point is farther away from the retina, the image here, as is seen in Fig. 264, will be appreciably larger than it would be in the emmetropic eye. With correcting spectacles, however, the opposite holds good and the image appears smaller and brighter.[2]

ACCOMMODATION is of little value to the myope, but rather increases his difficulties; he has no means of reducing his myopia or increasing his vision apart from " screwing up " his lids in the attempt to attain the advantages of a stenopæic aperture. At the same time, in the higher degrees of defect he may not be without accommodative difficulties. In these cases the range of accommodation is small: thus if a myope of − 5 D has a far-point at 20 cm. and a near-point at 10 cm., he has to vary his amplitude of accommodation by 5 dioptres to obtain a range of 10 cm. (Fig. 267).[3] It follows that in the higher degrees of uncorrected myopia, the slightest variation in the distance at which work is done may entail immense accommodative efforts if clear vision is to be maintained, so that even if convergence is eliminated and one eye only is used, fatigue of accommodation may be an important factor in inducing eye-strain.

As would be expected from the dissociation between accommodation and convergence, a considerable number of uncorrected myopic children develops strabismus.[4] In contrast to hypermetropes, divergence is relatively common but is by no means invariable; thus among 790 myopic children, Thomson (1919) found 65 squinters, of whom 27 diverged and 38 converged.

[1] p. 214.   [2] p. 214.   [3] p. 216.   [4] Vol. VI.

THE STRUCTURE OF THE MYOPIC EYE. Typically the myopic eye is large and somewhat prominent, with a deep anterior chamber (Raeder, 1922), and a large, somewhat sluggishly reacting pupil. In the simple (variational) type the fundus is normal, and the presence of a small negative angle alpha may suggest the presence of convergent squint (Fig. 177).[1]

THE VISUAL ACUITY IN MYOPIA

Visual acuity beyond the far point is seriously affected in uncorrected myopia, being reduced by about the same ratio as occurs in absolute hypermetropia (Eggers, 1945). It is impossible to predict accurately in any individual case what the uncorrected vision should be, but it has been found that the visual acuity and the error, in general, are closely correlated. Hirsch (1945) found in a study of 64 eyes with degrees of myopia varying from − 0·5 to − 13·5 D that the plot of the logarithm of visual acuity on the logarithm of the degree of myopia gave a coefficient of correlation of − 0·95, and Crawford and his colleagues (1945) in a study of 266 eyes obtained a correlation ratio of 0·834. Hirsch's (1945) figures are as follows (Fig. 310):

Myopia in D	− 0·5	− 1·0	− 1·5	− 2·0	− 3·0	− 4·0	− 5·0	− 6·0
Visual acuity	20/25	20/65	20/110	20/165	20/285	20/420	20/565	20/275

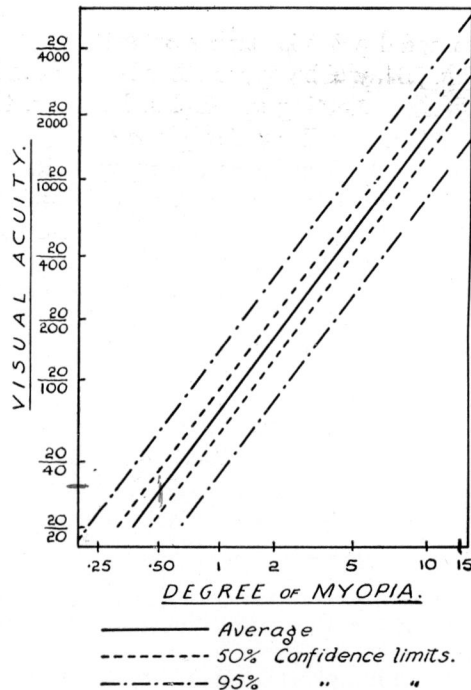

FIG. 310.—VISUAL ACUITIES PLOTTED FOR VARIOUS DEGREES OF MYOPIA (M. J. Hirsch).

[1] Vol. VI.

The *corrected visual acuity*, in the absence of degenerative changes, in contradistinction to the vision in hypermetropia is usually good, but it is to be remembered that individuals who use spectacles habitually see less well without them than do those who wear them intermittently or not at all (Jablonski, 1939)—the result not of physical but perceptual processes. For the same reason, if the spectacles are to be worn intermittently, better acuity and more comfort will be attained when they are not being worn if the error is under-corrected.

CLINICAL SYMPTOMS

Poor distant vision is the main symptom of myopia. Curiously, in its slighter degrees it may in many cases appear to be an advantage. Accustomed to defective vision from the time when he began to look upon the world intelligently, the myope frequently fails to recognize his limitations. Especially when his close attention is required largely for near work, as so often happens under civilized conditions of life, he accepts a blurring of distant objects as normal and neglects it. In middle life, when his accommodation fails, he has the added advantage that he does not require spectacles for reading; and in old age, as his contracting pupil cuts down his diffusion circles, and as the senile changes in his lens bring on a relative hypermetropia, he is in the happy position of finding his vision gradually improving. And so it happens that at 80 he is the envy of his hypermetropic contemporaries and the pride of his bespectacled presbyopic children.

In the smaller degrees of error symptoms of eye-strain may become evident, although generally not so obviously as in the case of the hypermetrope. The constant screwing of the lids in the attempt to secure clearer images may induce headache. The great accommodative adjustments required over short ranges may be fatiguing and annoying particularly if different working distances are constantly demanded, while the excess of convergence necessitated by close application to work disorientates the accommodation which is almost certainly not required in equal amount. The dissociation of the physiological synkinesis between the two related functions may have one of two opposite results. The accommodation may attempt to equal the convergence, thus producing ciliary spasm and artificially increasing the amount of myopia. Alternatively and more frequently, the attempt at convergence is given up, its latent insufficiency gives rise to the symptoms of muscular imbalance, until finally the advantages of binocular vision are abandoned, one eye alone is relied upon and the other deviates usually outwards, but in a proportion of cases inwards.

TREATMENT

The treatment of simple myopia merely demands the prescription of correcting spectacles, but it is first necessary to ensure that the condition is in fact simple. As we have seen, in the present state of our knowledge, to reach such a decision may be difficult : it may be if the measurement of axial length became a clinical routine that the problem would be further clarified. Apart from the elimination of any pathological changes in the fundus, the eyes should be examined at frequent intervals to assess the significance of any progress, particularly when a hereditary tendency to myopia is shown ; significant features in a particular case before the advent of degenerative changes and apart from *a hereditary history and rapid progress of the error, are an unaccountable loss of the visual acuity, an accentuated foveal reflex, and disproportionate degenerative changes in the vitreous* ; if any doubt exists the case should be treated as if it were potentially degenerative.

The prescription of spectacles for young myopic subjects is psychologically important. With their optical defect uncorrected, they develop in a limited world wherein they are at a considerable disadvantage in comparison with others, a handicap which may entail a seeming limitation of intelligence and a curtailment of interests which are frequently ascribed to stupidity and backwardness or to naughtiness, while they are really due to the physical defect. Much that is going on in the world—especially the more subtle things—escapes them ; avoiding outdoor sports and prone to introspection, debarred from free intercourse with their fellows and unable to enjoy a full appreciation of life, they frequently tend to grow up with introverted mental habits and peculiarities.

In the ordering of spectacles for young people, the question of a cycloplegic is discussed at a later stage[1] and, while the refractive error should never be over-corrected, as full a correction as can be comfortably worn should be ordered. The use of the duochrome test[2] is a valuable aid in this respect ; it is usually advisable to correct the defect only up to the point where the red objects are seen slightly more clearly than the green. A regime of six-monthly supervision should be adopted in low grades of myopia in adolescents until time has shown that it is not progressive. If it becomes clear that the refraction is stationary, the constant wearing of spectacles may be unnecessary, although their use is always wise when the eyes are used for any specific purpose. In adolescents who have not previously worn spectacles a full correction may not be acceptable for near work for the patient has been accustomed to read without exercising his accommodation ; he may, indeed, be more comfortable without spectacles or with weaker lenses. It should be impressed upon him, however, that in the matter of near work they are not intended to improve his vision but to allow him to use his eyes in their normal relationships. In adults, on the other hand, in whom visual habits have become stabilized, such care is unnecessary and the constant use of spectacles need not be insisted upon ; moreover, in the absence of a previous correction it will frequently be found that the ciliary muscle is not equal to the unaccustomed task of accommodating efficiently, so that a lens of slightly lower power may be prescribed with comfort for reading.

[1] p. 385.   [2] p. 437.

In the lower degrees of myopia the necessity for regular supervision once the condition is static is questionable; in general, low myopes change little after the end of adolescence and they may be confidently advised to return for further examination only if their spectacle frames or lenses become physically damaged or if they notice any deterioration in their corrected vision. They should be reassured that the latter event is unlikely in any event before the age of 40. Above the age of 40, of course, when accommodation fails physiologically, weaker lenses for near work are advisable or the spectacles can be removed.

In the higher degrees of myopia, the full correction can rarely be tolerated largely because the images formed by strong concave lenses are diminished and very bright and clear, and the patient, accustomed to interpret hazy diffusion circles, is intolerant of them. A compromise must therefore be adopted, and while an attempt is made to reduce the correction as little as is compatible with comfort for binocular vision, lenses are prescribed with which greatest visual acuity is obtained without distress. The amount which has to be deducted usually varies from 1 to 3 D, but in the highest grades spectacles even weaker than these will be found necessary. In these cases contact lenses may be of value if they are easily tolerated.

A plea has been made for the purposeful under-correction of myopia incorporating base-in prisms in the lenses (Cohn, 1871; Hay, 1914; and others); this is held to improve the condition by diminishing the accommodation-convergence reflex, the activity of which is believed by some to increase myopia. We shall see that there is no theoretical justification for this view; nor adequate evidence that such clinical improvement does in fact occur (Chance *et al.*, 1942).

Contact lenses, particularly of the corneal type, offer cosmetic and perhaps optical advantages over the wearing of spectacles, low myopia being perhaps the most widespread indication for their use. The subject, as well as the possible influence of wearing contact lenses on the progression of myopia, will be discussed in a later Chapter.[1]

A large school of thought does not agree with the principles enumerated here and would insist, sometimes vociferously, that young myopes—and sometimes adults—should wear their full correcting spectacles constantly (Cohn, 1883–92; and many others). Throughout his professional life an authority of the weight of Edward Jackson (1891–1935) insisted that " the constant wearing of full corrective lenses, no matter what their strength, with careful attention to other aspects of ocular hygiene, checks promptly and permanently the advance of myopia in the majority of cases ". Jackson was endowed with wisdom and long experience, and he has been by no means unsupported in his view, but such insistence is unjustified in simple myopia and its value is questionable even in the higher degrees associated with degenerative changes.

Apart from the optical correction, no specific treatment for simple myopia is indicated. There is no more evidence that the dioptric constitu-

[1] Chap. XVII.

ents of the healthy eye can be altered or its rate of growth in a healthy child regulated, no matter what its refractive condition may be, than that the growth of any other part of the body can be controlled. The whole question of optical or other treatment designed to arrest the progress of myopia is, of course, beset with problems, not the least of which is the uncertainty of its course if " untreated ". Thus Mandell (1965) in dismissing the value of bifocals indicated that subjects with less than 2 D myopia and over 14 years of age are very unlikely to progress in any event. Nor is there evidence that the simple myopic eye is unsound, as Donders (1864) claimed, deficient, or a victim of the disharmonies of an artificial civilization (Gullstrand, 1924; Keith, 1925). This question will be taken up more fully when we are considering myopia associated with degenerative changes[1]; but in the simple cases, as far as concerns the management of the patient whether adult or child, the extent to which spectacles are worn, the amount of near work done, peculiarities of diet or the administration of drugs are of small moment provided that hygienic conditions are good, overstrain is avoided and the general standards of health and development are maintained.

Regular Astigmatism

ASTIGMATISM is that type of refractive anomaly in which *no point focus is formed owing to the unequal refraction of the incident light by the dioptric system of the eye in different meridians.* It may be caused by irregularities in curvature or decentring of the optical surfaces of the eye, or by inequalities in the refractive index of the lens. In the healthy eye only the first of these factors is of practical importance.

Astigmatism ordinarily depends on the presence of toroidal instead of spherical curvatures of the refracting surfaces of the eye; the refractive power as a whole, therefore, instead of being equal in all meridians, changes gradually from one meridian to the next by uniform increments, and each meridian generally has a uniform type of curve. Such a condition was called REGULAR ASTIGMATISM by Donders (1864) and is correctable by a cylindrical lens. When, however, as in cases of corneal disease or lenticular sclerosis, there are irregularities in the curvature of the meridians conforming to no geometrical figure, the condition is called IRREGULAR ASTIGMATISM; such a defect cannot be compensated by spectacle lenses but sometimes can be, in so far as it is corneal, by contact lenses. Being pathological in nature it will be considered at a later stage.

As a rule, the major and minor meridians are at right angles; if they differ significantly from the vertical and horizontal, OBLIQUE ASTIGMATISM exists; if they are not at right angles, the optical condition is called BI-OBLIQUE ASTIGMATISM (Roure, 1896)[2].

[1] p. 300.   [2] p. 404.

THE COMPONENTS OF TOTAL ASTIGMATISM

Curvature astigmatism of the anterior surface of the cornea occurs physiologically and is thus responsible for the majority of cases of astigmatism. The average difference between the refractive powers of the two corneal meridians lies between 0·5 and 0·75 D; Donders (1864) gave a mean value of 1 D, Pfalz (1885) of 0·75 D, Sørensen (1944) of 0·75 to 0·5 D, Steiger (1895) and Gullstrand (1890) of 0·5 D, while Kronfeld and Devney (1930) suggested that any value over 1 D should be regarded as pathological. In about 90% of cases the section of least curvature is horizontal. If the meridian of least curvature makes an angle of less than 30° with the horizontal plane, the astigmatism is termed *direct* or " *with the rule* "; if it makes such an angle with the vertical plane so that the horizontal curvature is greater, it is termed *inverse* or " *against the rule*."

Corneal astigmatism is readily detected and its form analysed by keratophotometry.[1]   Figures 311 to 314 illustrate the regular forms; it is difficult for the observer to detect less than 2·5 D of regular astigmatism with the keratoscope (Levene, 1962), but it will be seen at a later stage that the method is extremely useful in demonstrating and recording changes in irregular astigmatism.

This physiological tendency has not yet been adequately explained. Snellen (1869) associated it with the pressure of the eyelids on the globe, a view which has received considerable support (Birch-Hirschfeld, 1922). To a certain extent this may be the case since, when the cornea is plastic as in keratoconus, the direct astigmatism increases considerably (Gullstrand, 1892–1922), a change which also occurs if the pressure of the lid is increased by forcible closure or by the weight of a chalazion or a tumour (Ormond, 1921; Safar, 1947; and others).   Conversely, when a raised intra-ocular pressure assumes the preponderant role in the conformation of the globe, as in glaucoma, inverse astigmatism may tend to develop, an effect, however, which although seen in the eyes of experimental animals (Laqueur, 1884; Eissen, 1888) is not of regular clinical occurrence (Martin, 1885; Pfalz, 1885; Eissen, 1888; Schoen, 1893; ten Doesschate, 1918; and others).   It seems likely, however, in view of the fact that the corneal curvature forms part of a similar deformation of the anterior segment of the globe including the sclera (Tron, 1925; Berg, 1930–32), that the cause is more fundamental, involving a peculiarity of growth.   This view is substantiated by the common occurrence of high astigmatism in deformities even of the posterior segment of the globe such as conus (Fuchs, 1882–1919; v. Szily, 1913–22).

Asymmetry of the skull has been suggested as a determinant of corneal astigmatism, particularly in cases of narrow orbits and maxillæ (Seggel, 1890–1903).   The evidence, however, would seem to be against this (Tron, 1925; Sorsby and Shaw, 1932).   Marked orbital asymmetry is not regularly associated with astigmatism and the growth of the orbit tends rather with conform with that of the globe.

[1] Vol. VII, p. 241.

FIGS. 311–314.—KERATOSCOPY IN ASTIGMATISM (M. Amsler).

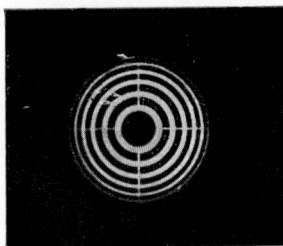

FIG. 311.—Keratoscopic image on an optically regular metallic "cornea" of 7·5 mm. radius of curvature (45 D refractive power).

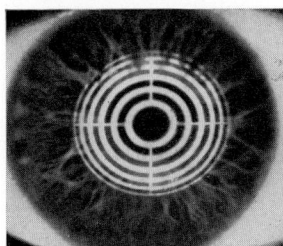

FIG. 312.—Keratoscopic image in physiological astigmatism.

—|—42 D
42·57 D

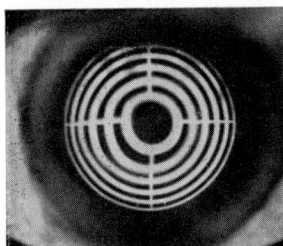

FIG. 313.—Keratoscopic image in marked direct astigmatism.

—|—40 D
45 D

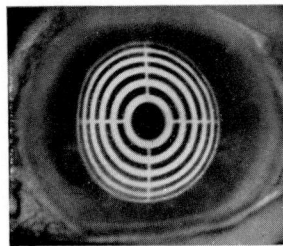

FIG. 314.—Keratoscopic image in inverse astigmatism—post-operative.

—|—45 D
42 D

It is to be noted that the healing of an incision along the upper limbus usually produces an inverse astigmatism after intra-ocular operations, particularly for cataract[1] (Fig. 314) and an alteration is sometimes seen to a less degree after a tenotomy or advancement operation (Snellen, 1869; Laqueur, 1884), or by the pressure of a finger or an orbital tumour on the globe (see Dascalopoulos, 1947).

The *posterior surface of the cornea* usually shows some astigmatic error; it is less than that of the anterior surface, varying from 0·25 to 0·5 D (Tscherning, 1904), but sometimes reaching 1·0 D, and is usually inverse in type, neutralizing to some extent the curvature of the anterior surface.

Curvature astigmatism of both surfaces of the lens is also a normal occurrence; its extent, however, is generally less than that of the cornea and its optical effect is usually in the reverse direction, the greatest curvature being in the horizontal meridian (Tscherning, 1898–1904; Awerbach, 1900; Lo Cascio, 1923). Tscherning's (1898) measurements for the radii in the optical zone were 10·2 mm. in the horizontal meridian and 10·1 in the vertical of the anterior surface, and 6·17 and 6·13 respectively for the posterior surface.

[1]p. 365. See Vol. XI, p. 280.

The outer surfaces, however, are not alone involved, for the laminated zones of the lens are not concentric. Such variations are normally small (0·5 to 0·75 D with a maximum variation of 2·0 D, Sørensen, 1944), but in deformations such as lenticonus their effect may be considerable.

Astigmatism from decentring of the optical system of the eye is again invariable and physiological. None of the surfaces is geometrically centred or has a true axis of symmetry. This particularly affects the lens which is not normally concentrically placed. According to Tscherning (1898) the deviation is made up of two components, a rotation of 3° to 7° round the vertical axis so that the temporal border lies behind the nasal, and 0° to 3° round the horizontal axis so that the upper border is in front of the lower. In consequence, the optic axis cuts the cornea not at its axial point but sometimes as much as 0·25 mm. below and to its inner side. This deviation however, is small (of the order of 0·25 D); such as it is, it tends to neutralize the physiological direct corneal astigmatism (Tscherning, 1904). On dislocation or subluxation of the lens, however, the effect is much increased. Moreover, considering the dioptric system as a whole, the fovea is not usually situated on the optic axis, but 1·25 mm. downwards to its temporal side,[1] while the central pupillary line is somewhat eccentric to the nasal side of the centre of the cornea[2]; accepting the usual angle of 5° between the pupillary line and the optic axis (Gullstrand, 1911), the resultant astigmatism is 0·1 D for a pupil of 2 mm. diameter.

Refractive astigmatism mainly concerns the lens for its many laminated zones may vary considerably in optical density. The evidence is that such astigmatic effects are small and are usually inverse in type; but in the normal sclerosis of age they may become clinically obvious and may be accentuated to produce extreme distortion or even polyopia in the grosser changes of cataract. It is probable that the variations in refractivity in different zones of the lens are chiefly responsible for the variations in refraction between different zones of the pupillary aperture (Stine, 1930).[3]

Since, therefore, every surface of curvature is optically imperfect in the eye and there is no true axis of symmetry, some degree of astigmatism is invariable (PHYSIOLOGICAL ASTIGMATISM). Usually, however, it is small and negligible from the visual point of view. The largest element of the TOTAL ASTIGMATISM is due to the anterior corneal surface while the other components (the RESIDUAL ASTIGMATISM, comprised of the astigmatism due to the posterior surface of the cornea, the surfaces of the lens, decentration and the variability of the refractive index of the lens) tend as a rule to neutralize this (Czellitzer, 1927).[4]

The residual astigmatism, however, is by no means to be neglected. Jackson (1932) found that in young adults the average corneal astigmatism

---

[1] p. 135.　　　　[2] p. 126.　　　　[3] p. 133.

[4] It is to be noted that the term *residual astigmatism* has a different connotation in the optics of contact lenses.

over a large series of cases was 1·04 D and the average residual astigmatism 0·61 D. Extreme values were 8 D of corneal astigmatism and 4·25 D of lenticular astigmatism. The extreme value of total astigmatism was 6 D, the less value being due to the neutralization of one component by the other. The significant degree of residual astigmatism is sufficient commentary on the inefficiency of the clinical correction of astigmatic errors estimated by keratometry alone. The residual astigmatism of an eye tends, however, to be similar to that of its fellow even although the total astigmatism may be quite different (Hofstetter and Baldwin, 1957).

Javal's rule is widely quoted, which gives an empirical relationship between total or subjective astigmatism (Ast) and the keratometric or corneal astigmatism (Asc) but is open to many exceptions:

$$\text{Ast} = k + 1\cdot25 \text{ Asc, where } k = 0\cdot5 \text{ D against the rule.}$$

The division between corneal and residual astigmatism was particularly stressed by Marquez (1909–42) who pointed out that the former could be measured directly and accurately by the keratometer, while the latter could only be estimated inaccurately and as a whole. He claimed more accurate measurement of the total astigmatism by assessing the two fractions separately in his technique of BI-ASTIGMATISM and better therapeutic results by their separate correction by crossed cylinders. The method has its advocates (Duque Estrada, 1942; Prado, 1943; Gonzales, 1943–47; and others), but its practical value is questionable (Crisp, 1930–31; Linksz and Triller, 1944). We shall return to this at a later stage.

The mode of inheritance of regular astigmatism is not entirely certain. Waardenburg (1963) suggested that transmission as an autosomal dominant with incomplete penetrance and variable expressivity is the commonest if the anomaly is significant in degree. Several pedigrees indicate this to be so (Leibowicz, 1928; Motolese and Berardi, 1936). Capalbi and Binchi (1955) believed that there may also be recessive forms. Studies of twins, however, confirm that dominant inheritance is the more important, showing a considerable concordance between both spherical errors and corneal curvature (Halbertsma, 1929; Wixson, 1959).

The variation of regular astigmatism with age is of considerable importance. As we have seen, a small degree of direct astigmatism is the usual condition in early life. The work of Marin Amat (1964) indicates that this astigmatism may not be present at birth but may develop during the first few years of life. The neonatal cornea is usually of nearly spherical shape and any alterations that occur in the less degrees of astigmatism are probably small (Blum *et al.*, 1959). Even if the astigmatism is marked it usually changes little during the school years (Hirsch, 1963).

From early adult life onwards there is a general tendency for the direct astigmatism to decrease or even to be converted into inverse astigmatism but, again, the changes are usually within narrow limits.[1] In some individ-

[1] Pomeroy (1867), Theobald (1885), Pfalz (1885–90), Schoen (1887), Jackson (1890), Steiger (1895–1920), Hess (1910), Stirling (1921), Kronfeld and Devney (1930), Sørensen (1944), Hirsch (1959).

uals there is little, if any, alteration in the corneal astigmatism (Exford, 1965) and any change that does occur may occasionally be in the opposite direction (Marin Amat, 1956). There is also some evidence that the change in the corneal refraction with age is less marked or slower in women than men (Forsius *et al.*, 1964). As a rule these alterations are essentially due to a decrease in the corneal astigmatism, the vertical meridian becoming flatter, and it can be shown that a flattening of the corneal curvature by 10% vertically produces almost 4 D of inverse astigmatism; but there is also an increase in the lenticular astigmatism which usually lies in the sense opposite to the corneal. Jackson's (1932) figures illustrating this are seen in Table XXI. It follows that a young adult aged 30 with a small amount of direct astigmatism may become stigmatic at 45 and is likely to show some inverse astigmatism at 60 years (Sørensen, 1944)[1]; among octogenarians inverse astigmatism is almost invariable.

TABLE XXI

ASTIGMATIC ALTERATIONS WITH AGE
(Jackson)

	Nil	*Horizontal*	*Vertical*	*Oblique*
Corneal astigmatism :				
before 25 years	52	24	910	32
after 50 years	84	118	737	86
Residual astigmatism :				
before 25 years	62	817	61	52
after 50 years	72	726	63	163

The cause of this change in corneal astigmatism is not certain; Marin Amat (1956) suggested that a combination of factors may be operative. The pressure caused by the lids in early life diminishes with progressive weakness of the orbicularis, an effect which he claimed was accentuated by the action of the extrinsic ocular muscles, particularly the medial rectus. The action of this muscle in convergence, however, could flatten the horizontal meridian of the cornea (and perhaps also make the vertical meridian more curved), a change which increases the direct astigmatism and is opposite to that actually found in old age. It has been suggested that the upper and lower portions of the cornea may suffer inadequate nutrition owing to their distance from the long posterior ciliary arteries, although there is no correlation between the development of an arcus senilis and inverse astigmatism. The cornea may also be influenced by contraction of the ciliary muscle which in old age is unable to alter the shape of the lens. The suggestion of Gullstrand (1922) that the configuration of the cornea in later life is related to a general increase in ocular rigidity is not borne out by studies of this factor (Forsius *et al.*, 1964).

[1] p. 132.

THE INCIDENCE OF ASTIGMATISM

Since physiological astigmatism is practically invariable, most eyes (95%) are clinically detectable as astigmatic in some degree. Estimates of *the frequency of significant astigmatism* therefore vary considerably with the starting point arbitrarily taken; this should be at least 0·5 D.

The following are some estimates in the literature: Mügge (1908) 10·56%; Lühl (1909) 7·47%; Cavara (1922) 44·39%; Zamora (1924) 75%; Menestrina (1925–26) 34%; Leibowicz (1928) 48·1%.

The *sex incidence* of astigmatism is difficult to assess. Some observers have found it more frequent and more marked in women than in men (Pflüger, 1890, 11 : 9; Zamora, 1924, 8 : 7); others have found the reverse (Pfalz, 1885—1900, 7 : 10; Lühl, 1909, 10 : 17; Axt, 1914, 7 : 10; Sergiewski, 1925, 2 : 3; Leibowicz, 1928, 11 : 12). It is probable that any difference is without much significance.

The *type of astigmatism* shows a fairly constant incidence, the most common forms being the compound myopic and hypermetropic forms. The farther the refractive state from emmetropia, the more common is the occurrence of astigmatism. The added figures of Lühl (1909) and Cavara (1922) are typical:

Compound hypermetropic astigmatism	27%
Simple hypermetropic astigmatism	13·72%
Mixed astigmatism	11·3%
Simple myopic astigmatism	9·62%
Compound myopic astigmatism	38·37%

The *degree of astigmatism* varies considerably, but in the great majority of cases it is less than 1 or 1·25 D (86%, Steiger, 1895; 84·76%, Seefelder, 1907). Above this the incidence falls rapidly and an astigmatism of over 6 D with the rule or 2·5 D against the rule is exceedingly uncommon in a non-pathological eye (Steiger, 1895; Lang, 1920; Leibowicz, 1928). Higher values, of course, occur (up to 18 and 20 D), but they are associated with such conditions as corneal trauma, keratoconus, ectasia and so on.

Cavara (1922) found the following incidence :—

astigmatism in D	>0·5	0·5–1	1–1·5	1·5–2	2–3	<3 D
% incidence	22·94	42·44	16·18	9·21	6·39	2·84

The *variational frequency of the degrees of corneal astigmatism in the different spherical refractive states* has received little attention (Menestrina, 1926; Kronfeld and Devney, 1930). The question is one of considerable importance for it forms the most rational statistical basis on which the biological significance of astigmatism can be determined. Its full elucidation is a task of formidable dimensions, particularly when small astigmatic errors are considered, and owing to the age variation would necessitate the enormous labour of investigating a significant amount of material in all age groups.   From Kronfeld and Devney's results (Fig. 315), however, it is evident that relatively small astigmatic errors (0·5 to 1·0 D)—much the most common group—are fairly evenly distributed among medium refractive states (+ 3·5 D to − 5·0 D); beyond these limits their incidence falls, slowly in

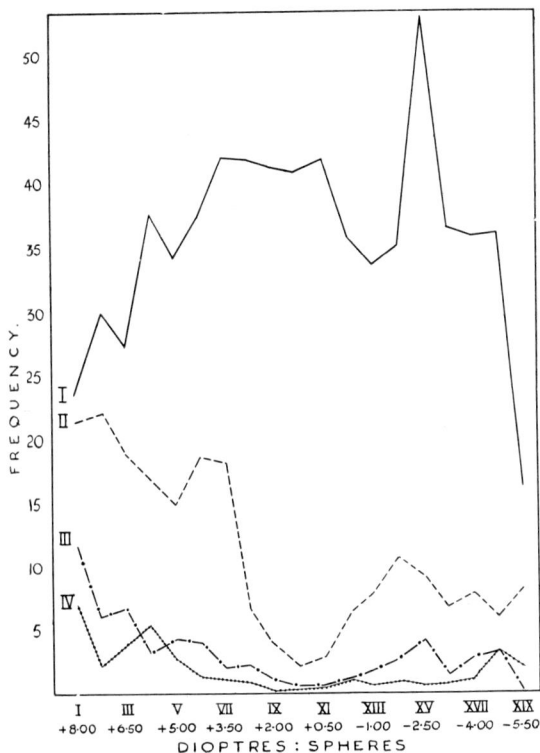

Fig. 315.—The Variational Frequency of Various Degrees of Corneal Astigmatism in the different Spherical Refractive States.

Curve I. Astigmatism of 0·5 to 1·0 D.
Curve II. Astigmatism of 2·0 to 2·5 D.
Curve III. Astigmatism of 5·0 to 5·5 D.
Curve IV. Astigmatism of 5·75 to 6·25 D.

It is seen that the distribution of the smaller astigmatic errors (Curve I) is entirely different from that of the larger errors. The first is (in general) most frequent in the region of the spherical emmetropia, the larger errors with the higher spherical errors (P. C. Kronfeld and C. Devney).

association with the higher hypermetropic spherical errors and abruptly with the myopic.   The distribution of astigmatism of more than 1·0 D, however, is very different: the minimum frequency is in association with + 1·25 D sphere—the commonest refractive state under cycloplegia (Fig. 000)—and as the spherical error increases, so does the tendency to higher astigmatism, more markedly on the hypermetropic side than the myopic.

This difference in distribution suggests a fundamental biological difference between the lower (physiological) degrees of astigmatism which may be classed as normal and the higher which would appear to be aphysiological and abnormal. We have already seen that emmetropia is the dominant refractive state in that it forms the peak in the incidence of spherical refraction; it is also the one at which there is the strongest tendency towards the absence of (aphysiological) astigmatism.

This tendency—the more the refractive state deviates from emmetropia, the more likely the occurrence of an astigmatic error—is well recognized. High astigmatic errors with high hypermetropia are readily understood in view of the fact that most such eyes are developmentally deformed. The occurrence of high astigmatism in high myopia—frequently inverse in type—is also a common observation (Mende, 1906; Seefelder, 1907; Cavara, 1922; and others). Menestrina (1926) found that inverse corneal astigmatism occurred in 1·93% of emmetropes and hypermetropes, but in 9·25% of myopes, and that 69% of all cases of astigmatism against the rule were myopic.

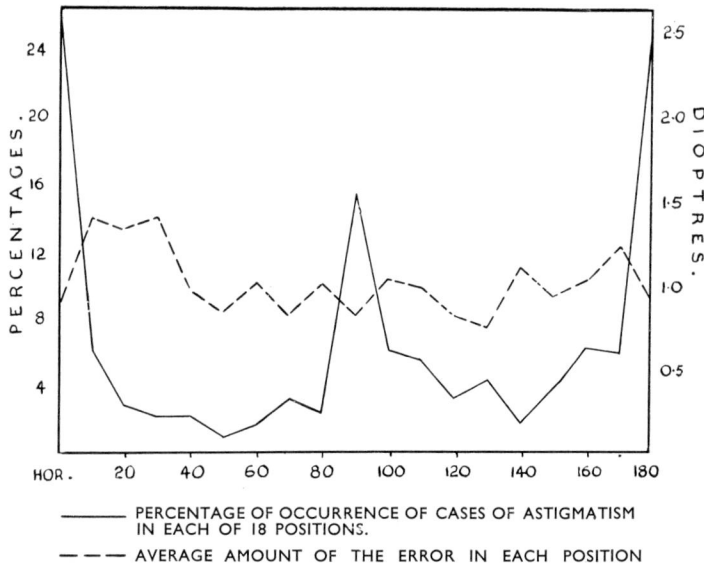

—— PERCENTAGE OF OCCURRENCE OF CASES OF ASTIGMATISM
IN EACH OF 18 POSITIONS.
— — — AVERAGE AMOUNT OF THE ERROR IN EACH POSITION

FIG. 316.—THE PERCENTAGE INCIDENCE OF THE DIRECTION OF THE AXIS
OF CORRECTING MINUS CYLINDERS.

It is seen that the most frequent occurrence is horizontal (or 180°); the next highest incidence is at 90° (B. T. Lang).

The *direction of the meridian of greatest curvature* has already been noted in dealing with the normal transference of a direct to an inverse astigmatism with age. In children and young adults of this meridian is vertical in most cases: Jackson's (1932) figures seen in Table XXI are typical and the relative incidence is seen graphically in Fig. 316. As age advances this preponderance gets less and less, and over the age of 50 oblique astigmatism becomes three times more common (Table XXI) and inverse astigmatism five or six times; eventually over the age of 80 the preponderance of inverse astigmatism over direct is almost as great as was the opposite relationship in youth (Schoen, 1893; Steiger, 1895; Hess, 1896–97; and others). Thus Cavara (1922) found that the incidence of direct astigmatism fell from 92·38% at the age of 10 to 14·3% at the age of 80, while inverse astigmatism rose correspondingly from 7·62% to 85·7%.

A *symmetry of astigmatism* between the two eyes is frequently seen with reference not only to the degree of the error, but also to the direction of the axis (1,307 compared with 458 cases, Risley and Thorrington, 1895). Aniso-metropia, however, is no rarity. Unilateral astigmatism occurs in about 30% of cases (Mügge, 1908; Lühl, 1909), but the degree of defect is usually less than when the error is bilateral (averages 2·99 : 3·41 D, Steiger, 1895).

THE OPTICAL CONDITION IN ASTIGMATISM

The manner of the refraction of parallel rays of light by an astigmatic system has already been described[1] and is indicated in Fig. 90. It will be recalled that two focal lines are formed lying at the focal points of the meridians of greatest and least curvature, separated by a focal interval, the length of which corresponds to the degree of astigmatism (that is, the differ-ence between the dioptric powers of the two meridians). It is of no optical consequence how many cylindrical or sphero-cylindrical refracting surfaces are combined with their axes in any position in respect to each other, for the resultant effect is always that of a sphero-cylindrical equivalent wherein the meridians of greatest and least curvature are always at right angles. So long, therefore, as the astigmatism is regular, and no matter at what oblique angle the meridians of the refractive surfaces in the eye intersect, the image of the retina can never be a point, but must always be either one of two lines at right angles (when it is distorted), a circle of least diffusion (when it is blurred) or an ellipse (when it is both distorted and blurred). The diameter of the circle of least diffusion varies directly with the degree of astigmatism and with the size of the pupillary aperture. The aim of optical correction is, first, the elimination of the focal interval by the use of a cylindrical lens which, acting in the plane of one meridian, so changes the refraction of the rays that they are brought to a focus at the same distance as those of the other meridian, when the whole image (theoretically) becomes a point; and second, the displacement (if it is necessary) of this stigmatic image to the plane of the retina by a suitable spherical correction.

Depending on the position occupied by the two focal lines, regular astigmatism may be classified thus (Figs. 317–18):

1. SIMPLE ASTIGMATISM, wherein one of the focal lines falls upon the retina when the eye is at rest. The other focal line may fall in front or

[1] p. 62.

behind the retina, so that while one meridian is emmetropic, the other is either hypermetropic or myopic. These are respectively designated SIMPLE HYPERMETROPIC and SIMPLE MYOPIC ASTIGMATISM.

2. COMPOUND ASTIGMATISM, where neither of the two focal lines lies upon the retina, but are both placed in front or behind it. The state of the

FIGS. 317 and 318.—TYPES OF ASTIGMATISM.

A cross with horizontal (HH_1) and vertical (VV_1) lines forms the object; the corneal curvatures (C_1C_2) differ in the two main meridans.

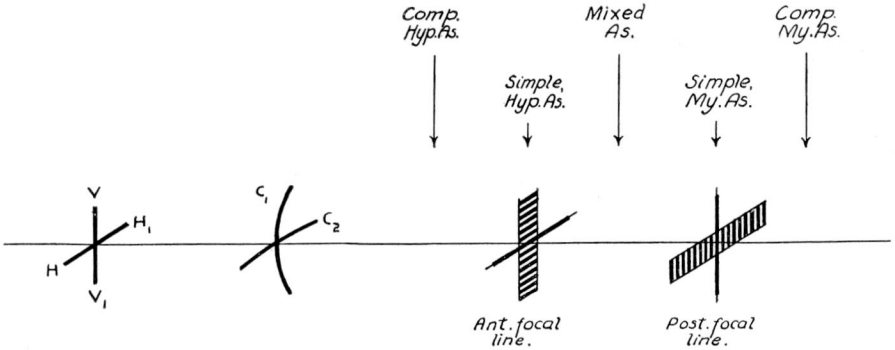

FIG. 317.—Direct astigmatism with the vertical meridian of greater curvature than the horizontal.

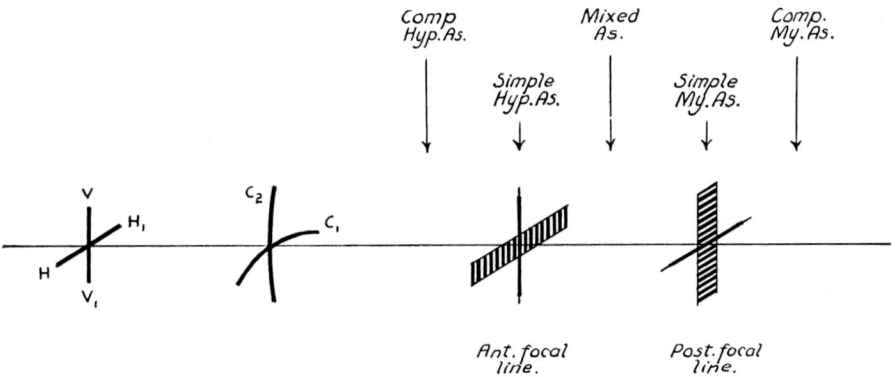

FIG. 318.—Inverse astigmatism with the horizontal meridian of greater curvature than the vertical.

refraction is then entirely hypermetropic or entirely myopic. The former is known as COMPOUND HYPERMETROPIC, the latter is COMPOUND MYOPIC ASTIGMATISM.

3. MIXED ASTIGMATISM, where one focal line is in front and the other behind the retina, so that the refraction is hypermetropic in one direction and myopic in the other.

ASTIGMATISM AND NEAR VISION

Accommodation may alter the nature of the image appreciably in astigmatism by varying the position of the focal lines so that a hypermetropic focal line may be focused on the retina. This is possible and is usually done in hypermetropic and mixed astigmatism when the most posterior focal line is usually imaged (Sallmann, 1930); but myopic astigmatism cannot be improved in this way except for distances less than the far-point.

Accommodative Astigmatism. It is an old and correct observation that an increase occurs in the amount of astigmatism and a change in its axis on accommodation, as can be demonstrated by measuring the refractive error before and after cycloplegia, or during the adjustment of the accommodation for distant vision and its employment in near-fixation (ACCOMMODATIVE ASTIGMATISM : NEAR ASTIGMATISM, Erggelet, 1925).[1] The increase in cylindrical power, whether convex or concave, has been found to be of the order of 10% when the fully accommodating eye is compared with the eye adjusted for distant vision (O'Brien and Bannon, 1947)—an amount relatively negligible for the smaller but important in the higher refractive errors. The change in axis is more irregular and seems sometimes to be in the direction of intorsion and sometimes of extorsion; O'Brien and Bannon (1947) found that the change bore no relationship to the cyclotorsional movements of the eyes in convergence and downward gaze. These alterations in the optical system are explicable by a variation in the pupillary diameter and by the differences not only of surface curvatures but perhaps also of tilt and rotation between the two states of the lens in relaxation and under strain. Moreover, the action of the extrinsic ocular muscles cannot be entirely ignored; horizontal flattening of the cornea during convergence in subjects of pre-presbyopic age was reported by Fairmaid (1959) and Löpping and Weale (1965).

In addition to the action of the extrinsic muscles, it has also been claimed that the intrinsic musculature may exert some influence on the shape of the cornea (Yamanaka, 1961–63), a finding, however, which has been denied (Fairmaid, 1959). It has even been suggested that the phenomenon of " aphakic accommodation " may be due to the action of the ciliary muscle on the shape of the cornea owing to its attachment to the termination of Descemet's membrane (Marin Amat, 1956).

The suggestion that the ciliary muscle may act in only part of its circumference to produce a DYNAMIC LENTICULAR ASTIGMATISM was put forward by Dobrowolsky (1868–69), and much has been written about the clinical importance of a hypothetical unequal contraction of the ciliary muscle which is said to induce a deformation of the lens, tending to neutralize the corneal astigmatism; it has even been claimed that this brings about symptoms of eye-strain by calling for constant accommodative efforts and eventually becomes a potent factor in the causation of cataract (Martin, 1886–91;

[1] Michel (1893), Hess (1897), Gradle (1897), Fick (1901), Belehrádek (1922), Sheard (1926), Hughes (1941), Sugar (1944), Beck (1965) and others.

Pflüger, 1890; Michel, 1893; Marquez, 1909–42; and others). There is no adequate evidence, however, that accommodation is employed to alter the degree of astigmatism. The claim was based upon the experimental work of Hensen and Völckers (1868–78), who showed that when a filament of the ciliary nerve was divided a local contraction of that part of the ciliary muscle supplied by the filament could be induced on stimulation. But this will occur if the local nerve supply of any muscle mass is separately stimulated, and such an isolated contraction under experimental conditions bears no relation to the normal action of the muscle in life. Such localized contractions have been seen clinically in partial recovery of the ciliary muscle after palsies such as in botulism (Lancaster, 1916), in cases of partial rupture of the zonule (Hughes, 1941) or (in monkeys) on the injection of drugs to a portion of the muscle (Bárány, 1966). All the evidence, however, indicates that in health the ciliary muscle always contracts as a whole.

THE VISUAL STATE IN ASTIGMATISM

The vision in astigmatism is characteristic. When the degree of astigmatism is appreciable, since in no circumstances can the eye form a sharply defined image upon the retina, the diminution of visual acuity may be very considerable. In his endeavour to see clearly the patient attempts

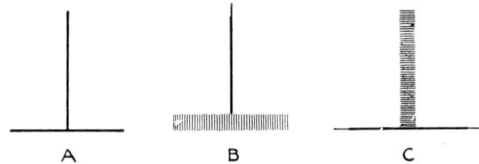

FIG. 319.—THE VISION IN ASTIGMATISM.

If two lines at right angles are regarded (A) and one focal line is focused, lines in one direction are seen clearly although elongated, while lines in the other are blurred (B, C).

to focus, not the central circle of least diffusion, but one or other of the focal lines so that the image is not blurred but distorted : such attempts, of course, can be made only in hypermetropic and mixed astigmatism. It is generally stated that the meridian most closely approaching emmetropia is usually chosen, or alternatively the focal line most suited to the shape of objects (such as the vertical lines in reading print), but Sallmann (1930) found experimentally that the most posterior focal line was usually preferred in practice. Since the focal line is made the object of attention, the vision of the astigmat shows peculiarities other than indistinctness on account of the elongated form of the diffusion circles which he has to interpret. Circles become elongated into ovals; a point of light appears tailed off; and a line, which consists of a series of points, appears as a succession of strokes fused into a blurred image (Fig. 319). Thus in every case of regular astigmatism there is one direction in which lines appear most distinct, and one in which they appear most confused. This is taken advantage of in the detection of astigmatism by a fan-shaped figure.[1]

[1] p. 439.

The consequent diminution of visual acuity may be very considerable and varies directly with the degree of astigmatism, a point brought out by a number of observers who have studied the average uncorrected visual acuity.[1] On the whole the diminution in acuity is about equal for corresponding degrees of simple hypermetropic and myopic astigmatism, and is considerably less than that caused by an equal degree of myopia or absolute hypermetropia; as measured by Snellen's types where vertical lines predominate it is

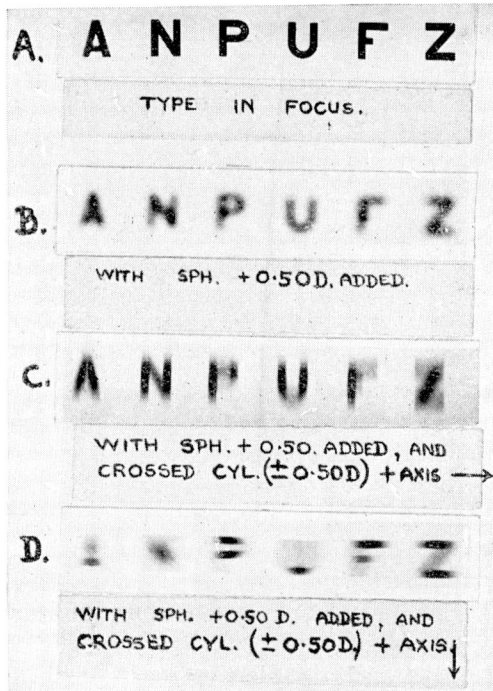

FIG. 320.—THE DIMINUTION OF VISUAL ACUITY WITH PLUS SPHERES AND CYLINDERS.

B shows the diminution of acuity of A with +0·5 D of absolute hypermetropia. In reading types the diminution of acuity with an astigmatic error is least when the axis of the cylinder is horizontal (C) and greatest when it is vertical (D) (F. A. Williamson-Noble).

greatest when the more positive axis is vertical, intermediate when it is oblique and least when it is horizontal, in which case the visual loss is about half that caused by a spherical error of equal power (Fig. 320).

Eggers's (1945) figures are seen in Table XXII.

The corrected visual acuity in the lower degrees of astigmatism can usually be brought up to normal standards or above, but in the higher degrees

[1] Steiger (1902), Seefelder (1908), Mügge (1908–18), Lühl (1909), Farid Bey (1919), Sergiewski (1925), Eggers (1945), and others.

TABLE XXII

APPROXIMATE VISUAL ACUITY IN ASTIGMATISM

Visual acuity	20/30	20/40	20/50	20/70	20/100	20/150	20/250
Astig. Ax. horiz.	1·00	1·50	2·00	2·50	3·00	4·00	5·50
Astig. Ax. oblique	0·75	1·00	1·50	1·75	2·25	2·75	4·25
Spher. Myopia or Abs. Hm.	0·50	0·75	1·00	1·25	1·50	2·00	3·00

this is by no means always the case, particularly if the optical correction is not made in early life and also if the astigmatism is oblique (Bonavolontà and de Simone, 1960). This deficiency is essentially perceptual and there may be a tendency for poor differentiation to be accentuated in the meridian of greatest astigmatism (*astigmatic amblyopia*) (Martin, 1890; Luedde, 1922). Amblyopia ex anopsia affecting all meridians is more common in the highest degrees, and there is a tendency to develop strabismus particularly in the presence of hypermetropic errors.[1]

CLINICAL SYMPTOMS

Apart from the visual defect in astigmatism, the constant effort to see clearly is a prolific cause of eye-strain. This is especially evident in hypermetropic and mixed astigmatism owing to the accommodative stress undergone and is particularly so in the case of small astigmatic errors for here the measure of success which the accommodative effort achieves stimulates it to greater endeavour. Considered as a whole, of course, in the great majority of cases these small errors give rise to no discomfort; they may be accepted as physiological and do not require treatment. In other cases, however, all the symptoms of eye-strain may be present—headaches varying from a mild frontal ache to violent explosions of pain, dizziness, neurasthenia, irritability, fatigue and a whole gamut of reflex nervous disturbances.[2]

A characteristic attitude is occasionally seen. If the axis of the cylinder is oblique, the head is frequently held to one side so as to reduce the distortion, a habit which may in children lead to the development of scoliosis; and in all cases there is a tendency to half-close the lids in order to make a stenopæic slit, so that by cutting out the rays of one meridian the object may appear more distinct.

TREATMENT

Provided they produce no serious deterioration of the visual acuity, and provided they are giving rise to no symptoms of asthenopia and eye-strain, the *smaller astigmatic errors* do not require correction; but if either of these two conditions is present, the error should be corrected by spectacles. It is obvious that in the correction of these small errors the utmost care is to be exercised, for any difference remaining is left for the patient himself to

[1] p. Vol. VI.   [2] p. 559.

attempt to correct, and if he is forced to do this the symptoms of asthenopia may continue or even be exaggerated.

The correction of the *larger astigmatic errors*, however, necessarily produces appreciable difficulties. Any asymmetry between the correction of the two eyes leads to an artificial heterophoria on looking in any direction other than through the optical centres of the two lenses. This considerable upset of binocular vision is further aggravated even in symmetrical corrections by inclinations and distortions in the retinal image and this in turn, as was first pointed out by Culbertson (1888) and Lippincott (1889), brings about errors in spatial localization. The correction of any ametropia of refractive (as opposed to axial) origin by a lens brings about a change in the size of the dioptric image on the retina which is magnified (or diminished) by an amount roughly proportional to the product of the ametropic error and the separation of the elements of the optical system (*i.e.*, the cornea and the spectacle lens). If the error is cylindrical a distortion is produced—an elongation of the image in the meridian of greatest power associated with rotatory displacements of the images of all lines in space not parallel with or perpendicular to the axis of the lens (Figs. 321–4). Two distortions are thus introduced—a meridional aniseikonic error and a declination error. This matter will be more fully discussed at a later stage,[1] but it is obvious that the greatest discomfort will arise from the correction of astigmatism with oblique axes which must introduce differences in the disparities of the images of the two eyes. In such cases uniocular vision may be tolerable and binocular vision intolerable. In some cases these declinations and size-differences may be partially compensated by cyclotorsions of the eyes, aniseikonic compensations in fusion and a compensating psychological mechanism ; in others the visual sensations are profoundly distressing.[2]

Such distortions may be minimized in several ways. They are mitigated by approximating the spectacle lens as closely as possible to the eye, and if the astigmatism is corneal they may be eliminated by a contact lens which abolishes the effect of the corneal astigmatism. Culbertson (1888) tried to decrease the spatial distortion by rotating the cylinders out of their true axis towards the horizontal or vertical meridian. Burian and Ogle (1945) obtained considerable comfort in a number of patients by meridionally iseikonic lenses[3]; but in many cases the easiest compromise—which is by no means successful—is under-correction of the refractive error.

As would be expected, these disturbances are more acute in subjects with high errors who have never worn glasses, in which case the unaccustomed effect of cylinders of considerable power may be intolerable. Moreover, in cases in which the error is not large but has been long uncorrected, for example, in the astigmatic presbyope who gets spectacles for the first time,

[1] p. 513.
[2] Declinations may be associated with (1) cylindrical lenses at oblique axes, (2) cyclophoria and (3) " basal meridional aniseikonia."
[3] p. 682.

FIGS. 321 to 324.—THE DISTORTIONS PRODUCED WHEN A WHEEL-LIKE CIRCULAR
FIGURE IS VIEWED THROUGH A CYLINDRICAL LENS.

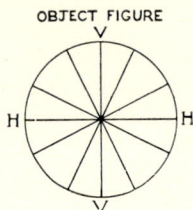

FIG. 321.

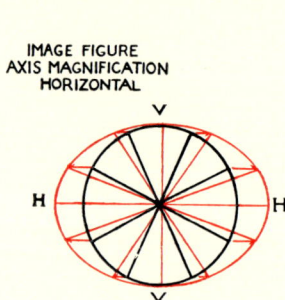

FIG. 322

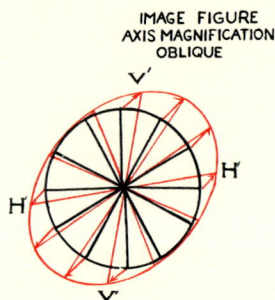

FIG. 323

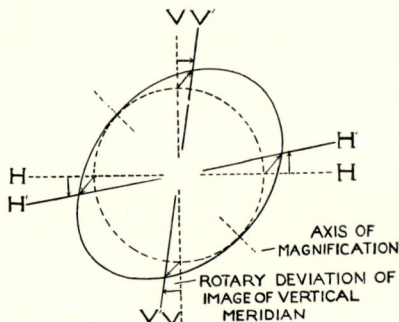

FIG. 324.

FIG. 321.—The object figure.

FIG. 322.—The rotatory deviation when Fig. 321 is observed through a cylindrical lens with the axis vertical.

FIG. 323.—The rotatory deviation produced when observed through a cylindrical lens with the axis oblique.

FIG. 324.—The vertical (VV′) and horizontal (HH′) declination by a meridional magnifier at an oblique axis (after H. M. Burian and K. Ogle).

the old, accustomed, uncorrected image may be preferable to a surprisingly sharp new picture. Since the purpose of the practice of refraction is to make patients comfortable and efficient rather than to strive after theoretical optical perfection, an under-correction of the cylinder may again be advisable.

In this endeavour, instead of eliminating the interval of Sturm and reducing the two focal lines to a point focus, the focal interval should be reduced so that the circle of least diffusion is reasonably small, and then the position of this circle should be moved so that it lies upon the retina. In order to do this, since the circle of least diffusion is approximately in the middle of the focal interval, half the deduction made from the cylindrical correction should be added algebraically to the spherical correction (Copeland, 1928; Prangen, 1941; Eggers, 1946).

Occasionally it may be expedient to omit the astigmatic correction entirely. When the cylindrical error of a compound lens system is totally uncorrected, the best optical correction will image the circle of least diffusion upon the retina. Such a correction is called the SPHERICAL EQUIVALENT of the system and is equal to *the algebraic sum of the spherical power of the lens system and half the power of the cylinder* (Copeland, 1928). A simple spherical correction in astigmatism is sometimes useful in cases of urgency, when supplies of lenses are scarce, or in the temporary correction of transitory astigmatic defects such as shortly after cataract extraction (Riddell, 1943); the partial correction of astigmatism is of much more widespread value.

Thus if the ideal correction is — 3·00 D sph. ⊃ — 5·00 D cyl. and it is decided to correct half the astigmatism, the prescription should read — 4·25 D sph. ⊃ — 2·50 D cyl. Similarly, + 6·00 D sph. ⊃ + 4·00 D cyl. becomes + 6·75 D sph. ⊃ + 2·50 D cyl. if a cylindrical reduction of 1·5 D cyl. is desired. If the astigmatism is to be neglected in a refraction of + 10·0 D sph. ⊃ + 2·0 D cyl., the prescription should be + 11·0 D sph.

The optical correction of astigmatism is usually made by sphero-cylindrical lenses; sometimes crossed cylindrical lenses are more appropriate, a matter which will be considered at a later stage.[1] Such lenses were advocated by Roure (1896) for the correction of bi-oblique astigmatism, and were preferred in all cases by Marquez (1909–42) who corrected the corneal astigmatism and the residual astigmatism separately by two cylinders ground on the anterior and posterior surfaces of the lens respectively. An alternative optical correction is by a contact lens which simply eliminates corneal astigmatism.

Re-examination of patients with significant degrees of astigmatism is advisable at intervals, perhaps yearly in children or more frequently if associated with an obviously changing spherical refractive error. In adult life " pure " astigmatism alters little until the later years, but re-assessment perhaps at two-yearly intervals will obviously be required in the presbyopic period. An important practical point relates to alterations in the axes of cylindrical corrections; extreme caution must be exercised in ordering a change of axis in a patient who has no ocular or visual complaints when a

[1] p. 674.

routine re-examination is being made. It is good practice to leave well alone even when the visual acuity can be significantly improved at a slightly different axis from that in the spectacles to which the patient has become accustomed; too often the ordering of a change in the axis to the "theoretically correct" position leads to a complaint of spatial disorientation such as has been already discussed, as well as to asthenopic symptoms. In many instances the patient has become mentally adjusted, perhaps over a long period, to the "incorrect" orientation of the cylinder in his old spectacles and it is often unwise to interfere unnecessarily with this situation by changing the axis. These arguments apply with less force to pathological refractive errors such as astigmatism developing in association with lenticular opacities. Here it is probably less hazardous to alter the axis and the power of corrections incorporating cylinders.

A more difficult situation arises when a patient has asthenopic symptoms which might be related to an incorrectly orientated cylindrical correction. If, on balance, it is decided to make the change to the axis found on subjective testing, it is always as well to warn the patient that symptoms of spatial distortion such as tilting of horizontal surfaces may be present for a short time after the new spectacles have been worn. We have noted that similar considerations apply to the introduction of a cylinder into a correction where none has been present before, particularly in presbyopes who have never worn spectacles. Some authorities, indeed, hold that the discovery in these cases of an astigmatic error, even if large, is best forgotten and spherical lenses alone should be ordered.

Apart from spectacles, however, the vision of astigmats can be improved by specific expedients. As in all refractive errors a stenopæic aperture is of great value[1] and in astigmatism a stenopæic slit serves equally well and allows the entry of more light (Gutzeit, 1924). Deformation of the globe by pressure on the eye may bring about a partial optical correction with visual improvement (Schiøtz, 1885), as also may screwing up the lids or pinching them together with the finger: Isakowitz (1912) improved the vision in a case of mixed astigmatism from 6/60 to 6/6 in this way.

Operative treatment has also been attempted. The usual occurrence of astigmatism after a cataract section suggested the therapeutic use of such a corneal section running perpendicular to the direction of the meridian of greatest refraction so that an opposite astigmatic tendency would be induced to neutralize that existing (Snellen, 1869; Schiøtz, 1885; A. Weber, 1899; Silex, 1906; Winselmann, 1909; Levinsohn, 1911; and others); alternatively, a partial section has been done, confined to the superficial layers of the cornea (Lans, 1898) or the same effect sought by the scar of a cautery (Wray, 1914; Clarke, 1914; O'Connor, 1933); Sato (1950–53) has used a posterior half-incision of the cornea. By such means 5 or 6 D of astigmatism may be neutralized, but the uncertainty of the results makes a premeditated procedure of this type more suitable for the treatment of marked irregular astigmatism due to progressive corneal disease than of a simple astigmatic error. Even in such cases the ready availability of contact lenses and the modern techniques of corneal grafting have largely obviated the need for this type of surgery. Alternatively, the technique of keratomileusis, to be noted later,[2] may be applied.

[1] p. 794.   [2] p. 853.

Awerbach. *Moscow ophthal. Soc., Wratsch,* **20.** See *Jber. Ophthal.,* **31,** 652 (1900).

Axt. *Statistische Zusammenstellung ü. d. Häufigkeit d. Astigmatismus,* (Diss.), Jena (1914).

Bárány. *Trans. ophthal. Soc. U.K.,* **86,** 539 (1966).

Beck. *J. opt. Soc. Amer.,* **55,** 1139 (1965).

Belehrádek. *Arch. int. Physiol.,* **20,** 52 (1922).

Benson. *Trans. ophthal. Soc. U.K.,* **2,** 55 (1882).

Berg. *Acta ophthal.* (Kbh.), **8,** 1 (1930); **10,** 212 (1932).

Birch-Hirschfeld. *Ber. dtsch. ophthal. Ges.,* **43,** 238 (1922).

Blum, Peters and Bettman. *Vision Screening for Elementary Schools,* Univ. Calif. (1959).

Bonavolontà and de Simone. *Ann. Ottal.,* **86,** 391 (1960).

Broekema. *Bijdrage tot de kennis der hypermetropie* (Diss.), Amsterdam (1909).

Brown. *Arch. Ophthal.,* **19,** 719 (1938).

Burian and Ogle. *Arch. Ophthal.,* **33,** 293 (1945).

Capalbi and Binchi. *Ann. Ottal.,* **81,** 1 (1955).

Cavara. *Boll. Oculist.,* **1,** 301 (1922).

Chance, Ogden and Stoddard. *Amer. J. Ophthal.,* **25,** 1471 (1942).

Clarke. *Trans. ophthal. Soc. U.K.,* **34,** 109 (1914).

Clausen. *Zbl. prakt. Augenheilk.,* **35,** 71, 72 (1911).

Cohn. *v. Graefes Arch. Ophthal.,* **17** (2), 305 (1871).
Die Hygiene d. Auges in den Schulen, Leipzig (1883).
Lhb. d. Hygiene d. Auges, Leipzig (1892).

Copeland. *Optom. Weekly,* **19,** 191 (1928).

Crawford, Shagass and Pashby. *Amer. J. Ophthal.,* **28,** 1220 (1945).

Crisp. *Amer. J. Ophthal.,* **13,** 906 (1930); **14,** 160 (1931).

Culbertson. *J. Amer. med. Ass.,* **11,** 622 (1888).
Amer. J. Ophthal., **5,** 117 (1888).

Czellitzer. *Berl. klin. Wschr.,* **47,** 557 (1910); **49,** 2070 (1912).
Klin. Mbl. Augenheilk., **79,** 301 (1927).

Daniel. *Zbl. prakt. Augenheilk.,* **7,** 193 (1883).

Dascalopoulos. *Ann. Oculist.* (Paris), **180,** 688 (1947).

Dobrowolsky. *Klin. Mbl. Augenheilk.,* **6,** Beil., 1 (1868); **7,** Beil., 141 (1869).

Dodd. *Trans. ophthal. Soc. U.K.,* **21,** 171 (1901).

ten Doesschate. *Klin. Mbl. Augenheilk.,* **61,** 411 (1918).

Donders. *v. Graefes Arch. Ophthal.,* **4** (1), 301 (1858).
On the Anomalies of Refraction and Accommodation of the Eye, London (1864).

Downing. *Arch. Ophthal.,* **33,** 137 (1945).

Duque Estrada. *Rev. bras. Oftal.,* **1,** 35 (1942).

Eggers. *Arch. Ophthal.,* **33,** 23 (1945); **35,** 346 (1946).

Eissen. *v. Graefes Arch. Ophthal.,* **34** (2), 1 (1888).

Erggelet. *Z. ophthal. Opt.,* **13,** 146 (1925).

Evens and Kuypers. *Bull. Soc. belge Ophtal.,* No. 147, 445 (1967).

Exford. *Amer. J. Optom.,* **42,** 685 (1965).

Fairmaid. *Brit. J. physiol. Opt.,* **16,** 2 (1959).

Farid Bey. *Z. Augenheilk.,* **42,** 55 (1919).

Fick. *v. Graefes Arch. Ophthal.,* **52,** 175 (1901).

Flom and Neumaier. *Amer. J. Optom.,* **43,** 732 (1966).

Forsius, Eriksson and Fellman. *Acta ophthal.* (Kbh.), **42,** 224 (1964).

Fuchs. *v. Graefes Arch. Ophthal.,* **28** (1), 139 (1882).
Klin. Mbl. Augenheilk., **62,** 433 (1919).

Gallati. *Z. Augenheilk.,* **51,** 133 (1923).

Gellzuhn. *Ueber ein Fall von höchstgradiger Uebersichtigkeit mit besonderer Berücksichtigung der Diagnostik* (Diss.), Berlin (1893).

Goldschmidt. *Acta ophthal.* (Kbh.) Suppl. 98 (1968).

Gonzales. *Arch. Oftal. hisp-amer.,* **2,** 56 (1943); **7,** 1169 (1947).

Gradle. *v. Graefes Arch. Ophthal.,* **43,** 252 (1897).

Gullstrand. *Skand. Arch. Physiol.,* **2,** 269 (1890).
Nord. ophthal. T., **4,** 142 (1892).
Einführung in d. Methoden d. Dioptrik d. Auges, Leipzig (1911).
Svenska Läk.-Sällsk. Handl., **48,** 103 (1922).
von Helmholtz's Treatise on Physiological Optics (ed. Southall), Opt. Soc. Amer., **1,** 380 (1924).

Gunn, Marcus. *Trans. ophthal. Soc. U.K.,* **15,** 136 (1895).

Gutzeit. *Dtsch. opt. Wschr.,* **10,** 102 (1924).

Halbertsma. *XIII int. Cong. Ophthal.,* Amsterdam, **1,** 272 (1929).

Harman. *Ophthal. Rev.,* **28,** 217 (1909).
Trans. ophthal. Soc. U.K., **33,** 202 (1913).
Proc. roy. Soc. Med., **8,** Sect. Ophthal., 3 (1914).

Hay. *Ophthalmoscope,* **12,** 20 (1914).

von Helmholtz. *Hb. d. physiologischen Optik,* Hamburg, **1** (1856).

Helveston. *Amer. J. Ophthal.,* **60,** 75 (1965).

Hensen and Völckers. *Experimental Untersuch. ü. d. Mechanismus d. Akkommodation,* Kiel (1868).
v. Graefes Arch. Ophthal., **19** (1), 156 (1873); **24** (1), 1 (1878).

Hess. *v. Graefes Arch. Ophthal.,* **42** (2), 80 (1896); **43,** 257 (1897).
Graefe-Saemisch. Hb. d. ges. Augenheilk. 2nd ed., Leipzig, **8** (2), 420 (1910).

Hirsch. *Arch. Ophthal.,* **34,** 418 (1945).
Amer. J. Optom., **36,** 395 (1959); **40,** 127 (1963); **41,** 137 (1964).

Hofmann and Carey. *Amer. J. Ophthal.,* **25,** 1495 (1942).

Hofstetter and Baldwin. *Amer. J. Optom.*, **34**, 388 (1957).

Holm. *Acta ophthal.* (Kbh.), **3**, 335 (1926).

Hughes. *Arch. Ophthal.*, **26**, 742 (1941).

Isakowitz. *Zbl. prakt. Augenheilk.*, **36**, 268 (1912).

Iwanoff. *v. Graefes Arch. Ophthal.*, **15** (3), 284 (1869).

Jablonski. *Klin. Mbl. Augenheilk.*, **68**, 560 (1922).
Arch. Augenheilk., **91**, 308 (1922).
Ophthalmologica, **98**, 56 (1939).

Jackson. *Trans. Amer. ophthal. Soc.*, **5**, 676 (1890).
Trans. Sect. Ophthal., *Amer. med. Ass.*, 113 (1891).
J. Amer. med. Ass., **98**, 132 (1932); **105**, 1412 (1935).

Jaensch. *Med. Klin.*, **35**, 69 (1939).

Jancke. *Klin. Mbl. Augenheilk.*, **106**, 264 (1941).

Jancke and Holste. *Klin. Mbl. Augenheilk.*, **107**, 373 (1941).

Keith. *Lancet*, **2**, 1047 (1925).

Krämer. *Arch. Augenheilk.*, **83**, 193 (1917).

Kronfeld and Devney. *Arch. Ophthal.*, **4**, 873 (1930).

Lancaster. *Trans. Amer. ophthal. Soc.*, **14**, 168 (1916).

Lang. *Brit. J. Ophthal.*, **4**, 126 (1920).

Lans. *v. Graefes Arch. Ophthal.*, **45**, 117 (1898).

Laqueur. *v. Graefes Arch. Ophthal.*, **30** (1), 99 (1884).

Leber. *Ber. dtsch. ophthal. Ges.*, **33**, 203 (1906).

Leibowicz. *Z. ophthal. Opt.*, **16**, 33 (1928).

Levene. *Brit. J. physiol. Opt.*, **19**, 123 (1962).

Levinsohn. *Münch. med. Wschr.*, **58**, 2613 (1911).

Linksz and Triller. *Amer. J. Ophthal.*, **27**, 992 (1944).

Lippincott. *Arch. Ophthal.*, **18**, 18 (1889).

Lo Cascio. *Ann. Ottal.*, **51**, 147 (1923).

Löpping and Weale. *Vision Res.*, **5**, 207 (1965).

Luedde. *Amer. J. Ophthal.*, **5**, 441 (1922).

Lühl. *Ueber d. Häufigkeit d. Astigmatismus u. seiner Beziehungen zur Sehschärfe* (Diss.), Marburg (1909).

Mackenzie. *Trans. ophthal. Soc. U.K.*, **4**, 152 (1884).

Mandell. *Contact Lens Practice*, Springfield (1965).

Marin Amat. *Bull. Soc. belge Ophtal.*, No. 113, 251 (1956).
Arch. Soc. oftal. hisp.-amer., **24**, 193 (1964).

Marquez. *XI int. Cong. Ophthal.*, Naples, 81 (1909).
Arch. Oftal. hisp.-amer., **12**, 474 (1912); **14**, 147 (1914); **21**, 573 (1921).
Klin. Mbl. Augenheilk., **51** (2), 756 (1913).
Clin. Ophtal., **20**, 221 (1914).
Amer. J. Ophthal., **25**, 1458 (1942).

Martin. *Ann. Oculist.* (Paris), **93**, 223 (1885); **96**, 5, 81, 217 (1886); **97**, 5, 141, 277 (1887); **103**, 5, 229; **104**, 101 (1890); **105**, 139 (1891).

van der Meer. *Onderzoek der oogen var de leeringen van het stedelijk gymnasium en van de middelbare scholen te Amsterdam gedurende 1898* (Diss.), Amsterdam (1901).

Mende. *Klin. Mbl. Augenheilk.*, **44**, Beil., 26 (1906).

Menestrina. *Boll. Oculist.*, **4**, 621 (1925); **5**, 106 (1926).
Arch. Ottal., **33**, 399 (1926).

Michel. *Klin. Mbl. Augenheilk.*, **31**, 223, 267 (1893).

Motolese and Berardi. *v. Graefes Arch. Ophthal.*, **136**, 27 (1936).

Mügge. *Klin. Mbl. Augenheilk.*, **46** (1), 474 (1908); **61**, 423 (1918).

Nettleship. *Trans. ophthal. Soc. U.K.*, **2**, 57 (1882).

Nottbeck. *v. Graefes Arch. Ophthal.*, **44**, 31 (1897).

O'Brien and Bannon. *Amer. J. Ophthal.*, **30**, 289 (1947).

O'Connor. *Amer. J. Ophthal.*, **16**, 337 (1933).

Ormond. *Brit. J. Ophthal.*, **5**, 117 (1921).

Pfalz. *v. Graefes Arch. Ophthal.*, **31** (1), 201 (1885).
Z. Augenheilk., **3**, 16 (1900).

Pflüger. *X int. med. Cong.*, Berlin, **4**, 10 (1890).

Pomeroy. *Trans. Amer. ophthal. Soc.*, **1**, 30 (1867).

Prado. *Arch. bras. Oftal.*, **6**, 100 (1943).

Prangen. *Amer. J. Ophthal.*, **24**, 413 (1941).

Raeder. *v. Graefes Arch. Ophthal.*, **110**, 73 (1922).

Riddell. *Brit. J. Ophthal.*, **27**, 302 (1943).

Risley and Thorrington. *J. Amer. med. Ass.*, **25**, 852 (1895).

Roure. *Arch. Ophtal.*, **16**, 241 (1896).
Ann. Oculist. (Paris), **115**, 99 (1896).

Safar. *Wien. klin. Wschr.*, **59**, 484 (1947).

Sallmann. *v. Graefes Arch. Ophthal.*, **124**, 605 (1930).

Sato. *Amer. J. Ophthal.*, **33**, 943 (1950); **36**, 462 (1953).

Schiøtz. *Arch. Augenheilk.*, **15**, 283 (1885).

Schoen. *v. Graefes Arch. Ophthal.*, **33** (1), 195 (1887).
Die Funktionskrankheiten des Auges, Wiesbaden (1893).

Schroeder. *Arch. Ophtal.*, **2**, 289 (1882).

Seabrook. *N.Y. med. J.*, **49**, 599 (1889).

Seefelder. *Klin. Mbl. Augenheilk.*, **45** (2), 486 (1907); **46** (2), 73 (1908).

Seggel. *v. Graefes Arch. Ophthal.*, **36** (2), 1 (1890).
Arch. Anthrop., **1**, 1 (1903).

Sergiewski. *Russ. oftal. J.*, **3**, 620 (1925).

Sheard. *Amer. J. physiol. Opt.*, **7**, 76 (1926).

Silex. *Z. Augenheilk.*, **16**, 516 (1906).

Smith, Priestley. *Trans. ophthal. Soc. U.K.*, **10**, 68 (1890).

Snellen. *v. Graefes Arch. Ophthal.*, **15** (2), 199 (1869).

Sørenson. *Acta ophthal.* (Kbh.), **22**, 341 (1944).

Sorsby. *Lond. Cty. Cncl. Ann. Rep.* (1933), **4** (3), 55 (1935).

Sorsby, Benjamin, Davey, *et al. Emmetropia and its Aberrations* (M.R.C. Spec. Rep. Series, No. 293), London (1957).

Sorsby and Shaw. *Brit. J. Ophthal.*, **16**, 222 (1932).

Spicer. *Trans. ophthal. Soc. U.K.*, **16**, 134 (1896).

Steiger. *Beitr. z. Physiol. u. Path. d. Hornhautrefraktion*, Wiesbaden (1895).

Arch. Augenheilk., **36**, 128 (1898); **44**, Erg., 15 (1902).

Die Entstehung d. sphärischen Refraktionen d. mensch. Auges, Berlin (1913).

Z. Augenheilk., **18**, 103, 223 (1907); **20**, 97 (1908); **43**, 144 (1920).

Stine. *Amer. J. Ophthal.*, **13**, 101 (1930).

Stirling. *Arch. Ophthal.*, **50**, 19 (1921).

Straub. *Ned. T. Geneesk.*, **35**, 570 (1899).

Sugar. *Arch. Ophthal.*, **31**, 34 (1944).

von Szily. *Ber. dtsch. ophthal. Ges.*, **39**, 265 (1913).

v. Graefes Arch. Ophthal., **110**, 183 (1922).

Theobald. *Trans. Amer. ophthal. Soc.*, **4**, 29 (1885).

Thomson. *Brit. J. Ophthal.*, **3**, 303 (1919).

Tirelli. *Rass. ital. Ottal.*, **16**, 85 (1947).

Tron. *Klin. Mbl. Augenheilk.*, **75**, 333, 623 (1925).

v. Graefes Arch. Ophthal., **132**, 182 (1934); **133**, 211 (1935).

Tscherning. *Optique physiologique*, Paris (1898).

Encycl. franç. Ophtal., Paris, **3**, 105 (1904).

Vereecken, Feron and Evens. *Bull. Soc. belge Ophtal.*, No. 143, 729 (1966).

Voipio, Tarkkanen and Koivusalo. *Duodecim* (Helsinki), **82**, 1207 (1966).

Waardenburg. *Klin. Mbl. Augenheilk.*, **84**, 593, 788, 795; **85**, 169 (1930).

Genetics and Ophthalmology, Oxon., **2**, 1201 (1963).

Weber, A. *IX int. Cong. Ophthal.*, Utrecht, 612 (1899).

Weber, E. *Klin. Mbl. Augenheilk.*, **107**, 47 (1941).

de Wecker and Jaeger. *Traité des maladies du fond de l'oeil*, Paris (1870).

Winselmann. *Z. Augenheilk.*, **22**, 426 (1909).

Wixson. *Amer. J. Optom.*, **36**, 586 (1959).

Wölfflin. *Z. mensch. Vererb. u. Konstit.-Lehre*, **29**, 243 (1949).

Wold. *Arch. Ophthal.*, **42**, 225 (1949).

Wray. *Trans. ophthal. Soc. U.K.*, **34**, 109 (1914).

Yamanaka. *Acta Soc. ophthal. jap.*, **65**, 1764 (1961); **67**, 475 (1963).

Zamora. *Arch. oftal. hisp.-amer.*, **24**, 491 (1924).

Zeeman. *v. Graefes Arch. Ophthal.*, **78**, 93 (1911).

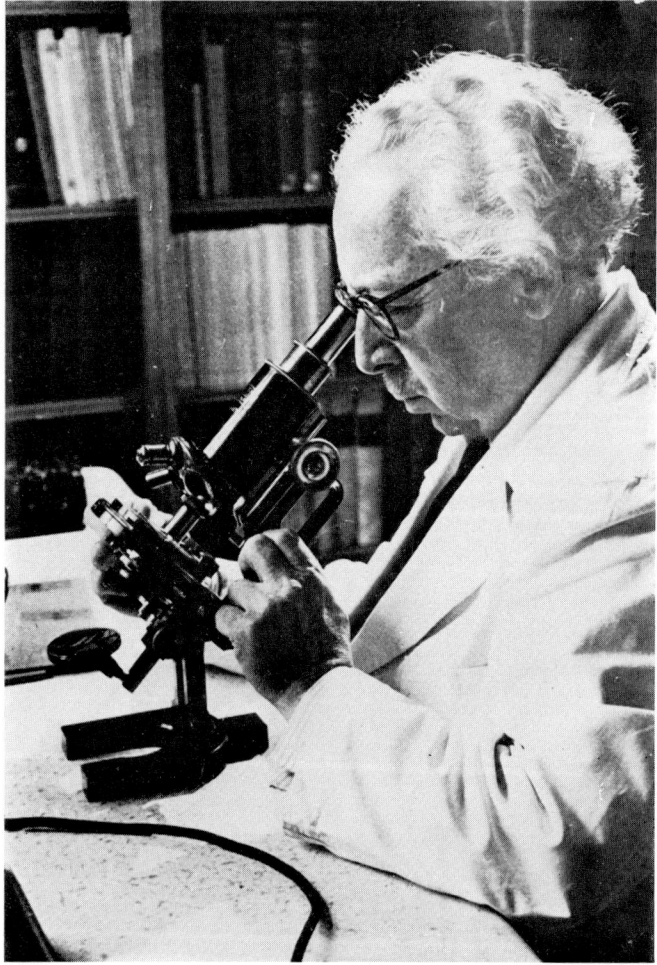

FIG. 325.—JACQUES MAWAS.
[1885 ——]

CHAPTER VII

PATHOLOGICAL REFRACTIVE ERRORS

JACQUES MAWAS [1885——] (Fig. 325) is one of the most colourful, endearing and delightful personages who has adorned ophthalmology. Born of a French family in Egypt, he started his medical apprenticeship in Alexandria and Beirut and then, migrating to France, studied in Montpellier, Lyons and eventually Paris. After serving in the first World War wherein he was gassed, he returned to Paris where he became chief medical officer of the Rothschild Foundation. He was also made Director of the Ophthalmological Laboratory of L'École Pratique des Hautes Études as successor to Emile Javal and Tscherning; this institute, transferred to the Rothschild Foundation, changed its traditional priority from ophthalmological optics to histology. This was Mawas's passion and he pursued it with unequalled enthusiasm and energy. Many of his 254 publications teemed with new ideas and were often illustrated by beautiful histological drawings done by his own hand. He studied a host of problems—embryology, the ciliary epithelium, the pigmentary epithelium, the innervation of the cornea, the development and structure of the vitreous, the histology of the retina and the anatomy and physiology of accommodation, while his histological work on intra-ocular tumours is classical. Because his outstanding contributions to the pathology of high myopia form the foundation of modern knowledge, his portrait introduces this Chapter. The affection and esteem in which he is held in our specialty was seen in the volume of contributions written by his friends and admirers in many countries of the world to commemorate his 80th birthday in 1966.

PATHOLOGICAL ERRORS OF REFRACTION may be defined as those refractive anomalies determined by the presence in the optical system of the eye of an element which lies outside the limits of the normal biological variations.

Pathological Hypermetropia

PATHOLOGICAL HYPERMETROPIA is relatively rare and is almost always caused by a deformation of the globe, usually a shortening of the axis but sometimes a flattening of the cornea, due to anomalous development. The hereditary transmission of the refractive error thus usually depends on that of the causal lesion. Cases have occurred without signs of microphthalmos or other defects and in these, as in most cases of high hypermetropia, in contradistinction to families with low hypermetropia, the inheritance has been recessive.[1] Some pedigrees, however, suggest an irregular dominance (Lambert and McDannald, 1931).

[1] Scherenberg (1900), Osterroht (1904), Schneideman (1906), Leber (1906), Clausen (1911), Vogelsang (1937), Knighton (1942), Biró (1951), Franceschetti and Klein (1956), Falls (1956), and others.

DEFORMATIONAL AXIAL HYPERMETROPIA

DEFORMATIONAL AXIAL HYPERMETROPIA is due to an abnormal shortening of the antero-posterior axis of the eye: each millimetre of shortening represents approximately 3 dioptres of refractive change. As a rule the condition is *developmental* and is typically seen in microphthalmos wherein very high refractive errors may occur. Even without gross deformity hypermetropia is the rule in these cases, sometimes of high degree (20 D, Osterroht, 1904; 18 D, Harman, 1909; 21 D, Zuccoli, 1951; and others), and a sagittal axis of 16·5 mm. has been noted (Dalén, 1904). It is to be remembered, however, that although they are small, microphthalmic eyes may be symmetrical so that emmetropia or even myopia may exist.[1] As a rule this is a curvature myopia due to changes in the cornea and lens, for in such cases the curvature, particularly of the cornea, tends to be increased (Friede, 1921–22); as a rarity, however, it may be axial, in which case there may be progressive and typical myopic changes in the fundus (Usher, 1921). Not uncommonly vision is subnormal, a disability probably associated with maldevelopment of the macula. Most eyes of this type which have been examined have been excised for absolute glaucoma and interpretation of the fine retinal structure has been difficult, but a thickening of the retina in the central area (Rahnenführer, 1917) and a hypoplasia of the fovea (Seefelder, 1930) or its absence (Grimminger, 1925) have been described.

Shortening of the antero-posterior axis of the globe may occur as a consequence of *disease*. An orbital tumour or inflammatory mass within the muscle-cone may indent the posterior pole of the eye or flatten it (Candian, 1922; S. S. and A. Brav, 1942; Jones, 1942), or an intra-ocular neoplasm or deposition of exudate may displace the retina forwards in the macular region; a progressive hypermetropia may be the first indication of the presence of such a lesion. Œdema at the optic nerve-head whether due to intracranial pressure or tumours of the optic nerve acts in the same manner, sometimes producing several dioptres of hypermetropia; a more pronounced condition may be caused by a detached retina which may be displaced almost to touch the posterior surface of the lens. These, of course, form pathological instances wherein the refractive error occupies the background of the clinical picture.

A *traumatic* hypermetropia may occur after a contusion in place of the more usual traumatic myopia. Grimsdale (1912) reported a case (+ 4 D) due to a rupture of the choroid and a raising of the retina with organized material; but other cases are not so easily explicable wherein a hypermetropia of 2 to 3 D occurs with undisturbed accommodation and apparently in the absence of any pathological change in the eye (Huber, 1929–32). A tendency to axial hypermetropia may be observed after an operation for

---

[1] −12 D, Brailey (1890), − 20 D, Pyle (1908), Rupprecht (1913), Frenzel (1920), Usher (1921), Pi (1929), Hermann (1958).

reposition of a detached retina by the extensive use of diathermy or a large scleral resection.

DEFORMATIONAL CURVATURE HYPERMETROPIA

Deformational curvature hypermetropia is rare and is usually due to an abnormally small curvature of the cornea: it is to be remembered that an increase of 1 mm. in its radius of curvature produces a hypermetropia of 6 dioptres. A *developmental* flattening is seen in cornea plana in which the refractive power of the cornea may be as low as 28·9 D (Friede, 1921). The total hypermetropia may not be very great (2 to 3 D); in other cases it may be high, in which case it is usually associated with a considerable degree of astigmatism (+ 7·0 D sph. ⊃ + 8·0 D cyl., Barkan and Borley, 1936).

An *acquired* flattening of the cornea may result from injury or disease usually associated with the contraction of wounds or central ulcers, but irregular astigmatic changes are more common (Mauthner, 1872; Axenfeld, 1893, a central hypermetropia of 5 D and a peripheral myopia of 7 D). Bayer (1913) noted a large hypermetropic change as a sequel to an interstitial corneal abscess. Percival (1911) observed its development in glaucoma, attributing it to a flattening of the corneal curvature with the increased intra-ocular pressure.

The other causes of pathological hypermetropia are incidental—the lenticular deformation resulting from internal ophthalmoplegia, the deep anterior chamber in iridocyclitis or subluxation of the lens, or a relative increase in the refractive index of the cortex of the lens so that the effective refractivity of this tissue is decreased, a change which may occur in cortical cataract.

The sudden development of hypermetropia will be subsequently discussed.

Axenfeld. *Klin. Mbl. Augenheilk.*, **31**, 33 (1893).

Barkan and Borley. *Amer. J. Ophthal.*, **19**, 307 (1936).

Bayer. *Ber. dtsch. ophthal. Ges.*, **39**, 374 (1913).

Biró. *Klin. Mbl. Augenheilk.*, **119**, 585 (1951).

Brailey. *Trans. ophthal. Soc. U.K.*, **10**, 139 (1890).

Brav. S. S. and A. *Amer. J. Ophthal.*, **25**, 82 (1942).

Candian. *Klin. Mbl. Augenheilk.*, **68**, 195 (1922).

Clausen. *Z. Augenheilk.*, **25**, 113 (1911).

Dalén. *Mitt. Augenklin. Carol. Inst.*, Stockholm, **5**, 53 (1904).

Falls. *Trans. Amer. Acad. Ophthal.*, **60**, 576 (1956).

Franceschetti. and Klein. *Encycl. méd.-chir Ophtal.*, Paris, **2** (1956).

Frenzel. *Ueber reinen Mikrophthalmus u. hochgradige Hypermetropie* (Diss.), Leipzig (1920).

Friede. *Klin. Mbl. Augenheilk.*, **67**, 192 (1921); **69**, 561 (1922).

Grimminger. *Z. Augenheilk.*, **55**, 144 (1925).

Grimsdale. *Trans. ophthal. Soc. U.K.*, **32**, 187 (1912).

Harman. *Ophthal. Rev.*, **28**, 217 (1909).

Hermann. *Arch. Ophtal.*, **18**, 17 (1958).

Huber. *Klin. Mbl. Augenheilk.*, **83**, 523 (1929); **88**, 230 (1932).

Jones. *Amer. J. Ophthal.*, **25**, 482 (1942).

Knighton. *Amer. J. Ophthal.*, **25**, 1376 (1942).

Lambert and McDannald. *Amer. J. Ophthal.*, **14**, 46 (1931).

Leber. *Ber. dtsch. ophthal. Ges.*, **33**, 203 (1906).

Mauthner. *Ber. naturw.-med. Ver. Innsbruck*, **2**, 184 (1872).

Osterroht. *Beitr. prakt. Augenheilk.*, **6** (60), 827 (1904).

Percival. *Ophthalmoscope*, **9**, 686 (1911).

Pi. *Nat. med. J. China*, **15**, 626 (1929).

Pyle. *Ophthal. Rec.*, **17**, 210 (1908).

Rahnenführer. *v. Graefes Arch. Ophthal.*, **92**, 76 (1917).

Rupprecht. *Münch. med. Wschr.*, **60**, 895 (1913).

Scherenberg. *Beitr. z. Lehre vom reinen Mikrophthalmus* (Diss.), Tübingen (1900).

Schneideman. *Ophthal. Rec.*, **15,** 468 (1906).

Seefelder. *Kurzes Hb. d. Ophthal.*, Berlin, **1,** 550 (1930).

Usher. *Brit. J. Ophthal.*, **5,** 289 (1921).

Vogelsang. *Klin. Mbl. Augenheilk.*, **99,** 539 (1937).

Zuccoli. *Atti Soc. oftal. Lombarda*, **6,** 20 (1951).

Pathological Myopia

DEGENERATIVE MYOPIA

To find a suitable name to indicate the class of case described in this section is somewhat difficult. The condition is frequently termed *progressive myopia*; but, as the habit of hypermetropia is to regress during development, so the majority of myopes —most of them of the simple type—progress. *High myopia* (for example, above 6 D) is also inappropriate, for myopes should be classified not by retinoscopy but by ophthalmoscopy; low myopes, and indeed, eyes with an axial length less than normal, may show the degenerative changes characteristic of myopia, while cases over − 17 D may show no abnormal changes in the fundus (Harman, 1913). *Malignant*, as opposed to *benign* myopia has too grave a connotation unless it is reserved for the worst cases— when, indeed, it is applicable. To complicate terminology, particularly in a well-known condition, is an almost unpardonable sin; but the term used here has the merit of describing what is meant.

DEGENERATIVE MYOPIA is that type of myopia which is accompanied by degenerative changes occurring particularly in the posterior segment of the globe; it is usually but not invariably associated with lengthening of the antero-posterior axis of the eyeball and is usually, but by no means always, progressive. It is probable that to some extent at any rate the two—the myopia and the degenerative changes—are independent but they are usually closely related. From the medical point of view degenerative myopia is the most important of all refractive errors for it is relatively common, leading frequently to much visual disability and not infrequently to eventual blindness; its economic and sociological implications are therefore considerable. Indeed, in England it is the commonest cause of " legal " blindness between the ages of 40 and 60 years (Sorsby, 1956), and in Canada accounts for 9% of these cases (MacDonald, 1965).

Incidence

The incidence of degenerative myopia is difficult to assess from the literature since the available statistics mainly deal with all types of short-sight. We have already seen that the incidence of simple variational myopia is high, since it occurs as a normal chance variant in the biological series which includes emmetropia and hypermetropia.[1] In comparison, high and degenerative myopia are relatively rare. It has been estimated that a myopia of over —6 D represents from 27 to 32% of the myopic population (Guttmann 1902; Blegvad, 1927) and of over — 8 D, 6 to 18% (Hertel, 1903; Betsch, 1929).

[1] p. 241.

Sex appears to have an influence on the incidence, for although in the lower degrees of myopia the sexes seem about equally affected, with a probable excess of males, females are more prone to the higher degrees and to degenerative changes. A considerable literature from many countries of the world bears this out.[1] To those who believe that myopia is caused by close work and study, particularly in youth, this inequality in the sexes follows from the healthy truancy of the young male.

Race, we have already seen, exercises a considerable influence over myopia[2]; high degrees with degenerative changes are very common in certain races such as the Chinese, Japanese, Arabs and Jews, more common in Central and Eastern than in Northern Europe, Britain and America, and are uncommon among Negroes, Nubians and Sudanese.[3] The variation is probably due more to heredity than habit.

Inheritance, as we have already noted, has a considerable influence in determining the lower degrees of myopia which are usually transmitted as a dominant trait; in the higher degrees which commence at a relatively early age inheritance is similarly important with the greater stress upon recessive transmission, but in this case care must be exercised to distinguish those cases wherein the refractive error exists in isolation from those in which high myopia is associated with other ophthalmic conditions which are themselves hereditarily determined, such as albinism or microphthalmos. In those subjects in whom a high myopia is not thus complicated, there appears to be various forms of the condition. Waardenburg (1963), for example, distinguished a benign infantile type, on the whole unprogressive and probably, although not certainly, different from congenital myopia. In most of these instances a recessive heredity is operative, but dominance has been recorded in a few families. In myopia which develops after the period of growth has passed, however, environmental factors probably exert some influence on its incidence (E. Goldschmidt, 1968).

In degenerative high myopia various forms of inheritance are encountered but the autosomally recessive mode has generally been found to be the most common, although the transmission is rarely completely characteristic[4]; consanguinity therefore leads to a high incidence (Bogatsch, 1911) and the children of two highly myopic parents tend to inherit their deformity (Fleischer, 1907–29; Jablonski, 1924; Clausen, 1938) (Fig. 326), although exceptions exist (Moutinho, 1931; Waardenburg, 1932). Harman (1937), analysing the family history of 547 high myopes, found a hereditary

---

[1] Horstmann (1880), Schleich (1882), Tscherning (1883), Proskauer (1891), Pflüger (1894), Widmark (1897), Guttmann (1902), Hertel (1903), Siebenlist (1911), Wilson (1913), Steiger (1913), Harman (1913), Blegvad (1918–27), Witte (1923), and many others.

[2] p. 236.   [3] p. 238.

[4] Stilling (1903), Fleischer (1907), Clausen (1921), Cholina (1925), Czellitzer (1927), Strebel (1941), Sabbadini (1951), and others.

element in 32·89%; among these, the father was myopic in 12·43%, the
mother in 17·36%, both parents in 3·1% and neither parent in 67·09%. This
is higher than the 25% incidence of expectation required of a recessive
characteristic. The recessive type of transmission appears particularly in
the axial myopia associated with ectodermal defects. This association with

FIGS. 326 to 329.—THE INHERITANCE OF HIGH MYOPIA.

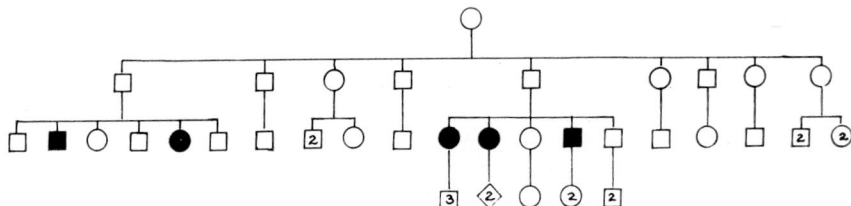

FIG. 326.—Recessive heredity (after J. François, 1959).

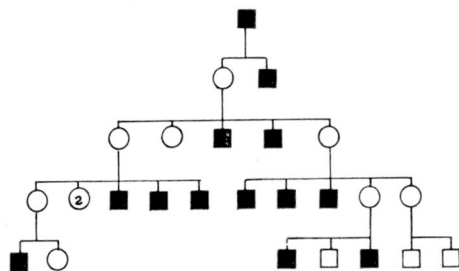

FIG. 327.—Sex-linked heredity (after C.
Worth, 1906).

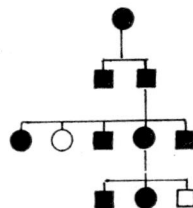

FIG. 328.—Dominant heredity, with nystagmus and poor vision (after A. Vogt, 1923).

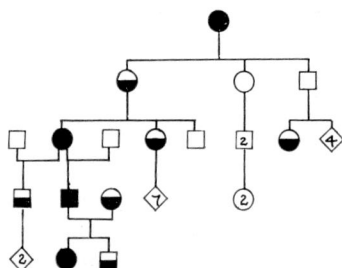

■ ● Myopia and detachment.

◨ ◒ Myopia only.

FIG. 329.—Myopia with retinal detachment (after P. Braendstrup, 1941).

retinal anomalies is typified in the occurrence of high myopia in the geneal-
ogies of such disorders as pigmentary retinal dystrophy (Usher, 1914; Bell,
1922; Raski, 1938) or the Laurence-Moon-Biedl syndrome (Cockayne et al.,
1935; Savin, 1935). A similar association occurs with such defects as night-
blindness; here again, although a dominant transmission is frequent in this
anomaly, in its association with high myopia it tends to exhibit a recessive
form (Nettleship, 1907; Vogt, 1923; Gassler, 1925, six generations); alterna-

tively a sex-linked form occurs, being transmitted through unaffected daughters of affected males to some of their sons[1] (Fig. 327). A sex-linked transmission of high myopia, not closely associated with night-blindness, was recorded by Worth (1906) and Wold (1949). An autosomally dominant inheritance, however, is far from uncommon[2] (Fig. 328); it is the most usual type of inheritance of high myopia associated with nystagmus and amblyopia (Vogt, 1924; MacGregor, 1946, Waardenburg, 1963) or with microphthalmos (Usher, 1921), and may be associated with a retinal detachment (Braendstrup, 1941) (Fig. 329).

Studies of myopic families over many generations often show a remarkable variation in the degree of myopia, however it may be inherited (Clausen, 1938; and others), a variation also found in the type and degree of the changes seen in the fundus associated with myopia. There is much to be said for the view of Vogt (1924), Meyer (1926) and Vontobel (1929) that axial length and myopia are phenomena genetically dissociated from, but frequently linked with, degenerative changes at the posterior pole of the eye which behave in a manner somewhat akin to senile or pre-senile degenerations about the disc or at the macula. It is obvious, however, that the whole of this difficult and complicated question must await much further work before it can be settled.

As occurs in other refractive states, monozygous as distinct from dizygous twins usually show a marked degree of concordance. The resemblance of the refraction in monozygous and its disparity in dizygous twins have been studied by Waardenburg (1930), who observed 31 pairs of monozygous twins and reviewed 137 monozygous and 55 dizygous pairs from the literature. His findings have been confirmed by others.[3] Discordance may occasionally be found between monozygous twins; indeed, one may be emmetropic and the other myopic (Orth, 1954). The differences, however, between dizygous twins may be much more marked, even exceeding 20 dioptres (Glatzel, 1931; Krüger, 1937; Lisch, 1941; Weekers et al., 1955).

The identity of the refractive errors, however, in monozygous twins may be very striking: Hofmann and Carey (1942) reported the refraction in such an instance at the age of 3 years (congenital myopia)—

(a) R.E. − 10·00 D sph. ⌒ − 1·00 D cyl. ax. 80°; L.E. − 11·00 D sph. ⌒ − 1·25 D cyl. ax. 90°.

(b) R.E. − 10·00 D sph. ⌣ − 1·25 D cyl. ax. 90°; L.E. − 10·5 D sph. ⌒ − 1·25 D cyl. ax. 90°.

In *degree* myopia may frequently attain an extent of − 20 D, and cases

[1] Donders (1855), Worth (1906), Oswald (1911), Nettleship (1912), Newman (1913), Kleiner (1923) six generations, Varelmann (1925), and others.
[2] Jablonski (1922), Paul (1938), Franceschetti (1953), Vogel and Balthaser (1956), François (1958).
[3] Jablonski (1926), Beckershaus (1926), Schmidt (1928), Jancke (1941), Weber (1941), Hofmann and Carey (1942), Burns (1949), Weekers et al. (1955), Vogel and Balthaser (1956), and others.

up to $-$ 30 D are not very unusual. The highest record we have found in the literature is R.E. $-$ 60 D, L.E. $-$ 24 D; apart from small myopic crescents both fundi were normal and vision with full correction was 3/60, 6/60 (Oliver, 1921, in a British soldier who served abroad in the First World War!). Cases of $-$ 40 D have been recorded by Harman (1914), Rehsteiner (1928), Erggelet (1932) and others; and many in the region of $-$ 35 D (Schweizer, 1890; and others). High degrees of astigmatism are not uncommonly associated with high myopia[1]—an association which has inspired the far-fetched theory that, owing to its irritating and " weakening " effect upon the retina, the astigmatism has caused the short-sight.

Binocular Inequality of Myopia. An unequal degree of high myopia in the two eyes is so common as to be almost the rule, but gross inequalities (greater than 3 D) are relatively rare (asymmetrical myopia, Frenkel, 1928). The most dramatic form of asymmetry is in the occurrence of *unilateral high myopia*, which is relatively rare.[2] An analysis of the figures from the literature tends to show a predominance for the higher degrees of myopia or for the unilateral myopia to be in the right eye. As in many other cases of marked anisometropia, in unilateral myopia the affected eye is often amblyopic and eccentric fixation is common; only a small percentage can be expected to attain useful binocular vision even with the aid of contact lenses and prolonged pleoptic treatment lasting for periods even up to three years (4 out of 16 cases, Bangerter, 1960; 3 out of 21, Priestley *et al.*, 1963).

The Types and Evolution of Degenerative Myopia

Degenerative myopia may take several forms. It occurs most commonly as an isolated developmental condition, but it may appear in association with other ocular disease or with general disease, and it may also present as a congenital anomaly.

CONGENITAL AXIAL MYOPIA

Congenital myopia of an axial type, first described by von Jaeger (1855), is not very uncommon. It is to be remembered, however, that cases do not usually come under observation until the second or third year of life. Mawas (1934), in France, found 32 congenital cases in 1,000 consecutive myopes; Feitelberg (1935), in Switzerland, 13 out of 200; Brown (1942), in America, found that 18 out of 97 eyes examined before the age of two showed a considerable degree of myopia; Cook and Glasscock (1951), also in America, obtained a figure of 25% in 1,000 neonatal subjects; Hosaka (1963) in Japan 5%; Mehra and his colleagues (1965) in India 9%; while Hiatt and his colleagues (1965) reported 120 cases. A hereditary influence is some-

---

[1] Steiger (1908), Harman (1913), Beckers (1920), Federici (1924), Oppenheimer (1924), Czellitzer (1927).

[2] Arlt (1876), von Reuss (1881), Seggel (1884), Martin (1894), Frenkel (1928), Venco (1935), Dellaporta (1948), Cambiaggi (1960), Proto (1964).

times marked (Brückner and Franceschetti, 1932); the condition may be hereditarily unilateral and an almost identical myopic refraction may be observed in monozygous twins (Hofmann and Carey, 1942, —10 sph. D with astigmatism at the age of 3). In a number of these congenital cases the myopia remains stationary, but in others it progresses and may result at an early stage in a double detachment of the retina. In some the vision is good; in others it is subnormal.

It is certain that all cases of congenital myopia do not form a homogeneous group. Some cases of high myopia occurring at this stage are almost certainly *extreme variants in the biological series* of distribution of refractive errors; and it is probable that among those are included cases of congenital myopia with relatively healthy fundi which do not necessarily progress (McCoy, 1927, — 15 D with astigmatism). Other cases must be classified as *congenital deformities*, particularly those which show a posterior staphyloma with signs of choroido-retinal atrophy (von Jaeger, 1855, — 19 D, R. and L., aged 2; Bartels, 1931, — 23 D, aged 3; Elwyn and Knighton, 1943, — 22 D, R. and L., aged 8 months). The association of such scleral ectasias with myopia as usually clinically recognized depends, of course, only upon their occurrence in the macular region.

The case illustrated in Plate I, Fig. 1 is an interesting example of such a localized staphyloma in an eye technically almost emmetropic: the macular refraction was — 2·0 D cyl. and the staphyloma below focused at — 10 D sph. It will be noted that the ectasia occurs in the portion of the sclera which is weakest ontogenetically, corresponding to the site of the fœtal fissure. Ectasias associated with colobomata are not uncommon and have already been described elsewhere.[1]

The axial anomaly may be associated with other congenital defects such as colobomata (Bartels, 1931); again, the myopia in cases of this type does not necessarily progress. Apart from its association with appearances of the fundus indicating some distortion of the globe, a congenital high myopia is also found in subjects with anomalies of pigmentation of the retina or choroid.

The most common appearance closely resembles partial albinism (Plate II, Fig. 1); although pigmentation of the remainder of the eye and body is normal, the pigmentary epithelium is defective so that the choroid underneath is visible, and in early life this tissue usually appears healthy and normal even although the myopia is high (— 20; — 22 D, Mawas, 1934). Such cases, however, usually progress and extensive choroidal atrophy and the formation of a posterior staphyloma are to be anticipated. Albinism itself, either ocular or generalized, is also often accompanied by high myopia (see Waardenburg, 1963).

Another type, of which Brückner and Franceschetti (1932) described a series of 25 with a myopia varying from — 3 to — 25 D, is characterized by a proliferation of the pigmentary epithelium taking the form of a mott-

[1] Vol. III, p. 541.

ling of the fundus particularly in the central area. The vessels are narrow, the disc small and nystagmus may be present, a hereditary tendency may be seen, and the myopia may remain stationary or may progress (Plate II, Fig. 2).

Mawas (1934) also described high myopia associated with widespread atrophy of the choroid and the optic nerve as well as with generalized anomalies in the growth of the body. This type of myopia commonly varies between − 7 and − 23 D and the condition may be progressive. Mawas considered it a disease of the fundus of the eye, of which the myopia was a symptom, forming part of a syndrome which included polyglandular deficiency, particularly of the pituitary and gonads.

While it is not certain that it is of axial origin, we must consider here the *myopia of prematurity*. This condition is almost certainly related to retrolental fibroplasia and possibly therefore to the administration of an overdose of oxygen to a premature infant.[1] Reese and Stepanik (1954) in their description of the degrees of development of this condition commented on the presence of myopia, an observation subsequently confirmed (Krause, 1955), but it has also been found that prematurity itself without anomalies in vascular growth is associated with myopia (Birge, 1955; Lomícková, 1964; and others). Fletcher and Brandon (1955) noted a variable degree of myopia in premature infants which regressed or disappeared in a few months, a transient change which may account for the negative findings of Castrén (1955) in prematurely born children reviewed at an older age; this transient myopia was attributed by Rivara and Gemme (1966) to the higher dioptric power of the incompletely developed lens. On the other hand, if retrolental fibroplasia has developed, a higher degree of myopia is common which persists although it may slightly decrease. Indeed, it has been noted in many cases that myopia associated with prematurity is often accompanied by lesions suggesting abortive retrolental fibroplasia (Weekers *et al.*, 1961), while exposure to unequal concentrations of oxygen may explain the occurrence of high myopia in one of monozygous twins (Vidal, 1959; Weekers *et al.*, 1961).

CONGENITAL TOXOPLASMOSIS has also been associated with myopia in the newborn (François, 1963) as well as the TOXÆMIA OF PREGNANCY in the mother (Gardiner and James, 1960).

MYOPIA ASSOCIATED WITH OCULAR OR SYSTEMIC ANOMALIES

ASSOCIATED MYOPIA

Many congenital anomalies may be associated with myopia, sometimes of a high degree. These include microphthalmos,[2] microcornea,[3] micro-

---

[1] See Vol. X, p. 187.

[2] − 12 D, Brailey (1890); − 20 D, Pyle (1908), Rupprecht (1913), Frenzel (1920), Usher (1921), Pi (1929), Hermann (1958).

[3] Biró (1935), Puglisi-Duranti (1936), Hohr Castán (1945), Batra and Paul (1967).

phakia, buphthalmos, ectopia lentis, and other deformities (Delmarcelle and Mans, 1965). In mongolism one third of the cases are myopic. In this connection hereditary external ophthalmoplegia may also be noted (Salleras and Ortiz de Zarate, 1950). Congenital nystagmus by itself or associated with other congenital or developmental retinal anomalies such as albinism, often inherited as dominant traits, may also be accompanied by high myopia (Vogt, 1924) (Fig. 328).

The tapeto-retinal dystrophies, such as choroideremia, gyrate atrophy and pigmentary dystrophy (François and Verriest, 1961), as well as Wagner's hyaloideo-retinal dystrophy (Alexander and Shea, 1965), may be accompanied by a highly myopic refraction; although such conditions are associated with a myopia which is not strictly speaking congenital, it is difficult to distinguish between this type of *associated myopia* and the truly congenital variety. Similarly, the high degree of myopia seen in essential night-blindness, sometimes in its autosomal recessive form but more usually in its recessive sex-linked form of transmission,[1] is also not strictly congenital; the night-blindness itself is congenital and static but the myopia appears in infancy and usually ceases to progress in adolescence.

DEVELOPMENTAL DEGENERATIVE MYOPIA

Most cases of myopia are developmental in origin. We have already seen that in the ordinary case of simple myopia the usual hypermetropia present at birth gradually diminishes, and from the refractive point of view a myopic tendency makes its appearance from the fourth to the seventh year of life. Progress thereafter is usually steady, but puberty, which in the simple case usually exerts a restraining influence, may have the opposite effect, so that the myopia increases more rapidly during adolescence between the ages of 12 and 20. Thereafter the axial increment tends to be slow, although a further increase may occur during the involutionary period of the mid-forties; in adult life the stage is monopolized rather by degenerative changes, resulting too frequently in a steady deterioration of vision which in a number of cases culminates in the loss of central vision or even in complete blindness from the occurrence of complications about the sixth decade. When the individual depends upon good vision for his livelihood, it is evident that high myopia of this type presents a serious economic problem.

MYOPIA ACQUIRED WITH DISEASE

It has long been observed that myopia has a habit of appearing or increasing in periods of ill-health or after disease: the common belief that it starts in youth with measles or some such childish febrile disease is not without truth, and the same type of incident occurring in adolescence may transform what appeared to have been a simple myopia which showed signs

[1] Vol. III, p. 660.

of stabilizing into a progressive condition (Priestley Smith, 1901; Sonder, 1920; and others). In this connection it may be apposite that Maurice and Mushin (1966) produced — 1 D of myopia in young rabbits by raising the body-temperature and increasing the intra-ocular pressure. Malnutrition may give rise to a relative myopia in infants in comparison with controls, a condition, however, which may be transitory if the marasmic state can be reversed (Halasa and McLaren, 1964; Sood and Gupta, 1966). The same tendency to develop myopia with illness may be seen in the adult, although when the growing period has passed the degree of elongation of the globe is usually small and ceases with the restoration of health. It was not uncommon to see the development of 2 or 3 D of myopia in an adult of 30 years, usually a woman, after a prolonged debilitating illness such as pulmonary tuberculosis used to be, while such increases have also been reported in malarial cachexia (Becker, 1883) and goitre (Wirtz, 1911). A change of this type can occur in non-myopic eyes, but is usually greater in those already short-sighted.

The sudden and frequently transient appearance of myopia in toxic, diabetic or other diseased states will be discussed at a later stage.[1]

Pathology

The gross appearance of the highly myopic eye is characteristic both in size and shape (Figs. 290–1). Instead of being globular it is egg-shaped; it is enlarged, but the elongation of the eye which results in myopia is almost entirely confined to the posterior pole, and the anterior half of the globe is usually normal. Heine's (1899) classical illustration of the two eyes of the same individual superimposed, one emmetropic and the other myopic (— 15 D), reproduced in Fig. 330, shows that the anterior segments are practically identical.

It is to be noted that the shape is entirely different from that of the buphthalmic eye which exhibits the reaction of the infantile globe to tension (Figs. 331–3). In this case the globe is enlarged in all dimensions equally—not only in the antero-posterior axis—and the anterior segment is correspondingly deformed with its enormously stretched cornea and its deep anterior chamber.

Although Antonio Scarpa,[2] the anatomist of Pavia, published a pathological account of two eyes with posterior staphylomata in 1801, he did not appreciate that the patient had been myopic; the first to present a full description of the histological changes in myopia and to correlate them with the ophthalmoscopic appearances was Albrecht von Graefe (1854). He attributed the changes to a chronic inflammation—*posterior sclerochoroiditis*—and since his time, although he himself modified his views at a later date, this term has frequently continued to be used. The difficulty, however, of attributing all the changes evident in myopia to inflammatory

[1] p. 368.   [2] Vol. VIII, Fig. 959.

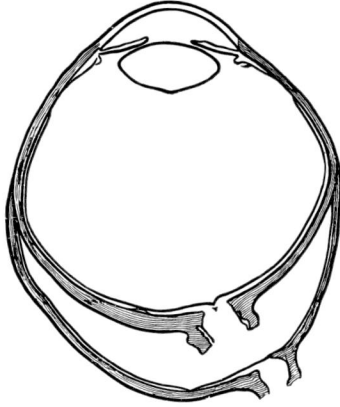

FIG. 330.—The two eyes of the same individual superimposed: the one emmetropic the other with —15 D of myopia (after L. Heine).

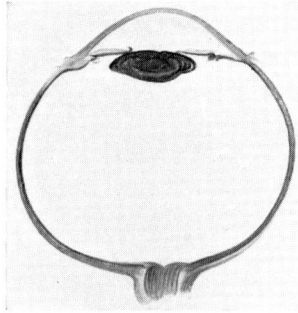

FIG. 331.

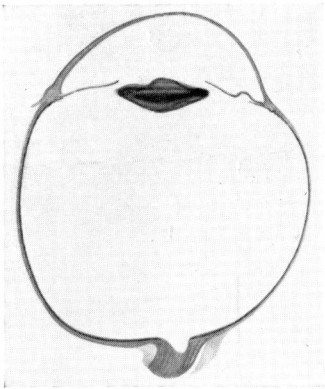

FIG. 332.

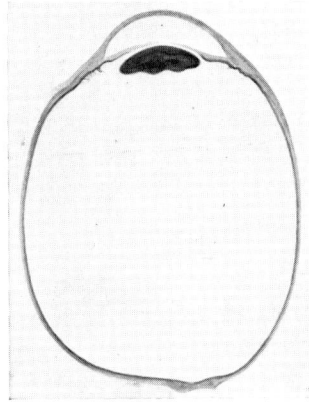

FIG. 333.

FIGS. 331 to 333.—A comparison between the shape of the typical emmetropic eye (Fig. 331), the buphthalmic eye (Fig. 332) and the highly myopic eye (Fig. 333) (modified from J. Mawas).

processes was soon pointed out by von Jaeger (1855) and Donders (1864); the latter suggested that a mechanical stretching of the coats of the globe caused capillary stasis and consequent secondary irritative and inflammatory changes which were eventually followed by atrophy. It is now establishd that *all the changes characteristic of myopia are those of degeneration, not of inflammation*. It is also of importance that *none of the changes is exclusively characteristic of myopia*, for all of them have been found in non-myopic eyes, particularly in senility.

The Sclera

That thinning of the sclera occurred in myopia, particularly in the posterior segment of the eye and very markedly so in staphylomata, is an old observation (Baas, 1893; Heine, 1900; Marschke, 1901; Stilling, 1904; and others) (Fig. 337). The thinning may occur on the nasal side of the optic disc (Plate VII, Fig 1), but ectasias are most common at the posterior pole, normally the thickest part of the sclera (Weiss, 1882; Mawas, 1934); the thinning may be localized (Hanssen, 1919–21), and occasionally dehiscences may be observed on the inner scleral surface into which the retinal tissues dip (Polatti, 1906; Plocher, 1919). Stocker (1943) found such a thinning in an early case of myopia, suggesting that it may be a precursor of stretching but, on the other hand, Stilling (1904) and E. Fuchs (1919) reported advanced cases of myopia in which the sclera was thicker than that of the average emmetropic eye.

The normal sclera gets progressively thicker from the equator backwards, becoming thickest at the posterior pole; the highly myopic eye gets progressively thinner posteriorly, particularly on the nasal aspect. Mawas (1934) found the following dimensions— normal (myopic): equator, temporal side 0·8 mm. (0·3 mm.), nasal 0·6 (0·35); posterior region, temporal (macular) 1·1 (0·2–0·3), nasal 0·7–0·9 (0·1) (Figs. 334–41).

In the fine structure of the sclera no great changes are involved. A flatter arrangement of the scleral fibres is characteristic, but the claim of Lange (1905) that elastic fibres are absent has been amply disproved (Birch-Hirschfeld, 1905; Hosch, 1905; Fuss, 1906; Krekeler, 1923; and others). Electron-microscopic studies of the sclera in high myopia, however, have shown a greater variability in the diameter of the scleral fibres than in the normal eye (Garzino, 1956). Thinning of the meridional bundles with separation and splaying of the cross bundles was found by Curtin and Teng (1958) who concluded that the changes were consistent with a slippage of the fibres. This variability of the size of the fibres was confirmed by Blach (1965), but he found that their general arrangement was normal even in staphylomatous areas where the thinning was confined to the inner lamellæ of the sclera (Figs. 342–5).

The cause of the thinning of the sclera has been disputed since von Graefe's (1854) original view that it was softened by an inflammatory choroido-retinitis. In the classical view the changes were due to mechanical

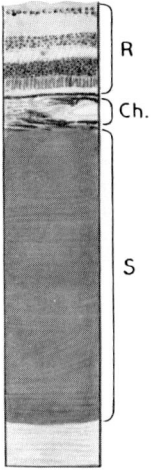

FIG. 334.

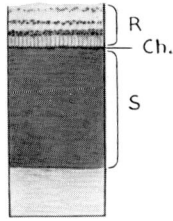

FIG. 335.

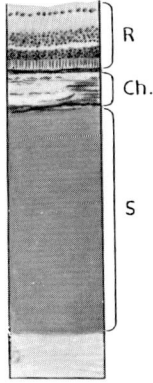

FIG. 338.

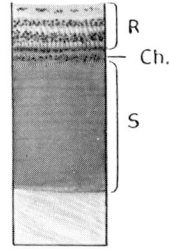

FIG. 339.

1 mm.

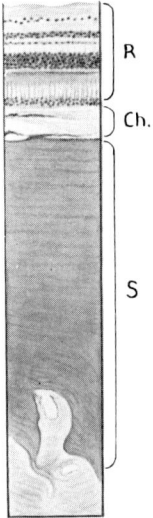

FIG. 336.

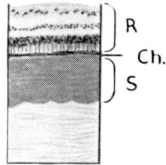

FIG. 337.

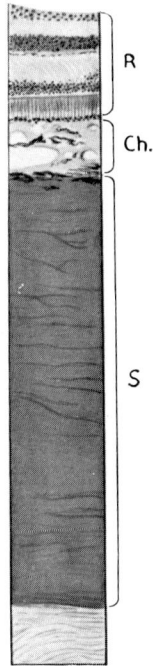

FIG. 340.

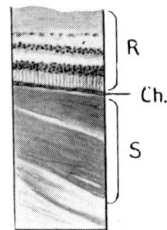

FIG. 341.

To compare the ocular coats in a normal and myopic eye. In both cases the eyes were subjected to the same sections and histological techniques. Scale × 50 : for comparison, see scale on the right. R, retina. Ch, choroid. S, sclera.

FIGS. 334–5.—Equatorial section, outer side, in a normal (Fig. 334) and myopic eye (Fig. 335).

FIGS. 336–7.—Equatorial section, inner side, in a normal (Fig. 336) and myopic eye (Fig. 337).

FIGS. 338–9.—Section through the macula in the normal (Fig. 338) and myopic eye (Fig. 339).

FIGS. 340–1.—Section through the inner part of the globe in the normal (Fig. 340) and myopic eye (Fig. 341).

Note in each case the thinning of the sclera and retina and the extreme atrophy or complete disappearance of the choroid (modified from J. Mawas).

FIGS. 342 and 343.—THE SCLERA IN HIGH MYOPIA (R. K. Blach).

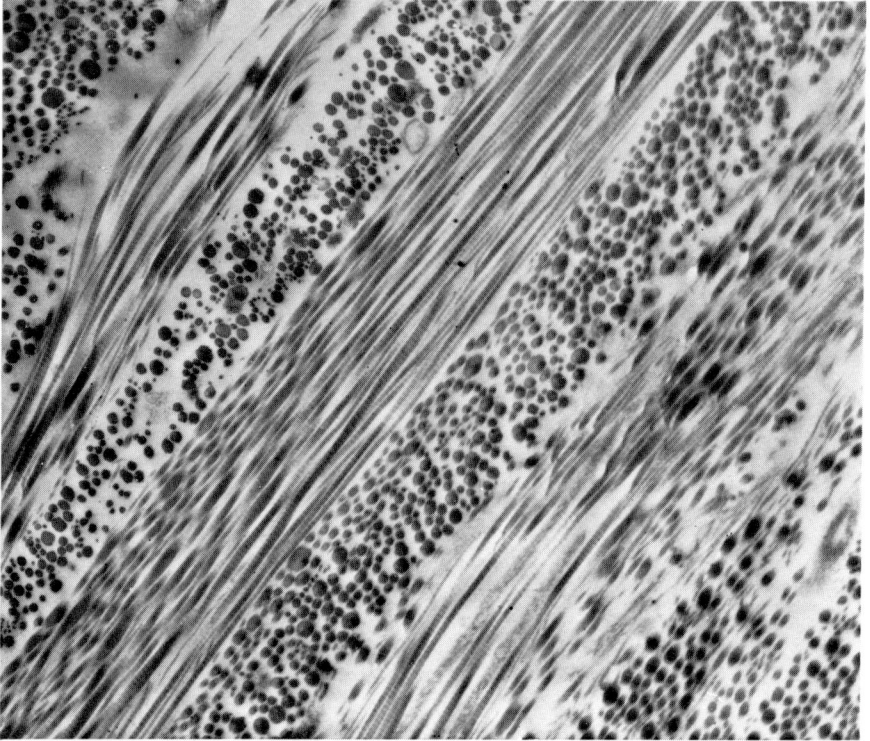

FIG. 342.—The general arrangement of the bundles of fibres in the posterior sclera.

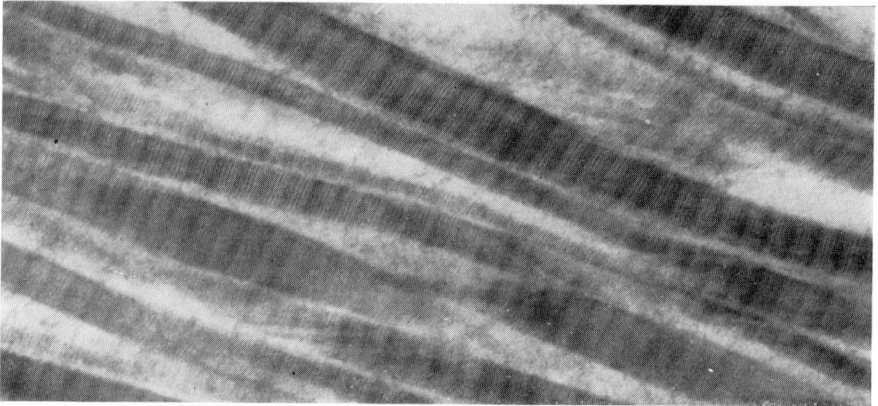

FIG. 343.—The collagen fibres are typical with an average periodicity of 460 Å.

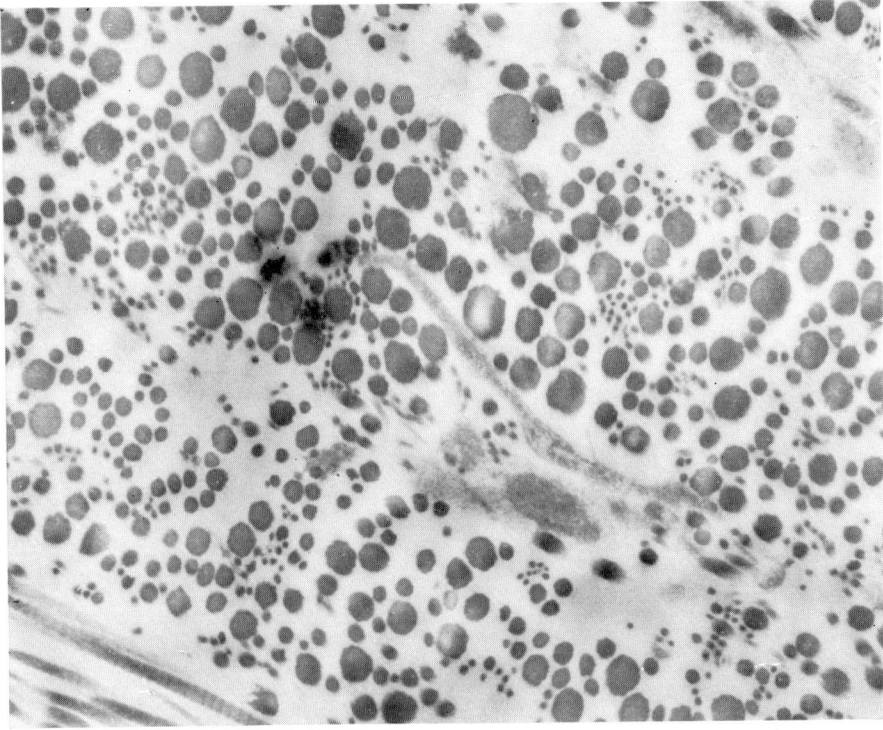

FIG. 344.—The variation in the cross-sectional diameter of the fibres in the posterior sclera (fixed in formalin; stained with phosphotungstic acid; × 26,000).

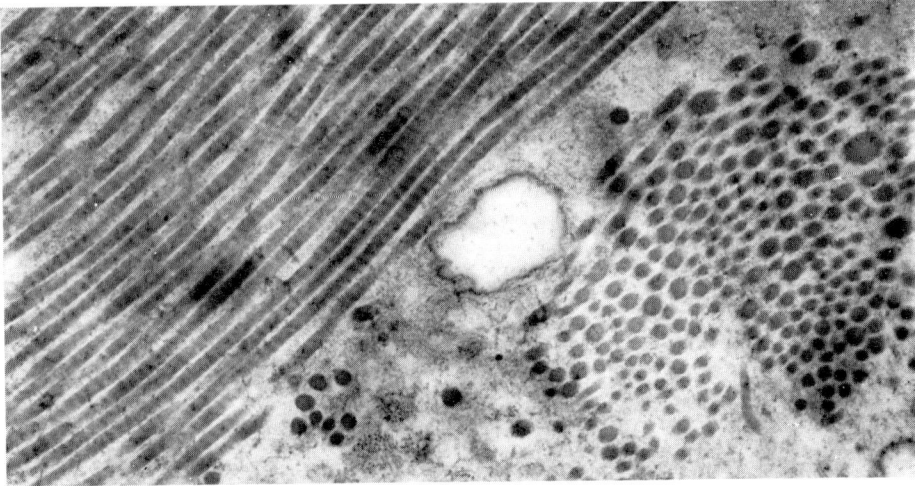

FIG. 345.—To show the elastic fibres (fixed in osmic acid; stained with phosphotungstic acid; × 32,000).

stretching (Donders, 1864); but the difference between the configuration of the sclera in myopia and buphthalmos and the preferential thinning at the posterior pole led Heine (1900) to postulate an atrophic element; this is now generally accepted. The cause of the atrophy is not clear and will be considered when the ætiological theories of myopia are discussed. That the preferential thinning in the posterior region is not mechanically determined seems certain, and it does not seem likely that the cause is intrinsic in the sclera itself: it would seem more probable that it is a phenomenon of growth imposed upon the sclera by other controlling influences.

The Choroid

The choroidal changes are essentially atrophic in nature (MYOPIC CHOROIDAL DEGENERATION) and in their consideration two facts must be kept in mind: first, in juvenile or commencing myopia the choroid is usually normal and shows no signs of atrophy (Stocker, 1943), and second, the atrophy does not usually occur until some considerable time after the elongation of the eye has ceased. The degeneration does not run *pari passu* with the degree of myopia, and the resemblance between the changes characteristic of myopic and senile degeneration is great (Vogt, 1924).

The chief change is a generalized thinning of the choroidal coat which may become very attenuated and may even disappear completely over large areas (Figs. 334–341). The first change is usually a disappearance of the lumina of the small vessels which may eventually appear as solid, sclerotic, white threads (Plate V, Fig. 2; Plate VI, Fig 1); the vessels which are patent may contain leucocytes which are not normally seen in histological sections. As the degeneration progresses the choriocapillaris fails completely and the larger vessels alone are left; finally these too become obliterated (Blach *et al.*, 1965) (Figs. 346–7). Coincidently with the vascular changes, the chromatophores lose their pigment and disintegrate, and last of all the elastic elements disappear.[1] Meantime splits appear in the elastic lamina, usually as clefts which may form branching or reticular figures resembling cracks in lacquer (Salzmann, 1902); through these tears connective tissue may proliferate from the choroid, fusing the choroid and retina together.

The Retina

Atrophic changes in the retina progress coincidentally with those in the choroid. Among the earliest evidences of atrophy are those involving the pigmentary epithelium which shows marked alterations in the posterior segment before atrophy of the rods and cones and chorioretinal fusion occur. The regular hexagonal pattern of the normal cells is replaced by an untidy layer with an irregular pattern of misshapen cells with much of the

[1] von Graefe (1854), Schweigger (1875), Heine (1899–1902), Krückmann (1905), Behse (1908), Gilbert (1920), and others.

FIGS. 346 and 347.—THE CHOROID AND PIGMENTARY EPITHELIUM IN A UNIOCULAR
MYOPE (R. K. Blach).

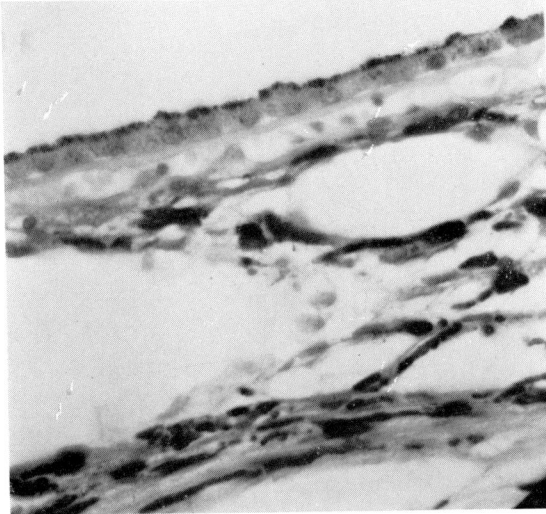

FIG. 346.—Section of the choroid and pigmentary epithelium in the normal eye
(Alcian blue; × 430).

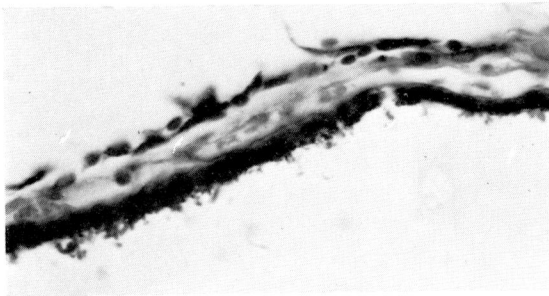

FIG. 347.—The choroid and pigmentary epithelium in the highly myopic eye
(× 430).

pigment lying extracellularly (Figs. 346–9). Sometimes, particularly in
association with the dehiscences in Bruch's membrane, the pigment proli-
ferates to form branched pigmented figures or large conglomerate masses.
It is a localized proliferation of this type which forms the circular Förster-
Fuchs black spot at the macula[1] (Lehmus, 1875) (Fig. 350). When the
elastic lamina is defective, fusion of the retina and choroid occurs, and this
with the consequent cicatrization and pigmentary proliferation produces a
picture identical with a late inflammatory lesion. Following the degeneration of the pigmentary epithelium and the choriocapillaris, the neuro-
epithelium also degenerates; the rods and cones and outer nuclear layer

[1] p. 328.

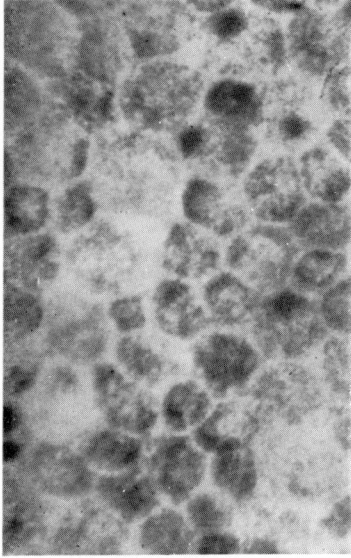 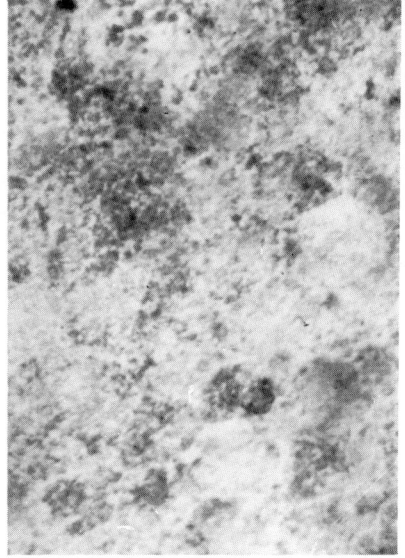

Fig. 348.   Fig. 349.

Figs. 348 and 349.—The Pigmentary Epithelium in the Normal (Fig. 348)
and in the Highly Myopic Eye (Fig. 349) (R. K. Blach *et al.*).

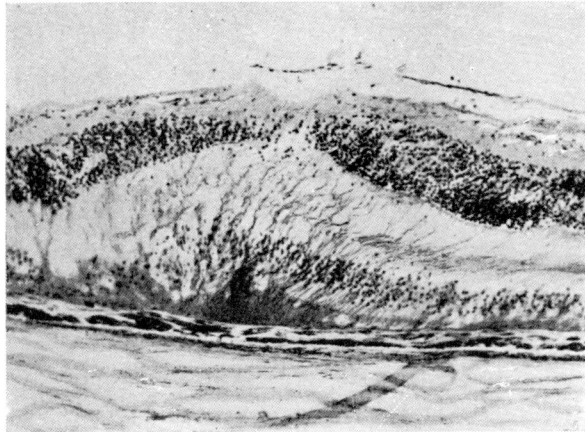

Fig. 350.—Macular Changes in Myopia (G. Coats).

gradually become attenuated, but the atrophy usually ceases at the inner
nuclear layer which has a retinal nutrient supply.   Only at the periphery
does retinal degeneration appear to run a separate course where the typical
picture of peripheral cystoid degeneration with the formation of Blessig's
cysts, so characteristic of a senile change, is frequent (Baas, 1893; Stock,
1908; Hanssen, 1925; Rehsteiner, 1928; and many others).[1]

[1] Vol. X, p. 549.

Changes at the Optic Disc

The striking changes at the optic disc have excited much attention and stimulated much controversy. The classical investigations of Heine (1899) showed that the myopic disc had a straight cribriform plate with a very thin layer of pre-cribriform glial tissue which Goldmann (1957) estimated at less than half the thickness of the non-myopic eye.

The optic disc is large in the myopic eye. It is interesting that the ratio of the optic cup to the optic disc has been found by Armaly (1967) to be genetically determined in a multifactorial pattern showing no influence of age or sex. Tomlinson and Phillips (1969) have found, however, that it does

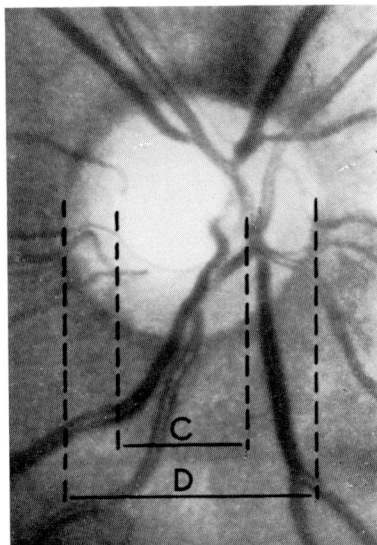

Fig. 351.—The Ratio of the Optic Cup, C, to the Optic Disc, D, in Myopia
(A. Tomlinson and C. I. Phillips).

vary with the axial length of the eye, the ratio tending to be high when this was long and the refraction myopic, but low in the short hypermetropic eye (Fig. 351). It would seem that the absolute area of the disc varies with the size of the eyeball but that the volume of nerve fibres congregated at the nerve-head is relatively constant.

The MYOPIC CRESCENT (CONUS MYOPICUS) has received elaborate and detailed histological descriptions from a number of observers.[1] The general configuration is seen in Figs. 352 and 353; the histology of an early crescent is illustrated in Fig. 354. The nerve fibres usually traverse the disc in an obliquely nasal direction (Fig. 353), and at the nerve-head many variations

[1] Schnabel (1874), Carl Theodore (1882), Weiss (1882–84), Schnabel and Herrnheiser (1895), Heine (1899–1900), Elschnig (1903–5), Siegrist (1906), Behse (1908), E. Fuchs (1919), Hanssen (1919–21), von Szily (1920–22), and many others.

FIGS. 352 TO 353.—THE CONFIGURATION OF THE DISC IN MYOPIA.

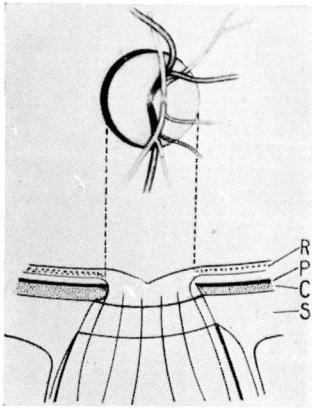

FIG. 352.

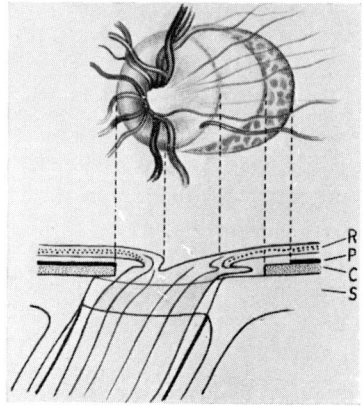

FIG. 353.

Fig. 352 shows the normal configuration; Fig. 353, the myopic. R, retina. P, pigmentary epithelium. C, choroid. S, sclera. On the temporal side the choroidal and scleral crescents are delineated. Note the temporal nerve-fibre loop, the oblique temporal direction of the optic nerve fibres and the overlapping on the nasal side resulting in supertraction.

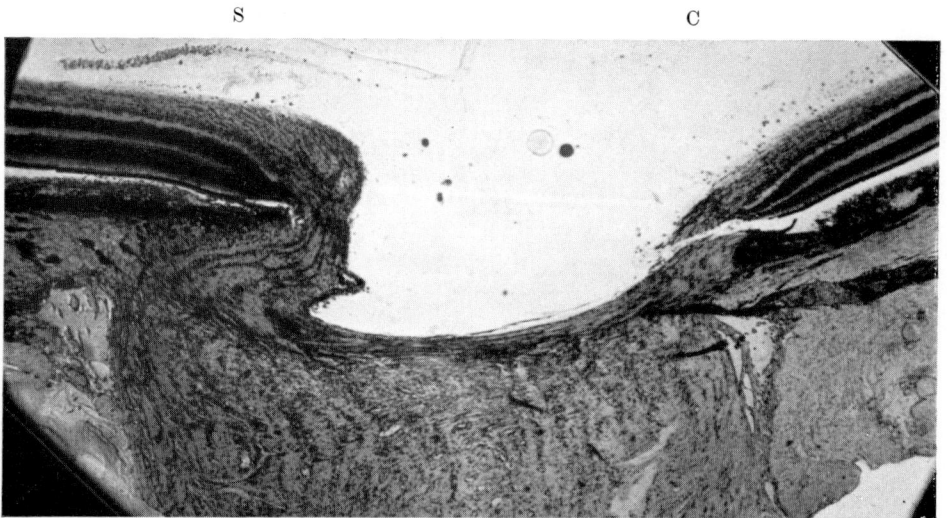

FIG. 354.—THE NERVE-HEAD IN MYOPIA.

Optic nerve-head of a 15-year-old myope. On the left, nasal supertraction (S), on the right, a crescent (C) (F. W. Stocker).

may be observed. The choroid usually terminates some distance from the margin of the disc and is completely or partially absent in the area of the crescent. Bruch's membrane may terminate with it; it may persist well towards the disc or, conversely, may end some distance from the edge of the choroid. The outer retinal layers and the pigmentary epithelium may be absent in the area of the crescent and only the inner layers continue. As they dip into the disc, where the retina overlaps the choroid the outer retinal nerve fibres often form a definite loop, running outwards beneath the retina

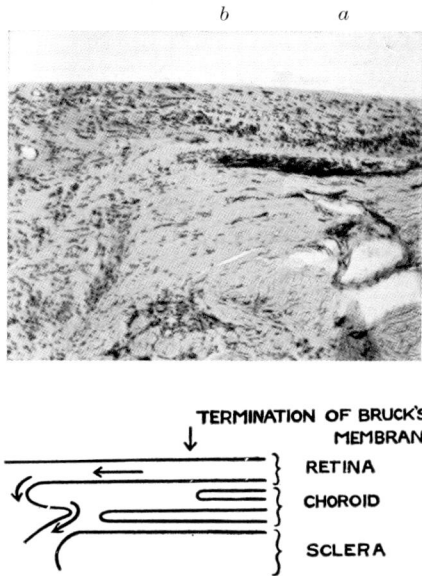

FIG. 355.—THE MYOPIC CRESCENT.

The temporal part of the optic nerve-head of a myopic patient aged 66. (a) termination of Bruch's membrane. (b) indicates the level of the nerve-fibre loop (F. W. Stocker).

and then turning back at a sharp angle to reach the optic nerve (Fig. 355) (Weiss, 1888; Heine, 1899; Stocker, 1943).

The rationale of the formation of the myopic crescent has stimulated many theories. It differs from a congenital conus which is a structural anomaly and non-progressive.[1] Schnabel (1874), Elschnig (1903–5) and von Szily (1922) believed that the crescent, like the conus, was determined in fœtal life, but this assumption lacks proof, and there is no evidence that the coloboma-like appearances formed in fœtal life develop into progressive defects in adults. In the classical view it is caused simply by stretching (Schnabel, 1874), the choroid being dragged back into the ectasia at the posterior pole of the eye (Fig. 356). Conversely, it has been interpreted as a result of an

[1] Vol. III, p. 674.

excessive response by the sclera to the stimulation of retinal growth so that a gap is left between the border of the choroid and the disc (Vogt, 1924; Stocker, 1943).   An alternative view is that it is due to localized atrophy (Salzmann, 1902).   It is barely necessary to mention more fanciful views—that it is due to a backward pull of the optic nerve (Weiss, 1882–84), to the pull of the superior oblique muscle (Stilling, 1885–1905) or of the ciliary muscle in accommodation (Iwanoff, 1869).

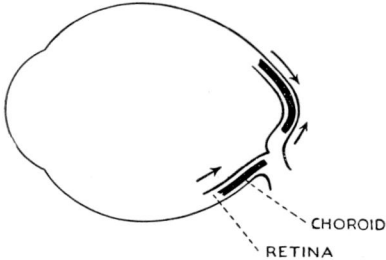

CHOROID

RETINA

Fig. 356.—The Development of Traction and Supertraction.

The arrows indicate the direction of stretching or, alternatively, of retinal overgrowth.

The TEMPORAL NERVE-FIBRE LOOP has been variously explained.   Heine (1899) considered that when Bruch's membrane was drawn back, its ramifications into the optic disc pulled back nerve fibres with it. It is questionable, however, if such ramifications do, in fact, occur (Inouye, 1925). Siegrist (1925) suggested that the connective-tissue fibres of the choroid on retraction would exert a similar pull.   Stocker (1943), on the other hand, emphasizing the occasional occurrence of such a loop in non-myopic eyes with senile peripapillary atrophy, suggested that the appearance was due to the neuroglial fibres from the retina which at the edge of the optic disc run temporally into the inner layers of the sclera participating in the eversion of the temporal side of the scleral canal; in this event the loop need not be associated with stretching.

SUPERTRACTION OF THE RETINA on the nasal side of the disc (or SUPER-VOLUTION, to avoid implied commitments as to its mechanism, Stocker, 1943) is in many ways the reverse of the myopic crescent.   The histological appearances are also variable.[1]   As a rule the choroid stops at the edge of the disc and the retina overlaps it, running out sometimes to the middle of the disc before the nerve fibres bend sharply backwards into the nerve (Fig. 357). At other times the choroid also overlaps the disc, but it is always less displaced than the retina.   The appearance suggests that the tissues are pulled over the nasal border of the disc as if they were dragged towards the posterior pole, and this is the classical interpretation of the phenomenon (von Jaeger, 1855; and others) (Fig. 356); alternatively, it can be argued that the overlapping is due to retinal overgrowth which on the nasal side finds no expansive outlet comparable with the posterior pole on the temporal side. It is to be remembered that supervolution of the retina, as is the case with most myopic changes, is also found in non-myopic eyes (Verhoeff, 1909).

The histological appearances of an inverse (nasal) crescent (Rønne, 1916; E. Fuchs, 1919; Salzmann, 1941) or an inferior crescent (Salzmann, 1902) are similar.

---

[1] von Jaeger (1855–61), Weiss (1882–84), Heine (1900), Salzmann (1902), Siegrist (1906), Stocker (1943), and others.

The *optic nerve* itself may show the characteristic changes of lacunar atrophy.[1] There is some doubt, however, whether this occurs without glaucoma; and the atrophy can in no sense be said to be characteristic of myopia.

Pathological changes in the *anterior segment of the globe* are less marked. Fleischer (1906) reported a rupture of Descemet's membrane—a characteristic of buphthalmos. Pigmentary degeneration with the accumulation of pigmented granules in the angle of the anterior chamber may be evident—a condition frequently seen in senile eyes. Most interest has centred around the condition of the *ciliary muscle* since the descriptions by Donders (1864)

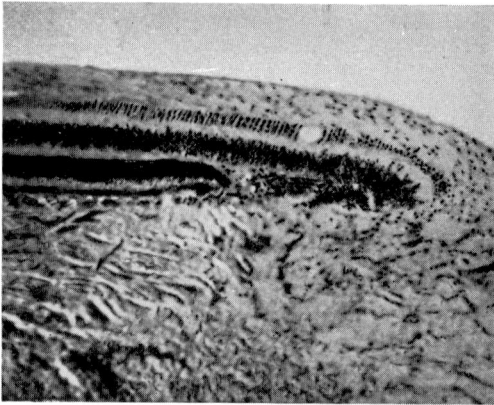

FIG. 357.—SUPERTRACTION IN MYOPIA.

The nasal part of the optic nerve-head in a myopic eye showing supertraction (superinvolution). The retina overlaps far onto the disc (F. W. Stocker).

and Heine (1900) pointing out that it was smaller than normal owing to an " atrophy of disuse." Iwanoff (1869) localized the atrophy to the circular fibres of Müller's muscle and found that the meridional fibres of Brücke's muscle represented the greater part of the entire ciliary muscle, being longer than in emmetropia and extending farther posteriorly; he claimed that the opposite relative proportions occurred in hypermetropia. These observations have not, however, been universally confirmed, for the circular fibres have been found by others to be equally or more highly developed in myopic compared with hypermetropic eyes (Arlt, 1876; Stilling, 1905; Hess, 1909; and others). There is no doubt that the configuration of the muscle is very variable even at birth.[2]

---

[1] Axenfeld (1905), Polatti (1906), Stock (1908), v. Hippel (1910), Fleischer (1912), and others.

[2] For the development of the ciliary muscle and the validity of the generally accepted anatomical subdivisions, see Vol. II, p. 149.

Clinical Features

Symptoms

The *visual disability* in high myopia is usually considerable. We have seen that in simple myopia the corrected visual acuity is generally good; in degenerative myopia it is frequently bad and, statistically, the higher the myopia and the longer it has existed the worse it tends to be (Schleich, 1882; Leininberg, 1886; Harman, 1913; and others) (Fig. 358). This diminution in acuity has been attributed to a spreading out of the cones on the expanded retinal surface, but it is probably accounted for by the atrophic changes in the sentient layer. The development of macular changes, of course, leads to the formation of an incapacitating central scotoma.

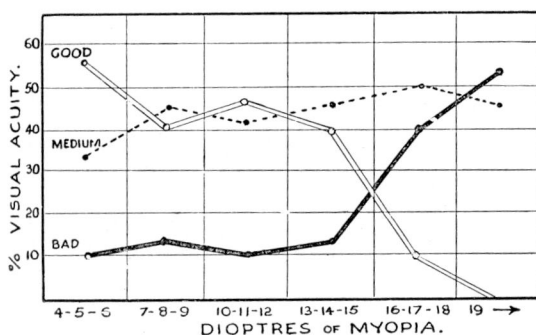

Fig. 358.—The Relation between the Visual Acuity and the Degree of Myopia.

Good vision is taken to be 6/6 to 6/12; medium, 6/18 and 6/24; bad, 6/36 or less (N. Bishop Harman).

Apart from the visual incapacity, the high myope is not usually comfortable in the use of his eyes. When corrected, the small, sharply defined and bright images are annoying; much use of the eyes brings about a feeling of strain and fatigue. The degenerated and liquefied vitreous gives rise to a multitude of muscæ volitantes and floating opacities and these, throwing abnormally large images upon the retina owing to its backward displacement, cause a great deal of distress and anxiety to the patient although their actual significance is small. Most of these patients are naturally anxious; their disability is obvious and may have excited sympathy, the memory of admonitions to care for the eyes in youth lingers into adult life, and not seldom the family history may contain more than one casualty from the same cause. Thus matters may tend to progress slowly and relentlessly, the patient all the while never using his eyes with comfort or without anxiety, until finally no useful vision may remain, or until the occurrence of a sudden calamity such as a gross macular lesion, a hæmorrhage or a retinal detachment, brings about a more dramatic crisis.

Associated Phenomena

Contraction of the *visual fields* for white and colours was noted in high myopes by the earlier observers (Otto, 1891), as well as the occurrence of ring scotomata; but these probably depend upon the degree of choroidal atrophy. Although perception of light is absent over the area of a crescent of any size (Donders, 1864), a regular enlargement of the blind-spot does not seem to be characteristic (von Graefe, 1854; Baas, 1893; Nicoletti, 1925). Jayle and Bérard (1955) classified the defects in the visual field in high myopes into typical and atypical; an enlargement of the blind-spot and a loss in the superior temporal quadrant of the peripheral field were considered typical, and cæco-central, hemianopic, nasal and annular defects atypical. Bitemporal defects have been noted (Odland, 1967), and occasionally the myopic scotomata resemble those seen in glaucoma (Kurozumi *et al.*, 1966). The optical aberrations of the uncorrected or corrected eye, however, frequently give rise to bizarre scotomata which can be largely eliminated by the use of contact lenses (Jayle and Ourgaud, 1953). Blach (1965) found that these defects in the fields, if contact lenses were worn during testing, were only as extensive as might be expected from the appearances in the fundus, while Blatt (1964) concluded that the changes in the fields depended as much on the depth as on the surface extent of the choroido-retinal lesions.

The *light sense* is generally considered to be subnormal in high myopes (Seggel, 1888–1906) and, while night-blindness occurs in a considerable number of patients, this tendency is by no means universal and is rarely applicable to the slighter degrees of short-sight (Stilling, 1888; Wölfflin, 1905; Stilling and Landolt, 1908; and others). Some authorities have attempted to relate the loss of rod-sensitivity to the extent of the myopic degeneration (Lohmann, 1907; Brändstedt, 1935; Jayle and Ourgaud, 1950), but no such correlation was found by Blach and his colleagues (1966).

The *colour vision* of high myopes usually shows a defect for blue (François and Verriest, 1957; Redi *et al.*, 1965). According to Blach (1965) the blue-yellow defect in such cases may be due to changes in the crystalline lens.

The *intra-ocular pressure* of the myopic eye has usually been considered to be normal or low (Caso, 1931; Kraupa, 1931) but it has interested many observers because of the possible relationship between myopia and glaucoma.[1] Lacroix (1922), for example, found that 30% of high myopes had raised tension and considered a low tension to be an unfavourable prognostic sign. It is now realized, however, that measurements of the intra-ocular pressure by means of indentation tonometry are unreliable (Goldmann, 1963).[2] Because the ocular rigidity of highly myopic eyes is low (Castrén and Pohjola, 1962), false low values for the tension are given by this method; in these cases applanation tonometry gives more reliable values. With this technique Blach and Jay (1965) found a normal distribution of applanation pressures in 77 high myopes (Fig. 359).

[1] Vol. XI, p. 404.   [2] See Vol. IV, p. 236.

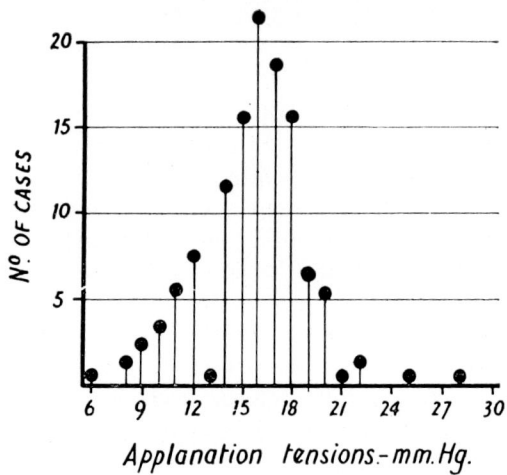

FIG. 359.—THE INTRA-OCULAR PRESSURE IN PATIENTS WITH DEGENERATIVE MYOPIA (R. K. Blach and B. Jay).

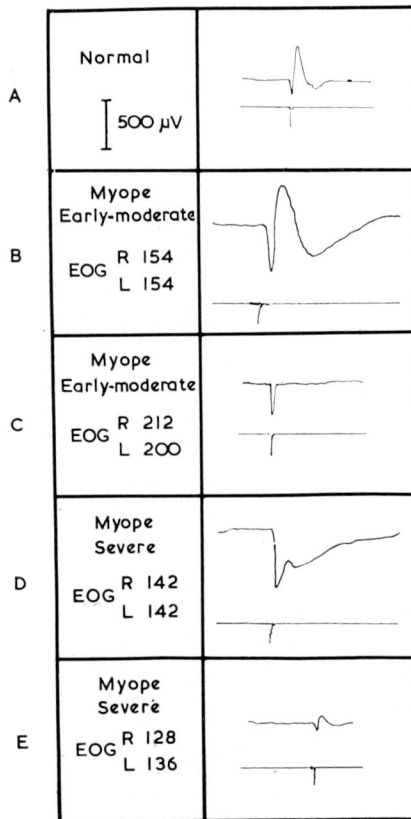

FIG. 360.—THE EOG AND ERG IN MYOPES.

A, normal eye. In myopes the ERG waveform varies in early moderate cases from supernormal (B) to negative (C). In severe myopes the wave-form can be negative with a very enlarged *a*-wave (D) or minute in amplitude (E) (R. K. Blach *et al.*).

Electrophysiological anomalies are frequently found in high myopia. The *electroretinogram* is usually subnormal (Karpe, 1945; François and De-Rouck, 1954; Franceschetti *et al.*, 1960; Ponte, 1962). There is some suggestion that the degree of reduction of the *b*-wave parallels the depression of visual function; high myopes show widely differing *a*-waves, but these are commonly of large size (Blach *et al.*, 1966) (Fig. 360). In general, these abnormalities are related to the degree of the chorioretinal atrophic changes and the degeneration of the pigmentary epithelium. Similarly, the *electro-oculogram* is often abnormal but there is little correlation between it and the

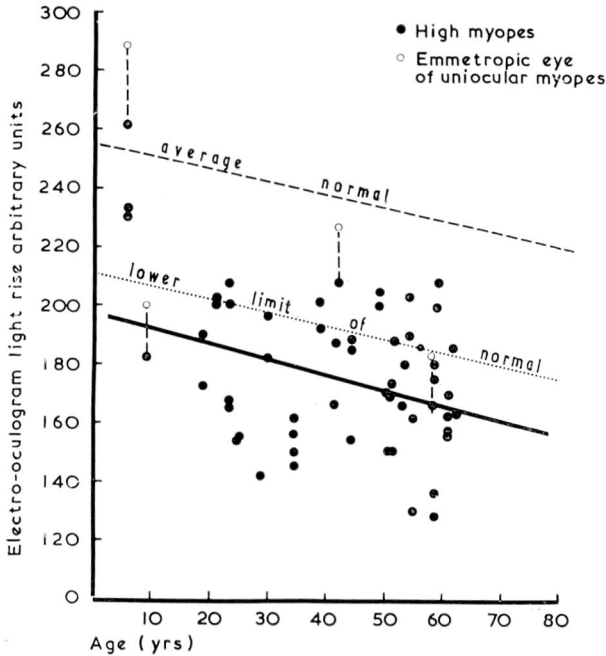

FIG. 361.—THE CORRELATION BETWEEN THE EOG RATIO AND AGE.

Normal limits indicated by the dashed line. Most of the myopes lie at or below the lower limit of normal, the average being indicated by the solid black line (R. K. Blach *et al.*).

ERG. The resting potential level may be normal (François *et al.*, 1956), but the light-rise is usually reduced, a change dramatically seen in uniocular myopia (Arden *et al.*, 1962; Blach *et al.*, 1966) (Fig. 361).

The *electro-encephalogram* has been found to show abnormalities in myopic macular disease (Frezzotti and Fois, 1958); Blach (1965) found paroxysmal activity in 6 out of 15 high myopes.

Clinical Signs

Clinically the eye generally appears obviously large and prominent, and when it is turned strongly inward so that the equatorial region appears in the outer part of the palpebral fissure, the flatness of its curvature is obvious. The cornea is usually abnormally flat (Mächler, 1928), counteracting to some extent the optical effect of the axial elongation. The anterior chamber is deeper than in emmetropia (Raeder, 1922) and the pupil usually dilated and somewhat sluggish, particularly in youth.

Ophthalmoscopically, degenerative myopia shows very characteristic changes : the essential features are :—

1. Changes at the optic disc—oblique entrance of the optic nerve, myopic crescent, nasal supertraction.

2. Atrophy of the choroid, sometimes generalized, frequently accentuated near the macula and often associated with vascular changes in this area.

3. Changes in the retina—atrophy of the pigmentary epithelium or its proliferation, particularly to form the Förster-Fuchs spot at the macula, cystoid degeneration at the periphery, and its total atrophy, particularly in the central area in association with choroidal atrophy.

4. Scleral ectasias usually seen at the posterior pole forming a posterior staphyloma.

5. Degenerative changes in the vitreous, detachments and the formation of hyaloid holes, and Weiss's reflex streak.

The changes at the optic disc are of great interest and are frequently the first organic signs to become clinically evident. It is to be noted that the thinness of the pre-cribriform glial tissue in the myopic eye may give the appearance of slight cupping which may sometimes suggest the presence of glaucoma.

The MYOPIC CRESCENT (Plate III, Figs. 1–3) may be present at birth (von Jaeger, 1855), but usually becomes evident about puberty ; at the age of 16 it is common and becomes almost invariable in later years in myopia over 6 D (Donders, 1864). It usually appears in the first place as a white, sharply defined area lying on the temporal side of the optic disc where the inner surface of the sclera or in some cases the scleral canal is directly seen. Sometimes the sharp edge towards the normal fundus is pigmented, and at other times there is a transitional region of brownish-red where the choroid is still partially present and its vessels are visible. The crescent may be narrow or considerably more than the diameter of the disc in breadth ; it is usually temporal but not uncommonly (13·43% of cases, von Szily, 1922) it lies somewhat superiorly or inferiorly, and occasionally, as we shall see presently, nasally ; not infrequently it becomes annular, surrounding the entire disc, sometimes spreading therefrom to include a large area of the fundus and envelop the whole macular area (Plate III, Figs. 4 and 5). The slow and gradual extension of the atrophic change can sometimes be followed when repeated ophthalmoscopic examination over a period of years reveals the migration of pigment temporally as the crescent progresses.

In 5,812 myopic eyes, Hertel (1903) found the following proportions:—

	% of all crescents	% of all myopes
Temporal . . .	79	69
Annular . . .	11	9·6
Inferior	6	5
Sup. and Sup.-nasal .	4	3·5

It is important to remember that a crescent is not exclusively confined to myopic eyes, for it occurs, although much more rarely, in emmetropia and hypermetropia (Schnabel, 1874; Seggel, 1890) in which event it is usually associated with astigmatism (Thomson, 1919; Kretz, 1929). Thus in 135 cases Schnabel found 99 myopic, 18 emmetropic and 18 hypermetropic. Among myopes astigmatism is a common association, with the meridian of greatest refraction lying in the direction of the crescent (Menestrina, 1926). Moreover, a very similar change is characteristic of senile eyes of any refractive denomination (senile circumpapillary choroidal atrophy, Bücklers, 1928).[1] The frequency of its occurrence, its extent and form (whether crescentic or annular) usually vary with the degree of myopia (Harman, 1913; Scheerer and Seitzer, 1929), but the relation is by no means close; it may be absent in the highest degrees or represented only by a narrow strip. While it has considerable significance, Harman's (1913) claim that the presence or extent of the crescent can be taken as an index of the seriousness of the myopia must be interpreted with great caution.

SUPERTRACTION (SUPERVOLUTION) of the retina over the nasal side of the disc was first described by von Jaeger (1861), wherein the retinal tissues appear ophthalmoscopically to encroach over the surface of the disc blurring its nasal border, the retinal vessels bending over the curved edge sometimes almost halfway across the papilla. The combination of this phenomenon with the temporal crescent may give the entire disc a deformed appearance, the structures at the nerve-head entering in an obliquely temporal direction (Plate III, Fig. 2).

While this is the most common arrangement at the optic disc, in a small number of myopic eyes there is an inverse arrangement wherein the myopic crescent is situated on the nasal side and sometimes supertraction appears on the temporal side (the *inverse crescent : inverse myopia*) (Rønne, 1916; E. Fuchs, 1882–1919; Salzmann, 1941; A. Fuchs, 1947): in these cases a nasal ectasia is common so that the nasal parts of the fundus show a higher degree of myopia than the macular region. A rarer occurrence is an inferior crescent associated with an ectasia in the lower part of the fundus (Salzmann, 1902; A. Fuchs, 1947).

ATROPHY OF THE CHOROID is an almost constant feature of the higher degrees of myopia, occurring simultaneously with pigmentary disturbances. A generalized appearance of " thinning " is common wherein

[1] Vol. IX, p. 673.

the pigment layer of the retina becomes attenuated and the choroidal vessels become clearly visible (Plate IV, Fig. 1). The smaller meshwork of vessels disappears leaving the larger trunks extant, and eventually the atrophic changes lead to the complete ophthalmoscopic disappearance of the tissues so that circumscribed white areas of sclera become visible. Simultaneously proliferation of pigment occurs in scattered areas, leading to the picture of extensive " myopic choroido-retinitis " which, however, despite its appearance, is degenerative in nature and not inflammatory (Plate IV, Fig. 2). These changes tend to be most marked and to occur most frequently in the central area and the periphery.

The *changes at the macula* are characteristic, common and, of course, incapacitating. Among 2,910 myopes Schweizer (1890) found such lesions in 6·3% of all myopes, in 14% of myopes above 3 D and 100% above 20 D. The choroid shows the first alterations, the origin of which is probably an atrophic sclerosis of the small vessels—a diffuse powdery pigmentation, the occurrence of small red spots which may show little or no change during prolonged observation and are probably tufts of dilated capillaries or thrombotic areas, hæmorrhages which may sometimes be extensive and multiple (Plate V, Fig. 1), and white spots of atrophy or branched white lines forming a net-like tracery said by Sattler (1907) to be due to sclerosis of small choroidal vessels (Plate V, Fig. 2 ; Plate VI, Fig. 1). Eventually large areas of atrophy may appear, usually with a considerable proliferation of pigment, until the choroid and retina may have disappeared over a wide area of the central region, sometimes so large as to include the disc within its boundaries (Plate IV, Fig. 2). Alternatively the peripapillary atrophy of an increasing crescent may spread from the disc and engulf the entire macular area (Plate III, Fig. 5).

A central circular dark spot—the FÖRSTER-FUCHS FLECK—forms an occasional characteristic feature at the macula (Plates III, Fig. 4, and V, Fig. 3). First described by Förster (1862), first anatomically examined by Lehmus (1875) and extensively studied by E. Fuchs (1901), it is due to proliferation of the pigmentary epithelium, possibly associated with a choroidal hæmorrhage. It usually appears somewhat suddenly in the 4th or 5th decade in moderately high myopes (about or above 12 D), first distorting central vision and later causing a central scotoma as it gradually develops into a raised, hard intensely black circle situated sometimes in a relatively normal fundus, at others in the midst of a large atrophic area. Occasionally it is bilateral (Kronfeld, 1925). A greyish-green epithelial proliferation has occasionally been observed at the macula (Butler, 1911 ; Stargardt, 1912 ; Bietti, 1912).

PERIPHERAL RETINO-CHOROIDAL ATROPHY (Plate VI, Figs. 2–4) is characterized by numerous small patches of atrophy and pigmentary proliferation anterior to the equator, but is not peculiar to this refractive

PLATES I TO VII

CHANGES IN THE FUNDUS IN MYOPIA

PLATE I
STAPHYLOMATA IN CONGENITAL MYOPIA

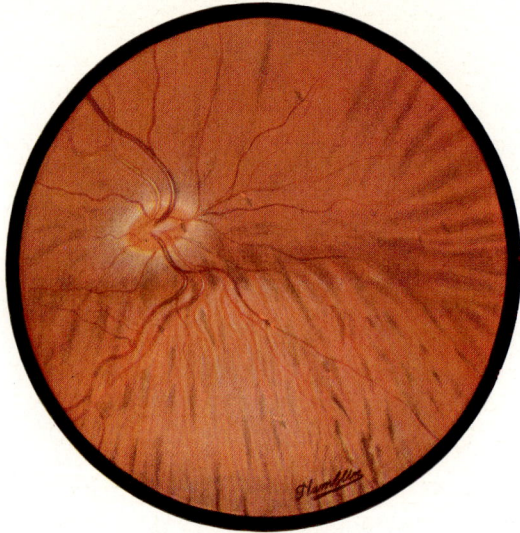

FIG. 1.—Congenital staphyloma in lower fundus showing no marked ridge. Note the deformity of the disc. In a woman of 26 in whom the refraction had remained stationary since early youth. Refraction at macula, — 2 D cyl.; in lower periphery, —10 D sph.

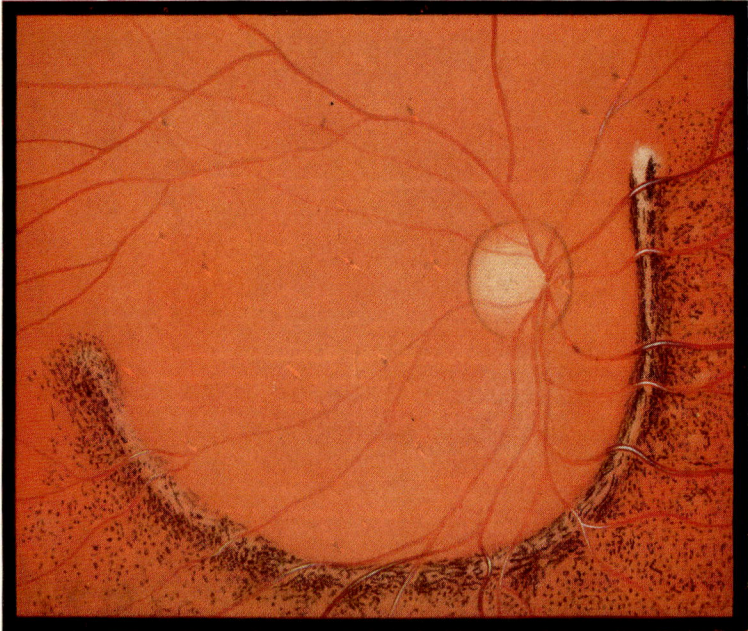

FIG. 2.—Congenital staphyloma in the central fundus with a marked ridge. The drawing was made when the patient (a girl) was aged 10. The refraction was unchanged 12 years later. Refraction at macula, — 9 D, outside the ridge, + 1 D.

PLATE II

Congenital Myopia

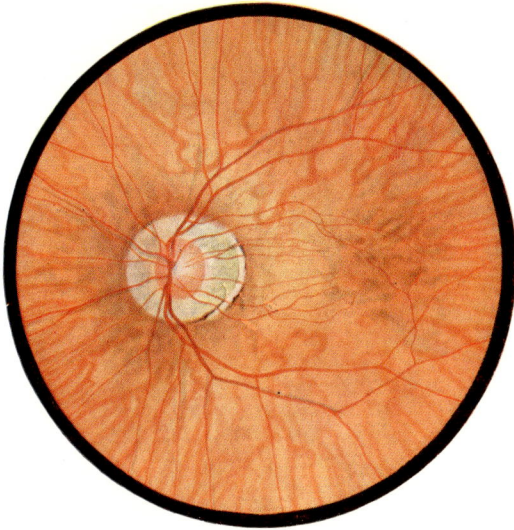

Fig. 1.—Congenital Myopia of the Albinoid Type.

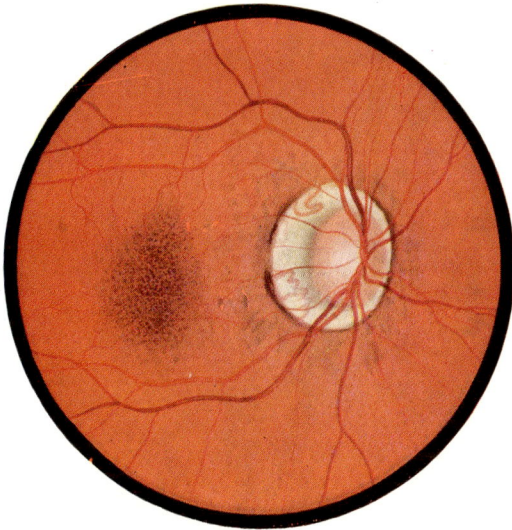

Fig. 2.—Congenital Myopia of the Pigmentary Type.

PLATE III

THE OPTIC DISC IN MYOPIA

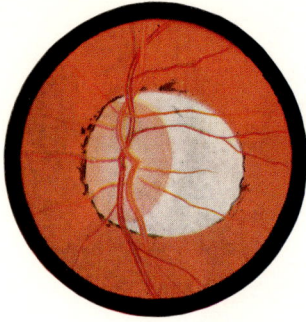

FIG. 1.—TYPICAL TEMPORAL
CRESCENT.

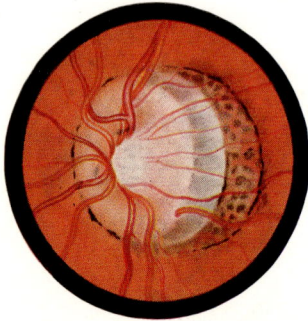

FIG. 2.—TEMPORAL CRES-
CENT; CHOROIDAL CRESCENT;
AND NASAL SUPERTRACTION.

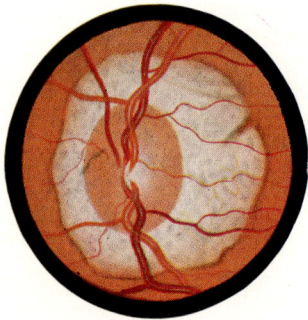

FIG. 3.—SPREAD OF THE CRES-
CENT TO AN ANNULAR FORM.

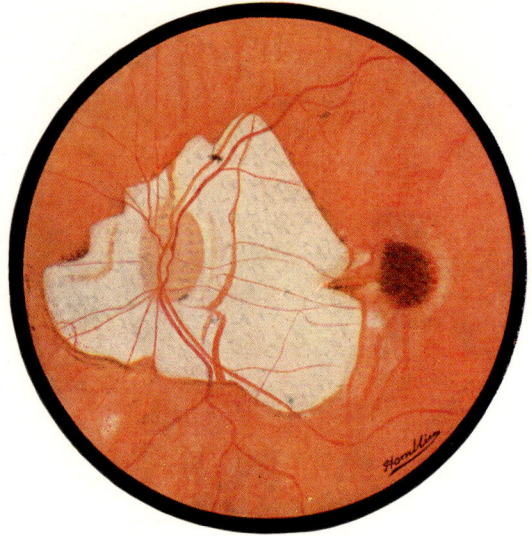

FIG. 4.—SPREAD OF DEGENERATION AROUND THE
DISC TOWARDS THE MACULAR AREA AT WHICH THERE
IS A FÖRSTER-FUCHS PIGMENTED SPOT.

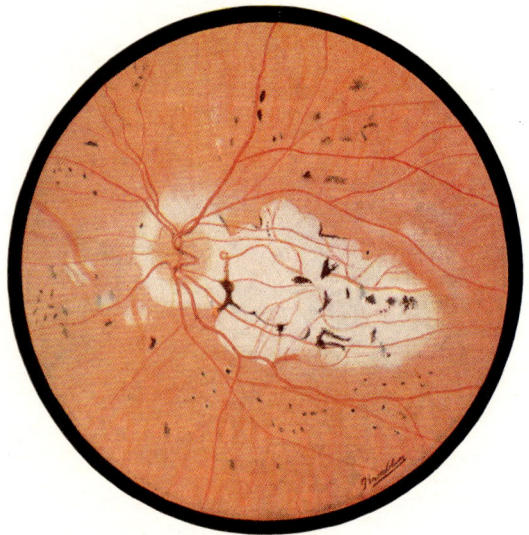

FIG. 5.—SPREAD OF DEGENERATION AROUND THE
DISC TO INCLUDE THE MACULA.

PLATE IV
Choroidal Atrophy in Myopia

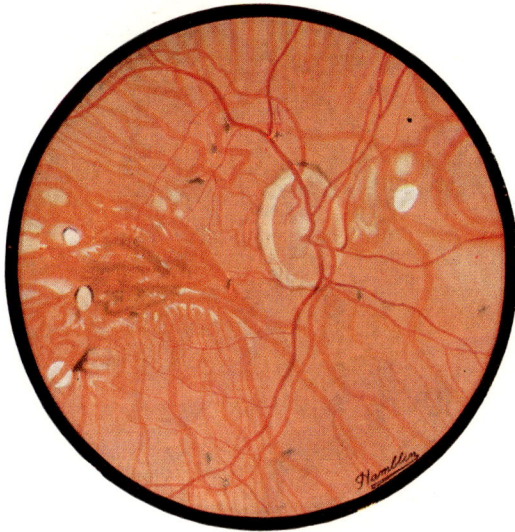

Fig. 1.—Early Atrophic Changes.

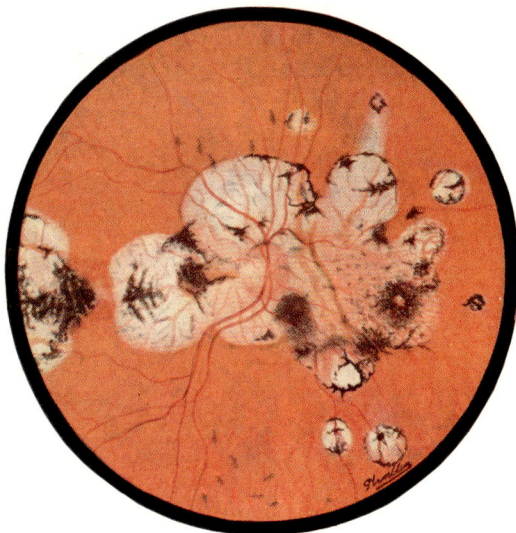

Fig. 2.—Advanced Degenerative Changes.

PLATE V
Macular Changes in Myopia

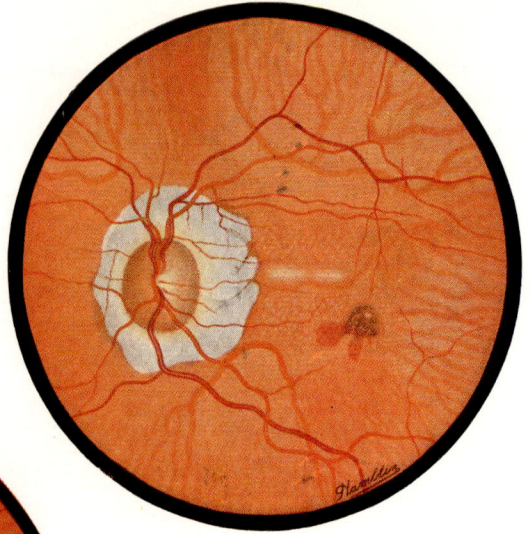

Fig. 1.—Choroidal Hæmor-
rhages at the Macula.

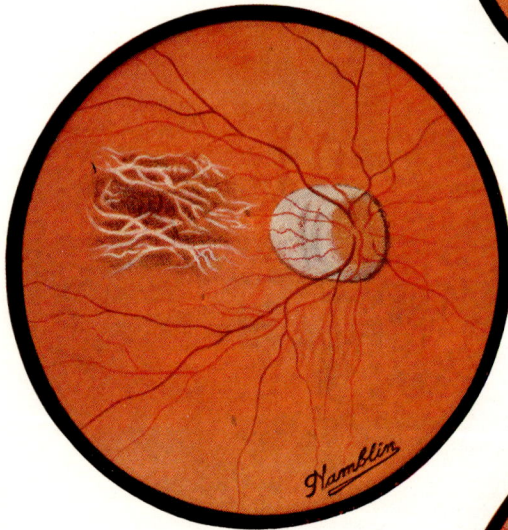

Fig. 2.—Streak Sclerosis of the
Choroidal Vessels.

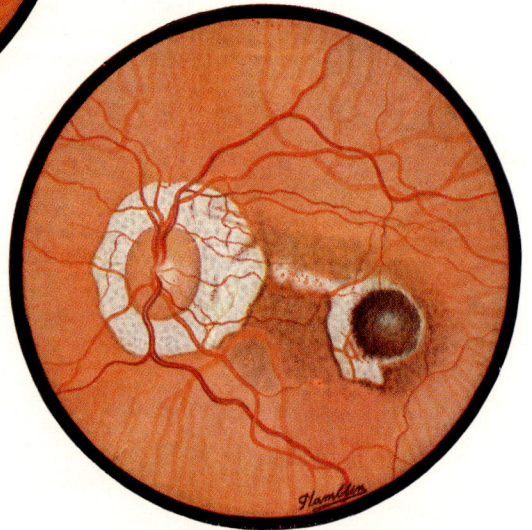

Fig. 3.—The Förster-Fuchs Spot
in Myopia.

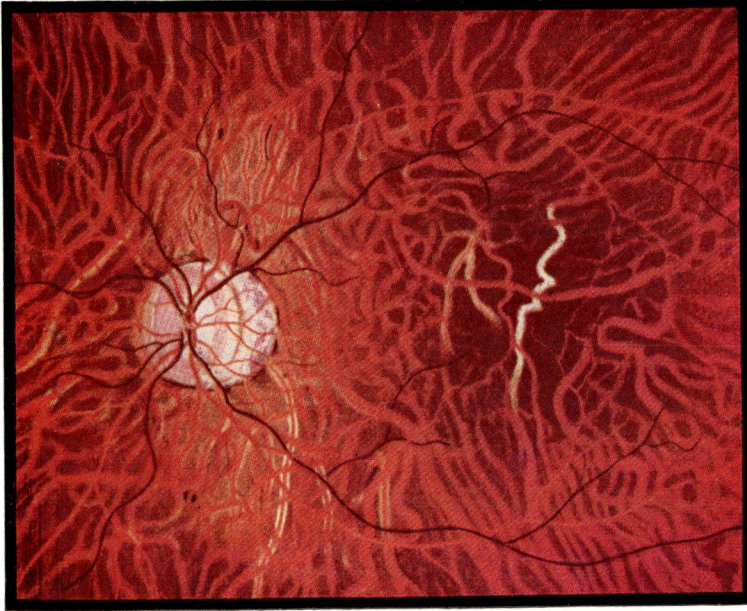

Fig. 1.—Diffuse Choroidal Atrophy with Sclerosed Vessels.

Fig. 2.—Peripheral Pigmentary Atrophy.

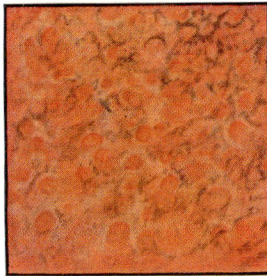

Fig. 3.—Peripheral Cystoid Atrophy of the Retina.

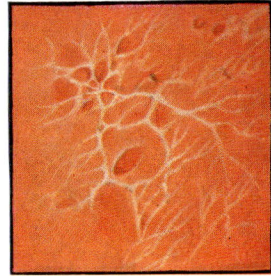

Fig. 4.—Peripheral Cystoid Atrophy with the Formation of Retinal Holes.

PLATE VII

Acquired Staphylomata in Myopia

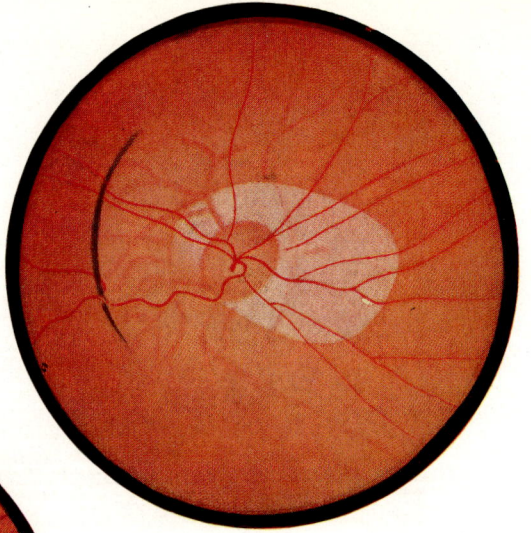

Fig. 1.—Posterior Staphyloma with a sharp Ridge on the Nasal Side.

A man, aged 49, R.E. — 30 D; L.E. — 38 D.

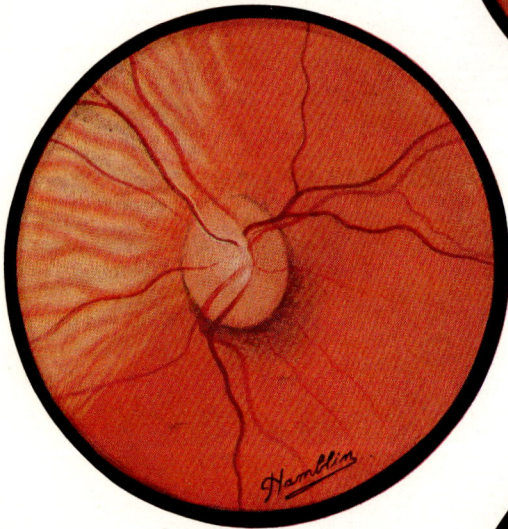

Fig. 2.—Nasal Staphyloma in a Woman, aged 36, showing no Acute Step.

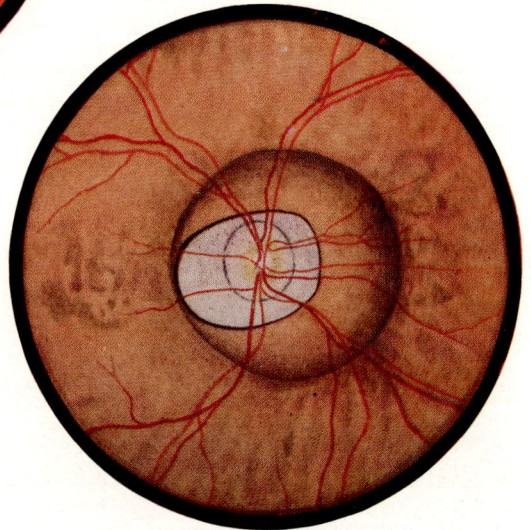

Fig. 3.—Complete Staphyloma Posticum Verum of the Entire Posterior Pole.

Refraction only — 5 D and the difference of refraction at the edge of the staphyloma only 2 D.

condition. The picture corresponds to that of *peripheral cystic degeneration* of the retina[1] which is an almost constant occurrence in senility and may also be seen in the young; it is a common feature of myopic eyes (Vogt, 1924; Hanssen, 1925; Rehsteiner, 1928) in which condition it may occur in comparatively early life (Ochi, 1927). Retinal holes may also occur (Hyams and Neumann, 1969) but such degenerative changes are by no means invariable (Zauberman and Merin, 1969).

SCLERAL ECTASIAS are relatively frequent in the higher degrees of short-sight (Fig. 362). Irregularities in the depth of the fundus so that differences of refraction exist in various localities are not very uncommon, particularly round the disc in the presence of a crescent, but the formation of a localized ectasia in the region of the posterior pole presents a striking ophthalmoscopic picture (Plate VII, Figs. 1 to 3). This was first described by von Graefe (1854) as STAPHYLOMA POSTICUM VERUM, but little attention was given to its occurrence and nature until interest was resuscitated by Weiss (1888), de Wecker and Masselon (1891), Otto (1891–98) and Caspar (1894); thereafter descriptions have been more frequent (Strebel, 1913; Harman, 1913; Haab, 1921; and others). Sometimes the fundus dips down into the ectasia gradually, but more usually there is a relatively abrupt edge, the shadow of which appears ophthalmoscopically as a dark line over which the retinal vessels bend and sometimes disappear from

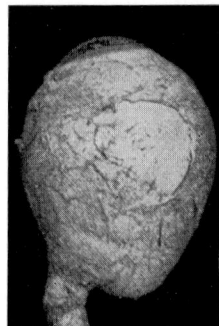

FIG. 362.—STAPHY-
LOMA IN MYOPIA
(after A. Elschnig).

view as at the edge of a glaucomatous cup. Occasionally the edge appears as a rounded ridge over which the vessels bulge (Plate VII, Fig. 1). Between the main levels of the fundus and the depths of the crater there may be a large dioptric difference, frequently of the order of 10 D and, while the texture of the fundus in general may be good, there may be much choroido-retinal atrophy in the staphyloma itself so that it has an albinotic appearance with the choroidal vessels distinctly delineated.

In the majority of cases the staphyloma involves the posterior pole of the eye, but the most common site for a sharp crescentic line of shadow is to the nasal side of the disc: the sharp shadow indicates an extension nasally of the ectasia at the posterior pole (Plate VII, Fig. 1): occasionally the line is duplicated as the depression descends in one or more steps (Sattler, 1907). In other cases where the staphyloma is more accentuated, a circular line may be apparent, circumscribing a pit at the bottom of which lies the optic disc usually surrounded by an annular crescent (Weiss, 1891; Rønne, 1916; Kraupa, 1936) (Plate VII, Fig. 3). Rarely an ectasia is limited to the nasal side of the disc (Weiss, 1891; Caspar, 1894) (Plate VII, Fig. 1). We

[1] Vol. X, p. 549.

have already seen that a congenital ectasia is not very uncommon, for which a typical site is below the disc (Plate I).

Changes in the vitreous are almost of constant occurrence in myopia, frequently appearing at an early stage and usually becoming more accentuated in later life. MYOPIC DEGENERATION OF THE VITREOUS closely resembles the senile type: the gel liquefies first at the posterior pole and the area immediately behind the lens is seen with the slit-lamp to be crowded with nodular interlacing filaments behind which fibrillar diaphanous membranes are visible (MICROFIBRILLAR DEGENERATION) (Fig. 363).[1] The opacities are aggregations of the colloid basis of the gel indicating its disruption without serious implications, but they give rise to distressing entoptic opacities.

FIG. 363.—MICROFIBRILLAR DEGENERATION OF THE VITREOUS IN MYOPIA.
Seen with the slit-lamp.

A POSTERIOR DETACHMENT of the vitreous is a common feature of myopia,[2] described by Iwanoff (1869) as a *detachment e vacuo*, the stretching of the globe leaving a space between the face of the vitreous and the posterior pole of the eye. On ophthalmoscopic examination the posterior surface of the gel gives rise to the reflex originally described by Weiss (1885–97) and the details of the detachment can be clearly seen with the slit-lamp aided by a contact lens (Kraupa, 1914–25; Pillat, 1922–36; and others) (Figs. 364–5).

The REFLEX STREAK OF WEISS was considered by him to be the first ophthalmoscopic sign of early myopia. He described it as a brilliant, crescentic, finely striated reflex on the nasal side of the disc, particularly evident by direct ophthalmoscopy (Fig. 366). It occurs in advanced myopia and is sometimes seen in non-myopic eyes when a detachment of the vitreous occurs. Although it is most readily seen on the nasal side of the disc, by manipulating the light it can be made to appear on the temporal side, and may, indeed, become evident as a circle anywhere around the posterior pole of the eye completely dissociated from the optic disc; this can be made particularly evident in fundus photography (Fig. 367). Stereoscopic photography shows it to be localized in front of the retina.

---

[1] Streiff (1924), Comberg (1924), Vogt (1924–25), Samuels (1930), Sallmann (1936), and others. See Vol. XI, p. 358.
[2] Vol. XI, p. 340.

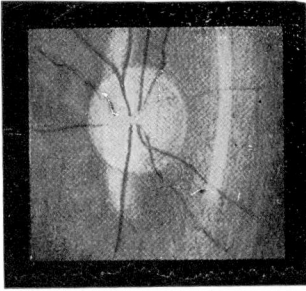

FIG. 364.—POSTERIOR DETACHMENT
OF THE VITREOUS IN HIGH MYOPIA
(H. Rieger).

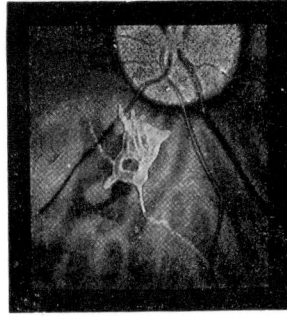

FIG. 365.—VITREOUS DETACHMENT
WITH CONDENSATION OPACITY IN
MYOPIA (H. Rieger).

A further appearance at the posterior pole is a condensation of the vitreous face into a grey membranous opacity, frequently taking the form of a ring indicating where it has become detached from the disc[1] (Fig. 365). The opacity floats about in front of the disc and may take on many shapes; but it is not characteristic of myopia, appearing as commonly in senility or in any part of the fundus associated with a localized patch of degeneration or inflammation.[2]

FIGS. 366 and 367.—THE REFLEX STREAK OF WEISS (H. Erggelet).

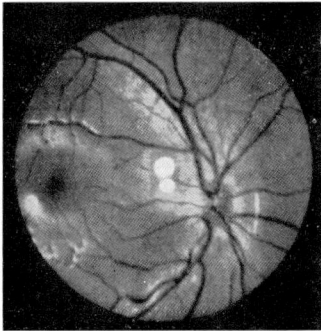

FIG. 366.—The reflex streak of Weiss seen as a crescent on the nasal side of the disc with the Zeiss-Nordenson camera in a 12-year-old child (−2·25 D sph. −0·5 D cyl.).

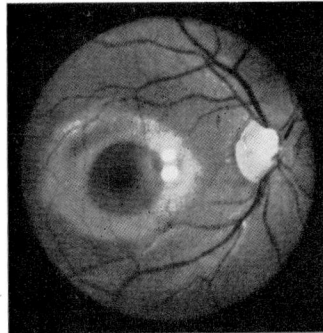

FIG. 367.—A ring-shaped reflex encircling the macula seen with the Zeiss-Nordenson camera in a 15-year-old girl (−6·5 D sph.).

Complications

The complications of degenerative myopia are numerous and grave, for the disability frequently results in blindness. As with the degenerative

[1] Brière (1875), Dimmer (1882), Dor (1898), Kraupa (1914–25), Pillat (1922–36), Vogt (1924–35), Rieger (1934–37), and many others.
[2] Vol. XI, p. 341.

changes themselves, the complications appear typically in adult life after the myopia has been fully established for some years.

CHOROIDAL THROMBOSES AND HÆMORRHAGES are not infrequent, as would be expected in view of the early obliteration of the small vessels. Such hæmorrhages may be recurrent, and when they occur in the central area, as they habitually do, each leading to the formation or extension of scarred atrophic areas, their cumulative effect upon vision is frequently disastrous, even if they are individually small. Larger hæmorrhages, of course, are correspondingly more tragic.

VITREOUS OPACITIES, always present in some degree in high myopia, may suddenly increase to become a serious complication. They may be either endogenous to the vitreous, a cloud of opacities or membranous veils appearing suddenly as the gel liquefies, or a leakage from a choroidal vessel may fill the vitreous with blood.[1] We have already noted that liquefaction and detachment of the vitreous are common occurrences.

RETINAL DETACHMENT is the most dreaded and one of the most common complications of myopia, occurring with considerable frequency in all degrees of the defect but showing a progressively greater tendency the higher the myopia. This association was first stressed by von Graefe (1857) who found that 50% to 60% of detachments occurred in myopic eyes. Summarizing the literature between 1879 and 1914, Leber (1916) found that 65% of retinal detachments occurred in myopes, and the estimate that two-thirds of all detachments occur in this refractive condition has been verified by the experience of surgeons from most countries since that time,[2] and in more than half of these cases no other cause can be found. Conversely it may be said that some 5% of myopes develop a retinal detachment.[3] Moreover, a retinal detachment occurs earlier in the myopic population than in those with other refractive conditions, it is more frequently bilateral and is relatively more common in eyes with the higher degrees of myopia.[4] It is interesting that Gonin (1934) found that the two commonest ocular degenerations, myopia and senility, were together responsible for 85% of retinal detachments.

The causes of retinal detachment in high myopia are discussed elsewhere,[5] and it is unnecessary to enter further into the question here except to note that the common ætiological factor is the formation of a retinal hole

[1] Vol. XI, p. 363.
[2] Uhthoff (1922) 61%, Arruga (1933) 58%, Shapland (1934) 62%, Gonin (1934) 66%, Dunnington and Macnie (1935) 66·6%, Thiel (1959) 53·3%, and many others.
[3] Horstmann (1879) 3·5%, Schleich (1882) 2·5%, Hertel (1903) 1%, Blegvad (1927) 1·2%, Arruga (1933) 5%, Böhringer (1956) 4%.
[4] Gonin (1920–34), Shapland (1934), Arruga (1933), Cambiaggi (1964), Schepens and Marden (1966), and many others.
[5] Vol. X, p. 779.

in an atrophic area, particularly in the periphery of the fundus where this process is facilitated by the occurrence of cystic degeneration and is aided by the adherence thereto of the framework of the degenerated vitreous (Plate VI, Fig. 4).

SIMPLE GLAUCOMA is a further complication of considerable importance in high myopia.[1] A significant percentage of cases of glaucoma usually of the slow, insidious and chronic type occurs in high myopes, most observers giving a figure of about 14% (Priestley Smith, 1879; Weinstein, 1934; Lehrfeld and Reber, 1937; Weekers et al., 1958), while others give a higher percentage (29%, Carvill, 1932; 43%, Lange, 1896; 33%, Lacroix, 1922; 56·6%, H. Goldschmidt 1923; 28%, Díaz-Dominguez, 1961; over 25%, Díaz-Dominguez and Marchena, 1966). Many cases have been recorded in high myopia (Ischreyt, 1910; Gilbert, 1912; A. Knapp, 1925; and many others). Thus Apollonio and Weigelin (1964) found simple glaucoma in 2·8% of cases of myopia in excess of − 10 D. It may be accepted that the incidence of simple glaucoma is certainly no less than in the non-myopic population. In fact, any insidious deterioration of vision in a case of high myopia, even in a relatively young patient, which is not otherwise explained should give rise to the suspicion of the presence of this disease. The relation between the two conditions is not clear. Some writers suggest that the raised intra-ocular pressure determines or accentuates the myopia (Wick, 1925; Poos, 1929; Estrada, 1947); others maintain that high myopia and glaucoma are of the same degenerative nature (Kraupa, 1917–31; Elschnig, 1922); while a third view is that the glaucoma is a sequel to a generalized atrophy of the choroid (Mawas, 1934). It is well known that the hypertensive response of the intra-ocular pressure to topical corticosteroids is hereditarily determined[2]; on the basis of finding a response in patients with high myopia (with no evidence of glaucoma in themselves or their families) similar to that found in glaucoma, Podos and his colleagues (1966) suggested that a genetic linkage existed between glaucoma and high myopia.

Whatever the relationship, the frequent occurrence of glaucoma in high myopia is clear, and the clinical importance of the association lies in the fact that the glaucoma is usually of an insidious type without high tension and therefore readily missed by indentation tonometry, partly because of the traditional association of glaucoma with hypermetropia and partly because the visual defects, the restrictions in the field and the atrophy of the optic nerve may readily be attributed to the myopia itself. With regard to the ocular tension, the importance of using applanation tonometry rather than the impression technique has already been emphasized owing to the low ocular rigidity. The appearance of the optic disc is also frequently mis-leading owing to the thinness of the pre-cribriform glial tissue. It is true that

[1] Vol. XI, p. 404.
[2] Vol. XI, p. 402.

a typical concave cup with overhanging edges may be present, but more frequently the cup is shallow with a sharp or even a gradually slanting edge giving the appearance that the disc is merely participating in the posterior staphyloma (A. Knapp, 1925; Goldmann, 1957; Blach and Jay, 1965) (Fig. 368). This shallowness of the cup, indeed, may resemble the appearance of the disc in myopia without glaucoma, so that a differentiation can be made only by further investigation to establish the presence of a raised tension.

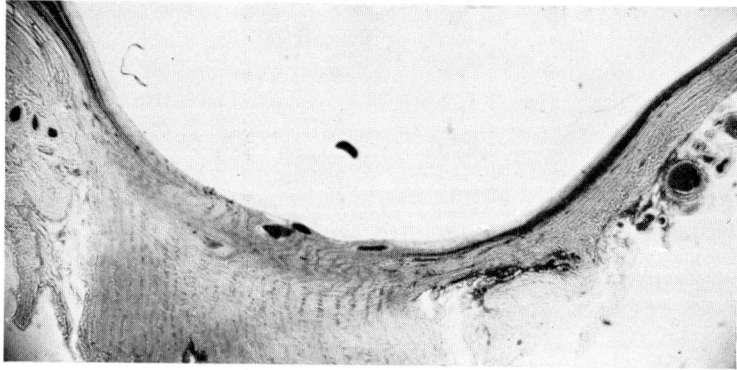

FIG. 368.—GLAUCOMATOUS CUPPING IN A HIGHLY MYOPIC EYE
(R. K. Blach and B. Jay).

CATARACT is a further complication of high myopia, occurring particularly in the higher degrees after mid-life; typically it is of the posterior polar type and is frequently associated with degenerative conditions of the choroid[1]. Nuclear lens changes may also occur, leading initially to a further aggravation of the myopic refraction.

In contradistinction to this unfortunate list of complications of high myopia, the reverse tendency tends to occur especially in certain vascular conditions. Thus, retinal venous thrombosis, hypertensive and diabetic retinopathies are rare in the highly myopic eye and in cases of unilateral myopia the pathological changes may be confined to the other eye. Arterial occlusions are slightly less frequent and papilloedema very rare, while owing to the configuration of the angle of the anterior chamber, closed-angle glaucoma is exceptional (Pallier et al., 1966).

The Ætiology of Degenerative Myopia

The ætiology of myopia has excited an immense amount of speculation and controversy ever since ophthalmology became a science, and the theories which have been put forward to explain its development are as

[1] Vol. XI, p. 225.

ingenious, fanciful and contradictory as have accumulated around any subject in medicine. Unfortunately their enthusiastic implementation in practice has too often involved far-reaching social and economic consequences, the rational basis for which has usually been insubstantial.

We have already seen that the most logical assumption is to suggest that two types of axial myopia exist, not necessarily completely independent since one may develop into the other—SIMPLE MYOPIA wherein there is a controlled degree of ametropia in a healthy eye, and DEGENERATIVE MYOPIA wherein axial elongation beyond the normal limits of growth occurs and degenerative changes are superimposed. If this assumption is correct, simple myopia is logically regarded as part of the biological series of ametropia, has no specific ætiology and requires no treatment beyond optical correction when this is necessary.

Viewed in the most general terms there are two principal and completely contradictory theories regarding the genesis of degenerative myopia which logically imply two schools of thought equally contradictory in every respect as to the ocular hygiene and the treatment desirable for the myope. The classical view—as suited the mechanistic philosophy of the last century—was the very simple hypothesis that axial myopia was due to mechanical stretching of the posterior part of the globe owing to weakness of the sclera. It depended on early anatomical observations that highly myopic eyes were egg-shaped and that the posterior part of the sclera was thin. Innumerable hypotheses were put forward to explain the occurrence of this weakening, but since myopia was seen to commence at the age when close work began to occupy attention and habitually progressed throughout the years of school life, near work and reading were popularly arraigned as the primary causal factors. Looked at in its broadest sense the essential feature of this conception was that the *degenerative changes in the myopic eye were secondary to and determined by a distension of the coats of the eyeball*, which itself was *due to influences in the internal or external environment determined either by the health of the individual or his habits*. Inconsistencies in this as a complete philosophy were, however, very obvious and it was generally admitted that, in addition, an inherent and often inherited tendency to weakness of the sclera must also be postulated.

During the last half-century, however, dissatisfaction began to grow with this purely mechanistic hypothesis. That it could not contain all the truth was suggested, on the one hand, by the accumulating evidence of the influence of heredity on the incidence of myopia and, on the other, by the apparent lack of the importance of environmental factors as seen in the occurrence of short-sight in favourable and its absence in unfavourable conditions, as well as its individualistic incidence or progression in the same environment and even in one of two eyes. Moreover, although it was tempting to explain the degenerative changes on the basis of mechanical stretching, a view so simple left many unanswered questions—why do they occur not at the times of active stretching but long thereafter? Why do the changes not run *pari passu* with the degree of stretching, for they may be absent in extreme degrees of axial elongation and may be present with an axial length shorter than the normal emmetropic eye? Why are all the characteristic changes—the choroidal atrophy, the myopic crescent, the supertraction, and so on—found, although less commonly, in all refractive states, having most of the characteristics seen in senile eyes? From out of these doubts there arose a completely divergent hypothesis adumbrated by Steiger (1913) and developed most enthusiastically by Vogt (1924) and his school: whereas in the majority of persons there exists enough co-ordination of growth between the ocular tissues to secure the development of an approximately emmetropic eye, high myopia is determined primarily by an overgrowth of the master-tissue—the retina; the stretching of the globe and the anatomical peculiarities of the myopic eye are secondary to this; and associated with these phenomena inherited degenerative factors play a prominent role. The philosophy of this view is *biological rather than mechanistic* and that *the environment plays a part of insignificant importance.*

We shall now proceed to examine briefly the main arguments put forward in defence of the more important theories. Most of them are imaginative, some are amusing, but all of them have been advocated with serious enthusiasm by their authors. They may be summarized as follows:

A. DISTENSION OF THE SCLERA.

    I. *Distension of normal sclera* as a result of:

        1. Increased intra-ocular pressure, due to:

            (a) the extra-ocular muscles
            (b) the intra-ocular muscles
            (c) insidious chronic glaucoma.

        2. Moulding of the globe by the extra-ocular muscles.
        3. Traction on the choroid by the intra-ocular muscles.
        4. Traction by the optic nerves.

    II. *Distension of sclera weakened by:*

        1. Ocular congestion due to:

            (a) posture
            (b) severe manual labour
            (c) blocking of the circulation at the disc or of the vortex veins
            (d) cardio-vascular diseases
            (e) visual difficulties
            (f) autolysis of the sclera.

        2. Choroido-retinitis.
        3. General deficiency disease.
        4. Endocrine disturbances.
        5. General debilitating disease.
        6. Intrinsic weakness.

B. GENETICALLY DETERMINED DISHARMONY IN GROWTH among the ocular tissues dominated by the retina, frequently combined with abiotrophic degenerations forming a multiple but usually related hereditary complex.

C. A TELEOLOGICAL explanation has been put forward to account for myopia on the grounds that it is a useful adaptation to the artificial environment of civilization: this has little to be said in its favour.

A. MECHANICAL AND ENVIRONMENTAL THEORIES

Mechanistic theories to explain the development of high myopia were the only popular explanation during the 19th century when the essential factor was considered to be a distension of the sclera, whether this tissue was normal or weakened by intrinsic influences.

I. DISTENSION OF A NORMAL SCLERA has been said to be caused by several factors:

1. By an *increased intra-ocular pressure*, which has been said to be caused by the action of the extrinsic or intrinsic ocular muscles or by the presence of a chronic glaucoma.

The Extra-ocular Muscles. von Graefe (1857) was the first to attribute the rise of pressure to the compression of the globe by the extra-ocular muscles, particularly the medial recti acting in convergence. The implication that excessive close work is partly responsible for myopia lies behind this as well as many other theories of the origin of the condition. Stilling (1885–1905) invoked the oblique muscles, postulating that deformation of the sclera is essentially determined by the configuration of the orbits. He and his pupils (Cohen, 1889; Romano-Catania, 1889; Krotoschin, 1891) measured large numbers of skulls and concluded that the myopic orbit is broad and low, one feature of a broad face, and surmised that the lengthening of the globe was due to the pressure of the superior oblique muscle sweeping over the top of the globe from an unusually low trochlea. This muscle is, of course, used in looking downwards at near work. Most other observers, however, have failed to find confirmatory evidence either by anatomical or radiological measurement (Schmidt-Rimpler, 1885–89; Weiss, 1885–88; Baer, 1888; Gamper, 1914; Favaloro, 1927; and others).

Mannhardt (1871–87) believed that in myopes the orbits were spaced far apart, so that anatomical configuration would involve an increased pupillary distance and therefore excessive convergence. His measurements were originally confirmed by Pflüger (1876–87), but subsequent observers have found no constant or significant relationship (Clarke, 1925; and many others).

The Intra-ocular Muscles. Dobrowolsky (1868–69) and Erismann (1871) attributed the rise in pressure to excessive accommodation, a suggestion amply disproved experimentally (Hess and Heine, 1898), while A. Wood (1916) suggested the opposite—that lack of accommodation discouraged the drainage of the aqueous through Schlemm's canal by failure of the pumping action of the ciliary muscle upon the scleral spur.

Insidious Chronic Glaucoma. A further school of thought considered that, apart from intermittent activities, the tension in the myopic eye is habitually higher than normal (Arlt, 1876; and others), and we have already noted the frequent association of myopia with glaucoma; high myopia in this view is essentially a type of chronic and insidious glaucoma (Stilling, 1905; Kraupa, 1917–31; Elschnig, 1922). It would seem obvious, however, that the distension of the sclera, with the preferential thinning at the posterior pole, particularly at the nasal side, and the vast difference between the globular buphthalmic globe and the egg-shaped myopic eye, cannot be explained by the mechanical factor of pressure alone. The suggestion that the muscles support the anterior segment of the globe so that the posterior part alone is distensible, does not seem convincing.

2. *The moulding action of the extrinsic ocular muscles*, together with their influence in raising the intra-ocular pressure or in causing venous congestion, was enthusiastically

acclaimed as a principal ætiological factor in the genesis of myopia following the lead of von Graefe (1857) and Donders (1864). As a rule, most stress was laid upon the horizontal recti, particularly the medial muscles which become especially effective on convergence when the eye is said to be pressed on the inner orbital wall, but others have arraigned the obliques which squeeze the globe between them (Dobrowolsky, 1868–69; Müller, 1894–1926; Gallus, 1906; Clarke, 1925; Jackson, 1932; and many others). No one has produced any positive evidence in favour of the theory and the sole experimenter (Ascher, 1895), who induced prolonged accommodation and convergence in rabbits by the use of eserine and advancement operations, had negative results. Finally, the contraction of the orbicularis muscle by the uncorrected myope in screwing the lids together was supposed by Burton (1942) to cause a raised ocular tension and distension of the sclera.

3. *Traction on the Choroid.* It was suggested by Iwanoff (1869) and Horner (1873) that the ciliary muscle in accommodation pulled on the choroid, tearing it away from the optic disc and inducing atrophy, but the classical experiments of Hensen and Voelckers (1868) disproved this possibility. On the other hand, van Alphen (1961) suggested that accommodation had the opposite effect of preventing an increase in the axial length of the globe, claiming that the traction exerted on the choroid by the tonus of the ciliary muscle tended to counteract the effect of the intra-ocular pressure in stretching the sclera.

4. *Traction by the Optic Nerve.* That a pull by the optic nerve on the posterior pole of the eye leading to scleral distension is effective particularly on convergence and downward torsion of the eyes on reading, was first suggested by Hasner (1874) to explain the origin of the myopic crescent. This view was supported by Paulsen (1882) and particularly by Weiss (1885), and at a later date by Jackson (1890–1935), Emmert (1905), Stock (1907–8) and others. Anatomical considerations, however, show this to be unlikely (Widmark, 1898–1909) and it has repeatedly been shown that relative or absolute shortness of the optic nerve has no relation to myopia, in the highest degrees of which the nerve may be found in a slack S-shaped configuration in the apex of the orbit (Stilling, 1905; Hanssen, 1921; and others). Moreover, myopia is not an accompaniment of exophthalmos, whether continuous or intermittent.

II. WEAKENING OF THE SCLERA has been suggested by many to be the cause of the ocular distension. The factors suggested as responsible for the weakening have been numerous.

1. *Congestion of the sclera* has been postulated as the ætiological factor and many theories have been offered to explain how this state may be produced. Levinsohn (1913–31) believed that the *dependent position of the head* during close work was the most important influence, since the position induced congestion while the effect of gravity pulled the globes upon the optic nerves. He backed these beliefs with experiments on apes, keeping them horizontally in boxes for long periods so that they had to look at the floor and converge upon their food. His results were confirmed by Essed and Soewarno (1928), but not by Behr (1919) and Marchesani (1929–31). Moreover, it has to be remembered that primates kept in captivity are frequently myopic (Young, 1961–65), that the conditions of the experiment do not tend towards normal development, that the usual myopic eye has a slack optic nerve, and that on depressing the head the eye moves forward a negligible amount or not at all (Dinger, 1919; Wick, 1923–25; Bartels, 1923–31; Comberg, 1928).

Severe manual labour, particularly in the stooping position or involving heavy lifting, has also been said to lead to congestion and scleral deformation. The most vocal advocate of this view was Edridge-Green (1924–25) who would thus account for high degrees of myopia among heavy workers. He ascribed the mechanism to venous congestion involving increased ocular tension and believed that " acute myopia " could be caused thereby.

Local muscular action has also been said to induce congestion of the eye by blocking the vortex veins, particularly in the acts of converging and reading. Arlt (1876) considered the medial rectus and inferior oblique the greatest offenders in this respect, Stilling (1885–1905) the superior oblique. Marlow (1935), on the other hand, laid the essential blame on the constant efforts expended by the ocular muscles to overcome the muscular imbalance which he found to be constantly present. The congestion determined by *general circulatory disturbances*, cardio-vascular disease or even inflammations of the nasal sinuses, has not been forgotten (Batten, 1892).

Visual difficulties have been said to exert an influence on the development and progress of myopia, perhaps by increasing ocular congestion. The prevalence of corneal opacities in myopes suggested this view to van Dyck (1904), Straub (1909), Meyerhof (1910–14) and E. Holm (1927), but it can hardly be maintained that these are more common in myopes than hypermetropes. Similarly, astigmatism has been credited with a causal role.[1] In the absence of visual defects, excessive convergence and strain have been said to cause myopia, an effect enhanced by reading or working in poor illumination (Cohn, 1883–92; Harman, 1919–23).

That weakness of the sclera is caused by a process of *tissue-autolysis* was suggested by Lindner (1939–41). Eye-strain, in his view, brings about a congestion of the choriocapillaris and autolytic enzymes in the albuminous exudation therefrom soften the connective tissue of the sclera. He claimed that normally the sclera is protected from this action by the suprachoroidea so that the localization of the distension to the posterior pole of the eye could be explained by the thinness of the suprachoroidea and the thickness of the choriocapillaris in this region. During the period of growth the sclera is softer than after maturity, so that myopia normally develops in youth, and a posterior staphyloma is due to the sudden localized disappearance of the suprachoroidea instead of its more usual gradual attenuation. Such a theory has obviously stimulated criticism (Weber, 1940; and others).

2. *Inflammation of the sclera* either by itself or by contiguity with the choroid and retina was a view first suggested by von Graefe (1854), and although he changed his ideas at a later date, the theory that a chronic and insidious uveitis was responsible for the degenerative changes was long maintained (Cowan, 1942; and others). It is, of course, true that choroiditis may occasionally precede the development of myopia, and is probably the cause of certain cases of rapidly developing myopia of low degree in previously emmetropic adults; and it has been argued that the atrophic condition of the myopic choroid may favour the incidence of inflammatory diseases; but overwhelming pathological evidence disproves a general relationship of cause and effect, particularly since the usual myopic changes are purely degenerative in nature. Tuberculous choroiditis has been particularly stressed in this respect (Feigenbaum, 1925; Hirsch, 1925).

3. *Scleral weakness* has been attributed to *dietary deficiency*. A calcium deficiency of the blood was claimed by D. J. Wood (1927) and Fleming (1934) to be a common condition in the years of rapid growth and this, governed perhaps by a parathyroid disturbance and deficiency of vitamin D, was said to lead to failure of the resistance of the sclera (Walker, 1932; Sorsby *et al.*, 1935). The development of myopia in this view has been compared with the onset of flat-foot and the stretching of other supportive tissues (Kuschel, 1923; Incze, 1929): it is, in a sense, scleral rickets. A. A. Knapp (1939–42) reported scleral œdema and weakness in dogs and rats fed on a diet deficient in calcium and vitamin D and marked clinical regression of myopia when the deficiency was made good.

The importance of dietary protein has often been emphasized. Gardiner (1956–58) held that myopic children more often refuse protein and found that a high dietary

[1] Mende (1906), Katel-Bloch (1906), Meyerhof (1910–14), Harman (1913), Steiger (1911–19), Clarke (1925), and others.

intake of animal proteins was beneficial in preventing the deterioration of myopia. At a later date (1960) he claimed that vegetable protein had a preventive influence against the progression of short-sight and that a high ratio of animal to vegetable protein had an adverse influence.

4. *Endocrine influences* have been thought by some authors to be responsible for scleral weakness. A disorder of growth determined by a disturbance of the pituitary gland has found its most authoritative exponent in Keith (1925). He contended that the growth of the fibroblastic tissues of the body was governed by this gland, the extent of its influence being seen in such diseases as acromegaly, and stressed the coincidence of the common onset or exacerbation of myopia at puberty, a period when the endocrine system is unusually active and unstable. He claimed that if the sclerotic fibroblasts lay sound material, all will be well whatever use or abuse the eyes be given; if the material is unsound or wrongly laid, these forces which leave the normal eye unaffected may cause damage. This view was supported by others, particularly Argañaraz (1922) who drew a parallel between the myopia and the ectasia of the cornea in keratoconus. Growth of the eye in association with growth of the skull was stressed by Rocha (1942). Besides the hypophysis, the thymus (Nicolato, 1929) and thyroid (Bothman, 1931) have also been implicated.

5. *General disease and debility* are widely thought to be responsible for the scleral weakness leading to myopia. It is a commonplace that in youth short-sight may start or become accentuated in periods of illness and debility and we have seen that it may appear in these circumstances even in adult life. Tuberculosis and syphilis have been credited with an ætiological significance (Fracassi, 1929), as has anæmia (E. Holm, 1925–28). Recent experimental evidence for the influence of a transient rise of temperature was given by Maurice and Mushin (1966) who found in rabbits that a permanent myopic change followed a rise in intra-ocular pressure if the body temperature were raised.

6. That distension of the sclera is due to a primary *intrinsic weakness* of this tissue (a scleromalacia) has been widely accepted since the original suggestion of Mauthner (1876) and its advocacy by Schnabel and Herrnheiser (1895), its popularity being essentially due to the difficulty of explaining the incidence of myopia on mechanical concepts alone. A recent supporter of such a theory is Sondermann (1950) who traced myopia as a consequence of the posterior sclerectasia which develops in fœtal life. Blach and his colleagues (1965) proposed a somewhat similar possible ætiology. This, of course, is little more than an introduction to the biological theory.

Throughout all this maze of theorizing, much of it mutually contradictory and most of it fanciful, there run two main threads of thought linking the onset and progress of myopia, whether simple or degenerative, with environmental and constitutional factors—EXCESSIVE CLOSE WORK and GENERAL DEBILITY. That ill-health and debility are factors in the progress of myopia is probably true although the likelihood that they play an adjuvant role only is suggested by the fact that most illness does not involve myopic changes while the occurrence of a unilateral defect becomes inexplicable. In any event if this view is accepted, the logical treatment of myopia by improving the general health is a very good thing. The importance of near work in the ætiology of myopia, however, must receive further examination if only because the consequences of its logical application in prophylaxis and therapeusis are very far-reaching.

The theory that excessive close work is a determining factor in the ætiology of myopia depends mainly on statistical evidence, and although such evidence by itself is always dangerous, it must be admitted to be impressive. Such a concept was suggested by Kepler (1611) and its general acceptance in the nineteenth century had great social consequences. We have already seen that from almost every country in the world figures have been produced proving that myopia is rare before school age, that it gradually increases during school life and that it reaches its highest point in the years of most concentrated study at the universities. The statistics of Cohn (1867–92)—the classical advocate of the occurrence of *school myopia*—may be taken as typical : a proportion of 1·4% of myopes in the lower grades of schools rising to 60% in the universities of Germany.

FIG. 369.—THE SO-CALLED "SCHOOL MYOPIA".

The typical attitude of Chinese children at school some years ago. The form of education which had persisted for 2,000 years consisted in memorizing and reproducing thousands of character-hieroglyphs while the children, aged 4 to 16, crouched at low stools. These habits are now almost entirely superseded by more modern methods (O. D. Rasmussen).

Several other observers have compared this tendency among academic populations.[1] The figures are clear; they appear to show that myopia was fostered and flourished in the schools; but it is by no means as clear that the deduction drawn from the statistics is correct, that the factors of growth and development are not the significant determinants and close work and study incidentals. The fact that the hygienically appalling habits of the Chinese of past generations coincided with a high racial incidence of myopia (Fig. 369) (Rasmussen, 1936) is offset by the fact that many and as high myopes are found among illiterate Arabs who know not of school (Butler, 1916) or the observation that myopia is non-existent equally among literate and illiterate primitive Negroes (S. Holm, 1937).

[1] Derby (1874–83), Ochapovsky (1935), Lindner (1947), Parnell (1951), Sato (1965), Riffenburgh (1965), Dunphy *et al.* (1968), E. Goldschmidt (1968).

Again, culture has been associated with myopia. If we take British figures alone, any conclusion can be reached. James Ware as early as 1813 claimed that among 10,000 British Guardsmen not a dozen had been rejected for military service for short-sight in the space of 20 years, while in one college at Oxford 32 out of 127 students examined were found to be myopic. Subsequently Lindner (1946) published somewhat similar statistics in Austria: the incidence of myopia in the general population is 3·5% whereas those engaged in close work show a much higher percentage (type-setters, 60%, cloth-darners, 70%). He found also that 60% to 65% of Catholic priests develop myopia in young adult life, a phenomenon which he compared to the late myopia he described occurring in college students in the United States of America—a phenomenon rare in Europe where children study closely all through their school days and not only towards the end. Since Ware's observations the most contradictory opinions have been expressed: that myopia is commonest among the educated and those engaged on near work (Doyne, 1923), and that it is equally common among farm labourers as among those who spend their life at the desk (Galloway, 1923); that it is essentially a disease of urban and industrial life (Kirk, 1921; Wanspa and Limpaphayom, 1965), and that it is more common in rural schools than urban schools (Thomson, 1919); that it abounds in the poorer, unhygienic schools (Harman, 1919–37), and that myopia is more common in the better lighted and ventilated schools (Lawson, 1898); that an improvement in school hygiene decreases myopia considerably (Moutinho and de Mattos, 1929), and that between its incidence in schools old or new with bad or good hygiene there is nothing to choose (Straub, 1909; Dinger, 1919). It is obvious that statistically any conclusion can be reached. Moreover, making international comparisons, we have already seen that the incidence of myopia is comparable in the cultured and industrial communities of Western Europe to that among the Arabs who do no close work and live in the desert spaces or the inhabitants of the West Indies where study is not prevalent and life more enclosed.

The converse argument may be raised. Largely as a result of Cohn's advocacy the hygiene of schools in many countries has been much improved over the last half century, but there is no clear evidence that myopia has decreased. This question has received considerable attention in the Scandinavian countries. Ask's (1910) figures for Sweden are better than those of Key (1885) by 2%; and Nordgren (1936) found that myopia had diminished in that country by one-third between 1894 and 1920. On the other hand, Heinonen (1923) could find no difference in Finland between 1910 and 1927, nor could E. Holm (1925) or E. Goldschmidt (1968) in Denmark between 1881 (Tscherning, 1883) and the time of their studies. In the complexities of changing social conditions, however, it would be difficult to derive any conclusions regarding near work and visual hygiene; but one would certainly expect a dramatic reduction in the incidence of myopia over a half-century which has seen (in some countries at any rate) a revolution in the care of the sight of children, an immeasurable improvement in hygienic measures and a revolution in lighting from the candle to kerosene and from gas to electric light. More conclusive is the mass of evidence of the favourable behaviour of some myopic eyes under the worst environmental conditions, the unfavourable behaviour of others under the best, the great difference in behaviour of many eyes in the same conditions and even the difference of behaviour of the two eyes of the same individual.

These arguments depended essentially on the concept that the progress of myopia was due to an increase in the axial length of the eye. Sato (1957–65), on the other hand, claimed that the increase of " school myopia " was essentially caused by an adaptive increase in the refractive power of the lens caused by continued close work, a view, however, not generally held.

B. BIOLOGICAL THEORIES

In contradistinction to these mechanistic concepts the theory adumbrated by Steiger (1913)[1] and elaborated and popularized by Vogt (1924) and his disciples (Meyer, 1926; Vontobel, 1929; and others) has a more biological significance. It follows from the observation of the hereditary determination of axial myopia, of the preferential thinning of the sclera at the posterior pole, of the fact that retinal degeneration occurs only secondarily to choroidal atrophy, and that atrophic changes occur separately in time and in degree from axial elongation and themselves are frequently hereditarily determined. In brief it is assumed that each coat of the eye, the retina, choroid and sclera, has its own growth potential; and just as the neural ectoderm determines the embryological growth of the eye and even when transplanted into mesodermal tissues will mould them to its requirements,[2] so in extra-uterine development the retina remains the master tissue. As a general rule there is enough co-ordination among the different tissues to achieve a result approaching emmetropia; in myopia an overgrowth of the retina—usually genetically determined—produces incongruence. As the retina enlarges it pushes towards the posterior pole, the sclera, adapting itself to this growth, becomes thinned and the various anatomical phenomena characteristic of myopia are produced (crescent, supertraction, etc.). The choroid, rendered susceptible by stretching, falls a ready prey to the influence of inherited degenerative tendencies with the development of atrophy resembling senile changes, and the retina, dependent upon the choroid for its nutriment, degenerates secondarily. The axial elongation and the degenerative changes are not therefore strictly a hereditary unity, but a combination of individually varying factors which mutually aid each other's development and need not necessarily become manifest together.

[1] p. 234.   [2] Vol. III, p. 49.

Vogt's view was that the determinant in developing myopia is the ecto-dermal tissue, the retina itself. Whether one or other of the components of the retina is the more important is not as yet a matter of debate. It has, however, been suggested that the retinal pigmentary epithelium may be paramount in this respect, a suggestion supported by its early degeneration and the electro-oculographic changes in high myopia (Blach, 1965). A parallel may be seen in the ectatic coloboma associated with a developmental failure of this layer.[1]

On the other hand, the influence of mesodermal structures has been stressed by Waardenburg (1963) who considered that the mesoderm sur-rounding the retina may be normal but stretched; it may, however, be defectively organized by the retina or simply developmentally inadequate. A more direct implication of the mesoderm was suggested by Poos (1950) who postulated that refractive errors originate in a disparity between the sclera and the muscles acting upon it; when the muscles cease to grow they exercise a restraining influence on the sclera, a stabilization which develops later in myopic subjects. On the other hand, an arrest of development of the sclera at the fifth fœtal month, for the posterior part of this tissue is the last to develop, might result in a thinness and weakness of this structure.

Basing his thesis on the lack of variation in the refraction among the inhabitants of Gabon in Equatorial Africa, one of the most ancient strains of the Negro race and a very pure racial group, S. Holm (1937) found support for the hereditary nature of refractive errors. It is usually accepted that " primitive " people show little variability from the characteristics of their primordial ancestors when compared with " progressive " peoples: this is taken to be the anthropological basis for their primitiveness. On this basis, high myopia, as well as other extreme refractive errors, is an exaggerated manifestation of the great qualities of variability characteristic of progressive peoples. As pointed out by Waardenburg (1963), however, myopes in a primitive community might be at a disadvantage if their survival depended on hunting or other activities requiring good distance vision.

Some authors would follow out this theory to its fullest implications. As an outpost of the brain, the retina in its overgrowth indicates advanced cerebral develop-ment and the myope is consequently an intelligent person (Steiger, 1913; von Moers-Messmer, 1940), a claim which has been contested (Young, 1963). If myopes as a class are, indeed, intelligent, it might be argued that their inability to compete equally with others at school in sport inclines them to studious and introverted habits (van Alphen et al., 1953; Young, 1967); but pressed to its logical extreme—as it has been—the suggestion that a high intelligence is associated with myopia, and that consequently Jews are more intelligent than Gentiles, and Americans (particularly Californians[2]) are more stupid than Europeans, would not meet with universal acceptance!

To summarize, it must be admitted that we are still to-day essentially ignorant of the ætiology of degenerative myopia. Two factors stand out clearly—the influence of heredity and the relation of the development of myopia to the processes of growth. We know that the condition is to a large extent hereditarily determined as are most growth processes; we may

[1] Vol. III, p. 613.   [2] p. 236.

suspect also that the heredity is multiple, axial length, degenerative changes and pathological complications being determined by different and frequently related genetic influences, a knowledge of the exact interplay of which must await future research. We know also that the development of the condition is largely bound up with the processes of growth. In general it may be said that the lengthening of the posterior segment of the eye commences only during the period of active growth, for elongation of an eye which has remained of normal dimensions up to the age of 20 is rare. The eye shares with the brain the peculiarity of having a precocious growth, for at the age of four the brain is 84% of its full size, the eye 78%, and the rest of the body only 21%. After this both eye and brain increase in size slowly until at about 20 years the adult dimensions have been reached. In a sense axial myopia may be interpreted as a continuation of this precocity, and a failure of the arresting influence to act. But we do not yet know what this influence is nor what tissue is primarily at fault, whether the ectoderm or the mesoderm.

Apart from predetermined hereditary influences it is natural to suggest other factors which may influence the processes of growth, one of which is undoubtedly nutrition, a second, salutary exercise and a balanced mode of life, and a third, the endocrine system. A further incidental factor which seems to have no inconsiderable influence is physical debility and illness. Of one thing, however, we can be reasonably sure—that the influence of close work is incidental in the ætiology of a condition which in children is primarily predetermined and constitutional and not environmental, effective, if at all, secondarily in so far as it is associated with a lack of full facilities for normal and healthy development. The possibility remains, however, that after the period of growth has passed some influence can be exerted by close work which involves constant visual strain (E. Goldschmidt, 1968).

Treatment

The treatment of degenerative myopia will naturally follow the ætiological view adopted by the practitioner, and it is not surprising that the multiplicity of theories regarding its causation has led to the adoption of equally numerous and equally contradictory methods of therapeusis. If myopia is regarded as a problem in mechanics involving the posterior pole of the eye, mechanical treatment is obviously appropriate; if it is looked upon as the result of near work and eye-strain, near work should be eliminated; if it is admitted that it is influenced by the processes of growth and development, everything should be done to ensure the healthy evolution of these processes; and if it is believed that it is essentially predetermined in the genes and once established cannot be influenced, then nothing in logic need be done and the only rational method of tackling the problem is by eugenic prophylaxis. The tendency for the disciples of each theory has been to be more royal than the king; and to the unbiased the difficulty in taking a reasoned and logical view is that all these theories are equally unproven and unsubstantiated.

The extremes to which the obsession that myopia was a mechanical problem has led ophthalmologists are extraordinary, sometimes within recent years. It was due to contraction of the extra-ocular muscles upon the globe, therefore the muscles had to be cut, at first the obliques (Phillips, 1841; A. Bonnet, 1842; Müller, 1926) and later, following von Graefe's advocacy, a crop of tenotomies involved the medial recti and sometimes both horizontal recti. Accommodation was at fault, therefore atropine or some other cycloplegic was given to abolish it[1] or, emanating from Donders's (1864) observation that watchmakers who use a uniocular loupe do not develop myopia, one eye was atropinized to discourage convergence (Luedde, 1932). An increased intra-ocular pressure was the cause and so an iridectomy (Dransart, 1884–85), or repeated paracenteses (Grunert, 1928–34) were performed, or enthusiasm was satisfied with the simple instillation of pilocarpine or eserine (Dianoux, 1912; Grunert, 1934) or adrenaline (Wiener, 1927). To stimulate an atrophic process or to remove congestion subconjunctival injections of saline, dionine or mercury salts were prescribed (de Bourgon, 1895; Hertel, 1910; and many others) or alternatively 10% saline injected intravenously (Filatov and Volokitenko, 1940). The sclera was weak, therefore the eye should be massaged (Dianoux, 1912); it was bulging and so should be compressed firmly into the orbit (Domec, 1912; Bourdeaux, 1914); it was congested and therefore it should be given rolling exercises (d'Ansan, 1926)— all of which expedients have their many exponents today.

Myopia is due to eye-strain and therefore full correcting spectacles should be worn constantly whereupon progression of the myopia will assuredly cease (Donders, 1864; Förster, 1885; Jackson, 1892–1935; Heine, 1901; Hertel, 1903; and others); it is accelerated by accommodation, therefore an under-correction must be given, or at the least, weak spectacles for near work (Cohn, 1871; Hirschberg, 1904); the maintenance of accommodation is necessary so that while distant correction is unimportant and should not be worn unless needed, fully correcting spectacles must always be worn for near work (Laval, 1941); it is due to the strain of astigmatic errors and these therefore must receive minute correction (Harman, 1913; Clarke, 1925); it is due to the strains of heterophoria making the extra-ocular muscles taut, therefore all latent muscular imbalance must be corrected with prisms (Marlow, 1935); it is due to lack of congruence between convergence and accommodation, therefore the myopia must be under-corrected or converging prisms worn for reading (Hay, 1914); its progress is not influenced by spectacles in any way so that it does not matter whether these are worn or not (Blegvad, 1918; Wätzold, 1924; Hansell, 1924; Cowan, 1942). It is due to a dependent posture of the head in reading, therefore myopes should read sitting erect, mechanical devices being employed to enforce this if necessary (Cohn, 1883–92). It is due to bad lighting or ventilation, therefore abundance of light and air must be provided (Cohn, 1871–92; Harman, 1919–37); it is due to the malign influence of too much light and this should therefore be regulated (Junius, 1920); it is due to physical effort and therefore manual labour and gymnastics must be forbidden (Edridge-Green, 1924–25); and finally—this being repeated all through the literature for over a century—it is due to study and close work and therefore close work should be banned, the school is its breeding ground and therefore the school as such must be abolished and education, so far as it is permissible, should be mediated by sound and touch rather than by sight (Ware, 1813; Cohn, 1871–92; Harman, 1913–37; and a host of others).

The general diet and medication of myopic subjects has again been at the whim of

---

[1] Derby (1874), Schultz-Zehden (1908), Pollock (1916), Lancaster (1953), Gostin (1962), Abraham (1966), and others.

the particular (and usually unfounded) theory as to the origin of the condition. It follows that vitamins B, D and E have all had their advocates. Regulation of the dietary protein in quantity and nature, calcium adjuncts, endocrine therapy (thyroid and placental implants), osmotherapy or anticoagulants have all their supporters, but no conclusive evidence exists of their value.

Conversely it is said that myopia is self-determined and amenable to no treatment but that complications should be minimized by treating associated ocular diseases (usually a low-grade uveitis, Cowan, 1942); and again that the degenerative changes are genetically determined abiotrophies, so that they, like the myopia, are outside the control of medicine (Vogt, 1924).

Amid this confusion of theorizing to steer a rational course is obviously difficult, and the easiest and only profitable course to adopt in this book is to give a summary of the principles on which our own practice is based. This, of course, will not meet with universal acceptance and, indeed, will be at variance with the convictions of many. We would therefore hasten to divest it of any claim to universally accepted authority.

In general terms the treatment of degenerative myopia should run along three general lines—the correction of the optical error, adequate visual hygiene and the building up of the general health. As a supplement to these, prophylactic measures should be considered, and as an appendix, the surgical measures occasionally practised will be noted.

Prophylaxis. We have already studied the question of the inheritance of myopia and the degenerations with which it is associated, and the evidence is without doubt sufficient to warrant the adoption of prophylactic eugenic measures. There need be no restraint on marriage and procreation among simple myopes; but a parent with degenerative myopia should be warned that any offspring will be liable to the same disability according to the laws of recessive Mendelian inheritance. Two highly myopic parents with degenerative changes should never—from the medical point of view—have children. The children of such parents should be closely supervised from their earliest years and if an increase in refractivity appears to evolve more rapidly than would normally be expected, they should be treated as if they were myopes, particularly if the early clinical signs suggestive of degenerative changes appear.

The Correction of the Optical Error. Although there seems little scientific justification for the claim commonly advanced that the constant wearing of precisely correct spectacles prevents the progress of the myopia or preserves vision, nothing but good can accrue from the elimination of visual strain and the proper training of visual habits, particularly in children; to them, however, the greatest value of spectacles is to aid mental and educational development by opening out the world to their observation. After the growing period has passed and visual habits have been established, if for any reason, æsthetic or otherwise, the spectacles are not worn continuously, and if a blank world is accepted without the constant output of visual strain to overcome the disability, it is difficult to imagine how medical harm can result. In the ordering of spectacles in high myopes we have already seen that the full correction can rarely be tolerated, and an under-correction, sometimes of considerable extent, is necessary to attain comfort: on the whole, the lenses which give the best vision with the greatest comfort are advisable.

In the higher degrees of myopia *contact lenses*[1] are more optically efficient than spectacles, since the distortions and aberrations associated with the latter are eliminated, while the close approximation of the lens to the cornea results in the formation of a larger image (by about 20% in the case of $-10\cdot0$ D). This enhances their value as an aid to vision in cases of myopic degeneration of the macula (Tower, 1947). Moreover, they largely eliminate the cosmetic disadvantages of spectacles. They are not universally tolerated, but many high myopes wear them with considerable comfort; in many sports their use is highly advantageous. In cases wherein degenerative changes have affected the macular area, further visual aids, such as *telescopic spectacles*, may sometimes be of value.

Ocular Hygiene. In his classical work on refraction, Donders (1864) stated categorically that for myopia, as such, there is no therapeutic treatment since it consists of an anomaly of form capable of no improvement for which only hygienic measures can prevent further development. Any high myope with degenerative changes should maintain as high a standard of ocular hygiene as possible. When close work is done illumination should be good and adequately arranged,[2] the posture should be easy and natural, the clarity of print should be suitably supervised and undue ocular fatigue should be avoided. Especially is this so in children, but it would seem reasonable to suggest that so long as the corrected visual acuity is adequate, proper care of visual hygiene is maintained and the general health is good, education need not seriously be curtailed. *The amount of work should be adjusted to the general physical and mental development of the child rather than to the degree of the myopia*, and only if the child appears strained under the forced or competitive stresses of school-life—which are sometimes considerable—should he be withdrawn from school or his study cut down. It is certainly the case that the regime of many modern schools imposes far too much application to books upon young children at an age when they require all their available vitality for physical growth and development, a generalization which applies particularly to girls at the age of puberty. In the exigencies of our artificial civilization, early application to work with a neglect of open-air pursuits may be an advantage in some respects, but it is an advantage sometimes gained at a cost. If there is evidence that increasing myopia is associated with physical debility, school-life should be temporarily abandoned and health with abundance of fresh air and exercise with adequately controlled study secured by a change to a good environment. Only when the visual acuity is inadequate for ordinary reading need the

[1] p. 774. [2] p. 589.

child be sent to a school where special non-visual educational methods are employed.

MYOPE SCHOOLS (" sight-saving classes ") were first started in London by Harman (1907) and were adopted in many countries of the world at the time when myopia was widely believed to be caused by excessive study (in the United States, Irwin, 1920–27; in Canada, MacDonald, 1923; in European countries such as Denmark, E. Holm, 1923). In these institutions an attempt was made as far as possible to provide individual tuition in a curriculum in which the cultivation of associative memory was made the first consideration, where the sense of touch was relied upon more than sight. Models which could be handled were used in place of pictures, and oral tuition largely took the place of reading out of books. These are irrelevant unless in the few cases of children in whom degenerative changes in the retina have rendered them visually handicapped and unable to participate in normal educative methods.

Similar considerations should be applied to adults, modified to meet the requirements of their case and their economic circumstances. In the choice of a career, if it seems possible that progressive changes will cause visual deterioration in later life, it is obviously economically unwise to choose a calling which involves the constant study of books or figures, and better that interest should be diverted to an avocation of a less visually exacting nature, preferably one which can, to some extent, be continued if the central vision eventually fails. The gravity of the economic problem thus presented is seen in Harman's (1922) figures: he found among 480 myopes between the working ages of 20 and 60, some 53% of those engaged in continuous fine work became seriously inconvenienced, the proportion increasing with the degree of myopia (33·7% of those between 3 and 3 D, 66·5% between 5 and 10 D, and 77·4% over 10 D), while only 9·4% of those whose occupation did not entail close work experienced a critical failure of capacity.

Supervision of the general health is of considerable importance, particularly in adolescent myopes. As we have seen, the competitive strains of school-life should be adjusted, if necessary, to meet the capacity of the child; relaxation and open-air exercise should be stressed, for few children should be asked to do what a fully developed man in the years of his discretion usually refuses to do—to work indoors all evening after working indoors all day. Convalescences from illness should be prolonged, the diet should be liberal and balanced and, especially in rapidly growing children and in those about the age of puberty, it seems not unreasonable, and it sometimes appears beneficial, to bulk up the available supply of calcium. With the calcium a liberal supply of vitamin D is necessary in order to promote absorption and to maintain the calcium-phosphorus ratio. The best sources of calcium and vitamin D are an abundance of milk and green vegetables, but these may be augmented, when necessary, by synthetic preparations.

Operative treatment for myopia, apart from the attempts to mould practice by theory which we have already considered, has run along two lines—the abolition of the optical defect by removal of the lens, and the amelioration of the refraction by plastic operations upon the globe.

Removal of the lens. Attention was first drawn to the visual advantages of removal of the lens in high myopia by Boerhaave (1708), and Janin (1772) of Lyons reported the change from short-sight to long-sight after the removal of cataract. Fukala (1890–96), of Vienna, however, was the first to popularize the operation. If an eye with an axial myopia of − 18 or − 20 D is deprived of its lens it will become emmetropic without any correcting lens, inasmuch as parallel rays of light will be focused upon the retina. The retinal images, moreover, will be larger than in emmetropia and much larger than in corrected myopia, but at the same time it must be remembered that accommodation is abolished. The immense improvement in vision which follows Fukala's operation in myopes—usually a needling was done followed in older people by an evacuation of the lens, if necessary—made it initially popular, but at a later date enthusiasm began to wane.[1] At a later date an intracapsular operation was performed in adults and the transparent lens removed (Poyales, 1953; Valerio, 1954; Salgado Gómez, 1958; and others). Technically, however, the removal of a clear lens in a young adult may be difficult and may not be without anxiety; it is to be remembered that the use of alpha-chymotrypsin (J. Barraquer, 1958) in young people is hazardous.[2] As a more serious factor when late end-results came to be studied, statistics showed that the tendency to retinal detachment is increased in such cases. If it is performed, such an operation, therefore, should always be confined to one eye and to adults who are in considerable difficulty (Hervouët, 1961). If there is a marked degree of peripheral degeneration of the retina, the risk of a subsequent detachment of this tissue may be diminished by light-coagulation or cryopexy.

Sclerectomy, a somewhat heroic procedure, consists of excising a strip of sclera and thus shortening the globe. Such an operation was originally suggested by L. Müller (1903) of Vienna for cases of retinal detachment in high grades of myopia, with the object of shortening the stretched sclera and bringing it back to the retina. The operation has been practised on several occasions, sometimes with remarkable success considering the desperate nature of the cases usually chosen (Lindner, 1933; Pischel and Miller, 1939; Borley, 1940; Pischel, 1945; and others). It has also been performed in cases of high myopia uncomplicated by detachment, but this has been rare. Holth (1911–13) and Grönholm (1921–22) claimed to produce a shortening of the globe with a pre-equatorial sclerectomy, and Hildesheimer (1937) excised loops of sclera with the electric cautery. Employing a modification of Müller's operation, Pischel (1945) and Borley and Tanner (1945) removed strips of sclera 2 or 3 mm. wide; but, although in each case vision was said to have improved, a change in the refraction does not seem to have occurred. Lamellar scleral resection has also been applied to myopic eyes even in the absence of detachment, but the results are uncertain (Salgado Gómez, 1956).

Newer procedures still in the experimental stage include surgical support to the sclera by strips of tendon (Malbrán, 1954) or fascia lata (Curtin 1961; Starkiewicz, 1965; Nesterov and Libenson, 1967–70) or donor sclera (Miller and Borley, 1963). Alteration of the corneal refraction has also been attempted. Sato (1952) and Sato and his colleagues (1953) claimed to attain a diminution of the axial refraction varying from 1·5 to 7·0 D by multiple radial incisions into the anterior and posterior surfaces of the cornea in the extrapupillary area extending in depth half-way into the stroma. Krwawicz (1964–65) removed lamellæ of the stroma to flatten it, and J. I. Barraquer

[1] Sattler (1898), Hertel (1899), Axenfeld (1903), Thompson (1910), Adam (1911), Lambert (1912), Elschnig (1916), Geyer (1920), Böhm (1921), Pesme (1927).
[2] Vol. XI, p. 286.

(1964–67) adopted the more drastic procedure of removing a portion of cornea, grinding it to a new shape while frozen, and then replacing it, claiming thereby a correction of up to — 15 D (*keratomileusis*[1]). Intra-ocular and intracorneal plastic materials have also been tried (Strampelli, 1954; de Almeida, 1963). The long-term results of all these manœuvres, however, are still too uncertain to allow their adequate evaluation; certainly the technical procedures devised are ingenious, but they are clearly attended by considerable risk, and in many cases it would seem better to remain myopic; moreover, while they change the refraction, they do not alter the degenerative process.

OTHER TYPES OF PATHOLOGICAL AXIAL MYOPIA

The remaining types of pathological myopia are rare and incidental to other ocular diseases, all of which have already been considered. A pathological axial myopia may occur when the coats of the eye are inflamed; *scleritis* has been recorded as producing a considerable degree of myopia (Gorse and Bergés, 1937); while a similar occurrence has been noted as a sequel of *choroiditis* (Tscherning, 1883; Kries, 1886; Priestley Smith, 1901).

In *glaucoma* a slight degree of myopia due to an antero-posterior stretching may occur, but it is neither common in incidence nor great in amount. An increase of tension rarely stretches the dense adult sclera. When it does so, it usually acts by making the whole globe more spherical, and the diminution of the curvature of the cornea which this brings about is sufficient to produce the slight degree of hypermetropia which is occasionally observed in glaucoma. The shallow anterior chamber and the forward displacement of the lens in the typical closed-angle glaucoma of adults probably have a more marked influence in determining the myopic changes which are encountered. Only in the congenital condition of buphthalmos, when the pressure makes itself evident before the tissues are fully consolidated, is a stretching effect apparent to any marked degree, but here the optical effect is largely neutralized by the flattening of the cornea and lens, the depth of the anterior chamber and the relative displacement backwards of the lens. In fact, if the cardinal points of the average buphthalmic eye are calculated it is found that in view of the optical changes introduced by these factors it would have to be 31 mm. long to be emmetropic (Parsons, 1920). Actually, a slight degree of myopia is the most common optical condition and hypermetropia also occurs, but high degrees of myopia up to — 15 D or — 16 D may develop. Astigmatism is also common, wherein, in contrast to adult glaucoma, the horizontal meridian is usually the more hypermetropic, a feature possibly explained by the pressure of the lids upon the plastic globe.

Finally, we have seen[2] that in previously emmetropic eyes an axial myopia may develop during constitutional disturbances which may undermine the strength of the sclera—dyscrasias of the pituitary gland, goitre, obesity, acute diseases such as malaria and the exanthemata, or chronic debilitating illnesses such as tuberculosis.

[1] p. 853.
[2] p. 340.

CURVATURE MYOPIA

PATHOLOGICAL CURVATURE MYOPIA may be due to corneal or lenticular deformations. Traumatic myopia will be discussed separately.

CORNEAL CONDITIONS

Inflammatory diseases of the cornea such as ulcers or keratitis, particularly syphilitic interstitial keratitis, may lead to a bulging of this tissue and an increase of its refractivity (Wilson, 1912; Bohnenberger, 1925–26); astigmatism also usually enters largely into the optical defect.

Conical cornea usually involves some degree of myopia, but since a considerable amount of astigmatism is also involved in this condition, it will be discussed at a later stage.[1] It is interesting that mongolism is frequently associated with myopia as well as keratoconus (Lowe, 1949).

LENTICULAR CONDITIONS

Increased lenticular curvature has a more varied ætiology. The temporary curvature myopia resulting from accommodative spasm, either functional or acquired, will be dealt with presently[2]; a permanent myopia occurs as a result of an increased curvature of the entire lens or of its axial portion only (lenticonus).

An increased curvature of the lens occurs in *microphakia (spherophakia)* wherein the lens is small and assumes a spherical shape[3]; such a condition may be part of Marfan's[4] or Marchesani's syndrome.[5] The myopia averages − 10 D (Franceschetti, 1930) or − 15 D (Meyer, 1930); Gnad's (1931) case had a refraction of − 14 D before and + 14 D after extraction of the lens. A similar globular lens may be seen in *microphthalmos* (Herrmann, 1927). The same condition occurs in the phakic part of the pupillary area in *ectopia lentis* (−15 D in the phakic part, +10 D in the aphakic part, Hess, 1911)[6] and in cases of *subluxation* or *dislocation* of the lens.[7]

In *anterior lenticonus (lentiglobus)* the anterior surface of the lens assumes a conical or spherical form while the nuclei remain intact and undisturbed[8]; as a consequence the central area may be highly myopic (− 20 D, Kienecker, 1929) while the periphery may be emmetropic. Sometimes there is a tendency for the myopia to increase (from − 5·5 D to − 10·0 D during six years, Feigenbaum, 1932). *Posterior lenticonus*[9] has a similar effect; the spheroidal elevation on the posterior surface of the lens produces a marked myopia in the axial region (− 29 D with a hypermetropia of + 4 D in the periphery, Colombo, 1924).

[1] p. 363.   [2] p. 469.
[3] Vol. III, p. 694.   [4] Vol. III, p. 1102.   [5] Vol. III, p. 1107.
[6] Vol. III, p. 710.   [7] Vol. XI, p. 300.   [8] Vol. III, p. 696.
                            [9] Vol. III, p. 700.

INDEX MYOPIA

INDEX MYOPIA is due to changes in the lens. The older writers ascribed a myopia of 1 to 2 D occurring in such conditions as iritis (Schapringer, 1893), jaundice (Moauro, 1893) and diabetes (Appenzeller, 1896) as due to an increased refractive index of the aqueous. The production of a change in the refraction of even 1 D from this cause would demand an increase in the refractive index far beyond the limits which occur in life or even experimentally—in diabetes, for example, it would require a concentration of approximately 20% of sugar—and any corresponding increase in the optical density of the vitreous, which must be assumed to accompany it, would counteract the effect. A vitreous index myopia due to a decrease in its refractivity has not been demonstrated. It follows, therefore, that index myopia is confined to changes in the lens.

An index myopia due to such changes may be of congenital origin. An *internal lenticonus* resulting from an abnormal convexity of the nucleus may have this effect (Møller, 1927) or an increased optical density of the axial portions of the lens (*false lenticonus*) (-14 D in the axial region, -3 D in the periphery, Doyne, 1889; Müller, 1894; Demicheri, 1895; Guttmann, 1898–1900; and others). The rare cases wherein the lens shows the peculiar optical phenomenon of a *double focal point*[1] has the same effect (v. Szily, 1903; Vogt, 1922; Kyrieleis, 1926; Hagen, 1929), as well as the more common cases of congenital *nuclear cataract*.[2]

Senile sclerosis of the nucleus of the lens, however, involving a relative increase of its optical density is the commonest cause of index lenticular myopia. In old age this change involves the gradual development of a relative myopia of 1 or 2 dioptres so that a person of over 70 may gradually and happily discard his presbyopic spectacles. Occasionally a myopia of 5 or 7 D may be attained. As was first pointed out by Henry (1790), however, the most dramatic and rapidly progressive change of this type occurs as an antecedent to nuclear cataract when a myopia up to -15 or -20 D may develop. The optical condition may change rapidly and variations in the index of refraction in different regions may involve correspondingly rapid astigmatic changes. These changes necessitate the frequent visual re-correction of such cases if their visual efficiency is to be maintained until operation is considered advisable.

A myopia due to the *position of the lens* may result from its forward displacement. This may be seen after trauma, with a shallow anterior chamber as occurs most dramatically after an intra-ocular operation; in the days following the operation the re-establishment of the chamber and the recession of the lens are accompanied by the gradual development of hypermetropia.

The *treatment* of curvature and index myopia is frequently difficult. In cases due to corneal curvature contact lenses offer a substitute for spec-

---

[1] Vol. XI, p. 159.   [2] Vol. III, p. 732.

tacles; but in cases wherein the lens is at fault, if a good visual result cannot be obtained with spectacles, a discission or extraction of the lens may occasionally place the patient in a more comfortable condition by rendering him aphakic.

TRAUMATIC MYOPIA

The occurrence of myopia after a concussion injury to the globe has been recognized since the original observation of Kugel (1870). After his paper observations accumulated rapidly (Aub, 1871; Manfredi, 1871; Just, 1872; and others): Frenkel (1905) collected 41 published cases and Fox (1942) gathered 60 others from the literature. Frequently the myopia is associated with hypotony,[1] an association noted by Schiess-Gemuseus (1881) and extensively studied by Magitot (1917–36). The two phenomena, however, do not necessarily occur together; hypertension, indeed, may be associated with concussion myopia (Frenkel, 1905; Marucci, 1936).

The extent of the myopia varies from 1 to 6 D, but its duration differs greatly from case to case, reports in the literature varying from 1 day (Bailey, 1921) or 2 weeks (Luntz, 1959) to over 30 years (Janson, 1935). In most cases the condition is transient, clearing up in a week or two; the refraction returns to normal in the great majority within a month. On the other hand, a proportion of cases shows a much longer duration—1 year (Fromaget, 1911; Morgan, 1940; Fox, 1942), 18 months (v. Grolman, 1896), 2 to 3 years (Sourdille, 1908; Fox, 1942) or apparently permanently (Bourgeois, 1904; Janson, 1935). The cause of the myopia in many cases is not clear and a considerable amount of ingenuity has been expended on devising ætiological theories in explanation. It is certain, however, that not all cases are due to a single cause. The two most important types are due, in the first, to ciliary spasm (or ciliary sympathetic paresis) and, in the second, to weakening or rupture of the zonule; more problematic ætiological factors are changes of a cataractous nature in the lens itself or a lengthening of the antero-posterior axis of the globe caused by trauma.

Spasm of accommodation initiated by the trauma is probably responsible for the majority of cases, particularly the transient variety. The characteristics of such a spasm will be discussed in a subsequent chapter, and it is sufficient to note here that a myopia of from 1 to 4 D is associated with a loss of accommodative amplitude and miosis (or sometimes traumatic mydriasis) and disappears under atropine. Tange (1914) and Morgan (1940) explained a prolonged spasm which lasted a period of a year as perpetuated by a functional element.

It has been suggested that a traumatic paresis of the radial fibres of Brücke's muscle allows the circular fibres of Müller's muscle to exercise an unopposed pull on the zonule, thus permitting the refraction of the lens to increase (Bolotte, 1934; Dejean and Guignot, 1938). The myopia, in this view, is caused not by irritative

[1] Vol. XI, Chap. X.

ciliary spasm, but primarily by paresis of the sympathetic moiety of the ciliary muscle allowing free play to the parasympathetic element.

Weakening and relaxation of the suspensory apparatus of the lens was considered an ætiological factor in certain cases by early writers (Aub, 1871; Schiess-Gemuseus, 1881; Darier, 1899; Guende, 1900). It seems very probable that a lenticular curvature myopia which shows no diminution with atropine accounts for a number of cases of longer duration than those caused by spasm (Damel, 1933; and others). More pronounced cases wherein the zonule is actually ruptured, associated with iridodonesis and showing a myopia of 5 to 6 D, seem possibly explicable in this way (Møller, 1926; Cosserat, 1938); while the ætiology of those showing an anterior dislocation of the lens is clear (Manfredi, 1871; Bourgeois, 1904; Janson, 1935). In such cases, of course, the myopia is permanent.

Cases which do not fall within these groups have excited considerable speculation, and several theories which have been advanced are less fully substantiated. Morgan (1940) observed transient subcapsular opacities in the lens which appeared to cause increased refractivity. Kugel (1870), in his original observation, postulated a lengthening of the antero-posterior diameter of the globe due to " inflammatory processes," but there is no evidence that this occurs; ruptures of Descemet's membrane (Bailey, 1921) or of the choroid have also been suggested. Finally, a lack of production of the aqueous has been claimed as an ætiological factor to account for both the hypotony and the myopia, the latter resulting from a consequent anterior displacement of the lens (Schiess-Gemuseus, 1881; Laws, 1897; Fox, 1942); cases have been observed wherein the anterior chamber has been temporarily abolished after concussion (H. Knapp, 1883; Fromaget, 1911).

There is no adequate treatment for traumatic myopia; but when spasm of accommodation is present atropine should be instilled. The prognosis should always be guarded, for although it may be permanent, even after a duration of a year or more the refraction may suddenly return to normal so long as no gross organic damage has been done.

Abraham. *J. pediat. Ophthal.*, **3**, 10 (1966).

Adam. *Zbl. prakt. Augenheilk.*, **35**, 164 (1911).

Alexander and Shea. *Arch. Ophthal.*, **74**, 310 (1965).

de Almeida. *Rev. bras. Oftal.*, **22**, 299 (1963).

van Alphen. *Ophthalmologica*, **142**, Suppl. (1961).

van Alphen, Lely, Nass and van Leeuwen. *Ophthalmologica*, **125**, 52 (1953).

d'Ansan. *C.R. Acad. Sci.* (Paris), **182**, 895 (1926).

Apollonio and Weigelin. *Boll. Oculist.*, **43**, 25 (1964).

Appenzeller. *Zbl. prakt. Augenheilk.*, **20**, 139 (1896).

Arden, Barrada and Kelsey. *Brit. J. Ophthal.*, **46**, 468 (1962).

Argañaraz. *Semana med.*, **29**, 1161 (1922).

Arlt. *Ueber d. Ursachen u. d. Entstehung d. Kurzsichtigkeit*, Wien (1876).

Armaly. *Arch. Ophthal.*, **78**, 35 (1967).

Arruga. *XIV int. Cong. Ophthal.*, Madrid, **2** (1), 5 (1933).

Ascher. *Beitr. Augenheilk.*, **2** (16), 19 (1895).

Ask. *III Cong. int. Hyg. scolaire* (Paris, 1910) (1911). See *Jber. Ophthal.*, **42**, 762 (1911).

Aub. *Arch. Augenheilk.*, **2**, 252 (1871).

Axenfeld. *Klin. Mbl. Augenheilk.*, **41** (1), 60, 176 (1903).

Ber. dtsch. ophthal. Ges., **32**, 303 (1905).

Baas. *Arch. Augenheilk.*, **26**, 33 (1893).

Baer. *Ueber das Verhalten d. Orbita-Index bei den verschiedenen Refraktionszuständen vom 10–19 Lebensjahr* (Diss.), Munich (1888).

Bailey. *Amer. J. Ophthal.*, **4**, 363 (1921).

Bangerter. *Amblyopiebehandlung*, Basel (1960).

Barraquer, J. *An. Méd. Cir.* (Barcelona), **38**, 255 (1958).

Barraquer, J. I. *An. Inst. Barraquer*, **5**, 206 (1964).
Int. Surg. (Chic.), **48**, 103 (1967).
Arch. Soc. Amer. oftal. optom., **6**, 21 (1967).
Bartels. *Klin. Mbl. Augenheilk.*, **71**, 465 (1923); **86**, 536, 770 (1931).
Batra and Paul. *Brit. J. Ophthal.*, **51**, 57 (1967).
Batten. *Ophthal. Rev.*, **11**, 1 (1892).
Lancet, **2**, 139 (1893).
Becker. *Ber. dtsch. ophthal. Ges.*, **15**, 77 (1883).
Beckers. *Berl. klin. Wschr.*, **57**, 254 (1920).
Beckershaus. *Z. Augenheilk.*, **59**, 264 (1926).
Behr. *Klin. Mbl. Augenheilk.*, **62**, 412 (1919).
Behse. *v. Graefes Arch. Ophthal.*, **67**, 379 (1908).
Bell. *Treasury of Human Inheritance*, London, **2** (1) (1922).
Betsch. *Klin. Mbl. Augenheilk.*, **82**, 365 (1929).
Bietti. *Klin. Mbl. Augenheilk.*, **50** (2), 529 (1912).
Birch-Hirschfeld. *v. Graefes Arch. Ophthal.*, **60**, 552 (1905).
Birge. *Trans. Amer. ophthal. Soc.*, **53**, 219 (1955).
Biró. *Klin. Mbl. Augenheilk.*, **94**, 239 (1935).
Blach. *The Nature of Degenerative Myopia* (Thesis), Cambridge (1965).
Blach and Jay. *Trans. ophthal. Soc. U.K.*, **85**, 161 (1965).
Blach, Jay and Kolb. *Brit. J. Ophthal.*, **50**, 629 (1966).
Blach, Jay and MacFaul. *Proc. roy. Soc. Med.*, **58**, 109 (1965).
Blatt. *Klin. Mbl. Augenheilk.*, **145**, 680 (1964).
Blegvad. *Klin. Mbl. Augenheilk.*, **60**, 155 (1918).
Acta ophthal. (Kbh.), **5**, 49 (1927).
Böhm. *v. Graefes Arch. Ophthal.*, **103**, 143 (1920); **104**, 157 (1921).
Böhringer. *Ophthalmologica*, **131**, 331 (1956).
Boerhaave. *De morbis oculorum*, Göttingen (1708).
Bogatsch. *Klin. Mbl. Augenheilk.*, **49** (2), 431 (1911).
Bohnenberger. *Klin. Mbl. Augenheilk.*, **74**, 770 (1925); **76**, 690 (1926).
Bolotte. *Arch. Ophtal.*, **51**, 662 (1934).
Bonnet, A. *Traité de sections tendineuses et musculaires*, Paris (1842).
Borley. *Arch. Ophthal.*, **23**, 1181 (1940).
Borley and Tanner. *Amer. J. Ophthal.*, **28**, 517 (1945).
Bothman. *Amer. J. Ophthal.*, **14**, 918 (1931).
Bourdeaux. *Bull. Soc. franç. Ophtal.*, **31**, 670 (1914).
Bourgeois. *Ann. Oculist.* (Paris), **132**, 267 (1904).
de Bourgon. *Ann. Oculist.* (Paris), **114**, 270 (1895).
Brändstedt. *Acta ophthal.* (Kbh.), Suppl. 5 (1935).
Braendstrup. *Acta ophthal.* (Kbh.), **19**, 272 (1941).

Brailey. *Trans. ophthal. Soc. U.K.*, **10**, 139 (1890).
Brière. *Ann. Oculist.* (Paris), **74**, 138 (1875).
Brown. *Arch. Ophthal.*, **28**, 845 (1942).
Brückner and Franceschetti. *Arch. Augenheilk.*, **105**, 1 (1932).
Bücklers. *v. Graefes Arch. Ophthal.*, **121**, 243 (1928).
Burns. *Brit. J. Ophthal.*, **33**, 491 (1949).
Burton. *Trans. Amer. ophthal. Soc.*, **40**, 340 (1942).
Butler. *Z. Augenheilk.*, **26**, 128 (1911).
Ophthalmoscope, **14**, 60 (1916).
Cambiaggi. *Ophthalmologica*, **140**, 259 (1960).
Amer. J. Ophthal., **58**, 642 (1964).
Carl Theodore. *Mitt. a. d. königl. Universitäts-Augenklinik München*, **1**, 233 (1882).
Carvill. *Trans. Amer. ophthal. Soc.*, **30**, 71 (1932).
Caso. *Lettura oftal.*, **8**, 287 (1931).
Caspar. *Arch. Augenheilk.*, **28**, 75 (1894).
Castrén. *Acta ophthal.* (Kbh.), Suppl. 44 (1955).
Castrén and Pohjola. *Acta ophthal.* (Kbh.), **40**, 33 (1962).
Cattaneo. *Boll. Oculist.*, **10**, 265 (1931).
Cholina. *Russ. oftal. J.*, **4**, 691 (1925).
Clarke. *Trans. ophthal. Soc. U.K.*, **45**, 373 (1925).
Clausen. *Münch. med. Wschr.*, **68**, 532 (1921).
Gütt's *Hb. d. Erbkrankheiten*, Leipzig, **5**, 223 (1938).
Cockayne, Krestin and Sorsby. *Quart. J. Med.*, **4**, 93 (1935).
Cohen. *Arch. Augenheilk.*, **19**, 41 (1889).
Cohn. *Untersuch. d. Augen v. 10,060 Schulkindern*, Leipzig (1867).
v. Graefes Arch. Ophthal., **17** (2), 305 (1871).
Die Hygiene d. Auges in den Schuler, Leipzig (1883).
Lhb. d. Hygiene d. Auges, Leipzig (1892).
Colombo. *Ann. Oculist.* (Paris), **161**, 363 (1924).
Comberg. *Klin. Mbl. Augenheilk.*, **72**, 692 (1924).
Ber. dtsch. ophthal. Ges., **47**, 126 (1928).
Cook and Glasscock. *Amer. J. Ophthal.*, **34**, 1407 (1951).
Cosserat. *Bull. Soc. Méd. mil. franç.*, **32**, 526 (1938).
Cowan. *Amer. J. Ophthal.*, **25**, 844 (1942).
Curtin. *Amer. J. Ophthal.*, **52**, 853 (1961).
Curtin and Teng. *Trans. Amer. Acad. Ophthal.*, **62**, 777 (1958).
Czellitzer. *Berl. klin. Wschr.*, **44**, 2070 (1912).
Klin. Mbl. Augenheilk., **79**, 301 (1927).
Damel. *Arch. Oftal. B. Aires*, **8**, 497 (1933).
Darier. *Clin. Ophtal.*, **5**, 85 (1899).
Dejean and Guignot. *Arch. Soc. Sci. méd. biol.* (Montpellier), **19**, 73 (1938).
Dellaporta. *Ann. Ottal.*, **74**, 567 (1948).
Delmarcelle and Mans. *Bull. Soc. belge Ophtal.*, No. 140, 414 (1965).

Demicheri. *Ann. Oculist.* (Paris), **113**, 93 (1895).

Derby. *Trans. Amer. ophthal. Soc.*, **2**, 139, 530 (1874–9); **3**, 456 (1883).

Dianoux. *Clin. Ophtal.*, **4**, 68 (1912).

Díaz-Dominguez. *Ann. Oculist.* (Paris), **194**, 597 (1961).

Díaz-Dominguez and Marchena. *Arch. Soc. oftal. hisp.-amer.*, **26**, 241 (1966).

Dimmer. *Klin. Mbl. Augenheilk.*, **20**, 259 (1882).

Dinger. *v. Graefes Arch. Ophthal.*, **100**, 78, 110 (1919).

Dobrowolsky. *Klin. Mbl. Augenheilk.*, **6**, Beil., 1 (1868); **7**, Beil., 138 (1869).

Domec. *Arch. Ophtal.*, **32**, 391 (1912).

Donders. *On the Anomalies of Accommodation and Refraction of the Eye*, London (1864).
Ann. Oculist. (Paris), **34**, 270 (1855).

Dor. *Ber. dtsch. ophthal. Ges.*, **27**, 321 (1898).

Doyne. *Trans. ophthal. Soc. U.K.*, **9**, 113 (1889).
Clin. J., **52**, 157 (1923).

Dransart. *Ann. Oculist.* (Paris), **92**, 30 (1884); **94**, 109 (1885).

Dunnington and Macnie. *Arch. Ophthal.*, **13**, 191 (1935).

Dunphy, Stoll and King. *Amer. J. Ophthal.*, **65**, 518 (1946).

van Dyck. *Statistisch onderzoek der niet door overlading met Schoolwerk ontstane byziendheid* (Diss.), Amsterdam (1904).

Edridge-Green. *Lancet*, **1**, 469 (1921); **2**, 883, 1209 (1924).
Brit. med. J., **1**, 48 (1925).

Elschnig. *v. Graefes Arch. Ophthal.*, **51**, 391 (1900); **56**, 49 (1903); **61**, 237 (1905).
Klin. Mbl. Augenheilk., **42** (2), 529 (1904).
Med. Klin., **12**, 527 (1916); **18**, 683 (1922).

Elwyn and Knighton. *Amer. J. Ophthal.*, **26**, 969 (1943).

Emmert. *X int. Cong. Ophthal.*, Lucerne, B79 (1905).

Erggelet. *Kurzes Hb. d. Ophthal.*, Berlin, **2**, 460 (1932).

Erismann. *v. Graefes Arch. Ophthal.*, **17** (1), 1 (1871).

Essed and Soewarno. *Klin. Mbl. Augenheilk.*, **80**, 56 (1928).

Estrada. *Bol. Hosp. oftal. N.S. Luz*, **3**, 313 (1947).

Favaloro. *G. Oculist.*, **8**, 37 (1927).

Federici. *Boll. Oculist.*, **3**, 487 (1924).

Feigenbaum. *Klin. Mbl. Augenheilk.*, **74**, 388 (1925).
Folia ophthal. orient., **1**, 103 (1932).

Feitelberg. *Étude statistique sur la variation de la réfraction chez le nouveau né* (Thèse), Geneva (1935).

Filatov and Volokitenko. *Vestn. oftal.*, **17**, 515 (1940).

Fleischer. *Klin. Mbl. Augenheilk.*, **44** (1), 64 (1906).
Ber. dtsch. ophthal. Ges., **34**, 238 (1907); **38**, 110 (1912).
Ergebn. Path., **21**, Erg.-Bel., 544 (1929).

Fleming. *Trans. ophthal. Soc. U.K.*, **54**, 286 (1934).

Fletcher and Brandon. *Amer. J. Ophthal.*, **40**, 474 (1955).

Förster. *Ophthalmologische Beiträge*, Berlin (1862).
Arch. Augenheilk., **14**, 295 (1885).

Fox. *Arch. Ophthal.*, **28**, 218 (1942).

Fracassi. *XIII int. Cong. Ophthal.*, Amsterdam, **1**, 83 (1929).

Franceschetti. *Klin. Mbl. Augenheilk.*, **85**, 285 (1930).
J. Génét. hum., **2**, 283 (1953).

Franceschetti, Dieterle and Schwartz. In *Electroretinographia* (Symposium, 1959), Brno, 247 (1960).

François. *L'hérédité en ophtalmologie*, Paris, 219 (1958).
La toxoplasmose et ses manifestations oculaires, Paris (1963).

François and DeRouck. *Bull. Soc. belge Ophtal.*, No. 107, 323 (1954).

François and Verriest. *Bull. Soc. belge Ophtal.*, No. 116, 351 (1957); No. 126, 1118 (1961).

François, Verriest and DeRouck. *Brit. J. Ophthal.*, **40**, 108 (1956).

Frenkel. *Ann. Oculist.* (Paris), **134**, 1 (1905).
Arch. Ophtal., **45**, 209 (1928).

Frenzel. *Ueber reinen Mikrophthalmus u. hochgradige Hypermetropie* (Diss.), Leipzig (1920).

Frezzotti and Fois. *G. ital. Oftal.*, **11**, 420 (1958).

Fromaget. *Bull. Soc. franç. Ophtal.*, **28**, 346 (1911).

Fuchs, A. *Arch. Ophthal.*, **37**, 722 (1947).

Fuchs, E. *v. Graefes Arch. Ophthal.*, **28** (1), 139 (1882).
Z. Augenheilk., **5**, 171 (1901).
Klin. Mbl. Augenheilk., **62**, 429, 433, 559 (1919).

Fukala. *v. Graefes Arch. Ophthal.*, **36** (2), 230 (1890).
Amer. J. Ophthal., **8**, 81 (1891).
Arch. Augenheilk., **24**, 161 (1892); **29**, 42 (1894).
Ber. dtsch. ophthal. Ges., **23**, 191 (1893); **25**, 265 (1896).
VIII int. Cong. Ophthal., Edinb., 181 (1894).

Fuss. *Virchows Arch. path. Anat.*, **183**, 465 (1906).

Galloway. *Brit. med. J.*, **2**, 46 (1923).

Gallus. *Klin. Mbl. Augenheilk.*, **44** (1), 398 (1906).

Gamper. *Die Stilling'schen Anschauungen ü. d. Entstehung d. Myopie unter besonderer Berücksichtigung des Röntgenbildes* (Diss.) Zürich (1914).

Gardiner. *Trans. ophthal. Soc. U.K.*, **76**, 171 (1956).
Lancet, **1**, 1152 (1958).
Proc. Nutr. Soc., **19**, 96 (1960).

Gardiner and James. *Brit. J. Ophthal.*, **44**, 172 (1960).

Garzino. *Rass. ital. Ottal.*, **25**, 241 (1956).
Gassler. *Arch. Klaus-Stift. Vererb.-Forsch.*, **1**, 259 (1925).
Geyer. *Beitr. zu d. Frage d. Myopieoperation mit Berücksichtigung d. Späterfolge* (Diss.) Breslau (1920).
Gilbert. *v. Graefes Arch. Ophthal.*, **82**, 389 (1912).
Arch. Augenheilk., **86**, 282 (1920).
Glatzel. *Z. klin. Med.*, **116**, 632 (1931).
Gnad. *Klin. Mbl. Augenheilk.*, **87**, 33 (1931).
Goldmann. *Biomicroscopie du corps vitré et du fond de l'oeil* (ed. Busacca *et al.*), Paris (1957).
Entwicklung u. Fortschritt in d. Augenheilkunde (ed. Sautter), Stuttgart, 361 (1963).
Goldschmidt, E. *Acta ophthal.* (Kbh.), Suppl. 98 (1968).
Goldschmidt, H. *Der Refraktionszustand beim Glaukom* (Diss.), Halle (1923).
Gonin. *Bull. Soc. franç. Ophthal.*, **33**, 1 (1920).
Le décollement de la rétine, Lausanne (1934).
Gorse and Bergès. *Ann. Oculist.* (Paris), **174**, 844 (1937).
Gostin. *Sth. med. J.* (Bgham, Ala.), **55**, 916 (1962).
von Graefe. *v. Graefes Arch. Ophthal.*, **1** (1), 390 (1854); **3** (1), 277 (1857).
Greeff. *Anleitung zur mikroskopischen Untersuchung d. Auges*, 2nd ed., Berlin (1902).
Grönholm. *v. Graefes Arch. Ophthal.*, **105**, 899 (1921); **107**, 489 (1922).
von Grolman. *Z. prakt. Aerzte*, **5**, 287 (1896).
Grunert. *Klin. Mbl. Augenheilk.*, **81**, 521 (1928).
Die Dehnsucht d. Auges (Myopie) u. ihre Behandlung, Munich (1934).
Guende. *Marseille-méd.*, **37**, 449 (1900).
Guttmann. *Zbl. prakt. Augenheilk.*, **22**, 193 (1898); **24**, 297 (1900).
v. Graefes Arch. Ophthal., **54**, 268 (1902).
Haab. *Klin. Mbl. Augenheilk.*, **66**, 231 (1921).
Hagen. *Acta ophthal.* (Kbh.), **7**, 174 (1929).
Halasa and McLaren. *Arch. Ophthal.*, **71**, 827 (1964).
Hansell. *Amer. J. Ophthal.*, **7**, 606 (1924).
Hanssen. *Klin. Mbl. Augenheilk.*, **63**, 295 (1919); **65**, 703 (1920); **67**, 171 (1921); **74**, 778; **75**, 344 (1925).
Harman. *Preventable Blindness*, London (1907).
Trans. ophthal. Soc. U.K., **33**, 202 (1913); **39**, 78 (1919); **42**, 20 (1922); **57**, 366 (1937).
Proc. roy. Soc. Med., Sect. Ophthal., **6**, 146 (1913); **8**, 3 (1914).
J. indust. Hyg., **4**, 371 (1923).
Brit. med. J., **1**, 129 (1933).
Hasner. *Vjschr. prakt. Heilk.* (Prague), **31**, 50 (1874).
Hay. *Ophthalmoscope*, **12**, 20 (1914).
Heine. *Ber. dtsch. ophthal. Ges.*, **27**, 33 (1898); **29**, 114 (1901); **30**, 333 (1902).

Arch. Augenheilk., **38**, 277 (1899); **40**, 160 (1900); **44**, 66 (1902).
Klin. Mbl. Augenheilk., **37**, 462 (1899).
Heinonen. *Finska Läk-Sällsk. Handl.* **65**, 172 (1923).
Henry. *Mem. lit. phil. Soc. Manchester*, **3**, 182 (1790).
Hensen and Voelckers. *Experimentaluntersuchung ü. d. Mechanismus d. Akkommodation*, Kiel (1868).
Hermann, P. *Arch. Ophtal.*, **18**, 17 (1958).
Herrmann. *Klin. Mbl. Augenheilk.*, **79**, 838 (1927).
Hertel. *v. Graefes Arch. Ophthal.*, **48**, 420 (1899); **56**, 326 (1903); **75**, 586 (1910).
Klin. Mbl. Augenheilk., **48**, Beil., 46 (1910).
Hervouët. *Ann. Oculist.* (Paris), **194**, 769 (1961).
Hess. *Arch. Augenheilk.*, **62**, 345; **63**, 88 (1909).
Graefe-Saemisch Hb. d. ges. Augenheilk., 3rd ed. (*Path. u. Ther. d. Linsensystems*), Leipzig, Kap. 9, 285 (1911).
Hess and Heine. *v. Graefes Arch. Ophthal.*, **46**, 243 (1898).
Hiatt, Costenbader and Albert. *Arch. Ophthal.*, **74**, 31 (1965).
Hildesheimer. *XV int. Cong. Ophthal.*, Cairo, **4**, 320 (1937).
von Hippel. *v. Graefes Arch. Ophthal.*, **74**, 101 (1910).
Hirsch. *Klin. Mbl. Augenheilk.*, **74**, 404 (1925).
Hirschberg. *Die Behandlung d. Kurzsichtigkeit*, Berlin (1904, 1910).
Hofmann and Carey. *Amer. J. Ophthal.*, **25**, 1495 (1942).
Hohr Castán. *Arch. Soc. oftal. hisp.-amer.*, **5**, 693 (1945).
Holm, E. *Acta ophthal.* (Kbh.), **1**, 273 (1923); **3**, 121, 234, 335 (1925); **6**, 157 (1928).
Hospitalstidende, **70**, 926 (1927).
Holm, S. *Acta ophthal.* (Kbh.), Suppl. 13 (1937).
Holth. *Ber. dtsch. ophthal. Ges.*, **37**, 293 (1911); **39**, 179 (1913).
Horner. *Klin. Mbl. Augenheilk.*, **11**, 488 (1873).
Horstmann. *Klin. Mbl. Augenheilk.*, **17**, 487 (1879).
Arch. Augenheilk., **9**, 208 (1880).
Hosaka. *Jap. J. Ophthal.*, **7**, 77 (1963).
Hosch. *v. Graefes Arch. Ophthal.*, **61**, 227 (1905).
Hyams and Neumann. *Brit. J. Ophthal.*, **53**, 300 (1969).
Incze. *Z. Augenheilk.*, **67**, 20 (1929).
Inouye. *Klin. Mbl. Augenheilk.*, **74**, 124 (1925).
Irwin. *Harvard Univ. Bull. on Education*, **7** (1920).
Methods of Teaching Sight-saving Classes, N.Y. (1926).
Sight-saving Classes, their Organisation and Administration, N.Y. (1927).

Ischreyt. *v. Graefes Arch. Ophthal.*, **73**, 566 (1910).

Iwanoff. *v. Graefes Arch. Ophthal.*, **15** (2), 1, 88; (3), 284 (1869).

Jablonski. *Klin. Mbl. Augenheilk.*, **68**, 560 (1922); **73**, 302 (1924).
Arch. Augenheilk., **97**, 369 (1926).

Jackson. *Trans. Amer. ophthal. Soc.*, **5**, 676 (1890); **6**, 359 (1892).
Amer. J. Ophthal., **14**, 719 (1931).
J. Amer. med. Ass., **98**, 132 (1932); **105**, 1412 (1935).

von Jaeger. *Beitr. z. Pathologie d. Auges*, Wien (1855).
Ueber d. Einstellungen d. dioptrischen Apparates im mensch. Auge, Wien (1861).

Jancke. *Klin. Mbl. Augenheilk.*, **106**, 264 (1941).

Janin. *Mém. et observ. anat. et physiol. sur l'oeil*, Lyons (1772).

Janson. *Klin. Mbl. Augenheilk.*, **94**, 517 (1935).

Jayle and Bérard. *Ann. Oculist.* (Paris), **188**, 431 (1955).

Jayle and Ourgaud. *La vision nocturne et ses troubles*, Paris (1950).
Bull. Soc. Ophtal. Fr., 513 (1953).

Junius. *Z. Augenheilk.*, **44**, 262 (1920).

Just. *Klin. Mbl. Augenheilk.*, **10**, 256 (1872).

Karpe. *Acta ophthal.* (Kbh.), Suppl. 24 (1945).

Katel-Bloch. *Klin. Mbl. Augenheilk.*, **44** (2), Beil., 66 (1906).

Keith. *Brit. J. physiol. Opt.*, **1**, 369 (1925).
Lancet, **2**, 1047 (1925).

Kepler. *Dioptrice*, Augsburg (1611).

Key. *Gutachten d. schwedischen Schul/commission*, Stockholm (1885).

Kienecker. *Klin. Mbl. Augenheilk.*, **82**, 55 (1929).

Kirk. *Brit. med. J.*, **2**, 8 (1921).

Kleiner. *Arch. Rassen- u. Gesellsch.-biol.*, **15**, 1 (1923).

Knapp, A. *Trans. Amer. ophthal. Soc.*, **23**, 61 (1925).

Knapp, A. A. *Amer. J. Ophthal.*, **22**, 1329 (1939); **25**, 850 (1942).

Knapp, H. *Arch. Augenheilk.*, **12**, 85 (1883).

Kraupa. *Zbl. prakt. Augenheilk.*, **38**, 129 (1914).
Z. Augenheilk., **31**, 149 (1914); **88**, 224; **90**, 276 (1936); **91**, 183 (1937).
Arch. Augenheilk., **82**, 67 (1917).
Klin. Mbl. Augenheilk., **66**, 735, 736 (1921); **70**, 716 (1923); **72**, 476 (1924); **75**, 707 (1925); **87**, 837 (1931).
v. Graefes Arch. Ophthal., **105**, 865 (1921).

Krause. *Arch. Ophthal.*, **53**, 522 (1955).

Krekeler. *Arch. Augenheilk.*, **93**, 144 (1923).

Kretz. *Boll. Oculist.*, **8**, 62 (1929).

Kries. *Ber. dtsch. ophthal. Ges.*, **18**, 26 (1886).
v. Graefes Arch. Ophthal., **32** (3), 15 (1886).

Kronfeld. *Z. Augenheilk.*, **55**, 193 (1925).

Krotoschin. *Arch. Augenheilk.*, **22**, 393 (1891).

Krückmann. *Ber. dtsch. ophthal. Ges.*, **32**, 291 (1905).

Krüger. *Zuillingsbefunde im gau Mecklenburg* (Diss.), Leipzig (1937).

Krwawicz. *Amer. J. Ophthal.*, **57**, 828 (1964).
Klin. oczna, **35**, 13 (1965).

Kugel. *v. Graefes Arch. Ophthal.*, **16**, 323 (1870).

Kurozumi, Matsuno and Kani. *Acta Soc. ophthal. jap.*, **70**, 2238 (1966).

Kuschel. *Z. Augenheilk.*, **51**, 339 (1923).

Kyrieleis. *Z. Augenheilk.*, **58**, 202 (1926).

Lacroix. *Ann. Oculist.* (Paris), **159**, 730 (1922).

Lambert. *J. Amer. med. Ass.*, **59**, 1007 (1912).

Lancaster. *Refraction and Motility*, Springfield (1953).

Lange. *Samml. zwangl. Abhandl. Gebiete Augenheilk.* (ed. Vossius), **1** (6) (1896).
v. Graefes Arch. Ophthal., **60**, 118 (1905).

Laval. *Amer. J. Ophthal.*, **24**, 408 (1941).

Laws. *Ophthal. Rev.*, **16**, 204 (1897).

Lawson. *Brit. med. J.*, **1**, 1614 (1898).

Leber. *Graefe-Saemisch Hb. d. ges. Augenheilk.*, 2nd ed., Leipzig, **7A** (2), 1595 (1916).

Lehmus. *Die Erkrankung d. Macula lutea bei progressiver Myopie* (Diss.), Zürich (1875).

Lehrfeld and Reber. *Arch. Ophthal.*, **18**, 712 (1937).

Leininberg. *Klinisch-statistische Beitr. zur Myopie* (Diss.), Würzburg (1886).

Levinsohn. *Ber. dtsch. ophthal. Ges.*, **39**, 217 (1913).
v. Graefes Arch. Ophthal., **88**, 452 (1914).
Z. Augenheilk., **35**, 243 (1916); **52**, 178 (1924); **56**, 351 (1925).
Klin. Mbl. Augenheilk., **62**, 794 (1919); **66**, 84 (1921); **68**, 574 (1922); **70**, 757; **71**, 205 (1923); **74**, 377 (1925).
Arch. Ophthal., **54**, 434 (1925).
Arch. Augenheilk., **99**, 569 (1928); **100–1**, 138 (1929); **102**, 308 (1930); **104**, 82 (1931).

Lindner. *Z. Augenheilk.*, **81**, 277 (1933).
Klin. Mbl. Augenheilk., **103**, 582 (1939); **105**, 113 (1940); **107**, 320 (1941).
Klin. Med., **1**, 1 (1946).
Wien. klin. Wschr., **59**, 265, 867 (1947).

Lisch. *Klin. Mbl. Augenheilk.*, **106**, 695 (1941).

Lohmann. *v. Graefes Arch. Ophthal.*, **65**, 365 (1907).

Lomícková. *Cs. Oftal.*, **20**, 195 (1964).

Lowe. *Brit. J. Ophthal.*, **33**, 131 (1949).

Luedde. *Amer. J. Ophthal.*, **15**, 603 (1932).

Luntz. *Brit. J. Ophthal.*, **43**, 566 (1959).

McCoy. *Amer. J. Ophthal.*, **10**, 610 (1927).

MacDonald. *Sight-saving Classes in Public Schools in Toronto* (1923).
Canad. med. Ass. J., **92**, 264 (1965).

MacGregor. *Ann. Eugen.*, **13**, 135 (1946).

Mächler. *v. Graefes Arch. Ophthal.*, **120**, 540 (1928).

Magitot. *Ann. Oculist.* (Paris), **154**, 667 (1917); **155**, 1 (1918); **157**, 680 (1920); **170**, 465 (1933); **173**, 785 (1936).

Malbrán. *Arch. Soc. oftal. hisp.-amer.*, **14**, 1167 (1954).

Manfredi. *Ann. Ottal.*, **1**, 189 (1871).

Mannhardt. *v. Graefes Arch. Ophthal.*, **17** (2), 69 (1871).

Klin. Mbl. Augenheilk., **25**, 217, 450 (1887).

Marchesani. *Klin. Mbl. Augenheilk.*, **83**, 338 (1929).

Arch. Augenheilk., **104**, 177 (1931).

Marlow. *Arch. Ophthal.*, **13**, 584 (1935).

Marschke. *Klin. Mbl. Augenheilk.*, **39** (2), 705 (1901).

Martin. *Ann. Oculist.* (Paris), **112**, 5 (1894).

Marucci. *Rass. ital. Ottal.*, **5**, 327 (1936).

Maurice and Mushin. *Lancet*, **2**, 1160 (1966).

Mauthner. *Vorlesungen ü. d. optischen Fehler d. Auges*, Wien (1876).

Mawas. *Bull. Soc. Ophtal. Paris*, 549 (1934).

Mehra, Khare and Vaithilingam. *Brit. J. Ophthal.*, **49**, 276 (1965).

Mende. *Klin. Mbl. Augenheilk.*, **44**, Beil., 26 (1906).

Menestrina. *Boll. Oculist.*, **5**, 106 (1926).

Meyer. *v. Graefes Arch. Ophthal.*, **116**, 553 (1926).

Klin. Mbl. Augenheilk., **84**, 525 (1930).

Meyerhof. *Zbl. prakt. Augenheilk.*, **34**, 193 (1910).

Klin. Mbl. Augenheilk., **48** (2), 220 (1910).

Ann. Oculist. (Paris), **151**, 257 (1914).

Miller and Borley. *Trans. Pac. Cst. oto-ophthal. Soc.*, **44**, 155 (1963).

Moauro. *Lav. Clin. Oculist. Napoli*, **3**, 100 (1893).

Møller. *Acta ophthal.* (Kbh.), **4**, 60 (1926); **5**, 258 (1927).

von Moers-Messmer. *Klin. Mbl. Augenheilk.*, **105**, 584 (1940).

Morgan. *Brit. J. Ophthal.*, **24**, 403 (1940).

Moutinho. *Bull. Soc. franç. Ophtal.*, **44**, 176 (1931).

Moutinho and de Mattos. *XIII int. Cong. Ophthal.*, Amsterdam, **1**, 84 (1929).

Müller, L. *Klin. Mbl. Augenheilk.*, **32**, 178 (1894); **41** (1), 459 (1903).

Wien. klin. Wschr., **39**, 321 (1926).

Nesterov and Libenson. *Vestn. Oftal.*, **80**, 15 (1967).

Brit. J. Ophthal., **54**, 46 (1970).

Nettleship. *Trans. ophthal. Soc. U.K.*, **27**, 269 (1907); **32**, 21 (1912).

Newman. *J. Genet.*, **3**, 25 (1913).

Nicolato. *Arch. Ottal.*, **36**, 453 (1929).

Nicoletti. *Ann. Ottal.*, **53**, 882 (1925).

Nordgren. *Nord. med. T.*, **12**, 2069 (1936).

Ochapovsky. *Arch. Ophthal.*, **14**, 412 (1935).

Ochi. *Amer. J. Ophthal.*, **10**, 161 (1927).

Odland. *Acta neurol. scand.*, **43**, 630 (1967).

Oliver. *Brit. J. Ophthal.*, **5**, 68 (1921).

Oppenheimer. *Amer. J. Ophthal.*, **7**, 530 (1924).

Orth. *Klin. Mbl. Augenheilk.*, **124**, 304 (1954).

Oswald. *Brit. med. J.*, **1**, 18 (1911).

Otto. *Ueber die hochgradige Myopie* (Diss.), Strassburg (1891).

v. Graefes Arch. Ophthal., **43**, 323, 543 (1897); **47**, 244 (1898).

Pallier, Proto and Risso. *Boll. Oculist.*, **45**, 231 (1966).

Parnell. *Brit. J. Ophthal.*, **35**, 467 (1951).

Parsons. *Brit. J. Ophthal.*, **4**, 211 (1920).

Paul. *v. Graefes Arch. Ophthal.*, **139**, 378 (1938).

Paulsen. *v. Graefes Arch. Ophthal.*, **28** (1), 225 (1882).

Pesme. *Clin. Ophtal.*, **16**, 334 (1927).

Bull. Soc. franç. Ophtal., **40**, 409 (1927).

Pflüger. *v. Graefes Arch. Ophthal.*, **22** (4), 63 (1876).

Kurzsichtigkeit u. Erziehung, Wiesbaden (1887).

Z. Schulgesdh. pfl. u. soz. Hyg., **7**, 346 (1894).

Phillips. *De ténotomie sous-cutanée*, Paris, 326 (1841).

Pi. *Nat. med. J. China*, **15**, 626 (1929).

Pillat. *Klin. Mbl. Augenheilk.*, **69**, 429 (1922); **96**, 396; **97**, 60 (1936).

Z. Augenheilk., **57**, 347 (1925).

Pischel. *Trans. Amer. Acad. Ophthal.*, **49**, 155 (1944–5).

Pischel and Miller. *Arch. Ophthal.*, **22**, 974 (1939).

Plocher. *Klin. Mbl. Augenheilk.*, **62**, 94 (1919).

Podos, Becker and Morton. *Amer. J. Ophthal.*, **62**, 1039 (1966).

Polatti. *Klin. Mbl. Augenheilk.*, **44** (1), 14 (1906).

Pollock. *Glasg. med. J.*, **86**, 214 (1916).

Ponte. *Boll. Oculist.*, **41**, 739 (1962).

Poos. *Arch. Ophthal.*, **2**, 66 (1929).

v. Graefes Arch. Ophthal., **150**, 245 (1950).

Poyales. *Arch. Soc. oftal. hisp.-amer.*, **13**, 777 (1953).

Priestley, Hermann and Bloom. *Amer. J. Ophthal.*, **56**, 926 (1963).

Proskauer. *v. Graefes Arch. Ophthal.*, **37** (2), 199 (1891).

Proto. *Boll. Oculist.*, **43**, 343 (1964).

Puglisi-Duranti. *Boll. Oculist.*, **15**, 535 (1936).

Pyle. *Ophthal. Rec.*, **17**, 210 (1908).

Raeder. *v. Graefes Arch. Ophthal.*, **110**, 73 (1922).

Raski. *Acta ophthal.* (Kbh.), **16**, 295 (1938).

Rasmussen. *Brit. J. Ophthal.*, **20**, 350 (1936).

Redi, Maselli and Miglior. *Ann. Ottal.*, **91**, 350 (1965).

Reese and Stepanik. *Amer. J. Ophthal.*, **38**, 308 (1954).

Rehsteiner. *v. Graefes Arch. Ophthal.*, **120**, 282 (1928).

von Reuss. *Wien. med. Presse*, **22**, 200 (1881).

Rieger. *v. Graefes Arch. Ophthal.*, **131**, 410 (1934); **136**, 119 (1937).

Riffenburgh. *Amer. J. Ophthal.*, **59**, 925 (1965).

Rivara and Gemme. *Atti Cong. Soc. oftal. ital.*, **23**, 395 (1966).

Rocha. *Ophtalmos*, **3**, 61 (1942).

Rønne. *Klin. Mbl. Augenheilk.*, **57**, 512 (1916).

Romano-Catania. *Sicilia med.* (Palermo), **1**, 593 (1889).

Rupprecht. *Münch. med. Wschr.*, **60**, 895 (1913).

Sabbadini. *Atti Soc. oftal. ital.*, **12**, 123 (1951).

Salgado Gómez. *Arch. Soc. oftal. hisp.-amer.*, **16**, 771 (1956).

Cirugia de la miopia, Barcelona (1958).

Salleras and Ortiz de Zarate. *Brit. J. Ophthal.*, **34**, 662 (1950).

Sallmann. *v. Graefes Arch. Ophthal.*, **135**, 593 (1936).

Salzmann. *v. Graefes Arch. Ophthal.*, **54**, 337 (1902); **143**, 547, 568 (1941).

Samuels. *Arch. Ophthal.*, **4**, 838 (1930).

Sato. *Rinsho Ganka*, **6**, 209 (1952).

The Causes and Prevention of Acquired Myopia, Tokyo (1957).

Trans. ophthal. Soc. N.Z., **17**, 109 (1965).

Sato, Akiyama and Shibata. *Amer. J. Ophthal.*, **36**, 823 (1953).

Sattler. *Ber. dtsch. ophthal. Ges.*, **27**, 207 (1898).

Trans. ophthal. Soc. U.K., **27**, 1 (1907).

Savin. *Brit. J. Ophthal.*, **19**, 597 (1935).

Scarpa. *Saggio di osservazioni e d'esperienze sulla principali malattie degli occhi*, Pavia (1801).

Schapringer. *N.Y. med. J.*, **58**, 465 (1893).

Scheerer and Seitzer. *Klin. Mbl. Augenheilk.*, **82**, 511 (1929).

Schepens and Marden. *Amer. J. Ophthal.*, **61**, 213 (1966).

Schiess-Gemuseus. *Klin. Mbl. Augenheilk.*, **19**, 384 (1881).

Schleich. *Mitt. ophthal. Klin. Tübingen*, **1** (3), 1 (1882).

Schmidt. *Klin. Mbl. Augenheilk.*, **80**, 553 (1928).

Schmidt-Rimpler. *v. Graefes Arch. Ophthal.*, **31** (4), 115 (1885); **35** (1), 200; (4), 249 (1889).

Schnabel. *v. Graefes Arch. Ophthal.*, **20** (2), 1 (1874).

Schnabel and Herrnheiser. *Z. Heilk.*, **16**, 1 (1895).

Schultz-Zehden. *Med. Klin.*, **4**, 1111 (1908).

Schweigger. *Hb. d. speciellen Augenheilk.*, 3rd ed., Berlin, 466 (1875).

Schweizer. *Ueber die deletären Folgen der Myopie, insbesondere die Erkrankung d. Macula lutea* (Diss.), Zürich (1890).

Seggel. *v. Graefes Arch. Ophthal.*, **30** (2), 69 (1884); **36** (2), 1 (1890); **56**, 551 (1903); **59**, 109 (1904).

Arch. Augenheilk., **18**, 303 (1888).

Shapland. *Trans. ophthal. Soc. U.K.*, **54**, 176 (1934).

Siebenlist. *Z. Augenheilk.*, **25**, 443 (1911).

Siegrist. *Klin. Mbl. Augenheilk.*, **44**, Beil., 1 (1906).

Refraktion u. Akkommodation d. mensch. Auges, Berlin (1925).

Smith, Priestley. *Glaucoma*, London (1879). *Ophthal. Rev.*, **20**, 331 (1901).

Sonder. *Arch. Ophtal.*, **37**, 290 (1920).

Sondermann. *v. Graefes Arch. Ophthal.*, **151**, 200 (1950).

Sood and Gupta. *Orient. Arch. Ophthal.*, **4**, 264 (1966).

Sorsby. *Blindness in England, 1951–4*, London (1956).

Sorsby, Wilcox and Ham. *Brit. J. Ophthal.*, **19**, 327 (1935).

Sourdille. *Gaz. méd. Nantes*, **26**, 945 (1908).

Stargardt. *Z. Augenheilk.*, **27**, 327 (1912).

Starkiewicz. *Klin. oczna*, **35**, 363 (1965).

Steiger. *Z. Augenheilk.*, **20**, 97 (1908); **25**, 41 (1911); **36**, 127 (1916).

Die Entstehung d. sphärischen Refraktionen d. mensch. Auges, Berlin (1913).

Klin. Mbl. Augenheilk., **57**, 588 (1916).

Berl. klin. Wschr., **56**, 419 (1919).

Stilling. *Arch. Augenheilk.*, **15**, 133 (1885); **22**, 47 (1891).

Untersuch. ü. d. Entstehung d. Kurzsichtigkeit, Wiesbaden (1887).

Schädelbau u. Kurzsichtigkeit, Wiesbaden (1888).

Z. Augenheilk., **9**, 1 (1903); **14**, 23 (1905).

Klin. Mbl. Augenheilk., **42** (1), 557 (1904).

Stilling and Landolt. *Klin. Mbl. Augenheilk.*, **46** (1), 490 (1908).

Stock. *Ber. dtsch. ophthal. Ges.*, **34**, 261 (1907).

Klin. Mbl. Augenheilk., **46** (1), 342 (1908).

Stocker. *Arch. Ophthal.*, **30**, 476 (1943).

Strampelli. *Ann. Ottal.*, **80**, 75 (1954).

Straub. *v. Graefes Arch. Ophthal.*, **70**, 130 (1909).

Strebel. *Beitr. Augenheilk.*, **9** (84), 305 (1913).

Klin. Mbl. Augenheilk., **107**, 179 (1941).

Streiff. *Klin. Mbl. Augenheilk.*, **73**, 703 (1924).

von Szily. *Klin. Mbl. Augenheilk.*, **41** (2), 44 (1903).

Ber. dtsch. ophthal. Ges., **42**, 200 (1920).

v. Graefes Arch. Ophthal., **106**, 195 (1921); **110**, 183 (1922).

Tange. *Arch. Ophtal.*, **34**, 463 (1914).

Terrien. *Arch. Ophtal.*, **26**, 737 (1906).

Thiel. *Ber. dtsch. ophthal. Ges.*, **62**, 206 (1959).

Thompson. *Ophthal. Rev.*, **29**, 321 (1910).

Thomson. *Brit. J. Ophthal.*, **3**, 303 (1919).

Tomlinson and Phillips. *Brit. J. Ophthal.*, **53**, 765 (1969).

Tower. *Arch. Ophthal.*, **38**, 521 (1947).

Tscherning. *v. Graefes Arch. Ophthal.*, **29** (1), 201 (1883).

Uhthoff. *Dtsch. med. Wschr.*, **48**, 115 (1922).

Usher. *Roy. Lond. ophthal. Hosp. Rep.*, **19**, 130 (1914).

Brit. J. Ophthal., **5**, 289 (1921).

Valerio. *Acta XVII int. Cong. Ophthal.*, Montreal-N.Y., **1**, 194 (1954).

Varelmann. *Arch. Augenheilk.*, **96**, 385 (1925).

Venco. *Ann. Ottal.*, **63**, 127 (1935).

Verhoeff. *Arch. Ophthal.*, **38**, 107 (1909).

Vidal. *Arch. chil. Oftal.*, **16**, 11 (1959).

Vogel and Balthaser. *Klin. Mbl. Augenheilk.*, **128**, 456 (1956).

Vogt. *v. Graefes Arch. Ophthal.*, **108**, 187 (1922).

Schweiz. med. Wschr., **53**, 161, 188 (1923); **59**, 301 (1929).

Ber. dtsch. ophthal. Ges., **44**, 67 (1924).

Klin. Mbl. Augenheilk., **72**, 212 (1924); **75**, 463 (1925); **95**, 94 (1935).

Vontobel. *v. Graefes Arch. Ophthal.*, **122**, 311 (1929).

Waardenburg. *Klin. Mbl. Augenheilk.*, **85**, 31 (1930).

Maandschr. Kindergeneesk., **1**, 451 (1932).

Genetics and Ophthalmology, Oxon., **2**, 1232 (1963).

Wätzold. *Ber. dtsch. ophthal. Ges.*, **44**, 71 (1924).

Walker. *Brit. J. Ophthal.*, **16**, 485 (1932).

Wanspa and Limpaphayom. *Trans. ophthal. Soc. N.Z.*, **17**, 106 (1965).

Ware. *Phil. Trans.*, **103**, 31 (1813).

Weber. *Klin. Mbl. Augenheilk.*, **105**, 111 (1940); **106**, 78 (1941).

de Wecker and Masselon. *Ophtalmoscopie clinique*, Paris (1891).

Weekers, Lavergne and Prijot. *Ann. Oculist.* (Paris), **191**, 26 (1958).

Weekers, Moureau, Hacourt and André. *Bull. Soc. belge Ophtal.*, No. 112, 146 (1955).

Weekers, Watillon and Thomas-Decortis. *Arch. Ophtal.*, **21**, 217 (1961).

Weinstein. *Klin. Mbl. Augenheilk.*, **93**, 794 (1934).

Weiss. *Mitt. ophthal. Klin. Tübingen*, **1** (3), 63 (1882); 69 (1884).

v. Graefes Arch. Ophthal., **31** (3), 239 (1885).

Klin. Mbl. Augenheilk., **26**, 349 (1888).

Arch. Augenheilk., **23**, 194 (1891).

Ueber d. Vorkommen v. scharfbegrenzten Ektasien im Avgengrunde . . . . bei hochgradiger Myopie, Wiesbaden (1897).

Wick. *Zbl. ges. Ophthal.*, **8**, 113 (1923).

Klin. Mbl. Augenheilk., **72**, 491 (1924).

Z. Augenheilk., **54**, 363; **56**, 356 (1925).

Widmark. *Nord. med. Ark.*, **8** (15), 1 (1897).

Mitt. Augenklin. Carol. med.-chir. Inst., Stockholm, **1**, 17 (1898); **4**, 61 (1902); **10**, 41 (1909).

Wiener. *J. Amer. med. Ass.*, **89**, 594 (1927).

Wilson. *Glasg. med. J.*, **77**, 241 (1912); **79**, 250 (1913).

Wirtz. *Wschr. Therap. Hyg. Auges*, **14**, 204, 238 (1911).

Witte. *Z. Augenheilk.*, **51**, 163 (1923).

Wölfflin. *v. Graefes Arch. Ophthal.*, **61**, 524 (1905).

Wold. *Arch. Ophthal.*, **42**, 225 (1949).

Wood, A. *Ophthalmoscope*, **14**, 302 (1916).

Wood, D. J. *Brit. J. Ophthal.*, **11**, 224 (1927).

Worth. *Trans. ophthal. Soc. U.K.*, **26**, 141 (1906).

Young. *Amer. J. Ophthal.*, **52**, 853 (1961).

Amer. J. Optom., **38**, 545 (1961); **40**, 257 (1963); **44**, 192 (1967).

E.E.N.T. Digest, **27**, 55 (1965).

Zauberman and Merin. *Amer. J. Ophthal.*, **67**, 756 (1969).

ACQUIRED AND IRREGULAR ASTIGMATISM

ACQUIRED REGULAR ASTIGMATISM is of little clinical importance. A considerable change of corneal astigmatism involving a reduction in curvature of the vertical meridian regularly follows a surgical cataract section, a subject which will be presently discussed.[1] A similar change may result as a sequel to surgery for squint, ptosis (Zamorani, 1960) or retinal detachment involving an infolding or resection of the sclera (Wolter, 1967). The presence of a pterygium frequently produces an astigmatism whereby the curvature of the horizontal diameter is decreased while its surgical removal usually results in the opposite effect, the vertical diameter in each case remaining unchanged; thus Melchionda (1966) reported the reduction of a pre-operative astigmatism to 2·32 D to 0·77 D, 40 days after surgery. Finally, changes in the corneal curvature may follow the prolonged use of contact lenses.[2]

[1] p. 365. [2] p. 757.

AN IRREGULAR ASTIGMATISM wherein the refraction in different meridians conforms to no geometrical plan and the refracted rays have no planes of symmetry, may be caused by anomalies in the cornea or the lens and very rarely by alterations in the retina.

IRREGULAR CORNEAL ASTIGMATISM

A marked degree of irregular astigmatism is most commonly found in pathological conditions of the cornea as a result of the softening or deformation associated with conical cornea or of inequalities in healing after trau-

FIGS. 370 to 373.—KERATOSCOPY IN ACQUIRED IRREGULAR ASTIGMATISM (M. Amsler).

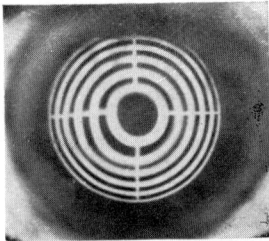

FIG. 370.—After herpes.

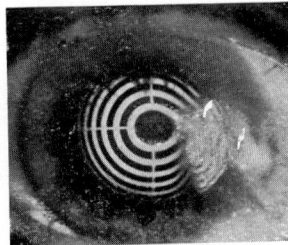

FIG. 371.—Pterygium.

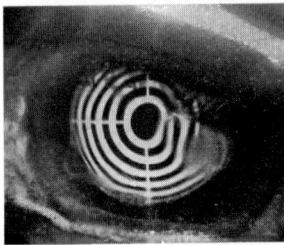

FIG. 372.—Phlyctenular keratitis.

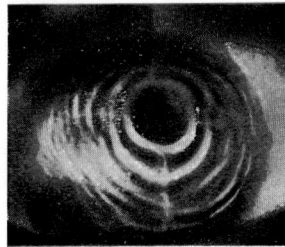

FIG. 373.—A chemical burn.

mata, inflammation or ulcerative processes or in degenerative conditions. In these cases the visual defect caused by the optical error is usually accentuated by the presence of opacities, and the combination of the two frequently makes any attempt to improve vision by spectacles difficult or impossible (Figs. 370–3).

CONICAL CORNEA

CONICAL CORNEA has already been fully described.[1] From the optical point of view the cornea is bulged forwards into the shape of a cone, the apex usually being slightly below the centre. The eye becomes myopic, but owing to the hyperbolic nature of the curvature, the refraction is irregular

[1] Vol. III, p. 964.

FIGS. 374 to 377.—KERATOSCOPY IN KERATOCONUS (Inst. Ophthal.).

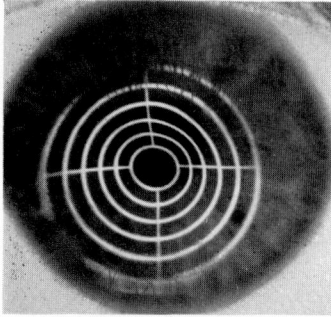

FIG. 374.—Keratoconus fruste. Note the depression of 4° in the horizontal axis.

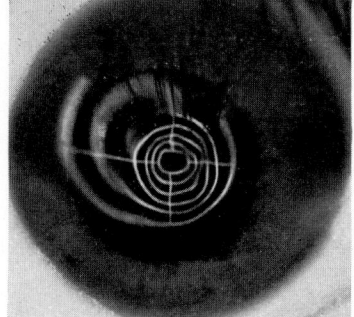

FIG. 375.—A well-developed eccentric case in a youth of 19.

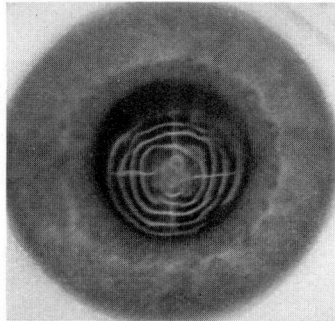

FIG. 376.—A marked symmetrical case in a man aged 21.

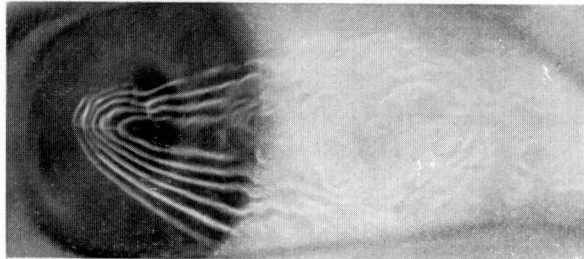

FIG. 377.—An advanced case in a man aged 55.

and a high degree of astigmatism is usually present. The difficulties of adequate correction are increased by the fact that the condition is progressive for a considerable time so that the optical condition tends constantly to change. In the initial stages or in mild cases, the astigmatic defect may be slight, and with keratoscopy relatively slight deflections from the normal may be evident (Amsler, 1930–46) (Fig. 374); in the more marked degrees the summit of the cornea may occasionally be remarkably regular but is often extremely irregular (Figs. 375–7).

In these marked cases when the eye is examined with the retinoscopic mirror at 1 metre distance, a ring shadow is frequently seen in the red reflex of the fundus, which alters its position on moving the mirror (Fig. 378). This ring appears dark because none of the rays from the fundus passing through it enters the observer's eye, the rays on the central side being convergent, and those on the peripheral side being divergent.

Treatment. Owing to the irregularity of the refraction, optical correction by spectacles may be very difficult and may lead to disappointing visual results. In such cases it is frequently found that the only satisfactory method of attaining good visual acuity is to eliminate the cornea from the refractive system by the use of a contact lens which frequently allows normal or even supernormal vision in a case in which spectacles will not allow an acuity of 6/60 (Fick, 1888; Strebel, 1937–43; Merigot de Treigny, 1938; von Györffy, 1940; Sverdlick, 1942; Jaensch, 1942; Ridley, 1956; and others). In the optical correction of this deformity contact lenses, both haptic and corneal in type, find their most

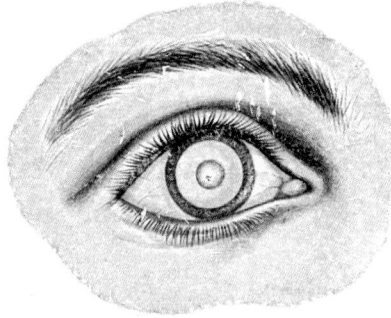

FIG. 378.—KERATOCONUS.

The retinoscopic appearance in a marked case.

useful and dramatic application; their failure, as in the presence of corneal opacities, is one indication for keratoplasty.[1]

THE HEALING OF CORNEAL WOUNDS

THE HEALING OF CORNEAL WOUNDS usually leaves an irregular astigmatism sometimes of a very gross degree (32 D, Aschheim, 1897), but in the case of operative sections the irregularity may be slight. Conversely, it has been known for the healing of a corneal injury to cause a pre-existing astigmatism to disappear (Burgos Fernandez, 1963). In the usual superior section for an iridectomy or cataract extraction a fairly regular inverse astigmatism usually results, a circumstance first noted by Donders (1864) and first accurately measured keratometrically by von Reuss and Woinow (1869) (Fig. 379). In 49 cases Treutler (1900) found the vertical curvature diminished in 88%, unchanged in 2% and increased in 10%, the highest diminution in radius being 1·5 mm. with a mean of 0·7 mm.; his conclusions have been generally substantiated by subsequent workers.[2]

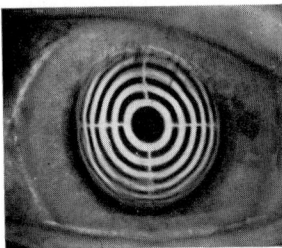

FIG. 379.—POST-OPERATIVE ASTIGMATISM.

[1] p. 780.
[2] van Lint (1914), Alexiadès (1920), Andreae (1923), Tron (1925), Alajmo (1950), Floyd (1951), Franco Lara (1958), and many others.

The astigmatism is greatest soon after operation and diminishes rapidly at first, and then slowly over a period of some 4 months. According to Cridland (1962) the alteration is exponential in character. The nearer the wound to the centre of the cornea, the more the resulting astigmatism, which is increased if complications such as a prolapse of the iris have occurred. The axis of the astigmatism also varies and may change by some ten degrees in the months following surgery.

Treatment. The treatment of all these varieties of irregular astigmatism is difficult, and at best unsatisfactory. Conforming to no optical system, the refraction must be estimated largely by a method of trial and error, a process which absorbs a large amount of time and patience and frequently leads to a poor optical result. The improvement which can be obtained will frequently be found to be disappointingly small; but considerable care

FIGS. 380 and 381.—THE OPTICAL EFFECT OF KERATOPLASTY AS DEMONSTRATED BY KERATOSCOPY (M. Amsler).

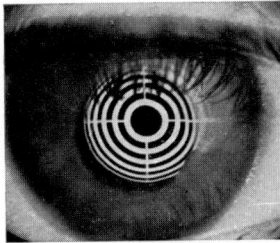

FIG. 380.—The corneal curvature is almost spherical.

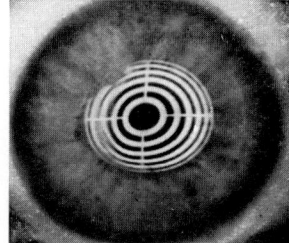

FIG. 381.—Some astigma-
tism is present after grafting.

should be expended in the attempt, if only because little benefit can be expected from other means. Even in cases with some corneal opacities an improvement may be attained by the use of contact lenses. In other cases operative measures may be indicated, all of which are dealt with elsewhere in this *System*. The most radical of these is penetrating or lamellar kerato-plasty in which the object is to excise completely the affected area of the cornea, in which case some residual astigmatism usually occurs although it may be slight (Figs. 380–1), but somewhat less drastic procedures may be of value in selected cases. For example, a thin translucent nebula situated in the centre of the pupillary area may be less incapacitating if made opaque by tattooing with platinum or gold chloride.[1] If light passes through the nebula it is refracted irregularly and renders the whole retinal image blurred; but a complete opacity prevents the passage of any rays, and since the rays from the periphery can reach the part of the retina directly behind the blocked-out area in the cornea, a more clearly defined image results, although

[1] Vol. VIII, p. 645.

the aberrations associated with the peripheral refraction lessen the optical value of the result (Fig. 382). Finally the technique of keratomileusis[1] wherein a corneal graft is removed, frozen and re-shaped may be undertaken if this tissue is clean.

IRREGULAR LENTICULAR ASTIGMATISM is usually *refractive* and is most commonly seen during the maturation of cataract owing to regional differences of refraction. An irregular curvature astigmatism occurs in congenital deformities such as coloboma or lenticonus, and is found in subluxation of the lens when the periphery occupies the axial region or when the lens itself lies obliquely; it may follow an intra-ocular operation such as iridectomy (Schiøtz, 1885). Since contact lenses are of no value in these conditions, their optical treatment involves either as adequate a correction as is possible with spectacles or removal of the lens.

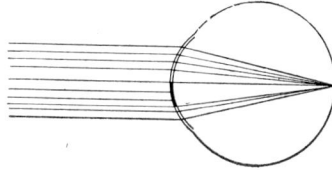

FIG. 382.—THE OPTICAL EFFECT OF A COMPLETE LEUCOMA.

Light falling upon it is not irregularly refracted and does not distort the retinal image.

RETINAL ASTIGMATISM is rare but may occur when the eye is deformed posteriorly as in a myopic staphyloma, or anteriorly as by a neoplasm at the posterior pole.

Alajmo. *G. ital. Oftal.*, **3,** 439 (1950).

Alexiadès. *Arch. Ophtal.*, **37,** 554 (1920).

Amsler. *Ber. dtsch. ophthal. Ges.*, **48,** 202 (1930).
  Bull. Soc. franç. Ophtal., **50,** 100 (1937); **59,** 120 (1940–6).
  Ophthalmologica, **96,** 77 (1938); **111,** 96 (1946).

Andreae. *Der postoperative Astigmatismus nach Staroperationen* (Diss.), Marburg (1923).

Aschheim. *Klin. Mbl. Augenheilk.*, **35,** 108 (1897).

Burgos Fernandez. *Arch. Soc. oftal. hisp.-amer.*, **23,** 418 (1963).

Cridland. *Trans. ophthal. Soc. U.K.*, **82,** 537 (1962).

Donders. *On the Anomalies of Accommodation and Refraction of the Eye*, London (1864).

Fick. *Arch. Augenheilk.*, **18,** 279 (1888).

Floyd. *Amer. J. Ophthal.*, **34,** 1525 (1951).

Franco Lara. *Arch. Asoc. evit. Ceg. Mex.*, **1,** 417 (1958).

von Györffy. *Klin. Mbl. Augenheilk.*, **104,** 81 (1940).

Jaensch. *Med. Klin.*, **38,** 131 (1942).

van Lint. *Bull. Soc. franç. Ophtal.*, **31,** 448 (1914).

Melchionda. *Atti Cong. Soc. oftal. ital.*, **23,** 273 (1966).

Merigot de Treigny. *Presse méd.*, **46,** 724 (1938).

von Reuss and Woinow. *Ophthalmometrische Studien*, Wien (1869).

Ridley. *Brit. J. Ophthal.*, **40,** 295 (1956).

Schiøtz. *Arch. Augenheilk.*, **15,** 283 (1885).

Strebel. *Klin. Mbl. Augenheilk.*, **99,** 30 (1937).
  Schweiz. med. Wschr., **73,** 1029 (1943).

Sverdlick. *Sem. méd.* (*B. Aires*), **49,** 938 (1942).

Treutler. *Z. Augenheilk.*, **3,** 484 (1900).

Tron. *Klin. Mbl. Augenheilk.*, **75,** 333 (1925).

Wolter. *J. pediat. Ophthal.*, **4,** 27 (1967).

Zamorani. *G. ital. Oftal.*, **13,** 67 (1960).

TRANSIENT CHANGES IN REFRACTION

TRANSIENT CHANGES IN REFRACTION may be due to local or general systemic causes.

CHANGES IN REFRACTION DUE TO LOCAL CONDITIONS are the most common and are practically all due to changes in the lens. The ciliary

[1] p. 853.

muscle is usually the agent responsible, inducing a temporary hypermetropia in accommodative paralysis or a temporary myopia in accommodative spasm : these conditions will be discussed subsequently. In *iritis* or *irido-cyclitis* a myopia has been observed of from 1 to 3 D or even 5 D, presumably from an irritative spasm of the ciliary muscle, possibly in some cases from relaxation of the suspensory ligament owing to turgidity and swelling of the ciliary body (Green, 1887; Hess, 1903; Davis, 1914; Sédan, 1922–26; Blatt, 1930; and others). We have already seen that a *contusion* may have a similar effect, the traumatic myopia being usually caused by lenticular deformation due to ciliary spasm or damage to the suspensory ligament.

That an acute transient myopia may develop as a sequel to *external inflammation*, such as conjunctivitis with episcleritis, was claimed by Gorse and Bergès (1937): the reaction may be a reflex ciliary irritation.

The occurrence of a transitory hypermetropia due to lesions in the fundus such as œdema or a retinal detachment is obvious.

Pressure on the eye from outside may bring about transient changes of refraction. Depending on its point of pressure an orbital tumour may bring about hypermetropia or hypermetropic astigmatism from axial pressure (Candian, 1922; S. and A. Brav, 1942; Jones, 1942) or myopia from equatorial pressure (Handmann, 1912). The same result may be due to an ethmoid mucocele (Seale, 1929) or may occur in exophthalmos. A scleritis (Evers, 1898) or an orbital inflammation has also been noted to induce a transitory myopia (Pascheff, 1914) or astigmatism (Latorre, 1947). Pressure from a tumour or swelling in the lids may also involve a transient astigmatic change (Ormond, 1921; Safar, 1947). A similar change may follow a tenotomy or advancement operation (Snellen, 1869; Laqueur, 1884), or surgery for ptosis (Yamanaka, 1965), while after scleral surgery for a retinal detachment the change in the refraction may be considerable (Wolter, 1967). A similar refractive change has been said to be associated with Quincke's œdema of the eyelids (Voisin, 1963).

CONSTITUTIONAL CONDITIONS provide a more interesting and speculative cause of transient refractive errors, the most important being diabetes and a number of toxic states.

CHANGES OF REFRACTION IN DIABETES MELLITUS

That sudden changes in the refraction occur in diabetes has been known since the original observation of Horner (1873), and a considerable literature has now accumulated on the subject (Duke-Elder, 1925). The essential features of the condition are that the changes of refraction come on suddenly and bilaterally, that a myopic change is associated with a rise, and a hypermetropic with a fall in the sugar concentration of the blood, and that the hypermetropic change seems not to occur as an initial phenomenon but to follow a myopic change. If the concentration of blood-sugar is made to vary, the refractive state of the eye may follow, changing over from hypermetropia to myopia and *vice versa*. The alteration in the refraction is frequently associated with astigmatic changes also ; it commonly involves an alteration of 2 to 3 dioptres, and sometimes of − 6 D and + 9 D in the highest meridians (Duke-Elder, 1925), and there is evidence that in terminal states of coma a much higher myopia may develop. It is interesting that in a large percentage the changes occur in patients over 50 years of age.

The *causation of these refractive changes* in diabetes has excited much speculation. Some of the earlier theories can be briefly dismissed. The old view that accommodative changes are responsible is discounted by the facts that atropine is without effect, that the refractive alterations usually occur in older people and that astigmatic changes are often marked. The suggestions that a shortening of the axial length of the eye results from a loss of intra-ocular fluid (Sourdille, 1900 ; Lichtenstein, 1906), or that its lengthening results from softening due to œdema do not bear examination ; nor does the theory of a change in the index of the refraction of the ocular fluids owing to an increased concentration of sugar since, as we have seen, concentrations far above levels compatible with life would be required to produce an alteration of refraction of 1 D (Hagen, 1921). Finally, the corneal curvature is found to be unchanged (Wölfflin, 1911 ; Lundsgaard, 1919 ; Enroth, 1922 ; Granström, 1933). From a process of exclusion, reasoning from the development of astigmatism and in view of a case of unilateral aphakia reported by Elschnig (1923) which showed changes only in the phakic eye, it would seem necessary to postulate that the lens is implicated.

The changes which occur in the lens have not yet been elucidated with certainty, and three theories require mention. The myopia associated with a rising sugar concentration has been ascribed to hydration of the cortical layers of the lens relative to the nucleus (Duke-Elder, 1925). As the blood-sugar rises, provided the available water-reserve is maintained, the osmotic pressure of the aqueous tends to decrease, largely owing to the reduction of osmotically active substances in the blood following the increased flow of relatively concentrated urine. In order to establish osmotic equilibrium, water tends to flow from the chambers of the eye into the lens, which tends to maintain its original molar concentration. It therefore swells and the optical density of its peripheral layers becomes diminished while the nucleus remains unaltered. On both counts its refractive power is increased, and the eye becomes myopic. If the inflow of fluid is rapid, actual droplets are formed under the capsule and eventually a cataract may be formed, sometimes with great rapidity. Conversely, with a fall in sugar concentration, a reverse osmotic flow is inaugurated, and a change to hypermetropia is induced.

Granström (1933), on the other hand, put forward the hypothesis that hydration of the nucleus of the lens was responsible for the hypermetropic change. He suggested that in hyperglycæmia there was a retention of salt in the tissues which, on diminution of the sugar, was followed by hydration ; the lens shared in these changes, the phenomena being more marked in the nucleus since the cortex attained rapid equilibrium with the aqueous.

One difficulty about both these theories is the impossibility of reproducing the changes in experimental animals by altering the fluid balance of the body either with sugar (Knapp, 1909) or salt (Weekers, 1941). Weekers was able, however, to induce myopic changes in animals by the ingestion or injection of galactose, and these were associated with early cataractous changes in the lens; such changes in these early stages are reversible, and the return of the lens to its normal state is associated with hypermetropia. He therefore concluded that the myopia was due to an increased refractive index of the lens due to changes of a pre-cataractous nature caused by a toxic agent; such changes are reversible and on their amelioration hypermetropia results.

Whatever the cause of the refractive changes, a sudden and seemingly inexplicable myopia should always suggest the possibility of diabetes and direct attention to the urine: occurring in a known diabetic it should suggest ineffective control of the disease. On the other hand, a rapid hypermetropic change points to treatment being too suddenly undertaken or too enthusiastically applied; the condition has certainly become more common since the general introduction of insulin in the treatment of this disease. In either case treatment should not be directed to the eye but rather to the constitutional condition, for the refractive change is transitory and invariably returns to normal provided metabolic equilibrium can be re-established. If spectacles are to be prescribed, they need be considered only as an emergency and temporary measure.

A TRANSITORY HYPERMETROPIA has been reported in other conditions: in *emaciation* from hepatic disease or pulmonary tuberculosis (Gallus, 1906) or in a non-diabetic woman (aged 63) undergoing a course of dietary reducing treatment in whom a transitory hypermetropia coincided on three occasions with the elimination of carbohydrates from the diet (Jensen, 1932).

A TRANSIENT MYOPIA, which probably has the same metabolic basis as that associated with diabetes in that a considerable disturbance of the water-and-salt balance is involved, has been reported in prolonged *diarrhœa* (Schieck, 1907), profuse *sweating* (Lindahl, 1938) and extreme *alkalosis* (in the Sippey regime: Thorson, 1933). Perhaps not unrelated to these changes is the transient myopia which has been reported in association with menstruation (Bergin, 1952; Jampolsky and Flom, 1953).

A TRANSIENT MYOPIA OCCURRING IN VARIOUS TOXIC STATES AND AFTER THE ADMINISTRATION OF DRUGS such as the arsenicals and sulphonamides is now well annotated in the literature. The mechanism is by no means clear, nor is it by any means certain that the cause in every case is the same. Most writers ascribe the phenomenon to an irritative ciliary spasm; but the myopia has frequently been found to be unchanged by atropine. A central toxic irritation of the parasympathetic nerves or centres is an alternative assumption. In most cases metabolic changes have not been investigated, but gross alterations in the salt and fluid balance have not been suggested. Whatever the mechanism, lenticular changes seem the best basis for an explanation. It is interesting that as a rule the myopia, varying in degree from 1 to about 4 D and in duration from a few days to a few weeks, is frequently the only toxic symptom.

The toxic diseases which have been reported include *jaundice* (Moauro, 1893), *influenza* (Lundsgaard, 1919) and the " mud fever," characterized by toxæmia and acute nephrosis, contracted by the German soldiers in the Baltic campaign in the Second World War (Techow, 1945–6; Freusberg, 1947).

Transitory myopia up to about − 4 D resulting from the administration of *arsenicals* has been recorded by several authors.[1] It has also been noted after the inhalation of arsenic fumes (Roggenkämper, 1931).

A similar transient myopia following one or other of the *sulphonamides* has been a common observation[2]; it has even followed the vaginal absorption of a cream containing sulphanilamide (Maddalena, 1968). As a rule, but with some exceptions, the myopia does not occur when the drug is initially taken but during a subsequent period of dosage. That atropine does not abolish the myopia indicates that it is not caused by ciliary spasm. Hornbogen (1941) believed it to be due to œdema of the lens, which in Blankstein's (1941) view might be caused by unequal distribution of the drug between the lens and the aqueous. An allergic reaction has also been suggested as a causal factor (Mattsson, 1952). Some disturbance of the salt and water balance of the lens probably takes place but its exact nature and its cause are not clear. As in some cases of traumatic myopia, the anterior chamber is occasionally found to be shallow, suggesting an anterior displacement or swelling of the lens, the vitreous or the ciliary body, sometimes resulting in acute closed-angle glaucoma (Maddalena, 1968).

A curious feature of the transient myopia occurring during sulphonamide therapy is that it has become much rarer since the introduction of more modern variants of these drugs. A similar phenomenon, however, has been more recently noted occurring as a complication of the use of some modern diuretics which are closely allied chemically to the sulphonamides.[3] Such diuretics fall roughly into two groups, the carbonic anhydrase inhibitors (Diamox, Cardrase, Daranide) and, more rarely, the thiazides (hydrochlorthiazide). A proportion of the cases seems to have occurred during pregnancy, perhaps against a background of the altered fluid and electrolyte balance already present. It is interesting that in addition to the myopia, retinal œdema has occasionally been noted (Beasley, 1961–62), shallowing of the anterior chamber (Garland *et al.*, 1962) and a rise in the intra-ocular

---

[1] Milian and Périn (1921), Bielschowsky (1922), Dupuys-Dutemps and Périn (1926), Jessner (1926), Casati (1927), Redslob and Lévy (1928), Terrien (1929), Milian (1930), Cerqueira-Falcão (1937), Sédan (1939) and others.

[2] Gailey (1939), Mattsson (1939), Landsberg (1939), Saba (1940), Hornbogen (1941), Blankstein (1941), Friedman (1941), Paez Allende (1941), Vázquez-Barrière (1941), Miranda (1942), von Fieandt (1942), Carlberg (1942), Granström (1949), and many others.

[3] Arentsen (1956), Back (1956), Binder and Steele (1957), Kronning (1957), Cristiansson (1958), Vitte (1959), Halpern and Kulvin (1959), Muirhead and Scheie (1960), Corcelle (1961), Mendle (1962), Michaelson (1962), Galin *et al.* (1962), Garland *et al.* (1962), Voisin and Lombard (1963), Ericson (1963), Hermann (1963).

pressure (Arentsen, 1956). Myopia has also been reported with a synthetic steroid (Spironolactone) used as a diuretic (Belci, 1968). It must be admitted that the mechanism by which this myopia occurs during therapy with diuretic drugs is as obscure as that produced by the sulphonamides from which they are derived.

The use of other drugs has also been complicated by the development of acute myopia: ACTH administration (Stern, 1955; Larsen, 1956), prednisone (Altenberger *et al.*, 1964), the autonomic blocking agents in a sympathectomized patient (Grossman and Hanley, 1960), antihistamines such as promethazine (Bard, 1964), a tranquillizer, prochlorperazine (Yasuna, 1962), penicillamine (Michiels *et al.*, 1962), tetracycline (Edwards, 1963) and even oral contraceptives.

A transient myopia has been reported as following *radium irradiation* (von Fieandt, 1941), and, associated with reversible pre-cataractous changes, in *parathyroid deficiency* following a thyroidectomy for Graves's disease (Weekers, 1941). In both of these, lenticular changes were involved.

Altenberger, Bromber-Sznek and Marciniak. *Pol. Tyg. lek.*, **19**, 769 (1964).
Arentsen. *Arch. chil. Oftal.*, **13**, 82 (1956).
Back. *Arch. Ophthal.*, **55**, 546 (1956).
Bard. *Amer. J. Ophthal.*, **58**, 682 (1964).
Beasley. *Arch. Ophthal.*, **65**, 212 (1961); **68**, 490 (1962).
Belci. *Boll. Oculist.*, **47**, 24 (1968).
Bergin. *Amer. J. Optom.*, **29**, 129 (1952).
Bielschowsky. *Ber. dtsch. ophthal. Ges.*, **43**, 245 (1922).
Binder and Steele. *J. Amer. med. Ass.*, **165**, 154 (1957).
Blankstein. *Amer. J. Ophthal.*, **24**, 895 (1941).
Blatt. *v. Graefes Arch. Ophthal.*, **125**, 125 (1930).
Brav, S. and A. *Amer. J. Ophthal.*, **25**, 82 (1942).
Candian. *Klin. Mbl. Augenheilk.*, **68**, 195 (1922).
Carlberg. *Acta ophthal.* (Kbh.), **20**, 275 (1942).
Casati. *Atti Cong. oftal. ital.*, 307 (1927).
Cerquiera-Falcâo. *Ann. Oculist.* (Paris), **174**, 847 (1937).
Corcelle. *Bull. Soc. Ophtal. Fr.*, **61**, 788 (1961).
Cristiansson. *Acta ophthal.* (Kbh.), **36**, 356 (1958).
Davis. *Trans. Amer. ophthal. Soc.*, **13**, 858 (1914).
Duke-Elder. *Brit. J. Ophthal.*, **9**, 167 (1925).
Dupuys-Dutemps and Périn. *Ann. Oculist.* (Paris), **163**, 123 (1926).
Edwards. *J. Amer. med. Ass.*, **186**, 69 (1963).
Elschnig. *Med. Klin.*, **19**, 17 (1923).
Enroth. *Acta med. scand.*, **56**, 500 (1922).
Ericson. *Acta ophthal.* (Kbh.), **41**, 538 (1963).
Evers. *Klin. Mbl. Augenheilk.*, **36**, 240 (1898).
von Fieandt. *Acta ophthal.* (Kbh.), **19**, 11 (1941); **20**, 24 (1942).
Freusberg. *Klin. Mbl. Augenheilk.*, **112**, 304 (1947).
Friedman. *Amer. J. Ophthal.*, **24**, 935 (1941).

Gailey. *Amer. J. Ophthal.*, **22**, 1399 (1939).
Galin, Baras and Zweifach. *Amer. J. Ophthal.*, **54**, 237 (1962).
Gallus. *Z. Augenheilk.*, **15**, 319 (1906).
Garland, Sholk and Guenter. *Amer. J. Obst. Gynec.*, **84**, 69 (1962).
Gorse and Bergès. *Ann. Oculist.* (Paris), **174**, 844 (1937).
Granström. *Acta ophthal.* (Kbh.), **11**, 1 (1933); **15**, 523 (1937); **27**, 59 (1949).
Green. *Trans. Amer. ophthal. Soc.*, **4**, 599 (1887).
Grossman and Hanley. *Arch. Ophthal.*, **63**, 853 (1960).
Hagen. *v. Graefes Arch. Ophthal.*, **105**, 243 (1921).
Halpern and Kulvin. *Amer. J. Ophthal.*, **48**, 534 (1959).
Handmann. *Z. Augenheilk.*, **28**, 542 (1912).
Hermann. *Bull. Soc. Ophtal. Fr.*, **63**, 719 (1963).
Hess. *Graefe-Saemisch Hb. d. ges. Augenheilk.*, 2nd ed., Leipzig, **8** (2), 284 (1903).
Hornbogen. *Amer. J. Ophthal.*, **24**, 323 (1941).
Horner. *Klin. Mbl. Augenheilk.*, **11**, 488 (1873).
Jampolsky and Flom. *Amer. J. Ophthal.*, **36**, 81 (1953).
Jensen. *Acta ophthal.* (Kbh.), **10**, 388 (1932).
Jessner. *Klin. Mbl. Augenheilk.*, **76**, 431 (1926).
Jones. *Amer. J. Ophthal.*, **25**, 482 (1942).
Knapp, P. *Z. Augenheilk.*, **21**, 420 (1909).
Kronning. *Acta ophthal.* (Kbh.), **35**, 478 (1957).
Landsberg. *J. Amer. med. Ass.*, **113**, 2260 (1939).
Laqueur. *v. Graefes Arch. Ophthal.*, **30** (1), 99 (1884).
Larsen. *Ugeskr. Læg.*, **118**, 807 (1956).
Latorre. *Arch. Soc. oftal. hisp.-amer.*, **7**, 1009 (1947).
Lichtenstein. *Z. Augenheilk.*, **16**, 330 (1906).

Lindahl. *Acta ophthal.* (Kbh.), **16,** 344 (1938).

Lundsgaard. *Klin. Mbl. Augenheilk.,* **63,** 349 (1919).

Maddalena. *Arch. Ophthal.,* **80,** 186 (1968).

Mattsson. *Acta ophthal.* (Kbh.), **17,** 314 (1939) ; **30,** 385 (1952).

Mendle. *Dapim Refuim,* **21,** 24 (1962).

Michaelson. *Amer. J. Ophthal.,* **54,** 1146 (1962).

Michiels, Laterre and Dumoulin. *Bull. Soc. belge Ophtal.,* No. 132, 552 (1962).

Milian. *Rev. franç. Derm. Vénér.,* **6,** 349 (1930).

Milian and Périn. *Paris méd.,* **41,** 388 (1921).

Miranda. *Arch. Soc. oftal. hisp.-amer.,* **1,** 305 (1942).

Moauro. *Lav. Clin. oculist. Napoli,* **3,** 100 (1893).

Muirhead and Scheie. *Arch. Ophthal.,* **63,** 315 (1960).

Ormond. *Brit. J. Ophthal.,* **5,** 117 (1921).

Paez Allende. *Sem. méd.* (*B. Aires*), **48,** 1273 (1941).

Arch. oftal. B. Aires, **17,** 46 (1942).

Pascheff. *Ann. Oculist.* (Paris), **151,** 426 (1914).

Redslob and Lévy. *Rev. Oto-neuro-ophtal.,* **6,** 801 (1928).

Roggenkämper. *Klin. Mbl. Augenheilk.,* **86,** 239 (1931).

Saba. *Rass. ital. Ottal.,* **9,** 708 (1940).

Safar. *Wien. klin. Wschr.,* **59,** 484 (1947).

Schieck. *Klin. Mbl. Augenheilk.,* **45** (2), 40 (1907).

Seale. *Brit. J. Ophthal.,* **13,** 503 (1929).

Sédan. *Marseille méd.,* **59,** 871 (1922).

Ann. Oculist. (Paris), **163,** 358 (1926).

Rev. Oto-neuro-ophtal., **17,** 112 (1939).

Snellen. *v. Graefes Arch. Ophthal.,* **15** (2), 199 (1869).

Sourdille. *Clin. Ophtal.,* **6,** 125 (1900).

Stern. *Arch. Ophthal.,* **54,** 762 (1955).

Techow. *Klin. Mbl. Augenheilk.,* **111,** 149 (1945–6).

Terrien. *Arch. Ophtal.,* **46,** 513 (1929).

Thorson. *Arch. Ophthal.,* **10,** 20 (1933).

Vázquez-Barrière. *Mem. Soc. Urug. Oftal.,* 31 (1941).

Vitte. *Bull. Soc. Ophtal. Fr.,* 923 (1959).

Voisin. *Bull. Soc. Ophtal. Fr.,* **63,** 497 (1963).

Voisin and Lombard. *Bull. Soc. Ophtal. Fr.,* **63,** 495 (1963).

Weekers. *Recherches expérimentales et cliniques concernant la pathogénie des cataractes* (Thèse), Liège (1941).

Wölfflin. *Klin. Mbl. Augenheilk.,* **49** (2), 426 (1911).

Wolter. *J. pediat. Ophthal.,* **4,** 27 (1967).

Yamanaka. *Acta Soc. ophthal. jap.,* **69,** 181 (1965).

Yasuna. *Amer. J. Ophthal.,* **54,** 793 (1962).

FIG. 383.—Benito Daza de Valdés.
[1591–1634].
(In his book, *Uso de los antojos*, 1623; by courtesy of Dr. A. Arruga).

CHAPTER VIII

APHAKIA

APHAKIA ($\dot{\alpha}$, privative; $\phi\alpha\kappa\acute{o}s$, lens), although the term suggests an absence of the lens from the eye, is usually taken to embrace those conditions wherein *the lens is absent from the pupillary area*. In the vast majority of cases the lens has been removed by operation, sometimes it has been lost through a perforating wound or ulcer, it may (very rarely) be absent as a congenital defect, or it may be displaced from the pupil by dislocation.

The condition of aphakia must have been known since the early days of operating on a cataract by couching in the medicine of India and classical times, but the optics of the eye deprived of its lens were first fully elucidated by von Helmholtz in 1856. It is almost certain that in early times the couched eye may have been aided with the use of magnifying glasses as were advocated by Roger Bacon, but the first to suggest the correction of aphakia by spectacles carrying strong convex lenses was BENITO DAZA DE VALDÉS [1591–1634] (Fig. 383). Born in Cordoba in 1591, he became a licentiate and notary of the Inquisition at Seville and wrote one of the earliest books on spectacles, *Uso de los antojos* (Seville, 1623) (Fig. 600). In this fascinating volume with its curious dialogues, reprinted with an introduction by Manuel Márquez of Madrid in 1923, not only did Daza de Valdés suggest aphakic spectacles but concave lenses for the short-sighted and convex lenses for hypermetropic adults at a time when lenses were considered to assist only the near vision of the aged. Full of originality he also advocated protective coloured and stenopæic spectacles (Fig. 790); it is interesting that it was not until a century had passed that the suggestion of aphakic spectacles was put in practice by Lorenz Heister [1683–1758] of Helmstadt, and not until after two centuries that stenopæic spectacles were used by the French ophthalmologist, Serre d'Uzès [1802–1870], and Frans Donders [1818–1889] in Holland.

THE OPTICAL CONDITIONS IN APHAKIA

An aphakic eye is strongly hypermetropic; in the absence of the lens, other things being normal, parallel rays of light are brought to a focus some 31 mm. behind the cornea, while the average antero-posterior diameter of the eye is only between 23 and 24 mm. The dioptric system must therefore be supplemented by a strong converging lens, usually, if the eye were originally emmetropic, of about + 10 or + 11 D. The optics of the eye is essentially that of the corneal system and the positions of the cardinal points are as has been previously indicated.[1]

It is to be remembered that +10 D does not represent the power of the crystalline lens (+ 19·11 D, Gullstrand, 1911)[2] or its effective power (total refractive power of eye + 58·64 D − power of cornea + 43·05 D = + 15·59 D, Gullstrand). The optical conditions are entirely altered by the difference in position of a correcting

[1] p. 70.   [2] p. 118.

375

spectacle lens and by the fact that it lies in air instead of aqueous humour. The refractive system of the aphakic eye is reduced to the refractive power of the cornea alone (+ 43·05 D) and the amount of correction necessary to render it emmetropic in each particular case will vary not only with the original ametropia of the phakic eye, but will also depend on whether this was one of curvature or was axial. Thus it can be shown that a pre-existing axial myopia of − 10 D will result in an aphakic hypermetropia of + 5·59 D, and a pre-existing curvature myopia of − 10 D will result in an aphakic hypermetropia of + 0·77 D. Conversely, a previous axial hypermetropia of + 10 D becomes an aphakic error of + 25·48 D and a previous curvature hypermetropia of + 10 D becomes an aphakic error of + 21·77 D (Haas, 1933–39). It is therefore quite impossible to predict the degree of post-operative ametropia which will result after removal of the lens unless the component elements of the dioptric system before the operation are known. Tables and empirical formulæ which have been worked out are therefore of statistical value only and cannot be applied to any particular case (Hirschberg, 1897; Treutler, 1900; and others). Thus after removal of the lens Bjerke (1902) found emmetropia in myopes whose previous refraction ranged from − 8 D to − 26 D, and Böhm (1920) from − 16 D to − 24 D. It is, however, possible to predict an aphakic correction with more certainty from keratometry and the ultrasonic determination of the length of the eye (Elenius and Sopanen, 1963).

Astigmatism, as we have seen,[1] is always present in such cases, usually against the rule. Eight to ten days after operation it is usually high, of the order of 8 or 10 D; it diminishes rapidly to average about 2 or 3 D in 6 weeks and then slowly during the next 3 months to a somewhat smaller value, the resultant astigmatism being, of course, added algebraically to a pre-existing error.[2] It is therefore safe to order a correction in aphakia some 6 weeks after the operation, but if spectacles are desired before this they will of necessity be temporary and a spherical equivalent[3] is practicable.

It is to be noted that since the nodal point of the eye has been moved forwards, the optical effect of the corneal curvature is not so strong as is indicated by the keratometer. Moreover, the astigmatism of the posterior surface of the cornea is neglected in this estimation. Since correcting lenses are worn some distance from the cornea, the corrective lens, whether spherical or astigmatic, must be weaker than the ametropia.

The *size of the image* is very considerably altered in corrected aphakia. It will be remembered that the size of the retinal image is uninfluenced by a correcting lens if it is placed in the anterior focal plane of the eye.[4] Even although it is placed at this point, however, the size of the image must vary in comparison with that of an emmetropic eye by an amount depending on the difference between their first focal distances, that is, they will be in the ratio of 23·22 : 17·05 or 1·36 : 1 (Figs. 384–5). If the correcting lens is worn at this point, therefore, the size of a distant image in the corrected aphakic eye will be about one-third larger than in an emmetropic eye; if the correcting lens is farther from the eye, then this difference will be increased (Fig.

[1] p. 365.
[2] Donders (1864), von Reuss and Woinow (1869), Treutler (1900), van Lint (1914), Alexiadès (1920), Andreae (1923), Tron (1925), and others.
[3] p. 651.   [4] p. 217.

276)[1]; if it is brought closer, the difference will be diminished, but if it were to become of equal size, the spectacle lens would have to be within the eye. At the usual spectacle distance the retinal image is about one quarter larger than in the phakic eye. In comparison with a hypermetropic or myopic phakic eye, this difference in the size of the image will be respectively increased or diminished.

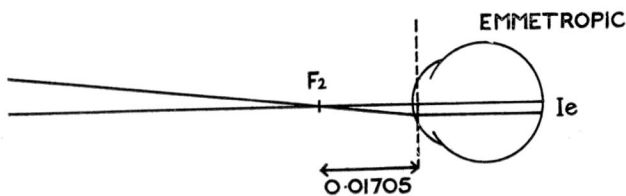

FIG. 384.

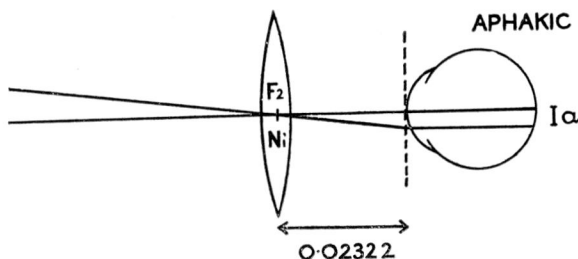

FIG. 385.

FIGS. 384 and 385.—THE SIZE OF THE IMAGE IN THE PHAKIC AND APHAKIC EYE.

The condition in the emmetrope is seen in Fig. 384; that in an aphakic eye, previously emmetropic, corrected by a lens in Fig. 385. The size of the retinal image of the aphakic eye (Ia) is related to that of the emmetropic eye (Ie) as are their respective focal distances, i.e., as 0.02322 is to 0.01705m, or 1.36 : 1 (after E. Haas).

THE VISION IN APHAKIA

Because of the enlargement of the image the visual acuity in aphakia corrected with spectacles is theoretically worse than is indicated by the usual clinical tests; when vision is interpreted in visual angles, a vision of 6/9 in a corrected aphakic eye corresponds to an acuity of only 6/12 in an eye with its optical system unaltered.

Accommodation is abolished, and consequently the patient should theoretically be provided with spectacles for every distance at which he desires to see clearly. In practice it is usually sufficient to provide a lens for distant vision, one for reading distance with, in addition in some cases, one for an intermediate position. In wearing these a certain amount of elasticity is more easily attained; since a convex lens becomes stronger if it is moved away from the cornea,[2] some artificial accommodation may be attained by the

---

[1] p. 222.   [2] p. 222.

patient if he moves the spectacles up and down his nose, whereby the far-point of clear distant vision is removed or brought nearer.

A considerable disadvantage of aphakia is the distortions produced when strong convex correcting spectacles are worn; these do not move with the eyes and in all positions other than the primary the prismatic and aberrational effects are great: indeed, a rotation greater than 3° is rarely tolerable (Erggelet, 1914; Ishihara, 1914). In these circumstances straight lines outside a small axial region become curved and a linear world becomes converted into parabolas which continually change their shape when the patient moves his eyes. Even although the distortions are mitigated by aspherical lenses,[1] the patient must learn to move his head rather than his

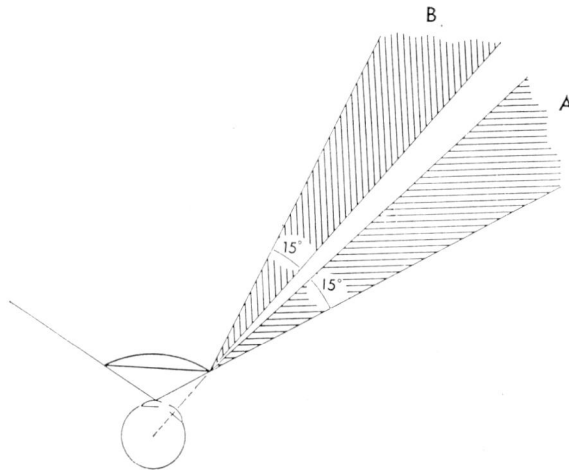

FIG. 386.—THE ROVING RING SCOTOMA IN CORRECTED APHAKIA.

With the eye in the primary position there is a ring scotoma (A) of approximately 15°. When the eye moves to the side the scotoma moves in the opposite direction (that is, towards the fixation point). It follows that if, while the eye is in the primary position, an object in the region B attracts attention and the eye is moved to fixate it, it thereupon disappears (R. C. Welsh).

eyes, especially on looking downwards, so that he always looks as nearly through the central portion of his lenses as possible.

A further disadvantage is the limitation of the visual field with an absence of peripheral vision in all directions vertically and horizontally. This is due to the ring scotoma of approximately 15° caused by the prismatic effect at the periphery of the correcting lens when it is placed a short distance in front of the eye and the eye is in the primary position. There is thus a circular area in the peripheral field which is invisible. A more disturbing phenomenon occurs when the eye is moved peripherally in any direction; in this case the spectacle-lens acts as a limited aperture so that the scotoma moves centrally, that is, in the direction opposite to that in which the eye

[1] p. 648.

is moved (the *roving ring scotoma* of Welsh, 1961) (Fig. 386). In this way when the eyes are moved to look at an object slightly to the periphery it suddenly disappears and when the eyes are moved again it as suddenly appears like a jack-in-the-box.

The adaptation of an aphakic to the use of strong convex lenses is thus difficult. If the other eye retains an effective amount of vision the degree of aniseikonia caused by a strong convex lens makes fusion impossible and the resulting diplopia is very disturbing, so disturbing, indeed, that the unnecessary removal of a uniocular cataract is usually inadvisable unless there happens to be perhaps an occupational reason for increasing the patient's visual field on the affected side. The difficulties thus experienced are subsequently discussed.[1] This situation, however, has altered somewhat in view of the wider use of contact lenses,[2] particularly corneal lenses, and in a more restricted sense because of the introduction of intra-ocular plastic lenses. It is true that rare cases wherein binocular vision has been attained in uniocular aphakics using correcting spectacles have been reported (Delogé, 1906), particularly in young people if the normal eye is over-corrected and the aphakic eye under-corrected (Berens *et al.*, 1933): but these must be considered very exceptional. Even in cases of bilateral aphakia corrected with spectacle lenses, their centring must be exact or the optical difficulties may be such that binocular vision cannot be attained or is maintained only with difficulty (Foster and Jackson, 1933).

In uniocular or binocular aphakics corrected by spectacles other diffi-culties are apparent which have been dramatically described by Woods (1952–64). Fortunately, many of these patients are old and sedentary and do not demand or require accurate visual judgements; some may be relatively comfortable from the start, but for those to whom accurate visual perceptions are necessary and who must be mobile, a considerable rehabilitation problem exists which must be intelligently tackled. Initially all objects seem larger than they were before so that distances are misjudged and, at the least, an annoying series of accidents apparently due to clumsiness tends to occur even in the smallest activities of life such as pouring a drink. The coordina-tion of manual movements with the new visual imagery is often a lengthy and difficult process which can be achieved only by practice and may be hastened by repetitive exercises such as with jig-saw puzzles. The distortion of straight lines into curved contours beyond the central area of the field, changing their shape with every movement of the eyes, brings other problems. Thus to the newly corrected aphakic a rectilinear doorway which he approaches becomes curved inwards so as to leave a space apparently only a few inches wide at the middle; it is true that if he approaches it boldly, the opening widens to admit him, but the illusion is disturbing. Only if he holds his eyes motionless and looks through the optical centre of his lens, and if he moves his head only and not his eyes to look at objects not straight in front

[1] p. 697.   [2] p. 776.

of him, do these objects assume their correct shape. Once this technique of orientation has become a habit, the effects of spherical aberration disappear and cease to worry him.

Finally, the peripheral roving scotoma gives rise to much inconvenience. For short distances (as for reading) this causes little distress and for distances beyond 20 feet (as for driving a car) the central area of clear vision is usually sufficiently large to allow adequate vision; but at intermediate distances between 2 and 10 feet the handicap presented is considerable. Thus within a room a relatively small area of clear vision is enclosed in a ring of fog, and on moving the eyes peripherally to fix an object of attention the patient suddenly does not see the person he is talking to, clumsily bumps into the furniture when he moves, stumbles on uneven ground or misses a step of the stairs with disastrous results. In time, it is true, the aphakic usually accommodates himself to these difficulties and acquires confidence, but the initial period is trying. Many of the difficulties can be soothed if they are explicitly pointed out to the patient before he gets his spectacles so that he knows what to expect and is not completely baffled by the new visual world in which he suddenly finds himself; and he will be less disturbed if the spectacles are prescribed as soon as possible and rehabilitation commences at once to train his reactions to the strange distances, the odd shapes and unexpected movements which confront him (see Hobbs and van Leuven, 1964; Liddy *et al.*, 1967).

These disadvantages are lessened but not eliminated by aspherical lenses, but in aphakia *contact lenses* present many advantages. With these, the limitation of the field, the peripheral distortion and the prismatic effects of spectacles are largely but perhaps not completely eliminated. Being very close to the eye a contact lens produces a retinal image considerably less in size than when spectacle lenses are used, so that even in uniocular aphakia binocular vision may be possible.[1] It must be remembered, however, that most aphakic patients are old, and to the aged the insertion and removal of a contact lens may be difficult; the most suitable type of patient is the young, or comparatively young.

We have already noted that the ideal situation for a lens to correct aphakia is actually within the eye. The realization of this has been brought about in recent years following the pioneer work of H. Ridley (1951) who described a technique for replacement of the human lens by a plastic lenticulus in the posterior chamber; at present the most popular technique is the insertion of a lenticulus in the anterior chamber, a method introduced by Strampelli (1954). The various techniques advocated, the indications for their use and the complications that may follow are discussed elsewhere.[2] The optics of the eye with an intra-ocular lens has, however, received little attention. A detailed investigation of the problems involved was under-

[1] p. 776.   [2] Vol. XI, p. 289.

taken by Troutman (1962–63) in the condition to which he applied the term *artiphakia*. He found that the resulting optics may be variable depending on the clarity of the retinal image and its size. The lenses used by Ridley tended to be too powerful, producing myopia and a relatively small image. In 41 cases of lenses inserted into the anterior chamber a wide range of anisometropia (− 5 to + 3 D) resulted, producing a considerable degree of aniseikonia ranging from 4% magnification required for the artiphakic eye to 6% for the fellow eye. Troutman concluded that artiphakia at present offers only a slight optical advantage over contact lenses, an opinion, however, not universally held (Choyce, 1964). Nevertheless, it may be that improvement in the design of intra-ocular lenses may lead to a minimal degree of aniseikonia and anisometropia.

The power required for the intra-ocular lens can be calculated from considerations of effectivity (Maria *et al.*, 1958; Simón, 1960; Le Grand, 1965). The last author gave the following formula:

$$D = \frac{R}{(1 - \delta D_c)\,(1 - \delta(D_c + R))}$$

where D is the power of the required lens, R the optical refraction of the eye, δ the reduced distance between the cornea and the lens (assumed to be thin) and D_c the power of the cornea.

Other visual symptoms in aphakia are of interest. The increased permeability of the ocular media to short-wave light after removal of the lens extends the spectrum in the ultra-violet region.[1] A larger proportion of infra-red rays also reaches the aphakic than the normal retina, making the liability to a retinal burn (as in eclipse blindness) theoretically greater. Coloured vision occasionally occurs, most commonly *erythropsia* (red vision), and more rarely and more transitorily, *chloropsia* (green vision) and *cyanopsia* (blue vision). These phenomena usually occur after exposure to bright light and particularly in cases wherein the pupil is widely dilated or a complete iridectomy has been performed. Although they frequently give rise to considerable subjective anxiety, they are of no organic importance.

The problems of attaining binocular vision in uniocular aphakic patients with good vision in the other eye are discussed in a later Chapter.[2]

Alexiadès. *Arch. Ophtal.*, **37**, 554 (1920).
Andreae. *Der postoperative Astigmatismus nach Staroperationen* (Diss.), Marburg (1923).
Berens, Connolly and Kern. *Amer. J. Ophthal.*, **16**, 199 (1933).
Bjerke. *Z. Augenheilk.*, **8**, 136 (1902).
Böhm. *v. Graefes Arch. Ophthal.*, **103**, 143 (1920).
Choyce. *Intra-ocular Lenses and Implants*, London (1964).
Delogé. *Anisométropie et vision binoculaire* (Thèse), Paris (1906).
Donders. *On the Anomalies of Accommodation and Refraction of the Eye*, London (1864).
Elenius and Sopanen. *Acta ophthal.* (Kbh.), **41**, 71 (1963).

Erggelet. *Klin. Mbl. Augenheilk.*, **52**, 240 (1914).
Foster and Jackson. *Brit. J. Ophthal.*, **17**, 98 (1933).
Gullstrand. *Einführung in d. Methoden d. Dioptrik d. Auges*, Leipzig (1911).
Haas. *Bull. Soc. Ophtal. Paris*, 29, 100 (1933).
   J. Physiol. Path. gén., **33**, 105 (1935).
   Traité d'ophtal., Paris, **3**, 281 (1939).
Hirschberg. *Zbl. prakt. Augenheilk.*, **21**, 65 (1897).
Hobbs and van Leuven. *Brit. J. Ophthal.*, **48**, 361 (1964).
Ishihara. *Klin. Mbl. Augenheilk.*, **52**, 247 (1914).

[1] Vol. IV, p. 454.
[2] p. 530.

Le Grand. *Optique physiologique*, Paris (1965).

Liddy, Carr and McCulloch. *Amer. J. Ophthal.*, **63,** 1793 (1967).

van Lint. *Bull. Soc. franç. Ophtal.*, **31,** 448 (1914).

Maria, Bonnet and Cochet. *Bull. Soc. franç. Ophtal.*, **71,** 521 (1958).

von Reuss and Woinow. *Ophthalmometrische Studien*, Wien (1869).

Ridley, H. *Trans. ophthal. Soc. U.K.*, **71,** 617 (1951).

Brit. J. Ophthal., **41,** 355 (1957); **44,** 705 (1960).

Simón. *Arch. Soc. oftal. hisp.-amer.*, **20,** 1191 (1960).

Strampelli. *Ann. Ottal.*, **80,** 75 (1954).

Treutler. *Z. Augenheilk.*, **3,** 484 (1900).

Tron. *Klin. Mbl. Augenheilk.*, **75,** 333 (1925).

Troutman. *Arch. Ophthal.*, **68,** 861 (1962).
Trans. Amer. ophthal. Soc., **60,** 590 (1962).
Amer. J. Ophthal., **56,** 602 (1963).

Welsh. *Amer. J. Ophthal.*, **51,** 1277 (1961).

Woods. *Amer. J. Ophthal.*, **35,** 118 (1952).
Brit. J. Ophthal., **48,** 349 (1964).

CHAPTER IX

CLINICAL METHODS OF ESTIMATING THE REFRACTION

MANY ophthalmologists have contributed much ingenuity to the techniques employed in the objective estimation of refractive errors, and from among them we are choosing EDMOND LANDOLT [1846–1926] to introduce this Chapter (Fig. 387). Born in Aarau in Switzerland, he had the good fortune to serve his apprenticeship in ophthalmology under Horner at Zürich and thereafter studied widely with Arlt in Vienna and von Graefe and von Helmholtz in Berlin. In 1870 when the Franco-Prussian war broke out, he went to France with a Swiss ambulance and afterwards to Snellen's clinic at Utrecht where he was a pupil of Donders. In 1874 he returned to Paris and worked for a time with Desmarres, with Charcot at the Salpêtrière, and with Javal at the Ophthalmological Laboratory at the Sorbonne. Here his interest in ophthalmic optics and muscular anomalies was thoroughly aroused. While becoming an authority on this subject, he was also an excellent clinician and an able surgeon. In surgery he devised many original instruments and introduced a number of operations, making this the subject of his Bowman Lecture (1911). But the most important of his many publications were concerned with ophthalmic optics. To this subject his contributions were immense: with Snellen he wrote the section on " ophthalmometrology " (the functional testing of the eye) (1874) in the 1st edition of the *Graefe-Saemisch Handbuch*, and the volume on the determination of refractive errors and ophthalmoscopy in the 3rd edition (1920). One of the great figures in French ophthalmology, the general appreciation of his professional achievements was rendered greater by his unusual charm and wide interests in life.

It must never be forgotten that the determination of a patient's refractive state is only one part, albeit an important one, of the general examination of the eyes. Certainly, no attempt should be made to correct an error of refraction until a full examination of the eyes has been undertaken and disease has been excluded. This is a principle which cannot be stressed too strongly, for if it is neglected not only does the refractionist bear the responsibility for allowing appropriate treatment to be postponed until an irreparable amount of damage may have been caused and the patient gravely injured, but he will frequently find that all his efforts to improve vision by optical appliances are unavailing and that his time has been lost in the attempt. It is only when this is done that optical correction can be undertaken with safety.

The methods adopted for the clinical investigation of the refractive state are legion and it is impossible to describe all of them in detail here. Most surgeons of experience (rightly) have their own individual techniques: many of them (wrongly) think that they are the only possible methods wherewith to attain accuracy. Most techniques are adequate provided they are applied with knowledge and precision— and above all, accuracy. The refractionist does not require genius; but he must be endowed with a capacity for taking pains. A useful routine, after taking the visual

FIG. 387.—EDMOND LANDOLT
[1846–1926].

acuity, is to determine the refraction by retinoscopy with cylinders and (as a routine in adults) without a cycloplegic; this is checked subjectively with test-lenses in a trial frame and Snellen's test-types, starting with the initial fogging of the neutralizing lenses found by retinoscopy, the spherical error being sometimes verified by the duochrome and the cylindrical always by cross-cylinders and sometimes with the astigmatic fan.

The theory and clinical routine of *testing the visual acuity* is discussed elsewhere[1] and need not detain us further. The value of the *pin-hole test*[2] should be remembered in determining whether any defect in acuity is due to an optical or pathological cause. In general, the stenopæic hole greatly improves visual defects due to refractive anomalies, to a less extent those due to abnormalities in the media, but does not ameliorate and may even aggravate those due to faulty perception. It should be remembered, however, that if the visual acuity is improved by a pin-hole in cases with opacities in the media, it may not be possible to attain the same acuity with lenses.

Before describing the technical methods of estimating the refraction we shall discuss the somewhat thorny question of cycloplegia.

Cycloplegia

The question as to whether accommodation for near vision should be paralysed before an estimation of the refraction has excited much controversy. Some writers consider the universal use of cycloplegics necessary at any rate until the age of 50 when accommodative activity becomes weaker; others claim that the practice is unnecessary except in the case of young children, while others again suggest that it is as a general rule inadvisable. There is no doubt that, properly used, a cycloplegic offers the most certain means of eliminating accommodative effects and of assessing the total refractive error; and it is also true that the accompanying mydriasis makes the clinical estimation easier and a full ophthalmoscopic examination possible, while it is the most satisfactory method of assessing the macular refraction.

At the same time the use of these drugs is attended with disadvantages, optical, medical and economic. The optical disadvantages are three. In the first place, under cycloplegia the lens is deformed so that after it has assumed its usual shape, minute errors cannot reasonably be transposed to the dioptric system in the ordinary conditions of use; we have seen[3] that there is often a considerable difference between the astigmatic error in an accommodated and a non-accommodated eye, and it therefore follows that the abnormal refraction under cycloplegia must be modified by a further determination of the refraction in normal conditions. In the second place the periphery of the pupillary aperture frequently has a refraction different from the central part which is alone employed in the normal circumstances of life, and in the former errors of aberration are an almost constant occurrence. The expert will be able to neglect the peripheral disturbances and confine his attention to the central area; or alternatively an artificial pupil can be used. In the third place cycloplegia affords no adequate recognition

---

[1] Vol. VII, p. 370.   [2] Vol. VII, p. 374.   [3] p. 285.

of accommodative anomalies or unusual accommodative habits, allowance for which is frequently advisable in the prescription of spectacles; again, a post-cycloplegic test is necessary. From the medical point of view there is an element of danger in patients predisposed to closed-angle glaucoma lest an acute attack be precipitated. It is true that in the normal eye such a danger is non-existent and that, where danger does exist, it is usually eliminated by a subsequent miotic. Before cycloplegic drugs are used, therefore, the possibility of such a complication should always be excluded, and when doubt is felt only transient agents should be employed and the patient should be kept under observation until the pupil is fully contracted by the instillation of a miotic. The rare occurrence of belladonna poisoning from the ocular instillation of atropine is to be remembered.[1] From the economic point of view the process of refraction under cycloplegia requires three examinations—a preliminary test, an examination under cycloplegia and a post-cycloplegic (or post-mydriatic) test at a later date. This may be an inconvenience to the surgeon and frequently is to the patient, particularly if the effect of cycloplegia is prolonged, although it can be mitigated by the subsequent use of a miotic, which should be a routine in all adult patients except, perhaps, myopes.

If sufficient time is available to the refractionist, however, a return visit for a post-cycloplegic test may be obviated by the following routine. After the preliminary examination, retinoscopy and subjective tests are carried out both for distance and near vision. A rapidly-acting cycloplegic is then instilled and after an appropriate interval the fundi are examined and the retinoscopy repeated. If this agrees reasonably well with that obtained before cycloplegia, spectacles may be ordered as indicated by the subjective tests previously performed. Only if there is considerable discrepancy between the retinoscopies before and after cycloplegia will it be necessary to bring the patient back on another occasion for a post-cycloplegic test.

It thus appears that the use of cycloplegics has definite indications and contra-indications. We must, however, remind ourselves that cycloplegia is necessary only when the patient cannot relax his accommodation sufficiently to allow an estimation of the total static refraction. Many refractionists consider it wiser to assume that all children are incapable of either relaxing their abundant accommodation or keeping their eyes still; and atropine cycloplegia is therefore considered mandatory. It is possible to argue that even in some children cycloplegia is unnecessary; this is particularly so in the case of myopes, but it should be remembered that a myopic refraction found by retinoscopy in a child not under the influence of a cycloplegic could be due to an excess of accommodation leading to pseudo-myopia. Accommodative spasm, however, is comparatively rare and can be excluded in most cases by comparing the retinoscopy before and after the administration of a short-acting cycloplegic. Certainly, once a child is established as

[1] Vol. VII, p. 546.

being myopic, there is little need for cycloplegia in subsequent examinations, provided he is sufficiently cooperative to keep his eyes still. The case, however, is quite different in children who may have anomalous ocular conditions, such as strabismus. Here cycloplegia, always atropine under the age of seven, is a necessity. Above that age cycloplegic refraction is legitimate using the newer synthetic short-acting but powerful drugs; indeed, these have replaced the time-honoured homatropine and cocaine both as mydriatic and cycloplegic in most circumstances.

Up to the age of 16 cycloplegia is usually advisable in non-myopic subjects. After the age of 20 cycloplegia need not be used as a routine unless there is a suspicion that the accommodation is abnormally active, unless the objective findings by retinoscopy do not agree with the patient's subjective choice, unless definite symptoms of accommodative asthenopia are present which do not seem to be explicable by the error found without a cycloplegic, or unless the pupil is so small that the refraction presents difficulties. Above the age of 40, except for the rare cases of excessive accommodation which occur at the commencement of presbyopia or in the presence of very small pupils, a cycloplegic is unnecessary. Several methods are available whereby the accommodation can be assessed with considerable accuracy so that the adult patients who require a cycloplegic are relatively few.

On the whole, where the optical conditions are good and the room large so that accommodation can be relaxed, when the surgeon is an expert and is prepared to spend a little time upon the estimation, and when the patient is reasonably intelligent and cooperative and is an adult who is not suffering from accommodative disturbances which cannot be otherwise assessed, there is no doubt that the ideal refraction is the one estimated in the absence of a cycloplegic. If, however, such drugs are employed with discrimination and provided correcting spectacles are prescribed thereafter not by rule of thumb but only after an adequate post-cycloplegic test, little can be said against their use.

The choice of cycloplegic depends on several considerations. Ideally the cycloplegia produced should be rapid in onset, total for a period of time appropriate to the performance of retinoscopy and ophthalmoscopy, and should subsequently wear off rapidly. Of the drugs classically employed, atropine and homatropine, neither satisfies these criteria.

Atropine is the most powerful cycloplegic but its effect persists for several days. It is given as drops or ointment (1·0%) and is best administered three times a day for 3 days before the examination to induce complete cycloplegia and mydriasis. This is more than is necessary but allows for inefficient administration at home. Full cycloplegia is usually attained after four instillations of 1·0% atropine; most patients can begin to read after the 3rd day and accommodation is normal after the 18th (Marron, 1940). It remains the principal cycloplegic for use in young children.

Hyoscine (*Scopolamine*) acts more rapidly and it has been found that satisfactory cycloplegia can be obtained shortly after the instillation of a 0·05% solution (Sorsby *et al.*, 1955).

Homatropine is weaker than atropine but has the advantage of wearing off more quickly. It may be used alone as drops in a watery solution (1 to 2%) in which case its instillation should be repeated two or three times at intervals of 10 minutes. The accommodation will be damped under its influence in one or one and a half hours; an alternative is a 5% solution administered once or twice; its action passes off to a large extent in 24 hours. When a cycloplegic examination is completed, a miotic such as 1·0% pilocarpine or 0·25% eserine should be instilled, but there is some residual impairment of accommodation which may occasionally persist for 2 or 3 days, and for this reason any post-cycloplegic test should be postponed for this interval.

The action of these drugs, particularly homatropine, is usefully augmented by *synergists* of the sympathomimetic group. The most common is *cocaine* hydrochloride (2% solution), which accelerates and reinforces its effect, a combination introduced by Lang and Barrett (1887) at Moorfields Eye Hospital and popularized by Cruise (1909) in England. The claims that *benzedrine* (Beach and McAdams, 1937) and *paredrine* (Tassman, 1938; Marron, 1940) act as effective synergists with homatropine, hastening and shortening the period of cycloplegia, have not been fully substantiated.

Of the large number of drugs both natural and synthetic which are known to possess useful cycloplegic action,[1] two in particular have come into widespread use in the modern practice of refraction—*cyclopentolate hydrochloride* (Cyclogyl, Mydrilate) (0·5 − 2%) and *bistropamide* (tropicamide, Mydriacyl) (1%).[2] The properties of these cycloplegics approach the ideal as defined above. In practice one drop is instilled in each eye, followed by a second five minutes later. After cyclopentolate, cycloplegia is complete in under an hour and usually wears off in 24 hours. Bistropamide is even faster, cycloplegia developing fully within half an hour and the total effect disappearing after about 6 hours. There have been reports of toxic reactions similar to those of atropine poisoning,[3] especially to the use of cyclopentolate, occurring particularly when the higher strengths are instilled as are often necessary to produce satisfactory cycloplegia in heavily pigmented eyes (Simcoe, 1962; Beswick, 1962; Mark, 1963; Binkhorst *et al.*, 1963).

The quantity and type of cycloplegic, however, should not conform to a blanket formula. Individuals vary considerably in the dosage needed to produce a satisfactory degree of ciliary paralysis and, as we have noted, those with pigmented irides, particularly in the dark races, generally require more than blondes. Even in the same individual the two eyes sometimes show a considerable variability in their response, a phenomenon called *anisocycloplegia* by Beach (1943) who found a difference of + 0·5 D in depth of cycloplegia common and exceptionally a difference of 10 D. The administration of these drugs should therefore be determined on an individualistic basis. In most cases, apart from young children, it is important from the economic point of view that the period of post-cyclo-plegic disability should be as short as possible and therefore no more of any drug should be given than is necessary. The adequacy of cycloplegia is usually indicated by the invariability of the findings of retinoscopy and, perhaps to a less degree, by the fixed dilatation of the pupils; certainly, if the pupils are active or the retinoscopy is changing, cycloplegia is inadequate

[1] Vol. VII, p. 541.

[2] Priestley and Medine (1951), Gettes and Leopold (1953), Stolzar (1953), Cher (1959), Robb and Petersen (1968).

[3] Vol. VII, p. 546.

and further instillations should be given, or another drug or combinations of drugs or even atropine should be used if a weaker cycloplegic has been given.

For adequate cycloplegia—if it is to be relied upon in the practice of refraction—a residual amplitude of accommodation of more than 1 D should not remain (that is, the line on the accommodation card[1] should become blurred at a distance of 1 metre). The depth of the cycloplegia should be tested in each case before the refractive examination is begun. After the refraction has been completed the state of the accommodation may again be verified: a + 3 D sphere is added to the full correction, when the far-point should be at 33 cm., and the near-point slightly over 25 but not over 28 cm. If this amount of cycloplegia does not remain and if the drug has been carefully administered, excessive accommodation should be suspected.

REFRACTIVE ERRORS can be estimated objectively and subjectively; both methods should be employed in every case but, wherever it is possible, the former should be the main basis of the test and reliance should substantially be placed upon it: subjective tests should never be started until the correction is already known. All methods of determining the STATIC REFRACTION—that is the refractive state during relaxation of accommodation—depend upon the fact that the fovea and the far-point are conjugate foci, that is, the retina is imaged at the far-point, and an object at the far-point is imaged at the fovea. In the objective methods the image of an illuminated area of the retina is located and imaged by the observer at the far-point; in the subjective methods the far-point is seen by the patient to be imaged on the retina; in both cases the far-point is brought to a suitable distance by adding to or subtracting from the refractivity of the eye by a lens system, if necessary.

Objective Methods of Refraction

THE OBJECTIVE METHODS of determining refractive errors are designed to determine the plane of the anterior of the two conjugate foci of the refracting system of the eye. It is to be remembered that in them all some slight inaccuracy is involved for the reflecting surface of the fundus —not the percipient elements—is taken as the posterior focus. Clinically these methods include ophthalmoscopy, retinoscopy, refractometry and keratoscopy, the last of which, it is to be noted, measures only the curvature of the anterior surface of the axial area of the cornea.

OPHTHALMOSCOPY

OPHTHALMOSCOPY is not of great value in the measurement of refractive errors because of its inaccuracy, but as a rough estimation is sometimes useful (Snellen and Landolt, 1874). The optics of ophthalmoscopy will be described in detail subsequently.[2] We shall see that in the direct method of

[1] p. 477.   [2] p. 832.

ophthalmoscopy[1] rays of light reflected from a point on the retina of an emmetropic patient are accurately focused on the retina of the emmetropic observer, the two retinæ being conjugate foci, and if this does not in fact occur, the lens in the ophthalmoscope necessary to bring the details of the retina into focus is a measure of the ametropia.   Any effort of accommodation on the part of the patient or the observer vitiates the result by adding to the apparent myopia or reducing the hypermetropia.   The patient's accommodation must therefore be relaxed, preferably by a cycloplegic or alternatively by voluntarily looking into the distance.   The observer should have his ametropia corrected and relax his accommodation by training.   Holding the ophthalmoscope as closely to the eyes as possible, the strongest convex or the weakest concave lens with which minute details of the fundus are clearly seen measures the spherical refractive error.   The astigmatism is measured by similarly focusing two retinal vessels at right angles to one another, the lens which makes each one clear being a measure of the ametropia in the meridian at right angles to it.

By using the indirect method the distance of the far-point can be calculated if the interposing lens has a known focal length.   If the patient's eye is emmetropic, rays emerging from it are parallel and an inverted real image will be formed at the focal plane of the lens.   If the eye is myopic, the emergent rays will be convergent and the image will be formed at a point nearer the lens by an amount corresponding to the myopia.   Conversely, if the eye is hypermetropic, the image will be at a point farther from the interposed lens than its focal distance by an amount depending on the hypermetropia.   It is obvious that no exact measure of the ametropia can be made in this way by the ordinary clinical methods of ophthalmoscopy, but the principle is used in optometry.[2]

RETINOSCOPY

Retinoscopy is the most generally satisfactory and accurate method for the objective determination of the refraction.   In the hands of a skilled and careful exponent a very high degree of accuracy can be attained, in favourable circumstances of the order of $0 \cdot 25$ D in power and $5°$ in the axis of astigmatism.   It is, however, an art which cannot be learned from books, for efficiency can be attained only by long, assiduous and painstaking practice.

The technique has been practised for almost a century.   It was originally used by Bowman (1859) to estimate the astigmatism in conical cornea, but first received general application at the hands of Cuignet (1873).   He attributed the phenomena to corneal reflection and suggested the name *keratoscopy*, but the true optical principles were first appreciated by Landolt, whose theories were published by Mengin (1878).   Landolt's more elaborate presentations appeared in 1883, 1886, 1904, 1920 and 1927.   Others who have contributed largely to our knowledge have been Parent (1880–82), Jackson (1885–1924), Gullstrand (1896–1911), Wolff (1903–17), Marquez (1922–27), Krämer (1922–27), Lindner (1926–27), Pascal (1930) and Klein (1944).   Several names have been suggested for the technique: the *shadow-test* or *skiascopy* (Landolt, 1886)

[1] p. 841.   [2] p. 408.

or, since the optical phenomena are referred to the pupillary plane, *pupilloscopy* or *korescopy* (Landolt, 1883).

The Optics of Retinoscopy

In retinoscopy an illuminated area of the retina serves as an object, and the image at the far-point of the eye is located by moving the illumination across the fundus and noting the behaviour of the luminous reflex in the pupil. The observer does not see the illuminated area of the patient's fundus, but only the rays emanating from it to form an illuminated area of the pupil. If the image is formed between the patient and the observer, the movements of the reflex and the external light are in opposite directions; if it falls outside this region, either behind the patient's eye or behind the observer's, the two move in the same direction. When the far-point of the patient's eye corresponds to the nodal point of the observer's eye, a *neutral point* (the *point of reversal* or *end-point*) occurs. If the eyes are separated by the convenient distance of, say, $\frac{2}{3}$ of a metre (the "working distance"), the far-point of the patient must be $\frac{2}{3}$ of a metre away, and therefore he must have $-1\cdot5$ D of myopia. The rationale of the method is therefore to add lenses to the dioptric system of the patient's eye until the point of reversal is seen by the observer; at that point the patient's refractive error is measured by the added lenses less the dioptric value of the working distance (*i.e.* $1\cdot5$ D assuming patient and observer are $\frac{2}{3}$ of a metre apart).

If the patient and the observer are separated by 2 metres, the point of reversal would be when the patient was corrected to $-0\cdot5$ D; if they were only $0\cdot5$ metre apart, the point of reversal would be at -2 D; and so on. The farther the surgeon is away the more theoretically accurate are the results obtained, but in practice this is counterbalanced by the difficulty in seeing clearly the play of lights in the pupil.

The detailed optics is most easily considered in three stages: first, the illumination of the subject's retina; second, the reflex imagery of this illuminated area formed by the subject's dioptric apparatus; and finally, the projection of the image by the observer. A crucial element in retinoscopy as a diagnostic procedure is the second stage wherein an image is formed of the illuminated retina and is therefore situated at the subject's far-point. The most convenient exposition is an examination of the conditions obtaining in the three principal refractive states. We shall first examine retinoscopy using a plane mirror and also assume that the illumination is by a point-source.

Retinoscopy in Emmetropia. In the accompanying figures the observer, to the left, rotates a plane mirror so that the image, S_I, of a point source, S_o, moves as indicated. S_I is referred to as the "immediate source", S_o being the "original source". In the first condition (Fig. 388) no light enters the subject's eye but with rotation of the mirror in the direction of the arrow (Fig. 389) some light enters through the subject's pupil and illuminates a patch of retina, P (the *illumination stage*). The site of this patch is deter-

FIGS. 388 to 391.—THE OPTICS OF RETINOSCOPY.
The determining ray is shown in red (R).   For explanation, see text.

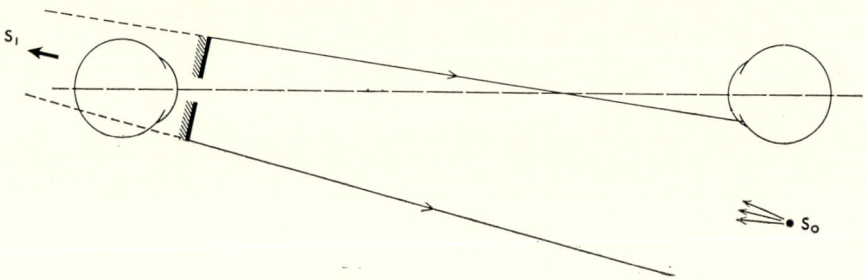

FIG. 388.—No light enters the subject's eye.

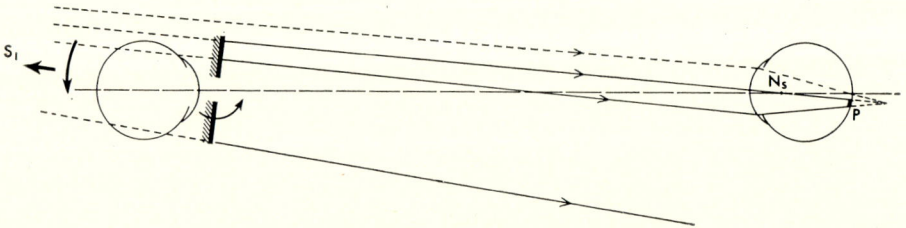

FIG. 389.—The illumination stage in emmetropia.

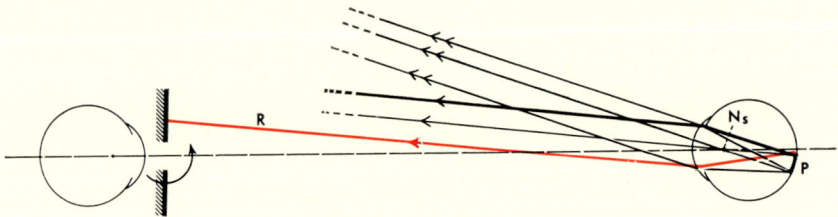

FIG. 390.—The reflex stage in emmetropia.

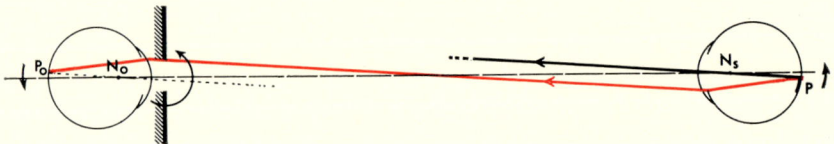

FIG. 391.—The projection stage in emmetropia.

mined by the line from S_I through the nodal point, N_s, of the subject's eye. As S_I is a finite distance from the subject and the eye is emmetropic, an image of S_I will be formed behind the retina.

The illuminated patch can now be considered as an object in its own right and will form an image at the far-point of the eye which in emmetropia is at infinity (the *reflex stage*—so called because the light is actually reflected from the fundus) (Fig. 390).

Even although the subject's retina is illuminated, the observer will not be able to see the reflex unless light enters the sight-hole of the mirror. In Fig. 390 the determining ray, R (in red), is that from the upper margin of P which just strikes the lower margin of the subject's pupil. With further rotation of the mirror, P moves upwards towards the principal axis of the eye. The ray R subtends a progressively smaller angle with the axis until it just enters the sight-hole (Fig. 391). At this point the reflex is seen by the observer. Its position is determined by projecting it in relation to the subject's pupil. It will be recalled that the ray R is one of a series of parallel rays formed by the dioptric apparatus of the subject's eye from the top edge of the illuminated patch, P. A ray parallel to R passing through the observer's nodal point will therefore strike the observer's retina at P_o where the parallel rays will be focused, presuming the observer to be emmetropic. As can be appreciated from the figure, the observer will project this to the lower border of the subject's pupil (the *projection stage*) (Fig. 391). As the mirror rotates further, P will move up and P_o moves downwards. The reflex seen by the observer appears as a light area with a shadow above it. These travel apparently upwards across the pupil in the *same* direction as the light moving across the eye externally. Thus in emmetropia a " with " movement is obtained.

Finally, the reflex disappears, the last ray to enter the observer's eye coming from the lower margin of the patch, P, which emerges close to the upper border of the subject's pupil and just passes the lower border of the sight-hole. The observer sees the reflex move as from Fig. 395 to Fig. 396.

Retinoscopy in Hypermetropia. The illumination stage is similar to that in emmetropia. The reflex stage differs because the patch of illuminated retina, P, forms a virtual image at the far-point behind the subject's eye (Fig. 392). Again, it is the ray from the upper margin of P emerging close to the lower border of the pupil that subtends the smallest angle with the principal axis, and as the mirror continues to rotate it will be the first to strike the sight-hole. The projection stage is the same as in emmetropia and therefore a " with " movement of the reflex is obtained.

Retinoscopy in Myopia. The illumination stage is again similar to that in emmetropia and hypermetropia. There is a slight difference since in high myopia the image of the immediate source may be in front of the retina (Fig. 394), but the illuminated blur-patch moves in the same way as in the other refractive conditions—in the *opposite* sense to the immediate source.

FIGS. 392 to 394.—THE OPTICS OF RETINOSCOPY.
The determining ray is shown in red (R).   For explanation, see text

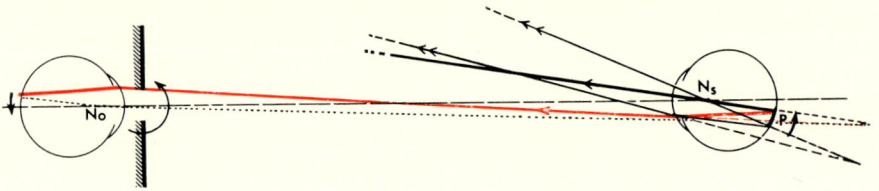

FIG. 392.—The reflex and projection stages in hypermetropia.

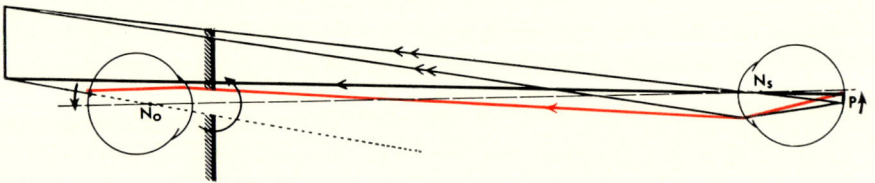

FIG. 393.—The reflex and projection stages in myopia less than 1.5 D.

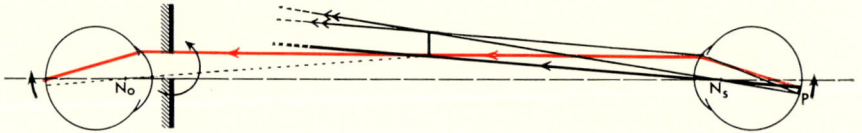

FIG. 394.—The reflex and projection stages in myopia greater than 1.5 D.

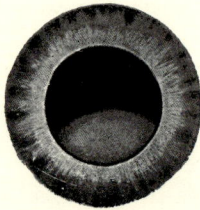   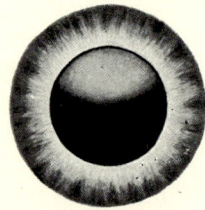

FIG. 395.   FIG. 396.

FIGS. 395 and 396.—THE SHADOWS IN RETINOSCOPY.

In the reflex stage a real image of the illuminated patch, P, is formed at the far-point in front of the subject's eye. Two situations must be considered. In the first (Fig. 393) the far-point is behind the observer—again, the determining ray is that from the upper edge of the area, P, which just passes the sight-hole and a " with " movement of the reflex is obtained as in emmetropia and hypermetropia. In the second situation (Fig. 394) the degree of myopia is higher and the image of the illuminated patch, P, is formed between the observer and the subject. As can be appreciated from the figure, the movement of the reflex is " against " that of the external movement of light across the subject's eye. The determining ray (shown in red) is that from the upper border of the patch, P, emerging through the upper border of the pupil, and this is the first to strike the sight-hole and therefore to be visible to the observer who consequently projects the reflex as if coming from the upper border of the subject's pupil, even although the light from the source strikes the lower border of the pupil first, thus giving rise to an " against " movement. The object of retinoscopy is to place lenses in front of the subject's eye so as to find the point of neutralization at which the direction of movement of the reflex is indeterminate. This occurs when the subject's eye is made myopic by lenses so that the image in the reflex stage is at the observer's nodal point—the situation obtaining somewhere between Figs. 393 and 394.

In practice the illuminated area of the pupil is not so readily observed as its border with the unilluminated area, for on movement this appears as a sharp contrast of advancing or receding light and shadow (Fig. 395).

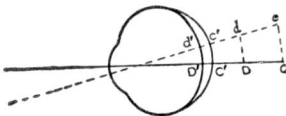   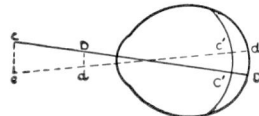

Fig. 397.   Fig. 398.

Figs. 397 and 398.—The Rate of Movement of the Illuminated Retinal
Area.

In each case the movement is referred to the punctum remotum of the eye. The greater the refractive error (D'd'), both in hypermetropia (Fig. 397) and in myopia (Fig 398), the nearer the punctum remotum (Dd), the shorter the excursion and the slower the speed of movement.

Moreover, the greater the degree of ametropia the shorter the excursion and the slower the speed of movement (Figs. 397–8); as the refractive error is being corrected, the area of the light-pencil becomes progressively smaller, and a small movement of the source makes it flit more rapidly across the pupillary aperture; at the neutral point the area of an image-element on the retina is so small that when it passes the aperture it passes entirely, so that the pupil appears at one moment uniformly light (but not brightly so), at the next uniformly dark. The accuracy of retinoscopy depends on the sharpness of this neutralization, but there is often no clearly defined neutral point but rather a *neutral zone*, since optical aberrations and irregularities of the retinal surface cause the conjugate focus to be formed not on a plane but in depth. Moreover, the issue is sometimes further confused by the appearance of irregular and scissor-like shadows as the neutral region is being approached.

The Methods of Retinoscopy

In the practice of retinoscopy a patch upon the retina is illuminated by a retinoscope. The classical combination is a separate source of light and a *reflecting retinoscope* (Fig. 400): this consists of a perforated mirror by which the beam is reflected into the patient's eye and through a central hole in which the emergent rays enter the observer's eye. Movements of the

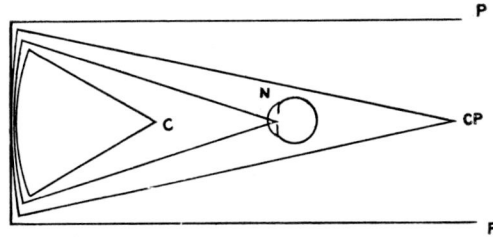

Fig. 399.—Reflection of Light by Mirrors of Different Curvatures in Retinoscopy.

If the source of light is approximately one metre from the mirror and a plane mirror is used, the vergence is zero and a pencil of parallel rays will be reflected (P). With a slightly concave mirror an image is formed behind the patient's eye (CP)—this concave mirror has a plane effect. With a greater concavity the image is formed at the patient's pupil (N) and no shadow movement occurs (the first neutral point). With a still more concave mirror the image is formed in front of the patient's eye.

illuminated retinal area are produced by tilting the mirror. Either a plane or a concave mirror can be used; with the former when the mirror is tilted, the image (the immediate source of light) moves in the opposite direction and the illuminated retinal area in the same direction as the tilt of the mirror; with a concave mirror, on the other hand, the illuminated area moves in a direction which depends on the focal length of the mirror in relation to the working distance.

There is no theoretical difference between the two types of mirror. In the concave type of mirror the source-image is projected between the patient's pupil and the mirror (C, Fig. 399); in the plane type (P, Fig. 399) (or in a weak concave mirror, CP, Fig. 399) the image is projected behind the patient's pupil. It is not the type of movement which matters but whether the image of the source of light falls in front of the patient's eye or behind it (or at infinity).[1] With a plane type of mirror the light and shadow are

[1] If a mirror with a convergence power of 1 metre were chosen the source-image would be projected into the patient's pupil and there would be no retinoscopic shadow no matter what the refraction of the eye (the FIRST NEUTRAL POINT of Marquez, 1925) (N, Fig. 399): Borschke (1905) made use of this in constructing astigmatic mirrors (*vide infra*).

FIG. 400.—PRIESTLEY SMITH
REFLECTING RETINOSCOPE.

One mirror is plane the other
concave.

FIG. 401.—LISTER REFLECTING
RETINOSCOPE.

The mirror has a focal length of
150 cm. thus having a plane action at
a distance of 1 metre.

probably more sharply accentuated; with a concave mirror a concentrated and more intense beam is formed. The best of both worlds can be obtained by using a slightly concave mirror the focal length of which is greater than the distance between the surgeon and the patient, that is, about 150 cm. (the Lister mirror) (Fig. 401). For purposes of retinoscopy it acts as a plane mirror and, converging the rays slightly upon the pupil, it increases the illumination. The larger the central hole, the more light can enter the observer's eye. With a plane mirror the advantages of a large hole are counterbalanced by the appearance of a circular dark patch in the centre of the reflection corresponding to the hole, which reduces the illumination in the pupillary area and confuses the retinoscopy. Again this difficulty is overcome by a slightly concave mirror which eliminates the shadow of the central hole so that a hole of 4 mm. diameter is suitable. Unless the source of light is very good the hole should be pierced and not be formed by a defect in the silvering of an imperforate mirror, since the glass reflects an appreciable fraction of the light which should enter the eye. If it is pierced, annoying reflexes may be formed at its edges, but these are avoided if the sides of the hole are blackened and are made to widen out posteriorly so that it is narrowest at the mirror end. If, however, a sufficiently bright source of illumination is employed a hole in the silvering only is sufficient as there is enough light to reach the observer's eye and also, reflected from the unsilvered glass, to eliminate the shadow of the hole.

FIG. 402.—
THE THOR-
INGTON
CHIMNEY
FOR RETI-
NOSCOPY.

With the reflecting retinoscope a source of light is necessary. This should be small, bright and enclosed, leaving only an approximately parallel beam. A frosted electric bulb in a Thorington chimney (1896) (an opaque cowl with an adjustable iris diaphragm) used to be the standard method (Fig. 402), but the source of light should always be larger than the sight-hole of the mirror. An electric bulb rendered opaque except for a window of ground glass is satisfactory (Fig. 403); a pointolite source is perhaps ideal (Williamson-Noble, 1928). When a plane mirror is used, the nearer the source is to the mirror the brighter the patch of light, and since the amount of light received by the pupil is determined by the size of the pupil and the distance from the source, the size of the mirror is immaterial. With a concave mirror, on the other hand, the beam of light is converged and the brightness of the pupil will therefore vary with the curvature and the size of the mirror. Moreover, the source of light must not be closer to the mirror than the focal distance of the mirror so that while it is an advantage to have the source of light close to a plane mirror, it should be immediately behind (and above) the patient's head when a concave mirror is used.

The *luminous retinoscope* introduced by Wolff (1893) (Fig. 404) is an alternative and more easily manipulated system with the advantage that the intensity and size

FIG. 403.—THE LISTER LAMP.

On the left is a ground glass window; on the right a clear glass window (Keeler).

of the beam can be readily controlled. The optical principles, of course, are identical (Fig. 405); in the portable instrument a strong convex lens and a mirror at 45° project the light on to the patient's eye. Both types of mirror-effect can be provided by moving the bulb to and from the condensing lens to vary the angularity of the light leaving the mirror, so that at one extreme the rays converge at a point close to the instrument (concave-type mirror) and at the other the rays are parallel (plane-type mirror).

FIG. 404.—THE ELEC-
TRIC RETINOSCOPE.

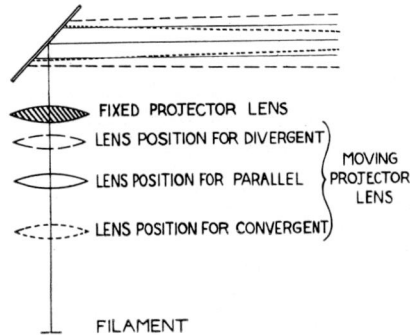

FIXED PROJECTOR LENS

LENS POSITION FOR DIVERGENT

LENS POSITION FOR PARALLEL

LENS POSITION FOR CONVERGENT

MOVING PROJECTOR LENS

FILAMENT

FIG. 405.—OPTICAL CONSTRUCTION
OF THE ELECTRIC RETINOSCOPE.

OBJECTIVE STIGMATOSCOPY is a modification of the classical technique introduced by Gullstrand (1896–1911). Using a powerful point-source of light (the Nernst ophthalmometric lamp with a small circular aperture), he reflected the light therefrom by a cover-glass set at an angle of 45° which served as a transparent mirror. This reflex acted as a bright point-source of light and the observer, looking through the cover-glass, sees a light reflex in the pupil; on moving his head in different directions, he notes a shadow moving similarly to that seen in retinoscopy with the plane mirror. Williamson-Noble (1924) used a similar technique with a pointolite lamp.

STREAK RETINOSCOPY. The classical source of light used in retinoscopy is circular, giving a cone-shaped beam and a circular image with spherical refractions and an elongated image in astigmatism. There are, however, considerable optical advantages to be gained from using a linear image. In this event in large spherical errors, the linear image is indistinct and its streak-like character barely recognizable; in small errors (or when large errors are nearly corrected) the streak-reflex gains in distinctness and becomes more linear; at the point of reversal the streak-reflex disappears and the pupil is filled now with light, now with shadow. In spherical errors the streak-reflex will be of equal distinctness in all meridians, but in the presence of astigmatism it will vary in thickness and when one meridian is neutralized the streak will be found recurring only in the direction of the other. This clear-cut directional character of the reflex is the greatest asset of streak

FIG. 406.—A STREAK RETINO-SCOPY MIRROR (M. Klein).

retinoscopy since it allows not only a greater facility in measuring the refraction in different meridians but still greater accuracy in determining the direction of the axis of astigmatism (see Clapp, 1924; Rundles, 1939; and others).

Historically, the importance of streak retinoscopy was first noted by Jackson (1896) in his description of the appearance of a band-shaped shadow in ordinary retinoscopy when one meridian is neutralized: when the observer's eye is at the point of reversal for one meridian the retinal image becomes greatly magnified in the direction of this meridian so that each point becomes a line of light. Wolff (1900–17) was the first to advocate these principles in practice in his self-luminous streak retinoscope in which a linear incandescent element of the electric bulb is rotatable. An alternative method is to use an ordinary circular light-source which is made to produce a linear image by a plano-cylindrical retinoscopic mirror (Borschke, 1905) or a slit-shaped retinoscopic mirror (Evans, 1940; Klein, 1942) (Fig. 406).

The Clinical Practice of Retinoscopy

The optical conditions in which retinoscopy is undertaken are important, particularly if a cycloplegic is not employed. It is necessary that accommodation be relaxed as much as possible, and therefore the room should be long and darkened: it is impossible for the majority of patients to relax their accommodation otherwise. Where a cycloplegic is not used, it is difficult in most cases to refract the macular region itself since the pupil contracts and the view is obscured by reflexes. A *slightly* eccentric position is therefore chosen, and the patient is instructed to look past the surgeon's head on the side opposite to that which corresponds to the eye under examination. Obviously, the less eccentric the gaze the better, for it is important to get as near to the macula as possible and essentially, the accommodation must be relaxed. The best way to ensure these two desiderata is to have two small spot lights fixed to the opposite wall at least 6 metres away, at which the patient can look steadily in the appropriate direction; or, alternatively, one light exactly opposite the patient can be employed, and the surgeon can orientate himself slightly to one side or other when the opposite eye is being refracted. If no fixation lights are available the subject is asked to gaze into the distance just past the examiner's ear but as close as possible to it. In either event, in cases of squint, one or other eye should be occluded. Ideally, the examiner should use his right eye for the patient's right eye and his left for the patient's left so that the eccentricity is minimal. When a cycloplegic is used the patient can look directly at the retinoscope.

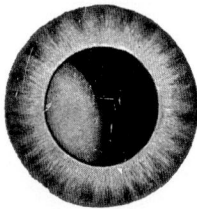

FIG. 407.—THE SHADOW IN RETINOSCOPY WITH A HIGH DEGREE OF SPHERICAL AMETROPIA WHEN THE MIRROR IS MOVED HORIZONTALLY.

The surgeon fits the trial frame on the patient's face with the trial lenses near at hand,[1] sits at his chosen distance in front of the patient, usually at arm's length which is equivalent to a working distance of $\frac{2}{3}$ metre, and directs the light from the retinoscope into the patient's pupil. We shall describe first plane-type retinoscopy with a circular mirror. He then slowly tilts the mirror from one side to the other and notes the appearance and movement of the light and shadow. If the patient has $-1 \cdot 5$ D of myopia, the pupillary area appears entirely illuminated or entirely dark. In the lower degrees of myopia and in emmetropia, the shadow is faint and has a straight border, while in the higher degrees of ametropia it is accentuated and dark with a curved edge (Fig. 407). When the mirror is moved, the greater the error of refraction the slower the movement. The direction of movement of the light and shadow is also noted: if they move in the same direction as the mirror the patient is more hypermetropic than $-1 \cdot 5$ D, if in the opposite direction he has a higher degree of myopia than this. The more horizontal meridian may be tested first, and then the more vertical. The effect of appropriate trial lenses on the reflex is then assessed. These lenses may be either inserted individually into a trial frame on the patient's face or held in the hand of the refractionist or, alternatively, they may be mounted in a rack. If movement occurs " with " the mirror, progressively stronger convex lenses are placed in the trial frame until no shadow can be seen; a slightly stronger lens ($+0 \cdot 25$ D) is then added, and the shadow should be reversed. At the point where there is no

---

[1] Trial frames and trial lenses will be described in the following section (p. 430).

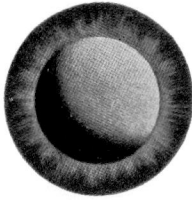

Fig. 408.

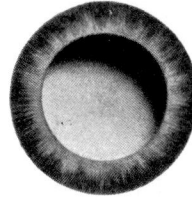

Fig. 409.

Figs. 408 and 409.—Retinoscopic Shadows in Oblique Astigmatism when
the mirror is moved horizontally.

shadow the refraction in this meridian is exactly neutralized, and the eye is rendered myopic to the extent of -1.5 D. When the points of reversal in all meridians are the same, the refractive error is spherical. When the points of reversal in different meridians are not the same, astigmatism is present; thus in hypermetropic or myopic astigmatism the edge of the illuminated area will move at different speeds, and in mixed astigmatism in opposite directions in the two meridians. Where the axis of the cylinder is oblique the edge of the illuminated area appears similarly oblique (Figs. 408–9).

The obliquity of the edge of this area depends on the direction of the axis of the cylinder, and is independent of the direction in which the mirror is tilted; this appearance is an optical illusion which is most easily explained pictorially (Fig. 410). If an oblique rule (AB) is slid across a circular opening in a horizontal direction (C) it will not seem to be travelling horizontally, but will appear to move obliquely (D) in a direction perpendicular to its own surface, and, no matter what the real direction of movement, this illusory direction will always be evident.

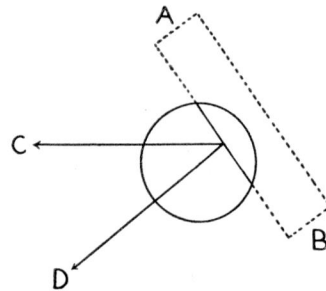

Fig. 410.—To Illustrate the
Apparent Direction of
Movement of an Oblique
Astigmatic Shadow.

If A B is slid across a circular opening in the direction of C it will appear to move obliquely in a direction (D) perpendicular to its own surface.

When the conditions which denote astigmatism are seen, the mirror is tilted in the two chief meridians which are respectively parallel and perpendicular to the edge of the illuminated area. The more emmetropic meridian is corrected first, and then the mirror is tilted at right angles and the more ametropic meridian corrected. When the first meridian is exactly corrected, the illumination of the pupil assumes a band or oval shape in astigmatic errors of some size (Fig. 411), and on tilting the mirror parallel to this band, a shadow appears coming from both edges of the pupil at once to meet in the centre, leaving the peripheral parts of the pupil illuminated (Fig. 412). This appearance is coincident with the exact neutralization of the meridian corresponding to the band; the effect is due to the retinal images as seen at the pupil being converted into the form of lines. The power of the cylindrical component is estimated by neutralizing the meridian in the direction of greatest movement or at right angles to the long axis of the band-shaped or oval reflex.

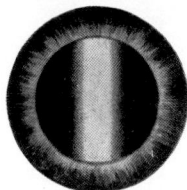 

Fig. 411.   Fig. 412.

Figs. 411 and 412.—When the more emmetropic meridian is neutralized, the illumination of the pupil appears as in Fig. 411; on tilting the mirror parallel to this band the appearance is as seen in Fig. 412.

Spherical lenses may be used throughout the examination and the final correcting lens found from the powers of the two principal meridians, the direction of the axis of the cylinder being assessed. It is more accurate (and ultimately saves time) however, if the first meridian is corrected with spherical lenses and the second with the addition of a cylindrical lens.

In order to read the axis of the astigmatism readily in the dark, Nelken (1959) suggested the use of a trial-frame and trial-lenses wherein the scale of the former and the cylindrical markings on the latter were painted with a reflecting substance which shows up brightly in the light used for retinoscopy.

Finally, with test lenses in place the strength of the combination can be verified by the surgeon altering his distance from the patient's eye. There is no shadow at $\frac{2}{3}$ metre distance since the far-point coincides with the surgeon's eye. If now the latter bends forward so that he approaches the patient's eye by (say) 25 cm., the far-point is now behind the surgeon's eye, and a shadow moving in the same direction as the tilt of the mirror should appear. If the surgeon then leans back so that the distance between the two is 1 metre, the far-point falls between them and a shadow moving against the tilt of the mirror should appear. If the expected change does not occur in both directions symmetrically, the spherical correction is wrong; if it occurs in one direction and not in the other, the cylindrical correction is wrong.

The position of the axis of the cylinder can be verified by the methods of cylindrical retinoscopy (*vide infra*).

Using *streak retinoscopy* the same principles are observed. When the streak is thrown into the pupil a light band is seen parallel to the axis of the streak (Fig. 413). The characteristics of the band-reflex are then noted. A wide indistinct band denotes high ametropia; the nearer to emmetropia (or to the point of reversal) the brighter and narrower it is; on the whole, the

FIGS. 413 to 419.—STREAK RETINOSCOPY.

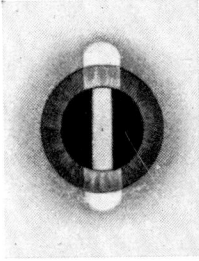 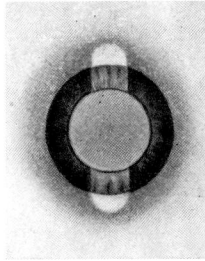 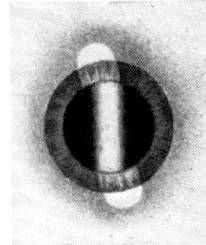

FIG. 413.—The streak reflex parallel to the retinoscopic streak.

FIG. 414.—The reflex at the point of neutralization.

FIG. 415.—The streak reflex in 90° axis of astigmatism when the retinoscopic streak is deflected.

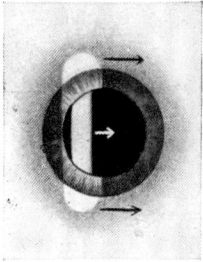 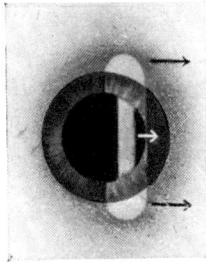 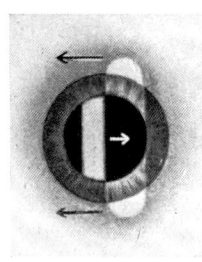 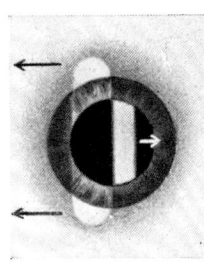

FIG. 416.   FIG. 417.   FIG. 418.   FIG. 419.

The reflex and streak in a "with" movement in hypermetropia (plane mirror).

The reflex and streak in an "against" movement in myopia (plane mirror).

band is narrower in hypermetropia, wider and less distinct in myopia. The streak is then rotated and if astigmatism is present it will vary in thickness in different meridians. The streak is then placed in the more emmetropic meridian and moved across the pupil. A " with " movement of the reflex indicates hypermetropia (with a plane-type mirror system), an " against " movement, myopia, and the slower the movement the greater the ametropia (Figs. 416–19). The first meridian is neutralized, at which point the streak disappears and the pupil becomes completely filled with light or completely dark (Fig. 414). If all meridians are similarly neutralized there is no astigmatism; if a band-shaped reflex appears in any meridian, astigmatism is present. When the first meridian is neutralized, therefore, the streak is turned through 90°; if it then passes exactly through the axis of astigmatism, a bright, sharply defined reflex band is seen which moves exactly parallel to the band of light outside the pupil, either " with " or " against ". If it does not pass exactly through the astigmatic axis (or if it is rotated a few degrees out) the reflex becomes more poorly defined and tends to remain fixed in the astigmatic meridian (Fig. 415), producing a break in the alignment between the reflex in the pupil and the band outside it and appearing to lie in a position intermediate between that of the latter and the true axis of astigmatism. The axis, even in the case of low astigmatic errors, can thus be determined by rotating the streak until it moves parallel to the reflex. The reflex in the astigmatic meridian is then similarly neutralized.

The strength of the correction is now verified by varying the working distance and obtaining reversals of the optical effects. It may also be verified by making use of the fact that if the point of reversal in one meridian has been reached, whatever the direction of the band of light the area of shadow in the pupil must travel in the direction of the other principal meridian (Fig. 410). The retinoscope is thus focused to give a broad light band (2 cm. width) on the patient's face and the streak turned to a wrong axis. If the power of the spherical lens is correct, the shadow movement will not change its direction but remains in the principal meridian. The axis of the cylinder may be verified by the methods of cylinder retinoscopy, and the final result deduced by adding algebraically to the correcting lenses employed a minus sphere representing the working distance.

CYLINDER RETINOSCOPY

In cylinder retinoscopy after the spherical error has been determined in the usual way, with the correcting sphere still in the trial frame the astigmatic error of the total refraction is measured by neutralization with cylindrical lenses as indicated in the previous section; the value of the method lies in that it allows the accurate estimation of bi-oblique astigmatism and that with ordinary astigmatic errors it offers a fine check on the correctness of the axis of the cylinder. The technique depends upon the utilization of the principles of obliquely crossed cylinders, and was first stressed by Jackson (1896) and later by Duane (1903), but was not popularized until the simple expositions of Krämer (1924–27) and Lindner (1925–27). In Jackson's words the technique " is the culmination and full development of skiascopy."

At this stage it is necessary to refer briefly to the principles of oblique cylinders. We have noted elsewhere[1] that if the axes of the two chief meridians in an astigmatic system are not at right angles, but are obliquely crossed, the combination can be resolved into another equivalent combination in which the two axes are at right angles. The sphero-cylindrical combination represented by such a system can be deduced by several methods which will be considered at a later stage[2]: it will suffice to mention here that:

(1) if the two obliquely crossed cylinders are of equal power and of the same denomination, in the resulting sphero-cylinder the axis of the cylindrical component will halve the angle formed by the axes of the obliquely crossed cylinders, and

(2) if the two obliquely crossed cylinders of the same denomination are of unequal power the angle formed by the axis of the resulting cylindrical component deviates from this position towards the axis of the stronger of the two by an amount which can be calculated since it is roughly proportional to its relative strength.

Thus a combination of $+$ 2 D cyl. $\smile$ $+$ 2 D cyl. separated by an angle of 15° results in a combination lying at an angle of 7·5°. If the cylinders are of opposite denominations the axis of the resulting cylinder will lie outside the axis of either component. A combination of $-$ 2 D cyl. ax. 40° $\frown$ $+$ 2 D cyl. ax. 90° acts astigmatically, if a $+$ 2 D sphere is added, as a combination of $+$ 2 D cyl. ax. 130° $\frown$

[1] p. 274.   [2] p. 673.

+ 2 D cyl. ax. 90°. The plus axis of the resulting combination (neglecting the spherical component) would be midway between the two—at 110°.

Considering the optical system formed by the combination of the astigmatic error in the eye and the astigmatic trial correction—

(a) If the trial cylinder is of the right power but at the wrong axis (that is, making the effect of two obliquely crossed cylinders of equal power corresponding to (1) above), retinoscopy will show the resulting effect to be an equally mixed astigmatism with its plus axis at right-angles to half the angle formed by the axes of the eye-cylinder and the trial cylinder. The light and shadow will therefore move, not at right-angles to the cylinder but obliquely, and the obliquity will be much exaggerated.

Thus if the eye is corrected by a + 2 D cyl. ax. 90°, its optical effect (uncorrected) is that of − 2 D cyl. ax. 90°. If the trial cylinder of + 2 D is at 75°, the position of the plus cylinder required to correct the resulting astigmatism (the plus axis) would be at 127·5°.

(b) If, however, the trial cylinder is of the wrong power and is at the wrong axis (corresponding to (2) above), an unequally mixed astigmatism will result. If the plus trial cylinder is too strong the resulting plus axis will fall farther away from the axis of the trial cylinder, if too weak, nearer to the axis. The greater the discrepancy between the eye-cylinder and the trial cylinder the stronger the shadow obtained but the less the deviation in direction. Percival (1928) suggested that the best check for the astigmatic axis in clinical practice is to use a trial cylinder of 7/8 of the power really required to neutralize the refractive error, in which case a misalignment of the trial cylinder will on retinoscopy be observed as an error six times as great.

For example, if in the above case where the correction is a + 3 D sph. ⊃ + 4 D cyl. axis 85°, a + 3 D sph. + 3·5 D cyl. is put up. Suppose the surgeon wrongly estimates that the direction of the axis is 90°, and he puts the cylinder vertically. On tilting the mirror in the horizontal direction he will find that the shadow does not move horizontally, as it should, but that it runs obliquely at about 150°, as indicated on the trial frame. This shows that the cylinder is not set correctly, and since the shadow is diverted 30° from the horizontal, he must rotate the cylinder through one-sixth of this angle in the corresponding direction. He must, therefore, rotate it through 5° and change the axis from 90° to 85°.

(c) Finally, if the trial cylinder is of the wrong power but at the correct axis the resultant combination will show no change in the axis of the astigmatism.

Since the obliquity of the shadow multiplies any error in the direction of the axis to such an extent, a very small deviation from the true axis is easily detected. The angle which the shadow makes with the axis of the cylinder can be roughly assessed, and the cylinder should be rotated through an angle one-sixth of this. The test should be again repeated, when any remaining error is as easily seen and corrected, until the final and correct position is attained. Such a test in practice takes very little time and is valuable and delicate, being especially useful where, for one reason or another, the subjective verification of the axis of the cylinder by the patient is not reliable.

FOGGING RETINOSCOPY. The practice of " fogging " vision by placing convex lenses in front of the eyes before the refraction is measured until distant vision is reduced to 6/60 was introduced by Sheard (1922) to discourage accommodative efforts in retinoscopy without a cycloplegic (*static non-cycloplegic retinoscopy*). In high hypermetropes the maximum convex lens and in high myopes the minimum concave lens which just allows this standard is used. Both eyes remain open as the patient fixes the test-card at a distance of 6 metres, and the refractive error is found by neutralizing with concave lenses.

Difficulties in Retinoscopy

The reading of the preceding paragraphs might give the impression that retinoscopy is a straightforward and easy technique characterized by mathematical accuracy. This is not always so and some special difficulties should be mentioned. Opacities in the optical media may reduce or abolish the reflex, a difficulty which may be mitigated by using a brilliant source of light and a large mirror while at the same time reducing the working distance. A small pupil may not always respond to mydriatics; and if accommodative changes occur, cycloplegia must be employed.

In the case of large refractive errors, as in aphakia or high myopia, the reflex obtained on retinoscopy may be faint until lenses of a power fairly close to the error are interposed. In this event when the media are known to be clear and the reflex is faint, a few lenses of high power (such as $\pm$ 8 D) should be tried first in order to establish the nature of the error. In many such cases this will be known if the patient is already wearing spectacles; these will give a clue to the appropriate lenses wherewith to start the examination.

Irregular astigmatism, whether caused by variations in curvature or refractivity, is a frequent source of trouble which becomes more accentuated as the neutral zone is reached so that it may be possible to attain only a rough approximation thereto. The ordinary aberrations of the eye contribute to this, an effect exaggerated by a large pupil. These are present to some extent in every eye, but may be so accentuated in some that it is necessary to study and differentiate the play of light and shadow in the various zones of the pupil.[1] Spherical aberrations tend to cause an increase of brightness at the centre or the periphery of the pupillary reflex depending on whether the aberrations are negative or positive (Figs. 420–1); the appropriate optics is illustrated in Fig. 422. These may be considerable even in the normal eye; thus von Szily (1903) found that only 16 out of 30 cases obtained equal vision through different parts of the periphery of the pupil and the optical zone, while Stine (1930) concluded that in normal eyes a positive aberration (wherein the peripheral zone is more strongly refracting and therefore more myopic than the central) up to $+7$ D may occur and a negative aberration (wherein the opposite relation obtains) up to -6 D. As a general rule the former is present and more attention should be given to the actual findings of retinoscopy. These aberrations in the same eye may be mixed, not only varying in degree in different quadrants but in type, and a variation between the two eyes is a regular occurrence. Stine found that the maximum difference between quadrants of a normal eye was 8 D;

---

[1] Jackson (1896), von Brudzewski (1900), Pi (1925), Lindner (1927), Stine (1930), and others.

FIGS. 420 to 422.—SPHERICAL ABERRATIONS.

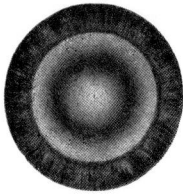 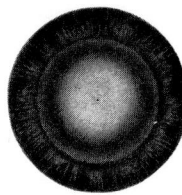

FIG. 420.   FIG. 421.

FIG. 420 shows positive aberration; FIG. 421, negative. The first appears near the point of reversal of the visual zone at the centre of the pupil, the second near the point of reversal for the extra-visual zone near the pupillary margin.

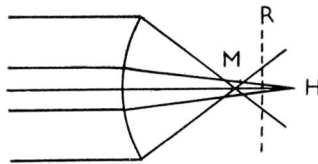

FIG. 422.—The optics of positive aberration. Two foci are indicated, and at the plane of observation (R) the appearance in Fig. 420 is seen wherein the peripheral zone is more myopic than the central.

and even in the axial zone itself the fine technique of stigmatoscopy will sometimes reveal considerable aberrations (Gullstrand, 1896). In pathological conditions, such as lenticular nuclear sclerosis, the differences may be much greater (14 D, Stine, 1930). In such cases attention should be given only to the central (visual) zone for it is through this part of the pupil that vision is normally conducted.

FIGS. 423 and 424.—SCISSOR-SHADOWS IN RETINOSCOPY.

 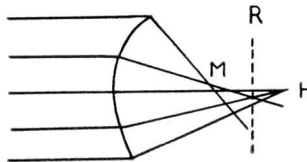

FIG. 423.—The appearance of scissor-shadows.

FIG. 424.—The optics of scissor-shadows wherein one part of the aperture is relatively myopic, the other relatively hypermetropic.

When a mixed aberration occurs so that one-half of the reflex differs in its refractivity considerably in character from the other, two band-reflexes appear which move toward and away from each other like the blades of scissors (*scissors-shadow*) (Jackson, 1887) (Fig. 423). This is due to differences in the curvatures of the cornea or lens in different areas so that at the same moment one part of the aperture shows the phenomena of myopia, the other those of hypermetropia (Fig. 424). Such an appearance may present itself only in the neighbourhood of the point of reversal. It is common in the presence of corneal scarring, the blades of the scissors pointing in the direction of the cicatrix. A somewhat similar scissors-movement may appear with a posterior staphyloma of the sclera when the blades point in the direction of the staphyloma (the *conical astigmatism* of Batten, 1897). A pendular movement of a single band of light with the fulcrum at the dark area of a corneal scar or conical distortion is another optical appearance. Sometimes the confusing shadows may be eliminated by varying the working distance or by altering the direction of the patient's gaze. In the case of scissor-shadows it may be possible to arrive at the approximate correction by finding the lens which causes the two bands of light to meet in the centre of the pupil, attention being directed to the central part of the pupil to the exclusion of the periphery. The practical point in the pendular swing of light and shadow is to determine the meridian of the band as it swings across the central visual zone which should locate the axis of the cylinder. In a markedly conical cornea the shadow is frequently triangular with its apex at the centre of the cone, and it appears to swirl round as the mirror is moved. In irregular astigmatism all sorts of distorted shadows may be apparent, which may move about in the most confusing manner. In such cases the small bright reflex of the pointolite is sometimes valuable in analysing the axial area, but frequently an approximate correction can only be guessed, and in many the greatest reliance must be placed upon subjective tests. A stenopæic slit may be placed in the trial frame and rotated into the position in which the patient sees best. This meridian is then corrected as far as possible with spherical lenses, and then the meridian at right-angles is treated similarly, and the two combined in the appropriate sphero-cylindrical lens. In all these anomalous cases, however, the estimation of the refraction must become a matter for experience rather than precept.

REFRACTOMETRY (OBJECTIVE OPTOMETRY)

Of the objective methods for measuring the refraction of the eye the most widely practised is retinoscopy, but other techniques of refractometry exist. For this purpose many special instruments have been designed which allow an observer to determine the degree of ametropia. These instruments —OPTOMETERS—are based on one of two principles.

In the first, a clear retinal image of a test-object is formed by an optical system and the degree of adjustment required gives a measure of the ametropia; the clarity of the retinal image is determined by ophthalmoscopic inspection. The adjustment giving maximum clarity, however, may not be easily defined. The method allows a comparison of subjective and objective findings, the observer's judgement of the clarity of the retinal image taken together with the subject's appreciation of it.

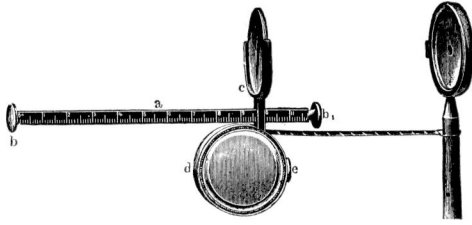

FIG. 425.—SCHMIDT-RIMPLER'S OPTOMETER.

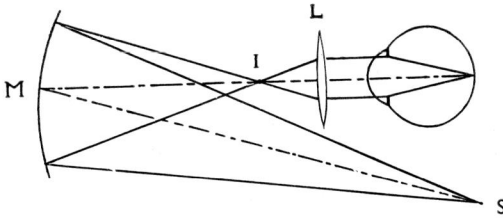

FIG. 426.—THE OPTICS OF SCHMIDT-RIMPLER'S OPTOMETER.

The source of light (S), with a trellis work serving as the object, is focused by the concave mirror (M) at I. The objective lens (L) is moved so that a sharp image of I is formed on the retina as verified by the observer looking through the hole in M. Since the distance MI is known, and the distance between I and the surface of the cornea is measurable, the far point of the eye can be calculated.

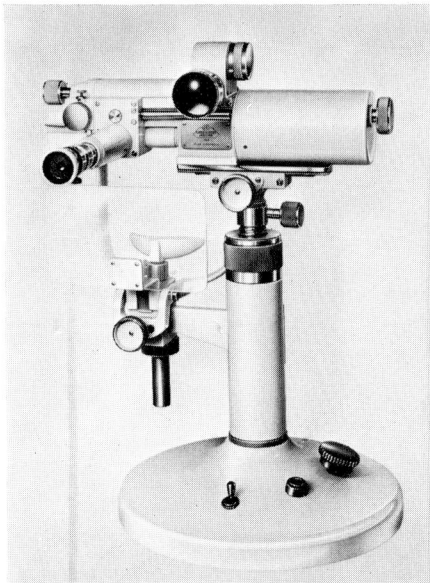

FIG. 427.—THE RODENSTOCK REFRACTOMETER.

The earliest of these optometers was that of Schmidt-Rimpler (1877) who used as an object a trellis-work traced on the lamp which served as the source of light, and an objective lens of + 10 D which, with the ophthalmoscopic mirror, was mounted on a calibrated arm (Figs. 425–6). Later and more refined versions of this type of instrument were designed to avoid troublesome reflexes and to use a greater area of the pupil as well as to obtain a more clearly defined end-point (see Zenker, 1929). The Rodenstock optometer designed by A. Kühl in 1922 (Kühl, 1927) (Figs. 427–8) and the

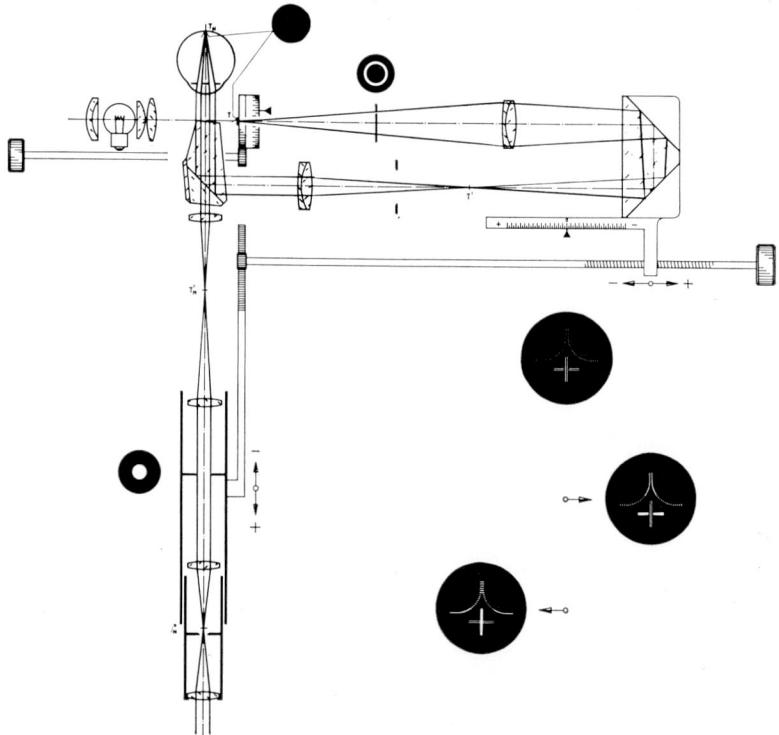

FIG. 428.—THE OPTICAL SYSTEM OF THE RODENSTOCK REFRACTOMETER.

The principle of the refractometer depends on the uniting of two separate paths of rays. The optometric system (horizontal) projects the measuring target onto the retina; its length is altered by means of an adjustable deviating prism. The resulting image is observed through the ophthalmoscopic system (vertical). Both systems are coupled in such a way that their focusing can be continually observed through the ophthalmoscope. The control for focusing connected to a measuring scale reads off in dioptres any deviation of the eye from emmetropia in terms of vertex power of the correcting lens required to correct the ametropic condition.

apparatus designed by Thorner (1922–28) and by Arnulf and his colleagues (1951–55) incorporate some of these improvements. The instrument designed by Arnulf is sufficiently sensitive to register tiny fluctuations of the order of one-tenth of a dioptre in the accommodated state of the eye.

In the second group of optometers, instead of a measurable adjustment being made to the rays entering the subject's eye, the vergence of the

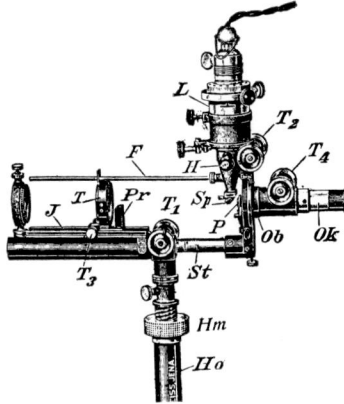

FIG. 429.—HENKER'S PARALLAX REFRACTIONOMETER (ZEISS).

It is essentially a modified Gullstrand ophthalmoscope .

L, source of light. T_2H, column containing the condenser system which forms within the slit, Sp, a slit-image of the lamp. An image of this and of the viewing diaphragm (P) are projected into the patient's pupil through the focusing lens. J is a rail calibrated in dioptres and T a test-disc transmitting light through four windows arranged cross-wise with a central point (Figs. 431–3). Each window contains a blackened linear mark interrupted in its centre. The visual image is viewed through the telescopic magnifier Ok. The patient's head is supported on a rest beyond the focusing lens and the instrument supported by a column (Hm, Ho). The illuminating tube can be swung in a semicircle to measure the refraction in any meridian. The coupling rod (F) allows the test-disc to participate in this movement.

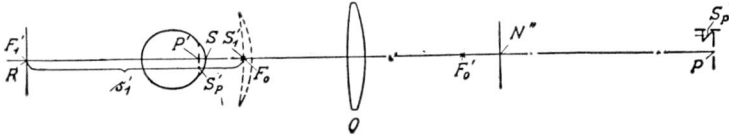

FIG. 430.—THE OPTICAL SYSTEM OF THE PARALLAX REFRACTIONOMETER.

The images of Sp and P, reduced by about four times, are projected into the patient's pupil ($S'p$ and P'). In the opposite sense the optical system of the patient's eye and the focusing lens O form an inverted magnified image of the retina at N''. Here also the focusing lens forms an image of the far point of the patient's eye (R). It is necessary to ascertain the position of N''. Viewed through the eye-piece, the test-disc and its shadow image (invariably at N'') coincide only when the former is also at the spot occupied by the retinal image. This is determined by the appearance of the test-disc.

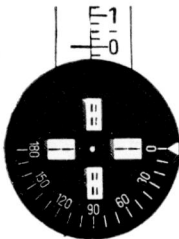
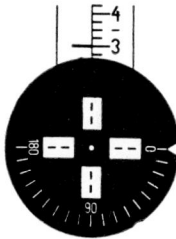
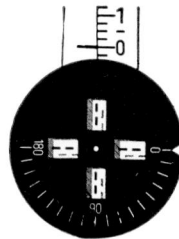

FIG. 431.   FIG. 432.   FIG. 433.

Fig. 432 shows the appearance when coincidence occurs, the shadow lines being coincident with the linear marks. Fig. 431 shows displacement towards the illuminating tube in axially symmetrical myopia. Fig. 433, the displacement in myopic astigmatism. Measurements are made by displacing the test disc on the calibrated rail until the primary and shadow images coincide.

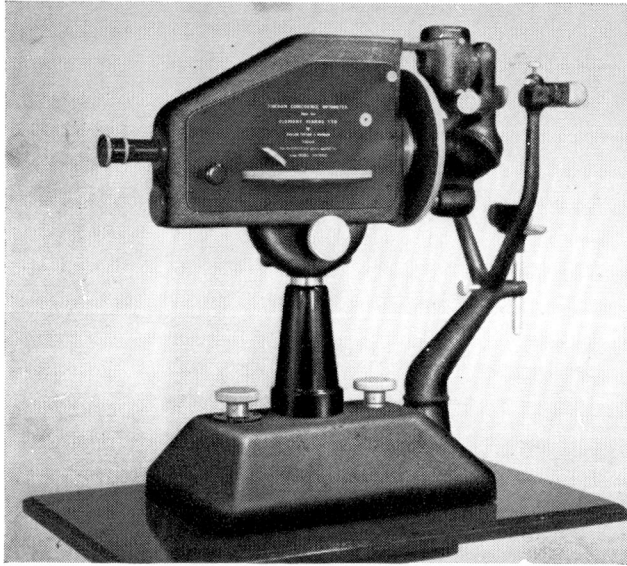

FIG. 434.—THE COINCIDENCE OPTOMETER OF FINCHAM.

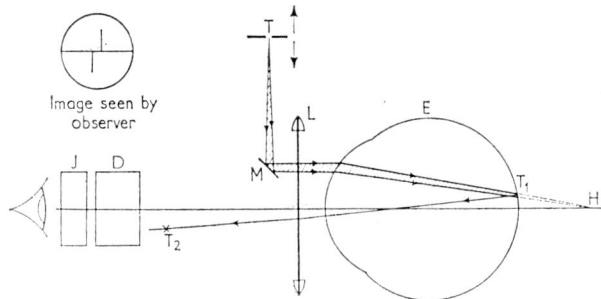

FIG. 435.—THE PRINCIPLE OF FINCHAM'S COINCIDENCE OPTOMETER.

Light from a slit, T, is reflected by a mirror, M, to pass through a lens, L, and into the subject's eye, E, through an eccentric part of the pupil. If the rays entering P are initially parallel, (in a hypermetropic eye) they converge to a point, H, on the optic axis, being intercepted by the retina to form a blur-patch at T_1. Light from T_1 emerges and after refraction by the lens, L, forms a blurred image of the test-object at T_2. If the object, T, is moved away from the mirror, M, so as to increase the convergence of the rays entering the eye, H moves towards the retina and therefore T_1 moves towards the axis; at the same time, T_2 is viewed through an eye-piece, J, and a doubling system, D, the latter being so arranged that T_2 is seen in its real position in one half of the field while the inverted image of it is seen in the other half (inset). When two images of the slit have been brought into alignment, T_1 must fall on the axis and the vergence of the in-going pencil is therefore a measure of the refractive error (after A. G. Bennett and J. Francis).

emergent rays is primarily determined. The principle is based on the method of indirect ophthalmoscopy wherein a condensing lens in front of the eye brings the emergent rays to a focus at a convenient distance. At the principal focus of the objective lens is placed a transilluminated test-object. The rays from this object are collimated by the lens, enter the pupil as a parallel beam and if the eye is emmetropic, are focused on the retina. From this image light emerges from the pupil again as a parallel beam and is focused by the objective lens at the position of the test-object. If the eye is myopic the emergent rays will be convergent and the image will be formed at a nearer point; if hypermetropic, the emergent rays will be divergent and the image will be formed farther away by an amount depending on the ametropia.

The accuracy of these instruments is greatly increased by employing the principle of displacement by parallax. This was utilized by Fick (1893) and was elaborated by Henker (1922–24) in his *parallax refractionometer* (Figs. 429–33). In this instrument, in order to utilize parallax to compare the distances of the test-object and that of the retinal image formed by the objective lens, the line of view of the examiner is displaced slightly to one side of the principal axis of the refracting system of the eye and the objective lens. If (as in emmetropia) the distances of the object and the image from the objective lens are equal, the image will be superimposed on the object and will not be seen. If (in myopia) the image is nearer the lens than the test-object, it will be displaced to the side next the illuminating tube. If (in hypermetropia) it is farther away, it will be displaced to the other side. When the two do not coincide the test-object is moved until coincidence is attained and the refraction is read from a scale (Figs. 431–3); in order to estimate astigmatism the system is rotated through 180°. Such an instrument gives a reasonably exact reading for the vertex value[1] of the refraction virtually in the visual line (that is, at the macula), but is not accurate in the case of small errors, particularly of astigmatism, and if it is used with a narrow pupil it cannot eliminate accommodation.

A more accurate principle was utilized by Fincham (1937) in his *coincidence optometer* (Figs. 434–5). In his instrument, when the target is not in a position which is conjugate to the subject's retina, the retinal image is displaced from the axis. The image is viewed through a system of prisms which divides the field into two and reverses one half, so that when the image is out of alignment the halves of the line-image move in opposite directions, and the setting is correct only when an unbroken line is formed (Fig. 435). In this system the accuracy of the instrument is doubled, and the most critical method of adjustment is employed—that of the alignment of a vernier. An optical fixation target is also incorporated in the instrument for the relaxation and control of accommodation (Reason, 1937; Briggs, 1937). A more modern instrument introduced by Hartinger is illustrated in Figs. 436–7.

An instrument wherewith the human element of observation was almost eliminated by using low-intensity infra-red radiation measured by a photo-electric cell suitably amplified by a thermionic valve and rectifier was introduced by Collins (1937) (Fig. 438); the refraction is measured by adjusting the focus until the maximum current is developed. A similar electronic instrument using a photo-electric cell with twin photo-sensitive surfaces was developed by Campbell (1956) and Campbell and Robson (1959) based on the Scheiner principle[2] so that an unequal stimulation of the cells indicates an out-of-focus effect. A single retinal image is formed in the emmetropic eye by two

[1] p. 639. [2] p. 155.

FIGS. 436 and 437.—THE HARTINGER OPTOMETER (from Degenhardt & Co.).

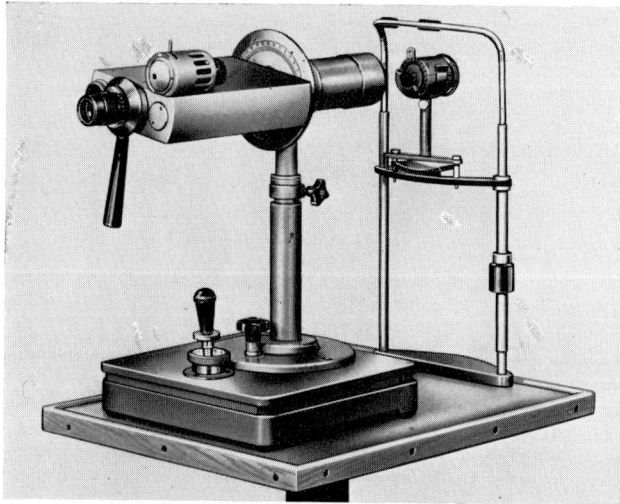

FIG. 436.—The instrument.

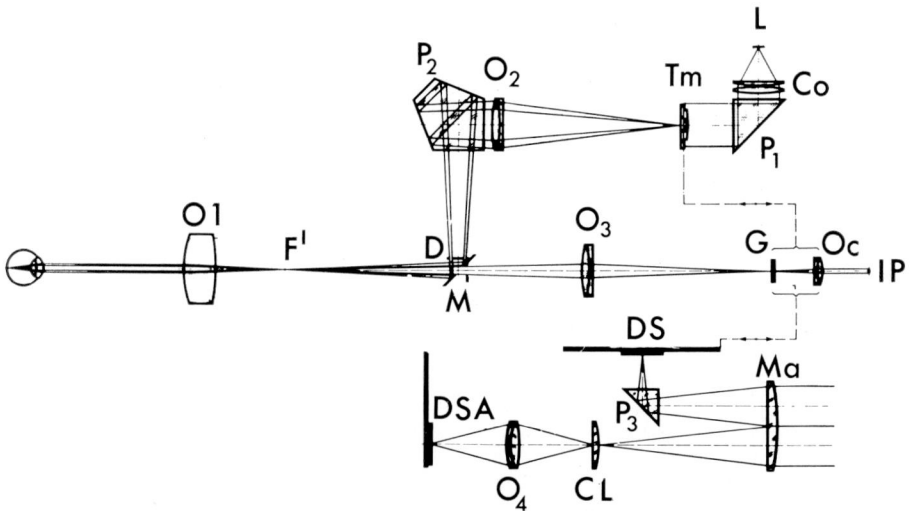

FIG. 437.—The path of the rays when adjusted for an emmetropic eye.

CL, collector lens.	IP, image-point.
Co, condenser.	L, light source.
D, diaphragm.	M, mirror.
DS, dioptric scale.	Ma, magnifier.
DSA, dioptric scale for axis.	O, objectives.
F′, point-focal length.	Oc, ocular.
G, graticule.	P, prisms.
	Tm, test-marker.

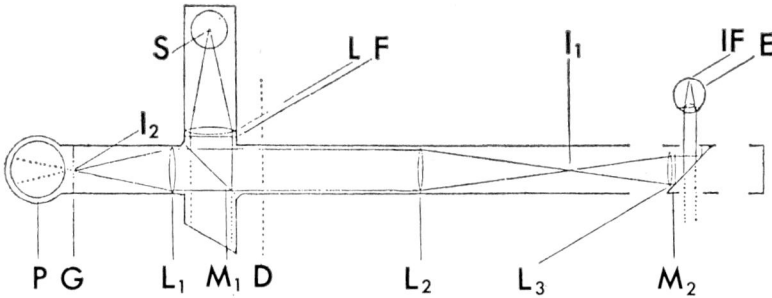

FIG. 438.—THE COLLINS ELECTRONIC REFRACTOMETER.

The radiation is reflected through 90° by a mirror which is made to vibrate at 100 cycles per sec. by an electromagnet. The beam returning from the retina oscillates as it is focused on a grating. If the image of the fundus is out of focus, the image returned to the plane of grating is blurred, whereas a sharp oscillating image will give rise to alternating stimulation of the photo-electric cell. The alternating signal is amplified by a thermionic valve and rectified, and changes in the current are indicated by a cathode-ray tube. A blurred image gives rise to a submaximal alternating current and the setting of the refraction is made by adjusting the focus until the maximum current is developed.

D, dividing plane for determining astigmatism.
E, eye being refracted (emmetropic).
F, filter.
G, grating.
I_1, image of filament which is caused to move by sliding L_2 towards or away from L_3, thus providing focusing adjustment to enable refraction to be measured.
I_2, final image upon grating.
IF, fundus image.

L, condenser for light from source.
L_1, condenser for light returning from eye.
L_2, focusing lens.
L_3, refractionometer lens.
M_1, vibrating mirror (transparent).
M_2, infra-red reflector.
P, photo-electric cell.
S, source of light.

narrow pencils of light but if the eye is ametropic the retinal image is doubled. From the responses of the two photo-cells, which are continuously recorded, doubling of the retinal image can be determined by alternately interrupting the two beams of light entering the eye. In some circumstances alterations of a refractive state of as small as 0·05 D can be discriminated.

Objective optometry is essentially a research technique. It is too complicated for routine clinical use and the conditions in which it is carried out, particularly in respect of accommodative activity and pupillary size, differ significantly from the circumstances of normal viewing.

KERATOMETRY (OPHTHALMOMETRY)

The KERATOMETER (OPHTHALMOMETER) is employed to measure the corneal astigmatism. The optical principles have already been fully described.[1] It will be remembered that the principle used is that the size of the image reflected from a mirror-surface (the cornea) depends on its curvature, variations of which are deduced by the device of doubling the image of an object. The type of instrument designed by Javal and Schiøtz (1881),

[1] p. 100.

using a Wollaston prism, has retained its popularity (Fig. 140); a later instrument was introduced by Littmann (1950).

It is to be recalled, however, that the ophthalmometer does not measure the refraction of the eye, but only the astigmatism of the curvature of the anterior surface of the cornea. Moreover, the refraction of the central part of the cornea is not estimated, but that of two points about 1·25 mm. or more on either side of it, and the reading does not give the cylinder required for correcting lenses but the value of the cylinder which when placed in contact with the cornea would correct the astigmatic curvature of its anterior surface. When the lenses are worn 13 or 15 mm. away from the eye their effective value is somewhat different. The residual astigmatism formed by the posterior surface of the cornea and the lens is neglected: we have already seen that the former frequently amounts to 0·5 D and the latter occasionally to 2 D or more. The method should therefore never be relied upon unless combined with retinoscopy except, perhaps, in aphakia. Its general popularity is due to the rapidity with which the measurement can be made, and if essential reliance is given to subjective methods of examination—which should never occur—a preliminary knowledge of the corneal astigmatism cuts short almost impossibly haphazard, hit-and-miss attempts to estimate the astigmatism. Its most useful function is to serve as an aid to the subjective refraction when the ocular media are so opaque as to obscure the reflex.

Arnulf, Dupuy and Flamant. *C.R. Acad. Sci.* (Paris), **232**, 349, 438 (1951).
Ann. Opt. ocul., **3**, 109 (1955).
Batten. *Ophthal. Rev.*, **16**, 1 (1897).
Beach. *Amer. J. Ophthal.*, **26**, 522 (1943).
Beach and McAdams. *Trans. Amer. ophthal. Soc.*, **35**, 221 (1937).
Trans. Amer. Acad. Ophthal., **42**, 179 (1937).
Beswick. *Amer. J. Ophthal.*, **53**, 879 (1962).
Binkhorst, Weinstein, Baretz and Clahane. *Amer. J. Ophthal.*, **55**, 1243 (1963).
Borschke. *Arch. Augenheilk.*, **52**, 161 (1905).
Bowman. *Roy. Lond. ophthal. Hosp. Rep.*, **2**, 154 (1859).
Briggs. *Proc. phys. Soc. Lond.*, **49**, 444 (1937).
von Brudzewski. *Arch. Augenheilk.*, **40**, 296 (1900).
Campbell. *J. Physiol.*, **123**, 357 (1954); **133**, 31 P (1956).
Campbell and Robson. *J. opt. Soc. Amer.*, **49**, 268 (1959).
Cher. *Trans. ophthal. Soc. U.K.*, **79**, 665 (1959).
Clapp. *Amer. J. Ophthal.*, **7**, 523 (1924).
Collins. *Brit. J. physiol. Opt.*, **11**, 30 (1937).
Cruise. *Trans. ophthal. Soc. U.K.*, **29**, 245 (1909).
Cuignet. *Recueil Ophtal.*, 14, 316 (1873).
Duane. *Ophthal. Rec.*, **12**, 420 (1903).
Evans. *Amer. J. Ophthal.*, **23**, 1159 (1940).
Fick. *Ann. Oculist.* (Paris), **110**, 356 (1893).
Fincham. *Proc. phys. Soc. Lond.*, **49**, 456 (1937).

Gettes and Leopold. *Arch. Ophthal.*, **49**, 24 (1953).
Gullstrand. *Photographisch - ophthalmometrische u. klin. Untersuchungen ü. d. Hornhautrefraktion*, Stockholm (1896).
Einführung in d. Methoden d. Dioptrik d. Auges, Leipzig (1911).
Hartinger. *See* Schober. *Klin. Mbl. Augenheilk.*, **125**, 194 (1954); **127**, 182 (1955).
Henker. *Ber. dtsch. ophthal. Ges.*, **43**, 87 (1922).
Dtsch. opt. Wschr., **9**, 375 (1923).
Z. ophthal. Opt., **12**, 34 (1924).
Jackson. *Amer. J. med. Sci.*, **89**, 404 (1885).
J. Amer. med. Ass., **9**, 645 (1887); **23**, 342 (1894).
Trans. Amer. ophthal. Soc., **5**, 141 (1888).
Skiascopy and its Practical Applications to the Study of Refraction, Phila. (1896).
Amer. J. Ophthal., **7**, 199 (1924).
Javal and Schiøtz. *Ann. Oculist.* (Paris), **86**, 5 (1881).
Klein. *Brit. J. Ophthal.*, **26**, 510 (1942); **28**, 157, 205 (1944).
Krämer. *Klin. Mbl. Augenheilk.*, **69**, 93 (1922).
v. Graefes Arch. Ophthal., **110**, 134 (1922).
Z. Augenheilk., **50**, 297 (1923); **54**, 177 (1924); **60**, 172 (1926); **61**, 276; **62**, 111 (1927).
Abderhalden's *Hb. d. biologischen Arbeitsmethoden*, Berlin, **5** (6) (1926).

Kühl. *Dtsch. opt. Wschr.*, **8**, 728 (1922).
Z. Augenheilk., **62**, 78 (1927).

Landolt. In de Wecker and Landolt's *Traité complet d'ophtal.*, Paris, **3** (1883). *The Refraction and Accommodation of the Eye and their Anomalies*, Edinb. (1886). *Graefe-Saemisch Hb. d. ges. Augenheilk.*, 2nd ed., Leipzig, **4** (1), 226 (1904); 3rd ed., Berlin, *Die Untersuchungsmethoden*, **1**, 118 (1920).
Arch. Ophtal., **44**, 65 (1927).

Lang and Barrett. *Roy. Lond. ophthal. Hosp. Rep.*, **11**, 219 (1887).

Lindner. *Ber. dtsch. ophthal. Ges.*, **45**, 284 (1925); **46**, 465 (1927).
Z. Augenheilk., **60**, 346 (1926).
Die Bestimmung d. Astigmatismus durch d. Schattenprobe mit Zylindergläsern, Berlin (1927).

Littmann. *Ber. dtsch. ophthal. Ges.*, **56**, 33 (1950).

Mark. *J. Amer. med. Ass.*, **186**, 430 (1963).

Marquez. *Arch. Oftal. hisp.-amer.*, **22**, 65 (1922); **26**, 189 (1926).
Bull. Soc. franç. Ophtal., **38**, 269 (1925).
Ann. Oculist. (Paris), **164**, 852 (1927).

Marron. *Arch. Ophthal.*, **23**, 340 (1940).

Mengin. *Recueil Ophtal.*, **5**, 122 (1878).

Nelken. *Brit. J. Ophthal.*, **43**, 444 (1959).

Parent. *Recueil Ophtal.*, **2**, 65, 424 (1880); **4**, 216 (1882).

Pascal. *Modern Retinoscopy*, London (1930).

Percival. *The Prescribing of Spectacles*, London (1928).

Pi. *Trans. ophthal. Soc. U.K.*, **45**, 393 (1925).

Priestley and Medine. *Amer. J. Ophthal.*, **34**, 572 (1951).

Reason. *Proc. phys. Soc. Lond.*, **49**, 469 (1937).

Robb and Petersen. *J. pediat. Ophthal.*, **5**, 110 (1968).

Rundles. *Arch. Ophthal.*, **21**, 833 (1939).

Schmidt-Rimpler. *Berl. klin. Wschr.*, **14**, 41 (1877).

Sheard. *Amer. J. physiol. Opt.*, **3**, 177 (1922).

Simcoe. *Arch. Ophthal.*, **67**, 406 (1962).

Snellen and Landolt. *Graefe-Saemisch Hb. d. ges. Augenheilk.*, 1st ed., Leipzig, **3**, 129 (1874).

Sorsby, Sheridan, Morris and Haythorne, *Lancet*, **2**, 214 (1955).

Stine. *Amer. J. Ophthal.*, **13**, 101 (1930)

Stolzar. *Amer. J. Ophthal.*, **36**, 110 (1953).

von Szily. *Klin. Mbl. Augenheilk.*, **41** (2), 44 (1903).

Tassman. *Amer. J. Ophthal.*, **21**, 1019 (1938).

Thorington. *Ann. Ophthal.*, **5**, 1027 (1896).
Retinoscopy, 2nd ed., Phila. (1898).

Thorner. *Ber. dtsch. ophthal. Ges.*, **43**, 75, 115 (1922); **46**, 419 (1927).
Dtsch. opt. Wschr., **13**, 576 (1927).
Arch. Augenheilk., **98**, 389 (1927).
Z. Augenheilk., **64**, 115 (1928).

Williamson-Noble. *Brit. J. Ophthal.*, **8**, 353 (1924).
Trans. ophthal. Soc. U.K., **48**, 210 (1928).

Wolff. *Klin. Mbl. Augenheilk.*, **31**, 439 (1893).
Ber. dtsch. ophthal. Ges., **28**, 180 (1900).
Ueber d. Skiaskopietheorie, Berlin (1903).
Arch. Ophtal., **24**, 213 (1904).
Arch. Augenheilk., **53**, 135 (1905); **60**, 210 (1908).
Skiaskopietheorie v. Standpunkt d. geom. Optik, Berlin (1905).
Z. Augenheilk., **16**, Erg., 91 (1906); **28**, 387 (1912); **38**, 318 (1917).

Zenker. *Arch. Augenheilk.*, **100-1**, 733 (1929).

Subjective Verification of the Refraction

We are introducing this Section with the portrait of EDWARD JACKSON [1856–1942] (Fig. 439). Jackson was a Quaker who started life as a civil engineer before studying medicine and ophthalmology. First associated with the University of Philadelphia, he spent the greater part of his professional life at Denver as professor of ophthalmology in the University of Colorado. Throughout his long and arduous life he interested himself in every branch of our specialty and in professional interests in the United States; thus he was chiefly responsible for forming the American Ophthalmic Board which set an academic standard for entrance into the specialty, an idea now extended to most subjects in medicine in that country; he started the Summer Teaching Courses in Ophthalmology (1923), now such a feature of American ophthalmology; and, among his many interests, his was the primary influence in forming the present 3rd Series of the *American Journal of Ophthalmology* (1918) as an amalgamation of six journals.

Perhaps his main interest was the study of refractive errors and his insistence on their clinical importance and accurate correction. He published many papers on this subject dealing both with the general principles on which refractive errors were measured and corrected and with improvements in the technique of their assessment. He was among the first to insist on the advisability of the full correction of ametropia,

FIG. 439.—EDWARD JACKSON
[1856–1942].

particularly of myopia, a practice at that time generally viewed with disfavour as tending to lead to visual deterioration; his classical papers on this subject appeared in 1891, 1892 and 1909. With regard to technique, his first contribution was the introduction of his refraction ophthalmoscope (1887); his first remarkable paper on retinoscopy appeared in 1885, and his book on the principles and application of skiascopy (1895) will remain one of the classics of American medical literature; his punctilious care in detail was exemplified in his insistence upon accuracy in such things as trial lenses and frames (1887); and his name will always be associated with the cross-cylinder, a device introduced by Stokes (1849) but exploited and popularized by no one more than Jackson (1907). It is to his great credit that, although an enthusiast, he maintained a sane and balanced attitude towards a subject which has excited almost hysterical exaggeration among some of its exponents.

SUBJECTIVE METHODS OF ESTIMATING THE REFRACTIVE ERROR depend upon the patient himself finding the position of the posterior conjugate focus of the refractive system of his eye by assessing the clarity of an image focused upon the retina. They are all subject to the grave objection that the accuracy of the results depends largely upon the intelligence, cooperation and observational ability of the patient. Many patients do not possess these three attributes to any great degree and therefore few subjective tests are wholly reliable. These methods should therefore be looked upon essentially as a means of verifying the refractive error as estimated objectively and form the means whereby the aim of refraction in most cases (that is, apart from certain pathological exceptions) is attained—*to provide the patient with the optical correction nearest to the optical ideal with which he sees best and is most comfort-*

FIG. 440.—JOHANN ZAHN'S POLYSPHERICAL LENS (from A. G. Bennett).

able. As a primary procedure, of course, they were the only methods available to the itinerant spectacle vendor and commonly used by oculists before the latter part of the last century (when they used to be known as " Donders's method "); as a primary procedure today, however, in a patient with clear ocular media, such purely subjective methods are unworthy of scientifically based professional practice. Nevertheless, retinoscopy is far from reliable in cases with any appreciable opacity of the media, and an improvement of acuity can occasionally be obtained by the subjective testing of patients with no recognizable retinoscopy reflex.

Historically Johann Zahn (1685) (Fig. 513) devised the first approach to a scientific technique by introducing his " polyspherical " lens with six different powers to be used for testing sight (Fig. 440). The plano-convex trial lens had a series of spherical curves ground and polished on different circular zones such that the central circular portion had the longest radius of curvature, while the plano-concave lens had the steepest curvature in the centre. Thus the patient observed which radius of curvature he preferred.

THE CLINICAL MEASUREMENT OF VISUAL ACUITY

During an examination of the refraction, subjective visual acuity is measured for distance vision. This topic is discussed elsewhere,[1] but is of

FIG. 441.—SNELLEN'S ORIGINAL CHART (1862) (about 2/9 size).

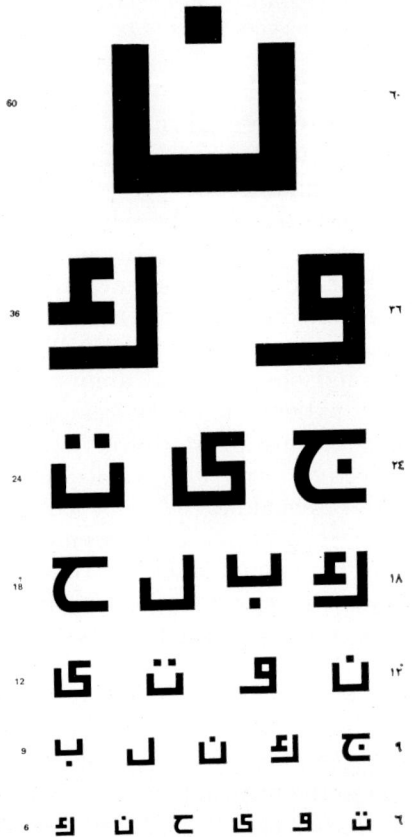

FIG. 442.—ARABIC TEST-TYPES BASED ON SNELLEN'S PRINCIPLES (M. H. M. Emarah).

such importance that some recapitulation in this Volume would seem appropriate. The testing of near-vision is discussed in a later Chapter.[2]

The usual test-object for distance vision is a test-type based upon the original *Optotypes* of Herman Snellen[3] of Utrecht (1862), which consists of

[1] Vol. VII, p. 370.   [2] p. 480.   [3] Vol. VII, Fig. 297.

a series of letters (Fig. 441).[1] Each letter is of such a shape that it can be enclosed in a square the size of which is five times the thickness of the lines composing the letter (Fig. 443). The size of the elements, that is, the breadth of the lines, is such that their edges subtend a visual angle of 1′ when the types are a certain specified distance away. Each entire letter therefore subtends an angle of 5′ at this distance, but in order to analyse its form completely and see its constituent parts, the eye must be able to resolve them down to the standard limit of 1′. The first line of type is so constructed that this angle is formed at a distance of 60 metres, the second at 36 metres, the third at 24, the fourth at 18, the fifth at 12, the sixth at 9, the seventh at 6, while additional lines are usually inserted which subtend the same angle at 5 and 4 metres (Fig. 444). These letters should thus be read by a person with standard vision at these distances away. Consequently, if a patient is placed at a convenient distance, which is usually taken as 6 metres,

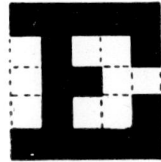

FIG. 443.

he should be able to read easily down to the line with a theoretical viewpoint 9 metres away, while the 6-metre line should just be distinct. If he cannot reach this limit his distant vision is defective; and if he can exceed it, it is above the standard. The results of the test are expressed as *Snellen's fraction*, the numerator of which denotes the distance at which the patient is from the type, and the denominator the line he sees at this distance. Thus if his vision is normal, and he sees the line which ought to be

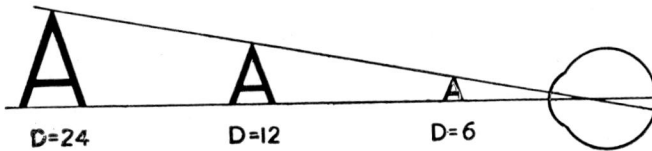

FIG. 444.

read at 6 metres when he is 6 metres distant, his visual acuity is 6/6; if, when he is at this distance, he can only see the line which a person with standard vision should see at 24 metres, his visual acuity is 6/24; while if he reads still further and reaches the line constructed to subtend the standard visual angle at 4 metres, his acuity is 6/4. These fractions, of course, should not be reduced since they are conventions giving numerical statements of specific conditions, indicating the actual types used and the distance away.

Underlying this conventional account of the Snellen chart there is a situation of considerable complexity. Several variable factors in the design of test-types must be considered if accurate and comparable measurements

[1] Snellen's optotypes were presented by Donders at the 2nd International Congress of Ophthalmology (1862). Curiously, at the same Congress, Giraud-Teulon presented a very similar test; Snellen's, however, became internationally popular.

of visual acuity are to be obtained. These factors are the methods of recording visual acuity, the distance, gradation in size and the illumination of the letters themselves.

The visual acuity is expressed according to Snellen's classical formula $V = d/D$, where d is the testing distance and D the distance at which unit squares of letters in the lowest line read subtend an angle of $1'$. The gradation in the size of letters used in the series of lines on the chart has not been absolutely standardized. The Snellen progression does not correspond to any mathematical series, but Monoyer (1875–1904) suggested the somewhat simpler method of a scale in arithmetical progression, where the relative sizes of the test-letters were 10/10, 10/9, 10/8, 10/7, ... and so on to 10/1, giving a relative visual acuity of 1·0, 0·9, 0·8, 0·7, ... and so on to 0·1; this method was advocated by Dufour at the International Congress of 1929 but has the disadvantage that it does not express the testing distance. Several other notations have been suggested (see Bennett, 1965)—for example, the oxyoptre of Blaskowicz (1914), which is the same as Monoyer's decimal multiplied by 60 and represents the reciprocal of the visual angle in degrees. Other authors have proposed a scale in geometrical progression wherein each smaller letter is multiplied by a constant factor to obtain the next larger (Green, 1869–1905; Javal, 1878; Nicati, 1894; Sulzer, 1899; Williams, 1905; L. Sloan, 1959; and others); but this is not generally used. In the United States of America the metric system is not usually employed (6 metres = 20 feet): vision of 6/6 is therefore 20/20. The conversion of the three most commonly used conventions for the clinical measurement of visual acuity are shown in Table XXIII.

TABLE XXIII

VISUAL ACUITY TRANSCRIPTION TABLES
(Adopted by the International Council of Ophthalmology, 1954)

Decimal V Notation	6-metre Equivalent	20-feet Equivalent	Visual Angle (minutes)
1·0	6/6	20/20	1·0
0·9	—	—	1·1
0·8	5/6	20/25	1·3
0·7	6/9	20/30	1·4
0·6	5/9	15/25	1·6
0·5	6/12	20/40	2·0
0·4	5/12	20/50	2·5
0·3	6/18	20/70	3·3
0·2	—	—	5·0
0·1	6/60	20/200	10·0

The *distance* at which the test-types are placed is usually 6 metres, for which Snellen designed many of his original charts. It is employed today in both Great Britain and America, in the former being expressed as 6 metres, in the latter as 20 feet. In Western Europe the testing-distance is more usually 5 metres, as used originally by Snellen himself for some charts but advocated principally by Monoyer (1875) and Landolt (1899) and accepted at the International Congress at Naples in 1909. This is the shortest distance which should be allowed. If 6 metres, or at least 5, are not obtainable, the required distance should be made up by using reversed test-types placed above the patient's head, and making him look at their reflection in a mirror hung on the opposite wall (Fig. 449); an alternative is the use of letters which are themselves reversible as in the Sheridan–Gardiner test-types (Fig. 445). In this case the light from the types travels to the mirror and then back to the patient's eyes, and thus an available room-space of 3 metres can be converted optically into 6. A distance of from 6 metres to infinity represents approximately the depth of focus in the eye, so that at the former distance the rays of light in the small bundle which enters the pupil suffer so little divergence that for most purposes they may be taken as parallel, that is, as coming from infinity.

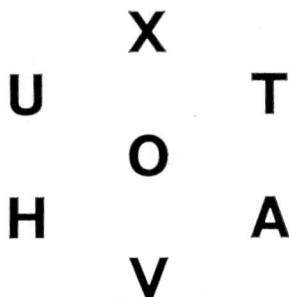

FIG. 445.—THE SHERIDAN-GARDINER TEST TYPES.
Seven reversible letters for use with a mirror.

In actual fact the divergence at this distance is equivalent to about $\frac{1}{6}$ of a dioptre, and in determining the absolute acuity allowance should be made for this in the adjustment of spectacle lenses.

The *test-letters* (*optotypes*) employed are clearly a factor of the greatest importance both with regard to their size and form. The strokes of the letter may subtend an angle of 1′ at the appropriate distance but the separation between these strokes may be less than this; Snellen's original H, for example, has a white T in its lower part of which the cross-piece subtends 1′ but the vertical much less (Fig. 446). In any case, the problem of the space between the components is really insoluble in cases of letters like H. As this last example has shown, the form of letters is therefore of some importance and the serifs originally used by Snellen have now been mostly abandoned as originally suggested by Green (1869). Some of the astonishing and ingenious varieties of these are shown in Fig. 446 taken from Bennett (1965). Further difficulties arise in the case of languages in which the letters themselves have strokes of variable thickness, some of which, however, have been largely overcome, as in the " Hirakana " letters in Japanese (Oshima *et al.*, 1965), or in the Arabic letters introduced by Emarah (1968) (Fig. 442).

The absolute size of the letters has also been subject to some dispute. Snellen's types were 5 units high by 5 or 6 units wide; later workers have used 5 × 5 or 5 × 4 or even irregular fractions of units for the horizontal or the vertical. Monoyer (1875) was the first to use a 5 × 4 non-serif system throughout and this is still widely accepted as in the chart recommended by the Council of British Ophthalmologists (1922) (Fig. 447).

The subject of the relative legibility of various letters has been extensively investigated since most test-charts have been designed with the principle of equal

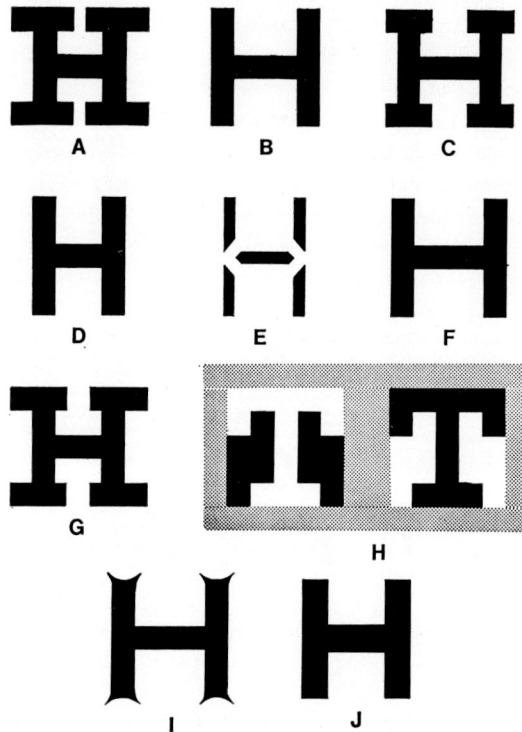

FIG. 446.—THE LETTER H (AND T) IN A VARIETY OF VISUAL TESTS.

A, Snellen (1862); B, Green (1868); C, Green (1872); D, Monoyer (1875); E, Dennett (1885); F, Hay (1919); G, Cowan (1928); H, Walker (1942); I, Prince (1954); J, Gill Sans Bold.

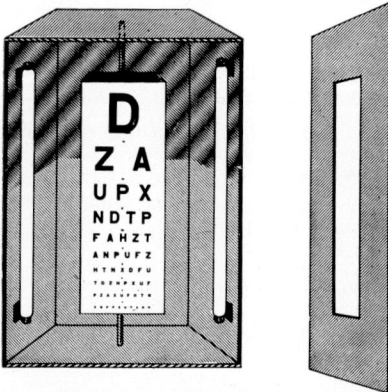

FIG. 447.—BOX TEXT-TYPES FOR CLINICAL USE.

Four different sets of letters are arranged on a revolving box, the movements of which are controlled by pulleys or electrically. This is contained within another box with two strip lights on the sides which illuminate the surface of the test-types. The cover on the right fits in front of the box to obscure the light from the patient. The reduction of this figure corresponds to the Snellen distance chart reduced to 1/17 of its usual size.

legibility in mind. Hartridge and Owen (1922) found that increasing difficulty in recognition occurred in the following series:

L A J E | N H X P F Z U T D | Y V K C B O R S
         | selection recommended |

Elschnig and Gnad (1930) found the following groups: (1) easily recognized—A C L D V O U 7 1 4; (2) intermediate—T P Z I G E F K N W R 6 2 3; and (3) difficult—H M Y X S Q B 5 8 9. Sloan and her colleagues (1952) found ten letters of somewhat similar legibility (Table XXIV), and Sloan (1959) based her chart on these. The situation is, however, far from simple and there is little agreement on it: the letter H was considered as easily recognizable by Hay (1919), of medium difficulty by Hartridge and Owen (1922), and of considerable difficulty by Sheard (1921). Hay (1919) suggested that the most legible letters to decipher should be used; Sheard (1921), following the recommendation of the Ophthalmological Section of the American Medical Association, advised letters presenting different degrees of difficulty; Hartridge and Owen (1922) advised letters of medium difficulty; and Banister (1927) and Arndt

TABLE XXIV

TABLE OF RELATIVE LEGIBILITIES
(Results of Sloan, Rowland and Altman)

Letter	Percentage of correct responses at the threshold	Deviation from the mean percentage
Z	94·0	+12·0
N	91·6	+ 9·6
H	89·3	+ 7·3
R	86·3	+ 4·3
V	84·6	+ 2·3
K	82·1	+ 0·1
D	79·5	− 0·5
C	71·4	−10·6
O	71·0	−11·0
S	70·6	−11·4
	Mean 82·0	

(1949) advocated the use of confusion letters such as C D G O Q and H K M N W; as we have seen, Sloan (1959) recommended letters of similar legibility, while Bennett (1965) chose the series of medium legibility already indicated. The British Standard[1] in 1968 advised the use of D E F H N P R U V Z (5 × 4) without serifs. The frequency with which the different letters incorporated in 12 test-charts currently used in Britain are employed is as follows:

A, 11; B, 5; C, 7; D, 7; E, 10; F, 6; G, 4; H, 10;
I, 2; J, 1; K, 2; L, 9; M, 3; N, 10; O, 10; P, 6;
Q, 1; R, 4; S, 2; T, 12; U, 9; V, 5; W, 2; X, 7;
Y, 5; Z, 7.

The absolute size of the letters in a single line of the chart has been varied so as to compensate to some extent for their differing legibilities (Dennett, 1885). Although the vast majority of charts has been based on the principle that the breadth of the strokes

[1] British Standard 4274 (1968).

should be such as to subtend an angle of 1′ of arc at specified distances, even this has been departed from by some authorities (Sulzer, 1904; Thorington, 1921). A further complication recently added to the whole question of testing visual acuity with test-types is that the recognition of single letters, particularly by children, is often easier than their recognition in a line of letters. This appears to be especially true if there has been any suggestion of amblyopia or eccentric fixation in the eye being investigated, a subject which will be discussed in the following Volume.[1]

Apart from the difficulty of choosing the most suitable test-letters, it must be stressed that the recognition of letters is a perceptual process with a strong personal factor. For this reason, many alternatives have been proposed, alternatives even more necessary in countries which do not have Roman script, and quite essential when the subject is illiterate. Arabic numerals provide possible substitutes. The counting of lines (Burchardt, 1869), the configuration of dots, the counting of concentric circles (Verhoeff, 1933), the recognition of the direction of the opening in a Snellen's prong (U) or a capital E, and many other devices have been suggested (see Ewing, 1920). Of the more scientific suggestions, that of Ives (1910–16) should be noted: he superimposed two finely-ruled gratings which could be rotated one over the other, presenting a pattern of contracting and expanding figures. Perhaps the most popular suggestion which does not depend upon letters is that of Landolt (1888) in which a ring with a gap in it which subtends an angle of 1′ at the prescribed distance (of 5 metres) is presented and the subject is asked to indicate in which segment of the ring the gap lies (Fig. 448). This was approved as a standard international test by the International Congress held in Naples (Hess, 1909) and again at Amsterdam (Dufour, 1929). It is probably the case that the gap is recognized by the increased illumination in its situation before its form is clearly discerned so that a higher value is obtained than exists and the test measures the light sense rather than the form sense; but possibly owing to the fact that it requires some considerable time to explain to patients how to indicate the position of the gap, and because it lacks the interest of reading letters, it has not been generally adopted in practice. Some modern test-charts, however, incorporate it, such as the Freeman–Archer unit (1955) (Fig. 449).

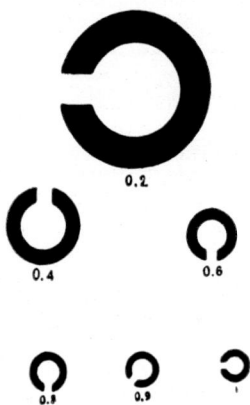

FIG. 448.—LANDOLT'S RINGS.

Whatever letters are employed, they should be clearly and boldly printed in black on a white ground in a setting on which they can be uniformly illuminated and changed; Fig. 447 is an example. The minimum illumination recommended in British Standards[2] is 120 candelas/sq. m. (35 foot-Lamberts) and for new equipment

[1] Vol. VI.   [2] British Standard 4274 (1968).

150 cd/m² (44 ft-L) to allow for deterioration. The use of a projection lantern has been advocated; indeed, instead of projecting lines of letters diminishing in size, the suggestion was put forward by Contino (1923), Ricci (1923) and Györffy (1948) of employing optical arrangements which permit a fine gradation of the size of the letters. To a considerable extent, however, the accuracy of any optically projected test is vitiated by the gradually increasing dark adaptation, the dilatation of the pupil, and the sharpness of the contrast between the test-field and dark surroundings in addition to the tendency for inaccurate focusing (Ferree and Rand, 1940; Monjé and Schober, 1950).

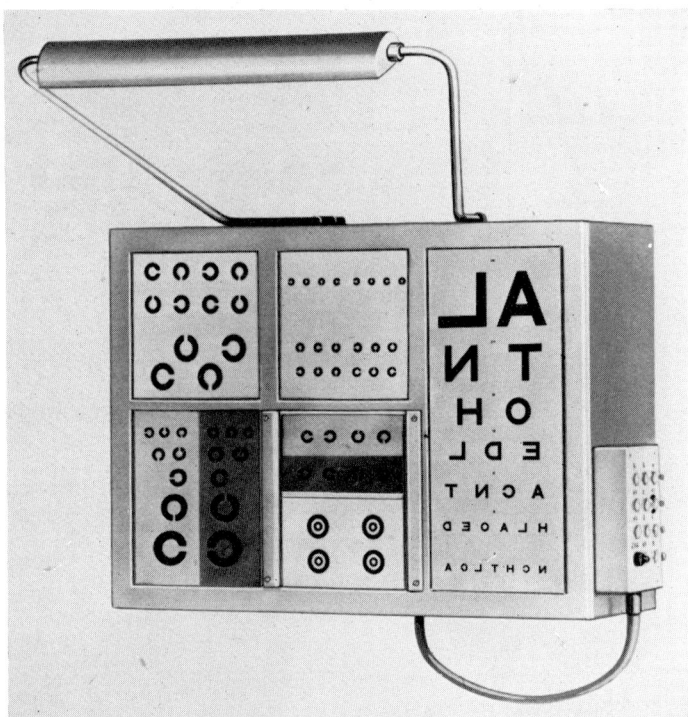

Fig. 449.—The Freeman-Archer Visual Testing Unit (Archer-Elliott Ltd.).

The provision of *test-types for children* is less satisfactory since reliability depends so much on the degree of interest excited as well as on their understanding the test. Many suggestions have been made, the majority consisting of pictures of well-known objects the parts of which correspond to the standard angle. In most cases blocked-in figures are best, and it is too often forgotten that the outline of an object should not subtend an angle of less than 1′; thus although a horse (for example) is drawn to the size of a Snellen's letter of 6/60, no part of the outline by which it is recognized should be less than 1/5 of this in thickness, whereas the outline in many tests on the market corresponds to a letter of 6/6. It is therefore better to make the test depend on one or more individual features which can be made of standard

size. This is followed in a chart such as Fig. 450 wherein the funnels of
ships drawn to a size conforming to Snellen's principles are counted. In all
these cases any approach to accuracy must be very approximate, but one
of the most effective ideas is the E-TEST of Albini (1885) which is applicable
to children of 3 years of age and upwards (Fig. 451). With one eye tied
up the child is shown the letter E on a card held at varying positions, directed

FIGS. 450 to 452. CHILDREN'S TESTS.

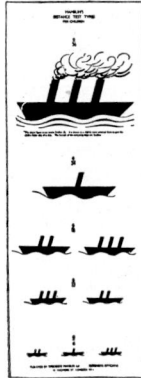

FIG. 450.—TEST-TYPES CONSTRUCTED ON   FIG. 451.—THE E-TEST OF ALBINI.
         SNELLEN'S PRINCIPLES

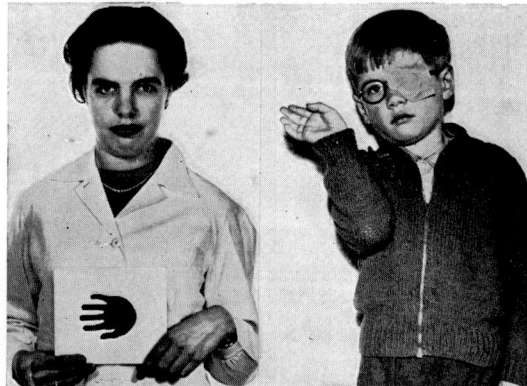

FIG. 452.—SJØGREN'S HAND TEST. In conducting the test the examiner (facing
the child) holds the card in a specific direction while the child orientates his hand
accordingly (T. K. Lyle and A. G. Cross, *May and Worth's Diseases of the Eye*,
Baillière, Tindall and Cassell).

up, down, to the right or left. He is given a wooden E to hold and asked to
put it in the same direction as the demonstration letter. In such a test
young children are usually very cooperative, and if it is carried out under
Snellen's principles with letters of different sizes held at the appropriate
distance a reasonably exact record of the acuity can be obtained. Sjøgren's

HAND-TEST (1939) is equally effective. The picture of a hand is printed in varying sizes on cards, the fingers corresponding to Snellen's notation, and as the examiner holds them in progressively smaller sizes in different directions the child is encouraged to orientate his own hand correspondingly, the entire procedure being treated as a game (Fig. 452). A further simple test was devised by ffooks (1965) consisting of squares, triangles and circles.

OBJECTIVE METHODS may be employed to determine the visual acuity based on the elicitation of optokinetic nystagmus, an involuntary reflex occurring when moving objects are passed in front of the eye so long as they are visually resolved.[1] This test is usually made with vertical stripes on a rotating drum (Bach, 1935; Reinecke and Cogan, 1958) or a moving checkerboard (Goldmann, 1943–50). By exhibiting progressively smaller images, the phenomenon can be used to assess the visual acuity of young children (even infants a few days old, Gorman *et al.*, 1957), uncooperative or malingering adults or even of animals.

Test-objects for astigmatic corrections will be noted subsequently.[2]

TRIAL LENSES AND FRAMES

Historically, the first author to write of trial lenses was Johann Zahn (1685) (Fig. 513). In addition to his polyspherical lens (Fig. 440) of which we have already spoken,[3] he recommended that various lenses of different curvature, both convex and concave, should be at hand for subjectively testing the vision. In his researches on this subject, however, Bennett (1966) found that although cases of trial lenses and trial frames had been in use for some time in France (see Theis, 1843), the first publication on this subject was that of the Bavarian ophthalmologist, Georg Tobias Cristoph Fronmüller (1843), whose suggestions, however, were largely unnoticed; the first trial case of loose lenses offered for sale was that of G. Merz and Sons (1848) of Munich (see Binard, 1849). An improvement was suggested by Donders (1864) that instead of biconvex and biconcave lenses, plano lenses be used for cylinders, while Zehender (1866) advocated the same for spheres; but the first major attempt to produce such a set was by Edward Jackson (1887) (Fig. 439) who introduced a specially designed trial frame and a set of trial lenses in which the spherical lenses were of the plano type. To the trial case F. H. Smith (1899) of Chicago added a prism-bar. The adoption of the dioptric notation (Monoyer, 1872) and the necessity for numbering the lenses by their back-vertex power,[4] insisted on by von Rohr (1912), allowed Kellner (1918) to put these ideals into practice with the production of plano-spherical and plano-cylindrical lenses, the former being of the same thickness irrespective of power, notated with their back-vertex powers along with a specially designed trial frame wherein the axes of the cylinders were accurately controlled by a milled head. Since then many improvements have been made which were summarized in the recommendations of the British Ministry of Health in 1956 in which the principle of additive vertex power is retained but the cylinder is (inconveniently) placed behind the sphere so that the effective power of the combination remains the same for distant and near vision.

Test Lenses. A sufficiency of test lenses should be at hand so that any reasonable combination of sphere, cylinder and prism can be put before the patient's eyes. This will include spheres and cylinders in pairs (say) every eighth dioptre to 1, every fourth to 4, every half to 6 cylindrical and 8 spherical, and every one to 10 cylindrical and 20 spherical. By combinations within such a series,

---

FIG. 453.—TRIAL CASE CONTAINING THE NECESSARY LENSES, PRISMS AND ACCESSORIES.

FIG. 454.—SPHERICAL TEST-LENS.

FIG. 455.—CYLINDRICAL TEST-LENS.

alterations of eighths of a dioptre up to 10 D spherical or cylindrical can be obtained, fourths up to 24 D and halves up to 28 D spherical. For a complete examination, prisms up to 10, with an additional two of 15 and 20 prism dioptres are also required, and accessories such as plano lenses, opaque discs, pin-hole and stenopæic discs, Maddox rods, red and green glasses and so on. All these are enclosed in a trial case (Fig. 453).

For the sake of lightness and thinness the lenses should be of small aperture (down to 15 mm. diam.) and for ease of manipulation so that almost instantaneous changes can be made, they should be surrounded by a light plastic or metal rim preferably (in the case of spheres) provided with suitable handles: the rotation of cylinders is often impeded by handles (Figs. 454–5).

The type of test lenses employed does not usually receive the attention its importance warrants. In the interests of practical accuracy the effective power of the trial lenses should conform as closely as possible, particularly in the higher powers, to the type of lens which is to be used in the spectacles.[1] It is obvious that this ideal cannot be attained, but practical convenience should involve as few departures from theoretical accuracy as possible. Biconvex and biconcave lenses are therefore unsatisfactory, and plano-convex and plano-concave lenses should be used, annotated with their back vertex powers.

In the trial frame the plane surface of a convex lens and the concave of a concave lens should when practicable be next the eye, and the plane surfaces of the two component lenses should be in apposition. To allow this apposition to be close, as suggested by Green (1880), the rim of the lens should be mounted so that it is as nearly as practicable in the plane of the plano surface (Fig. 456).

Trial frames should be primarily light and comfortable and be provided with three cells which fit the trial lenses and prisms exactly and carry them firmly and in close apposition. They must be readily adjustable and allow accurate

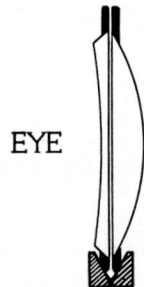

FIG. 456.—THE CORRECT ARRANGEMENT OF LENSES IN THE TRIAL FRAMES (− 4 D CYL. + 10 D SPH.).

---

[1] It is to be remembered that

an 11·5 D plano-convex = 12 D biconvex
14·0 ,,   ,,   = 15 ,,   ,,
17·5 ,,   ,,   = 20 ,,   ,,

centring vertically and horizontally for each eye in an asymmetric face, efficient angling, stability on the face, and the carriage of the lenses in a position corresponding to that to be occupied by the spectacles—all of which necessities are not easy to attain. Since the times of Green (1880) and Schultze (1893), an immense amount of ingenuity has been expended on this problem, and the tendency has been to allow complications in construction to diminish lightness and comfort—the most important consideration in any subjective test if the patient's attention is not to be distracted. The perfect trial frame has not been designed (Fig. 457).

FIG. 457.—TRIAL FRAME.

Accurate centring when the lenses are in the trial frame so that the optical centre of any lens lies in the visual axis is important. To adjust the trial frames with reference to the middle of the pupil is inaccurate, for this point need not necessarily be upon the visual axis; the *interaxial*, not the interpupillary distance should be determined. Many devices have been suggested to ensure this, one of the simplest of which is to insert in the frames in front of each eye a plane glass with two cross-markings meeting in the centre (Fig. 458). The patient looks straight forward at a light in the distance, and the surgeon notes its reflection upon the cornea. The frames are then adjusted so that the cross-lines meet in the centre of the reflection.

It is also important to fit the trial frame so that the spherical lens can be inserted as nearly as possible at the spectacle-distance from the eye. In practice the lens in the back-cell of the trial frame should just clear the lashes. This is of little significance when the correction is small but is especially important in the case of the higher corrections, for in these slight variations in the position significantly alter the effectivity of the lens. To a first approximation the effect of each millimetre of difference in the distance between the lenses and the cornea on the back-vertex power can be assessed from the simple formula $F^2/1,000$, where F denotes the power of the lens. Thus a $+16.00$ D lens will change in effective power by approximately 0.25 D on being moved 1 mm. towards or away from the eye.

FIG. 458.—CENTRING DEVICE.

Devices are in use for determining the distance between the back lens in the trial frame and the eye. The simplest is the measurement of the distance between the back of the lens and the closed lids, either by a narrow ruler inserted through a stenopæic slit or with a caliper-type gauge and adding 2 mm. thereto for the thickness of the lids; a more accurate optical device is the keratometer of Wessely (Fig. 459). Where several lenses of high power are used, the back-vertex power of the combination in the trial frame should be determined by means of a focimeter, a subject which will be subsequently discussed.[1] In all cases the lenses to be worn should be ordered with reference to their vertex power[2] (Henker, 1915).

OPTICAL UNITS. It has been suggested that ease of manipulation may be attained and time saved if the trial lenses were incorporated in a mechanical unit. The simplest form of such a system is a bracket containing a series of spherical lenses held in the hand as is sometimes used in retinoscopy. A more complicated type of apparatus mounts the whole series of lenses in circular chains which can be rotated before the eye with axial adjustments for the cylinders. Most modern optical units combine such a system of lenses with many of the various pieces of apparatus used in the testing of muscle balance. The instruments on the market vary, but most of them reflect more than ordinary ingenuity in combining an incredible number of possibilities—a spirit level for horizontal adjustment, a lever adjustment for pupillary distance, large batteries of plus and minus spherical and cylindrical lenses, multiple Maddox rods, a Stevens's phorometer for measuring right and left hyperphoria, esophoria and exophoria, rotatory prisms for measuring prismatic deviation and for testing duction and

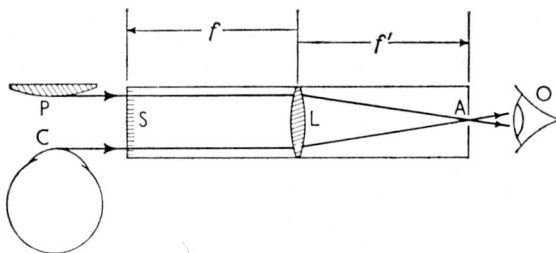

FIG. 459.—THE WESSELY KERATOMETER.

A positive lens, L, has a millimetre scale, S, at its first principal focus and a pinhole aperture, A, at its second. The observer, O, looking through the aperture, A, can read off the distance between the patient's cornea, C, and the posterior vertex of the trial lens, P, without parallax. With a negative lens in the trial frame the separation of C and the edge of the lens is obtained, the "sag" of the surface of the lens being added to deduce the full vertex distance (after A. G. Bennett and J. L. Francis).

exercising with prisms, a septum for use in stereoscopic work, a drum calibrated in centimetres and dioptres for reading and testing muscle balance at close range, cross-cylinders, prisms giving a vertical separation for testing muscle balance, complementary red and blue filters, and so on (Fig. 460). There is no doubt that such units look impressive and permit the performance of a large number of tests in a short space of time, but their value depends entirely on the personal habits and ideas of the surgeon.

SENSITOMETRIC REFRACTION

An alternative to the usual method of subjective testing with test-types which depends upon the resolution of the minimum visible while the brightness and contrast of the object with its background remain constant was suggested by Luckiesh and Moss (1940–43). In this procedure the size of the test-object remains constant while its contrast and brightness are simultaneously varied by placing filters of decreasing density before the eyes until the threshold of visibility is reached. The process is repeated with trial lenses of various powers until an ultimate threshold is reached. It is claimed that in this way the stimulus to accommodate is avoided (Luckiesh and Moss, 1937), but the technique has not become popular.

[1] p. 641.   [2] p. 639.

FIG. 460.—A REFRACTING UNIT.
Above is a phorometer, on the side a refractionometer with test-lenses below
(London Optical Company).

The standing wave-pattern generated by lasers has also been used to estimate refraction subjectively (Knoll, 1966). The visibility of this pattern depends on the optical state of the eye. It has even been suggested that such a technique may be used as a mass screening device.

THE MANIFEST REFRACTION WITH TEST-TYPES

The object of SUBJECTIVE MANIFEST REFRACTION is to obtain the best possible vision with lenses. Each eye is tested separately while an opaque disc is placed in the other compartment of the frames, and then the two are finally tested together. With the trial frames in place, properly centred and containing the correction found objectively (less the amount deducted for the working distance in retinoscopy), the patient sits 6 metres away from the illuminated test-types and the surgeon makes such alterations in the spherical and cylindrical correction as elicit the maximum acuity. The alterations should be done quickly to provide easy contrasts and it should be impressed on the patient that improvement in distinctness only (not in size) is wanted. It is usual to begin with alterations in the spherical correction. Spheres of small power are held in front of lenses in the trial frame, or the sphere in the trial frame is itself exchanged for one of greater or less power. There are no hard and fast rules about the steps in which these changes should be made. An experienced refractionist takes into account a number of factors, such as the acuity obtained with the first correction and the power of the sphere in it; gradations of 0·25 D or 0·5 D are usual.

FIG. 461.—THE STENOPÆIC SLIT.

When the best vision is obtained by altering the sphere, attention is directed to the cylinder and we shall examine some of the specialized tests for astigmatism at a later stage. It is, however, possible to manage without these, altering by small degrees the power and the axis of the cylinder in the frame. If a small degree of astigmatism is indicated by retinoscopy and the subject finds little difference in acuity on rotating the cylinder freely, an astigmatic correction may be unnecessary, and the best sphere by itself should be sought. A constant check of the cylindrical axis should be maintained throughout the subjective refraction; ideally it should be confirmed each time the power of the cylinder is altered. When the cylindrical correction has been finally determined, the sphere should again be checked.

In discovering astigmatism and finding the axis of the cylinder, however, a stenopæic slit (20 × 1 mm.) may be useful (Donders, 1864; Snellen, 1869) (Fig. 461). When it is rotated with the optimal spherical correction in place it will not affect the vision of a stigmatic eye, but will improve the acuity, particularly in one meridian, if astigmatism is present, since it shortens the elongated diffusion circles in the direction perpendicular to that of the slit. The slit is then turned at right angles to this direction and spherical lenses added until the acuity is as good as that obtained in the first place. The correcting cylinder will have the power of the lens added and lie at an axis corresponding to that of the first direction of the slit.

In occasional instances a correction in the trial frame based upon an accurate retinoscopy may result in a poor acuity. A common case of this is the hypermetrope who relaxes his accommodation during retinoscopy but on subjective testing will accept only a much reduced convex sphere. In this circumstance it may be advantageous to keep the fellow eye fogged by a high plus lens (sometimes combined with a base-down prism, Emerson,

1965) rather than being screened out by an opaque disc during subjective testing; in any event, hypermetropes will often accept a somewhat higher spherical correction binocularly. In a young myope inadequate improvement with the expected lenses is sometimes due to the retinoscopy not being axial. Some of these subjects have an oblique optic disc perhaps characterized by a " rolled " nasal edge and a retinoscopy at the macula shows them to be more myopic than indicated by a conventional refraction near the disc.

In the great majority of cases the refractionist should aim at improving the vision to the standard of 6/5, and if this is not attained he should satisfy himself that he is able to account for the visual defect. This, however, is a counsel of perfection. It is well known that high hypermetropes or subjects with pronounced astigmatic errors and organically healthy eyes may fail to attain a corrected vision approaching 6/5, a circumstance particularly so when the wearing of spectacles has been unduly delayed. Indeed, the difficulties experienced by wearers of high astigmatic corrections may in many cases outweigh the slight improvement in visual acuity which they obtain. When the vision of such a patient does not correct to better than 6/18, as occasionally happens, a difficult diagnostic problem may arise. It is as well, therefore, to be aware of this condition which has been termed *bilateral ametropic amblyopia* (Abraham, 1964).

The method of estimating the refraction *ab initio* in this way, by simply adding convex spheres to the highest possible or concave spheres to the lowest possible consonant with good vision, and thereafter (or if these make no great visual improvement) trying convex and concave cylinders through all meridians, is merely farcical, as well as being quite impractical. Some modification of this procedure is, however, necessary on occasions when retinoscopy is impossible or unreliable.

Purely subjective tests cannot be based on blind trial-and-error throughout the box of lenses. Some clue will be given by the nature of the visual complaint, the unaided visual acuity, the age of the patient, the spectacles previously worn, and also by the ophthalmic diagnosis. Thus a child of 12 complaining of difficulty in seeing the blackboard at school is likely to be myopic, with unaided vision of 6/18 about -1.5 D, of 6/60 about -2.5 D; a man in his fifties with previously good but now slightly impaired unaided distance vision is likely to be hypermetropic; while an elderly patient with a poor retinoscopic reflex because of cataract may benefit from a correction slightly more myopic than before.

A purely subjective technique of refraction is, of course, the diametrical opposite of that indulged in by a select few of ordering a spectacle correction on the basis of retinoscopy alone. This is unjustified save where subjective tests are impossible because of the youth of the subject, a lack of comprehension, or because spectacles are being ordered as part of the optical treatment of strabismus.

Various techniques are in common use as refinements of subjective testing; they may be divided into three categories: (1) Tests to induce a relaxation of accommodation when a cycloplegic is not used (the fogging test and cyclodamia); (2) tests to correct the power of the correction (bichromatic tests); and (3) tests to correct the strength or axis of the astigmatism (the cross-cylinder and astigmatic figures).

1. *Methods to eliminate accommodation.*

It is to be remembered that the accommodation is very considerably relaxed in the dark (Mauthner, 1876; Sasiain, 1947) or by the simple expedient of closing the eyes for a few minutes (Lancaster and Williams, 1914).

(*a*) THE FOGGING METHOD. In order to induce a relaxation of accommodation in the absence of a cycloplegic it has long been advocated to make the eyes artificially myopic by adding convex spheres, a technique elaborated particularly by Sheard (1922). When the refraction has been estimated objectively and the corrected vision determined (say 6/6, 6/6), the correcting lenses are left in place, and with both eyes uncovered, sufficient spheres (say +4 D) are added to each eye to make the acuity less than 6/60. The patient remains wearing these added lenses for some time, relaxing his accommodation by looking at the distant test-objects. The strength of the added lens before one eye is then gradually lessened by small fractions (0·5 D) until the maximum acuity is just reached, the first lens not being removed until the next is in position to prevent the accommodation from becoming active. The completely fogging lens (+4 D) is then replaced in front of the first eye and the same process repeated in the second; the maximum correction allowing full vision is ordered. The entire examination must be done slowly and leisurely.

(*b*) CYCLODAMIA (κύκλος, the circular ciliary muscle; δαμνάω, subdue or tame) is a technique evolved by Dorland Smith (1926) with a view to attaining the maximum control of accommodation; it differs from the fogging test in that vision is kept low all the time. Convex lenses are added to the correction determined objectively until the vision in each eye with both open is just 6/60 and is maintained at this level. A similar test is then made so as to fog the vision in each eye to 6/12. The lenses allowing 6/60 vision less 1·5 D and those allowing 6/12 less 0·5 D measure the total spherical error; if these two deductions mutually agree and corroborate the retinoscopic findings, the result is considered reliable.

2. *Chromatic tests to verify the power correction.*

These tests make use of the chromatic aberration of the eye by which the short blue rays are brought to a focus in front of the red rays. Theoretically if the image coincides with the percipient retinal elements, the middle yellow-green range of the spectrum is focused at this plane; the blue rays will come to a focus in front of this as if in a myopic refraction and the red behind as if in a hypermetropic refraction (Fig. 462).

(*a*) *Successive colour transformations* on this principle form the basis of the COBALT-BLUE TEST of Landolt (1887). Cobalt-blue glass transmits only red and blue light, and consequently if the patient is hypermetropic he sees a blue central light with a red halo, if myopic, a red central light with a blue halo (Fig. 462). Adjustments should be made until the chromatism is abolished.

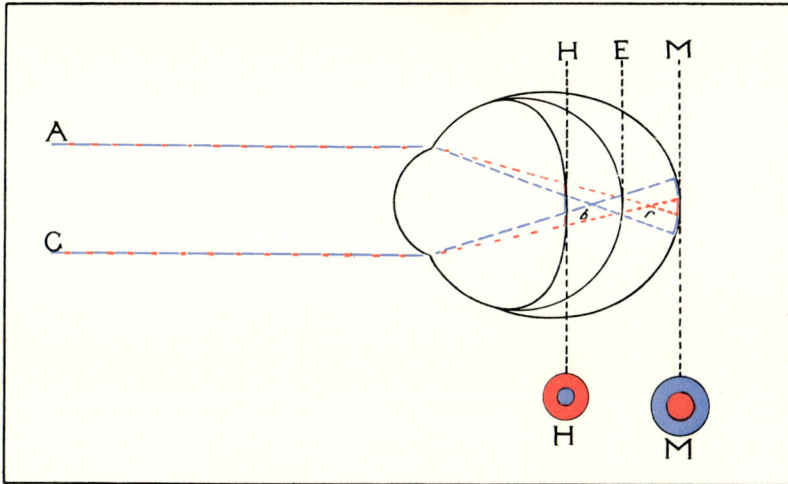

FIG. 462.—CHROMATIC TEST FOR REFRACTION.

The blue rays are focused at *b*, the red at *r*. In the emmetropic eye (E) the yellow-green rays are in focus and the red and blue equally unclear. In hypermetropia (H) the blue rays are more in focus, in myopia (M) the red. The appearances in the cobalt-blue test are seen below.

Rössler (1927–31) adapted this method to test astigmatism, and Fileti (1928) used the same principle by filtering light through a solution of methylene blue.

(*b*) *Simultaneous contrast* in colours provides an equally good test (the DUOCHROME TEST) (Imbert, 1929; Pech, 1930; Haas, 1931; and others). Opaque test letters are set in two illuminated glass panels, one of red glass and one of blue, set side by side or one above the other. These the patient compares. When the letters on the blue glass are more distinct than those on the red, the patient is relatively hypermetropic; in the reverse he is myopic, and adjustments are made until they are equal. An easier alternative is to have a word which can be readily divided, such as FRIEND, with FIN in green and RED in red, or SHOE, SO being in red and HE in green (Fig. 463). The method can be applied to astigmatism by utilizing coloured fan-shaped lines (*vide infra*). The simultaneous presentation of the

FIG. 463.—Snellen's test-types on a movable scroll in a box, provided also with a spotlight and a duochrome test below, *SO* being in red and *HE* in green.

two foci to one eye tends to abolish the desire to accommodate and adjustments to 0·25 D or less are usually readily made. Extensive use of chromatic tests is a feature of Freeman's technique of purely subjective refraction (Freeman and Hodd, 1955, (Fig. 449). The bottom left-hand panel is a series of Landolt rings, 6/24 to 6/6 in size, on either a green or red background; the sphere is estimated by the correction with which the two sets appear equally distinct.

It may be noted that chromatic tests are also of considerable value in the assessment of binocular balance.

3. *Astigmatic Tests.*

(*a*) The CROSS-CYLINDER is a simple refinement and is of extreme practical value to check both the power and the strength of the cylindrical correction. It was first described by Gabriel Stokes (1849), an Irish mathematician of Cambridge and known as the STOKES'S LENS; it was used ophthalmologically by Javal (1866–78), Snellen (1873) and Dennett (1885); but it owes its general popularity today to the enthusiastic advocacy of Edward Jackson (1893–1929). The principles involved have received extensive study.[1] The cross-cylinder (Fig. 464) is a mixed cylindrical combination of varying strengths in which the spherical component is one half the power of the cylindrical with the axes at right angles. With its use the cylindrical correction can be altered at the same time as the spherical correction is proportionately changed in the opposite sense. It is carried on a handle set at an angle of 45° from the axes of the cylinders so that when it is held before the combination in the trial frame and rapidly rotated around the axis of the handle the cylinder is changed from one direction to the other at right-angles.

FIG. 464.—THE CROSS-CYLINDER.

The most useful cross-cylinder is probably the combination of $- 0.25$ D sph. $\subset + 0.5$ D cyl., but many combinations are in use involving a cylindrical strength varying from 0.12 D to 1.0 D. The strength employed in any particular case depends on the visual acuity and on the cylindrical correction which is being assessed.

To check the strength of the cylinder the cylindrical axis is first placed in the same direction as the axis of the cylinder in the trial frame and then perpendicular to it. In the first position it enhances the effect of the cylinder, in the second it diminishes it by the same amount. If the visual acuity is unimproved in either of these positions, the cylinder in the trial frame is correct. If the visual acuity is improved by any of these, the change should be made and the verification repeated with the new combination by running through the cycle again.

To check the axis of the cylinder the principles of obliquely crossed cylinders are applied.[2] A moderately strong cross-cylinder (± 0.5 or ± 1.0) is held before the eye so that each axis lies 45° to either side of the axis of the trial cylinder. If visual improvement is attained in one alternative in comparison with the other, the correcting cylinder is turned slightly in the direction of the axis of the cylinder of the same

[1] Schneideman (1900), Crisp (1923–43), Hurst (1926), Danielson (1929), Pascal (1940), Friedman (1940) and others.

[2] p. 673.

denomination in the cross-cylinder. The test is then repeated several times until the position of the trial cylinder is found at which rotation of the cross-cylinder gives no alteration in distinctness in either position.

It is to be remembered that when tested on test-types in which vertical lines are more important than horizontal, the patient when partially fogged tends to choose a cylinder favouring the former, that is, too great a cylinder against the rule (Friedman, 1940; Williamson-Noble, 1943) (Fig. 465).

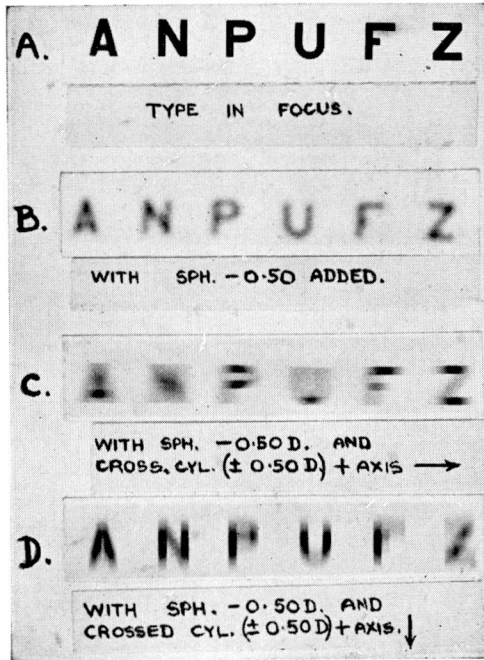

FIG. 465.—To show the Tendency towards Preferential Fogging with a Cross-cylinder having its Axis Horizontal (C) when contrasted with the Position with the Axis Vertical (D) when Test-letters are used.

A photographic reproduction. The effect would be somewhat similar in an eye totally without accommodation. Compare also Fig. 320.

The cross-cylinder can also be used with great value in conjunction with the astigmatic fan (Wilson, 1942; Crisp, 1943).

(b) *Astigmatic Figures.* In regular astigmatism lines which run in the same direction as the meridian of the greatest refractive error appear sharply defined[1]; lines which run at right angles to this are blurred, and lines running intermediately vary progressively between the two extremes (Figs. 466–8). A line therefore appears sharply outlined when it is accurately refracted in the meridian at right angles to it. This principle is used in a test for astigmatism when the patient observes suitably constructed figures.

[1] p. 63.

Many such figures have been devised, most of which have been derived from the ingenious and original work of John Green (1866–69), who used radiating lines, blocks of lines at right angles and acute angles, red and green lines and rotating dials to aid in the determination of the strength and the direction of the axis of astigmatic errors. Fixed charts depend on radiating lines arranged either in circular form as in the Lancaster chart (1915) (Fig. 470) or in a fan-shaped figure as was devised by Purkinje (1819–23) and is employed in the charts of Landolt (1909) and Pergens (1909) (Fig. 469). The lines have been duplicated (Green, 1866; the Wallace chart, 1889) (Fig. 471) or dotted (Green, 1866; Sheard, 1923), but this is generally confusing. Lancaster

FIGS. 466 to 468.—THE OPTICAL EFFECT OF A STAR-SHAPED FIGURE SEEN THROUGH AN ASTIGMATIC LENS.

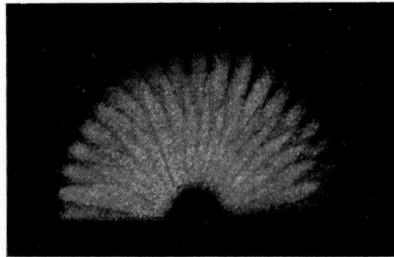

FIG. 466.

FIG. 467.

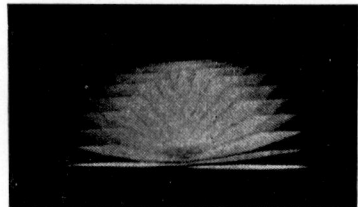

FIG. 468.

FIG. 466.—The entire fan is seen equally fogged through a spherical lens. In Fig. 467 the vertical line is most clearly defined, in Fig. 468 the horizontal, and the others progressively ill-defined, the effect in each case being obtained by photographing through a cylindrical lens with its axis at right angles to the sharply focused line (after E. Landolt).

(1915) believed the ideal combination to be very black lines on a white background; Friedenwald (1924–26) used black lines with white borders set on a background of grey into which the blurred lines might become lost and disappear (Fig. 472). In such tests one line stands out most sharply in regular astigmatism and the line at right angles is blurred; in bi-oblique astigmatism the blurred line is not at right angles to the clearest line; and in irregular astigmatism two lines not at right angles may be clear and the intervening ones are blurred.

The rotating type of chart is ideal to determine the exact axis of the cylinder after its appropriate direction has been found by a chart incorporating radiating lines. The lines on a rotating chart may be at right angles or at an angle, both of which principles

FIGS. 469 to 472.—ASTIGMATIC FAN FIGURES.

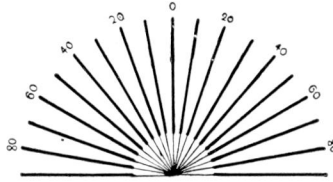

FIG. 469. LANDOLT'S CHART.

FIG. 470.—LANCASTER'S CHART.

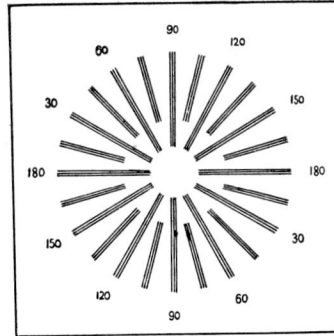

FIG. 471.—WALLACE'S CHART.

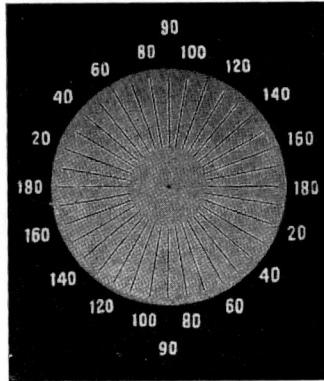

FIG. 472.—FRIEDENWALD'S CHART.

were employed by Green (1866); the simplest example of the first is Verhoeff's cross (see Friedenwald, 1924) (Fig. 473); complicated examples of the latter are Verhoeff's original charts (1899) (Figs. 474–5); and the simplest is Maddox's V-test (1921) or his arrow-test (1924) (Fig. 477). Verhoeff's chart is rotated until one of the main cross-lines is distinct, and the line at right angles is blurred; these points are accentuated by the fact that the small lines at right angles to the cross-lines are in the first case blurred, in the second distinct. In Maddox's test the arrow is rotated towards the sharpest radiating line and a fine adjustment made by comparing the relative intensities of the limbs of the head and the barbs of the arrow. By rotating the arrow-head slightly

FIGS. 473 TO 477.—ROTATING ASTIGMATIC TESTS.

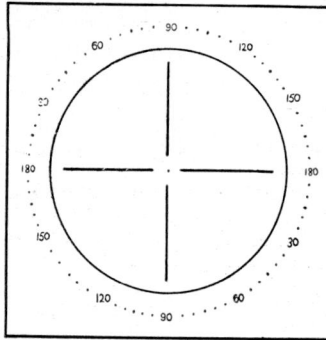

FIG. 473. VERHOEFF'S SIMPLE CROSS.

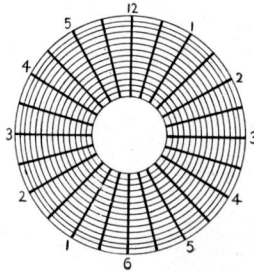

FIG. 474.

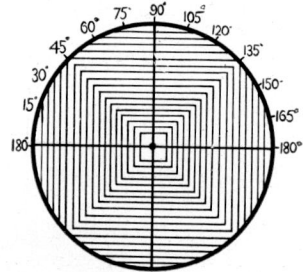

FIG. 475.

FIGS. 474 AND 475. VERHOEFF'S ROTATING ASTIGMATIC TESTS.

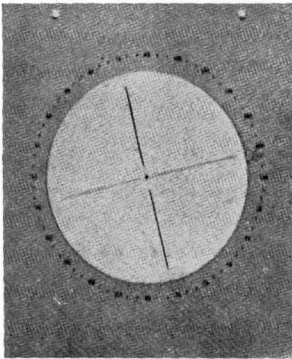

FIG. 476.—A ROTATING CROSS ON A GREY BACKGROUND SHOWING THE DIFFERENCE IN DISTINCTNESS IN SLIGHT ASTIGMATISM.

FIG. 477.—MADDOX'S ROTATING ARROW TEST.

in the direction of the blacker limb, an intermediate position is reached when the two limbs appear equally distinct. This denotes the direction at right angles to the axis of the correcting cylinder. The points of maximum definition and maximum blurring may be further checked by matching the two sets of parallel lines incorporated in the chart. Such a test is of very considerable accuracy (Verhoeff, 1923). Raubitschek (1929) modified the straight lines of the arrow-head into curved lines in a test which became popular.

As a clinical routine the test should be carried out with the patient slightly fogged by an amount sufficient to over-correct every meridian by 0·5 D; he is then asked to observe if any of the lines stand out more clearly than the others. If not, there is no astigmatism or the astigmatic correction is exact—or, as frequently happens, he is a poor observer. If astigmatism is present he will see one or a neighbouring group of lines more sharply defined by a degree depending on the amount of the astigmatism (Fig. 476). Concave cylinders are now added, their axes lying at right angles to this line, until all the lines—including that at right angles to the first—are equally clear, additional convex spheres being added meantime to maintain the fogging if necessary.

These tests are made at 6 metres distance. Oppenheimer (1924) suggested that in high myopes they should be conducted at the far-point.

The recognition of angular figures (such as the Maltese cross, Beach, 1928) in the test-types is of value in verifying the astigmatic correction.

4. Binocular tests

The final stage of any subjective examination of the refraction is a reassessment of the results found for each eye separately in conditions of normal binocular viewing. It is usually found that the binocular visual acuity is slightly better than that obtained with either eye alone if their corrected acuities are approximately equal. In order to confirm that the acuities of each eye are maximal and reasonably similar in binocular conditions, several techniques have been devised. The simplest is to cover one and then the other eye of the patient with the two uniocular corrections in the trial frame; the vision of the two eyes is compared subjectively and related to the uniocular acuity previously obtained. This is not, of course, a test of true binocular viewing but if carried out rapidly gives some idea of the equality or otherwise of the acuities. The two eyes may also be dissociated by the influence of vertical prisms to allow a more direct comparison between them. The results of the duochrome test on the two sides may be compared and equalized by adjustment of one or other correction, usually leaving the patient seeing the red test-object slightly more clearly than the green.

More elaborate devices are, however, in use in order to investigate the binocular balance and to allow some estimation to be made of any muscle imbalance that may exist; these have been summarized by Gentsch and Goodwin (1966). In his *infinity-balance test* Turville (1946–51) used an opaque strip 30 mm. wide placed vertically between the patient and the chart or down the mid-line of a reflecting mirror through which the test-types are viewed in such a manner that the chart is effectively divided into vertical halves seen exclusively by the right or left eye. Any difference between the two halves of the lines of test-types is thus obvious and the visual acuity can be balanced; uniocular vision is thus tested in binocular conditions without fusion. This technique may be combined with a bichromatic test (Freeman and Hodd, 1955). Instead of their mechanical divorce in this way, the images of the two eyes may be separated during binocular viewing either by a polarizing screen in front of the test-chart (Wilmut, 1951) or by the use of optotypes of polarizing material (Cowen, 1955); the dissociation is brought about by polarizing analysers at right angles to one another placed in the trial frames. Here again the testing may incorporate the dichromatic technique (Cowen, 1959). Using the latter in the form of the word " Friend " in alternate red and green letters with red and green filters in front of the eyes, Banks (1954) in his *foveal lock test* dissociated the two eyes while the periphery of the chart was seen by both, thus constituting a " lock ". It is probably fair to say, however, that while they are undoubtedly of established validity (Amigo, 1968), complex procedures for assessing the binocular balance do not have an extensive part to play in the routine of clinical refraction.

SUBJECTIVE OPTOMETRY

Many techniques have been devised to allow a subject to determine his own refractive error (*autoretinoscopy,* Sheard, 1926). The defect with most of these methods is that in approximating a piece of apparatus to the eye, a stimulus to accommodation is given which vitiates the result, a fault which remains even if efforts are made to keep the fellow eye unaccommodated by fixing a distant object. The subjective responses upon which these instruments are based are of two types, depending either on the clarity of a test-object or a doubling effect.

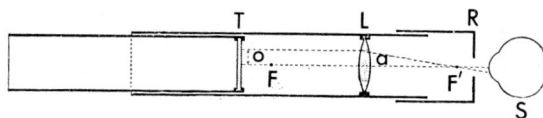

FIG. 478.—THE OPTOMETER OF BADAL.

In a tube which carries a convex lens, L, of foci, F, F', a second tube is introduced carrying a transparent test-type, T, which is viewed by a subject, S, through an aperture in a regulatable sleeve, R. Whatever the position of the test-type, the object, o, is always seen at the same angle, a, from the focal point F' of the lens.

Those instruments based on the ability to recognize the clarity of a test-object vary considerably in complexity; one of the simplest is that designed by Badal (1876) (Fig. 478). With the *differential optometer* of de Gramont (1934), based on the same principle, it is possible to estimate the astigmatism and to measure this during accommodation. In another instrument, the *variator* of Thorner, the two eyes may be simultaneously tested.

The methods depending on the doubling effect are based on the classical experiment of Scheiner (1619). It will be remembered (Fig. 479) that Scheiner held a needle before a card pierced with two holes at a distance apart less than the pupillary diameter. If the eye were focused on the needle it was seen single; if it were not so focused the needle was seen double. It is clear from the figure that if the rays of light from the object (O) are parallel, a clear image will be formed on the emmetropic retina (E), two images (or a blurred image) will be focused on the hypermetropic (H), and two (or a blurred inverted image) on the myopic retina (M). Only when the object is conjugate with the retina is a single clear image seen.

This principle was first utilized optometrically by Porterfield (1759), whose method was improved by Thomas Young (1801); by its use with characteristic ingenuity he first demonstrated the existence of astigmatism in the human eye. The *optometer of Thomas Young* was simply a card with two stenopæic holes through which a line was observed, a + 10 D spherical lens being interposed to approximate the far-point; if the line were seen single, emmetropia existed; in ametropia it appeared double, the image being either direct or crossed depending on the ametropia, and the alteration of the distance between the needle and the eye required to abolish the doubling was read off on a measured scale. By setting the two holes in different meridians, Young estab-

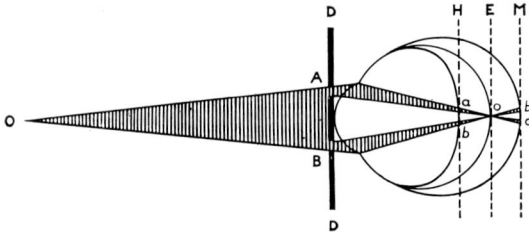

FIG. 479.—SCHEINER'S EXPERIMENT.

lished that his refraction was − 3·94 D in the vertical meridian and − 5·62 D in the horizontal (1·68 D of inverse astigmatism), and thus made the first clinical measurement of this optical defect. His optometer was again modified and improved by several others, more particularly by Tscherning (1898).

von Helmholtz (1866) utilized another aspect of the same principle by passing a card slowly in front of the pupil so as to cover it progressively while the patient looked at a light. It is obvious from Fig. 479 that if the card moves downwards, A, *a*, *a′* will be successively cut off; in emmetropia a sharp image of the light will remain (although it will be reduced in intensity); in hypermetropia a shadow will move down the retina, and in myopia a shadow will move up the retina. Since these movements are reversed subjectively, the patient will see a shadow thrown across the light directly or inversely depending on whether the eye is myopic or hypermetropic. Holth (1902) made this observation more exact in his technique of *skiakinescopy* in which a stenopæic hole was moved across the pupil: in emmetropia a source of light viewed through the moving hole remains immobile, and it is displaced directly or inversely depending on whether the eye is myopic or hypermetropic.

VELONOSKIASCOPY (νελόνη, a needle, σκία, shadow), a technique elaborated by Trantas (1921), is a further more sensitive development of Scheiner's original experiment. A rod somewhat thicker than a needle (a 3 or 4 Bowman lacrimal probe)—hence Krämer's (1927) suggested term RHABDOSCOPY (ῥάβδος, a rod)—is moved in front of the eye: if the eye is emmetropic it casts no shadow, if the eye is ametropic it projects on the source of light a shadow moving directly or inversely depending on whether the eye is myopic or hypermetropic. By moving the bar across the pupil and in different meridians, astigmatism can be explored and, given a patient of observational ability, considerable accuracy in verifying the exactness of a refractive correction can be attained (Sheard, 1926 ; Krämer, 1927 ; Müller, 1933 ; and others).

FIGS. 480–485.—LINDNER'S TECHNIQUE OF VELONOSKIASCOPY.

FIG. 480.—The trial disc. Arms of the cross-wire are 0.75 mm. wide; the centre must coincide with the centre of the patient's pupil and the arms with the principal meridians of astigmatism.

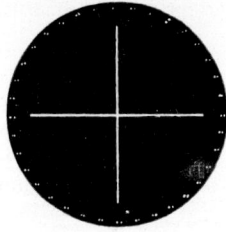

FIG. 481.—The wall chart. The two white lines are 4 mm. thick.

FIG. 482.—A. A line seen in focus. B. A line seen out of focus.

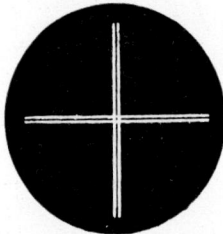

FIG. 483.—The appearance with a spherical but no astigmatic error.

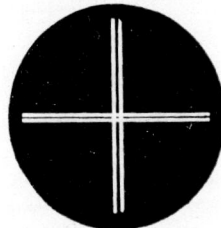

FIG. 484.—Unequal intervals and square-cut ends indicate the presence of astigmatism the axis being correct. The broader shadow indicates the meridian still astigmatic.

FIG. 485.—Unequal intervals and obliquely cut ends indicate that the axis of the astigmatism does not correspond to the axes of the cross-wire and the limbs of the white cross.

A further refinement in the verification of astigmatic correction was practised by Lindner (1927) using the principles of velonoskiascopy and a cross in place of a needle. A cross-wire is inserted centrally in front of the patient's pupil in the trial frame behind the trial lenses (Fig. 480). When a white cross on a black background is regarded (Fig. 481), if the trial lenses are correct so that the object-cross is exactly focused on the retina, the presence of the wire cross does not alter its appearance but merely reduces its brightness (Fig. 482, A). If, however, the object-cross is out of focus, a dark shadow will be seen down the white line as Fig. 482, B. A $+1$ D fogging sphere is now put into the trial frame to restrain accommodation and an interval of shadow appears in the limbs of the white cross. If the astigmatism is properly corrected the shadows will be of equal breadth with square-cut edges

(Fig. 483). If a vertical or horizontal astigmatism remains, the shadows are of unequal breadth and the ends square-cut (Fig. 484). If an oblique astigmatism remains, the ends become sloping, the slope indicating the direction in which the cross lines must be rotated to adjust the axis (Fig. 485). To correct any remaining astigmatic effect, minus cylinders are added with the axis parallel to the broadest shadow until their widths become equal, and the spherical strength made more myopic until the shadows disappear. This test is very delicate both for a spherical and a cylindrical error but requires co-operation and good powers of observation on the part of the patient (Morsman, 1928; Dobson, 1929; and others).

SCREENING TESTS

There is a considerable need for mass screening tests by relatively unskilled persons to test the visual performance of numbers of people so large that individual examination by an expert with suitably complicated apparatus is impracticable; it is usually accepted

FIGS. 486 and 487. VISION SCREENERS.

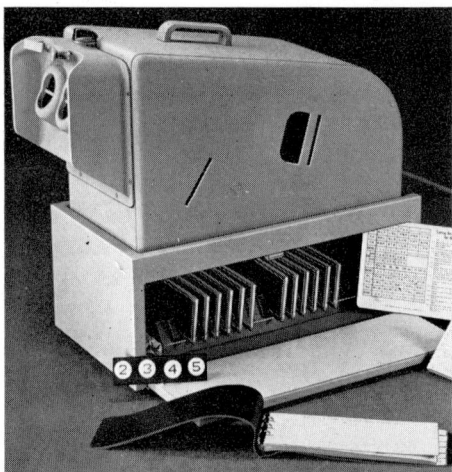

FIG. 486.—THE ORTHORATER (BAUSCH AND LOMB).

FIG. 487.—THE MAVIS SCREENER (BRITISH-AMERICAN OPTICAL COMPANY).

that those failing to pass the test are advised to seek further investigation by a specialist or, alternatively, not to undertake a particular type of work requiring good visual performance. Such groups may comprise schoolchildren, students or workers in factories. It is probably the case that in order to be comprehensive many of these techniques were too complicated, including uniocular and binocular distant and near vision, distant and near fusion, stereoscopic vision and muscular imbalance, the tests being frequently contained in a convenient portable box fitted with suitable optical adjustments. In the screening of children the tests can be converted into games; thus in the Maddox test the red line may run centrally through the front door of a house, through a side window or outside it, or alternatively through the door, through the upper windows or in the sky.

The *Massachusetts test*, introduced for the screening of schoolchildren, was among the first of these (Sloane, 1940) which has been subsequently simplified (Sloane and Gallagher, 1943–52; Turner and Potter, 1950; Yasuna and Green, 1952; Benton, 1953); it comprised tests for uniocular and binocular visual acuity, a fogging test with

+ 1.5 D, and tests for heterophoria for distance and near vision using Maddox rods. Other similar tests have been produced in America such as the *orthorater* (Fig. 486) (Bausch and Lomb, 1944; Davis, 1946; ten Doesschate, 1956) or various types of screeners, such as the *sight-screener* or the *telebinocular* (Schumacher and Lauer, 1955; Cutler and Davey, 1965). Similar British instruments are the *stereometer*, and the *master vision screener* (MAVIS) (Fig. 487). The latter checks 14 visual functions with a single knob-control and the individual screening time is claimed to be under three minutes. A typical European instrument is the Rodenstock Vision Screener. It must be remembered, however, that all tests of this type are merely indicative of the attainment or failure to attain certain standards of visual capacity and are in no sense a substitute for a complete ophthalmic and optical examination.

Abraham. *J. pediat. Ophthal.*, **1**, 57 (1964).
Albini. *Tavoli ottimetriche*, Napoli (1885).
Amigo. *Amer. J. Optom.*, **45**, 511 (1968).
Arndt. *Klin. Mbl. Augenheilk.*, **115**, 157 (1949).
Bach. *Klin. Wschr.*, **14**, 1505 (1935).
Badal. *Ann. Oculist.* (Paris), **75**, 101 (1876).
Banister. *Brit. J. Ophthal.*, **11**, 49 (1927).
Banks. *Brit. J. physiol. Opt.*, **11**, 216 (1954).
Bausch and Lomb. *Bausch and Lomb Mag.*, **20**, 6, 14 (1944).
Beach. *Amer. J. Ophthal.*, **11**, 209 (1928).
Bennett. *Brit. J. physiol. Opt.*, **22**, 238 (1965).
  Ophthal. Optician, **6**, 964, 1011, 1035, 1061 (1966).
Benton. *Amer. J. Ophthal.*, **36**, 363 (1953).
Binard. *Ann. Oculist.* (Paris), **21**, 175 (1849).
Blaskovicz. *Klin. Mbl. Augenheilk.*, **53**, 552 (1914).
Burchardt. *Berl. klin. Wschr.*, **6**, 516 (1869).
Contino. *Ann. Ottal.*, **51**, 863 (1923).
Cowen. *Optician*, **130**, 479 (1955).
  Brit. J. physiol. Opt., **16**, 60 (1959).
Crisp. *Amer. J. Ophthal.*, **6**, 209 (1923); **15**, 729 (1932); **26**, 571 (1943).
  Trans. ophthal. Soc. U.K., **51**, 495 (1931).
Cutler and Davey. *Brit. J. physiol. Opt.*, **22**, 53 (1965).
Danielson. *Amer. J. Ophthal.*, **12**, 903 (1929).
Davis. *J. appl. Psychol.*, **30**, 596 (1946).
Dennett. *Trans. Amer. ophthal. Soc.*, **4**, 106 (1885).
Dimmer. *Klin. Mbl. Augenheilk.*, **29**, 111 (1891).
Dobson. *Proc. roy. Soc. Med.*, **22**, 1453 (1929).
ten Doesschate. *Ophthalmologica*, **132**, 282 (1956).
Donders. *On the Anomalies of the Refraction and Accommodation of the Eye*, London (1864).
Dufour. *XIII int. Cong. Ophthal.*, Amsterdam, **4**, 1 (1929).
Elschnig and Gnad. *Arch. Augenheilk.*, **102**, 475 (1930).
Emarah. *Brit. J. Ophthal.*, **52**, 489 (1968).
Emerson. *Amer. J. Ophthal.*, **59**, 1048 (1965).

Ewing. *Amer. J. Ophthal.*, **3**, 5 (1920).
Ferree and Rand. *Amer. J. Ophthal.*, **23**, 882 (1940).
ffooks. *Brit. J. Ophthal.*, **49**, 312 (1965).
Fileti. *Ann. Ottal.*, **56**, 289 (1928).
Freeman. *Arch. Ophthal.*, **2**, 48 (1929).
Freeman and Hodd. *Brit. J. physiol. Opt.*, **12**, 8 (1955).
Friedenwald. *Amer. J. Ophthal.*, **7**, 8 (1924).
  J. opt. Soc. Amer., **13**, 621 (1926).
Friedman. *Arch. Ophthal.*, **23**, 720, 1175; **24**, 490 (1940).
Fronmüller. *J. Chir. Augenheilk.*, 174 (1843). See *Ann. Oculist.* (Paris), **10**, 283 (1843).
Gentsch and Goodwin. *Amer. J. Optom.*, **43**, 658 (1966).
Giraud-Teulon. *II int. Cong. Ophthal.*, Paris, 97 (1862).
Goldmann. *Ophthalmologica*, **105**, 240 (1943); **107**, 55 (1944).
  Schweiz. med. Wschr., **78**, 937 (1948).
  Klin. Mbl. Augenheilk., **117**, 570 (1950).
Gorman, Cogan and Gellis. *Pediatrics*, **19**, 1088 (1957).
de Gramont. *Bull. Soc. franç. Ophtal.*, **47**, 57 (1934).
Green. *VII Ann. Rep. Netherlands ophthal. Hosp.*, Utrecht (1866).
  Trans. Amer. ophthal. Soc., **1** (4), 68, 131 (1869); **2**, 467 (1878); **3**, 133 (1880); **10**, 644 (1905).
Györffy. *Orv. Lapja* (Budapest), **4**, 489 (1948).
Haas. *v. Graefes Arch. Ophthal.*, **126**, 528 (1931).
Hartridge and Owen. *Brit. J. Ophthal.*, **6**, 543 (1922).
Hay. *Trans. ophthal. Soc. U.K.*, **39**, 240 (1919).
von Helmholtz. *Hb. d. physiologischen Optik*, Hamburg (1866).
Henker. *Z. ophthal. Opt.*, **2**, 21, 129 (1915).
Hess. *XI int. Cong. Ophthal.*, Naples, 5 (1909).
Holth. *Ann. Oculist.* (Paris), **127**, 241 (1902).
Hurst. *Texas St. J. Med.*, **21**, 704 (1926).
Imbert. *La chromoptométrie*, Lyon (1929).
Ives. *Elect. Wld.*, **55**, 939 (1910).
  J. Franklin Inst., **182**, 539 (1916).

Jackson. *Trans. Amer. ophthal. Soc.*, **4**, 595 (1887).
Ophthal. Rec., **2**, 464 (1893); **16**, 378 (1907).
Amer. J. Ophthal., **10**, 266 (1927); **12**, 897 (1929).
Jackson and O'Rourke. *J. Amer. med. Ass.*, **94**, 81 (1930).
Javal. *Ann. Oculist.* (Paris), **55**, 5 (1866); **79**, 97, 241; **80**, 135, 143, 201 (1878).
Klin. Mbl. Augenheilk., **6**, 372 (1868).
Kellner. *Ophthalmic Test Lens Set* (U.S. Patent No. 1,265,671) (1918).
Knoll. *Amer. J. Optom.*, **43**, 415 (1966).
Krämer. *Z. Augenheilk.*, **62**, 111 (1927).
Lancaster. *Trans. Amer. Acad. Ophthal.*, **20**, 167 (1915).
Lancaster and Williams. *Trans. Amer. Acad. Ophthal.*, **19**, 170 (1914).
Landolt. de Wecker and Landolt's *Traité complet d'ophtalmologie*, Paris, **3** (1887).
Bull. Soc. franç. Ophtal., **6**, 213 (1888); **7**, 157 (1889).
Arch. Ophtal., **19**, 465 (1899).
XI int. Cong. Ophthal., Naples, 614 (1909).
Lindner. *Ber. dtsch. ophthal. Ges.*, **46**, 465 (1927).
Luckiesh and Moss. *Amer. J. Ophthal.*, **20**, 469 (1937); **24**, 423 (1941).
Arch. Ophthal., **23**, 941 (1940); **29**, 968; **30**, 489 (1943).
Amer. J. Optom., **18**, 249, 313 (1941).
Maddox. *Amer. J. Ophthal.*, **4**, 571 (1921); **7**, 163 (1924).
Brit. J. Ophthal., **8**, 318 (1924).
Mauthner. *Vorlesungen ü. d. optischen Fehler d. Auges*, Wien (1876).
Merz. *Ueber den Gebrauch eines neuen Brillenbestekes für Augenärzte*, Munich (1848).
Ministry of Health. *Trial Case Lenses*, London (1956).
Monjé and Schober. *Klin. Mbl. Augenheilk.*, **117**, 561 (1950).
Monoyer. *Ann. Oculist.* (Paris), **68**, 101 (1872).
C.R. Acad. Sci. (Paris), **80**, 1137 (1875).
X int. Cong. Ophthal., Lucerne, C50 (1904).
Morsman. *Amer. J. Ophthal.*, **11**, 433 (1928).
Müller. *Z. Augenheilk.*, **80**, 113 (1933).
Nicati. *Ann. Oculist.* (Paris), **111**, 413 (1894).
Oppenheimer. *Amer. J. Ophthal.*, **7**, 530 (1924).
Oshima, Shinoda, Enomoto *et al. Rinsho Ganka*, **19**, 315 (1965).
Pascal. *Arch. Ophthal.*, **24**, 722 (1940).
Pech. *Arch. Ophthal.*, **47**, 363 (1930).
Pergens. *XI int. Cong. Ophthal.*, Naples, 312 1909).
Porterfield. *A Treatise on the Eye*, Edinb. (1759).
Purkinje. *Beobachtungen u. Versuche z. Physiologie d. Sinne*, Prague (1819–23).
Raubitschek. *Klin. Mbl. Augenheilk.*, **83**, 221 (1929).

Reinecke and Cogan. *Arch. Ophthal.*, **60**, 418 (1958).
Ricci. *Ann. Ottal.*, **51**, 965 (1923).
Rössler. *Ber. dtsch. ophthal. Ges.*, **46**, 328 (1927); **47**, 374, 457 (1928).
Klin. Mbl. Augenheilk., **87**, 323 (1931).
von Rohr. *Das Auge und die Brille*, Leipzig (1912).
Sasiain. *Arch. Soc. oftal. hisp.-amer.*, **7**, 351 (1947).
Scheiner. *Oculus*, Innsbruck (1619).
Schneideman. *Ophthal. Rec.*, **9**, 169 (1900).
Schultze. *Klin. Mbl. Augenheilk.*, **31**, 342 (1893).
Schumacher and Lauer. *Amer. J. Optom.*, **32**, 647 (1955).
Sheard. *Amer. J. physiol. Opt.*, **2**, 168 (1921); **3**, 177 (1922); **4**, 163 (1923); **7**, 76 (1926).
Sjøgren. *Acta ophthal.* (Kbh.), **17**, 67 (1939).
Sloan, L. *Amer. J. Ophthal.*, **48**, 807 (1959).
Sloan, L., Rowland and Altman. *Quart. Rev. Ophthal.*, **8**, 4 (1952).
Sloane, A. E. *Arch. Ophthal.*, **24**, 924 (1940).
Sloane, A. E. and Gallagher. *Amer. J. Ophthal.*, **26**, 1076 (1943); **35**, 819 (1952).
Arch. Ophthal., **31**, 217 (1944).
Smith, Dorland. *Amer. J. Ophthal.*, **9**, 896 (1926); **14**, 498 (1931).
Smith, F. H. *Pocket-case for Opticians' Lenses* (U.S. Patent No. 620,984) (1899).
Snellen. *Letterproeven tot Bepaling der Gezigtsscherpte*, Utrecht (1862).
Test-types for the Determination of the Acuteness of Vision, Utrecht (1868).
v. Graefes Arch. Ophthal., **15** (2), 199 (1869); **19** (1), 78 (1873).
Stokes. *Rep. Brit. Ass. Advancement Sci.*, 10 (1849).
Sulzer. *Ann. Oculist.* (Paris), **121**, 445 (1899).
Bull. Soc. franç. Ophtal., **21**, 1 (1904).
Swann. *Diopt. Rev.*, **41**, 250 (1939).
Theis. *Ann. Oculist.* (Paris), **10**, 283 (1843).
Thorington. *Amer. J. Ophthal.*, **4**, 740 (1921).
Trantas. *Bull. Soc. franç. Ophtal.*, **34**, 273 (1921).
Ann. Oculist. (Paris), **158**, 458 (1921).
Tscherning. *Optique physiologique*, Paris (1898).
Turner and Potter. *Ill. med. J.*, **97**, 151 (1950).
Turville. *Outline of Infinity Balance*, London (1946).
Trans. int. opt. Cong., London, 299 (1951).
Verhoeff. *Ophthal. Rec.*, **8**, 541 (1899).
Amer. J. Ophthal., **6**, 908 (1923).
Arch. Ophthal., **10**, 226 (1933).
Wallace. *Univ. med. Mag. Phila.*, **2**, 13 (1889–90).
Williams. *Ophthal. Rec.*, **14**, 400 (1905).

29

Williamson-Noble. *Brit. J. Ophthal.*, **27**, 1 (1943).

Wilmut. *Optician*, **122**, 37 (1951).

Wilson. *Arch. Ophthal.*, **28**, 490 (1942).

Yasuna and Green. *Amer. J. Ophthal.*, **35**, 235 (1952).

Young. *Phil. Trans.*, **91**, 34 (1801).

Zahn. *Oculus artificialis teledioptricus sive telescopium*, Würzburg (1685).

Zehender. *Klin. Mbl. Augenheilk.*, **4**, 1 (1866).

CHAPTER X

ANOMALIES OF ACCOMMODATION

It is fitting to introduce a chapter on the anomalies of accommodation with a portrait of the American ophthalmologist, ALEXANDER DUANE [1858–1926] (Fig. 488). His first monograph on this subject was published in 1901 and, after Donders, it is due essentially to his labours continued over the following quarter of a century that our views on the normal variations and the abnormalities of accommodation have become stabilized. His first publication in ophthalmology, entitled " Some New Tests for Insufficiency of the Ocular Muscles ", was published in the N.Y. med. J., of August 3rd, 1889 ; over a long and intensely industrious life he contributed generously to all aspects of the problems of the motility of the eyes and physiological optics, and when he died he left uncompleted manuscripts on both these branches of ophthalmology. His name will live in our literature not only because of the size and importance of his offerings to our science, but also because of the accuracy and precision with which he marshalled his clinical observations on a somewhat complicated subject which, before his time, greatly required clarification.

The essential physiological feature of accommodation is the faculty of focusing of the dioptric mechanism of the eye and rapidly adjusting it to the existing visual situation and maintaining it in that state. The anomalies of accommodation therefore largely consist of conditions in which the focus of the dioptric mechanism is either inappropriate or is changing in an undesirable direction or cannot be maintained or altered with the required facility.

The cardinal symptom of these troubles is *blurring of vision* and although additional complaints are often present, it will be useful to consider at the outset the characteristics of this visual affection and its differential diagnosis. An inappropriate accommodative state will be attended by a relatively fixed optical anomaly so that the visual disability is constant ; when, however, the accommodative state is changing—at one instant appropriate, at another either excessive or inadequate—the symptoms may be of an intermittent visual disturbance. Herein arises the difficulty in differential diagnosis since a host of ophthalmic conditions also gives rise to intermittent blurring of vision.

It may be that at the time of examination such a patient will evince no abnormal physical signs so that great importance attaches to the history of the complaint. In accommodative anomalies vision is not totally obliterated as it might be in those conditions giving rise to the phenomenon of amaurosis fugax due, perhaps, to some vascular affection of the retina. The visual disturbance of accommodative anomalies affects the whole visual field but generally for one distance only, far or near, a limitation which may give a clue to the type of the disturbance ; moreover, ancillary visual phenomena

Fig. 488. Alexander Duane
[1858–1926].

such as photopsiæ, teichopsiæ, auras or haloes are absent. Symptoms of eye-strain including perhaps a dull aching pain may be present, sharp pain rarely, if ever. General symptoms are most unusual save in a neurotic or highly strung patient for functional anomalies of accommodation may be only a manifestation of a disturbed mind. The state of the patient's general health, physical as well as mental, is also of great importance, for systemic disease or its treatment may have a profound influence on the availability of accommodative adjustment.

We shall now proceed to consider the major anomalies in the adjustment of the optical system of the eye.

Fatigue of Accommodation

On the whole, in the normal eye it is difficult to fatigue accommodation and in a considerable proportion of cases its excessive use leads to the development of a greater amplitude (Lancaster and Williams, 1914). If, however, visual tasks are continued at a range near the punctum proximum over a considerable length of time, fatigue appears in the normal emmetropic and orthophoric individual. In its occurrence age is an important consideration, as well as the state of general fatigue and the amount of accommodative effort called for in proportion to the total available (Sédan, 1947; Dubois-Poulsen and Rozan, 1947); this is seen dramatically in myasthenia gravis (Manson and Stern, 1965). Two other factors which deserve a special note and tend to influence the onset of accommodative fatigue are the refractive state of the eye and the power of convergence.

Accommodative Strain and the Refractive State

We have already seen[1] that differences in the refractive state entail great variations in accommodation. The emmetrope has clear distant vision and uses his accommodation only for near work. The hypermetrope, in order to see clearly at a distance, has to exert an amount of accommodation equivalent to the amount of his hypermetropia, and to see close at hand must supplement his accommodation still further. While, therefore, he has the advantage that he can compensate for his refractive error by accommodative effort, this faculty brings with it the disadvantage that if he is to see distinctly he must be making continual use of it and when he does near work the demands made upon the ciliary muscle must be still greater. A myope cannot see distant objects clearly by any effort of accommodation, but has the advantage that he can see near work with considerably less effort than the emmetrope or the hypermetrope. On the other hand, while a young emmetrope or a low hypermetrope with active accommodation is able to see distinctly over all ranges which may be considered to exist in practical life without much accommodative effort, a high hypermetrope may

---

[1] p. 215.

be incapacitated from all near work without the artificial aid of spectacles, while a myope may have his far-point so close to his near-point that within an exceedingly limited range he may have to apply his total amplitude of accommodation to attain clear vision, a circumstance which may entail considerable strain. Again, in hypermetropic or mixed astigmatism the desire to attain a clearer image involves constant accommodative effort. Finally, since the accommodative effort of the two eyes cannot be dissociated, the error of an anisometrope cannot be corrected by his accommodation, so that when correcting spectacles are not worn, the image of one eye is always blurred. Especially when the error is small, however, the slight difference acts as an incentive for its correction, and since the end is never achieved and the stimulus is always there, just as occurs in astigmatism, a considerable amount of accommodative strain may result. In all refractive states, therefore, accommodative effort plays a large part in the causation of asthenopia, and the development of accommodative fatigue varies with the type and degree of ametropia.

Accommodative Strain and Convergence

We have seen that the two synkinetic functions of accommodation and convergence are normally closely interrelated. The relation between them, however, is elastic, and either can be separately exercised. Thus fixation upon and clear vision of a distant object may be maintained if weak convex or concave lenses are placed in front of the eyes, in which case an effort of accommodation is made without convergence. Conversely, if weak prisms are employed, convergence can be called upon without involving accommodation to eliminate diplopia. When accommodation fails in age, convergence is retained, and when the ciliary muscle is paralysed by atropine, convergence is still possible. It is indeed fortunate that this is so, for a dissociation of the two is necessary in all forms of ametropia. The hypermetrope has to use his accommodation in excess of his convergence, and the myope his convergence in excess of his accommodation. The amount of dissociation which is possible is not, however, unlimited; it can be increased by practice, and it varies with different individuals and in the same individual at different times. The effort to dissociate the two may give rise to no trouble while, on the other hand, it may be the cause of considerable distress; indeed, the necessary amount of dissociation may on occasion be impossible to attain and, since a clear image is usually of more immediate advantage than the retention of binocular vision, fusion may be discarded and one eye may eventually deviate.

The amount of accommodation which it is thus possible to exert while the convergence remains fixed is called the RELATIVE ACCOMMODATION: the amount in excess of the convergence is called *positive*, that below, *negative* (Fig. 489). The first is measured by the highest concave lens, the second by the highest convex lens with which an object can be seen distinctly. It is obvious that the nearer the object is to the eye, the smaller will be the positive and the larger the negative range of accommodation. In the ultimate, if the eyes are emmetropic, when the object of fixation is at infinity, there will be no negative accommodation, and it will be found that no convex lens can be tolerated and at the same time good vision obtained. Similarly, if the object is at the near-point, the positive fraction will have become nil, for here no concave lens can be tolerated since it requires all the accommodative effort possible to see an object at this distance. Thus while

Fig. 489.—Relative Accommodation.

The subject is emmetropic with the far-point (R) at infinity. Looking at an object (A) situated 33 cm. away, he exercises 3 D of accommodation and 3 m.a. of convergence. If convex lenses of + 2 D just blur the object, he has relaxed his accommodation by 2 D from 3 D to 1 D and the relative far-point (R′) is at 1 metre. If concave lenses of − 3 D just blur the object, he has augmented his accommodation from 3 D to 6 D and his relative near-point (P′) is at 16.6 cm. For 3 m.a. of convergence, therefore, the relative far-point is at 1 m., the relative near-point at (approx.) 17 cm., the relative range of accommodation 83 cm. (R′P′) of which 67 cm. (R′A) are negative and 16 cm. (AP′) positive. The relative amplitude is 5 D (6 D − 1 D), of which 2 D are negative and 3 D positive.

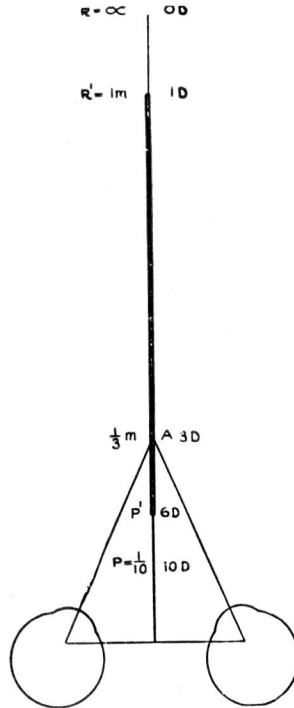

there is one *absolute* far-point, one *absolute* near-point, and one *absolute* range of accommodation, there is a different *relative* far-point, near-point and range for every degree of convergence.

The importance of this relationship is that *it is essential for comfort that the positive portion of the relative accommodation should be as large as possible*: it should be greater than the negative portion. When it is large, the patient has a correspondingly large amount of accommodation in reserve, but in the opposite case he will be working too near the limit of his capacity for comfort since, like all other muscles, the ciliary muscle becomes fatigued if, instead of working in relays, all its fibres are called upon to contract for any length of time. Landolt (1903) estimated that in such circumstances two-thirds of the accommodation could be made available, and that about one-third of the total accommodative power must be held in reserve : Scrini and Fortin (1922) concluded that one-fourth and Lagrange (1903) one-fifth ought to be in reserve. If for any reason the amplitude of accommodation is diminished, and the near-point recedes to the region of the working distance so that the positive accommodation becomes small, prolonged near work can be undertaken without distress only if convex lenses are provided which bring the range of accommodation nearer to the eye.

In a similar manner, as we have seen,[1] if the accommodation is kept constant, the convergence may be made to vary. The amount of convergence which can thus be exerted or relaxed is called the RELATIVE CONVERGENCE. We have already discussed how this is measured and seen that if comfort is to be maintained the positive portion of the relative convergence should be greater than the negative, and that in practice only the middle third of the relative convergence can be exercised for any length of time. If, in his near work, a patient has habitually to go outside this limit, either in a positive or negative direction, he should be provided with prisms so that his work is kept within his area of comfort.

Oxygen deficiency, as in a low-pressure chamber or at high altitudes, brings about a rapid fatigue of accommodation (Wilmer and Berens, 1918; Berens and Stark, 1932). This was of importance in aviation for a considerable decrease in the range of accommodation occurs above 5,000 metres (16,400 feet) (Furuya, 1937); a similar decrease is seen in mountaineering at about the same altitude (McFarland, 1937, in the Andes). After a 60-minute period at this height the accommodation requires 40 minutes to return to its normal activity.

The Symptoms of Accommodative Fatigue—Accommodative Asthenopia. Donders (1864) was the first to insist that most of the symptoms of eye-strain were due to " the fatigue of the muscular system of accommodation " and thus introduced the concept of ACCOMMODATIVE ASTHENOPIA. On the onset of fatigue the patient fails to maintain good vision for the near objects he is studying; they become indistinct and blurred and are clarified only with an effort, the periods of blurring being at first intermittent but gradually increasing in duration until vision becomes impossible unless the patient increases his working distance or ceases to work (Ferree, 1914). On resuming work the intervals of effective vision become smaller until eventually it has to be abandoned. These functional symptoms are frequently associated with a dull headache referred to the brows rather than the eyes.

The treatment of such a condition, in so far as it is impossible to vary the type and amount of near work and the general conditions of ocular hygiene, should first involve the adequate correction of the refractive error. The accuracy with which this is done is of great importance and should be associated, if necessary, with the correction of any muscular imbalance. In cases of high ametropia it may be necessary to prescribe an over-correction for hypermetropia, an under-correction for myopia and an adjustment of the

---

[1] p. 197.

astigmatic correction to suit the working distance since, as we have seen, the static and dynamic astigmatism may differ[1]; moreover, special spectacles centred and angled for the particular distance of work may be advisable.[2] In no case should these be ordered by rule of thumb, but each particular individual and his working distance must be studied. The total amplitude of accommodation is obtained by subtracting the dioptric value of the far-point from that of the near-point; one-third of this is kept in reserve, and lenses are added to give the amplitude required in the particular case. The convergence should also be carefully examined; if it is excessive a stronger spherical correction should be worn than might otherwise seem advisable, for by relieving the effort to accommodate the stimulus to converge is lessened; if there is insufficiency, a weaker lens acts in the reverse way, but if the patient is habitually working outside the area of comfort of convergence the addition of prisms may add to his comfort. In many of these cases where convergence is a complicating factor, orthoptic exercises are of great value.[3]

Finally, if work must be done at very close range in the interests of visual acuity, *orthoscopic lenses*[4] correcting both accommodation and convergence may be advisable. This occurs in certain industrial processes wherein minute detail must be studied at close range for long periods; by such means occupations of this sort may be undertaken in comfort and without strain (Weston and Adams, 1927–29).

Failure of Accommodation for Near Vision

FAILURE OF ACCOMMODATION FOR NEAR VISION, apart from the factor of justifiable fatigue, may be due to two factors: (*a*) physical changes in the lens rendering its deformation difficult or impossible, and (*b*) functional incapacity or paralysis of the ciliary muscle in so far as its parasympathetic activity is concerned. If the lens becomes sclerosed and hard, as it does with advancing age or in cataract so that it is no longer sufficiently plastic to allow its deformation, accommodation cannot be effected no matter how great the contraction of the ciliary muscle. On the other hand, a weak or paralysed ciliary muscle will not be able to induce changes in a normally elastic lens. There are thus two distinct considerations entering into the mechanism of accommodation, called by Fuchs (1922) *physical* and *physiological accommodation*.[5] These two elements are fundamentally distinct, and although they usually correspond during the first half of life, they may become dissociated, and when they do so they entail different pathological effects. Physical accommodation fails in presbyopia so that accommodation becomes difficult; on the other hand, the available power of the ciliary

---

[1] p. 285.   [2] p. 679.
[3] Vol. VI.   [4] p. 703.
          [5] p. 193.

muscle may decrease in states of debility at any age, diminishing or abolishing accommodation, although the lens is eminently deformable. In the first case the failure of accommodation is static, in the second dynamic.

FAILURE OF STATIC ACCOMMODATION

PRESBYOPIA

We have already seen that because of changes in the lens the power of accommodation becomes progressively smaller with advancing age. This loss of accommodation is not to be considered as abnormal; it proceeds gradually throughout the whole of life without any sudden alterations and is in no wise to be looked upon as a disease. At first no difficulty is experienced, but eventually a time comes when the near-point has receded beyond the distance at which the individual is accustomed to read or to

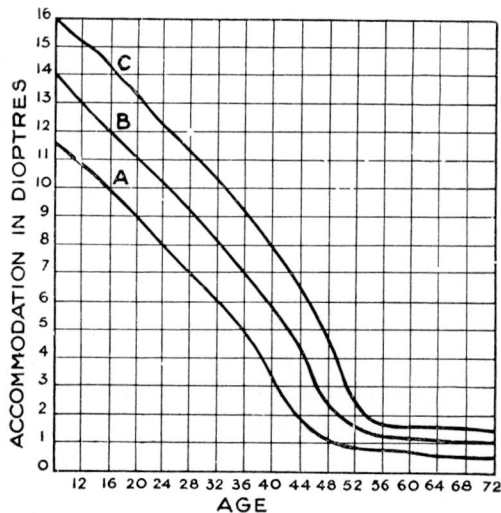

Fig. 490.—The Amplitude of Uniocular Accommodation at Different Ages (A. Duane).

A. Lowest physiological values.   B. Average values.
C. Highest physiological values.

work and then he becomes inconvenienced. When it has progressed to this stage the condition is called PRESBYOPIA (πρέσβυς, old; ὤψ, the eye). This condition was first differentiated from hypermetropia by Stellwag von Carion in 1855[1].

The variation in the power of accommodation with age was recognized in classical times as a weakness in the sight only of the aged but was first adequately assessed by Donders (1864). Large-scale statistical studies were subsequently undertaken by Jackson (1907) and even more extensively by

[1] p. 209, Fig. 252.

Duane (1908–31) whose findings are summarized in Fig. 490, and agree with the later work of others (Clarke, 1924; T. D. Allen, 1930; Gross, 1931; Hirose, 1968; and others).

As we shall note subsequently, a subject's ability to accommodate can be measured in various ways. An assessment by the subjective method of approximating the object until it appears blurred may give a falsely high value for the actual change in dioptric power because of the effect of the depth of focus of the eye. The binocular accommodation is also usually somewhat greater than when one eye alone is employed.

From Duane's figures it will be seen that in the early years of life the amplitude of accommodation is about 14 D, so that the near-point in the emmetrope is situated at 7 cm. distance. Thereafter it gradually and uninterruptedly recedes; at the age of 36 it has reached 14 cm., when the amplitude has become halved and is now 7 D instead of the original 14 D. At the age of 45 it has reached 25 cm., and the amplitude of accommodation is only 4 D; at the age of 60 only about 1 D of accommodation remains. According to Slataper (1950) the descent of accommodation occurs more rapidly in women than in men. In the majority of cases near work is done at an average distance of 28 to 30 cm. away from the eyes, and therefore in the emmetrope the actual limit of clear vision is reached at 45 years, when an amplitude of 3·5 to 4 D of accommodation remains. This, however, would entail working at the near-point continuously and thus exercising the whole of the accommodation to obtain useful vision, a condition of strain which we have seen cannot be tolerated over any length of time. It follows that when the near-point is at a distance of some 22 cm., presbyopia may be said to have set in. In the emmetrope this occurs at or soon after 40 years of age.

It has been suggested that Duane's figures for the amplitude of accommodation over the age of 40 may be too low (D. G. Allen, 1961) and that the precise age at which presbyopic symptoms occur may be a matter not only of individual but also of racial variation (Rambo, 1960, in Indians; Raphael, 1961, in Israelis; and others). This has, however, been denied (Fukuda et al., 1962, and Kajiura, 1965, in Japanese), and Coates (1955) concluded that geographical rather than racial considerations are more important; thus South African Europeans but not the natives were found to have lower amplitudes of accommodation than would be suggested by Duane's figures. Hofstetter (1963), however, found no difference between ethnic groups in South Africa in the presbyopic additions required at various ages but reported (1968) that there were significant differences between Ghanaians and Fijians; there are, however, difficulties in comparisons, not least of which is the uncertainty of the age of the subjects.

A hypermetrope starts life with his near-point considerably farther away than that of an emmetrope, and since the decline in accommodative power is approximately the same in both, the symptoms of presbyopia will come on earlier. In a myope, on the other hand, the opposite conditions hold, and if he has an error of −4 D, presbyopia will never occur. Presbyopia is thus a *relative* term, depending not only on the age but also on the

refraction.   It also varies with the individual and with his habits.   A person
who has the habit of reading with his book on his knees complains of discomfort later than one who is used to reading more closely ; and the carpenter
or book-keeper or the musician will be comfortable at his work at 30 or 40
cm. or over, while the seamstress, the compositor or the engraver of the
same age and with the same refractive error will have been forced to use
spectacles in order to see at the working distance of 20 cm.

The ætiology of presbyopia is a problem intimately related to theories
of accommodation and has already been discussed.

The premature onset of presbyopia, due regard being paid to the
refractive condition, should always excite suspicion that factors other than
physiological are involved.   The failure of accommodation may be due to a
premature sclerosis of the lens or the development of cataract.   Lederer
(1927–29) found a similar premature presbyopia among furnace workers.
An early failure of the accommodation may suggest a premature tendency
to senility (Bernstein, 1931 ; Blatt, 1931 ; Steinhaus, 1932): indeed, it has
been said that the development of presbyopia bears a statistical relation to
the expectation of life (Bernstein, 1932–45 ; Heidemann, 1932).   Presbyopia
is said to appear early after suppression of the ovarian functions (Guillot,
1932): but otherwise accommodative failure is usually due to lack of the
effectivity of the ciliary muscle.

Symptoms.   The failure of accommodation becomes evident gradually,
and as a rule becomes apparent first in reading.   Small print becomes
indistinct, and in order to get within the limits of his receding near-point,
the patient tends to hold his head back and his book well forwards, until a
distance is reached when clear vision in any circumstances is difficult.
Trouble is experienced at first in the evening when fatigue comes on easily,
the light is dim and the pupils are dilated, permitting the formation of large
diffusion circles.   The presbyope consequently likes to read by brilliant
illumination so that his pupils may be forced to contract and diminish the
aperture.   For this reason also, in more advanced years when the pupils
become smaller, an old person with no accommodation may see near
objects with a fair degree of detail.   Complaint is usually made of visual
failure rather than visual fatigue.   The eyes tire rapidly, so that print becomes indistinct after reading a few minutes : the lines run together, letters
overlap and become double, and finally reading becomes impossible. Sooner
or later symptoms of eye-strain appear.   The ciliary muscle working near
its limit becomes fatigued and the accommodative effort, strained to its
limit and acting in excess of convergence, gives rise to distress—the eyes
feel tired and ache, headaches come on, and eventually near work becomes
an impossibility.   Since the loss of accommodation with age is progressive,
any reading spectacles the patient has gradually become inadequate and
these symptoms recur until in the late 50's when the condition becomes
static.

Very occasionally, early presbyopia manifests itself as a functional spasm of accommodation, the ciliary muscle being violently stimulated as a reaction to its failing effectivity as if suffering from a " fatigue cramp ".[1] A patient in the early forties may thus present as a case of *pseudo-myopia*. Minor degrees of the same phenomenon are sometimes in evidence when performing retinoscopy on such a patient who may find it impossible to relax his accommodation ; in such cases a cycloplegic is indicated.

Treatment. The treatment of presbyopia is to provide the patient with convex lenses so that his accommodation is reinforced and his near-point brought within a useful working distance. To do this adequately we must first know the working point of the individual, estimate his refraction, determine the amplitude of his accommodation, and then supplement this by the appropriate strength of lens allowing him a sufficient reserve accommodation. The clinical methods for determining these will be discussed presently, as also will the problems arising in the prescription of spectacles for near work.

Presbyopia is one of those conditions wherein a monocle—that somewhat derided article—or a lorgnette may be of service : on the many little occasions in everyday life when taking out of a pair of spectacles and putting them on for a moment becomes irksome, the more easily manipulated monocle may save much time and not a little annoyance.

FAILURE OF DYNAMIC ACCOMMODATION FOR NEAR VISION

A FAILURE OF DYNAMIC ACCOMMODATION FOR NEAR VISION may be either incomplete or total ; although we shall discuss these separately it should be realized that the differences are in many cases only a matter of degree and many conditions causing partial dynamic failure can, if more severe, lead to a complete paralysis.

PARTIAL FAILURE OF DYNAMIC ACCOMMODATION

PARTIAL FAILURE OF DYNAMIC ACCOMMODATION occurs in one of three forms : *insufficiency of accommodation* wherein the accommodative power is consistently poor, *ill-sustained accommodation* wherein accommodation, perhaps normal initially, cannot be maintained over any length of time, and *inertia of accommodation* wherein difficulty is experienced in altering its range.

In the condition of INSUFFICIENCY OF ACCOMMODATION *the accommodative power is constantly below the lower limit of what may be accepted as the normal variation for the patient's age.* It is a relatively common condition occurring in young and middle-aged adults, which, although long known, has received little attention. It was stressed at the turn of the last century by such American writers as Theobald (1891–1913), Huizinga (1899), Suker (1903) and Gould (1905), and particularly at a later stage by Duane (1916–25) who, in his last paper, discussed 175 cases in his own practice. Because

[1] p. 471.

of its fugitive nature and because the range of accommodation is rarely tested as a routine in young adults, there is no doubt that it is frequently missed.

The condition has been frequently called *premature presbyopia*; but this term is better kept to describe the early onset of a static (lenticular) accommodative loss rather than a dynamic (muscular) failure. It may be due to local conditions in the eye or more commonly to general factors. It is possible, moreover, that the same result may follow a spasm of the sympathetic mechanism of accommodation for distance, a factor which may be of importance in functional cases of accommodative failure for near vision or in the recession of the near-point in Graves's disease.

Of the local ocular conditions causing accommodative insufficiency, simple glaucoma is said to be important, for the early or rapid onset of " presbyopia " may be a significant sign in this disease.[1] Muscular failure may also be associated with cyclitis, particularly the development of sympathetic ophthalmitis (Blatt, 1930). Curi (1942) reported a case of a perforating injury in the ciliary region in a young patient who lost all accommodation in the uninjured eye until the injured eye was removed.

That refractive errors were responsible for a state of accommodative insufficiency is a view held by many writers, and much stress has been paid to the effects of small astigmatic errors in this connection since the writings of Martin (1888). The reflex effect of nasal sinusitis has also been inculpated, particularly inflammations of the sphenoidal cells (Berens and Stark, 1932; Berens et al., 1933), as well as dental infections (Prangen, 1931; Brownell, 1941).

The general state of health is also frequently responsible for ciliary weakness. It has been noted with weakness of the other muscles in conditions of general debility, malnutrition, anæmia, diabetes, lactation, and in general toxæmias due to intestinal disturbances, tuberculosis and other chronic and acute infections; it has also been described in association with endocrine anomalies, the induction of the menopause or arteriosclerosis.[2] Daniels (1927) found accommodative failure in chronic alcoholics, and it has been reported in women shortly before and after childbirth (Alpers and Palmer, 1929). In general, however, the condition is characteristic of asthenic debilitated persons and is also seen in neurotic or neurasthenic individuals and may be a symptom of hysteria.

The *symptoms* may be productive of much discomfort and, although the condition may be mild and fugitive, they may be incapacitating for near work. All the features of asthenopia and eye-strain may be present, with headaches, fatigue and irritability of the eyes. Near work is blurred and becomes difficult or impossible, and the accommodative failure is frequently accompanied by a disturbance of convergence. Sometimes the attempt to accommodate brings on an excessive amount of convergence, but more often

[1] See Vol. XI. p. 443.
[2] Veasey (1919), Holloway (1919), Wood (1920), White (1921), Sumner (1921), Perrin (1928), Bistis (1929), Rosenberg (1931), Blatt (1931), Ruedemann (1931), Prangen (1931), and many others.

this associated function also fails and becomes deficient. When near work is not attempted the patient is usually comfortable. The duration of the condition is usually dependent upon the cause; with an improvement of the exciting factors, a betterment in the general health, or a relaxation from over-work or worry, the ocular condition may improve considerably, only to relapse at a later date if the same conditions again recur.

When the accommodative failure is associated with general debility, its cause is reasonably clear; when it is not and particularly (as is often the case) if it is accompanied by normal and brisk pupillary responses, the mechanism is more difficult to explain. Suker (1903) postulated a peripheral muscular weakness, but the presence of an active pupil in many cases as well as the bilaterality of the affection suggested to Duane (1925) and Blatt (1931) that a nuclear or more central disturbance was responsible. The matter cannot be said to be satisfactorily clarified.

ILL-SUSTAINED ACCOMMODATION is essentially the same condition as insufficiency but of a less degree. The range of accommodation is normal, but on any attempt to use the eyes for near work over a prolonged period the accommodative power weakens, the near-point gradually recedes and the near vision becomes blurred (Fig. 499). Frequently it is the initial stage of a true insufficiency. The causes of the condition are the same as those just reviewed, but it is characteristic of convalescence from debilitating illnesses. Such a condition in a mild form is relatively common in those who read in the evening when they are tired, or in bed when they are physically relaxed. This, of course, is by no means surprising. The ocular muscles share in any general state of fatigue, and when the other muscles are tired and have demanded and have obtained relaxation, it would be strange if the former should be prepared to carry on uncomplainingly. In these circumstances, and in convalescence from illness, it is too often forgotten that reading or sewing entails muscular work in as true a sense as any other exercise, and activities should be regulated on this understanding.

Treatment. Optical treatment should be the first consideration. Any refractive error should be corrected with accuracy, and if vision for near work is seriously blurred and reading is therefore difficult, spectacles correcting the refractive error should be supplemented by an additional correction for reading, the procedure adopted being the same as that described for presbyopia. If there is an associated convergence excess, such spectacles should be prescribed unhesitatingly, for by relieving the effort to accommodate, much of the stimulus to converge is removed. On the other hand, in cases with convergence insufficiency a decision should be made as to whether this is primary or whether it is consequent upon the failure of accommodation. Such a decision may not be easy and no hard-and-fast rule can be given as to the appropriate treatment; the alternatives are convergence exercises, convex lenses with or without base-in prisms, or a combination of these. The only practical solution is by trial and error, which will show which is most successful for any particular patient. If it is decided that the accommodative weakness is primary it is as well to start off with weak convex lenses but without incorporating prisms; in many such cases the renewed clarity of the image of near objects given by these lenses stimulates binocular vision and consequently improves the convergence. In all these cases only the weakest convex lens which will allow clear vision should be ordered, so that the accommodation may be exercised and stimulated rather than abrogated. For the same reason, as soon as recovery takes place, the additional correction for reading should be made progressively weaker from time to time.

Meantime, the condition may be much improved by the practice of *accommodation exercises* at short periods throughout the day, the patient wearing his correcting spectacles for distance. The accommodation card[1] is held a considerable distance away and then brought closer to the eye until the line appears blurred and indistinct; by repeating this he should be encouraged to attempt to bring his near-point as close as possible, and to maintain his accommodative effort as long as he can with comfort. Such exercises will defeat their own ends unless they stop short of producing fatigue and distress, and should be undertaken only in those cases which are the result of ciliary under-activity, and in patients who are not in a state of general debility. When there is an excess of convergence, one eye only should be used at a time and the other should be covered; when convergence also is deficient, both eyes should be exercised simultaneously, and exercises should be undertaken for the stimulation of this function also.[2]

At the same time, treatment should be directed to the cause of the condition, if that is discoverable. Work, and the conditions of work, should be regulated, the general health should be improved in every way, and any suggestive toxic condition should be dealt with upon its merits.

ACCOMMODATIVE INERTIA is a somewhat rare condition wherein the patient experiences some *difficulty in altering the range of his accommodation.* Normally the focus is altered readily and accurately within 1 second (Vierordt, 1857; Aeby, 1861; Barrett, 1885; Seashore, 1893); in the condition of inertia it takes some time and involves some effort for him to focus a near object after looking into the distance. It rarely assumes serious proportions, but on occasion may give rise to some trouble and annoyance. Most cases are functional and probably depend upon insufficiency of accommodation. A somewhat similar phenomenon is seen on looking into the distance after removing presbyopic spectacles.

The *speed of adjustment of accommodation* from far to near and near to far is of some importance in certain industrial tasks and in aviation. Methods of its measurement have been devised by Guglianetti (1923) and Ferree and Rand (1918–36). The latter workers devised a *tachistoscope* wherein distant and near objects are presented alternately to the eyes by means of a timed rotatory mechanism. Some research has been done on this subject in America by E. B. Goodall (1920), Tefft and Stark (1922)

---

[1] p. 477.   [2] Vol. VI.

and Robertson (1934–37), and in England by Whiteside (1957).   Age has a marked influence on the inertia of accommodation, which becomes accentuated after 30 years; physical fatigue has an important bearing; among ocular factors, heterophoria, ametropia and inequality of vision are the most important.

PARALYSIS OF ACCOMMODATION FOR NEAR VISION

PARALYSIS OF ACCOMMODATION FOR NEAR VISION, whether due to a congenital anomaly, to the action of drugs, or to infective, toxic, nervous or traumatic causes, is not uncommon. It may be unilateral or bilateral; the onset may be sudden or it may start insidiously, being an extension of a partial failure of accommodation. It may be associated with a paralytic mydriasis—the other function mediated by the parasympathetic elements in the IIIrd nerve—or with an oculomotor palsy. If the loss of accommodation occurs as an isolated lesion it is probable that it is nuclear in origin or located within the eye; a lesion in the brain-stem or the trunk of the nerve usually involves other palsies.

The *symptoms* are characteristic. The near-point recedes and approximates the far-point and the enlarged pupil which usually accompanies the condition accentuates any optical defects the eye may already have and tends to produce an uncomfortable amount of dazzling. The resulting disability depends largely on the refractive state: the emmetrope can see in the distance but near objects are blurred; the myope may be little inconvenienced; to the hypermetrope everything is blurred, and the greatest inconvenience is experienced in hypermetropic astigmatism when the entire world is both blurred and confused. Age also alters the drama of the symptoms, for the emmetropic presbyope may find little alteration in his visual state. The phenomenon of *micropsia* is also evident; it is the reverse of the macropsia which occurs in accommodative spasm. Objects appear smaller than they really are owing to a delusion of distance. To see an object distinctly a great accommodative effort is made, and thus it is taken to be nearer than it actually is and consequently, judged from this standpoint, it is assumed to be unnaturally small.

We have already emphasized that the distinction between partial failure and complete paralysis of accommodation is one only of degree and the conditions now enumerated may lead to either.

The *causes* of accommodative failure may be summarized as follows:

1. Congenital defects.

2. Cycloplegic drugs. Such drugs may be applied topically to the eye, the cycloplegia produced being intentional or incidental; systemically administered medications may also produce accommodative failure or insufficiency as side effects.

3. Infections and toxic conditions.

4. Degenerative conditions affecting the brain-stem.

5. Metabolic toxæmias.

6. Exogenous poisons. The most interesting are lead (Blatt, 1931; Jakovleva, 1931), ergot (Stepka, 1929), snake venom from bites (Gonzalez, 1922; Blatt, 1923), a bee sting at the limbus (Szeghy *et al.*, 1963), arsenicals given by injection (Makrocki, 1911; Milian and Périn, 1921; Milian, 1930) and caesosan (Sklarz and Massur, 1921).

7. Involvement of the IIIrd nerve trunk in any part of its course— neoplasms or hæmorrhages in the brain-stem, aneurysms, particularly of the subclinoid type, neoplasms of the base of the skull, cavernous sinus thromboses or arterio-venous fistulæ, disturbances either neoplasic or inflammatory at the superior orbital fissure or in the orbit itself or affecting the posterior group of nasal sinuses.

8. Diseases of the eye affecting the ciliary muscle (cyclitis, glaucoma).

9. Concussion injury[1] to the eye, usually associated with a traumatic mydriasis. The accommodative failure may be due to small injuries to the ciliary muscle; the same effect may result from more gross disturbances involving the zonule or lens, particularly the lodgement therein of a small foreign body, in which case it may be of very long duration or permanent; but the opposite condition of ciliary spasm is the more common sequel to trauma leading to a temporary traumatic myopia.[2] Trauma to the head may also be followed by accommodative failure (Wescott, 1936).

10. Hysteria in which paralysis of accommodation is rarer than a functional spasm.

11. A *congenital defect* in the ciliary muscle may be responsible for a lack of accommodation but such a condition is very rare.

These conditions will be fully annotated in the volume on neuro-ophthalmology[3] but the action of drugs concerns us here.

Paralysis by *cycloplegic drugs* is the most common ætiological factor, and it is to be noted that this does not apply only to the instillation of drugs into the conjunctival sac, but also to accidental contamination by the fingers from an ointment containing atropine or, as was first noted by Lussana (1852), to the effects of the drug taken systemically (Beyer, 1898; Passow, 1926; Müller, 1952). Hamilton and Sclare (1947) found that in acute belladonna poisoning (from the ingestion of 4·3 mg. of alkaloid) accommodative symptoms appeared within $\frac{1}{2}$ hour while the general symptoms became apparent in 3 hours. Cycloplegia is a feature of the activity of all anticholinergic drugs. Their pharmacology, particularly that of atropine and the naturally occurring alkaloids of a similar nature, as well as the various synthetic drugs, has already been studied,[4] as also has their use in refraction and as mydriatics.

It is, however, of interest that the action of these cycloplegics may in rare and exceptional cases be unduly prolonged and even permanent (Jackson, 1925); this has

[1] Vol. XIV.   [2] Vol. XIV.
[3] Vol. XII.   [4] p. 387.

been reported even with homatropine (Decker, 1924). It may also be noted that general belladonna poisoning has (rarely) followed the instillation of atropine into the eye (Métivier, 1935; Duggan, 1937) or even the use of 1·0% ointment (Hughes, 1938); Hopkins and Robyns-Jones (1937) recorded a case following a wash-out of the conjunctival sac with atropine after the operation of iridectomy, and death in convulsions has resulted (H. G. Morton, 1939; Heath, 1950).

Many systemic medications may interfere with accommodative activity. Although this effect is frequently transitory and may not be profound, a knowledge of those which are particularly liable to behave in this way is clearly essential both for the ophthalmologist and for those in general medical practice.

Preparations containing atropine or its derivatives are obviously prone to this undesirable side-effect. But many drugs which have a similar activity pharmacologically may also produce blurring of vision due to their influence on accommodation. Thus many of the agents used in the treatment of parkinsonism—quite apart from the time-honoured derivatives of belladonna—including such as Artane, Parpanit and Lysivane, may have this effect. The antihistamines are recognized as having some atropine-like activity and they may also occasionally lead to a mild impairment of accommodation.

Of the drugs used in the treatment of hypertension the ganglion-blocking agents may adversely influence the activity of the ciliary muscle, presumably by interfering with transmission through the ciliary ganglion. Such agents as the hexamethonium compounds have now been largely supplanted by other drugs such as guanethidine, the activity of which is on the post-ganglionic sympathetic effector mechanism. These latter drugs may produce blurring of vision but this may be due rather to accommodative spasm. In any event, the postural hypotension commonly experienced with many hypotensive drugs could itself lead to episodes of blurred vision irrespective of their effect on the ciliary muscle.

Insufficiency of accommodation has also been reported from the use of central nervous stimulants such as Imipramine and Desipramine (Maim and Heseltine, 1963; Hollister, 1964), and of massive doses of tranquillizing drugs such as the phenothiazine derivatives; thus Isayama and Yasui (1967) found that the power of accommodation was reduced in all the 39 schizophrenic patients treated thus whom they examined (Bonnet et al., 1964, 10 in 24; and others).

Treatment of paralysis of accommodation should be initially directed to the cause of the lesion, and when this is amenable to therapeutic relief the ocular condition requires little attention. Strychnine injections were frequently advised as a direct stimulant to accommodative power, but their effect is illusory. Miotics (particularly pilocarpine) may be of some assistance, particularly in cases of partial paresis, their value lying not only in the ciliary stimulation, but also in the optical improvement of a small pupil. When, however, recovery is delayed, the prognosis is bad or near work must be done despite the disability, spectacles which allow the patient to read or work in comfort should be prescribed, most conveniently in the form of bifocals. The correction should not, however, be over-strong so that some exercise of the accommodation within the limits of fatigue is allowed. In uniocular cases the patient may neglect or occlude the affected eye, but frequently gains sufficient comfort to use both with the help of a weak convex lens.

PARALYSIS OF ACCOMMODATION FOR DISTANCE

The occurrence of such a condition is problematical, but it has been said to follow a destructive lesion of the cervical sympathetic. In this event, the palsy should lead to an increased amplitude of accommodation for near vision, the parasympathetic mechanism for which will act unimpeded by its physiological antagonist. Such a condition involves little functional disability but becomes apparent in unilateral cases. An inequality of accommodation whereby an increased amplitude for near vision and an approximation of the near-point 1 to 4 cm. to the eye on the affected side was reported in soldiers by Cobb and Scarlett (1920), and in a series of cases as part of Horner's syndrome after the operation of cervical sympathectomy by Cogan (1937). Few observations on this interesting clinical condition have, however, been recorded.

Aeby. *Z. rat. Med.*, **11**, 300 (1861).
Allen, D. G. *Amer. J. Ophthal.*, **52**, 702 (1961).
Allen, T. D. *Arch. Ophthal.*, **4**, 84 (1930).
Alpers and Palmer. *J. nerv. ment. Dis.*, **70**, 465 (1929).
Barrett. *J. Physiol.*, **6**, 46 (1885).
Berens, Connolly and Kern. *Amer. J. Ophthal.*, **16**, 199 (1933).
Berens and Stark. *Amer. J. Ophthal.*, **15**, 216, 527 (1932).
Bernstein, F. *Zbl.–Z. Opt. Mech.*, **52**, 321 (1931).
  Forsch. u. Fortschr., **8**, 272 (1932).
Bernstein, F. and M. *Arch. Ophthal.*, **34**, 378 (1945).
Beyer. *Zbl. Nervenheilk. Psychiat.*, **9**, 262 (1898).
Bistis. *Z. Augenheilk.*, **67**, 158 (1929).
Blatt. *Z. Augenheilk.*, **49**, 280 (1923).
  v. Graefes Arch. Ophthal., **125**, 236 (1930).
  Arch. Ophthal., **5**, 362 (1931).
  Klin. Mbl. Augenheilk., **86**, 482 (1931).
Bonnet, Leopold and Istre. *Bull. Soc. Ophtal. Fr.*, **64**. 433 (1964).
Brownell. *Arch. Ophthal.*, **26**, 1057 (1941).
Clarke. *Errors of Accommodation and Refraction of the Eye*, 5th ed., London (1924).
Coates. *Brit. J. physiol. Opt.*, **12**, 76 (1955).
Cobb and Scarlett. *Arch. Neurol. Psychiat.* (Chic.), **3**, 636 (1920).
Cogan. *Arch. Ophthal.*, **18**, 739 (1937).
Curi. *Rev. bras. Oftal.*, **1**, 53 (1942).
Daniels. *Z. Augenheilk.*, **62**, 288 (1927).
Decker. *Amer. J. Ophthal.*, **1**, 443 (1924).
Donders. *Arch. Holländ. Beitr. Natur- Heilkunde*, Utrecht, **10** (1861).
  On the Anomalies of Accommodation and Refraction of the Eye, London (1864).
Duane. *Trans. Amer. ophthal. Soc.*, **11**, 634 (1908); **20**, 132 (1922).
  Ophthal. Rec., **18**, 403 (1909).
  Ophthalmoscope, **10**, 486 (1912).
  J. Amer. med. Ass., **59**, 1010 (1912).
  Arch. Ophthal., **45**, 124 (1916); **54**, 566 (1925); **5**, 1 (1931).
  Amer. J. Ophthal., **5**, 865 (1922); **8**, 196 (1925).

Dubois-Poulsen and Rozan. *Ann. Oculist.* (Paris), **180**, 206 (1947).
Duggan. *Brit. med. J.*, **1**, 918 (1937).
Ferree. *Ophthalmology*, **10**, 622 (1914).
Ferree and Rand. *Trans. Amer. ophthal. Soc.*, **16**, 142 (1918).
  Arch. Ophthal., **15**, 1072 (1936).
Fuchs. *Arch. Ophthal.*, **51**, 21 (1922).
  v. Graefes Arch. Ophthal., **120**, 733 (1928).
Fukuda, Hamada and Makuo. *Acta Soc. ophthal. jap.*, **66**, 181 (1962).
Furuya. *Acta Soc. ophthal. jap.*, **41**, 142, 680 (1937).
Gonzalez. *Int. Cong. Ophthal.*, Washington, 81 (1922).
Goodall. *Air med. Serv.*, **6**, 70 (1920).
Gould. *Amer. Med.*, **9**, 103 (1905).
Gross. *Z. Sinnesphysiol.*, **62**, 49 (1931).
Guglianetti. *Arch. Ottal.*, **30**, 25 (1923).
Guillot. *Bull. Soc. belge Ophtal.*, No. 64, 92 (1932).
Hamilton and Sclare. *Brit. med. J.*, **2**, 611 (1947).
Heath. *Brit. med. J.*, **2**, 608 (1950).
Heidemann. *Presbyopie u. Lebensdauer* (Diss.), Göttingen (1932).
Hirose. *Rinsho Ganka*, **22**, 523 (1968).
Hofstetter. *Amer. J. Optom.*, **40**, 3 (1963); **45**, 522 (1968).
Hollister. *Clin. Pharm. Ther.*, **5**, 322 (1964).
Holloway. *Trans. Amer. ophthal. Soc.*, **17**, 440 (1919).
Hopkins and Robyns-Jones. *Brit. med. J.*, **1**, 663 (1937).
Hughes. *Trans. ophthal. Soc. U.K.*, **58**, 444 (1938).
Huizinga. *Ophthal. Rec.*, **8**, 163 (1899).
Isayama and Yasui. *Rinsho Ganka*, **21**, 635 (1967).
Jackson. *Calif. St. J. Med.*, **5**, 163 (1907).
  Amer. J. Ophthal., **8**, 207 (1925).
Jakovleva. *Russ. oftal. J.*, **13**, 330 (1931).
Kajiura. *Jap. J. Ophthal.*, **9**, 85 (1965).
Lagrange *Précis d'Ophtal.*, 2nd ed., Paris, 33 (1903).
Lancaster and Williams. *Trans. Amer. Acad. Ophthal.*, **19**, 170 (1914).

Landolt. *Graefe-Saemisch Hb. d. ges. Augen-heilk.*, 2nd ed., Leipzig, **4** (1) (1903).

Lederer. *Klin. Mbl. Augenheilk.*, **78**, 97 (1927); **82**, 656 (1929).

Lussana. *Ann. Univ. di Med.*, Milan, **140**, 514 (1852).

McFarland. *J. comp. Physiol.*, **23**, 227 (1937).

Maim and Hesseltine. *Canad. med. Ass. J.*, **88**, 1102 (1963).

Makrocki. *Berl. klin. Wschr.*, **48**, 1417 (1911).

Manson and Stern. *Lancet*, **1**, 935 (1965).

Martin. *Ann. Oculist.* (Paris), **99**, 24 (1888).

Métivier. *Lancet*, **2**, 1232 (1935).

Milian. *Rev. franç. Derm.*, **6**, 349 (1930).

Milian and Périn. *Paris méd.*, **41**, 388 (1921).

Morton, H. G. *J. Pediat.*, **14**, 755 (1939).

Müller. *Wien. klin. Wschr.*, **64**, 38 (1952).

Passow. *Arch. Augenheilk.*, **97**, 432 (1926).

Perrin. *Bull. Soc. franç. Ophtal.*, **41**, 191 (1928).

Prangen. *Arch. Ophthal.*, **6**, 906 (1931).

Rambo. *Proc. All-India ophthal. Soc.*, **17**, 263 (1960).

Raphael. *Brit. J. physiol. Opt.*, **18**, 181 (1961).

Robertson. *U.S. Nav. med. Bull.*, **32**, 275 (1934); **33**, 187 (1935).

Arch. Ophthal., **14**, 82 (1935); **15**, 423 (1936); **17**, 859 (1937.)

Rosenberg. *Z. Augenheilk.*, **73**, 207 (1931).

Ruedemann. *J. Amer. med. Ass.*, **97**, 1700 (1931).

Scrini and Fortin. *Manuel pratique pour le choix des verres de lunettes et l'examen de la vision*, 2nd ed., Paris (1922).

Seashore. *Stud. Yale psychol. Lab.*, 56 (1892–3).

Sédan. *Rev. Oto-neuro-ophtal.*, **19**, 114 (1947).

Sklarz and Massur. *Med. Klin.*, **17**, 346 (1921).

Slataper. *Arch. Ophthal.*, **43**, 466 (1950).

Steinhaus. *Arch. Augenheilk.*, **105**, 731 (1932).

Stellwag von Carion. *Accommodations-Fehler d. Auges*, Wien (1855).

Stepka. *Cas. Lék. ces.*, **1**, 305 (1929).

Suker. *Amer. J. Ophthal.*, **20**, 208 (1903).

Sumner. *Amer. J. Ophthal.*, **4**, 356 (1921).

Szeghy, Pápai and Vas. *Ophthalmologica*, **146**, 74 (1963).

Tefft and Stark. *Amer. J. Ophthal.*, **5**, 339 (1922).

Theobald. *Trans. Amer. ophthal. Soc.*, **6**, 127 (1891); **7**, 138 (1894).

Johns Hopk. Hosp. Bull., **24**, 282 (1913).

Veasey. *Trans. Amer. ophthal. Soc.*, **17**, 436 (1919).

Vierordt. *Arch. physiol. Heilk.*, **1**, 17 (1857).

Wescott. *Amer. J. Ophthal.*, **19**, 385 (1936).

Weston and Adams. *Indust. Hlth. Res. Bd.*, London, Rep. No. 40 (1927); No. 49 (1928); No. 57 (1929).

White. *Amer. J. Ophthal.*, **4**, 276 (1921).

Whiteside. *The Problems of Vision in Flight at High Altitudes*, London (1957).

Wilmer and Berens. *J. Amer. med. Ass.*, **71**, 1394 (1918).

Wood. *Brit. J. Ophthal.*, **4**, 415 (1920).

Spasm of Accommodation

SPASM OF ACCOMMODATION FOR NEAR VISION

In ACCOMMODATIVE SPASM, first adequately described by von Graefe (1856), the tone of the ciliary muscle is increased and a constant accommodative effort is expended by the parasympathetic nervous system so as to bring both the far-point and the near-point closer; a *spurious* or *pseudo-myopia* (Liebreich, 1861) is thus induced wherein the hypermetrope becomes apparently less ametropic, the emmetrope myopic and the myope more short-sighted (Agrawal, 1965; Bessière and Vérin, 1965). In its less accentuated degrees wherein ciliary tonus is functionally increased, usually intermittently and accentuated by near work, it is common; in its more marked manifestations wherein the muscle is in permanent spasm sometimes increasing the dioptric power of the eye by 25 or even 30 D, it is rare. In general the condition is an expression of excessive parasympathetic activity, and it may be that sympathetic under-activity or paresis may sometimes enter into its ætiology.

The *symptoms* of ciliary spasm are typical. Vision is not seriously impaired unless the condition is marked. The distant vision is blurred because of the pseudo-myopia, to which may be added the occurrence of accommodative astigmatism[1] if an optical correction is worn; near vision, on the other hand, is unimpaired although in marked cases close work may be done at very short range. Added to this is the phenomenon of *macropsia*: objects appear larger because of an illusion of distance. Since little additional accommodative effort is required to see a near object it is judged to be some considerable distance away and its apparent size at that distance is necessarily unusually great. Subjectively all the symptoms of accommodative astheno-pia are present and usually become accentuated with close work—pain usually referred to the brows, headache, early fatigue and inability to main-tain visual or mental concentration. The pain may sometimes be consider-able as is typically seen after the instillation of eserine (*asthenopia dolorosa*) and tenderness may be elicited on pressure upon the globe; gastric disturb-ances and vomiting have been observed (Irvine, 1947). The accommodative disturbance is sometimes associated with a spasmodic miosis if it depends upon an organic cause; in functional cases this combination is unusual. An excess of convergence may also be seen, sometimes involving the appearance of an internal squint; but convergence insufficiency is also a common accompaniment.

The *diagnosis* of accommodative spasm is usually easy, but too often it is missed and the pseudo-myopia optically corrected. The correction im-proves the vision for a time until increasing spasm demands an increase in correction; in this way not a few people wear myopic lenses for the greater part of their lives, sometimes being periodically augmented in strength, to compensate a functional and permanent ciliary spasm which has, on occasion, involved a myopic correction of -22 D in an emmetrope (Hambresin, 1939). The condition should be suspected whenever subjective and objective tests of the refraction give differing or variable results, when the range of accom-modation is abnormal for the age of the patient, and when fogging tests or remaining in the dark betrays difficulty in its relaxation, or when weak cycloplegics appear to be ineffective. It is also suggestive if in the subjective test with test-letters the successive addition of small concave spherical lenses (in steps of -0.25 D) does not diminish the visual acuity, nor does their neutralization with convex spheres (Leplat, 1908). The essential basis of diagnosis, however, is the establishment of a difference between the refraction with and without complete cycloplegia greater than that accounted for by the normal ciliary tone (about 1 D). In suspected cases atropine should always be used and tests should ensure that cycloplegia is complete.

The ætiology of accommodative spasm divides itself into two main categories: (*a*) a functional spasm which is essentially a response to fatigue and over-strain, and (*b*) an organic spasm due to irritation of the para-sympathetic nerve supply.

[1] p. 285.

FUNCTIONAL ACCOMMODATIVE SPASM

FUNCTIONAL ACCOMMODATIVE SPASM is a relatively common response to accommodative fatigue resembling the fatigue-cramp of other muscles; it is an alternative response by an over-worked ciliary muscle to insufficiency of accommodation.[1] It is essentially a condition of irritability due to asthenia (Prangen, 1922–37; Alexander, 1940): the tired muscle forces itself to continued activity, but can act only in a spasmodic and inefficient manner whereas in accommodative insufficiency the muscle gives up its efforts. Such a reaction is usually precipitated by three factors—over-work sometimes in bad hygienic conditions, optical or muscular anomalies rendering vision difficult, and a physical and mental background favourable for the development of functional irregularities.

The conditions of work are frequently of considerable importance, prolonged close work in inadequate illumination being a common exciting cause. Exposure to intense and glaring light may precipitate a spasm (Thomson, 1898). Unaccustomed work may excite the condition and for this reason it is not infrequently seen in the child starting school, the candidate preparing for an examination, or the adolescent who leaves the changing and careless activities of youth for the responsibilities and imprisonment of the office.

Optical difficulties are the most common immediate association, a circumstance particularly seen in early myopes and astigmats during adolescence when accommodation has a large available amplitude, but met with in adults with all types of refractive error (Walker, 1946). The perceptual irritation caused by anisometropia may be an association. It is relatively common in early presbyopia when strenuous efforts to maintain the visual capacity for close work result in disordered function, and it has been observed in patients of 60 years and over (Leplat, 1927; Prangen, 1937); in such cases a rapid decrease of hypermetropia or increase of myopia should always give rise to the suspicion that excessive accommodation may be the fault rather than the static refraction. An imbalance of the extra-ocular musculature may also be a causal factor, particularly convergence insufficiency or excess, and Marlow (1922) maintained that a peculiarly effective influence was a latent hyperphoria which could be elicited only on prolonged occlusion.[2]

The constitutional make-up of the individual enters into the ætiological picture. Typically those affected are tense and emotional, anxious in mind and unstable in their reactions, and sometimes afflicted with a more or less marked functional neurosis.

The functional element in accommodative spasm is well exemplified in the traumatic neuroses in which it is occasionally a prominent feature. Inability to read is a common sequel of head injuries and may persist for a considerable time (Wescott,

[1] p. 461.   [2] Vol. VI.

1943). Functional influences are seen, however, in their most marked degree in hysteria wherein accommodative spasm, sometimes associated with spasm of convergence, miosis, and reinforced by blepharospasm, is not uncommon and may accompany contraction of the visual fields and amblyopia (Borel, 1886; Morax, 1905; Plantenga, 1908; Sollom, 1966; and others).

The *treatment* of functional accommodative spasm may be difficult. Any exciting cause in the occupation, the environment or in the general health should be eliminated in so far as this is possible, but the essentially important factors are properly correcting glasses and visual rest. Sometimes a holiday may be sufficiently effective, but in the more marked and persistent cases complete accommodative rest under atropine cycloplegia may be necessary for 3 or 4 weeks. Even then the spasm not infrequently returns after the influence of the drug has passed off, when a further period of atropinization should be prescribed. Correcting spectacles should be worn immediately the eyes are used again. The optical correction must, of course, be accurate, astigmatic errors being corrected with particular care : this, indeed, is an effective cure in itself in many of the milder cases. At first the true correction may cause blurring of distant vision, but usually the eyes relax after a little time so that the spectacles are eventually worn with relief and gratitude, but sometimes the occasional administration of a mild cyclo-plegic such as homatropine may be indicated initially to help the patient to change his visual habit. Finally, if close work tends to cause further relapses, stronger lenses for work may bring relief while, by aiding ocular relaxation, orthoptic training of the stereoscopic vision and convergence may be of considerable value (Irvine, 1947).[1]

When pain is severe on attempting near work, Grunert (1928) and Frieberg (1929) advocated the use of pilocarpine. The administration of antispasmodics such as injections of acetylcholine has been suggested by Bari (1933); while Green and Sluder (1923) suggested anæsthesia of the sphenopalatine ganglion when pain was a prominent symptom.

ORGANIC ACCOMMODATIVE SPASM

Accommodative spasm of organic origin is rare. There is little reason to distinguish between partial and complete spasm; indeed, many cases of mild transitory myopia are probably best considered in this category.

1. Ciliary spasm is seen after the use of miotic drugs such as the cholinergic stimulants (physostigmine, prostigmine and their allies, the alkyl fluorophosphonates such as DFP or echothiopate, demecarium, pilocarpine, muscarine, choline, acetylcholine and related esters). This condition may be quite distressing to a patient commencing miotic therapy for glaucoma for, apart from the discomfort, the visual difficulties due to the varying myopic shift of the refraction may be considerable.[2] In the case of pilo-carpine, the effect tends to be minimal and within 2 to 3 weeks the

---

[1] Vol. VI,   [2] See Vol. XI. p. 515.

refractive change usually settles so that the final optical state becomes little different from that before using the drug; this is especially so in older patients. The administration of the more powerful miotics such as echothiopate to a young subject with active accommodation, however, may not be attended by rapid stabilization and the distress of a constantly changing refraction may be protracted.

Accommodative spasm may also be associated with over-dosage of such drugs as morphia, aconitine, hydrastinin and the digitalis group. Violent accommodative spasm has been noted after smoking " ersatz " tobacco (due to solanine or other toxins liberated in combustion) (Sédan, 1947).

2. In irritative lesions of the brain-stem and the oculomotor trunk, as in epidemic encephalitis (Cords, 1920) or in the crises of tabes (Blatt, 1930), meningitis and inflammatory conditions of the orbit or of the ocular coats (scleritis, Gorse and Bergès, 1937).

3. Reflex irritation as in trigeminal neuralgia (Pereyra, 1898).

4. In intra-ocular inflammations when the ciliary body is irritated (Oliver, 1892; Blatt, 1930).

5. It has been reported after infections such as diphtheria (Davids, 1961), following the extraction of a tooth (Krudysz, 1962) or in helminthic infestations (Indeikin, 1960).

6. The transitory myopia which may follow the administration of many drugs such as the sulphonamides[1] may be due to a spasm of the ciliary muscle, as well as that occurring with toxic states such as jaundice, influenza or mud fever.

7. An increase of accommodative power after the injection of large doses of vitamin B_1 (aneurin) has been reported by Sysi (1946).

8. A periodic spasm of accommodation occurs in cyclic oculomotor spasm.

9. A ciliary spasm may be a cause of traumatic myopia and may be seen as a sequel to head injuries (Girling, 1958; Anderson, 1961; Murrah, 1965).

SPASM OF ACCOMMODATION FOR DISTANT VISION

A SPASM OF ACCOMMODATION FOR DISTANT VISION owing to stimulation of the sympathetic is a possible clinical entity as yet unestablished and unexplored. Such a condition would oppose accommodation for near vision and cause a recession of the near-point. Heath (1936) and Cogan (1937) have brought forward evidence that the sympathomimetic drugs act in this way. Grancher (1880) reported a similar recession of the near-point in thyrotoxicosis and Cogan (1937) in an irritative condition of the cervical sympathetic which may have been susceptible to a similar explanation.

Agrawal. *Orient. Arch. Ophthal.*, **3,** 89 (1965).

Alexander. *Trans. ophthal. Soc. U.K.*, **60,** 207 (1940).

Anderson. *Brit. orthopt. J.*, **18,** 117 (1961).

Bari. *L'occhio e il meccanismo della visione,* Bologna (1933).

Bessière and Vérin. *Bull. Soc. Ophtal. Fr.*, **65,** 91 (1965).

Blatt. *v. Graefes Arch. Ophthal.*, **125,** 236 (1930).

Borel. *Arch. Ophthal.*, **6,** 181 (1886).

Cogan. *Arch. Ophthal.*, **18,** 739 (1937).

Cords. *Münch, med, Wschr.*, **67,** 627 (1920).

[1] p. 371.

Davids. *Med. Welt*, **48**, 2526 (1961).
Frieberg. *Hosp. tid.*, **1**, 15 (1929).
Girling. *Acta XVIII int. Cong. Ophthal.*, Brussels, **2**, 1550 (1958).
Gorse and Bergès. *Ann. Oculist.* (Paris), **174**, 844 (1937).
von Graefe. *v. Graefes Arch. Ophthal.*, **2** (2), 364 (1856).
Grancher. *Gaz. Hôp. Paris*, **53**, 1060 (1880).
Green and Sluder. *Trans. Sect. Ophthal.*, *Amer. Med. Ass.*, 147 (1923).
Grunert. *Klin. Mbl. Augenheilk.*, **81**, 44 (1928).
Hambresin. *Traité d'ophtalmologie*, Paris, **3**, 268 (1939).
Heath. *Arch. Ophthal.*, **16**, 839 (1936).
Indeikin. *Vestn. Oftal.*, **73** (1), 41 (1960).
Irvine. *Brit. J. Ophthal.*, **31**, 289 (1947).
Krudysz. *Klin. oczna*, **32**, 437 (1962).
Leplat. *Le Scalpel*, 512 (1908).
   Bull. Soc. belge Ophtal., No. 55, 62 (1927).

Liebreich. *v. Graefes Arch. Ophthal.*, **8** (3), 259 (1861).
Marlow. *Arch. Ophthal.*, **51**, 223 (1922).
Morax. *Encycl. franç. Ophtal.*, Paris **4**, 546 (1905).
Murrah. *Sth. med. J.* (Bgham, Ala.), **58**, 1135 (1965).
Oliver. *Ophthal. Rev.*, **11**, 397 (1892).
Pereyra. *Boll. Oculist.*, **7**, 191 (1898).
Plantenga *Ned. T. Geneesk.*, **1**, 795 (1908).
Prangen. *Trans. Sect. Ophthal.*, *Amer. Med. Ass.*, 283 (1922).
   Arch. Ophthal., **18**, 432 (1937).
Sédan. *Rev. Oto-neuro-ophtal.*, **19**, 65 (1947).
Sollom. *Brit. orthop. J.*, **23**, 118 (1966).
Sysi. *Acta ophthal.* (Kbh.), Suppl. 25 (1946).
Thomson. *Med. Times and Gaz.*, **26**, 711 (1898).
Walker. *Brit. J. Ophthal.*, **30**, 735 (1946).
Wescott. *Ill. med. J.*, **83**, 170 (1943).

TONIC ACCOMMODATION

This is a rare but noteworthy phenomenon, first noted by Axenfeld (1919), whereby *an accommodative posture is prolonged* so that the change in focus from distant to near objects or *vice versa* is delayed; indeed, the inconvenience may be so great that the patient, even although young, may find it advisable to wear bifocal lenses. The site of the causal lesion is unknown, but it has occasionally been reported in measles, diabetes, alcoholism, migraine, Graves's disease, after trauma, and also in syphilis (Jess, 1920–22; Gehrcke, 1921; Karpow, 1923; Erggelet, 1932).

Axenfeld. *Klin. Mbl. Augenheilk.*, **62**, 59 (1919).
Erggelet. *Kurzes Hb. d. Ophthal.*, Berlin, **2**, 703 (1932).
Gehrcke. *Neurol. Zbl.*, **40**, Erg., 93 (1921).

Jess. *Klin. Mbl. Augenheilk.*, **64**, 114 (1920); **69**, 837 (1922).
Karpow. *Klin. Mbl. Augenheilk.*, **71**, 218 (1923).

METHODS OF ESTIMATING THE ACCOMMODATION

The full clinical assessment of the accommodation involves a measurement of its range, amplitude and fatiguability, its positive and negative moieties relative to the convergence, as well as an estimation of the dynamic refraction—that is, the refraction of the eyes focused for objects at the working distance. Most commonly subjective methods are employed in these investigations, but objective methods are also available.

Objective Methods

DYNAMIC RETINOSCOPY

DYNAMIC RETINOSCOPY (DYNAMIC SKIASCOPY) is a method of investigation introduced by Cross (1903–11) and Sheard (1922) in America and elaborated by Nott (1925–26), Ketchum (1926), Lea (1928), Pascal (1929–41), Swann (1939) and others, wherein instead of the eyes being relaxed as much as possible as in static retinoscopy, their refractivity is measured while they are actively accommodating and converging. The refractive power in this state of binocular activity can thus be measured, differences in the accommodation of the two eyes can be estimated and the near-point can be assessed. The optical principles are the same as in static retinoscopy except that the anterior conjugate focus is sought, not at infinity but at the working distance.

The technique requires greater experience and skill than static retinoscopy, but unfortunately there is not complete agreement as to the interpretation of the results.

The practical technique is to use a refracting mirror, or more conveniently a self-luminous retinoscope, to which is attached a fixation chart below the level of the beam of light (Fig. 491). Wearing his distance correction with both eyes uncovered, the patient is asked to fix and focus the chart which is held at the working distance, and the refraction is estimated again, the maintenance of convergence being controlled by the central position of the corneal reflexes. Instead, however, of obtaining a neutral shadow with a patient of ample accommodative power, as would be expected to occur if his retina and the mirror were conjugate, a " with " movement is obtained (using a plane mirror) and a neutral reflex is normally found only if the patient fixes and accommodates for an object a short dis-

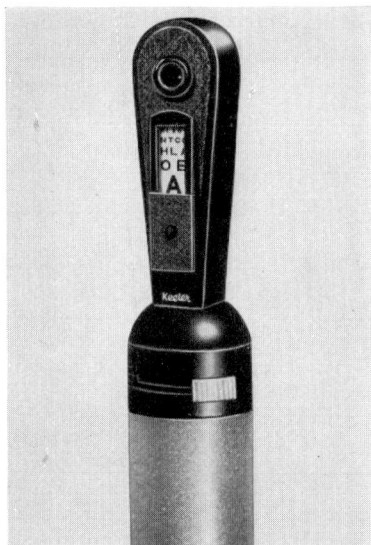

FIG. 491.—DYNAMIC RETINOSCOPE (KEELER).

tance in front of the mirror or if plus lenses are added binocularly ($+0.5$ to 0.75 D at a distance of 33 cm.). This " lag of accommodation " (Sheard, 1922) occurs normally but its rationale is not understood; various explanations depending on a lag of accommodation behind convergence, spherical aberration, and so on, have been advanced. When this " with " movement has been neutralized (the *low neutral point*) convex lenses are added binocularly. No rapid reversal of the shadow is obtained, however, as occurs in static retinoscopy, but as accommodation gradually relaxes a wide *neutral zone* is traversed until eventually the shadow is reversed, marking the *high neutral point*. It is generally agreed that the high neutral point represents an objective finding of the negative relative accommodation, that is, the amount of accommodation which can be relaxed while convergence remains fixed. The strength of the lenses at this point—that is, the highest convex lenses that give neutrality of shadow—is generally stated to indicate the point of association between convergence and accommodation which brings about a comfortable adjustment between them; in practice the lenses will be found to be somewhat strong for comfort.

Our knowledge of the problems raised in this way, however, is not yet sufficient to allow dogmatic conclusions to be drawn from the results or to assess their real significance. The method is of distinct value in that, just as static retinoscopy gives an objective basis for the appropriate correction for distant vision, dynamic retinoscopy provides an objective basis for the optical correction when the eye is focused for near vision, a matter which had hitherto been left entirely to subjective testing. Retinoscopy with the eye accommodating also allows an objective reassessment of the astigmatism and occasionally reveals a significant difference between the powers of the necessary cylindrical corrections at distant and near vision. Such changes can be confirmed by subjective testing. Objective estimation of the binocular balance for near vision is also possible. Because of the difficulties in the practice and interpretation of dynamic retinoscopy, however, it has found only a limited place in the routine estimation of the refraction.

Several variations of the technique of dynamic retinoscopy have been advocated, particularly in relation to the nature and position of the fixation object (see Giles, 1956–60); for example, a position closer to the patient than the retinoscope is employed by Hodd for part of his technique (1951). It is, of course, difficult to be certain that the patient is clearly focusing the test-object and bichromatic targets have been used so that the retinoscopy can be performed while the patient states whether the red or green is dominant (Cockerham, 1954).

REFRACTOMETRY. Some optometers, such as that of Fincham,[1] can be fitted with an optical device to approximate fixation, and used to estimate the refraction during accommodation. This and the more recent methods of continuous optometry are of research rather than of clinical importance.

Subjective Methods

THE MEASUREMENT OF THE NEAR-POINT

The assessment of a subject's near vision involves one of two types of investigation. The first is a formal measurement of the near-point of accommodation; the second, a procedure which is more widely practised clinically, is to test the subject's ability to read progressively smaller print at his normal reading distance, usually taken to be about 30 cm.

The power of accommodation which, apart from its bearing on refractive problems, is often of value in the investigation of neurological cases, is frequently roughly measured by approximating the near test-types to the patient's eye and, while he looks at the smallest, noting the distance at which it gets blurred. This test is, however, inaccurate since a failure in convergence inducing diplopia may bring about a blurring of the letters indistinguishable from that due to accommodative insufficiency. A more accurate measurement can be made by the *hair-optometer of Donders* (1864),

[1] p. 412.

an instrument resembling a small harp in which the strings are replaced by fine hairs; this is held against a white background and approximated to the eye until the hairs cannot be distinguished. *Scheiner's experiment* (1619)[1] provides a basis for another useful test suitable for uniocular observations: a card pierced with two small pin-holes situated close together is placed in front of the eye and the patient looks through the holes at a pin held about a metre away. At this distance the pin is easily seen as a distinct image, but as the pin is brought near to the eye a point is reached at which it appears double—this marks the near-point of accommodation (Fig. 479). A rapid and useful test is the ACCOMMODATION CARD OF DUANE (1909) on which is

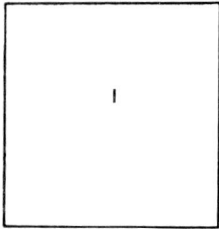

FIG. 492.—THE ACCOMMODATION CARD OF DUANE.

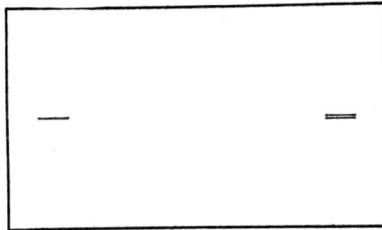

FIG. 493.—THE ACCOMMODATION CARD OF SLATAPER.

engraved a single line 0·2 mm. thick by 3 mm. long (Fig. 492); this is brought near to the eye and the point at which it becomes blurred (not duplicated) is recorded. Slataper (1926–45) modified this by adding two lines similar to those of Duane separated by an interval equal to the width of either (Fig. 493): blurring is easily noted by the fusion of the two lines into one. Colenbrander (1937–40) employed a test-card in which the essential feature was the recognition of the direction of triangles of diminishing size somewhat after the principle of a Landolt C.

Different authorities have used different bases for measurement. Donders (1864) measured from the anterior nodal point; Landolt (1903) from the anterior principal point; and Duane (1922)—who is now generally followed—from the anterior principal focus (15·7 mm. in front of the cornea). The distance is measured in cm. and thence translated into dioptres. It will be remembered that the dioptric value of the reading distance is the reciprocal of the length expressed in metres: thus a distance of 25 cm. represents 100/25, or 4 dioptres.

A considerable amount of ingenuity has been expended in designing instruments to make such measurements easy and rapid. The convenient *Prince's rule* is calibrated in both dioptres and centimetres. In practice the distance is measured by a tape held at the outer canthus of the eye: looking from the side, the surgeon estimates the level of the anterior summit

[1] *Oculus*, Innsbruck (1619). See p. 444.

FIG. 494.—LIVINGSTON'S BINOCULAR GAUGE.

The left-hand end of the wooden rule (36 cm. long) fits against the infra-orbital margins. It is marked in cm. from the anterior corneal surface. The shield on the left can be used (when attached to the instrument) in the estimation of uniocular accommodation. The central rod, running in a slot, is slid towards the eyes until the limit of convergence, when one eye diverges. The convergence can then be measured subjectively by sliding the attachment at the right-hand end towards the eye. There is a black vertical line in the centre of the vertical limb of the cross. At the limit of convergence the line is seen to go into the right or left arm of the cross according to whether the left or right eye has diverged. By replacing this with small print the near-point of accommodation can be measured at the point at which the print becomes blurred.

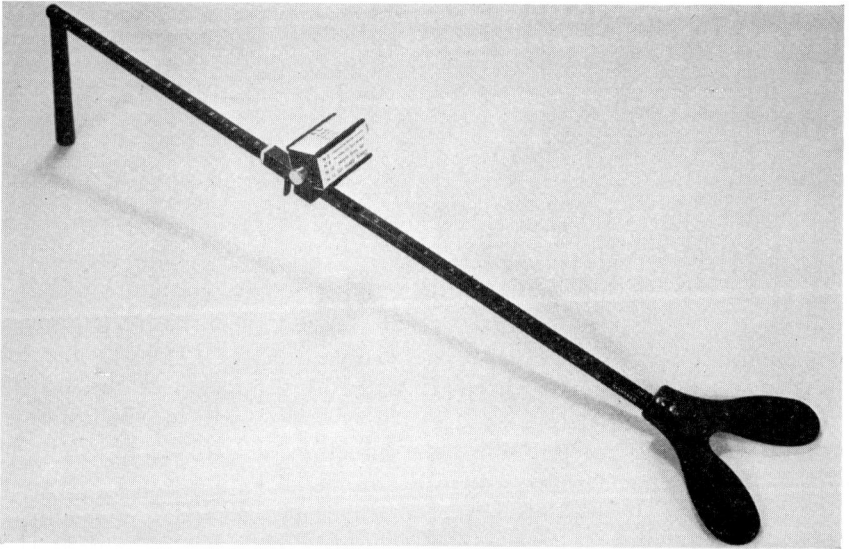

FIG. 495. A NEAR-POINT RULE.

The instrument is 50 cm. long, marked on the top in centimetres and on the two sides with dioptres. The quadrilateral metal slide can be rotated to present 4 white plastic faces showing appropriately reduced Snellen's types, reading types, reproductions of lines from a telephone directory, and a vertical line with a central dot for convergence fixation (J. C. Neely).

of the cornea and, deducting this distance plus 15·7 mm. from the total measurement to the accommodation card, he obtains the measurement to the near-point. Duane's (1921) accommodation rule is a modification of Prince's rule, consisting of a straight wooden ruler placed between the eyes with a groove cut at the end to fit the bridge of the nose. It is calibrated along the top and down the sides to serve binocular and uniocular measurements, and is marked in centimetres to register the near-point and in dioptres to register the amplitude of accommodation, the scale commencing at a distance of 14 mm. in front of the cornea. As the accommodation card is approximated to the eye its distance can be read off in centimetres, and translated simultaneously into dioptres of accommodative power. Somewhat similar rules have been designed by Nicolai (1922), Berens (1923), Lee (1927), Thorne (1928), Livingston (1935), Abbott (1941), Simpson (1941), Neely (1956), Giles (1960), and many others (Figs. 494–5).

It was claimed by Luckiesh and Moss (1940–43) that their sensitometric technique[1] offered unusual advantages of accuracy over subjective methods of estimating the refraction in the accommodated state.

The AMPLITUDE OF ACCOMMODATION—that is, the difference between the refractivity of the eye when at rest with a minimal refraction and when fully accommodated with a maximal refraction—can be calculated from measurements of the range (since the refracting power is the reciprocal of the focal distance in metres) or it may be measured directly by subtracting the dioptric value of the far-point from that of the near-point.

The RELATIVE ACCOMMODATION AND CONVERGENCE should be investigated at the working distance, that is, the amount of accommodation or convergence which can be additionally exerted or relaxed by the one function while the other remains constant. The amount of accommodation which can be thus relaxed while the patient still fixes (the negative relative accommodation) is determined by adding further plus lenses until the object becomes blurred. The positive relative accommodation (that is, the amount by which accommodation can be augmented) is similarly found by adding concave lenses to the normal reading correction.

Tests of accommodative balance have been suggested by various authors. Maddox (1928) claimed to determine the point at which the accommodative far-point tends when at ease to coincide with the point of intersection of the visual lines. The device —black lettering on a blue and red ground in juxtaposition (Fig. 496)—is held at the working position and convex lenses are added to the static refraction until the two sets of lettering are equally clear. If the lettering on the red shows best, the accommodative correction is too high. Since the two sets of lettering

FIG. 496.—MADDOX'S ACCOMMODATIVE BALANCE TEST.

The word "Now" is printed with black lettering on a blue and red ground.

are looked at simultaneously the test is effortless in contradistinction to the usual tests which demand the maximum expenditure of accommodation. Subjective bichromatic tests for near vision have also been advocated by Freeman (1953–54), polaroid glass being employed to present separate test-objects to the two eyes.

The investigation of the optical condition in accommodation is rendered complete by checking the astigmatic error of refraction in the accommodated

[1] p. 432.

state, an advisable procedure in higher errors of astigmatism since, as we
have seen, significant changes in the strength or axis of the cylinder may
occur. This may be done objectively by dynamic retinoscopy or subjectively
using cross-cylinders with test-types or an astigmatic fan held at the near-
point (O'Brien and Bannon, 1947).

THE NEAR VISUAL ACUITY

The determination of the near visual acuity is carried out by asking the
patient to read a near-vision test-chart at his normal reading distance.

Reading tests for near vision have been used from very early times
(Daza de Valdés, 1623; Chevallier, 1815; Tauber, 1815; Himly, 1843; and
others). The first scientific test, however, was due to SNELLEN (1868) who
constructed reading script on the same basis as his distance types, each
letter being a square subtending an angle of 5′ when held at the ordinary

N.5 renaissance

N.8   accession

N.12   examiner

N.18   passion

N.36 blood

FIG. 497.—THE BRITISH FACULTY OF OPHTHALMOLOGISTS' TEST-TYPES.

reading distance. These have been modified by several ophthalmologists,
notably by Nieden (1882) and Oliver (1885). In Oliver's test groups of
words are chosen, each having no relation with the other so that the factor
of guessing from the context is eliminated; in addition, each word is specially
chosen so that its component letters are of value in the detection of astigmatism. Letters based on Snellen's principle, however, have an unfamiliar
appearance and are not quite so easily read as ordinary type. For this
reason the earlier test proposed by E. VON JAEGER (1854–67) of Vienna became much more commonly used: this consisted of a card on which are
printed paragraphs written in the ordinary printer's founts of type of varying
sizes, each of which is numbered (nonpareil, minion, etc.). The near vision
was then recorded according to the serial number (J.1, J.2, etc.).

These types, however, have gone out of commercial use so that for a
number of years the printers of test-types have used approximations, thus
invalidating comparison of records. The British Faculty of Ophthalmologists (Law, 1951–52) therefore proposed that standard reading test-types

should be adopted to conform with modern usage in the style of print known as " Times Roman ", the notation being based on the printer's " point " system (Fig. 497). A point (1/72 in.) indicates the size of the block upon which individual letters are cast and is constant for any given style. Thus a 5-point type is one in which each letter is cast upon a block

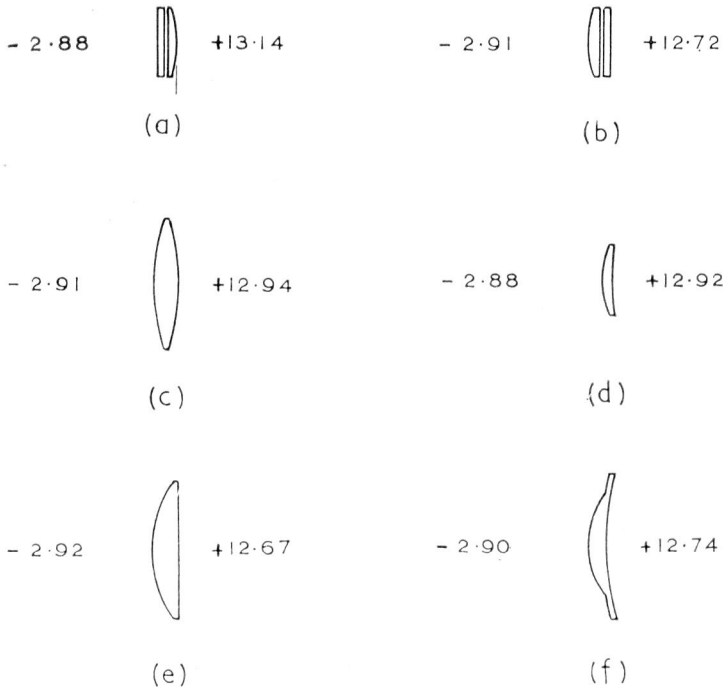

FIG. 498.—THE EFFECTIVE POWER OF TEST-LENSES FOR NEAR VISION.

These various lenses or combinations of lenses all have a back vertex power of + 16.00 D. (a) is an additive vertex power arrangement with a plane glass in place of a cylinder placed in front, and (b) the same combination seen with the cylinder behind; (c) is a symmetrical lens, (d) a curved lens, (e) a plano-convex spectacle lens, and (f) a solid lenticular. The eye is looking at a near object 35 cm. from the back vertex of the lens or combination. The numerals in front of the lenses denote the vergence of a paraxial pencil from the object at the first lens surface; the numerals behind, the vergence of the pencil at the last lens surface. This last is seen to vary from 12.67 to 13.14 D. It will be seen that the effective power for near vision of the combination (b) most nearly corresponds to that of the two spectacle lenses (e) and (f) (after A. G. Bennett).

5/72 in. tall so that in any one type the maximum distance between the head of an ascending letter (e.g., h) and the foot of a descending letter (e.g., q) will be slightly less than 5/72 in. The Faculty notation recommended was N (indicating " near "), followed by the point-number varying from 5 to 48. In America, Louise Sloan (1959) introduced a reading test based on the same principles as recommended by the American Medical Association for distant vision.[1] Whatever test is used, the print should be upon a durable and cleansable material, either plastic or a varnished white card, lest the dirt accumulating with continued use spoil the contrast of the print with its background.

In making the test the patient remains seated in the chair, and with a good light over his shoulder he is given the card with the test-types to hold and asked to read them. The near vision is recorded as the smallest type which he can comfortably read together with a note of the approximate distance at which the card is held (e.g., N.5 at 30 cm.).

In testing the visual acuity for near work the complication arises that lenses having the same back-vertex power are not equally effective for near vision, a fact first pointed out by Mayer (1909). Because their thickness in the centre is negligible this complication may be neglected for concave lenses and for convex lenses of low power, but for convex lenses of high power the difference becomes significant. Allowance for this should therefore be made in the form and arrangement of the trial lenses. Bennett (1966) has calculated the effectivity for near vision in various types of trial lens and spectacle lenses all of which have a back-vertex power of 16 D (Fig. 498). It is seen that the additive vertex power of the combination of a spherical lens and cylinder each with a plano-surface is practically identical with two forms of spectacle lenses; this combination of a spherical lens in front and a cylindrical lens behind it with their plano-surfaces in apposition therefore represents the ideal solution.

THE MEASUREMENT OF ACCOMMODATIVE FATIGUE

The diagnosis of accommodative fatigue is usually made on the history of an inability to continue near work or reading for more than a short time without the on-set of dimness of near vision and evidences of distress which may disappear allowing the patient to resume his task. This was first stressed by Donders (1864) as a factor of importance in the incidence of eye-strain. An attempt to measure the onset of fatigue was first made by Lancaster and Williams (1914) who used a small test-object and measured the shortest distance from the eye at which it could be seen without blurring for periods up to an hour. As a general rule they found little evidence of accommodative fatigue even after long periods of continuous fixation—in fact, the power of accommodation tended to increase. A more accurate method was initiated by Lucien Howe (1916) who adapted Mosso's classical technique of studying fatigue in striated muscle to the function of accommodation as he had already done to con-vergence,[2] and his work was extended and amplified by Berens (1929) and Berens and Stark (1929–32) in America and Dubois-Poulsen and Rozan (1947) in France. In brief, the method consists in repeatedly approximating to the eye a target carrying as object a dot or minute type until it becomes blurred, the excursion of the target being recorded automatically on a drum and kymograph (Fig. 499). There should be no evidence of diminution of the excursion in 15 minutes whereafter the factor of general fatigue may make itself obvious (Figs. 500–1). It is to be noted that the response of the two eyes may be different and either may differ from binocular records (Howe, 1917); when one eye only is used, the other shows signs of fatigue although less in degree (Berens

---

[1] p. 425.   [2] Vol. VI.

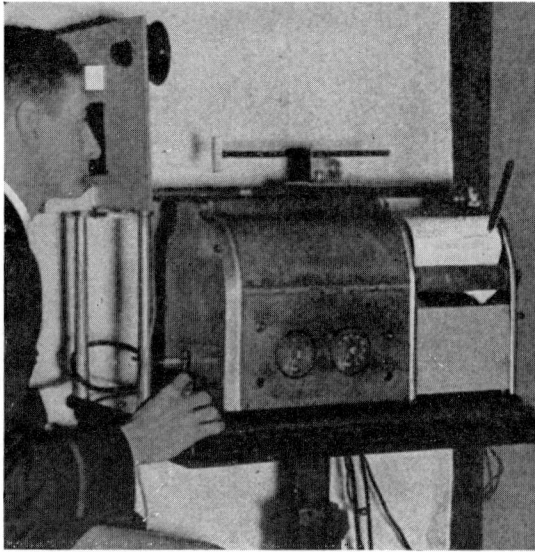

FIG. 499.—THE OPHTHALMIC ERGOGRAPH (C. Berens *et al.*).

FIGS. 500 and 501.—ERGOGRAPHIC TRACINGS OF THE ACCOMMODATIVE POWER
(C. Berens).

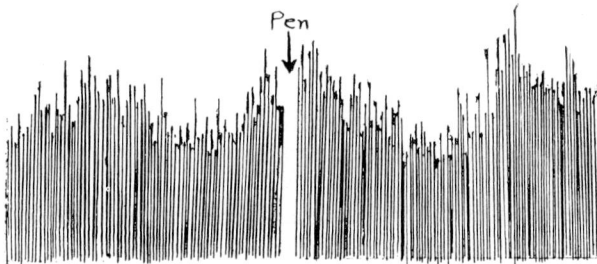

FIG. 500.—THE NORMAL ACCOMMODATIVE POWER.

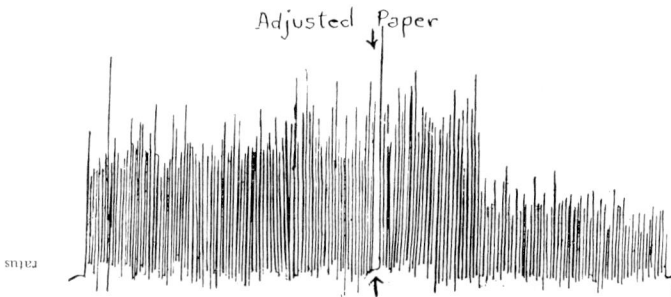

FIG. 501.—THE RESPONSE IN ILL-SUSTAINED ACCOMMODATION, SHOWING THE EARLY
ONSET OF ACCOMMODATIVE FATIGUE.

and Sells, 1944), and the curve of accommodative fatigue is frequently very different from that of fatigue of convergence so that these two factors in the ætiology of asthenopia can be differentiated.

The Determination of Spectacles for Near Work

In theory, the determination of spectacles for near work requires a knowledge of the static refraction, any refractive change in accommodation, the uniocular and binocular amplitude of the accommodation, and the positive and negative portions of the relative accommodation for the distance of work. In practice, a knowledge of the patient's static refraction and the distance at which near work is to be performed is sufficient to allow the refractionist to proceed to a subjective test of near vision with the additions of appropriate convex lenses and to prescribe on the basis of the tests already described.

The appropriate strength of these additions raises important questions. It is certainly true that presbyopic spectacles should never be prescribed mechanically by ordering an appropriate addition based on the age of the patient. Each patient should be tested individually and, as was pointed out by C. G. Hertel (1716), those lenses should be ordered in each case which give the most serviceable and comfortable, not necessarily the clearest, vision for the particular work for which the spectacles are intended. Nevertheless, there is not a great variation between individuals in the way that their accommodation declines. While it is wrong to give a dogmatic rule such as the addition of 1 dioptre for every 5 years above 40, most refractionists formulate their own loose relationship between the age and the presbyopic correction needed by the average patient. It is customary to start with an addition of $+0.75$ D to the distance correction in the first reading spectacles prescribed for a presbyope showing the typical early symptoms of difficulty with newsprint in the evenings or in poor illumination, and it is a safe rule to be wary of increasing a reading addition by more than this amount (0.75 D) for the presbyope whose near correction is no longer adequate.

In all cases *it is better to under-correct than to over-correct* since, if the lenses tend to be too strong, difficulties will be experienced with the association of accommodation and convergence and the range of vision will be inconveniently limited. Short of a formal determination of the positive and negative relative accommodation, a good practical hint is to make sure that with the reading correction it is intended to prescribe the patient is able to read the near-vision chart satisfactorily not only at his reading distance but also some 12 to 15 cm. further away. This will guard against over-correction.

The average subject's accommodation declines so that in the late fifties an addition of about $+2.50$ D becomes necessary and thereafter little further change is required. In any case, a lens which brings the near-point closer than 28 cm. is rarely tolerated (that is, a total power of 3·5 D), and if for any reason the demands of fine work require a higher correction, the convergence should be aided with prisms as well as the accommodation with spheres. Unequal or very powerful additions for near work are often indicated in the presence of medical lesions causing poor visual acuity in one or both eyes. Thus patients with early cataract will often be enabled to read more comfortably with a $+3.5$ D or $+4$ D addition. Even higher additions may be considered as visual aids.[1]

In the normal subject, however, it cannot be too strongly emphasized that the usual cause of strain and discomfort following the prescription of spectacles for presbyopia is over-correction. If the lenses can be reduced in strength without causing a serious deterioration in visual acuity for work at the required range, they should be so reduced; but if this is impossible, the discomfort is usually relieved by adding to the lenses a prism with the base inwards or, alternatively, by decentring the lenses by a corresponding amount.[2] Thus, while the sphere relieves the accommodation, the prism relieves the convergence.

If near work with the reading spectacles still gives rise to trouble which cannot obviously be explained, the relative accommodation and convergence for the working distance must be further considered. It is to be remembered that the positive portion of the relative accommodation (that is, the amount in reserve) must be as large as possible, certainly larger than the negative portion. Similarly, the positive portion of the relative convergence should also be large. If the relative accommodation is deficient, the spherical addition for the working spectacles should be altered; if the patient is working outside the " area of comfort " of his convergence orthoptic exercises should be prescribed or a prismatic correction should be ordered which brings his convergence within it.[3]

Even if there is no astigmatic change in the accommodated state, *the optical value of a spectacle lens used for near work* differs from its value when used for distant vision owing to the fact that in the first case the incident rays of light are parallel, while in the second they are divergent. In order that the latter may be converged to the same focus so that they fall upon the retina, a stronger correction is required than is indicated by the refraction. If the same correction is required for distant and near vision by a non-presbyope for a working distance of (say) 30 cm., the strength of the distance lens must therefore be increased by a factor of about 9% (Percival, 1928). Thus a $+3.0$ D sphere for infinity is optically equivalent to a $+3.27$ D sphere for 30 cm., while the wearer still uses 3·3 D of accommodation (see Appendix Table XXXII). In a presbyope, however, the additional spherical element required for near work has the effect of making the incident light more nearly parallel, and consequently a smaller correction factor is required. When a $+1.0$ D sphere is added, the correcting factor is 6%, when a $+2.0$ D sphere is added the correction is 3%, and when $+3.0$ D sphere is added the incident rays become parallel and no correction is required.

The practical importance of this lies in cases of high cylindrical corrections; for in many of these, if the same spectacles are used for reading as for distant vision, the

[1] p. 796.   [2] p. 674.
            [3] Vol. VI.

result is unsatisfactory. Thus if a +5·0 D cylinder is required for distance, a +5·5 D cylinder is required for near work. To secure adequate centring we shall see later[1] that a special pair of reading spectacles is usually advisable when the astigmatic error is high, even in non-presbyopes, and the opportunity should be taken of incorporating this correction in them.

A slight amount of cyclophoric extorsion usually occurs when the eyes are converged.[2] A slight rotation of a high cylinder, particularly if it is oblique, can be made in the reading lenses in order to neutralize this, thus adding considerably to the comfort of the patient, as well as increasing his visual acuity for close work.

The form of lens which the reading correction may take will be discussed at a later stage.[3]

Abbott. *Arch. Ophthal.*, **25**, 331 (1941).

Bennett. *Ophthal. Optician*, **6**, 1011 (1966).

Berens. *Amer. J. Ophthal.*, **6**, 26 (1923).
Trans. Amer. Acad. Ophthal., **34**, 472 (1929).

Berens and Sells. *Arch. Ophthal.*, **31**, 148 (1944).

Berens and Stark. *XIII int. Cong. Ophthal.*, Amsterdam, **1**, 119 (1929).
Amer. J. Ophthal., **15**, 216, 527 (1932).

Chevallier. *Le conservateur de la vue*, Paris (1815).

Cockerham. *Optician*, **128**, 58 (1954).

Colenbrander. *Klin. Mbl. Augenheilk.*, **99**, 213 (1937).
Ophthalmologica, **99**, 402 (1940).

Cross. *A System of Ocular Skiametry*, N.Y. (1903).
Dynamic Skiametry in Theory and Practice, N.Y. (1911).

Daza de Valdés. *Uso de los antojos para todo genero de vistas*, Sevilla (1623).

Donders. *On the Anomalies of Accommodation and Refraction of the Eye*, London (1864).

Duane. *Ophthal. Rec.*, **18**, 358 (1909).
Motor Anomalies of the Eye, N.Y. (1910).
Arch. Ophthal., **49**, 349 (1920).
Trans. Amer. ophthal. Soc., **19**, 178 (1921).
Amer. J. Ophthal., **5**, 865 (1922); **8**, 196 (1925).

Dubois-Poulsen and Rozan. *Ann. Oculist.* (Paris), **180**, 206 (1947).

Freeman. *Optician*, **126**, 453, 503, 615, 645, 667 (1953–4).

Giles. *Brit. J. physiol. Opt.*, **13**, 190 (1956).
The Principles and Practice of Refraction, London (1960).

Hertel. *Vollständige Anweisung zum Glass-Schleiffen*, Halle (1716).

Himly. *Die Krankheiten u. Missbildungen d. mensch. Auges*, Berlin (1843).

Hodd. *Trans. int. opt. Cong.*, London (1951).

Howe. *J. Amer. med. Ass.*, **67**, 100 (1916).
Trans. Amer. ophthal. Soc., **15**, 145 (1917).

von Jaeger. *Schriftskalen*, Wien (1854); 4th ed. (1867).

Ketchum. *Amer. J. physiol. Opt.*, **7**, 543 (1926).

Lancaster and Williams. *Trans. Amer. Acad. Ophthal.*, **19**, 170 (1914).

Landolt. *Graefe-Saemisch Hb. d. ges. Augenheilk.*, 2nd ed., Leipzig, **4** (1) (1903).

Law. *Brit. J. Ophthal.*, **35**, 765 (1951); **36**, 689 (1952).

Lea. *Optician*, **75**, 469, 478 (1928).

Lee. *Arch. Ophthal.*, **56**, 351 (1927).

Livingston. *Proc. roy. Soc. Med.*, **29**, 59 (1935).

Luckiesh and Moss. *Arch. Ophthal.*, **23**, 941 (1940); **30**, 489 (1943).
Amer. J. Ophthal., **24**, 423 (1941).
Amer. J. Optom., **18**, 249 (1941).

Maddox. *Brit. J. Ophthal.*, **12**, 374 (1928).

Mayer. *Ann. Oculist.* (Paris), **142**, 333 (1909).

Neely. *Brit. J. Ophthal.*, **40**, 636 (1956).

Nicolai. *Ned. T. Geneesk.*, **66**, 1748 (1922).

Nieden. *Zbl. prakt. Augenheilk.*, **6**, 89 (1882).

Nott. *Amer. J. physiol. Opt.*, **6**, 490 (1925); **7**, 366 (1926).

O'Brien and Bannon. *Amer. J. Ophthal.*, **30**, 289 (1947).

Oliver. *Test Words for Determination of the Power of Accommodation*, Phila. (1885).

Pascal. *Optician*, **1**, 399 (1929).
Amer. J. Ophthal., **12**, 29 (1929).
Modern Retinoscopy, London (1930).
Arch. Ophthal., **25**, 859 (1941).

Percival. *The Prescribing of Spectacles*, London (1928).

Sheard. *Amer. J. physiol. Opt.*, **3**, 177 (1922).

Simpson. *Arch. Ophthal.*, **25**, 483 (1941).

Slataper. *Texas St. J. Med.*, **21**, 536 (1926).
Arch. Ophthal., **34**, 389 (1945).

Sloan. *Amer. J. Ophthal.*, **48**, 807 (1959).

Snellen. *Test-types for the Determination of the Acuteness of Vision*, Utrecht (1868).

Swann. *Dynamic Retinoscopy*, London (1939).

Tauber. *Anweisung f. auswärtige Personen wie dieselben a. d. optisch-okulistischen Institut zu Leipzig Augengläser bekommen*, Leipzig (1815).

Thorne. *Amer. J. Ophthal.*, **11**, 555 (1928).

[1] p. 678. [2] Vol. VI.

[3] p. 679.

CHAPTER XI

MALINGERING

THE detection of malingering provides intriguing problems for the ophthalmologist when he meets a patient who denies the presence or absence of vision for no accountable organic reason and has to decide whether he is dealing with a sick hysteric or a wilful cheat. The result may be a battle of wits between the examiner and the examinee wherein the former requires as much subtlety and skill as the latter has determination and shrewdness. As ammunition for this a host of ingenious tests has been evolved, a knowledge of which is essential.

These tests have been devised for many years, and the first to turn his mind pragmatically to the question and introduce several tests was ALFRED CARL GRAEFE [1830–1899] (Fig. 502), a cousin of the great Albrecht von Graefe. He did not rise to the professional heights of his cousin but he carved for himself a place so distinguished in his specialty that the Graefe Medal was established in his memory. He introduced Lister's technique of sterilization into ophthalmology, was the first to observe and remove a cysticercus from the eye, worked enthusiastically and wrote prolifically, his most important contributions being on the disorders of motility of the eyes. He also established the *Klinische Monätsblatter für Augenheilkunde*, at first as a private publication, and shared the editorship of the first edition of the *Graefe-Saemisch Handbuch der gesammten Augenheilkunde* with Theodor Saemisch. Always a frail and sickly individual constantly nursed by his wife, he was nevertheless an amiable and charming companion and no mean poet.

TO MALINGER is *to mislead wilfully with regard to the existence or the seriousness or the origin of a disease or disability in order to gain a desired end.* Several types of malingering may be recognized. SIMULATION is the feigning of a non-existent disease or disability. EXAGGERATION or AGGRAVATION is the pretence that a condition is worse than it is. FALSE ATTRIBUTION is the assignment to a disease or injury of an origin other than the real. DISSIMULATION is the pretence that a disease or disability does not exist, or that its effects are less than they really are. Simulation, exaggeration and false attribution are all aspects of *positive malingering*; they are practised by the same type of person with the same objects in view and will therefore be considered together. Dissimulation is the opposite reaction—a *negative malingering*—and will be noted separately. All of these have important ophthalmological implications.

SIMULATION

POSITIVE MALINGERING—either SIMULATION, EXAGGERATION or FALSE ATTRIBUTION—is usually undertaken to avoid the duties of citizenship (national service, jury service, and so on), to escape unpleasant or dangerous

Fig. 502.—Alfred Carl Graefe
[1830–1899].

tasks (particularly applying to soldiers in war) or to receive or increase financial compensation for a disability. It is a common manifestation of human weakness and is found in three types of person characterized respectively by a normal, a degenerate or a psychopathic mentality (Dufestal, 1888; Jones and Llewellyn, 1917; Spaeth, 1930).

Among normal people SIMULATION is by no means unknown; it may be regarded, indeed, as the logical sequel to the make-believe of the child who may transpose the " let's pretend " of the nursery to shamming a headache to stay away from school. As a rule normal people are bad and inefficient malingerers who lack pertinacity and cold-bloodedness in their deceit, are ashamed of their fabrication and are clumsy in its execution. They present a problem relatively easy to deal with and when confronted with the facts they readily break down. The degenerate malingerer, on the other hand, is secret, solitary and self-contained in his duplicity, logical, obstinate and exceedingly shrewd in carrying it out, and as persistently bent upon his purpose as falling rain, so that to break down his disguise is frequently difficult. The psychopathic malingerer presents an even more difficult problem, for his pretence, frequently assuming hysterical characteristics, may become almost involuntary and is usually consistent: he is found in the hospital ward and provides a puzzling problem in diagnosis.

In general terms the malingerer differs from the hysteric in that the former deliberately deceives others with amoral intent, but not himself, while the latter, without design or malice and without conscious motive, deceives himself (and sometimes others). The former is wicked or lazy; the latter is psychoneurotic. The former hates and tries to escape from examination and may be unco-operative in it to the extent of abuse; the latter revels in it and enjoys it, and does everything to help and show how dramatically bad things are. Moreover, on extended observation the malingerer usually overplays his part when under examination and will frequently lower his defences when he is apparently alone, but the hysteric consistently maintains his attitude while both off and on the stage. Finally, on " recovery " from the symptoms, the hysteric is usually delighted, but the malingerer is shamed in confusion or fights on to the end even when cornered.

The *ocular symptoms* evoked in simulation are protean, their variability depending only on the ingenuity of the individual concerned. The most common expedients used in simulation are as follows:

1. *Self-inflicted injuries*—conjunctivitis, blepharitis or keratitis, or wounds of the lids. These are discussed in a subsequent volume[1] and are particularly common in the evasion of military service; they vary in type from the introduction of irritant chemicals into the eye to deliberate auto-inoculation with a disease so potentially disabling as trachoma, and in results from incidental and temporary harm to permanent blindness.

[1] Vol. XIV.

2. *Visual disturbances*, involving either inability to see owing to amaurosis or amblyopia, either unilateral or bilateral, night-blindness, a defect in colour vision, difficulty in the use of the eyes owing to weakness of sight, photophobia, dazzling, dizziness, and changes in the visual fields. Diplopia is uncommonly simulated.

3. *Motor disturbances* : ocular palsies and blepharospasm. Paralytic cycloplegia may be induced by mydriatics. A spasm of convergence with intermittent nystagmus may be simulated (Elschnig, 1917).

EXAGGERATION is usually applied to a visual defect due to an organic cause, when a severe degree of amblyopia or even amaurosis may be feigned ; vociferous complaints of vertigo, headaches or asthenopia come into the same category.

FALSE ATTRIBUTION usually finds expression in the assertion of a relationship of an existent defect to an industrial or military injury with a view to gaining financial reward : interstitial keratitis, optic atrophy, retrobulbar neuritis, developmental amblyopia, or a pre-existing strabismus, nystagmus or ptosis are the commonest disabilities chosen.

The *diagnosis* of simulated ocular defects is sometimes ludicrously easy for the expedients adopted may be naïve in their transparency ; sometimes it may be extremely difficult, demanding ingenuity and patience on the part of the examiner equal to that of the malingerer. As a rule in clinical work the veracity of a patient is accepted, and it probably often happens that the simulator gets away with his designs ; the real malingerer is detected only if suspicion is excited and the routine clinical examination is supplemented by special tests which serve as dodges to trap the unwary. A very large number of such tests has been devised, many of which will expose both simulated and functional conditions of a hysterical type, all of which are in essence trickery to match trickery, either conscious or subconscious. One point is important : the examiner should know thoroughly the tests he proposes to carry out, for the most important feature in such testing is rapid and sure manipulation ; few succeed unless they are well prepared.

It goes without saying, of course, that in such cases the clinical examination must be done with considerable care, for nothing could be more unfortunate than that organic disease should be stigmatized as functional or treated as if it were pretence. Moreover, functional disturbances and true malingering may co-exist with organic disease ; the two are sometimes difficult to differentiate and it may be deplorable if the latter is missed. Prolonged observation and repeated examinations are sometimes advisable before a final decision is made.

DISSIMULATION

DISSIMULATION, or NEGATIVE MALINGERING, is more rare than its opposite. It is exemplified in the enthusiastic volunteer for military service who memorizes the visual chart or peeks with a better eye while the worse one is being tested, by the candidate for insurance, by the aspirant for a job which necessitates a certain standard of visual acuity or colour vision, or by the convalescent who wishes to return to work. Reasonable care in the ordinary routine clinical testing should make the position plain.

Tests for Functional and Simulated Defects

A. Tests for functional *total blindness* must be objective in nature.

(i) The PUPILLARY REFLEXES may give a valuable clue (v. Graefe, 1855; Heddaeus, 1886–89). If the direct and consensual REACTIONS TO LIGHT are maintained, it is clear that the integrity of the lower visual paths is unimpaired as well as the efferent pupillary paths. The retention of the reflexes, however, does not exclude cortical or subcortical blindness, nor does it exclude hysteria, for in maximal mydriasis or extreme miosis due to spasm the response to light may not be elicited; it does, however, exclude malingering. If the test is made suddenly with strong focal illumination in a dark room, flinching may indicate the presence of vision. Conversely the REFLEXES TO DARKNESS may be usefully employed, for the pseudo-anisocoria sign of Kestenbaum[1] may be used to distinguish a functional blindness in one eye from an organic retrobulbar neuritis. In the application of these tests the possible use of mydriatics by the patient should always be remembered.

(ii) The MENACE REFLEX can frequently be elicited if an object is suddenly approximated to the eye if carried out sufficiently vigorously and abruptly, but it may be suppressed by a determined and practised malingerer.

(iii) The ATTITUDE of the patient in traversing a room with obstacles may be suggestive. A blind man goes carefully and knocks into things naturally; the hysteric often circumnavigates them with success, seeing them, as it were, subconsciously; while the malingerer seems to bump purposefully into them as if to prove his blindness. Again, the simulator will probably sign his name too well or much too badly, and a constant and prolonged watch over his movements usually leads to a breakdown.

(iv) The SCHMIDT-RIMPLER TEST (1871–76). The patient is asked to look at his hand. The blind will look at it (in the absence of corporeal agnosia); the simulator will usually look in any other direction. Similarly the request to touch the two index fingers is readily carried out by the blind with accuracy but causes the malingerer embarrassment (Burchardt, 1894).

(v) A. Graefe's (1867) OBJECTIVE FIXATION TEST may be employed. A light is placed in front of one eye, the other being covered and a 6 Δ prism quickly inserted, base out, in front of the eye. It is extremely difficult for the subject not to fix the light for a short time at least, and on the insertion of the prism the eye will automatically assume fixation by a movement to counteract the deviation caused by the prism if vision is present.

(vi) In the OPTOKINETIC NYSTAGMUS TEST of Bach (1935), nystagmus is automatically elicited when the striped drum of an optokinetoscope is revolved before the eyes.[2] If one eye is examined ophthalmoscopically while the drum revolves before the other a slight nystagmus will be easily observed. This test unmasks both hysterical and simulated blindness.

(vii) HEAD-ROTATION NYSTAGMUS TEST. If the head is passively rotated about 30° alternately to the right and left, the presence of vestibular nystagmus indicates blindness; if the eyes tend to remain in their original position in space a fixation mechanism exists.

[1] Vol. XII.   [2] Vol. XII.

(viii) ELECTRO-ENCEPHALOGRAPHY has been employed in such tests, the assumption being that the normal Berger rhythm is damped down or ceases when light or an object is seen (Lemere, 1942). It would seem, however, from the extended observations of Callahan and Redlich (1946) that while most persons with a normal occipital rhythm as recorded electro-encephalographically and with a normal visual apparatus do show evoked responsive changes in the occipital rhythm when the retina is stimulated by light, there are exceptions, particularly in persons with fast rhythms. Sufficient is not yet known about this subject to allow us to understand the significance of this, but it seems evident that the method cannot differentiate true from false blindness with certainty and cannot have any medico-legal significance.

(ix) The PSYCHO-GALVANIC REFLEX after visual stimulation has been suggested by Callahan and Redlich (1946) as a possible test for simulated blindness. The galvanic skin response is the bio-electric current accompanying the secretion of the sweat glands and vasomotor activity induced by sensory stimuli and various types of psychological situations, and has had considerable applications in criminology as a lie-test, particularly in America (Landis, 1932): it has been applied to distinguish between organic and hysterical anæsthesia of the skin. Stimulation of the eye with an intense light normally produces a deflection, while if the eye is blind, no response is elicited.

B. Tests for simulation of *uniocular blindness*.

While the blindness of the hysteric is usually bilateral, that of the malingerer is usually unilateral. In testing for its functional nature the good eye may be covered up and the tests indicated for bilateral blindness may be carried out with equal applicability. It is to be noted that if the pupils of both eyes react equally to stimulation by light one eye is probably not blind; moreover, if the pupil of the suspected eye is as wide or wider than the other and remains inactive when the eye is exposed to light but contracts on accommodation-convergence, the existence of unilateral amaurosis is likely.

FIXATION TESTS can be made more elaborate. Several tests may be employed depending on the fact that if the visual axis of one eye is deviated by a prism when both are seeing, an automatic rotation of the eye occurs in the opposite direction to avoid diplopia (an *antidiplopic movement*). Such tests prove the presence of binocular fixation and presuppose the existence of binocular single vision. In von Welz's original test (A. Graefe, 1867), while the subject is reading, a prism (10° to 20°) base-out is placed before the alleged blind (or amblyopic) eye. If the patient has appreciable vision this eye will deviate inwards and on removal of the prism, deviate outwards. Smith and Jackson (1900) employed a point source of light at 6 metres for fixation and Duane (1924) suggested that the subject be asked to read aloud rapidly whereupon, if a 4° prism base-down were placed before the suspected eye, his reading would falter owing to the vertical diplopia.

A refinement may be introduced in Schmidt-Rimpler's test of fixating the hand. Both eyes are kept open and the finger which is being fixed is approximated to the eyes until one eye deviates: this should be the allegedly blind eye. Immediately it does, a card is put in front of the fixing eye, whereupon the " blind " eye at once automatically resumes fixation (Falta, 1915).

In addition the following objective test should be noted.

VESTIBULAR TEST. In stimulating the labyrinth by the caloric test, nystagmus is elicited[1] and giddiness occurs. The degree of spatial disorientation and giddiness is

[1] Vol. VI.

counteracted to a considerable extent by vision. If therefore a past-pointing test and an equilibration test are done after labyrinthine stimulation on the side of the allegedly blind eye, these tests should show equal results whether the eye is open or covered if it is blind; if it is not blind, the tests will show more dramatic anomalies if the eye is shut (Goldmann, 1917).

A large number of subjective tests is available for this type of functional defect or simulation, but in all of them the examiner must make certain that both eyes are kept open throughout and that the shrewd malingerer does not momentarily close the " blind " eye to discover what he should see if he is to maintain his deceit.

(i) DIPLOPIA TESTS. Several tests wherein binocular diplopia or triplopia is induced by prisms are of considerable value. In A. Graefe's test (1867) the suspected eye is covered and uniocular diplopia elicited in the good eye by bisecting the pupil with the base (or preferably the edge) of a strong prism. The suspected eye is then quickly uncovered and simultaneously the prism slipped over the whole pupil of the other; if diplopia is still confessed, malingering is proved. A great many modifications of this test have been suggested. Galezowski (1877) used a double refracting lens of Arago to induce diplopia; Fröhlich (1895) used a double refracting prism; Baudry (1897) constructed a special box containing a triangular prism so that the subject could not know what was before his good eye; Todd (1913) used a double prism; and many more. An effective practical test is to make the subject run up and down a stair with a vertical prism in front of his allegedly bad eye.

(ii) Physiological diplopia was utilized by Wessely (1908). A distant object is regarded through two short slightly converging tubes held close to the eyes; then, while distant fixation is maintained, the examiner places a finger immediately in front of the

FIG. 503.—
WESSELY'S TUBES.

tubes, asking how many fingers the subject sees (Fig. 503). The presence of the tubes makes physiological diplopia irresistible if both eyes are being used.

(iii) The transposition of images so that one eye sees the image which should apparently be seen by the other forms the basis of a number of PSEUDOSCOPIC TESTS which can be very effective provided watch can be maintained that the subject does not momentarily close one eye. Ingenious devices (PSEUDOSCOPES) have been designed to exploit this, using mirrors or screens as a basis. The first pseudoscope, depending upon a mirror arrangement whereby the images are reflected so that the patient believes he is seeing with his good eye what he is actually seeing with his allegedly blind eye, was devised by Fles (1860) (*Fles's box*) (Fig. 504), while screens were employed in *Chauvel's box* (1885); many modifications have appeared since (Mareschal, 1879 (Fig. 505); André, 1882; Froidbise, 1883; Bertin-Sans, 1885; and others). Worth's amblyoscope may be used in the same way with the tubes approximated so that the images are crossed. The patient sees that the tubes themselves do not cross and is frequently misled; and his confusion may be increased by using combinations of letters and words to produce different possible results (Snell, 1940). The synoptophore can be used for the same purpose (Singer, 1963).

The same principle can be employed using converging tubes as in the classical Prato's box (Fig. 506) or Gratama's tubes (Koster, 1906; Thies, 1930) (Fig. 507).

The *Bishop Harman diaphragm apparatus*[1] (1910) has a similar application. As

[1] Vol. VI.

the subject looks through the diaphragm the middle portion of an object card is seen binocularly and the ends by the two eyes singly, the right end by the left eye and the left by the right. If the subject reads an entire line he is using both eyes; if he is simulating he rarely appreciates the crossing of vision and may choose to read the print only on the side of the good eye.

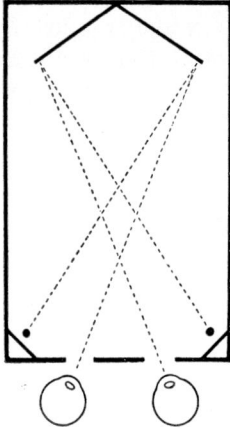

FIG. 504.—FLES'S Box.

Making use of a mirror arrangement.

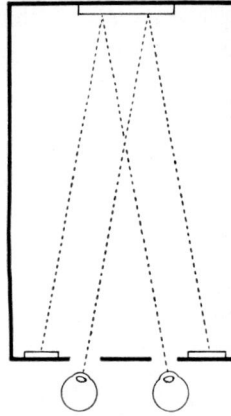

FIG. 505.—MARE-schal's Box.

Making use of a mirror with an arrange-ment different from that suggested by Fles.

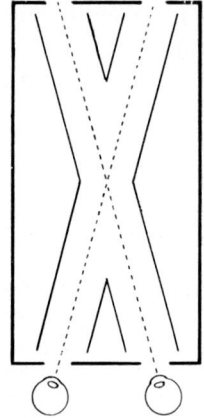

FIG. 506.—PRATO'S Box.

Making use of cross-ing tubes.

Rémy's *diploscope*[1] can be used in the same way.

(iv) FOGGING TESTS are numerous. They depend on obstructing the vision of the good eye while both are kept open; but their success implies that the subject does not close the " defective " eye to find out what he should see. A strong spherical lens, either convex or concave, may be used in this way, slipped in front of the good eye in addition to the refractive error if it is significant, and if reading at a distance continues,

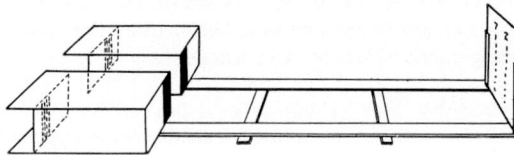

FIG. 507.—GRATAMA'S TUBES.
As modified by Koster.

vision with the other eye is proved (Schenkl, 1875). In Harlan's test (1882) a $+6\cdot0$ D sphere is placed before the corrected good eye and the subject asked to read a card 17 cm. away; as he reads the card is slowly withdrawn; if he continues he must be using the other eye. Similarly in Jackson's cylindrical test (1898) a $+5\cdot0$ D cyl. and $-5\cdot0$ D cyl. are placed in the trial frame with axes vertical; the eye is then suddenly

[1] Vol. VI.

fogged by changing the axes to 15° apart. In Gradle's polaroid test (1937) two polaroid discs are placed in front of the good eye and one in front of the other all with the polarizing axis horizontal; by rotating one of the pair in front of the good eye at right angles the passage of light to this eye is stopped.

(v) *Coloured lenses and charts* or printing with some of the lines or letters in the complementary colours provide a useful means of fogging. Snellen's test (1877) makes use of a red and green lens in front of either eye with red and green writing. The subject sees the red letters only through the red glass, and if he reads them with the red glass in front of the " bad " eye he is malingering. Again, many modifications of this have been made; thus in the Wagner chart the letters are white and black on a pink background, so that, if the red glass is in front of the good eye, the white letters should be obliterated. Bakker (1938) used coloured lights (red, green and yellow) which were suddenly turned on to illuminate the test chart, and Eisner and Haldimann (1966) manipulated the coloured lights of Worth.

The same principle with the test-chart bisected, one half with vertical and one half with horizontal polaroid glass while the subject wears dissimilar polaroid glasses, was suggested by Brackup (1963).

(vi) The BAR TEST of Javal (1868) and Cuignet (1870) depends on the interpolation of a vertical ruler 1·25 in. wide 4 to 5 in. away and midway between the two eyes. If

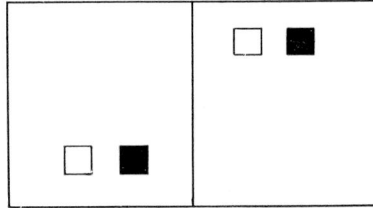

FIG. 508.—ARMAIGNAC'S STEREOSCOPIC PICTURES FOR MALINGERING.

the subject reads from a card with lines 4 in. long without hesitation he must be using both eyes provided the head and the book are kept still; otherwise a portion of the field would be missing. This test has been elaborated among others by Armaignac (1906) and Roth (1907).

(vii) STEREOSCOPIC TESTS have been employed for many years, the patient being tricked into making a composite picture out of uniocular constituents (Rabl-Rückhard, 1874; Roth, 1902). Many types of pictures may be used from simple diagrams (Armaignac, 1906) (Fig. 508) to more complicated devices such as paragraphs of print with an occasional word left out on one or other of the two pictures presented (Figs. 509–10). In the first case the description of the composite diagram or in the second continuous reading betrays the use of the two eyes (Fazio, 1928).

(viii) The VISUAL FIELDS may be utilized for tests for malingering. The blind-spot may be used to trap the unwary in von Szily's test (1920). In alleged uniocular blindness the field is plotted at 2 metres distance on the screen with both eyes open; if blindness does not exist a small target will be seen on the blind-spot of the seeing eye.

In Cuignet's field test (1870) a light is passed across the binocular field; in many cases of alleged uniocular blindness the subject denies vision in one half of the field. In a binocular field test the malingerer will rarely admit to the loss of not more than the temporal crescent.

(ix) DARK ADAPTATION was employed in testing by Beckmann (1912). The test depends on the fact that if one eye is occluded after dark adaptation it retains its adaptation. If in these circumstances the good eye is light adapted and the subject

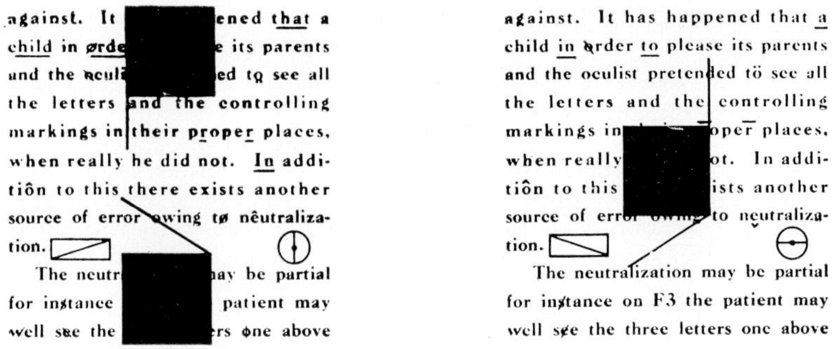

against. It ...ened that a
child in orde... its parents
and the ocul... ed to see all
the letters and the controlling
markings in their proper places,
when really he did not. In addition to this there exists another
source of error owing to neutralization.

The neutr... may be partial
for instance ... patient may
well see the ...rs one above

against. It has happened that a
child in order to please its parents
and the oculist pretended to see all
the letters and the controlling
markings in ...oper places,
when really ...ot. In addition to this ...ists another
source of err owing to neutralization.

The neutralization may be partial
for instance on F3 the patient may
well see the three letters one above

FIG. 509.

In using this plate one begins   spelling.
The reader must also ... able to define
all   small marks w...ch   above or
below the letters. E...ryone who has
already learned to see the ...mer series correctly
will   be able to read the title of this   . ⊙
SHOULD   STILL FAIL WITH THE
SMALL PRINT, ONE MUST BEGIN AGAIN
with   title or pass on to one of the
with larger type. --
After having spellt this line   carefully one starts
again at   beginning.

If one is convinced, that the first word is seen with both eyes, the patient must at once glance from here to the first word of the   or lower line, now this will be seen also with binocular vision and reading can   continued. As soon as notices, by not seeing one   control marks, that one eye deviates, one must begin the experiment just described all over again.

In using this plate   begins by spelling.
The reader must ...so be able to define
all the small mark   which are above or
the lett s.   Everyone who
already learned to see ...e former series correctly
will also be able to read the title   this plate.-O
SHOULD ONE STILL FAIL WITH
SMALL PRINT, ONE MUST BEGIN
with the title or pass   to one of the
lines with larger type. --
After having   this line out carefully one starts
again   the beginning.

If one is convinced, that the   word is seen with both eyes, the patient must at once glance from   to the first word of the upper or lower line, now this will be seen also with binocular vision   reading can be continued. As soon as one notices, by   seeing one of the control   that one eye deviates, one must begin the experiment just described all over again.

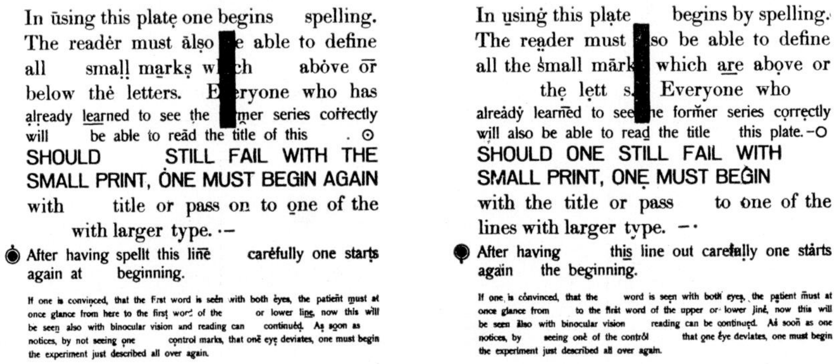

FIG. 510.

FIGS. 509 and 510.—INTERRUPTED READING.

Types of interrrupted reading. Fig. 509 is a stereogram in Javal's series and was included in Sattler's. Fig. 510 is of graded difficulty.

returned to a dark room and the other eye then uncovered, he must be using his supposedly bad eye if he orientates himself rapidly and well.

C. Tests for the simulation of *amblyopia.*

Binocular amblyopia is not uncommonly simulated and is sometimes difficult to detect. Many have learned that the top line or two lines of the test-chart can safely be read, and on the presentation of charts with the upper two lines corresponding to 6/24, 6/18 instead of 6/60, 6/36 they will readily read them. Again tests of vision at 1·5, 3 and 6 metres may reveal that the subject may be able to read the same upper lines at all distances; it is rare for the malingerer to maintain an exact limiting visual angle in these circumstances, for if the distance is reduced by half, letters one half the size should be read. By making the subject look through a tube at the letters he loses his appreciation of distance and is more readily fooled. By means of a reversed chart and a mirror which multiplies the optical distance by two, he may read the same letters at 3 and at 6 metres (Peltzer, 1879; Bichelonne and Cantonnet, 1925). In the same way the magnifying effect of binoculars may not be admitted. The size of the letters may also be varied and charts may be used with the letters not in size-sequence, but intermingled.[1] Thibaudet (1923) used the ingenious method of confusing by testing with figures so constructed that the largest have the smallest optical components; the malingerer analyses these before he admits to seeing the larger constituent elements of a smaller figure (Fig. 511).

Lytton (1942) suggested the use of cylinders in the trial frame. In addition to the correcting lenses $+1 \cdot 0$ D cyl. axis 90° is put in the trial frame together with $-1 \cdot 0$ D cyl. axis 45°, the subject is asked to rotate one of them until vision is clearest. An honest person will arrive at the neutralizing position of 90°, and a dishonest one will rarely admit to the normal decrease of about 50% of vision when the cylinders are at

FIG. 511.—THE MALINGERING TEST OF THIBAUDET.

The malingerer claims to resolve the detail of the larger figure on the right and not of the smaller figure on the left, although the former subtends the smaller visual angle.

right angles. Whatever vision the subject claims when the two cylinders are at right angles cannot be less than half his real corrected vision.

Baudry (1897) asked the subject to read, and if he said he was unable, placed $+6 \cdot 0$ D sphere in front of his eyes. The malingerer might be persuaded to read now holding the print close. Saying he was now to double the strength of the glasses, he neutralized the convex spheres with corresponding concave spheres, at the same time drawing the print away. If the malingerer continues to read, a measure of his acuity may be obtained.

Occasionally good vision with spectacles is admitted, but little or none without correction—a matter sometimes of importance in relation to military service. There is a definite correlation between uncorrected vision and the refractive error, a subject already discussed[2] (Agatston, 1944; Eggers, 1945); if this relationship is not adhered to, malingering should be suspected and the above tests can be made.

Electro-encephalography may be able to detect simulated amblyopia since in simulated blindness the electroretinogram and the evoked visual responses in the electro-encephalogram are normal, although it must be remembered that some hysterical patients may be able to cause a block in the flow of visual information at a subcortical level (Adams *et al.*, 1969). It must also be remembered that these responses may be

[1] Adler (1896), Roth (1906), Terson (1909), Kern and Scholz (1912), Bjerke (1917), Lindberg (1930), Casanovas (1963), Chen (1963), Pelz (1964), and others.
[2] pp. 261, 270.

normal in cases of apparent blindness associated with extreme mental retardation (Harcourt, 1969) (Fig. 512).

Simulated *amblyopia in one eye* can be investigated with many of the tests used for uniocular blindness, and many of them—the fogging tests, the Cuignet bar test, pseudoscopic tests, the Bishop Harman test, and others —may be employed to determine the actual visual acuity of the "amblyopic" eye provided the subject can be tricked into the belief that he is using the good one at the time. The pseudoscopic mirror test, using letters printed on glass at the back of the box, lends itself well to this (Chauvel, 1885).

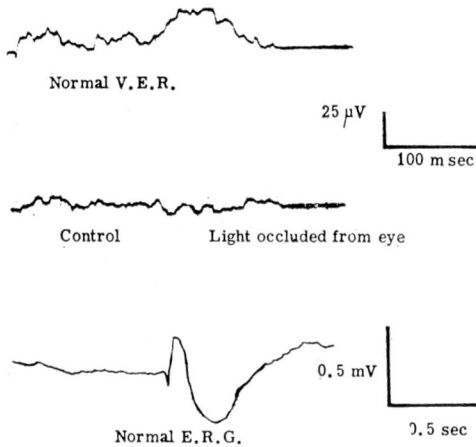

Normal V.E.R.

25 µV

100 m sec

Control   Light occluded from eye

0.5 mV

Normal E.R.G.   0.5 sec

Fig. 512.—Apparent Blindness due to Mental Retardation in a Micrencephalic Child.

The ERG and VER are normal but there is no clinical response to visual stimulation (R. B. Harcourt).

D. The simulation of *night-blindness* is frequent in war when it may spread like an epidemic disease and is notoriously difficult to prove apart from prolonged observation. Tests by different photometers may reveal inconsistencies greater than can be explained by the inaccuracies of these instruments.

An ingenious test was devised by Epstein and Lesser (1945) applicable to individuals with normal macular function. After a period of dark adaptation the subject is tested on an adaptometer[1] showing a red light of wave-length 680–720mμ obtained by the use of a Dufay-Chromex filter. Since light of this wavelength stimulates the macular cones and not the rods, the threshold is normal in the night-blind; the malingerer, however, regarding it as a test of night-vision, will not usually admit to this.

A further test depends on the fact that Purkinje's phenomenon[2] is reversed in essential nyctalopia. If a blue and a red disc are viewed in equal intensity of illumination and the illumination gradually diminished, to the normal person the red becomes more rapidly black than the blue; to the night-blind without retinal lesions the reverse

[1] Vol. IV, p. 557.   [2] Vol. IV, p. 627.

occurs; the simulator will either give the normal sequence or more probably say that they both disappear simultaneously.

A third useful test depends on the elicitation of optokinetic nystagmus using a revolving black drum painted with white strips in very dim illumination. If the subject sees the drum the involuntary movements of the eye can be observed by red light or by the use of a contact lens with spots of luminous paint.

E. The simulation of *abnormalities in the visual fields* usually involves the claim of concentric contraction or a hemianopia, frequently affecting the lower quadrant (Klein, 1907; Pichler, 1917; Goldstein, 1918; and others). The simulation of a central scotoma is rare (Klauber, 1917). It is to be remembered that a true constriction of the field to 10° is incompatible with normal orientation, and a loss of the lower field with walking about and escaping obstacles or going readily down stairs. The menace reflex coming from a " blind " portion of the field will also frequently expose simulation. As a rule such defects are easily exposed by repeated tests on various instruments, perimeters and screens, in which case the malingerer can rarely adhere consistently to a constant relationship of the visual angle if the size of the targets and the distance of testing are suitably varied; thus the field may remain constant whatever the size of test-object (Lincoff and Ennis, 1956), or the contour varies between centripetal and centrifugal displacement of the test-object (Kluyskens, 1958). The appreciation of distance can also be varied by the use of convex lenses (Schmidt-Rimpler, 1892).

The fixation point may also be varied: thus if the field is taken in the ordinary way and then taken with a new fixation point placed eccentrically, an organic constriction is orientated as before concentrically around the new fixation point, but in a functional or simulated field the tendency to keep to the old centre is almost irresistible so that the new fixation point becomes eccentric in the second field (Klein, 1907; Klauber, 1917). Schmidt-Rimpler (1871–76) deceived the malingerer by the use of a prism. Several tests are available by this means. The binocular fields may be taken ordinarily and then retaken with a prism before one eye to distort the seeing area: the increase in binocular field is not readily admitted by the simulator. In the case of uniocular constriction or if the fields are unequal, the test-object may be put just outside the limits of the smaller field and within the larger; both eyes are now opened and a strong prism placed in front of the affected eye. In an organic constriction the patient will see two fixation points and one test-object; in a functional case the subject may claim he sees only one of both (in which case he is untruthful) or two of both (in which case the smaller field is larger than was claimed).

Optically elicited movements may be of great value in elucidating a functional constriction of the field in hysteria or malingering when the patient denies seeing anything in the periphery. An object is held in the periphery, the patient denies seeing it, but when asked to look at it, does so directly, thus proving he had seen it since he knows where it is. Such a test can frequently be done without the patient realizing that his field is in fact being tested.

Conversely *acoustically elicited movements* may detect malingering. The patient is asked to turn his eyes towards a noise; this a blind man will do accurately, but sometimes a malingerer will not.

F. The simulation of *diplopia*, or usually the persistence of diplopia, is generally exposed by repeating several times the classical tests with coloured lenses before the eyes and noting inconsistencies.[1]   A simple expedient is to put a prism in front of one eye and ask how many images are seen : confronted with a real diplopia the malingerer frequently claims that he sees three or four objects.

Adams, Arden and Behrman.   *Brit. J. Ophthal.*, **53**, 439 (1969).

Adler.   *Ber. dtsch. ophthal. Ges.*, **25**, 325 (1896).

Agatston.   *Arch. Ophthal.*, **31**, 223 (1944).

André.   *Recueil Mém. Méd. Chir. Pharm. milit.*, **38**, 627 (1882).

Armaignac.   *Ann. Oculist.* (Paris), **135**, 142 (1906).

Bach.   *Klin. Wschr.*, **14**, 1505 (1935).

Bakker.   *v. Graefes Arch. Ophthal.*, **139**, 267 (1938).

Baudry.   *Arch. Ophtal.*, **17**, 550 (1897).

Beckmann.   *Woenno med. J.*, **233**, 120 (1912).

Bertin-Sans.   *Ann. Hyg. publ.* (Paris), **14**, 340 (1885).

Bichelonne and Cantonnet.   *Le simulateur devant l'ophtalmologiste-expert*, Paris (1925).

Bjerke.   *Z. ophthal. Opt.*, **5**, 55 (1917).

Brackup.   *Amer. J. Ophthal.*, **56**, 659 (1963).

Burchardt.   *Praktische Diagnostik d. Simulation*, 3rd ed., Berlin (1894).

Callahan and Redlich.   *Amer. J. Ophthal.*, **29**, 1522 (1946).

Casanovas.   *Med. clin.* (Barcelona), **41**, 92 (1963).

Chauvel.   *Arch. Méd. Pharm. milit.*, **6**, 129 (1885).
    Recueil Ophtal., **8**, 225 (1886).

Chen.   *Trans. ophthal. Soc. Sin.*, **2**, 56 (1963).

Cuignet.   *Recueil Mém. Méd. Chir. Pharm. milit.*, **26**, 320 (1870).

Duane.   *Fuchs's Text-book of Ophthalmology*, 8th ed., Phila., 241 (1924).

Dufestal.   *Des maladies simulées chez les enfants*, Paris (1888).

Eggers.   *Arch. Ophthal.*, **33**, 23 (1945).

Eisner and Haldimann.   *Ophthalmologica*, **152**, 411 (1966).

Elschnig.   *Klin. Mbl. Augenheilk.*, **58**, 142 (1917).

Epstein and Lesser.   *Brit. med. J.*, **2**, 644 (1945).

Falta.   *Wschr. Ther. Hyg. Auges*, **18**, 177 (1915).

Fazio.   *Arch. Ottal.*, **35**, 31, 72, 133 (1928).

Fles.   *Arch. belge Méd.*, **25**, 170 (1860).

Fröhlich.   *Klin. Mbl. Augenheilk.*, **33**, 263 (1895).

Froidbise.   *Arch. méd. belg.*, **23**, 239 (1883).

Galezowski.   *Gaz. Hôp. Paris*, **50**, 75, 115 (1877).

Goldmann.   *Z. Augenheilk.*, **37**, 77 (1917).

Goldstein.   *Dtsch. Z. Nervenheilk.*, **59**, 198 (1918).

Gradle.   *Amer. J. Ophthal.*, **20**, 300 (1937).

von Graefe.   *v. Graefes Arch. Ophthal.*, **2** (1), 266 (1855).

Graefe, A.   *Klin. Mbl. Augenheilk.*, **5**, 53 (1867).

Harcourt.   *Proc. roy. Soc. Med.*, **62**, 556 (1969).

Harlan.   *Trans. Amer. ophthal. Soc.*, **3**, 400 (1882).

Harman.   *Trans. ophthal. Soc. U.K.*, **30**, 56 (1910).

Heddaeus.   *Die Pupillarreaktion auf Licht, ihre Prüfung, Messung u. klin. Bedeutung*, Wiesbaden (1886).
    Klin. Mbl. Augenheilk., **26**, 410 (1888).
    Arch. Augenheilk., **20**, 46 (1889).

Jackson.   *Phila. med. J.*, **1**, 695 (1898).

Javal.   *Du strabisme dans ses applications à la théorie de la vision* (Thèse), Paris (1868).

Jones and Llewellyn.   *Malingering*, Phila. (1917).

Kern and Scholz.   *Sehprobentafeln*, Berlin (1912).

Klauber.   *Wien. klin. Wschr.*, **30**, 1170 (1917).

Klein.   *Arch. Psychiat. Nervenkr.*, **42**, 359 (1907).

Kluyskens.   *Bull. Soc. franç. Ophtal.*, **71**, 64 (1958).

Koster.   *v. Graefes Arch. Ophthal.*, **64**, 502 (1906).

Landis.   *Psychol. Bull.*, **29**, 693 (1932).

Lemere.   *J. Amer. med. Ass.*, **118**, 884 (1942).

Lincoff and Ennis.   *Amer. J. Ophthal.*, **42**, 415 (1956).

Lindberg.   *Finska Läk.-Sällsk. Handl.*, **72**, 840 (1930).

Lytton.   *Brit. J. Ophthal.*, **26**, 512 (1942).

Mareschal.   *Recueil Mém. Méd. Chir. Pharm. milit.*, **35**, 437 (1879).

Peltzer.   *Dtsch. militärärztl. Z.*, **8**, 604 (1879).

Pelz.   *Klin. Mbl. Augenheilk.*, **145**, 329 (1964).

Pichler.   *v. Graefes Arch. Ophthal.*, **94**, 227 (1917).

Rabl-Rückhard.   *Dtsch. militärärztl. Z.*, **3**, 172 (1874).

Roth.   *Das Stereoskop u. d. Simulation einseitiger Sehstörungen*, 4th ed., Berlin (1902).
    Verwechselungs-Sehproben z. Nachweis d. Vortäuschung v. Schwachsichtigkeit, Leipzig (1906).
    Ueber Simulation v. Blindheit u. Schwachsightigkeit u. d. Entlarvung, Berlin (1907).

Schenkl.   *Ärztl. Korresp.-Bl. Prague*, 205 (1875).

---

[1] Vol. VI.

Schmidt-Rimpler. *Berl. klin. Wschr.*, **8**, 526 (1871).
   Klin. Mbl. Augenheilk., **14**, 173 (1876).
   Dtsch. med. Wschr., **18**, 561 (1892).
Singer. *Cs. Oftal.*, **19**, 366 (1963).
Smith and Jackson. Norris and Oliver's *System of Diseases of the Eye*, Phila., **4**, 801 (1900).
Snell. *Treatise on Medicolegal Ophthalmology*, St. Louis, 231 (1940).
Snellen. *Klin. Mbl. Augenheilk.*, **15**, 303 (1877).

Spaeth. *Arch. Ophthal.*, **4**, 911 (1930).
von Szily. *Klin. Mbl. Augenheilk.*, **65**, 1 (1920).
Terson. *Arch. Ophtal.*, **29**, 453 (1909).
Thibaudet. *Arch. Ophtal.*, **40**, 105 (1923).
Thies. *v. Graefes Arch. Ophthal.*, **123**, 691 (1930).
Todd. *Ophthalmology*, **9**, 81 (1913).
Wessely. *Ber. dtsch. ophthal. Ges.*, **35**, 339 (1908).

SECTION III

BINOCULAR FACTORS IN REFRACTION

Fig. 513.—Johann Zahn

[?1641–?1707].

(In his book, *Oculus artificialis teledioptricus sive telescopium*, 1685, by courtesy of the Library of the British Optical Association.)

CHAPTER XII

ANISOMETROPIA

History

Although the existence of differences in refraction in the two eyes must almost certainly have been known for many years, the usual way of dispensing spectacles was to have identical lenses in each eye based essentially on the subject's age since in the vast majority of cases they were given for presbyopia. We shall see in a subsequent Chapter that these were usually sold by itinerant and peddling spectacle-dealers and the presbyopic subject chose the strengths which he thought suited him best; much the same method of choice, of course, was commonly employed in multiple stores until recent years—a practice, however, now not permitted in Britain. Although Kohlhans (1663) and Dechales (1674) pointed out that frequently one eye needed a concave and the other a convex lens, the first study of the condition of anisometropia was by an obscure German monk, JOHANN ZAHN (?1641–?1707) (Fig. 513), a member of the Premonstratensian Order in Herbipolis (Würzburg). He published an important treatise on optics in 1685–6 comprising three volumes written in Latin, Vol. 3, Chapter 1, being devoted to spectacle lenses. Zahn undoubtedly practised the craft of an optician, testing the sight of his patients and grinding the lenses they needed as indicated by subjective tests. He insisted that the two lenses of a pair must correspond in material and form but pointed out that the same lens is not always suited to both eyes of the same ageing person. In any event, when Donders (1864) wrote his classical book introducing refraction to the medical profession as an art and a science, he noted that opticians, when necessary, put two different lenses in the same spectacle frame.

In this Section we shall discuss those factors which must be considered in the correction of refractive errors if efficient and comfortable binocular vision is to be attained. They comprise a difference in the refraction between the two eyes (*anisometropia*), a difference in the sizes of the images formed on the two retinæ (*aniseikonia*) and a *disturbance in the muscular balance* so that the two images do not readily fall on corresponding retinal areas. It will be remembered that the condition of aphakia involves a high degree of both anisometropia and aniseikonia so that the correction of uniocular aphakia must receive special notice.

Absolute Anisometropia

ANISOMETROPIA (ASYMMETROPIA) is the term applied to that condition wherein the total refractions of the two eyes are unequal. As was pointed out by Donders (1864) it is found in every possible variety: one eye may be emmetropic and the other of any other denomination, hypermetropic, myopic or astigmatic, or both eyes may be ametropic, the refraction differing in degree or in kind. Joseph (1936) proposed the following classification:

1. One eye emmetropic, the other hypermetropic or myopic—SIMPLE HYPERMETROPIC or MYOPIC ANISOMETROPIA.

2. Both eyes unequally hypermetropic or myopic—COMPOUND HYPER-METROPIC or MYOPIC ANISOMETROPIA.

3. One eye hypermetropic, the other myopic—MIXED ANISOMETROPIA (ANTIMETROPIA).

4. One eye emmetropic, the other astigmatic—SIMPLE ASTIGMATIC ANISOMETROPIA.

5. Both eyes unequally astigmatic—COMPOUND ASTIGMATIC ANISO-METROPIA.

THE ÆTIOLOGY OF ANISOMETROPIA

Apart from the uncommon instances of uniocular disease or injury anisometropia is clearly genetically determined (Steiger, 1913; Gallus, 1924; Lebensohn, 1924; Mächler, 1928; Waardenburg, 1930; Cattaneo and Romagnoli, 1960; and others). The hereditary factors which act on the two eyes determining the differing refractions are as obscure as those which in other subjects dictate that the refractions will be similar. It is doubtful if the development of anisometropic myopia should be considered in a separate category from congenital anisometropia since it is very likely that the development of myopia is largely influenced by heredity.

As far as the actual components of refraction are concerned, the axial length is the most significant factor in determining anisometropia (Mauthner, 1876; Steiger, 1913; Waardenburg, 1930; Tron, 1935); both the cornea and the lens exert considerably less influence and of the two the latter is the more important, but in some cases the cornea may even counteract the anisometropic influence of the axial length (Sorsby et al., 1962).

THE INCIDENCE OF ANISOMETROPIA

In the strictly mathematical sense anisometropia is almost invariable. In the clinical sense, however, the two eyes are usually very much alike considering the variability of the optical components in the refractive system and their developmental evolution, the symmetry extending not only to the degree of ametropia, but to the direction of astigmatic axes (Risley and Thorington, 1895). Particularly in the higher degrees of refractive errors, however, differences up to 3 D are common and disparities up to 34 D (Joseph, 1936) or 36 D (Oliver, 1921) have been recorded.

Estimates of *the percentage incidence of anisometropia* of significant degree vary considerably; Hess (1896–97) found 50% and Gallus (1924) 20%. van der Meer (1901) found the following incidence among high hypermetropes: bilateral high hypermetropia, 121; emmetropia associated with high hypermetropia, 73; different degrees of hypermetropia, 18; and hypermetropia associated with myopia, 3. Joseph (1936) found that for inequalities greater than 3 D the most common association was an unequal degree of myopia: compound myopic anisometropia, 38%; simple myopic anisometropia, 26%; compound hypermetropic anisometropia, 6%; simple hypermetropic, 4%; mixed anisometropia, 26%.

The vision in anisometropia of significant degree may be binocular, alternating or exclusively uniocular.

Binocular vision is the rule in the smaller degrees of the defect. Each 0·25 D difference between the refraction of the two eyes, however, causes 0·5% difference in size between the two retinal images, and a difference of 5% is probably the limit which can usually be tolerated with ease.[1] Moreover, since the uncorrected image of one eye is always blurred, binocular vision is rarely perfect, and attempts at fusion frequently, although by no means always, bring on symptoms of accommodative asthenopia. The symptomatology of this group thus resembles that of small refractive errors.

With the higher grades of error, fusion is usually impossible, and one of two alternatives offers itself.

Alternating vision may result, in which case each of the two eyes is used one at a time. This is especially apt to occur when they both have good visual acuity, and when one is emmetropic or moderately hypermetropic and the other is myopic, in which case, as was pointed out by Donders (1864), the patient falls into the easy and legitimate habit of using the former for distant vision and the latter for near work; thereby he may remain very comfortable and, indeed, be quite unaware of his defect and, if the anisometropia is mixed, require no optical correction for any distance at any time in life. On the other hand, if the defect in one eye is high, and more especially if its visual acuity is not good, it may be excluded altogether from vision, the other and better eye alone being relied upon in uniocular vision. In this event the defective eye may become amblyopic and not uncommonly deviates.

Theoretically, the ideal treatment is the full optical correction of each eye in order to produce a distinct image on the retinæ of both. In practice, this course is satisfactory and usually advisable when dealing with small refractive differences, but in the case of the higher grades difficulties present themselves when ordinary spectacles are employed, associated particularly with the difference in size of the images and irregularities of peripheral distortion. These frequently necessitate a modification of this simple procedure. The adult usually has difficulty in wearing ordinary spectacles when the difference between the two eyes is greater than 2 D. The difference in size of the images may be diminished by the optical correction, but the patient's difficulties are enhanced by the appreciation of two sharply defined and unequal images whereas before one of them was blurred and therefore easily neglected. The greatest discomfort, however, is due to the artificial heterophoria created whenever the eyes move from the primary position:

[1] p. 516.

with 2 D difference in optical correction, 1 prism dioptre of deviation is incurred if the gaze deviates 5 mm. from the optic axis. In hypermetropic anisometropia these prismatic effects may lead to a narrowing of the effective field of binocular vision thereby encouraging the development of amblyopia in children, a result not necessarily seen in myopic anisometropia (Ruben, 1965). Theoretically these difficulties may be overcome by the use of *iseikonic*[1] or *contact lenses*,[2] or systems of multiple lenses with all of which considerable differences may be reconciled. If these optical compromises fail to give comfort or are not obtainable, binocular correction of the anisometropia must be abandoned.

It follows that the treatment of these patients cannot be standardized. Each case must be considered separately, attention being paid to the amount of discomfort and the disability from which the patient is suffering without correction and the amount he is likely to experience with it, always bearing in mind the advantages of binocular vision, and the importance in young people of retaining the potentialities of an eye for vision.

In children (under the age of 12) every attempt should be made to induce the full correction to be worn; the younger the child the more persistent should be the attempt, the easier it will prove, and the more successful will be the result. There is evidence, for example, that a significant improvement in the reading age of young children can thus be obtained (Eames, 1964). When binocular vision is weak or muscular imbalance is marked, orthoptic exercises should be undertaken, and when a squint has developed this should receive the proper treatment. Even in the absence of a squint the more ametropic eye may become amblyopic and occlusion of the better eye may be necessary to improve the vision; the type of occlusion should depend on the degree of suppression, for it should be remembered that there is a risk of a latent squint becoming manifest if one eye is occluded for any length of time so that an unstable binocular relationship may be disrupted.

In adults with small grades of anisometropia and any degree of binocular vision—certainly in those with a difference of 2 D—an attempt should be made to wear the full correction, and the spectacles should be used constantly. In these circumstances, after a few weeks' difficulty, the symptoms of strain will happily disappear. It occasionally happens that a marked anisometropia with good vision when corrected in each eye is discovered in middle age, perhaps during a refraction for presbyopia. If spectacles have never been worn it is frequently difficult to decide whether the anisometropic correction is desirable or whether it is preferable merely to correct the less ametropic eye. No hard and fast rules can be given but it is sometimes worth a trial period with the full anisometropic correction; most of such patients will, however, be unable to tolerate it. In an adult with alternating vision—one eye being hypermetropic and used for distance and the other myopic and

[1] p. 682.   [2] p. 782.

used for near work—unless there are definite symptoms of eye-strain the condition is usually best left alone or, if it is indicated, he should be provided with spectacles which enable each eye to perform its separate functions comfortably; in most adult cases this will be found the best plan to adopt.

Several ancillary expedients may be tried to aid the tolerance of anisometropic spectacles before deciding to abandon the binocular correction. Thus the differences in size of the retinal images may to some extent be compensated by varying the base curve of the two lenses.[1] The stronger plus lens or the weaker minus should have a relatively flat back surface, while the back surface of the weaker plus or stronger minus lens should be deeply curved: thus a plus lens on a −12 D base-curve magnifies the size of the image 1·6% as compared with a flat lens. The lenses may be placed at

unequal distances from the eyes (Eggers, 1937; Zoubek et al., 1963; Polásek and Zoubek, 1967), an effect which can be attained to a small extent by making one flat and the other toric. If, however, despite optical devices, symptoms of eye-strain, headache or dizziness persist, and if the alternative of iseikonic lenses is not available, some compromise will be necessary, such as an under-correction of the more ametropic eye, in which case a small reduction will often bring comfort; alternatively, the eye habitually used (usually the more emmetropic) may be corrected and the other provided with the same lens. At the same time attention should be given to the correction of the artificial heterophoria in deviations of gaze to prevent diplopia. The patient should be instructed to turn his head instead of his eyes in looking to the

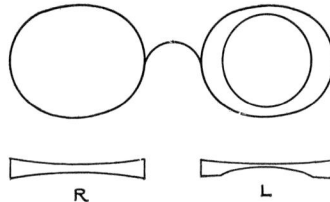

FIG. 514.—ANISOMETROPIC SPECTACLES.

In myopia in which the left eye has a higher myopic refraction than the right. The periphery of the lens of the left eye has the same correction as the lens of the right.

side in order to avoid the prismatic effect produced by the periphery of the lenses. This annoyance may be minimized by making the margin of the stronger lens weaker, so that it is equal to that of the other lens, as in Fig. 514, and thus, when the patient looks to the side, both eyes are corrected equally. The prismatic action of the periphery of lenses may be very evident in near work, for on looking down through the lower part of the lens, a convex lens acts as a prism base-up and a concave lens as a prism base-down, so that diplopia is thereby produced. When a myopic eye and a hypermetropic eye are thus associated, a certain amount of comfort in reading binocularly may sometimes be obtained on neutralizing this action by cementing a correcting prism onto the lower portion of each lens as a bifocal; but it is usually wiser to prescribe a separate pair of reading spectacles carefully centred and tilted so that the visual axes in the reading position pass normally through them.[2]

Many of the problems associated with anisometropia are resolved by the use of *contact lenses*.[3] Both the artificial heterophoria due to dissimilar spectacle lenses and also the aniseikonia appear to be largely eliminated. Thus we shall see that in uniocular aphakia where there is marked hypermetropic anisometropia, contact lenses have an important part to play. It is somewhat surprising but nevertheless well established that the aniseikonia

[1] p. 655.　　　　　　[2] p. 679.
[3] Littwin (1947), Comberg (1950), Alajmo (1953), Zamorani et al. (1964), Spaeth and O'Neill (1960), Ruben (1965).

of myopic anisometropia is also considerably ameliorated by contact lenses (Littwin, 1947; Phillips, 1959). A relative magnification of the retinal image in a myope is to be expected when the correcting lens is closer to the eye than the spectacle point. It is, however, possible that the retinal cones are spread out in highly myopic eyes and that this may act as a compensating factor. It is to be noted that the increasing use of contact lenses in childhood and even in infancy[1] offers hope that gross anisometropes, if discovered early, may avoid amblyopia in the more ametropic eye, and may allow the development of full binocular functions (Ruben, 1965).

FIGS. 515 and 516.—ANISOMETROPIC SYSTEMS.

Point focal anisometropic systems giving an equal-sized image at the fovea with an emmetropic eye free from oblique astigmatism for rotations of 25° from the direction of the axis (M. von Rohr and H. Boegehold).

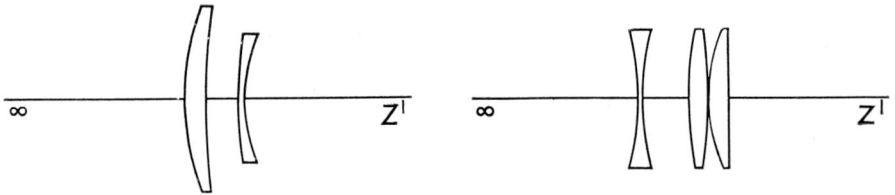

FIG. 515.—For a − 7·00 D.S. vertex refraction.

FIG. 516.—For a + 13·00 D.S. (aphakic) vertex refraction.

In marked anisometropia a *compound lens system* may be of value when other expedients such as varying the curvature of the lens, its thickness or its distance from the eye or even the use of iseikonic lenses fails to attain binocular vision. Such a system requires a combination of three lenses but the expedient has not been popularized because of the weight and cumbersomeness as well as the expense of the spectacles, their optical limitations and the difficulty of their computation.[2] von Rohr's system for myopia is seen in Fig. 515; the reversed Galilean system for aphakia is seen in Fig. 516. The computation is such that equal retinal images are received free, or nearly so, from oblique astigmatism up to a marginal angle of 25° of field for aphakia (+13 D) and myopia as high as −20 D, each associated with an emmetropic fellow eye.

Relative Anisometropia

By the term RELATIVE ANISOMETROPIA we are designating that type of refractive anomaly wherein, although the total refraction of the two eyes is equal, or approximately so, the component elements in each show relatively large differences. Reuss (1877–80), using the Helmholtz ophthalmometer, was the first to draw attention to the essential differences which may occur in isometropic eyes, and we have already seen, for example, that emmetropia has occurred both with an axial length of 22·42 mm. associated with a refractive power of 64·12 D and an axial length of 27·30 mm. with a refractive power of 52·59 D (Tron, 1934–35). In the two eyes of the same individual of equal total refraction (+10 D), Tron found a difference in axial length of 0·65 mm.

[1] Sato and Saito (1959), Cassady (1963), Blaxter (1963), Girard (1964).
[2] von Rohr and Stock (1912–13), Wolff (1912–19), Hegner (1912), Löwenstein (1913), Erggelet (1916), von Rohr (1917–21).

and in refractive power of 1·79 D. It is true that such combinations will give equally clear retinal images, but it is also obvious that the differences in optical construction will result in differences in the size of the retinal images and in the diameter of the diffusion circles. This subject will be considered more fully in the Chapter on aniseikonia, as well as the problem of the attainment of binocular vision in the uniocular aphakic patient who retains good vision in his phakic eye.

Alajmo. *G. ital. Oftal.*, **6**, 436 (1953).

Bennett. *Optician*, **150**, 395, 422 (1965). *Ophthalmic Optician*, **8**, 301 (1968).

Blaxter. *Trans. ophthal. Soc. U.K.*, **83**, 41 (1963).

Cassady. *Amer. J. Ophthal.*, **56**, 305 (1963).

Cattaneo and Romagnoli. *Ann. Ottal.*, **86**, 261 (1960).

Comberg. *Klin. Mbl. Augenheilk.*, **116**, 18 (1950).

Dechales. *Cursus seu mundus mathematicus*, Lugdunum (1674).

Donders. *On the Anomalies of Accommodation and Refraction of the Eye*, London (1864).

Eames. *Eye, Ear, Nose, Thr. Monthly*, **43**, 36 (1964).

Eggers. *Arch. Ophthal.*, **17**, 328 (1937).

Erggelet. *Z. Sinnesphysicl.*, **49**, 326 (1916).

Gallus. *Klin. Mbl. Augenheilk.*, **73**, 491, 771 (1924).

Girard. *Corneal Contact Lenses*, St. Louis (1964).

Hegner. *Klin. Mbl. Augenheilk.*, **50** (2), 273 (1912).

Hess. *v. Graefes Arch. Ophthal.*, **42** (2), 80 (1896); **43**, 257 (1897).

Joseph. *Bull. Soc. Ophtal. Paris*, 421 (1936).

Kohlhans. *Admiranda optica seu tractatus opticus*, Leipzig (1663).

Lebensohn. *Illinois med. J.*, **46**, 254 (1924).

Littwin. *Arch. Ophthal.*, **38**, 259 (1947).

Löwenstein. *Z. ophthal. Opt.*, **1**, 97 (1913).

Mächler. *v. Graefes Arch. Ophthal.*, **120**, 540 (1928).

Mauthner. *Vorlesungen ü. d. optischen Fehler d. Auges*, Wien (1876).

van der Meer. *Onderzoek d. oogen van de leeringen van het stedelijk gymnasium en van de middelbare Scholen te Amsterdam gedurende 1898* (Diss.), Amsterdam (1901).

Oliver. *Brit. J. Ophthal.*, **5**, 68 (1921).

Phillips. *Brit. J. Ophthal.*, **43**, 449 (1959).

Polásek and Zoubek. *Augenoptik*, **84**, 52 (1967).

Reuss. *v. Graefes Arch. Ophthal.*, **23** (4), 183 (1877); **26** (3), 1 (1880).

Risley and Thorington. *J. Amer. med. Ass.*, **5**, 852 (1895).

von Rohr. *Arch. Augenheilk.*, **82**, 31 (1917). *Graefe-Saemisch Hb. d. ges. Augenheilk.*, 3rd ed., *Die Brille als optisches Instrument*, Berlin (1921).

von Rohr and Stock. *v. Graefes Arch. Ophthal.*, **83**, 189 (1912); **84**, 152 (1913).

Ruben. *Proc. roy. Soc. Med.*, **58**, 112 (1965).

Sato and Saito. *Contacto*, **3**, 419 (1959).

Sorsby, Leary and Richards. *Vision Res.*, **2**, 43 (1962).

Spaeth and O'Neill. *Amer. J. Ophthal.*, **49**, 548 (1960).

Steiger. *Die Entstehung d. sphärischen Refraktionen d. mensch. Auges*, Berlin (1913).

Tron. *v. Graefes Arch. Ophthal.*, **132**, 182 (1934); **133**, 211 (1935).

Wolff. *Z. Augenheilk.*, **28**, 149 (1912); **40**, 235 (1918). *Z. ophthal. Opt.*, **7**, 10 (1919).

Waardenburg. *Klin. Mbl. Augenheilk.*, **85**, 169 (1930).

Zahn. *Oculus artificialis teledioptricus sive telescopium*, Würzburg (1685–6).

Zamorani, Merlin and dal Fiume. *Ann. Ottal.*, **90**, 479 (1964).

Zoubek, Polásek and Hamák. *Sborn. ved. Praki lék. Fak. Hradci Králové*, **6**, Suppl., 523 (1963).

Fig. 517.—Adelbert Ames
[1880–1955].
(Courtesy of Dr. Paul Boeder, Iowa).

CHAPTER XIII

ANISEIKONIA

ANISEIKONIA (ἀ, privative; ἴσος, equal; εἰκών, an image), a term coined by Walter B. Lancaster in 1932, is the condition wherein *the images presented to the cortex from the two eyes are abnormally unequal in size or shape*. The difference in size is relative and aniseikonia becomes apparent only in binocular vision.

HISTORY

That equal retinal images could not be formed on the two retinæ in anisometropia was recognized by Donders (1864) and in the latter half of the last century a number of ophthalmologists proved experimentally the asymmetry of such images and discussed the possible clinical bearing of their discrepancy—Wadsworth (1876) of Boston, and Culbertson (1888) who investigated the effect of a concave cylinder held before one eye, Wadsworth (1883) who investigated the distortions caused by prisms, Lippincott (1890) of spheres and Green (1889) of different types of spectacle lens. Subsequently Risley (1899), Duane (1901) and Delogé (1906) pointed out the optical difficulties presented by anisometropia, and the impossibility of its correction to attain equality of the retinal images was demonstrated by Erggelet (1914). Although the placing of correcting lenses at the anterior focal points of the eyes equalizes optical differences in the sizes of the images due to the presence of spectacles in axial ametropia (Cattaneo, 1927), a proper understanding of the whole problem of size-differences was prevented by lack of adequate methods of clinical measurement. This, and the enthusiasm to persevere with a difficult piece of research, were provided by Ames and his associates in the Dartmouth Eye Institute (1932–45) where, for the first time, an adequate attempt was made to elucidate the theoretical importance of this subject and to equalize the dioptric images in clinical practice.

ADELBERT AMES [1880–1955] (Fig. 517) was a New Englander who obtained a degree in law at Harvard University but, after practising this profession for four years, he turned to painting, an activity which focused his interest on visual problems on which he did research in Clark University from 1914 to 1917. In the first World War he served as an aerial observer, whereafter, in 1919, he went to Hanover in New Hampshire to resume his studies on binocular vision and visual perception. From these resulted the foundation in 1937 of the Dartmouth Eye Institute, largely financed by the Rockefeller Foundation and the American Optical Company, a clinical and research organization housing some 40 research workers, of which he became director and professor of physiological optics (1921). The main interest of the institute, apart from other problems in ophthalmic optics, was the development of instrumentation and techniques for the measurement of aniseikonia and the binocular perception of space, a subject which demanded as much patience as optical ingenuity. Although the Dartmouth Eye Institute closed in 1949, its contributions to visual science both in its optical and psychological aspects, exerted a significant influence on the development of this branch of physiological optics not only in America but throughout the world; for a time W. B. Lancaster and A. Bielschowsky worked there, and in its relatively short life it was responsible for stimulating such distinguished researchers as R. E. Bannon, H. M. Burian, S. H. Bartley, A. Linksz and K. N. Ogle.

The clinical importance of aniseikonia is thus a comparatively late concept in ophthalmological thought. A great deal of work was done upon both the theoretical and practical aspects of Ames's teaching in America and little elsewhere, and no significant advances have emerged during the last two decades. The theoretical implications of aniseikonia, particularly with regard to spatial perception, are profound and clear; the practical importance of its clinical application is not so fully established, and since the investigation of the optical defects involved is a time-consuming business demanding elaborate apparatus, and their correction necessitates lenses which are difficult and expensive to manufacture and are not generally available, it is natural that widespread control investigations in different countries have been few. The position is further complicated by the fact that the response of patients to treatment must be judged subjectively rather than objectively, and in America itself agreement has by no means been reached on the value of the technique.[1] It follows that this chapter must be written in a somewhat tentative way. Theoretically, however, it would seem reasonable to assume that if comfortable binocular vision requires the suitable presentation to consciousness of two approximately equal images, the clarity of focusing the images (the refraction) and their formation on corresponding retinal points (the muscle balance) should not only be considered to the exclusion of their relative size.

THE CAUSES OF ANISEIKONIA

A difference in the size and shape of the retinal images of the two eyes occurs normally. This *physiological aniseikonia* (or *retinal disparity*) is of a very small order and the slight differences which necessarily exist between the two images because of the lateral separation of the eyes are responsible for the stereoscopic interpretation of space. Such a difference is increased when objects are laterally placed and is particularly marked when the objects are close; indeed, in asymmetrical convergence it may become of the order of 5 to 10% or more. This discrepancy, however, is compensated psychologically and gives rise to no symptoms, being used as the perceptual basis whereon our judgments of the position and distance of the object are formed (Herzau and Ogle, 1937; Lancaster, 1942). Moreover, it will be

---

[1] See among others Hughes (1935), Ludvigh (1936), Jackson (1937), Berens and Loutfallah (1939), Post (1942–46), Burian (1943), Crisp (1943), Hicks (1943), Cushman (1945), Macnie (1948), Linksz (1959), Berte and Harwood (1961), Bourdy (1961), Berens and Bannon (1963).

remembered that the retinal images are normally asymmetrically distorted in the horizontal meridian relative to the axis of vision, usually increasing progressively in size across the visual field, being smaller on the nasal side and larger on the temporal, a condition which shows itself in the Hering-Hillebrand horopter deviation.[1]

Luminance Aniseikonia. A perceptual aniseikonia can be produced with two normal eyes if the size of the retinal image in one is changed by altering the apparent luminance of an object as seen by one of the eyes, for the size of the retinal image depends not only on the size of the object and the effects of diffraction and aberration but also on its luminance. Of two equally large objects the brighter will appear to be the larger (Weale, 1954). Thus in Fig. 518 if AB is a white object on a dark background and a neutral density filter (F) is placed before the right eye, the image (a_o) as seen by this eye appears to be smaller than that seen by the left (a_u) owing to the reduction of retinal irradiation. It follows that the projection into space of the boundaries of the two images will intersect at A′ and B′ instead of at A and B, resulting in a distortion of space.

ANOMALOUS ANISEIKONIA, on the other hand, can theoretically be caused by one of two distinct factors : it may be an optical phenomenon depending on a difference in the size of the dioptric images formed on the retinæ, or it may be anatomically determined by a difference in distribution of the retinal elements. With regard to the first factor, the difference between the dioptric images may depend on a difference between the refraction of the two eyes, and is therefore present in some degree in most cases of *anisometropia*. The size of the image is governed essentially by the distance of the second nodal point from the retina, and consequently a further degree of aniseikonia may be determined by differences in the magnification effectivity of any correcting lenses, and is varied by the power, shape, and the position at which they are worn and, if the anisometropia is astigmatic, the correction of the refractive error may increase an asymmetrical aniseikonia. Even if the anisometropia is relative and the same degree of ametropia is compounded of a different combination of axial and refractive elements, the sizes of the retinal images are unequal. With regard to the second factor, it is quite obvious that even if dioptric images of exactly the same size were formed on the retina, they would be appreciated as such only if the distribution of

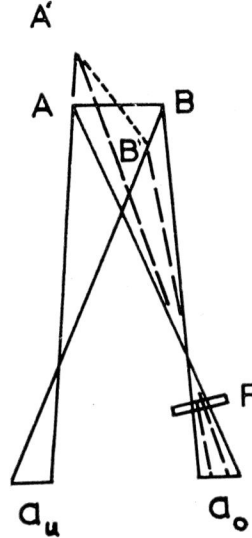

FIG. 518.—LUMINANCE ANISEIKONIA.

AB is a white object on a dark background. a_u and a_o are the images in the unobstructed and obstructed eyes respectively. The filter, F, in front of the right eye reduces the apparent size of AB owing to the reduction of retinal irradiation. The projection of the boundaries of the smaller image at a_o will intersect those of the image from the left eye at A′ and B′ respectively, thus distorting space (R. A. Weale).

[1] Vol. IV, p. 680.

rods and cones were identical; if, for example, the visual elements were more widely separated in one eye than the other, the image received by the brain would appear to be smaller in the first since fewer end-organs were stimulated. Little is known about this, but it is presumed that anatomical considerations explain the occurrence of aniseikonia in cases wherein the dioptric mechanism cannot account for the phenomenon (Ames *et al.*, 1932).

Ætiologically, therefore, abnormal aniseikonia may be classified as:

(*a*) Optical aniseikonia.
> (i) Inherent—depending on the dioptric system of the eye.
> (ii) Acquired—depending on the correcting lenses worn, their power, position, thickness and form.

(*b*) Anatomical—depending upon the density of the retinal mosaic and perhaps other factors at a perceptual level concerned with the simultaneous perception of the two visual images—a matter about which little is known.

The *incidence* of aniseikonia is difficult to assess and must depend upon the degree of difference in size which may be considered abnormal and may therefore be presumed to give rise to symptoms. From work on horopter settings and on aniseikonic differences it would appear that the threshold for the discrimination of size-differences between the ocular images is of the order of 0·25%.[1] The difference which may give rise to symptoms is presumably larger than this. The amount which gives rise to symptoms, as occurs with refractive errors and heterophoria, varies greatly with the sensitivity, the state of health and the occupation of the patient, and it is generally stated that a difference of 1% is potentially significant. Measurements have shown that significant differences of size are relatively common even in emmetropia (Hughes, 1937). Burian (1943) found that 93% of air cadets in the United States had 0·5 per cent. or less size-difference between their retinal images and 100% 1 per cent. or less. In contradistinction to this highly selected population, 33% of students showed 0·5 per cent. or less, 70% measured 1 per cent. or less, 23% showed 1 to 2 per cent. and 7% had over 2 per cent. In England Gillott (1957) found that in an unselected population of 100 subjects, 42% had a size-difference greater than 0·8 per cent, and 7% greater than 3 per cent; it is likely that the incidence in ophthalmic patients would be higher than this. It is probable that a discernible amount of aniseikonia occurs in from 20 to 30% of people who wear spectacles and the greatest degrees are seen in corrected uniocular aphakia where a difference of 33 per cent.[2] makes binocular vision intolerable.

The *types of size-difference* embraced under the generic term aniseikonia have been classified by Ames and his colleagues (1932) as follows:

---

[1] von Kries (1909), Fruböse and Jaensch (1923), Fischer (1924), Tschermak (1924), Herzau (1929), Ames and Ogle (1932), and many others.

[2] p. 376.

FIGS. 519–526.—TYPES OF ANISEIKONIA.

Representing superimposed ocular images presented to the brain.

Images presented by the Right Eye

FIG. 520.—Overall enlargement.

FIG. 521.—Horizontal meridional enlargement.

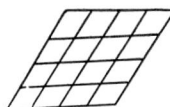

FIG. 522.—Oblique meridional enlargement.

The image presented by the Left Eye

FIG. 519.

FIG. 523.—Meridional enlargement horizontally and diminution vertically.

FIG. 524.—Asymmetrical enlargement in one direction (horizontal).

FIG. 525.—Asymmetrical enlargement in all directions.

FIG. 526.—Asymmetrical diminution in all directions.

1. SYMMETRICAL DIFFERENCES (differences in size).

(a) *Overall*, the retinal image of one eye being symmetrically larger or smaller than that of the other (Figs. 519–20).

(b) *Meridional*.

(i) The retinal image of one eye being symmetrically larger or smaller in one meridian than that of the other (Fig. 521). This meridional difference may be oblique (Fig. 522).

      (ii) The retinal image of one eye being symmetrically larger in one meridian and smaller in another than that of the other eye (Fig. 523).

2. ASYMMETRICAL DIFFERENCES (differences in shape).

(*a*) There is a progressive increase or decrease in size across the visual field (Fig. 524). This is the effect produced by an ordinary flat prism (Ames *et al.*, 1932).

(*b*) There is a progressive increase or decrease in size in all directions from the visual axis (pin-cushion or barrel distortion) (Figs. 525–6).

(*c*) Irregular distortions or warping may occur, or combinations of any of the above.

So far only regular incongruities have been investigated and measured, but there is evidence that irregular incongruities exist determined either by the dioptric condition of the eye or the pattern of the retinal mosaic. Irregularities in the dioptric mechanism may produce irregular incongruities of the images, and these may vary at different angular distances. Again, the images from the nasal side of the retinæ may be greater than those from the temporal producing an anomalous horizontal incongruity. In such a case a flat surface normal to the observer may appear convex towards him or flat and nearer. If, on the other hand, the incongruity is greater temporally than nasally, the surface may appear concave or flat and farther away (Ames, 1945).

Data on the clinical *incidence of the various types* of aniseikonia are scanty. Rayner (1966) reviewed some 682 patients who had iseikonic lenses prescribed by the American Optical Company, classifying the various types as spherical, cylindrical or axial anisometropia; much the most common anomaly was a combination of all three.

SYMPTOMS

The symptoms of aniseikonia may be classified as visual and subjective; the visual symptoms concern binocular vision and stereoscopic spatial perceptions, while the subjective symptoms are those of eye-strain.

Binocular Vision. We have already seen that small differences in size (under 0·25%) are not generally appreciated and it would seem likely that these do not impair binocular vision. As a general rule differences up to 5% can be compensated by the plasticity of the visuo-perceptive processes, but the fact that such compensation impairs the effectiveness of perception of depth is suggested by the finding that after the correction of such disparities stereopsis has been found to be markedly improved (Burian, 1943). When the difference is in excess of this, binocular vision becomes difficult or impossible (Hosaka, 1955; Gillott, 1957; Bourdy, 1961). Ordinarily, escape from such a situation is attained by suppression in one eye at an early stage in life and comfort is obtained in uniocularity; but if binocular vision has already been well established and a sudden marked aniseikonia is introduced (as occurs typically in aphakia), diplopia results. It is significant that differences of the order of 5 to 15% have been found in cases of strabismus and it is not improbable that the difficulty of fusion in such circumstances —or even the aversion to fusion described as " horror fusionis "[1]—may have not a little to do with the causation, the perpetuation and the difficulties of treatment in such cases (Bielschowsky, 1935–36).

Spatial Perception. We have already seen[2] that our perceptions of space are mediated by two mechanisms, one of an extrinsic nature based on perceptual judgments derived from past experiences and the other of an

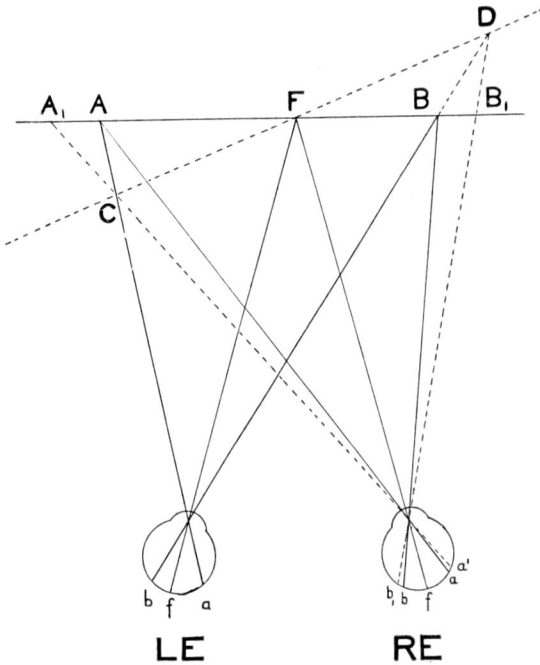

FIG. 527.—TO ILLUSTRATE SPATIAL DISTORTION IN ANISEIKONIA (see text).

intrinsic nature based on the stereoscopic effect derived from the slightly dissimilar images received by the two eyes on account of their lateral separation. In the first mechanism spatial perceptions may be appreciated by one eye alone; the second depends on the association of the two eyes. It is obvious that if normal binocular spatial localization is based on a system of normal incongruity of the ocular images, when the incongruity of the ocular images differs from normal, anomalous spatial localization must necessarily occur involving apparent changes in the environment.

Figure 527 will make this clear wherein a meridional size-lens magnifying the image in the horizontal meridian is placed before the right eye of an iseikonic individual.

[1] Vol. VI.   [2] Vol. IV, p. 691.

Before such a lens is placed in position, if the eyes are converged on an object F, two objects A and B on the horopter will be imaged on corresponding retinal points a and b. After the size-lens has been placed before the right eye all sizes in the horizontal meridian will be magnified to this eye (AB appearing as A_1B_1) and the retinal image in the right eye will be represented by $a'\ b'$, while that in the left eye has remained unaltered. Since the only object which can simultaneously stimulate the two retinal points a in the left eye and a' in the right is C, A will appear to have moved forwards to C. Since the only object which can stimulate the two retinal points b in the left eye and b' in the right is D, B will appear to have moved backwards to D. The horizontal disparity thus created results in a stereoscopic distortion and the plane AB appears to be rotated around the fixation point F to CD.

The angle of such notation (ψ) is given by Ogle's (1932–38) formula:

$$\psi = \frac{(m-1)\ b}{(m+1)\ a}$$

when m is the magnification, b the fixation distance and a one-half the inter-pupillary distance.

If the horizontal disparity of the retinal images which is responsible for stereoscopic effects is disorientated in this way, well-defined effects are produced which can readily be experienced by anyone by holding an iseikonic lens of zero power magnifying in the horizontal meridian before one eye (say the right). If two vertical rods in a frontal plane are looked at, one appears farther away than the other. Objects in the right half of the field appear larger and yet farther away than objects of the same size and at the same distance in the left field. A flat surface such as a table slants down on the right and up on the left, and the ground seems to show the same tilt to the observer who imagines he is walking on a hill. Objects will be correspondingly distorted; the right hand is larger than the left, the face is asymmetrical with the right side protruding, squares become rectangles, circles ellipses, and the top of the table a trapezoid. If such an experiment is maintained over a length of time these unusual experiences gradually wear off. Burian (1943) found that if such a lens were worn for 3 or 4 days these distortions gradually disappeared provided the subject stayed in the ordinary surroundings to which he had been habituated, or remained in surroundings abundant in perspective, but they returned again if he entered an environment with few rectilinear perspective factors to guide his visual judgments. It would seem that if there were perspective clues in sufficient quantity, the perceptual mechanism of spatial perception based on judgments derived from experience would be sufficiently potent to dominate the stereoscopic factors causing disorientation, allowing a re-interpretation of the retinal stimuli; but when these aids became few and scanty and so less effective, the disorientation returned. As would be expected, there is a considerable individual difference in this reaction, for in some persons the uniocular perceptual factors quickly dominate the disorientated localization derived from retinal disparity, while in others the stereoscopic mechanism appears to relinquish its hold much more slowly. The same phenomenon is seen every day in the varied reaction of different individuals to new spectacles, particularly in the case of anisometropic astigmatic errors, and the differences in the time taken to become accustomed to the spatial disorientations which they necessarily cause.

The *induced effect* of Ogle (1950) is an astonishing reaction which is not yet understood. When a vertical disparity of the retinal images is produced and studied experimentally, the magnification of the retinal image in the vertical meridian of one eye produces a sense of spatial distortion identical with that caused by the magnification of the retinal image of the fellow eye in the horizontal meridian. This observation accounts for the fact that the lens producing over-all magnification leads to comparatively little spatial distortion since the vertical component in front of one eye leads to an induced horizontal effect as from the fellow eye, thus balancing the horizontal " geometrical " effect of the lens in front of the original eye. The process of gradual adaptation to artificially induced aniseikonia in the horizontal meridian described by Burian (1943) is similarly seen as aniseikonia in the vertical meridian. An induced obliquely orientated aniseikonia, however, may excite little adaptation even after a prolonged period of time (Miles, 1948).

From these experimental observations it follows that patients with aniseikonia and binocular vision do not ordinarily experience spatial disorientations owing to prolonged adaptation; the retinal disparity is disregarded and reliance is placed upon perspective clues. If, however, they become fatigued or if they are transposed to surroundings in which there is a minimum of uniocular perspective clues such as in aviation or, in certain circumstances, in motoring, distortions in space become evident with resulting errors in the judgment of distances. This condition of instability is comparable to a latent heterophoria which becomes manifest when fusion is lost; in both cases the defect is present all the time but is elicited only in special circumstances.

Such a divorce from perceptual aids in the judgment of distances has been made the basis of two tests to demonstrate aniseikonia: they depend upon the creation of conditions which eliminate perceptual clues in the formation of spatial judgments and call for stereoscopy alone. The " tilting field " test comprises a flat plane with an irregular pattern of detail on its surface free to rotate in all directions on a pivot (Fig. 528). A screen arrangement allows one eye to see the tilting field only and the other eye its frame and surroundings, and the test lies in setting the tilting surface parallel to its frame (Ames, 1935).

The " leaf room " forms a very dramatic demonstration (Ogle, 1943). This is a rectangular box open at one end, to the black walls, ceiling and floor of which are stapled artificial vines with leaves individually adjusted so that they stand out from the surface. When properly illuminated the leaves provide many contours to stimulate binocular stereoscopy and a minimum of perspective clues, and as he looks into the box the aniseikonic (or artificially aniseikonic) observer describes apparent positions, shapes and sizes of the walls and leaves in gross distortions which are characteristic of each type of incongruity. The normal observer has merely to look into such a room wearing a size-lens to convince himself of the reality of aniseikonia. Hosaka and Kato (1965) have used a similar technique in measuring aniseikonia.

The *subjective symptoms* of aniseikonia have given rise to some controversy. They are generally described as those typical of asthenopia[1]—ocular discomfort with burning and itching of the eyes, blurred vision and fixational difficulties, visual fatigue particularly evident at close work or in watching moving objects (exemplified in the cinema, motoring and travelling in trains), headaches of various types and photophobia (Hughes, 1935–37; Berens, 1937; Berens and Loutfallah, 1939; Macnie, 1948; and others). To these have been added general symptoms of fatigue, irritability, lack of concentration, nervous tension, gastric disturbances, nausea and indigestion.

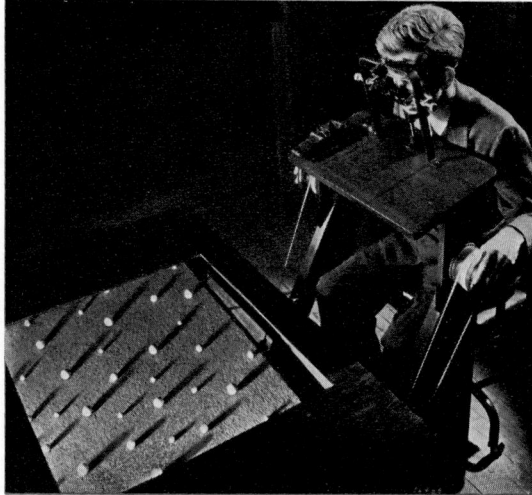

FIG. 528—THE TILTING FIELD (American Optical Co.).

It will be noted that none of these is distinctive or specific to the condition, all of them are common to the general state of eye-strain and most of them may well have a large functional element in their motivation. In some hypercritical patients, however, whose occupations demand absolutely accurate space perception, such as artists or engineers, spatial disorientation may be a presenting symptom, but this is surprisingly uncommon. Finally, in this discussion of symptoms relevant to aniseikonia, it is to be remembered that many normal subjects who have significant and measurable degrees of aniseikonia may be completely free of symptoms.

The evaluation of the significance of these symptoms except, perhaps, the last, is obviously a matter of elimination. Aniseikonia as a clinical anomaly, however, should be considered in a patient complaining of typical asthenopic symptoms which persist after a satisfactory correction of his refractive error or muscular imbalance. If the symptoms are unrelated to the use of the eyes, they are unlikely to be due to aniseikonia. If doubt is

[1] p. 559.

felt, therapeutic criteria may be applied, for example, the effect of a suitable iseikonic correction given as a clip-on lens can be noted. The essentially binocular nature of the problem in aniseikonia is illustrated by a uniocular occlusion-test in which genuine aniseikonic symptoms are said to be relieved. Unfortunately, in neither of these cases is the result really conclusive.

CLINICAL MEASUREMENT

The initial method proposed for the measurement of aniseikonia was the theoretically simple expedient of presenting two images, one to each eye, in a reflecting stereoscope; fusion was prevented by employing dissimilar objects of the same size of such a design that discrepancies between them could be readily assessed.

The simpler type of instrument—the original EIKONOMETER of Ames and his colleagues (1932)—was essentially a haploscope. Two targets were presented, one to each eye, reflected in mirrors (MM₁), as seen in Fig. 529; the targets (Fig. 530) had identical circles at the centre which were fused, while peripherally the dots on one target should lie in the centres of the dash lines on the other (Fig. 531). Any enlargement will appear as a disalignment as seen in Fig. 531. The difference in size was then

FIGS. 529–531.—THE ORIGINAL EIKONOMETER OF AMES.

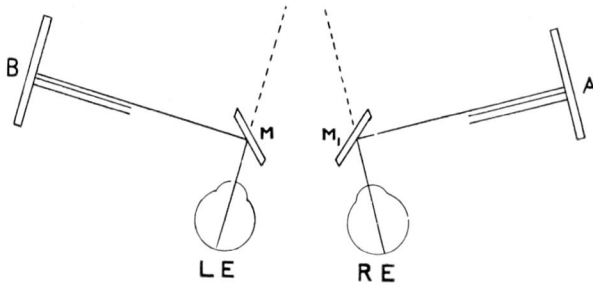

FIG. 529.—The haploscopic arrangement of the instrument.

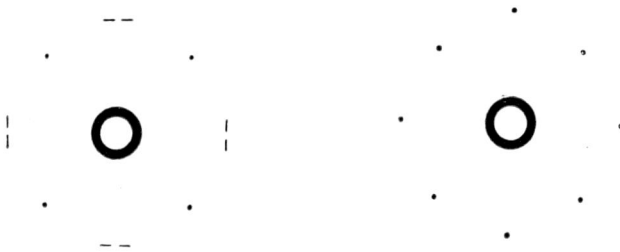

FIG. 530.—The targets presented to the two eyes.

FIG. 531.—On the left, coincidence of the elements in each target denotes iseikonia; on the right disalignment denotes aniseikonia.

FIGS. 532–536.—THE STANDARD EIKONOMETER (A. Ames *et al.*)

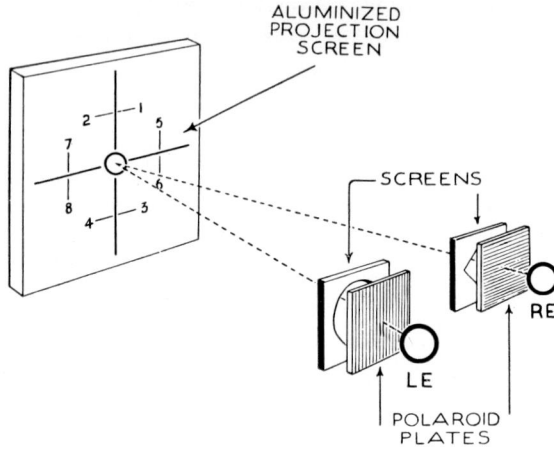

FIG. 532.—The general principle of the eikonometer.

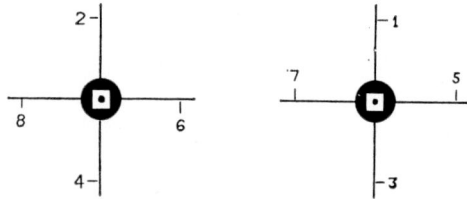

FIG. 533.—The targets, polarized in different directions, presented to the two eyes.

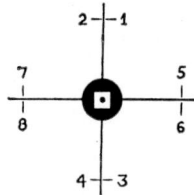

FIG. 534.—The binocular appearance in iseikonia.

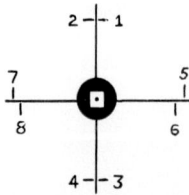

FIG. 535.—The appearance in horizontal disparity.

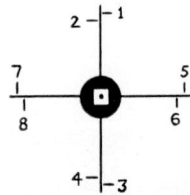

FIG. 536.—The appearance in horizontal and vertical disparity.

measured by neutralizing with zero power iseikonic lenses which magnify the image either over-all or meridionally as the case required (Ames *et al.*, 1932).

In a later model—the *standard eikonometer* (Fig. 532)—the target used is composed of four pairs of lines arranged round a central fixation mark (Fig. 533). The central fixation mark is seen by both eyes; the light from the lines bearing even numbers is polarized in one direction so that they are seen by one eye through the appropriate polarizing filter; the light from the lines bearing odd numbers is polarized in

FIG. 537.—THE STANDARD EIKONOMETER.

Side view showing
A. Forehead-rest control.	F. Inter-pupillary adjustment.
B. Chin-rest control.	G. Dioptre test-lens cells.
C. Chin-rest.	H. Eikonic lens-unit cells.
D. Corneal aligning device.	I. Apertures.
E. Housing for near target.	J. Slots to hold polarized plates.

(American Optical Co.).

the other direction so that they are seen by the other eye. When there is no aniseikonia the target appears as in Fig. 534; different types of aniseikonia appear as in Figs. 535–6.

The standard instrument with its necessary fittings for support of the head, placement for the optical correction and the necessary adjustments, is seen in Fig. 537 (Ogle, 1942; Ogle and Ames, 1943). A more complicated instrument—the OPHTHALMO-EIKONOMETER—measures not only the aniseikonia but also the refractive error by stigmatoscopy and the heterophoria.

By such instruments errors of less than 0·25% can be measured subjectively and are repeatable on the same patient at different times with considerable accuracy (Ogle *et al.*, 1940). The method, however, necessitates eye movements 4° out from the fixation point in all directions, and is unsatisfactory for patients with marked heterophoria, the presence of which may, indeed, vitiate the measurements. To obviate this, other techniques have been introduced, such as a modification of Hering's horopter apparatus (Ames *et al.*, 1932), or the comparator (Field, 1943), but probably the most convenient and simple technique so far devised is the space eikonometer of Ames (1945). It has the advantages of being satisfactory in the presence of heterophoria or poor fixation and can be employed even in the absence of good central stereoscopic vision provided peripheral stereopsis is present.

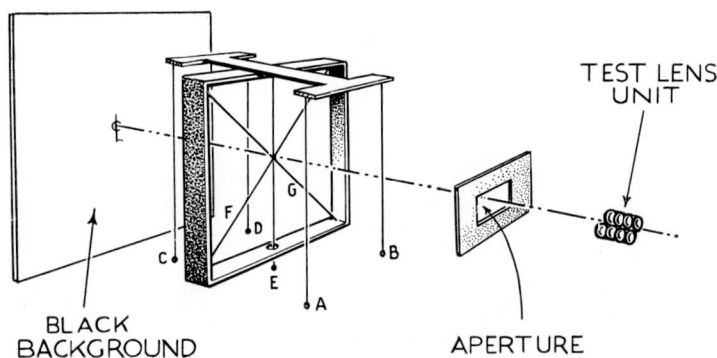

FIG. 538.—THE GENERAL PRINCIPLE OF THE SPACE EIKONOMETER.

The SPACE EIKONOMETER (Fig. 538) is based upon the fact that when the incongruity of the ocular image differs from normal, anomalous spatial localization must necessarily result. If spatial localization is removed from accessory aids and uniocular clues, and the patient has to rely solely upon disparities of the images of the two eyes, it can be used satisfactorily as a measure of aniseikonia (Ogle *et al.*, 1943–45; Ames, 1945; Burian and Ogle, 1945; Ogle and Madigan, 1945).

The principle of the space eikonometer is seen in Fig. 538. It consists of four vertical plumb lines (A, B, C, D) arranged two in front and two behind a cross consisting of two cords at right angles (F, G). A fifth vertical plumb line (E) passes through the centre of the cross. The whole is viewed through a test-lens unit upon a uniform background. When no anomalous incongruity of the ocular images is present, the elements of the eikonometer appear in their normal relationships, all of them lying in planes normal to the binocular line of sight; if an anomalous incongruity exists the elements will appear to be displaced by an amount proportional to the degree and in a direction corresponding to the type of incongruence, and this can be measured by neutralizing the displacement by the appropriate iseikonic lenses set in the trial test-unit.

Figs. 539–543.—The Appearances seen with the Space Eikonometer.
(The arrows indicate the direction of observation) (after A. Ames).

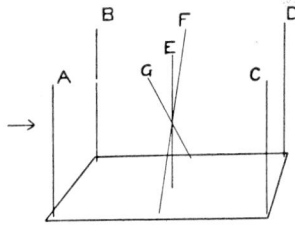

Fig. 539.—Normal localization, normal ocular images.

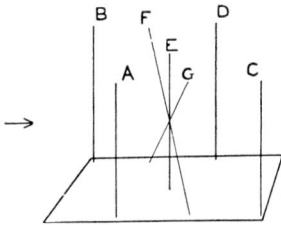

Fig. 540.—Anomalous localization; horizontal disparity.

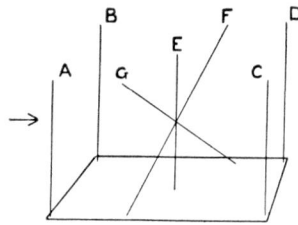

Fig. 541.—Anomalous localization; vertical disparity.

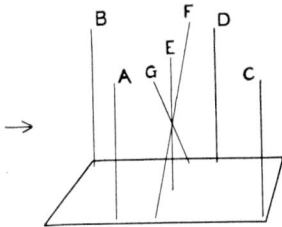

Fig. 542.—Anomalous localization; overall size difference.

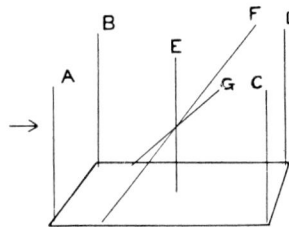

Fig. 543.—Anomalous localization;
size difference at an oblique axis.

Thus while the normal appearance is as in Fig. 539, with a horizontal size-difference there is an apparent displacement of the front and back vertical cords and the cross seems turned around a vertical axis in the same direction (Fig. 540). A rotation of the cross with correct orientation of the vertical cords indicates incongruence in the vertical direction (Fig. 541). Rotation of the vertical elements and not the cross indicates overall discrepancies (Fig. 542), and tilting of the cross indicates meridional discrepancies (Fig. 543).

It is interesting that Ogle (1943) found a high correlation between measurements taken with the standard eikonometer and those obtained on the space eikonometer.

In clinical examination three measurements are made (Ogle and Ellerbrock, 1945). The image size-difference in the horizontal meridian is determined by finding what magnification must be introduced before one eye in the horizontal meridian to make the two front cords of the instrument appear equidistant from the subject: in this measurement the sensitivity is of the order of 0·05% in magnification of the images of the two eyes. The image size-difference in the vertical meridian is then determined by finding what magnification must be introduced before one eye in the vertical meridian in order to correct any apparent rotation of the cross about a vertical axis: the standard deviation is of the order of 0·07% in magnification of the images of the two eyes. Finally, the declination error, which is indicative of a meridional aniseikonic error at an oblique axis, is determined by finding the angle through which the geared size-lenses must be turned to correct any apparent inclination of the cross about a horizontal axis: in this measurement the sensitivity is of the order of 1°.

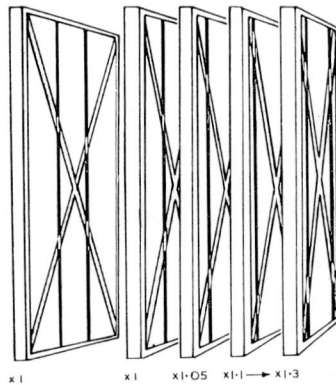

x 1   x 1   x1·05   x1·1 ⟶ x1·3

FIG. 544.—STEREOSCOPIC AND ANISEIKONIC SLIDES.
Used in determining the degree of aniseikonia in unilateral aphakia (C. M. Ruben).

In spite of the passage of some 20 years since the closure of the Dartmouth Eye Institute, only a few advances have been made in the measurement of aniseikonia. Several screening devices have been suggested based on the techniques or targets in the standard or space eikonometers (Charnwood, 1952; Malin, 1955; Burnside and Langley, 1957; Cohen *et al.*, 1957; the Keystone Apparatus; Berg, 1967). Perhaps the most valuable of these has been one of the methods devised by Ruben (1962) for use with the major amblyoscope; the targets are based on Ames's cross and verticals, with the subject fusing the two slides while the arms of the synoptophore are slowly diverged. At a certain point the images begin to break apart but always in a definite manner; the first to split are the verticals on the side of the eye with a larger image, a phenomenon sensitive to a size-difference of about 0·5%. The technique, as we shall see, is of particular value in the assessment of binocular function in cases of uniocular aphakia[1] wherein stereoscopic and aniseikonic slides may be employed (Ruben, 1962) (Fig. 544). For patients without fusion, Fisher and Ludlam (1963) have presented

[1] p. 532.

a method of estimating aniseikonia based on an intra-ocular transfer of the after-images produced by a xenon flash-tube. This technique may be of value in assessing the part played by aniseikonia in the ætiology of those cases of strabismus wherein a loss of binocular vision is due to " horror fusionis ".

TREATMENT

The first question to be settled about the treatment of aniseikonia is whether any specific therapy is required, a problem somewhat similar to the treatment of anisometropia, itself the most important cause of aniseikonia. Generally speaking, the younger a patient for whom an anisometropic correction is prescribed, the more likely is it that comfortable binocularity will normally develop so that no treatment will be necessary. In later life the decision for specific therapy will depend on an evaluation of the patient's symptoms, particularly after correction of any refractive errors and hetero-phoria. On the whole, non-ocular symptoms are rarely cured by treating aniseikonia, and patients who give inconsistent readings on repeated clinical measurements as well as those with measurable aniseikonia but without symptoms should not receive specific treatment. There may, however, be some adults who initially require anisometropic optical corrections for occupational reasons ; aniseikonic symptoms in such patients should usually be treated.

The treatment of relatively small degrees of aniseikonia is the correction of the disparity in size of the retinal images with iseikonic lenses, that is, lenses which cause magnification without introducing any appreciable refractive power by changing the direction of the pencils of light passing through them. It is, of course, possible to correct aniseikonia wholly or partially by altering the form or the position of a patient's spectacle lens or lenses. Generally speaking, an increase in the base curve or thickness of a lens will lead to magnification, as also will an increase in the vertex distance of a convex lens or a decrease in the case of a concave lens. The vertex distance of the lens is clearly dependent on its form and the position of the spectacle frame holding it ; these are factors which can be significantly modified so as to minimize or eliminate relatively small degrees of aniseikonia.

Alternatively, specific iseikonic lenses may be prescribed, the optics of which will be discussed subsequently.[1] Briefly, the size of the image of an object can be varied by altering the thickness or curvature of the lens. Viewed through a plane parallel glass plate an image is displaced towards the plate by an amount approximating one-third the thickness of the plate ; it follows that the image will suffer a corresponding angular magnification, which, however, is small. If, however, the glass plate is curved, the magnifi-cation which depends on the refractive power of the front surface (and the

[1] p. 682.

thickness of the lens) can be much increased. This refractive power of the
front surface is neutralized by an appropriate refractive power of the back
surface so that the image of the object is situated at the location of the
object itself—that is, the lens becomes of zero refractive power. Magnifications in one or all meridians can be incorporated in the lens to suit the
regular types of aniseikonia. Such lenses can be worn as an additional fit-
ment to the spectacles—a suitable temporary expedient (Fig. 684)—or in
most cases there can be incorporated into the size-lens the refractive correction and, if necessary, prisms, even in bifocal form.

Using such treatment some writers have reported considerable success
in the relief of patients with visual troubles; on an average it would
appear that some 50 to 60% of aniseikonic patients are relieved of their
symptoms and a further 10 or 15% experience considerable improvement.[1]
As a general rule the patients received in clinics are those who have obtained
no relief after repeated trials of visual correction by routine methods. It
has been argued that the extreme care lavished upon the visual correction
may account for the successful results in some cases, and that the psychological effect of a prolonged, impressive and expensive examination is the
determinant factor in others, the " cure " being essentially by suggestion;
and finally, that iseikonic correction may bring sufficient relief to allow inadequate refractive or heterophoric corrections to be tolerated and therefore
is itself unnecessary. However that may be, iseikonic correction has
relieved of distressing symptoms some patients who have been able to obtain
relief by no other means, and it would seem that, although the technique of
correction is unfortunately skilled, time-consuming and expensive, the
correction of a visual fault which can be shown to cause considerable visual
disability cannot be completely unsound; its proper place in ophthalmic
therapeusis, however, while yet to be fully evaluated, is probably real
although small. In uniocular aphakia its significance is undoubted and its
evaluation is important in the post-operative case, no matter how it is
optically corrected, even by intra-ocular or contact lenses. There is little
doubt, however, that the widespread and general use of contact lenses has
had important repercussions in the field of aniseikonia; these will be discussed more fully at a later stage,[2] as also will be the use of compound
lenticular systems.[3]

Binocular Vision in Uniocular Aphakia

We have already pointed out the gross difference between the refraction
of the phakic and the strongly hypermetropic aphakic eye which makes the
attainment of binocular vision when a correction with spectacles is attempted

[1] Carleton and Madigan (1932–37), Hughes (1935–37), Doane (1935–41), Hardy (1937),
Berens (1937), Fisher (1938–40), Berens and Loutfallah (1939), Bannon (1941–54), Lancaster
(1942), Hicks (1943), Burian (1943), Cushman (1945), Linksz (1959), Berens and Bannon (1963),
Linksz and Bannon (1965), and others.
[2] p. 713.   [3] p. 682.

so difficult that diplopia results with all its disastrous consequences.[1] These difficulties are increased by the difference in size of the image in the corrected aphakic eye, and they are so great as to make the extraction of an opaque lens from an eye when its fellow retains reasonably good vision inadvisable unless strong indications exist such as the necessity for a full visual field or the imminent hypermaturity of the cataract.

It is true that the increasing use of corneal contact lenses or, still more effectively, of intra-ocular plastic implants (if the surgeon has the courage to indulge in this rarely practised procedure)[2] has mitigated the disabilities arising from anisometropia and aniseikonia. It is also true that exceptional cases have been reported wherein uniocular aphakic patients have attained binocular vision, particularly in young people if the phakic eye is over-corrected and the aphakic eye is undercorrected (Delogé, 1906; Berens et al., 1933). Other expedients have been attempted to attain binocular vision in corrected uniocular aphakia as by fitting the lenses in spectacles so that their distances from the eyes are unequal (Eggers, 1937; Zoubek et al., 1963; Polásek and Zoubek, 1967), or by incorporating a reversed Galilean telescope[3] partially in a contact lens placed in front of the aphakic eye and using its negative element in the spectacle frame (Enoch, 1968); these expedients may achieve some success in a few cases, particularly in young people who had recently lost binocular vision, but they are inconvenient and the problem still remains.

In the attainment of binocular vision in patients with uniocular aphakia, *contact lenses* have many advantages; being close to the eye such a lens produces a retinal image considerably smaller than that formed by a spectacle lens. Some residual aniseikonia, varying between 4 and 10%, however, still exists (Burian, 1962). This, together with the absence of accommodation as well as difficulties often experienced with wearing such a lens particularly by old people, may result in failure in a proportion of cases owing to diplopia and a lack of binocular vision. Widely differing results are in fact reported in the literature, varying from the unfavourable[4] to the enthusiastic.[5] Indeed, the presence of fusion in some uniocular aphakics wearing contact lenses is somewhat surprising in view of the existence of an aniseikonia which may still be far from negligible (Ogle et al., 1958). Burian (1962) suggested that this may be explained by taking into account Panum's fusional areas[6] in the retinæ or by assuming that the peripheral retinal images are disparate but can be ignored.

The state of the binocular vision may be assessed when wearing a contact lens combined with orthoptic investigation in uniocular aphakic patients

[1] p. 379.   [2] Vol. XI, p. 289.   [3] p. 804.
[4] Mann (1947), Cross (1949), Budde and Mackensen (1963).
[5] Little (1934), Williamson-Noble (1938), Town (1939), Girardet (1948), Hirtenstein (1950), Blum (1952), Ridley (1953), Lyle (1953), Constantine and McLean (1954), Goar (1955), Györffy (1955), Spaeth and O'Neill (1960), Zoldan (1964), Gerhard and Bronner (1965), Riehm and Thiel (1965), May and Woolliscroft (1968).
[6] Vol. IV, p. 682.

(Ridley, 1953; Lyle, 1953). For this purpose Ruben (1962) devised a valuable method of assessing the state of binocular vision without the use of a contact lens, using a synoptophore with aniseikonic lenses. The results of such tests indicate that a contact lens is more likely to lead to good binocular vision if the correction is given as soon as possible after the interruption of binocular vision; thus in a case of traumatic uniocular cataract the best chance of restoring binocularity is by early operation followed by rapid fitting of a contact lens (Ridley, 1953; Lyle, 1953; May and Woolliscroft, 1968). Delay is likely to lead to suppression of the image in the aphakic eye, particularly in younger patients. In those of advancing years the insertion and toleration of a contact lens present greater problems. It is therefore commonly found that the uniocular aphakic subjects who react satisfactorily to contact lenses are young adults with a short history of disruption of binocular vision.

It has been suggested that the simultaneous wearing of a contact lens by the phakic eye as well as the aphakic may be of advantage to the uniocular aphakic subject. In this case Boeder (1938) suggested that the aniseikonia may be still further reduced if the unoperated eye is made 3 D hypermetropic, the artificial error being then corrected by spectacles, while it is possible that the bilateral contact lenses may reduce the heterophoria caused by the relative immobility of a scleral contact lens worn in the aphakic eye alone (Ridley, 1953). It would seem, however, that many patients are most comfortable wearing a contact lens only for their aphakic eye. With the use of intra-ocular implants,[1] however, these difficulties are further decreased and binocular vision is usually attained, particularly in young subjects.

The fact remains, however, that many uniocular aphakic patients who wear spectacles prefer to remain with uniocular vision. If the phakic eye is good it is used preferably since if the aphakic eye is uncorrected the dim unfocused image is usually neglected after some time and the visual field is retained. This habit may well be continued while the aphakic eye may be employed when the patient is not moving about and requires acute vision as in reading or viewing the television. On the other hand, if the vision of the phakic eye is poor and reliance must be placed on the aphakic eye, the vision of the other is usually obscured by a strong convex lens which balances the aphakic eye or by an opaque lens. Similarly, many of these who wear a contact lens in the aphakic eye are more comfortable with it alone corrected, neglecting the vision in the phakic eye.

Ames. *Amer. J. Ophthal.*, **18**, 1014 (1935); **28**, 248 (1945).

Ames, Gliddon and Ogle. *Arch. Ophthal.*, **7**, 576 (1932).

Ames and Ogle. *Arch. Ophthal.*, **7**, 904 (1932).

Ames, Ogle and Gliddon. *J. opt. Soc. Amer.*, **22**, 538, 575 (1932).

Bannon. *Amer. J. Optom.*, **18**, 145 (1941). *Clinical Manual on Aniseikonia*, Buffalo, N.Y. (1954).

Berens. *Brit. J. Ophthal.*, **21**, 132 (1937).

Berens and Bannon. *Arch. Ophthal.*, **70**, 181 (1963).

[1] Vol. XI, p. 289.

Berens, Connolly and Kern. *Amer. J. Ophthal.*, **16**, 199 (1933).
Berens and Loutfallah. *Amer. J. Ophthal.*, **22**, 625 (1939).
Berg. *Acta ophthal.* (Kbh)., **45**, 2 (1967).
Berte and Harwood. *Brit. J. physiol. Opt.*, **18**, 108 (1961).
Bielschowsky. *Amer. J. Ophthal.*, **18**, 925 (1935).
    Arch. Ophthal., **15**, 589 (1936).
Blum. *Ophthalmologica*, **123**, 284 (1952).
Boeder. *Arch. Ophthal.*, **19**, 54 (1938).
Bourdy. *Ann. Oculist.* (Paris), **194**, 1048 (1961).
Budde and Mackensen. *Klin. Mbl. Augenheilk.*, **143**, 729 (1963).
Burian. *Arch. Ophthal.*, **29**, 116; **30**, 645 (1943).
    Trans. Amer. Acad. Ophthal., **66**, 285 (1962).
Burian and Ogle. *Arch. Ophthal.*, **33**, 293 (1945).
Burnside and Langley. *Amer. J. Ophthal.*, **43**, 620 (1957).
Carleton and Madigan. *Arch. Ophthal.*, **7**, 720 (1932); **18**, 237 (1937).
Cattaneo. *Ann. Ottal.*, **55**, 345 (1927).
Charnwood. *Optician*, **124**, 598 (1952).
Cohen, Forman and Milan. *Amer. J. Optom.*, **34**, 184 (1957).
Constantine and McLean. *Arch. Ophthal.*, **51**, 212 (1954).
Crisp. *Amer. J. Ophthal.*, **26**, 1329 (1943).
Cross. *Brit. J. Ophthal.*, **33**, 421 (1949).
Culbertson. *J. Amer. med. Ass.*, **11**, 622 (1888).
Cushman. *Arch. Ophthal.*, **33**, 9 (1945).
Delogé. *Anisométropie et vision binoculaire* (Thèse), Paris (1906).
Doane. *Trans. Amer. Acad. Optom.*, **9**, 31, 179 (1935).
    Amer. J. Optom., **18**, 393 (1941).
Donders. *On the Anomalies of Accommodation and Refraction of the Eye*, London (1864).
Duane. *Arch. Ophthal.*, **30**, 621 (1901).
Eggers. *Arch. Ophthal.*, **17**, 328 (1937).
Enoch. *Amer. J. Optom.*, **45**, 231 (1968).
Erggelet. *Z. Psychol. Physiol. Sinnes.*, **49**, 326 (1914–15).
Field. *Arch. Ophthal.*, **29**, 981 (1943).
Fischer. *Pflügers Arch. ges. Physiol.*, **204**, 203, 234, 247 (1924).
Fisher. *Trans. Amer. Acad. Optom.*, **12**, 52 (1938).
    Amer. J. Optom., **17**, 367 (1940).
Fisher and Ludlam. *Amer. J. Optom.*, **40**, 653 (1963).
Fruböse and Jaensch. *Z. Biol.*, **78**, 119 (1923).
Gerhard and Bronner. *Bull. Soc. Ophtal. Fr.*, **65**, 633 (1965).
Gillott. *Brit. J. physiol. Opt.*, **13**, 122, 218 (1956); **14**, 43 (1957).
Girardet. *Ophthalmologica*, **116**, 226 (1948).
Goar. *Arch. Ophthal.*, **54**, 73 (1955).

Green. *Trans. Amer. ophthal. Soc.*, **5**, 449 (1889).
Györffy. *Ophthalmologica*, **130**, 329 (1955).
Hardy. *Amer. J. Ophthal.*, **20**, 599 (1937).
Herzau. *v. Graefes Arch. Ophthal.*, **121**, 756 (1929).
Herzau and Ogle. *v. Graefes Arch. Ophthal.*, **137**, 327 (1937).
Hicks. *Arch. Ophthal.*, **30**, 298 (1943).
Hirtenstein. *Brit. J. Ophthal.*, **34**, 668 (1950).
Hosaka. *Ochanomizu Igak. Zas.*, **3**, 325 (1955).
Hosaka and Kato. *Acta Soc. ophthal. jap.*, **69**, 943 (1965).
Hughes. *Amer. J. Ophthal.*, **18**, 607, 715 (1935); **19**, 686 (1936); **20**, 887 (1937).
    Arch. Ophthal., **14**, 156 (1935); **17**, 944 (1937).
Jackson. *Amer. J. Ophthal.*, **20**, 16 (1937).
von Kries. *Z. Psychol. Physiol. Sinnes.*, **44**, 165 (1909).
Lancaster. *Trans. Amer. ophthal. Soc.*, **40**, 82 (1942).
    Arch. Ophthal., **20**, 907 (1938); **28**, 767 (1942).
Linksz. *Amer. J. Ophthal.*, **48**, 441 (1959).
    Trans. Amer. Acad. Ophthal., **63**, 117 (1959).
Linksz and Bannon. *Int. Ophthal. Clin.*, **5**, 515 (1965).
Lippincott. *Trans. Amer. ophthal. Soc.*, **5**, 560 (1890).
Little. *Arch. Ophthal.*, **11**, 646 (1934).
Ludvigh. *Amer. J. Ophthal.*, **19**, 292 (1936).
Lyle. *Trans. ophthal. Soc. U.K.*, **73**, 387 (1953).
Macnie. *Arch. Ophthal.*, **40**, 326 (1948).
Malin. *Amer. J. Optom.*, **32**, 30 (1955).
Mann. *Brit. J. Ophthal.*, **31**, 565 (1947).
May and Woolliscroft. *Canad. J. Ophthal.*, **3**, 231 (1968).
Miles. *Amer. J. Ophthal.*, **31**, 687 (1948).
Ogle. *J. opt. Soc. Amer.*, **22**, 665 (1932); **26**, 323 (1936); **30**, 145 (1940); **32**, 143 (1942).
    Pflügers Arch. ges. Physiol., **239**, 748 (1938).
    Arch. Ophthal., **20**, 604 (1938); **30**, 54 (1943).
    Researches in Binocular Vision, Phila. (1950).
Ogle and Ames. *J. opt. Soc. Amer.*, **33**, 137 (1943).
Ogle, Burian and Baum. *Arch. Ophthal.*, **59**, 639 (1958).
Ogle and Ellerbrock. *Arch. Ophthal.*, **34**, 303 (1945).
Ogle, Imus, Madigan et al. *Arch. Ophthal.*, **24**, 1179 (1940).
Ogle and Madigan. *Arch. Ophthal.*, **33**, 116 (1945).
Polásek and Zoubek. *Augenoptik*, **84**, 52 (1967).
Post. *Sth. med. J.* (Bgham., Ala.), **35**, 649 (1942).

Amer. J. Ophthal., **26**, 321 (1943); **29**, 742 (1946).

Rayner. *Amer. J. Optom.*, **43**, 617 (1966).

Ridley, F. *Trans. ophthal. Soc. U.K.*, **73**, 73, 373 (1953).

Riehm and Thiel. *Klin. Mbl. Augenheilk.*, **146**, 589 (1965).

Risley. *Ophthal. Rec.*, **8**, 389 (1899).

Ruben. *Brit. orthopt. J.*, **19**, 39 (1962).

Spaeth and O'Neill. *Amer. J. Ophthal.*, **49**, 548 (1960).

Town. *Arch. Ophthal.*, **21**, 1021 (1939).

Tschermak. *Pflügers Arch. ges. Physiol.*, **204**, 177 (1924).

Wadsworth. *Trans. Amer. ophthal. Soc.*, **2**, 342 (1876); **3**, 481 (1883).

Weale. *Brit. J. Ophthal.*, **38**, 248 (1954).

Williamson-Noble. *Trans. ophthal. Soc. U.K.*, **58**, 535 (1938).

Zoldan. *Atti Soc. oftal. Lombarda*, **19**, 23 (1964).

Zoubek, Polásek and Hamák. *Sborn. ved. Praki lék. Fak. Hradci Králové*, **6**, Suppl., 523 (1963).

CHAPTER XIV

MUSCULAR IMBALANCE

THE clinical effects of a lack of balance between the extrinsic ocular muscles were first clearly recognized to give rise to discomfort ("asthenopia muscularis") by von Graefe (1862) and Donders (1864), but their observations were confined to the action of the medial rectus muscles, ailments of which were designated as "insufficiency". The subject, however, was not pursued until the activities of the six pairs of muscles were fully analysed in the fundamental and classical researches of George T. Stevens (1887) of New York. He proposed the term *orthophoria* for the condition wherein the visual axes were parallel while looking into the distance, and the generic term *heterophoria* when they attained parallelism only under stress with the aid of the fusion reflexes, and designated inward, outward, upward and downward deviations as *eso-*, *exo-*, *hyper-* and *hypo-phoria*. Shortly thereafter, G. C. Savage (1891) of Nashville introduced the term *cyclophoria* for similar torsional deviations. At the same time Stevens introduced a similar terminology for ocular deviations that could not be controlled by the urge for fusion—*heterotropia*, divided into *eso-*, *exo-*, *hyper-* and *hypo-tropia*.

GEORGE THOMAS STEVENS [1832–1921] (Fig. 545) was thus a pioneer in the rational study and treatment of muscular imbalance. Born in New York, he started in general practice after medical qualification, and served in the Army of the Potomac in the American Civil War; thereafter, having resumed general practice, he became professor of physiology and diseases of the eye in the Albany Medical College (1870). In 1880 he returned to New York and confined himself to ophthalmology. But his interests were wide and he wrote of his experiences in war, on functional nervous diseases, on travelling (his book, *Coaching through North Wales*, was published in 1895), and on botany on which at the age of 78 he wrote a classical book illustrated by himself. His greatest contribution to knowledge, however, concerned the subject of this Chapter; his ingenuity is seen in the design of many instruments which became standard pieces of equipment such as the phorometer, the tropometer and the clinoscope; and at the age of 86 he still retained his deftness as a surgeon. It is interesting that in his office Alexander Duane learned about the intra-ocular muscles, and in his turn he trained J. W. White who subsequently trained H. W. Brown (of "Brown's syndrome")—an interesting pedigree of America's leading strabismologists.

The subject of imbalance of the extra-ocular muscles is so extensive that it merits a separate volume in this *System* on the motility of the eyes.[1] It is a subject, however, which it is impossible to divorce entirely from the refraction of the eye, and here we shall confine ourselves to the somewhat restricted theme of *the muscular balance in its relation to the refraction*, and discuss shortly only those particular aspects of the subject which con-

[1] Vol. VI.

Fig. 545.—George Thomas Stevens
[1832–1921].

cern the investigation of the optical efficiency of the two eyes and the prescription of spectacles. The aim of the refractionist is to allow the patient to attain binocular vision by fusing together two similar and reasonably clear images, one from each eye; although he may be primarily concerned with the optical defects of the two eyes, the effectivity of binocular vision therefore comes within his province. Defects in binocular vision may be due to an impairment of the retinal image in an eye so that binocular vision is not stimulated or is impossible; it follows that we must first consider how optical defects may interfere with the afferent limb of the binocular reflexes and their central organization. Moreover, a failure in binocular vision may be due to a defect in the effector limb of these reflexes and it is the duty of the refractionist to alleviate or compensate for this in so far as it can be done by optical means. We have also noted the close association between the optical state and the muscle balance in the relationship between accommodation and convergence[1]; here again the refractionist can play an important part.

The Relation of the Muscle Balance to Refraction

CONCOMITANT STRABISMUS

It is well recognized that a refractive error is a frequent accompaniment of some types of manifest squint. Of these, much the most important is the association of hypermetropia with a concomitant convergent strabismus arising in childhood usually between the ages of 2 and 4, since in a significant proportion of these cases the cause of the deviation is wholly or partially accommodative as a result of which convergence is stimulated. It is to be remembered, however, that this abnormal relationship between accommodation and convergence in a hypermetropic subject is not the sole factor in the ætiology of convergent deviations. Indeed, in cases of congenital alternating convergent squint, excessive hypermetropia is not a feature; conversely, in subjects with a non-accommodative convergent squint, a hypermetropic refraction is often found. Again, a congenital high myope may develop a convergent deviation, but here an excessive convergence is exerted in order to look at objects at or near the far-point which is close to the eyes. The general association between hypermetropia and concomitant convergent squint, however, appears to be in accord with the mutual relationship between accommodation and convergence. It would be reasonable, therefore, to expect that a divergent deviation should usually be associated with a myopic refraction and, in fact, if a simple myope shows an anomaly of binocular vision, the deviation is usually of this type. Nevertheless, the great majority of subjects with divergent concomitant squint are not myopic; they either have no significant refractive error or they sometimes show a high degree of astigmatism.

[1] p. 196.

Anisometropia of any variety is of considerable potential importance in relation to the muscle balance and may play a significant part in the genesis of a uniocular squint. If not a primary factor it may determine which eye deviates ; it is thus common to find the greater refractive error in the deviating eye of a case of concomitant convergent strabismus. It is as if the brain chooses to reject the more blurred of the two retinal images and the deviation occurs so that the eye used for fixation has the clearer image. By itself anisometropia does not lead to any particular type of deviation but the refraction of the dominant eye may itself be significant. If, for example, this is myopic, the prevailing background of diminished accommodation may lead to a divergent deviation.

We have already noted the importance of anisometropia as a cause of amblyopia, even in a subject with no strabismus. A deviating anisometropic eye may therefore be amblyopic for two reasons. The exact sequence of events is not always certain, but anisometropic amblyopia may have some causative relationship to strabismus, and when the deviation has occurred the amblyopia may be accentuated.

Vertical deviations do not often have any direct association with refractive errors, but in some cases a gross anisometropia may be a causal factor of the ocular misalignment. This is particularly so in cases with a uniocular high myopia, when the more myopic (or less hypermetropic) eye becomes hypotropic with a head-tilt towards the side of the depressed, myopic eye (Fig. 546) (Bagshaw, 1966 ; Ward, 1967). A deviation of this type was called the *heavy eye phenomenon* by Ward (1967). Such an eye is frequently limited in vertical excursions (Fig. 547); for this reason R. Hugonnier and Magnard (1960) suggested the designation " the nervous syndrome of high myopia " which, because of the muscular ætiology, was changed to " myopic myositis " by R. and S. Hugonnier (1965).

In addition to this, insuperable hypertropia may precipitate horizontal dissociation of the two eyes if a suitable refractive background is present. Indeed, some authorities believe that many cases of horizontal concomitant strabismus arising in childhood may owe their origin to a primary but apparently trivial vertical deviation due to a muscular anomaly.

In all cases of manifest strabismus in a child it is essential that the refraction be undertaken with a cycloplegic drug and in most cases atropine is indicated because of the age of the patient. The technique of refraction may be varied to suit the particular subject. Thus in a young child it may be wise to avoid the use of trial frames during the retinoscopy ; the trial lenses can be held in the hand and this may be done so that the palm occludes the fellow eye while the subject looks directly at the light of the retinoscope. This will ensure that a macular refraction of each eye is obtained, provided the fixation is central in both eyes. Should this not be so, the refractionist may have to guess the whereabouts of the visual axis of the deviating eye while the other eye fixes a distant object. Alternatively, the refraction of an eye that has lost central fixation may be deferred until after a trial period of direct occlusion has been carried out.[1] Occasionally a completely unco-operative child may have to be examined under general anæsthesia if a gross refractive error is to be eliminated.

If trial frames are not used in estimating the refraction, difficulties may arise in deciding the axis of any astigmatic error. This is particularly important in the refraction of patients with strabismus upon whom a sub-jective test is often impossible; indeed, the ordering of a high astigmatic

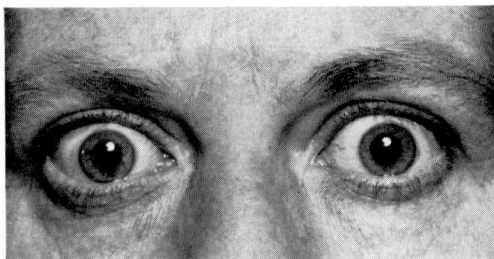

FIG. 546.

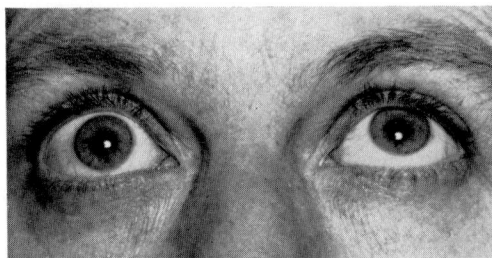

FIG. 547.

FIGS. 546 and 547.—THE HEAVY EYE PHENOMENON.

The patient has −10 D of right myopia with an emmetropic left eye. In the primary position (Fig. 546) there is 20△ deviation left over right with a head-tilt to the right and bilateral lid retraction. On elevation (Fig. 547) there is a limitation of movement of the right eye (D. M. Ward).

correction at an incorrect axis may aggravate rather than ameliorate the amblyopia of a deviating eye. In such cases the best method of identifying the axis is to use a cylinder with a power of about $\frac{7}{8}$ of that required for neutralization; during retinoscopy this will exaggerate any misdirection of the reflex in an incorrect axis.[2]

In ordering spectacles for a child with a manifest squint on the basis of a retinoscopy with atropine it is customary to deduct an extra 1 D from the values at which neutralization of the reflex occurs to allow for the "tone" of

[1] Receptor amblyopia
[2] p. 404.

the ciliary muscle; if the retinoscopy is carried out at arm's length a subtraction of 2·5 D is required. In the case of patients with a convergent accommodative squint a smaller deduction may well be made in the hope that the hypermetrope will relax his accommodation and in so doing tend to reduce the angle of strabismus; such a result, however, is somewhat doubtful and may occur at the expense of clear distant vision so that the child will decline to wear the spectacles. In this event or in children with the type of accommodative strabismus which is more marked for near vision (" convergence excess "), bifocal spectacles have been advocated by some authorities; in this event the increased correction for near vision may so reduce the accommodative requirement that binocular vision can be maintained.

In the early stages of the management of a concomitant strabismus re-examination of the refractive state should be performed at least every 6 months, and improved cooperation with the child as well as a more normal mode of fixation will usually facilitate the subsequent tests and enhance their validity. A reassessment of the refraction is also advisable after surgery although the usual recession-resection procedure has little or no effect on the optical state of the eye, and then perhaps only for a short time. The continued wearing of spectacles for a long period may not be necessary as, for example, in the case of a child with a small hypermetropic correction when the convergent squint has been eliminated by surgery so that he has become fully binocular. A reduction in the strength of a hypermetropic correction may also be indicated when surgical over-correction of the convergence has occurred; in such cases, however, there is no mathematical relationship between a residual strabismus and the uncorrected hypermetropia. In these circumstances the expedient of "clip-on" minus lenses is often valuable. At the same time the use of prisms may be considered advisable in order to correct a residual deviation. Prisms may also occasionally be used as a primary measure to correct a manifest deviation if it is of small degree and perhaps of recent origin. Unfortunately, in both these cases the neuromuscular condition may simply alter so as to perpetuate the ocular deviation.

PARALYTIC STRABISMUS

The optical state of the eye is not related to the development of paralytic squint but the prescription of spectacles in such a case may require the ordering of a prismatic correction. In a horizontal paralytic squint prisms may be introduced so as to avoid diplopia without recourse to occlusion, if they can ensure an area of comfortable binocularity. In cases of pareses rather than paralyses this may prevent the development of a deviation of the head. If the degree of paresis is likely to change, prisms can be employed as " clip-ons " and their strength appropriately varied. In order to reduce the weight of the lenses, it is best to divide the prismatic correction between the two eyes, for prisms of $10\triangle$ or more are poorly tolerated.

The effects of an incomitance due to a weakness of a vertical muscle is less easily aided by prisms, placing the prisms base-up before the hypotropic eye and base-down in front of the other. For obvious reasons, diplopia occurring in the primary position of the eyes and in downward gaze causes much greater inconvenience than that produced by upward movement. Occasionally, however, a patient may be helped by having the bases of the prisms in the same direction on each side. If, for example, there is considerably more vertical deviation on looking downwards than in the primary position, unequal base-down prisms may be ordered before each eye, the stronger being before the hypertropic eye so that the difference between the two represents the degree of hypertropia; the gaze of the two eyes is thus kept to a part of the field where the hypertropia is less marked.

LATENT STRABISMUS—HETEROPHORIA

As we have seen, heterophoria may be defined as the condition wherein the eyes in their conjugate movements are maintained on the fixation point only under stress with the aid of the fusion reflex. There is often no clear dividing line, however, between manifest and latent strabismus, either of the concomitant or incomitant variety. In either case the corrective fusional reflex may be adequate only part of the time and may maintain binocular vision for one distance but not for another. In cases of constant manifest strabismus the complaint of the patient is usually either of double vision or of the appearance of the deviation itself or of both; in heterophoria, on the other hand, further symptomatology may arise from the effort required to maintain the binocularity. These symptoms will merely be outlined and will be more fully discussed under the heading of eye-strain.[1]

Such symptoms may be of two types. The vision occasionally becomes blurred, especially when the patient is fatigued. There is difficulty in gazing steadily at any object, and the discomfort is increased on any attempt to follow a moving object; sudden bewilderments are thus apt to occur, when objects, especially in motion, become jumbled. In all cases vision is improved and relief is obtained by closing one eye. There is frequently a tendency towards adopting eccentric poses of the head, while an associated blepharospasm or a wrinkling of the forehead is characteristic. The most acute distress is associated with high degrees of cyclophoria wherein vertical lines appear deviated, the houses on either side of the street, for example, appearing to fall down upon the unfortunate patient, a sensation sometimes associated with pronounced reflex and labyrinthine disturbances.

The reflex symptoms are usually marked. Headache of any kind is common, and may come on a few minutes after near work is commenced and may make its continuation difficult or impossible. An associated labyrinthine upset gives rise to vertigo which may lead to nausea and

[1] Chapter XV.

occasionally result in vomiting. Restlessness is frequently apparent in children, and in adults of unstable temperament and neurotic tendencies a neurasthenic condition may be induced or, if it is already present, its symptoms may be accentuated. Muscular imbalance, especially when associated with an error of refraction, may thus give rise to a host of varying symptoms; but, like the effects of errors of refraction, it is to be remembered that in the literature the subject has not been exempt from unfortunate exaggeration.

The degree of muscular imbalance certainly tends to determine the severity of the symptoms. Indeed, a mild degree of heterophoria may not give rise to any symptoms; on the other hand, a marked latent strabismus may at times become fully manifest, leading to diplopia. The symptomatology of heterophoria is also dependent on the type of deviation; hyperphoria and cyclophoria are more likely to give symptoms than purely horizontal latent deviations. Thus a horizontal heterophoria of less than $6\triangle$ is unlikely to cause subjective trouble, although a sensitive or neurotic individual may suffer distress from a minor imbalance and a normal individual may periodically experience symptoms at times of mental stress or general physical upset. It is frequently a difficult problem, however, to decide whether the symptoms of a particular patient are primarily due to his muscle imbalance since many subjects show evidence on routine testing of a similar imbalance without apparent ill-effect.

As we have seen to occur in manifest strabismus, heterophoria is frequently associated with errors of refraction. Thus many hypermetropic subjects demonstrate esophoria and many myopes are exophoric. In these cases the strong synkinesis of convergence and accommodation is, of course, the determining factor, and the wearing of an appropriate refractive correction may alter the degree of heterophoria and sometimes even its direction.

A considerable amount of PSEUDO-CYCLOPHORIA is frequently associated with astigmatism wherein the principal axes are not vertical and horizontal. When a patient suffering from this condition looks at a vertical or horizontal line, the image formed on the retina will lean in the direction of the maximal corneal meridian (Figs. 321–4). To bring the image into its proper alignment, the patient may attempt a corrective torsion and this tends to become a life habit. It probably explains to some extent the distressing symptoms to which this uncorrected astigmatism so frequently gives rise, as well as the great discomfort which may result from an error in the direction of the axis of a cylinder in spectacles. With the proper correction of any oblique astigmatism, of course, all symptoms of this nature disappear.

The iatrogenic heterophoria produced by certain types of spectacle correction has already been noted and will be discussed further in the section devoted to spectacle optics.

The Clinical Examination of the Muscle Balance

The investigation of the state of the binocular cooperation should never be regarded as an isolated technique; as with the refraction itself, it must be a part of a complete ophthalmic examination. It must be admitted, however, that this is often a counsel of perfection. In most patients with symptoms suggestive of an optical anomaly, the examination of the muscle balance is rarely as extensive or as thorough as in a case of suspected strabismus. Few ophthalmologists would suggest, for example, that examination with the major amblyoscope should always supplement a routine refraction. The investigation of any muscle imbalance in such cases will usually be confined to the following manœuvres: inspection of the corneal reflexes, the

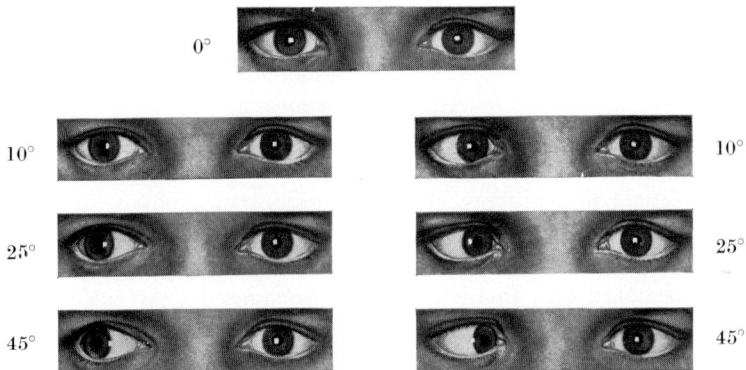

Fig. 548.—THE CORNEAL REFLEX TEST.

Estimation of the deviation by the position of the corneal reflex. Above, the normal position. Left-hand column, divergent strabismus. Right-hand column, convergent strabismus.

cover-test with and without the appropriate spectacle correction for near or distant vision, a study of the ocular movements and, in appropriate cases, the measurement of heterophoria for near and distance and occasionally of the vergence power.

The methods of performing these tests will be dealt with in detail in another volume,[1] but a brief recapitulation is given here so that the task of the refractionist may be complete.

The *corneal reflections* are inspected as the patient looks directly at a light held by the observer immediately in front of him, a procedure first suggested by Hirschberg (1874). The pin-point images of the light as reflected by the two corneæ are compared with respect to their position in relation to the pupil and to the cornea as a whole (Fig. 548).

[1] Vol. VI.

The *cover-test*, used by Donders (1864) and Stilling (1885) and popularized by Duane (1889–1919), is carried out on the basis of the corneal reflections. If the latter suggest that one eye, say the left, is deviating, the patient continues to fix a near or distant object and the right eye is covered by the hand or by a card. If the left eye is deviating and if its vision is adequate it will move to take up fixation indicating a manifest strabismus. On removing the card if the left eye remains fixing and the right stays in the deviated position, the squint has an alternating character. If, however, on removing the card the left eye returns to its former position and the right resumes fixation, a left (uniocular) manifest strabismus is present. If on covering either eye the other does not deviate, a manifest squint is absent. In this event the cover-test should be similarly repeated but the behaviour of the covered eye is observed when the cover is removed. It may be found to have deviated while covered and to return to its fixing position on uncovering, while the other eye keeps its fixation and moves neither on covering nor uncovering. In this instance, a latent strabismus is present. If no movement of either eye occurs, any deviation that appears to exist is an apparent squint (pseudo-strabismus).

This method of performing the cover-test—the method of binocular uncovering—may not always elicit a latent strabismus. The examiner should then proceed to the *alternate cover-test*—the method of uniocular uncovering. Here each eye is covered in turn, the behaviour of each on uncovering is noted and finally both are uncovered. Attention should be paid to the speed of recovery to the binocular state. Even this may fail to break down the patient's binocular vision and it may be supplemented by making the patient follow a light in several directions with one eye, the other being covered, before proceeding to the alternate covering.

The examination of the ocular movements should be carried out in all the principal positions of the gaze and may be supplemented by the performance of the cover-test in these positions. Any defective movement or complaint of diplopia should be noted.

Of particular importance is the examination of convergence since an absolute or relative weakness of this function can be a potent cause of the symptoms of eye-strain. The ætiology of this condition and its treatment will be discussed elsewhere,[1] but it is always to be remembered that convergence and accommodation are interconnected and weakness of one should direct attention to the other.

The degree of heterophoria for distant vision is usually estimated by means of the *Maddox rod* (1890) which depends on the effect of a cylindrical lens in converting the image of a point-object into linear form. As generally used, the apparatus consists of one or several cylinders of red glass placed side by side in a frame (Fig. 549); in the latter case the cylinders should be thin and there should be no chinks between them (Maddox, 1929). A

[1] Vol. VI.

similar optical effect is produced by glass bevelled to the same general configuration so that it acts as parallel rows of double prisms—the *Maddox groove* (Fig. 550). When a spot of light is regarded through either of these the image is formed as a focal line running perpendicular to the axes of the cylinders, so that with the rod before one eye this eye sees a red line running perpendicularly to the direction of the cylinders while the other eye sees the

FIG. 549.—THE MADDOX ROD.

FIG. 550.—THE MADDOX GROOVE.

spot of white light (Figs. 551–3). In orthophoric projection the red line runs through the white light; with a latent or manifest deviation it does not. With the cylinders running in a horizontal direction a deviation to the right or to the left indicates a lateral deviation; with the cylinders vertical, a deviation above or below indicates a vertical deviation; if the red line runs obliquely when the Maddox rod is vertical, a cyclophoria is indicated which

FIGS. 551–553.—THE MEASUREMENT OF DEVIATIONS WITH THE MADDOX ROD.

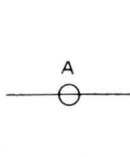

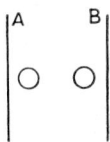

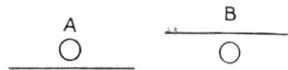

FIG. 551.   FIG. 552.   FIG. 553.

FIG. 551.—Orthophoria in the vertical (A) and horizontal (B) direction.
FIG. 552.—With the rod in front of the right eye. A, exophoria; B, esophoria.
FIG. 553.—With the rod in front of the right eye. A, right hyperphoria; B, left hyperphoria.

can be more easily recognized if two Maddox rods are used, one before each eye, in which case the absence of parallelism when they are both set vertically becomes more evident. The degree of deviation can be read off directly on a tangent scale (Fig. 554), or may be estimated by correcting the displacement with prisms so that the red line is made to run through the point of light: in the first case, if the angle of deviation is measured objectively on the scale, the angle of anomaly is determined directly.

This test, in every way practical, easy and accurate, may be employed with the Maddox rod in one cell of a trial frame and prisms in the other; for accurate results it is well to repeat the examination with the rod in

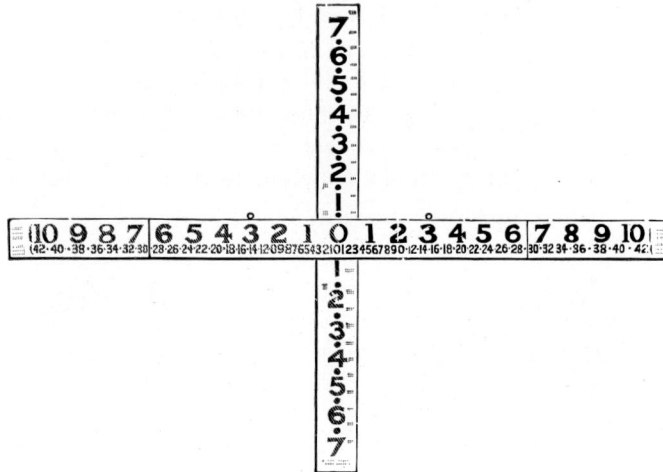

FIG. 554.—THE TANGENT SCALE.

front of the other eye since the tendency to deviation of the two may not be equal (Grimsdale, 1929). A variable prism forms a rapid method of measurement (Prince, 1893–98; Jackson, 1893): the combination is seen in the *Maddox hand-frame* (1929) (Fig. 555), a neat and simple instrument wherein a rotating prism is placed before the fixing eye, the deviation being measured by rotating the prism. It is recommended by some authorities that true

FIG. 555.—THE MADDOX HAND-FRAME.

In front of the right eye is a multiple Maddox groove; in front of the left, a rotating prism calibrated in degrees of deviation.

fusion-free heterophoria can be measured more accurately by using the Maddox rod if alternate covering of the two eyes is carried out at the same time.

The clinical measurement of cyclophoria is not commonly carried out as part of a simple examination of the refraction. It can, however, be estimated by the use of the Maddox rod. In cyclophoria when this instrument is horizontal the line of light is not vertical but oblique and the extent of torsional imbalance can be estimated by the number of degrees through which the rod has to be rotated from the horizontal position in order to make it appear vertical. For this purpose many other means are available and perhaps more accurate, such as the *Maddox double prism* (1890–98);

FIGS. 556 and 557.—THE MADDOX DOUBLE PRISM.

FIG. 556.

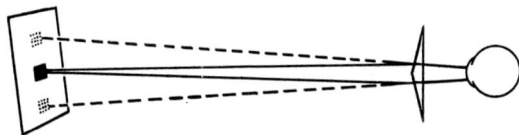

FIG. 557.—The optical effect of the double prism.

this method consists in presenting the doubled image of a horizontal line to one eye which is then compared with the single image of the same line seen by the other eye lying midway between the two (Fig. 556–7). If parallelism is maintained, cyclophoria is not present; if the centre line declines to the temporal side, intorsion is present, if to the nasal side extorsion, the amount being measured by the degree of rotation necessary to attain parallelism (Fig. 558).

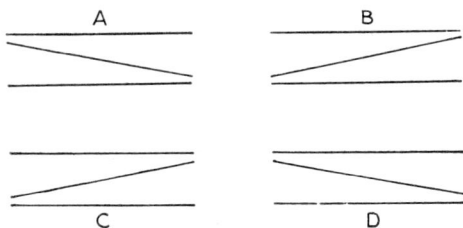

FIG. 558.—THE MADDOX DOUBLE PRISM TEST IN CYCLOPHORIA.

With the Maddox double prism placed in front of the right eye: A, insufficiency of the left superior oblique. B, insufficiency of the left inferior oblique. With the Maddox double prism placed in front of the left eye: C, insufficiency of the right superior oblique; D, insufficiency of the right inferior oblique.

von Helmholtz's indicator (Figs. 559 to 562) is useful for studying cyclic deviations. A card with a horizontal line and central spot is supported on a horizontal rod, the proximal end of which is held in the patient's teeth (Fig. 559). In cyclo-vertical deviations due to affections of the oblique muscles, double images are seen on tilting the head (Figs. 560 to 562).

For near vision, heterophoria is most simply estimated by means of the *Maddox wing* (1913) (Fig. 563). Here the dissociation of the two eyes is not produced by distorting one image, as with the Maddox rod, but by

FIGS. 559–562.—VON HELMHOLTZ'S HEAD-TILTING TEST (J. Ringland Anderson).

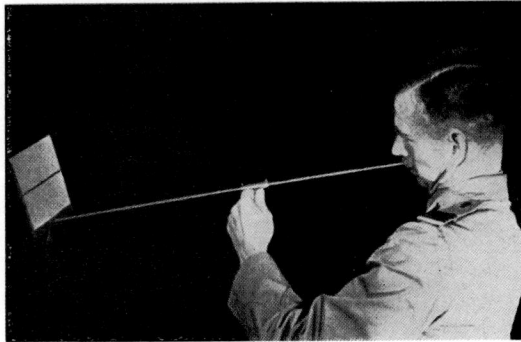

FIG. 559.—The test being made with the head tilted to the left.

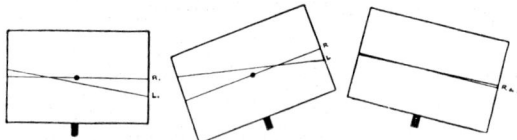

FIG. 560.   FIG. 561.   FIG. 562.

In paresis of the left superior oblique the appearance of the images of the horizontal line:

FIG. 560.—When the head is erect.

FIG. 561.—On tilting the head to the left the image of the left eye rises and tilts more.

FIG. 562.—On tilting the head to the right the images tend to fuse.

mechanically presenting two different parts of the field to each of the two eyes. When the patient looks through the two slit-holes in the eye-pieces of the instrument, the fields which are exposed to each eye are separated by a diaphragm in such a way that they glide tangentially into each other. The right eye sees a white finger pointing vertically upwards and a red arrow pointing horizontally to the left. The left eye sees a horizontal row of figures in white and a vertical row in red; these are calibrated in degrees of deviation. The finger pointing to the horizontal row of figures and the arrow pointing to the vertical row should both be at zero, and the amount of any deviation can be read off on the scale. The patient is also asked to move the red arrow so as to appear parallel to the white line (Fig. 563). A measurement of the near cyclophoria is thereby obtained. The diploscope of Rémy (1901–8) is constructed on similar principles.

FIG. 563.—MADDOX WING TEST (Hamblin).

The descriptions just given apply only to specific simple tests performed in a particular way, but many others are available. Among the instruments which can be used for these measurements, mention should be made of the Stevens *phorometer* (1888). It consists of two rotating cells, each carrying a prism of 5°, which rotate in unison under the control of a gear-wheel, and a scale measures the strength of the

FIG. 564.—THE PHOROMETER.
Consisting of a rigid mounting of a trial frame, two rotatable multiple Maddox grooves, an $8^\triangle$ or $10^\triangle$ prism which can be placed, base down, before the right eye, and calibrated rotatory prisms (American Optical Company).

refracting angle used. The whole is set on a levelling arm, and through it the patient looks at a light or a cross-line chart. When the instrument is set so that the prisms are base-down before one eye and base-up before the other, two images are seen on the same vertical line if there is no heterophoria; the absence of alignment indicates esophoria or exophoria, which can be measured by increasing the prismatic effect in the direction of base-out for esophoria and base-in for exophoria. Similarly, for measuring hyperphoria the prisms are rotated so that a horizontal displacement is created by setting the prisms base-in before both eyes. If one image is higher than the other the prisms are rotated until the images are made level, the pointer indicating on the scale the amount of manifest hyperphoria. The same test can, of course, be made for distant and for near vision.

The phorometer, rotatory prisms, and the Maddox rods can all be combined in one instrument (Fig. 564); or, as we have already seen, practically the entire outfit of visual testing can be condensed together in a refracting unit[1] which makes these tests easier and more rapid of accomplishment. Alternatively, the deviations of muscular imbalance can be rapidly and accurately measured on the more complicated types of major amblyoscope which, by dissociating the fields of view presented to the two eyes, constitutes the most accurate method of measuring the various types of heterophoria including cyclophoria (Fig. 565).

FIG. 565.—THE SYNOPTOPHORE (Clement Clarke).

As we have noted,[2] the principle of dissociating the fields of the two eyes has been used in the Turville infinity balance, a technique which also allows estimations to be made of the muscle balance.

The fusional reserves or *vergence power* gives a measure of the ability of the eyes to maintain binocular single vision when forced into disjugate movements (vergences).

Should such a measurement be indicated during clinical refraction it is most simply carried out by *prisms*. An object is fixated by both eyes and a deviation is induced by gradually increasing prisms either on a prism-bar or as a rotatory prism (as in the Maddox prism verger) which is introduced

---

[1] p. 432.　　　　[2] p. 443.

before one eye until diplopia occurs. With base-out prisms a blur-point and then a break-point occur, the former due to the stimulation of accommodation by the increasing convergence, the latter denoting the appearance of diplopia, a value quoted as the *prism vergence*. A marked interval between the two indicates a considerable ability to dissociate accommodation and convergence. The recovery-point to binocular vision should also be noted as the strength of the prism is gradually reduced; this is usually slightly below the break-point; blinking and changing the fixation will accelerate the recovery. Again, the most accurate method is with the major amblyoscope. In testing the various vergences, convergence, divergence and vertical vergence (sursum-vergence), it is wise to leave a short interval between each procedure in order to allow recovery from the effort previously made.

The following are average figures for the fusional reserves:

Divergence

Negative horizontal fusional reserve	Distance	7–8 △ base-in
	Near	16–18 △ base-in

Convergence

Positive horizontal fusional reserve	Distance ⎫ Near ⎬⎭	25–35 △ base-out (the point at which blurring occurs is about 12 △)
Vertical	Distance and near	3–4 △ base-up or -down.

Torsional vergence, the ability to fuse together two torsionally disparate images, is not of great clinical importance as far as the routine refractive examination is concerned. Normal values are difficult to establish because the conditions in which the test is performed and the nature of the test-objects greatly influence the results. In any case, where cyclovertical movements are suspected to be important, a full orthoptic investigation should be carried out, employing a major amblyoscope such as the synoptophore (Fig. 565).

An ample fusional reserve is some indication that adequate compensation is made for a heterophoria. In assessing these reserves in a patient with heterophoria, however, it is as well to take into account the " starting point ", which is the fusion-free position of the eyes. For example, the ability to overcome up to 25 △ of base-out prisms in a subject with 5 △ of exophoria means that the actual fusional convergence is 30 △.

The Treatment of Heterophoria

The incidental finding of heterophoria in a patient during refraction raises the difficult clinical question as to whether or not it is causing symptoms. No general statement can be made and much will depend on the nature of the patient's symptoms, his personality, environment, general health, and his refractive error, as well as the degree and type of heterophoria. If, for example, the symptoms are such as might be expected from the refractive error alone, the heterophoria should be ignored; thus a myope complaining of poor distant vision may be found to have exophoria but in such a case the latter needs no specific treatment and his complaint will probably be abolished when spectacles are worn for the refractive error. The first guiding principle, therefore, is not to treat the heterophoria itself unless there are positive indications to do so.

A more perplexing situation arises when the patient's symptoms are those of eye-strain, in which case it may be impossible to decide on the importance of any muscle imbalance; here the clinician's experience must dictate his approach to treatment. As far as the visual symptoms of eye-strain are concerned it is usually wisest first to correct the refractive error with the greatest accuracy, particularly hypermetropia or astigmatism, and to adopt an expectant policy with regard to any heterophoria which may be present. In this instance a small refractive error such as might be ignored in the absence of heterophoria should be corrected. In most cases the correction of the refractive error alone will abolish the symptoms. It is, of course, possible, particularly when referred symptoms of eye-strain such as headache are prominent, that the heterophoria found at the refractive examination is responsible for the symptoms and requires treatment. This is particularly so if there is the slightest hint that at times the heterophoria becomes decompensated, giving symptoms such as blurring of the vision or diplopia.

The precise degree of heterophoria is not usually of great help in deciding whether treatment is necessary. Certainly, horizontal deviations of $6 \triangle$ or less can usually be ignored but vertical heterophoria even of 1 or $2 \triangle$ may well be responsible for symptoms; in many such cases a full orthoptic examination will be helpful, particularly if any incomitance is evident.

A particularly difficult situation arises when the refractive error and the heterophoria are, so to speak, in conflict; thus a myope may demonstrate esophoria or a hypermetrope may be exophoric. It should still be the general rule that the refractive error takes precedence, but here it may be felt that slightly weaker correcting lenses are necessary; a full correction may give rise to a fresh symptomatology if the muscular imbalance is aggravated. Apart from the power, the form of the spectacle correction may to some degree be selected so as to take into account any existing heterophoria. This applies, for example, to a choice of segment in bifocal spectacles.

If it is decided to treat the patient specifically for the muscular imbalance, the spectacle correction may, in appropriate cases, incorporate *prisms* or, alternatively, strong lenses may be decentred[1] (Figs. 566–7); in these cases it is usual not to correct more than half of the horizontal heterophoria but for vertical heterophoria the correction should be the full value

[1] p. 676.

of the latent deviation although difficulties may arise in patients if slight
incomitance is present. In such instances attention is paid particularly to
the straight-ahead and straight-down position. The prescription of relieving
prisms, a practice adumbrated by Wells (1792) and clinically substantiated
by Donders (1847) and von Graefe (1857), may not only compensate for the
imbalance but by relieving strain and producing relaxation may stimulate
fusion and aid in establishing and producing normal habits of binocularity.
The effects of prisms, however, are not uniformly beneficial; in some cases
they result in a compensatory alteration of muscular activity, which itself
leads to a perpetuation of the original error or even exaggerates it. In

FIGS. 566 and 567.—THE CORRECTION OF HETEROPHORIA WITH PRISMS.

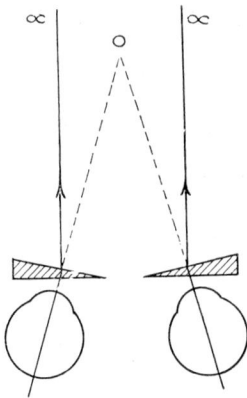

FIG. 566.—Esophoria. The conditions determining esophoria tend to direct the visual
axes towards O; fusion impulses maintain
their direction upon the fixation object
(infinity). Prisms, base out, maintain this
direction without fusional effort.

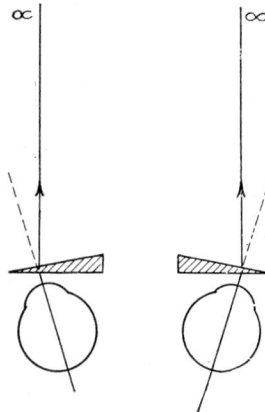

FIG. 567.—Exophoria. The conditions
determining exophoria tend to diverge the
visual axes in the direction of the dotted lines;
they are maintained upon the fixation point
(infinity) by fusional reflexes and may be so
maintained by prisms, base in.

stationary deviations, however, particularly those of small degree, prisms
may not have these ill-effects, and are greatly appreciated by old patients
in whom exercises or surgery of the extra-ocular muscles cannot be considered.

Orthoptic exercises will be fully discussed elsewhere,[1] but particularly
suitable cases for such treatment are those of convergence insufficiency and
small degrees of horizontal heterophoria, especially divergence; vertical
deviations are much less responsive to this form of therapy. At the same
time any improvement of defective binocular vision which may be derived
from exercises may allow the patient to control his deviation with less effort
and will give him greater ocular comfort.

The treatment of cyclophoria is difficult either by optical means or by exercises.
The adequate correction of the refraction is essential and it is significant that if

[1] Vol. VI.

hyperphoria is present, as is often the case, its correction frequently brings relief of all the symptoms. Apart from this, the distress of the effects of torsion can be alleviated by using " rest cylinders " of small power (say 0·5 D) placed at an angle between 45° and 90° in the right eye and between 90° and 135° in the left in non-astigmatic cases, and by moving the cylinder in astigmatic cases in a similar direction (about 5° for each 1 D cyl.). This expedient, however, has much to be said against it. As with the use of prisms, the introduction of cylinders does nothing to strengthen the muscles involved and, if anything, tends to perpetuate the deformity. Moreover, if a vertical deviation is overcome, it is done at the cost of disturbing horizontal lines and, in addition, the astigmatic effect blurs the vision. An incorrect cylinder may, indeed, bring on all the symptoms of eye-strain, with the result that a greater evil is treated by introducing a less.

An attempt can be made to exercise the torsion of the eye by using two Maddox rods placed perpendicularly, one in front of either eye; in this case two red lines are seen and, instead of running horizontally, they are inclined at an angle the size of which varies with the degree of the defect. One of the rods is then rotated until the two lines are fused, and then it is moved alternately backwards and forwards in an appropriate direction, the patient meantime trying to keep the line of light from doubling. According to the same principles, exercises may be carried out with two lines drawn on stereoscopic cards and inserted into an amblyoscope so that they can be rotated round in opposite directions. Both these procedures the patient can practise at home.

In specific cases combinations of the above treatments may be indicated for any type of heterophoria; indeed, a policy of trial-and-error may have to be adopted. If, for example, spectacles cannot (or will not) be worn, exercises may be substituted for them. In the worst cases wherein the imbalance is marked, recourse should be had to surgery. Finally, it is worth bearing in mind that all methods of treatment act as placebos, an effect which depends to some extent on the interest, the time and the care the examiner devotes to the patient; the favourable response of a neurotic individual to therapy for his heterophoria is not necessarily an indication of the relevance of his physical signs to his symptoms.

In summary, heterophoria found at routine refraction should be ignored unless there are strong indications for treatment. These indications include an overall assessment of the patient's personality, his environment, his general health, both physical and mental, his visual task and optical state, supplemented, if necessary, by a complete orthoptic examination. Treatment is directed primarily to the refractive error, but may also consist of relieving prisms, orthoptic exercises and surgery in appropriate cases.

Bagshaw. *Brit. orthop. J.*, No. 23, 75 (1966).
Donders. *Ned. Lancet*, **2**, 227, 233 (1847).
   On the Anomalies of Accommodation and Refraction of the Eye, London (1864).
Duane. *N.Y. med. J.*, **50**, 113 (1889); **73**, 890 (1901).
   Arch. Ophthal., **24**, 258 (1895); **48**, 1 (1919).
   Ann. Ophthal., **14**, 301 (1905).
von Graefe. *v. Graefes Arch. Ophthal.*, **3** (1), 177 (1857); **8** (2), 314 (1862).

Grimsdale. *Trans. ophthal. Soc. U.K.*, **49**, 33 (1929).
Hirschberg. *Arch. Augenheilk.*, **4**, 273 (1874).
Hugonnier, R. and Magnard. *Bull. Soc. franç. Ophtal.*, **73**, 80 (1960).
Hugonnier, R. and S. *Strabismes*, 2nd ed., Paris (1965).
Jackson. *J. Amer. med. Ass.*, **21**, 737 (1893).
   Ophthal. Rec., **3**, 105 (1893).
Maddox. *Ophthal. Rev.*, **9**, 129, 287 (1890).

Tests and Studies of the Ocular Muscles, Bristol (1898); 2nd ed., Phila. (1907).

Trans. ophthal. Soc. U.K., **33,** 220 (1913); **49,** 2 (1929).

Parsons. *Ophthal. Rev.,* **33,** 321 (1914).

Prince. *Arch. Ophthal.,* **22,** 372 (1893).

J. Amer. med. Ass., **30,** 197 (1898).

Rémy. *Recueil Ophtal.,* **23,** 385 (1901); **28,** 520 (1906); **30,** 203, 350, 438 (1908).

Savage. *Ophthal. Rec.,* **1,** 228 (1891).

Arch. Ophthal., **20,** 105 (1891).

Stevens. *Arch. Ophthal.,* **16,** 149 (1887).

Med. Rec., **33,** 511 (1888).

A Treatise on the Motor Apparatus of the Eyes, Phila. (1906).

Stilling. *Arch. Augenheilk.,* **15,** 73 (1885).

Ward. *Trans. ophthal. Soc. U.K.,* **87,** 717 (1967).

Wells. *An Essay upon Single Vision with Two Eyes,* London (1792).

SECTION IV

EYE-STRAIN AND VISUAL HYGIENE

FIG. 568.—SILAS WEIR MITCHELL
[1829–1914].
(Courtesy of the Wellcome Trustees.)

CHAPTER XV

EYE-STRAIN

A VERY suitable introduction to a Chapter devoted to the subject of eye-strain is the photograph of SILAS WEIR MITCHELL [1829–1914] (Fig. 568) of Philadelphia, one of the greatest neurologists that America has produced. After studying in Paris with Claude Bernard he returned to Philadelphia and there in a long life-time reported an amazing series of original observations. Among the first to investigate the properties of the venoms of snakes from which he isolated the diffusible constituents, he pointed out the coordinating functions of the cerebellum, during the American Civil War he investigated the effects of injuries of the peripheral nerves, giving the earliest account of ascending neuritis and the traumatic neuralgias, and was the first to inculpate eye-strain as a cause of headaches. For his treatment of nervous diseases by prolonged rest in bed (the " rest cure ") he became famous, a view for which there is considerable justification and is seen in its most modern form in the " sleep centres " of Russia or the Hypnotron of America. In his sobriety and versatility, and his excellent writing full of quaint phrases, Mitchell was a typical survival of the American gentleman of the Colonial type.

In health the use of the eyes ought to be a subconscious function: EYE-STRAIN may be defined as *the symptoms experienced in the conscious striving of the visual apparatus to clarify vision by ineffectual adjustments,* and when we reflect on the tasks constantly demanded from the eyes and the degree of accuracy to which they are required to adjust themselves, the importance of eye-strain in a civilized economy becomes obvious. The treatment of eye-strain is so to modify the vocational demands upon sight and to assist the eyes that such adjustments which may be required are within the visual capacity of the individual—to convert seeing into easy seeing.

It should be remembered that biologically the eyes were adapted for relatively simple purposes—to look for enemies and for food; and although, from long custom, we accept the conditions in which we live today as normal, it by no means follows that the eyes have evolved sufficiently to fulfil the exorbitant demands of unremitting close work imposed upon them by a highly complex and artificial civilization. The more is this understandable when we remember the functional minutiæ required for the attainment of accurate vision and the high degree of coordination necessary between the movements of the two eyes so that they can fulfil the requirements of binocular vision. It is understandable that this complexity of the visual apparatus tends to make it less capable of withstanding long-continued strain than a cruder and less highly specialized mechanism. The visual apparatus of man is also a relatively recent development in evolutionary history, and the newer the function the more liable it is to break down under stress. Thus convergence, so constantly required for near work, with the exception of its presence to a slight degree in the higher apes, is a new function unique to man and is frequently one of the first to break down in conditions of strain. Indeed, that the eyes are able as a rule to meet the demands constantly made upon them is a compliment of no mean order to our adaptability, and it is not surprising that of all human ailments, eye-strain of one type or another is one of the most common.

Historical. Eye-strain or " weak-sightedness," as befits a condition of common incidence and incapacitating effects, has long been known. To Demosthenes " atonicity of the eyes " (ἀτονία ὀφθαλμῶν) occurred on looking at " brightness " and particularly on reading when the lids readily close and the eyes water: the treatment he recommended was sound—walking, running and gymnastic exercises. In order to preserve sight, and at a later date, Johann Zahn (1685) (Fig. 513) warned against doing fine work in twilight and bending too closely over the book when reading. William Mackenzie (1843), enumerating a score of symptoms that may result therefrom, adopted the term *asthenopia* (ἀ, privative; σθένος, strength; ὤψ, eye): the treatment he advocated was abstention from near work, purgatives, tonics, hot and cold drinks, tenotomy of the medial recti to relieve accommodation, cauterization of the urethra to stop spermatorrhœa or diminish masturbation—and only very rarely and in the aged, convex lenses. In the event of failure of these measures the disease was considered incurable and Mackenzie was constrained to advise the relinquishment " of a sedentary trade " in order to " drive a horse and cart," or " to those in better circumstances," to emigrate and " follow the pastoral pursuits of an Australian colonist." It was not until the work of Donders (1864) that the optical and accommodative basis of eye-strain was appreciated and the importance of its rational treatment stressed. To the early writers it was a type of amaurosis associated later with a deficiency in focusing; von Graefe (1862) suggested that owing to an insufficiency of the medial recti, a defect of convergence might give rise to symptoms, and Donders (1864), pointing out that the condition depended on the hypermetropic structure of the eye, claimed that with optical aids " the condition (of asthenopia) need now be no longer an inconvenience to anyone."

Stimulated by Donders's work, ophthalmologists in many countries of the world bent their energies to the study of refractive errors in their relation to the relief of eye-strain and in this respect the most minute errors were endowed with significance. In this development, under the stimulus of Edward Jackson's work (1885–95), American writers were prominent (Norton, 1887; Gould, 1891–1906; Risley, 1892; White, 1894; and others); they had, however, their disciples in other countries, as Martin (1888) and Javal (1891) in France and Leonard Williams (1918) in England. At the same time, to ametropia and accommodative anomalies as causes of asthenopia were added the disturbances caused by muscular imbalance, and to the " muscular asthenopia " of von Graefe and Donders, who envisaged only the medial recti and ciliary muscles as a cause of distress, there was superimposed the concept of strain arising from heterophoria, a view largely deriving from the work of Stevens (1887–1906), Savage (1891–1902) and Duane (1896–1904) in America and Maddox (1898) in England. Finally, in recent years, the further complication of aniseikonia has been added (Ames and others, 1932–45).

As ideas on the ætiology of eye-strain have grown so also has the scope of the associated symptoms. Dimness of vision, watering of the eyes and headaches were the essential clinical evidences to early writers such as Mackenzie (1843); for them the essential problem was presbyopia, and in this defect visual failure was more prominent than asthenopic symptoms. Later in the nineteenth century the importance

of referred nervous symptoms impressed itself on a number of American ophthalmologists, prominent among whom was William Thompson (1879) of Philadelphia,
with whom was particularly associated Weir Mitchell. Mitchell (1874), impressed by
the fact that a patient of his on whom he lavished all his skill in vain, even going to the
length of cauterizing the spine, was completely cured by spectacles of all his symptoms,
none of which was referable to the eyes, became the world's greatest advocate cf
the widespread reflex effects attributable to refractive errors and eye-strain, a role
in which he was surpassed in the prolific output of his pen only by George M. Gould
(1891–1906). To Gould, who wrote and re-wrote everything he thought with evan-
gelical enthusiasm rather than with critical restraint, most ills in the world from
migraine and Ménière's disease to insomnia and suicide could be evaluated in terms
of eye-strain. The case was over-exaggerated and his zeal stimulated the contrary
view of therapeutic nihilism; but the end-result was that the syndrome of eye-strain
has now a balanced and permanent place in medicine. It is unfortunate, however,
that in a problem which concerns the environment as much as the individual, ophthalmologists have in general bent their energies almost exclusively to improving visual
capacity by optical correction to the neglect of the equally important factors of environmental conditions and the vocational demands made upon the eyes. By the middle
of the twentieth century we were just beginning to see the establishment of a due
balance in this respect.

THE CAUSES OF EYE-STRAIN

The manifestations of eye-strain depend partly on the use to which the
eyes are put, partly on the efficiency of the visual apparatus and partly on
the capacity of the individual to withstand sustained effort. The subject is
indeed a complex one involving the interplay of physical, physiological,
psychological and social factors and illustrates the innumerable aspects in
which ophthalmology bears upon the activities of everyday life. In an
assessment of the ætiology of the condition it is to be remembered that
comfort is subjective and not susceptible to objective measurement; it is
negative as well as positive, depending upon the absence of things that are
annoying and irksome as much as on the presence of circumstances which
are conducive to smooth and easy function.

Following the teaching of Donders (1864) it is said that the visual
factors causing eye-strain are those which induce muscular fatigue and that
eye-strain is itself essentially muscle-strain; the most important element
is accommodative asthenopia due to over-taxing of the ciliary muscle, and
to this is added strain of the neuro-muscular control of the ocular movements
in order to maintain convergence and compensate for heterophoria.
Lancaster (1932) suggested that the strain lay, not in the total expenditure
of muscular effort, but in constantly shifting and changing adjustments of
the intra- and extra-ocular musculature in futile groping after a more
satisfactory but unattainable ideal. It would seem, however, that this
cannot explain the whole case if eye-strain be regarded in its widest sense.
Just as constant attention to a faint sound induces fatigue, so we would
expect constant efforts to perceive an indistinct image to be equally tiring.
It is said that inadequate illumination or minutiæ in the object cause strain

by exciting accommodative efforts to clarify the image; this is undoubtedly true, but it does not altogether explain the symptoms which exist in the myope, in the emmetrope when distant objects are regarded, or those which appear to be relieved by the correction of aniseikonia or occur in diplopia. It would seem that retinal fatigue (using the term with its usual connotation) is unknown in ordinary conditions; but much of the symptom-complex of eye-strain is probably due to tiring of the higher perceptual processes such as interest and attention when the call is made upon them continuously to interpret blurred and indistinct images. This effect is seen dramatically in the readiness with which fatigue becomes evident in post-traumatic states, many of the symptoms of which are referred to the eyes although the causal lesion had been entirely cerebral and the eyes themselves are unaffected. It is also seen in ordinary circumstances when visual effort is maintained while interest flags.

In this connection the question of the strangeness or familiarity of the visual task is important—a factor which applies to all mechanisms involving delicate neuro-muscular co-ordination and necessitating interpretive judgments. Habitual muscular adjustments acquire a quality of smoothness and ease in the expert unknown to the novice provided they are within the margin of functional capacity. Visual acuity itself may be improved by exercise and facilitation in the case of amblyopic eyes or in the visual efficiency resulting from the establishment of full and easy convergence. The visual efficiency of the trained look-out at sea or the stalker who spots his quarry on the hillside, although invisible to the novice, is proverbial; and considerable strain and fatigue are experienced by the child starting school, the adolescent commencing office-work or the worker transferred to a task demanding the resolution of minute detail—all of which disappear with prolonged experience.

This is well seen in reading. The habitual reader provided with good lighting, good print on good paper, good vision and muscular balance can read almost indefinitely —provided he is not called upon to think too much—without strain and fatigue (Vernon, 1931). He glances along the lines, fixates no letters nor even each word but interprets groupings as a whole, filling in large blanks readily and easily. A child, on the other hand, fixates at first each letter and then each word, and slowly and laboriously expends an enormous visual effort on the same task. So the adult, reading the same letters in unaccustomed groupings in a strange language fatigues more readily, or learning a new script, as Greek or Arabic, relapses to the strains of childhood. Or again, faced with an accustomed task in unfavourable conditions, with poor illumination, bad print on shiny paper, having a refractive error giving muzzy images and phorias which make fixation difficult, the adult readily breaks down.

ENVIRONMENTAL FACTORS CAUSING EYE-STRAIN

The principal environmental factors responsible for eye-strain are concerned with the illumination provided and the nature of the task imposed on vision (its size, movements, contrast with its surroundings, and so on).

That the ILLUMINATION, not only its quantity and quality but its distribution, has a direct bearing on the incidence of eye-strain is undoubted.

It is, of course, relative rather than absolute, for the insensitive, fit person with good vision will get along happily with a level of illumination such as would make work impossible to the sensitive, the ailing or those with ocular defects. It depends also on the nature of the work, for form vision is defective in poor conditions of lighting and it also varies with the fineness in detail required in the work in hand. This subject is considered at length in the subsequent Chapter.

THE NATURE OF THE OBJECT is a second factor of first-class importance in the ætiology of eye-strain. The strain involved depends upon *the size of the details* which must be resolved—not their actual size but the visual angle they subtend. Minute objects, of course, the detail of which subtend an angle approaching the limits of visual acuity, are necessarily viewed closely in order to enlarge the retinal image, thereby adding accommodation-convergence strain to the difficulties of seeing. To many people with decreased visual acuity small print comes into this category; while processes involving fine detail such as in the electronics industry are a source of strain to the most efficient eyes. With the methods of mass-production necessitated by the progressive mechanization of industry whereby individual workers specialize in one narrowly circumscribed task, the factor of strain becomes more evident. Again, to the child, who in his difficulty in reading and enthusiasm to master a strange task, pores closely over his book, the same conditions apply.

In addition to size, *lack of contrast* frequently induces strain, for objects are seen only by dissimilarities in brightness and colour. Associated with this should be remembered poor definition of the object and its lack of contour, a disadvantage seen commonly in the illegibility of print. Finally, *constant movement* of the object of attention necessitates constant and rapid ocular adjustments, a factor seen in reading while travelling as well as in many industrial processes. Frequently as distressing is the need for prolonged fixity of the gaze necessitated by a demand for concentrated attention on a small detail for a period of time.

THE OCULAR FACTORS CAUSING EYE-STRAIN

The ocular factors causing eye-strain have already been fully discussed and need not detain us further here. They may be briefly recapitulated:

(i) Uncorrected ametropia, leading to the formation of indistinct images, difficult to interpret and frequently involving accommodative strain for their correction.

(ii) Accommodative difficulties, either insufficiency or excess.

(iii) Heterophoria, leading to difficulties in making the muscular effort necessary to maintain fusion.

(iv) Convergence difficulties, a prolific cause of strain particularly when the synkinesis with accommodation is disturbed.

(v) Fusional inadequacy when the fusional reflexes are not sufficiently potent to maintain easy and sustained binocular vision.

(vi) Aniseikonia, the influence of which is still somewhat difficult to assess.

As a general rule gross visual errors do not give rise to the typical symptoms of eye-strain but merely result in a failure of visual function. Thus a high refractive error entails a loss of acuity with its social and economic consequences to which the patient reconciles himself without attempting to improve the condition and the matter begins and ends with visual impairment; a gross muscular imbalance or aniseikonia involves loss of binocularity which is frequently symptomless. In these cases the diagnosis is apparent and the treatment obvious. But when the error is small the patient is able to rectify it to a greater or less extent by muscular effort; this he continually attempts to do to the best of his ability, and the constant strain thus unconsciously imposed upon him brings on muscular and nervous fatigue with its attendant train of reflex symptoms. It is not the error itself which causes the trouble so much as the continuous effort called forth automatically in the attempt to correct it. The physician may suspect that a symptom-complex may be attributable to the eyes, and on his suggestion the patient will protest that his vision is excellent; but examination may show that an unsuspected small error of refraction, or a slight degree of muscular imbalance is present, and its correction will frequently result in an equally unexpected and dramatic relief.

THE CONSTITUTIONAL FACTORS CAUSING EYE-STRAIN

PHYSICAL FACTORS. Since the occurrence of eye-strain is determined essentially by muscular fatigue so far as the eyes are concerned and mental fatigue at the interpretive level, it is obvious that the breaking-point will be reached more readily in the feeble than in the robust. Symptoms therefore tend to appear in the debilitated and in those convalescing from an acute illness, or in women after a confinement and during lactation when fatigue, which in normal circumstances would be barely appreciated, readily manifests itself, and an optical error which would give rise to no symptoms of discomfort were the individual in robust health may become acutely felt, and may necessitate the use of spectacles which may frequently be discarded at a later date in happier circumstances. Indeed, in some cases the ciliary muscle may not be able to perform a normal amount of work without showing signs of distress, and symptoms of eye-strain may make themselves evident in the presence of satisfactory environmental conditions and the absence of any error in the optical system. To do hard eye-work the individual must be physically fit; overwork, malnutrition, exhaustion, insufficient sleep, anxiety and emotional strain may bring about a condition of ocular decompensation even in the otherwise healthy.

FUNCTIONAL FACTORS. In an activity requiring extreme delicacy of neuro-muscular coordination, involving intimately complex reflexes of the autonomic system and necessitating perceptual integrations of a high order, it is not surprising that the symptoms of eye-strain are so characteristic of psychogenic states that some authorities with a varying degree of emphasis consider nervous instability to be a primary factor in their ætiology.[1] Few, however, would agree whole-heartedly with Best (1934) who bluntly asserted that " all asthenopias are psychogenic conditions." Notoriously the symptoms do not appear in proportion to the gravity of the causal defect; they vary from individual to individual in the most surprising degree without any apparent reason, this one showing no sign of trouble, and that one, with apparently equal cause and seemingly equally constituted, bitterly complaining. The explanation of many such cases lies in the fact that it is the individual who is asthenic rather than the eyes. The alacrity with which neurotic symptoms are referred to the eyes is well recognized. To the victim of an anxiety state eye-strain with its imagined injury to the sight—the prelude to blindness—can appear the most fearsome thing with a potential threat to happiness and economic security. To the neurotic, stressed by overwork, emotional strain or illness, the eyes provide a convenient substitute for more deeply seated maladjustments, and around vision, through which most contacts with life are made, a screen from the outer world can readily be erected behind which is found a convenient escape. It is to be remembered that it is not the neurotic alone who suffer thus: those also succumb whose nervous system is too highly organized and unstable or are spending themselves too lavishly, sometimes to the considerable enrichment of society, to sustain additional strain without cost. Finally, the victims of eye-strain include those capable people to whom achievement counts too much, who are over-sensitive to the dictates of exaggerated and exacting duties, who keep their minds under the lash and meet fatigue not with rest but with further applications of the lash.

The functional factors in eye-strain therefore arise from the interrelationship of personality and environment. Fatigue and conflict are part of everyday life, and the element of conflict is certainly present when the desirable visual performance may not be obtainable. In the susceptible individual these factors need not be in any way excessive to produce symptoms such as eye-strain; when fatigue and conflict occur to an extreme degree, even a normal individual may succumb.

THE SYMPTOMS OF EYE-STRAIN

The symptoms ascribed to eye-strain are protean in their character and individualistic in their incidence. They may be classified as visual, ocular, referred and functional. Sometimes the visual symptoms predominate accompanied by little or no further disturbances, as occurs typically in

---

[1] Murrell (1893), Hobby (1894), Carpenter (1898), Woods (1907), Emerson (1919), Derby (1930), Rutherford (1932), and many others.

presbyopia; at other times the referred symptoms are exclusively present, a circumstance which may leave the ocular ætiology unsuspected; frequently the functional manifestations dominate the picture; and occasionally all four types of symptoms run concurrently, in which case the activities of the individual may be much curtailed.

VISUAL SYMPTOMS

As a general rule the visual capacity forms no true guide to the assessment of eye-strain, for the condition is caused essentially by the effort to compensate for optical and muscular imperfections and if such compensation is impossible, no sustained effort is attempted. The symptoms thus tend to be most marked in those cases wherein the vision remains good. One person will live placidly and comfortably with a small degree of astigmatism and proportionately reduced vision, while another more highly organized, suffering the same disability, will attain normal or supernormal sight—and pay for it. There frequently comes a time, however, either in periods of unusual strain, or during a temporary deterioration of the general health or vitality, when fatigue comes on and the visual acuity fails. A sense of confusion and a temporary blurring of vision is experienced, the letters when reading, for example, appearing to become blurred. Here the ciliary muscle gives up any attempt to focus or goes into spasm and the image becomes indistinct, the extrinsic muscles slip back into their original condition of rest and transient diplopia results, or convergence fails and the letters run together. This may be momentary and pass off, to recur again at more frequent intervals, the eyes gradually becoming tired and the lids heavy, while a sensation of weariness or drowsiness makes itself progressively felt and renders continued attention difficult or impossible. A relaxation of attention brings relief, but a resumption of the matter at hand induces a repetition of the trouble, until ultimately the individual is constrained to give up the attempt from annoyance or exhaustion.

OCULAR SYMPTOMS

The ocular symptoms associated with eye-strain are directly due to the increased muscular work which the defect invokes and the discomfort of the resultant muscular fatigue, to which are added the effects of a condition of more or less permanent vascular engorgement determined by this state of sustained and forced activity. Subjectively, especially after long periods of close application to work, the eyes feel tired, hot and uncomfortable; temporary relief is obtained by resting or by rubbing them, but if the work is continued, the vague discomfort gives place to a feeling of actual strain and this develops into pain. Pain in the eyes unconnected with inflammation is almost invariably due to eye-strain, and rarely to any deep-seated disease. It usually is mild and dull and aching, but may on occasion be severe and acute; it may be situated in the eyes themselves or be located more deeply in the orbits or, spreading therefrom, become referred as a general headache. Eventually every attempt to use the eyes may be associated with discomfort and the constant recurrence of repeated attacks may eventually lead to a condition of neurosis.

The ocular pain associated with eye-strain is muscular in origin and is due to fatigue. It is difficult, however, to be more specific about the nature of this fatigue or, indeed, about which muscle or muscles are involved. The ciliary muscle is usually incriminated, but fatigue as a physiological phenomenon is rare and spasm of accommodation is usually painless. Similar considerations cast doubt upon the significance of the extra-ocular muscles in the problem of the ocular pain in eye-strain, and any detectable muscular imbalance is often quite disproportionate to the symptoms (Heaton, 1968). Lancaster (1932) suggested that constantly altering levels of ciliary and extra-ocular muscular activity may be the fatiguing factor.

On the other hand, the pain may be comparable to that which occurs in other organs, the musculature of which is controlled by the autonomic nervous system. A close parallel can be drawn between it and cardiac pain (Ramsay, 1931): in both cases continued activity is compatible with comfort so long as the effort is within the physiological margin of balanced activity between the two components of this system; in both cases if the margin is over-stepped and the parasympathetic innervation is forced to employ more than a reasonable modicum of muscle fibres in relays over a period so that a resting interval is not afforded each for recuperation and all suffer fatigue at the same time, pain which may be acute on occasion may result, precipitated by effort and passing off with rest. The pain of tonic and sustained ciliary contraction often passing into a general headache is well exemplified after the instillation of eserine but this is not pain of the kind occurring in eye-strain, and such pain is not dispelled by cycloplegia. That pupillary contraction on exposure to excessive illumination can give rise to the same type of pain was demonstrated by Ernst Fuchs who found that gazing at the brilliance of a dazzling snowfield in the high Alps excited considerable ocular pain which was banished (although the dazzling was increased) after the instillation of a mydriatic. Indeed, Cowan (1955) suggested that asthenopic symptoms could be pupillary in origin, the stimuli to pupillary activity arising from accommodation and from light being in conflict. The mechanism of the pain is not thoroughly understood—an ignorance not confined solely to ocular pain.

Objectively, the eyes frequently have a typical appearance and lacrimation is common. The continued state of irritability and congestion is said eventually to bring about an unhealthy condition of the lids and conjunctivæ so that low-grade infections tend to establish themselves and become chronic in spite of the usual local medicaments, the eyes having a characteristic look, watery, suffused and bleary. This is especially notable in children, in whom low-grade infections may possibly be accentuated and prolonged by the child constantly rubbing his eyes with his fingers; the eyes feel strained and sore, and a child's hands are rarely clean.

Eye-strain has at one time or another been credited with a share in the ætiology of almost every ophthalmic disease. Frequent mention has been made of it in association with iritis and iridocyclitis, with glaucoma and even with cataract. The factors determining the incidence of these diseases are usually complex and often not a little obscure, but there is no scientific evidence to support the view that eye-strain plays an important or determining part in the ætiology of any of them.

REFERRED SYMPTOMS

The referred symptoms arising from eye-strain are headaches, vertigo and a host of other manifestations, some of which may be digestive.

The mechanism of the causation of these reflex symptoms is interesting. The headaches, for example, cannot easily be explained on the basis of intracranial events, for cerebral sources causing pain are considered to be traction or distension of the intracranial venous sinuses or arteries, inflammation in or about the coverings of the cranium or the large intracranial vessels, and inflammation or pressure affecting the cranial nerves containing afferent pain fibres—the Vth, IXth, Xth and upper three cervical nerves. Nor does the pain of eye-strain correspond to the type or distribution of intracranial pain. In this connection the work of Penfield and McNaughton (1940) throws an interesting light on headache and referred pain to and from the eye: during an intracranial operation stimulation of the dura and dural vessels in the frontal and occipital regions in man, a common distribution of ocular headaches (Hobbs, 1964), produced a sensation of ocular pain. The alternative explanation that the pain is a reflex neuralgia spreading through the branches of the Vth nerve cannot meet every case, since many of the referred symptoms are experienced outside its distribution. A more rational explanation draws an analogy between ocular pain and the types of visceral pain long recognized in other organs such as the heart or the intestinal tract, the musculature of which is controlled by reciprocal innervation between the two components of the autonomic nervous system (Ramsay, 1926–31; Michaelson, 1932). It has long been known that visceral muscular disturbances give rise to pain—the *referred pain* of James Ross (1887)—which is experienced in the area of skin supplied by the segment of the central nervous system receiving a sympathetic supply from the viscus in question. The irritability excited in this segment is appreciated by the brain as if the visceral stimulation originated from the area of the peripheral distribution of the afferent somatic nerve involved; pain is therefore referred to the region supplied by this nerve, hyperæsthesia is evident over this region and in the area supplied by the corresponding efferent somatic nerve a muscular contraction appears (Head, 1893–96; Sherrington, 1906; J. Mackenzie, 1923).

The homologous segmental reference of visceral pain, originally suggested by Martyn (1864), by which pain of visceral origin is referred to the area which shares a common segmental innervation with the viscus, must now be accepted as an established physiological principle, but the mechanism of the pain is not yet understood. The metamere is the phylogenetic unit of the organism, and since the pain fibres in the cord, brain-stem and thalamus are arranged segmentally, it would seem probable that all pain impulses from one segment—visceral or peripheral—reach a functionally related area of the sensorium (Cohen, 1947); when integrated into the cortical pattern of the body-image they will be localized in that segment. The hypothesis of Penfield (1925) and Davis and Pollock (1932) that sensations of pain are due to changes

(vascular or metabolic) in the periphery excited by abnormal activity of the autonomic nerves of the segment is disproved by the referred pain in a " phantom "
limb after amputation (*e.g.*, the arm in angina) (Cohen and Jones, 1943).   It may,
indeed, be that there is little distinction between visceral and somatic pain (Lewis
and Kellgren, 1939), and that the sensorium appreciates pain and localizes it in a
particular segment whenever the stream of impulses from that segment, either the
somatic tissues or their homosegmental viscera, exceeds a liminal value (Lewis, 1942;
Harman, 1948).

In the same way, therefore, as over-strain of the cardiac muscle produces angina
which spreads over the shoulder, down the arm and up the neck, so ciliary pain is
referred to the region corresponding to the cervical segments which connect with
the superior cervical ganglion; from these segments the somatic outflow is represented by the bulbo-spinal root of the trigeminal and the upper cervical nerves.   It
will be remembered that the primitive metameric arrangement of the Vth nerve is
maintained in man by which the ophthalmic division is represented most caudally[1]
so that ciliary pain is primarily frontal and occipital in distribution.   The hyperæsthesia of the frontal and occipital regions of the scalp not infrequently encountered in
cases of eye-strain has a parallel with the hyperæsthesia in the segment corresponding
to an affected viscus; while the tonic contraction of the corrugator supercilii and
frontalis muscles responsible for the constant frown of the subject of eye-strain, is
analogous to abdominal rigidity in peritoneal inflammation or the retracted testicle
in renal colic.   The same irritability spreads to the nearby vagus centres, and tachy-
cardia and gastric disturbances result.

Headache is the commonest symptom associated with eye-strain.   This
occurs in almost every possible variety, and may be referred to any part of
the area of distribution of the first division of the Vth or upper cervical
nerves.   It may be localized around the region of the eyes; it is usually
frontal, is sometimes occipital, and perhaps less commonly temporal or
vertical.   On occasion the pain may extend down the neck or even into the
arms.   It may remain limited to any part, being associated frequently with
a tender area in the vertex or the temple, but as a general rule, when thus
limited, it occurs as a " brow ache " over the immediate neighbourhood of
the eyes or more rarely in the temples.   Alternatively, originating in one
region, it may extend, sometimes remaining strictly unilateral but, more
usually developing a cumulative and expansile character, it becomes generalized.   It varies widely in nature: sometimes it is superficial and resembles
a cutaneous hyperæsthesia, sometimes deep-seated and boring or full and
throbbing; it may be a dull and heavy ache difficult to describe or to localize
accurately, or it may be neuralgic in nature, sharp, shooting and lancinating.
In its incidence it may be permanent or periodic, or it may come on at quite
irregular intervals.   It may or may not be definitely associated with the use
of the eyes; usually it is so, and makes itself most evident in the evening
after a day's work.   On the other hand, it may come on in the morning after
a night's rest and sleep.   Occasionally, appearing at periodic intervals, it
has all the characteristics of a typical attack of true migraine.   Usually,
however, of a mild nature, giving rise to annoyance and exasperation rather

[1] Vol. II, p. 783.

than actual pain, it may be completely incapacitating on occasion, or by its constancy and persistence it may suggest an organic lesion.

Conforming thus to no type and simulating many general diseases, mental as well as physical, the headache of eye-strain is difficult to diagnose with certainty; the only rational course to adopt is to examine the eyes as a routine in all cases wherein such an origin might be suspected. Certainly no case of obscure headache should be treated on general medical lines without first eliminating the possibility of eye-strain as being one at least of the factors in its ætiology. In this knowledge it has become a common practice of many physicians to refer every case of obscure headache for an ocular examination, and in this the ophthalmologist bears a responsibility beyond that of the elimination of eye-strain as the relevant agent. Having satisfied himself that environmental factors, the refractive state, the muscular balance and perhaps aniseikonic defects are not likely to be responsible, he should proceed with a full ocular examination, paying special attention to the intra-ocular pressure, the visual fields, the appearance of the optic discs and the retinal vessels. Upon him lies the responsibility of answering two questions: first, are there any ocular abnormalities liable to give rise to headaches? and second, are there any ocular findings suggesting the existence of a systemic disease of which headache may be a symptom?

Hyperæsthesia of the scalp is a less common finding in eye-strain, usually associated with headache; it may be so severe as to make it painful and difficult to comb the hair.

Vertigo was defined by Isaac Jones (1918) as the subjective sensation of a disturbed relationship of one's body to surrounding objects in space; it arises if different sensations of space are experienced which cannot be reconciled with each other. It is different from the more indefinite feeling of *dizziness*, a loss of co-ordination and balance, as in fainting.

Spatial sensations are derived essentially from the eyes and the labyrinths (as well as the deep muscle-sense). Thus, with regard to the eyes themselves, a peripheral paresis of the extra-ocular muscles disorientating the spatial impressions received from the two eyes will cause vertigo; a conjugate palsy will not. When exteroceptive visual stimuli cannot be reconciled with proprioceptive labyrinthine impressions, vertigo again occurs. Thus stimulation or disease of a labyrinth producing a sense of rotation induces vertigo. When a normal person is rotated, at first no vertigo is caused since visual and labyrinthine impressions correspond, but after some time the endolymph of the labyrinth rotates gravitationally with the body and no stimulation occurs; consequently since the visual impression persists, vertigo is experienced. If, however, the rotation is carried out in the dark the visual evidences of rotation are also lacking, no discrepancy between the visual and labyrinthine impressions exists, and there is no vertigo.

Vertigo in its severe manifestations is rarely of ocular origin—these are usually due to disease of the ear or labyrinth, of the brain, particularly the brain-stem or cerebellum, or of the circulatory system; we have also seen that it may be a feature of migraine. Dioptric conditions are not generally associated with giddiness except when distortion or a sudden change in the relative size of the retinal images is produced as may occur when spectacles are worn for the first time. The correction of oblique astigmatism of some magnitude may produce the same effect; but severe vertigo of ocular origin is associated essentially with muscular anomalies, particularly cyclophoria and pareses, a circumstance not surprising in view of the close relationship between the ocular motor and octavus systems. Apart from these conditions, if it occurs in any severity in the absence of disease of the labyrinths and their central connections, vertigo is usually a manifestation of a neurosis.

Occasionally *gastric disturbances* may form part of the clinical picture of eye-strain —chronic indigestion, dyspepsia, nausea and even vomiting. It is this symptom-complex, when it occurs periodically associated with an acute and incapacitating headache, which resembles a true migraine. The near association of the bulbo-spinal root of the Vth nerve with the nucleus of the vagus in the medulla may be responsible for accentuating these gastric disturbances, and tend to perpetuate a condition of anorexia and mild dyspepsia.

A constant and involuntary *frown* with wrinkling and puckering of the brow is also typical: to a large extent this is an automatic accompaniment of forced attention but, as we have seen, it may to some extent be a segmentally referred muscular spasm.

Muscular spasms may have a similar explanation. Reflex irritability of the VIIth nerve may occur, which may be manifested in spasmodic movements of the facial muscles, especially those associated with the lids. Rarely, the disturbance may spread to involve the upper cervical segments of the cord and give rise to a spasmodic torticollis. This is most frequently seen in children in whom such habit-spasms, tics and choreiform movements may be associated with an error of refraction or muscular imbalance, and can be cured by its correction in combination with suitable measures directed against any other concomitant sources of irritation. Sympathetic disturbances also occasionally occur, such as a vasomotor upset or, more rarely, a hyperhidrosis which may be limited to one or other side of the head.

There is a somewhat fanciful tendency among some writers to ascribe to errors of refraction very much more profound effects than these. They are spoken of as being the cause of migraine, chorea and epilepsy; as being an important factor in the ætiology of constipation, gastric ulcer, and even in the liability to succumb to tuberculous or any other infection; as or having a determining influence in the occurrence of alcoholism, depression, suicide and crime.[1] It is true that eye-strain may cause much worry and unhappiness, and it is certainly the case that it may lower the general vitality considerably; it may reasonably occur that a person is placed in circumstances with which normally he may just be able to deal, but the additional distress of an optical error carries matters to the breaking-point. In these cases, however, the influence of the optical defect is incidental and occasional rather than primary and essential.

FUNCTIONAL SYMPTOMS

We have already noted that a neurotic temperament is frequently a causal factor in the development of marked symptoms of eye-strain; the converse relationship also holds wherein, in susceptible cases, eye-strain

[1] p. 561.

may be the means of the aggravation and prolongation of such psychopathological states. It also happens, particularly, although not exclusively, in women, that functional troubles which are without any reasonable organic basis are referred definitely and persistently to the eyes. Such patients will insist that they cannot use their eyes for any length of time, or that when they attempt to do so they cannot see at all. Frequently they see spots floating about in front of them. Sensitivity to light is especially marked, and they are quite unable to bear illumination of any unusual intensity; even in diffuse daylight they prefer to go about in dark glasses. Headache is a common association, the neurotic origin of which can frequently be recognized from the sensations they describe. A patient with a true organic headache rarely hesitates to describe his sensations as those of pain pure and simple: they, on the other hand, with no evidence of emotion, will describe a sense of pressure, of emptiness, of the head opening or shutting, or of its being bored through by a nail, or being constricted by a band. These, and many more; but whatever it is, the impression is given that it is indeed unpleasant. There may be an optical anomaly, or there may not; if there is, the constant repetition of attacks leads to a permanent state of neurosis in which the patient shuns the light, becomes unable to read or apply visual attention to any task until, thinking and speaking of little else than ocular troubles, he (or usually she) abandons the attempt to take any active part in life and becomes completely absorbed in the observation of the symptoms. A host of spectacles, each of which has been worn punctiliously, makes no difference to the condition. Certainly any optical error or muscular anomaly should be corrected with scrupulous care; but the real trouble is a pathological attitude of mind, none the less real, it is to be noted, because it is so, and treatment should be directed towards that. Frequently in these cases psychological treatment directed not to the eyes but to the psychogenic factor will result in disappearance of the visual troubles.

The DIAGNOSIS of eye-strain is frequently difficult because, in the first place, the symptoms are often referred and seem to bear little or no relation to an ocular origin; in the second place, in a great many cases the vision, as judged by the patient's own standard, may be unimpaired or, indeed, may be considered above the normal. It is always to be remembered that in many cases the most distress is caused by errors so slight that they readily escape detection unless they are looked for with care. Too often in the diagnosis of such cases the ocular cause of the trouble is neglected or thought of ultimately as a last expedient, when frequently it should have been considered and remedied first.

THE TREATMENT OF EYE-STRAIN

There is no evidence that use of the eyes, provided they are normal, the conditions of ocular hygiene are good and the person is healthy, is in any way deleterious. Like all other organs they, and the perceptual processes which interpret their imagery, become tired with over-use, but in general the rational treatment of eye-strain involves not the cutting down of the amount of visual work (within broad limits), but the elimination of all deleterious factors in an ætiology which may well be composite. Optical efficiency is necessary, but treatment should never degenerate into a routine correction of the optical defect with spectacles; it should include in addition a survey of the patient's environment, the nature and amount of work he does, his physical ability to undertake this work and his psychological reactions to life as a whole.

Nothing is more pernicious than the routine correction of optical defects by rule-of-thumb methods. Not only is the eye to be treated as an optical instrument, but it ought always to be considered as an integral part of the body, sharing with other organs in its constitutional variations and in the effects of the ills with which it may be afflicted. The prescription of optical devices should always be regulated by the physician's grasp of the organic condition underlying the trouble, no less than by his understanding of the demands made upon the patient and his ability to meet them. Many symptoms which are apparently caused by refractive errors or muscular anomalies would give no trouble in the ordinary course of events, and become apparent only because of ill-health or on the attempt to do more work than the individual is capable of accomplishing with safety. If optical aids alone are prescribed, and the warning of overwork as manifested in the eyes is neglected, the spectacles may provide the patient with the means wherewith to struggle on until he suffers a much more serious breakdown. In many of these cases the eyes thus form a valuable index of the general state of fatigue, and from a study of their condition the work and conduct of the patient can usefully be regulated. The provision of suitable lenses is not sufficient treatment in itself; the refractionist must take into account the whole life and activities of his patient—his habits, his diet, his exercise, the manner and amount of his work, as well as his personality and intelligence. We have seen that there is little pathognomonic in the symptoms of eye-strain and that frequently, when they simulate constitutional disease, their origin in the eyes is overlooked. So conversely, symptoms which may appear obviously to be due to a refractive anomaly may be the result of an entirely different cause, mental or physical; and the ophthalmologist should be one who is competent to appreciate and recognize this and allow his treatment and advice to be guided by his knowledge.

For this purpose it may be well to refer the patient to a general physician or psychiatrist. In this connection we should remember that the symptoms of eye-strain, ocular or referred, particularly headaches, may in many cases be primarily psychogenic rather than physical in origin; treatment, along the lines we shall indicate by spectacles and exercises may, by acting as placebos produce a relief of the symptoms, particularly so after an elaborate diagnostic procedure.   Awareness of this factor should lead to a critical appraisal of certain therapeutic measures supposed to be of value for eye-strain.   The prescription of optical devices in this way is as far along the psychotherapeutic road as most ophthalmologists would like to venture. There is always, however, at our disposal the powerful weapon of reassurance, which is frequently sufficient to dissipate a patient's anxiety and to alleviate and sometimes even dispel his symptoms of eye-strain.

When the history and the ocular examination indicate some form of treatment directed specifically to the eyes and to vision, this may take a variety of forms and we shall complete our review of this subject by a brief reference to two of its main aspects—the optical correction of the ocular anomaly and the use of exercises ; visual hygiene in the environment, often a matter of great importance, will be discussed in the following Chapter.

THE OPTICAL CORRECTION OF VISUAL DEFECTS

The optical correction of visual defects involves an examination of the refractive condition, the accommodation and the convergence and their mutual relationships, the state of muscular balance, the degree of binocular vision, and finally, if it is possible and indicated, the size-relationship of the retinal images.   The thorough investigation of these functions involves a considerable expenditure of trouble, but when practice becomes routine and long custom makes the execution of the various tests automatic and their interpretation instantaneous, they can be performed with surprising rapidity and at the same time with accuracy.

Stress has been repeatedly laid upon the large part played in the symptomatology of refractive errors by the smaller defects, but it should be pointed out that every small error by no means requires correction.   There has undoubtedly been a tendency to do this in the past and to provide a large proportion of the population with unnecessary spectacles,   and unfortunately the tendency still survives.   Sometimes the habit is pernicious, as in the provision of convex lenses to young hypermetropes with small errors, thereby depriving them of the stimulus to accommodate, or to patients with a refractive error requiring no correction, particularly young people who are commencing studies and are suffering from a muscular deficiency which requires treatment by exercises.   The wholesale correction of small errors of astigmatism is a more negative evil.   It has been pointed out that an absolutely normal refraction is so rare as to be considered abnormal, for a small astigmatic error is present in the vast majority of people.   Moreover, the eye is neither an accurately centred nor corrected optical system, but is characterized by inaccessible errors of spherical, chromatic, diffractive and astigmatic aberration, so that in no case is an optically perfect image formed.   It is, in fact, doubtful if the eye really focuses more accurately than about ± 0.25 D.   To correct a minute symptomless error, especially when it is measured in the pathological condition of cycloplegia and transposed to the eye in its normal dynamic state, and when it is further warped by the optical defects inseparably associated with the fitting of spectacles, is to misinterpret the whole economy of living organisms. Where an error is found, however, and with it are associated symptoms, the case is different, and its correction must depend upon the ophthalmologist's assessment of the patient's visual requirements and personality.

In the treatment of these ocular conditions the greatest essential is accuracy. We have seen that the smaller errors tend to give rise to the greatest systemic disturbance, and when their correction becomes advisable, unless this is done with punctilious care, a small error will be perpetuated, perhaps in another form, and the symptoms will be unrelieved. The discomfort on first wearing spectacles experienced by a patient with a marked refractive anomaly may occasionally be caused by a slightly inadequate correction, the residual small error resulting in eye-strain. It is fortunate that of all the branches of medicine, refraction work lends itself to the highest degree of objective accuracy. The same punctiliousness must, of course, be observed in the fitting and centring of spectacles, for inaccuracies in this have the same effect as inaccuracies in determining the prescription. But the worst treatment of all is the firmer fixation of a neurosis by the prescription of successive optical corrections each differing from the other in alterations of insignificant minutiæ.

EYE EXERCISES

Orthoptic Exercises. There is no question that orthoptic exercises designed to remedy bad habits of binocularity, to develop fusional reflexes, and to endow by means of repetitive tutoring a skill to an imperfect neuro-muscular mechanism so that binocular habits are learned and performed easily and smoothly, have a very definite place in the therapeusis of some types of eye-strain. Their value is fully discussed elsewhere,[1] particularly in those common and distressing cases wherein the disability depends on exophoria and convergence deficiency.

Visual Exercises. We have already seen in the fourth volume of this *System* that vision includes not only the formation of retinal images by the dioptric system of the eyes and their transference by physiological processes to the cortex, but also the perceptual appreciation of their presentation as a pattern endowed with meaning. In the interpretation of such patterns the memories of past experiences play a dominant part and the ease and efficiency of the process of seeing depends in very large measure on the facilitation of the cortical processes involved. Orthodox ophthalmology has devoted itself almost entirely to the events occurring at the lower level and has confined its interest to the means of attaining suitable dioptric images on corresponding retinal areas to the relative exclusion of the con-

[1] Vol. VI.

sideration of events at the higher level; and it must be admitted that this
unequal division of interest is without reason. Difficulties of interpretation
at the higher level can be as much a cause of strain as disturbances at the
lower, and in the easement of visual strain the oculist should give consideration to them both. The facilitation of the processes of seeing is exemplified
in a comparison between the efforts of the child who fixes each letter in his
early attempts at reading with the practised reader who can interpret print
with a glance which does not require fixation even of each word: it is the
difference between the facile ease of the practised golfer or skater and the
strained efforts of the tiro. Again, the skilled steel worker sees half a dozen
tints where the untrained observer sees only a uniform glow. Indeed,
practised efficiency at the upper level can compensate for a considerable
degree of failure at the lower, for the same minute and unresolved image on
the retina will appear as a smudge to the landsman and as a particular type
of ship to the trained look-out at sea.

Repetitive exercises, by facilitation of the perceptual processes and the
provision of an accumulated fund of memories and associations to aid
interpretation, are of immense aid in the art of seeing. It is unquestioned
that the efficiency of macular vision can thereby be improved to a dramatic
extent in cases of amblyopia ex anopsia[1]; and innumerable instances are on
record wherein an improvement in visual acuity can be attained amounting
to a line or two in Snellen's test-types by assiduous practice which improves
the interpretative faculties leaving the dioptric imagery unchanged. The
differences in acuity obtained some weeks after discarding long-worn
spectacles is a further example. Similarly it has been shown in properly
controlled conditions that the efficiency of peripheral vision can be increased
some 16% with training (Low, 1943). In the same way it is probable that
with much practice the tricks of a test for colour vision can be learned and
the interpretation of similar tests facilitated sufficiently to enable an examinee to qualify without his colour vision being fundamentally improved—
always provided he is only asked to interpret a similar combination of
tricks (Bridgman and Hofstitter, 1943; Gallagher et al., 1947; McCord,
1947).

The lack of legitimate professional interest in these matters has left a clear field
for their exploitation by the illegitimate practitioner; the opportunity has been
seized with considerable enthusiasm, but in order to make the rather tedious business
of eye-exercises more palatable and make their inherent simplicity sufficiently impressive to convert the credulous, an irrelevant and usually ridiculous pantomime of
accessories has been added (Bates, 1920; Corbett, 1938; Ross and Rehner, 1943;
and many others). The best and most readable exposition is that of Aldous Huxley
(1942–43).

In all these systems the fundamental concept is sound—that visual interpretation
can be improved and strain eased by repetitive exercises alternating with periods
of relaxation. The childish and somewhat undignified accompaniments of palming

[1] Vol. VI.

(covering the closed eyes with the palms of the hands and imagining a beautiful scene), butterfly blinks, relaxed breathing, sunning (" letting go and thinking looseness " and turning the eyes to the sun), swinging (rhythmic swaying of the body to make the mind " friendly to movement " and " soothe " it " as do the movements of the womb or the cradle "), nose-writing (writing with an imaginary pencil conceived to be attached to the nose), flashing with dominoes, shifting, rubbing and kneading the upper part of the nape of the neck and a host of other procedures, are in the main innocuous if there is nothing else to do with time, and add sufficient mystery to make effective therapeusis to the psychopath. To this type of patient such treatment is as valuable as any other autosuggestive system of Yoga or Coué-ism. The foundation of its popularity lies in the possibility of doing away with the abhorrent " crutch " of spectacles; its greatest value in psychopathic states wherein a host of troubles is displaced to and fixated upon the eyes, is to reinstate visual self-confidence in a person emotionally insecure; its danger lies in the acceptance by the credulous of its infallibility in the cure of all ills to the exclusion of any other—and possibly very necessary—method of therapeutics.

Ames. *Amer. J. Ophthal.*, **18,** 1014 (1935); **28,** 248 (1945).

Ames, Gliddon and Ogle. *Arch. Ophthal.*, **7,** 576 (1932).

Bates. *Perfect Sight without Glasses*, N.Y. (1920).

Best. *Zbl. ges. Ophthal.*, **30,** 321 (1934).

Bridgman and Hofstitter. *Optom. Wkly.*, **34,** 471 (1943).

Carpenter. *J. Amer. med. Ass.*, **30,** 198 (1898).

Cohen. *Lancet*, **2,** 933 (1947).

Cohen and Jones. *Brit. Heart J.*, **5,** 67 (1943).

Corbett. *How to Improve your Eyes*, Los Angeles (1938).

Cordes and Harrington. *Amer. J. Ophthal.*, **22,** 1343 (1939).

Cowan. *Amer. J. Ophthal.*, **40,** 481 (1955).

Davis and Pollock. *Arch. Neurol. Psychiat.* (Chic.), **27,** 282 (1932).

Derby. *J. Amer. med. Ass.*, **95,** 913 (1930).

Donders. *On the Anomalies of Accommodation and Refraction of the Eye*, London (1864).

Duane. *Ann. Ophthal.*, **5,** 969 (1896).
Arch. Ophthal., **28,** 261 (1899).
Ophthal. Rec., **13,** 562 (1904).

Emerson. *J. Amer. med. Ass.*, **72,** 1817, 1828 (1919).

Gallagher, J., Ludvigh, Martin and Gallagher, C. *Arch. Ophthal.*, **37,** 572 (1947).

Gould. *J. Amer. med. Ass.*, **17,** 432 (1891); **31,** 632 (1898); **47,** 734 (1906).

von Graefe. *v. Graefes Arch. Ophthal.*, **8** (2), 314 (1862).

Harman. *Brit. med. J.*, **1,** 188 (1948).

Head. *Brain*, **16,** 1 (1893); **17,** 339 (1894); **19,** 153 (1896).

Heaton. *The Eye. Phenomenology and Psychology of Function and Disorder*, London (1968).

Hobbs. *Trans. ophthal. Soc. U.K.*, **84,** 637 (1964).

Hobby. *J. Amer. med. Ass.*, **23,** 377 (1894).

Huxley. *The Art of Seeing*, London (1942). *Collier's*, **111,** 24 (1943).

Jackson. *Amer. J. med. Sci.*, **89,** 404 (1885). *Skiascopy and its Practical Application to the Study of Refraction*, Phila. (1895).

Javal. *Mémoires d'ophtalmométrie*, Paris (1891).

Jones, Isaac. *Equilibrium and Vertigo*, London (1918).

Lancaster. *Amer. J. Ophthal.*, **15,** 783 (1932).

Lewis. *Pain*, N.Y. (1942).

Lewis and Kellgren. *Clin. Sci.*, **4,** 47 (1939).

Low. *Science*, **97,** 586 (1943).

McCord. *J. clin. Psychol.*, **3,** 197 (1947).

Mackenzie, Sir J. *Angina Pectoris*, London (1923).

Mackenzie, W. *Edinb. med. surg. J.*, **60,** 73 (1843).

Maddox. *Tests and Studies of the Ocular Muscles*, Bristol (1898).

Martin. *Ann. Oculist.* (Paris), **99,** 24 (1888).

Martyn. *Brit. med. J.*, **2,** 296 (1864).

Michaelson. *Brit. J. Ophthal.*, **16,** 202 (1932).

Mitchell. *Med. surg. Reporter*, Phila., **31,** 67 (1874).

Murrell. *J. Amer. med. Ass.*, **21,** 642 (1893).

Norton. *Amer. J. Ophthal.*, **4,** 297 (1887).

Penfield. *Amer. J. med. Sci.*, **170,** 864 (1925).

Penfield and McNaughton. *Arch. Neurol. Psychiat.* (Chic.), **44,** 43 (1940).

Ramsay. *Glasg. med. J.*, **106,** 337 (1926). *Lancet*, **2,** 1063 (1931).

Risley. *Ann. Ophthal.*, **1,** 143 (1892).

Ross, J. *Brain*, **10,** 333 (1887–8).

Ross and Rehner. *How to get and keep Good Eyesight*, N.Y. (1943).

Rutherford. *J. Amer. med. Ass.*, **99,** 284 (1932).

Savage. *Ophthal. Rec.*, **1,** 228 (1891); **10,** 453 (1901).
Ophthalmic Myology, Nashville (1902).

Sherrington. *The Integrative Action of the Nervous System*, London (1906–47).

Stevens. *Arch. Ophthal.*, **16,** 149 (1887). *Med. Rec.*, **33,** 511 (1888); **37,** 108 (1890).

Ophthal. Rec., **1**, 215 (1891); **3**, 294 (1893).
A Treatise on the Motor Apparatus of the Eyes, Phila. (1906).

Thompson. *Med. News Libr.*, Phila., **38**, 81 (1879).

Vernon. *Experimental Study of Reading*, London (1931).

White. *Trans. Amer. ophthal. Soc.*, **7**, 153 (1894).

Williams. *Minor Maladies*, London, 78 (1918).

Woods. *J. Amer. med. Ass.*, **49**, 211 (1907).

Zahn. *Oculus artificialis teledioptricus sive telescopium*, Würzburg (1685).

CHAPTER XVI

VISUAL HYGIENE AND THE ENVIRONMENT

VISUAL HYGIENE may be defined as *the promotion of a correct relationship between the visual task, the environment in which it is performed and the person performing it.* Of the environmental factors the most important is illumination.

Illumination

History

The story of man's appreciation of light dates back to the time when he first awoke to the consciousness of the existence of the all-dominating sun; the natural result was that he worshipped it and centred myths around it. In classical mythology the light of the sun was distributed by the Greek god, Helios, who drove his four-horsed chariot daily across the sky from east to west (Fig. 569). On earth, the immortal Prometheus ascended to the top of Mount Olympus to steal some sparks from the wheel of the sun and, carrying them down hidden in a giant fennel, presented them to man, an exploit for which the jealous Zeus chained him to a rock where a monstrous eagle tore at his liver unceasingly until he was freed by Heracles. In Jewish and Christian mythology light was created by God who, as depicted on the ceiling of the Sistine Chapel by Michelangelo, on the first day divided the light from the darkness that " in the beginning " was upon the face of the waters (Fig. 570).

Fire and flaming faggots were undoubtedly the first means of lighting used by primitive man, a source which survived in the flambeaux of the Middle Ages. It is probable, however, that the specialized technique of illumination consisted of some type of combustible material placed in crudely hollowed pieces of stone such as were used by Neanderthal man in the Mousterian Age which flourished as the glaciers of the Ice Age receded northwards. This was followed by the terracotta vessels found in the plains of Mesopotamia dating from 8–7000 B.C., and later in the copper and bronze lamps of Persia and Egypt in 2700 B.C.; in 1000 B.C. these were supplied with a wick and contained olive or nut oil, to be evolved by the Romans in 5–400 B.C. into cylindrical lanterns eventually, according to Pliny (A.D. 50), containing mineral oil. The efficiency of these was vastly improved by Leonardo da Vinci in 1490, and particularly by Aimé Argand of Geneva in 1784, to be aided by the discovery of petroleum by Edwin Drake in 1859. In the meantime, the use by the Greeks and Romans of candles consisting of flax threads coated with pitch dates from the beginning of the Christian era, and wax candles were introduced by the Phœnicians about A.D. 400, a source of lighting which became standardized when the early whalers brought spermaceti into use.

In addition to these standard methods, unusual sources of artificial illumination have been employed. One example of this is the use of wicks drawn through the carcases of various animals copiously rich in fat; in this the penguin was perhaps most frequently used. Another example of artificial illumination was the confinement in lanterns in the West Indies or the imbedding in wax in Java of glow-worms, beetles or fireflies.

Combustible gases from the earth formed a second source of light which, brought

FIG. 569.—HELIOS, GOD OF THE SUN, IN HIS CHARIOT.

At dawn, as he rises from the sea. The boys diving into the sea before his chariot represent the fading stars. An Attic calyx-krater, *c.* 420 B.C., from Apulia, Italy (courtesy of the British Museum).

FIG. 570.—GOD DIVIDING LIGHT FROM DARKNESS.

From the fresco by Michelangelo on the ceiling of the Sistine Chapel, Rome.

from deep beds of rock-salt in bamboo tubes to the surface, were used as illuminants by the Chinese some centuries before the Christian era. The extraction of coal gas by distillation experimentally accomplished by John Clayton in England in 1739 introduced a new technique which was used for lighting by Jean Pierre Minckelers in 1874, to be improved by the introduction by Carl Auer von Welsbach of the incandescent gas-mantle exhibited in London in 1887. In the meantime, Sir Humphry Davy demonstrated that strips of platinum could be heated electrically to incandescence (1809), a discovery which eventually culminated in the introduction by the American inventor, Thomas A. Edison, of a practical incandescent electric lamp with a carbonized thread for a filament (1879), the first commercial installation of which was in the steamship " Columbia " in 1880. This was followed by the use of the osmium filament by Welsbach in 1899 and tungsten filaments in 1907. Simultaneously, lamps based on electric discharges were evolved. About 1850 Henrich Geissler of Germany demonstrated the luminosity accompanying the discharge of electricity through rarefied gases, in 1860 John T. Way in England constructed the first mercury arc, an innovation followed by the use of other gases in the Cooper-Hewitt lamp in the United States in 1903 and the development of low-voltage fluorescent tubes in 1934 and high-intensity sodium-vapour lamps about the middle of the century.

In the practical application of illumination both of natural and artificial light as an art and a science to decrease eye-strain and increase efficiency, no organizations have been more effectual than the Illuminating Engineering Societies, first founded in the United States of America (1906), followed by similar organizations in Britain (1909), Germany (1913), Japan (1915), Austria and Hungary (1915), the Netherlands (1926) and other countries, while the International Commission on Illumination was founded in 1913 and first functioned in Paris in 1921, the purpose of which was to standardize illumination and suggest desiderata for the home, schools, offices and factories. But the individual who acted as a pioneer in converting the world to the belief that good and scientific illumination was a worthwhile aim in the interests of visual health and efficiency was MATTHEW LUCKIESH [1888–1967] (Fig. 571), a native of Iowa who was associated with the General Electric Company from 1910, and became director of its Lighting Research Laboratory at Cleveland in 1924. His researches extended over 20 years, the main trend of which was the concept and design of many lamps and developments in lighting so that artificial lighting should become a competitor of daylight. This truth was told to the scientific world in hundreds of scientific and technical papers and to the lay world in 24 fascinating and readable books; he did more than any other to spread the gospel that effective illumination was medically, scientifically and economically worth while. Some years later his work was taken up in Britain by H. C. Weston, at one time director of the Group for Research in Occupational Optics at the Institute of Ophthalmology in London and president of the Illuminating Engineering Society, whose researches were summarized in his two volumes, *Sight, Light and Efficiency* (1949) and *Sight, Light and Work* (1962), both of which received wide international recognition.

A study of illumination in its relation to the performance of visual tasks must be concerned with the intensity, the distribution and the quality of the lighting provided.

THE INTENSITY OF THE ILLUMINATION

In this respect the standards used in photometry are of importance.[1] The classical unit of luminous intensity was an arbitrary unit, the *foot-candle*. The International

---

[1] See also Vol. IV, p. 457.

Fig. 571.—Matthew Luckiesh
[1888–1967].
(Courtesy of Mrs. Luckiesh.)

Candle was set up by agreement between Britain, the United States and France in 1909, as a sperm candle weighing $\frac{1}{6}$ lb. which burned 120 grains of wax per hour. The flux emitted in a unit solid angle by a source of 1 candle-power constituted a *lumen*. The unit employed was the density of luminous flux of one lumen falling on a specific area, in Britain and America 1 unit per square foot (*foot-candle*), in France 1 unit per square metre (*metre-candle*) or per sq. cm. (*phot*).

In the Procès Verbaux de la Commission Internationale d'Éclairage (C.I.E.) in 1946, international agreement was obtained to change the unit to the *candela* (cd); the radiation emitted per sq. cm. at the opening of a hollow tubular furnace (that is, of black-body radiation) operated at the temperature of solidifying platinum (2,042°K) represents 60 candelas of luminous intensity. In this standardization the *lumen* is the luminous flux emitted within a unit solid angle by an idealized uniform point-source of 1 candela. The illumination of a surface is measured in lumens per sq. foot or per sq. centimetre (the *phot*) or per sq. metre (the *lux*)[1]; the luminance emitted by a surface (its reflectance) used to be measured in *foot-lamberts* (*i.e.*, the illumination in lumen/sq. ft. × the reflection factor) but is now assessed as candelas per sq. foot or as candelas per sq. metre (cd/sq. m., or the *nit*)[2] or sq. cm. (the *stilb*).[3]

The QUANTITY OF ILLUMINATION has a direct bearing on the incidence of eye-strain; it is, of course, relative rather than absolute, depending on the individual, his age, and on the nature of the work, particularly the fineness of the detail which must be resolved. As a rule the fault with illumination is its inadequacy. It is to be remembered that the eyes of man were evolved to function in daylight and that the temperature of the surface of the sun is of the order of 6,000°K; in England direct summer sunlight at noon has an intensity of the order of 100,000 lux, under an overcast sky the intensity is from 5,000 to 1,000 lux, and indoors near a window it varies from 1,000 to 2,000. Yet in all civilized countries today illuminations of 10 or 20 lux are sometimes regarded as adequate in the study, the office or the workshop, and the illumination on the coal-face provided by the miner's oil-lamp was 0·05 lux and by the electric head-lamp only 0·34 lux (Barber *et al.*, 1933). In Britain the application of regulations (1947) is rapidly improving the general illumination of coal mines. It has, of course, to be remembered that excessive light as is experienced in reading in the open air at noon can reduce form vision and be equally distressing (*veiling glare*) (Bell *et al.*, 1922; Stiles, 1929; Albers and Sheard, 1936).[4] Such an excess of light, causing *blinding glare*, not only makes vision more difficult by reducing the sensitivity of the retina and altering the conditions of spatial and temporal induction, but is psychologically disagreeable and often physically painful. The pain appears to be partly due to sustained maximal pupillary contraction, since under mydriasis the glare, although more blinding, is less distressing.

In assessing the quantity of illumination required for any particular task, the visual acuity required to do the task at all (the *basic acuity*) should

[1] 1 lumen/sq. ft. = 10·764 lux.
[2] 1 foot-lambert = 3·426 cd/sq. m., 1 cd/sq. in. = 1,550 cd/sq. m.
[3] 1 stilb = 10,000 cd/sq. m.
[4] Vol. IV, p. 614.

not be made the criterion of measurement, but the standard required for easy and efficient performance of the task (the *efficient acuity*). This can be determined by performance tests wherein accuracy, speed and absence of fatigue are the accepted criteria (Fig. 572). If the ordinary liminal visual standards depending on the angular subtense of the objects viewed are employed, the only results which can legitimately be expected are inefficiency and eye-strain; the criteria should correlate optimum illuminations with visual capacity on a broad statistical basis.

While a considerable amount of work has been done on the relation between visual acuity and illumination,[1] comparatively little attention has been given to visual efficiency, and widely divergent views have been expressed thereon. One reason for this lack of agreement is the immense

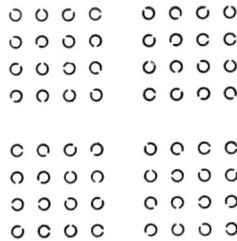

FIG. 572.—A TEST FOR EFFICIENCY OF VISUAL ACUITY.

Sheets of Landolt's broken rings are presented arranged as in the figure and the examinee is required to indicate by a line the position of the gaps. The number of correctly cancelled rings expressed as a fraction of the total number which should have been cancelled is a measure of accuracy. If the number of rings correctly cancelled per minute is multiplied by the accuracy factor the result is *an index of performance*, taking into account both speed and accuracy. The test can be carried out with many variables, as in varying illumination, with print giving different contrasts, with rings of different sizes; and so on (H. C. Weston).

adaptability of the human eye which can function with a considerable degree of efficiency over ranges of illumination between 10,000 : 1.[2]

The relation of basic visual acuity (Ba) to illumination has already been shown to be logarithmic (Ba = K log I, where I is the illumination),[3] wherein the rise in acuity with the illumination is very rapid until a maximum is reached about 20 lumen/sq. ft. (Ferree and Rand, 1920; Lythgoe, 1932; and many others). The degree of illumination required, however, to ensure a worker's efficiency is of a much higher order and must depend upon three factors: (1) the size of the detail in the task considered, (2) the reflectance of the working material, and (3) the amount of contrast in its detail.

[1] Vol. IV, p. 611.
[2] In complete dark adaptation the sensitivity of the retina may be increased by a factor varying from 50,000 to 100,000 times. See Vol. IV, p. 559.
[3] Vol. IV, p. 611.

The *relation of the intensity of illumination to the size of detail* has only recently excited much attention. The early work was done on " ordinary " tasks of which reading was taken as the essential example. Katz (1896) concluded that illuminations 25 times as intense as the threshold standard was a fair average (that is, 0·4 lm/sq. ft. for reading). Most authors at the beginning of this century recommended 2 to 4 lm/sq. ft. as the optimum for reading or average industrial work and Troland (1931), in a most comprehensive review of the subject, suggested 10 lm/sq. ft. For ordinary tasks it is probable that 5 lm/sq. ft. should be taken as a minimum and 10 as a reasonable average. More recent work has shown that with variations in size of the object, efficiency can be retained only with the employment of much wider ranges (Beuttell, 1934; Weston, 1935–62; and others). Weston (1935–62), for example, showed that as the size of detail diminishes, the illumination required for efficient performance increases rapidly at an approximate rate inversely proportional to the third power of the apparent size of the detail to be seen. Thus if 10 lm/sq. ft. are required for an " ordinary " task, 80 are required for work presenting detail of half the size, and if the size were again halved, the necessary illumination for efficiency would be increased to 8 times 80 = 640 lm/sq. ft. Such sizes, which lie near the absolute threshold of resolution, are not uncommon in industry, as in inspection processes, making thermo-couples for instruments measuring radio-frequency, and so on; and when it is remembered that illuminations of this order are not found industrially except occasionally when working in daylight, the reason for the occurrence of eye-strain is obvious.

In these circumstances Weston (1935) found that the efficient acuity (Ea) is a logarithmic function of the base acuity (Ba), the equation being of the form Ea = n log Ba + k, when n = 1·5 and k = 2·22. It would seem, therefore, that depending on the size of the detail of the task, extremes of the range of efficient illumination should be of the order of 100:1.

A very large literature has recently accumulated on recommended scales of illumination and many studies of job-analyses have been published, the best of which are those prepared by the Illuminating Engineering Societies of Great Britain and America. Of these, the recommendations in America are considerably higher than those in Britain and France; those obligatory in Russia vary from 10 lm/sq. ft. to 300 lm/sq. ft. for the most exacting. Examples of the recommendations of the Illuminating Engineering Societies of Britain and America are seen in Table XXV.

In England, the Education Act (1944) provided for regulations governing school lighting. The Regulations (1945) prescribed 10 foot-candles (lm/sq. ft.) as the working level in teaching classrooms; the British Illuminating Engineering Society (1961) now recommends that the level in schools should be at least 30 lm/sq. ft. and up to 70 lm/ sq. ft. in embroidery or sewing rooms.

Suggestions for illumination for domestic activities are seen in Table XXVI.

TABLE XXV

RECOMMENDED LEVELS OF WORKING ILLUMINATION

	I.E.S. BRITAIN (1968) (lux)*	I.E.S. U.S.A. (1965) (foot-candles)*
Offices		
General office work	400	100
Business machine work	600	150
Drawing offices (boards)	600	200
Assembly work		
Rough to very fine work	200–2,000	30–1,000
Inspection (engineering)		
Rough to fine	200–900	50–200
Very fine to minute	2,000–3,000	500–1,000
Machine shops		
Rough bench and machine work	200	50
Medium bench and machine work	400	100
Fine bench and machine work	900	500
Printing plants		
Machine composition	200	100
Presses	400	70
Composing rooms	600	100
Proof reading	900	150
Textile mills		
Cotton:		
Carding and spinning	200	50
Weaving	400–900	100
Cloth inspection	1,300	100
Silk and synthetics:		
Winding, twisting, etc.	400	50–200
Warping	400	100
Weaving	900	100
Woodwork shops		
Rough sawing and bench work	200	30
Sizing, planing, etc.	400	50
Fine bench and machine work	600	100

* 1 foot-candle = 10·76 lux.

TABLE XXVI

RECOMMENDED LEVELS OF DOMESTIC ILLUMINATION

	BRITAIN (lux)	U.S.A. (foot-candles)
Living rooms:		
General	100	10
Reading (casual)	200	30–50
Desk and prolonged reading	400	50–70
Sewing and darning	600	30–200
Bedrooms:		
General	50	10
Bed-head	200	30–50
Kitchens (working areas)	200	30
Bathrooms	100	30
Halls, landings, stairs	100	10

The importance of *the reflection factor of the work*—that is, its ability to reflect incident light—is frequently forgotten. It is to be remembered that a simple statement of the illumination emitted by the source of light or as an intensity incident upon the work in hand may be quite illusory. The eye sees any object by means of the light reflected from it and if most of the light is absorbed or transmitted by the object, a higher level of illumination is required for efficiency in seeing. This is illustrated diagrammatically in Figs. 573–4. The brightness of any object, as we have seen, is equal to its illumination multiplied by its reflection factor. With the same degree of

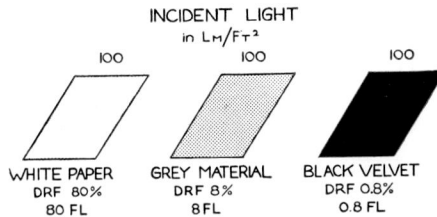

Fig. 573.—To Illustrate the Amount of Light Reflected from Different Materials when the Incident Light is Constant.

When the incident light is 100 lm./ft.², white paper reflects 80%, grey material 8% and black velvet only 0·8% (after M. Luckiesh).

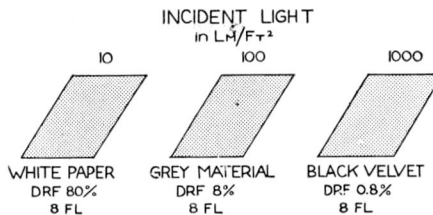

Fig. 574.—To Illustrate the Amount of Incident Light necessary to give Equal Reflected Illumination from Different Surfaces.

If a reflected illumination of 8 foot-lamberts is desired, an incident illumination of 10 lm./ft.² is necessary on white paper (diffuse reflection factor 80%), of 100 lm./ft.² on grey material (diffuse reflection factor 8%), and of 1,000 lm./ft.² on black velvet (diffuse reflection factor 0·8%) (after M. Luckiesh).

illumination, therefore, white paper, with a reflection factor of 80%, has 10 times the brightness of grey cloth (reflection factor 8%) and 100 times the brightness of black velvet (reflection factor 0·8%). If efficiency and ease of seeing demand a specific brightness, the illumination required for reading on white paper should be increased by one fourth, that required for sewing grey cloth should be 10 times greater than this, and that required for working on black velvet 100 times greater. For the attainment of uniform efficiency it would thus appear that even with homely tasks variations of intensity of illumination of the order of 1 to 100 are necessary. Table XXVII gives typical reflection factors for different colours.

The *relation of the intensity of the illumination to the contrasts* provided in the detail to be analysed is of equal importance. The ease of seeing any object depends largely on its contrast with neighbouring objects, that is, on the differences it presents in brightness and colour from these. Such a measurement, of course, is relative depending on the illumination falling upon the objects concerned and their reflection factors. Thus in reading, if the ink reflects 4% of the incident light and good white paper 80%, the contrast is 4 : 80 or 95%. If the ink is bad and the paper is poor, yellow or smudged, the contrast is lessened and more illumination is required for equal efficiency. With equal illumination, however high its value, equal performance of tasks presenting different contrasts cannot be obtained, for performance with a poor contrast can never equal the maximum performance

TABLE XXVII
TYPICAL REFLECTION FACTORS

REFLECTION FACTOR PER CENT	MATERIALS	COLOURS BRITISH STANDARD (1930)
80–89	White tile	
	Good white paper	
70–79	White plastics	
	White paper	Pale cream
	Polished brass	
60–69	" White " newsprint	Deep cream
	Aluminium	Lemon
	Polished copper	Golden yellow
50–59	Portland stone	Light buff
40–49	Concrete	Middle buff
	Poplar, deal	Grey
30–39	Dull brass	Salmon pink
	Yellow brick	Deep buff
20–29	Dull copper	Turquoise blue
	Bright steel	Golden brown
10–19	Cast iron	Sage green
	Galvanized iron	Grass green
Less than 10	Black velvet	Crimson

when this is good. For a wide range of illuminations the effect of a change of contrast on performance is greater the smaller the size involved. In general, performance varies directly with the contrast in brightness and the illumination required varies inversely with it. As a rough approximation it may be said that increasing the illumination from 1 to 100 increases the visual acuity 70%, the speed of seeing 230%, and the contrast-sensitivity 350% (Nutting, 1916; Lythgoe and Tansley, 1929; Luckiesh and Moss, 1934; Ferree and Rand, 1934). Nevertheless, both brightness contrast and colour contrast should not be excessive; symptoms of visual fatigue and eye-strain may result from this just as from inadequate contrast.

The value of designing contrasts as a visual aid is becoming recognized in industry. Thus, a study of the effect of providing a suitable light background to a fine assembly process was found by Mitchell (1936) to increase output by 19·5%. While it is still common to do minute tasks with dull-coloured metal upon an equally dull-coloured bench, it is much easier and very much more profitable (and much more gay) to work upon, say, a pale yellow and green bench of washable plastic material. The immense differences involved are exemplified in Fig. 575. Apart from the visual task itself, environmental colour can be employed to good effect by creating a psychologically pleasant working background; here again, contrast is important, for a large area of one strong colour is undesirable (Weston, 1962).

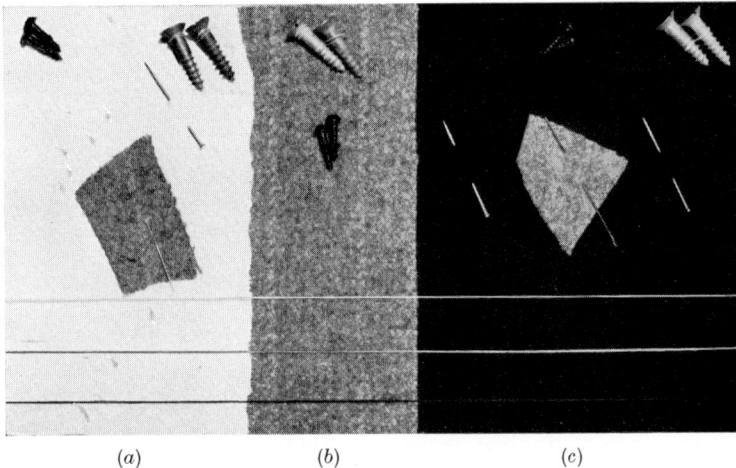

(a)   (b)   (c)

FIG. 575.—THE IMPORTANCE OF CONTRAST.

The importance in the contrast of the background is well seen. Thus the black tacks are well seen in (a) and (b) but are almost invisible in (c) (top middle). The screws are seen much better in (a) and (c) than in (b). The needle is well seen on a white background in (a) but hardly at all in the small square of grey cloth, but is well seen in (c). The white thread (upper) is clear in (b) and (c) but not in (a); the grey thread clear in (a) and (c) but not in (b); and the black thread in (a) and (b) but not in (c).

THE DISTRIBUTION OF THE ILLUMINATION

The distribution of the illumination is as important as its intensity. As early as 1685, Johann Zahn (Fig. 513) stressed that in reading the candle should be placed so that no direct light can enter the eyes, but positioned so that it falls from behind or from the side and preferably from above. Too much illumination in the peripheral field of view lowers the visual efficiency by reducing the acuity and perpetuating after-images and thus causes distress (*dazzling glare*) (Cobb, 1913–19; Holladay, 1926; Cobb and Moss, 1928; Luckiesh and Moss, 1933). This result is seen in exaggerated form in the effect of motor headlights and occurs more commonly with unshaded lights in a room or workshop. *Specular glare* is a further cause of distress. Specularly reflected light from an object which is being studied cannot be focused on the retina, since if it were focused it would form an image of the source of light, not of the reflecting object. So long as the object is focused, therefore, the light of specular reflection forms an overlay of unfocused light upon the image, blurring it and hampering and embarrassing vision (Hardy and Rand, 1945). For this reason the illumination,

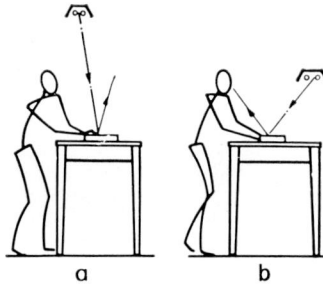

FIG. 576.—THE PLACEMENT OF SUPPLEMENTARY LIGHTING.

a, a good position which prevents reflected glare. *b*, a bad position when reflected light coincides with the angle of view.

FIG. 577.—SUPPLEMENTARY ILLUMINATION.

The lamp is in a good position to avoid specular reflexes (General Electric Company).

daylight or artificial, particularly by inadequately shielded lamps mounted close to the task, should not be directly in front but to the side (Figs. 576–7), and a bench should run at right angles to a window. This type of glare is seen in an exaggerated form in the reflection of the sun on snow or a body of water, and is a common result of the reflection of lights on shiny paper or polished metal surfaces.

It is undesirable that there should be any great contrast in illumination between the area under observation and neighbouring areas, for a brilliantly illuminated working area in a dark room requires rapid changes of adaptation which are abolished by a moderate amount of general illumination; worse is a higher illumination in the surrounding field than on the object. The great advantage of daylight for working indoors is its diffusion, for the room is lit not usually by the sun but by a considerable area of sky, an arrangement most closely attained artificially by the combination of direct and indirect lighting.

FIG. 578.—FOREHEAD SHIELD
FOR PROTECTION AGAINST
GLARE.

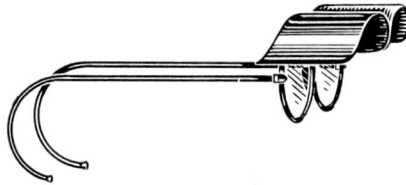

FIG. 579.—FLANGED SPECTACLES FOR
PROTECTION AGAINST GLARE.

The distribution of the light is therefore important in two respects— the avoidance of glare and the provision of a balanced illumination in the background and the surrounds. To avoid glare from the source of light itself all intense sources of light should be as far as possible outside the line of vision; if that is impossible protection for the eyes can be obtained in many cases by wearing a peaked cap, a large forehead shield (tennis shade) (Fig. 578) or flanged spectacles (Fig. 579). To avoid reflected glare from specular reflection the source of light (or the position of the worker) should be moved so that the eye receives no light reflected directly from the source but only diffused light. If this is impossible the light source should be made as extensive as possible.

Rhoads (1913) suggested a useful test for this type of glare. A mirror is placed on the working plane or in the position of a book to be read; if any light source can be seen in the mirror, some specular glare must exist.

A balanced illumination is equally important for comfort and efficiency. When the surroundings are of a markedly different brightness from the working (or reading) area there is a great reduction of visual acuity (Lythgoe, 1932—36), the speed of vision (Lythgoe and Tansley, 1929), the contrast

sensitivity (Cobb, 1916) and the accuracy of visual judgments (Cobb and
Moss, 1925). The acuity, for example, improves as the surrounding illumination is raised to the level of a little below the test-object; if the surrounding
illumination is raised above this point, there is a very rapid decline in performance (Fig. 580). To work in a small pool of light surrounded by gloom
is therefore bad; but it is worse to work in shadow surrounded by light.

To avoid eye-strain and attain ocular comfort, therefore, efficient
lighting requires not only candelas but engineering and design. The visual
task should be a little lighter than the surroundings, and this can best be
attained by a combination of diffuse roof lighting (direct or semi-direct)

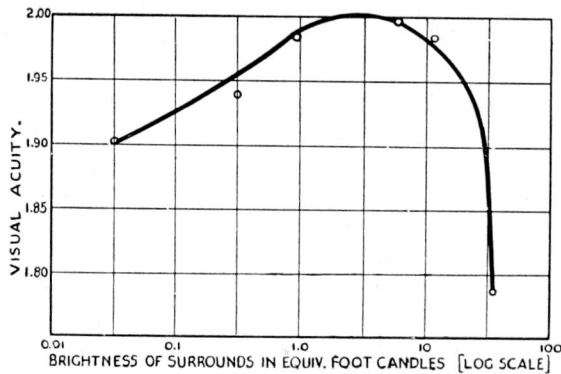

Fig. 580.—The Influence of Brightness of the Surrounds on Visual
Acuity with a Constant Brightness of the Test-object.

At a constant illumination of the test-object at 130 lux (13 f.c.) the visual acuity
improves slowly as the surrounding illumination is raised to just below the level of that
of the test-object; when it is raised beyond this point there is a rapid fall in performance
(R. Lythgoe).

attained by diffusing bowls of louvered units by which some 40 to 60% of
the light is emitted upwards and the remainder downwards, together with
shaded supplementary lighting placed relatively close to the task in such a
way that specular glare does not arise (Figs. 581–3).

As opposed to *panoramic lighting*, this, the *ergoramic lighting* of Weston
(1962), wherein other local sources of light are provided in addition to
the general illumination, is of particular value when work of great precision
is required, when cavities exist or shadows cannot otherwise be eliminated.
It is to be remembered, of course, that in some industrial processes such as
certain types of inspection for defects the formation of shadows is a necessity.

A useful test for an adequate distribution of light was suggested by Lancaster
(1937). A pencil is held parallel to and 3 in. above a sheet of paper upon which light
from the main source falls perpendicularly; a sharp and clear-cut shadow indicates too
concentrated a light, while a blurred shadow indicates adequate diffusion.

The illumination can be much enhanced by suitable *colouring in the environment*. Much work has been done on this subject to determine the most satisfactory contrasting colours for use on ceilings, walls, floors, benches and machines. The ceilings, as a rule, should be light and have as high a reflection factor as possible; the upper walls should have a reflectance of 50 to 60% and the lower not more than 30 to 40% if dark furniture and machines are in view. The colour employed should be non-aggressive, of medium tone without harsh contrasts. Similarly, the painting of large expanses of drab machinery with light-tinted durable paints increases the

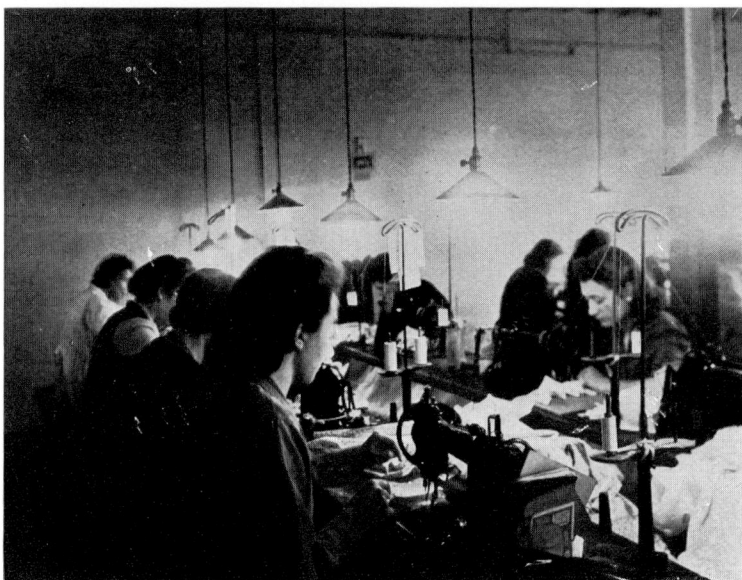

FIG. 581.—BAD LIGHTING.

Bad lighting in a clothing factory. The light-sources are inadequately screened so that they cause considerable glare, which is uncomfortable and detrimental to visual efficiency. The light is badly distributed and produces heavy shadows which reduce the visibility of the work. The surroundings are poorly illuminated and the general appearance of the interior is grim.

amount of light reflected to the shadowed sections of the machines. A marked contrast, for example, between the stationary and moving parts of a machine not only makes it easily seen in three dimensions but also provides a high safety factor. To these advantages of increased efficiency and decreased danger there is added the psychological effect of brightness and cheerfulness—so sadly and unnecessarily lacking in many industrial plants.

THE QUALITY OF THE ILLUMINATION

A further important factor which must be considered is the *type of light*—its flickering nature and colour, that is, its spectral composition. A

FIG. 582.—A WELL-LIT FACTORY.
Lit by 780 Lucalox lamps (General Electric Company).

FIG. 583.—GOOD LIGHTING.
The knitting machine room of a hosiery factory. The artificial light is fluorescent.
The light is well distributed and gives good visibility everywhere—even on the floor
(compare Fig. 584).

flickering light, such as may be seen with moving machinery, with fluorescent light out-of-phase, or as was common in the early days of the cinema, excites rapid changes of adaptation and considerable psychological annoyance. Sunlight, to which the eyes are adapted by evolution, is richer by reason of its temperature in short wavelengths (blue and violet) than any artificial illuminant, but there is no evidence that the excess of longer wavelengths in the latter, if adequate in intensity and properly distributed, gives rise to strain. The efficiency of vision is highest with white light, and fatigue has been said to come on more readily with red and yellow than with blue and

FIG. 584.—To Illustrate the rapid Fall of the Illumination
DERIVED FROM SIDE WINDOWS IN A LARGE ROOM.
The fall to 1% is rapid. Compare Figs. 582 and 583.

green (Bockoven and Wilcox, 1937). The vagueness and psychological disturbance caused by a highly fluorescent light, as seen in radar tubes, is usually a prolific cause of fatigue.

NATURAL DAYLIGHT is generally accepted to be the best lighting from the practical and psychological point of view, but if it is to be effective the windows must not be obstructed by other buildings, they must be adequate in number and distribution and they must be kept clean—an important detail which seldom receives enough attention in industry. With side windows it is often impossible to light satisfactorily all parts of a large floor space without subjecting some of the workers to objectionable glare (Fig. 584); the most satisfactory method wherewith to provide a uniform illumination is through an abundance of skylight windows high up, near or in the roof. It is to be remembered, also, that even in sunny climates daylight provides an inadequate illumination for a surprisingly large percentage of the time; artificial lighting is usually necessary everywhere at some time.

The *daylight factor* is the fraction of the outside illumination which reaches any particular area inside a building. A minimum value of 4% will lead to a satisfactory level of internal illumination of work-rooms— giving a level of 70 cd/sq. m. if the outside illumination does not fall below 1,000 cd/sq. m. (Figs. 585–6).

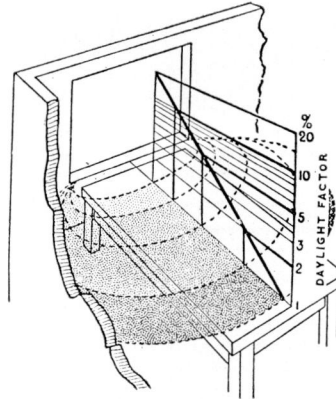

FIG. 585.—THE VARIATION OF THE DAYLIGHT FACTOR AT DIFFERENT POINTS ON THE WORKING PLACE IN A ROOM LIGHTED BY WINDOWS IN ONE WALL (H. C. Weston).

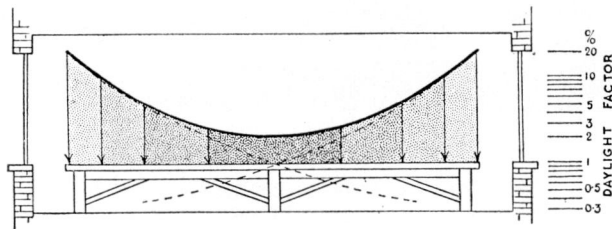

FIG. 586.—THE VARIATION OF THE DAYLIGHT FACTOR ACROSS A ROOM LIGHTED BY WINDOWS IN OPPOSITE WALLS (H. C. Weston).

Nearly all ARTIFICIAL LIGHTING is now by electricity and two different types of source are used, incandescent and discharge lamps. It should be remembered, however, that with this type of lighting no lamp is immortal for they all slowly deteriorate throughout their lives (Figs. 587–8). The initial planning of the illumination should therefore make allowance for this and the lamps should be renewed before they become half spent. The loss of efficiency, of course, depends not only on the decrease of the output of light from the lamps with age but also with the rate at which dirt accumulates, a factor which depends largely on design.

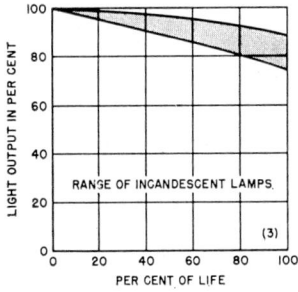

FIG. 587.

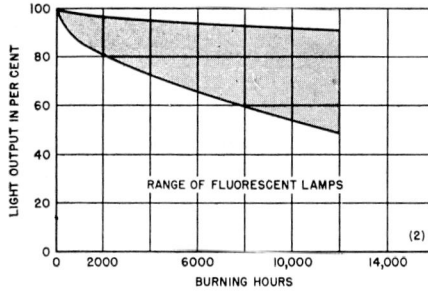

FIG. 588.

FIGS. 587 and 588.—LAMP-LUMEN DEPRECIATION.

The shaded area indicates the range of the curves for 25 to 1,000 watt general service lamps for incandescent (Fig. 587) and fluorescent lamps (Fig. 588) (General Electric Company).

Incandescent lamps with filaments of tungsten provide a continuous spectrum with a psychologically pleasing predominance of the longer wavelengths giving a " warm " tone (Fig. 589). A tungsten filament, however, is of limited life and its efficiency is not outstandingly great. Recently quartz iodine bulbs, which are of greater efficiency, have been introduced in which, as the tungsten vaporizes, it combines with iodine to form tungsten iodide;

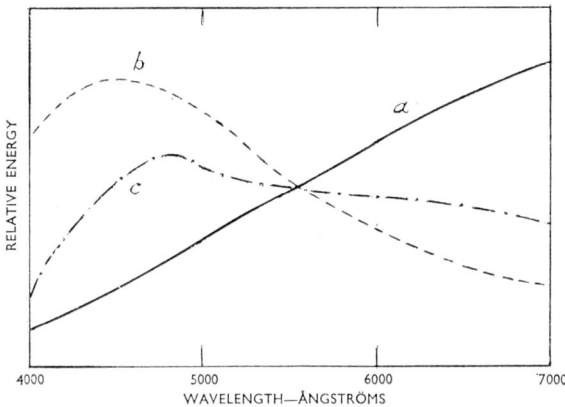

FIG. 589.—SPECTRAL ENERGY DISTRIBUTION FOR DIFFERENT LIGHTS (H. C. Weston).

(*a*) Tungsten filament light; (*b*) north sky light; (*c*) noon sunlight, on basis of equal energy at wavelength 555 mμ.

this then decomposes at the very high prevailing temperature, depositing the tungsten on the filament again. The quartz incorporated in the wall of the bulb withstands the high temperature, and the overall size of the lamp is smaller than ordinary filament lamps. They are of particular value for public lighting and also for car headlights.

Electric discharge lamps are of two types. In the first a discharge occurs in a gaseous atmosphere. Neon, sodium vapour and mercury vapour lights are of this type, the latter two being widely used for street lighting. The light they emit is not in the form of a continuous spectrum (Fig. 590), and colour rendering is poor. Sodium and mercury vapour lamps were formerly of a type which operated only at low pressures, but now higher pressures up to 10 atmospheres and beyond are employed. The importance of this is that the higher the pressure the greater is the proportion of the radiation emitted in the visible spectrum.

Fluorescent lighting is a second type of electric discharge lamp which has become increasingly popular since it was commercially employed in 1938. In this type of lighting an arc is produced by a current flowing through

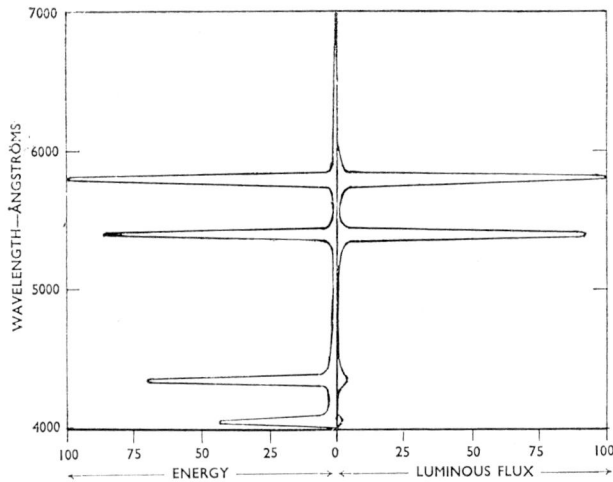

FIG. 590.—THE DISTRIBUTION OF ENERGY AND LUMINOUS FLUX IN THE VISIBLE SPECTRUM OF HIGH-PRESSURE MERCURY VAPOUR LAMPS (H. C. Weston).

mercury vapour contained at a low pressure within a tube; the arc generates some light and much ultra-violet radiation which excites fluorescent chemicals (the phosphor) coated on the inside of the tube and these convert this radiation to light. Such an illuminant is not harmful to the eyes (Taylor, 1945; Hardy, 1945; and others), nor is any appreciable degree of ultra-violet light emitted (Fig. 591). These lights have a high efficiency, giving out little heat, and are particularly suitable for lighting large areas. Nevertheless, they frequently make people psychologically unhappy, possibly because of the preponderance of short rays, their high intrinsic brightness, the extent of the light source, the occurrence of flicker and the fact that the lights are frequently badly arranged (Collins, 1956). The flicker is probably due to a small fluctuation of 50 cycles/sec. superimposed on the 100 cycles/sec. on which the tubes run, but appropriate design should render this modulation negligible (Collins and Hopkinson, 1954). Although they emit a continuous spectrum, the relative deficiency of long wavelengths from which the early type suffered made colour-rendering poor, but in later types the red end of the spectrum has been augmented giving a more " natural " hue.

Apart from industries wherein colour discrimination is important, however, variations in the quality of light have little practical effect on visual acuity (Luckiesh and Moss, 1936; Woodside and Reinhardt, 1937). In all cases the brightness of fluorescent tubes should be controlled by a central louvre or be otherwise shaded, they should be high above the level of the eyes against a ceiling which itself should be bright; deteriorated lamps which flicker and thus cause psychological annoyance and visual fatigue should be discarded, and multiple out-of-phase tubes should be used. Even so, an unpleasant stroboscopic effect is obtained with moving machinery.

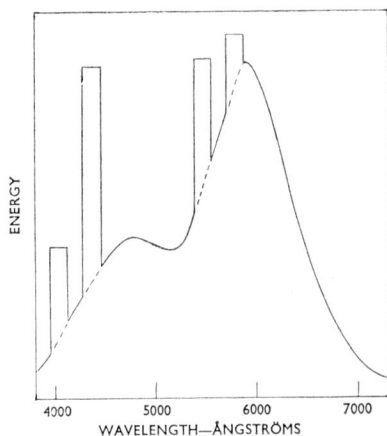

FIG. 591.—SPECTRAL ENERGY DISTRIBUTION CURVE OF AN 80-WATT FLUORESCENT "NATURAL" TUBE (H. C. Weston).

The Visual Task

There is no doubt that some visual tasks are more taxing than others. It would therefore seem logical to expect eye-strain more frequently in those whose work demands great attention to fine detail over a prolonged period of time. Apart from the peripheral muscular effort required there is certainly an element of what, for want of a more specific term, we may call mental fatigue.

In comparing one visual task with another, several factors must be considered: the viewing distance, the detail or visual size, any required perception of motion, the contrast of the object with its environment, and the influence of reflection of light from the object.

The viewing distance and the visual size are obviously interrelated. Visual tasks were conveniently classified by Weston (1949) according to the viewing distances into three types: *teloramic* (τῆλε, far; ὅραμα, a view), over six feet (steel-rolling or viewing a blackboard are examples); *mesoramic* (μέσος, middle), one foot to six feet, including most indoor occupations and reading; and *ancoramic* (ἄγχι, near), less than one foot, such as fine embroidery. The greater the required perception of detail, the closer the working distance and the greater the effort of convergence and accommodation required, the more is the liability to eye-strain.

The apparent size of the object of regard is therefore of prime importance and there are three ways in which this can be increased so that the visual task becomes easier: by the use of large objects, by the approximation of the object to the eye, and by the employment of optical magnification. Of these the first and last are the most useful.

Increasing the apparent size of the objects comprising the visual task is a much more rewarding method of improving the visual efficiency and reducing eye-strain than any method directed primarily to environmental factors. Weston (1962) found that a tenfold increase of the illumination produced an improvement of 30% in the performance of a simple visual task, whereas increasing the apparent size ten times produced a 200% improvement in performance. The employment of optical aids to magnification has become standard industrial practice and we shall be examining some of these devices and their optical principles when discussing optical appliances in a later Chapter.

It may be noted here, however, as was originally suggested by Brücke (1859) for dissecting, that in many industrial tasks involving minute accuracy at close range, visual fatigue can frequently be relieved, even if the eyes are normal, by spectacles wherein spheres are combined with prisms (*orthoscopic spectacles*). Weston and Adams (1927–29) showed that with such optical aids, in addition to the comfort thereby attained, efficiency in the production of linkers, menders in a wool-mill, and steel-ball examiners increased automatically up to 25%. The combined aid to accommodation and convergence thus obtained allows the approximation of the object to the eye, thus increasing its apparent size without strain.

A brief note on two common activities may be desirable—reading and viewing television.

Reading

Reading is a complex act and advice for the avoidance of strain and discomfort should involve a multiplicity of factors, physical, psychological and interpretive, which have not yet been satisfactorily correlated. The most important requirement for ease and comfort is sufficient illumination arranged so that direct light does not enter the eyes; a light of 200 to 400 lux should be placed behind and to the side (the left side for writing by right-handed people so that the shadow of the hand is avoided). The worst possible arrangement is in front so that the specular reflection from glossy paper is seen. These considerations obviously apply to reading in bed for which a bright central ceiling light should be banned.

Considering the great importance of reading in modern life, it is surprising that the visibility of different forms of type has received so little attention from physiologists. Historically these were derived from manuscripts and were modified for technical reasons, but further changes have been almost entirely empirical and even in the best printing presses more care has been expended on obtaining æsthetic effects than in fostering legibility. It is to be remembered that the eyes read a line of print in a series of small jumps (saccades)[1] and in the pauses between, a group of about ten letters is more or less accurately visualized; when ocular movements occur they are too rapid to allow the letters to be seen. The only smooth movement is between the end of one line and the beginning of its successor. The number of saccades remains the same irrespective of the distance at which the book is held. A child or an adult reading a strange language or the proof-reader makes more and shorter jumps than the practised reader of a well-known language and he directs his attention chiefly to the commencement of words, reading them not by letters but their general configuration. In this the legibility of the typing is important.

In English printed characters all capital letters extend above the line and in the ordinary page of print about 85% of the ordinary long letters extend above the line and only 15% descend below. In the short letters the most characteristic features are in their upper parts which attract the greatest attention; thus if the lower half of a line of print is covered by a card, the context is easily read, a feat difficult or impossible if the upper half is covered. Legibility is considerably increased if the lines in the letters are emphasized by serifs, probably an empirical introduction which counteracts irradiation and thus increases definition. The tendency of printers, however, to attain uniformity of appearance by equalizing the thickness of heavy and slender strokes which formed a feature of writing by quills or pens, considerably diminishes legibility, but the slender strokes must not transgress the limits of visibility at the reading distance and their terminations should be accentuated by serifs. Similarly, the modern tendency to minimize the differences between letters diminishes visibility. Thus round letters have been flattened laterally and square letters rounded; the loops of b, d, p, and q, have been equalized to o, and the similarity of the top curves of a, c, e, o, and s, of n and r, of h and b, or of n and p, as now printed, is much greater than it used to be. It is probable, however, that these physiological disadvantages will continue to be sacrificed to æsthetic considerations.

Television and the *cinema* have always given rise to anxiety lest they damage the eyes by causing strain. There was some justification for this in the early evolution of

[1] Vol. VI.

these media at the period when the jerky and the stroboscopic effect was considerable, but now that the succession of stationary pictures is sufficiently rapid to give an effect of continuous movement this criticism does not arise. Acceptable conditions are obtained with 50 frames per sec., a surprisingly low figure rendered possible by the finite decay-time of the screen phosphor (Haantjies and de Vrijer, 1951). Provided the general lighting is adequate to obviate a sharp differentiation between a dark surround and brightly lit screen to avoid the annoyance of rapid and frequent changes of adaptation, and provided the viewer is at least some 10 feet away so that the screening is invisible, these media cause no damage to the eyes particularly if, with any significant refractive error corrected, he relaxes and refrains from continually straining to see minute detail. The spectral emission by television tubes for non-coloured screening shows peaks in the blue and yellow and it has been suggested that this might give rise to accommodative difficulties; the wearing of blue or yellow tinted spectacles to overcome this has little to recommend it.

The Individual and the Environment

It is clear that visual comfort in the environment, with its accompaniment of efficiency, healthfulness and lack of strain, is a complex subject demanding much study and experience, for it is measured subjectively as well as objectively, and the requirements are not susceptible to universal legislation but must be modified to suit the particular task and the individual (or low average) worker. Defective illumination can readily be recognized and in most cases eradicated—despite popular prejudice—with considerable economic profit. The human element, however, is not so readily manipulated. The visual capacity of the person concerned is also of importance. This depends not only on his work and his condition of work but also on his visual skill, innate or acquired, which is naturally a matter of great individual variation. The trained worker is able to appreciate defects so minute as to be invisible to the untutored eye, or can pick out subtle differences in colour. Nevertheless, whatever his innate or acquired skills, they can be profoundly influenced by environmental factors, particularly the illumination. A task requiring a " normal " acuity, that is, involving the resolution of details subtending a visual angle of 1 min., cannot be done over a long period with efficiency by a person of " normal " vision (6/6). Weston (1943) found that efficiency required an acuity double this (6/3). Lighting standards are generally fixed on the basis of the needs of the average worker, suggested (usually in a vague way) by experience or experiment. The performance of all workers with increasing illumination increases with improvement in the illumination up to high levels of the order of 5,000 lux, but the improvement is relatively greater among those with inferior than with superior visual capacity. The level of efficiency in any work-room is therefore higher if the illumination meets the needs not of the average but of the " average inferior " worker.

It is to be remembered, also, that *age* is an important factor since more light is required by those past mid-life than the young if the same visual efficiency is to be maintained. It has been shown that the retinal illumination at the age of 60 is about one-third that at the age of 20 (Weale, 1961) and that the visual resolving power begins to fall after the age of 50 years (Slataper, 1950; Weale, 1963) (Fig. 592). This question has not been fully explored, nor have its implications been realized, but Weston (1947) has shown that there is a steady diminution of visual efficiency after the age of 20 sometimes involving an *annual* loss of as much as 3 to 4%. This loss of the speed and acuity of vision is additional to the loss of accommodative power and is still evident when presbyopic spectacles are worn; it is of insidious onset and may in part be due to decreasing transparency of the ocular media, a decrease in muscular reaction-time and a decrease in the speed and efficiency of the higher ocular reflexes. Whatever the cause, it is most pronounced if the visual task is made more difficult by decreasing the

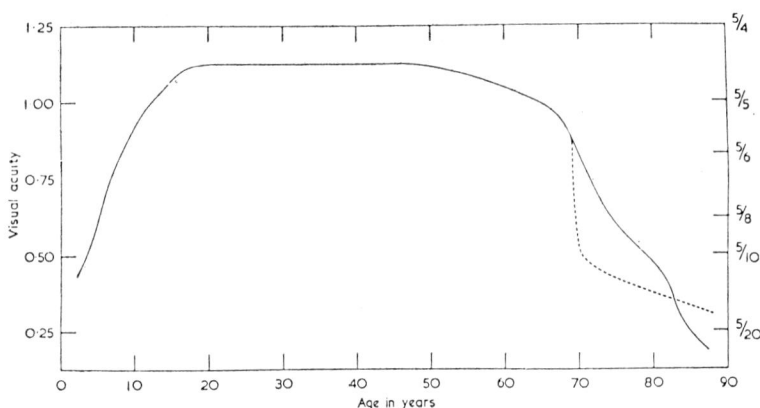

FIG. 592.—THE AGE-VARIATION OF VISUAL RESOLVING POWER.

The continuous line refers to normal observers; the dotted line includes observers with incipient cataract (after F. J. Slataper).

illumination, the angular size of the objects, or their contrast with the background, but to a considerable extent it can be offset by increasing the illumination. As age advances a given increment of illumination (for example, a doubling) is relatively more effective, giving a greater percentage improvement of visual efficiency at the age of 45 than 35. It follows that middle-aged and older workers should have considerably brighter levels of illumination than the young, but it is to be remembered that no matter how much the illumination be improved, it cannot nullify the toll of time.

From the prophylactic point of view, however, much could be done by the adoption of adequate pre-selection for jobs requiring specific visual skills, effective ocular supervision and, when necessary, the provision of optical aids. In view of the fact that a very high proportion of the population has ocular defects (some 40% of industrial workers, Luckiesh and Moss, 1930; Sydenstricker and Britten, 1930; Rainey, 1937; or of students,

Thacker, 1939; Kuhn, 1941; and many others), the selection of workers for particular industries is of importance. Apart from certain special services such as transport and the fighting services, as a general rule the young worker on entering industry is guided in his choice of work rather by chance or inclination than by his physical fitness for it, for relatively few firms require a visual test for potential employees; but there is no doubt of the benefits which would accrue—in comfort, and in lack of eye-strain, in safety to the worker and in increased efficiency to industry—if young men and women starting work were guided (not necessarily directed) into jobs for which they were physically suited—or at any rate, not markedly unsuited. The selection of applicants for jobs is becoming more important as an increasing social conscience and paternal legislation make haphazard " hire and fire " a difficult procedure. As a general rule a slow process of natural selection occurs, for the apprentice in a machine shop never becomes a lathe-hand if his sight is unequal to the job. The problem is intensified today because the complications and speed of machines are greatly increased, and to tend the machines faster reactions and keener vision are required. The handicapped worker necessarily becomes a misfit, he is uneasy in his decisions, slow in his judgments, and all the while strained, fatigued and unhappy, as well as being in many cases a danger to himself and his fellows.

The ideal, of course, is systematized testing in school, not only at the stage of leaving school, but also at the stage when the adolescent may be forming ambitions for his future, in order to avoid the wastage of unsuitable specialist education and the disappointment of a frustrated career. It is, however, to be remembered that the usual test of reading letters at a certain distance practised in many schools and services today is quite inadequate; data not only on distant vision are required, but also on near vision, convergence and the muscular balance of the eyes, the stereoscopic sense and colour vision, as well as an indication of the probability of the maintenance of this standard throughout the working life. Finally, in many occupations a test for speed of vision is of great value, assessing both the efficiency of vision and of the mental reaction thereto (Weston, 1945) (Fig. 572).[1] Some jobs require perfection in the retinal image, others fine discrimination of movement, others stereopsis, others good adaptation, and others attention and expectancy rather than visual discrimination. The clerk should have at least 6/12 vision in one eye and, if binocular, he should have good convergence. A crane operator must have good distant vision and depth perception; the operator of a strip mill requires good distant vision to read his dials; in machine tool operations and machine feeding operations depth perception is necessary; inspection of tin plate requires good near vision; small-parts assembly requires good near vision and good convergence. Other specific jobs have other visual requirements and the employee (or potential employee) not meeting one requirement may meet another and be put on the job for

[1] This may be done rapidly by the various visual screening devices (p. 447).

which he is best suited. Indeed, as a practical definition " good " industrial vision should not connote the ability to see in the distance ; " good " vision for a specific job may be said to be *the visual ability which is adequate to perform the visual task in question comfortably and efficiently*. Such a procedure of selection would not result in the establishment of a pool of unemployables, for there are tasks in plenty for all types of vision—and, indeed, for the blind.

The systematic care of the eyes as a prophylactic against eye-strain should not cease when the individual commences work. Changing conditions and changes in work as well as the gradual deterioration of vision with age make it advisable that periodic examination of the eyes should be made, not only in school life, but at intervals all throughout the working life, and if advisable, optical aids adjusted for special working distances or if necessary a change of activity advised (see Andrew, 1936 ; Slyfield, 1937 ; Mayer, 1942 ; and many others).

Albers and Sheard. *Amer. J. Ophthal.*, **19**, 407, 460 (1936).

Andrew. *The Eyes in Industry* (Nat. Soc. Prev. Blindness, U.S.A.) (1936).

Barber, Emmett and Jones. *Trans. Inst. mining Engrs.*, **85**, 155 (1933).

Bell, Troland and Verhoeff. *Trans. illum. Engng. Soc. Amer.*, **17**, 743 (1922).

Beuttell. *Illum. Engineer*, **27**, 5 (1934).

Bockoven and Wilcox. *Arch. Ophthal.*, **17**, 1024 (1937).

Brücke. *v. Graefes Arch. Ophthal.*, **5** (2), 180 (1859).

Cobb. *Trans. illum. Engng. Soc. Amer.*, **8**, 292 (1913).
Psychol. Rev., **21**, 23 (1914) ; **26**, 428 (1919). *J. exp. Psychol.*, **1**, 540 (1916).

Cobb and Moss. *J. Franklin Inst.*, **199**, 507 (1925) ; **205**, 831 (1928).

Collins. *Ophthalmologica*, **131**, 83, 377 (1956).

Collins and Hopkinson. *Trans. illum. Engng. Soc. Lond.*, **19**, 135 (1954).

Ferree and Rand. *J. exp. Psychol.*, **3**, 243 (1920).
Trans. illum. Engng. Soc. Amer., **29**, 296 (1934).

Haantjies and de Vrijer. *Philips' Techn. Rev.*, **13**, 55 (1951).

Hardy. *Illum. Engineer*, **40**, 287 (1945).

Hardy and Rand. *Arch. Ophthal.*, **33**, 1 (1945).

Holladay. *J. opt. Soc. Amer.*, **12**, 271 (1926).

Katz. *Wratsch*, **17**, 509, 567 (1896).

Kuhn. *Trans. Amer. Acad. Ophthal.*, **45**, 208 (1941).

Lancaster. *Amer. J. Ophthal.*, **20**, 1221 (1937).

Luckiesh and Moss. *Trans. illum. Engng. Soc. Amer.*, **25**, 15 (1930) ; **29**, 296 (1934) ; **31**, 655 (1936).

J. gen. Psychol., **8**, 455 (1933).

Lythgoe. *Med. Res. Cncl., Spec. Rep. Series*, London, No. 173 (1932).
Trans. illum. Engng. Soc. Lond., **1**, 3 (1936).

Lythgoe and Tansley. *Med. Res. Cncl., Spec. Rep. Series*, London, No. 134 (1929).

Mayer. *Arch. Ophthal.*, **27**, 375 (1942).

Mitchell. *Human Factor*, **10**, 341 (1936).

Nutting. *Trans. illum. Engng. Soc. Amer.*, **11**, 1 (1916).

Rainey. *Amer. J. Ophthal.*, **20**, 930 (1937).

Rhoads. *Ophthal. Rec.*, **2**, 416 (1913).

Slataper. *Arch. Ophthal.*, **43**, 466 (1950).

Slyfield. *Nat. safety News*, **39**, 201 (1937).

Stiles. *Sci. indust. Res. techn. Papers*, London, **8** (1929).

Sydenstricker and Britten. *Publ. Hlth. Rep.*, **45**, 1927 (1930).

Taylor. *Illum. Engineer*, **40**, 77 (1945).

Thacker. *Amer. J. Ophthal.*, **22**, 1003 (1939).

Troland. *Trans. illum. Engng. Soc. Amer.*, **26**, 107 (1931).

Weale. *Trans. illum. Engng. Soc. Lond.*, **26**, 95 (1961).
The Ageing Eye, London (1963).

Weston. *Indust. Hlth. Res. Bd.*, London, Jt. Rep. (D.S.I.R.) (1935) ; Rep. No. 87 (1945).
Trans. ophthal. Soc. U.K., **63**, 348 (1943).
Proc. roy. Soc. Med., **40**, 824 (1947).
Sight, Light and Efficiency, London (1949).
Sight, Light and Work, London (1962).

Weston and Adams. *Indust. Hlth. Res. Bd.*, London, Rep. 40 (1927) ; No. 49 (1928) ; No. 57 (1929).

Woodside and Reinhardt. *Trans. illum. Engng. Soc. Amer.*, **32**, 365 (1937).

Zahn. *Oculus artificialis teledioptricus sive telescopium*, Würzburg (1685).

SECTION V

OPTICAL APPLIANCES

FIG. 593.—THE SPURIOUS TOMBSTONE OF SALVINO D'ARMATO IN FLORENCE.

Long accepted as the inventor of spectacles, it is, indeed, doubtful that Salvino ever lived; the bust is derived from an unknown Graeco-Roman warrior of about A.D. 100, cut from a sarcophagus intended for the Pitti Palace in Florence (from the Museo Nazionale (Bargello), by courtesy of Prof. M. Focosi, Florence).

CHAPTER XVII

SPECTACLES

HISTORY

The origin of spectacles has given rise to many conjectures, many of them based on insecure evidence. It has been suggested that they were used by the Chinese from the earliest times: indeed, a Chinese emperor is said to have used lenses to observe the stars in 2283 B.C. (Cuming, 1855; Horner, 1885; Pansier, 1901); it has also been said that when he visited the court of Kublai Khan from 1271 to 1295, Marco Polo reported that convex lenses were worn by the elderly to assist them to read. It is true that rock crystal, quartz and other transparent minerals were found in considerable quantity in China and there is evidence that lenses made of these were worn probably for their coolness as sun-glasses and as a therapeutic measure for conjunctivitis (Confucius, 551–479 B.C.); but for the claim that at this time they were used for visual purposes there would appear to be no authentic evidence (Hirschberg, 1908; Oliver, 1913; Greeff, 1918). It has also been suggested that spectacles originated in India and thence travelled to China through Turkestan during the Mongolian migrations (Laufer, 1907); certainly during the Mongolian Dynasty in the 14th century spectacles for old people were used in China, but the evidence suggests that they came from Europe, by which route is unknown, whether through Central Asia along the trade-routes opened by Genghis Khan's conquests that to some extent unified Eurasia, or by ship through the early Portuguese explorers. Although spectacles, probably from China, may have been in use in the 15th century in the Buddhist temples in Japan, they were taken to that country by St. Francis Xavier [1506–1552], the Spanish missionary (Hukushima, 1963).

To the Classical Greeks, the Romans and the Arabians lenses as a visual aid were unknown and even in the middle years of the Roman Empire literary figures such as Cicero and Suetonius perforce had a slave to read to them when they grew old. Sun-glasses, however, were described by Pliny and Seneca, and the former records that Nero [A.D. 54] wore an emerald or beryl attached to his thumb at the Roman circus.[1] It has been suggested that the Emperor was myopic and hence looked through a concave lens; but in the same passage Pliny made it clear that the green stone was used by Nero to protect his eyes from the glare of the arena:

[1] Beryllus, a greatly valued precious stone, a relatively soft and easily polished silicate of beryllium and aluminium, includes the emerald and aquamarine: the green varieties depend for their colour on chromoxide. Hence the Dutch " Bril ", the old French " béricle " and the German " Brille ". See G. ten Doesschate (1946).

" There is no colour more agreeable to the eye than that of the emerald. . . . It is the only precious stone the contemplation of which satisfies the eye without ever tiring it, nay, when our eyes are tired through strenuous and fine work, they are refreshed and strengthened again by looking at the emerald. The lapidaries have no other means to rest their tired eyes. The agreeable colour of the emerald strengthens their power of seeing."

It is, however, the case that a roughly shaped convex lens, the segment of a transparent sphere or a spherical bottle filled with water was used by the ancient peoples as a burning glass; and probably as an accidental discovery their magnifying properties were occasionally appreciated. In the ancient ruins of Nineveh about the time of Ashur Nasir-Pal [9th century, B.C.] and elsewhere there is evidence that lapidaries used them as hand magnifiers in the engraving on stone of hieroglyphics so minute as to preserve them as secrets from the curious. There are also casual references to the use of magnifying lenses at an early date as by Wynfrith [Saint Boniface] [680–754], the English monk who organized Germany for the Papacy. We have also noted[1] that Ptolemy [c. 90–160] and more particularly Al-Hazen [965–1038] in Egypt understood something about this power of magnification; the latter particularly, in his *Opticæ thesaurus*, knew that the segment of a sphere had this property, but their interpretation of the dioptrics concerned was incorrect.[2] This knowledge, however, was not generally assimilated but was passed on to the Franciscan school of Oxford[3] where Robert Grosseteste [c. 1175–1253] and Roger Bacon [1214–1294] described these magnifying properties, while John of Peckham [c. 1228–1294] disseminated this knowledge throughout Europe in his *Perspectiva communis*.

Of these English scholars, ROGER BACON (Fig. 4) was the most famous and the most original observer, and in his *Opus majus*, written while incarcerated in Paris, he wrote the following description of this phenomenon. His appreciation of the optics involved, however, was incorrect; as is illustrated in Fig. 6, it is essentially taken from the writings of Al-Hazen.

" If anyone examine letters or other minute objects through the medium of crystal or glass or other transparent substance, if it be shaped like the lesser segment of a sphere, with the convex side towards the eye, and the eye being in the air, he will see the letters far better, and they will seem larger to him. For according to our canon (Fig. 6) concerning a spherical medium beneath which the object is placed, the centre being beyond the object, the convexity being towards the eye, all causes agree to increase the size, for the angle in which it is seen is greater, the image is greater, and the position of the image is nearer, because the object is between the eye and the centre. For this reason such an instrument is useful to old persons and to those with weak eyes, for they can see any letter, however small, if magnified enough."

" For we can so form glasses and so arrange them with regard to our sight and to objects that the rays are refracted and deflected to any place we wish, so that we see the object near at hand or far away beneath whatever angle we desire. And so we can read the smallest letters or count grains of sand or dust from an incredible distance owing to the magnitude of the angle beneath which we see them, and again the largest

---

[1] p. 4.   [2] p. 5.   [3] p. 9.

objects close at hand might be scarcely visible owing to the smallness of the angle beneath which we see them; for it is on the size of the angle on which this kind of vision depends, and it is independent of distance save per accidens. So a boy can appear a giant, a man seem a mountain, and in any size of angle whatever, for we can see a man under as large an angle as though he were a mountain and make him appear as near as we desire. So a small army might seem very large, and though far away appear near, and conversely: so, too, we could make sun, moon and stars apparently descend here below, and similarly appear above the heads of our enemies, and many other similar marvels could be brought to pass, that the ignorant mortal mind could not endure the truth." (*Opus Majus*, Part 5.)

Although Bacon in 1267 sent a specimen of his segmented sphere to the Pope as a reading glass, such an instrument cannot legitimately be termed a spectacle; even when such a lens was carried on a handle to bring it close to the eye, the same criticism can be applied although the approach to spectacles is now nearer. The evidence is conclusive that the first convex lenses mounted on a frame to form a pair of spectacles came from Venice somewhere between 1270 and 1280, for this opulent city was the world-centre of the glass trade at that period; the manufacture was soon moved outside the city to the island of Murano owing to the danger of fire. It has been conjectured that Bacon's knowledge was taken to northern Italy by Heinrich Goethals, a close friend whom he commissioned to travel to the Pope in 1285 to intercede for him. The identity of the inventor, however, is not clear, if indeed one existed. It may be that they derived from the chance use of plano-convex glass towards the end of the 13th century in windows by one or several persons unknown, or that they evolved from the magnifying lenses described by Bacon. The first reference to them as an aid to old people would appear to be in a collection of minstrels' ballads (Minne-sänge) in 1280, and they were probably well known in 1300 in Europe. However that may be, in the archives of the monastery of St. Catherine in Pisa, where died a Dominican friar, Alexandro de Spina, it is recorded that he made spectacles in 1305 copied from those made by another who would not divulge the secret of their manufacture. Who the secretive inventor was is not known, but in the church of Santa Maria Maggiore, on the tomb of Salvino d'Armato of Florence who was said to have died in 1317, the following inscription is said to have been engraved: " Qui diace Salvino d'Armato degli Armati di Firenze, Inventor degli occhiali; Dio gli perdoni la peccata. Anno D. MCCCXVII" (Fig. 593).[1] So goes the story, but it is to be remembered that these claims rest merely on the unsupported evidence of a patriotic and enthusiastic Florentine historian, Domenico Manni.[2] It is questionable, however, if such an individual ever existed and the figure portrayed is the bust of an unknown Graeco-Roman dating from about

[1] " Here lies Salvino d'Armato of the Armati of Florence, Inventor of Spectacles; May God forgive him his sins."
[2] *Degli occhiali da naso inventati da Salvino Armati, Gentiluomo Fiorentino*, Florence (1738).

A.D. 100.[1] It is recorded in the Palatine and Riccardi codices at Florence that Giordano da Rivalto, a renowned preacher of the same monastery, said in one of his sermons delivered on February 23rd, 1305:

" It is barely 20 years since the art of making spectacles which enable us to see better was introduced, one of the most useful arts in the world. I have myself seen and spoken to the man who first made them ".[2]

As would be expected, spectacles were originally scarce and expensive, but throughout the 14th century the *perspicille* (*ocularia* or *beryllia*) of Venice became more common until the invention of printing in the 15th century, in which small letters succeeded the luxuriously written manuscripts of the scribes, made their wider use obligatory. Although Venice long retained its hegemony, its privileged position was eventually shared by Nuremberg, Regensburg and Augsburg in Germany, Rouen and Flanders. But for some time they remained scarce and expensive[3]: they were left as legacies in wills (as by Kings John and Charles V of France), and when the Elector of Saxony sent his servant to Augsburg for spectacles to relieve his presbyopia he could not obtain them and was obliged to complete his mission in Venice. At first they were used for presbyopia to aid the weakened sight of the aged and they were prescribed merely by engraving the appropriate age of the patient upon them; their use for hypermetropia naturally followed. Although Roger Bacon wrote of concave lenses in 1276, the first mention of the use of such lenses for myopia was by Nicolaus Cusanus [1401–1464] in his book, *De beryllo*[4]; the earliest picture of them is in Raphael's portrait of Pope Leo X (1517) in the Palazzo Pitti in Florence; the reflex betrays the concavity of the lenses, and the myopic pontiff boasted that with them he could see to hunt better than his companions. The introduction of astigmatic lenses, however, had to wait until the time of the English astronomer, Sir George Biddell Airy [1801–1892], who had them made by an optician, Fuller of Ipswich, in 1827. They were ground independently by McAlister of Philadelphia in 1828 at the request of a very observant clergyman, Mr. Goodrich, who subjectively diagnosed his own astigmatism,[5] and by Suscipi of Rome in 1844 for the painter Cassas. Prisms were introduced by Kepler (1611), and although pioneer clinical work on their use had been done by William Wells (1792), it was left to Donders (1848–64) and particu-

[1] See Rosen. *J. Hist. Med.*, **11**, 13, 1956; Gasson, *Ophthal. Optician*, **9**, 924 (1969).

[2] Dr. Franciscus Redi in a letter to Paul Falconeri, a Roman, said he had a manuscript dated 1299 which says: " I find myself so oppressed with years that without the glasses known as spectacles, I have strength neither to read nor write. These have lately been invented for the convenience of poor old people who are weak-sighted " (Oliver, 1913).

[3] The expense depended largely on the frames. In the 16th century those with leather frames were sold wholesale at one penny per pair and those in gilt or horn at 3d. The artist, Albrecht Dürer, paid 9½ farthings for his in 1521; Henry VII paid 4d. each for 10 pairs; and the Venetian spectacles with gold mountings purchased by Prince August, the Elector of Saxony about 1570, cost 12 guineas (see K. Müller, *Klin. Mbl. Augenheilk.*, **137**, 104 (1960)).

[4] *Opuscula*, 2 *De beryllo*, Norimbergæ (1441).

[5] See Noyes, *Amer. J. med. Sci.*, **63**, 355 (1872); Flaxman, *Arch. Ophthal.*, **16**, 78 (1936).

Fig. 594.—Guy de Chauliac [1300–1368] giving a Lecture on Surgery.

A miniature in the letter "P" from the manuscript, *Chirurgie*, of Guy de Chauliac (Vatican Library; courtesy of the Wellcome Trustees).

larly von Graefe (1857–62) to appreciate their value, while Charles Chevalier of Paris advocated their use for squint in 1844.

The early development of spectacles is most easily derived from their mention in literature and the form they took in mediæval art. In literature, wherein they were regarded as one of the wonders of the age, their first traceable mention was by the German poet, Heinrich Frauenlob [1250–1318]; thereafter followed references by Dante [1265–1321] in his *Inferno*, and by Petrarch [1304–1374]. In medical writings the first three authors to describe them were associated with Montpellier. Bernard de Gordonio was the first to describe them as *oculus berrelerius* (along with the first description of a truss) in his *Lilium medicinæ* (1305).[1] Arnold of Villenova [1235–1311], a doctor of theology, law, philosophy and medicine in Montpellier and also an alchemist who sought the elixir of life and introduced tinctures and brandy into the pharmacopeia, wrote of them as *vitrea vocata conspicilia*.[2] GUY DE CHAULIAC [1300–1368] (Fig. 594),

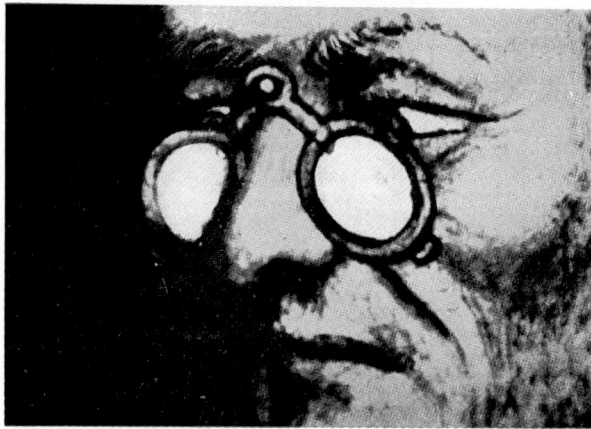

FIG. 595.—PORTRAIT OF CARDINAL HUGO DE TREVISO BY TOMMOSO DA MORENA
IN THE CHURCH OF SAN NICOLO AT TREVISO.
The oldest extant pictorial representation of spectacles in Europe (1352).

the best early medical historian and the greatest authority in surgery in the 14th and 15th centuries who studied at Montpellier among other places and practised in Auvergne where he was the first to take the operation for cataract out of the hands of charlatans, described them at length and advocated their use should his collyria fail.

In art their first pictorial representation is to be seen in the portrait of Cardinal Hugo de Treviso by Tommoso da Morena in the Church of San Nicolo at Treviso in Northern Italy, dated 1352 (Fig. 595). Another picture of much the same date by a painter of the Giotto school is in the Figdor Gallery in Vienna; another is a miniature in a Bible dated 1380 in the Bibliothèque Nationale in Paris; and a fourth dated 1404 by Conrad van Soost is in the Church in Niederwildung. Thereafter from the 15th century their appearance was common, frequently appearing as a sign of dignity and learning (Fig. 596). Interestingly there are many pictures in which spectacles are obviously anachronistic, such as in a Spanish tapestry depicting the Creation of Eve in the Garden of Eden, in Schoneus's engraving of the circumcision of Jesus wherein the

[1] Published in Venice, 1496.
[2] *Breviary of Practice*, published in Milan (1843).

operating rabbi wears spectacles, or in the tapestry in Rheims Cathedral depicting the presentation of the infant Jesus at the temple (Fig. 597), in Dürer's painting of the Christ-child in the Temple, Jan van Eyck's Madonna at Bruges, Martin Schöngauer's engraving of the death of Mary, and Joerg Syrtin's wood-carving of St. Luke. They also figure in caricatures, such as Sebastian Brant's picture of the Book-worm (1494) (Fig. 598), or as worn by the Devil (Fig. 599).[1] Saint Jerome, the patron saint of the optical guilds, is usually portrayed with spectacles.

FIG. 596.—"LES LUNETTES."
A lithograph by L. Boilly (1821).

Apart from the first work of Nicolaus Cusanus, the earliest books on spectacles were the *Uso de los antojos* of Benito Daza de Valdés (Seville, 1623) (Fig. 383), a notary of the Inquisition at Seville who first advised spectacles for aphakia, the title-page of whose book is seen in Fig. 600,[2] and the *L'occhiale all'occhio* of Carlo Antonio Manzini (Bologna, 1660).

[1] See Sacken (1879), Gunther (1923–45), Reis (1928), Disney *et al.* (1928), Greeff *et al.* (1929), Clay and Court (1932), ten Doesschate (1946), and others.
[2] *Uso de los antojos y comentarios a propósito del mismo* (1623). On the 300th anniversary of its publication the book was republished, edited by Manuel Márquez in Madrid (1923), forming Tome IV of the *Biblioteca Clásica de la Medicina Española* for the Real Academia Nacional de Medicina.

Spectacle frames have a long history and have evolved from crude and heavy contrivances to the comfortable devices of modern times. The oldest picture of them seen in Fig. 595, dating from 1352, shows early " nail eye-glasses ", virtually two monocles with metal frames joined by a nail. The oldest pairs extant, according to Greeff (1913), are preserved in the museum at Nuremberg, one found in an old volume and the other in a cranny of the wall of the house of Wilbrand Perkheimer [1470–1530],

FIG. 597.—THE CIRCUMCISION OF JESUS.
From a tapestry in the cathedral of Rheims, showing the Rabbi wearing spectacles (from the Spectaclemakers Company, London).

the burgomaster of Nuremberg; both have round lenses bound together by a solid bow of leather. Such spectacles of leather were gradually replaced by those in which the mountings were of metal (iron, silver or gold) or horn (Fig. 601). Many expedients were adopted to fix their position—first the slight adjustability of the " nail eye-glasses " on the nose, to be replaced considerably later by a light metal spring (Fig. 602), fixation to the cap (as was advised by Savonarola in one of his sermons), by a cord around the occiput or behind the ears sometimes hanging down over the chest to provide a counterweight, by temple-springs to grip the temples to form " spectacles " (in the modern sense of the word) as were made by Ayscough of London in 1752 (Fig. 603),

FIG. 598.—THE BIBLIOMANIAC.
A satire by Sebastian Brant (1494).

FIG. 599.—THE DEVIL IN SPECTACLES.

A detail from a wood sculpture by Thaddäus Stammel (*c.* 1760) from the Benedictine Monastery in Admont, Austria (W. Reis).

and eventually ear-pieces running behind the ears, at first as crude right-angled brackets but finally as flexible or adjustable ear-pieces, an innovation introduced by Edward Scarlett of London in 1728 and made more useful by the invention of hinged folding sides by James Ayscough in 1752. In the meantime, the spectacles, first of a crude type generally sold by itinerant pedlars throughout Europe (Fig. 604), gradually became the prerogative of reputable opticians organized in Guilds, in 1465 in France and in 1563 in England where Charles I gave the Spectaclemakers Company a Royal Charter in 1628. In the latter part of the 15th and in the 16th century the metal frames

FIG. 600.—THE TITLE-PAGE OF DAZA DE VALDÉS'S BOOK

conformed with the dressing habits of the time and became elaborate and ornamental, often being kept in costly cases of exquisite handicraft decorated with gold, silver and precious stones (Fig. 605); while the dandy affected a monocle with a handle and the lady a lorgnette, carried more often for fashion than for visual purposes (Heymann, 1911). The more restrained customs of later times led to the adoption of simple and pliable metal frames of gold or steel while, at the time of George III in England, the tortoiseshell frame, originally worn by the Chinese since the tortoise brought fortune and long life, was adopted in place of metal, a type made fashionable by King Edward VII, to be replaced more recently by simple frames of plastic material. The antithesis of the elaborate frame was achieved by Waldstein of Vienna in 1840 who introduced rimless eye-glasses which appeared in England about 1850. It is interesting that European glasses were imported into America until 1867, but after that date their

FIGS. 601–603.—OLD SPECTACLES.

FIG. 601.—Spectacles of the older period, before 1600, with flattened bows (from the Regensburg Manuscript).

FIG. 602.—Spectacles of the London Spectaclemakers' Company about the time of Queen Anne (1st quarter of the 18th century). The rims of tortoiseshell are riveted to a steel spring bow (A. von Pflugk's collection).

FIG. 603.—Spectacles with temple-pieces. Scarlett's shop print, *c.* 1728 (D. Blaxandall).

manufacture rapidly spread in the United States and after 1870 innumerable devices were patented in that country, some of them impractical gadgets but others innovations of great value and ingenuity, particularly in the design of eye-glasses (see Hill, 1915).

For a myopic dog, Boden (1910) used the appropriate lenses inserted into a modification of motoring goggles strapped to the animal's head (Fig. 606).

FIG. 604.—THE ITINERANT PEDLAR OF SPECTACLES.
(From Mme. Heymann's "Lunettes et Lorgnettes de Jadis", Paris, 1911).

The *lenses* were at first crude and made of scarce " pebbles " of quartz or relatively transparent semi-precious stones such as topaz or emerald (beryl) or the Chinese " tea-stone ", but their development on a large scale necessarily depended on the development of *glass* of a type which could be optically worked. The existence of glass dates back to very remote times, possibly 5000 B.C. The Egyptians, who had a well-established industry in 1500 B.C., claimed to have been taught the art by Hermes. The

FIG. 605.—SILVER NOSE SPECTACLES.

Italian 18th century (from the collection of the British Optical Association).

Phœnicians also found that nitre mixed with sand was melted by the sun's rays into a coarse glass, and the finding of glass in the ruins of Pompeii established its use on a considerable scale before A.D. 79. When glass was introduced for spectacle-making in Europe, the centre of its manufacture was Venice, where the thick and heavy lenses made at Murano achieved a high reputation (Fig. 607). In the archives of Venice

FIG. 606.—SPECTACLES ON A DOG.

Motoring goggles adapted as spectacles strapped onto the head of a myopic dog (R. Boden).

in 1300 and 1331 edicts appeared forbidding the manufacture of spectacles from any material other than crystal glass. At the end of the 16th century a German industry was set up at Augsburg, Regensburg and particularly at Nuremberg, where glass was blown and the lenses were thinner, lighter and cheaper; it was these " Nueremberg glasses " which formed the stock-in-trade of the itinerant Jewish pedlars of the time. The development of the telescope by Galileo in 1608 gave a marked impetus to the technique of the grinding of lenses and the art rapidly spread throughout Europe, particularly in France, Holland and England. In the middle of the 19th century, Faraday and Stokes in England and Fraunhofer and Guinard in Germany began to improve the quality of glass by adding various oxides in the manufacturing process, and in 1838 the English firm of Chance commenced making a large range of optical glass. Half a century later, developing from the researches of Abbé and Schott, the German firm of Zeiss again added considerable improvements to the process of manu-

FIG. 607.—THE WORKSHOP OF THE VENETIAN OPTICIAN, BIAGIO BURLINI
IN THE 18TH CENTURY.
(From the collection of the British Optical Association.)

facture of crown glass (1885 onwards) and rapidly gained what amounted to a world monopoly (von Pflugk, 1913–41), a proud position, however, now widely shared.

The effectiveness of spectacle lenses also rapidly improved. In 1756 the English optician, John Dollond, the son of a Huguenot refugee, first made achromatic lenses by grinding, combining flint and ground glass into a single lens. Benjamin Franklin, the great American politician and scientist, designed bifocal lenses for himself probably about 1775, while John Isaac Hawkins of London introduced trifocal lenses in 1826. At the same time great advances were made in designing improved optical forms of lenses, particularly to avoid the astigmatism of oblique pencils. The initial meniscus shape suggested by Kepler in his *Dioptrice* (1611) was greatly improved by the English scientist, W. H. Wollaston (1804–12), who introduced *periscopic* lenses, an idea modified to conform with the centre of rotation of the eye by A. Müller (1889) of Germany and more elaborately by F. Ostwald (1898) of France; finally the *orthoscopic* lenses of Tscherning (1908) corrected distortion and curvature in the periphery in eccentric vision, an idea, however, anticipated by Sir George Biddell Airy (1827). Meantime, Allvar Gullstrand (1899–1911) developed his aspherical *katral* lenses to correct spherical aberration, a problem of considerable importance in the thick lenses used for aphakic patients, and brought forward a solution to the problem of oblique astigmatism in his *point-focal* lenses. Gullstrand's treatment of the subject was further elaborated by Moritz von Rohr (1908–21) and as a result of his work, Zeiss produced thin *punktal* lenses. H. Boegehold (1916–21) was mainly responsible for the theory of astigmatic correction by toric surfaces.

All these matters will be discussed in the following pages, but in the meantime it is appropriate here to include a note of three of the most important innovators— Franklin who introduced bifocal lenses, Wollaston who designed periscopic lenses and Airy who elaborated astigmatic lenses. The portraits of Kepler (Fig. 11), Tscherning (Fig. 191), Gullstrand (Fig. 131) and von Rohr (Fig. 653) are found elsewhere.

BENJAMIN FRANKLIN [1706–1790] (Fig. 608), the American son of an English dyer, was the youngest of ten children born in Boston, and had one of the broadest and most creative minds of his age and at the same time one of the most fascinating. While still a youth he published the " first sensational newspaper " in the United States and, such a production being unpopular in New England at the time, he went to London to learn printing. Returning to America at the age of 20, he started a printing house in Philadelphia and published the *Pennsylvania Gazette*, a newspaper so entertaining that its circulation became the largest in America, while he printed the first novel in America (Richardson's *Pamela*). Established in Philadelphia, he rapidly became wealthy and socially influential and took a prominent part in politics as a radical and progressive figure. He paid frequent visits to England when he strove to see America develop within the British Empire, was the American minister to France and was ultimately President of the Commonwealth of Pennsylvania. He always took a versatile and original interest in science, founding the American Philosophical Society and the Academy ultimately to become the University of Pennsylvania, while he was a Fellow of the Royal Society of London, and a member of the French Academy of Sciences. His first invention was an open stove, and he took an intense interest in the infant science of electricity, framing a new theory of its nature, first introducing the terms positive and negative electricity, proved its identity with lightning and invented the lightning conductor to counter its disastrous effects. " What is the use of electricity? ", a lady asked him. " Madam ", replied Franklin, " what is the use of a newborn baby?"

The idea of bifocal lenses was probably conceived by Franklin about 1775, and was expressed in a letter to George Whateley, a friend in Philadelphia, written in 1784 and preserved in the Library of Congress, in which he remarked on the nuisance of two pairs of spectacles which required to be constantly changed. " Finding this change troublesome, and not always sufficiently ready, I had the glasses cut and a half of each kind associated in the same circle. By this means, as I wear my spectacles constantly, I have only to move my eyes up or down, as I want to see distinctly far or near, the proper glasses being always ready. This I find more particularly convenient since my being in France, the glasses that serve me best at table to see what I eat not being the best to see the face of those on the other side of the table who speak to me; and when one's ears are not well accustomed to the sounds of a language, a sight of the movements in the features of him who speaks helps to explain; so that I understand French better by the help of my spectacles."

Fig. 608.—Benjamin Franklin
1706–1790].
(Courtesy of the Royal Society.)

Fig. 609.—William Hyde Wollaston
[1766–1828].
Drawn by Sir Thomas Lawrence, PRA.

Fig. 610.—Sir George Biddell Airy
[1801–1892].
(Courtesy of the Royal Society.)

WILLIAM HYDE WOLLASTON [1766–1828] (Fig. 609), a chemist and natural philosopher of Cambridge, eccentric, reserved and secluded, had a personality the reverse of Franklin's. He studied medicine but, failing to obtain a suitable hospital post, spent his life on private research on which he was strangely uncommunicative. He died of a thalamic tumour which caused an intermittent homonymous hemianopia from which he deduced the partial decussation of the nerve fibres in the optic chiasma; his last days were spent calmly dictating discoveries which he had not revealed but were posthumously published. He made notable contributions to chemistry, optics, acoustics, mineralogy, astronomy, botany and art. He discovered how to work platinum from which he made a fortune (£30,000, at that time an immense sum), he detected palladium and rhodium in crude platinum, proved the elementary character of columbium and titanium, discovered cystine, proposed the use of chemical equivalents, invented the slide-rule, first observed the Fraunhofer lines in the solar spectrum, and introduced a revolution in mineralogy and crystallography by evolving a reflecting goniometer—all in addition to his designing periscopic lenses.

SIR GEORGE BIDDELL AIRY [1801–1892] (Fig. 610) was one of the most outstanding mathematicians and astronomers that England has produced. He was professor of mathematics (1826) and then of astronomy (1828) at Cambridge and finally went to Greenwich where he became Astronomer Royal (1835). In our present subject he will always be remembered for his studies on the nature of light and the phenomenon of diffraction,[1] his design of an astigmatic lens and his elaboration of the mathematics of best-form lenses to overcome the astigmatism of oblique pencils. In astronomy his most remarkable contributions included the discovery of an inequality in the motions of Venus and the earth, which becomes apparent over a period of 240 years, his new method of treating lunar theory, his investigations into the mass of Jupiter and his determination of the mean density of the earth by experiments with pendulums at the top and bottom of a mine 1,256 feet deep.

LITERATURE

Interesting books and monographs on the history of spectacles are as follows.

Böck. *Die Brille und ihre Geschichte*, Wien (1903).

Chevalier. *Manuel des myopes et de presbytes contenant des recherches historiques sur l'origine des lunettes ou bésicles*, Paris (1841).

Greeff, Hallauer, Weve, *et al. Katalog der Bilderausstellung zur Geschichte der Brille. XIII Int. Cong. Ophthal.*, Amsterdam (1929).

Heymann. *Lunettes et lorgnettes de jadis*, Paris (1911).

Hirschberg. *Graefe-Saemisch Hb. d. ges. Augenheilk.*, 2nd ed., Leipzig, **13**, 265 (1908).

Horner. *Ueber Brillen aus alter und neuer Zeit*, Zürich (1885).

Münchow. *Geschichte der Brille*, in Velhagen's *Der Augenarzt*, Leipzig, **7**, 474 (1967).

Oliver. *A History of the Invention and Discovery of Spectacles*, London (1913).

Pansier. *Histoire des lunettes*, Paris (1901).

von Rohr. *Acht Vorlesungen zur Geschichte der Brille*, Berlin (1921).

Airy. *Trans. Camb. phil. Soc.*, **2**, 267 (1827). *Edinb. J. Sci.*, **7**, 322 (1827).

Boden. *Arch. verg. Ophthal.*, **1**, 195 (1910).

Boegehold. *Z. ophthal. Optik*, **4**, 161 (1916); **5**, 129 (1917); **6**, 14, 60, 119 (1918); **8**, 10 (1920). *Naturwissenschaften*, **9**, 273 (1921).

Clay and Court. *The History of the Microscope compiled from Original Instruments and Documents up to the Introduction of the Achromatic Microscope*, London (1932).

Cuming. *J. Brit. Archæol.*, **11**, 144 (1855).

Disney, Hill and Baker. *Origin and Development of the Microscope as Illustrated by Catalogues of the Instruments and Accessories, in the Collections of the Royal Microscopic Society*, London (1928).

[1] p. 80.

ten Doesschate. *Brit. J. Ophthal.*, **30**, 660 (1946).

Donders. *Holländ. Beitr. anat. physiol. Wiss.*, **1**, 105, 384 (1848).
On the Anomalies of Accommodation and Refraction of the Eye, London (1864).

von Graefe. *v. Graefes Arch. Ophthal.*, **3** (1), 177 (1857); **8** (2), 314 (1862).

Greeff. *Z. ophthal. Optik*, **1**, 11, 46 (1913); **2**, 7 (1914); **4**, 142 (1916); **5**, 42, 65 (1917); **6**, 1, 36, 97 (1918); **11**, 98 (1923).
Die Erfindung der Augengläser, Berlin (1921).

Gullstrand. *v. Graefes Arch. Ophthal.*, **49**, 46 (1899).
Einführung in d. Methoden d. Dioptrik d. Auges d. Menschen, Leipzig (1911).

Gunther. *Early Science in Oxford*, 14 vols., Oxford (1923–45).

Hill. *Amer. Encycl. Ophthal.*, Chicago, **7**, 4894 (1915).

Hukushima. *Amer. J. Ophthal.*, **55**, 612 (1963).

Kepler. *Dioptrice*, Augsburg (1611).

Laufer. *Mitt. z. Gesch. d. Med.*, Leipzig, **6**, 379 (1907).

Müller, A. *Brillengläser u. Hornhautlinsen* (Diss.), Kiel (1889).

Ostwald. *C.R. Acad. Sci.* (Paris), **126**, 1446 (1898).

von Pflugk. *Z. ophthal. Optik*, **1**, 106 (1913); **11**, 33 (1923); **13**, 103 (1925); **14**, 138 (1926); **16**, 2 (1928); **29**, 20 (1941).

Reis. *Arch. Augenheilk.*, **98**, 192 (1928).

von Rohr. *Ber. dtsch. ophthal. Ges.*, **35**, 25 (1908).
Z. ophthal. Optik, **5**, 1, 33, 78 (1917); **12**, 14, 28, 46, 120 (1924); **13**, 42, 107, 111 (1925); **19**, 33, 65 (1931).
Die Brille als optisches Instrument, Graefe-Saemisch Hb. d. ges. Augenheilk., 3rd ed., Berlin (1921).

Sacken. *Archaeol.-Epigr. Mitt. aus Oesterreich*, **3**, 151 (1879).

Tscherning. *Arch. Optik*, **1**, 401 (1908).

Wells. *Two Essays*, London (1792).

Wollaston. *Phil. Mag.*, **17**, 327; **18**, 165 (1804).
Phil. Trans., **102**, 370 (1812).

The Making and Dispensing of Spectacles

THE MAKING OF SPECTACLE LENSES

OPTICAL GLASS. Glass, a mixture of silicates and metallic oxides, is not an amorphous substance as had been thought until recently, but contains minute crystals (10^{-6} mm.) scattered at random in a non-crystalline matrix. Although about 80 different types of glass are employed for optical purposes, the glass mainly used for ophthalmic lenses is a *crown glass* of a refractive index of 1·523. Its manufacture is difficult, demanding extreme care and skill, for many properties are required of it—homogeneity, freedom from striæ, bubbles, milkiness or strain (which causes double refraction), and specified optical constants.

The ingredients—sand[1] (as free from iron as possible), to which is added potassium, calcium, lead, aluminium, barium and boron, generally as pulverized oxides—are mixed and placed in a dome-shaped crucible with an opening to allow for stirring. The mixture is then raised to a temperature of approximately 900°C, when the mass liquefies. The temperature is kept steady for 2 or 3 days until the mixture has finished " gassing " and stirring is continued until all the bubbles are removed. When cooling, the glass tends to split into pieces of varying size ; these are re-heated, pressed into slabs of the required thickness and examined for striæ, bubbles, bad metal and other faults. From these slabs often only about a quarter are selected and these are re-heated and " annealed." The annealing process allows the glass to cool very slowly over several days, thus preventing the outer portion of the slab from cooling before the inner. The two opposite surfaces of the slab are

[1] Only a few known deposits on the world's surface are ideally suitable.

finally flattened and polished and turned out in discs of approximately the required thickness, either flat in shape or curved ("*blanks*").

These blanks are subjected to "*grinding*," a process by which the surfaces are shaped by electrically driven tools of finely grained cast iron of appropriate curvature, the necessary abrasion being effected by a hard powder such as carborundum or emery ("*surfacing*"). The abrasives used become finer and finer with each process of "roughing" and "smoothing" until the lens surface is very smooth when it is polished with rouge (oxide of iron) and water. The process is finally completed by "*polishing*," in which a covering of cloth or wax is substituted for the powder. The product forms the "*uncut*" *lens*, and the spheres and cylinders and toric forms employed in ordinary use are kept in stock in quantity in this state, their further treatment being dependent upon the requirements of the individual prescription.

Flint glass (refractive index 1·62) is sometimes used when a glass of a higher refractive index is wanted, as in the making of bifocal or achromatic lenses. It contains lead which is absent from crown glass.

Safety (*reinforced*) *glass* is sometimes used to obviate the danger of injury to the eye on breakage, for ordinary glass is liable to splinter. The principle of such lenses is the mounting of laminæ of a non-splintering substance (cellulose acetate, xylonite, etc.) between two sheets of glass, the three being made to adhere with cement with sufficient adhesiveness that if it is shattered it cracks into fragments but does not splinter and break away.[1] Exposure to daylight, however, tends eventually to discolour most of the materials used for the inserted lamina, a process which shortens the useful life of the lenses.

A further method of avoiding splintering is the use of *case-hardened* (or *toughened*) *lenses* of glass with a minimum central thickness of 3 mm. The lens is heated to 1330°F in an oven and rapidly cooled by an air draught or oil immersion. This temperature is just not sufficient to distort the glass but yet adequate to anneal it so that when it is rapidly cooled the outer shell hardens more quickly than the inner mass. The resulting pressure generated within the lens makes the outer layer crumble on an impact without the lens fracturing or breaking into pieces.

QUARTZ—the original material generally used by the Chinese and early Europeans for lenses—is a naturally-occurring rock crystal of oxide of silicon. To-day it is rarely used in "pebble" lenses. Its spectral transmission is greater than that of glass since it allows relatively short ultra-violet and long infra-red rays to pass through it, and it is harder, more difficult to work and less easily scratched than glass. It is, however, doubly refracting and polarizes the transmitted light.

PLASTIC LENSES

The disadvantages and the dangers of glass owing to splintering have stimulated research into the optical uses of plastics. In 1935 a polymerized form of methylmethacrylate, a derivative of acrylic acid and one of the thermo-plastic group of plastics,[2] was evolved under the trade name of

---

[1] *Triplex*, *Salvoc* and various trade names are applied.
[2] A thermo-plastic material can be softened and resoftened indefinitely by heat and when cooled possesses its original properties.

Perspex. Its refractive index is 1·495, it is very light, is more transparent to visible and ultra-violet light than ordinary glass but has approximately the same transmission for infra-red, does not break easily and when it does resolves into large, blunt-edged pieces. Perspex has, however, two disadvantages, its susceptibility to scratching and its tendency to warp when heated or put under pressure. These handicaps, however, have been largely overcome by the use of a hard thermosetting resin, allyl diglycol carbonate, which compares well with glass in resistance to scratching and is, indeed, superior to it in resisting pitting (as when used at a grinding wheel or when welding or sand-blasting) because of a difference in impact resistance ; it does not fog up as quickly as glass in changing temperatures since it warms up more rapidly. Such lenses can also be dyed to reduce their transmission of light and surface-coated to eliminate annoying reflections.

The making of ophthalmic plastic lenses is a relatively simple process. A sheet of Perspex is cut into circular discs which are then turned on a lathe to a curvature near to that finally required. These are heated by steam to a temperature depending upon the form and thickness of the lens. The lens blank is placed between two steel dies with surfaces accurately shaped and polished to the required optical form and pressed for several minutes while the temperature is maintained. The lens leaves the press with its surfaces brightly polished and is then subjected to a hardening treatment whereby a fine film of silica, a few wavelengths in thickness, is deposited on the surfaces.

Owing to its lightness plastic is particularly advantageous in the case of high-power lenses (as in aphakic prescriptions)[1] as well as in contact lenses.

THE DISPENSING OF SPECTACLE LENSES

In the dispensing of an ophthalmic prescription the uncut lens is " checked " for surface and material blemishes, such as scratches, veins, bubbles, striæ, greyness or waves, and its power verified.

The various techniques employed for optical verification will be discussed presently.[2]

Having been checked (or " set "), that is, with its optical centre and axis marked with glass pencil, the lens is then placed upon a protractor (Fig. 611) with its axis along the required direction and a horizontal line drawn through the optical centre. The geometrical centre is found by measurement and any decentring verified.

The actual fitting of lenses into frames is known as *glazing* and this also denotes one or two necessary prior procedures such as cutting and edging. In the classical procedures of *cutting*, a lens-cutting machine engraves a deep

---

[1] For example, a lens of power of $\dfrac{+12\cdot00 \text{ DS}}{+\ 1\cdot00 \text{ DC}}$ edged 42 × 39 PRO weighs 14·1 gm. in full aperture glass, 9·7 gm. in a lenticular glass and only 4·5 gm. as a plastic lenticular.

[2] p. 629.

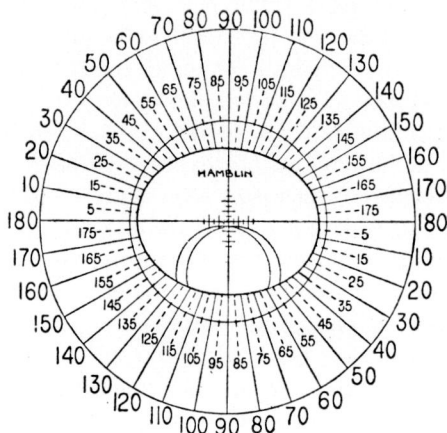

FIG. 611.—THE LENS PROTRACTOR.

line with a diamond upon the glass of the required size and shape. The glass is then broken off at this line by nippers and subjected to *edging* by which the edge is smoothed and, if necessary, bevelled by a rotating carborundum wheel. Some of the commoner forms of lens-edge are shown in Fig. 612.

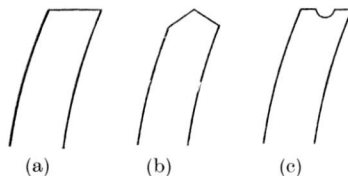

(a) (b) (c)

FIG. 612.—COMMON EDGE-FORMS OF LENSES.
(a) flat edge ; (b) bevelled edge ; (c) grooved edge (A. G. Bennett).

Hand-glazing is now, however, only a small part of modern manufacturing practice. The whole procedure of reducing the lens-blank to the required shape and size with an edge of the required design is automated to a greater or less degree. Cutting as a distinct process can be eliminated because diamond-impregnated grinding wheels remove surplus glass much more rapidly than carborundum wheels and can be used for producing a flat-edged or bevel-edged lens of the final form from the uncut blank. By employing a " former " or " template ", lenses of different sizes but similar shape can be produced by modern automated machines. Lastly, in the process of glazing the lenses are inserted and fitted into the frames.

A final checking completes the process. The optical centres in relation to the two visual axes (the *interaxial* not the interpupillary distance) are verified and the axis of the cylinder checked. Faults or scratches on the lenses are eliminated and any strain in the glass detected by special means.

In the process of glazing, strains may be put on the lenses which render them liable to crack sometimes with explosive force. Such strains induce the phenomenon of double refraction which can be detected by a " strain-tester " whereby the lens is examined by a polarizing apparatus.

The Size and Shape of Lenses. Different methods are employed in the standardization of the size and shape of lenses. The Optical Society (1904) differentiated varying shapes as round, round oval, long oval, and pantoscopic (an oval with a flattened top), and indicated the sizes by the circumferential measurement. The American notation indicates the shape of the oval by a number which denotes the difference in millimetres between the long and the short axes. In practice most opticians do not adhere to these, but adopt the much freer procedure of varying the size and shape to conform to the requirements of the prescription, the size of the frames chosen and the configuration of the face. Although some shapes have a semi-official terminology applied to them (" upswept ", " contour ", etc.), most are now designated by trade names.

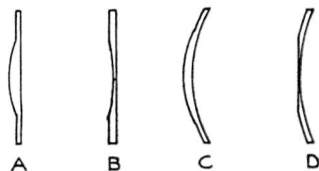

FIG. 613.—LENTICULAR LENSES.

A. Plano-convex.   C. Convex-meniscus.
B. Plano-concave.   D. Concave-meniscus.

LENTICULAR LENSES. In lenses of high power it is of great value to reduce the size and weight to the minimum. To attain this end the sighted area is reduced in *lenticular lenses* which are ground only in the centre or, after grinding, the periphery is further ground down to a plano form (Fig. 613). Although the field is reduced in this way, peripheral vision is not of great value owing to optical aberrations and distortions in lenses of high power, and the added comfort of lightness and the improved appearance usually compensate for the loss. Their optical efficiency can be improved by grinding them in meniscus form.[1]

Lenticular lenses may be employed to reduce the peripheral distortions and prismatic effects inseparable from high-powered lenses by grinding the peripheral rim with less curvature than the central area. We have already discussed their use as applied to the more ametropic eye in cases of anisometropia,[2] but although they may reduce the discomforts of peripheral vision associated with gross optical differences between the two eyes, they do not by any means provide a perfect solution to the problem.

THE VERIFICATION OF OPHTHALMIC LENSES

A lens may be verified by the somewhat inaccurate method of neutralization or more exactly by special instruments; these methods, however,

[1] p. 56.   [2] p. 509.

indicate only the correctness of the form of the lens and not its effective power—a subject which will be considered presently.[1]

The Method of Neutralization. If a convex lens is held close to the eye[2] and a distant object is regarded through it, when the lens is moved from side to side, the image is seen to move in the opposite direction owing to the prismatic effect (Fig. 96). Conversely, with a concave lens the image moves in the same direction (Fig. 97). The method of neutralization consists in imposing upon the spectacle lens a series of lenses of known strength in succession until one is obtained which is equal and opposite, at which point the image regarded through the combination will not be displaced, but will appear as if looked at through a glass plate with parallel sides.

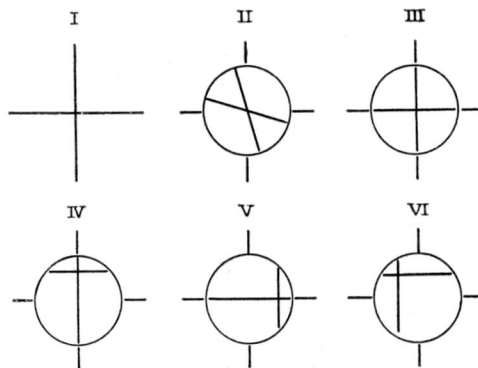

FIG. 614.—THE NEUTRALIZATION OF LENSES (see text).

In practice a cross some distance away is regarded through the lens (Fig. 614, I). If the cross appears skewed in a scissors movement as the lens is rotated round (II), it is rotated until there is no deformation of the cross-lines (III). The lens is now moved in a direction parallel to one of the lines, say up and down, when a deviation of the horizontal lines will be noticed (IV); this movement is exactly neutralized by the appropriate lenses, and the dioptric value in this meridian is thus obtained. The lens is then moved in the meridian at right angles: if no deviation of the line occurs, the lens is a sphere; if one does appear (V), it is neutralized in the same way by placing cylinders with their axes in the appropriate direction: this gives the value of the cylindrical element. These meridians are marked with glass pencil: the point at which they meet is the optical centre. Finally, a prism may be present. When the exact neutralizing lenses are combined with the glass, the combination should ordinarily act as a glass plate, and on movement in any direction the cross should appear unaltered. If, however, a

---

[1] p. 639.
[2] Within the focal length of the convex lens; if it is held farther away (beyond the focal length) the opposite movement occurs.

prism is present, on moving the lens there is no relative movement of the arms of the cross, but a displacement of the entire cross in one direction (VI). Prisms should now be combined with the lens until this effect also is neutralized.

During the process of neutralization the lenses should be held with their optical centres opposite each other, and they should be approximated as closely as possible, for any degree of separation introduces an error. When some degree of separation does exist, a condition which must obtain to a certain extent, a convex lens appears slightly stronger than it actually is, so that when strong lenses have to be employed in the process of neutralization,

FIG. 615.—LENS CENTRING MACHINE.

the convex element predominates in the combination. Such errors can only be eliminated by the measurement of the vertex power, a matter which will be dealt with later.[1]

Special instruments—*centring machines, axometers*—have been devised to estimate the centring quickly and accurately (Fig. 615). The lens is placed in the centre of the instrument and cross lines on a target placed in the correct axis observed through it. The lens is then moved until the cross lines are continuous and the centring, axis marking and " laying-off " accomplished in one operation.

The *Geneva lens measure* (Fig. 616) is a rapid and somewhat inaccurate method of verifying the power of a lens. It is provided with a fixed support on each side and a movable one placed centrally, so that, when placed upon a lens, the movable leg is deflected by an amount depending on the curvature of the surface. The deflection is recorded after the manner of

[1] p. 640,

an aneroid barometer on a scale marked in dioptres, and thus the dioptric value of the lens in any meridian may be read off directly (Fig. 617). It is graduated for glass of a refractive index of 1·523 (ordinary crown glass), so that if any other glass is employed a correction factor must be applied.

FIGS. 616–618.—THE GENEVA LENS MEASURE.

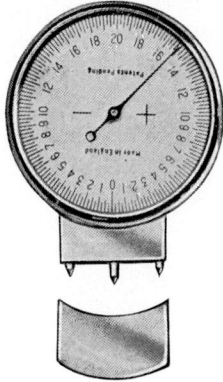

FIG. 616.—The instrument.

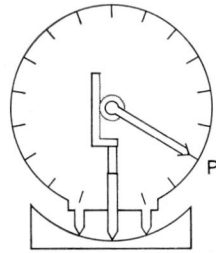

FIG. 617.—The principle of registration.

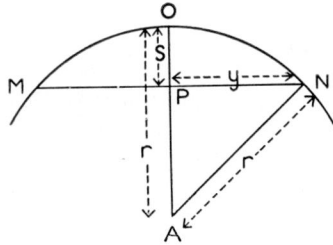

FIG. 618.—The theory of calculation.

The theory of the instrument can be derived from Fig. 618. Let MON be the curvature of the lens surface of radius (r) AO = AN; MN represents a chord of the circle of which one-half PN = y. OP (s) represents the *sag* of the curvature at that diameter, which is measured by the instrument.

$$\text{Then } r^2 = y^2 + (r - s)^2$$

$$\therefore r = \frac{y^2 + s^2}{2s} \text{ or } R = \frac{2s}{y^2 + s^2}$$

Since in most spectacle lenses s^2 is so small as to be neglected,

$$r = \frac{y^2}{2s} \text{ or } R = \frac{1}{r} = \frac{2s}{y^2} \text{ approximately.}$$

Since in a given instrument y = constant, *the curvature is directly proportional to the sag*. A recent version of the lens measure reads the sag directly and this is then compared with the findings on a series of master curves.

The axis of a cylinder in the glazed spectacles may be rapidly and effectively verified by the *axis finder* (Fig. 619)—a pendulum which indicates the direction of the axis when the spectacles are held in contact with the top edge and rotated until the cross-lines of the test-chart are continuous.

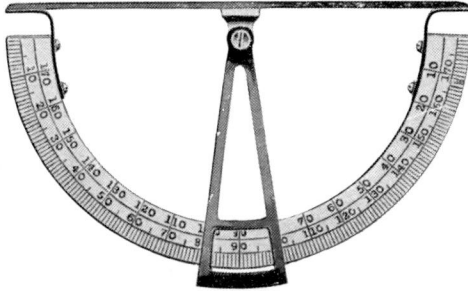

FIG. 619.—THE LENS AXIS FINDER.

The spectacles are held against the overhanging ledge (above) and the combination tilted so that the pendulum lies in the axis of the cylinder, the angle of which can then be read off (Dixey).

SPECTACLE FRAMES

The suitability and accurate fitting of spectacle frames involve many considerations; they must satisfy several interests which are frequently conflicting—optical accuracy, the compensation of facial asymmetry and æsthetic demands. They should be rigid, strong and light, fitting securely, yet lightly and easily, and causing no irritation to the points of the skin whereon they rest. They should hold both lenses firmly and constantly in a place perpendicular to the direction of regard, for any tilting introduces optical errors which are not negligible in lenses of high power. Spectacles for distance should therefore sit vertically, but since the eyes tend more frequently to be directed downwards than upwards, especially in tall people, they may be canted slightly downwards: an upward tilt is inadmissible for ordinary purposes. Spectacles for reading should be slightly lowered, they should converge slightly, and they should be angled downwards at an angle of from 10°, depending on the wearer's habit.[1] The frames should hold the lenses so that their optical centres are opposite the centres of the pupils for the particular visual task. Finally, the lenses should remain at the same distance in front of the cornea (about 12 mm.) since their effectivity varies with their distance from the eye.[2]

Spectacle frames are made of metal, tortoiseshell, plastic material or combinations of these. The metals that have been used are stainless steel, solid or rolled gold, anodized aluminium, and nickel; of these, only the last three are in extensive use today. Tortoiseshell, derived not from the tortoise but from the back-plates of the hawk's bill turtle, is available in various shades; it is cosmetically attractive, durable and has

[1] p. 679.   [2] p. 639.

the property of being bonded by heat and pressure to similar material. Plastics such as cellulose nitrate (xylonite), cellulose acetate and Perspex are widely used. Cellulose nitrate has the advantage over the acetate of being harder and more rigid but has the distinct disadvantage that it is inflammable, a property which should forbid its use. Attractive patterns in spectacle frames can be introduced by the use of laminates of coloured acetate material. Many modern spectacle frames are of all-metal or all-plastic construction, the latter sometimes being intentionally bulky in design (the " library frame "). In others there is a combination of various types of material as, for example, where the metal is covered with plastic (the " Windsor frame ") or the metal reinforces a predominantly plastic part of the frame.

Different portions of the frame may be of differing materials. Thus the rims may be of plastic and the bridge of metal. In rimless spectacles, introduced in 1840 by

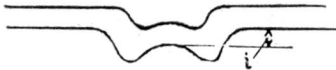 

Fig. 620.—Projection of Inset Bridge.   Fig. 621.—Projection of Saddle Bridge.

i, inset (negative projection).   *p*, projection (after L. S. Sasieni).

Walstein in Vienna, the lenses have no supporting rim, being connected to one another by the bridge, the side-pieces being attached either to the lenses by screws or to an extension of the bridge along the top of the lenses. A modern type of frame giving a partly rimless appearance is the " nylon supra ", in which the lower part of each lens is held to the frame by a nylon cord instead of a solid rim, or alternatively by a steel wire. In some designs the lens is either glued or screwed to the frame along its upper border.

The design of the various elements of the frame—rims, bridge, side-pieces and joints—has shown many variations. The sides, for example, usually have an angled " hockey-end " or occasionally a " curl-end " encircling the ear, a type particularly useful for children or sportsmen to prevent them slipping off, but sometimes the sides may be straight. The bridge in most modern frames is of the padded type having two supports for the sides of the nose, but in plastic frames a key-hole shape is a widely used design formed by the combination of a pad and the bridge itself. In some metal frames, however, the W bridge is still in use where the support is given by the bridge of the nose. Such a " regular " bridge is occasionally found in plastic or shell frames and further refinements of this are the " saddle " or " inset " varieties (Figs. 620–1). Special reversible or swivel bridges are used in reversible spectacles. Numerous ingenious devices are used in the joints of spectacle frames and many methods are used to conceal them. In very young children who wear spectacles for the treatment of squint, ear-pieces may be inadvisable; and if the side-pieces terminate in a metal loop, a tape arranged over the head, as in Fig. 622, broken with a small length of elastic, provides an effective and admirable means of fixation.

Fig. 622.—Spectacle Frames for Young Children.

The weight of the spectacles rests on the side nose-pads and the ear-pieces are replaced by a tape.

Most refractive errors are corrected by lenses in spectacle frames in which the side-piece is an integral element. The spectacle frame has almost but not completely ousted *nose-glasses* (*pince-nez*), the sole support of which is upon the

bridge of the nose. It is obvious that the former are a more adequate optical instrument than the latter and should always be preferred. Nose-glasses are found useful by
some on account of the ease with which they are put on and taken off. It is to be
remembered[1] that if they are placed obliquely so that one lens is nearer to the eye than
the other, considerable optical errors are introduced, and if they are canted out of the
perpendicular plane a spherical lens becomes sphero-cylindrical, while the cylindrical
element in an astigmatic lens becomes magnified. For this reason they should not be
used in the case of large refractive errors, particularly in astigmatism, or in conditions
of hetcrophoria wherein a minutely adjusted and rigidly supported correcting lens is
necessary.

The *monocle*, the most difficult ornament to wear, is of little serious ophthalmological value; it has been caricatured in many ways (Fig. 623). As has already been
mentioned, however, it is frequently of service to presbyopes, to whom it is useful for

FIG. 623.—"LIVING MADE EASY".

Revolving hat with eye-glass, cigar, scent-box, spectacles, hearing trumpet, etc.:
a caricature of 1830 (from a coloured print in the Wellcome Institute of the History of
Medicine, by courtesy of the Wellcome Trustees).

rapid reference. *Lorgnettes* which are held in the hand may serve a similar purpose.
In cases of marked astigmatism, however, these are rarely satisfactory since the
adjustment of the glass is largely a matter of chance.

The fitting of spectacle frames is a highly skilled procedure. A basic
measurement required for this is the interpupillary distance (p.d.), to
measure which several special instruments have been devised (Fig. 624).
It is frequently important to measure the interpupillary distance not only
for distant vision but also for reading, and although the centration for the
latter is often calculated by rule of thumb from the former, this simple
procedure may be inaccurate not only because the rule is not applicable in
every case but also because the centration distance (c.d.) for near vision is
not the same as the interpupillary distance (Fig. 625). The importance of
the accuracy of these measurements must be stressed; thus, in an assess-

[1] p. 639.

ment of 3,616 cases, Garrigosa and Pérez Irisarri (1968) found that the average p.d. was 63 mm. for adult males and 61 for females, whereas the measurement of the spectacles revealed that the distances between the centres varied respectively from 67 to 72 mm. and 66 to 70 mm., a discrepancy which entails prismatic effects and difficulty with convergence.

Estimates or measurements are also made of the size and shape of the bridge of the nose, the temple-width, and the distance from the spectacle plane to the top of the ear. Again, there are many ingenious devices for

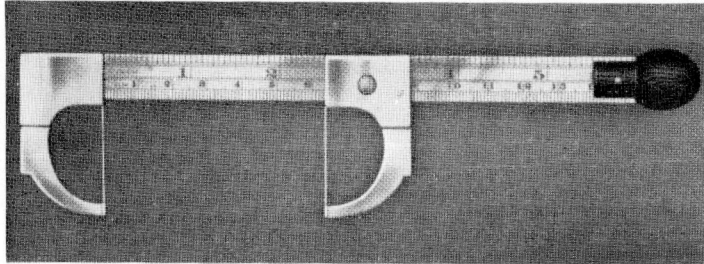

FIG. 624—A SIMPLE P.D. RULE (Hamblin).

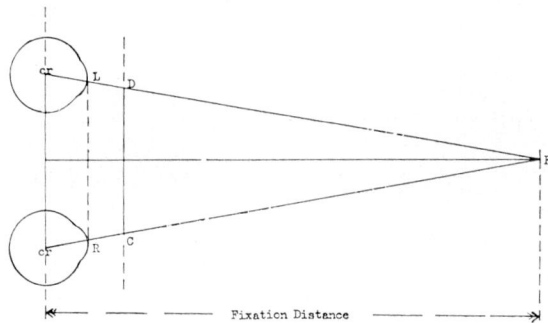

FIG. 625.—THE CENTRATION DISTANCE FOR NEAR.

The line joining the centres of rotation, *cr*, is taken as the base of an isosceles triangle. CD, the centration distance, is drawn parallel to this in the spectacle frame and is the distance between the visual axes there. RL is the actual near pupillary distance (L. S. Sasieni).

these purposes, particularly relating to the shape of the bridge. Any significant degree of facial asymmetry may present considerable problems when fitting the frames and must be carefully studied. Thus the two halves of the interpupillary distance may differ, one eye may be higher than the other, the bridge of the nose may be irregular, or the ears may not have symmetrical relationships to their respective eyes. A skilful optician will be able not only to overcome the optical problems presented by such cases but, in addition, to contribute a cosmetic improvement by disguising the facial asymmetry with suitably designed frames.

SPECTACLE DERMATITIS

A contact dermatitis excited by the materials of which the spectacles are made is not uncommon in sensitive persons. All stages of eczematous dermatitis are met with—erythematous, papular, vesicular and even pustular —which become particularly evident where the frames contact or chafe the skin on the bridge of the nose, the temples and behind the ears. Every case of dermatitis encountered is not necessarily allergic; such a condition may be due to a traumatic irritation such as occurs when newly acquired spectacle frames bear heavily on the skin or where the surface of old spectacles has become dirty, encrusted with other material, or rough. Allergic reactions are seen particularly in the case of spectacles made of nickel or plastic.

Spectacle dermatitis caused by *nickel* is similar to that seen in nickel-plating workers in industry or in the wearers of nickel-plated articles, such as watches. The spectacle dermatitis was first noted by Lain (1931) and has since been recorded by several authors.[1] The condition affects the areas in contact with the metal—the bridge of the nose, the inner canthus, a horizontal band across the temples, and the post-auricular region—and may assume the characteristics of an acute weeping eczema ultimately developing into a chronic infiltrated stage if contacts are maintained, and spreading to the neighbouring areas of the eyelids and cheeks. Susceptibility was at one time considered to be greater if the nickel content of the frames were below 15%, and for this reason most metal frames contain not less than 14% of metal. There is, however, no convincing evidence for the concept of a critical content of nickel below which there is an increased risk of sensitization.

A sensitivity to nickel causing dermatitis has never been recorded on a first contact; it is presumably brought about by some alteration by the nickel ions in the tissue cells which thereafter become sensitized so that subsequent contacts lead to further changes. Spread of the dermatitis is direct in the skin itself only; nickel dermatitis is therefore a " true " contact dermatitis in contradistinction to others, such as rag-weed dermatitis which can be induced by pulmonary or alimentary absorption. As a rule the reaction remains local and only in rare instances becomes generalized, a circumstance which is correlated with the fact that the skin hypersensitivity as indicated by the patch test (8% solution of nickel chloride) may be positive locally and negative elsewhere (Cormia and Stewart, 1935). The corrosion of spectacles containing nickel may produce a highly irritant greenish compound composed of nickel and copper salts (Gaul, 1958).

A dermatitis has also been said to arise from *plastic spectacles* (Mac-Cormac, 1931) (Figs. 626–7). Sutton (1927), who first noted the condition, attributed the irritation to dyes or faulty curing of the xylonite; Kristjansen

---

[1] A. W. and A. W. McAlester (1931), Fox (1933), Urbach (1935), Foster and Ball (1935), Cormia and Stewart (1935), Hollander and Baer (1935), Urbach (1935), Löwenstein (1938), Taylor (1944), Taylor *et al.* (1945), and others.

Figs. 626 and 627.—Plastic Spectacle Dermatitis.

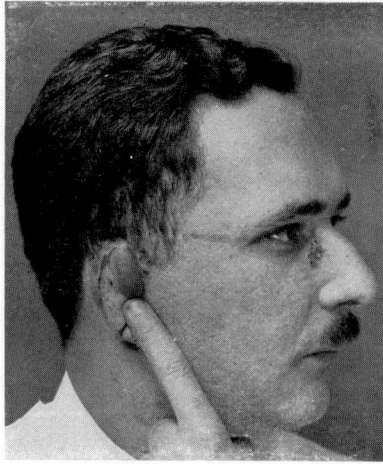

Fig. 626.—Chronic stage (MacCormac).

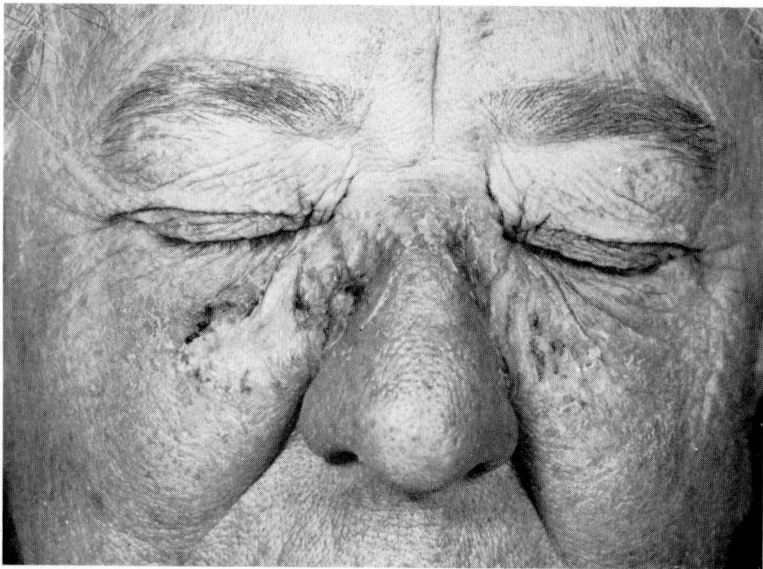

Fig. 627.—Acute stage (D. Calnan).

(1937) attributed it to artificial resins; and it has been said that the fault
may lie with the plasticizers or softeners used in manufacture (tricresyl or
triphenyl phosphate) rather than with the basic material (cellulose acetate)
or with the dyes used in manufacture (Berkoff, 1938; Thistlethwaite, 1943;
Gray, 1943). The cases reported by Wilde (1959) apparently all resulted
from wearing the formaldehyde polymer type of frame which is now obso-

lete. Finally, from a critical review of some 20 cases of spectacle dermatitis by Smith and Calnan (1966) it was concluded that modern plastics were very unlikely to cause allergic reactions; they found that patch tests carried out with rigid criteria were negative to many of the substances—basic plastics, plasticizers or colouring material—previously incriminated as the cause of spectacle dermatitis. A further significant fact was the high incidence of forms of eczema affecting other parts of the body in those said to be allergic to their plastic spectacle frames. It is therefore possible that the development of spectacle dermatitis in those wearing plastic frames depends on a constitutional predisposition.

Berkoff. *Arch. Derm. Syph.* (Chic.), **38**, 746 (1938).

Cormia and Stewart. *Canad. med. Ass. J.*, **32**, 270 (1935).

Foster and Ball. *Arch. Derm. Syph.* (Chic.), **31**, 461 (1935).

Fox. *J. Amer. med. Ass.*, **101**, 1066 (1933).

Garrigosa and Pérez Irisarri. *Arch. Soc. oftal. hisp.-amer.*, **28**, 541 (1968).

Gaul. *Arch. Derm.* (Chic.), **78**, 475 (1958).

Gray. *Brit. med. J.*, **1**, 648 (1943).

Hollander and Baer. *Amer. J. Ophthal.*, **18**, 616 (1935).

Kristjansen. *Acta derm.-venereol.* (Stockh.), **18**, 519 (1937).

Lain. *J. Amer. med. Ass.*, **96**, 771 (1931).

Löwenstein. *Allergische Augenerkrankungen*, Basel (1938).

McAlester, A. W. and A. W. *Amer. J. Ophthal.*, **14**, 925 (1931).

MacCormac. *Proc. roy. Soc. Med.*, **24**, 518 (1931).

Smith and Calnan. *Trans. St. John's Hosp. derm. Soc.*, **52**, 10 (1966).

Sutton. *J. Amer. med. Ass.*, **89**, 1059 (1927).

Taylor. *Brit. J. Ophthal.*, **28**, 493 (1944).

Taylor, Fergusson and Atkins. *Brit. med. J.*, **2**, 40 (1945).

Thistlethwaite. *Brit. med. J.*, **1**, 493 (1943).

Urbach. *Klinik u. Therapie d. allergischen Krankheiten*, Wien (1935).

Wilde. *Derm. Wschr.*, **140**, 1089 (1959).

SPECTACLE OPTICS

THE EFFECTIVITY AND EQUIVALENCE OF LENSES

We have seen that if an object is imaged on the retina, it must occupy a position conjugate to this structure, that is, it must be situated at the far-point of the eye. We have also seen that in order to correct an optical defect in the eye, a correcting lens (for distance), when placed in a suitable position, must be such that its second focal point corresponds to the remote point of the eye and the image of the remote point is brought to a focus on the retina by the dioptric system of the eye. The combination of the two will thus focus parallel rays upon the retina. It is therefore obvious that *the factor of primary importance in a spectacle lens is its posterior focal length* (or BACK VERTEX POWER). It also follows that the shape and thickness of the lenses and their distance from the eye must be considered for these factors influence the value of the vertex power.

With the second point in view, the trial frames should be maintained at the same distance from the eyes as the spectacle lenses will eventually be; otherwise a correction for effectivity should be applied if the optical error is large. "Ideal" optical conditions are attained when the optical centre of the lens lies in the anterior focal plane of the eye (15·706 mm. in front of the

cornea). As a rule, however, a closer plane is chosen—the *spectacle plane*—
just clear of the lashes, which averages about 12 mm. in front of the cornea,
and if the visual test has not been conducted with the trial lenses in this
position a corrective factor must be applied. With regard to the first point,
the back vertex power varies with the form of the lens (or combination of
lenses). Thus thick lenses and thin lenses of the same surface powers are
not equivalent, and a combination of lenses in the trial frame has not the same
optical effect as a single lens ground to represent the sum of their surface
powers. Moreover, a biconvex lens cannot be replaced by a meniscus lens
of the same power, or either of these by a toric lens since their equivalent
focal lengths are not equal. In all these cases, particularly if the error is
large, equivalent spectacle lenses of the same effectivity should be supplied.

It is for these reasons that, as we have already indicated,[1] the test lenses should
be as thin as possible, with plano surfaces so that they can be closely apposed, and the
trial frames should be so constituted that they are held securely in apposition. The
frames should also be adjustable so that the lenses are at a known distance from the
cornea.

In spectacle optics the problem which usually arises is, given the back
vertex power (BVP), the thickness and the inside or base curve, to
determine the curve which must be worked on the anterior surface of the
lens. For this it is easier in this case to trace the ray of light backwards
from the focus. Thus from the equations on p. 75, if the BVP (F'_v) is
$+5\cdot00$ D, the thickness of the lens (d) is 3 mm., the back surface power (F_2)
is $-6\cdot00$ D, and the refractive index (n) is $1\cdot5$, tracing the rays back from
the second focus f', the vergence at the back surface is $-5\cdot00$ D. After refraction by the back surface the vergence is $-11\cdot00$ D and the light appears
to diverge from a point $1{,}000/11$ mm. from the back surface. It now goes
through 3 mm. of glass which is equivalent to $3/1\cdot5 = 2$ mm. of air, so that
its vergence at the front surface is $-10\cdot76$ D. Therefore the front surface
must have a power of $+10\cdot76$ D to make the rays parallel. The general
formula for the power of the front surface is then:

$$F_1 = \frac{F'_v - F_2}{1 + d/n\,(F'_v - F_2)}$$

and since the surface power (F_1) is equal to $\dfrac{n-1}{r_1}$, the radius of curvature
to be ground on the front surface (r_1) can easily be calculated.

The Practical Determination of the Vertex Power

The method of neutralization, while accurate for thin lenses, obviously
breaks down in the measurement of combinations of lenses of some thickness, but the vertex power is readily determined by direct measurement
(Fig. 628). The general principle of the method is that the image of a

[1] p. 429.

target as seen through a telescope is focused by a standard lens; the unknown lens is then inserted into the system and its power is measured by the change in the position of the target required to bring it again into focus.

The first such instrument was patented by Zeiss in 1914 as the *vertex refractionometer*; other trade names include the *vertometer, lensometer, vertex dioptrescope, ultimeter* and the *focimeter* (Fig. 628). Its optical principle is seen in Fig. 629. Before

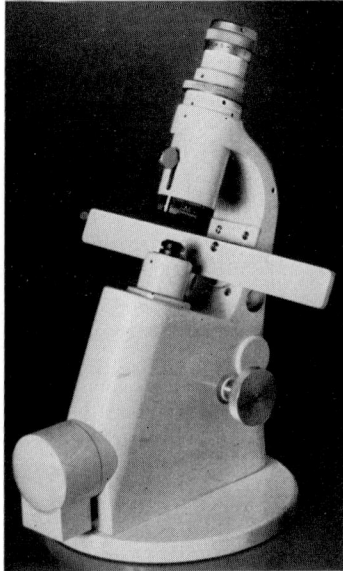

FIG. 628.—ZEISS VERTEX REFRACTIONOMETER (Degenhardt).

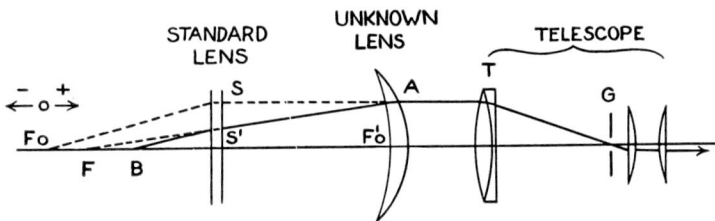

FIG. 629.—THE OPTICAL PRINCIPLES OF VERTEX REFRACTIONOMETERS (see text).

the lens to be tested is inserted, when the telescope is focused for parallel light, a clear image of the target (B) will be seen where it coincides with the focal point (F_0) of the standard lens. This point is therefore the zero position and at this point the light between the standard lens and the telescope (SAT) is parallel. The lens or combination of lenses to be tested is now inserted at A with the back surface facing the standard lens. If the lens is positive, the light from the standard lens will no longer be parallel but convergent so that the target will no longer be focused at G. The image of B will now be formed at F, the focal point of the unknown lens, and when the target is moved from F_0 to F the pencil of light emerging from A will again be parallel and B will once more be sharply focused at G. The excursion of the target towards F (in the case of convex lenses) or away from F (in the case of concave lenses) is in direct proportion to the back vertex power of the lens under test.

In order to measure the back vertex power of meniscus lenses of small diameter and high curvature, such as corneal contact lenses, it may be necessary to modify the instrument used for this purpose, reducing considerably the diameter of the circle of contact between the test lens and the contact lens. Failure to do this will give a false reading. It is also quite invalid to turn the lens upside down thereby assessing the front vertex power unless measurements are also taken of the surface powers and the thickness.

The same instrument determines the optical centres, locates cylindrical axes and measures the power and locates the direction of prisms. The ideal method of verification of an ophthalmic lens is undoubtedly to make these measurements on such an instrument, and by inserting the test-lenses in the trial frame into it and then the spectacle lens, to compare directly the back vertex power of each.

The Optical Defects of Spectacles and their Correction

There are many optical defects associated with spectacle lenses, some—but not all—of which are susceptible to correction or partial correction. These defects include the disability arising from the use of a lens fixed with respect to the head in conjunction with an eye which moves independently of the head, as well as a number of aberrations inherent in the optical properties of lenses themselves which concern mainly the refraction of oblique rays.

THE ROTATION OF THE EYE

Since the eye and the spectacle lens do not move together in unison it is obvious that if the optical system is accurate for axial rays when the eye is in the primary position it will be inaccurate when the eye looks eccentrically and the head is kept still, for then the eye moves and the lens remains stationary. In its movements the eye moves round a variable centre of rotation (Z, Fig. 630) which experimental measurements have located on the axis about 13 mm. behind the vertex of the cornea. On looking eccentrically to view an object not situated straight in front, therefore, the pupil of the eye and the macula rotate around the centre of rotation. If a sharp image of the object is to be obtained, we have already seen that an image at the remote point must be brought to a focus on the macula. The remote point, which is conjugate with the macula, must therefore similarly move over a spherical surface which, as is seen in Figs. 630 and 631, is a *real* sphere lying in front of the eye in myopia and a *virtual* sphere lying behind the eye in hypermetropia. If the object-point rotates on this sphere concentric to the centre of rotation, it follows that in all positions on this sphere, all the pencils of light entering the pupil will have the same convergence and the course of the rays will be the same as if a stationary aperture (or *stop*) existed at Z (Figs. 630–1). Assuming the power of accommodation is absent, objects can be seen distinctly only if they lie on this *sphere of sharp definition*.

If, however, the eye can accommodate there will be a sphere of sharp definition concentric to Z corresponding to each state of accommodation

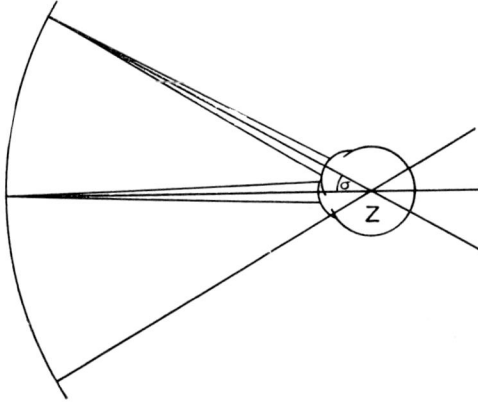

FIG. 630.—THE REAL CIRCLE OF SHARP DEFINITION FOR A MYOPIC EYE REVOLVING AROUND Z.

All pencils of light entering the pupil from points on this circle are equally divergent. The angle σ measures the obliquity of vision to the horizontal axis. If the plane of this circle were rotated around the axis of the eye, it would trace the *sphere of sharp definition*.

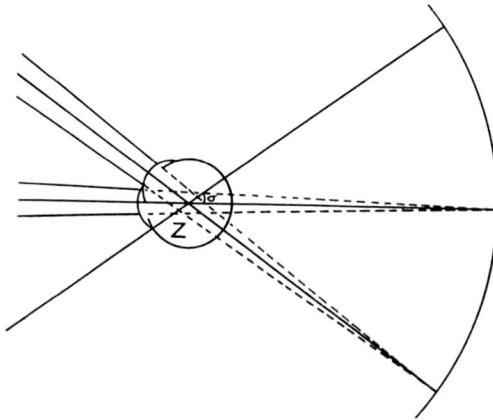

FIG. 631.—THE VIRTUAL CIRCLE OF SHARP DEFINITION FOR A HYPERMETROPIC EYE REVOLVING AROUND Z.

All pencils of light entering the pupil from points on this circle are equally convergent.

with two limiting positions, the *proximate sphere of sharp definition* at the near-point and the *remote sphere* at the far-point. The construction for the myopic eye is seen in Fig. 632 and for the hypermetropic eye in Fig. 633. If, in hypermetropia, the power of accommodation can compensate for all the refractive error, the conditions of emmetropia will be reproduced and the remote sphere will be at infinity (in the *plane of infinite distance*); and if the amplitude of accommodation is greater than the degree of hypermetropia the proximate sphere (as in emmetropia) will be situated as a real concept in front of the eye.

It is obvious that the three-dimensional space lying between the two boundary surfaces corresponding to the remote sphere and the proximate sphere contains all the points at which an object can be seen clearly without moving the head. This has been called by Gullstrand the *space of sharp definition*. As accommodation fails the proximate sphere approaches the remote sphere, and the space of sharp definition contracts until it is ultimately reduced to the surface area of the remote sphere.

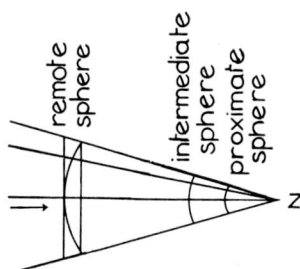 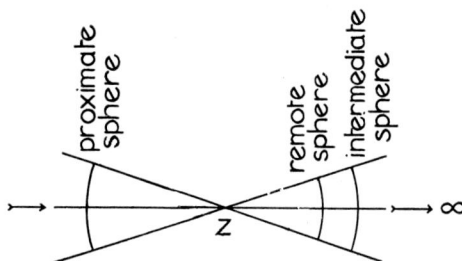

FIG. 632.   FIG. 633.

FIGS. 632 and 633.—THE SPHERES OF SHARP DEFINITION IN AN ACCOMMODATING EYE.

In each case the eye rotates around Z, and the direction of incident light is denoted by arrows. Fig. 632 shows the condition in the myopic eye (where two tangent planes are represented at the vertex). Fig. 633 shows the condition in a hypermetropic eye wherein the amplitude of accommodation is greater than the amount of hypermetropia so that, while the remote sphere is behind, the proximate sphere is real and lies in front of the eye. Between the proximate and the remote spheres (*i.e.*, on any intermediate sphere) all points can be brought to a focus on the retina.

Let us now consider the case of a spectacle lens which remains stationary while the eye rotates behind it (Fig. 634). From some points of view (such as the magnification of the image) the best optical results would be obtained if the principal point of the (thin) lens were placed at the anterior focal point of the eye (that is, 15·7 mm. in front of the vertex of the cornea according to Gullstrand's measurement).[1] In practice, however, the inner vertex of the lens (S_1) is placed closer to the eye so that it just clears the lashes, at an average distance of 12 mm. from the cornea. The eye now rotates around Z'.[2] In the fitting of the spectacles, of course, the new centre

---

[1] p. 120.

[2] Z' lies in the " *image space* "—that is all points, virtual and real, reached by rays after refraction. These are conveniently denoted by dashes to distinguish them from the corresponding points in the *object space* so that

$$S_1Z' = S_1S + SZ'$$
$$= 12 + 13 = 25 \text{ mm. (or 1 inch)}.$$

of rotation (Z′) must fall in the axis of the spectacle lens, that is, it must be *centric* in position.

The system in the case of a spectacle lens is thus seen in Fig. 635 wherein the course of the rays can be traced by substituting an axial stop P′ for Z′, $S_1P′$ being 25 mm. The obliquity of an eccentric bundle of rays before traversing the lens (σ), that is, their apparent obliquity in the object space now corresponds to their real obliquity ($\sigma′$) in the image space. The difference between the two angles ($\sigma-\sigma′$) represents a deviation inherent in

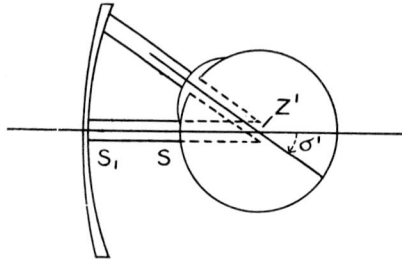

FIG. 634.—THE EYE ROTATING AROUND Z′ AT AN OBLIQUITY $\sigma′$ IN THE PRESENCE OF A SPECTACLE LENS.

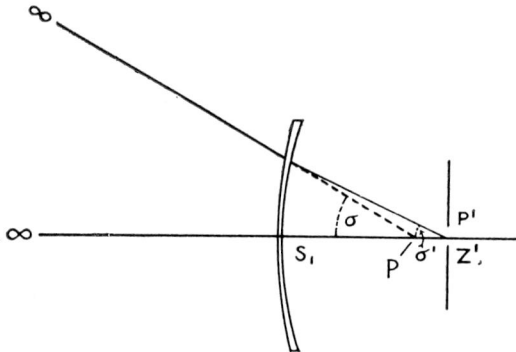

FIG. 635.—THE OPTICAL SYSTEM OF A ROTATING EYE PROVIDED WITH A SPECTACLE LENS, AN AXIAL STOP P′ COINCIDING WITH THE CENTRE OF ROTATION, Z′.

the use of lenses, for the value σ cannot be appreciated by the eye which only rotates around $\sigma′$. This is called the *prismatic difference* of the spectacle lens at the corresponding eccentric point. The obliquities ($\sigma′$) seen behind the lens are larger with converging lenses and smaller with diverging lenses than the obliquities (σ) in the object space. It follows that eccentric objects or parts of objects are larger to the corrected hypermetropic eye than to the emmetropic eye and those in the corrected myopic eye smaller.

Whereas a photographic lens is designed to produce sharp images on a flat plate, *the problem in the design of a spectacle lens is therefore to produce sharp images of the plane of infinite distance on a remote sphere concentric to the centre of rotation* (Z') assuming an axial distance of 25 mm. between the inner vertex of the spectacle lens and the centre of rotation. We shall see presently that this can be done by varying the radii of the two surfaces of the lens, that is, by bending it. Much of the design of best-form spectacle lenses has been carried out to correct this aberration, but clearly, if other criteria are taken into account such as a variable axial distance and varying object-distances, compromise forms must be sought.

THE DEFECTS OF IMAGES

We have already seen that certain optical defects are associated with optical imagery, some of them unavoidable, others correctable to a certain extent. Their summated effect makes it inevitable that *no point-focus of light is ever formed*. The theory of refraction by lenses worked out by Gauss more than a century ago is a beautiful example of the imagery of mathematics. It conceives the refraction of homogeneous light by an imaginary perfect lens occurring at one plane surface and involving rays perpendicular to that surface; it ignores—as can be done in mathematical reasoning—all the awkward exceptions, such as the aberrations of obliquity, which occur in life. It is true that for small obliquities up to 10° these effects are scarcely perceptible from the practical point of view, but for angles greater than this —and these are constantly occurring in life—their effects are profound so that, despite the apparent exactitude of the optical diagram in all text-books, all images are formed of blurred circles of light.

These optical defects of images can be summarized thus:

A. Aberrations depending on the nature of light.
    1. Diffraction of light.
    2. Chromatic aberration.

B. Aberrations depending on the nature of lenses.
    3. Spherical aberration.
    4. Coma.
    5. Oblique (radial) astigmatism.
    6. Curvature of the image.
    7. Distortion of the image.

In the theory and practice of spectacles lenses, among the first class of aberrations the blurring of the image due to the DIFFRACTION OF LIGHT cannot be overcome, but the resolving power of the eye due to the retinal mosaic is not sufficiently fine to endow this defect with importance. That due to CHROMATIC ABERRATION, by which the short waves of light are retarded and therefore more acutely bent as they travel through a refractive medium so that they come to an axial focus in front of the longer waves (Fig. 109), can theoretically be overcome by the use of achromatic lenses.[1] This aberration, however, does not inconvenience the wearer of spectacles,

[1] p. 82.

for the eye itself is uncorrected for chromatic aberration and accommodates itself to the phenomenon. Moreover, in ordinary spectacle lenses the error is slight and assumes importance only in compound spectacle systems; since this aberration cannot be corrected except in such systems, this is fortunate. The *chromatic difference in magnification*[1] for oblique pencils (Fig. 110) is not evident in spectacle lenses owing to the narrowness of the pupillary diameter, but is very noticeable in compound spectacle lens systems with a wide field. It can, however, be overcome partly by choosing suitable dispersions for the component types of glass forming the various lenses, and partly by bending the object lens so that oblique rays subtend a relatively constant angle at the centre of rotation of the eye.

We have already seen[2] that in a lens of any thickness and considerable aperture SPHERICAL ABERRATION is evident since the periphery has a higher refracting power than the central parts because of the greater obliquity of its

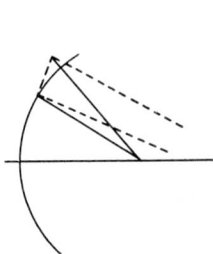
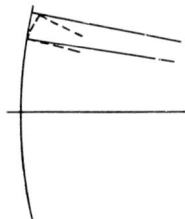
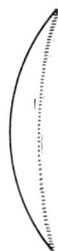

FIG. 636.   FIG. 637.   FIG. 638.

FIGS. 636–638.—CORRECTION FOR SPHERICAL ABERRATION (M. von Rohr).

The alteration of a spherical surface to compensate for spherical aberration. A converging lens (Fig. 636) must have its surface flattened, a diverging lens (Fig. 637) its surface deepened to counteract the aberration. The initial sphere and the normals to it are in continuous lines, the aspherical surfaces and the normals to them are in dotted lines. Fig. 638. A strongly spherical lens (cataract lens of the Katral type) with an aspherical surface.

surfaces so that the peripheral rays are brought more quickly to a focus than the central rays (Fig. 115). It follows that the highest definition possible is a circle of least confusion and not a point-focus. This aberration, however, is not of great consequence in spectacle lenses because of the smallness of the pupillary diameter. We have also seen that the neutralization of this aberration may be accomplished partly by altering the form of the lens. This is best done when the more convex surface faces the incident rays. The form of spectacle lenses should therefore be such that a plane or preferably a concave surface is next the eye and a convex surface away from it.

This expedient, of course, minimizes but does not abolish spherical aberration. To do so the curvature of one of the surfaces of the lens must

[1] p. 81.   [2] p.82.

be continuously altered from the axial portion to the periphery (*aplanatic lenses*). For example, a convex spherical surface may be flattened by the addition of material in the periphery (Fig. 636) and a concave surface deepened to obtain a point-focus (Fig. 637). The form of such a lens with an aspherical surface so that its power is progressively reduced towards the periphery is seen in Fig. 638. Such lenses are difficult and expensive to make and are unnecessary in practice unless in the case of strong spectacles, as in aphakia.[1]

The ABERRATION OF COMA,[2] whereby oblique rays from an object in the peripheral field come to a focus on one side of the central ray so that the image of a point so situated is drawn out like the tail of a comet is essentially a phenomenon of wide-apertured systems and therefore in spectacles is of little importance.

OBLIQUE ASTIGMATISM

In discussing the optics of oblique astigmatism[3] we have seen that when a pencil of light strikes a lens obliquely, two focal lines are formed, the meridional and the sagittal. An indication of what occurs in the case of a spectacle lens is seen in Fig. 639. By joining with a curve all the points (F'_m) of the meridional focal lines and all the points (F'_s) of the sagittal focal lines we shall obtain two curves outlining the points at which each focal line is situated. These considerations, of course, will apply to any axial plane and if Fig. 639 is rotated around the optic axis of the lens, the curves for the

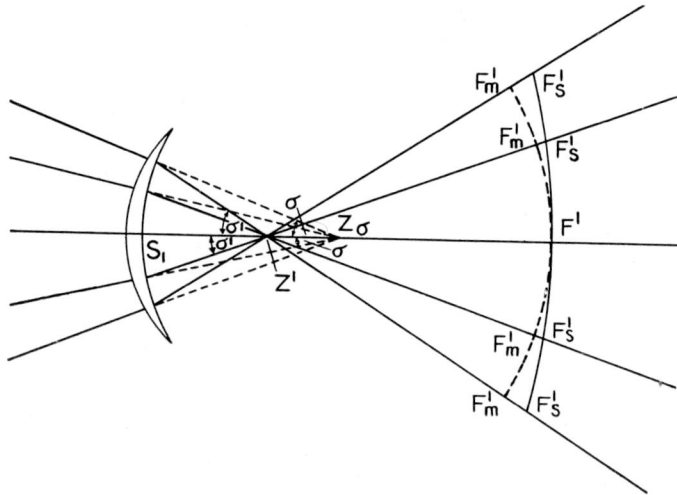

FIG. 639.—THE ASTIGMATIC SURFACES OF A CONVEX LENS.

Z' represents the centre of rotation and Zσ the apparent centre of rotation. F'_m F' F'_m and F'_s F' F'_s represent the two focal planes coming into contact at the axial point F'. If these planes are rotated around the optic axis of the lens they will trace out the *m*- and *s-surfaces* of the lens as the loci for some approximation to an image.

[1] p. 697.　　　　[2] p. 86.　　　　[3] p. 87

focal lines will trace out the *astigmatic image surfaces* of the lens as the loci for image-formation (*meridional and sagittal planes*; the *m*- and *s*- *surfaces*).

It will be seen that these two surfaces are related to each other somewhat as a cup and saucer. The cup (F'_m) represents the converging point of rays lying in the plane of the paper containing the optic axis and the principal ray (or the peripheral object point): it is therefore called the

FIGS. 640—642.—THE FOCUSING OF OBLIQUE PENCILS BY A LENS (M. von Rohr).

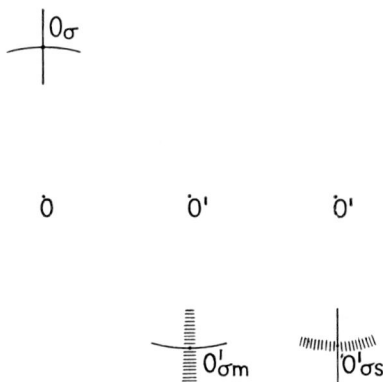

FIG. 640.—The focusing of a cross near the principal ray of an oblique pencil ($O\sigma$) with regard to O, the axial point of the plane focused. On the meridional surface ($O'\sigma m$) the vertical arm is muzzy since every point is drawn out to a peripheral line, but the horizontal arm is clear since these lines overlap. Conversely, on the sagittal surface ($O'\sigma s$) the vertical arm is sharp and the horizontal muzzy.

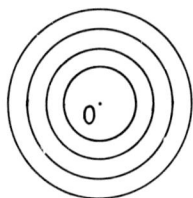

FIG. 641.—The depictable lines in the object plane in focus on the meridional surface, all the points being drawn out peripherally.

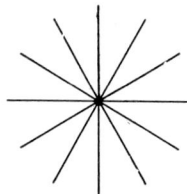

FIG. 642.—The depictable lines in the object plane in focus on the sagittal surface, all the points being drawn out radially.

primary or *tangential* or *meridional focal surface.* The saucer (F'_s) represents the converging point of rays in the plane perpendicular to this and may be called the *secondary, sagittal* or *equatorial focal surface.* If, for example, a cross serves as the eccentric object (Fig. 640) on the tangential surface the vertical image line is blurred, and on the sagittal surface the cross-line is blurred; and between the two surfaces will be a third plane whereon lie the circles of least confusion. Neglecting other aberrations, if the lens is spherical it follows that a point on the axial line is clearly imaged (at F', Fig. 639);

on the sagittal plane clear images are depicted of all radial lines drawn in
the object plane through its axial point (Fig. 642); while in the tangential
plane concentric circles are similarly focused (Fig. 641). Such lines were
called by Gullstrand the *depictable lines* of a lens traversed by oblique pencils.

It will be noted that this clarity applies only to lines. Points in the
object plane are depicted as strokes, and the overlapping of these allows
lines in one direction to be depicted distinctly. In order to obtain the ideal
condition wherein points in the object space are imaged as points in the
image space (*stigmatic* or *punctiform* images of Gullstrand), both focal planes
must coincide and conditions must be arranged so that

$$F'_m = F'_s = F'_\sigma.$$

This can be done by altering the form of the lens by bending it for it is
obvious that as the lens is bent so that its outer surface is convex, obliquely
incident rays will become more normal. It will be observed that the same
form neutralizes spherical aberration and the solution of this question in
the construction of stigmatic or point-focal lenses will be considered presently.

The Astigmatism of Tilted Lenses. It follows as a corollary to the
argument of the previous paragraph that the same astigmatic phenomena
will apply to the axial rays if a spherical lens is tilted. In both cases the
astigmatic effect is due to the obliquity of the incident light upon the lens.
The phenomena can be simply demonstrated by focusing the light from a
point-source upon a screen. When the lens is held vertically, the focus is a
small circle; if the lens is tilted upon a horizontal axis, the circular patch
becomes a hazy vertical line which comes sharply into focus if the source is
brought near to the lens; further approximation to the screen leads to the
formation of a circle of least confusion and then to a sharply focused horizontal line. It thus appears that a tilted spherical lens is converted into
a sphero-cylindrical combination with the spherical component slightly
increased and a cylindrical component added with its axis parallel to the
axis of rotation of the lens. The tilting of cylindrical lenses, of course,
produces the same effect.

If the tilt is represented by θ and the power of the sphere by F, the power of the
resulting sphero-cylinder is given by the following expressions (Martin, 1929):

$$\text{sphere} = F \left(1 + \frac{1}{3} \sin^2\theta\right)$$

$$\text{cylinder} = F \tan^2\theta$$

Table XXVIII gives Percival's (1928) values for the tilting of a $+10\cdot00$ DS when the
refractive index is $1\cdot523$.

If the lens is not $+10$ D sphere, but some other value, the figures in Percival's
(1928) table are multiplied by the tenth part of the power of the lens. Thus if the
strength of the sphere is 9 D or 11 D, they are multiplied by $0\cdot9$ or $1\cdot1$.

It is thus evident that the tilting of the lenses in spectacles with reference to the
incident rays—quite a common error in fitting and a necessary occurrence in reading
with lenses designed primarily for distance—is very considerable if they are not bent

TABLE XXVIII

Obliquity	Spherical value	Cylindrical value
10°	10·101 D	0·314 D
15°	10·228 D	0·734 D
20°	10·409 D	1·379 D
25°	10·648 D	2·315 D
30°	10·948 D	3·349 D
35°	11·314 D	5·547 D

to the proper form. Conversely, the effect may be useful to patients who require a horizontal cylinder. Thus it may be useful in aphakic patients shortly after operation who frequently have in the horizontal axis a cylinder which must be gradually decreased in strength after some time, a change which can be effected by merely straightening the spectacles. Another advantage of the method is that the lenses are lighter without the cylindrical addition.

Thus if an effect of $+11·5$ DS $\subset$ $1·5$ DC ax. $180°$ is required,

$$\text{since } 1·1 \times 10·409 = 11·5$$
$$\text{and } 1·1 \times 1·379 = 1·5$$

the effect can be obtained by prescribing a $+11$ DS tilted downwards at $20°$.

Similarly, a myope of -20 DS $\subset$ $-2·5$ DC ax. $180°$ can be treated in the same way by prescribing a lens of -19 DS inclined at $20°$.

$$\text{Since } 1·9 \times 10·409 = 19·78$$
$$\text{and } 1·9 \times 1·379 = 2·62$$

the effect is that of $-19·78$ DS $\subset$ $2·62$ DC ax. $180°$.

CURVATURE OF THE IMAGE

We have already seen that in refraction through lenses, even although all the aberrations we have considered have been eliminated so that the image is stigmatic, the surface upon which the images lie may be curved, so that a flat object will appear curved (*Petzval's curvature*).[1]

The mathematical treatment of the curvature of the image was worked out at an early date by G. B. Airy in 1827, H. Coddington in 1829 and J. Petzval in 1843.[2] For point-focal lenses corrected for oblique astigmatism the curvature of the sharp image is given by the formula

$$\frac{1}{r} = -\frac{1}{n_1 f'_1}.$$

Consequently the radius of curvature in the neighbourhood of the axis, $r = -n_1 f'_1$, when n_1 is the refractive index of the glass. In a spectacle lens, however, as we have seen, the optimum condition is that the image should not be flat but that all its constituent points should lie on the remote sphere concentric with the centre of rotation ($F'F'$, Fig. 643). Since for thin lenses $S_1 F' = f_1$ it is seen that, in general, the radius of curvature of point focal images is less than $Z'F'$ (Fig. 639).

This is clear from Figs. 643 and 644 where it is seen that, away from the axial region, the radius of curvature of point-focal images is longer than

[1] p. 89.   [2] p. 89.

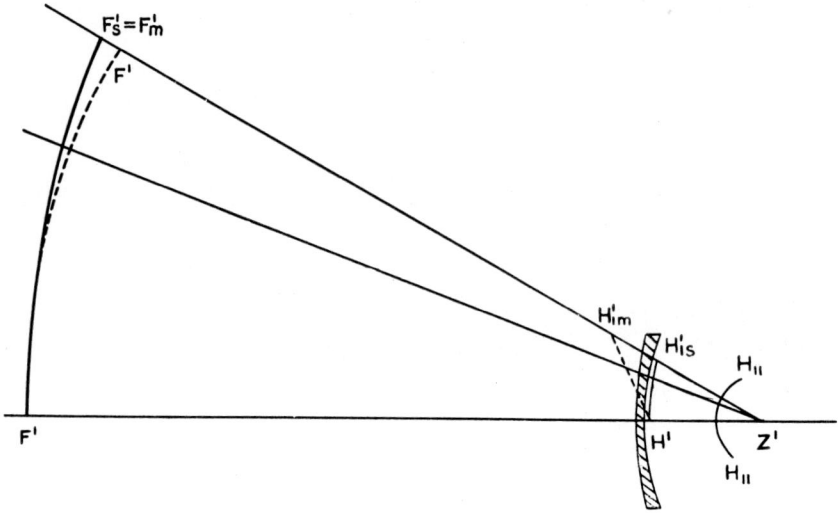

FIG. 643.—THE REMOTE SPHERE (F′F′) OF A MYOPIC EYE AND THE SURFACE OF POINT-FOCAL IMAGES (F′F′$_m$ = F′F′$_s$) WITH A CONCAVE LENS.

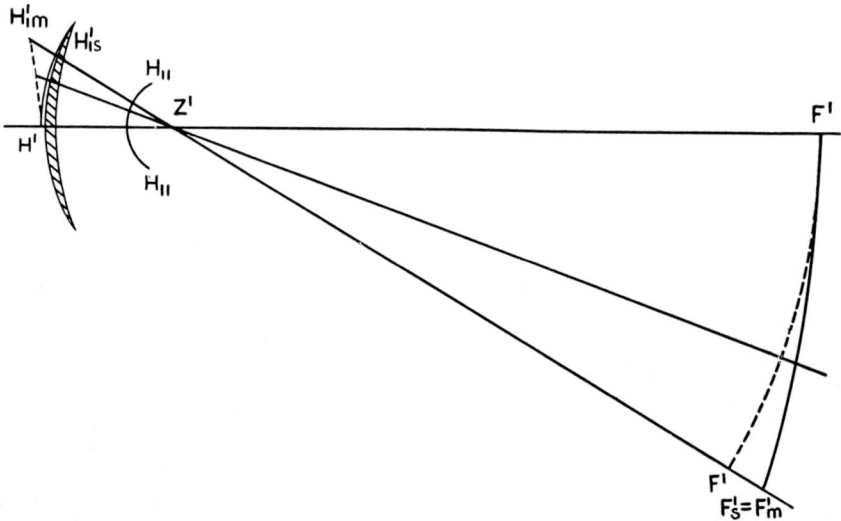

FIG. 644.—THE REMOTE SPHERE (F′F′) OF A HYPERMETROPIC EYE AND THE SURFACE OF POINT-FOCAL IMAGES (F′F′$_m$ = F′F′$_s$) WITH A CONVEX LENS.

Z′F′ (the radius of curvature of the remote sphere of the eye). If any accommodative power is left, it is easy to advance the surface of point-focal images to the remote sphere in hypermetropic eyes and thus eliminate this defect for oblique vision if the amount of accommodation required is small (v. Rohr *et al.*, 1934). But in myopic eyes such an adjustment is impossible;

and for this reason Gullstrand (1911) suggested that myopic eyes should be slightly over-corrected in the direction of the axis so as to include the remote sphere within the scope of sharp definition.

DISTORTION BY LENSES

In addition to the previous aberrations, the final aberration of distortion of the image[1] must be considered, whereby the images of peripheral points are different in size from those of central points. We have already dealt with the cause of this phenomenon: in spectacle lenses it may be illustrated

FIGS. 645 and 646.—PERIPHERAL MAGNIFICATION OF LENSES.

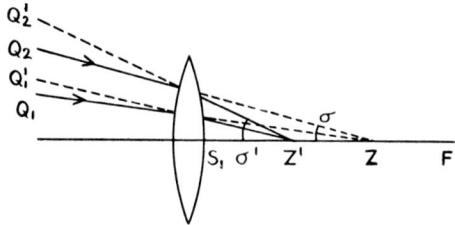

FIG. 645.—Positive peripheral magnification by a convex lens. The angle (σ) subtended by the object Q_1Q_2 is less than the angle (σ') subtended by the image $Q'_1Q'_2$. Since $Q_2Q'_2$ is therefore greater than $Q_1Q'_1$, the peripheral parts of the image are magnified (Fig. 125).

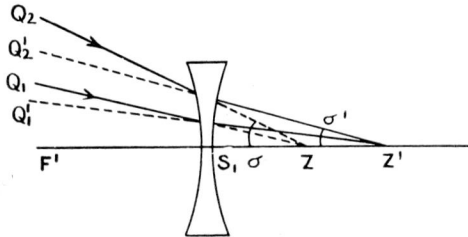

FIG. 646.—Negative peripheral magnification by a concave lens. The angle (σ) subtended by the object Q_1Q_2 is greater than the angle (σ') subtended by the image $Q'_1Q'_2$. Since $Q_2Q'_2$ is therefore greater than $Q_1Q'_1$, the peripheral parts of the image are reduced (Fig. 124).

simply. It is seen (Fig. 645) that in the case of a convex lens if an object of considerable extensity (Q_1Q_2) is regarded, its obliquity (σ) in the object space is considerably less than its obliquity (σ') in the image space. The eye behind the lens will therefore see Q_1Q_2 at $Q'_1Q'_2$, and since QQ' is progressively greater the farther away from the axis, the converging lens magnifies the more peripheral parts of objects to a progressively greater degree (the *peripheral magnification of lenses*). With convex lenses the magnification is positive, the peripheral magnification being greater than the axial (*pin-cushion distortion*) (Fig. 125): with concave lenses the opposite

[1] p. 91.

condition obtains (Fig. 646) and the magnification is negative, giving a *barrel-shaped distortion* (Fig. 124). The effect involves an astigmatic deformation so that lateral circles become ellipses. It was shown by Airy (1827) that this effect was eliminated and an *orthoscopic image* produced if (*a*) spherical aberration is abolished and (*b*) the ratio between the tangents of the corresponding angles (σ and σ') is constant for all inclinations of the rays (Airy's *tangent condition*). Such a condition is impossible to attain in spectacle lenses but the phenomenon becomes much less pronounced with bent than with flat lenses.

With lenses of high power this distortion may be considerable: lines in an object viewed eccentrically will appear curved, an effect seen markedly in respect to the floor which appears to rise or fall away, and when the visual axis is changed objects will appear to move owing to the variation of this curvature when different portions of the lens are employed for vision. This movement is superimposed on that caused by the varying prismatic effect of the lens with the disturbing effects rendered all the more marked when there is also a considerable cylindrical element with axes at different angles in the two eyes.

In an assessment of the effect of these aberrations on the optics of spectacle lenses we must remember that minute aberrations can be neglected because the resolving power of the eye as determined by the retinal mosaic is finite: the *tolerance* of the eye is therefore considerable. Moreover, the degree of acuity possible in the periphery of the retina is sufficiently low to make the resolution of pencils eccentric from the macula relatively unimportant. Again the smallness of the pupillary aperture rules out the consideration of those aberrations such as coma which depend on marked peripheral refraction. Finally the physiological mechanism of the eye is adapted to compensate chromatic aberrations so long as the chromatic difference of oblique pencils is not excessive. The most important remaining conditions, therefore, which it is desirable to satisfy are:

1. That when the eye rotates objects at the far-point (*i.e.*, at infinity in the corrected eye) be imaged on a remote sphere concentric with the centre of rotation.

2. That oblique images be as sharp as axial images, thus correcting the astigmatism of oblique pencils.

3. That oblique images be of the same size as axial images, thus correcting distortion.

The design of spectacle lenses into a " best form " so as to correct these aberrations allows very few variables by which their optical character can be varied. The lens must be single, light and thin; moreover, ophthalmic lenses are generally made of glass so that the refractive index is relatively constant; and, finally, the distance from the cornea is also fixed. The single variable quantity left is the relation between the curvatures of the two surfaces. The total power of the lens is fixed by the prescription; and since the total power of a (thin) lens is represented by the formula

$$F_1 + F_2 = (n-1)\left(\frac{1}{r_1} - \frac{1}{r_2}\right),$$

it is permissible to vary the individual values of r_1 and r_2 provided the factor $\left(\dfrac{1}{r_1} - \dfrac{1}{r_2}\right)$ remains constant. This in effect means bending the lens from the flat shape into a curve in which the two surfaces may have a variable but related curvature. Since in this computation there is a single variable quantity, only one of the aberrations can be accurately corrected. Fortunately if the lens is bent so that the astigmatism of oblique pencils is eliminated (and this is usually considered the most distressing of the aberrations) objects regarded obliquely are reasonably sharp and the first of our three important conditions is also very nearly fulfilled for the curvature of the image formed by such a lens is approximately that of the remote sphere and the image is usually readily brought upon that sphere by accommodation. At the same time the bending of the lens goes a considerable way to mitigate distortion although some must remain as the price of clear images. The same configuration also tends to minimize spherical and other aberrations. We shall therefore proceed to consider the characteristics of a " best-form " lens upon this basis.

The Form of Lenses

History. Originally lenses were treated only in combination with a stationary eye looking along the axis of the lens, and the form, whether symmetrical, asymmetrical or plano, did not matter very much; but even the Venetian opticians at the beginning of the 17th century knew that plano-convex lenses gave a larger field of view than biconvex lenses. In his *Dioptrice* in 1611, Kepler was the first to consider rotation of the eye around the *centrum oculi* and for this reason he introduced the *meniscus* form of lenses, bent with the concavity next to the eye (μηνίσκος, dim. of μήνη, the moon). At that time optical science was not sufficiently advanced to conform to mathematical designs, but as early as 1645 the moon-shaped lenses, confined at first to the convex type, were known in Paris and later in the century were sold in London and Germany as an expensive high-grade product (see Heymann, 1911). Meniscus lenses were advocated, more, however, for fanciful than for scientific reasons by the Parisian optician, Jacques Bourgeois (1745), spectacle-maker to Louis XIV.

The first mathematical discussion of the question was undertaken by W. H. Wollaston (1804–12) in England who introduced deep "*periscopic*" lenses (περί, around, and σκοπêιν, to look) designed to overcome the astigmatism of oblique pencils (Figs. 647–51). Although his views excited some controversy (W. Jones, 1804–13), they were elaborated analytically by Airy (1825–27) and Coddington (1829) who published formulæ for oblique pencils. Towards the end of the century the centre of rotation was similarly introduced into the theory of spectacle design in a precise mathematical manner first by A. Müller (1889) and then more extensively by F. Ostwald (1898). From his calculations the latter introduced a periscopic lens of much shallower design than Wollaston's (Figs. 648 and 650); these, being less conspicuous, are generally favoured in spectacle design although they do not satisfy curvature con-

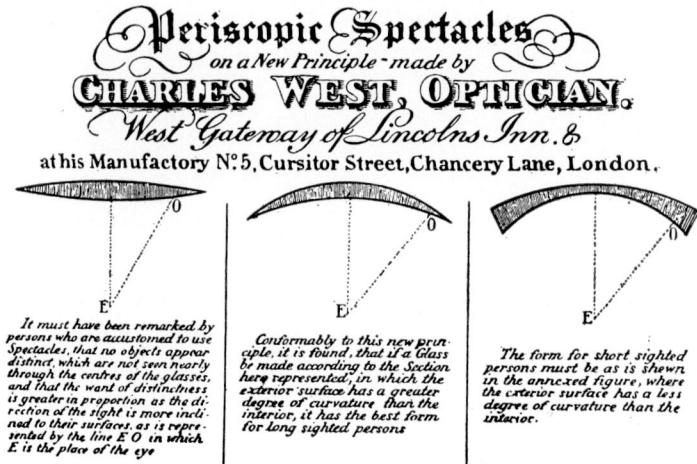

FIG. 647.—AN ADVERTISEMENT FOR PERISCOPIC LENSES OF H. W. WOLLASTON'S ORIGINAL FORM, DATED ABOUT 1818 (M. von Rohr).

ditions so well as the Wollaston type. Ostwald, however, confused the centre of rotation of the spectacled eye (Z') and its apparent position (Z), a problem correctly solved shortly thereafter by Tscherning (1904). At a later date Tscherning (1908) showed that for a large range of lenses (+7·23 to −22·22 DS) oblique astigmatism can be entirely abolished by two forms of meniscus, the shallow form of Ostwald and the deep form of Wollaston; he showed that the two forms were related to each other graphically as an ellipse (Fig. 652); and he published a series of computations showing

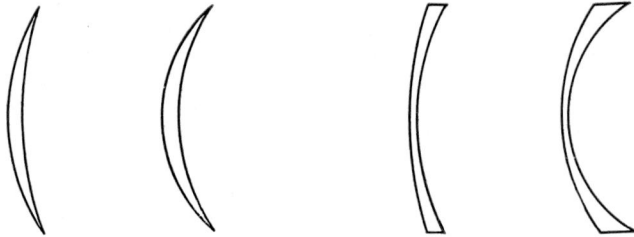

FIG. 648.   FIG. 649.   FIG. 650.   FIG. 651.

FIGS. 648 and 649.—Two lenses of + 5·00 DS. Fig. 648 shows Ostwald's form, and Fig. 649 Wollaston's.

FIGS. 650 and 651.—Two lenses of − 5·00 DS. Fig. 650 shows Ostwald's form, and Fig. 651 Wollaston's.

the form of thin " orthoscopic " lenses wherein the distortion and curvature in the peripheral parts of the field on eccentric vision are corrected as far as possible, both for distant and near vision.

At the same time, Gullstrand (1899–1911) became interested in the problem and developed aspherical lenses to correct spherical aberration and brought forward a solution to the problem of oblique astigmatism in his *point-focal lenses*. His work was extended by von Rohr (1908–21) and Boegehold (1916–21) with the result that the firm of Zeiss produced their *punktal lenses*.

Other solutions to the problem have been advanced. A. S. Percival (1901) considered it unnecessary to calculate resolution in the peripheral field with such nicety since it was not in any case observed with accuracy, and contented himself with a circle of least confusion in the macular area of a diameter of 0·002 mm.—the diameter of a macular cone. On these bases he produced tables for the surface power of " best-form " lenses, correcting them in 1914 and 1926 for the thickness of the lens and a greater angle of rotation. Thereafter, A. Gleichen (1922–23) published a series of computations and dealt elaborately with the prescription of sphero-cylinders in periscopic (toric) form, a problem also developed extensively by A. Whitwell (1924–28).

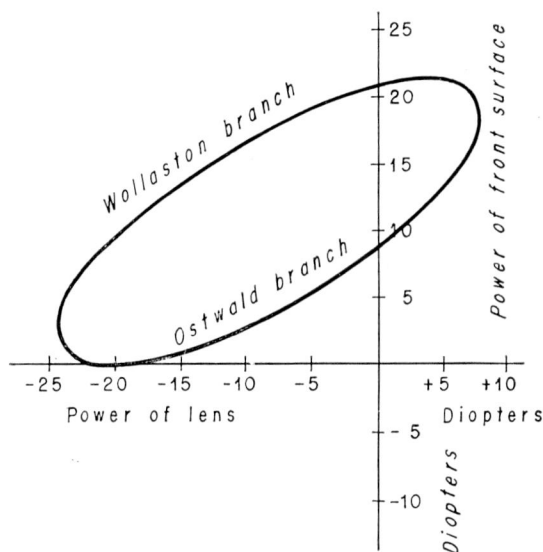

FIG. 652.—TSCHERNING'S ELLIPSE.

The approximate base curve required if an ophthalmic lens is to have no astigmatism for rays at an oblique incidence, assuming that the lens has zero thickness, the object is at infinity, the oblique angle is small and the vertex distance from the lens to the centre of rotation is 25 mm. The curve shows the relationship between the power of the front surface of the lens and the power of the lens itself; the part utilizing the higher powers of the front surface (Wollaston branch) is little used since the base curves are too high; the part of the ellipse utilizing the lower powers of the front surface (Ostwald branch) is widely used as the basis for the design of ophthalmic lenses.

Most of the great figures who have contributed to our knowledge of the best form of spectacles have already been commemorated in this Volume, but a notable exception is LOUIS OTTO MORITZ VON ROHR [1868–1940] (Fig. 653). He worked for the firm of Carl Zeiss in Jena from 1895 to 1935 and was professor of optics at the University of Jena from 1913 to 1940, spending most of his life in the perfection of optical instruments. Working initially under the inspiration of his teacher, Ernst Abbé,[1] he was greatly assisted by his colleagues, H. Boegehold and H. Hartinger. Optically his main interests lay in photographic optical systems (1899), binocular instruments (1907–20) and spectacle lenses (1908–34), the design of which he did much to revolutionize largely owing to his ability to translate theory into practice so that he became a unique authority. But his greatest love was the history of optics; thus in his first great work

[1] Vol. II, Fig. 43.

Fig. 653.—Louis Otto Moritz von Rohr
[1868–1940].
(From A. H. Degenhardt.)

on photographic lens systems the theoretical part occupies 80 pages and the historical 320 pages. So elaborate was his study of historical detail, indeed, that the readability of his writing was sometimes impaired and the interrelation of the argument difficult to follow in the wealth of the story of its development.

SPHERICAL LENSES

We have seen that in the design of lenses the most important aberration to eliminate is the astigmatism of oblique pencils so that the wearer of the spectacles can see distinctly when he ranges his eyes from side to side. We have also seen that for a considerable range of lenses (from $+7\cdot23$ DS to $-22\cdot22$ DS) there are two forms for each power by which this astigmatic effect is eliminated, one with a shallow curvature (Ostwald type) and the other a deep meniscus (Wollaston type) (Tscherning, 1908). Fortunately, as we have seen, point-focal (or stigmatic) lenses designed on this basis which allow the coalescence of the tangential and sagittal spheres (F'_m, F'_s, Fig. 643), also produce an image-plane nearly coincident with the remote sphere ($F'F'$, Fig. 643), and moreover to a considerable extent minimize distortion curvature and chromatism, reducing them to such proportions as to be within the tolerance of the eye. This form of lens is thus generally taken as a basis in design.

The effect of different forms of lenses on the astigmatism of oblique pencils is seen in Figs. 654–9, wherein the imagery is constructionally derived. In Figs. 654–6 three forms are given for a $+8\cdot0$ DS when the object is at infinity showing the curves derived for an obliquity of the refracted rays up to 30°. In the symmetrical form (Fig. 654) the astigmatic difference (MS) is very great when the obliquity is appreciable. As the lens is bent to the best form (Fig. 655) the two curves of the image surfaces approximate even at high obliquities, but if the lens is bent farther, the astigmatic difference increases (Fig. 656). A similar variation is seen in the case of concave lenses (Figs. 657–9), and the same kind of variation can be derived for all corrections within the limits we are considering.

A graphical representation of the residual errors in lenses of different form can be derived from Fig. 660. In the figure the obliquity of the pencil involved is σ', and the vertex refraction for $\sigma' = 0$ is given by $1/S_1F'$. It is necessary to find a relation for F'_m and F'_s in comparison with S_1F'. For this purpose a *vertex sphere* is described around Z' with a radius $Z'S_1$ cutting the oblique ray at S_σ. If we now measure the distances $S_\sigma F'_m$ and $S_\sigma F'_s$, the reciprocals of these ($1/S_\sigma F'_m$ and $1/S_\sigma F'_s$) give vertex sphere refractions corresponding to σ' exactly comparable with the vertex refraction $1/S_1F'$ for $\sigma' = 0$.

Figures 661–2 show the horizontal plot of the angles σ' of the obliquities in the image space, and the vertical plot of the vertex sphere refraction in dioptres when S_1Z' is 25 mm. The horizontal line represents the performance of an ideal lens, and it is seen that the aberrations of biconvex or biconcave lenses are considerable, the marginal astigmatism for obliquities of 35° in the first case being $3\cdot0$ D and in the second of 30° being $2\cdot0$ D.

The photographic performances of such lenses are compared in Fig. 663.

FIGS. 654–659.—THE EFFECT OF LENS FORM ON THE ASTIGMATISM OF OBLIQUE
PENCILS.

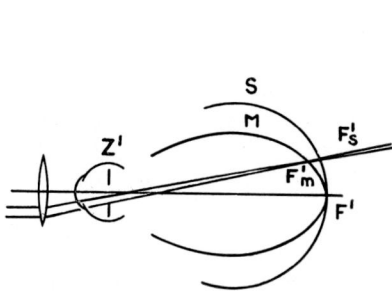

FIG. 654.

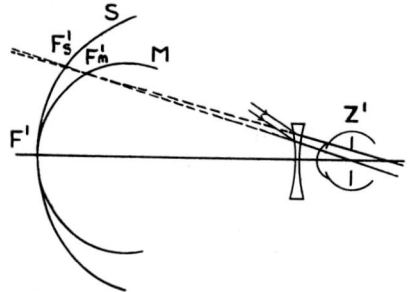

FIG. 657.

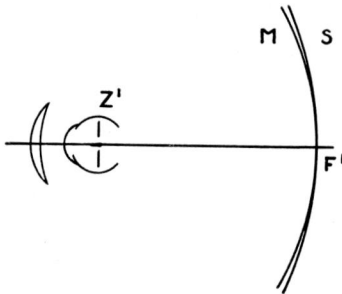

FIG. 655.

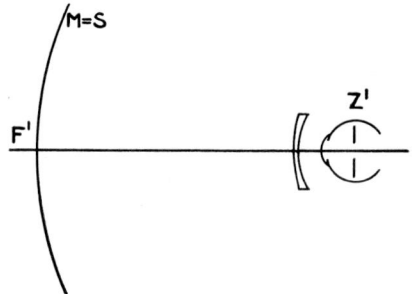

FIG. 658.

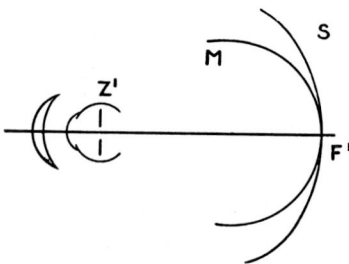

FIG. 656.

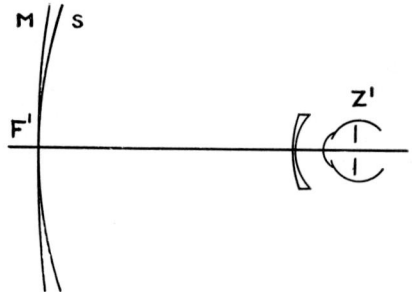

FIG. 659.

FIGS. 654–656.—With a biconvex lens (Fig. 654) the oblique astigmatism is considerable and the curvatures of the m and s surfaces are very different. With a lens of meniscus form with the concave surface next the eye (Fig. 655) the two surfaces nearly coincide. If the bending is overdone (Fig. 656) the astigmatic difference again increases.

FIGS. 657–659.—With a biconcave lens (Fig. 657) the oblique astigmatism is high and there is a great astigmatic difference between the m and s surfaces. In the lens of meniscus form with the more concave surface next the eye (Fig. 658) the two surfaces can be made to coincide. Again, if the bending is overdone (Fig. 659) the m and s surfaces separate again and may interchange.

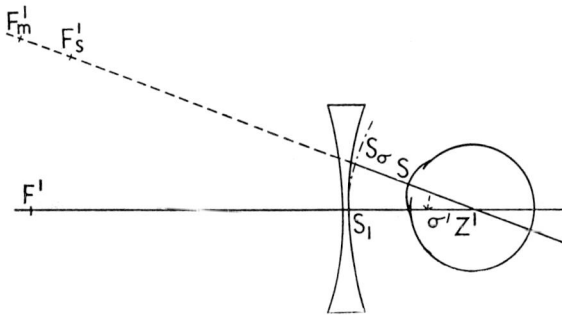

FIG. 660.—VERGENCES ALONG PERIPHERAL RAYS OF FINITE OBLIQUITY REFERRED
TO THE VERTEX SPHERE ($S_1 S\sigma$).

FIGS. 661 and 662.—THE ABERRATIONS OF SPECTACLE LENSES (M. von Rohr).

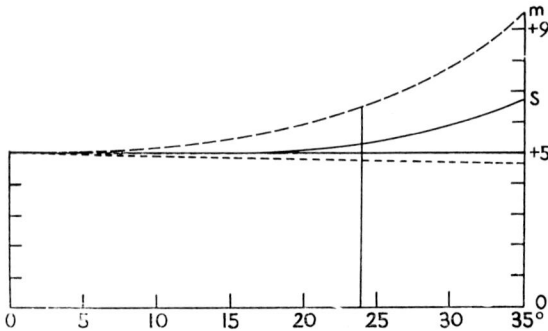

FIG. 661.—A convex lens of + 5·00 DS. The unbroken horizontal line through
+ 5 gives the character of an ideal lens having the same refraction (+ 5·00 DS) for
any angle of obliquity of the rays between 0° and 35°. The curve ———— denotes the
aberrations for a well-formed point-focal lens giving an oblique astigmatism at 35° of
less than 0·5 D. The great aberrations of a biconvex lens of + 5·00 DS are seen in
divergence of the m-curve (———) and the s-curve (————) showing an astigmatic
difference of 3 D at 35°.

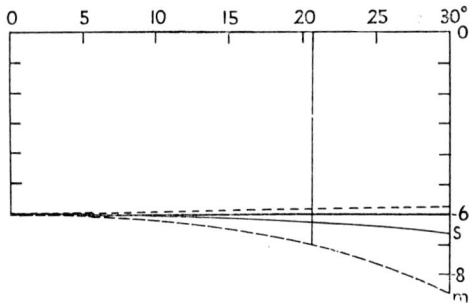

FIG. 662.—Similar aberrations for a biconcave spectacle lens of − 6·00 DS. The
ideal curve is indicated by the horizontal line ending at 6. The curve ———— denotes the
aberrations of a well-formed point-focal lens giving an oblique astigmatism of 0·25 D.
The aberrations of a biconcave lens (m-curve ———; s-curve ————) show an
astigmatic difference of 2·0 D at 30°.

The determination of these " best-form " lenses by trigonometrical computation as accomplished by von Rohr (1921) is a complicated procedure varying with the vertex distance, the lens thickness and the refractive index of the glass and cannot be gone into fully here. It depends on the basic relationship defining the distances of the two image planes containing the focal lines of an obliquely refracted pencil from a refracting surface. If t' and s' are the distances of the focal lines from the refractive surface measured along the peripheral ray of the pencil, the relationship is defined by the formula:

$$\frac{n'}{s'} - \frac{n}{l} = \frac{n \sin (I - I')}{r \sin I'} = \frac{n' \cos^2 I'}{t'} - \frac{n \cos^2 I}{l}$$

when the light is incident on a spherical surface of radius r separating two refracting media of refractive indices n and n', the light being derived from an object a distance

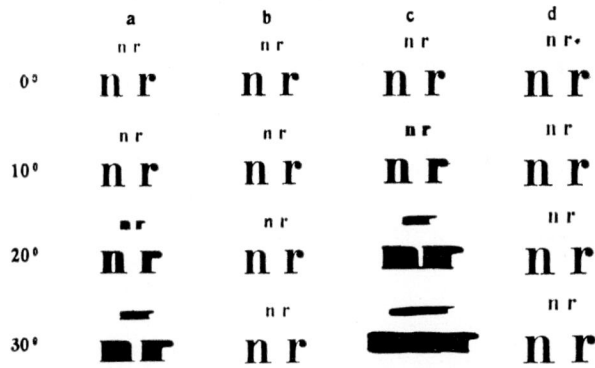

FIG. 663.—PHOTOGRAPHIC REPRESENTATION OF THE IMAGES FORMED BY DIFFERENT LENSES AT DIFFERENT OBLIQUITIES (M. von Rohr).

Each horizontal line is photographed at obliquities (o) of 0°, 10°, 20° and 30°.

Column a gives the images of a biconvex lens of + 5·00 DS ; at 30° the image is not decipherable. Column b gives the images of a well-formed point-focal lens of + 5·00 D.S. ; at 30° the image is as clear as at 0°.

Column c gives the images of a biconvex (cataract) lens of + 13·00 D.S., the image of which becomes indecipherable at an obliquity of 20°. Column d gives the well-formed images with an aspherical lens even at 30°.

l from the surface as measured along the chief ray of the pencil, and I and I' are the angles of incidence and refraction at the surface. These computations must be undertaken not only for each surface, but for different thicknesses, back vertex distances from the cornea and for distant and near vision. Full details with tables for the best form of lenses of different power will be found in the writings of Tscherning (1908), v. Rohr (1908–12), Gleichen (1922), Whitwell (1924–25), v. Rohr et al. (1934) and Emsley and Swaine (1946).

It is, of course, impossible from the manufacturing point of view to have tools in stock to grind the immense number of surfaces which optimum performance would require and so in practice the compromise is generally adopted of utilizing certain curves which have become more or less standard commercially and are relatively suitable for groups of powers between +7·0 DS and −20·0 DS. These groups are seen in Table XXIX.

TABLE XXIX

Power of lens in dioptres	Nearest standard base curve
From 0·0 to + 7·0	— 6·0 (back surface)
— 0·12 to — 5·0	+ 6·0 (front surfac)
— 5·0 to 9·0	+ 3·0 (front surface)
— 10·0 to 15·0	+ 1·25 (front surface)
— 15·0 to 20·0	plano (front surface)

The actual form of the lens supplied to a prescription, however, is usually left to the manufacturers, and unfortunately many of them are retained as confidential. The best form of lenses recommended by various authorities is given in Table XXXIII in the Appendix.

Of the two curvatures the flatter is called the *base curve* (or lower curve) and the steeper, the *second surface*. The base curve is usually fixed and the second surface is specially determined and ground for the particular case whence it may be known as the *combining surface*. A lens with a base of 6 D is called a *deep meniscus lens*: one with a base of 1·25 is called a *periscopic lens*. For positive lenses a negative base curve is used, and for negative lenses a positive base curve, and in the fitting of the spectacles the concave surface is always placed next the eye. The base curve of a positive meniscus is therefore the back surface, of a negative meniscus, the front surface.

Outside the range we have just considered (−22·22 D to +7·23 D) no single lenses with spherical surfaces will eliminate oblique astigmatism, a matter of considerable importance in high myopes and aphakia; but at the same time a " best form " in which the oblique astigmatism is at a minimum can be computed. It will be remembered[1] that to fill this want Gullstrand proposed the use of lenses with aspherical surfaces (v. Rohr, 1908), but the difficulty of their manufacture and hence their cost prevent their general adoption. A very useful compromise is to retain the spherical surface and curve the lens to such an extent that both its surfaces are approximately concentric with the centre of rotation of the eye.

ASTIGMATIC LENSES (TORIC SURFACES)

To a large extent astigmatic lenses are amenable to the same treatment as spherical lenses, but the computation of their form is more complicated. We have seen that the only device available for minimizing aberration is to bend the lens. When a sphero-cylindrical lens is bent the astigmatic surface takes on the form of a *toric surface*. The term is derived from *torus* which described the moulding of the base of an Ionic column which had such a curvature, and is seen in the shape of a motor tyre. It is generated by the revolution of a circular arc (ASB, Fig. 664) of radius AC around the central

[1] p. 656.

axis OO' which does not pass through its centre C. We thus have two curvatures in the vertex (S, Fig. 665), one *meridional* with a radius r_1 and the other *rotational* with a radius r_2 each lying in *symmetrical planes* orientated at right angles to each other. If $r_2 > r_1$ a tyre-shaped toric surface results (Fig. 666): if $r_2 < r_1$ a barrel-shaped surface (Fig. 667).

In order to trace the passage of rays through such a lens let us take the simplest case when the symmetrical planes are horizontal and vertical (Fig. 668). At the centre of the lens the two vertex powers (found by

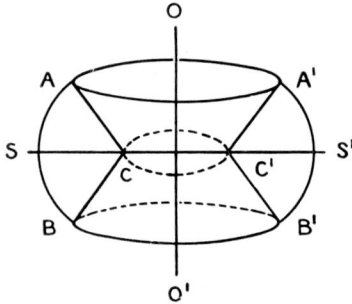

FIG. 664.—The generation of a toric surface by the revolution of ASB around OO'.

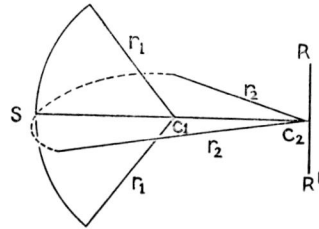

FIG. 665.—The two symmetrical planes in the vertex (S) of a toric surface. The meridional (radius r_1) is in an unbroken line, the rotational (r_2) in a dotted line. RR' is the axis of rotation.

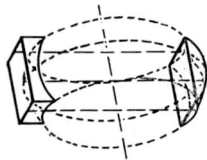

FIG. 666.—The "tyre-shaped" toric surface as a diverging (left) and collecting system (right).

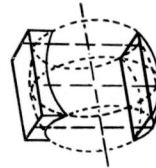

FIG. 667.—The "barrel-shaped" toric surface as a diverging (left) and converging system (right).

visual testing) are represented by M and A. Rays with an upward obliquity coming through a peripheral portion of the lens in the vertical meridian suffer the defect of oblique astigmatism as well as the required (axial) astigmatism ($M - A$) so that the values of M^m and A^m will be different. Similarly the values of M^a and A^a in the horizontal plane will differ. If the lens is to have a perfect form all these astigmatic differences should be equal and the effective axial astigmatism should equal the effective astigmatism in oblique vision both in the vertical and horizontal meridians; *i.e.*,

$$M - A = M^m - A^m = M^a - A^a$$
$$\text{or} \quad M^m = M^a = M \text{ and } A^m = A^a = A.$$

When these conditions are not fulfilled an *astigmatic error* appears in each meridian representing the difference between the peripheral and the axial astigmatism (called Y_1 and Y_2 by E. Weiss, 1918–21).

Thus for the vertical meridian

$$Y_1 = (M^m - A^m) - (M - A)$$

and for the horizontal

$$Y_2 = (M^a - A^a) - (M - A).$$

In the perfect lens

$$Y_1 = Y_2 = (M - A).$$

The errors thus arising are considerable as is seen graphically in Fig. 669 taken from v. Rohr and his colleagues (1934).

With one variable quantity—the bending of the lens form—at our disposal it is impossible to satisfy the four primary variable conditions (M^m, M^a, A^a, A^m) and astigmatic errors must remain so that *lenses of expedient form* only can be obtained wherein the astigmatic errors in all meridians cannot be equalized.

A simplified diagram of the image-surfaces produced by such an astigmatic lens is impossible to construct in two-dimensional co-ordinates, for the simple cup-and-saucer relationship characteristic of spherical surfaces (Fig. 639) assumes a complicated and twisted three-dimensional configuration. The problem can only be usefully solved mathematically; but the delight of mathematics—and its advantage over fiction —is its ability to solve analytically with complete assurance and exactitude examples of a general law no matter what the dimensional complexities introduced, and no matter how far they lead us into the realms of purely imaginative speculation. The mathematical treatment of the subject will be found in the writings of Weiss (1917), Boegehold (1917–21) and Whitwell (1924–26).

FIG. 668.—The tract of four marginal pencils (M^m, A^m, M^a, A^a), the principal rays of which lie within the symmetrical planes of an astigmatic spectacle lens.

The ideal of an equality of the effective powers of the astigmatic lens over its entire area being unattainable, some compromise must be adopted. For example, the single variable available might allow the satisfaction of one of the following conditions:

(a) The astigmatism in the vertical and horizontal meridians might be equalized.

(b) The primary oblique power in one meridian may be equalized to the secondary in the other.

(c) The secondary oblique power in one meridian may be equalized to the primary in the other.

(d) The circles of least confusion in the two meridians might be made to lie on a sphere concentric with the centre of rotation of the eye.

Whitwell (1924) suggested the useful compromise of selecting the lens

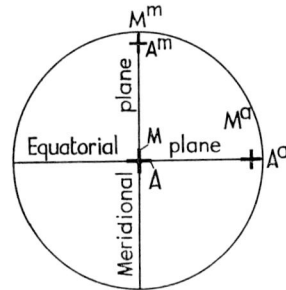

in which none of the powers had an error greater than 0·1 D, and if all could not be satisfied simultaneously, preference should be given to the lens with the best performance in the horizontal meridian. On this basis he (1924–25) calculated tables covering a range of powers from +10 D to −25 D with axial astigmatic differences of 0, 1, 2, 3 and 4 D. Plotted in graphic form, a curve resembling the profile of a nose is obtained (*nose graph*), which over much of its extent resembles Tscherning's ellipses for spherical lenses, suggesting some similarity between the optimum form of

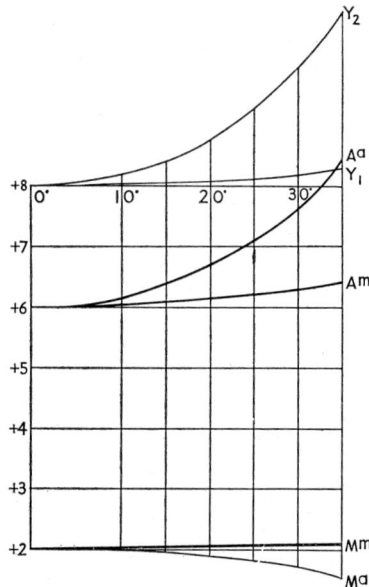

Fig. 669.—Aberrations suffered by Oblique Pencils with a Sphero-cylindrical Lens.

The spectacle lens is + 6·00 DS + 2·00 DC. The four values, M^m, M^a, A^m, and A^a, are recorded as well as the astigmatic errors, $Y_1 Y_2$ for obliquities from 0° to 35°.

At $\sigma = 35°$
$$Y_1 = 0.27 \text{ D} = 6.7\%$$
$$Y_2 = 2.85 \text{ D} = 71.25\%$$
$\left.\right\}$ of M − A = 4 D.

(M. von Rohr *et al.*).

lenses correcting spherical and astigmatic errors. Other computations have been advanced by Percival (1928), by Zeiss (von Rohr *et al.*, 1934) and by the manufacturers of Ultor lenses in England.

The modern design of lenses has been considerably influenced by the development of computers which are a valuable aid to the involved mathematics required. Complex ray-tracing is so facilitated by this means that once the criteria of the design have been agreed, a range of the best forms of lenses can be rapidly produced. A further factor influencing the design is the realization that the centre of rotation of the eye occupies a less fixed position than had been presumed by previous workers. There appears to be a considerable variation in the distance between the lens of the spectacles and the optical " stop " at the centre of rotation, a distance which is commonly between 27 and 33 mm. (Fig. 670); moreover, in the same individual this distance may vary for the different positions of the gaze. Taking these facts into account, Davis and his colleagues (1965) of the American Optical Company have commenced the design of a new series of lenses with negative toric base curves. In this series the preoccupation with oblique astigmatism which had been a feature of many previous designs is less evident and attention is given to chromatic effects contributing to total blur. The lens-forms are also intended to embrace a wide range of object-distances as well as

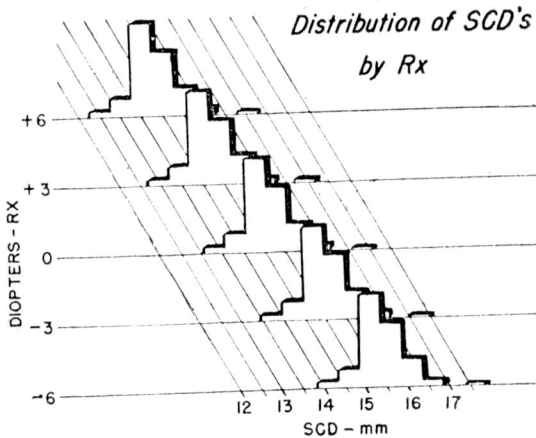

FIG. 670.—THE INFLUENCE OF THE CENTRE OF ROTATION.

The distribution of the distances from the cornea to the optical "stop" of the rotating eye, that is, the sighting centre distances (SCD), are seen to vary with the correction for the ametropia. The variations in the position of the sighting centre for different angles of view are smaller and more consistent than the differences between individuals (J. K. Davis et al.).

taking into account the variation in the position of the centre of rotation in about 90% of the population. Preliminary clinical results with these lenses suggest that they are in some degree superior to previous designs.

The Disadvantages of Bent Lenses

Although their advantages are very great in the increase of an effective field of view by the diminution of distortion and movement of objects in the periphery—matters of great importance particularly when moving about and in reading—they have certain disadvantages. Economically, the difficulty in their manufacture increases their cost and, practically, disturbing reflections are superimposed upon the visual field particularly in artificial light. Thus light from a source in front is reflected by the back surface of the lens and reflected again by the inner aspect of the front surface and so into the eye; the direct reflection of lights behind have a similar effect. The corneal reflex (and sometimes the sclera) may originate a similar set of reflections from one or both surfaces of the lens into the eye. Finally, if the lens is in lenticular form, disturbing reflections tend to arise from the bevelled edges.

THE TRANSPOSITION OF LENSES

The process of computing the change from one form of a lens to another equivalent form is called TRANSPOSITION. This subject may be considered under three headings—simple, toric and vertex transposition.

SIMPLE TRANSPOSITION occupies itself largely with the alteration of the form of lenses in cases of astigmatism, and with the production of periscopic or meniscus lenses or of forms which produce some of their advantages. It is simply a matter of the algebraic addition of the powers of the two surfaces.

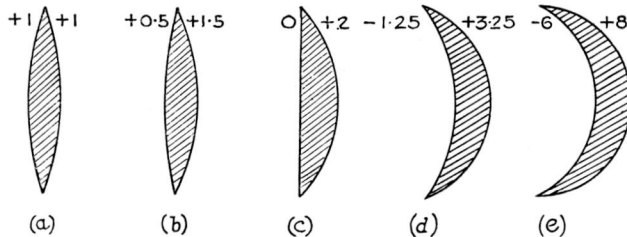

FIG. 671.—TRANSPOSITION OF LENSES.

Simple transposition of a lens of + 2·00 DS from a symmetrical (a) to an asymmetrical (b) biconvex form, (c) plano, (d) periscopic (to the base − 1·25 D), and (e) deep meniscus form (to the base − 6·00 D).

The *transposition of spheres* to different forms is seen in Fig. 671; in the transposition to periscopic and deep meniscus forms it is to be remembered that the given power is combined with a base curve of the opposite sign.

Thus a +2 DS converted into periscopic form has curvatures of −1·25 and +3·25 DS. A −2 DS similarly converted has curvatures of +1·25 and −3·25 DS.

In the same way a +2 DS converted into a deep meniscus form has curvatures of −6 and +8 DS, while a −2 DS is transposed to +6 and −8 DS.

In the *simple transposition of cylinders* two desiderata are always to be kept in view: an attempt should be made to keep the lenses as light as possible, and it is desirable to maintain the axes of the cylinders in the two eyes in approximately the same direction to avoid unequal meridional distortions. The three simple steps in such a transposition are these:

(a) The new spherical surface is given by adding algebraically the powers of the sphere and the cylinder.

(b) Retain the power of the cylinder but change the sign.

(c) Rotate the axis of the cylinder through 90°.

Some examples will make this clear.

$+2 \cdot 0$ DS $\subset +1 \cdot 0$ DC ax. 90° transposed equals $+3 \cdot 0$ DS $-1 \cdot 0$ DC ax. 180°.

If a refraction is $-0 \cdot 5$ DS $\subset -1 \cdot 0$ DC ax. 180° and it is desired to add $+1 \cdot 5$ DS as a presbyopic correction, the effect is gained by transposing to a simple $+1 \cdot 0$ DC ax. 90°.

In some cases a cross-cylinder is preferable to a sphero-cylinder in that it is lighter and provides a wider field. Thus a $+3 \cdot 0$ DS $\subset -4 \cdot 0$ DC ax. 180° might well be transposed to $+3 \cdot 0$ DC ax. 90° $\subset -1 \cdot 0$ DC ax. 180°.

Again, if the refraction is given as

R.E. $+2 \cdot 0$ DC ax. 90° $\subset -1 \cdot 0$ DC ax. 180°.
L.E. $-3 \cdot 0$ DC ax. 180°,

the transposition R.E. $-1 \cdot 0$ DS $\subset +3 \cdot 0$ DC ax. 90°, would be correct, but the presence of two cylinders in the two eyes at right angles would be borne with difficulty. The better transposition would therefore be

R.E. $+2$ DS $\subset -3$ DC ax. 180°.

Here, however, a thicker glass is involved, and for this reason the combination had best be left in the cross-cylinder form.

TORIC TRANSPOSITION. Toric transposition, although it appears a more complicated process, depends on the same principles and is as simple. The toric formula is written as a fraction, the numerator of which is a sphere, and the denominator comprises both the base curve and the cylinder necessary to give the required combination.

The steps in the transposition may be summarized thus:

(a) Transpose the given prescription to one having a cylinder of the same sign as the base curve which is to be used.

(b) The spherical surface is given by subtracting the base power from the sphere in (a). This is written as the numerator of the fraction.

(c) Fix the cylindrical base curve with its axis at right angles to the cylinder in (a).

(d) Add to the base curve the cylinder in (a) with its axis at right angles to that of the base curve.

The toric surface is given by (c) and (d) which form the denominator of the fraction of the formula.

An example will make this clear.

To transpose $+3$ DS $\subset -1$ DC ax. 90° to a toric formula to the base -6;

(a) is already done;
to get the effect of $+3$ DS the spherical surface must have a curvature of $+9$ DS, *i.e.*, the base power subtracted from the original sphere, $+3$ D $- (-6$ D$)$;
the base curve required for (c) is -6 DC ax. 180°;
the other toric power to give a resultant of -1 DC ax. 90° is -7 DC ax. 90°, that is, -6 D added to -1 D;
this gives a combination on the one surface of

-6 DC ax. 180° $\subset -7$ DC ax. 90°, or -6 DS $\subset -1$ DC ax. 90°.

The formula is written thus:

$$\frac{+9 \cdot 0 \text{ D sph.}}{-6 \cdot 0 \text{ D cyl. ax. } 180° / -7 \cdot 0 \text{ D cyl. ax. } 90°.}$$

In the same manner the transposition of $+5 \cdot 0$ DS $\subset$ $-2 \cdot 0$ DC ax. 180° to the toric form to the base $+6$ is accomplished thus.

Transposing the sign of the cylinder to correspond to that of the base, the prescription becomes:

$$+3 \cdot 0 \text{ DS} \subset +2 \cdot 0 \text{ DC ax. } 90°.$$

A similar series of steps is now gone through, giving as a result:

$$\frac{-3 \cdot 0 \text{ D sph.}}{+6 \cdot 0 \text{ D cyl. ax. } 180° / +8 \cdot 0 \text{ D cyl. ax. } 90°.}$$

VERTEX (ACCURATE) TRANSPOSITION. These methods of transposition, of course, assume that the lenses are thin and deal only with the form of the lens and not with its optical effect on the eye. It is obvious, however, that accuracy can be obtained only if the new lens has the same vertex power as the original. This is particularly important in thick lenses and meniscus lenses, and assumes its greatest importance when these properties are combined in aphakic lenses. Since the principal points of a diverging meniscus are outside the glass on its concave (ocular) side, the meniscus acts as if it were a lens placed slightly closer to the eye, and hence must not be as strong as the correcting biconcave lens. Similarly, since the principal points of a converging meniscus are situated in front of the lens, it also must not be as strong as a correcting biconvex lens. In thin lenses of weak power and periscopic shape the errors introduced are of little practical effect; but otherwise the surface powers found by simple transposition must be modified. The problem usually presented is to find the combining surface, given the back vertex power, the base curve and the thickness. These values can be computed directly from the equations on page 640.

Thus to take a simple case, given a back vertex power of $+10 \cdot 0$ DS, a base of $-6 \cdot 0$ DS, and a thickness of 4 mm.:

(a) Perform simple transposition for the front surface $= +16 \cdot 0$ DS.

(b) To obtain the focal length in millimetres,

take the reciprocal of (a) $\times 1000 = \dfrac{1000}{+16} = +62 \cdot 5$ mm.

(c) To obtain the reduced thickness divide the thickness in millimetres by the

refractive index $= \dfrac{4}{1 \cdot 523} = 2 \cdot 63$.

(d) To obtain the focal length of the front surface,

add (b) and (c) algebraically $= 65 \cdot 13$ mm.

(e) To obtain the power of the front surface (in dioptres),

take the reciprocal of (d) $\times 1000 = \dfrac{1000}{65 \cdot 13} = 15 \cdot 35$ D.

THE TRANSPOSITION OF CROSSED CYLINDERS

The optical properties of crossed cylinders are readily understood if their axes are parallel or at right angles when the rules of simple transposition apply.

1. If two cylinders are combined with their axes parallel the resulting cylinder is the algebraic sum of their powers with the axis in the same direction. Thus $+1\cdot0$ DC ax. $180° \subset +2\cdot0$ DC ax. $180° \equiv +3\cdot0$ DC ax. $180°$. Again the two cylinders of equal and opposite power thus placed produce no effect.

2. If two crossed cylinders are combined with their axes at right angles the combination may be resolved in two ways.

(a) In the resulting sphero-cylindrical combination the power of the sphere can be that of the smaller of the two cylinders and the power of the cylinder the difference between the smaller subtracted from the greater with its axis parallel to the axis of the greater cylinder.

Thus $+2\cdot0$ DC ax. $90° \subset +4\cdot0$ DC ax. $180° \equiv +2\cdot0$ DS $\subset +2\cdot0$ DC ax. $180°$.

(b) Alternatively in the resulting combination the power of the sphere can be the power of the larger cylinder, and the power of the cylinder the difference between the greater subtracted from the smaller with its axis parallel to the axis of the smaller cylinder.

Thus $+2\cdot0$ DC ax. $90° \subset +4\cdot0$ DC ax. $180° \equiv +4\cdot0$ DS $\subset -2\cdot0$ DC ax. $90°$.

It follows that if the cylinders are of equal size the equivalent lens will be a sphere of power equal to either cylinder.

Thus $+2\cdot0$ DC ax. $90° \subset +2\cdot0$ DC ax. $180° \equiv +2\cdot0$ DS.

Conversely any given cylinder can be replaced by a sphere of the same power and a cylinder of equal but opposite power with its axis perpendicular to the first.

Thus $+4\cdot0$ DC ax. $180° \equiv +4\cdot0$ DS $\subset -4\cdot0$ DC ax. $90°$.

Obliquely crossed cylinders, however, present a more difficult problem in transposition. If the prescription contains two cylinders not crossed at right angles, it is possible to prepare a lens with each surface bearing the appropriate cylindrical curvature so that a crossed cylindrical form is maintained (Roure, 1896; Márquez, 1912–42). As a rule, however, the more practical expedient is adopted of transposing the combination into another in which the two axes are at right angles. That this can always be done is readily seen if two cylindrical lenses are taken from the trial case and held with their axes at various angles before a small point of light; it will be seen that in all positions of the lenses the optical effect is the production of two focal lines at right angles to one another. These, of course, can be exactly reproduced by a pair of cylinders at right angles, or by an ordinary sphero-cylindrical combination.

The general optical effect of the curvature of a cylindrical surface in an oblique meridian is seen in Fig. 672. In the plane FAE the surface of the cylinder is circular (of radius r); in the plane of the axis MN the curvature is zero, and in all intermediate positions it varies gradually between the two. In the intermediate position ABCD inclined at an angle θ to the axis, the surface is an ellipse of which the semi-minor axis CA $= r$ and the semi-major axis CB $= r/\sin\theta$, while the curvature along an arc AB increases gradually from a minimum at A to a maximum at B.

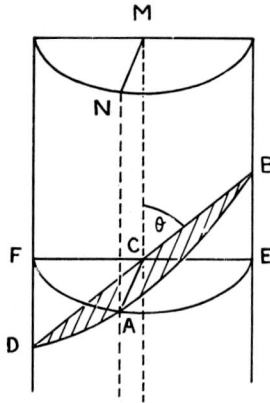

Fig. 672.—The Curvature of a Cylinder in an Oblique Meridian (see text).

The laws governing this variation can be deduced from Euler's theorem of curved surfaces.

The curvature of the cylinder along FAE

$$R = 1/r$$

The curvature in the neighbourhood of A along the oblique meridian DAB

$$R_\theta = R\sin^2\theta$$

The curvature at A along a meridian at right angles to DAB

$$R_{(\theta + 90°)} = R\sin^2(\theta + 90°) = R\cos^2\theta$$

Hence $R_\theta + R_{(\theta + 90°)} = R(\sin^2\theta + \cos^2\theta) = R.$

That is, *the sum of the curvatures along any two mutually perpendicular directions of a cylindrical surface is equal to the maximum curvature.* It also follows that the power of a cylinder in dioptres (C) set at an angle θ from the horizontal meridian has the power (in dioptres) $C\sin^2\theta$ in the horizontal meridian and $C\cos^2\theta$ in the vertical meridian.

To take an example, the power of a cylindrical lens of -4 D at an angle of 150° would be

$-4\sin^2 150°$ in the horizontal meridian,

and $-4 \sin^2 (\theta - 90°)$, or $-4 \cos^2\theta$, $i.e.$, $-4 \cos^2 150°$ in the vertical meridian. $-4 \sin^2 150° = -4 (\tfrac{1}{2})^2 = -1$ D,

and $- 4 \cos^2 150° = - 4 \left(\dfrac{\sqrt{3}}{2}\right)^2 = - 3$D.

The theory of transposition in this case, given the powers of the cylinders, and the angle of their inclination, was suggested by Stokes (1849) and elaborated by S. P. Thompson (1900). In Fig. 673 draw OA on any agreed scale to represent the power of the stronger cylinder (F_1) and OB to represent the power of the weaker (F_2) so that they are included at an angle *twice* the given angle a between their axes. Then, on completing the parallelogram, the diagonal OC (C) represents the strength of the resultant cylinder, and the angle COA represents twice the angle (θ) at which it is inclined to the meridian of greater power. For positive cylinders the directions OA

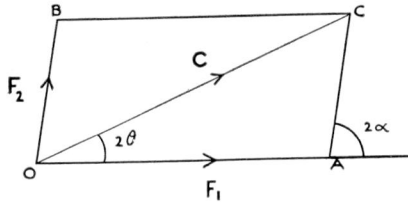

FIG. 673.—THE TRANSPOSITION OF OBLIQUE CYLINDERS (see text).

and OB are chosen: for negative cylinders the opposite directions. The actual value of these can easily be obtained by measurement to scale. Since, as we have just seen derived from Euler's theorem, the sum of the refractive powers of the original combination must equal that of the resultant combination, the strength of the spherical component (S) of the new system can easily be deduced from a simple formula.[1]

In the resultant sphero-cylindrical combination the curvature of the meridian of minimum power will be S dioptres, while that of the maximum will be $S + C$ dioptres. Since the sum of the powers of the new combination must equal that of the old, we can obtain the value of this sphere from the formula :—

$$S + (S + C) = F_1 + F_2$$
$$2S + C = F_1 + F_2$$
$$S = \frac{F_1 + F_2 - C}{2}$$

The values of C and θ may also be derived from the following formula which can be deduced from the geometry of Fig. 673.

When C is the strength of the cylindrical component in the resultant spherocylindrical combination

$$C = \sqrt{F_1{}^2 + F_2{}^2 + 2F_1F_2 \cos 2a}$$

[1] Following from Euler's theorem concerning curved surfaces.

Where θ is the angle at which the required cylinder lies with reference to F_1,

$$\tan 2\theta = \frac{F_2 \sin 2\alpha}{F_1 + F_2 \cos 2\alpha}$$

Emsley (1926) simplified the practical application of these formulæ by tabulating the values for a large number of combinations and constructing a graph from them, from which the strength of the resultant cylinder and the direction of its axis can be read off directly. He also suggested an ingenious instrument which consists of two rotating protractors by means of which such transpositions can be done with great rapidity and ease.

To take an example. If in the refraction it is found that there are two principal meridians, one of $+4$ D at an axis of $20°$ and another of $+2$ D at an axis of $60°$, we then draw to scale, OA $= 4$, OB $= 2$, and angle BOA, which is twice the angle between them (i.e., twice $40°$), $80°$. Then on completing the parallelogram the resultant cylinder (C) is found on measurement to be $4\cdot7$ D and the angle COA $24°$. The required cylinder, therefore, lies inclined at an angle of $12°$ to the direction of F_1, that is, at an angle of $32°$ in the accepted notation.

The spherical component $S = \frac{1}{2}(F_1 + F_2 - C)$
$$= \tfrac{1}{2}(4 + 2 - 4\cdot7)$$
$$= 0\cdot615 \text{ D.}$$

Instead of the graphical construction the formula can be used:

$$C = \sqrt{16 + 4 + 2 \times 4 \times 2(0\cdot1736)} = 4\cdot77$$

and
$$\tan 2\theta = \frac{2 \times 0\cdot9848}{4 + 2 \times 0\cdot1736} = 0\cdot453$$

$$\therefore \theta = 12° \ 12'.$$

That is, expressed to the nearest 1/8 dioptre, the original combinations of obliquely crossed cylinders,

$$+4 \text{ D cyl. ax. } 20° \supset +2 \text{ D cyl. ax. } 60°$$

is optically equivalent to

$$+0\cdot62 \text{ D sph. } \supset +4\cdot75 \text{ D cyl. ax. } 32°,$$

a form in which the lens can be easily ground.

It follows, of course, that if the cylinders are at right angles $\alpha = 90°$, $\theta = 0°$, $C = F_1 - F_2$ and $S = F_2$, which are the findings of simple transposition. Moreover, if they are at right angles and equal, $F_1 = F_2$ and the combination is equivalent to a sphere of power F.

Naylor (1968), proceeding along lines indicated by Stokes and by Emsley, gave formulæ and tables making it possible to express astigmatic differences in refractive errors which have changed over a period of time, both in power and in the axis of the cylinder.

PRISMATIC EFFECTS AND DECENTRATION

Since a lens may be looked upon as a series of prisms,[1] it follows that when light passes through any part outside its optical centre, the effect is that of a prism with its base directed towards the thickest part of the lens (Fig. 674). The importance of the accurate centring of spectacle lenses is therefore obvious.

[1] p. 56.

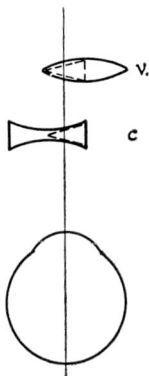

FIG. 674.—THE DECENTRATION OF LENSES

If the eye figured is the right, displacement of a convex lens (*v*) outwards or a concave lens (*c*) inwards produces the action of a prism, base out.

FIGS. 675–678—THE DECENTRATION OF LENSES.

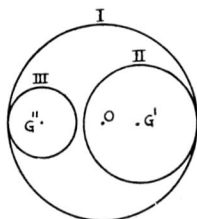

FIG. 676.—A normally centred lens wherein the optical (O) and geometrical centres (G) coincide.

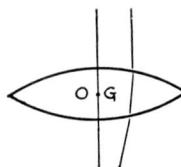

FIG. 675.—I, a large lens symmetrically centred when the optical centre (O) and the geometrical centre coincide (Fig. 676). From I may be cut II and III (seen in Figs. 677–8). Since the optical and geometrical centres of these do not coincide they act as prismospheres.

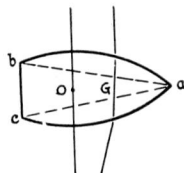

FIG. 677.—The optical centre (O) is placed eccentrically as in II, Fig. 675. Rays passing through the geometrical centre (G) are deviated.

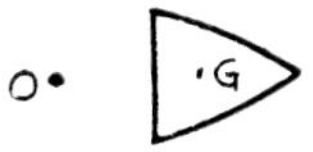

FIG. 678.—The optical centre (O) is outside the lens as in III, Fig. 675. The deviation of rays is greater.

In this connection two definitions must be borne in mind. The *optical centre* is the centre of the optical system formed by the lens, and all rays passing through it are undeviated. The *geometrical centre*, on the other hand, is the point in the middle of the lens, and is merely a relation of the placement of the lens in its frame. The two need not coincide since, depending on the shape of the orbits and the asymmetry of the face, the lens may be displaced in any direction, provided the optical centre is kept in the correct position. For cosmetic reasons it is usually advisable that the geometrical centre of the lens is opposite the centre of the pupil.

The clinical methods of determining the optical centre have already been described: it is not sufficient only to measure the interpupillary distance, as is often done, since owing to the variability of the angle kappa the visual axes may not coincide with the centres of the pupils; moreover, each eye must be measured separately from the centre of the nose, for a face is rarely symmetrical.

A prismatic effect can be introduced into a lens purposely by two methods: the lens itself may be decentred or the curved surfaces are ground on the faces of a prism of the required refracting angle.

THE DECENTRING OF LENSES

Lenses may be decentred in one of two ways. The optical centre and the geometrical centre may be allowed to coincide in the centre of the frame, and the frame may be displaced as a whole by lengthening or shortening the nose-piece. Alternatively, the lens may be displaced in its rim. Both methods give the same prismatic effect. The action of the first is seen in Fig. 674, but for practical cosmetic reasons the second is usually to be preferred. In it lenses are cut eccentrically out of a larger lens as is seen in Fig. 675. Here the large lens (I) is normally centred, for its optical and geometrical centres coincide (OG, Fig. 676). The smaller lens (II), however, will have its optical centre at O and its geometrical centre at G', and will appear as in Fig. 677; while the smallest (III), which has its geometrical centre at G'', will have its optical centre at O outside it altogether, assuming the form seen in Fig. 678. In each case the optical effect will be the same as if a prism had been interpolated into the substance of the lens. Such a lens becomes a *prismosphere*. The quantitative effects of decentration will vary with the dioptric strength of the lens: it is found that *there is a prismatic effect of 1 prism dioptre for every dioptre of power in the lens for every centimetre of decentration which is effected.*

This can be shown mathematically from Fig. 679, wherein O is the optical centre of the lens OB and F' is the second focal point. The ray incident at B distant c cm. from the optical axis is deviated c cm. in f metres.

Hence the prismatic deviation in prism dioptres

$$P = \frac{c}{f} = cD$$

when D is the power in dioptres.

It follows that the amount of decentration

$$= \frac{P}{D} \text{ cm.} = \frac{10\,P}{D} \text{ mm.}$$

Thus if a prismatic effect of 1·0Δ is required, a lens of +2·0 DS must be decentred

$$\frac{1·0}{2·0} = 0·5 \text{ cm.} = 5 \text{ mm.}$$

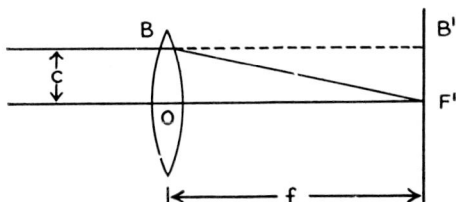

FIG. 679.—DECENTRATION AND PRISMATIC EFFECT.

If the lens in question is spherical, the above reasoning applies for decentration in any direction. If, however, it is cylindrical, the amount of decentration depends on the relation of the direction of decentration with that of the axis of the cylinder. As far as the cylinder is concerned, any decentration in the direction of its axis has no optical effect: any decentration in the direction perpendicular to its axis has the same effect as in the case of a sphere. Thus a combination of +2 D sph. +3 D cyl. ax. 90°, if decentred upwards, acts as a +2 D sphere, if decentred inwards or outwards, as +5 D sphere.

If, however, the cylinders are oblique, or if an oblique decentration is required in a vertical or horizontal cylinder, the effect is more complicated. It can, however, be readily deduced from the construction in Fig. 672 wherein it was shown that if θ is the angle made by the axis of the cylinder with the meridian which is to be considered for prismatic effect, the power of the lens in that meridian in dioptres is represented by the expression $C \sin^2 \theta$ when C is the strength of the cylinder (at right angles to its axis). The decentration is then calculated on this basis in the manner already described.

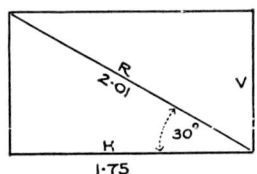

FIG. 680.—THE MEASUREMENT OF AN OBLIQUE PRISMATIC EFFECT.

When the prismatic effect required is oblique, the extent of the defect is usually calculated clinically as two components at right angles. Thus a patient may require a correction of 2 prism dioptres for a right hyperphoria, and of 3·5 for an exophoria. In such a case, as Percival (1928) pointed out, it is unsatisfactory to correct the vertical defect in one eye with a vertical prism and the other with a horizontal prism. The two components should be resolved into one oblique deviation, the effect being equally divided between the two eyes.

This can be accomplished graphically (Fig. 680). If the horizontal (H) and vertical (V) components of the deviation are drawn to scale at right angles and the parallelogram completed, the length of the diagonal will represent the strength of the resultant prism (R) and its direction will be indicated by the angle between it and the horizontal.

Thus if a deviation of 1·75 cm. (exophoric) in the horizontal direction and 1·0 cm. (rt. hyperphoric) in the vertical is required (in each eye), graphical construction will show that a resultant prism of 2·01 prism dioptres is necessary base down and in (for the right eye) at an angle of 30° with a corresponding correction base up and in for the left.

If drawing to scale is objected to, the result can be found on calculation, for it is obvious that $R = \sqrt{H^2 + V^2}$, and the angle of direction = tan V/H. In the present case, therefore, a correction of 2 prism dioptres pointing upwards and outwards at 30° in the right eye and a similar correction downwards and outwards for the left eye would be prescribed. The lenses are therefore decentred in these directions by an amount in millimetres represented by 10P/D. If the refractive error is 4 D, for example, the decentration would be 10 × 2/4 = 5 mm.

WORKED PRISMATIC LENSES. It is obvious that the prismatic effect attainable by the decentration of lenses is limited, particularly if they are of low dioptric power. If the required effect is greater than can thus be obtained, specially worked prismatic lenses must be made by grinding the necessary curved surfaces on the faces of a prism. The prismatic effect is determined by measuring with calipers the difference in thickness at the two opposite ends of the lens. In this case the required difference in thickness in millimetres is obtained by the product:

diam. of lens in mm. × required deviation in prism dioptres × 0·02
or, diam. of lens in mm. × required decentration in cm. × power of lens × 0·02.

The Uses of Decentration

Decentration may be required for three main purposes.

1. For mechanical reasons, when no prismatic effect is desired, difficulties may be encountered in making the geometrical centres of the lenses fit the wearer; this may occur in the case of an asymmetrical face or in the fitting of large lenses to suit a small interpupillary distance. In such cases the blank lenses are cut asymmetrically so that the optical centres coincide with the visual axes, and in this way no prismatic effect is produced.

2. In the correction of a heterophoria or to overcome a deficiency or excess of convergence.[1]

3. To avoid a prismatic effect when the essential direction of regard is not in the primary position. This arises in shooting or in some games as billiards wherein the necessity for eccentric sighting would normally introduce a prismatic effect. The most important instance, however, is spectacles for close work or reading when the visual axes are converged and directed downwards. The amount of convergence varies with the interpupillary distance and the distance from the eye at which the spectacles are worn; and on the average it will be found that the centres for reading should be 6·0 or

[1] Vol. VI.

6·5 mm. below the horizontal, the distance depending on the habit of the individual. As a rule, when reading, the head is lowered about 20° to 30° while the visual axes are further depressed by a downward rotation of the eyes through an angle of approximately 15°.

In Fig. 681, if R and R′ denote the centres of rotation of the eyes, RS and R′S′ the visual axes when the eyes are directed straight forwards, and RN and R′N the distance from the visual axes of the eyes to the central point of the nose, the visual axes will assume the positions RO and R′O when they are directed upon a near object

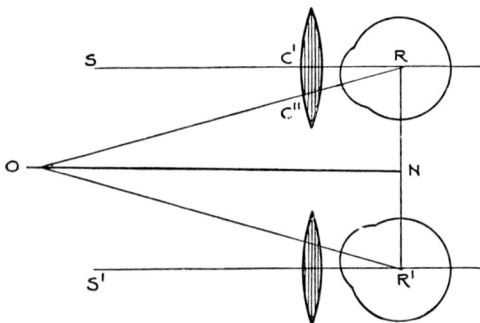

Fig. 681.—Decentration inwards for Reading.

(O). In the right eye C′ will denote the position of the optical centre of a lens for distance, and C″ that of one for reading. C′C″ can be calculated thus:

$$\frac{RN}{NO} = \tan RON = \tan C'RC'' = \frac{C'C''}{C'R}$$

hence
$$C'C'' = \frac{RN}{NO} \times C'R.$$

RN is measured: suppose it is 30 mm.
NO = the distance of the object from the plane of the lens + the distance of the lens from the centre of rotation of the eye, say, 300 mm. + 25 mm. = 325 mm.; and C′R is also 25 mm.

$$C'C'' \text{ therefore} = \frac{30}{325} \times 25 = 2·3 \text{ mm.}$$

RELATIVE PRISMATIC EFFECTS

Since the prismatic effect of decentring a lens depends upon its power, differences are introduced between the two eyes in all cases of anisometropia on eccentric regard (RELATIVE PRISMATIC EFFECTS). This may bring about considerable discomfort, particularly in reading, for a vertical imbalance of more than 1 Δ is not readily tolerated. Thus if the two eyes have a refraction of R + 3·0 DS and L + 6·0 DS and the wearer looks downwards so that the visual lines intersect the lenses 1 cm. below their optical centres, the prismatic deviations (at the lenses) are 3 Δ and 6 Δ respectively. The deviation itself is troublesome since vision becomes blurred, but the relative prismatic effect of 3 Δ may be insupportable and lead to diplopia. In such cases, therefore, the two lenses should be decentred accordingly.

The problem becomes more acute in bifocal lenses with reading segments. From a practical point of view a suitable correction can be made from the following simple formula suggested by Percival (1928). If D and d represent the dioptric strengths of the distant lens and the reading addition respectively, then if the centre of the segment is to be 6·5 mm. below the mid-horizontal line, the vertical decentration required (V) is represented by $\dfrac{D}{d} \times 6\cdot5$.

Similarly, if the centre of the segment is to be converged 2·5 mm., its horizontal decentration (H) will be $\dfrac{D}{d} \times 2\cdot5$.

When the lenses are convex the decentration is downwards and inwards respectively: when they are concave, the decentration is upwards and outwards.

Thus in the above case, if to a distance refraction of R + 3·0 DS and L + 6·0 DS a reading correction of +3·0 DS is added,

$$V \text{ (R.E.)} = 3/3 \times 6\cdot5, \text{ and } H = 3/3 \times 2\cdot5.$$
$$V \text{ (L.E.)} = 6/3 \times 6\cdot5, \text{ and } H = 6/3 \times 2\cdot5.$$

Hence the segment for the right eye is decentred 6·5 mm. downwards and 2·5 mm. inwards, while that for the left eye must be decentred 13 mm. downwards and 5 mm. inwards.

LENS FORM AND MAGNIFICATION

We have already seen that the size of the retinal image alters with the distance from the eye at which a correcting lens is placed. Consideration must now be given to the effect upon magnification produced by altering the form of the lens. It should be realized at the outset that magnification of the retinal image can be produced by lenses of certain surface curvatures which have no focusing power for distant objects and, indeed, the properties of magnification and focusing power are to a certain degree independent.

It may be recalled that the angle subtended by an object at the nodal point of the eye determines the size of the retinal image. From each extremity of a distant object the rays of light striking the eye are parallel and the size of the retinal image therefore depends on the angle of incidence of these rays with the optic axis of the eye. There are several optical devices which can change this angle but do not alter the vergence of the light. In other words, parallel rays of light enter and emerge from the system still parallel, in which case the optical device is afocal; this optical system is seen in telescopic systems, afocal contact lenses and some iseikonic lenses.

We have already noted that an object at a finite distance viewed through a thick glass block may appear to be magnified. Assume that an object AB (Fig. 682) is regarded through a glass plate CD held before the eye E. The image A′B′ is displaced towards the plate by an amount depending on its refractive index. The decreased image distance B′E compared with the object distance BE produces an angular magnification increasing with the thickness of the plate. It is to be noted that the magnification decreases as the distance of the object from the plate increases. If now the plate is curved, a considerably greater magnification is introduced, depending not only on the thickness of the plate but on the refractive power of the front surface: the more curved the front surface—and the thicker the plate—the greater the magnification. In this case also the magnification would increase the farther the plate was removed from the eye.

Afocal lenses do not have accurately parallel curved surfaces but the precise relationship between the surfaces can be derived very simply from the optics of thick lenses and the magnification produced is similar to that of a telescopic system.[1]

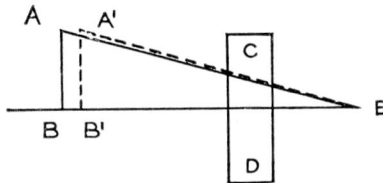

Fig. 682.—The Effect of Lens Thickness on the Size of the Image.
(Applicable to virtually parallel rays.)

We have seen that the back vertex power of a thick lens is given by the formula:

$$\frac{F_1 + F_2 - F_1 F_2 \, d/n}{1 - F_1 \, d/n}$$

where F_1 and F_2 are the surface powers. If we are to say that this is nil, as it must be if incident parallel rays of light emerge still parallel, then $F_1 + F_2 - F_1 F_2 \, d/n = 0$. Furthermore, by analogy with the telescopic system, the angular magnification $M = - F_2/F_1$, and in this case

$$M = \frac{1}{1 - F_1 \, d/n}.$$

The magnification thus depends on the curvature of the front surface of the lens and its thickness. The factor $\dfrac{1}{1 - F_1 \, d/n}$ is, as we have noted previously,[2] the " shape factor " of a thick lens, which, when the latter is afocal, is the same as the angular magnification. If therefore we wish to produce pure magnification without any focusing power, we shall determine the most suitable front curvature and thickness from the magnification formula and then determine the back curvature so as to make the lens afocal.

Lenses of power greater than $+18$ D on the front surface and of thickness greater than 8 mm. are not practical and even these are extreme values. As a result, an afocal lens of magnification no greater than 5% is about the most powerful iseikonic lens in use.

[1] p. 804. [2] p. 77.

Iseikonic lenses, therefore, are designed so that the refractive power of the surface of the lens towards the object is neutralized by a refractive power imposed on the surface next the eye. They can be ground as *over-all size lenses*, having the same magnification in all meridians, or as *meridional-size lenses*, having a magnification in one meridian only and none in the meridian at right angles. In addition, of course, a refractive correction can also be imposed on the lens; and they can even be made in bifocal form.

FIGS. 683 and 684.—ISEIKONIC LENSES.

FIG. 683.—A bitoric lens; doublet lens (cut to show air space); laminated bitoric bifocal lens.

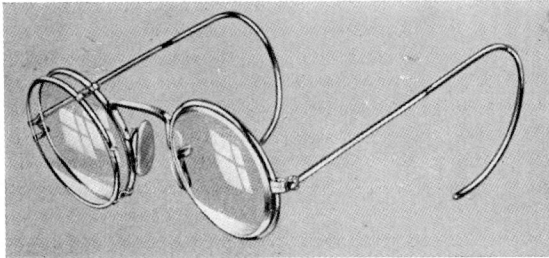

FIG. 684.—A fit-over lens for the correction of aniseikonia (American Optical Co.).

They are, however, expensive, requiring special machinery, and for this reason when required for a trial period a supplementary iseikonic lens may be used clipped on to an ordinary spectacle lens correcting the ametropia (Figs. 683–4).

If a lens has a dioptric power, the effect of its form upon the magnification is again related to the shape factor. In refractive ametropia the magnification of a distant object is given by

$$M = \frac{1}{(1 - F_1 \, d/n)} \times \frac{1}{(1 - F_{v_1} \, h)}$$

F'_v being the back vertex power and h the distance between the back vertex of the lens and the site of the abnormal refractive element.

In axial ametropia the form of the lens will again influence the magnification produced. Thus, if the back vertex of a convex meniscus lens is at the anterior focal point, the second principal plane is considerably anterior to this and the magnification will be larger than that produced by a thin lens of the same power at the anterior focal point. It follows that the more curved the anterior surface of a lens of given power, the more can the shape factor influence magnification. This, as we shall see, is of particular importance in aphakia where it is advisable not to order highly bent forms of the lenses and to keep the spectacle distance as short as possible.

The form of lenses used to correct simultaneously both ametropia and aniseikonia can be derived from expressions such as the formula seen on p. 682. The degree of ametropia will determine F'_v, the required back vertex power, and the magnification can be altered by choosing an appropriate front curvature F_1 or the thickness, d, of the correcting lens; alternatively, its distance from the eye may be varied.

BIFOCAL AND MULTIFOCAL LENSES

The lenses we have been considering up to the present are ideally adapted for one distance only. To the presbyope whose accommodation is failing, in states of insufficiency or paralysis of accommodation, and sometimes in cases of convergent squint, particularly of the partially or wholly accommodative variety, a combination of lenses for distant and near vision is convenient. Most such combinations consist of a correction for distance and a correction for near vision in the lens before each eye, a combination first suggested by Benjamin Franklin[1] about 1775 (bifocal lenses); other more elaborate designs have multiple optical focusing properties suitable for three or more distances.

THE OPTICAL FUNCTION OF BIFOCAL SPECTACLES

In the common variety the upper portion of the spectacle lens subserves distant vision and the lower, smaller segment corrects for near work. In addition to lightness and inconspicuousness, the requirements from the optical point of view are three:

(a) The two portions should provide equally clear vision free from aberrations. Bending to a toric form can usually satisfy this requirement although some oblique astigmatism is inevitable because of eccentric viewing through the lower segment.

(b) There should be no sudden change in the prismatic effect at the junction of the two segments so that, when the eye changes from one to the other, objects do not appear to " jump ". This requires that the optical centres of both distant and reading portions should be located at or near

[1] p. 622.

the junction of the two segments; the ideal is a *monocentric bifocal* wherein they are coincident.

(*c*) The centring of the two portions should be exact for their different purposes and therefore separately controllable, a matter which is far from straightforward.

In distant vision the visual axis of the eye passes through the spectacle lens at a point referred to as the *distance visual point* (DVP), which should coincide with the optical centre. On reading, each eye moves so that its visual axis now passes through the lens at a point approximately 8 mm. below and 2 mm. nasal to the DVP at a point known as the *near visual point* (NVP) (Fig. 685). In a bifocal spectacle it is optically advantageous if the effective centre of the combined distance lens and the segment coincides with the near visual point; should it not do so there will be a prismatic

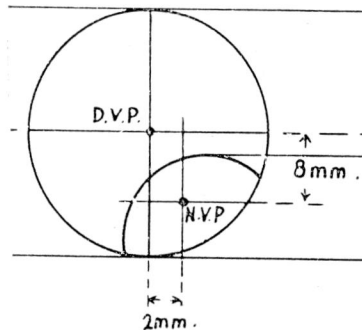

FIG. 685.—A BIFOCAL LENS.

The distance visual point (DVP) corresponds to the optical centre. The near visual point (NVP) of the reading segment is approximately 8 mm. below and 2 mm. nasal to the former (C. M. Ruben).

effect when the eye looks through this point. If this is slight and symmetrical between the two eyes it may be of little consequence, but when there is a significant anisometropia or when the prismatic effect is marked because of high ametropia, a muscular imbalance may be precipitated or there may be manifest displacement of objects in the near field leading to intolerance of the bifocals. Moreover, it is an incomplete description of the optical situation to discuss the prismatic effect merely at the near visual point. In reading, the eyes move laterally and vertically over a short distance and any prismatic effects due to anisometropia will therefore vary, making tolerance even more difficult. It is thus obvious that the optical conditions required to eliminate " jump " and attain coincidence of the optical centres of the portions used for near and distant vision are incompatible with an absence of a prismatic effect at the near visual point which clearly cannot coincide with the optical centres of both parts of a bifocal lens.

The important dimensions of a bifocal lens are indicated in Fig. 686. The top of the segment is usually placed $1\frac{1}{2}$ to 2 mm. below the distance visual point (DVP) of the main lens but may be varied slightly for some occupational requirements, being increased to 3 to 4 mm. if spectacles are continuously worn. They are often fitted with the segment-top at the level of the lower lid in straight-ahead gaze. The horizontal orientation of the

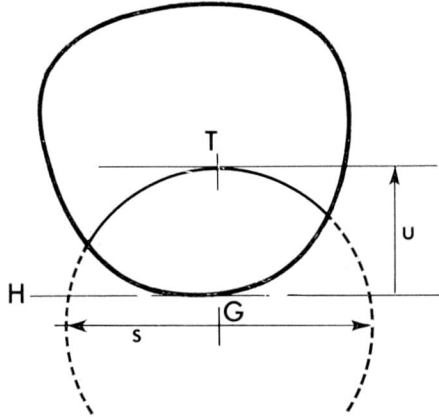

FIG. 686.—THE DIMENSIONS OF A BIFOCAL LENS.
G, mid-point of diameter of segment; H, horizontal tangent at lowest point of periphery of lens; S, diameter of segment; T, top of segment; U, height of segment.

segment is also a matter of some variation; in general it is arranged to take account of the position of the near visual point which is usually about 2 mm. nasal to the distance visual point, but some adjustments may be required depending on the subject's interpupillary distance and any horizontal prismatic effect induced by lenses of high power. A useful device for assessing the size and position of bifocal segments is indicated in Fig. 687.

The form of the segment determines the site of its optical centre and

FIG. 687.—DEVICE FOR ASSESSING THE SIZE AND POSITION OF BIFOCAL SEGMENTS
(I. Shoot).

therefore the site of the combined optical centre of the segment and the part of the distance lens it overlies (known collectively as the *near portion*). The degree of " jump " is proportional to the power of the addition for near vision and to the vertical distance between the top of the segment and its optical centre. The prismatic effect at the near visual point is partly determined by the distances, both vertical and horizontal, of this point from the *near optical centre* (the combined optical centre of the distance portion and the segment). It depends also, of course, upon the optical power of the near portion (distance lens plus segment) in both vertical and horizontal directions. The most important component of the prismatic effect is the vertical and it is possible to estimate this for corrections which incorporate obliquely orientated cylinders. It follows that any difference in the prismatic effect at the near visual points of the lenses for the two eyes must be considered in anisometropic corrections.

It is clear that the prismatic effects, both vertical and horizontal, to which wearers of bifocals are subject are considerable; clinically, it is therefore of importance to make a complete assessment of the muscle-balance both for near and distant vision during the refraction so that account can be taken of this when deciding upon the type of bifocal to be ordered.

In order to reconcile to some degree these optical incompatibilities, many types of bifocal lenses represent compromises the range of which reflects not only the particular problems presented by various refractive errors but also widely differing occupational requirements. In addition, many people wearing them insist that the dividing line between the two parts of the lens should be barely noticeable, if at all, and to secure this a design may be tolerated with a considerably inferior optical performance. Properly fitted bifocal spectacles should be designed so that the optical disadvantages we have mentioned will be minimized and at the same time the size and shape of the distance and reading segments give a reasonable field of clear vision in the tasks for which the wearer employs them.

THE TOLERANCE OF BIFOCALS

Intolerance to bifocals is unfortunately all too common and there are some patients in whom they are best avoided. To some extent the wearer must learn to move his head appropriately for near and distant viewing, that is, upwards for near and downwards for distant vision, in a fashion opposite to the way to which he has become accustomed. Some instability while walking is initially common because of the unaccustomed blur on looking downwards. Although to obviate this some designs have a strip for distant vision below the near segment this may be inadequate so that nervous subjects wearing bifocals may have difficulty in walking downstairs or stepping off a kerb. Particularly in old people, it is inadvisable to prescribe bifocals if they have not been worn previously and a considerable added correction for near vision is required; a stumble or a fall can so often have a catastrophic effect in the aged or in those with physical disabilities that cause difficulty in walking. Similarly, bifocals are best avoided in anyone prone to vertigo, whether organic or functional in origin. Moreover, some occupations, such as working at heights, also contra-indicate their use. Finally, experience has shown that some refractive anomalies such as marked anisometropia and high oblique astigmatism are particularly ill-suited for bifocal spectacles. The highly anisometropic myope is sometimes best suited by spectacles correcting the more myopic eye for near and the other for distance,[1] while astigmatic subjects may be more comfortable with " drop-ins " (" grab fronts " or " hook fronts ") for close work.[2]

TYPES OF BIFOCAL

Since Franklin's time several methods have been devised to con-summate his idea with as few optical disadvantages as possible. The earliest types of bifocal were composite. His suggestion consisted merely

FIGS. 688–691.—TYPES OF BIFOCAL LENS.

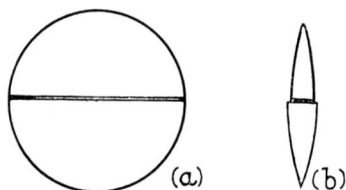

FIG. 688.—Franklin bifocal lenses.
(a) front; (b) side view.

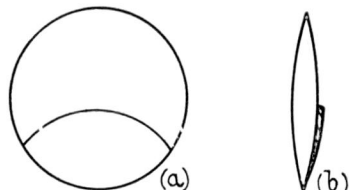

FIG. 689.—The supplementary wafer.
(a) front; (b) side view.

FIG. 690.—The inserted wafer.

FIG. 691.—Fused bifocal lens.

of two separate segments held together in a frame (the *split* or *two-piece bifocal*) (Fig. 688); the dividing line between them was horizontal and very conspicuous. More modern versions have been developed with both straight and curved dividing lines, which have the advantage of easy placement of the two optical centres; if both are on the dividing line no " jump " is experienced.

The feat of grinding a lens in two curvatures was achieved by I. Schuster in 1836, but the more simple plan, suggested by Samuel Gregg in 1866, of using a supplementary lens or " wafer " which was cemented onto the surface of the main glass (*cemented*

[1] p. 508.   [2] p. 691.

bifocal) became widely adopted (Fig. 689). One surface of the wafer is worked to correspond to the spherical or cylindrical lens upon which it is to lie, while the other supplies the necessary additional curvature; thus if it were proposed to add an additional correction of $+3$ D to a distance lens of $+2$ D sphere, a wafer with surfaces ground to -2 D and $+5$ D would be necessary. The wafer is usually attached to the posterior surface of the lens, the latter being of spherical form. The cement employed is Canada balsam, which has the same refractive index as glass, but it suffers from the disadvantage that it may dry and crystallize, or may soften and allow some degree of movement. Such a lens, however, has the advantages that the wafer is easy to make, is inexpensive, is scarcely noticeable, is easily centred and can be removed and altered when the presbyopic error increases; it is also a simple matter to incorporate a prism into it if necessary. An improvement in stability and in appearance was introduced by inserting the wafer into the middle of the lens which had been split where it was cemented (Fig. 690). The split and wafer types of bifocal are now obsolete, most modern bifocals being of the fused or solid variety.

Fused bifocals, introduced about 1890 by J. L. Borsch of Philadelphia, were a considerable improvement on earlier types. These "invisible" bifocals were made by combining a lens of crown glass with a segment of

FIGS. 692 and 693.—UNIVIS BIFOCAL SEGMENTS.

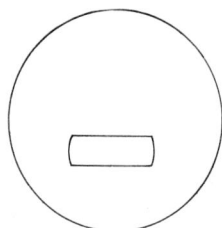

FIG. 692.—B-shaped segment.

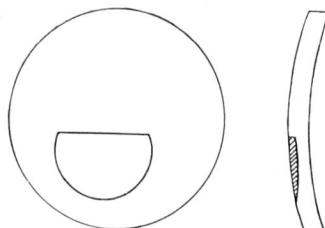

FIG. 693.—D-shaped segment.

flint glass of higher refractive power so that the increase in refractivity is obtained by virtue of the difference in refractive index. A depression is ground in the lens of crown glass, and a "button" of flint glass, similarly polished and ground, is laid upon it; the two are then clipped together and heated in a furnace to 600°C until they fuse together (Fig. 691). The fusion is made on to the face of the lens with a spherical curve so that any cylindrical power will be the same in both portions, and the same curvature is ground all over the combined "segment" surface. This usually means that the segment is inserted into the spherical front surface of the glass, the posterior concave surface being toric if required. The optical performance of fused bifocals is good although with higher-powered segments some chromatism is experienced because of the differing dispersions of the two types of glass. A degree of "jump" is inevitable but is somewhat lessened in the more modern designs of the Univis type, many of which have a flat-topped segment allowing the optical radius to be smaller (Fig. 692–3).

The fused bifocal lens has a good cosmetic appearance with no visible or palpable line of demarcation; but, inasmuch as the exacting conditions of refractivity, transparency, hardness and expansion are difficult to fulfil, the optical effect is not invariably perfect. A lens of this type must be handled carefully since the segment is readily scratched.

The determination of the design of a fused bifocal is somewhat complicated. The difference in power of the two segments is made up partly of the difference in refractive index and partly of the power of the surface of contact between the two lenses. The additional optical effect which will result in any particular lens must be calculated in each case.

The total difference in power between the distance and reading portions is made up of:

(a) The difference in power on the segment side between the reading (F_3) and the distance (F_1) portions. (b) The difference between the powers of the contact surfaces (F_c). The total addition (F_A) is therefore ($F_3 - F_1$) + F_c.

If n is the refractive index of the crown glass, n_s the refractive index of the flint segment and R_1 the curvature of the segment surface,[1]

then
$$F_3 - F_1 = (n_s - 1) R_1 - F_1 = (n_s - 1) \frac{F_1}{n-1} - F_1$$
$$= F_1 \times \frac{n_s - n}{n-1}.$$

The amount of addition to be provided by the contacting surfaces is therefore:
$$F_A - F_1 \times \frac{n_s - n}{n-1}.$$

Where R_c is the curvature of the contacting surface, this becomes
$$(n - n_s) R_c = F_A - F_1 \times \frac{n_s - n}{n-1}$$
$$i.e., R_c = \frac{F_1}{n-1} - \frac{F_A}{n_s - n}.$$

If the contact curve is formed by a tool which produces a power F on ordinary spectacle glass

the curvature required (F) $= F_1 - \frac{n-1}{n_s - n} \times F_A$

The fraction $\frac{n-1}{n_s - n}$ is the ratio between the two glasses, crown and flint, and is therefore constant for the glasses used: it can be represented in the formula by k.
$$i.e., F = F_1 - kF_A$$

For example, if a prescription reads $+2 \cdot 00$ DS $\subset$ $+1 \cdot 00$ DC axis $180°$, reading addition $+3 \cdot 00$ DS, in toric form, and the refractive indices are, crown $1 \cdot 523$, flint $1 \cdot 654$, the bifocal would be made thus:

$$\frac{+9 \cdot 00 \text{ DS}}{-6 \cdot 00 \ -7 \cdot 00}$$ with the segment on the $+9 \cdot 00$ sphere side.

The addition provided by the segment side is
$$F_3 - F_1 = F_1 \times \frac{n_s - n}{n-1} = 9 \times \frac{1 \cdot 654 - 1 \cdot 523}{1 \cdot 523 - 1} = +2 \cdot 25 \text{ DS}.$$

[1] In this section R_1 and R_c are the reciprocals of the corresponding radii of curvature.

The addition to be provided by the contacting surface is therefore

$$+3{\cdot}00 - 2{\cdot}25 = +0{\cdot}75 \text{ DS}$$
$$\text{hence } (n - n_s)\, R_c = +0{\cdot}75 \text{ DS}$$
$$R_c = \frac{+0{\cdot}75}{-0{\cdot}131} = -5{\cdot}73 \text{ DS}$$

and the power of the tool to work this is

$$(n - 1)\, R_c = 0{\cdot}523 \times (-5{\cdot}73)$$
$$= -2{\cdot}99 \text{ DS}.$$

Solid (or *one-piece*) *bifocals*, on the other hand, introduced in England in 1906, are made in one piece of glass, two distinct curves being ground upon one spherical surface, the segment side (usually the posterior except in some high ametropias), any cylinder being ground on the other (Fig. 694). The production of such a combination, however, if it is to be free from optical defects, is not without technical difficulties.

FIG. 694.—SOLID ONE-PIECE BIFOCAL.

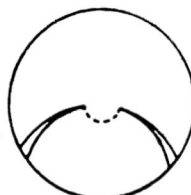

FIG. 695.—SEMI-VISIBLE CENTRE CONTROLLED SOLID BIFOCAL LENS.

A palpable break, sometimes even a step, is always present which allows solid bifocals to be distinguished readily from the fused variety. " Jump " is present in a degree proportional to the additional correction for near vision and the optic radius; the latter is half the diameter of the segment since in most varieties of solid bifocal this is circular. Chromatism is negligible and much larger segments can be employed than those used in a fused bifocal, but the cosmetic factor is not generally as good as in the latter. Nevertheless, where there is no significant anisometropia it is often possible to provide an invisible solid bifocal since the circumference of the segment lies flush against the distance portion of the lens. The position of the optical centre is therefore fixed for any particular power and size of segment, leading to a limited control over the optical defects of " jump " and prismatic displacement. A greater or less degree of visibility, however, is inevitable in those types of solid bifocal in which a prism is incorporated in order to eliminate or minimize these optical defects. Once the feature of invisibility is abandoned, the variety of optical design available is considerable. In the commonest type of *solid visible bifocal* a prismatic effect is introduced by tilting the segment, part of which no longer lies flush with the distance portion of the lens.

If, in addition, the bifocal lens is so designed as to allow some selection of the sites of the optical centres, it is known as a *centre-controlled solid bifocal*. The term " prism-controlled bifocal " is sometimes used to describe any design, not necessarily solid, in which an attempt is made to control the intrinsic prismatic effects of bifocal spectacles; it is, however, also used in a more restricted sense to describe a solid visible bifocal lens incorporating a prismatic correction solely for this purpose. Apart from these intrinsic prismatic effects, a solid bifocal, in this case invariably visible, may also incorporate any prismatic corrections judged necessary in cases of latent or manifest strabismus, for near or distant vision or both.

If both the distance and reading portions are negative in power, the ridge at the top of a solid visible bifocal can be ground away giving a small arc referred to as an invisible " witness " (Fig. 695); such a *semi-visible* (or *semi-invisible*) *solid bifocal* can also be centre-controlled. With this design the base-down effect of the reading portion in solid bifocals correcting medium and high myopia can be considerably reduced.

As an alternative to bifocals, the additional correction for reading may be supplied as a separate pair of spectacles placed in front of the distance lenses (" hook-fronts "). It is more useful if these are pantoscopic with ∪ shaped lenses, so that it is easy to look over them for distant vision. To a simple presbyope lenses shaped in this way are extremely useful for reading, while the unaided eye looking over the lens is used for distance. A low myope will frequently read most comfortably through the converse arrangement, a kidney-shaped omission, corresponding in size to an ordinary bifocal segment, being cut from the lower half of a pair of rimless distance spectacles.

MULTIFOCAL LENSES

Trifocal lenses were introduced in 1826 by John Isaac Hawkins of London; their designs vary and they offer some advantages over bifocals, particularly when the amplitude of accommodation has declined to the point where intermediate distances are significantly blurred (Figs. 696–8).

FIGS. 696–698.—TRIFOCAL LENSES.

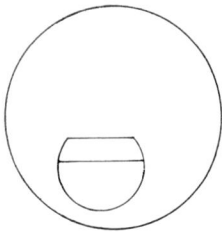

FIG. 696.—Univis trifocal lens.   FIG. 697.—Trivis trifocal lens.   FIG. 698.—Executive trifocal lens.

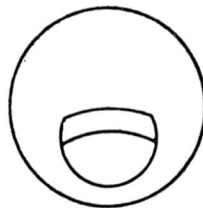

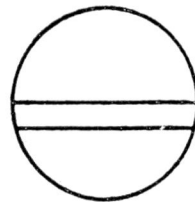

In addition, the " jump " effect of bifocals may be somewhat ameliorated. They have, however, some limitations. They are not suitable for aniso-metropes or when a special prism is indicated for close work; moreover, they cannot usefully be worn by those who need very small segments for occupational reasons. The strength of the intermediate addition varies in different designs but, within limits, it is usually about half the full addition required for close work.

Several attempts have been made to design a *multifocal lens* in which the reading portion of the lens has a continuously variable curve, there being a gradual accretion of power from the upper periphery to the lower reading segment where the limit of the addition ordered is attained. There are thus embodied in the one lens powers for intermediate distances from infinity to the working distance, and the sharp jump from a distance to a near focus is eliminated, the multiple range thus counterbalancing the restriction of the range for close work. One of the first was the " Ultifo " introduced by Gowland of Montreal in 1922. More recently the " Varilux " lens of Maitenaz (1961–66) and the " Omnifocal " of Volk and Weinberg (1962) have been introduced (Figs. 699–700). In the Varilux lens the upper portion is for distant

FIGS. 699 and 700.—MULTIFOCAL LENSES.

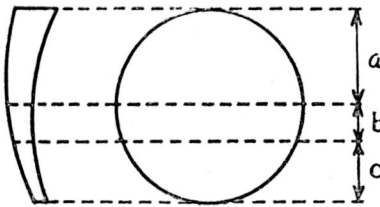

FIG. 699.—The Varilux lens.

There is a gradual and controlled addition of power with three main areas : (a) for distant vision, (b) progressive power, (c) maximum reading addition.

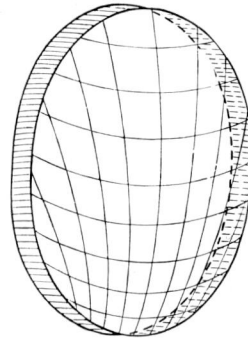

FIG. 700.—The Omnifocal lens.

The lines drawn on the front surface represent the principal directions of convergence of the area of greatest power.

vision below which there is a 12mm. vertical segment of increasing power until a fixed reading area is reached. If they are tolerated, the advantages of such lenses are clearly considerable, but difficulties may arise because of restricted visual field ; the lateral parts of the lenses are subject to considerable aberration on account of their non-spherical curvatures which may lead to a sense of gross distortion on looking to the side, an effect exaggerated if there is more than a very moderate amount of astigmatism particularly at an oblique axis.

VARIABLE FOCUS SPECTACLES have recently been invented by Wright in London in 1968. They have hollow lenses, with one thin flexible wall, filled with a liquid of refractive index approximating to that of glass (about 1·50) (such as a saturated solution of calcium bromide with glycerol). The volume of the lenses is changed by pumping the liquid in and out of the cavity in the lens so as to change the curvature of the flexible wall at will. The variable part of the lens is in the form of a circular cell of 25 mm. diameter set in the optical centre of a conventionally shaped lens which lies in front and a flexible glass coverslip behind, the two being separated peripherally by a sheet of plastic material (Fig. 701). The adjustment of the volume is effected by means of a simple cylinder (3 mm. × 20 mm.) and piston with a rubber ring seal operated by a slide in one side-piece of the spectacles (Fig. 702).

FIGS. 701 and 702.—VARIABLE FOCUS SPECTACLES (B. M. Wright).

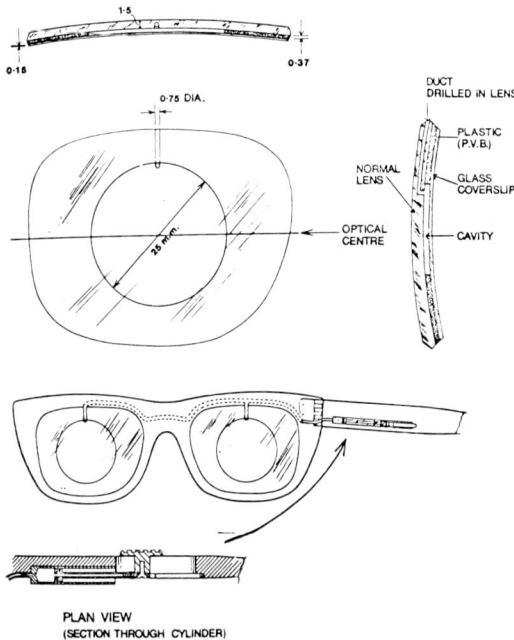

FIG. 701.—Diagram of the constitution of the lens. In front is a conventionally shaped lens and behind a glass cover slip with a central cavity between. This is connected by ducts to an adjustable cylinder in the side-piece; movements of the piston adjust the amount of fluid in the cavity.

FIG. 702.—B. M. Wright adjusting his variable focus spectacles for focal length.

THE SELECTION OF THE FORM OF BIFOCAL AND MULTIFOCAL LENSES

The factors which should determine the selection of such lenses are of interest and importance. Optically the nature of the refractive error and the strength of the addition or additions for close work are the first consideration. Fused bifocals, while cosmetically excellent, are preferably avoided in subjects with high refractive errors and for the higher additions of 2 D or more. Centre-controlled solid bifocals are especially valuable for the higher refractive errors particularly when there is any significant anisometropia, while, as we have seen, the semi-visible variety is available for high myopia.

Anisometropia of any degree calls for special care in the selection of the segments to be used. Here the important factor is anisometropia in the vertical meridian which is responsible for a difference of prismatic effect at the near visual points of the two eyes since more than 1Δ is usually intolerable. There are no hard and fast rules about this, however, and some patients may overcome prismatic effect by slightly tilting the head. Several optical designs are available to overcome this prismatic disparity if it is necessary to do so.

One suggestion is to provide segments, perhaps of the solid invisible variety, with different diameters for the two eyes. To calculate the difference in segment diameter the vertical difference in power of the two eyes is multiplied by 8 (the distance in millimetres between the reading and distance centres); this is divided by the reading addition (which gives the needed decentration of the segment centre); and this is multiplied by 2 (to complete the diameter). The final figure gives the difference in millimetres of the diameters of the two circles. The larger segment is used on the lens with the greater positive or less negative power in the distance portion.

For example, if the prescription is R.E. +2·00 DS and L.E. −1·00 DS with a reading addition of +2·00 DS,

the vertical difference is then 3;

the difference in size of the circles is $\dfrac{3 \times 8}{2} \times 2 = 24$ mm.

This method is limited by the availability of the different sizes of segment. Recourse may also be had to prism-controlled bifocals in cases of anisometropia, usually of the solid visible or semi-visible variety. A further alternative is the use of differing shapes of segment such as the fused variety of the Univis R range where the optical radius, the distance from the optical centre of the segment to the flat top, differs between the two eyes. Technically, the lenses are denoted by a numeral (4 to 10) after R, indicating this distance in millimetres.

In other anisometropic cases the effect of a prism base-up in the segment can be introduced by the design known as *bi-prism* (or *slab-off*) (Fig. 703). For this a flat-top fused bifocal is generally used, the front surface being ground in two parts at an angle to one another, the flat top of the bifocal being at the apex. Such a design can be employed in one or both lenses.

The size of the segment is closely related to the type of bifocal, to the refractive error and especially to the visual task for which the spectacles are intended. If close work is the major activity and provision is required only for an occasional glance to the distance, larger segments are indicated and

FIGS. 703–706.—SPECIAL TYPES OF BIFOCAL LENS.

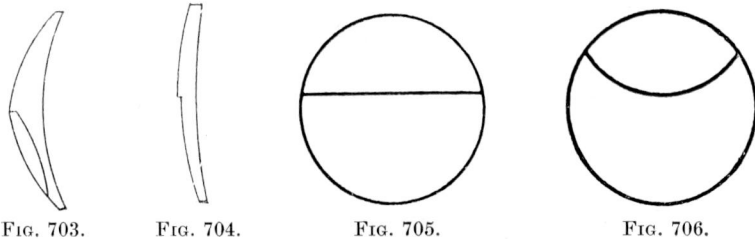

FIG. 703.   FIG. 704.   FIG. 705.   FIG. 706.

FIG. 703.—Bi-prism fused bifocal.
FIGS. 704 and 705.—Executive bifocals.
FIG. 706.—Upcurve bifocal.

this, particularly if a large field is desired, excludes the fused type. Typists, book-keepers and secretaries generally come into this category; solid bifocals with a 45 mm. segment are most suitable. A slightly more expensive version is the " executive bifocal ", a flat top variety with the segment anteriorly (Fig. 704–5). This is a one-piece version of the Franklin bifocal and gives a minimal " jump ". If a very extensive field for near vision is required, an " upcurve bifocal " can be given (Fig. 706), but in this the distance segment is prone to those defects, " jump " and displacement of the object, which are a feature of the near portion in a conventional bifocal. Where only occasional close work is done when using the bifocals, as with the golfer or theatre-goer, a smaller segment may be appropriate, perhaps of the fused variety and with a strip for distant vision below. For general purposes an ample field for reading is provided by an area in the page of

FIGS. 707–710.—RISING-FRONT BIFOCALS (F. A. Williamson-Noble).

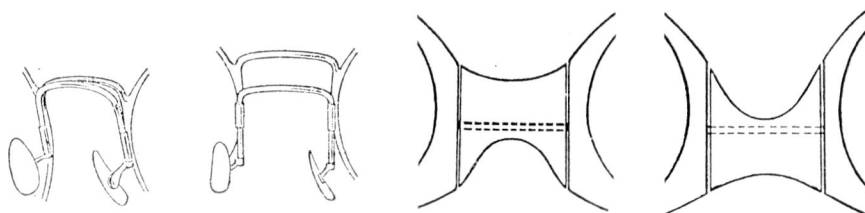

FIG. 707.   FIG. 708.   FIG. 709.   FIG. 710

FIG. 707.—The frame in the normal position with the reading segment depressed.
FIG. 708.—The frame raised by depressing the back bridge so that the reading segment is raised.
FIGS. 709 and 710.—The raising and depression of the reading segment is obtained by rotating the nose-piece mounted on a decentred axle.

15 cm. long and 10 cm. high, and if the book is held at a distance of 33 cm. from the eye, this will be covered by a segment which measures only 12·5 mm. × 9 mm. In many such cases, however, it will be found helpful to prescribe separate reading spectacles in addition; this facilitates reading the newspaper, for example, or reading in bed when a large vertical field is required, sometimes difficult to obtain with bifocals because of the necessary elevation of the head.

A further technical device which is frequently of considerable use is the so-called " *rising-front* " *bifocals* (Williamson-Noble, 1935). In these an adjustable step is incorporated in the nose-piece so that the spectacles can be raised or lowered (Figs. 707–10). In the first position the reading segment is almost straight in front of the pupil, so that the wearer can read without having to hold the written matter well below the horizontal; and in the second position the reading segment is well below the visual axis so that the wearer is less handicapped in walking about.

Other considerations relating to the visual task must be carefully elucidated from the patient. Apart from the size and general shape, displacement of the segments downwards or to the right or left may be indicated according to the orientation of the close work required. The distances of the task to be focused need not necessarily be for far distances and near work. In some occupations, such as a librarian, dentist, radiologist, shopkeeper or gardener, a combination for intermediate and near vision will be in order. An orchestral musician who does not wish to see his instrument may have a distance segment over an intermediate, the latter of the strength necessary to see his music. Where it is appropriate, all these tasks can be accommodated in a trifocal or other multifocal.

Individual susceptibility to the sensation of jump is very variable but a design minimizing this effect is important in certain occupations, such as a waitress or a bus conductor, where the subject has to move about a great deal. We have already noted that the wearing of bifocals is inadvisable in those working at heights or in a physically unstable environment; in such a person as an architect or a surveyor, if it is vital to wear a double correction, a small segment with a distance portion extending below the near portion should be ordered, the Univis B type being very suitable. In all cases wherein high corrections are involved (as well as in the low ametropias), the bifocal lens may be made of plastic material.

Airy. *On a Peculiar Defect in the Eye and a Mode of Correcting it* (1825). See *Trans. Camb. phil. Soc.*, **2**, 267 (1827); **3**, 1 (1830).

Boegehold. *Z. ophthal. Opt.*, **4**, 161 (1916); **5**, 129 (1917); **6**, 14, 60, 119 (1918); **8**, 1, 10 (1920).
Naturwissenschaften, **9**, 273 (1921).

Bourgeois. *Advis aux curieux de la conservation de leur veue sur les lunettes*, Paris (1745).

Coddington. *A Treatise on the Reflexion and Refraction of Light*, Camb. (1829–30).

Davis, Fernald and Rayner. *Amer. J. Optom.*, **42**, 203 (1965).

Emsley. *Proc. opt. Convent.*, London, **1**, 415 (1926).

Emsley and Swaine. *Ophthalmic Lenses*, 5th ed., London (1946).

Gleichen. *Zbl.-Z. Opt. Mech.*, **43**, 253, 275, 289, 307, 324, 340 (1922).
Arch. Augenheilk., **92**, 202 (1923).
Optician, **64**, 267, 345, 363, 393; **65**, 52, 125, 140 (1923).

Gullstrand. *Skand. Arch. Physiol.*, **2**, 269 (1891).
v. Graefes Arch. Ophthal., **49**, 46 (1899); **53**, 185 (1901).
Arch. Optik, **1**, 2, 81 (1907).
Einführung in d. Methoden d. Dioptrik d. Auges, Leipzig (1911).

Heymann. *Lunettes et lorgnettes de jadis*, Paris (1911).

Jones, W. *Phil. Mag.*, **18**, 65, 273 (1804); **41**, 247; **42**, 464 (1813).

Maitenaz. *Trans. int. ophthal. Opt. Cong.*, London, 533 (1961).
Amer. J. Optom., **43**, 441 (1966).

Márquez. *Arch. Oftal. hisp.-amer.*, **12**, 474 (1912); **14**, 147 (1914); **21**, 573 (1921).
Amer. J. Ophthal., **25**, 1458 (1942).

Martin. *Applied Optics*, London, **1** (1929).

Müller. *Brillengläser u. Hornhautlinsen*, Kiel (1889).

Naylor. *Brit. J. Ophthal.*, **52**, 422 (1968).

Ostwald. *C.R. Acad. Sci.* (Paris), **126**, 1446 (1898).
v. Graefes Arch. Ophthal., **46**, 475 (1898).

Percival. *Arch. Ophthal.*, **30**, 520 (1901); **32**, 367 (1903).
Ophthalmoscope, **12**, 390 (1914).
Brit. J. Ophthal., **10**, 369 (1926).
The Prescribing of Spectacles, Bristol (1928).

von Rohr. *Ber. dtsch. ophthal. Ges.*, **35**, 25 (1908); **37**, 51 (1911); **38**, 94 (1912).
Ergebn. Physiol., **8**, 541 (1909).
v. Graefes Arch. Ophthal., **75**, 561 (1910); **89**, 408 (1915).
Z. ophthal. Opt., **1**, 137 (1913); **2**, 33, 97 (1914); **3**, 1 33, 65, 73, 111, 145 (1915); **4**, 22, 85 (1916); **5**, 1 (1917); **8**, 33 (1920); **9**, 1 (1921).
Klin. Mbl. Augenheilk., **53**, 408 (1914); **57**, 529 (1916); **60**, 145 (1918).
Naturwissenschaften, **5**, 5 (1917).
Arch. Augenheilk., **82**, 31 (1917).
Zbl.-Z. Opt. Mech., **37**, 44, 211, 227, 243, 348, 361, 375, 387, 402, 417, 430, 444, 459 (1916); **40**, 137, 146, 156 (1919); **41**, 31, 41, 53, 383, 393, 405, 416, 429, 443, 456, 472 (1920).
Graefe-Saemisch Hb. d. ges. Augenheilk., 3rd ed.: *Die Brille als optisches Instrument*, Berlin (1921).
Trans. ophthal. Soc. U.K., **58**, 359 (1938).

von Rohr, Boegehold and Hartinger. *Das Brillenglas als optisches Instrument*, Berlin (1934).

Roure. *Arch. Ophtal.*, **16**, 241 (1896).
Ann. Oculist. (Paris), **115**, 99 (1896).

Stokes. *19th Meet. for Advancement of Science, Brit. Ass. Trans.*, 10 (1849).

Thompson. *Phil. Mag.*, **49**, 316 (1900).

Tscherning. *Encycl. franç. Ophtal.*, Paris, **3**, 105 (1904).
Arch. Optik, **1**, 401 (1908).

Volk and Weinberg. *Arch. Ophthal.*, **68**, 776 (1962).

Weiss. *Z. ophthal. Opt.*, **2**, 69 (1914); **5**, 153 (1917); **6**, 40, 88 (1918).

Zbl.-Z. Opt. Mech., **38**, 184 (1917); **39**, 225, 235 (1918); **41**, 321, 337, 354, 369 (1920); **42**, 159 (1921).

Whitwell. *Optician*, **67**, 3, 56, 167, 240, 307, 360, 415; **68**, 77, 113, 163 (1924); **70**, 17, 75, 369, 419 (1925–26); **71**, 105, 357, 362 (1926); **72**, 421, 439; **73**, 137, 319, 325, 403, 419; **74**, 89, 203 (1927); **1**, 63, 223; **2**, 33, 315 (1928).

Williamson-Noble. *Brit. J. Ophthal.*, **19**, 165 (1935).

Wollaston. *Phil. Mag.*, **18**, 165 (1804); **42**, 387 (1813).
Phil. Trans., **102**, 370 (1812).

Wright. *See* Sasieni *Ophthal. Optician*, **8**, 592 (1968).

Best-form Lenses for Special Purposes

THE SPECTACLE CORRECTION OF APHAKIA

We have examined elsewhere the optical condition of the aphakic eye and the problems involved in its correction.[1] As we have seen, the use of highly convex lenses has several disadvantages: a limitation of the effective field of view due to peripheral aberrations of the spectacle lens, true restriction of the field because of the prismatic effect at the edge of the lens, and the roving ring-scotoma with the associated " jack-in-the-box " phenomenon produced on moving the eye; to these must be added the excessive weight and unsightliness of the lenses. A further problem is raised by the intrinsic magnification of the condition of aphakia itself, and this may be further compounded with astigmatic corrections which may add a meridional magnification to the overall increase in the size of the retinal image. Finally, difficulties with near vision and with binocularity may be not inconsiderable. The simultaneous complete resolution of all these problems is impossible and in all cases some type of compromise is necessary. Their seriousness can, however, be ameliorated in several ways (Welsh, 1961).

Although the advantage of a full-aperture lens is its potentially large field of vision, no spherical form of a lens of the power required to correct aphakia will satisfactorily eliminate oblique astigmatism, but it is possible to choose spherical surfaces which minimize this optical defect by bending the lens. The bulging of a highly bent lens, however, is unsightly and the magnifying properties are increased. As an optimal requirement, Benton and Welsh (1966) recommended a curvature of the anterior surface of $+12$ to $+14$ D.

The weight of such lenses often passes unnoticed by the patient in his gratitude for the restoration of his sight; nevertheless, it is objectionable to many subjects, an inconvenience which can be mitigated by several expedients. A small-aperture lens may be employed so that it is thin over as large a part of its circumference as is feasible (the *minimum effective diameter*,

[1] p. 377.

Benton and Welsh, 1966). Alternatively, the lens can be made of plastic material, either polymethylmethacrylate or allyl diglycol carbonate; the advantage of the smaller weight of these materials is, however, somewhat lost since lenses of steeper curvature are necessary because of their lower refractive index compared with the crown glass usually used for aphakic corrections. The excessive curvature and thickness thus make them cosmetically unacceptable, particularly in the higher powers.

The optical properties of full-aperture lenses can be improved by using aspherical surfaces in either glass or plastic material. The glass Katral lenses of Gullstrand's design (1899–1905) produced by Zeiss (von Rohr, 1919–21) were of this type; these, however, are no longer obtainable. Modern varieties of aspherical lens (the lenses of Volk, 1961, and the Pan-aspheric lenses manufactured by Bausch and Lomb) are now available but they are relatively expensive.

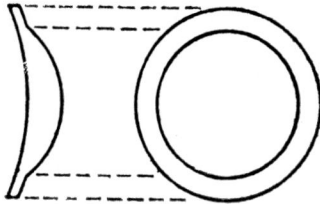

FIG. 711.—CONVEX SOLID LEN-
TICULAR LENS.

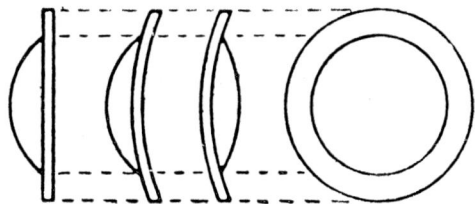

FIG. 712.—CONVEX UNISEAL LENTICULAR
LENSES.

Lenticular lenses[1] which eliminate the peripheral portion of the lens which, in any case, is of no optical value, are a thinner and lighter alternative to the full-aperture lens in aphakia. The optically effective button occupies a central position in the peripheral " carrier " which is usually afocal or nearly so. The segment which usually has a plano or concave posterior surface may be of any size from 25 to 40 mm., commonly 32 to 34 mm. This reduction in the effective size of the lens is not particularly serious as may be gathered from Benton and Welsh's (1966) estimate that at a spectacle distance of 12 mm. a circle of a diameter of 25 mm. for a +10 D lens and 15 mm. for a +15 D lens is all that is available for clear central vision. For peripheral vision the corresponding areas would be a 35 mm. circle for a +12 D lens and a 25 mm. circle for a +15 D lens.

The segment is commonly positioned on the anterior surface alone as part of a solid lens or cemented on (unisealed) (Figs. 711–12). Lenticulars with a button of glass of high refractive index fused into the anterior surface have also been widely used but there is no great reduction in weight in comparison with full-aperture lenses. It is also possible to have the lenticular button on the posterior surface of the lens and in some designs both the anterior and posterior surfaces have lenticular forms as in the " Rotoid " (Fig. 713) and " Alphakat " types (Fig. 714). In Rotoid lenticulars

[1] p. 629.

a standard outside base-curve of $+28\cdot00$ D is used for a segment of 28 mm.; the Alphakat is a cemented lenticular, the central area of the posterior surface being of a curvature of about $-8\cdot0$ D. Lenticular lenses can also be constructed in plastic, and aspherical surfaces may be utilized in the lenticular portion.

For near vision many aphakics are happy to change to a separate pair of reading spectacles but carefully prescribed and dispensed bifocals are worth considering in most cases. For this purpose the range of bifocal and aphakic spectacle lenses is wide, as might be expected from the various forms and materials available. Although aphakic bifocal spectacles can be made with a full aperture, most are of the lenticular type. Fused and solid bifocal segments are also available, the former being of the conventional round-top or of flat-top shape. A popular design is the Bilentic in which a segment of the Univis type D is fused into the posterior surface of a solid lenticular; the Univis B segment may also be employed and is said to be valuable in

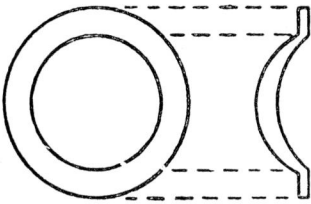

FIG. 713.—ROTOID LENS.   FIG. 714.—ALPHAKAT   FIG. 715.—CONOID APHAKIC
                                LENS.   BIFOCAL LENS.

binocular cases (Figs. 692–3). Other fused bifocals may have the segment in the anterior surface or even occasionally in the substance of the lens as in the Volk conoid aphakic bifocal (Fig. 715). A solid aphakic bifocal can be fashioned from a standard solid bifocal with a 38 or 45 mm. segment, on the front of which is unisealed a lenticular segment of sufficient power. Most one-piece bifocals, however, are of plastic either with nearly flat tops or with the standard circular tops.

The addition required for near vision in uniocular cases is usually higher than that suitable for binocular aphakics. In the latter, the strong base-out prismatic effect of the lens on converging the eyes is minimized by making the additional correction as small as is convenient and using the thinnest possible lens. The in-setting of segments must be exaggerated in binocular cases for the same reason.

The selection of the segment depends to some extent on the technique of the surgery. After an extraction leaving a round pupil some authorities believe that most patients prefer flat-top segments, while those with a complete iridectomy are happier with round-top segments; since the steno-pæic optical effect of miosis is lost in the second type of case a stronger reading addition may be required. The top of the segment should always be close to the optical centre for distance vision, preferably not more than 1 to 2 mm. below, so as to minimize the effect of oblique astigmatism on looking downwards.

Temporary spectacles may be prescribed for use during the first six weeks after the operation in the interval which is usually allowed to elapse before the corneal wound is finally sealed and a definitive prescription is given. They can be glass spheres of appropriate power for distance and the patient with the usual type of post-operative astigmatism can provide himself with slightly clearer vision by tilting the lens to give the effect of a horizontal cylinder; by increasing their distance from the eye by pulling down the nose the effectivity is increased to allow clearer near vision. Various forms

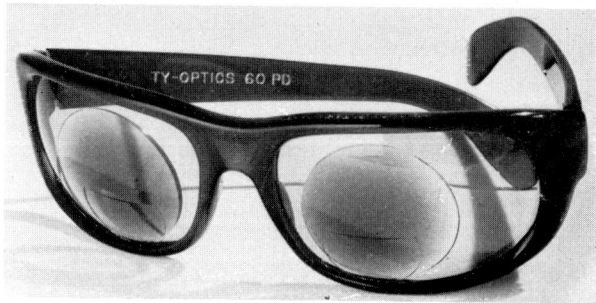

FIG. 716.—TEMPS WITH TINTED LENSES (P. J. Fenton).

of temporary lens exist in glass or plastic, some with cylinders and some tinted; an example is a tinted plastic spherical lenticular lens, incorporated in which is a flat-top bifocal (the " Temps ", Fenton, 1968) (Fig. 716). The shape of the lens and the frame offer some physical protection to the recently operated eye, and the total weight of the frame and the lenses of 1 ounce is considerably less than the maximum readily tolerable (about $1\frac{3}{4}$ ounces for a man and $1\frac{1}{2}$ ounces for a woman).

The use of *tinted spectacles* for aphakics is considered by most surgeons to be unnecessary, but some feel that the increased transmission of short-wave light should be counteracted. Tinted spectacles may also provide an initial relief for the photophobia associated with a complete iridectomy, the degree of sunlight in the patient's normal environment, and the possible temporary occurrence of erythropsia which theoretically calls for a yellow tint, as well as sometimes being a cosmetic asset to cater for the patient's wish to conceal the magnification of his eye by the powerful convex spectacle glass. For this purpose isochromatic tinting is advisable and in some lenticulars this can be done by tinting the carrier only (Fig. 717).

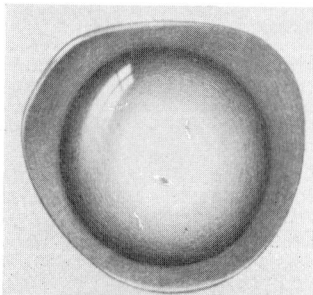

FIG. 717.—ROTOID GRADATONE APHAKIC LENS.

Whatever type of lens is employed, accuracy in prescribing the correction is essential, and the back vertex power of the lenses in the trial frame should be measured with a focimeter as well as the vertex distance from the rearmost lens to the cornea. The lenses should be fitted as closely to the eye as is practicable and the patient should be discouraged from selecting bizarre shapes of spectacle frame which tend to accentuate an already difficult problem; indeed, the choice of frame may be related to the form of the lens to be used if, for example, the weight of the correction is to be minimized (Benton and Welsh, 1966). However theoretically perfect the form of the spectacle lens, all aphakic patients require an initial period of mental readaptation and rehabilitation during which most require encouragement, a subject we have already discussed.[1] Particular difficulties arise in depth perception and the patient should be advised to move his head, not his eyes, when looking to the side; but even so, he will be disturbed by the apparent relative movement of objects in the peripheral field owing to the prismatic effect of the lenses.

In uniocular aphakia with good vision in the phakic eye, if correcting lenses are worn in spectacles correcting each eye the resulting diplopia is usually sufficiently disturbing to make the correction of only one eye desirable. Attempts, however, have been made to obtain binocular vision by this means, the lens for the aphakic eye being as thin and flat as possible with the shortest convenient vertex distance while the vertex distance and base-curve of the lens for the phakic eye are manipulated so as to make the size of the image as great as can be obtained and the patient's phoria being balanced by prisms (usually base-in) (Lubkin *et al.*, 1966–69). With excellent fusion and good cooperation this may sometimes be successful so far as central vision is concerned, but better results are more easily attained with contact lenses.

LENSES FOR HIGH MYOPIA

The usual precautions must be taken when ordering spectacles for high myopia; where indicated a measurement of the back vertex power of the lenses in the trial frame should be made with a focimeter and the back vertex distance estimated.

Highly concave spectacle lenses cannot be made of a form which eliminates all the optical disadvantages inherent in this type of lens, but the most appropriate form is determined initially by the need to minimize oblique astigmatism (see Table XXXIII in the Appendix). Full-aperture lenses for the higher degrees of myopia are therefore often best in a plano-concave form. Apart from their weight, highly concave lenses also have the disadvantage in that the thick edge may be very conspicuous and gives rise to so-called *power rings* due to internal reflections in the region of the bevelled edge. Special glazing techniques can be used for the edge in order to minimize these effects; an example of these is seen in Fig. 718.

The use of a lenticular form eliminates some of the peripheral aberrations and reduces the weight of the lens as well as diminishing the power rings. The lenticulus may be of any aperture—decreasing with increasing minus

[1] p. 379.

power; it may be round, oval or fashioned by hand to follow the shape of the final spectacle lens. The carrier part of the lenticular lens is convex in power in the simplest designs, but some reflections still arise from the periphery of the lens in this type. Several patterns are now available, however, in which the carrier is afocal or nearly so. In the solid lenticular the anterior surface is flat or has only a cylindrical correction on it; the spherical lenticular portion stands above the level of the posterior surface (Fig. 719). In other designs the sharp edge of the lenticulus is avoided (Myotor, Myodisc), but here the edge is inevitably thicker (see Fig. 720).

Both full-aperture and lenticular forms are made in plastic material as well as in glass. As with highly convex lenses the advantageous decrease in weight—sometimes of the order of a half for comparable prescriptions—is to a certain degree offset by the increased thickness necessary owing to the lower refractive index of the plastic.

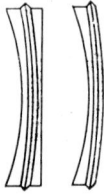

Fig. 718.—Stigmat-edge Lenses. Fig. 719.—Flattened Lenticular Lens. Fig. 720.—Myotor Lenticular Lens.

Near vision in the corrected high myope may be disturbed by the necessity for using an eccentric portion of the lens. This can be avoided by tilting the head, but in the presence of marked anisometropia the slab-off (bi-prism) design of the lens may be indicated with upper and lower portions of identical power but having separate optical centres. In high myopes of presbyopic age, bifocal lenses are an alternative to a separate pair of reading spectacles, but certain optical difficulties present themselves. Down-curve segments larger than 22 mm. in invisible solid bifocals give rise to a considerable base-down prismatic effect and should be avoided; indeed, both fused and invisible solid bifocals of any type should not be used in powers above $-12 \cdot 00$ D. For this class of patient the semi-invisible solid bifocal is particularly well suited, either in full-aperture or in lenticular lenses. Up-curve bifocals, however, present fewer optical problems and the solid up-curve lenticular bifocal known as the " Bilentic " is a particularly valuable design.

DIVERS' SPECTACLES. Since the refractive power of the cornea is largely abolished when it is immersed in water, divers become so hypermetropic that clear vision is impossible. It has been recorded that visitors to the Persian Gulf saw pearl fishers wearing transparent tortoiseshell spectacles in 1331 (Dugan, 1956). About 1490 Leonardo da Vinci described and sketched glasses for coral and pearl divers, and they appear in

FIG. 721.—THE CORAL FISHERS.

From *Venationes Ferarum, Arium, Piscium. Pugnae Bestiariorum et mutae Bestiarum, depictae*, by A. Ioanne Stradano (Jan van der Straet), Antwerp, 1578. Courtesy of the British Museum.

a copperplate drawn by the Dutch artist, Jan van der Straet, about 1600 (Fig. 721). In 1865 Francis Galton used to amuse himself by reading under water in his bath using as a spectacle lens the two objectives of his opera glass in combination. Some years later R. E. Dudgeon (1870–71) introduced spectacles for " subaqueous vision " consisting of two meniscus plano lenses enclosing between them a bi-concave lens of air. Out of water such a system is afocal, but under water the air-lens has a convergent effect, the power being determined by the curvature of the glass lenses (von Rohr, 1921) (Fig. 722). Duane and his colleagues (1959) devised a $+64$ D lens system in air placed 7·5 cm. from a clear window with which a field of 28° and a reasonable range of accommodation could be obtained. An underwater contact lens has been devised incorporating an air-space with a flat front allowing the swimmer good vision in and out of water (Mosse, 1964).[1]

ORTHOSCOPIC SPECTACLES[2] are prismo-spheres wherein equal spherical and prismatic (base-in) powers are combined, to which may be added any ametropic correction desirable. They are worn with advantage in performing extremely fine tasks (Weston and Adams, 1927–29).[3] Such work is held close

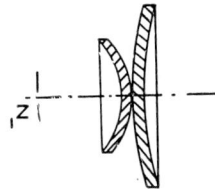

FIG. 722.—DIVERS' SPECTACLES.

[1] p. 791.
[2] This is to be distinguished from orthoscopic lenses, p. 656.
[3] p. 600.

to the eye to attain the necessary magnification, and in such an attitude strain is avoided since the spheres relieve the accommodation and the prisms the convergence.

PRISMATIC SPECTACLES enable a patient to read in the completely supine position (Reid, 1935) (Fig. 723). The prisms are so designed that the incident light is reflected twice and emerges from the third surface free from chromatism and without inversion of the image. Differences in the angles of the prisms allow for any degree of reflection desired so that while lying supine or semi-recumbent the patient can read with both the eyes and hold the book in a normal and comfortable position (Fig. 724).

FIG. 723.

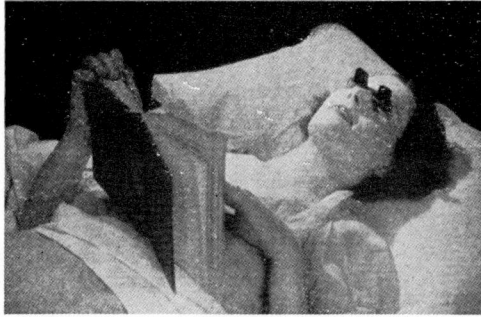

FIG. 724.

FIGS. 723 and 724.—PRISMATIC RECUMBENT SPECTACLES.

HEMIANOPIC SPECTACLES may be of assistance to allow a patient with homonymous hemianopia to see objects in his blind half-field. This is attained by affixing to the spectacle lens furthest from the blind field a prism up to a strength of 8Δ. Braunschweig (1920) found that with a prism of 7Δ an area 40 cm. to the blind side is gained at a distance of 5 metres and an area of 3 to 4 cm. at reading distance; Strebel (1923) found that one-third of his cases was helped in this way. Wiener (1926) and Young (1929), on the other hand, used a right-angled reflecting prism (Fig. 725); if the prism is placed out of the direct line of sight the patient may look into the prism when he wants to see to the side as one looks into the mirror of a motor car. The same effect can be obtained by an adjustable mirror suspended from the nose-piece of the spectacles (Bell, 1919; Burns *et al.*, 1952; Walsh and Smith, 1966) (Fig. 726).

ADAPTATION GOGGLES

In order to induce a state of dark adaptation in ordinary circumstances a wait in the dark of at least 10 to 15 minutes, and preferably of 30 minutes or more, is necessary[1] —a tedious process at best and a great disadvantage in certain activities—photographic

[1] Vol. IV, p. 558.

and experimental work, fluoroscopic work in radiology, and so on—and sometimes impracticable, for example, to the driver at night, the aviator or the look-out at sea who must make reference to the chart room. It has been established that the rods (which mediate night-vision) are very insensitive to red light, for at 6,220 Å.U. the scotopic visibility curve falls to below the 5% level (Hyde *et al.*, 1918; Hecht and Williams, 1922–23; and others). It follows that if a red filter is worn in well-fitting goggles which allow no stray light to enter, cone vision can be employed for ordinary activities and the rods, being unstimulated, will adapt as readily as if all light were excluded; indeed, there is some evidence that they adapt more quickly (Miles, 1943).

FIGS. 725 and 726.—HEMIANOPIC SPECTACLES.

FIG. 725.—Prismatic optical correction (C. A. Young).

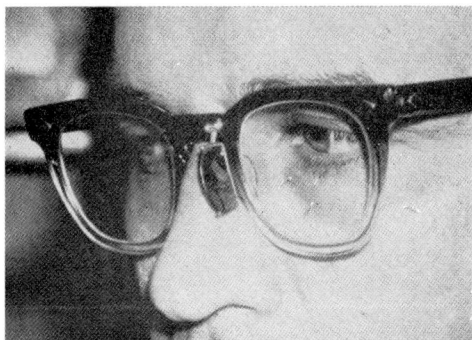

FIG. 726.—A mirror is affixed to the nasal part of the frame of the left eye (T. J. Walsh and J. L. Smith).

Suitable filters are commercially available: a 2 mm. glass Corning filter (No. 2403), for example, gives a sharp cut-off and passes no visible radiation shorter than 6,200 Å.U. (Carson, 1943; Miles, 1943). With such goggles the period of waiting in darkness for adaptation to develop can be usefully employed, and a means is provided whereby activities in the dark can be interrupted at will and a return to lighted areas can be made without the loss of dark adaptation.

PROTECTIVE GLASSES

Although protective glasses are not strictly speaking optical appliances, the combination of a protective and optical function is so common in spectacles that a short discussion of their main principles will not be out of place.

Such glasses may be of two types, (*a*) those giving protection against radiation, either generally against an excess of light or preferentially against harmful wavelengths in the long- and short-wave bands of the spectrum, and (*b*) those affording mechanical protection against flying particles.

One of the earliest expedients adopted for the former purpose was the simple one of cutting down the amount of radiation incident on the eye by using a *stenopœic opening* (see Skinner, 1815). It is interesting that this expedient has long been made use of, usually in the form of a horizontal stenopæic slit in a crude " spectacle " of wood, by the primitive Eskimos as a protection from the ultra-violet radiation reflected from the snow.

PROTECTIVE GLASSES AGAINST RADIATION

The discomforts of glare and brilliant sunlight have inspired the idea from very early times that too much light was deleterious to the eyes. Nero's emerald[1] may have been used for this purpose and coloured glasses to cut down glare were known to Daza da Valdés (Fig. 383), a notary of the Inquisition of Seville who wrote the first treatise on spectacles in a modern language in 1623 : the subject was discussed at some length by an anonymous author in the *Phil. Trans.* of the Royal Society, London, in 1668, and later attracted a considerable amount of attention (Martin, 1760; Beer, 1813; Bernstein, 1819; and others). At a later stage the value of the exclusion of noxious parts of the spectrum (the ultra-violet and infra-red rays) began to be realized, and a considerable amount of research was undertaken on the development of glasses which would exclude these preferentially (Fieuzal, 1885–87; Hallauer, 1907; Schanz and Stockhausen, 1908; and others). The most elaborate series of experiments was undertaken by Sir Wm. Crookes (1914) who worked on the problem of the protection of glass workers from the development of cataract.

The technical methods employed in cutting down the transmission of glass have varied. They may act in one of two ways, the unwanted rays being either absorbed or reflected. Most glasses belong to the first class and are prepared by combining the glass with some chemical substance or substances with special absorbing properties. For this purpose Crookes (1914) investigated the effects of iron, chromium, cobalt, cerium and many other metallic oxides, and found that the absorption of ultra-violet light is increased by cerium and iron oxide particularly in the ferrous form, and its transmission enhanced by silica and boric oxide, while the absorption of infra-red was diminished by ferrous oxide. As would be expected, all these substances are coloured so that all such glasses are tinted. Glass itself, of course, absorbs a considerable amount of ultra-violet while quartz readily transmits the longer ultra-violet rays (Fig. 727).

The simplest method of using such substances is to incorporate them in the material during manufacture, but this process has the disadvantage that the depth of the (" solid ") tint varies with the thickness of the lens. Thus a convex lens will be deeply tinted in the centre, while a concave one will have its maximum intensity in the periphery, the central and essential part remaining more or less clear. This disadvantage may be overcome

[1] p. 609.

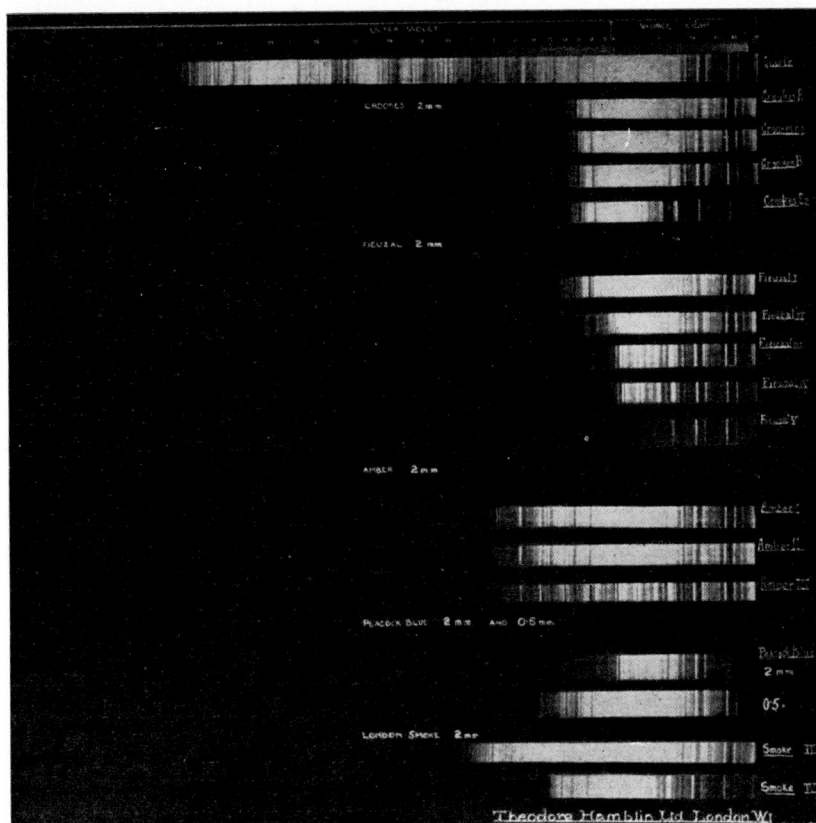

FIG. 727.—THE SPECTRAL TRANSMISSION OF VARIOUS GLASSES.

Upper Spectrum—Quartz.
The next four—Crookes's glasses, α, A₂, B, B₂.
The next five—Fieuzal glasses, I, II, III, IV, V.
The next three—Amber glasses, I, II, III.
The next two—Peacock blue, 2 mm., 0·5 mm.
The lowest group—London smoke glass, II, IV.

in two ways in *isochromatic lenses*. A thin layer (equitint) of the protective material of uniform thickness may be cemented or fused onto the (back) surface of the spectacle lens, glass or plastic, or, as was suggested in 1911 by Schreiner, an American optician, the ordinary spectacle lens may be split and a protective lamina cemented or fused between the two halves. Alternatively, as was suggested by G. Henkel in Germany in 1912, the spectacle lens is dipped into a gelatine solution of the required substance which is set in a special way to form a uniform film; the tinting of plastic lenses may be similarly effected. A surface deposit of metallic oxides in a high vacuum (vacuum coating) has also come into widespread use in recent years. The Umbral glasses of Zeiss are made as a solid tint for plano sun-glasses or alternatively are fused onto the prescribed lens in such a way as to give an equitint effect, and may also be vacuum-deposited.

Tinted lenses may be made to vary in the density of their colour in different parts (*gradutint lenses*): thus the periphery may be tinted and the centre left clear to exclude peripheral rays, the upper part may be darker than the lower to provide shade from the sun, and so on. Such a gradation can be produced by deposition or selectively grinding an equitinted lens.

The cheap dark glasses sold popularly at the seaside are usually made in the form of blown *globular lenses*. Glass of the appropriate tinted type is blown into large spheres from which lenses are cut, the thickness being about 2 mm. and the radius of curvature varying from 4·5 cm. (*coquille*) to 9 cm. (*mi-coquille*). The two surfaces should be concentric, resulting in the development of a very slight negative power, but they frequently show a wavyness or distortion due to the unequal contraction of the glass when it cools, resulting in cylindrical effects. Such deformed lenses should be discarded. Only occasionally are the lenses to some extent surfaced on the appropriate tool (*worked globular lenses*).

The second method of dealing with the problem is the use of REFLECTING GLASS. The accumulation of heat by the absorption of infra-red rays by the first type of lens raises the temperature of the lens sometimes uncomfortably, and in certain conditions it may be advisable to allow the transmission of short waves which are also absorbed by the heat-absorbing ferrous oxide usually employed as a protection against infra-red. These objections can be met by depositing layers of a metal, such as gold, silver or platinum, of such extreme thinness (of the order of 10 to 15μ) that they remain to a large extent transparent to luminous rays; the delicate lamella is then protected by incorporating it within the substance of a split lens, where it is cemented or fused.

During the last half-century a very large number of types of glasses has been placed upon the market from time to time, all of which have been widely exploited: most of them are commercial propositions rather than scientific productions, and few of them have anything in particular to recommend them. It can be reasonably understood that as a general rule the manufacturers are reluctant to liberate data concerning the chemical constitution of their products, and in some cases the mixtures appear to be indefinite, giving discordant results for their spectral analyses and transmission intensities. A further difficulty has arisen in agreement upon methods of comparison. In Great Britain there are now recognized standards for evaluating the tinted media used for spectacle lenses consisting of a transmission curve derived from 2 mm. and at least one other stated thickness of the material over the spectral range 3,000 to 10,000 Å.U. and an integrated visible transmission-factor (IVT) for C.I.E. Standard Illuminant A.

The range of visible radiation for 4,000 to 8,000 Å.U. is well within the range suggested and published data have therefore given an indication of the effectiveness of the material in absorbing not only visible light but also ultra-violet (2,550 to 2,000 Å.U.) and some of the infra-red spectrum (8,000 to 600,000 Å.U.). Figure 728 and Table XXX show the appropriate data for Crookes's glass (Chance-Pilkington) of various tints which are among the most reliable and efficient available, particularly for the ultra-violet end of the range. Crookes's B not only excludes the ultra-violet but also

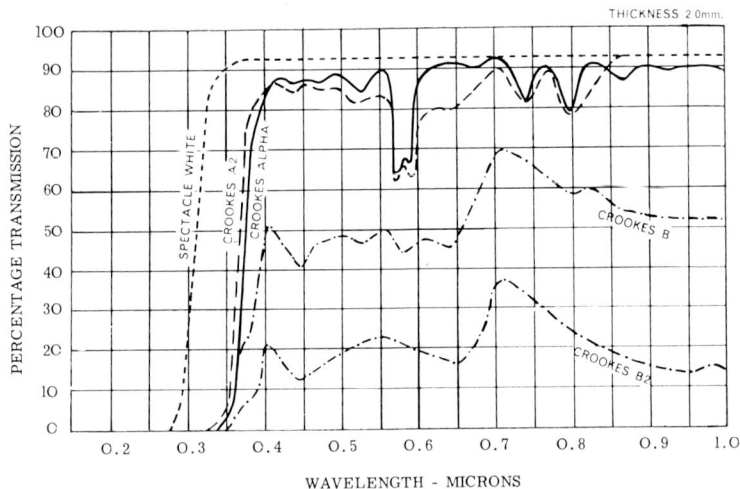

FIG. 728.—THE TRANSMISSION OF LIGHT BY CROOKES'S GLASSES.

The percentage transmission of daylight (6500°K) by these glasses of different thickness is as follows:

Alpha—for 2 mm. thickness, 82·5; for 3 mm. thickness, 77·0.
A2—for 2 mm. thickness, 76·5; for 3 mm. thickness, 73·0.
B—for 2 mm. thickness, 47·0; for 3 mm. thickness, 34·0.
B2—for 2 mm. thickness, 19·5; for 3 mm. thickness, 10·0.

gives considerable protection against infra-red radiation and at the same time cuts down excessive light throughout the whole range of the spectrum without seriously impeding the luminous rays. The Chance-Pilkington SG (sage-green) range is also valuable in absorbing ultra-violet and infra-red radiation but relatively less so against the visible radiations.

TABLE XXX

THE TRANSMISSION OF DAYLIGHT (6500°K) BY CHANCE-PILKINGTON CROOKES GLASSES

Chance Crookes	% of light transmitted by 2 mm. thickness	% of light transmitted by 3 mm. thickness
Alpha	82·5	77·0
A2	76·5	73·0
B	47·0	34·0
B2	19·5	10·0

The choice of the colour of tinted spectacles, grey, brown, blue, green or pink, is, however, not often made upon scientific grounds alone and the æsthetic factor often predominates. The nature of the refractive error probably has little bearing upon the colour to be selected although it has been suggested that myopes prefer brown tints and hypermetropes green. It is obviously desirable that the tint should interfere as little as possible with the subject's evaluation of colours.

Many types of tinted lenses are available in different intensities, the selection of which is again a matter of personal choice superimposed on the appropriate visual requirement. It is clearly inadvisable to prescribe very deep shades for solid tints, especially in the higher degrees of ametropia.

PHOTOCHROMIC GLASS (Bestlite Corning Glass) alters its colour on exposure to ultra-violet light, a property imparted to it by incorporated submicroscopic crystals of silver halides; such lenses darken in sunlight and lighten in the shade. The theoretical advantage of being able to wear them for all conditions of illumination is, however, not as great as it seems because the full degree of darkening may take about an hour.

POLAROID LENSES incorporate a different principle. They consist of a film mounted between two pieces of glass as in an ordinary laminated lens, the film being a matrix of minute dichroic crystals about 10^{12} per square inch, orientated so that the whole acts as one large crystal which polarizes light in one direction. In protective glasses it is used as an analyser so as to arrest horizontally polarized light. Reflected light is partially polarized in a plane parallel to the reflecting surface so that the glare from extensive smooth surfaces such as a concrete road or an expanse of water, which has a significant component of horizontally polarized light, is lessened. Because of this, polaroid spectacles may be of value to motorists, yachtsmen and fishermen and since they are coloured they tone down the ordinary light in addition.

The use of tinted contact lenses will be described in a subsequent Chapter.[1]

The uses of protective glasses, legitimate and illegitimate, are varied and may be classified thus.

(a) *Protection against visible radiation* is advisable when the sun is unusually strong or where its intensity is increased by the reflection of light from a large mirror surface as the sea, the plains of the tropics, the desert or a snow-field. In ordinary illumination, however, they are unnecessary for the healthy eye, and the frequency with which they are employed in temperate climates depends partly upon fashion and erroneous ideas of the action of light upon the eye and partly upon the demands of neurasthenics and psychoneurotics actuated by fear either of their vision or of the outside world. In pathological conditions they are useful when prolonged dilatation of the pupil by atropine is necessary, in albinos who are provided with an inadequate supply of pigment to absorb an excess of scattered light, in early axial cataract where the irregular dispersion of light diminishes vision by dazzling, and in cases of cataract extraction where the removal of an opaque lens has subjected the eye suddenly to unusual conditions. The strength of the converging lenses usually necessary in these last cases provides an additional reason for the employment of some tint, since spheres of high power tend to concentrate the light after the manner of a burning glass. In some diseases of the retina and choroid also, it is well that the light entering the eye should be cut down to a minimum. In most of these cases, and in all of them where the eye itself is healthy, the ideal glass is that which cuts off as little of the light as is necessary for comfort, and cuts it off throughout the spectrum uniformly so that colour appreciation is interfered with as little as possible thus minimizing their depressant effect.

(b) *Protection against Infra-red Radiation.* Infra-red rays are harmful to the eye, and when absorbed in quantity may produce cataract and retinal lesions of the nature of burns. Sunlight contains a large quantity of these heat rays, but rarely enough to do harm unless the sun is looked at directly,

[1] p. 790.

when the lesions of eclipse blindness are produced.[1] In some industries there
is a considerable exposure to infra-red, as, for example, in the smelting of
metals and the making of glass. Crookes's sage-green glass, as we have
seen, which eliminates 95% of the infra-red as well as the ultra-violet and
a proportion of the luminous spectrum, forms an ideal protection in this
respect.

(c) *Protection against Ultra-violet Rays.* These rays are not present in
ordinary sunlight in sufficient intensity to give any trouble except at high
altitudes or when they are reinforced by the reflection from snow or some
extensive surface which acts as a mirror. In this case they give rise to the
extremely painful condition of photophthalmia on account of the desquama-
ting effect upon the cornea.[2] In some industries also, such as electric welding
or in those wherein arc lamps are used, in film studios and in ultra-violet light
clinics, provision against short-wave light must also be made.

PROTECTION AGAINST MECHANICAL INJURY

For protection against minor injury as against dust, wind or flying particles,
globular lenses of blown glass are frequently fitted into goggles provided with side-
shields to add further protection; alternatively, plano lenses may be employed. A
protective side-piece may with advantage be fitted to ordinary spectacle frames in cases
wherein exposure to as little light or dust as possible is desired, as in lagophthalmos,
chronic epiphora or lacrimation and in cases of corneal anæsthesia. The more elaborate
types of goggle advisable to use in many industrial processes are discussed at length in
a subsequent Volume.[3]

Despite the immense number of people who now wear spectacles, ocular injuries
from broken glass are relatively rare.[4] In many cases these are caused by flying objects
which would damage the globe if spectacles were not worn; nevertheless, the end-result
may be serious even although such wounds are usually aseptic; thus, of 36 injuries due
to broken lenses, Keeney (1960) found that 10 resulted in legal blindness.

To provide protection against injury from flying particles that would splinter
ordinary glasses, a REINFORCED or LAMINATED LENS may be used; such lenses are
also useful for motorists and aviators, for children or those who play games wearing
their spectacles. A great many such types of safety glass are commercially available (Triplex, Salvoc, and so on), but in all cases the principle involved is the
same. Two pieces of glass enclose between them a lamina of cellulose acetate or
some related material and the three are cemented together by a wet process or
fused by a dry process carried out under heat and pressure. In some types the edges
are sealed with an enamel to protect the interior from damp, but in most cases there
is a tendency for the organic material in the middle to become discoloured after long
exposure to sunlight. Such lenses can be worked into optical form, but are thicker
than ordinary lenses since at least 0·7 mm. thickness of glass must be left on either
side of the lamina to give stability to the finished lens. Toughened glass[5] also provides
an efficient protection. PLASTIC LENSES, of course, are breakable only with great
difficulty and do not shatter, but disintegrate into large fragments with blunt edges
and are therefore an efficient protection.

[1] Vol. XIV.   [2] Vol. XIV.   [3] Vol. XIV.
[4] Five cases in 150,000 ocular accidents, Lauber (1923); 11 out of 133 consecutive incised
wounds of the globe, Moncreiff and Scheribel (1945); 9 cases in 1,099 industrial ocular injuries,
Kaufmann (1956).
[5] p. 626.

Beer. *Das Auge*, Wien, **8**, 158 (1813).

Bell. *J. Amer. med. Ass.*, **140**, 1024 (1919).

Benton and Welsh. *Spectacles for Aphakia*, Springfield, 35, 119 (1966).

Bernstein. *Prakt. Hb. f. Wundärzte*, Leipzig, **3**, 551 (1819).

Braunschweig. *Klin. Mbl. Augenheilk.*, **65**, 535 (1920).

Burns, Hanley, Pietri and Welsh. *Amer. J. Ophthal.*, **35**, 1489 (1952).

Carson. *J. aviat. Med.*, **14**, 10 (1943).

Crookes. *Phil. Trans. A*, **214**, 1 (1914).

Duane, Emrich and Shepler. *Arch. Ophthal.*, **61**, 561 (1959).

Dudgeon. *Nature* (Lond.), **3**, 121, 387 (1870–71).

Phil. Mag., **41**, 350 (1871).

Dugan. *Man under the Sea*, N.Y. (1956).

Fenton. *Trans. ophthal. Soc. U.K.*, **88**, 451 (1968).

Fieuzal. *Ann. Oculist.* (Paris), **94**, 260 (1885); **98**, 87 (1887).

Galton. *Rep. Brit. Ass.* (Birmingham), **35**, Trans., 10 (1865).

Gullstrand. *v. Graefes Arch. Ophthal.*, **49**, 46 (1899).

Ann. Physik (Drude), **18**, 941 (1905).

Hallauer. *Ber. dtsch. ophthal. Ges.*, **34**, 334 (1907).

Hecht and Williams. *J. gen. Physiol.*, **5**, 1 (1922–23).

Hyde, Forsythe and Cady. *J. Franklin Inst.*, **185**, 829 (1918).

Kaufmann. *Canad. med. Ass. J.*, **75**, 284 (1956).

Keeney. *Surv. Ophthal.*, **5**, 405 (1960).

Lauber. *Hb. d. ärztlichen Berufsberatung*, Berlin (1923).

Lubkin, Linksz and Chamby. *Amer. J. Ophthal.*, **67**, 547 (1969).

Lubkin, Stollerman and Linksz. *Amer. J. Ophthal.*, **61**, 273 (1966).

Martin. *An Essay on Visual Glasses, Vulgarly called Spectacles*, London, 24 (1760).

Miles. *Fed. Proc.*, **2**, 109 (1943).

Mosse. *Brit. J. physiol. Opt.*, **21**, 250 (1964).

Moncreiff and Scheribel. *Amer. J. Ophthal.*, **28**, 1212 (1945).

Reid. *Brit. med. J.*, **2**, 259 (1935).

von Rohr. *Zbl.-Z. Opt. Mech.*, **40**, 137, 146, 156 (1919).

Die Brille als optisches Instrument; Graefe-Saemisch Hb. d. ges Augenheilk., 3rd ed., Berlin (1921).

Schanz and Stockhausen. *Electrotechn. Z.*, **29**, 777 (1908).

Skinner. *Phil. Mag.*, **45**, 461 (1815).

Strebel. *Klin. Mbl. Augenheilk.*, **71**, 236 (1923).

Volk. *Amer. J. Ophthal.*, **51**, 615 (1961).

Walsh and Smith. *Amer. J. Ophthal.*, **61**, 914 (1966).

Welsh. *Postoperative-Cataract Spectacle Lenses*, Miami (1961).

Weston and Adams. *Indust. Hlth. Res. Bd.*, London, Rep. No. 40 (1927); No. 49 (1928); No. 57 (1929).

Wiener. *Arch. Ophthal.*, **55**, 362 (1926).

Young. *Arch. Ophthal.*, **2**, 560 (1929).

CHAPTER XVIII

CONTACT LENSES

HISTORY

THE germ of the idea of contact lenses was conceived by Leonardo da Vinci about 1508[1] who suggested immersing the eye (or eyes) in a hollow glass bowl containing water (Fig. 730). A somewhat similar suggestion was made by Descartes (1637) who wrote : " . . . if one applies directly against the eye a tube full of water . . . at the end of which there is a glass whose shape is exactly like that of the skin [cornea] . . . there will no longer be any refraction at the entry of this eye " (Fig. 731). It is interesting that Descartes recognized that his idea was impracticable owing to the difficulties arising from obtaining the correct radius of curvature of the glass at the end of the tube and of applying it completely filled with water to the eye and supporting it there ; he therefore abandoned the idea in favour of a simple glass cone anticipating the mid-nineteenth century Steinheil cone.[2] This idea was greatly improved by the French mathematician, de la Hire (1685), who suggested the use of a concave " glass " upon the eye, the inner surface having the same convexity as the cornea so that the corneal refraction was eliminated and " the aqueous humour and the glass were considered as one humour "[3] (Fig. 732).

The first careful observations were made by that great pioneer of physiological optics, Thomas Young (1801), who sought to abolish the optical disadvantages of the corneal curvature by an ingenious although crude home-made apparatus formed by sticking with wax a lens from an old botanical microscope onto a glass tube $\frac{1}{4}$ in. long, filling the tube with water and applying it to his eye. His concept was the simple expedient of eliminating the cornea with its frequently irregular optical properties from the dioptric system of the eye and substituting for it a regularly ground lens, an easy matter since aqueous humour, cornea and water have virtually the same refractive index and therefore act as a single optical medium. It is interesting that almost a century later the same idea was taken up in the HYDRODIASCOPES of Lohnstein of Berlin (1896–97) and Siegrist of Switzerland in 1897 (see 1916). The later form of this device was a shallow metal cup filled with water, fitting closely to the orbital margin by a rubber rim and strapped round the head with an elastic band, and provided with a suitably ground window of glass in front (Fig. 733) : at its best it was, of course, unwieldy and impracticable.

After Thomas Young, the next suggestion came from Sir John Herschel (1830), the English astronomer who, commenting on Airy's invention of lenses to correct astigmatism, speculated on the possibility of eliminating this defect by applying to the eye a glass capsule containing a transparent animal jelly in contact with the cornea, the glass being moulded to correspond to the shape of the eye. Apart from the suggestion of William White Cooper (1859) that symblepharon after a lime burn might be prevented by placing a "glass mask" in the eye and filling the fornices, there is no record of any attempt to put this idea into practice until more than 60 years had passed when, in 1887, Saemisch suggested to A. C. Müller (Fig. 729), one of the famous family of glass-blowers and artificial eye-makers of Wiesbaden, that he make a protective shell

---

[1] Codex D of Leonardo's notebooks; see Ravaisson Mollien, *Les manuscrits de Leonard de Vinci*, Paris (1881–91); Hofstetter and Graham, *Amer. J. Optom.*, **30**, 41 (1953).

[2] p. 818.   [3] See Levene, *History of Science*, **6**, 90 (1967); *Contacts*, **25**, (2), 13 (1969).

FIG. 729.—ALBERT CARL MÜLLER
[1864–1923].

FIGS. 730–732.—EARLY IDEAS ON CONTACT LENSES.

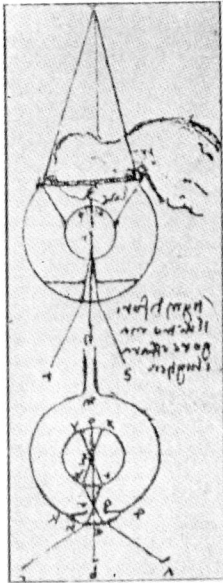

FIG. 730.—Leonardo da Vinci (c. 1508).

FIG. 731.—René Descartes (1637).

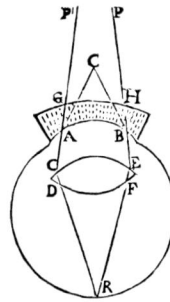

FIG. 732.—Phillipe de la Hire (1685).

FIG. 730.—A ball of glass is made with a diameter of ⅜ of a braccia; from one side of it a piece should be cut so that the face can be put into it as far as the ears. The ball is filled with clear luke-warm water. In the glass there is a smaller ball of thin glass and "you will see that this instrument sends out images to your eye, as the eye sends them to the visual sense". The optical system depicted below is, of course, not correct (Manuscript D, folio 3 V, Institut de France).

FIG. 731.—Descartes's draw-tube full of water applied to the eye having a glass at its far end fashioned to conform to the curvature of the cornea (from *La dioptrique*, 1637 edition).

FIG. 732.—A contact glass is placed directly on the cornea.

for a patient who had complete lagophthalmos after operative removal of the lid for malignant disease (see F. A. and A. C. Müller, 1910): the patient wore the device for 21 years until his death, retaining his corneal transparency.

In the following year three ophthalmologists independently and simultaneously produced contact lenses in different ways for different purposes—A. E. Fick (1888) of Zürich, who introduced the term *contact lens* (*Kontaktbrille*) and used a blown glass from a plaster mould taken from the eye for the optical treatment of conical cornea, E. Kalt (1888) of Paris, who used a moulded lens as an orthopædic splint in the same condition to mould the cornea into a more normal shape, and A. Müller of Gladbach (1889) who devised the first ground glass and used it to correct his own myopia of 14 D. A. Müller also experimented with the use of the

FIG. 733.—THE HYDRO-DIASCOPE OF SIEGRIST.

recently introduced cocaine as a local anæsthetic and suggested but never successfully carried out the process of taking a mould of the human eye; none of the many lenses produced for him by Himmler, an optician in Berlin, could be tolerated for more than half an hour.

Thereafter experience began to accumulate rapidly. In the case of scleral lenses this involved the development of ground and moulded lenses instead of the original blown types; there followed the use of plastic materials instead of glass and the introduction of corneal contact lenses. Originally, before the introduction of sulphonamides and antibiotics, the fear of a corneal abrasion with the tragic consequences it might entail made it advisable unless for clamant reasons to use a large scleral lens with a wide interspace filled with fluid between it and the corneal surface; but when infection could be readily controlled the more easily manipulated corneal lens rapidly became popular and many varieties were introduced. It is obvious, however, that the story of the development of contact lenses has not yet been completed and much more research is required before finality is reached on the subject. Today the subject is changing so rapidly and there are so many individual methods of practice that it is inevitable that many of the suggestions made in this chapter will be contradicted by some authorities.

Descartes. *La dioptrique*. In *Discours de la méthode*, Leyden (1637).

Fick. *Arch. Augenheilk.*, **18**, 279 (1888).

Herschel. *Encyclopædia metropolitana*, London, **2**, 398 (1830).

de la Hire (1685). See *Mem. Acad. roy. Sci. depuis* 1666–1699, Paris, **9**, 530 (1730).

Kalt. *Bull. Acad. Méd. Paris*, **19**, 400 (1888).

Lohnstein. *Klin. Mbl. Augenheilk.*, **34**, 405 (1896); **35**, 97, 132, 266 (1897).

Müller, A. *Brillengläser und Hornhautlinsen* (Diss.), Kiel (1889).

Müller, F. A. and A. C. *Das künstliche Auge*, Wiesbaden, 68 (1910).

Siegrist. *Klin. Mbl. Augenheilk.*, **56**, 400 (1916).

Young. *Phil. Trans.*, **92**, 23 (1801).

CONTACT LENSES AND CORNEAL PHYSIOLGY

The basic principles of the physiology of the cornea have been fully discussed in a previous Volume[1] where it was pointed out that the thickness and transparency of this tissue are maintained by a process of active dehydration mediated largely by the epithelium and endothelium. We have also noted that of the two important metabolites, glucose and oxygen, the latter enters the cornea normally from the atmosphere after being dissolved in the tear-film. A contact lens must therefore be expected to have a considerable effect on the functioning of the corneal epithelium by acting as a barrier to the reoxygenation of the tear-film beneath it. There are, however, other physiological problems to be considered such as effects on the corneal metabolism, changes in the reaction, the flow and the temperature of the tears, and alterations in the corneal sensitivity. Unfortunately, in all these problems our knowledge is still incomplete but their study is necessary before we consider the optical and mechanical problems associated with the wearing of contact lenses.

The most important and dramatic problem is the occurrence of *corneal œdema* which may lead to considerable damage to this tissue and may occur with any type of contact lens, particularly scleral lenses and tightly fitting corneal lenses. This condition was first noted by Fick (1888) and A. Müller

[1] Vol. IV, p. 339.

of Gladbach (1889), but since it was extensively studied by C. H. Sattler of Königsberg (1931–46) it has frequently been referred to as *Sattler's veil*. Corneæ appear to vary in their thresholds for the occurrence of œdema, but veiling usually commences with an (unventilated) scleral lens from 40 minutes to 14 hours after it has been inserted and tends to progress until the lens is removed, in the meantime giving rise to blurring of the vision and the appearance of haloes around lights. The phenomenon is essentially due to anoxia aided by the stagnation of the fluid beneath the lens (Anderson, 1944; Dallos, 1946; Bier, 1947), to which may be added the element of negative hydrostatic pressure (Ruben, 1967; Ridley, 1967), and if unrelieved it may lead to exfoliation of the epithelium and the occurrence of considerable damage.

It has been amply shown that such an anoxia is caused by a scleral lens (Langham and Taylor, 1956). It was demonstrated by Hill and Fatt (1963) that there is normally a progressive decrease in oxygen-tension across the cornea from without inwards; in the closed eye the tension falls to about $\frac{1}{3}$ of its previous value at the epithelial surface, the atmospheric oxygen being replaced to some extent by a supply to the tear-film from the tarsal capillaries (Langham, 1952), but under a flush-fitting scleral lens no alternative source is available and the oxygen-tension becomes very low indeed. The insertion of a hard corneal lens has been found in experimental animals to lead to a depletion of oxygen within 30 to 60 seconds (Hill and Fatt, 1964), an effect seen also with a hydrophilic lens (Hill, 1967). With a corneal lens, however, the movements on blinking lead to some exposure of the cornea and renewal of the tear-film beneath it so that the seriousness of the depletion of oxygen is reduced. The anoxia as well as the stagnation of fluid can be largely obviated in a scleral lens by *ventilation*, a suggestion made by Dallos (1946), either by holes (*fenestrated lens*) or by a groove (*channelled lens*) communicating with the perilimbal fluid. Owing to its free movement a corneal lens requires this expedient less frequently; here also fenestrations may increase the transfer of air and fluid even although some depression of the oxygen-uptake still occurs (Ruben, 1967). The appropriate techniques for dealing with this will be subsequently discussed.

Metabolic changes also occur, but these are more indefinite and of less serious import. Glucose is available to the cornea both from the tears and the aqueous humour and is metabolized by both aerobic and anaerobic pathways.[1] It is not known if a contact lens interferes with the first source of supply, but a deprivation of oxygen favours the anaerobic route of metabolism with an accumulation of lactic acid and CO_2 as end-products. An increase in lactic acid was demonstrated in the fluid beneath a contact lens by McCulloch and Morley (1961) and of CO_2 by Hill and Fatt (1963) with a consequent alteration in its reaction. It may be noted that no corresponding

[1] Vol. IV, p. 357.

increase in the CO_2 in the aqueous humour was found in rabbits fitted with a contact lens by McCulloch and Fielding (1963).

Although no evidence is forthcoming, it is possible that epithelial damage may alter the stroma by damaging the dehydrating mechanism mediated by this layer of cells; it may thus be that metabolic changes combine to some extent with mechanical factors in altering the shape of the cornea.

A minimal rise in the *temperature* of the corneo-lenticular fluid probably occurs. Hill and Leighton (1963–65) found that the slight rise in temperature in human and animal eyes stabilized within 3 or 4 minutes after the insertion of a lens as it does during closure of the lids, and that the maximal sensation of pressure was related to the maximum height of the temperature. The sensation of heat experienced by some patients cannot be correlated with this and requires a very high stimulus (Kenshalo, 1960). The effects of this hyperthermia are unknown but it is theoretically possible that a reduced solubility of oxygen and an increased demand for it by the epithelium may result.

The changes in *corneal sensitivity* are of more importance. Although it has been claimed that a fall in sensitivity occurs only with poorly fitted lenses (Moore and McCollum, 1967), most observers have established that this is a common although not an invariable phenomenon.[1] The hypo-æsthesia may be of value in the process of adaptation to the lens, particularly in aphakic patients fitted soon after the surgical operation when the corneal sensitivity is low, but it has the disadvantage that corneal complications may not be noticed by the patient.

Disturbances of the tears are also noteworthy. The adequate production of tears is essential for the preservation of as normal a physiological state as possible when contact lenses are being worn; if there is any doubt about this a Schirmer's test[2] may be advisable as a preliminary to the procedure of fitting. Moreover, the free mobility of tears under the lens allowing a replenishment of oxygen and perhaps of glucose as well as facilitating the removal of carbon dioxide is a physiological necessity; with corneal lenses the movements of blinking are also important in this respect. A copious flow of tears is deleterious; it leads to increased mobility and lack of centration of the lens, causing new stimuli and leading to spasm of the lids. Excessive lacrimation will also alter the chemical composition of the tears, making them relatively hypotonic. The lipids in the tears normally coat the epithelium, preventing drying of this layer and an abnormal relationship may induce œdema (Mishima and Maurice, 1961); an excess of lipids, however, as occurs with excessive meibomian secretion, leads to discomfort and also blurs the vision. It has also been claimed that

---

[1] Boberg-Ans (1955–6), Bronner and Gerhard (1958), Cochet and Bonnet (1960), Hamano (1960), Bryon and Weseley (1961), Schirmer and Mellor (1961), Schirmer (1963), Dixon (1964).
[2] Vol. XIII.

the proteins in the tears, perhaps conjugated with polysaccharides, may play a part in the adequate wetting of the ocular surface membranes as well as of a contact lens (Ridley, 1967 ; Dabezies, 1967). There is a suggestion that a deficiency of lysozyme or of other protein components may be associated with a poor tolerance of corneal lenses (Halberg, 1967). It is also possible that the slight increase in the leucocytes in the tears while a contact lens is being worn may augment the bacteriostatic activity of lysozyme (Dixon, 1964). Finally, the physical properties of the tear-film must be considered. Tears are more viscous than water and their high surface tension plays an important part in determining the position adopted by a corneal lens ; moreover, the pre-corneal film shows some elasticity and compressibility. These properties are most readily judged by the appearance of the marginal strips along the lids where the lacrimal film is retained by the lipids of the meibomian secretion ; it would seem that a thick elastic and mobile film favours rapid adaptation to the wearing of a corneal lens.

Anderson. *Technic of Fitting Contact Lenses*, Minneap. (1944).
Bier. *Amer. J. Optom.*, **24**, 611 (1947).
Boberg-Ans. *Brit. J. Ophthal.*, **39**, 705 (1955). *Acta ophthal.* (Kbh.), **34**, 149 (1956).
Bronner and Gerhard. *Bull. Soc. Ophtal. Fr.*, Nos. 7/8, p. i (1958).
Byron and Weseley. *Amer. J. Ophthal.*, **51**, 675 (1961).
Cochet and Bonnet. *Clin. ophtal.*, **4**, 1 (1960).
Cooper. *Wounds and Injuries of the Eye*, London (1859)
Dabezies. *Corneal and Scleral Contact Lenses* (ed. Girard), St. Louis, 347 (1967).
Dallos. *Brit. J. Ophthal.*, **30**, 607 (1946).
Dixon. *Amer. J. Ophthal.*, **58**, 424 (1964).
Fick. *Arch. Augenheilk.*, **18**, 279 (1888).
Halberg. *Corneal and Scleral Contact Lenses* (ed. Girard), St. Louis, 167 (1967).
Hamano. *Contacto*, **4**, 41 (1960).
Hill. *J. Amer. optom. Ass.*, **38**, 181 (1967).
Hill and Fatt. *Science*, **142**, 1295 (1963). *Amer. J. Optom.*, **41**, 678 (1964).
Hill and Leighton. *Amer. J. Optom.*, **40**, 427 (1963) ; **42**, 9, 72 (1965).
Kenshalo. *J. appl. Physiol.*, **15**, 987 (1960).

Langham. *J. Physiol.*, **117**, 461 (1952).
Langham and Taylor. *Brit. J. Ophthal.*, **40**, 321 (1956).
McCulloch and Fielding. *Amer. J. Ophthal.*, **56**, 57 (1963).
McCulloch and Morley. *Arch. Ophthal.*, **66**, 379 (1961).
Mishima and Maurice. *Exp. Eye Res.*, **1**, 39 (1961).
Moore and McCollum. *Corneal and Scleral Contact Lenses* (ed. Girard), St. Louis, 408 (1967).
Müller, A. *Brillengläser und Hornhautlinsen* (Diss.), Kiel (1889).
Ridley. *Corneal and Scleral Contact Lenses* (ed. Girard), St. Louis, 200 (1967).
Ruben. *Trans. ophthal. Soc. U.K.*, **87**, 27, 643, 661 (1967).
Sattler. *Dtsch. med. Wschr.*, **57**, 312 (1931). *Klin. Mbl. Augenheilk.*, **100**, 172, 482 (1938) ; **111**, 184 (1945–6).
Schirmer. *Brit. J. Ophthal.*, **47**, 488, 493 (1963).
Schirmer and Mellor. *Arch. Ophthal.*, **65**, 433 (1961).

Scleral Contact Lenses

A SCLERAL CONTACT LENS overrides the cornea and rests upon the sclera ; it consists of two portions, the OPTICAL (corneal) central part and the HAPTIC[1] (scleral) part. Apart from the effectiveness of the optical correction, the suitability of the fitting to the sclera (haptics) is most important for upon this the comfort of wearing the lenses and therefore their practical value largely depend.

[1] ἅπτω, to bind together.

BLOWN CONTACT LENSES

The original work on blown contact lenses by A. C. Müller in 1887 was continued in Wiesbaden and, in 1909, a contact lens was produced rather like an artificial eye with an opaque scleral portion and a transparent corneal region (Fig. 734). Since, however, it is not practicable to blow glass so that the inside and outside curvatures are optically exact, blown lenses can eliminate the corneal curvature but cannot achieve optical accuracy, for any attempt to grind a focal lens on its corneal portion presents great technical difficulties owing to the high internal strains of blown glass. The selection of the correct blown contact lens for a particular patient was therefore a tedious and difficult task and reproduction was not possible should the lens be lost or broken. Blown lenses therefore remained out of favour until the firm of Müller-Welt of Stuttgart (1935) announced the development of more accurate lenses which were blown over pre-formed toric castings to form

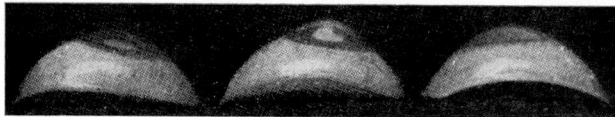

FIG. 734.—THE BLOWN CONTACT LENSES OF F. E. MÜLLER.
They are afocal and have no corneo-scleral shoulder.

the scleral portion; the corneal segment was later ground and polished to whatever refraction was required. The use of a pre-formed toric casting followed from the investigations of Dallos (1933) on the shape of the sclera as determined by castings of the human eye. This work led naturally to the idea of moulded lenses.

GROUND CONTACT LENSES

After the preliminary experiments of A. Müller, the firm of Zeiss, at the suggestion of Sulzer (1892), first turned their attention to ground contact lenses in 1892 and in 1911 they turned out a systematized series (Fig. 735). The lenses were ground in two segments of different spherical curvatures, the outer portion resting on the sclera and the inner arching over the cornea (Fig. 736). At first they were afocal, but the expedient was adopted by Heine (1929–30) of varying the radii of curvature of the corneal portion so as to vary the strength of the effective fluid lens between the glass and the cornea; the focal point of the system was thus moved forwards or back-wards according to whether hypermetropia or myopia was to be corrected and any necessary residual correction was ground on the outer surface of the glass. Corneal astigmatism, of course, was automatically eliminated. For many errors of refraction, however, the limitations of this method make accurate optical correction impossible and a large number of standard types was required to attain suitable combinations of scleral and corneal curvatures (500 according to Heine). To obviate this, Gualdi (1931–34) suggested that the scleral radii alone should be made variable for fitting, that one continuous curve should be ground on the back surface and that the front surface should be specifically ground to suit the refraction, thus eliminating a multitude of combinations of scleral and corneal curvatures. The technical difficulties of adding a high corrective power (−20 to −18 D) to the central area of the contact lens were eventually solved by Dallos (1933). The technique then developed into the fitting of the patient from a standard set with a comfortable lens which matched the sclera and cleared the cornea, determining the refraction at this stage, and grinding the required spherical correction onto the front surface. Although these lenses were used with some success[1] and although a toric scleral curvature was introduced by

FIG. 735.—THE GROUND CONTACT LENSES OF ZEISS.

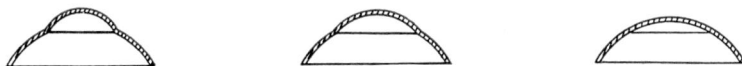

FIG. 736.—DIFFERENT COMBINATIONS OF CURVATURE IN THE CORNEAL AND SCLERAL SEGMENTS OF A ZEISS CONTACT LENS.

In the three lenses illustrated the corneal curvature has a different optical efficiency while the scleral curvature is the same.

Feinbloom (1940–41) allowing for differences between the horizontal and vertical scleral radii, as a general rule they were uncomfortable owing to the fact that the scleral curvature is extremely variable and frequently astigmatic, following no mathematically expressible curve (Erggelet, 1930; Strebel, 1937; Bruce, 1937; and others). It thus became clear that simple curves for the corneal and scleral parts were inadequate.

MOULDED CONTACT LENSES

Fick (1888) had originally experimented with plaster moulds, first on the eyes of rabbits, then of cadavers, of himself and finally of patients, but it was not until von Csapody (1929–30) hit upon the hydrocolloid dental impression material " Dentacoll " that the method became clinically practicable. The credit for the development of the technique is essentially due to J. Dallos (1932–38), first of Budapest and later of London who, using Poller's "Negocoll", a preparation made for dental work in 1928, was able to make practicable negative casts of the eye. By pressing the glass into a positive

---

[1] Strebel (1937), Reid (1938), Sattler (1938–46), Eggers (1939), and many others.

metal mould fashioned from such a cast he made an asymmetrical and individually fitting scleral portion, and subsequently ground both surfaces of the corneal portion as was required for optical purposes (Fig. 737).

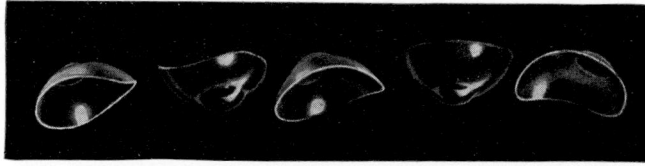

FIG. 737.—THE MOULDED GLASS CONTACT LENSES OF DALLOS.

The Dallos moulded contact lens made of glass represented a major advance in the subject but its production, modification and reproducibility were far from straight-forward. The firm of Zeiss in Jena, however, produced moulded contact lenses of glass from individual castings for an experimental period before the second World War. The principle of moulding was further developed by Feinbloom (1937) who introduced plastic materials into the field of contact lenses in America; he originally employed plastic for the (opaque) scleral part only, while the corneal portion was of optical glass. The early versions of such a lens had a haptic portion which was moulded from indi-vidual castings, but Feinbloom abandoned this in favour of standardized " scleral " matrices of spherical or toric shape; the scleral portions of such lenses were again opaque. Thereafter, he (1945) abandoned the concept of overall contact of the scleral portion

FIG. 738.—OBRIG'S PLASTIC CONTACT LENS.

of the lens with the globe and designed an all-plastic *pre-formed lens*, the *tangent cone* or Feincone, in which the corneal segment was joined onto a conical rim, the latter being in contact with the sclera only by tangential touch. Lenses of celluloid (Teissler, 1937) and pre-formed lenses made of an acrylic resin (Thier, 1939; Fritz, 1939) were tentatively developed in Europe about the same time that Feinbloom began using plastic material in America.

The *all-plastic lens* moulded from individual castings was first introduced in 1938 in Europe by von Györffy (1940–64) and in America by Obrig (1942) of New York (Fig. 738). Obrig chanced upon the value of fluorescein in determining areas of contact between a lens and the globe; where the lens is not in contact the green colour of the fluorescein was easily seen, particularly when viewed through cobalt-blue glass. During his work on the fitting of the Zeiss moulded contact lenses of glass it became clear that the corneal portion was too small and that their weight led to their exerting pressure on part of the limbus. Györffy and Obrig realized that the plastic polymethyl methacrylate developed about 1936 had many qualities which make it eminently suitable for contact lenses. Apart from its lightness it is inert to bodily secretions and retains its transparency which is as high as that of optical glass; moreover, it is unbreakable to practically all the usual traumata that a patient might experience. A different method was suggested by Ridley (1946) who described plastic lenses cut on a lathe from a solid block of plastic (methyl methacrylate; Transpex) which could be prepared (in spherical or oval shape) to any corneal or overall diameter; these were made on the Zeiss principle. In the early 1940's, therefore, the plastic contact lens had established itself and schools of thought were emerging which continue today. First was the concept of individual moulding, against which was set the idea of the pre-formed lens.

To a minor extent this dichotomy has depended upon the availability of local anæsthesia for the technique of moulding, since in some countries the use of local analgesics by those who are not medically qualified is forbidden; pre-formed fitting has therefore often been favoured because it can be carried out without local anæsthesia and is more rapid than the moulding technique. It may also be the only method applicable to some children (Lake, 1964). Moulding is, of course, a procedure which needs considerable skill and time, but there seems little doubt that in principle it is the correct approach to the fitting of scleral lenses.

Whatever type of scleral lens was worn, the phenomenon of *veiling*[1] was beginning to be understood. It had become apparent that the facilitation of the interchange of fluid under the lens and therefore the avoidance of pressure on the limbal region were important and desirable factors in the design of scleral lenses and the introduction of the *ventilated lens* by fenestration (Dallos, 1946; Bier, 1947–48) or by channelling (Ridley, 1948) markedly reduced the incidence of this undesirable phenomenon. Before the employment of ventilated lenses, much attention had been paid to the type of solution used to fill the space between the lens and the cornea, in the (forlorn) hope that adjustments in its composition might have some influence on veiling. With the realization that the nature of this fluid was not of such importance as its potential stagnation, a trend was established towards minimizing its volume. The modern scleral contact lens, whether of the pre-formed or moulded type, is therefore most usually a ventilated lens with minimal apical clearance (about 0·1 mm.); it has a smooth transition between the corneal and scleral portions and adequate clearance of the limbus. Should the latter feature not be present the limbal tissues are traumatized and may swell with the result that the fluid under the lens is sealed off and becomes stagnant.

[1] p. 717.

MODERN SCLERAL CONTACT LENSES

PRE-FORMED SCLERAL LENSES of standard shapes are of two types, geometrical or anatomical. We have already noted one type of *geometrical lens*, the Feincone,[1] but it never became popular although several of its successors which owe something to it in design have been widely used.

Such lenses are based upon simple geometrical concepts; their parts and dimensions are shown in Figs. 739–40. The least sophisticated designs have one spherical curvature on the back haptic surface and one spherical curvature on the back optic portion. A typical specification of such a lens would give the radii of curvature of the haptic and optic portions, the overall size or lengths of the longest and shortest axes if oval, and any displacement of the optic portion and the dioptric power. The back optic surface is occasionally of two curvatures, central and peripheral, the latter being flatter. The transitional zone between the two may be spherical as in the " transcurve " design of Bier and Cole (1948) or conical as in the original Feincone lens and later in the Nissel wide-angle lens (Fig. 741). The haptic portion may be toroidal instead of spherical and designs are employed which incorporate multiple haptic curvatures such as the offset blended curves of Forknall (1959) and the double offset curves of Biri (1968) (Figs. 742–3).

Anatomical pre-formed lenses are of designs which are obtained by vast

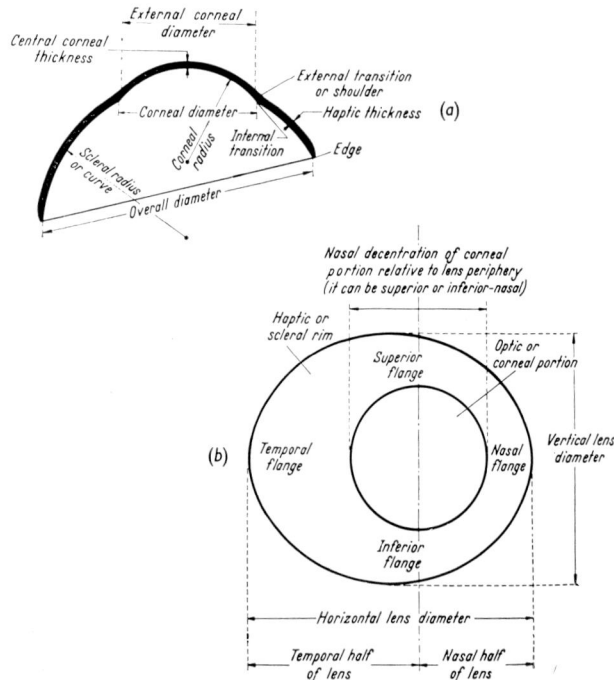

FIG. 739.—ONE SYSTEM OF NOMENCLATURE OF A SCLERAL CONTACT LENS.
(a) Section, and (b) plan view (N. Bier).

[1] p. 722.

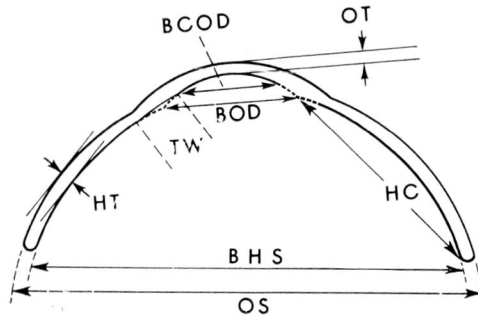

FIG. 740.—PARTS OF A SCLERAL CONTACT LENS.

BHS, back haptic size; BOD, back optic diameter; HC, haptic chord; HT, haptic thickness; OT, thickness of optic portion; OS, overall size; TW, transition width (British Standards terminology).

experience of the mouldings of normal eyes, with particular reference to the corneal, scleral and limbal zones: Dallos, Treissman, Cottereau, and Dudragne have all assembled trial lenses based on this principle (Fig. 744).

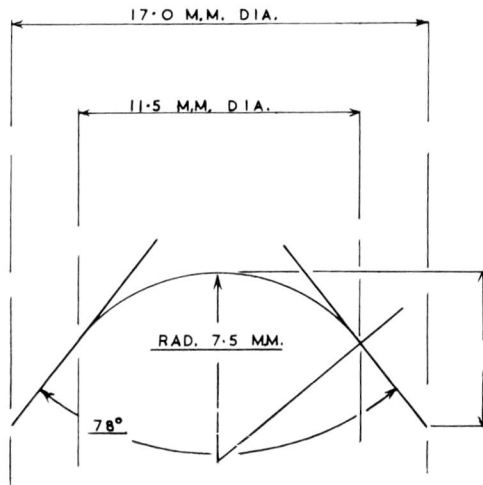

FIG. 741.—THE CONE ANGLE OF THE NISSEL WIDE-ANGLE SCLERAL CONTACT LENS.

MOULDED SCLERAL LENSES are based on castings taken from the individual patient's eye. These are carried out by introducing into the palpebral aperture a readily impressionable material in the melted form which sets rapidly and firmly to form a negative cast. To find a substance for the initial negative cast which combines adequate ease of preparation, absence of irritation, ready melting and setting properties with sufficient elasticity to maintain its shape during removal from the eye, has caused some difficulty and excited many suggestions.

FIGS. 742 and 743.—SCLERAL LENSES BASED ON GEOMETRICAL DESIGNS.

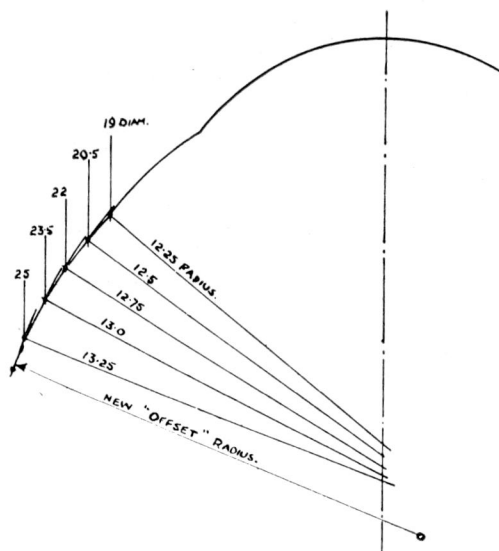

FIG. 742.—Forknall's lens. Progressive flattening of the scleral portion produced by zones of increasing radii of curvature with offset radius.

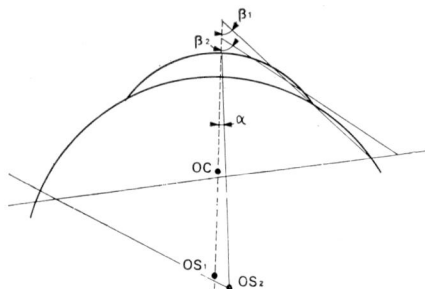

FIG. 743.—Biri's lens. Selective flattening of the scleral portion obtained by two surfaces of different spherical curvature, OS_1 and OS_2, giving angles a, β_1 and β_2. OC, centre of the corneal curvature.

The first was a material used for dental impressions (Dentacoll) by von Csapody (1930); thereafter Negocoll, a hydrocolloid formulated by Poller of Vienna, the base of which was agar to which cotton fibres imparted internal strength, was introduced by Dailos (1933) but it must be used hot and takes some time to prepare. These features prompted a search for more suitable materials and other substances were suggested such as Zelex, (Boshoff, 1943) ophthalmic Moldite,[1] Cosmet, Optimold, Super-Kromopan; the latter has a coloured constituent which changes to indicate that setting is occurring. The chief advantages of these materials over Negocoll are that they can be inserted cold and that they set rapidly.

Special plastic shells are employed to apply the material to the eye (Figs. 745).

[1] Moldite is made of gypsum, light magnesium carbonate, dental plaster, trisodium phosphate and sodium alginate.

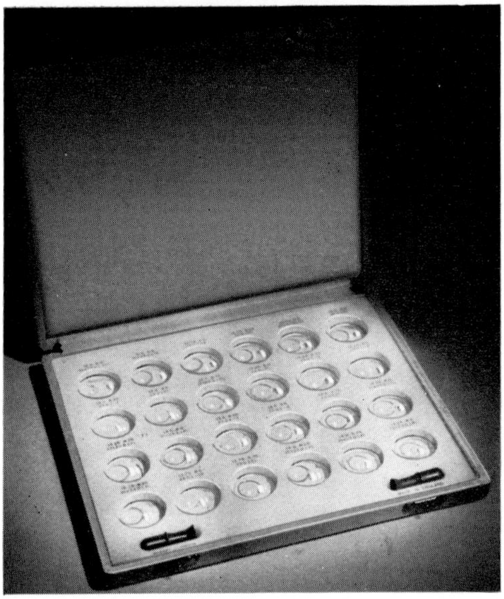

FIG. 744.—PRE-FORMED SCLERAL LENSES.
Trial case of 24 wide-angle lenses (G. Nissel).

These vary according to the technique adopted but all have holes in them so that the excess casting material can flow out, locking the mould once it is set. The two principal techniques employed are the insertion method or the injection method. In the former the casting material is applied to the shell which is then inserted between the subject's lids and gently pressed onto the globe. In the injection method the moulding shell is first put into position under the lids and then the material is injected through the hollow handle of the instrument.

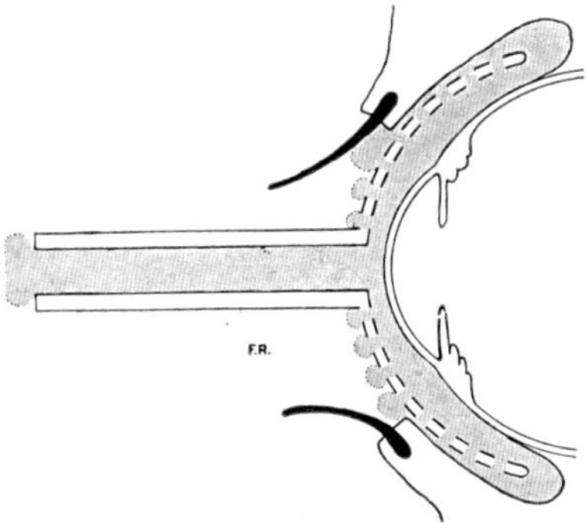

FIG. 745.—THE MOULDING TRAY *in situ*.
It is filled with the moulding material, inserted beneath the lids and the excess material escapes through the perforations (F. Ridley).

Both methods produce good results but skill and practice are required. In the insertion method the placement of the " loaded " shell is difficult. In the injection method it is not easy to ensure that the material has spread evenly over the globe and it is more difficult to remove the cast when it is set without breaking the impression. Subjectively, however, the patient notices little difference between the two techniques. In both the eye is anæsthetized and it is usual to take the mould with the eye in a slightly convergent (10°) and depressed (30–40°) position, some convenient target being fixed by the other eye, but account must be taken of any latent or manifest ocular deviation. In this position the temporal and superior portions of the eye will be suitably represented and the convergent position avoids a false impression produced by the greater bulk of the medial rectus relative to that of the lateral (Marriott, 1966).

The process of moulding may itself alter the shape of the globe, particularly the haptic portion, and part of the skill in taking an impression consists of a knowledge of the correct pressures at which to inject the material or how firmly to hold the shell against the eye. It is also important to avoid trapping air or pools of tears. In the best hands, however, the mould provides a reasonable reproduction of the shape of the anterior segment of the globe. It has in fact been shown that keratometric readings taken from the corneal segment of a mould are very similar to those of the patient's cornea.

From the impression a model of the anterior segment of the globe is made in one of the many substances, usually dental plasters, that are available (Albastone, Celestone, Celsta, Castite, Kaffir D). A shell is now fashioned by pressing a sheet of heated plastic onto the model. Before fitting the shell its back optic surface is usually cut or ground so as to give the lens minimal apical clearance from the cornea, and although some sealed (non-ventilated) lenses are still in use, most are ventilated either by fenestration or channelling. Some intended for therapeutic use, however, are of the flush-fitting type in which the lens closely follows the anterior surface of the cornea.[1] If a minimal apical clearance is desired, the back surface of the optical portion should be ground to a slightly flatter curve than that of the subject's cornea. The shell is then assessed as to its fit.

THE FIT OF SCLERAL CONTACT LENSES

To a large extent *the criteria of a satisfactory fit* are empirical, for experience has demonstrated that certain features of the lens–eye relationship signify how the patient will tolerate the lens or whether damage to the globe will occur. It follows that some features of the physical fit are still controversial; moreover, our imperfect knowledge of the physiological effects produced by the wearing of contact lenses frequently allows only *ad hoc* explanations to be provided for a patient's intolerance to a particular lens.

A properly fitting and well-designed scleral contact lens has the following features. The haptic (scleral) portion lies in even contact with the globe to within 2 to 3 mm. of the limbus with no very tight or loose areas, its temporal and superior regions being as large as possible and the nasal flange fitting moderately loosely to encourage the through-flow of tears and the outflow of debris.

The limbal region is cleared and there is no sharp transition between the haptic and optic portions. The optic is well centred on the cornea and,

---

[1] p. 786.

save in the flush-fitting variety, clears the apical region perhaps in its axial two-thirds by about 0·1 mm. The problem of the precise relationship between the lens and the corneal apex is unresolved. Although a minimal apical clearance is the theoretical ideal, it is likely that light central touch is present even in the primary position. The good tolerance of corneal lenses clearly indicates that such contact by scleral lenses need give rise to no undue alarm, and may even be desirable. In the peripheral zone of the cornea clearance becomes progressively greater until the limbal region is reached where it is at its maximum.

These relationships, however, cannot be accurately maintained because the physical fit of a scleral contact lens is not static but is altered on the

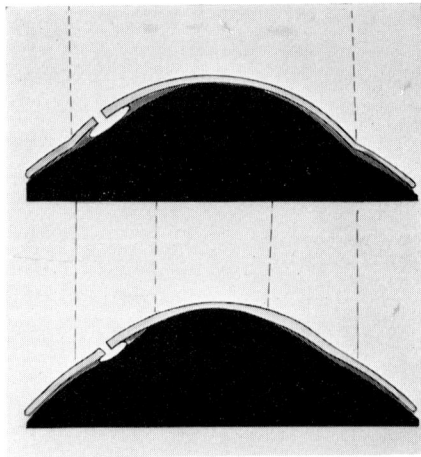

Fig. 746.—The Fenestrated Scleral Lens.
Above is a lens with a single back optic curve ; below a lens with two back optic curves (C. M. Ruben).

movements of the eye, a change which should be minimized. There must be no excessive lag of the lens on ocular movements, nor must it sag under its own weight ; some relative movement, however, is inevitable and probably desirable in order to encourage the exchange of fluid under the lens. Because of the progressive clearance towards the periphery of the cornea a concave meniscus of fluid exists between the lens and the eye, and when ventilated the fenestration or channel (groove) must communicate with this perilimbal meniscus (Fig. 746).

A fenestration is placed in the palpebral aperture, usually the temporal border of the optic and slightly above or below the mid-point of the pupil, and a bubble of air forms beneath the lens at this point (Fig. 747). In a well-fitted scleral lens the bubble is bean-shaped, about $\frac{1}{4}'' \times \frac{1}{8}''$ wide, in the primary position and with the movements of the eye it moves round the limbus. It may alter in size as air is sucked in or forced out ; the increase in

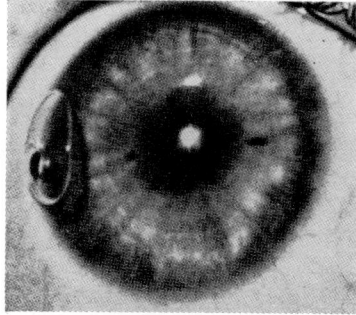

FIG. 747.—THE BUBBLE TEST.

The size of the bubble at the limbus in a fully-centred scleral contact lens when the eye is in the primary position (N. Bier).

the size on extreme ocular movements should never be so great that on return to the normal position there is undue delay in the refilling of the chamber between the lens and the eye. The bubble should remain confined to the limbal region and preferably the temporal portion; in the nasal or infranasal region it may interfere with vision.

A single channel usually suffices but occasionally more are employed; they are essentially gutters along the inner aspect of the haptic portion of

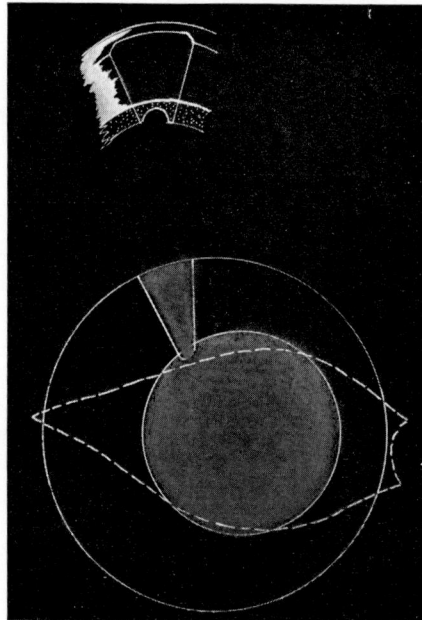

FIG. 748.—THE PLAN OF A CHANNELLED SCLERAL LENS.

The channel should have a wide shallow mouth at the periphery and should be narrower and deeper at the corneo-lens interspace (C. M. Ruben).

the lens and may conveniently be sited along already loose areas of the flange. Since they communicate externally with areas under the lids they are probably not as efficient as fenestrations (Ruben, 1967). Their shape is indicated in Fig. 748.

Scleral lenses designed and fitted in accordance with these principles will not unduly traumatize the eye and will allow adequate nutrition to the cornea by the facility of the interchange of fluid and perhaps of air beneath the lens. The fit of a scleral lens, however, alters not only with the movements of the eye but also with the passage of time, a process sometimes referred to as *settling*; to some extent this may be a moulding of the ocular tissues in association with the development of local œdema or a " herniation " forwards of the corneal apex.

A fenestrated lens tends to be more mobile and a relatively larger haptic portion may therefore be indicated. A sealed (non-ventilated) lens should have a looser haptic fit in order to encourage the through-flow of fluid; both this and the channelled lens rely more on negative hydrostatic pressure to keep their position than does the fenestrated type where such pressure does not exist, save temporarily on movements of the eyes. Again, a more markedly distinct degree of " settling " is a feature of the fenestrated lens and allowance must be made for this in the initial fitting; failing this, the initial minimal clearance may in time become an excessive apical touch.

The procedure adopted for the *clinical assessment and adjustment of the fit* varies with different practitioners. The fit may be inspected after inserting the lens dry but more commonly it is inserted with fluid to which a drop of fluorescein is added. The lens is marked to indicate the horizontal diameter either before it is inserted (by comparison with the mould) or when it is *in situ*.

The factors to be considered after insertion are the overall size and shape of the lens, its movement with the eye, the haptic bearing relationship, the transitional zone between the haptic and optic portions, the clearance and centring of the optic, and the behaviour of the bubble if the lens is of the non-sealed variety. If the lens is too small it may be cosmetically unacceptable because the edges of the haptic are visible; if it is too large it can be reduced in size at the appropriate site. Rotation indicates a gross error in the fitting and makes it impossible to mark areas which require modification; if it is present it may be necessary to carry out a fresh moulding, but some modification to any tight areas of the haptic seen by the blanching of the underlying conjunctival vessels, or to its edge if this is loose, may be effective in abolishing it.

Once the approximate overall size and stability are established it is advisable to make any desired fenestration and then to re-examine the fit. The position and mobility of the lens are assessed in white light, tight areas in the haptic are noted and marked, and the behaviour of the bubble is observed.

Apart from showing some undesirable features of size, position and mobility there may be a tendency for the bubble of air to break up into a froth with a disturbing effect on vision; excessive sebaceous material under the lens may have a similar effect. In the early stages froth or multiple bubbles are more common with ventilated than with sealed lenses; their presence may be an indication for an increase in corneal clearance or further ventilation. At the same time, loose areas of the haptic should receive attention since these allow an excessive entry of air which may not easily escape; the entry and escape of bubbles occurring with a loosely fitting lens may give rise to an unpleasant clicking sensation. Much sebaceous secretion is also common with ventilated lenses and, indeed, may be so marked as to preclude the use of any kind of contact lens.

The examination of the fluorescein pattern is carried out in light filtered through cobalt blue glass or in ultra-violet black light (wave-length 248 mμ)

Fig. 749.   Fig. 750.

Figs. 749 and 750.—Ultra-violet Black-light Lamp (G. Nissel).

(Figs. 749–50). These show loose areas in the haptic as pools of yellow-green fluorescence and positions of corneal touch as dark areas in the pattern. About the limbal region there should be a ring of fluorescence some 2 to 3 mm. in width if the clearance there is adequate (Plate IX). It is important to assess the fluorescein pattern not only in the primary position but also on movements of the eyes. Digital pressure on the lens may give some indication of the freedom or otherwise with which fluid can enter and leave the space behind it.

Any areas requiring modification are marked and the lens is removed. The precise details of the procedures used in modification are not within the scope of this book but, in principle, tight areas are ground out and polished and the region surrounding a loose zone is similarly treated. Heavy apical touch of the cornea requires increased clearance which can be gained by grinding the posterior surface of the optic.

Once the physical fit is satisfactory a refraction is carried out and the centre of the pupil is marked with the eye in the primary position. The lens is then finally adjusted for optical power and for haptic thickness, which is usually about 0·6 mm.

FACTORS IN THE SUCCESSFUL WEARING OF SCLERAL CONTACT LENSES

The wearing of a contact lens throughout the day is an ideal state which is probably less often obtained with scleral lenses than with the corneal type; nevertheless, wearing-times of 8 to 15 hours per day are not uncommon with the former provided they are properly fitted; particularly with the almost routine use of ventilation, such lenses can continue to be worn thus for many years. As with all types of contact lens, however, motivation is a potent factor in their toleration, since the initial and sometimes persistent discomfort is outweighed by cosmetic and considerable visual advantages. When the lenses are being worn for optical defects, three principal considerations are important: maximum clarity of vision, comfort in wearing them over prolonged periods, and the absence of damage to the eye or its adnexa. The patients most likely to conform to these criteria are those fitted in accordance with the principles we have enumerated; it is obvious, however, that these cannot be fully assessed initially for certain features such as, for example, poor vision due to the presence of too large an air-bubble or froth may be improved with continued use; in this knowledge the practitioner should encourage the patient to persevere.

The most important factor in obtaining good vision, however, is the accuracy of the *optical correction*. The objective and subjective refraction is usually examined with the contact lens in place, either an afocal or powered trial lenses or a shell obtained by moulding onto which a suitable back optic surface has been ground. The appropriate optical power is then worked on the front surface of the lens. In the majority of cases the refraction of a subject wearing a contact lens with a spherical anterior surface will show a simple spherical correction since the lens eliminates the corneal astigmatism; in some instances, however, a significant degree of residual astigmatism is found and this can be corrected by modifying the front surface of the optical part of the lens to a toroidal form. In ordering the incorporation of an optical correction it is usual to err in under-correcting myopia or over-correcting hypermetropia since in subsequent modifications it is easier to make the correction more myopic or less hypermetropic than the reverse.

A second factor in the visual performance of the scleral lens is the accurate centring of the optical portion which must be ensured during the procedure of fitting. It may be necessary to decentre the optic in relation to the haptic; but the former should not be tilted since this would produce unwanted prismatic effects. If, however, the incorporation of a prism is desirable this is possible up to about 3 △.

The question of the *tolerance* of scleral contact lenses raises difficult problems that are incompletely understood. During the process of adaptation the initial symptoms caused by the presence of a foreign body and many of the reflex responses to it become much less marked. Thus pain, lacrimation, blepharospasm and conjunctival injection which may be present in the early stages later disappear, while the sensation of a foreign body, the burning feeling and the sensation of stretching of the eyelids also markedly diminish. It should be realized, however, that a strongly motivated patient may adapt himself to wearing contact lenses even if their fit is not ideal; indeed, tolerance may in some cases be satisfactory in spite of the evidence of traumata to the globe.

Although clearance of the cornea is desirable with most scleral lenses it is likely that contact occurs in many cases with some movements of the globe. The nature of corneal touch is uncertain. In some instances there may still be a film of lacrimal fluid present between lens and corneal epithelium; in others this is not so and actual damage may occur. The degree of touch has been subdivided into " heavy " or " light ", and some practitioners regard the latter in certain positions of gaze as acceptable; others would go further and take no active steps even in the presence of fluorescein staining of the cornea, if the patient is seeing well, feels comfortable and shows no other signs of ocular irritation. In marked cases associated with persistent œdema, vascularization of the cornea may occur, but even in such instances the patient may have no particular discomfort since a degree of corneal anæsthesia undoubtedly develops after wearing a contact lens over a long period. The situation is, of course, quite the reverse when manifest damage such as frank ulceration of the cornea has occurred, since in this case symptoms and signs such as pain, photophobia, lacrimation, circumcorneal injection arise and persist. When tolerance is good it is likely that during the intervals when the lens is removed the corneal epithelium heals, but in others the re-insertion of the lens into an eye with an insufficiently healed epithelium may further aggravate the condition, symptoms will be experienced and intolerance will result.

Bier. *Amer. J. Optom.*, **24**, 611 (1947).
  Optician, **116**, 497 (1948).
Bier and Cole. *Optician*, **115**, 605 (1948).
Biri. *Cah. Verres Contact*, No. 16, 8 (1968).
Boshoff. *Arch. Ophthal.*, **29**, 282 (1943).
Bruce. *Amer. J. Ophthal.*, **20**, 605 (1937).
von Csapody. *Klin. Mbl. Augenheilk.*, **82**, 818 (1929); **85**, 116 (1930).
Dallos. *Klin. Mbl. Augenheilk.*, **89**, 108 (1932); **91**, 640 (1933).
  Arch. Ophthal., **15**, 617 (1936).
  Trans. ophthal. Soc. U.K., **57**, 509 (1937).
  Brit. J. Ophthal., **30**, 607 (1946).
Eggers. *Arch. Ophthal.*, **21**, 647; **22**, 403 (1939).
Erggelet. *Klin. Mbl. Augenheilk.*, **52**, 240 (1914).

Ber. dtsch. ophthal. Ges., **48**, 199 (1930).
Feinbloom. *Amer. J. Optom.*, **9**, 78 (1932); **14**, 41 (1937).
  J. Amer. optom. Ass., **12**, 88, 148, 175, 203, 244, 272, 351, 371 (1940–1); **13**, 69, 105, 223 (1941–2).
  Optom. Wkly., **36**, 1159 (1945).
Fick. *Arch. Augenheilk.*, **18**, 279 (1888).
Forknall. *Brit. J. physiol. Opt.*, **16**, 96 (1959).
Fritz. *Bull. Soc. belge Ophtal.*, No. 78, 71 (1939).
Gualdi. *Boll. Oculist.*, **10**, 486 (1931); **11**, 1093 (1932).
  Klin. Mbl. Augenheilk., **92**, 775 (1934).
von Györffy. *Klin. Mbl. Augenheilk.*, **104**, 81 (1940).
  Brit. J. physiol. Opt., **21**, 291 (1964).

Heine. *XIII int. Cong. Ophthal.*, Amsterdam, **1**, 232 (1929).
    Münch. med. Wschr., **77**, 6, 271 (1930); **80**, 885 (1933).
Lake. *Brit. J. physiol. Opt.*, **21**, 287 (1964).
Marriott. *Brit. J. physiol. Opt.*, **23**, 1 (1966).
Müller-Welt. *Klin. Mbl. Augenheilk.*, **94**, 108 (1935).
Obrig. *Arch. Ophthal.*, **19**, 735 (1938).
    Contact Lenses, Phila. (1942).
Reid. *Trans. ophthal. Soc. U.K.*, **58**, 434 (1938).
Ridley. *Proc. roy. Soc. Med.*, **39**, 842 (1946).

Trans. ophthal. Soc. U.K., **68**, 385 (1948).
Ruben. *Trans. ophthal. Soc. U.K.*, **87**, 643 (1967).
Sattler. *Klin. Mbl. Augenheilk.*, **100**, 172, 482 (1938); **111**, 184 (1945–6).
Strebel. *Klin. Mbl. Augenheilk.*, **99**, 30 (1937).
Sulzer. *Bull. Soc. franç. Ophtal.*, **10**, 113 (1892).
Teissler. *XVI int. Cong. Ophthal.*, Cairo, **4** (2), 297 (1937).
Thier. *Klin. Mbl. Augenheilk.*, **102**, 724 (1939).

Corneal Lenses

To write a short and comprehensive account of the development of corneal contact lenses is difficult and almost impossible, partly because of the astonishing diversity of the methods of approach adopted among those who are engaged in this field, and partly because of the incredible frequency with which new techniques and materials appear and disappear. As a consequence there is now an enormous literature on the subject which makes any critical evaluation extremely difficult. All that can reasonably be done is to enunciate the general principles of the problems involved and in particular their relation to the practice of ophthalmology.

The impetus to the development of corneal lenses arose from certain undesirable features of scleral lenses when these were used to correct low degrees of ametropia. The cosmetic advantage which was often a motivating factor in their use was largely offset by the protracted process of fitting required and by limited tolerance of the lens. Even in the early years of their development, however, attempts had been made to reduce their overall size making them virtually " corneal " in dimensions (Kalt, 1888). It was not until 1948 that Tuohy in America produced an all-plastic corneal lens with a standard overall diameter of 11·5 mm. which lay just within the limbus, the posterior surface being slightly flatter than that of the cornea; a peripheral bevel of 0·5 mm. was also incorporated on the posterior surface which therefore had a central optical portion 10·5 mm. in diameter (Fig. 751). The Tuohy lens, however, was well tolerated by relatively few subjects since it gave rise to pressure on the corneal apex as well as intermittent limbal interference because of its large size so that veiling developed. Although the lens of Tuohy's original design soon became obsolete, an important principle had been established—or rather broken. It was realized that corneal touch, anathema to the fitter of the scleral lens, was not necessarily harmful.

The next stage of development followed the realization that a reduction of the overall diameter and thickness frequently led to improved tolerance. Along these lines the MICROLENS was developed by Sohnges, Neill and Dickenson (see Neill, 1954 and Dickenson, 1954) and the greater success obtained with it stimulated a host of new ideas in design with the object of increasing their tolerance. *Contour-fitting* of the cornea with the central posterior curvature the same as that of the flattest corneal meridian was employed by Bier (1956–57), while in other subsequent designs the curvature of the optical zone has been made steeper than that part of the cornea on which the lens lies, giving rise to considerable apical clearance; the extent of this zone has been the subject of much variation. This was followed by

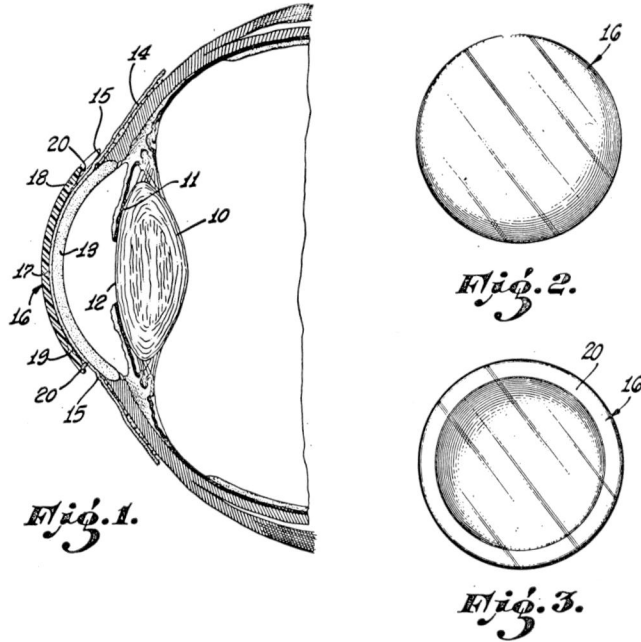

FIG. 751.—THE TUOHY CONTACT LENS.

FIG. 1.—Vertical section of the eye.
FIG. 2.—Anterior surface of the contact lens.
FIG. 3.—Posterior surface of the contact lens.

10 and 12, posterior and anterior surfaces of the crystalline lens; 11, iris; 13, cornea; 14, sclera and conjunctiva; 15, limbus; 16, anterior surface of contact lens and, in Figs. 2 and 3, the outer rim of the lens; 17, area of contact between the lens and the cornea; 18 and 19, areas where there are clearance spaces; 20, bevel on the posterior surface of the lens.

The main innovations are the close fitting, flatter than "K", and the diameter of the lens which lies just within the limbus (U.S. Patent 2,510,438, of 1948).

the use of multiple curvatures outside the optical zone, the original simple flange of the Tuohy lens being replaced by two or three zones of decreasing curvature to conform to the flattening of the periphery of the cornea. More subtle geometrical designs are now being developed, departing from spherical curvatures in the periphery or combining spherical curvatures in complex fashion.

With the development of technical resources which allow innumerable variations in design, more attention is being paid to the measurement of the cornea as a guide to the parameters and design of the lens—*custom-fitting*, as it is known in the United States—a topic on which, however, some controversy still exists. Devices to prevent rotation and the use of bifocal lenses are now established. More recently, a new material has come into use in the soft hydrophilic lenses of Dreifus and Wichterle (1964). Finally, a rather more speculative feature of the corneal lens is its increasing use as a therapeutic device in an attempt to influence the course of myopia or keratoconus.

THE DESIGN OF CORNEAL CONTACT LENSES

Nomenclature. A working knowledge of the nomenclature of corneal lenses is an essential preliminary to the understanding of their design and of the methods used to

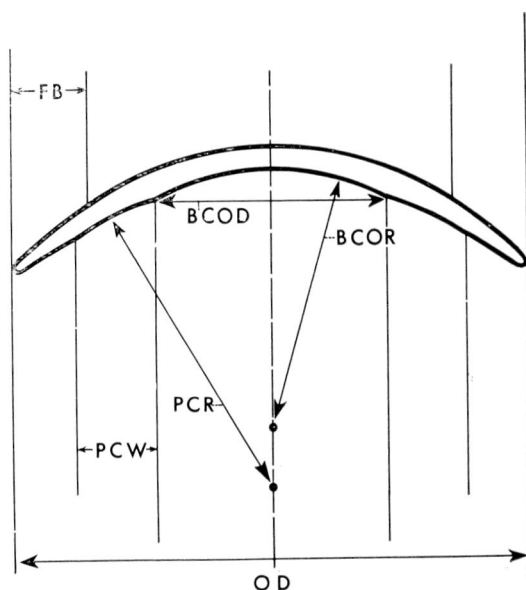

Fig. 752.—Parts of a Corneal Contact Lens.

BCOD, back central optic diameter; BCOR, back central optic radius; FB, front bevel; OD, overall diameter; PCR, radius of peripheral curve; PCW, width of peripheral curve.

fit them. An essential feature of the design of most types of corneal lens is that the posterior surface must conform to a greater or less degree with the shape of the cornea; any significant disparity in this respect will lead to a lack of adhesion between the lens and the eye, or in some cases to the precise opposite.

We have already examined the problem of the shape of the cornea in some detail,[1] and it will be remembered that it has usually an axial region of varying size and of largely spherical curvature, peripheral to which there is a band of progressively decreasing curvature (Fig. 752). *Monocurve* corneal lenses which have a single spherical curvature

[1] p. 125.

on the posterior surface have never been successful and they have now been largely abandoned. The central portion of the posterior surface of a corneal lens is, therefore, the most steeply curved, the curvature being spherical and occupying a proportion varying from one case to another; in the British terminology the *back optic zone* thus has a spherical curvature measured as the *back central optic radius* (BCOR) and an extent known as the *back central optic diameter* (BCOD). Some of these terms are often abbreviated: thus the word " central " is often omitted and the expression " back optic " is used for the back central optic surface. In America the back central optic surface is frequently referred to as the " optical zone " and the back central optic radius is described as the " central posterior curve ", the " optical zone radius " or the " base curve radius ", and the back central optic diameter is known as the " optical zone diameter ".

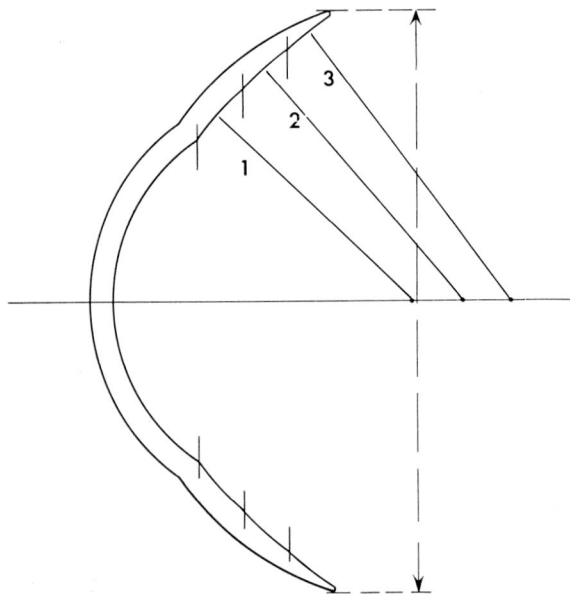

FIG. 753.—MULTICURVE CONTACT LENS.
The areas of different curvature of the periphery are indicated.

The peripheral part of the posterior surface of a corneal lens again follows the corneal topography in being less curved than the axial region but the design has shown great variety. In its simplest form there is a single peripheral curvature, the radius of which is greater than that of the optic zone; such a lens is known as a *bicurve*. In more complex designs there may be two or more peripheral curves—*tricurve* or *multicurve* lenses (Fig. 753). In all of these the centre of curvature of the peripheral curve lies on the axis of symmetry of the whole lens. The curvatures of the peripheral zones or bands progressively decrease; their width is a matter of great variation, the most peripheral usually being narrow and forming part of the edge. The inevitable discontinuities at the junctions between the zones of different curvatures can be eliminated to some extent by the process of *blending*, but a more recent solution of the problem is the introduction of lenses in which the two curvatures have a common tangent at the point of intersection (Figs. 754–5). Such offset lenses are usually of bicurve design. Other innovations include *continuous curve lenses* which flatten in non-spherical fashion from the axis outwards; the precise geometrical details of these are still unpublished. The design of the edge of the lens is also very important and several shapes have been suggested; too sharp an edge may dig into the cornea or the limbal tissues; too thick an edge may irritate the lids.

The form of the anterior surface depends on the ametropia to be corrected which determines the curvature of the axial region of the lens. A peripheral zone may be incorporated on the anterior surface (sometimes referred to as a *front bevel*) but this is part of the edge. An intermediate zone is present on the anterior surface in lenticular lenses, a design sometimes necessary in order to reduce the thickness of the edge in a highly myopic correction or to diminish the weight in high hypermetropia or aphakia.

FIGS. 754 and 755.—DESIGN OF THE POSTERIOR SURFACE OF "OFFSET" CORNEAL LENSES.

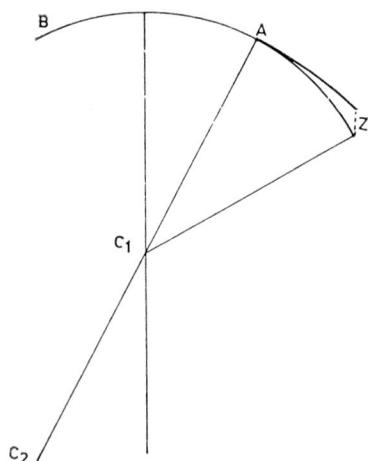

FIG. 754.—AB, optic zone; C_1, centre of curvature, and AC_1 radius of curvature of the optic zone; C_2, centre of curvature, and AC_2 radius of curvature of the multicurved periphery. Z, flattening factor (P. Cochet *et al.*).

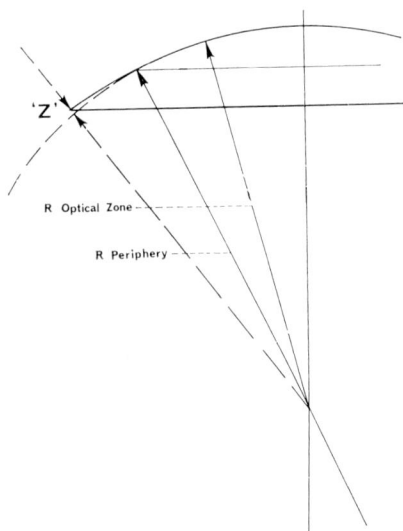

FIG. 755.—To show a different interpretation of the term "flattening factor Z" (after M. Ruben).

The important gross dimensions of the lens are its overall diameter, its back central optic diameter and its central thickness. The overall diameter of the lens varies considerably between different individuals and also according to the technique of fitting; in hard plastic corneal lenses it is usually below 10 mm. and may be as little as 6 mm. The lighter the lens the better, but the central thickness cannot be reduced to less than about 0·1 mm. in myopic corrections for reasons of structural stability; the precise thickness will depend on the type of ametropia.

THE IDEAL CORNEAL LENS

The criteria for an ideal corneal lens are the comfort of the patient, ocular health and perfect optical correction; these are, of course, interrelated. Many designs of corneal lenses meet this standard to a greater or less degree. It must, however, be stressed that the patient's symptomatology or lack of it is frequently an unreliable guide to the state of the eye, for many patients are so strongly motivated to wear corneal lenses that minor discomforts which may be an indication of a relatively more serious corneal disorder are ignored. The assessment of the suitability of a lens must therefore take into account not only the patient's subjective symptoms and the degree of his comfort as well as its optical performance, but also an objective appraisal of the state of the eye after wearing it for a reasonable period. Applying these criteria, a body of empirical knowledge has accumulated concerning desirable features of the relationship between the lens and the patient's eye.

POSITION AND MOBILITY. Ideally the lens should be well centred on the cornea and its optic axis should coincide with that of the eye; from the practical point of view this means that the position of the corneal lens should be such that its geometrical, which is usually its optical, centre is opposite the mid-point of the pupil. We have already noted that the optical zone of the cornea (apical zone or corneal cap) may be decentred in relation to the geometry of the cornea as a whole; furthermore, the relationship of the mid-pupillary point to the corneal landmarks may also vary. A certain degree of optical decentration of the lens may therefore be a consequence of a decentred apical zone over which even a well-designed lens will tend to position itself.

Whenever a lens is significantly decentred its optical function suffers in some degree. This impairment is small in low degrees of ametropia and if some part of the optical portion of the lens remains opposite the visual axis, the degree of oblique astigmatism may be negligible; if the decentration is gross, however, the optical functions through the edge of the lens may be poor. Nevertheless, an eccentrically located lens which remains on the cornea may be optically acceptable but, if the eccentricity is such that the lens permanently positions itself over the limbus at one point, discomfort may arise whatever the optical state. At the same time, many such lenses continue to be worn with few ill-effects although there is no doubt that in fitting the lens accurate centration should be attempted.

The precise mechanism by which a corneal lens remains adherent to the globe and, in the best circumstances, tends to position itself over the corneal apex and to reposition itself centrally, is a complex biophysical problem. The forces acting on a corneal lens are numerous and Miller (1963) summarized these as hydrostatic pressure behind, atmospheric pressure in front, the weight of the lens, the surface tension and viscosity of the tears, the force exerted by the upper and the support given in some cases by the lower lid. The surface tension of the pre-lens tear-film may be an adhesive force of special importance. The form of the lens in relation to its centre of gravity and to the shape of the cornea must also be taken into account. Centration of a corneal lens is related to the form of the meniscus at its periphery when the eye is adapted and tear-flow is at a minimum, as well as to changes in the volume of fluid entrapped under it. There is in addition the factor of the mechanical action of the lids (Mackie, 1969).

The eyelids are thus of importance. A corneal lens of large diameter, 9 mm. and upwards, often lies with its upper edge covered by the upper lid for 2 to 3 mm.; this exerts some backward pressure keeping the lens in place. In this connection it should be noted that there is a tendency for

FIGS. 756–758.—LENS LAG.

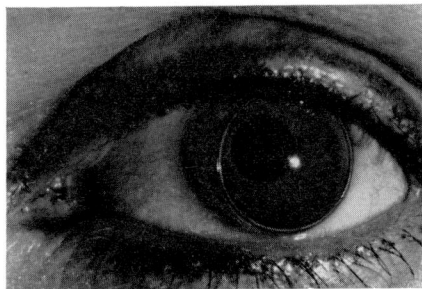

FIG. 756.

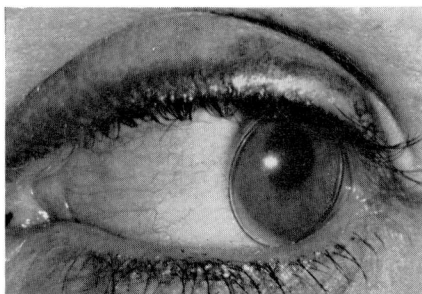

FIG. 757.

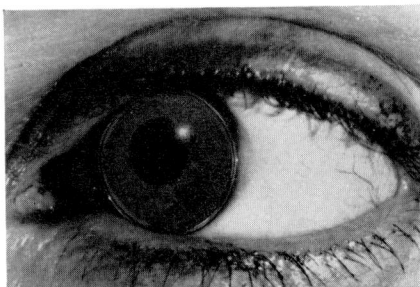

FIG. 758.

FIG. 756.—Primary position. FIG. 757.—Eye abducted. FIG. 758.—Eye adducted (I. Mackie).

corneal lenses incorporating myopic corrections to ride high because of the increase of thickness towards the periphery, while the lids combine with gravity to act in the opposite sense in the case of high hypermetropic corrections wherein the lens often tends to ride downwards. The lower lid usually exerts no supporting influence on the lens except when in contact with its lower margin. While undesirable, this may have no untoward consequences, but a situation wherein the lower lid actually covers the lower margin of the lens is usually thought to be unacceptable since it causes pooling of tears between the lens and the lower part of the cornea.

It is a curious fact that the claim made for the optical superiority of

contact lenses over spectacles is often supported by a statement to the
effect that they " move with the eye ".　This is certainly largely true of
scleral lenses, but the position with regard to a corneal lens is somewhat
less straightforward.　Indeed, some degree of relative movement between
it and the eye is inevitable; rotation without actual translation is therefore common and may not cause any optical disability, or lead to
any discomfort.　Thus with temporal movements of the eye the lens
approaches the nasal limbus; the precise degree of such movement (the
excursion lag of Mandell, 1965) that is acceptable is difficult to define, but in
horizontal movements it should not be greater than 1–2 mm. for a lens of
a total diameter of 9 to 9·5 mm. (Figs. 756–8).　Anything more than a very
slight overlap of the limbus during ocular movements is usually not well
tolerated.

More important are the movements which occur on blinking.　A
properly fitted lens moves downwards relative to the cornea with the descent
of the upper lid, is taken rapidly upwards to a level above its static position
as the upper lid ascends, and finally settles down again more slowly to its
initial position.　Any undue delay in this may give rise to a temporary
blurring of the vision.　This mobility during blinking is believed to be of
importance for the continued health of the cornea, giving the part of this
tissue which physically supports the lens in its central position temporary
relief and allowing the tear-film under the lens to be renewed.　Any theoretical optical advantages that might arise from a lens remaining fixed in the
centre of the cornea are considerably outweighed by the damage which
would occur as a result of immobility and the stagnation of tears.

The overall picture of the mobility of a corneal lens is sometimes characterized by
the terms *tight* or *loose fitting*, based on the criteria we have just discussed.　A tight lens
will move little in blinking or on ocular movements; it may even resist movement if
pushed externally and may be so tight as to leave an imprint of its edge on the cornea.
Some consequences of a tight fitting lens have already been noted.　Loose fitting lenses
besides having optical disadvantages lead to excessive awareness of their presence
because of their free mobility; this may be of such degree that gross displacement of
the lens may occur onto the conjunctiva, into one or other fornix or even off the eye
altogether (Fig. 764).　In this connection the amount of tears in the eye is of great
importance since a relative insufficiency is required to maintain adequate centration
(Mackie, 1970).

THE BEARING RELATIONSHIP.　It is a matter of speculation and debate
as to whether a corneal lens is supported directly on the corneal epithelium
at any point or whether a minute film of tears with admixed lipid material
always intervenes.　However this may be, it is widely believed that the
maximum support for a corneal lens should be neither at its periphery nor
at its apex but somewhere between.

As with scleral lenses, fluorescein instilled onto the superior conjunctiva
plays an invaluable part in the evaluation of the bearing relationship.
Naked-eye inspection with light filtered through cobalt-blue glass or ultra-

violet black light (Figs. 749–50) will indicate the proximity of the cornea to the lens at various sites as shown by the degree of fluorescence. Slit-lamp microscopy of the lens–cornea interspace with a narrow beam may provide additional information (Soper, 1963; Girard, 1964; Schlegel, 1967). The fluorescein pattern is not static since the tear-film in the interspace alters with every movement of the lens; it is examined initially with the lens centred and the lids retracted. The relationship generally favoured is indicated in Plate VIII. A uniform film of tears intervenes between the optical zone of the lens and the apical zone of the cornea, thinning somewhat so that the green pattern becomes darker in the intermediate zone where most support is given to the lens. At the extreme periphery the

FIGS. 759 and 760.—AREA OF CONTACT BETWEEN A CONTACT LENS AND THE CORNEA.

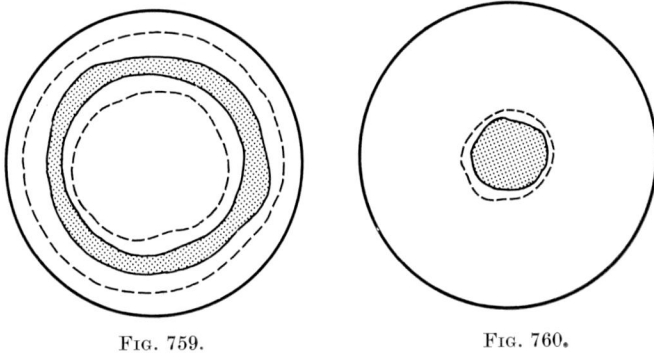

FIG. 759.   FIG. 760.

FIG. 759.—The usual relationship. The hatched area shows the position of contact with the lens centred, this area extending between the limits shown by the dotted lines during relative movement of the lens and the eye.

FIG. 760.—The situation when apical contact exists indicating that in such a case the load-bearing is undertaken by a very much smaller and relatively unchanged area of the cornea.

green colour again becomes more intense; this indicates greater clearance of the cornea allowing free access of tears to the interspace and counteracting stagnation therein. A progressive dilution of the fluorescein in the lens–cornea interspace should be seen to occur, indicating that the tear-film under the lens is being constantly renewed.

Much experience is required in the interpretation of the fluorescein patterns which vary with the technique of examination and the parameters of the lens. Thus the pattern just described indicates that in the mid-periphery there is an annular area which has the greatest load-bearing function. It will be appreciated from Figs. 759–60 that such an annular area will be even greater because of movement of the lens, thereby " spreading " any force exerted on the cornea.

How peripherally this area is situated and its breadth will vary with the design of the lens; in some it will be at the periphery of the back central optic zone, in others it will be at an intermediate area of flatter curvature. Again, the part of the lens receiving this maximal support will depend on the degree to which its back central optic zone and the apical zone of the cornea are matched, intentionally or otherwise, in curvature and diameter. These factors, although seemingly complex, follow logically from simple geometrical principles. Unfortunately, as we have already seen, the geometry of the cornea itself is not simple, even in principle. Because of this, corneal lenses based on simple geometry not infrequently require modification before an optimal adaptation to the patient's cornea is obtained.

Since we are dealing with biological material, even with an apparently perfectly fitting lens, corneal œdema and corneal staining may not be completely absent but should be negligible after it is removed from the eye; the conjunctiva and the lids, however, should show no signs of inflammation and the patient should have no symptoms relating to ocular irritation or trauma. Finally, the patient's visual function wearing spectacles should be as good as it had been before wearing contact lenses.[1]

FITTING TECHNIQUES

The manner in which corneal lenses are fitted is related to their design, the facilities available to the practitioner, the type of eye under consideration both anatomically and optically, and perhaps most of all on the outlook of the practitioner. A wide range of methods exists and these can only be outlined. In principle, the main distinction between them is the degree to which the topographical features of the cornea are considered prior to the wearing of a trial lens. At one extreme no assessment is made of the shape of the cornea, and trial lenses are fitted successively from a standard set until one is obtained which as far as possible fulfils the criteria of the ideal lens as indicated above. These lenses may be optically powered but examination of the refraction is usually carried out with the optimally fitting trial lens in place. A final lens is then ordered and this is reassessed and any modifications required undertaken to improve either its fit or its optical function.

Trial corneal lenses whether used alone or in combination with other methods are available with innumerable variations of their parameters. Every single factor discussed in the section on the design of these lenses is a possible variable and from the permutations and combinations of these a selection is often made of perhaps twenty lenses as a basic fitting set. Such a small number of necessity implies a certain pre-selection of one principal parameter.

Thus the design of the posterior surface and the number of zones of different curvature outside the back central optic zone may be fixed, or the total diameter may be restricted within a certain range. The trial set may be based on one particular overall diameter, one design of posterior surface and one back central optic diameter,

---

[1] See *spectacle-blur*, p. 757.

PLATES VIII AND IX

FLUORESCEIN PATTERNS WITH CONTACT LENSES
(Ian Mackie)

To face p. 744.

PLATE VIII

(Corneal Lens)

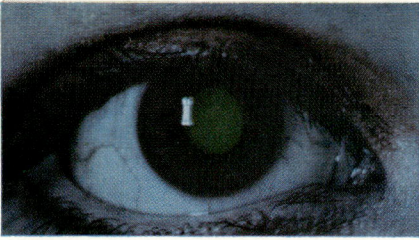

FIG. 1.—Normal fluorescence of the crystalline lens without the instillation of fluorescein. This is a source of confusion to the novice in assessing the fit.

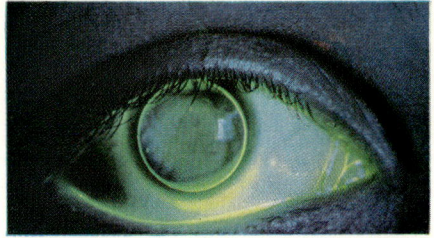

FIG. 2.—Minimal apex-clear fitting in a corectopic patient with the pupil at the limbus at 12 o'clock. Note that a more apex-clear lens would show a broader dark band of contact adjacent to the peripheral curve.

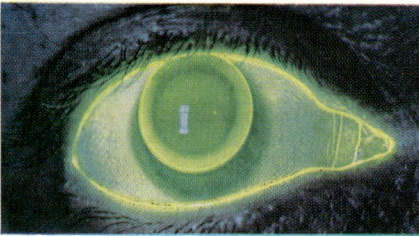

FIG. 3.—The apex-clear pattern in the normal eye. Note the fluorescence of the crystalline lens within the pupil.

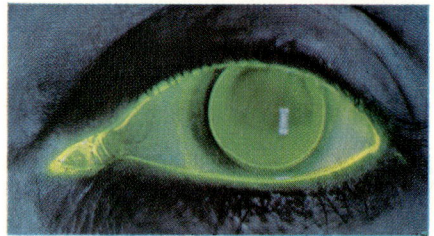

FIG. 4.—Flat-fitting lens. There is touch at the apex of the lens.

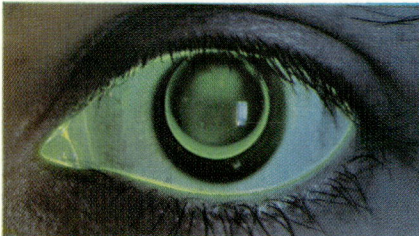

FIG. 5.—Flat-fitting lens. A pool of fluorescein with a curved lower limit is seen above the central touch.

FIG. 6.—Flat-fitting lens. A pool of fluorescein with a curved upper limit is seen below the central touch.

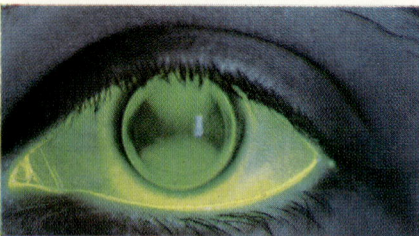

FIG. 7.—Flat astigmatic picture. The other eye of the patient with corectopia seen in Fig. 2.

FIG. 8.—Apex-clear astigmatic pattern in a normal eye.

PLATE IX
(FIGS. 1–5 CORNEAL LENS; FIGS. 6–8 SCLERAL LENS)

FIG. 1.—Keratoconus. A hard touch in the area of the cone, lifting off the lens in other areas.

FIG. 2.—Keratoconus. A thin small lens fitted to the flattest keratometry reading. This lens proved satisfactory.

FIG. 3.—Same case as in Fig. 2, with the lens in a lower position showing a completely different fluorescein pattern.

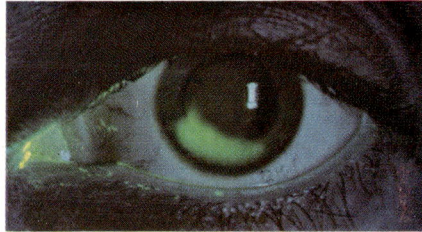

FIG. 4.—Asymptomatic corneal stain of a superficial punctate type 6 days after cessation of corneal lens wear.

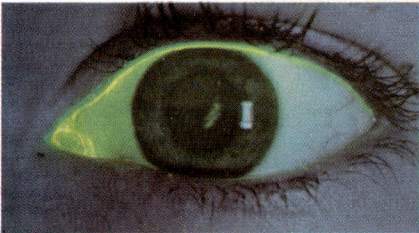

FIG. 5.—Transient crescentic staining of a granular or punctate type with a corneal lens, differing from that resulting from central corneal œdema and not giving rise to any serious complications.

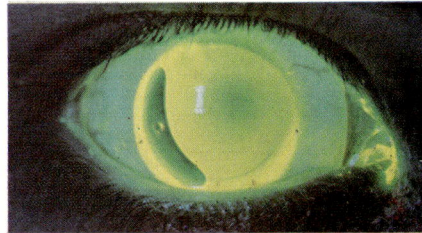

FIG. 6.—Normal eye, scleral lens. There is a light corneal touch with adequate limbal clearance and a sausage-shaped bubble associated with the fenestration.

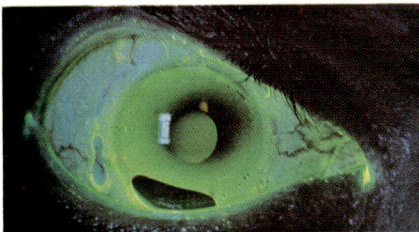

FIG. 7.—Central corneal touch. Poor limbal clearance.

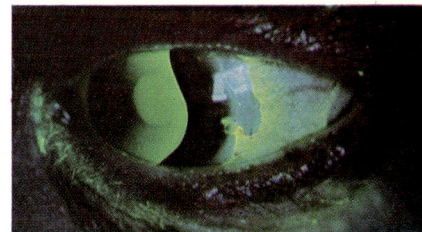

FIG. 8.—Nasal corneal touch and enlargement of the bubble on adduction.

while the variables relate to the curvatures of the back central optic zone and the peripheral zone or zones. In many cases the relationship between these curvatures is also pre-determined; thus a bicurve fitting set may have a fixed overall diameter of 9·5 mm., a fixed back central optic diameter of 6·7 mm. and a difference of 0·08 mm. between the back central optic radius and the peripheral zone radius. The matter can thus be complex, as may be seen from Table XXXIV in the Appendix, which is the specification of a set of 23 lenses of multicurve design. It may be noted that each lens in such a set has an identical back central optic diameter, the same width of peripheral zone and the same overall diameter; if it should be desirable to vary these also it would clearly call for an enormous number of different sets of trial lenses. The most useful variable in addition to radius is the back central optic diameter.

The art of *fitting corneal lenses from a trial set* of limited range depends on the ability of the practitioner to recognize the faults of any particular one and to replace it rapidly by another giving optimal features. If an optimally fitting lens cannot be found in the trial set, it may still be possible to infer what the dimensions of such a lens should be and this may be ordered, assessed and modified as necessary. The choice of the back central optic radius when fitting purely from a trial set is arbitrary, but an intelligent guess is frequently successful. Thus in the low myope a start might be made with a radius of 7·7 or 7·8 mm., and as a general rule the smaller the palpebral aperture the steeper the radius.

The employment of trial lenses may be regarded as an unscientific approach without an accurate evaluation of the dimensions of the cornea but this may be time-consuming and cause unnecessary discomfort. A preliminary measurement of the curvature of the apical zone of the cornea by the classical method of keratometry is thus a very useful procedure to give an indication of the most suitable radius of the optical zone, while the degree of corneal astigmatism may influence the lens selected for trial. It is, in fact, possible to proceed to the *ordering of a corneal lens solely on the basis of keratometry*. As in the selection of a lens from a trial set, the corneal diameter and radius, the palpebral aperture and the tension of the lids are guides to the overall diameter to be ordered. The average size of the pupil and the radius of curvature of the cornea (which is usually related to the size of the corneal cap) are pointers to the desirable extent of the back central optic diameter of the lens. The refraction to be ordered may be simply the back vertex power of the spectacle refraction, corrected for the change in effectivity related to the spectacle distance.[1] The relationship between the keratometric findings and the back central optic radius to be ordered is varied by different practitioners.

In the type of fitting known as " on K ", the back central optic radius of the lens is made the same as that of the flattest meridian of the apical zone of the cornea. It should be noted that the terms " flatter than K ", " on K " and " steeper than K " relate to fitting by the keratometer. The descriptions of the fit of a corneal lens as " flat ", " alignment " and " apex clear " are based on appearances obtained with

---

[1] p. 639.

fluorescein and ultra-violet black light, and are by no means synonymous with those relating to " K ".

Relating to these principles of fitting there are many empirical methods of ordering, particularly if a significant corneal astigmatism is shown by the keratometer. If the apical zone is toric a lens steeper than " K " is more readily tolerated and something between the flattest and steepest meridians is often ordered. With more than 3 to 4 D of astigmatism, lenses of special design may need to be employed.[1] Again, a spherical cornea may require the curvature of the optic zone to be slightly flatter than " K " in order to encourage the through-flow of tears. It will also be appreciated that

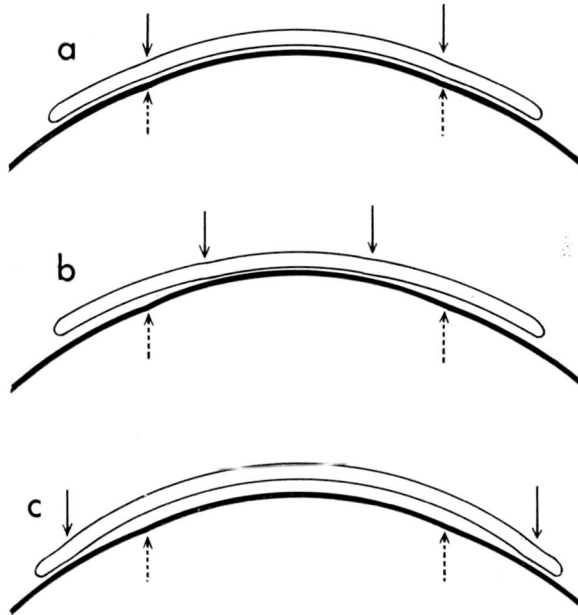

Fig. 761.—The dependence of the apical clearance of a contact lens upon the relationship between its back central optic diameter and the diameter of the optical zone of the cornea.

In (a) the alignment is good, the BCOD matching the cornea. In (b) clearance is unsatisfactory since the BCOD is relatively too small. In (c) apical clearance is excessive owing to the opposite relationship.

if the corneal lens is designed with a large optic zone the curvature of this zone must be made slightly flatter than " K ", otherwise the peripheral flattening of the cornea will lead to excessive apical clearance by the lens (Fig. 761).

The final factor to be decided in ordering a lens based only on keratometric readings is the form of the posterior surface, that is, the number of peripheral zones and their curvatures; there are no rules about this but experience and the commercial availability of proven designs are the principal considerations. The number of zones is dictated to some degree by the overall size of the lens, and their curvatures may bear standard relationships

[1] p. 778.

one to another or, in the case of the most peripheral zone, a standard curvature may be employed.

All the facts taken into consideration when ordering a lens without using trial lenses apply equally to the selection of a lens from a trial set when keratometry is used as a preliminary guide to this method of fitting. *The combination of keratometry and trial lenses* is probably the better method since keratometry alone is sometimes misleading as, indeed, is to be expected when we recall the limitations of this technique and the vagaries of corneal topography (Bier, 1964; Mandell, 1965). There is, however, an increasing practice of making more refined measurements of the shape of the cornea in order to produce a lens the posterior surface of which accurately parallels this configuration. The many sophisticated techniques devised for this purpose have already been discussed in the section on the optics of the corneal periphery,[1] and we shall now briefly examine their application in the present context.

In spite of its somewhat questionable scientific basis, *eccentric keratometry* carried out with standard instruments is employed to indicate the size of the apical zone. A modification of the classical procedure consists in changing the patient's fixation in regular fashion so that the curvature of areas close to the corneal apex can be measured. One of the most widely used devices is the *topogometer*, a movable fixation light used in combination with the Bausch and Lomb keratometer (Soper *et al.*, 1962) (Fig. 762). With this it is claimed that within the apical zone of the cornea an area may be found of greater curvature than that at the visual centre as measured by classical keratometry. By measuring in various meridians the limits of eccentric fixation over which the keratometric reading does not show significant flattening, an estimate can be obtained of the size of the apical zone. The longest diameter of this was used by Girard and his colleagues (1964) as the basis for the total diameter of the lens which is calculated as being 2 mm. larger. The back central optic diameter of the lens is 1 mm. larger than the longest diameter of the apical zone of the cornea. The back central optic radius is usually " on *K* " for lenses over 9 mm. overall total diameter, or steeper by a quarter of the corneal astigmatism. For lenses under 9 mm. total diameter, the average of the flattest and steepest apical zone curvatures is taken, or 0·5 D is added to " *K* ", whichever is the steeper. The two millimetres of the diameter beyond that corresponding to the apical zone are added empirically, the inner millimetre for stability and movement, the outer for the design of the edge and the peripheral curvatures.

An even more sophisticated approach to the design of contact lenses is that based upon the *specific keratometry* of Bonnet[2]; this makes use of a very small area of the cornea and is carried out at 5° intervals along the two principal meridians. From the radii of curvature at various degrees of eccentricity, the flattening factor, " *K* "[3], can be determined either from a nomogram or from the formula

$$K = \frac{1}{\alpha_2 - \alpha_1} \; \log \frac{R_2 - R_0}{R_1 - R_0}$$

where α_1 and α_2 are the angular eccentricities of two corneal points in the same semi-meridian in relation to the ophthalmometric axis, and R_0, R_1 and R_2 are the radii of curvature at the ophthalmometric pole and at these two points respectively.

[1] p. 126.   [2] p. 131.
[3] The use of the term K for the flattening factor is confusing because of the other interpretations given to this letter. The term " flattening factor " has also other interpretations; see Z Figs. 754–5.

The apical zone of the cornea is examined by classical and specific keratometry; if these differ the result of specific keratometry at 10° of eccentricity is taken for the curvature of the optical zone of the lens to be ordered. The back central optic diameter varies from 5 to 6·5 mm. according to the difference of specific keratometry at the apex and at 10° of eccentricity; the smaller the difference the larger the diameter. There are usually four peripheral zones each of 0·5 mm. width. The innermost is based upon the smallest specific keratometric reading at 20° of eccentricity; it is between 0·15 and

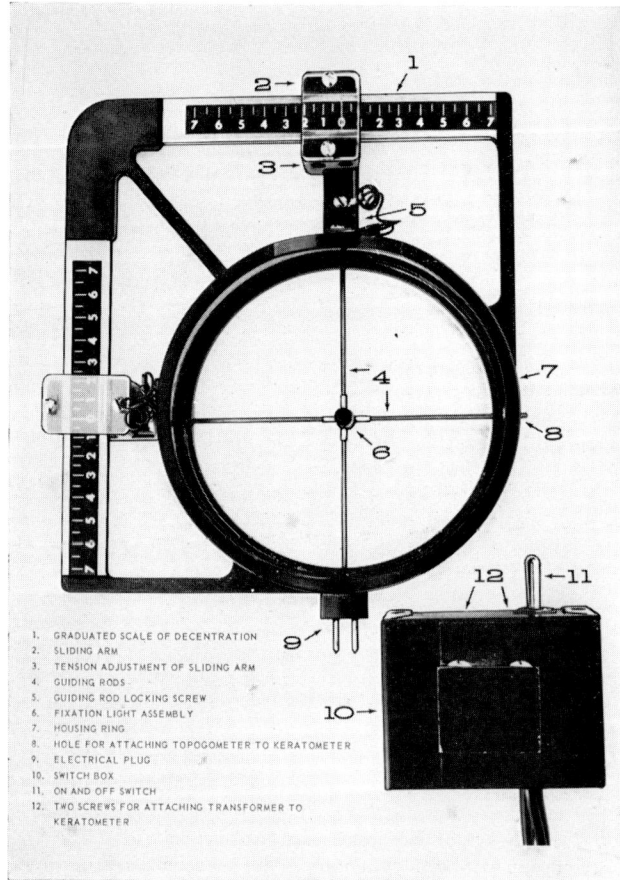

1. GRADUATED SCALE OF DECENTRATION
2. SLIDING ARM
3. TENSION ADJUSTMENT OF SLIDING ARM
4. GUIDING RODS
5. GUIDING ROD LOCKING SCREW
6. FIXATION LIGHT ASSEMBLY
7. HOUSING RING
8. HOLE FOR ATTACHING TOPOGOMETER TO KERATOMETER
9. ELECTRICAL PLUG
10. SWITCH BOX
11. ON AND OFF SWITCH
12. TWO SCREWS FOR ATTACHING TRANSFORMER TO KERATOMETER

FIG. 762.—GIRARD'S TOPOGOMETER.

0·4 mm. larger in radius than the back central optic radius. The curvatures of the other peripheral zones are determined by the flattening factor and the curvatures of the optic and first peripheral zones, as well as by their width.

Photokeratoscopy has also been used as a means of determining the curvature of many regions of the cornea. Cochet and Amiard (1966) devised an instrument which allows a fairly direct computation of the peripheral posterior curvatures required, the design of the lens being determined graphically from the coaxial radii given by the instrument for the particular angles concerned (Cochet *et al.*, 1967) (Fig. 763). A photographic profile of the cornea taken with the apparatus devised by Collignon-Brach and her colleagues (1966) and by Bitonte and Keates (1967) can also be used to estimate the flattening of the periphery of the cornea. It may be a useful preliminary to the fitting of quasi-conoidal lenses (Ruben, 1966), although these are usually fitted merely with classical keratometry.

It must be admitted that the fitting of custom-designed corneal lenses involving specialized investigation of the patient's cornea requires considerable resources and time and thus must remain somewhat limited in its application. Corneal topography clearly has a place in their general design

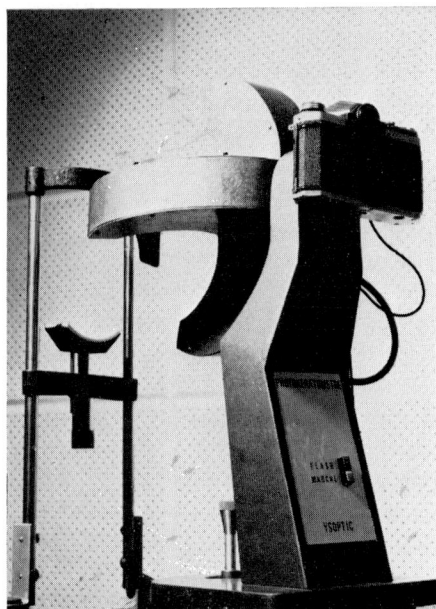

FIG. 763.—THE PHOTOKERATOMETER OF COCHET AND AMIARD.

but faithful reproduction of the shape of the cornea in the posterior surface of the lens is neither possible nor may it be physiologically desirable. Theoretical advantages have been claimed for corneal lenses fashioned from mouldings of the cornea (Dallos, 1964).

Comparisons have been made between rule-of-thumb prescribing from nomograms on the basis of classical keratometry and the more complex techniques of eccentric keratometry; no significant difference in results was found (Dyer, 1968). In fact, however elaborate or simple the preliminaries to the ordering of a corneal lens may be, there are limitations to the type that the patient will subsequently try, due partly to the physical dimensions, optical requirements and design of the lens imposed by ease of manufacture and reproducibility and partly to the nature of the material of which the lens is made. When the patient comes to wear the lens ordered for him, it is hardly surprising that, however scientifically well founded the procedure of fitting, some modification may be necessary. It is obviously desirable that such modifications be minimized, and new fitting techniques are often directed to the development of a system whereby the optimal lens is initially obtained. If, however, the patient of the future is to be subjected to a lengthy and tedious procedure based on esoteric instruments operated perhaps only by their inventors, the gain may be small, and if modifications to the lens are subsequently deemed necessary the value of the whole elaborate technique is put into question.

Whichever approach is adopted to the fitting of corneal lenses, a bewildering assortment of designs is available either for use as trial sets or for ordering. Some are the exclusive products of particular schools of thought, institutions or manufacturers; others not so exclusive are based upon the original ideas of individual practitioners. The principal features of some of these designs have been mentioned previously. A comparative assessment of the value of these various techniques is difficult owing to the impracticability of obtaining adequate controls, and it is undesirable simply to experiment with several types of lens in a single patient. Moreover, the degree of tolerance, influenced as it is by different degrees of motivation, varies between patients, and different practitioners accept different criteria of success.

One feature of corneal lenses about which there is still considerable debate is the overall size, and the designs can be roughly divided into those having diameters above or below 8·5 mm. Although some practitioners confine their practice to small or large lenses, this rigidity is unnecessary and patients will be encountered in whom the large or the small lens will be best tolerated. The very small, extremely thin corneal lens is often intended to lie entirely in the palpebral aperture, in contradistinction to a large lens of which about one-fifth is covered by the upper lid. In general terms, the smaller the lens the better the tolerance to be expected, partly because it gives rise to less of the sensation of a foreign body, and partly because less of the cornea is covered and thereby deprived of its normal milieu. The optical performance, however, may be interfered with by the distorting effect of the periphery which is more likely to position itself over the pupil during some movements of the eye and during blinking; the smaller the lens the more easily is it misplaced and the more difficult it is for the patient to manipulate. A very thin lens may be of poorer optical quality and may tend to ride high. On the whole, fitting is less critical the smaller the lens, but the use of trial lenses is almost mandatory and their manufacture must be of great technical excellence, particularly with respect to the finishing of the edge and the thickness.

The general indications for the use of small lenses include a narrow palpebral aperture which is often found together with a steep radius, perhaps in a patient having a backward head-tilt when he uses a large lens. Other indications include a cornea which develops œdema rapidly, the presence of high convex corrections, and the difficulties arising with large lenses from poor centration or irregularity of the peripheral cornea.

CLINICAL ASPECTS

A full ocular history and examination as well as a review of the patient's general health are essential before a decision can be taken whether to attempt to fit corneal lenses; moreover, it is important to elicit the reason why the patient desires them. In most cases in young adults this is purely cosmetic, but the greater the patient's motivation the more likely is he to use them successfully (Edmund, 1967). No dogmatic rules can be laid down as to the *contra-indications* for the use of corneal lenses, but some general guidance may be given. Certain of the conditions mentioned may be temporary or amenable to treatment. Others, while not constituting absolute contra-indications, may be factors militating against wearing them successfully over periods of years.

Age itself is immaterial; there are innumerable examples of the very young successfully wearing them, usually for medical rather than optical indications, while at the other end of the scale an increasing number of the elderly are wearing corneal lenses as their optical correction after a cataract extraction. Active ocular disorders are usually definite contra-indications; these include inflammatory diseases of the lids, conjunctiva, cornea or anterior uveal tract, whether bacterial or allergic in nature, squamous or rosaceal blepharitis, styes and chalazia, or any condition wherein excessive sebaceous secretion is formed. Lacrimal anomalies must also be considered; excessive lacrimation will lead to instability and difficulty in fitting, as also does the defective secretion of tears associated with kerato-conjunctivitis sicca. Patients demonstrating " dry-spots "—areas of cornea which appear dark when fluorescein is instilled—may be unsuitable for corneal lenses (Girard, 1967). Small pingueculæ need not be a contra-indication, but a pterygium is. Trachomatous corneal scarring does not preclude them if the corneal vascularization is light nor does old interstitial keratitis.

Glaucoma, either simple or closed-angle, need not necessarily be considered as a contra-indication but in this case scleral lenses are probably best avoided; special techniques may be adopted if a drainage bleb is present. Endophthalmitis has been observed to result from injury to a filtering bleb by a lens (Wild, 1962; Ashline and Ellis, 1968). A history of retinal detachment or a liability to it raises some problems particularly in high myopes. There is no evidence that the wearing of any type of corneal lens increases the likelihood of this complication, but it is obvious that a patient who is apt to be clumsy in manipulating the lens into and out of the eye is unsuitable; in these cases an examination of the fundus including its periphery in a high myope under full mydriasis is advisable prior to the wearing of any type of contact lens. Corneal surgery itself is no contra-indication to wearing a contact lens, scleral or corneal; indeed, it may be helpful, the scleral lens both optically and in healing, or the corneal lens subsequently but also as an aid to splinting the graft (Desvignes, 1966).

General conditions may also have a bearing on the ability to tolerate contact lenses. Allergic diseases of the upper respiratory tract such as asthma, hay fever, and vasomotor rhinitis are often reflected in sufficient conjunctival hyperæmia and irritability to make wearing the lens difficult. Similarly, a history of contact dermatitis should be regarded with suspicion in view of the possibility of allergy to plastic material. It is, however, very unlikely that there is a true allergy to the best grades (Controlled Quality: " CQ ") of Perspex; in material of an inferior quality the persistence of small quantities of the chemicals used in its manufacture may be responsible for irritative phenomena (Ridley, 1967). Allergy to tinted plastic is, however, possible. The fitting of a lens should not be attempted during an acute upper respiratory disease such as coryza. Endocrine conditions are coming into increasing prominence as factors in the wearing of contact lenses. Diabetics are said to be somewhat unsuitable subjects because of the liability to infection and the fragility of the corneal epithelium, a view, however, not generally accepted. Fitting is also inadvisable during pregnancy since this is believed to be associated with changes in the corneal shape, possibly due to œdematous swelling. Post-menopausal endocrine changes, perhaps in the tear-film, may also have an adverse influence; at this time psychological factors also complicate the picture. The taking of contraceptive pills has been blamed for poor tolerance of contact lenses (Koetting, 1966).

Apart from the patient himself, the conditions in which he is to wear the lenses must also be considered. Hot, dusty atmospheres are unsuitable and those engaged in dirty occupations or exposed to chemical conjunctival irritation will probably be unable to tolerate the lenses. Similarly, high altitudes as in flying may give rise to discomfort owing to changes in the atmospheric pressure (Diamond, 1967; Raygada, 1967).

In the absence of contra-indications, a *tolerance trial* is usually carried out at an early stage. The trial lenses, preferably powered to approximate the patient's refraction, are inserted and the patient is allowed to retain them for a period of time, perhaps half an hour; thereafter the fit of the lens is assessed as we have already described. It is usual for the practitioner to insert the lenses himself initially, with or without the use of local anæsthesia. The main advantage of analgesia is to cut down the flow of tears, and a sense of confidence is also given to the patient; but at the same time it is impossible to observe the reaction of the eye and it is necessary for the patient to learn at an early stage how to insert the lens without anæsthesia. The reaction, which usually lasts 15 minutes or less, consists of a foreign-body sensation accompanied by blinking and lacrimation, symptoms relieved by looking downwards and relaxing the lids, and there may be a reactionary hyperæmia of the conjunctiva. The fluorescein test and slit-lamp examination, if deemed necessary, are delayed until the phase of profuse lacrimation is over. Refraction through the trial lens is also carried out. If powered lenses are being tried, the patient's vision as well as the fit of the lens will be investigated before and after the tolerance trial. On the basis of these findings a definitive lens may be ordered.

Once the practitioner is satisfied with the fit and optical performance of the modified lens he has ordered, the patient is instructed in a wearing schedule, possibly a progressive build-up at the rate of one or more hours per day, starting with two to four hours, and after a period of three to four weeks wearing them throughout the day may be indicated. During the early period supervision is essential to reassess the optical function and the fit of the lens as well as the condition of the eye as a whole and in particular the state of the cornea as judged by the slit-lamp and keratometer. Again, modifications of the lens may be indicated and the wearing-schedule may be appropriately altered, being speeded up or retarded according to the findings.

SYMPTOMS AND COMPLICATIONS

It must be remembered that the symptoms and signs experienced on wearing corneal contact lenses do not necessarily go hand in hand; evidence of trauma to the cornea may be present in a symptomless patient and in certain circumstances this would be an indication to modify the lens while, in the absence of evidence of corneal injury, the mere fact that the pattern of fitting does not conform to the optimum is no indication to alter the lens in the absence of symptoms.

The *non-visual symptoms* are important. Many patients rapidly become hardly conscious of wearing corneal lenses; they are the fully adapted wearers. It is true that in the initial stages there is an inevitable awareness of the presence of the lens lasting for a few minutes accompanied by the symptoms and signs met with at the first insertion every time the lens is inserted, but as the wearer becomes adapted the time taken for these to disappear shortens to a mere few seconds. Awareness of the presence of the lens developing at a variable period after its insertion associated with increasing discomfort may be caused by an anomaly in fitting; this may be of various forms and usually consists of stinging, burning and itching sensations. In addition, acute pain may be felt with or without the actual presence of a foreign body if the corneal epithelium is abraded on the insertion of the lens.

Some indications as to the causation of the various symptoms will be given by the pattern of their development not only after wearing the lens for a single day but also from day to day. Thus, anomalies in fitting may tend to produce symptoms which are mild on insertion and become subsequently worse, a period which becomes shorter if the anomalies are not corrected. Unfortunately, the type of discomfort experienced with a badly fitting lens may mimic that normally experienced, and disappear as the lens continues to be worn because of corneal anæsthesia associated with developing œdema. Apart from its shape a lens may give rise to discomfort because it is rough, chipped or scratched, because the design is bad or the edge is poorly polished, or because dried debris is adherent to it. In such cases as the discomfort increases there is associated blinking and spasm of the lids and this may also result from a conscious effort to clear the vision which is often blurred. A sense of tightness and fullness of the lids together with lacrimation and conjunctival hyperæmia may also be accompanied by flushing on the affected side of the face and even by rhinorrhœa. Meantime, a mounting desire to remove the lens is experienced by the wearer.

Photophobia is not infrequent and is thought to be associated with some definite change in the cornea; this may take the form of punctate staining but the basis of it is almost certainly œdema. Tinted lenses are often prescribed in such cases.

Visual symptoms may be due to faulty optics in the lens–eye relationship or to some abnormality of the cornea developing on wearing the lens. The lens may fail to correct the patient's refractive error; if the spherical correction incorporated is inadequate, small modifications are usually possible such as a correction of -0.75 D. The correction of residual astigmatism is a more difficult problem but may be dealt with by such expedients as the incorporation of a toric surface. The altered accommodative requirement compared with spectacles may give rise to visual difficulties with close work. This applies particularly to a high myope whose distant vision is much better with contact lenses than with spectacles but who reads comfortably when the latter are removed.

Other optical visual symptoms may also arise from the effects of the peripheral curves, the edges of the lens or from the meniscus at this site, if and when they obtrude over the pupil. This condition is described as " flare " or " ghost " images and may even give rise to uniocular diplopia or polyopia. The lens as a whole or its back central optic diameter may be too small, the mobility of the lens may be excessive, it may centre poorly, or the size of the pupil may be larger than had been assumed.

Visual symptoms may be due to abnormalities of the cornea, particularly œdema which is the common cause of all the pathological changes in this tissue that result from wearing corneal lenses; these have already been described.

Other causes of visual impairment are the accumulation of debris or sebaceous secretion on the lens–corneal interspace, debris on the anterior surface, warping of the shape of the lens, putting the lens into the wrong eye, and displacement of a lens off the cornea, sometimes into the upper fornix where it may become implanted sub-conjunctivally even to the extent of its being regarded as " lost " (Long, 1963; Green, 1963; Lippmann, 1965) (Fig. 764).

Among the *clinical signs* which might be found in patients with such symptoms are anomalies of blinking, either frequent or deficient, corresponding to spasm of the orbicularis or levator respectively, arising from a desire to reduce the discomfort. Excessive blinking may be accompanied by an abnormal tilt of the head so as to minimize the discomfort arising from the movements of the lens. On the other hand, a failure to blink resulting in a staring appearance may lead to the stagnation of tears under the immobile lens; such patients should be taught to exercise their blinking, as also should those who close their lids incompletely in this reflex. An incorrect movement of the lens when the patient blinks normally may indicate a deficient fit. If the lens is relatively fixed it may be too steeply curved or too large; the opposite holds for a too mobile lens when irritation of the lids may occur and occasionally the lens may be completely displaced. It is possible to modify a lens to correct some of these defects either by altering the overall size or the curvature of the optical zone or occasionally by adding more intermediate posterior curves.

Corneal anomalies are particularly important and of these, as we have just seen, œdema is the most common pathological sign. This arises in a variety of circumstances, but the factors in its genesis include mechanical trauma to the cornea, negative hydrostatic pressure under the lens, hypoxia of the epithelium and anomalies of the tear-film, particularly its lipid layer,

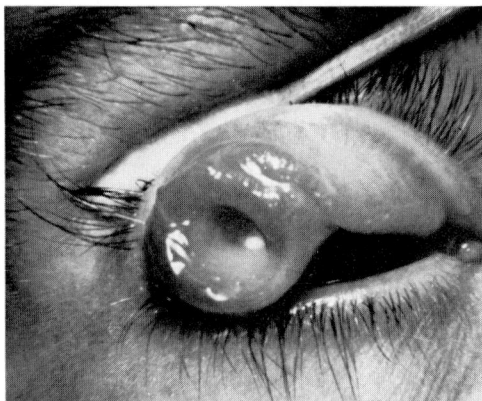

FIG. 764.—A "LOST" CONTACT LENS.

It became embedded in the conjunctiva of the upper lid and was discovered only when the lid was doubly everted (W. R. Green).

as well as the effect of drying (see Ruben, 1967). Generalized œdema to a degree sufficient to produce veiling[1] is uncommon, but localized œdema seen as microbullæ by retro-illumination with the slit-lamp is frequent and may be associated with corneal staining. Less degrees of œdema are made evident by the technique of sclerotic scatter[2] wherein the limbal region of the sclera is illuminated; this type of œdema is said to be the earliest change in the cornea and with it there may be no associated staining.

Where it is present corneal staining is frequently difficult to define; whether it is due to an actual loss of epithelial cells or to some alteration in the cells themselves, disappearance of the stain is often remarkably rapid, so rapid, indeed, that it has been suggested that it is caused merely by a destruction of the normal lipid-cellular relationship. On the other hand, some simple stains may take days to disappear, especially those developing after œdema. "Dimple veiling," a form of corneal staining associated with

---

[1] p. 717.　　　　　　　　[2] Vol. VII, p. 255.

the trapping of small bubbles of air under the lens, may occur centrally or peripherally; since it is very transient, it is of little pathological significance.

Mechanical trauma often presents as punctate stains where undue pressure is exerted by the lens on some area of the cornea; this will clearly be aggravated by spasm of the lids. Imperfect blending between two of the curves on the posterior surface of the lens or poor polishing may lead to an arcuate area of staining. A similar pattern may occur as an abrasion caused on insertion and may also follow repeated recentring of the lens. Limbal staining on the upper part of the cornea may be due to the edge of the lens either riding high or being of poor shape. The staining at 3 and 9 o'clock described by Mackie (1966) may be traumatic in nature or it may be related to drying of the cornea when the lens prevents contact between the lids and the

FIGS. 765 and 766.—TRAUMATIC LIMBAL STAINING (I. Mackie).

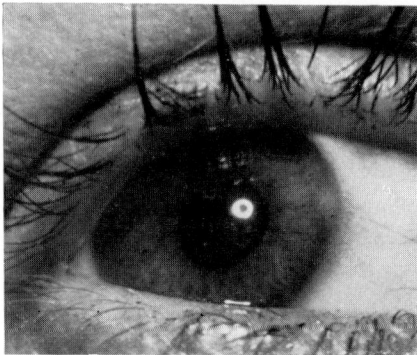

FIG. 765.—There is slight staining at 3 o'clock.

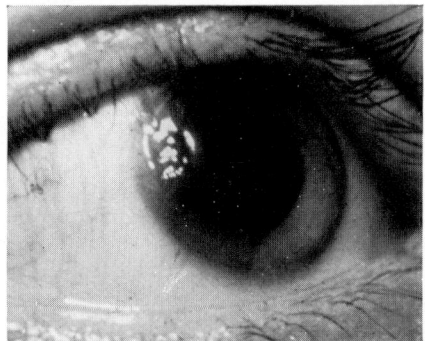

FIG. 766.—More extensive staining at 9 o'clock.

globe (Figs. 765–6). This is a serious type of pathological change following the wearing of corneal lenses and is associated with œdema and inadequate blinking. Excessive movement of the lens during blinking may also be associated with vertical wrinkles in the epithelium. Staining will, of course, occur if a foreign body gets under the lens from which an abrasion may result. The symptomatology may, however, be minimal and a linear track stain may be the only evidence.

Chronic erosions can also occur and these may be acutely painful as well as being slow to heal; they may become recurrent if the lens is reinserted and may lead to continuing disability even if the lens is abandoned. Gross loss of the corneal epithelium is possible if the patient continues to wear a lens for some time after the onset of the œdema. Symptoms of the loss of epithelium often do not come on until some time after removing the lens when the patient experiences intense blepharospasm, pain, watering and the sensation of a foreign body (the " over-wearing syndrome " of Girard, 1964) (Lansche and Lee, 1960; Cassady, 1961; Wohlrabe and Moore, 1967).

If the œdema is severe it can also involve the corneal stroma. Vascularization of both the epithelium and the stroma may follow, a complication to which patients with aphakia or keratoconus are particularly prone; fortunately, regression frequently occurs if use of the lens is discontinued. In all cases, however, the presence of œdema and vascularization may be followed by scarring and a permanent opacity; there is also the danger of the secondary infection of epithelial bullous lesions. The development of some degree of corneal anæsthesia is another consequence of prolonged and perhaps repeated epithelial œdema (Boberg-Ans, 1955; Schirmer, 1963).

Analysing the records of 10,000 patients who had worn contact lenses over a period of one year in the United States, Dixon and his colleagues (1966) found that 14 eyes were blinded or removed and 157 cases of permanent scarring occurred attributed to wearing the lenses. Less serious and temporary damage followed abrasion in 5,194 cases, deep corneal opacities in 276, corneal ulceration in 468, stromal œdema in 845, traumatic iritis in 107, wrinkling of Descemet's membrane in 101, and in 616 cases the lenses seemed to be responsible for the reactivation of corneal disease. From this it is obvious that all patients wearing contact lenses should receive periodical medical examinations. The 10,000 patients consulted doctors about their eyes after wearing contact lenses. Since some 25% of ophthalmologists in the United States were involved in the study, the true population wearing contact lenses from which these figures were derived may be of the order of 2,000,000; the incidence of complications quoted in a sample of this size is thus not so alarming as it would appear.

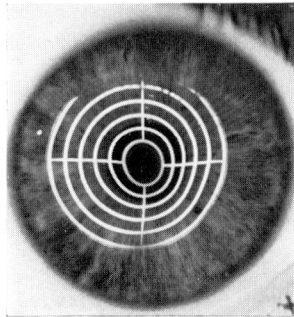

FIG. 767.—PSEUDO-KERATOCONUS FOLLOWING THE WEARING OF A CORNEAL LENS
(I. Mackie).

The influence of a corneal lens on the shape of the cornea is interesting. An extremely common phenomenon among wearers of corneal lenses is that of *spectacle-blur*, an indistinctness of vision experienced when using the spectacle correction after removing the lenses. This is due to two factors: in addition to the element of œdema there may be some degree of warping or distortion of the cornea to allow it to conform to the shape of the posterior surface of the lens, particularly if the latter is steeply fitted, and sometimes there is an increase in the thickness of the cornea.[1] In association with these changes the visual disturbance may or may not be correctable

[1] Smelser and Ozanics (1952), Kinsey (1952), Miller and Exford (1967).

by optical means. The œdema often clears rapidly after removal of the lens but the warping effect on the cornea may persist for long periods[1]; it may change the patient's refractive error considerably, even to the point of giving good unaided vision. Induced astigmatism, direct, indirect or irregular, is also common and marked forms have been reported, even the development of keratoconus (Fig. 767). Over the long term, a corneal flattening is said to occur, particularly marked in lenses fitted " on *K* ", a change which may persist for some weeks or months after wearing of the lens is discontinued. In any event, during keratometry to determine a flattening or otherwise of the corneal apex after wearing a corneal lens, distortion or indistinctness of the mires may be observed, due to œdema or to irregularities of the corneal surface. It would thus seem that the precise changes which may occur in the cornea cannot be accurately predicted.

The complications of wearing a corneal lens are therefore numerous and unpredictable and modifications of the lens or its replacement are often necessary. Table XXXI shows some of the possible modifications and the indications for their application.

TABLE XXXI

LENS MODIFICATIONS (R. B. MANDELL)

Lens variable	Modification possible	New lens necessary
Total diameter (T.D.)	Decrease	Increase
Optical zone diameter (O.Z.D.)	Decrease	Increase
Peripheral curve radius	Increase (Flatten)	Decrease (Steepen)
Peripheral curve width (P.C.W.)	Increase (Must also decrease O.Z.D.) Decrease (Must also decrease T.D.)	Decrease (Must also increase O.Z.D.)
Intermediate curve radius	Increase (Flatten)	Decrease (Steepen)
Intermediate curve width (if present)	Increase (Must also decrease O.Z.D. or P.C.W.)	Decrease (Must also increase O.Z.D.)
Blend width	Increase	Decrease
Front bevel width	Increase	Decrease
Power change	$< \pm 1 \cdot 00$ D.	$> \pm 1 \cdot 00$ D.
Surface polish	Yes (Minor)	Yes (Extensive)
Thickness increase or decrease	No	Yes
Change optical zone radius	No	Yes

The modifications of a corneal lens which are possible, however, are limited, whether it is desired to improve the fit or the optical performance or to eradicate some technical flaw. Polishing can eliminate minor scratches on the surfaces and the edge can be reworked, thus improving comfort and optical efficiency. For practical reasons many of the dimensions of a corneal lens can be changed only in one direction; thus the total diameter or the back central optic diameter can only be decreased. The back central optic radius of a lens cannot be altered so that a poor bearing relationship which

[1] Sabell (1961), Fontana (1962), Rengstorff (1965), Pratt-Johnson and Warner (1965), Hartstein (1965), Hodd (1965), Soper (1967), Ruben (1967), Miller (1968).

requires a change in this parameter calls for a completely new lens. The width of the intermediate or peripheral zones can be increased or extra zones sometimes introduced at the expense of the diameter of the back central optic zone and they can be made flatter but not steeper. The indications for carrying out such changes follow from the bearing relationship of the lens; thus, a flattening or widening or increasing the number of peripheral curves may allow a lens which shows a steep fit in the back central optic zone to settle to a more normal relationship, an effect which can also be obtained by reducing the total diameter of the lens and reworking the peripheral curves as they were before. The mobility of the lens also depends on the bearing relationship; thus a flat-fitting lens has often to be rejected as steepening of the central curvature is not feasible. Faulty centration may also call for a different design of lens, particularly with reference to the back central optic diameter and the thickness, but certain high-riding lenses can be corrected simply by reducing the overall diameter if the trapping effect of the upper lid is the responsible factor (Steele, 1964). A prism can be incorporated to bring down a lens while having little optical effect. Refractive alterations are also possible, usually up to about ± 1 D, but distortion of the optic may be introduced especially if the alteration is large. It is particularly difficult, however, to alter the power of aphakic corneal lenses. Finally, persistent corneal œdema may occur even after a poorly fitting lens has been appropriately modified in shape or dimensions and in such instances fenestration by one or several perforations, which must be 0·3 mm. in diameter to be effective, may be incorporated (Boyd, 1965). Such perforations should be suitably smooth and polished to avoid the accumulation of mucus within them. It has, in fact, become established practice by some authorities to fenestrate corneal lenses routinely or at their first modification.

The question of deciding whether modifications can make the lens suitable or whether a new fitting is necessary is often difficult in any individual case, overshadowed as it may be by the doubt whether the patient will tolerate any type of corneal lens. The problem is not made easier by the constant stream of new designs being introduced. It is thus possible that a proportion of patients who were unable to tolerate corneal lenses, however modified, ten years ago can comfortably be fitted today with lenses of a more modern design, the product of more sophisticated technology. In this connection the controversy about the advantage of a very small overall diameter is particularly relevant for many patients previously unsuccessfully fitted can wear small thin lenses; it is interesting in this respect to note the frequency with which, for a diversity of complaints, the most appropriate modification is a reduction in overall diameter or thickness.

LATE CONTACT LENS INTOLERANCE AND ITS MANAGEMENT

If at some stage refitting is considered necessary, a problem immediately arises in that the corneal topography may have been altered by the previous lens and discontinuation of the latter may lead to temporary alterations in corneal curvature, which may persist over a prolonged period. It is particularly important that no definite decision be made on the fit in a patient who has been continuously wearing a lens.

Another aspect relates to optical corrections when contact lenses are discontinued temporarily or permanently. Here any spectacle correction may be exasperatingly temporary in value—a significant alteration in the correction required occurring even in the short interval between the examination of the refraction and the receipt of the spectacles.

If a patient who has been wearing contact lenses comfortably for some time wishes spectacles for occasional use, it may be inadequate to allow merely an interval of, say, seven days after removal before refracting him. We have already noted that among the criteria of an ideal corneal lens is the ability to see clearly with spectacles when the contact lens is not used. It is true that many wearers of corneal lenses no longer possess spectacles, but this is undesirable; it is particularly these who may experience difficulties when for any reason their corneal lenses have to be discontinued.

LENSES OF SPECIAL MATERIALS

Contact lenses of special materials appear periodically but have not yet offered sufficient or adequately proven advantages over polymethyl methacrylate to justify the replacement of the latter. Clearly it would be helpful to have a material with as high a refractive index as possible and many have been investigated. " Hyfrax ", for example, is a polycarbonate plastic with a refractive index of 1·58 compared to 1·49 for polymethyl methacrylate (Morrison, 1962); the latter is, however, mechanically more rigid and less soluble than Hyfrax.

The most widely popularized of the new materials is the soft HYDROPHILIC PLASTIC introduced by Wichterle (Wichterle et al., 1961; Dreifus and Wichterle, 1964); this hydrogel is a tridimensional copolymer of ethylene glycol monomethacrylate with the addition of a little triethylene dimethacrylate. Its hydrophilic nature is in marked contrast to the hydrophobic properties of polymethyl methacrylate, and its free permeability to water, oxygen and the other constituents of tears with low molecular weights would appear to offer considerable metabolic advantages; moreover, it is also said to be resistant to the enzymic action of the tears.

Contact lenses of this soft material are easily manufactured in a wide range of optical powers. They are paraboloidal in shape with an overall diameter somewhat larger than that of the cornea; since their softness allows the lens to mould itself to the shape of the cornea, their fitting is a simple procedure and the lens which gives the clearest vision is ordered. The minimal corneo-lenticular tear-film encourages its adhesion and reduces the likelihood of the entry of a foreign body. Tolerance of such lenses is generally good and prolonged, and they have been reported to be without apparent ill-effects (Chiaravazza and Dossi, 1967).

Nevertheless, they have disadvantages. The tendency of the lens to adopt the shape of the cornea inevitably leads to a distortion of its posterior and anterior surfaces, the effect on the latter being complex and to some extent unpredictable (Wichterle, 1967). As might be expected, therefore, their optical performance is not uniformly good, particularly where there is significant corneal astigmatism (greater than 2 D), regular or irregular, or where the corneal surface itself is distorted. Optical verification of the lenses is also somewhat difficult. Moreover, despite the theoretical advantages of permeability, there is some evidence of stagnation of the tears since water and gases do not pass freely into the atmosphere as was initially hoped so that veiling appears in a proportion of patients (Ruben, 1966); corneal œdema and induced astigmatism may therefore occur and corneal staining is common. In spite of their softness, anomalies of the edge occasionally give rise to abrasions of the cornea. The lenses must be kept moist, otherwise they become dry and shrink and are then liable to split or fragment. They must also be boiled for five minutes twice a week in order to destroy invading fungi; since their porosity tends to retain antiseptic solutions this should be done with water. Late discoloration of the plastic material has also occurred. These lenses require a special technique of removal, most readily by pinching the lens with dry fingers; a sucker is ineffective due to the porosity of the material.

Clearly soft contact lenses present problems, but the search for a soft permeable material in which contact lenses with good optical properties can be fashioned will undoubtedly continue.

Ashline and Ellis. *Amer. J. Ophthal.*, **66**, 960 (1968).

Bier. *Brit. J. physiol. Opt.*, **13**, 79 (1956); **21**, 224 (1964).

J. Amer. optom. Ass., **28**, 394 (1957).

Bitonte and Keates. *Corneal and Scleral Contact Lenses* (ed. Girard), St. Louis, 301 (1967).

Boberg-Ans. *Brit. J. Ophthal.*, **39**, 705 (1955).

Boyd. *Amer. J. Ophthal.*, **60**, 726 (1965).

Cassady. *Arch. Ophthal.*, **66**, 356 (1961).

Chiaravazza and Dossi. *Ann. Ottal.*, **93**, 391 (1967).

Cochet and Amiard. *Bull. Soc. Ophtal. Fr.*, **66**, 1094 (1966).

Cochet, Marechal-Courtois and Prijot. *Bull. Soc. belge Ophtal.*, No. 145, 1 (1967).

Collignon-Brach, Papritz and Prijot. *Bull. Soc. belge Ophtal.*, No. 144, 971 (1966).

Dallos. *Brit. J. Ophthal.*, **48**, 510 (1964).

Desvignes. *Symposium on Contact Lenses* (Munich, 1966), Basel, 103 (1967).

Diamond. *Aerospace Med.*, **38**, 739 (1967).

Dickenson. *Amer. J. Optom.*, **31**, 378 (1954),

Dixon, Young, Baldone *et al. J. Amer. med. Ass.*, **195**, 901 (1966).

Dreifus and Wichterle. *Cs. Oftal.*, **20**, 393 (1964).

Dyer. *Contact Lens med. Bull.*, **1**, 8 (1968).

Edmund. *Acta ophthal.* (Kbh.), **45**, 760 (1967).

Fontana. *Optom. Wkly.*, **53**, 991 (1962).

Girard. *Corneal and Scleral Contact Lenses*, St. Louis, 45 (1967).

Girard, Soper and Samson. *Corneal Contact Lenses*, St. Louis (1964).

Green. *Arch. Ophthal.*, **69**, 23 (1963).

Hartstein. *Amer. J. Ophthal.*, **60**, 1103 (1965)

Hodd. *Contacto*, **9** (3), 18 (1965).

Kalt. *Bull. Acad. Méd. Paris*, **19**, 400 (1888).

Kinsey. *Amer. J. Ophthal.*, **35**, 691 (1952).

Koetting. *Amer. J. Optom.*, **43**, 268 (1966).

Lansche and Lee. *Arch. Ophthal.*, **64**, 275 (1960).

Lippmann. *Amer. J. Ophthal.*, **60**, 1104 (1965).

Long. *Amer. J. Ophthal.*, **56**, 309 (1963).

Mackie. *Symposium on Contact Lenses* (Munich, 1966), Basel, 66 (1967).

Brit. J. physiol. Opt. (1970) in press,

Mandell. *Contact Lens Practice*, Springfield
    (1965).
Miller. *Arch. Ophthal.*, **70**, 823 (1963); **80**,
    430 (1968).
Miller and Exford. *The Contact Lens*, **1**, 5
    (1967).
Morrison. *Amer. J. Optom.*, **39**, 252 (1962).
Neill. *Amer. J. Optom.*, **31**, 411 (1954).
Pratt-Johnson and Warner. *Amer. J.
    Ophthal.*, **60**, 852 (1965).
Raygada. *Acta med. venez.*, **14**, 75 (1967).
Rengstorff. *Amer. J. Optom.*, **42**, 153 (1965).
Ridley. *Corneal and Scleral Contact Lenses*
    (ed. Girard), St. Louis, 222 (1967).
Ruben. *Brit. J. Ophthal.*, **50**, 642 (1966).
    Proc. roy. Soc. Med., **59**, 531 (1966).
    Trans. ophthal. Soc. U.K., **87**, 27 (1967).
Sabell. *Trans. int. ophthal. Opt. Cong.*,
    London (1961).

Schirmer. *Brit. J. Ophthal.*, **47**, 493 (1963).
Schlegel. *Klin. Mbl. Augenheilk.*, **151**, 716
    (1967).
Smelser and Ozanics. *Arch. Ophthal.*, **49**, 335
    (1952).
Soper. *Highlights of Ophthal.*, **5**, 81 (1963).
    Corneal and Scleral Contact Lenses (ed.
    Girard), St. Louis, 445 (1967).
Soper, Samson and Girard. *Arch. Ophthal.*,
    67, 753 (1962).
Steele. *Brit. J. physiol. Opt.*, **21**, 205 (1964).
Wichterle. *Corneal and Scleral Contact
    Lenses* (ed. Girard), St. Louis, 247 (1967).
Wichterle, Lím and Dreifus. *Cs. Oftal.*, **17**,
    70 (1961).
Wild. *Amer. J. Ophthal.*, **54**, 847 (1962).
Wohlrabe and Moore. *Corneal and Scleral
    Contact Lenses* (ed. Girard), St. Louis,
    159 (1967).

CONTACT LENS TECHNOLOGY

The precise details of the manufacture and modification of contact lenses are of no immediate concern to the general ophthalmologist but some knowledge of the basic principles is advisable. Manufacture is almost entirely in commercial hands but modification, while largely so, is still to some degree undertaken by fitters themselves. Practice varies between manufacturers, but the following is a representative summary.

Modern corneal lenses are fabricated from a rod or sheet of Perspex cut into small discs which are edge-turned to about 11 mm. in diameter, and the back central optic surface with the selected radius is then cut with a diamond tool on a lathe. Subsequently this surface is polished on an automatic polishing machine and checked for accuracy and regularity by means of a radiuscope and Newton's rings. Thereafter the peripheral curves are produced by one of several techniques such as by cutting on a lathe or by grinding with a diamond-impregnated tool; the first of these curves is of great importance because its extent delimits the back central optic diameter. Subsequent curves are similarly generated and all the peripheral curves are polished. The front surface is then cut with a diamond tool so as to impart the appropriate power and central thickness to the lens, which is then polished. Finally, the edge is attended to so as to bring the diameter down to the required dimension and to fashion a suitable contour, whereafter it is polished. There are many methods for producing the edge, as by applying a cutting tool to the rotating edge, by buffing or grinding.

Much ingenuity has gone into the technology and this is particularly so in relation to the many modern designs of lens where non-spherical surfaces are generated for the peripheral curvatures of the back surfaces; for this purpose special lathes may be designed or grinding tools as for producing toric peripheral surfaces.

Modification techniques are basically similar and those practitioners who are personally involved in such procedures usually have available a modification unit consisting of a vertical spindle on which can be mounted tools, grindstones and polishing lathes; thus modifications of the peripheral curves can be carried out by means of a wax tool placed on a spindle. Blending, in which any transition between two curvatures on the posterior surface is smoothed out, can be performed with a polishing lap having a radius intermediate between those of the zones concerned. Modification of power is more usually undertaken by the manufacturing laboratory.

Although ground spherical scleral lenses were originally cut with a lathe from solid

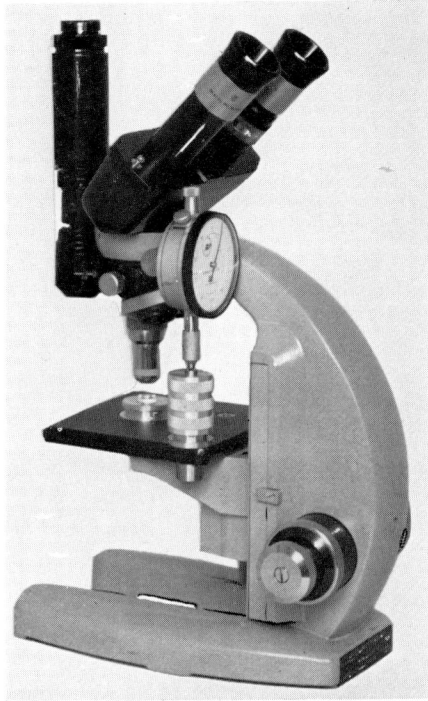

FIG. 768.—BINOCULAR RADIUSCOPE (G. Nissel).

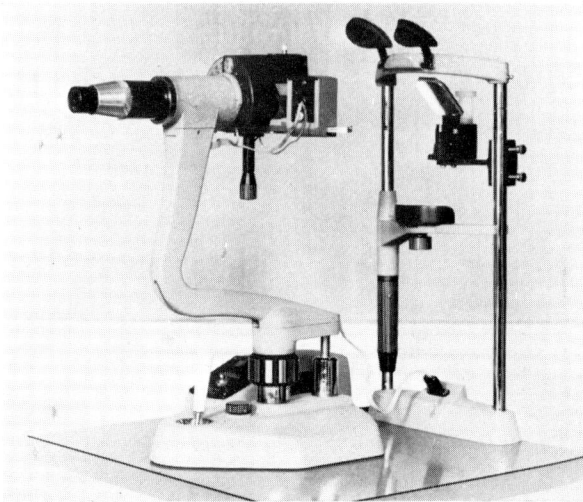

FIG. 769.—CONTA-CHECK ON GUILBERT-ROUTIT KERATOMETER (I. Mackie).

Perspex, a common modern practice is to produce pre-formed lenses by moulding heated Perspex material over jigs which are themselves lathe-cut and polished. A diamond-impregnated tool is used only to grind the optic portion to the required accuracy. This and the haptic portion are polished and the transition between them is also ground off and polished; the front surface is then cut to the appropriate power on a lathe with a diamond tool, the limbal shoulders are ground off and polishing is carried out.

Scleral lenses produced by mouldings from a cast of the eye also have a back optic curve ground on and polished so as to give apical clearance; they are then cut to the

FIG. 770.—STANDARD DIALGAUGE FOR MEASURING THE THICKNESS OF A CONTACT LENS
(G. Nissel).

indicated size and filed. At this stage the shell may be reassessed for fit or the lens may be completed by cutting the front surface to the appropriate power and polishing it.

Modification of scleral lenses is very frequently required, the optic portion perhaps requiring to be raised, altered in power or position; occasionally a peripheral optic curve is added. Tight areas of the haptic portion must frequently be ground away. As with pre-formed lenses, those made by moulding from casts also frequently require modification to the transitional zone.

It is obvious that both the manufacturer and the practitioner must have accurate instruments with which to determine the dimensions of contact lenses. The first essential is a device for estimating curvatures, such as the radiuscope which is essentially a microscope (usually binocular) which measures curvature on the Drysdale principle[1] (Fig. 768); the keratometer can also be adapted for this purpose (Fig. 769). Devices are also necessary to measure the central thickness, the overall diameter and the band-width (the extent of the peripheral zones); two of these are illustrated in Figs. 770 and 771. The technique of using moiré fringes has also been employed for the measurement of radii of curvature and for assessing the homogeneity of the surface of contact lenses.

FIG. 771.—THE BAND-MEASURING MAGNIFIER OF NISSEL.

THE HANDLING AND STORAGE OF CONTACT LENSES

The *insertion* of a scleral lens is simple although it requires some practice, Figs. 772–4. The early scleral lenses with their wide clearance required first to be filled with fluid, a manœuvre not necessary with a fenestrated lens. The lens is held with the first three fingers of one hand and the lower lid is held down with the other. With the face in the horizontal position the lens is then inserted into the upper fornix, and the lower lid eased over the lower edge of the lens with the second hand. If an air bubble is included with a sealed lens the process must be repeated. The lens is removed by easing its edge from one or other fornix (usually the upper) using the finger held against the lid margin. Mechanical aids such as suckers may be used, as advocated by Heine (1931).

A corneal lens (of the hard type) is inserted by the patient as represented in Figs. 775–9. The lens, cleaned in wetting solution and rinsed, is placed on the tip of the right forefinger while the upper eyelid is retracted by the left hand and the lower lid is drawn downwards by the other fingers of the right hand. The lens is brought gradually up to the cornea as the patient looks steadily at it; when in place the lower lid and then the upper lid are gently released. After a little time the patient acquires a ready facility for this manœuvre and often a remarkable skill which approaches sleight-of-hand. A novice may find it easier to perform this looking into a mirror laid on the table with the head in a horizontal position. The initial sensation on insertion is reduced by looking slightly downwards for a few moments. As with scleral lenses, insertion can also be carried out with the aid of a

[1] p. 127.

Figs. 772–774.—The Insertion and Removal of a Scleral Contact Lens
(I. Mackie).

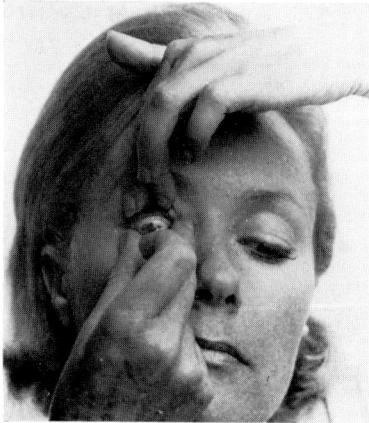

FIG. 772.—The lens is held by its edge with the thumb and second finger and orientated for its position on the eye. The forefinger steadies the lens. The eyes look downwards while the first two fingers of the other hand pull up the upper lid. The lens is slipped under this lid.

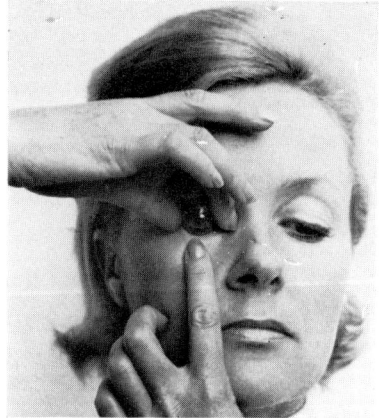

FIG. 773.—The second hand then releases the upper lid and moves below to pull down the lower lid so that it slips over the lens. (For photographic purposes the first hand has been lifted.)

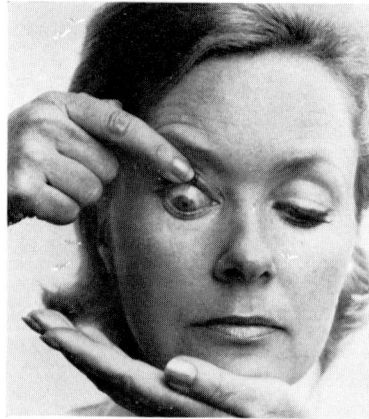

FIG. 774.—The lens is removed by looking down and pulling up the upper lid with the forefinger so that its edge engages the edge of the lens. A little downward push then releases the lens from the eye and it is caught in the other hand.

rubber sucker to hold the lens, perhaps self-illuminated in order to facilitate the manœuvre if the unaided vision is very poor.

A binocular aphakic patient is often helpless without some optical correction and may find location of the lens difficult. The insertion of the first lens may be aided if the patient wears his cataract spectacles with one eye, say the right, corrected and the lens and the lower rim removed from the other side to allow free access to the left. Into this latter eye the contact lens is inserted with the visual control of the right.

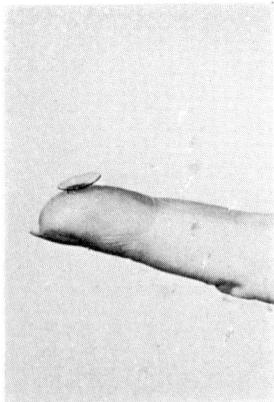

FIG. 775.

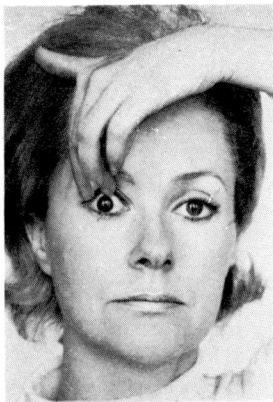

FIG. 776.

FIG. 777.

FIG. 778.

FIG. 779.

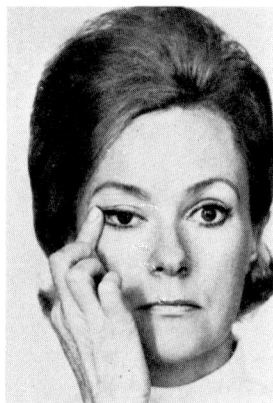

FIG. 780.

FIG. 775.—The wetted lens is placed on the forefinger of one hand, where it will be retained.

FIG. 776.—The ball of the thumb of the other hand is placed on the forehead with the fingers facing down and the first two fingers holding up the upper lid and its eyelashes. The head is held straight and both eyes are kept wide open.

FIG. 777.—The middle finger of the hand holding the lens pulls down the lower lid and its eyelashes. The eye looks straight at the lens on the finger. The lens is brought gently towards the eye until it meets the cornea.

FIG. 778.—When the lens is on the cornea it is important to release the lower lid first and then the upper.

FIG. 779.—Recentring. Should the lens be displaced onto the sclera the following procedure should be adopted. Turn the head in the direction of the lens while looking at a mirror located directly in front. This produces maximal exposure of the lens and applies whether the lens is under the upper or lower lid or displaced laterally. The lens can be replaced on the cornea by using the finger to push the lid against the lens. The tendency to blink should be resisted.

FIG. 780.—Removal. The head is held straight and the eyes, which are opened as widely as possible, look straight ahead. The forefinger is held vertically and the tip of it is placed on the outer corner of the eye, touching both lids and also the sclera at this point. The finger is pulled outwards causing the lens to be caught between the lids. It will then pop out or stick to the lashes, whence it is easily removed. The left forefinger is used for the left eye. If it should be necessary to blink to remove the lens, the pull of the index finger should not be relaxed.

In order to *recentre a lens* it is maximally exposed by the patient looking straight in front and then turning the head in the direction of the displacement. The recentring is then carried out by pushing the lens with the forefinger held against the lid margins.

Removal of a corneal lens is performed by the patient placing an index finger at the outer canthus and then stretching both lids laterally, while the eye looks straight ahead; thereupon the lens drops onto the lashes or out altogether, to be caught on the palm of the other hand held directly underneath (Fig. 780). Removal of a lens by the practitioner is usually performed by exerting pressure through the eyelids using both his forefingers.

The *fluid* used with a contact lens excited much attention in the early days when scleral lenses maintained a wide clearance of the cornea and many suggestions were advanced such as glucose, saline, sodium bicarbonate, Ringer's or Tyrode's solution. With the modern closely fitting scleral lenses or with a corneal lens this problem does not exist for the lacrimal solution suffices to occupy the retrolental space.

We have noted that polymethyl methacrylate is hydrophobic and it is believed that some of the initial discomfort of wearing a lens composed of this material may be obviated if it is wetted before insertion. The lens is usually cleansed in a *wetting solution* by manipulation between finger and thumb of the wearer's well-washed hand or by using the special cleansing devices available. Wetting solutions, and there are many proprietary brands, usually incorporate methylcellulose or polyvinyl alcohol and an antiseptic such as benzalkonium chloride, chlorbutol or an organic mercurial. Their constitution is subject to some variation as far as concentrations are concerned, and also in relation to pH, most being slightly acidic. It is usually advisable to rinse off the wetting solution before the lens is inserted since some components such as the higher concentrations of benzalkonium chloride may be irritative (Dabezies *et al.*, 1966). Cetrimide is an effective wetting agent but must be washed away before inserting the lens.

The method of *storage of contact lenses* has aroused some controversy (Allen, 1962). The advocates of dry storage point to the occasional cases of the storage fluid acting as a source of infection to the eye, but this should not occur if the lenses are handled in a sanitary fashion and the solution is changed at least twice a week. Wet storage has the advantage of keeping the plastic material hydrated, tears being absorbed into the lens when it is worn and subsequently evaporated if kept dry (Hind and Sezekely, 1959). Wet storage tends to prevent scratching while the lens is carried in a box. A cleansing action on the lens during soaking is also claimed in that chemicals and secretions which have been deposited on the surface will dissolve away. In addition, wet storage offers the possibility of some antiseptic action, but this whole subject is clouded by argument as to how effective are the incorporated preservatives, particularly against the more virulent organisms such as *Pseudomonas pyocyanea*.[1] The preservatives most frequently employed are one or more of the following: benzalkonium chloride, chlorbutol, chlorocresol, cetrimide or phenyl mercuric nitrate. A chelating agent, disodium ethylenediamine tetra-acetate, is sometimes used to potentiate their antibacterial action. On the other hand, some practitioners recommend storage in tap-water which should be changed daily.

[1] Vol. VII, p. 499.

Allen. *Arch. Ophthal.*, **67**, 119 (1962).

Dabezies, Naugle and Reich. *Eye, Ear, Nose, Thr. Monthly*, **45**, 78 (1966).

Heine. *Fortschr. Ther.*, **7**, 11 (1931).

Hind and Sezekely. *Contacto*, **3**, 65 (1959).

The Optics of Contact Lenses

The correction of ametropia by means of contact lenses does not involve any fundamental departure from the optical principles we have already discussed. In evaluating the importance of the position of a correcting lens,[1] the optical function of contact lenses has been mentioned in relation to considerations of effectivity, magnification and the accommodation, but in this discussion we ignored the form of the contact lens, treating it as a thin lens and applying paraxial optics. Although this forms a convenient approach to the subject, it is unjustified because of the high curvature of such lenses.

THE CORRECTION OF AMETROPIA

When a contact lens is in place, four media of different refractive indices must be taken into account (Figs. 781–2). Following the direction of the incidence of the light, these are air of refractive index 1, the contact lens

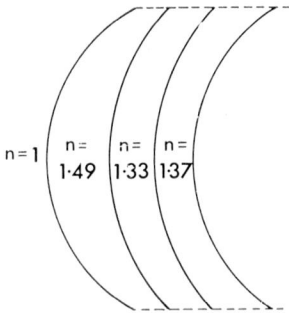 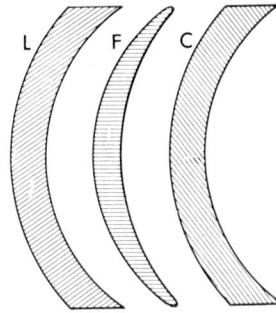

Fig. 781.   Fig. 782.

FIGS. 781 and 782.—THE OPTICS OF CONTACT LENSES.

C, cornea; F, fluid lens; L, contact lens.
n, refractive index of L, F and C.

material usually polymethyl methacrylate of refractive index 1·49, the tears of refractive index 1·33, and the corneal substance of refractive index 1·37. It is clear from the similarity of the refractive indices of the last three media that the most significant refractive power lies in the interface between the air and the lens, the front surface of which optically replaces the front surface of the cornea. The curvatures of the interfaces obviously have equal importance in the refractive properties of the system, and in this respect the two basic principles of correcting ametropia by contact lenses must be reviewed.

[1] p. 639.

In the early scleral lenses made of glass the lens itself was afocal, that is, of no dioptric power in air. Here the correcting properties of the optical system were imparted by the different curvatures of the surfaces of the " fluid lens " which is bounded by the posterior surface of the contact lens and the anterior surface of the cornea; the optical principles involved received considerable attention.[1] It is perfectly valid to regard the three elements, contact lens, fluid lens and cornea, as separated by infinitely thin air-spaces (Fig. 782). We can easily appreciate that if the contact lens is afocal the correction of the ametropia is due to the back vertex power of the fluid lens in air. Regarding the latter as thin, this power will be the sum of its front and back surface powers, that is, $F_{LA} + F_{LP} = K$, the ocular refraction.[2] Now F_{LA} is $\dfrac{1 \cdot 336 - 1}{r_A}$, and F_{LP} is $-C$, where r_A is the radius of curvature of the anterior surface of the fluid lens and C is the corneal power as measured by the keratometer. Since r_A is also the posterior radius of curvature of the contact lens, we can calculate this from $r_A = \dfrac{0 \cdot 336}{K + C}$ in metres. The required posterior radius of curvature of an afocal contact lens can therefore be calculated from the ocular refraction and keratometry if we assume that the fluid lens is thin.

Afocal contact lenses are now outdated therapeutically (but not for diagnostic purposes). Too many base curves are required to cover all the possible types of ametropia, and the necessary added power required on the anterior surfaces of these lenses makes them no longer truly afocal. Even more important is the limitation of the fitting technique allowed by such an optical system.

In modern practice both corneal and scleral lenses are designed with the posterior surfaces of their optical zones differing in curvature relatively little, if at all, from the anterior surface of the cornea. In these circumstances the correction of the ametropia is fundamentally due to the difference in curvature of the anterior and posterior surfaces of the contact lens. Once the curvature of the posterior surface is known, the optical problem is to decide on the curvature of the anterior surface; this has an empirically decided relationship to the corneal curvature which is determined.

If again we regard the optical system of the eye corrected by a contact lens as if each element were separated by a thin air-space from its neighbour, it will be seen that in this case the refractive error is eliminated because the back vertex power of the contact lens in air is equal to the ocular refraction provided its posterior surface parallels the apical zone of the cornea as is approximately the case in modern practice. Thus a myope requiring a —6·00 D lens in a spectacle frame 12 mm. in front of the corneal vertex requires a contact lens of back vertex power of —5·6 D. If the radius of curvature of the optical zone of the cornea is 7·5 mm., then the anterior surface of the appropriate contact lens must have a radius of curvature of 8·2 mm. on the basis of the optics of a thin lens. This is illustrated in Tables XXXV to XXXVII in the Appendix, taken from A. G. Bennett (1966).

[1] Hartinger (1930), Gualdi (1931), Boeder (1938), Pascal (1939), Strebel (1943), Bennett (1948), Bürki (1948), and others.
[2] The use of the terms K and C in this connection is unfortunate since in modern terminology K also refers to keratometry readings and to the flattening factor (p. 747).

THE IMPORTANCE OF THE THICKNESS OF THE CONTACT LENS

In the simple example of a myopic contact lens given above, we are assuming not only that the lens is thin but also that the fluid lens has no effective power. In practice neither of these assumptions is correct.

In spite of the efforts made to reduce the axial thickness of a contact lens to the minimum, it should be considered as a thick lens because of the relatively marked curvatures. The optical zone of a modern contact lens is therefore a thick meniscus lens. In such a lens the formula for the back vertex power in air can be related to the surface powers by the formula[1]

$$BVP = \frac{F_1}{1 - F_1 \, d/n} + F_2$$

where F_1 and F_2 are the surface powers, d the distances between the surfaces and n the refractive index. Given the posterior surface power which will be determined by the fitter on the basis of keratometry, and deciding upon the minimum value for the thickness of the lens based on other considerations not purely optical, a calculation of the required anterior surface curvature is easily made.

In practice the refraction is often estimated with the trial lens in place; such a lens may be afocal or powered and the spectacle refraction is determined to give maximum acuity. It is usually adequate to add to the back vertex power of the trial lens the effective power at the cornea of the supplementary lens required in the spectacle plane; for lenses of power less than 4 D the effectivity at the cornea is only slightly altered and the change can be ignored. This may, however, give rise to a slight error if high powers are involved or if the thickness of the trial lens is excessive. The more accurate method of calculating successive vergences may occasionally be necessary in such cases, but this is usually left to the manufacturer who should know both the power and the thickness of the trial lens. Even so, it is clearly preferable to assess the fit and the refraction with a lens as close as possible in power to the final one.

It should be remembered that even an afocal lens has some influence on the vergence of light which is not parallel. In examining the refraction during the fitting of a contact lens, a lens in the spectacle plane must necessarily produce non-parallel rays at the trial lens. When it is necessary to take into account the optical effect of an afocal lens this can be calculated from its surface powers by the formula:

$$F_1 = \frac{-F_2}{1 - F_2 \, d/n},$$

where d and n are the thickness and refractive index of the material. This formula, based on the property of the lens to allow incident parallel rays to emerge parallel from it, derives from the formula for back vertex power which in this instance is nil. The formula also gives the relationship between the radii of curvature.

$$r_1 = r_2 + \left(\frac{n-1}{n} \right) d.$$

[1] p. 77.

THE INFLUENCE OF THE FLUID LENS

Two variable factors concerning the fluid lens that bear upon its optical properties are its *thickness* and its *surface curvatures*. The thickness is usually of no great optical significance, being generally less than 1·0 mm. In certain techniques of fitting scleral lenses it may, however, be of some consequence and, if it is necessary to take it into account, the method of successive vergences is applicable. It can be shown that for average curvatures of the cornea and the contact lens, the converging power of the liquid lens in air increases (or its diverging power decreases) by about 0·12 D for every 0·1 mm. increase in its thickness.

Several factors in the design of a contact lens influence the thickness of the fluid lens. Thus, increasing the optic diameter of a scleral lens or of a steeply fitting corneal lens will increase this thickness. The interdependence of the characteristics required in fitting and the optical properties of the fluid lens are demonstrated by some empirical rules for the power of the latter in the case of scleral lenses; it is probable that if a good fit and tolerance are to be expected, this should be about −3·5 to −5·0 D (Jenkin and Tyler-Jones, 1964).

The curvatures of the surfaces bounding the fluid lens are those of the cornea and the posterior surface of the contact lens. It is easy to compute the optical power of the fluid lens imagined in air based upon these curvatures and the refractive index of tears, 1·33. For a contact lens with a back central optic radius of 7·5 mm., the anterior surface of the fluid lens will be $\dfrac{1·336 - 1}{0·0075} = +44·80$ D. The posterior surface of the fluid lens on a cornea

of apical curvature of 7·9 mm. has a power of $-\dfrac{1·336 - 1}{0·0079} = -42·53$ D.

Ignoring the thickness, the power of the fluid lens itself is therefore +2·27 D in air. From these figures it can be appreciated that a change of 0·1 mm. in the radius of curvature of the optical zone of a contact lens, whether arrived at by accident or design, leads to an alteration of about 0·5 D in the power of the fluid lens. For this reason manufacturing tolerances are rigid and the radii of curvature are expected to be accurate to within ±0·02 mm.

ASTIGMATISM

The problems presented by the astigmatic cornea and astigmatic corrections in relation to the fitting of contact lenses have already been mentioned and will be discussed in further detail later. The optical correction of such an eye by means of contact lenses of spherical surface curvatures is not difficult. If the posterior surface is approximately " on K ", the spherical correction required in the lens is that of the appropriate effectivity transposed to the negative cylindrical form. Thus for a correction of −7 D sph. −1·5 D cyl., the sphere incorporated in the contact lens would be − 7D, and for a correction of $+3$ D sph. $+2$ D cyl., it would be $+5$ D. In these circumstances the corneal astigmatism is largely eliminated by the fluid lens which is spherical on its anterior surface and toroidal on its posterior in a sense opposite to that of the cornea.

The fluid lens may have a further influence when toric back optic surfaces are used in contact lenses either to fit a markedly toroidal cornea or to attempt to ensure rotational stability when an astigmatic correction is ground on the anterior surface. Because of the differing refractive powers in the various meridians it is no longer possible to simplify the optics by considering the fluid lens in air. In such cases some astigmatism is introduced into the system because of the difference in the refractive indices of the material of the lens and the tears. The posterior surface of the lens can be modified in order to correct residual astigmatism; in this event it is necessary to grind a surface with an astigmatic power about three times that of the astigmatic correction (Williamson-Noble *et al.*, 1940).

Prismatic effects with contact lenses are in principle optically similar to those obtained with spectacle lenses. In practice their value depends on the accuracy of centration and the degree of relative movement between the lens and the eye, and in these respects properly fitted scleral lenses give more satisfactory results than corneal lenses. With the latter, disturbances may occur during and after blinking until the lens centres again. The slight decentration of a corneal lens may not have any adverse effect but with lenses of high power discomfort may arise from muscular imbalance, particularly if the centration differs between the two eyes. A prismatic effect, however, may be introduced by the fluid lens beneath a sagging scleral lens (Bennett, 1966). Prisms as a means of orientating the lens (prism ballast) are discussed elsewhere; their optical power is believed by some authorities to be reduced when incorporated in contact lenses as compared to that in air, but this has been denied (Mandell, 1967). In any event their employment as purely optical devices in corneal lenses is not practicable.

Related to the problem of prismatic effects is the question of convergence when wearing contact lenses as distinct from spectacle lenses. In this case, movement of the lens with the eye is a disadvantage to the myope who when wearing spectacles gets the effect of a base-in prism which is lost when wearing contact lenses. On the other hand, the hypermetrope requires less convergence when wearing contact lenses than with spectacles.

We have already dealt with the question of *magnification* when discussing the correction of ametropia, treating the contact lens as a thin lens[1]. So as to assess the effect of this unwarranted assumption we can divide the equivalent power of the lens into its back vertex power by the equation:

$$\frac{F_v{'}}{F} = \frac{1}{1 - F_1\,d/n}.$$

This is the *shape factor*[2] and depends solely on the thickness and the curvature

[1] p. 862.   [2] p. 77.

of the front surface; if either of these increases, the shape factor increases and the magnification likewise, as is seen in Table XXXVIII in the Appendix.

Bennett. *Brit. J. Ophthal.*, **32**, 257 (1948).
　Optics of Contact Lenses, London (1966).
Boeder. *Arch. Ophthal.*, **19**, 54 (1938).
Bürki. *Das Haftglas als optisches Instrument*, Basel (1948).
Gualdi. *Boll. Oculist.*, **10**, 486 (1931).
Hartinger. *Z. ophthal. Opt.*, **18**, 135 (1930).

Jenkin and Tyler-Jones. *Theory and Practice of Contact Lens Fitting*, London (1964).
Mandell. *Amer. J. Optom.*, **44**, 573 (1967).
Pascal. *Arch. Ophthal.*, **22**, 399 (1939).
Strebel. *Schw. med. Wschr.*, **73**, 1029 (1943).
Williamson-Noble, Dallos and Mann. *Brit. J. Ophthal.*, **24**, 43 (1940).

The Clinical Uses of Contact Lenses

THE CORRECTION OF OPTICAL ANOMALIES

The widespread use of both types of contact lens for the correction of optical anomalies calls for a summary of the advantages and disadvantages of each, particularly since some empirical and to a large extent unsubstantiated restrictions used to be placed upon the use of corneal as opposed to scleral lenses. From the cosmetic point of view, corneal lenses are the better, they are easier to fit and to replace and are more easily tolerated than the scleral type, largely because they are lighter in weight (25 mg. as opposed to 500 mg., Stone, 1968). The relative mobility of a corneal lens, however, may give rise to unwanted and variable prismatic effects if the correction is high but the increased weight of a scleral lens may give rise to a constant hypophoria since it may depress the eye. In addition, as it sags the scleral lens may create a base-down prismatic effect from the fluid lens. Veiling and frothing are less of a problem with corneal than with scleral lenses; the latter, however, are easier to see and manipulate and are less liable to be lost. The possibility of loss is usually taken into account by a remoulding of the posterior surface of the lens as finally modified and keeping this for record purposes. Scleral lenses do not rotate, an optical advantage of some consequence and, as we shall see, they are applicable for use with markedly misshapen corneæ.

MYOPIA

The corneal contact lens finds its most widespread clinical application in the correction of myopia; the vision obtained when the error is less than −2 D usually makes the use of such a lens unnecessary. The main advantage is cosmetic; spectacles are avoided and the appearance of the small eye produced by myopic spectacle lenses is also abolished and a large and attractive globe is seen instead. To this are added the optical advantages of the increased size of the retinal image obtained with contact lenses, an effectively wider field of vision, and the elimination of the distortion experienced when looking through an eccentric portion of a spectacle lens. A counterbalancing factor to these advantages is the relatively greater effort of accommodation and convergence required in the myope when wearing contact lenses; this may be of no consequence in young subjects but is important in presbyopic patients in whom difficulties in near vision may be precipitated (Robertson *et al.*, 1966).

Moderate degrees of myopia are ideally corrected by corneal lenses and a variety of fitting techniques and designs is available, the choice of which depends on the personal fancy and experience of the individual practitioner. In the higher degrees the optical advantages of contact lenses are correspondingly increased but problems arise in their fitting. Such lenses are relatively heavy and every effort is made to fashion them to be as thin as possible; a central thickness of 0·1 mm. or slightly less is about the minimum that can be produced consistent with mechanical stability. The inevitable thickness of the edge of the lens leads to difficulties with the upper lid since its movements over the edge may be partially obstructed and once over the lens the latter may be gripped and in consequence rides high. This difficulty may be overcome by bevelling the peripheral part of the anterior surface of the lens, an expedient, however, which effectively reduces the optical portion (Fig. 783).

Fig. 783.—Bevelled Lens for Myopia (R. B. Mandell).

Although it may be thought that the prescription of a corneal lens of small diameter might be advantageous in high myopia by reducing its weight, the opposite is usually the case since the loss of adhesion due to the small overall size more than offsets the advantage of a decrease in weight. The problem may make it desirable that scleral lenses should be used in the higher degrees of myopia; indeed, some practitioners make use of this type of lens in these cases without a trial of corneal lenses.

At the present time a debate is taking place on the effect on the progression of myopia of wearing contact lenses, either scleral or corneal. There have been many reports suggesting that such a progression is arrested or slowed down and that the prescription of contact lenses, particularly corneal lenses for young myopes, is therefore a good thing.[1] It has also been shown that an increase in myopia may occur in some cases after the use of contact lenses has been discontinued (Rengstorff, 1968). On the other hand, it is certain that myopia may progress in spite of wearing such lenses (Stewart, 1963; Nakajima, 1966; Elie *et al.*, 1966). At the present time no definitive statement can be made whether or to what extent the progress of myopia may be influenced in this way, for prolonged studies on a large scale with adequate controls and extensive follow-ups, taking into account the practical difficulties of a refraction at the time of the removal of contact lenses and its subsequent changes, are lacking. It must be shown that any check on the progress of the myopia that may be found is not at the expense of some permanent pathological change in the cornea.

[1] Morrison (1956–58), Dickenson (1957), Bier (1958), Barksdale (1960), Neill (1961), Miller (1962), Nolan (1964), Kelly and Butler (1964), Elie *et al.* (1966), G. and A. de Ocampo (1968), Kelly (1970).

It is certainly a common experience for the practitioner to find that subsequent alterations of contact lenses are not usually required in young myopes, but this does not necessarily signify an arrest of the progression of the condition; it is possible that an over-correction was given initially, perhaps as a result of the accommodative spasm associated with the procedures of fitting, while many of the reports of the favourable effects of contact lenses in this respect refer to refractions carried out without cycloplegia. Moreover, it has not always been made clear at what stage after removal of the lenses the refraction was carried out and whether it was performed with the lenses in place. It is well recognized that the unaided vision of the myope may be very much better for a period after the removal of contact lenses, sometimes to the extent that the previous spectacle correction may make the vision worse. The whole problem is related to the factor of spectacle-blur and the contribution made by the change in corneal curvature produced by wearing the lenses. This has been said to be particularly true with flat-fitting corneal lenses with which the flattening effect on the cornea may last as long as some weeks or months (Soper, 1967). Any effect on the axial length of the myopic eye is completely speculative and the techniques available to measure this, as by ultrasonography, are not of sufficient accuracy to make a precise assessment.

Various other explanations have been offered for the control of myopia by contact lenses, such as an increased depth of focus because of the smaller pupil (Morrison, 1957–58), the difficulties of near vision because of the additional accommodation and convergence required (Neill, 1961), the effects on the intra-ocular pressure (Kelly and Butler, 1964) or interference with the corneal metabolism (Ruben, 1967).

HYPERMETROPIA

On the whole, the incentive to wear contact lenses is much less in the hypermetrope than in the myope, for most young hypermetropes do not need a constant optical correction and older patients are not so concerned with cosmetic considerations. In any event, the optical advantages of contact lenses in preference to spectacles are marginal. There may be a reduced requirement for accommodation and convergence resulting from the approximation of the optical correction to the eye, as well as the avoidance of the prismatic effect of strong convex spectacle lenses. The size of the retinal image is smaller in hypermetropia with a contact lens than with spectacles.

APHAKIA

The aphakic patient corrected with a high convex spectacle lens experiences several untoward effects which we have already discussed[1]: when a spectacle correction is worn the size of the retinal image is one-third larger than in the phakic eye, involving an intolerable aniseikonia, peripheral vision is accompanied by distortion due to oblique astigmatic effects and other aberrations, and the prismatic effect of the edge of the lens leads to a roving ring scotoma in the field of vision which in any event is restricted. Many of these undesirable optical effects can be eliminated by wearing contact lenses either of the corneal or scleral type, a mode of correction now being increasingly employed for binocular as well as uniocular aphakia.

The fitting of corneal lenses in such patients poses special problems.

[1] p. 530.

If the whole of the anterior surface is of uniform curvature, the lens will be of excessive central thickness and heavy, a so-called *single-cut lens*, and it will tend to ride downwards. Lenses of small overall diameter, although recommended by some practitioners (Girard, 1964), may also not centre well so that special designs are often employed for the anterior surface of larger lenses (9·4 to 10·4 mm.) which are believed by some writers to centre more satisfactorily. A lenticular form is widely used but must be of a high quality of manufacture (Welsh, 1960–61) (Fig. 784). If the patient has a complete iridectomy, however, lenticular corneal lenses may give rise to considerable " flare " arising from the non-optical peripheral portion of the anterior surface; a tinted lens may be indicated. The posterior surface of the lens is usually designed with the back central optic zone " on K " or steeper than " K " according to the amount of corneal astigmatism and with a sufficiently large diameter to combat " flare ". Decentration of the lens may also result if it tends to lie over a corneal apex which may be markedly displaced as a result of surgery; corneal deformation may also be found in association with traumatic aphakia. In these instances it may be found simpler to fit the scleral type of contact lens (Ridley, 1953–63) or one extending only minimally over the limbus (Bagshaw *et al.*, 1966 ; Mills,

CARRIER ———>

FIG. 784.—LENTI-
CULAR LENS FOR
APHAKIA
(R. B. Mandell).

1967). The procedure of fitting is best carried out with a trial set of lenses closely similar in design to that which it is proposed to order, the refraction being corrected through a suitable lens.

The period after surgery when fitting should first be attempted is a matter of debate. In uniocular traumatic cases fitting ought to be considered as a matter of urgency. The usual interval is between three and ten weeks, but it is possible to assess the most favourable time from the general signs that the eye is quiet and from the invariance of successive examinations of the refraction and keratometry. It is said that hydrophilic lenses can be fitted within five days after cataract surgery (Wichterle, 1967).

Several features of the aphakic eye are important in relation to the procedures of fitting. As we have noted, corneal hypo-æsthesia is frequently present and, although it allows relatively early fitting without discomfort, it is an indication for close supervision thereafter. Vascularization of the cornea has been said to occur in aphakics wearing corneal lenses (Mandelbaum, 1964) but they usually tolerate them well. Elderly patients, particularly those subjected to bilateral surgery or with one blind eye, may have difficulty in handling corneal lenses and special aids for the former such as a spectacle frame with one aphakic lens in place may be necessary.[1] The atonic lids of these subjects often add to the difficulties since the lens may

[1] p. 766.

be poorly retained. Curiously, many aphakic patients wearing contact lenses for distance are able to see sufficiently well with this correction to read without the aid of reading spectacles.

There are now many reports of the successful fitting of contact lenses, both ventilated scleral and corneal as well as those of intermediate designs with a small haptic portion, to patients with unilateral and bilateral aphakia[1]; this applies also to infants and children[2] with aphakia, either traumatic or following surgery for congenital cataract.

ASTIGMATISM

It is evident that if the total astigmatism of the eye were entirely due to the anterior surface of the cornea and if the refractive indices of the tear-fluid and the corneal substances were identical, a properly centred corneal lens of appropriate power with spherical surfaces would fully correct the ametropia. This theoretical situation is rarely seen for a variety of reasons, so that the optical system of an eye corrected by a spherical corneal lens almost invariably shows some astigmatism.

Residual astigmatism is the term used in this respect to describe the astigmatic error found when refracting a patient wearing any type of contact lens, particularly a spherical lens from a trial set. It is made up of two elements: the true residual astigmatism of the eye itself, largely lenticular in origin, and factors caused by the contact lens. These include the astigmatic effect caused by the difference in the refractive indices of the sphero-toroidal tear-film and the cornea, the tilt, eccentricity or warping of the corneal lens, and intended or accidental toroidicity of its surfaces. These factors cannot be easily assessed and it is therefore impossible to estimate the residual astigmatism from a keratometric reading or from the patient's refraction. Fortunately it is usually small (about 0·5 D against the rule) and has little effect on the visual acuity so that it can be ignored, but in its higher degrees spherical corneal lenses may not give an adequate acuity. It is frequently found that the keratometric readings differ from the spectacle refraction in the cylindrical component. If the spectacle lenses show some astigmatism and none is found by keratometry or an astigmatism in the opposite direction, residual astigmatism is usually present. If, however, a marked corneal astigmatism is seen with the keratometer in the absence of a cylindrical correction in the spectacle lenses, there is usually no residual astigmatism.

The physical fit of a spherical corneal lens on an astigmatic cornea is a further important consideration. We have already seen that in the fitting of such lenses the selection of the curvature of the back central optic zone is usually made in close relation to the curvature of the flattest

[1] Hirtenstein (1950), Ridley (1953), Rosenbloom (1953), Dyer and Ogle (1960), Neill (1962), Figueroa and Barreau (1963), Abel (1963), Torres (1964), Riehm and Thiel (1965), Davies and Panter (1968), MacDiarmid (1968), May and Woolliscroft (1968), and many others.
[2] Blaxter (1963), Lake (1964), Baldone (1966), Saraux (1966).

meridian of the cornea. When the astigmatism is small the moderate lack of coaptation between the lens and the corneal surface is of physiological value in encouraging the flow of tears through the interspace, but in higher degrees difficulties may arise. Thus discomfort may occur if the lens rocks or becomes decentred and the corneal periphery in the flatter meridian may be unduly traumatized; moreover, flare may interfere with the vision and spectacle-blur may be a problem. Some of these difficulties can be minimized if, when fitting a significantly astigmatic cornea, a small lens with a small back central optic diameter is used. It may be possible to use a spherical lens with success in cases showing up to 4 D of corneal astigmatism or even more, and a thin flexible lens may be particularly advantageous.

Difficulties with spherical corneal lenses may to a certain extent be anticipated and avoided if contact lenses of special design are used. The patient's spectacle correction, keratometry and the pattern obtained with fluorescein characteristic of high corneal astigmatism (Plate IX) are indications that such a design may be necessary, but many practitioners make a trial of a spherical lens before embarking on more complex fitting techniques.

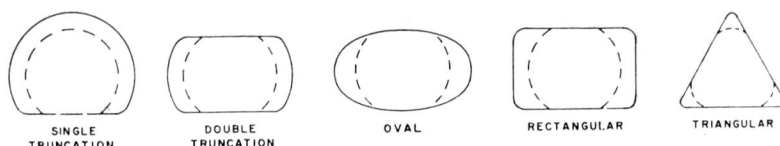

FIG. 785.—VARIOUS OPTIONAL LENS SHAPES USED TO DISCOURAGE ROTATION.
Single truncation is the most commonly employed (after R. Mandell).

If the residual astigmatism results in a significantly inadequate visual acuity, *a lens which does not rotate* or does so minimally may be indicated. For this purpose many ingenious designs exist wherein the anterior surface of the lens has a toric instead of a spherical configuration. The devices used to prevent rotation are a toric posterior peripheral curve, prism ballast usually of 2 prism dioptre power, and truncation which is frequently combined with prism ballast (Fig. 785). If such a non-rotating corneal lens cannot be tolerated, a scleral lens which has orientational stability may be substituted, particularly if the residual astigmatism is more than 4 dioptres (Ridley, 1963). Alternatively, spectacles with an astigmatic correction can be worn when a maximal visual acuity is required, or a compromising spherical correction may be adopted as a substitute for a sphero-cylinder (*e.g.*, —5·50 D sphere in place of —4·75 D sphere —1·50 D cylinder).

A toric posterior surface is also of some value in the *optical* management of residual astigmatism, as well as being of widespread application in obtaining an optimal fitting when corneal toroidicity is present. One such design employs a spherical back central optic zone with toroidal peripheral zones, a form which derives from the fact that the peripheral cornea may demonstrate a different toroidicity from that of the apical zone, but in some instances a lens with a toroidal back central optical curvature is advisable. Although the principles of fitting based on keratometry and trial sets are the same as with purely spherical lenses, in practice considerable experience is required to fit these lenses satisfactorily and their manufacture and modification are far from simple. Moreover, if the back central optic curvature is toroidal, this itself may induce a significant degree of residual astigmatism because of the difference between the refractive indices of the tears and of the plastic material of the lens; in such cases a toric curvature may have to be generated on the anterior optical surface also, making a *bitoric lens*, the production of which requires considerable technical refinements.

In summary, therefore, it may be said that astigmatism of low or moderate degree creates no extraordinary problems in the fitting of a corneal lens with a spherical curvature. Higher degrees of astigmatism associated with marked corneal toroidicity, however, present problems in the physical fit of the lens but these can be overcome by spherical lenses with special features or by lenses of toroidal curvature. The optical problem presented by residual astigmatism may be ignored if slight or it can be overcome by non-rotating lenses, either corneal or scleral in design, a toric front surface being generated at the appropriate axis.

KERATOCONUS

The clinical features of this condition have been described in a previous Volume[1] where it was noted that contact lenses play a significant part in its optical treatment. There are, however, several highly contentious aspects of their use, particularly in relation to the type and form of lens and the manner in which it is fitted and its associated therapeutic effects.

At various times all types of contact lens have been advised for this condition. Scleral lenses were originally employed and, indeed, the treatment of keratoconus was among the earliest successes obtained with them.[2] A large fluid lens was a feature of those early scleral lenses, the corneal portion of which vaulted over the apex of the cone. Scleral lenses continue to be used successfully today. Thus Ridley (1956–66) used moulded scleral lenses with the posterior surface ground so as to give a flatter curvature than that of the subject's cornea so that the resulting lens just cleared the apex of the cone; ventilation was provided by channelling in preference to fenestration for with the latter technique the bubble formed interfered with vision if the keratoconus were marked. Using such lenses Ridley reported substantial improvements in the vision in a representative sample of 100 out of 500

---

[1] Vol. VIII, p. 964.

[2] Fick (1888), Strebel (1937–43), Merigot de Treigny (1938), von Györffy (1940), Sverdlick (1942), Jaensch (1942), and others.

cases fitted at all stages of the disease save for the presence of hydrops; keratoplasty was necessary in only four patients. In early cases Bier (1957) and others found it possible to fit preformed fenestrated scleral lenses, the posterior surface of which comprised several zones with curvatures decreasing from the axis outwards.

At the same time there are many reports of the satisfactory employment of corneal lenses in this condition.[1] Their design, however, has been controversial. It has been claimed that the lens should fit flat on the apex of the cornea, thereby exerting some pressure on it with a view to retarding the progress of the disease (Fonda, 1961); but against this is the frequent occurrence of an abrasion or ulceration of the apex of the cone if such lenses are worn for a considerable time. On the other hand, lenses fitted steeply to the cornea with some apical clearance are not entirely satisfactory. As a compromise several solutions have been investigated. Some apical touch and pressure may be acceptable in association with a further bearing area in the non-conical periphery of the cornea.[2] Again, attempts have been made to contour the apex and the remainder of the cornea, a procedure which frequently requires a multicurve design with a relatively small optical zone of high curvature surrounded by up to five progressively flattening peripheral zones (Kemmetmüller, 1966). The overall size of the lens has also given rise to argument. Large lenses are said to be more static and therefore less liable to ulcerate the cornea. It has been claimed that smaller lenses may be satisfactory in the early stages of the disease (Mandell, 1965), but this has been denied (Buxton et al., 1967).

The technique of fitting is liable to be protracted. Classical keratometry is often unreliable in other than very early cases; eccentric keratometry or the specific keratometry of Bonnet[3] may be required, while photokeratoscopy may provide added information (Figs. 374–7), but none of these procedures gives perfect guidance in deciding the optimum shape of the lens. Trial sets of corneal lenses of bicurve, tricurve and multicurve design specifically made for keratoconus are available, but the vagaries of shape of the cornea are numerous in this disease. Subsequent modification of the lens ordered from the results of these methods is often necessary and " custom fitting " may proceed by the introduction of a number of peripheral curves until the desired degree of coaptation is obtained. Close observation and further modification as required must form part of the follow-up of all such patients.

Although contact lenses of either type may be of great optical value in cases of keratoconus, it is uncertain whether they have any beneficial effect other than purely optical. It has often been claimed that by exerting some pressure on the apex of the cornea the progress of the disease is arrested or retarded, but this belief is far from universally held. In any event, the con-

---

[1] Zekman and Krimmer (1955), Redmond (1957), Bier (1957), D. Fonda (1961), Kemmetmüller (1961–66), Hall and Thomson (1962).
[2] Moss (1959), Chiquier-Arias (1959), Filderman and Isen (1960).
[3] p. 131.

dition is of such unpredictable course, many cases progressing to a certain extent and thereafter remaining static, that conclusions are difficult. The decision to abandon contact lenses in favour of surgery may have to be taken because of intolerance of the lenses or failure to obtain satisfactory vision with them, perhaps because of apical scarring. A further important factor is the rate of the progression of the disease which may be either acute or only detectable by repeated observations over a long period. In such cases Girard (1967) felt that if the area of thinning of the cone exceeds 5 mm. in diameter surgery is indicated since the technical hazards of keratoplasty beyond this stage become substantial. It is possible that the prior wearing of contact lenses makes the surgeon's task more difficult; thus scleral lenses have been said to encourage a broadening of the base of the cone necessitating a larger corneal graft.

The diverse and in many instances contradictory approaches to the subject of the place of contact lenses in the treatment of keratoconus can be related in some degree to the stage of the disease. In the earlier stage spectacles suffice; in the more advanced stages corneal or scleral lenses are suitable and it may be possible to make use of standard designs if the fitting has been undertaken before significant progression has occurred. In still more advanced cases, custom-fitting of corneal lenses or moulded scleral lenses are indicated, the latter being particularly applicable to those instances of marked eccentricity of the cone. Finally, contact lenses of any type may be unsuitable and surgery must be undertaken; there is no consensus of opinion when this stage is reached, but extreme views on this issue are at present unjustified.

ANISOMETROPIA

Contact lenses are of value in this condition because they abolish the prismatic effects obtained with spectacles when the eyes look through parts of the lenses other than their optical centres. Moreover, the size of the retinal image when contact lenses are worn differs from that obtained with spectacle lenses so that they may diminish the aniseikonia. There is some dispute whether this applies to all types of anisometropia. Theoretically the advantages of contact lenses over spectacles should be most marked in refractive rather than axial anisometropia and in the reverse condition spectacle lenses should be preferable. In view of the complex interrelationships of the components of the refraction, however, it is not possible to determine clinically whether the eyes of a subject with anisometropia have refractive or axial anomalies and it is likely that many such subjects have a combination of both. It thus follows that a trial of contact lenses is clinically justified in any type of anisometropia, certainly if a correction by spectacles is not acceptable. The use of contact lenses as part of a compound optical system in this condition will be noted at a later stage.[1]

[1] p. 818.

PRESBYOPIA

Contact lenses are only exceptionally the primary optical correction for presbyopia in the emmetrope; on the other hand, several choices are available for a patient wearing contact lenses for ametropia who has become presbyopic. The simplest expedient is to use a spectacle correction for near work in addition to the lens; alternatively, dissimilar contact lenses can be used, one for distance and one for close work, often with surprisingly little disturbance of binocularity (Woodworth, 1961; G. Fonda, 1967). A third possibility is bifocal contact lenses, but the number of designs of these now available is unfortunately some indication that as yet none is entirely satisfactory (Moss, 1962; Bier, 1967). It follows from considerations of effectivity that the power of the near addition needs to be slightly greater in a bifocal contact lens than in bifocal spectacles.

The two principal types of BIFOCAL CORNEAL LENS are the rotating and the segment variety. In the *rotating* or *annular type* the optical centres of

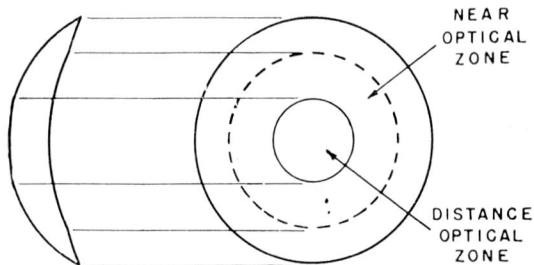

FIG. 786.—ANNULAR BIFOCAL CONTACT LENS (R. Mandell).

the distant and near corrections are the same and the two are thus concentric with the latter in an annulus round the periphery (Fig. 786). The lens rotates freely and a change from one type of vision to the other is effected by the relative vertical movement of the eye and the lens, the lower lid pushing the near annulus up so that it is opposite the pupil when gaze is directed slightly downwards. When the design is deliberately intended to produce either distant or near vision at any instant the lens is said to operate on the *alternating* principle, but it is doubtful whether even the best fitted or designed of these ever produces ideally alternating vision. The acceptance of this fact has been incorporated into the *bivision* principle or the principle of simultaneous vision, where it is left to the patient to disregard the blurred and pay attention only to the clear image, both being visible at the same time. The annular zone of increased power may be ground onto the front (Wesley and Jessen, 1958), the back (de Carle, 1959–60) or both surfaces of the lens and the portion of the back central optic zone given to distant or near vision depends on the principle to be utilized. Thus a distance portion of relatively small diameter so that a small part of the peripheral annulus is permanently opposite the pupil is a feature when simultaneous vision is the objective. Attempts to employ a lens with simultaneous vision but with a small reading segment in the axial position have not been successful. Continuously variable corneal lenses with steadily increasing power from the axial region outwards have also been described (Bier, 1967).

Some of the difficulties which may be encountered in fitting bifocal corneal lenses of the annular type may be anticipated from our knowledge of the ideal features of a single-vision lens. Thus the mobility and the design of the posterior surface are of great importance in the tolerance of the lens and any attempt to subordinate these features to the requirements of bifocal vision sometimes leads to a poorly tolerated lens of indifferent optical function. We have already noted how the mobility of the lens is of importance in facilitating a bifocal effect. If alternating vision is intended the lens must be reasonably mobile and the opposite is the case for the lens intended to give simultaneous vision. Various compromise designs are available as, for example in the *biprofile* lens wherein the intermediate curves of the posterior surface contribute some increased power which is supplemented by an annulus on the anterior surface (Moss, 1963). In such a type an attempt is made to retain the orthodox features in the design of the posterior surface while allowing this surface to contribute to the bifocal effect.

The other group of bifocal corneal lenses has a particular *segment of increased power*. They usually incorporate a feature designed to prevent rotation thus maintaining this segment in an inferior orientation; for this purpose prisms, metallic ballast and truncations of various types, as well as unusual shapes for the whole lens such as triangular, have all been employed. The segment itself may be ground on a section of one surface, usually the front, a solid or one-piece bifocal, or it may be incorporated as a fused bifocal in the posterior surface using a plastic of higher refractive index. An inserted wafer and even a completely separate segment have been described (Breger, 1964; Bier, 1967). Many shapes are available for the segment, almost as great as those among bifocal spectacles. At the time of writing a particularly popular design is the upcurve fused bifocal described variously by Jessen (1970) and Morrison (1970). Prism ballast and inferior truncation are other features of this lens.

The fitting of such lenses is directed to producing alternating vision wherein the lower segment comes opposite the pupil only on downward gaze. The centration of the lens as a whole and the demarcation between the two optical components and their relative sizes are features of particular importance. Some degree of simultaneous vision, however, frequently occurs and with this as with the rotating type the patient needs considerable practice before being able to position the lenses readily for the clearest distant or near vision.

Abel. *Optom. Wkly.*, **54,** 1647 (1963).

Bagshaw, Gordon and Stanworth. *Brit. orthop. J.*, **23,** 19 (1966).

Baldone. *Symposium on Contact Lenses* (Munich, 1966), Basel, 15 (1967).

Barksdale. *Contacto*, **4,** 349 (1960).

Bier. *Contact Lens Routine and Practice*, 2nd ed., London (1957).
Optician, **135,** 427 (1958).
Amer. J. Optom., **44,** 687 (1967).

Blaxter. *Trans. ophthal. Soc. U.K.*, **83,** 41 (1963).

Breger. *Optom. Wkly.*, **55,** 22 (1964).

Buxton, Hoefle and Koverman. *Corneal and Scleral Contact Lenses* (ed. Girard), St. Louis, 116 (1967).

Camp. *Ann. Meeting Contact Lens Soc. Amer.*, St. Louis (1961).

de Carle. *Contacto*, **3,** 5 (1959); **4,** 185 (1960).

Chiquier-Arias. *Contacto*, **3,** 393 (1959).

Davies and Panter. *Brit. orthop. J.*, **25,** 75 (1968).

Dickenson. *Optician*, **133,** 263 (1957).

Dyer and Ogle. *Amer. J. Ophthal.*, **50,** 11 (1960).

Elie, Zenatti and Hudelo. *Bull. Soc. Ophtal. Fr.*, **66,** 1081 (1966).

Fick. *Arch. Augenheilk.*, **18,** 279 (1888).

Figueroa and Barreau. *Arch. chil. Oftal.*, **20,** 58 (1963).

Filderman and Isen. *J. Amer. opt. Ass.*, **31,** 623 (1960).

Fonda, D. *Contact Lens Management* (ed. Raiford), Boston, 83 (1961).

Fonda, G. *Corneal and Scleral Contact Lenses* (ed. Girard), St. Louis, 276 (1967).

Girard. *Corneal Contact Lenses*, St. Louis (1964).
Corneal and Scleral Contact Lenses, St. Louis (1967).

von Györffy. *Klin. Mbl. Augenheilk.*, **104,** 81 (1940).

Hall and Thomson. *Contacto*, **6,** 207 (1962).

Hirtenstein. *Brit. J. Ophthal.*, **34,** 668 (1950).

Jaensch. *Med. Klin.*, **38,** 131 (1942).

Jessen. *Brit. J. physiol. Opt.* (1970) in press.

Kelly. *Brit. J. physiol. Opt.* (1970) in press.

Kelly and Butler. *Brit. J. physiol. Opt.*, **21,** 175 (1964).

Kemmetmüller. *Wien. med. Wschr.*, **111,** 863 (1961).
Symposium on Contact Lenses (Munich, 1966), Basel, 43 (1967).

Lake. *Brit. J. physiol. Opt.*, **21,** 287 (1964).

MacDiarmid. *Trans. ophthal. Soc. N.Z.*, **20,** 83 (1968).

Mandelbaum. *Arch. Ophthal.*, **71,** 633 (1964).

Mandell. *Contact Lens Practice*, Springfield (1965).

May and Woolliscroft. *Canad. J. Ophthal.*, **3,** 231 (1968).

Merigot de Treigny. *Presse méd.*, **46,** 724 (1938).

Miller. *Contacto*, **6,** 196 (1962).

Mills. *Trans. ophthal. Soc. U.K.*, **87,** 729 (1967).

Morrison. *Optom. Wkly.*, **47,** 1487 (1956).
J. Amer. opt. Ass., **28,** 711 (1957).
Contacto, **2,** 20 (1958).
Brit. J. physiol. Opt. (1970) in press.

Moss. *J. Amer. opt. Ass.*, **30,** 570 (1959).
Amer. J. Optom., **39,** 653 (1962).
Optom Wkly., **54,** 801 (1963).

Nakajima. *Symposium on Contact Lenses* (Munich, 1966), Basel 139, (1967).

Neill. *Trans. int. ophthal. Opt. Cong.*, London, 191 (1961).
Amer. J. Optom., **39,** 169 (1962).

Nolan. *Contacto*, **8,** 25 (1964).

de Ocampo, G. and A. *Orient. Arch. Ophthal.*, **6,** 156 (1968).

Redmond. *Trans. ophthal. Soc. Aust.*, **7,** 85 (1957).

Rengstorff. *Amer. J. Optom.*, **45,** 364 (1968).

Ridley. *Trans. ophthal. Soc. U.K.*, **73,** 73, 373 (1953).
Brit. J. Ophthal., **40,** 295 (1956).
Arch. Ophthal., **70,** 740 (1963).
Symposium on Contact Lenses (Munich, 1966), Basel, 163 (1967).
Corneal and Scleral Contact Lenses (ed. Girard), St. Louis, 109 (1967).

Riehm and Thiel. *Klin. Mbl. Augenheilk.*, **146,** 589 (1965).

Robertson, Ogle and Dyer. *Amer. J. Ophthal.*, **64,** 860 (1966).

Rosenbloom. *Amer. J. Ophthal.*, **30,** 536 (1953).

Ruben. *Trans. ophthal. Soc. U.K.*, **87,** 27, 649 (1967).

Saraux. *Bull. Soc. Ophtal. Fr.*, **66,** 1069 (1966).

Soper. *Corneal and Scleral Contact Lenses* (ed. Girard), St. Louis, 481 (1967).

Stewart. *J. Amer. opt. Ass.*, **34,** 1223 (1963).

Stone. *Amer. J. Optom.*, **45,** 528 (1968).

Strebel. *Klin. Mbl. Augenheilk.*, **99,** 30 (1937).
Schweiz. med. Wschr., **73,** 1029 (1943).

Sverdlick. *Sem. med.* (B. Aires), **1,** 938 (1942).

Torres. *Arch. port. Oftal.*, **16,** 137 (1964).

Welsh. *Arch. Ophthal.*, **64,** 251 (1960).
Int. Ophthal. Clin., **1,** 401 (1961).

Wesley and Jessen. *Optom. Wkly.*, **49,** 583 (1958).

Wichterle. *Corneal and Scleral Contact Lenses* (ed. Girard), St. Louis, 104 (1967).

Woodworth. *Ann. Meet., Contact Lens Soc. Amer.*, St. Louis (1961).

Zekman and Krimmer. *Arch. Ophthal.*, **54,** 481 (1955).

THE THERAPEUTIC USES OF CONTACT LENSES

Apart from their questionable value in arresting the progress of myopia and keratoconus, corneal contact lenses have little place in ophthalmic therapeutics; this aspect of the subject is therefore essentially concerned with scleral lenses. It should be realized, however, that corneal lenses can be used as optical devices in scarred and diseased corneæ.

We have seen that historically the first use of a contact lens was therapeutic—the protection of the cornea in lagophthalmos. Even before the introduction of moulded plastic lenses the therapeutic potential of contact lenses was widely recognized. They have been used in neuroparalytic keratitis (Sattler, 1938), in entropion and trichiasis (Strebel, 1943), pemphigus (Whiting, 1937; Phillips, 1939), degenerating corneal scars, descemetocele (Procksch, 1932), recurrent erosions (Sattler, 1931) and mustard gas keratitis (Moore, 1929; Ridley, 1936; Mann, 1944); in this last condition they were not only protective but also optical in function. A contact glass was also used as a post-operative protection to cover a corneal graft (Prister, 1933) and when fitted with an opaque periphery as an anti-glare measure in cases of aniridia (Streiff, 1932; Reid, 1938; Strebel, 1943) and albinism (Ascher, 1930; Friede, 1931). In most of these instances the lenses were of the preformed variety and made of glass.

The advent of plastic scleral lenses was marked by a period of neglect of their possible therapeutic value, interest in these initially being largely non-medical. A further factor in their temporary eclipse was the introduction of corneal lenses which in many instances totally replaced scleral lenses for optical purposes; the latter were regarded as outmoded and investigations which might extend their therapeutic range almost ceased. Interest in this subject, however, was kept alive by the work of Frederick Ridley and his team in Moorfields Eye Hospital,[1] but it was slow in being appreciated. His principal contribution was his advocacy of the *flush-fitting shell* for a diversity of corneal conditions including most of those noted above (Fig. 787). The shell was fashioned in plastic polymethyl methacrylate and ideally its shape followed precisely that of the anterior segment of the globe as determined by moulding. As therapeutic devices these may be worn continuously for long periods or they may be removed and re-inserted daily or even more frequently. If, as a result of their therapeutic effect, the shape of the eye changes, as for example by the filling of a crater of an ulcer, a fresh moulding may be carried out and a new shell fashioned, a process which may be repeated as often as necessary.

Various technical refinements of this therapeutic approach are possible. It is desirable to keep the shell in close contact with the cornea in all positions of gaze but some clearance of the nasal region of the haptic flange should be left to allow for alterations in the shape of the eye during movement. It

---

[1] Ridley (1954–67), Ruben (1967), and others.

may be necessary to grind the posterior surface of the haptic flange in order to encourage the optical portion to settle into close overall contact with the cornea. Irregularities in the back surface of the axial region of the shell may preclude good vision, but to obtain this is not the primary object of the device; modifications are nevertheless possible to provide an optical flush fit (Miller *et al.*, 1966–68; Ruben, 1967). Optical modification of the front surface is, of course, always possible but the improvement in vision thus obtained may not be great if the cornea is grossly diseased. It may nevertheless be of considerable benefit in patients with corneal scarring in

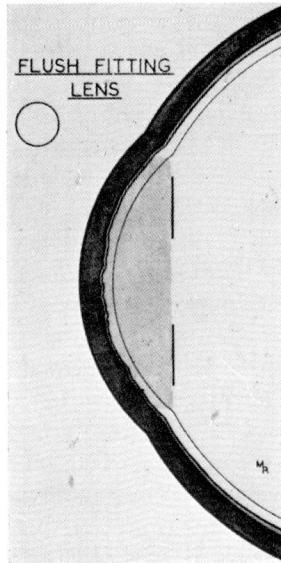

FIG. 787.—THE FLUSH-FITTING LENS.

The posterior surface is made directly from a cast of the impression of the eye and copies the surface of the globe; under it a film of tears is always maintained (F. Ridley).

which case, however, the lens need not be of the flush-fitting type. Ventilation may be introduced, either by a channel for the removal of debris (Ruben, 1967) or a fenestration (Gould, 1967).

There is some debate as to the necessity for an accurate reproduction of the shape of the cornea and for this purpose various techniques have been used to produce the shell. Girard and Soper (1966) and Ridley (1967) considered that a high degree of accuracy is necessary and to attain this they used different materials; Ridley used a plastic sheet pressed over the mould while the former workers used powdered plastic. Gould (1967) also used plastic sheet but he was more concerned with speed of production of the shells so that they could be rapidly replaced if necessary and he used a more elementary process than Ridley's with perhaps some loss of accuracy. It will thus be appreciated that considerable technical resources must be available to support the use of scleral lenses as therapeutic devices.

The factors responsible for the beneficial effect of flush-fitting shells are probably multiple and may differ from one case to another. In some a good flow of tears, the even capillarity of the film and the prevention of the gathering of stagnant pools of lacrimal fluid probably play a part. The protective factor is also important by which damage to the corneal epithelium arising from movement of the lids is largely eliminated. In addition, the smooth inner surface of the shell acts as a base for the overgrowth of proliferating epithelial cells since the elimination of dead spaces by the shell prevents the accumulation of debris over which the epithelium will not grow. Finally, the increase in temperature beneath the shell is possibly also beneficial.[1] It will be obvious that these conditions are similar to the effects of a tarsorrhaphy with the advantage that the diseased cornea is readily seen. It seems, however, that the oxygen-tension behind closed lids, while lower than at the epithelial surface of the cornea in the open eye, is higher than that behind a flush-fitting corneal contact lens (Hill and Fatt, 1963). In other instances the therapeutic benefits of scleral lenses depend on specific mechanical effects such as the separation of two inflamed conjunctival surfaces, thus preventing their abnormal adhesion while at the same time acting as a surface under which re-epithelialization can occur.

The considerable variety of cases in which benefit is thus obtained includes most of those previously noted as having benefited by glass preformed lenses, but there is little doubt that the modern techniques using the moulded plastic shell give much better results. The therapeutic objectives vary, however, from one type of case to another.

The use of flush-fitting shells may lead to cure or considerable amelioration of active disease of the cornea or conjunctiva, such as indolent ulceration and chemical burns. In the latter condition before the lens is fitted there may be a period during which it is desirable to irrigate the affected eye, a process which can be carried out by a specially ventilated scleral lens or with a moulding shell. In other instances the objective may be to stabilize the clinical condition, at the same time giving the patient symptomatic relief; in this group of diseases are included descemetocele and bullous keratopathy. In chronic epithelial œdema of the cornea from whatever cause, particularly the Fuchs type or a post-cataract dystrophy characterized by painful rupture of the vesicles, a flush-fitting shell not only relieves the distressing symptoms but may also effect some visual improvement. Other anomalies of corneal shape, such as ectasia or keratoconus, can be similarly managed; the latter is a special problem and has already been discussed.

The protective effect of a therapeutic shell is dramatically seen in neuroparalytic keratitis and in other conditions characterized by corneal epithelial fragility: corneal erosions, recurrent ulceration and insensitivity due to herpes, keratitis associated with lagophthalmos, rosacea, previous

[1] Girard (1967) gave figures for this increase, averaging 2·75°C.

exposure to mustard gas and some types of corneal dystrophy (see Gould, 1967). When the corneal fragility is already high, however, the improper fitting or wearing of such therapeutic shells may be dangerous; it is obvious that close observation of such patients is necessary in a clinic where rapid modification or replacement of the device can be undertaken. Perforation is a real danger.

The flush-fitting shell may be used as an adjunct to some other forms of treatment. Apart from the prevention of symblepharon in the primary treatment of ocular burns it can be employed after dividing an established symblepharon resulting from trauma, whether chemical, mechanical or surgical, or diseases such as trachoma, bullous eruptions of the conjunctiva as in the Stevens-Johnson syndrome or benign mucous membrane pemphigoid. In this last group of cases the prevention of drying of the cornea is an added advantage conferred by the flush-fitting shell which is used in conjunction with artificial tears. Other cases wherein lacrimal secretion is defective, for example, keratitis sicca and the syndrome of Riley-Day, respond to similar management.

Some work has also been carried out on the use of shells as splints for corneal grafting with or without some additional means of fixing the graft (Ridley, 1958–62), and also tentatively in cataract extraction. For these cases a shell is prepared pre-operatively. Optical benefit may, of course, be derived from the use of contact lenses of either the corneal or scleral type after corneal grafting, but in addition a flush-fitting shell may be of some value in restoring a graft to a more normal position if it becomes elevated in the early post-operative period and may also be used to influence the final corneal curvature.

The most important anomaly of the lids in which scleral lenses may be useful is lagophthalmos whether caused by chronic disease or by injury of the lids; they may also be of value in intractable trichiasis and entropion. It is also possible to support a ptosed upper lid by a bar over the upper part of the corneal portion of such a lens (Cochet et al., 1967).

EPIKERATOPROSTHESIS, whereby the corneal epithelium is replaced by gluing on a protective and optically correct layer of plastic material, may be useful in patients with abnormal or damaged epithelium such as occurs in bullous keratopathy or the Stevens-Johnson syndrome (Dohlman et al., 1968; Gasset and Kaufman, 1968). This, however, is largely a surgical problem and has little relevance to a book on optics.

Ascher. *Klin. Mbl. Augenheilk.*, **85**, 829 (1930).

Cochet, Marechal-Courtois and Prijot. *Bull. Soc. belge Ophtal.*, No. 145, 1 (1967).

Dohlman, Refojo, Carrol and Gasset. *Arch. Ophthal.*, **79**, 360 (1968).

Friede. *Klin. Mbl. Augenheilk.*, **86**, 649 (1931).

Gasset and Kaufman. *Amer. J. Ophthal.*, **66**, 641 (1968).

Girard. *Corneal and Scleral Contact Lenses*, St. Louis (1967).

Girard and Soper. *Amer. J. Ophthal.*, **61**, 1109 (1966).

Gould. *Corneal and Scleral Contact Lenses* (ed. Girard), St. Louis, 177 (1967).

Hill and Fatt. *Science*, **142**, 1295 (1963).

Illig. *Klin. Mbl. Augenheilk.*, **60**, 701 (1918).

Mann. *Brit. J. Ophthal.*, **28**, 441 (1944).

Miller, Carroll and Holmberg. *Arch. Ophthal.*, **76**, 309 (1966).

Miller, Holmberg and Carroll. *Arch. Ophthal.*, **76**, 422 (1966); **79**, 311 (1968).

Moore. *Brit. med. J.*, **1**, 497 (1929).

Phillips. *Proc. roy. Soc. Med.*, **32**, 756 (1939).

Prister. *Boll. Oculist.*, **12**, 149 (1933).

Proksch. *Wien. med. Wschr.*, **82**, 758 (1932).

Reid. *Trans. ophthal. Soc. U.K.*, **58**, 434 (1938).

Ridley. *Proc. roy. Soc. Med.*, **29**, 962 (1936). *Trans. ophthal. Soc. U.K.*, **74**, 377 (1954); **78**, 171 (1958); **79**, 533 (1959). *II Curso int. de Oftal.* (Symposium on Corneal Grafting, Inst. Barraquer), Barcelona (1958).

Int. Ophthal. Clin., **2**, 687 (1962). *Practitioner*, **190**, 611 (1963). *Arch. Ophthal.*, **70**, 740 (1963). *Corneal and Scleral Contact Lenses* (ed. Girard), St. Louis, 109, 222 (1967).

Ruben. *Trans. ophthal. Soc. U.K.*, **87**, 27, 649 (1967).

Sattler. *Dtsch. med. Wschr.*, **57**, 312 (1931). *Klin. Mbl. Augenheilk.*, **100**, 172, 482 (1938).

Strebel. *Schweiz. med. Wschr.*, **73**, 1029 (1943).

Streiff. *Klin. Mbl. Augenheilk.*, **89**, 625 (1932).

Whiting. *Brit. J. Ophthal.*, **21**, 529 (1937).

CONTACT LENSES WITH SPECIAL FEATURES

TINTED CONTACT LENSES, either scleral or corneal in type, may be advisable on medical grounds as in albinism or aniridia; in the case of scleral lenses the haptic portion may be opaque and an artificial iris may be painted on the corneal portion. As we have noted, photophobia is sometimes a prominent symptom with a corneal lens for which tinted lenses may provide relief, but before proceeding, corneal œdema as a cause of the photophobia must be excluded. The tint may be provided by the use of tinted plastic material or by a surface coating although this may not be durable. Wearing anything more than moderately tinted corneal lenses may be disadvantageous in darkness and additional lenses of clear materal are often ordered for use in poorer illumination (Fletcher and Nisted, 1963).

The transmissivity of tinted and clear corneal lenses is somewhat variable and some may well allow the passage of ultra-violet radiation (Ball, 1964). Even when this is not so, it is obvious that the tinted corneal lens offers no protection from ultra-violet to the conjunctiva, as for example, during skiing. Tinted lenses may also be employed for purely cosmetic reasons in order to alter the colour of a patient's eye.

Totally or partially OCCLUSIVE LENSES have also been employed. Totally occlusive lenses made of black plastic material may be of value in strabismus either in the relief of intractable diplopia or in the treatment of amblyopia in children. Catford and Mackie (1968) have employed high plus lenses for this purpose with good effect. Partially occlusive devices may be of value as optical aids, as in irregular astigmatism. A pin-hole contact lens may be

(a)   (b)   (c)   (d)

FIG. 788.—A STENOPÆIC CONTACT LENS.

The lens (a) is made up of a grooved contact lens on the surface of which is a perforated disc of black opaque glass (b). (c) and (d) are sections of (a) and (b) (F. A. Williamson-Noble).

of several designs, the pin-hole itself being a plug of clear plastic in a black plastic disc, or a gap in a dark coating or lamination (Williamson-Noble, 1960) (Fig. 788). The pattern of the iris can be painted on the periphery of the anterior surface of an occlusive lens, either partial or total. Such a *cosmetic shell* of the scleral type may be of value in disguising an unsightly eye or one grossly disfigured by disease; the scleral portion is either clear or of white plastic and the iris is appropriately coloured. Such shells if flush-fitting may alleviate some of the chronic irritability to which these eyes may be prone (Espy, 1968).

A contact lens can also form part of a VISUAL AID, usually based upon the principle of the Galilean telescope. Thus a contact lens with a high minus power of either the corneal or scleral variety acts as the eye-piece, the objective being worn as a spectacle lens. This is discussed elsewhere.[1]

OCCUPATIONAL USES of contact lenses require little further comment. The misting and fogging of spectacle lenses that may occur from rain or steam in certain occupations are indications for attempting to wear contact lenses. Where they are required for sports they may be fitted with particular criteria in mind; thus the tendency to dislodgement may be minimized by ordering a very thin corneal lens. Corneal lenses of large diameter and special designs with small scleral flanges are recommended by some practitioners. The hydrophilic lens may be of value in sports. Such lenses, of course, may be exchanged for spectacles in ordinary life. A scleral lens is much less easily displaced during sport, and is the only lens that can be used for swimming, an activity during which many corneal lenses have been lost. An ingenious *underwater contact lens* has been devised which incorporates an air space with a flat front allowing the swimmer good vision both in and out of the water (Nagel and Monical, 1954; Grant, 1963; Mossé, 1964).

The use of contact shells as a protection in *radiotherapy* has been discussed elsewhere.[2]

Ball. *Brit. J. physiol. Opt.*, **21**, 219 (1964).

Catford and Mackie. *Brit. J. Ophthal.*, **52**, 342 (1968).

Espy. *Amer. J. Ophthal.*, **66**, 95 (1968).

Fletcher and Nisted. *Ophthal. Opt.*, **3**, 23 (1963).

Grant. *Opt. J. Rev. Opt.*, **100**, 22 (1963).

Mossé. *Brit. J. physiol. Opt.*, **21**, 250 (1964).

Nagel and Monical. *Amer. J. Optom.*, **31**, 468 (1954).

Williamson-Noble. *Brit. J. Ophthal.*, **44**, 679 (1960).

[1] p. 818. [2] Vol. VII, p. 775.

FIG. 789.—GALILEO GALILEI
[1564–1642].

CHAPTER XIX

VISUAL AIDS

No book on optics would be complete without a tribute to GALILEO GALILEI [1564–1642] and, since many of the most efficient visual aids are based on the Galilean telescopic system, this seems the most suitable place for the insertion of his portrait (Fig. 789). Born of a noble but impoverished Florentine family, he went to the University of Pisa to study medicine but soon mathematics and physics excited his interest to the exclusion of all else. Starting with observations on the motion of pendulums (as seen in the swing of a lamp hung in the cathedral of Pisa) and noting the fact that bodies of different weights fell with the same velocities (as seen by dropping objects from the Leaning Tower of that city), he first established physics, both statics and dynamics, as an experimental science founded quantitatively on mathematics just as Johannes Kepler was contemporaneously establishing the science of optics. The next generation saw the observations of Kepler and the dynamics of Galileo combined by Isaac Newton in his theory of universal gravitation.

In the present connection the principles of the telescope arose as a chance by-product of the manufacture of lenses by Dutch opticians about 1600. Their haphazard combinations of lenses were put on a scientific basis by Kepler who used two convex lenses, an arrangement improved by Galileo who introduced the more effective combination of a concave eye-piece and a convex object-lens. Overcoming the difficulties of grinding and polishing his lenses, he constructed a large number of these, his first telescope magnifying by 3 diameters and his last by 33. With them he made an extraordinary number of outstanding astronomical observations, the revolutionary character of which he immediately realized and as a result he demolished from the scientific point of view the ancient cosmology founded on Aristotelian-Ptolemaic dogma which had been accepted for more than 2,000 years, and established the correctness of the new theory of Copernicus. To the Church, however, the view that the earth was not especially created by God as the centre of the Universe but rotated around the sun in the company of other planets was heresy, and he was warned in 1616 and was eventually denounced by the Inquisition in Rome in 1633; he thereupon recanted his views and thereafter lived in retirement. Nevertheless, his prodigious mental activity remained undiminished and he continued to produce work which was enthusiastically acclaimed throughout the scientific world, persisting even after he became blind in 1637 until the year of his death, during which he was dictating to his disciples a new theory of impact.

When defective vision is due to some cause other than an optical anomaly of the eye, the first therapeutic consideration will always be whether medical or surgical treatment is available which might be beneficial. When improvement is not possible or, perhaps because of fear or ignorance, when such treatment is refused, optical devices may alleviate the patient's visual disability to some extent. The devices employed in these circumstances are commonly known as VISUAL AIDS.

Many of these are difficult to manage so that the patient's cooperation, adaptability, intelligence and motivation are of prime importance in learning to use them. The apathetic and the old with minimal incentives rarely succeed as well as an active person to whom a visual aid may make all the difference to his being able to continue his gainful employment or his pleasurable activities. The attitude of the practitioner is also important ; clearly he must be skilled in the application of his optical knowledge but in addition he must be enthusiastic in encouraging the patient to tolerate or overcome the inevitable disadvantages of most of these devices. In this respect there are psychological hurdles to be overcome. The idea is held by many such patients that the use of the eyes is harmful so that the poor sight remaining to them will thereby be further damaged. This wish to " conserve " vision is associated with a reluctance to adopt unusual ocular postures such as a very short reading distance. Such notions should be tactfully dispelled and the patient should be encouraged to use his eyesight as much as he can. Sometimes the idea is inadvertently conveyed to the patient by the practitioner that visual aids are very much a final despairing effort to retain some useful sight ; the feeling of hopelessness thereby engendered is strongly to be deprecated since it militates against the patient's persistence with the device.

Whatever the nature of the ocular disorder, the more nearly the patient approaches complete blindness—lack of the perception of light—the less likely is it that visual aids will be of value. From the practical viewpoint it is improbable that a patient with a visual acuity of less than 3/60 will be materially helped. The converse is also true, that patients with only slightly subnormal corrected vision often derive the greatest benefit from a visual aid ; the most favourable are those with an acuity of 6/18 who require aid in reading print. The central visual acuity is, however, only a general guide to the likelihood of success. The precise pathology, duration and course of the lesion are also of importance and may also indicate the type of visual aid which is appropriate.

Non-refracting Devices

Disorders of the ocular media associated with irregular astigmatism and the presence of numerous small opacities may lead to the formation of multiple blurred retinal images ; in these cases a pinhole device will be found helpful, sometimes markedly more so than ordinary spectacles.

STENOPÆIC " SPECTACLES " have been known as a visual aid from early times ; they were advocated and their optical principles explained by Daza de Valdés in 1623 (Fig. 790), and were first employed clinically by the French ophthalmologist, Serre (1857), and Frans Donders (1864). The main disadvantage of a stenopæic hole is that it provides a very small visual field and, since it does not move with the eye, it is of little advantage to the wearer when walking about. The expedient is useful, however, in reading, when it is best held in the hand following the line of print. When it is required for general purposes, a disc composed of several such openings bored in a sheet of opaque material may prove better than nothing (Fig.

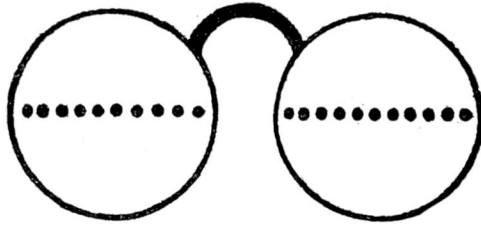

FIG. 790.—DAZA DE VALDÉS'S STENOPÆIC SPECTACLES.

791). Guthrie (1934) found that the most useful spacing between the holes was about 4 mm., and that with ordinary illumination the optimum size was 1·5 mm. for distant and 0.3 mm. for near vision (Figs. 792–3). Hoitash (1934) used a stenopæic slit, 1·5 to 2·0 mm. wide; it may be widened by a

FIGS. 792 and 793.—C. C. GUTHRIE'S STENOPÆIC SPECTACLES.

FIG. 791.—STENO-PÆIC "SPECTACLE".

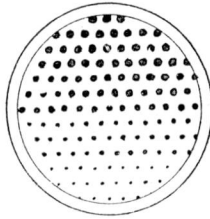

FIG. 792.—The gradua-tion of the holes in the disc which progressively diminish in size from above downwards.

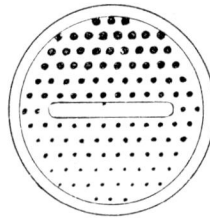

FIG. 793.—The addition of a central stenopæic slit to allow distant vision.

semicircular opening either in the centre or towards the side according to the need for distant or near vision (Fig. 794). Any of these expedients can be used uniocularly or binocularly, with or without a correcting spectacle lens. The visual benefit obtained can sometimes be increased by varying the number or position of the perforations. Such devices are now

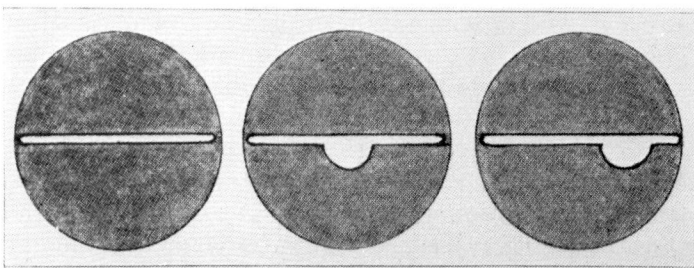

FIG. 794.—HOITASH'S STENOPÆIC DISCS.

Showing three types of stenopæic slit. The middle disc shows an enlarged segment centrally; that on the right is peripheral.

almost obsolete, but a place may still be found for them in a patient with considerable corneal irregularity who refuses or is unsuitable for surgery or contact lenses or for those with early cataract. It is interesting that a narrow slit cut in a wooden " spectacle " strapped to the head has long been used by Eskimos as a protection against snow-blindness.

A similar optical effect is to some extent provided for himself by a patient with a permanently miotic pupil, thus perhaps partially accounting for the occasional patient operated on for cataract who finds it possible to read with his distance spectacles.

It is to be noted that a stenopæic opening will prove equally useful in any error of refraction, and in the event of loss or breakage of a pair of spectacles a pinhole in a sheet of dark paper will enable an ametrope or a presbyope to read or write in an emergency.

The use of a *reading-slit* cut in dark cardboard or plastic material placed immediately over print with dimensions of $\frac{1}{4}''$ to $\frac{1}{2}''$ by $3''$ to $7''$ so that only one or two lines are visible is also sometimes found helpful by patients with early lens opacities. In such cases reflected light from the page is decreased and the contrast is thereby increased thus allowing greater clarity in reading (Leinbach, 1960) (Fig. 795).

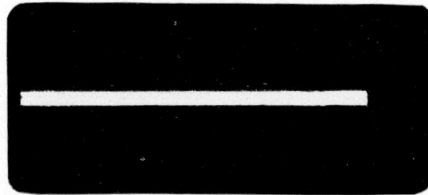

FIG. 795.—LEINBACH'S READING SLIT.

Magnifying Devices

Non-refracting devices have little part to play in disorders of the retina, optic nerve or visual pathway; indeed, they may significantly impair the vision in these cases because of the associated reduction in illumination. In this group of diseases considerable benefit may be derived from magnification of the retinal image and this is also true of other types of visual defect such as those associated with opacities of the media or nystagmus. Magnification is of the greatest value, however, in certain varieties of macular disease. Visual aids thus find their commonest application in senile macular degeneration, particularly of the " dry " pigmented type; the exudative form is frequently so extensive that any practical degree of magnification will fail to bring recognizable portions of the image onto normally functioning retina. The advantages of magnification are less manifest in patients with disorders restricting the visual fields such as advanced glaucoma and the tapeto-retinal dystrophies or other diffuse retinal diseases such as diabetic retinopathy. An attempt to improve the vision in such cases by visual aids, however, is always worth while.

THE OPTICAL PRINCIPLES OF MAGNIFICATION

It will be recalled that the size of the retinal image depends upon the angle subtended by the object at the nodal point of the eye and the simplest manœuvre which provides magnification is to approximate the object of regard to the eye. A visual aid, therefore, not only produces optical magnification of the object but also takes advantage of the effect of approximation. Indeed, the patient may be able to inspect an object at a very close distance without an optical adjunct, depending upon his available amount of accommodation and the refractive error. Thus a child with superabundant accommodation or a highly myopic patient may well be able to read with reasonable facility in spite of macular degeneration, merely by holding the print close to his eyes.

This magnification is the basis of the commonly used test for the integrity of central vision in a high myope with cataract for whom surgery is being considered. Such a patient with a corrected distance vision of less than 6/60 may, unaided, be able to read N 5 on a well-illuminated reading chart held very close to the eye, the magnification compensating for the poor quality of the retinal image.

For distance vision, approximation may be considered by definition to be impossible and here the only optical devices that are of assistance are telescopic arrangements, the optical principles of which will be discussed later.[1] The most important optical aids are those intended to assist reading and close work. These fall into four groups: magnifiers held some distance from the eye, for convenience referred to as hand-magnifiers; spectacle-magnifiers made up either of a single lens or a combination of lenses; telescopic devices; and finally, forms of projection apparatus.[2]

THE OPTICS OF SIMPLE MAGNIFYING DEVICES

In all these a powerful converging lens (or combination of lenses) is interposed between the eye and the object so as to produce an erect optically magnified image. The device is positioned so that the object is between the lens and its focal point, usually close to the latter.

Consider first the optical situation wherein the eye is very close to the lens as in a *spectacle-magnifier* or a simple magnifying glass held close to the eye (Fig. 796). Since the size of the retinal image is determined by the angle subtended at the nodal point, the magnification produced by the lens will be θ_2/θ_1, where θ_1 is the angle subtended by the object at the nodal point and θ_2 the angle subtended at the nodal point by the image formed by

---

[1] p. 804.
[2] A certain confusion in terminology exists with regard to the term " loupe ". In Great Britain this term is used for a magnifying device held close to the eye. In the United States, however, a loupe means a magnifying device used some distance away from the eye usually, of course, less than arm's length (Linksz, 1955). This terminological distinction highlights some important aspects of the optics of the use of magnifiers, as we shall now investigate. For this purpose we shall avoid the use of the term " loupe " where possible and refer to one instrument as the hand-magnifier and to the other as a spectacle-magnifier.

the interposed lens. It requires emphasis that θ_2/θ_1 is always greater than 1, but only to a small extent if the eye is close to the lens; the shorter the eye-lens distance (in geometrical terms, the nearer the nodal point is to the optical centre, C, of the lens) the more nearly does the fraction approach unity, and no change occurs in the size of the retinal image as a result of interposing the lens. This may seem extraordinary but it follows from the fact that the image formed by the lens is larger the further it is from the eye, an effect which is physiologically advantageous since the image can be positioned so that it is within the range of the accommodative power of the eye. In an old subject without accommodation the image can be placed at infinity by having the object at the anterior focal point of the lens; in a subject with active accommodation the image may still be clearly focused if it is anywhere between infinity and the near-point. The main optical effect of a magnifier used in this way is therefore to allow a clear retinal image to be obtained of an object so close that the unaided eye is incapable of the

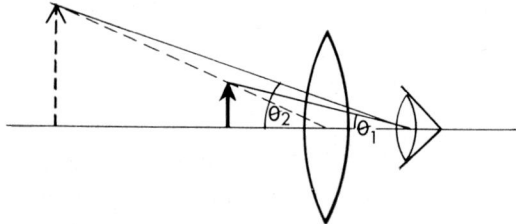

Fig. 796.

necessary accommodative effort; were the subject able to accommodate for this position there would be little optical advantage in interposing a convex lens.

In order to standardize the power of magnification (M) it is customary to denote magnifiers as being $8\times$, $10\times$, etc., and an artificial convention is adopted in order to calculate this (Figs. 797–8). The magnifier is assumed to produce an image at infinity, the object being at the anterior focal point and the apparent size of this image is compared to the apparent size of the object if it were at the accepted near-point of distinct vision, which is taken to be 25 cm. from the nodal point. Thus

$$M = \frac{\text{Apparent Size of Image}}{\text{Apparent Size of Object were it 25 cm. from the eye}}.$$

As can be seen from this, tan θ_2 is o/f, and tan θ_1 is $o/25$. When θ_2 and θ_1 are small their tangents can be considered to be equal in value to the angles themselves. Therefore:

$$M = \theta_2/\theta_1 \simeq \tan\theta_2/\tan\theta_1 = o/f \div o/25 = 25/f$$
$$\text{or } M = F/4$$

Thus in these particular circumstances with the object at the anterior focal point, applying the paraxial optics of a thin lens, the magnification defined as indicated above, is seen to be a quarter of the dioptric power of the lens (F). When the object is located here the position of the eye is immaterial since the image formed by the lens is at infinity.

It will be appreciated that with magnification defined in this way much depends on the accepted near-point of distinct vision and there is some indication that the distance of 25 cm. might be too short, 40 cm. being more appropriate (Sloan and Habel, 1956). For this reason it has been suggested that in defining magnification it is probably more reliable to give the equivalent power (Sloan and Jablonski, 1959).

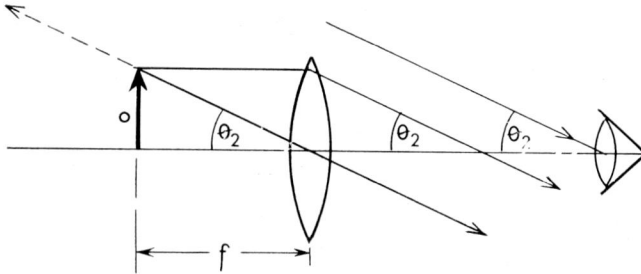

FIG. 797.

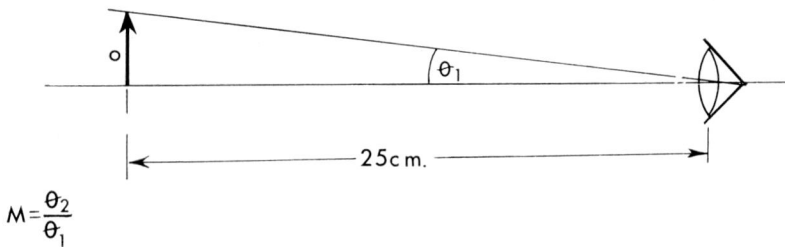

$$M = \frac{\theta_2}{\theta_1}$$

FIG. 798.

HAND MAGNIFIER

The optics of a *hand-magnifier* is somewhat more complex since the eye-lens distance and the lens-object distance may vary. In all cases the object is within the anterior focal distance of the lens, usually being close to but not precisely at the anterior focus. The optical conditions we have assumed in order to find the power of a magnifier do not apply to this situation. In discussing the practical application of a magnifier we are concerned with its value as a means of enlarging the retinal image and with its effect in allowing the eye to focus clearly the object of regard. In other words, the image formed by the magnifier must be within the range of the accommodation of the eye.

The magnification depends upon the relationship between the angles subtended at the eye by the object and that subtended at the eye by the optically magnified image formed by the lens. Because of the separation of the eye and the lens this image subtends a smaller angle at the eye than it would if the eye and the lens were closely approximated. Nevertheless, this angle will always be greater than that subtended by the object at the eye except when the eye is very close to the lens; save in this instance, therefore, enlargement of the retinal image, true magnification, is produced.

Where the eye-object distance is fixed and the lens is moved, as the latter approaches the eye from a position close to the object the magnification which was originally unity increases until the lens is sited so that the object is at its anterior focus (Fig. 799). As the lens approaches this position the angle subtended at the nodal point by the image formed by it increases

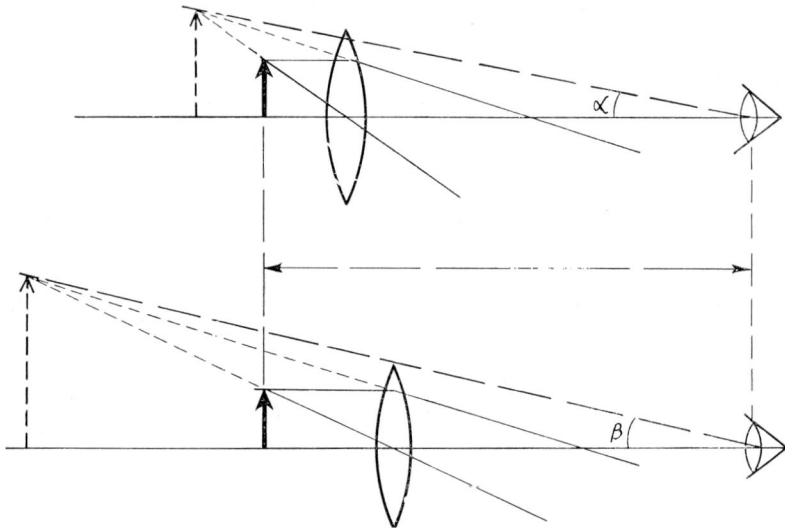

Fig. 799.—The Eye-object Distance is Fixed ($\beta > \alpha$).

slightly; there is, however, a marked displacement of the image away from the lens and the eye towards infinity so that less accommodation is required. It follows that the closer the magnifying glass to the eye, the less is the accommodative requirement for any given object-distance. Moreover, the stronger the magnifying glass the further away from the eye can it be held so as to give a magnification equivalent to that of a weaker lens for a fixed eye-object distance.

In many magnifiers the distance between object and lens is predetermined, as in a *stand-magnifier*. The distance can be arranged so that the object is close to or at the anterior focus of the lens (Fig. 800). The image is then so far distant that it subtends an angle at the nodal point which does not greatly vary whatever the position of the eye, the size of the retinal image remaining virtually constant and little accommodative effort being required. This remarkably unrestricted situation, however, may alter if a presbyopic correction is worn when using such a stand-magnifier because far distances

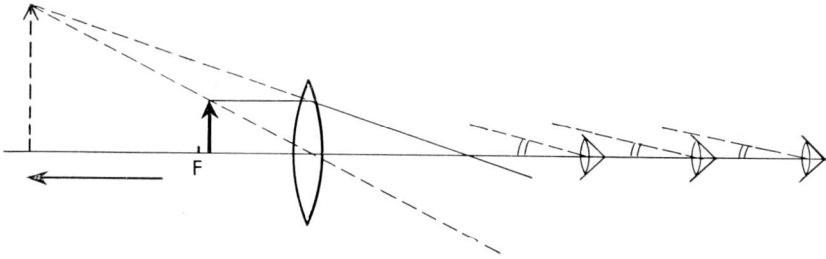

FIG. 800.—STAND-MAGNIFIER: THE OBJECT-LENS DISTANCE IS FIXED.

cannot be focused. There may, however, be circumstances in which, by altering the object-lens distance, a subject wearing a presbyopic correction can get the advantage of approximation.

Although the size of the retinal image changes little with the position of the eye, if the lens-object distance is kept fixed, the field of vision does vary since this depends both on the eye-lens distance and on the diameter of the lens; the advantage of bringing the lens-object close to the eye is the increase in visual field thus obtained (Fig. 801). In practice many stand-magnifiers are arranged so that the print is well within the focal distance, and the size

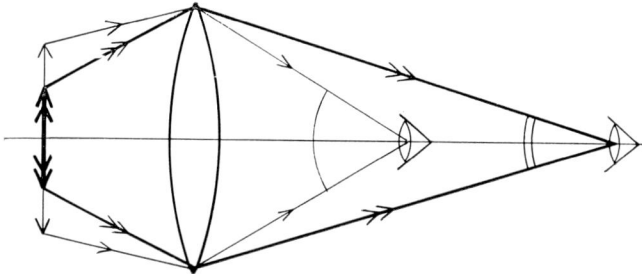

FIG. 801.—THE FIELD OF VIEW IS INCREASED BY APPROXIMATING THE EYE
TO THE LENS.

of the retinal image therefore depends on the position of the eye. As this is approximated to the lens both the field and the size of the retinal image increase.

The mental impression of size, however, is closely related to the eye-lens distance, even when the lens-object distance is constant. Thus when the object is at the anterior focal point of the lens, the image is formed at infinity and, if the eye is moved backwards from a position close to the lens to one some distance away, the image appears to get larger even although the size of the retinal image remains constant. This illusion, first explained by Robert Smith (1738), is because the observer adjusts his notion of size in the belief that the image formed by the lens is a certain finite distance behind it and withdrawing from it should therefore make it seem smaller; as the retinal image actually remains static in size, an impression of magnification results.

SPECTACLE-MAGNIFIERS

In *spectacle-magnifiers* the distance between eye and lens is constant and small. They are usually of high power and focusing is therefore critical, the object being of necessity placed at the anterior focal point. Thus when a $+20$ D lens is placed close to the eye, an object need be moved forwards from the focal point only 8 mm. to bring its image from infinity to 25 cm. from the eye, the near-point of distinct vision.

In comparing the sizes of retinal images for various object-distances with a fixed eye-lens distance, the relationship of the posterior focal point of the lens to that of the nodal point of the eye is crucial. As can be seen from Fig. 802, when these two points coincide the size of the retinal image is the same wherever the object; its clarity, however, depends upon the ability of the eye to accommodate for the distance at which the lens forms its image,

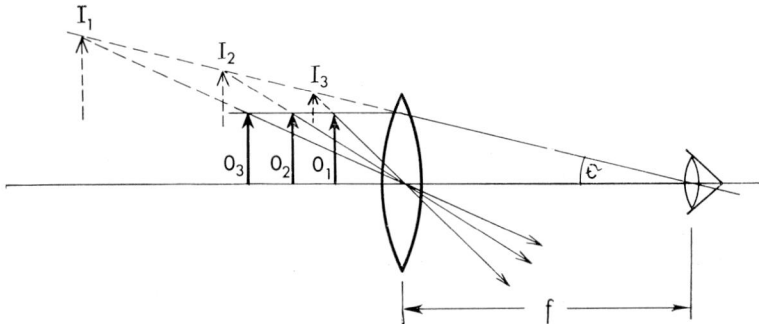

FIG. 802.—SPECTACLE MAGNIFIER: THE EYE-LENS DISTANCE IS FIXED.

which in turn, of course, depends on the position of the object. In the spectacle-magnifier the posterior focal point is usually behind the nodal point of the eye. The short distance of clear vision through which the object can be moved from the anterior focus to the point where its image is produced at the near point of distinct vision brings with it a slight increase in the size of the retinal image (Fig. 803). For a near point of distinct vision of 25 cm. and with the eye very close to the lens, the magnification is $F/4 + 1$, numerically slightly greater than that of the conventional definition, $F/4$ (Fig. 804).

The opposite situation occurs when holding a hand-magnifier a fixed distance from the eye so that its posterior focus is in front of the nodal point of the eye. Approximation of the object now leads to a steady decrease in the size of the retinal image until with the object at the lens itself the magnification is unity.

It is worth noting that at all object-distances, when the nodal point of the eye and the posterior focus of the lens coincide, the size of the retinal image is the same as that obtained when the object is at the anterior focal point whatever the position of the eye may be, and in the conventional definition of magnification it is the size of this retinal image which is compared with that produced by the object at the near-point of distinct vision (Figs. 798 and 802).

One additional factor to be considered in this account of magnification is the patient's refractive state; thus an uncorrected hypermetrope may be able to focus the image of an object slightly outside the anterior focus of the lens.

The usefulness of magnification cannot be indefinitely extended for numerous practical reasons. Unlimited magnification of print may lead to difficulties in interpretation because the restricted field allows only parts of

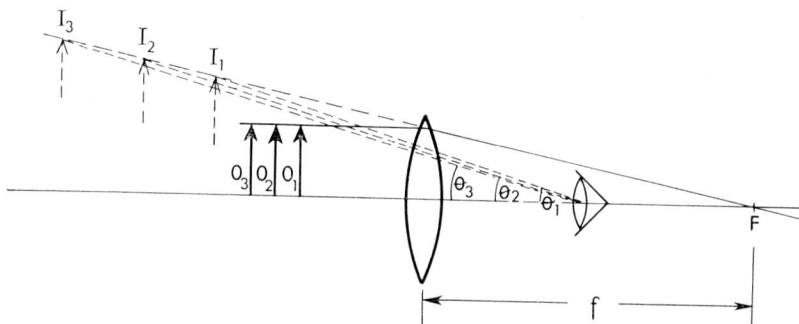

Fig. 803.—If the posterior focus is behind the eye, approximating the object leads to an increase in the size of the retinal image; $\theta_1 > \theta_2 > \theta_3$.

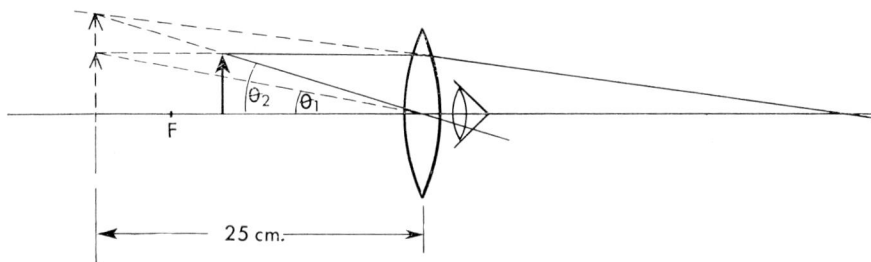

Fig. 804.—Magnification with the eye close to the lens and the image at 25 cm.

$$M = \theta_2/\theta_1 = v/u$$
$$1/v - 1/u = 1/f$$
$$1/v - 1/u = 1/f$$
$$1 - v/u = v/f$$
$$1 - M = -25/f \qquad \therefore M = F/4 + 1.$$

words or sentences to be visible at the same time; reading may therefore be irritatingly slow and difficult. In addition, strong lenses are prone to cause distortions which act as restrictions to their effective field. High magnification is also liable to be accompanied by instability of the field, a factor aggravated if there is any unsteadiness of the head or hand of the patient. The depth of focus is also poorer with greater magnification and this again is accentuated by involuntary motions of the head or hand. Taking all these factors into consideration, it is thus desirable to prescribe the weakest magnification that is adequate for the required visual task.

It should be noted that some authorities make a distinction between spectacle-magnifiers with which the object is always at the anterior focal point and other magnifiers placed some distance away from the eye with the object within the anterior focal distance, in which case the image is formed at a finite distance from the eye. As we have seen, this is not a fundamental consideration but it must be remembered when taking into account the degree of accommodation available to the patient.

TELESCOPIC SPECTACLES

The advantage to the high myope of employing the Galilean telescope for distant vision has long been known. Small Dutch telescopes were used in the 17th century for this purpose: Gustavus Adolphus in 1631 had one, and Father Eschinardi tried to compute lenses for such a glass for reading in 1667; H. Dixon (1785) introduced a reflecting telescope for the same purpose. Kitchiner (1824), also of London, produced a treatise on the subject and L. Seidel in 1846 succeeded in correcting the optical aberrations to some extent,[1] but owing to lack of the optical knowledge to deal effectively with aberrations, little progress was made towards a satisfactory solution of the problems involved until Hertel (1910) of Strasbourg, exercised at the serious end-results in patients operated on for myopia by Fukala's operation,[2] turned his attention to optical methods of improving the vision in aphakia. As a result of his interest the study of the technical requirements was undertaken at Jena (von Rohr, 1910–21), and since then the efficiency of such instruments has grown apace due to optical research principally in Germany[3] and England[4] and in America by the Kollmorgen Optical Company.

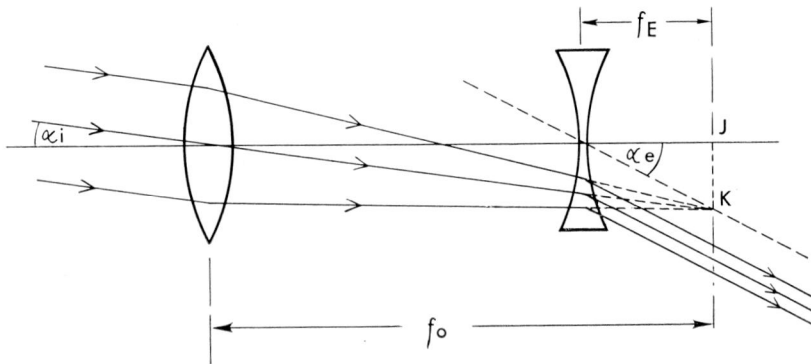

FIG. 805.—THE OPTICAL SYSTEM OF A GALILEAN TELESCOPE.

The *Galilean system* (Fig. 805) is much the most suitable optical arrangement to meet the problems involved. In this an erect image is obtained by two simple lenses, a positive objective and a negative eye-piece, separated by the difference of their focal lengths (not their sum as in positive telescopic systems), so that lightness and compactness are attained. Moreover, the combination of a positive with a negative lens provides a tolerably flat field without much astigmatism.

[1] Unfortunately, no details of his work are available.
[2] p. 350.
[3] Wagenmann (1911), Nitsche and Günther (1914), Stock (1916), Henker (1916), Erggelet (1916–20).
[4] Levy (1928–29), Keeler (1956), Moffatt (1958).

Telescopes are theoretically *afocal* in the sense that parallel rays of light entering the system emerge parallel.[1] The magnification in such cases depends on the angles of incidence and emergence of these rays. Thus in Fig. 805:

$$M = \frac{\alpha_e}{\alpha_i} \backsimeq \frac{\tan \alpha_e}{\tan \alpha_i} = \frac{JK}{f_E} \div \frac{-JK}{f_o}$$

$$= \frac{-f_o}{f_E} = \frac{F_E}{F_o} = \frac{1}{1 - F_o S}$$

where α_i is the angle of incidence and α_e the angle of refraction, S is the distance between the objective and the eyepiece, f_o and f_E the focal lengths of the objective and the eye-piece, and F_o and F_E their respective powers. Magnification is thus the ratio of the power of the eye-piece to that of the objective. It will be appreciated that the shorter the telescope the less the

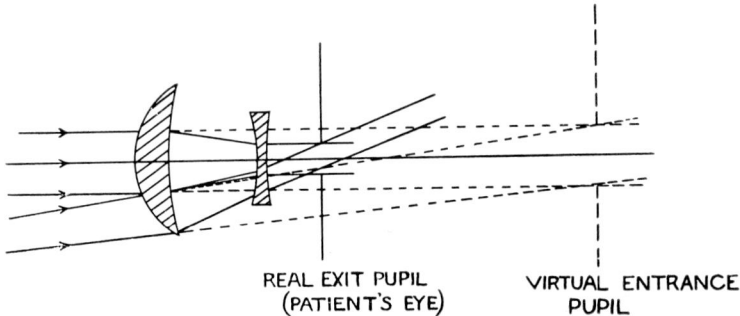

REAL EXIT PUPIL   VIRTUAL ENTRANCE
(PATIENT'S EYE)   PUPIL

FIG. 806.—THE APERTURES OF THE GALILEAN SYSTEM.

magnification. If, therefore, it is to be worn in a spectacle frame, one factor restricting the magnification obtainable is the necessity to limit its length.

The aberrations of such a system can be reasonably well minimized. These depend largely on the width of the aperture of the entrance pupil. Since the observer's pupil limits the pencil available for vision, it may be taken as the exit pupil situated (when the eye is as close to the eye-lens as possible) some 15 mm. behind the eye-piece; its image cuts the entrance pupil, and it is seen from Fig. 806 that the tracery of the rays sites the virtual entrance pupil behind the exit pupil. It is seen that the enforced position of the exit pupil allows the passage of very oblique rays from a large field, which is undesirable but unavoidable. The entrance pupil, however, is not large; for if the pupil averages 4 mm. in diameter, with a magnification of 1·8, the aperture will be 7·3 mm. at the objective.

With such an aperture the axial aberrations (spherical and chromatic) do not seriously interfere with the efficiency of the system. The peripheral aberrations (chromatic difference of magnification, coma, oblique astigmatism, curvature and

[1] This, however, is not strictly true when they are used for improving reading vision.

distortion), however, should be neutralized, and since the aperture is fixed as well as the distance between the lenses within a small margin (for practical reasons), the computer has at his disposal only three degrees of freedom—the bending of the two constituent lenses and the choice of their relative dispersions. If the objective is made of glass of much lower dispersion than the eye-lens, achromatism of magnification is almost eliminated. At the same time, since a low dispersion is associated with a low refractive index, astigmatism and curvature are simultaneously reduced. By using an objective of glass of sufficiently low dispersion (such as fluor-crown) and an eye-lens of as high dispersion as is compatible with durability and efficient transmission, a tolerable correction of chromatism can be achieved in the two-lens system. The type of glass having been fixed, computations are made for each of the peripheral aberrations when the lenses are a fixed distance apart, and curvatures calculated to determine the form of the lenses which gives the least combined aberration. They cannot all

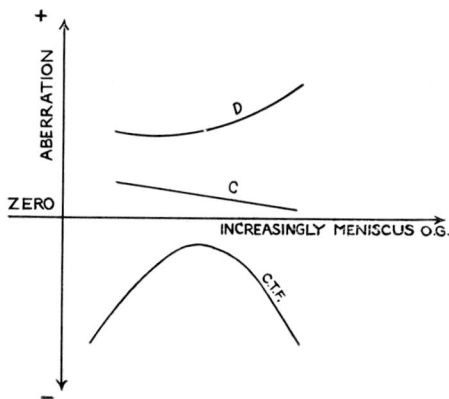

FIG. 807.—THE ABERRATION OF TELESCOPIC SYSTEMS.

A typical set of curves showing the effect of bending the objective lens in a particular telescopic spectacle. The coma (C) falls with increasing bending. The distortion (D) and the curvature of the tangential focus (C.T.F.), however, never reach zero and increase rapidly with increasing the meniscus form. The computer must therefore adopt the best compromise after surveying the whole series of curves (A. H. Levy).

be simultaneously eliminated since they vary at different rates and a suitable compromise is effected; an example is illustrated in Fig. 807. If this is not easy, some adjustment can be made by small variations in the separation of the lenses, their thickness, their composition or the magnification. Alternatively, greater freedom can be obtained at the expense of weight and light transmission by having two lenses cemented together in the eye-piece, thus admitting as variables two types of glass, two thicknesses and three curves. Finally, at the still greater expense of more complicated and weighty mounting and lessened contrast owing to the haze produced by secondary images formed by internal reflections, an uncemented doublet lens may be introduced in the eye-piece allowing the further degrees of freedom offered by two independent curvatures separated by an air-gap.

PROJECTION DEVICES

Apparatus designed to project an enlarged image of reading material is helpful in those with extremely poor vision. Magnification up to $20 \times$ is obtainable with some devices ("Megascope", Urban Electric Company).

Closed-circuit television has been considered for the same purpose (Potts et al., 1959; Genensky, 1969).

The same effect is given by the provision of printed matter in larger type than that customarily employed (Ulverscroft, etc.).

Daza de Valdés. *Uso de los antojos*, Seville (1623).

Dixon. *Certain considerable Improvements in the Construction of Telescopes, Microscopes, Spectacles and all Instruments of Vision*, London (1785).

Donders. *On the Anomalies of Accommodation and Refraction of the Eye*, London (1864).

Erggelet. *Z. Sinnesphysiol.*, **49**, 326 (1916). *Z. ophthal. Opt.*, **8**, 146 (1920).

Genensky. *Amer. J. Optom.*, **46**, 519 (1969).

Guthrie. *Arch. Ophthal.*, **11**, 254 (1934).

Henker. *Z. ophthal. Opt.*, **4**, 43 (1916).

Hertel. *v. Graefes Arch. Ophthal.*, **75**, 586 (1910).

Hoitash. *Arch. Ophthal.*, **12**, 101 (1934).

Keeler. *Trans. ophthal. Soc. U.K.*, **76**, 605 (1956).

Kitchiner. *The Economy of the Eyes*, London (1824).

Leinbach. *Amer. J. Ophthal.*, **49**, 1401 (1960).

Levy. *Brit. med. J.*, **2**, 438 (1928). *Brit. J. Ophthal.*, **13**, 593 (1929).

Linksz. *Amer. J. Ophthal.*, **40**, 831 (1955).

Moffatt. *Acta XVIII int. Cong. Ophthal.*, Brussels, **2**, 1567 (1958).

Nitsche and Günther. *Z. ophthal. Opt.*, **3**, 54 (1914).

Potts, Volk and West. *Amer. J. Ophthal.*, **47**, 580 (1959).

von Rohr. *v. Graefes Arch. Ophthal.*, **75**, 561 (1910). *Ber. dtsch. ophthal. Ges.*, **37**, 51 (1911). *Arch. Augenheilk.*, **82**, 31 (1917). *Graefe-Saemisch Hb. d. ges. Augenheilk.*, 3rd ed., *Die Brille als optisches Instrument*, Berlin (1921).

Serre. *Ann. Oculist.* (Paris), **38**, 223 (1857).

Sloan and Habel. *Amer. J. Ophthal.*, **42**, 863 (1956).

Sloan and Jablonski. *Arch. Ophthal.*, **62**, 465 (1959).

Smith, Robert. *A Compleat System of Opticks*, Camb. (1738).

Stock. *Ber. dtsch. ophthal. Ges.*, **40**, 281 (1916).

Wagenmann. *v. Graefes Arch. Ophthal.*, **79**, 160 (1911).

Clinical Aspects of Visual Aids

The clinical assessment of patients for visual aids must be based upon a full history with details of the visual task for which optical assistance is required combined with a thorough ocular examination which should include an accurate measurement of the refraction modified or extended in order to take into consideration the low visual acuity. It may be necessary to assess the visual acuity using special charts at a distance closer than 6 metres; for near vision special reading charts are available which indicate the degree of magnification which is necessary for any particular function.[1] The Keeler chart is read at 25 cm. with the patient's distance correction and a +4 D addition. These and other charts are often designed to be used in conjunction with special sets of trial optical devices, either spectacle magnifiers or telescopes.

The correspondence which usually exists between the standard of distant and near vision may no longer be present in certain types of ocular pathology. The diminution of the size of the pupil may be an advantage for reading when irregular astigmatism or peripheral opacities of the media are present, but a disadvantage with axial opacities. Nystagmus may be more or less severe according to the distance of fixation. Defects in the

[1] Lebensohn (1936), Keeler (1956), Sloan and Habel (1956), Stimson (1957), Keeney and Duerson (1958), Sloan (1959), Sloan and Brown (1963).

central field may selectively impair near vision. Nevertheless, the distant vision may be a guide to the required addition for reading, and Kestenbaum and Sturman (1956) suggested that the reciprocal of the distance visual acuity gives the addition required in order to read J5 which is somewhat larger than N6 and is roughly the size of normal newsprint. Correspondingly larger magnifications would be required for smaller type such as a telephone directory, J3, N5, and even more in order to read J1, N4, which is the size

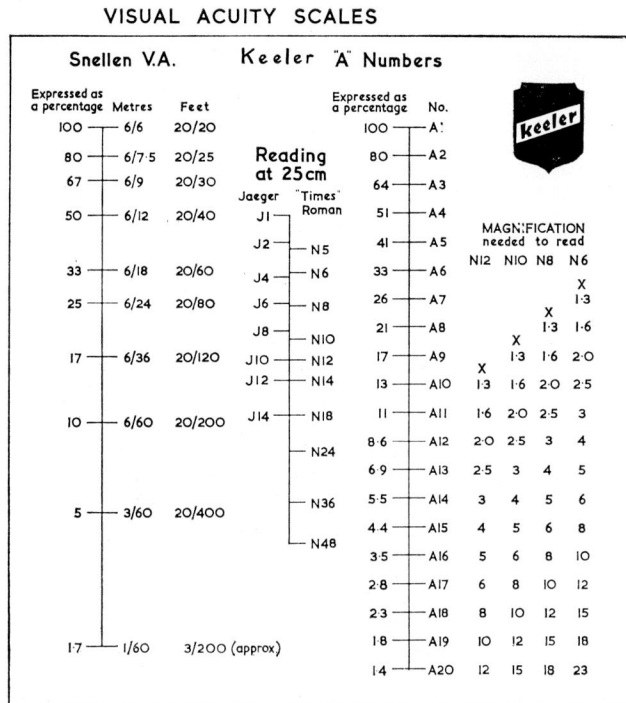

VISUAL ACUITY SCALES

Fig. 808.

of small bible-type. An indication of the magnifications required with variations in the visual acuity for distant and near vision is seen in Fig. 808.

The standard of visual acuity as assessed by routine and specialized tests and the precise ophthalmic diagnosis are of prime importance. The visual task must be fully discussed with the patient, paying special attention to any requirements for a particular working distance or field. In addition, the selection of the type of visual aid is no simple matter. The age, intelligence, cooperation and educability of the patient, as well as the general state of health must also be taken into account. Hand-held devices may be excluded if both hands are required to be free for the subject's employment; a marked tremor of the head would likewise eliminate such a device, while instability of the head would preclude a head-borne aid. Finally, the expense and the simplicity or otherwise of handling the apparatus are not to be forgotten.

The *hand-magnifier* is the simplest and most widely used visual aid for near vision in order to obtain magnification not only by patients with poor vision who wish to see ordinary tasks but also by those with normal vision engaged in occupations which require considerable magnification of detail (watch-making, diamond-cutting, examination of fabrics, stamp collecting, etc.). Low magnifications can be obtained in this way by an ordinary spherical reading lens (about $+13 \cdot 0$ or $+15 \cdot 0$ D) with a handle, but outside the central portion of the field definition is poor owing to distortion, the best form being plano-convex with the plane surface towards the eye. Moreover, the working distance between the lens and the object is limited so that considerable steadiness is required in holding it. If the aperture of a hand-magnifier is adequate, binocular vision may be possible.

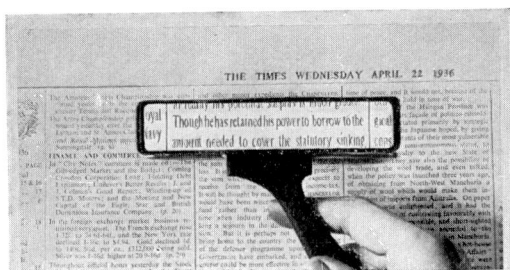

Fig. 809.—A Reading Magnifying Lens.
($+ 5 \cdot 50$ D.S. $+ 9 \cdot 0$ D.C. ax. 180°) (Hamblin).

The flexibility of the hand-magnifier derives, however, from the control by the patient over its position in relation to the eye or the object of regard. When such a simple device is used for reading it is sometimes advisable to sacrifice this flexibility and to mount it on a stand so that the object-lens distance is kept fixed, higher magnifications then being practicable. The optical advantage of a *stand-magnifier* is, as we have noted, the relative constancy of the size of the retinal image if the object is very close to the anterior focal point of the magnifier, although in most cases it is significantly within the focal distance. The eye may be positioned either close to the lens giving a large field or some distance away. The further the subject is away from the hand- or stand-magnifier, the more likely is it that useful binocular vision will be possible.

There are many variants of the hand-held and stand-magnifiers. For reading, a useful lens is a sphero-cylinder (*e.g.* $+5 \cdot 5$ DS $\supset +9 \cdot 0$ DC ax. 180°) magnifying preferentially in the vertical direction and of rectangular shape so that it takes in a line of type (Fig. 809). An additional or optional

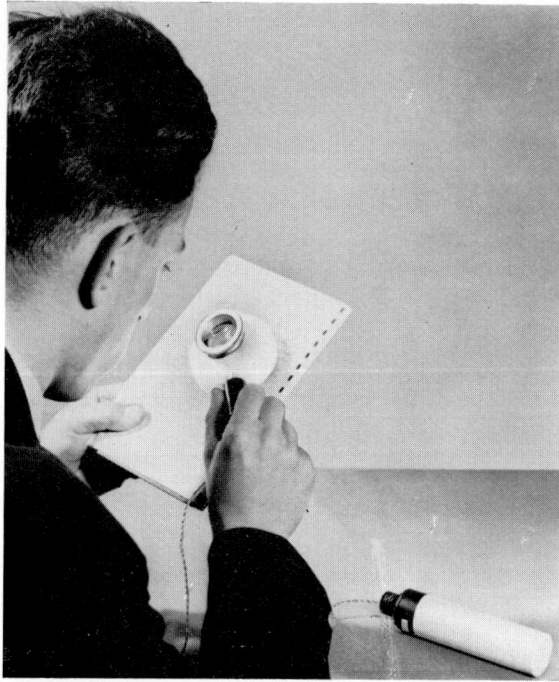

FIG. 810.—SELF-ILLUMINATED HAND-MAGNIFIER (Keeler).

FIG. 811.

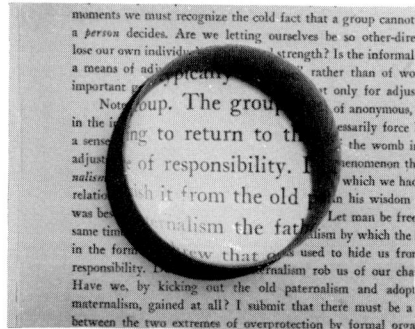

FIG. 812.

FIGS. 811 and 812.—PAPERWEIGHT PLANO-CONVEX LENSES (Keeler).

feature in some stand- and hand-held varieties is the incorporation of illumination into the devices, this being particularly helpful if the working distance
is short (Fig. 810). Their lightness and optical properties have been improved by fashioning them in plastics and taking advantage of aspherical
surfaces, thereby increasing the useful field. Another single lens magnifier is
the " paperweight " plano-convex glass (Figs. 811–12); binocular magnifiers

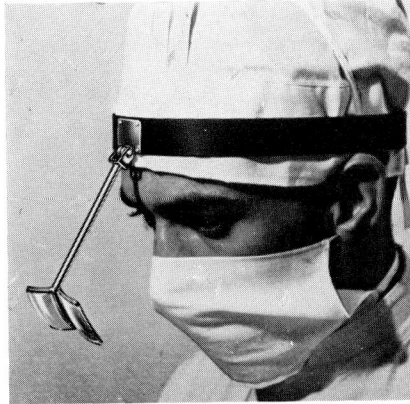

FIG. 813.—HEAD-BAND LOUPE (Keeler).

such as the head-band loupe (Fig. 813) require the incorporation of base-in prisms.

Combinations of lenses are also extensively used in magnifiers (Fig. 814). Focusable stand-magnifiers of doublet design up to +53 D in power, with which the patient does not need to wear his spectacle correction, offer some advantages in certain types of ametropia (Sloan, 1964).

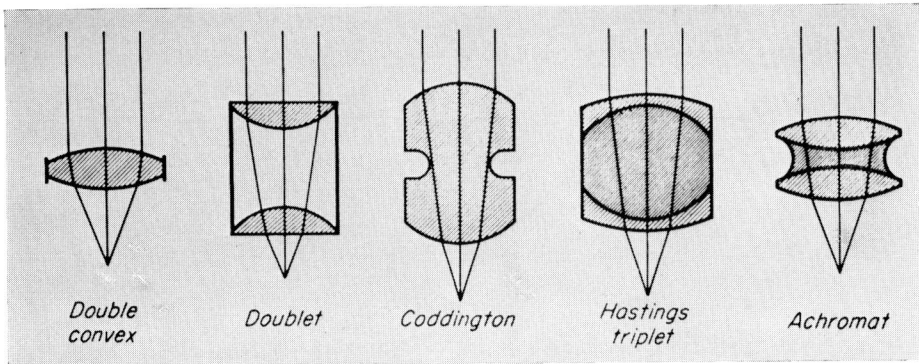

FIG. 814.—COMMON TYPES OF MAGNIFIER.

Stepped lenses were proposed by the Comte de Buffon in 1748 who suggested that instead of consisting of a solid piece of glass, concentric zones should be cut in order to reduce the thickness to a minimum; the Marquis de Condorcet in 1773 and David Brewster in 1811 designed similar lenses built of stepped annular rings. Such a lens was introduced for lighthouses by Augustin Fresnel in 1822 in which only the central part was spherical and centres of curvature of the outer rings were arranged so that spherical aberration was practically eliminated. Subsequently, in 1827, he designed for the outermost zones rings of reflecting prisms so constructed that rays from a point-source at the focus of the lens emerged in a horizontal direction (Fig. 815). The optics of such a projection system was analysed by W. Hampton (1928–29).

FIGS. 815 and 816.—THE FRESNEL LENS.

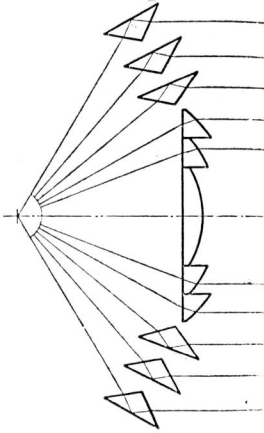

FIG. 815.—With peripheral catadioptric prisms.

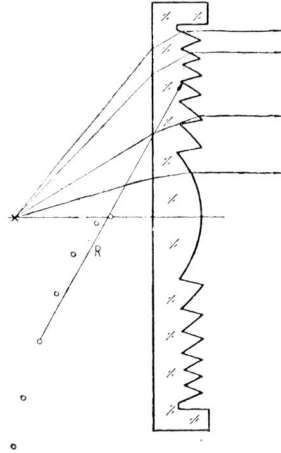

FIG. 816.—The stepped lens.

A stepped lens of this type has recently been introduced as a magnifier (Fig. 816) It is essentially a plastic sheet with concentric ridges on its surface forming a series of prisms of increasing power from the axis to the periphery and has the great advantage of eliminating the thickness and marked aberration that would be unavoidable in a single large lens with a continuous surface.

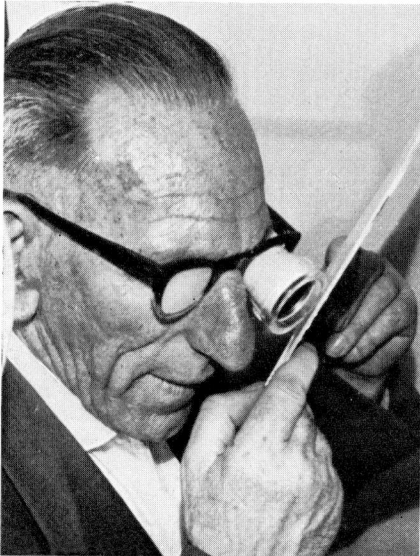

FIG. 817.—SPECTACLE-BORNE VISUAL AID (Keeler).

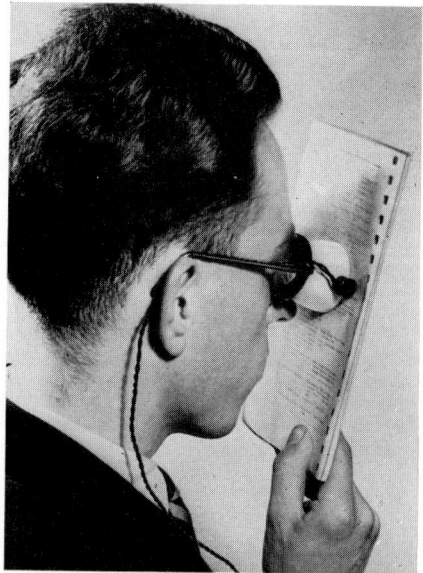

FIG. 818.—SELF-LUMINOUS SPECTACLE-BORNE VISUAL AID (Keeler).

Most of the visual aids just reviewed are employed with only a minor degree of approximation of the object to the eye during close work. In those devices worn in spectacle frames, apart from telescopic spectacles, a considerable degree of approximation is usually necessary, and much encouragement is often required to induce the patient to read with the print " at the nose ". In most of these *spectacle-borne visual aids* the object is to all intents and purposes placed at the anterior focal point of the device and not, as in the case of hand-held and stand-magnifiers, within the anterior focal distance. We have already noted that focusing is critical and some means of maintaining print in a fixed position such as a " distance post " is necessary (Figs. 817–8).

Single or multiple lens units, both microscopic and telescopic devices, can be built into spectacle frames and some of these optical arrangements incorporate an illuminating device.

FIG. 819.—WATCHMAKER'S LOUPE.

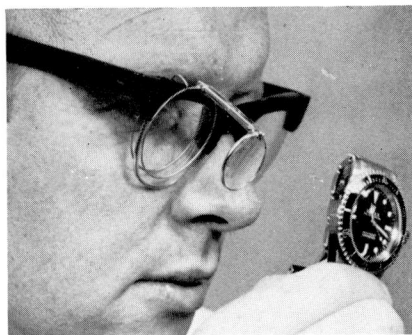

FIG. 820.—WATCHMAKER'S FIT-ON MAGNIFIER

Single lenses may be conventional or best-form convex glasses (Lederer, 1954) occupying a spectacle frame or monocle, or be fitted as a " clip-on " over the required correction; jewellers' and watchmakers' loupes can be similarly employed (Figs. 819–20). There are also various aspherical designs offering less aberration peripherally and therefore a larger field—glass " conoid " lenses (Volk) up to $+100$ D and plastic lenses (Aolite and Igard) up to $+48$ D. The original Katral aspherical glass cataract lenses based on Gullstrand's designs[1] are no longer extant.

Bifocal arrangements are quite feasible and additions may be fused, ground or cemented on; powers up to 32 D are practicable and even higher in some cases; the distance portion may merely be a cut-out.

Multiple lens systems, doublets with or without an air-space or triplets (such as the Hastings) can also be used as spectacle magnifiers (Fig. 814). Powers up to $+80$ D are possible with doublets and these can also be built in to form a bifocal correction. Modern compound reading spectacles (such as the Bier-Hamblin type) make use of plastic materials and have aspherical surfaces.

Binocular corrections are not usually practicable with high-powered spectacle magnifiers so that a frosted glass is worn before the fellow-eye. With relatively lower corrections up to an addition of approximately $+10$ D in bifocals, or slightly more

[1] p. 622.

in a single lens, a binocular correction is possible. In such cases insetting of the seg-ments or in single lenses nasal decentration as well as high base-in prisms may be necessary. A binocular correction offers a larger field and a greater depth of focus.

Telescopic spectacles (Figs. 821–5), as we have noted, offer the possi-bility of uniocular and binocular corrections for both distance and reading,

FIGS. 821 and 822.—TELESCOPIC SPECTACLES.

FIG. 821.—Uniocular for distant vision (2× or 2·5×) and binocular for near vision (1·6× or 2×) (Keeler).

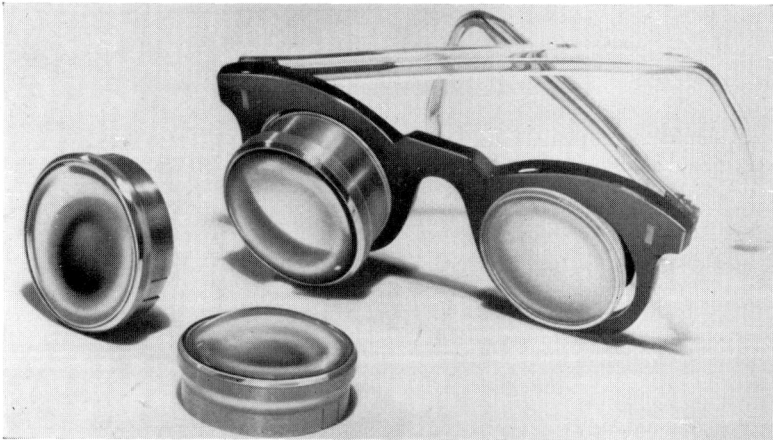

FIG. 822.—For distant (2×), intermediate (2×) and near vision (2·5×) (Keeler).

the latter activity being at a greater working distance than other head-borne devices, but the field of view is more restricted. It is obvious for optical reasons that the fitting of such spectacles must be scrupulously correct and the frames should be rigid. They should be worn as close to the eyes as possible so that the approximation of the exit pupil to the eye-lens provides the maximal attainable field. They must be centred with un-usual care and any tilt is quite inadmissible for in this case all the aberrations

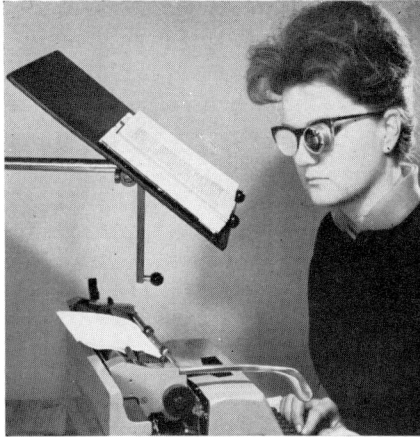

FIG. 823.—UNIOCULAR READING TELESCOPIC SPECTACLES (Keeler).

FIG. 824.—LOW-POWERED BINOCULAR
READING TELESCOPIC SPECTACLES
(Keeler).

FIG. 825.—HIGH-POWERED BINOCULAR
READING TELESCOPIC SPECTACLES
(Keeler).

of the periphery become effective in the central area. For this reason binocular telescopic spectacles for distance cannot comfortably be used for near work, for both telescopes must be angled to allow their optic axes to meet at the working distance. In the Keeler binocular reading telescopes a specially angled P.D. bar is used.

A suitable test for the accuracy was described by Levy (1928). A cross test-card is regarded. If the fitting is considerably wrong two crosses will be seen. A lack of alignment leads to displacement in one or other direction of the image: the spectacles should be moved in the direction opposite the direction of the displacement. Tilting is betrayed by the appearance of coloured rings at the boundaries of the black lines; the spectacles should be tilted towards the yellow edge.

The clinical uses of telescopic spectacles are, of course, restricted. Optically the simplest problem is the correction of high myopia when macular degeneration is present. The magnification of the image may also be of value in any refractive state when vision is indistinct owing to opacities in the media, amblyopia, and particularly in localized macular disease.

For myopia the optical arrangement designed by von Rohr (1938) is simple wherein the light entering the objective is made to diverge as it emerges from the eye-lens (Fig. 826); and a system of two lenses of different

FIGS. 826–829.—THE DESIGN OF TELESCOPIC SPECTACLES (M. von Rohr).

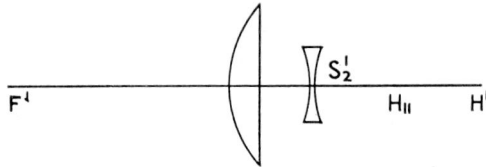

FIG. 826.—A telescopic spectacle system for high myopia. On the image side, H′ is the posterior principal point and H′F′ the focal length, H″ the anterior principal point of the eye. In this system $1/S'F' = -18$ D; $1/H'' F' = -14.64$ D; $1/H'F' = D_{12} = -11.42$ D.

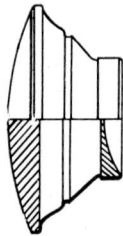

FIG. 827.—A telescopic spectacle system for high myopes.

FIG. 828.—An auxiliary lens to be put in front of the lens of Fig. 827 for reading.

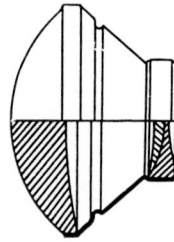

FIG. 829.—The more complex system required for small degrees of ametropia and hypermetropia.

dispersions suffices (Figs. 827–8). To overcome oblique aberrations in inconsiderable degrees of ametropia, however, and in hypermetropia when it is necessary for the emergent pencils of light to have an approximate parallelism or a convergence, the problem is more difficult and the eye-lens is composite (Fig. 829). Astigmatism is corrected by means of an additional astigmatic lens next the eye. Near vision presents difficulties. With ordinary spectacles in the unaided eye, the accommodation required for reading is equivalent to the dioptric power of the working distance. Since the angle of convergence of the incident light with telescopic spectacles is increased approximately in proportion to the magnification, the accommodation required must be multiplied by the degree of magnification. Such an amplitude is beyond the power of the individual without a special addition which may be added to the objective (Figs. 826–9) or, with advantages in weight and definition of the image, to the eye-piece. If the patient has marked astigmatism a cylindrical correction can be incorporated into the eye-piece.

The disadvantages of telescopic spectacles are nevertheless considerable. They are difficult to wear and uncomfortable in many cases, and the magnification cannot be indefinitely extended owing to cumbersomeness, the restriction of the field and the depth of focus, which vary directly with the magnification and the unsteadiness of objects with movements of the head.

Modern telescopic spectacles incorporate plastic lenses to minimize their weight and may be employed as uniocular or binocular corrections. A variety of designs is available and magnification up to tenfold is possible in uniocular telescopes, about half of this if binocular. The advantage of the telescopic correction for near vision is that in certain cases it can provide a magnification adequate for reading at a somewhat greater working distance than obtainable with other head-borne visual aids. The working distance is, however, yet another factor adversely affected by increasing magnification : the greater the latter the closer must the object be viewed.

The practical value of telescopic spectacles for distant vision is decidedly limited. Few patients are able to learn to walk about wearing them because of relative movement of the field which is in any event restricted to about $15°$ with a binocular telescope giving twofold magnification. If the subject is stationary, however, the prospects for useful employment of a telescopic aid for distant vision are better. This may be hand-held or used as a clip-on purely as a temporary measure in order to inspect a particular object such as a place-name or the indicator of the destination of a bus. Telescopes with a variable focus are also useful in some circumstances, and maximum magnification is obtainable with a prismatic telescope which is simply one half of a pair of binoculars. These are of necessity somewhat bulky and must be held in the hand.

Both distance and reading telescopes may be adapted for the opposite purpose by the use of caps of appropriate power. Either or both of these may be so incorporated in a spectacle lens in bifocal fashion. Thus both a distance and reading telescope may be inserted in one lens of a uniocular correction, the reading portion being much the larger ; such a combination may be of great value to a partially sighted child in the classroom.

Telescopic spectacles so arranged to give an enlarged stereoscopic image at the working distance while the hands are left free are extremely valuable as an aid to the ophthalmic surgeon himself in operating or for any other close inspection work. The spectacles can be small so that a full field is obtainable by a slight movement of the head and they may be affixed if desired to the ordinary spectacles. The same Galilean system wherein the magnification is obtained by a wide separation of the objective from the eye-lens can be made equally effective by incorporating a small negative lens

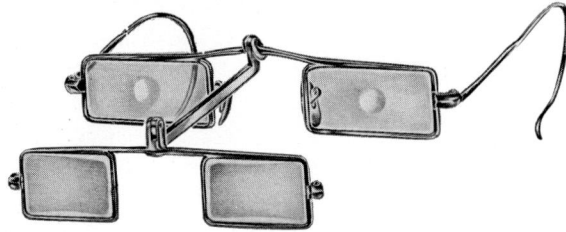

FIG. 830.—THE GALILEAN SYSTEM MODIFIED AS OPERATING SPECTACLES.

in the centre of the spectacles and a relatively weak convex lens in a light objective combined with appropriate prisms, bases-in (Fig. 830).

STEINHEIL'S CONE (Fig. 831) is a similar Galilean system made of solid glass of length varying with the required magnification, the front surface being convex and the eye-surface being steeply concave. It was constructed about 1866 by Steinheil of Munich at Donders's suggestion and is useful as a hand instrument. A modern version of this has been introduced by Univis.

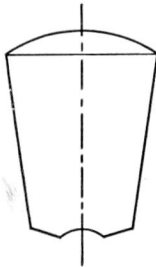

FIG. 831.—
STEINHEIL'S CONE.

The optics of the telescope can be applied to eyes which are markedly hypermetropic, whether naturally so or as a result of cataract surgery. Such patients can obtain distance magnification by holding a weak convex lens some distance from the eye (Fig. 832) (Lebensohn, 1956; G. and D. Fonda, 1962). This principle can be extended to the emmetrope by incorporating a -12 D segment in a spectacle lens and holding a $+3$ D lens some distance away; if it is held at 10 inches a fourfold magnification of distant objects results.

Some specially designed *contact lenses* allow both normal and magnified vision. The magnified vision is subserved by a small axial concave area on the anterior surface of the contact lens in combination with a convex spectacle lens; when the spectacles are removed normal vision is obtained through the periphery of the optical zone of the contact lens (Fig. 833). In the Telecon system of Filderman (1959–64) a special spectacle lens gives the alternation of magnified or normal vision depending on whether

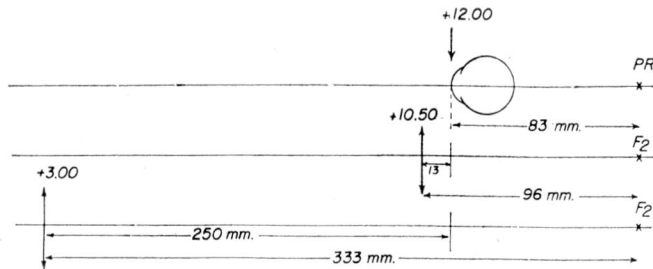

FIG. 832.—CORRECTION FOR APHAKIA.

The diagram represents an aphakic eye the far point of which (PR) lies 83 mm. behind the cornea so that the hypermetropia is $+12$ D. A convex lens placed 13 mm. in front of the cornea would require a focal length of 96 mm. to correct this error and therefore must be $+10·5$ D. The same refractive error may be corrected by a lens of $+3$ D (focal length 333 mm.) at a distance of 250 mm. in front of the cornea (G. and D. Fonda).

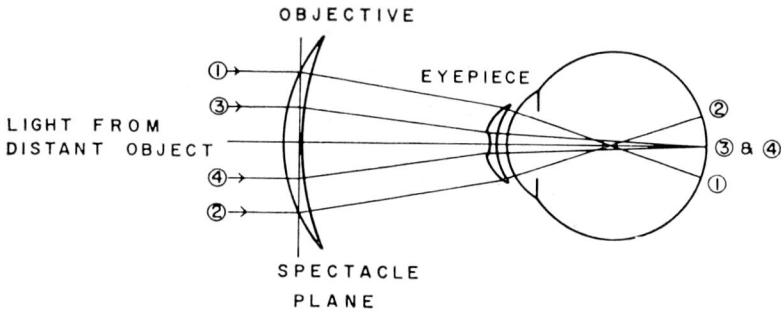

FIG. 833.—THE BIVISUAL CONTACT-SPECTACLE TELESCOPIC SYSTEM.

The concave area on the anterior surface of the contact lens in combination with the convex spectacle lens gives magnified vision. When the spectacles are removed, normal vision is attained from the peripheral zone of the contact lens (R. Mandell).

FIGS. 834 and 835.—THE TELECON SYSTEM OF FILDERMAN (R. Mandell).

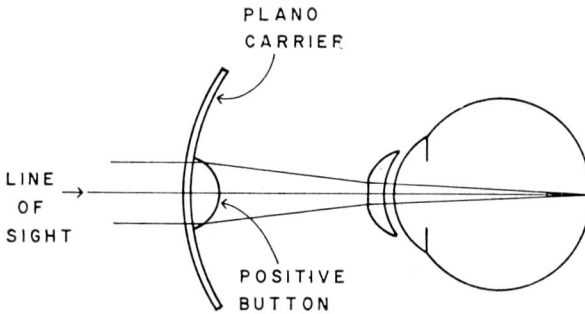

FIG. 834.—The highly convex axial button gives magnified vision in the direct line of sight.

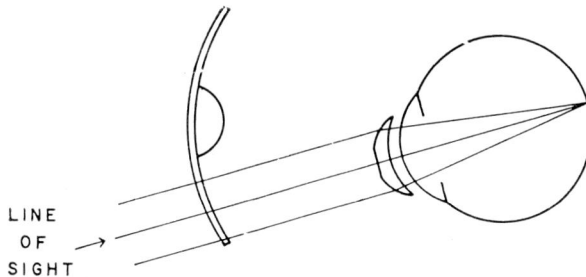

FIG. 835.—When the line of sight is through the plano-periphery, normal vision is attained.

the subject directs his line of vision through its highly convex axial button (Figs. 834–5) or through its periphery; again, a contact lens is worn with a bivisual function, a small highly concave axial optical zone being surrounded by a conventional optical periphery.

Ingenious as these optical systems are, they still show the disadvantages of telescopic systems such as restriction and relative movement of the visual field. The mobility of the corneal lens aggravates the sensation of relative movement so that a scleral lens is often to be preferred in telescopic devices.

The role of the eye-piece of a telescopic system can also be subserved by an intra-ocular lenticulus (Choyce, 1964).

There is therefore a wide choice of the type of visual aid to be recommended, particularly for reading. If the patient can learn to accustom himself to a close working distance, a head-borne device, provided illumination is adequate or can be arranged, and provided the print can be maintained steadily in the correct position, will prove suitable. Such an arrangement may be satisfactory even for higher magnifications but here a stand-magnifier is often best in older patients. The fixed object-lens distance allows an optimal optical situation and the eye can be moved as near to or as far from the device as the patient desires.

From the clinical point of view there is some debate as to the value of telescopic spectacles particularly for distance but even for close work; some authorities hold that their optical disadvantages are outweighed by the advantages of optically less sophisticated devices provided the patient can be taught to alter his reading habits. Moreover, many of the more elaborate visual aids, such as telescopic aids and projection devices, are relatively expensive; economic considerations and the fact that in many instances such advanced designs may be ineffective dictate that a prolonged trial should be the routine practice before purchase is undertaken. The interchangeability of components in some of the more complex optical systems is a further factor limiting their ultimate expense.

A considerable literature has accumulated over the past 20 years evaluating the performance of various types of visual aid.[1] Most practitioners who take a particular interest in this subject are acquainted with the value of each of the various devices and order them appropriately. This attitude is not universal and a certain partisan feeling is sometimes evident. G. Fonda (1965), for example, evinces an antipathy to telescopic devices apparently favouring very high-powered spectacle magnifiers; Sloan and her collaborators (1959–64) appear more impressed with non-spectacle devices such as the stand-magnifier. There is certainly something to be said for proceeding from the less to the more optically complex as required.

The reported series of cases give variable degrees of success and the various publications are difficult to compare because of such differing features as the diagnosis and age of the patients which they include. In general, however, there is a substantial proportion, usually a minority, of patients who are unable to manage with any visual aid. As we have seen,

[1] Levi and King (1955), Keeler (1956), Stanworth (1956), Kestenbaum and Sturman (1956), Lebensohn (1956), Sloan and Habel (1956), Moffatt (1956–58), Fonda and Snydacker (1959), Pameijer (1959), Sloan and Jablonski (1959), Gunstensen (1960), Willetts (1960), G. Fonda (1961–65), Weiss (1963), Sloan and Brown (1964), and many others.

among the features responsible for failure are restriction of the visual field, the working distance and the depth of focus, the weight or the unsightliness of the appliance and possible expense, as well as the age and mental adaptability of the patient; indeed, some are so wedded to their " blindness " or partial sight that they offer a considerable psychological resistance to anything which might improve their vision. It is noteworthy, however, that any attempt to forecast which type of patient will benefit from any particular optical device is hazardous and not necessarily unfavourably so. The determined subject with an unpromisingly low degree of acuity may respond surprisingly well to a visual aid when fully instructed in its use. We may end this Chapter by reiterating that optimism and enthusiasm on the part of the prescriber are likely to be matched by persistence and ultimate success in the wearer.

Choyce. *Intra-ocular Lenses and Implants*, London (1964).

Filderman. *Amer. J. Optom.*, **36**, 135 (1959). *Contacto*, **3**, 94 (1959). *Brit. J. physiol. Opt.*, **21**, 195 (1964).

Fonda, G. *Amer. J. Ophthal.*, **51**, 433 (1961); **55**, 247 (1963). *Management of the Patient with Subnormal Vision*, St. Louis (1965).

Fonda, G. and D. *Trans. Amer. Acad. Ophthal.*, **66**, 790 (1962).

Fonda, G. and Snydacker. *Trans. Amer. Acad. Ophthal.*, **63**, 79 (1959).

Gunstensen. *Brit. J. Ophthal.*, **44**, 672 (1960).

Hampton. *Trans. opt. Soc. Lond.*, **30**, 185 (1928–9).

Keeler. *Trans. ophthal. Soc. U.K.*, **76**, 605 (1956).

Keeney and Duerson. *Amer. J. Ophthal.*, **46**, 592 (1958).

Kestenbaum and Sturman. *Arch. Ophthal.*, **56**, 451 (1956).

Lebensohn. *Amer. J. Ophthal.*, **19**, 110 (1936). *Sight Sav. Rev.*, **26**, 201 (1956).

Lederer. *Nature* (Lond.), **174**, 977 (1954).

Levi and King. *Amer. J. Ophthal.*, **40**. 29 (1955).

Levy. *Brit. med. J.*, **2**, 438 (1928).

Linksz. *Amer. J. Ophthal.*, **40**, 831 (1955).

Moffatt. *Trans. ophthal. Soc. U.K.*, **76**, 589 (1956). *Acta XVIII int. Cong. Ophthal.*, Brussels, **2**, 1567 (1958).

Pameijer. *An Investigation of Optical Corrections for enabling Patients with Low Visual Acuity to Read*, Amsterdam (1959).

von Rohr. *Trans. Ophthal. Soc U.K.*, **58**, 359 (1938).

Sloan. *Amer. J. Ophthal.*, **48**, 807 (1959); **58**, 604 (1964).

Sloan and Brown. *Amer. J. Ophthal.*, **55**, 1187 (1963); **58**, 594 (1964).

Sloan and Habel. *Amer. J. Ophthal.*, **42**, 863 (1956).

Sloan and Jablonski. *Arch. Ophthal.*, **64**, 465 (1959).

Stanworth. *Trans. ophthal. Soc. U.K.*, **76**, 619 (1956).

Stimson. *Optical Aids for Low Acuity*, Los Angeles (1957).

Weiss. *Amer. J. Ophthal.*, **55**, 255 (1963).

Willetts. *Brit. J. Ophthal.*, **44**, 547 (1960).

FIG. 836.—THE SPECTACLE PEDLAR.

An etching without a title, signed Rahcued A. v. Ostade. A modified version
from A. von Ostade's "Spectacle Dealer" by David Deuchar (Rahcued reversed).
Deuchar was a Scottish engraver who lived from 1743–1808 in Edinburgh, and who
copied from Rembrandt and other Netherlandish artists (from the Wellcome Institute
of the History of Medicine, by courtesy of the Wellcome Trustees).

CHAPTER XX

THE PRESCRIPTION OF SPECTACLES

DURING the last century we have progressed far from the original method when the patient himself chose what he imagined to be the best spectacles from the variety the itinerant pedlar carried (Fig. 836), a practice only recently made illegal in Britain. It is astonishing that 126 years ago there was no medical refractionist in the world. English (and other) textbooks up to the first half of the 19th century advised the patient to go to an optician, try a series of spectacles and select those which suited him best. On the contrary, most ophthalmologists deprecated their use. It is true that the great French surgeon, Guy de Chauliac [1300–1368] (Fig. 594) advocated them when his collyria failed to restore the sight, but most regarded them as a means of weakening the eyes, a belief still widely existing today (Bartisch, 1583[1]; Beer, 1813–17[2]; Karl H. Weller, 1821, of Dresden,[3] and many others).

The first to advocate openly the use of spectacles in England was William Rowley [1743–1806], an extraordinary charlatan who practised many branches of medicine and founded the first (partially) eye hospital in London, the St. John's Hospital for Diseases of the Eyes, Legs and Breast, which, however, had a short life (1771–1773). His advice on the value of spectacles was in the only original part of his book (1790)[4] which was a blatant and thoroughly bad plagiarism from Plenck's *Doctrina de morbis oculorum*, Wien (1777). The attitude of hostility, however, was broken down about the middle of the 19th century by the teaching of two authorities—Fronmüller (1843),[5] whose work was largely ignored, and Donders (1864)[6] whose ideas changed the entire outlook of the ophthalmological world on the importance of the correction of refractive errors. It is true that these ideas have been grossly exaggerated by some writers[7] but, on the whole, they are still generally maintained. Today the fear of correcting errors of refraction has largely disappeared; thus in the United States it is estimated that 60% of the population between the ages of 15 and 79 years have spectacles and that 32% wear them constantly.[8]

Donders has been annotated elsewhere,[9] but a note on GEORG TOBIAS CHRISTOPH FRONMÜLLER [1809–1889] may be of interest. Born at Fürth in Bavaria, he studied widely at Erlangen, Würzburg, Munich, Vienna and Paris before settling down to practice in Fürth, at that time one of the great centres for manufacturing spectacles in Europe. Here he wrote condemning the prescription of spectacles on the basis of age and stressing the need for a careful examination of each patient, for which purpose he was one of the earliest to use trial lenses and trial frames.

---

[1] Ὀφθαλμοδουλέια, *Das ist, Augendienst*, Dresden (1583).

[2] *Lehre von den Augenkrankheiten*, Wien (1813–17).

[3] *Diätetik für gesunde und schwache Augen*, Berlin (1821).

[4] *A Treatise on one hundred and eighteen Principal Diseases of the Eyes and Eyelids*, etc., London (1790).

[5] *J. Chir. Augenheilk.*, 174 (1843).

[6] *On the Anomalies of Accommodation and Refraction of the Eye*, London (1864).

[7] p. 560.

[8] *Vital Health Statistics*, Series, 11 No. 28 (1968).

[9] p. 255. Fig. 305.

THE CLINICAL EXAMINATION

An adequate clinical examination of the eye for any visual appliance should, after the history has been taken and disease excluded, include a determination of the visual acuity for distant and near objects, an objective assessment of the refractive state and its subjective verification, a measure of the accommodation and its relation to convergence, of the muscular balance and of the degree of binocular vision. Aniseikonia seldom requires special attention in routine practice. All these have been discussed in detail in earlier chapters of this Volume, the reading of which may suggest that their practical application is an extremely complicated and time-consuming process. A short routine, however, which becomes habitual and its interpretation instantaneous, resolves it into a rapid and enjoyable exercise. In the first place, the nature of the defect will determine the type of optical appliance to be used. If the visual acuity can be improved to 6/12, spectacles are usually indicated; if the defect is a gross or irregular corneal astigmatism, or if spectacles will not be worn either because of social reasons or owing to the patient's work or sport, contact lenses may be considered; if the acuity is less than 6/18, visual aids may be necessary.

1. External examination of the eye in diffuse light.
2. Examination of the power of fixation and general mobility of the eyes.
3. The cover test to elicit heterophoria and squint.

This is best done at this stage, before the trial frames are put on. It saves them being taken off subsequently and, in addition, the detection of a squint may account for a marked deficiency of vision in the deviating eye which, if it is not recognized early in the examination, may give rise to some concern.

4. Examination of the eyes by focal illumination with the loupe and, if any suspicion of disease exists, with the slit-lamp; thereafter with the plane mirror, and ophthalmoscopic examination by the direct and indirect methods.

The trial frames are put on and centred.

5. The testing of visual acuity, uniocularly and binocularly.
6. Retinoscopy, and its verification with the sphero-cylindrical combination (or refractionometry).
7. Verification of the retinoscopy with the test-types and then with the cross-cylinder (and astigmatic fan).
8. With the full correction in place, the testing of the ocular balance for distance both visual and muscular.
9. With the full correction in place, the determination of the near-point of accommodation and convergence.
10. The addition of the correction for near work and the testing of the acuity for near vision, uniocularly and binocularly.

11. With the additional correction for near work an estimation of the muscle balance for near vision.

12. If it is indicated by the symptoms and the results of 8, 9, 10 and 11, a testing of the vergence power.

13. Determination of the degree and type of binocular vision and the amplitude of fusional movements (if indicated).

14. Testing for aniseikonia if this is indicated—and possible.

This routine should vary with the age of the patient.

(*a*) In all children less than 7 years or a few years older in cases of accommodative squint, (1) to (4) are done; trial frames are usually inadvisable and the visual acuity is tested by one of the tests for children. The patient is then sent home to be given 1·0% atropine ointment three times a day for 3 days. On the second visit the ophthalmoscopic examination is repeated, (6) the retinoscopy is done, and spectacles are prescribed with the appropriate deduction for cycloplegia.

(*b*) If the patient is between 7 and 15 years of age the entire examination can be done in one sitting and trial frames should be used; cyclopentolate or bistropamide can be used as a cycloplegic, or weak hyoscine in the younger group.

(*c*) If the patient is between 15 and 20 years of age a cycloplegic is usually not necessary (if it is used a post-cycloplegic test may be advisable), and (1) to (10) should be done with (13) if indicated.

(*d*) If the patient is between 20 and 40 years of age a mydriatic need only be given if the smallness of the pupil makes the ophthalmoscopic examination or the refraction difficult; after it a miotic (1·0% pilocarpine) should be instilled. (1) to (10) should be done as a routine, with (13) if indicated.

(*e*) If the patient is above 40 years of age the same routine is adhered to and (1) to (12) should be performed.

PRACTICAL ASPECTS OF THE PRESCRIPTION OF SPECTACLES

In the preceding pages we have dealt at some length with refractive errors and muscular imbalance and the optical devices for their correction. At the cost of repetition, it may be well to summarize them as a whole and to note some further troubles that may arise from the prescription of spectacles and how they may best be avoided.

THE PRESENTING SYMPTOMS

The prescription of spectacles should be correlated with the patient's symptoms. Where there is an obvious refractive error associated with a visual defect, the indication to order spectacles is clear; apart from such an obvious indication, however, there is a whole range of less definite complaints in which this decision may be made in the realization that the ametropia discovered is of a kind or degree that is unlikely to be the sole cause of the trouble. We have mentioned elsewhere the effects of spectacles as a placebo; such mild psychotherapy should, however, be cautiously undertaken lest the ocular symptomatology is merely the most obvious feature of a more profound mental or physical disturbance. Nevertheless, even in these cases the prescription of spectacles, while it may not be beneficial, does no mental or physical harm. In children, however, the prescription of spectacles for slight degrees of hypermetropia or astigmatism is to be avoided; so often a child complains of defective vision out of the desire to wear spectacles when a class-mate has recently acquired them. If a minimal or non-existent refractive error is found in association with normal fundi and media, all that is required in such cases is a tactful word of explanation to the parents and a reassessment of the case in, perhaps, three months.

Many refractions are carried out on patients who already have spectacles but merely come for a routine check-up without symptoms and in deference to the prevailing myth that " neglecting the eyes " or wearing wrong spectacles does harm. It must be admitted that in many cases this is unnecessary; indeed, while there may be a place for pre-symptomatic diagnosis in ocular conditions such as glaucoma, such an attitude about these routine assessments of optical errors is without doubt grossly inflated. Apart from the established facts concerning age-changes in the refractive state, the refraction of children, adolescent myopes and hypermetropes clearly needs reviewing at intervals and it may be advisable not only to suggest re-examination in six months or a year but also in certain cases to indicate the likely future progression of the condition; this will forestall the frequent complaint that spectacles have " made the eyes worse " or made the patient dependent on them.

Most subjects between the ages of 20 and 40, however, have static refractions. When a patient in this age-group requires a new pair of spectacles, his present pair being in poor physical condition with the lenses scratched and the frame-joints loose or broken, it is reasonable to check that the refraction is indeed static; otherwise re-examination is likely to be superfluous at this time of life unless the optical anomaly is severe.

If a slight change in refraction is found at a routine re-examination, the examiner must be chary of invariably altering the correction; minor changes in refraction in the absence of symptoms can well be ignored, particularly small alterations in the axis of a cylindrical correction or the introduction of a small cylinder where none was previously present; the result may well be the development of symptoms which were not present with the old prescription and the claim by the patient that he sees better with his old spectacles—a circumstance entailing considerable chagrin to the examiner. Even if the patient has ocular or visual complaints, the finding that his present spectacles are in some marginal degree incorrect should not always be taken as an indication to alter them, and in all cases the question should be asked whether the symptoms can reasonably be related to the change in refraction. The importance of a knowledge of the correction the patient is wearing is obvious, being of value not only in assessing the necessity for any alteration but also facilitating the examination of the refraction.

INTOLERANCE TO SPECTACLES

The reasons for the inability of a patient to use with comfort the spectacles prescribed for him are varied, some of them due to the patient himself, some to the prescriber and some to the dispenser.

The patient's ocular condition may be one in which it is inherently difficult to correct the vision with spectacles. In the higher degrees of ametropia the best form of lenses does not entirely eliminate their disadvantages— optical, physical or cosmetic—as we have noted, for example, in discussing the correction of aphakia and high myopia; moreover, the correction of astigmatism and anisometropia may be accompanied by anomalies of the muscle balance and of spatial orientation. Even in the lower degrees of ametropia, however, some disturbance is usual on wearing spectacles for the first time, perhaps a sensation of "pulling" the eye and "tightness" in the temples; this is possibly associated with the need to establish a new relationship between accommodation and convergence and is usually short-lived. The complaint of some patients that they can see reflections from their lenses can be dealt with by anti-reflective coating. The persistence of symptoms when wearing spectacles may simply be due to the irrelevance of the optical anomaly, although the converse is not necessarily true. It is certainly advisable in the presence of organic disease such as, for example, opacities in the ocular media, to anticipate the patient's possible dissatisfaction by giving a warning that vision will not be perfect even with the spectacles.

As far as the prescriber is concerned in the intolerance to spectacles, he may have carried out a poor refraction and ordered the wrong prescription; in other cases, while the refraction itself has been impeccable in its accuracy, the spectacles ordered may have been injudicious. Thus, the sudden prescription of a high correction to a patient who has not previously worn spectacles is inadvisable and it is wiser to advise an under-correction which can be gradually strengthened over a period of months. Perhaps the most common fault is to prescribe too strong an addition for reading in patients with presbyopia; occasionally the opposite situation occurs and the patient returns saying he still cannot read adequately. For this no rules can be firmly laid down and few refractionists have escaped trouble from presbyopic prescriptions. It should be emphasized again that the nature of the task for which near vision is required must be carefully elucidated in each individual case, in particular the position in which a book is habitually held or the working distance and the fineness of the objects being inspected at work.

Bifocal lenses frequently give rise to trouble in this respect and, in addition, complaints of dizziness on looking down while wearing them are common; in this event attention should be paid to the power, type, size and position of the segment and where appropriate these should be adjusted or, alternatively, it is frequently necessary to advise that bifocals be discontinued.

Re-examination in cases of intolerance should always include a further assessment of the muscular balance; if it is deranged the prescription of prisms or the use of orthoptic exercises may be advisable. Finally, the prescriber may have been less than careful to eliminate organic disease during the general ophthalmic examination or, where reading difficulties seem to persist in spite of the proper optical correction, the possibility must be eliminated that the cause is not a defect of the visual field such as an unsuspected hemianopia, a small paracentral scotoma, or some alexic or dyslexic anomaly.

The dispensing of the spectacles is occasionally at fault and may be responsible for some cases of intolerance. These may relate solely to the frame or other aspect of the fitting. In practice, the form of the lenses is often left to the manufacturer, but the prescriber can and should indicate the need for any special form of lens in certain cases. The centring of the lenses and the degree of pantoscopic tilt must also be extremely accurate. A tactful suggestion to the effect that certain shapes of frame are unsuitable in the higher degrees of ametropia may prevent future trouble such as complaints of the restriction of the field. Many of these considerations apply with equal force to the changing of spectacles; a high myope, for example, may not welcome an alteration in the form of the spectacles, even if the new lenses are of the same dioptric power as those previously worn.

So far as the lenses themselves are concerned, points of importance are the occurrence of a small change in the posterior vertex distance in strong lenses; a change in the base curve from previous lenses; a change from flat lenses to meniscus or toric forms; and finally, a difference in the base curve in two eyes of approximately equal refraction,

To some extent this may appear difficult and somewhat gloomy; nevertheless, the adequate correction of refractive errors is in itself interesting and brings more happiness and eliminates more disabilities both in work and in play than any other single medical technique.

CHAPTER XXI

THE OPTICS OF CLINICAL OPHTHALMIC INSTRUMENTS

GREAT progress has been made in the methods of examining the eye since the homely and happy technique practised a century ago (Fig. 837). In the interval, ophthalmic examination and diagnosis have become the most accurate and detailed in their minutiæ in the whole of medicine. The optics of the instruments used in the determination of the optical properties of the eye and its refraction have been described in the previous pages; the appliances used in the ophthalmic investigation of the eye are described and illustrated together with their clinical application in another Volume[1] to which the reader is referred, so that their optical properties are all that we need consider in the present context.

Examination of the Anterior Segment of the Eye

THE CORNEAL MICROSCOPE AND SLIT-LAMP

A MICROSCOPE is designed to provide magnification of a near object, as distinct from a telescope which acts similarly for a distant object. Strictly speaking, any magnifying glass, such as we have mentioned in the Chapter on Visual Aids, should be classified as a simple microscope. Compound microscopes of which the corneal microscope is one example provide higher magnification than simple magnifiers and are a combination of two magnifying systems separated from one another. In its most elementary form the microscope consists of two convex lenses, one of very short focus, the objective lens, and the other of longer focus, the eye-piece or ocular.

The optical arrangement is shown in Fig. 838. The objective and eye-piece are separated from one another by a fixed distance and the interval between the posterior focus of the objective and the anterior focus of the eye-piece is known as the optical tube-length (s). With the eye close to the eye-piece, the whole is then moved so that the object (1) is just outside the anterior focus of the objective which forms the image of it at (2) close to the anterior focus of the eye-piece. The linear magnification (m_o) of this image can be calculated from the formula derived on page 61:

$$\frac{1}{v} - \frac{1}{u} = \frac{1}{f_o}$$

Multiplied by v, this becomes

$$1 - \frac{v}{u} = \frac{v}{f_o}, \text{ hence } 1 - m_o = \frac{f_o + s}{f_o}, \therefore m_o = \frac{-s}{f_o}$$

[1] Vol. VII, pp. 233 *et. seq.*

829

FIG. 837.—EXAMINATION OF THE EYE A CENTURY AGO
(from Professor M. Amsler, Zürich).

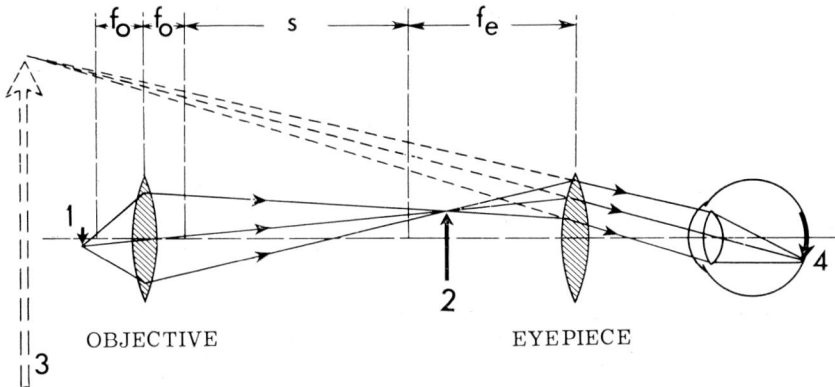

FIG. 838.—THE OPTICS OF THE MICROSCOPE.

Magnifications up to $40\times$ are obtained with corneal microscopes. For details see text.

The eye-piece now provides angular magnification of this image to the eye and, as in the conventional definition of magnification,[1]

$$m_e = \frac{F_e}{4} = \frac{250}{f_e}$$

where F_e is the power of the eye-piece in dioptres and f_e is its focal length in milli-metres. The overall magnification (M) is therefore:

$$m_o \times m_e = \frac{-s}{f_o} \times \frac{250}{f_e}.$$

If the observer relaxes his accommodation, image (3) is at infinity; if this is not so the magnification may differ slightly.

In practice such a simple system of two lenses gives rise to imagery of poor quality and the eye-piece and objective should each be composed of systems of lenses so as to eliminate chromatic aberration, spherical aberration and coma.

Eye-pieces based on the design of both Huygens and Ramsden have been employed in corneal microscopes (Figs. 839–40). Each consists of two lenses, a larger aperture field-lens distant from the eye and a smaller aperture eye-lens to which the eye is nearest. In more advanced designs the field- or the eye-lens or both may be replaced by doublets which eliminate further the aberration, particularly the chromatism of the Ramsden eye-piece. The power of eye-pieces is conventionally expressed in the same way as that of magnifiers, *i.e.* $10\times$, $16\times$, etc. The field-lens and eye-lens are usually of equal power in the Ramsden eye-piece, but in the Huygens type the field-lens is 1·5 to 3 times the stronger.

No great complexity is required in the objective of a corneal microscope. As the movement of the eye limits the magnification which is of practical

[1] p. 798.

FIGS. 839 and 840.—EYE-PIECES IN OPTICAL INSTRUMENTS.

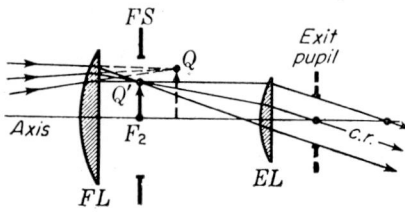

FIGS. 839 and 840.—EYE-PIECES IN OPTICAL INSTRUMENTS.

FIG. 839.—The Huygens's eye-piece.

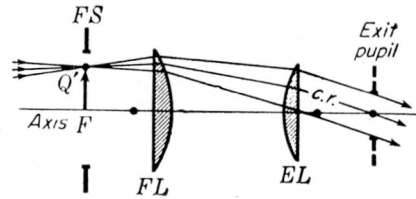

FIG. 840.—The Ramsden eye-piece.

Rays from an objective (unseen on the left) converge to a real image point, Q. The field-lens, FL, refracts these rays to a real image at Q' where a field-stop, FS, is often located; from this they diverge again to be refracted by the eye-lens, EL, into a parallel beam, $c.r.$ The exit pupil is therefore the image of the objective formed by the eye-piece located at the position marked in the figure (F. A. Jenkins and H. E. White).

value in inspection of the anterior segment of the eye, a simple achromatic doublet is the usual form. Objectives may be denoted either by their magnification or by their focal length in millimetres or inches. As an example of how weak the objectives are in corneal microscopes it may be noted that in the Haag Streit 900 instrument the magnification of the objective is $1 \times$ or $1 \cdot 6 \times$. All modern instruments employ the principle of independent fields of view with two eyes as first embodied in the Czapski microscope. The independent microscopes have eye-pieces with an adjustable focus to allow for the observer's refractive error, their axes converge $13°$ or $14°$ and each incorporates a pair of Porro prisms (Fig. 841) between objective and eye-piece so as to give an erect image and also to shorten the tube-length.

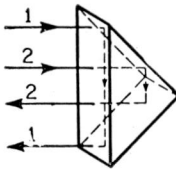

FIG. 841.—THE PORRO PRISM

(F. A. Jenkins and H. E. White).

The ILLUMINATION SYSTEM of the slit-lamp is seen in principle in Fig. 842. Essentially it has three components: a condensing lens (C), a slit and a projecting lens (P). The light from the condensing lens forms a focus on the back vertex of the projecting lens. The aperture of the slit (which acts as the object) and the illuminated image of the slit in the observed eye are conjugate points; this image can be viewed through the microscope from either side.

The optics of the GONIOSCOPE are indicated elsewhere.[1]

Examination of the Fundus

OPHTHALMOSCOPY

The history of the development of the ophthalmoscope, the general principles of its optics and its clinical use are described elsewhere[2]; here we

[1] Vol. VII, p. 269.   [2] Vol. VII, p. 290.

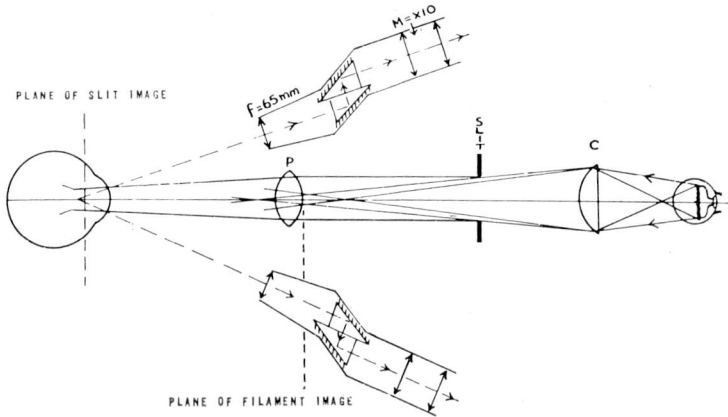

FIG. 842.—THE PRINCIPLE OF THE ILLUMINATION OF THE SLIT-LAMP AND CORNEAL
MICROSCOPE.

The illuminating system has a condensing lens, C, a slit, and a projecting lens, P;
the light from the former lens forms a focus on the back vertex of the latter so that the
filament of the lamp does not form a real image in the eye. The slit aperture which
serves as an object, the projecting lens and the image of the slit are conjugate points.
(C. M. Ruben).

shall discuss the optical principles involved in the illumination and observation of the fundus.

From the historical point of view, the optics of the original " eye-mirror " of von
Helmholtz is of interest. The principle he adopted was essentially that of Galileo's
telescope, illustrated in Fig. 843. Light from a source (L) is allowed to fall upon a
number of superimposed glass plates (M). The greater proportion of the light passes
through the glass plates and, suffering a slight deflection, is lost in the direction NN'.

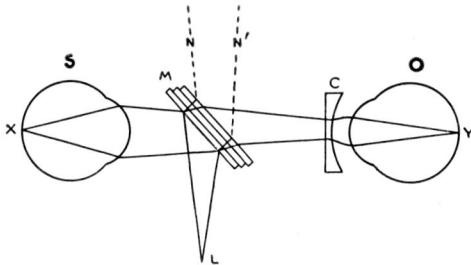

FIG. 843.—THE OPTICS OF THE OPHTHALMOSCOPE OF VON HELMHOLTZ.

A considerable proportion, however, is reflected at each surface and will pass to the
subject's eye (S) where it can be brought to a focus at X. Reflected back, these rays
again meet the glass plates when some of the light will be reflected back to L and thus
be lost, but a considerable amount will pass through to the observer's eye (O). The
rays reflected from the subject's eye will, depending upon the refraction of his eye, be
convergent; but, by the interposition of a concave lens (C) held at the appropriate
distance from O, they can be given the proper divergence so that the observer by

accommodating can bring them to a focus on his retina at Y. In this way the image of X is formed at Y and a detailed picture of the fundus can be seen. From this has been evolved the *direct method of ophthalmoscopy*.

THE ILLUMINATION SYSTEM

THE FIELD OF ILLUMINATION

The area of the observed fundus which is illuminated, that is the FIELD OF ILLUMINATION, varies with (1) the extensity of the source of light, (2) the nature of the mirror employed, (3) the distance of the source of light from the mirror, and (4) the state of refraction of the eyes.

(*a*) *When a plane mirror* is employed the optical conditions may be represented in Fig. 844, where L is the source of light. When the light from L (*the original source*) is reflected by the mirror the rays will diverge as if they came from L', the image of the source of light (the *immediate source*), and will enter the eye accordingly. If L (or L') were at infinity these rays would be parallel and would therefore come to a point-focus on the retina of the emmetropic eye (E). But if L (or L') is a finite distance away

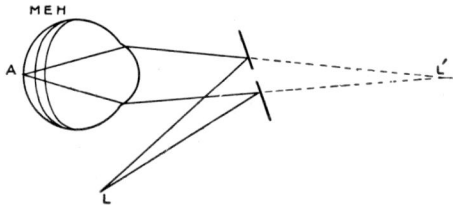

FIG. 844.—THE FIELD OF ILLUMINATION WITH A PLANE MIRROR IN DIRECT OPHTHALMOSCOPY.

the rays will be divergent and can only come to a focus (A) on the retina of a myopic eye (M). It therefore follows that with the plane mirror the field of illumination is least in myopia, greatest in hypermetropia, and inter-mediate in emmetropia. Moreover, if the light is moved farther from the eye, the divergence of the rays becomes less and more nearly approaches paral-lelism, in which case the field in the hypermetropic eye becomes less, in the myopic eye it increases, while in the emmetropic eye it approximates to the theoretical consummation of a point. In this last case the size of the field is therefore independent of the size of the aperture of entry (that is, the size of the subject's pupil), but when the field is formed by an area of diffusion its extent depends directly upon the size of the pupil.

(*b*) *When a concave mirror* is employed the extent of the field varies with the distance of the mirror from the source of light. If the source of light is at a distance from the mirror equal to its focal length, the reflected rays will be parallel and will come to a focus on the retina of the emmetropic eye. The field of a point-source would therefore be a point in emmetropia and a diffusion circle in hypermetropia and myopia. If the mirror is nearer than its focal length to the light, the reflected light will be divergent, producing the same result as a plane mirror, the field being smallest in myopia and largest in hypermetropia. If, however, as is always the case in ophthalmoscopy, the mirror is somewhat farther off from the light than its focal length the rays will be convergent and, being brought to a focus by the dioptric system of the eye in the vitreous body, they will form a diffusion circle on the retina of considerable size, such that the field in myopia is the greatest and that in hypermetropia is the least (Fig. 845). But if the mirror be still farther removed so that the reflected rays come to a focus between the mirror and the eye, the rays entering the eye will be divergent, and the same conditions will be obtained as with a plane mirror. In all these cases, of course, if astigmatism is present the difference in refraction in two meridians will result in a difference in the size of the field in the two corresponding directions, with the result that, instead of being circular, it is oval in shape.

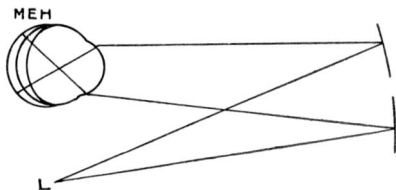

FIG. 845.—THE FIELD OF ILLUMINATION WITH A CONCAVE MIRROR IN DIRECT OPHTHAL-MOSCOPY.

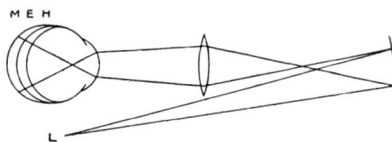

FIG. 846.—THE FIELD OF ILLUMINATION IN INDIRECT OPHTHALMOSCOPY.

Figure 845 represents the optical path of the illuminating system in direct ophthalmoscopy. In the indirect method a convex lens is interposed between the eye and the mirror, and since this always ensures that the entering rays are convergent, the optical conditions represented in Fig. 846 are found, wherein the field of illumination is least in hypermetropia, greatest in myopia, and intermediate in emmetropia.

THE INTENSITY OF THE ILLUMINATION

The *quantity* of light falling upon the retina depends in the first place upon the luminosity of the source and the reflection factor of the mirror, and in the second place upon the area of the pupil, or the extent to which its aperture is occupied by the incoming rays. When these factors remain constant the *intensity* of the light falling upon the retina will depend upon the same factors which determine the size of the field of illumination, for since the total quantity of light in all sections of the cone of light traversing the eye is the same, the greater the section of the cone forming the field, the less must be the intensity. Thus in the case of parallel rays entering the emmetropic eye, the apex of the cone coincides with the retina, the field for a point-source is also a point, and all the light is concentrated here. When the source has some extension the retinal image is considerably smaller than it. In all cases, therefore, when the subject can accommodate for the immediate source of light so that a clear retinal image is formed, the intensity is the same no matter what type of mirror (plane, concave or convex) be used.

If, however, a diffusion area is formed, the intensity varies. With parallel rays in myopia and hypermetropia, since the same amount of light is distributed over a circle of diffusion as was before concentrated to a point, the intensity is less than in emmetropia. In the direct method when a plane mirror is employed, so that slightly diverging rays enter the eye and are converged upon the retina, the whole of the light passing through the pupil is concentrated into a relatively small but very brilliant field and the intensity of illumination is greater in myopia than in hypermetropia (Fig. 844). When a concave mirror is employed so that a diverging cone falls upon the retina, the illumination of the large field is relatively low, and is less in myopia than hypermetropia (Fig. 845), a relation which is met with in every case with the indirect method.

THE MOVEMENT OF THE ILLUMINATED FIELD WITH MOVEMENTS OF THE
    IMMEDIATE SOURCE

If a point of light is placed in front of the eye, the rays entering the pupil will be refracted so that they are brought to a focus, or a partial focus, upon the retina, thus illuminating a circular area of the fundus. If a point of light is represented by A in Fig. 847, whatever the refractive condition

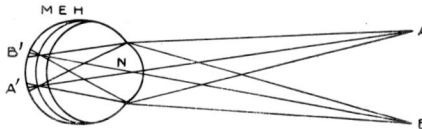

FIG. 847.—THE MOVEMENT OF THE ILLUMINATED RETINAL FIELD WITH THE SOURCE
OF LIGHT.

of the eye, a luminous area will be formed at A′. If we now imagine that A moves downwards to B, the centre of the illuminated field must still lie along the line which connects the object (B) to the nodal point (N), and therefore the image on the retina must be displaced upwards to B′. Accordingly, *if the source of light is moved, the illuminated retinal field always moves in the opposite direction whatever the condition of the refraction of the eye.* Movements of the immediate source of light are most readily brought about by tilting the mirror. If a concave mirror is used, the image formed by it lies in front of the mirror and, as is seen in Fig. 848, when the mirror is tilted in one direction (from AB to A′B′), the image moves in the same direction (from O′ to O″). When a plane mirror is used, however, the image appears to be formed behind it. Thus if the source of light is represented by O (Fig. 849) the image is formed at O′. If, now, the mirror is tilted from the position AB into the position A′B′, the image will appear to have moved so that it will lie in the position O″. When a plane mirror is tilted in any direction the image therefore moves in the opposite direction. It follows that *when a plane mirror is used the illuminated area on the fundus moves in the same direction as the tilt of the mirror*, and when a *concave mirror is used, it moves in the opposite direction* if the immediate source lies between the concave mirror and the illuminated eye. It is obvious from Fig. 847 that the *rate of movement in the myopic eye is greatest and in the hypermetropic eye least.* We have already noted the importance of these phenomena in discussing the optics of retinoscopy.

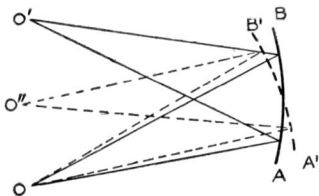

FIG. 848.

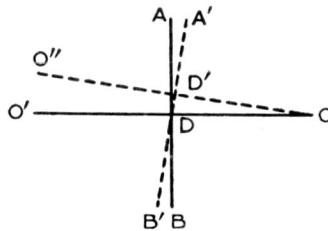

FIG. 849.

THE OBSERVATION SYSTEM

THE OPHTHALMOSCOPIC FIELD OF VISION

The entire field of illumination does not necessarily become visible to the observer, for only those rays can reach his retina which pass through his own pupil. The area of the retina from which these rays come and which the observer can therefore see is called the OPHTHALMOSCOPIC FIELD OF VISION, and it is determined by *the projection of the image of the observer's pupil upon the subject's retina*. It follows, therefore, from our previous reasoning that, when the light is not brought accurately to a focus upon the retina, the field of illumination is dependent upon the size of the pupil of the subject's eye; while the ophthalmoscopic field of vision depends not only upon this but upon the size of the observer's pupil (or the size of the sight-hole of the mirror, whichever is the smaller).

THE EXTENT OF THE FIELD

In a system with diverging rays, as in the direct method of ophthalmoscopy (Fig. 850), if S represents the subject's eye and O the observer's eye, then parallel rays entering S will be brought to a focus on the emmetropic retina E, and diverging rays on a point behind this. Consequently the image of the observer's pupil CD will be found at C′D′, and the extreme rays will determine the ophthalmoscopic field of vision (*xy*) on the retina. CD may therefore be treated as an object and C'D' as an image. From the laws of refraction it follows that they will be of the same size when the two anterior foci of the subject's and the observer's eye coincide, that is, when CD is twice the focal distance of S from the subject's eye. If the observer's eye is farther away than this C'D' diminishes, from which it follows that *the ophthalmoscopic field by the direct method of observation diminishes as the distance between the eyes increases.* Moreover, since the myopic retina is nearer C'D' than the hypermetropic, *the field in myopia is least, that in*

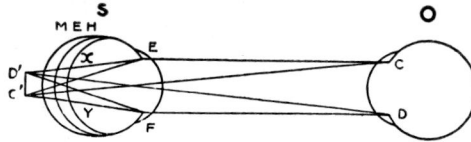

FIG. 850.

hypermetropia is greatest, while the emmetropic field is intermediate in size. Finally, dilatation of either pupil increases the area of the field. In all cases, however, *the field of vision is smaller than the field of illumination,* for the former is determined by the size of the pupil of the observer's eye, while the latter is determined largely by the size of the immediate source of light, which is the larger of the two in all practical cases.

In a system with converging rays, as in the indirect method of ophthalmoscopy (Fig. 851), if a convex lens is held at its own focal distance from the

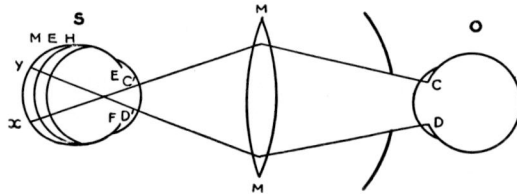

FIG. 851.

pupil of the subject's eye EF, the lens will form an image of CD in the plane of EF, and the projection of this image of the observer's pupil upon the subject's retina will delimit the ophthalmoscopic field of vision (*xy*). If CD is farther from the lens than is C'D', the image C'D' will be smaller than the object, and will therefore be smaller than the average pupil. It follows that *the ophthalmoscopic field is independent of the size of the observed pupil* (so long as this is greater than the reduced image of the observer's pupil formed by the lens). Further, the field is greatest when the lens is at its principal focal distance from the pupil of the subject's eye; and it increases (within the limits imposed by spherical aberration) directly with the size of the lens and inversely with its focal distance. So far as the refractive condition is concerned, *the field is greatest in myopia, least in hypermetropia, and intermediate in emmetropia*; and the field can be increased (at the cost of diminished illumination) by the use of a plane mirror. In the conditions wherein the method is usually employed, the image of the observer's pupil is in the pupillary plane, and the image of the immediate source of light is formed in the vitreous body (Fig. 846). Since the divergence of the rays at the plane of the retina is greater in the former case, it follows that *the ophthalmoscopic field is greater than the field of illumination.*

THE BRIGHTNESS OF THE FIELD

When the direct method is used (Fig. 852) the rays from one point (z) on the emmetropic retina will include the rays from every point of $C'D'$ of the image (*cf.* Fig. 850), and will fill the whole of the observer's pupil (CD);

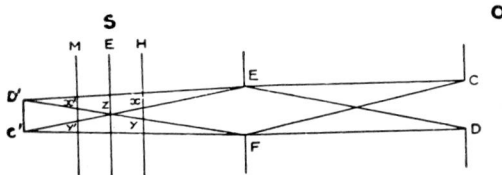

FIG. 852.

the rays from every point between x and y on the hypermetropic retina will similarly fill CD; whereas in the myopic eye no point between x' and y' can send out a cone of rays which will cover the whole of the pupil CD. It follows that *the image is brightest in hypermetropia, less bright in emmetropia, and least bright in myopia.* Moreover, it is obvious that it varies with the size of both pupils and with the distance between them.

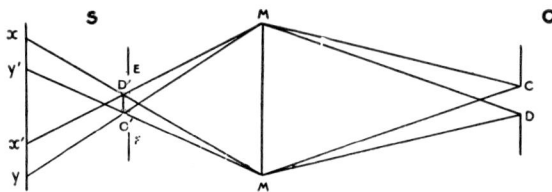

FIG. 853.

In the indirect method, on the other hand (Fig. 853), every point between x' and y' will emit a cone of light which will entirely cover the pupil CD, while the light emitted from points between x and y' and x' and y will not do so. The illumination of the ophthalmoscopic field will therefore be unequal, for the peripheral zone will be less bright than the central zone, but *the entire area of the latter is of maximum brightness.*

THE MOVEMENT OF THE OPHTHALMOSCOPIC FIELD WITH THE FIELD OF
    ILLUMINATION

The Direction of Movement. The direction of movement of the ophthalmoscopic field varies with the state of the refraction of the subject's eye and
the position of the observer.

(*a*) If the subject is emmetropic (Fig. 854) the retinal point X will emit
a parallel bundle of rays DE; these will be projected by an observer as
coming from the punctum remotum of the eye, that is, from infinity. They
are thus projected in the direction A. If the point X is moved to X′ the
bundle of rays emanating from it will be similarly projected as if coming

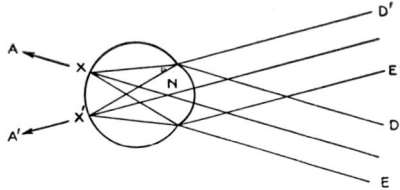

FIG. 854.

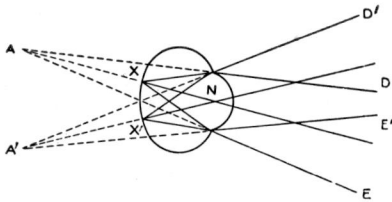

FIG. 855.

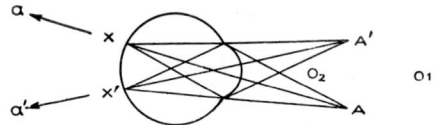

FIG. 856.

FIGS. 854–856.—THE DIRECTION OF MOVEMENT OF THE OPHTHALMOSCOPIC FIELD.

from A′. It follows that *the apparent movement of the illuminated retinal area
is in the same direction as its actual movement.*

(*b*) If the subject is hypermetropic (Fig. 855), an illuminated point (X)
on the retina will emit a cone of diverging rays (DE) which will be projected
by the observer as if coming from the punctum remotum of the eye (A). If
now the point X is moved downwards to X′, X′ will similarly be projected to
A′; *the movement of the ophthalmoscopic field is therefore in the same direction
as that of the field of illumination.*

(*c*) In myopia (Fig. 856) the emergent rays from X are convergent and
come to a focus at the punctum remotum of the eye (A) which lies in front
of the eye, between it and infinity. The *apparent movement of the image will
now depend upon the position of the observer relative to the punctum remotum.*
If the myopia is high so that the punctum remotum lies between the observer
and the subject, the former (being situated at O_1) will see the image of X

at A and of X' at A'; consequently the movement of the ophthalmoscopic field is in the direction opposite to that of the field of illumination. If the myopia is low so that the punctum remotum lies behind the observer (who may be considered at O_2), its projection will again be in the direction aa' as in Fig. 854, that is, in the same direction as the movement of the field of illumination. It follows that when the observer is situated at the remote point itself, no movement of the field of illumination can be seen: on one side of this point a virtual erect image is observed, the movement of which is in the same direction as the movement of the illuminated retinal field; on the other side a real inverted image is seen, the movement of which is in the opposite direction; but at this point, which is called the POINT OF REVERSAL, the whole pupil appears either bright or dark.

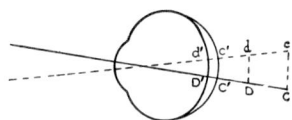

FIG. 857.

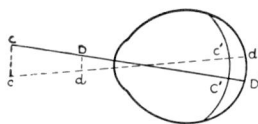

FIG. 858.

FIGS. 857 and 858.—THE RATE OF MOVEMENT OF THE OPHTHALMOSCOPIC FIELD.

The Rate of Movement. Since in each case the movement is determined as referred to the punctum remotum of the eye, the excursion depends upon the apparent displacement at this plane. Hence *the greater the refractive error* (D'd') both in hypermetropia (Fig. 857) and myopia (Fig. 858) the nearer the punctum remotum (D*d*), *the shorter the excursion, and the slower the speed of movement.* The dependence of the apparent movement of an illuminated area of retina upon the refraction of the eye is the basis of retinoscopy.[1]

METHODS OF OPHTHALMOSCOPY
Direct Ophthalmoscopy

THE FORMATION OF THE IMAGE

When the direct method of examination is employed and light is thrown into the eye by a mirror, we have already seen that in the normal condition, when the subject and the observer are separated by some considerable distance (*e.g.*, 1 metre), an image of one point only of the retina can be seen when the observer's eye is in line with the source of light. The optical conditions are represented in Fig. 859. Since the whole of the pupillary aperture of the subject's eye is filled by the cone of light from one point, no image of a retinal area is seen, but his pupil appears uniformly illuminated. If we consider the path of light emitted by two points (*x*, *y*, Fig. 860), it is evident that they form two diverging and parallel bundles. If the observer's

---

[1] p. 390.

eye is at O, rays from these two points cannot enter his eye simultaneously; no clear image is therefore formed since light from one point only (z) can be seen. It is only when the observer's eye is brought up so close to the subject that it enters into a region common to both beams (O'), that rays from two points on the retina can enter his pupil; and the closer the two eyes are together the larger will be the number of these points, and therefore the larger the available image.

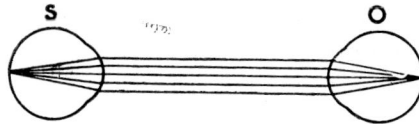

FIG. 859.

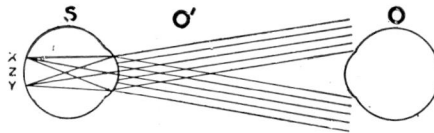

FIG. 860.

If there is a large refractive error, however, the case is different. In the case of a hypermetropic eye (Fig. 861) the rays from two retinal points (x, y) will appear to come from x' and y' and will leave the eye in two diverging beams, a proportion of both of which can be received simultaneously through the observer's pupil. The observer thus sees an erect virtual image of the fundus. If the observer moves towards one side more of the bundle of rays coming from the opposite side of the retina enters his pupil and less from

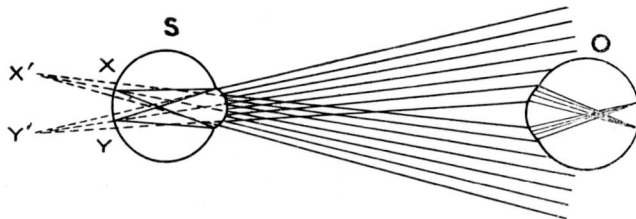

FIG. 861.

the same side. He, however, refers the apparent movement of the fundus (whereby more from the opposite side appears and some from the same side disappears) to the pupil as a fixed reference frame, and the appearance is therefore mentally interpreted as a movement of the image in the same direction as his own movement.

Similarly a myopic eye (Fig. 862) will emit convergent beams to form a real inverted image in front of the eye; but continuing from this image the rays will deviate in two diverging bundles, part of each of which can simultaneously enter the observer's pupil. It will therefore be possible for the observer to see a small inverted image of the fundus. Since the image is inverted, if the observer moves he will see more of the fundus on the same side and less upon the opposite side, so that the image will appear to move in the opposite direction. If, however, the eyes of the subject and the observer are brought close together, and in the event of the myopia being very high, the remote point of the subject's eye may be situated in space so close to the observer's eye that it is impossible for him to accommodate for it; in this case no clear image can be seen.

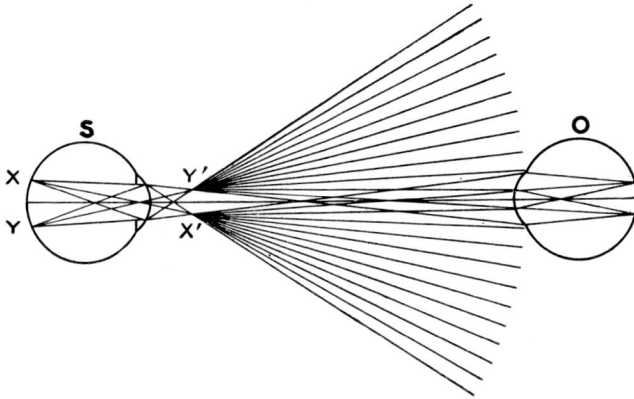

FIG. 862.

It follows that with the direct method of observation, employing a mirror alone, if the observer's eye is situated some distance away an illuminated area of the retina without any clear image is seen, except in the presence of high refractive errors; in which case, if the error is one of hypermetropia, an erect and virtual image, or if the error is one of myopia, an inverted real image of the retina may be seen. If, however, the observer's eye is brought close to the eye a retinal image can be seen in all cases except those of very high myopia. The first optical system is that which as we have described is employed in the objective estimation of the refraction by retinoscopy; the second system is employed in the direct method of ophthalmoscopy.

The Formation of the Image in Emmetropia

If the subject's eye is emmetropic rays emitted from it are parallel (Fig. 863). The image of any point (B) on the retina as seen by an observer (O) in front is therefore formed at infinity at the apparent meeting place of two rays: DF, which, after running parallel (BD) to the optic axis XY, passes through the anterior principal focus F; and BN which, passing through the nodal point, is unrefracted. The image of AB is therefore an enlarged virtual erect image at infinity (A'B'). It is this image which O observes. If O is placed directly in front of S so that their anterior foci and optic axes coincide, and if O is also emmetropic, two rays from B' will meet in B'', the one N'B'

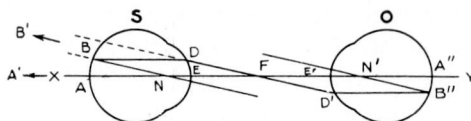

FIG. 863.—THE FORMATION OF THE IMAGE IN EMMETROPIA IN DIRECT
OPHTHALMOSCOPY.

passing unrefracted through the nodal point, and the other B'FD'B'' passing through
the principal focus and running parallel to the optic axis. The image on the observer's
retina is therefore A''B'', and from the similarity of the triangles DFE and D'FE', it
is equal in size to the object AB.

The Formation of the Image in Hypermetropia

If the subject's eye is hypermetropic (Fig. 864) the rays issuing from B (DF and
BN) are divergent: a virtual erect image of AB is therefore formed at a finite distance
behind S at A'B'. Now since the rays from A'B' are not parallel but divergent, they

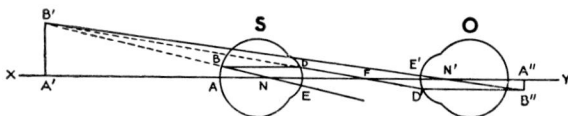

FIG. 864.

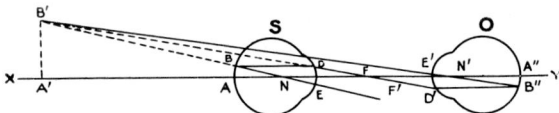

FIG. 865.

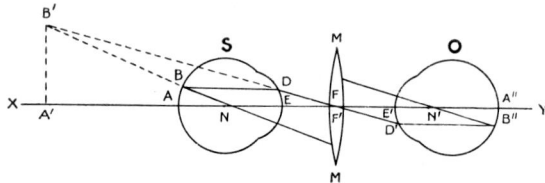

FIG. 866.

FIGS. 864–866.—THE FORMATION OF THE IMAGE IN HYPERMETROPIA IN
DIRECT OPHTHALMOSCOPY.

form an image A''B'' behind the retina of O, if this eye is emmetropic. Again, from the
similarity of the triangles DFE and D'FE', the image A''B'' is the same size as the
object AB; but it cannot be clearly seen unless the refractive power of O is increased
by an effort of accommodation, or unless the rays entering it are rendered parallel by
placing a convex lens in front of the eye.

In the first event, if O accommodates (Fig. 865) the principal focus F' will approach
O and will no longer coincide with F, and since the refraction of O is now dynamically
increased, D'B'' is now no longer parallel to XY. It follows that A''B'' is less than
E'D' and is therefore less than AB, that is, the image formed on the retina is less than

the object. On the other hand, if a convex lens (M, Fig. 866) is placed in the path of the entering rays in such a position that its optic centre coincides with the principal foci of O and S, and of such a strength that its principal focus coincides with A'B', the image of A'B' formed by such a lens will be at infinity. The rays issuing from it will therefore be parallel, so that an image of A'B' will be formed upon the retina of O at A''B''. Here again, provided the lens is situated at F, the image A''B'' is equal in size to the object AB.

The Formation of the Image in Myopia

In the case when S is myopic, the image of AB is formed at A'B' behind the observer's eye so that he can catch the convergent rays (Fig. 867). The ray N'B' will pass unrefracted, but F'D' will be refracted parallel to XY and will therefore cut N'B' in B''. A''B'' will therefore form the image of A'B', that is, of AB, and it will be of the same size as AB. The only way in which such an image can be seen is by placing a concave lens in front of O of such a strength as to render the rays issuing

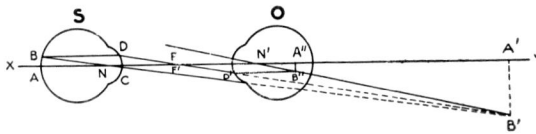

FIG. 867.

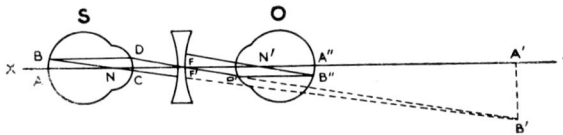

FIG. 868.

FIGS. 867 and 868.—THE FORMATION OF THE IMAGE IN MYOPIA IN DIRECT OPHTHALMOSCOPY.

from S parallel. If a lens be placed in such a position that its optical centre coincides with the two anterior focal points of the eyes, and of such a strength that its principal focus coincides with A'B', the rays issuing from it will be parallel, the image A''B'' will lie upon the retina and will be of a size equal to AB (Fig. 868). If, however, the degree of myopia is so great that the punctum remotum is situated between O and S, no image can be formed by any correcting lens.

In astigmatism there are two anterior foci to the subject's eye, and it is obvious that they cannot both be occupied by the correcting lens simultaneously. It follows that in astigmatism no clear image of the whole field can be formed, but only lines perpendicular to the meridian which if corrected can be clearly seen.

It follows that in all these cases an inverted image of the subject's fundus falls upon the observer's retina, and since the image is inverted psychologically, *an erect image is invariably appreciated. If the subject's eye is emmetropic an image of equal size to the object is formed on the retina of the emmetropic observer when his accommodation is relaxed; but if the subject is ametropic, such an image is formed in these circumstances only if a correcting lens equivalent to the amount of ametropia is placed behind the mirror of the ophthalmoscope in the anterior focal plane of each eye,* except in the case of very high myopia.

This forms a means of estimating the refraction, but since it is difficult to approach the subject's eye so closely that the lens lies in its anterior focal plane, the correcting lens is usually weaker than the true amount of hypermetropia and stronger than the true amount of myopia.

THE MAGNIFICATION OF THE IMAGE

When viewing the fundus of the emmetropic eye, the rays enter the observer's eye in a parallel direction and, as we have seen, the image formed on the retina of the latter is of the same size as the object. This image, however, is projected by the observer to the distance of distinct vision behind the subject's eye and appears to him to be situated there (Fig. 869).

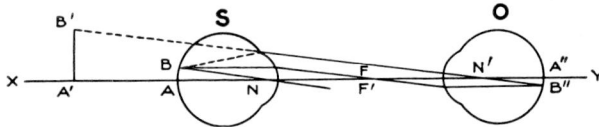

Fig. 869.—THE MAGNIFICATION OF THE IMAGE IN DIRECT OPHTHALMOSCOPY.

This distance is necessarily arbitrary so that the apparent magnification is also arbitrary. If the image is assumed to be at the near-point of distinct vision (25 cm.), then the magnification

$$M = i/o = A'B'/AB = A'N'/N'A''$$

where $N'A''$ is the posterior nodal distance which, being equal to the anterior focal distance expressed in metres, is the same as the reciprocal of the ocular power in dioptres.

Therefore $i/o = 0.25$ m. $\div$ 1 m./60 = 15.

The calculation simply regards the dioptric system of the eye (of 60 D power) as a magnifier and, as we have noted before, magnification is expressed conventionally as one quarter of the dioptric power. Hence in emmetropia the subject's fundus is seen magnified about 15 times.

In axial ametropia if a lens is placed at the principal foci of the two eyes it will have no effect on the direction of the rays, so that the magnification will be the same in all cases. But if, as is usually the case, the correcting lens is placed beyond the anterior focus of the subject's eye, the rays diverge less in hypermetropia and more in myopia; consequently the magnification is less in hypermetropia and greater in myopia than in emmetropia. In astigmatism (unequal curvature ametropia), since the magnification is greatest in the relatively myopic meridian and least in the hypermetropic, the magnification will be unequal, being greatest in the meridian of greatest refraction. It follows that the image will be distorted, the optic disc, for example, appearing oval with a major axis of the ellipse in the meridian of greatest refraction.

Differences in level in the fundus may be estimated by parallactic displacement, for a movement of the observer's eye will result in an apparent displacement of a point on the subject's retina in the opposite direction when compared with a point situated behind it. The difference of level can be measured by finding the correcting lens which, when held at the anterior focal plane, is necessary to bring each point into accurate focus. When the ophthalmoscope is held in this plane (that is, 15·706 mm. in front of the cornea), the axial length represented by a difference in focusing may be obtained from the equation, $l_1 l_2 = f_1 f_2$. When f_1, the anterior focal length, is 17·054 mm., f_2, the posterior focal length, is 22·785 mm., l_2 is the distance of an object from the posterior principal focus (the fundus) and l_1 the distance of its image from the anterior principal focus, then

$$l_2 = f_1 f_2/l_1 = 17 \cdot 054 \times 22 \cdot 785/l_1 = 388 \cdot 575/l_1.$$

It follows that in the emmetropic eye each dioptre of change of focus is equivalent to an axial length of 0·388 mm. (or approximately 0·4 mm.); or a difference in focusing between two points on the fundus of 3 D indicates a difference of level of 1·17 mm. (*i.e.*, approximately 1 mm.). In the case of the aphakic eye, on the other hand, the ophthalmoscope must be held at a distance of 23·227 mm. in front of the cornea, and $l_2 = 23 \cdot 227 \times 31 \cdot 031/l_1 = 720 \cdot 757/l_1$. It follows that in the aphakic eye each dioptre of focusing is equivalent to an axial length of 0·72 mm., or a difference in focusing between two points on the fundus of 3 D indicates a difference in level of 2·16 mm. (that is, approximately 2 mm.).

Indirect Ophthalmoscopy

THE FORMATION OF THE IMAGE

We have already seen that when the illuminated fundus of a highly myopic eye is observed from a considerable distance so that the punctum remotum falls between the eyes of the subject and of the observer, details of the fundus can be seen so long as the observer can accommodate for the image formed at the punctum remotum (Fig. 862). The principle of the indirect method of ophthalmoscopy is to make every eye highly myopic by placing in front of it a convex lens of sufficient strength to form a real image of the fundus in this position.

The optical principles determining the formation of this image are evident in the following construction. In the emmetropic eye (Fig. 870) rays from AB will leave in a parallel direction and are therefore brought to a focus as an inverted image (*ab*) at the principal focus of the lens, between the lens and the observer's eye. In hypermetropia the emerging rays will diverge, and they will thus appear to come from a virtual enlarged, erect image situated behind the eye (A′B′, Fig. 871). The lens, using this as an object, forms an inverted image of it (*ab*), and since the rays are divergent this final image will be situated in front of its principal focus. In the myopic eye, on the other hand, the rays coming from the fundus are convergent, and therefore an inverted image is formed in front of the eye (A′B′, Fig. 872). The lens then forms a second smaller image of this at a point (*ab*) within its focal length. The relative position of these images will be evident from Fig. 873.

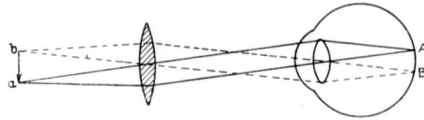

FIG. 870.

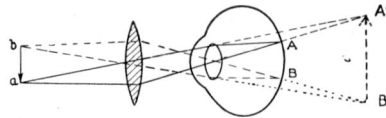

FIG. 871.

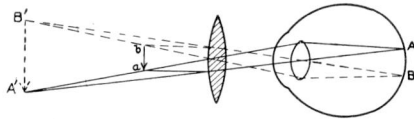

FIG. 872.

FIGS. 870–872.—THE FORMATION OF THE IMAGE IN INDIRECT OPHTHALMOSCOPY.

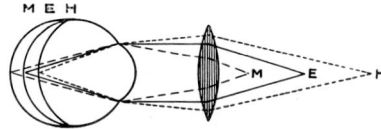

FIG. 873.—THE POSITION OF THE IMAGE IN INDIRECT OPHTHALMOSCOPY.

THE MAGNIFICATION OF THE IMAGE

The magnification of the image varies primarily with the dioptric strength of the lens employed and its position relative to the eye. Consider the case of an emmetropic eye (Fig. 874). Since the triangles ABN and abO are similar, the magnification $= i/o = ab/AB = a$O$/$AN. If the value of AN is 15 mm., it follows that *the linear magnification is equal to the focal length of the lens divided by* 15. The lens usually employed in practice is $+13$ D, in which case the magnification is $75/15 = 5$. *If a stronger lens is employed the image is smaller and brighter; and if a weaker lens is employed the magnification is greater and the illumination less.* The actual size of the image formed on the observer's retina will, of course, depend on his distance from the real aerial image of the subject's fundus. This is usually about 33 cm. but may vary. It is quite simple, however, to calculate angular magnification on a basis similar to that used for other magnifying devices as the ratio between the angular subtense of this aerial image of the subject's fundus and the angular subtense of the subject's fundus itself if it were 25 cm. from the observer.

In the case of the emmetropic eye the emitted rays are parallel: consequently no matter where the lens is placed the image is always formed in the principal plane. It follows that in Fig. 874 the angle aOb is constant, so that ab always bears the same relation to AB. Consequently *in the emmetropic eye the size of the image remains unchanged for all positions of the lens.*

In the ametropic eye, however, the relations are different. When the lens is held at such a distance that its principal focus (f) corresponds to the anterior focus of the eye (F), rays parallel to the optic axis, as represented in Fig. 875, will run parallel after passing through the lens. The size of the image is therefore the same in hypermetropia and myopia as in emmetropia. If, however, the principal focus is nearer to

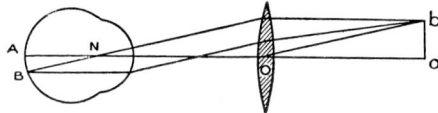

FIG. 874.

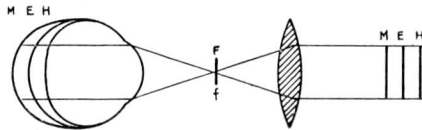

FIG. 875.

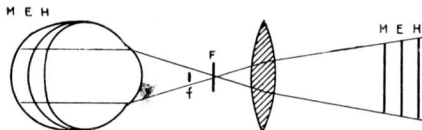

FIG. 876.

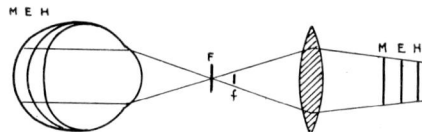

FIG. 877.

FIGS. 874–877.—THE MAGNIFICATION OF THE IMAGE IN INDIRECT OPHTHALMOSCOPY.

the eye than this, such rays will leave the lens in a divergent direction. In this case it is seen from Fig. 876 that, since the image of the myopic fundus is nearer the lens, and the image of the hypermetropic farther than that of the emmetropic, the image of the first must be smaller and that of the second larger. Conversely, when the principal focus of the lens is farther from the eye than the anterior principal focus, these rays converge after leaving the lens, and the opposite relation will be produced (Fig. 877).

It follows that *when the lens is at its own focal distance from the anterior focus of the eye, the magnification is the same in all refractive conditions; if the lens is less than its own focal distance from the anterior focus of the eye the magnification is greater in hypermetropia and less in myopia than in emme-*

tropia; and if the lens is farther from the eye than this, the magnification is greater in myopia and less in hypermetropia than in emmetropia. Consequently when the lens is moved towards the observer from this position, the image remains the same size in emmetropia, diminishes in hypermetropia, and increases in myopia, while with the reverse movement the opposite conditions obtain. In the case of astigmatism there are two anterior foci but only one principal point at the anterior pole of the reduced eye. When the lens is at its focal distance from this point it will refract all rays in a direction parallel to the axis. It follows that when the lens is at its focal distance from the cornea the magnification is the same for all meridians and the image is undistorted. If the lens is nearer the eye than this an unequal magnification occurs, being greatest in the least refractive meridian; and if the lens is farther from the eye the magnification is greater in the more refractive meridian.

Differences in level in the fundus can be made evident by parallactic displacement in this method of examination also. In Fig. 878 if A and B represent two spots at unequal levels on the fundus, when the lens is moved from O_1 to O_2 the respective

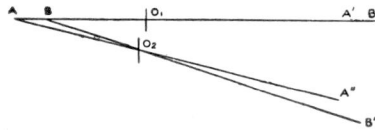

FIG. 878.—PARALLACTIC DISPLACEMENT IN INDIRECT OPHTHALMOSCOPY.

images will move from A'B' to A''B''. When the lens is moved, therefore, objects closer to the observer will appear to move more rapidly and over a greater excursion than those farther away.

BINOCULAR INDIRECT OPHTHALMOSCOPY is of particular value for determining differences in level. Rubin (1964)[1] has shown that the axial magnification upon which the sensation of depth depends is equal to the square of the linear magnification. We have previously remarked that in indirect ophthalmoscopy the observer's pupil is imaged in the subject's pupillary plane; in binocular indirect ophthalmoscopy it is necessary for both the observer's pupils to be projected onto that plane. This is effected by optical reduction of the interpupillary distance (Fig. 879) and by employing maximal mydriasis during the examination. Greater magnification can be obtained in indirect ophthalmoscopy by the use of prism binoculars which act as a telescopic device to inspect the aerial image instead of the usual simple 3 D lens incorporated to facilitate accommodation onto this image (L'Esperance, 1959).[2] More powerful condensing lenses are often used in binocular indirect ophthalmoscopy; in addition to the +13 D lens, +20 D and +30 D lenses are available.

[1] *Surv. Ophthal.*, **9**, 449 (1964).
[2] *Arch. Ophthal.*, **63**, 1096 (1959).

Lenses of aspherical form have the advantage of offering a larger field free of aberration and attention has also been paid to features of design which minimize the annoying reflections that are a feature of this technique.

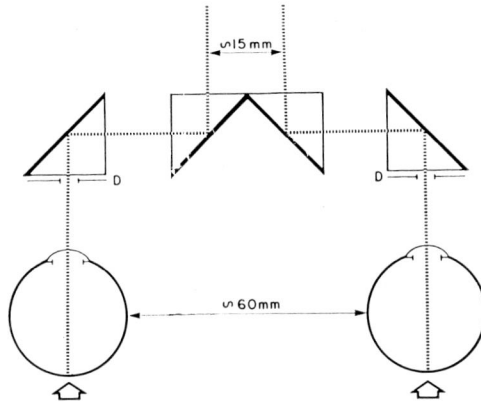

FIG. 879.—THE OPTICS OF BINOCULAR OPHTHALMOSCOPY.

The observer's true pupillary distance is reduced to a fixed 15 mm. by the prism binocular. D is the exit pupil of the binocular viewing system for each eye. This pupil is imaged in the patient's pupil (M. L. Rubin).

Focal Illumination of the Posterior Vitreous and Fundus

In order to view the posterior part of the vitreous and the fundus with the slit-lamp, their images must come within the focusing range of the microscope.[1] This problem has been solved in three ways: by abolishing

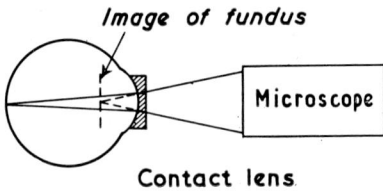

Image of fundus

Microscope

Contact lens

FIG. 880.

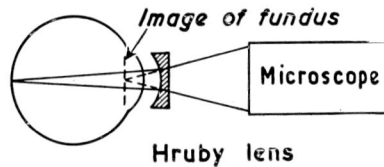

Image of fundus

Microscope

Hruby lens

FIG. 881.

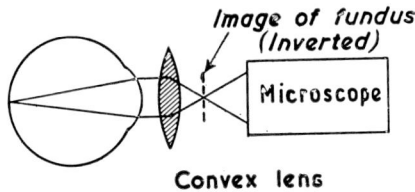

Image of fundus (Inverted)

Microscope

Convex lens

FIG. 882.

FIGS. 880–882.—BIOMICROSCOPY OF THE FUNDUS.

The diagrams show in a simplified manner the optical arrangements for examination of the fundus with the slit-lamp, with a contact lens (Fig. 880), a concave Hruby lens (Fig. 881) and a strong convex lens (Fig. 882).

[1] Vol. VII, p. 265.

the refraction of the cornea by means of a contact lens with a flat anterior surface, or by introducing a strong concave or convex lens into the optical system, in all cases maintaining the illuminating beam and the microscope as nearly coaxial as possible. The general optical principles are seen in Figs. 880 to 882.

The most useful and plastic instrument for the first technique is the gonio-lens introduced by Goldmann[1] which is fitted with three mirrors which reflect the incident light to different degrees so that the entire periphery of the fundus can be explored as well as the angle of the anterior chamber (gonioscopy). By interposing a strong concave lens into the incident beam close to the cornea (−58 D, Hruby[2]) the corneal microscope is converted into a telescope (Fig. 881). Alternatively by interposing a strong convex lens (+55 D, El Bayadi[3] and Rosen[4]) in a similar position, a real inverted image of the fundus is formed between it and the microscope some 16 mm. in front of the supplementary lens, on which the microscope, removed some distance away from the patient's eye, can be focused (Fig. 882); this technique therefore resembles that of indirect ophthalmoscopy.

[1] *Ophthalmologica*, **96,** 90 (1938).
[2] *Klin. Mbl. Augenheilk.*, **108,** 195 (1942); *Wien. klin. Wschr.*, **63,** 699 (1951).
[3] *Brit. J. Ophthal.*, **37,** 625 (1953).
[4] *Amer. J. Ophthal.*, **48,** 782 (1959).

ADDENDUM

THE OPTICS OF KERATOMILEUSIS

KERATOMILEUSIS[1] cannot by any means be called an ophthalmic appliance, but although it is not yet an established procedure the interest it is exciting merits a short note as an addendum about the optics involved. In the procedure devised by J. I. Barraquer (1964–67) to alter the ocular refraction by surgery, a deep lamella of the anterior portion of the cornea is removed, frozen and its posterior surface ground to a new curvature. When this is replaced on the bed from which it was removed, the lamella is bent and the curvature of the anterior surface becomes altered. The consequent change in refractive power reduces or abolishes the ametropia.

In order to calculate the curvature appropriate for the posterior surface of the lamella, Barraquer originally relied simply on the refractive power of the anterior surface of the eye before and after surgery as indicated by the conventional keratometric scale, but as Littman (1967) pointed out, this is inadequate since the thickness of the cornea before and after surgery is also important. Taking this into account, he gave the formula:

$$ r = \frac{r_a}{\dfrac{r_a D}{376} + 1} - 0.273 \, (d_a - d) $$

where r is the post-operative radius of the curvature of the anterior corneal surface in millimetres, r_a the pre-operative value, D the ocular refraction in dioptres, d_a and d the pre- and post-operative thickness of the cornea in millimetres.

It will be appreciated that the surgical technique involves a bending of the reshaped lamella as it is replaced on the corneal bed from which it was originally removed, a situation somewhat analogous to that occurring in a soft contact lens when in place on the cornea. The optical changes are, however, not entirely predictable but, making some elementary assumptions about the geometry of the lamella before and after bending, attempts have been made to estimate its effects (Kaplan, 1966; Kaplan et al., 1968).

Barraquer. *An. Inst. Barraquer*, **5**, 206 (1964).
Int. Surg. (Chic.), **48**, 103 (1967).
Arch. Soc. Amer. oftal. optom., **6**, 21 (1967).
Kaplan. *Amer. J. Optom.*, **43**, 795 (1966).

Kaplan, Elstein, Fehgal and Katzin. *Amer. J. Optom.*, **45**, 806 (1968).
Littman. *Arch. Soc. Amer. oftal. optom.*, **6**, 103 (1967).

[1] p. 351.

APPENDIX

TABLE XXXII

Lenses of Same Effectivity for Near and Distant Work
(A. S. Percival, 1928)

$F\infty$ = lens for distant vision.
Fn = lens for near vision (30 cm.).
K = equivalent lens placed in contact with the cornea (corneal contact lens).

Convex			Concave		
$F\infty$ $p = \infty$	K $p = \infty$	Fn $p = \cdot 3$	$F\infty$ $p = \infty$	K $p = \infty$	Fn $p = \cdot 3$
+ 1	+ 1·014	+ 1·092	− 1	− 0·987	− 1·093
+ 2	+ 2·056	+ 2·183	− 2	− 1·947	− 2·184
+ 3	+ 3·128	+ 3·272	− 3	− 2·882	− 3·288
+ 4	+ 4·230	+ 4·360	− 4	− 3·794	− 4·382
+ 5	+ 5·365	+ 5·447	− 5	− 4·682	− 5·481
+ 6	+ 6·533	+ 6·532	− 6	− 5·549	− 6·581
+ 7	+ 7·737	+ 7·616	− 7	− 6·392	− 7·682
+ 8	+ 8·877	+ 8·699	− 8	− 7·215	− 8·785
+ 10	+ 11·574	+ 10·860	− 10	− 8·803	− 10·995
+ 12	+ 14·340	+ 13·016	− 12	− 10·316	− 13·210
+ 14	+ 17·292	+ 15·167	− 14	− 11·761	− 15·431
+ 16	+ 20·540	+ 17·313	− 16	− 13·141	− 17·658
+ 18	+ 23·835	+ 19·453	− 18	− 14·460	− 19·890
+ 20	+ 27·473	+ 21·588	− 20	− 15·723	− 22·127

TABLE XXXIII

BEST-FORM LENSES FOR DISTANCE (SPHERICAL)

BACK OR OCULAR SURFACE POWERS

(Emsley and Swaine)

Total Power of Lens s =	Tscherning		Tscherning		Whitwell		Percival	Gleichen	Ultor	Ortho
	O.	W.	O.	W.	O.	W.	O.	O.	O.	O.
	20 mm.		25 mm.		27 mm.		27 mm.	25 mm.	Various	?
+14	—	—	—	—	—	—	—	—	—	—
13	—	—	—	—	—	—	−5·75	—	—	—
12	—	—	—	—	—	—	6·2	—	—	—
11	—	−14	—	—	—	—	6·75	—	—	—
10	−14	17	—	—	—	—	6·75	—	—	—
9	12·5	18·5	—	—	—	—	7	—	—	—
8	11·5	19·5	−11	−11	−8·8	−10·6	7	−7·7	−6·75	−8·5
7	12·2	21	9·5	14	7·5	12·9	7	6·7	7·75	8·2
6	11	22	9	15·2	7·5	13·9	7	6·2	7·5	7·6
5	11	23	8·7	16·5	7·4	15	6·75	6·2	7	7
4	11	24	8·7	17·5	7·4	16	6·5	6·2	7	7
3	11	25	8·5	18·7	7·5	16·9	6·5	6·5	6·75	6·7
2	11	−25·7	8·7	19·5	−7·7	−17·7	6·5	6·5	6·75	6·2
+1	−11·2		−8·7	−20·5			−6·5	−6·7	−6·5	−6·2
0	−11·5	−26·5	−9	−21	−8	−18·5	−6·5	−7	−6·75	−8·7

—	—	—	—	—	—	—	—	—	—	—
1	9	7·75	7·2	7·0	19·2	8·2	21·7	9·2	27·2	11·7
2	9	8·25	7·7	7·7	19·9	8·5	22·5	9·5	27·7	12
3	9·2	8·5	8	8·2	20·6	8·8	23·2	10	28·5	12·3
4	9·5	8·75	8·5	8·7	21·2	9·3	24	10·5	29	12·7
5	9·7	9	9	9·2	21·8	9·7	24·5	11	29·5	13
6	10·7	9·25	9·5	9·7	22·3	10·1	25·2	11·5	30	13·5
7	11	9·75	10·5	10·2	22·9	10·6	25·5	11·7	30·5	13·7
8	11·2	10·25	11	10·7	23·4	11	26·2	12·2	31·2	14·2
9	12·2	10·75	11·7	11·5	23·8	11·6	26·7	12·7	31·5	14·7
10	13	11·37	12·2	12	24·2	12·1	27·2	13·2	32	15·2
11	13·2	12	13	12·5	24·6	12·7	27·7	13·7	32·5	15·5
12	14	12·7	13·7	13·2	25	13·4	28·2	14·5	33	16
13	14·5	13·5	14·5	14	25·3	14·1	28·5	15	33·5	16·5
14	15·2	14·2	15·2	14·7	25·7	14·7	29	15·5	34	17
15	15·7	15	16		26	15·5	29·5	16·2	34·5	17·5
16	16·7	16	16·7		26·2	16·25	29·7	17	34·7	18·5
17	17		17·7		26·4	17·1	29·7	17·5	35	19
18	18		18·5		26·4	18	30	18·5	35·5	19·5
19	19		19·7		26·4	19	30	19·2	35·7	20·5
20	20				26·3	20	30	20	36	21
21					25·9	21·7	29·7	21	36·5	21·5
22							29·5	22	36·7	22·5
23							29	23	36·7	23
24							25	24·5	37	24
25								25	37	25
26									37	26
28									37	28
30									36	31

Note. O = Ostwald   W = Wollaston

APPENDIX

TABLE XXXIV

STANDARD TAPERED MULTICURVE TRIAL SET OF 23 CORNEAL CONTACT LENSES
(Nissel)

Specification:

Back optic diameter 6·50 mm.
1st peripheral band diameter 7·50 mm.
2nd peripheral band diameter 8·50 mm.
Overall diameter 9·50 mm.
Trial lenses −2·00 D ±0·12 D.
Blended transitions.
Lenses engraved 1 to 23.

Range of Radii

No.	Radius	1st Peripheral Radius	2nd Peripheral Radius	3rd Peripheral Radius
1	7·20	7·70	8·20	8·70
2	7·25	7·75	8·25	8·75
3	7·30	7·80	8·30	8·80
4	7·35	7·85	8·35	8·85
5	7·40	7·90	8·40	8·90
6	7·45	7·95	8·45	8·95
7	7·50	8·00	8·50	9·00
8	7·55	8·05	8·55	9·05
9	7·60	8·10	8·60	9·10
10	7·65	8·15	8·65	9·15
11	7·70	8·20	8·70	9·20
12	7·75	8·25	8·75	9·25
13	7·80	8·30	8·80	9·30
14	7·85	8·35	8·85	9·35
15	7·90	8·40	8·90	9·40
16	7·95	8·45	8·95	9·45
17	8·00	8·50	9·00	9·50
18	8·05	8·55	9·05	9·55
19	8·10	8·60	9·10	9·60
20	8·15	8·65	9·15	9·65
21	8·20	8·70	9·20	9·70
22	8·25	8·75	9·25	9·75
23	8·30	8·80	9·30	9·80

TABLE XXXV

RADII AND CORRESPONDING SURFACE POWERS
(A. G. Bennett)

F_1 = front surface power of contact lens
F_2 = back surface power of contact lens (in air)
F_{L1} = front surface power of liquid lens (in air)
F_{L2} = back surface power of liquid lens (in air)
$F_2 + F_{L1}$ = power of lens/liquid contact surface

Radius (mm.)	Surface Powers (dioptres)			Radius (mm.)	Surface Powers (dioptres)		
	F_1 or F_2 (n = 1·490)	F_{L1} or F_{L2} (n = 1·336)	$F_2 + F_{L1}$		F_1 or F_2 (n = 1·490)	F_{L1} or F_{L2} (n = 1·336)	$F_2 + F_{L1}$
7·00	± 70·00	± 48·00	− 22·00	8·00	± 61·25	± 42·00	− 19·25
7·05	± 69·50	± 47·66	− 21·84	8·05	± 60·87	± 41·74	− 19·13
7·10	± 69·01	± 47·32	− 21·69	8·10	± 60·49	± 41·48	− 19·01
7·15	± 68·53	± 46·99	− 21·54	8·15	± 60·12	± 41·23	− 18·89
7·20	± 68·06	± 46·67	− 21·39	8·20	± 59·76	± 40·98	− 18·78
7·25	± 67·59	± 46·35	− 21·24	8·25	± 59·39	± 40·73	− 18·66
7·30	± 67·13	± 46·03	− 21·10	8·30	± 59·03	± 40·48	− 18·55
7·35	± 66·67	± 45·72	− 20·95	8·35	± 58·68	± 40·24	− 18·44
7·40	± 66·22	± 45·41	− 20·81	8·40	± 58·33	± 40·00	− 18·33
7·45	± 65·77	± 45·10	− 20·67	8·45	± 57·99	± 39·76	− 18·23
7·50	± 65·33	± 44·80	− 20·53	8.50	± 57·65	± 39·53	− 18·12
7·55	± 64·90	± 44·50	− 20·40	8·55	± 57·31	± 39·30	− 18·01
7·60	± 64·48	± 44·21	− 20·27	8·60	± 56·98	± 39·07	− 17·91
7·65	± 64·06	± 43·92	− 20·14	8·65	± 56·65	± 38·84	− 17·81
7·70	± 63·64	± 43·64	− 20·00	8·70	± 56·32	± 38·62	− 17·70
7·75	± 63·23	± 43·36	− 19·87	8·75	± 56·00	± 38·40	− 17·60
7·80	± 62·82	± 43·08	− 19·74	8·80	± 55·68	± 38·18	− 17·50
7·85	± 62·42	± 42·80	− 19·62	8·85	± 55·36	± 37·96	− 17·40
7·90	± 62·03	± 42·53	− 19·50	8·90	± 55·05	± 37·75	− 17·30
7·95	± 61·64	± 42·26	− 19·38	8·95	± 54·74	± 37·54	− 17·20
8·00	± 61·25	± 42·00	− 19·25	9·00	± 54·44	± 37·33	− 17·11

TABLE XXXVI

SPECTACLE AND OCULAR REFRACTION: EFFECTIVITY CORRECTIONS IN HYPERMETROPIA
(A. G. Bennett)

Spectacle Refraction	Effectivity correction when vertex distance is				
	8 mm.	10 mm.	12 mm.	14 mm.	16 mm.
D	D	D	D	D	D
+ 2·00	+ 0·03	+ 0·04	+ 0·05	+ 0·06	+ 0·07
+ 2·50	+ 0·05	+ 0·06	+ 0·08	+ 0·09	+ 0·10
+ 3·00	+ 0·07	+ 0·09	+ 0·11	+ 0·13	+ 0·15
+ 3·50	+ 0·10	+ 0·13	+ 0·15	+ 0·18	+ 0·21
+ 4·00	+ 0·13	+ 0·17	+ 0·20	+ 0·24	+ 0·27
+ 4·50	+ 0·17	+ 0·21	+ 0·26	+ 0·30	+ 0·35
+ 5·00	+ 0·21	+ 0·26	+ 0·32	+ 0·38	+ 0·43
+ 5·50	+ 0·25	+ 0·32	+ 0·39	+ 0·46	+ 0·53
+ 6·00	+ 0·30	+ 0·38	+ 0·47	+ 0·55	+ 0·64
+ 6·50	+ 0·36	+ 0·45	+ 0·55	+ 0·65	+ 0·76
+ 7·00	+ 0·42	+ 0·53	+ 0·64	+ 0·76	+ 0·88
+ 7·50	+ 0·48	+ 0·61	+ 0·74	+ 0·88	+ 1·02
+ 8·00	+ 0·55	+ 0·70	+ 0·85	+ 1·01	+ 1·17
+ 8·50	+ 0·62	+ 0·79	+ 0·97	+ 1·15	+ 1·34
+ 9·00	+ 0·70	+ 0·89	+ 1·09	+ 1·30	+ 1·51
+ 9·50	+ 0·78	+ 0·99	+ 1·22	+ 1·46	+ 1·70
+ 10·00	+ 0·87	+ 1·11	+ 1·36	+ 1·63	+ 1·90
+ 10·50	+ 0·96	+ 1·23	+ 1·51	+ 1·81	+ 2·12
+ 11·00	+ 1·06	+ 1·36	+ 1·67	+ 2·00	+ 2·35
+ 11·50	+ 1·16	+ 1·49	+ 1·84	+ 2·21	+ 2·59
+ 12·00	+ 1·27	+ 1·64	+ 2·02	+ 2·42	+ 2·85
+ 12·50	+ 1·39	+ 1·79	+ 2·21	+ 2·65	+ 3·13
+ 13·00	+ 1·51	+ 1·94	+ 2·40	+ 2·89	+ 3·42
+ 13·50	+ 1·64	+ 2·11	+ 2·61	+ 3·15	+ 3·72
+ 14·00	+ 1·77	+ 2·28	+ 2·83	+ 3·41	+ 4·04
+ 14·50	+ 1·90	+ 2·46	+ 3·06	+ 3·70	+ 4·38
+ 15·00	+ 2·04	+ 2·65	+ 3·29	+ 3·99	+ 4·74
+ 15·50	+ 2·19	+ 2·84	+ 3·54	+ 4·29	+ 5·11
+ 16·00	+ 2·35	+ 3·05	+ 3·80	+ 4·62	+ 5·51
+ 16·50	+ 2·51	+ 3·26	+ 4·07	+ 4·95	+ 5·92
+ 17·00	+ 2·68	+ 3·48	+ 4·36	+ 5·31	+ 6·35
+ 17·50	+ 2·85	+ 3·71	+ 4·65	+ 5·68	+ 6·81
+ 18·00	+ 3·03	+ 3·96	+ 4·96	+ 6·06	+ 7·28

Above corrections to be added.

Example: spectacle refraction + 13·50 D, vertex distance 14 mm.
Ocular refraction = + 13·50 + 3·15 = + 16·65 D.

TABLE XXXVII

SPECTACLE AND OCULAR REFRACTION : EFFECTIVITY CORRECTIONS IN MYOPIA
(A. G. Bennett)

Spectacle Refraction	Effectivity correction when vertex distance is				
	8 mm.	10 mm.	12 mm.	14 mm.	16 mm.
D	D	D	D	D	D
− 2·00	+ 0·03	+ 0·04	+ 0·05	+ 0·05	+ 0·06
− 2·50	+ 0·05	+ 0·06	+ 0·07	+ 0·08	+ 0·10
− 3·00	+ 0·07	+ 0·09	+ 0·10	+ 0·12	+ 0·14
− 3·50	+ 0·10	+ 0·12	+ 0·14	+ 0·16	+ 0·19
− 4·00	+ 0·12	+ 0·15	+ 0·18	+ 0·21	+ 0·24
− 4·50	+ 0·16	+ 0·19	+ 0·23	+ 0·27	+ 0·30
− 5·00	+ 0·19	+ 0·24	+ 0·28	+ 0·33	+ 0·37
− 5·50	+ 0·23	+ 0·29	+ 0·34	+ 0·39	+ 0·44
− 6·00	+ 0·27	+ 0·34	+ 0·40	+ 0·47	+ 0·53
− 6·50	+ 0·32	+ 0·39	+ 0·47	+ 0·54	+ 0·61
− 7·00	+ 0·37	+ 0·46	+ 0·54	+ 0·62	+ 0·70
− 7·50	+ 0·42	+ 0·52	+ 0·62	+ 0·71	+ 0·80
− 8·00	+ 0·48	+ 0·59	+ 0·70	+ 0·81	+ 0·91
− 8·50	+ 0·54	+ 0·66	+ 0·78	+ 0·90	+ 1·01
− 9·00	+ 0·60	+ 0·74	+ 0·88	+ 1·01	+ 1·13
− 9·50	+ 0·67	+ 0·83	+ 0·97	+ 1·12	+ 1·26
− 10·00	+ 0·74	+ 0·91	+ 1·07	+ 1·23	+ 1·38
− 10·50	+ 0·81	+ 1·00	+ 1·18	+ 1·35	+ 1·51
− 11·00	+ 0·89	+ 1·09	+ 1·28	+ 1·47	+ 1·65
− 11·50	+ 0·97	+ 1·19	+ 1·39	+ 1·60	+ 1·79
− 12·00	+ 1·05	+ 1·29	+ 1·51	+ 1·73	+ 1·93
− 12·50	+ 1·14	+ 1·39	+ 1·63	+ 1·86	+ 2·08
− 13·00	+ 1·22	+ 1·50	+ 1·75	+ 2·00	+ 2·24
− 13·50	+ 1·32	+ 1·61	+ 1·88	+ 2·15	+ 2·40
− 14·00	+ 1·41	+ 1·72	+ 2·01	+ 2·29	+ 2·56
− 14·50	+ 1·51	+ 1·84	+ 2·15	+ 2·45	+ 2·73
− 15·00	+ 1·61	+ 1·96	+ 2·29	+ 2·60	+ 2·90
− 15·50	+ 1·71	+ 2·08	+ 2·43	+ 2·76	+ 3·08
− 16·00	+ 1·82	+ 2·21	+ 2·58	+ 2·93	+ 3·26
− 16·50	+ 1·93	+ 2·34	+ 2·73	+ 3·10	+ 3·45
− 17·00	+ 2·04	+ 2·47	+ 2·88	+ 3·27	+ 3·64
− 17·50	+ 2·15	+ 2·61	+ 3·04	+ 3·44	+ 3·83
− 18·00	+ 2·26	+ 2·75	+ 3·20	+ 3·62	+ 4·02
− 18·50	+ 2·38	+ 2·89	+ 3·36	+ 3·80	+ 4·22
− 19·00	+ 2·51	+ 3·03	+ 3·53	+ 3·99	+ 4·43
− 19·50	+ 2·63	+ 3·18	+ 3·70	+ 4·18	+ 4·64
− 20·00	+ 2·76	+ 3·33	+ 3·87	+ 4·37	+ 4·85

Above corrections to be added algebraically.

Example: spectacle refraction −5·25 D, vertex distance 12 mm.
Ocular refraction = −5·25 + 0·31 = −4·94 D.

APPENDIX

TABLE XXXVIII

The Relative Magnification produced by Contact and Spectacle Lenses

The percentage increase (or decrease) in the size of the retinal image afforded by contact lenses in comparison with orthodox spectacles fitted at 12 mm. from the cornea. The figures were compiled by J. L. Francis and published by A. G. Bennett.

In the computation the following values were assumed:

Corneal radius	7·8 mm.
Posterior optic radius of contact lens	8·0 mm.
Central thickness of contact lens	0·5 to 1·0 mm. according to power
Thickness of fluid	0·5 mm.
Refractive index of lens material	1·4900
Refractive index of fluid	1·336

Spectacle Refraction	Equivalent Power of Spectacle Lens $F(a)$	Ocular Refraction	Equivalent Power of Contact Lens System $F(b)$	$\dfrac{F(a)}{F(b)}$	Percentage Increase afforded by Contact Lens
− 20	− 20·00	− 16·13	− 15·73	1·272	27·2
− 18	− 18·00	− 14·80	− 14·41	1·248	24·8
− 16	− 16·00	− 13·42	− 13·06	1·225	22·5
− 14	− 14·00	− 11·99	− 11·65	1·201	20·1
− 12	− 12·00	− 10·49	− 10·19	1·178	17·8
− 10	− 9·99	− 8·93	− 8·66	1·153	15·3
− 8	− 7·99	− 7·30	− 7·07	1·129	12·9
− 6	− 5·99	− 5·60	− 5·42	1·105	10·5
− 4	− 3·98	− 3·82	− 3·69	1·078	7·8
− 2	− 1·98	− 1·95	− 1·88	1·054	5·4
+ 2	+ 1·98	+ 2·05	+ 1·96	1·012	1·2
+ 4	+ 3·92	+ 4·20	+ 3·99	0·983	− 1·7
+ 6	+ 5·81	+ 6·47	+ 6·10	0·953	− 4·7
+ 8	+ 7·68	+ 8·85	+ 8·29	0·926	− 7·4
+ 10	+ 9·52	+ 11·36	+ 10·62	0·897	− 10·3
+ 12	+ 11·27	+ 14·02	+ 13·07	0·862	− 13·8
+ 14	+ 12·93	+ 16·83	+ 15·64	0·827	− 17·3

INDEX

PRINTED IN GREAT BRITAIN BY THE WHITEFRIARS PRESS LTD.
LONDON AND TONBRIDGE